SOCIETY FOR INDUSTRIAL AND ORGANIZATIONAL PSYCHOLOGY

JobNet

Welcome to SIOP JobNet
What Is the SIOP JobNet?
How Does the SIOP JobNet Work?
What Are the Benefits of Subscribing
to the SIOP JobNet?
> Employers
> Job Seekers
> Positions Available

HOW TO CHOOSE A GRADUATE TRAINING PROGRAM

Standard Criteria
> Compliance with Guidelines
> Ratio of applicants to acceptances
> % of students completing degrees

- Intern/Externship requirements
- Quality of Faculty
- Student/Faculty interaction
- Student satisfaction

DESCRIPTION OF A GRADUATE PROGRAM

Contact Person:
E-Mail:
Program: Ph.D., MA/S, or both
Description:
Primary Focus: Applied or Research
Requirements:
Students: Number, Gender, Race
Undergrad Major:
Admissions Requirements:
Faculty: Number, Gender, Race
Financial Aid:
Degrees Granted per Year:

WORK IN THE 21ST CENTURY

WORK IN THE 21ST CENTURY

AN INTRODUCTION TO INDUSTRIAL AND ORGANIZATIONAL PSYCHOLOGY

Frank J. Landy
SHL North America

Jeffrey M. Conte
San Diego State University

Boston   Burr Ridge, IL   Dubuque, IA   Madison, WI   New York
San Francisco   St. Louis   Bangkok   Bogotá   Caracas   Kuala Lumpur
Lisbon   London   Madrid   Mexico City   Milan   Montreal   New Delhi
Santiago   Seoul   Singapore   Sydney   Taipei   Toronto

Higher Education

WORK IN THE 21ST CENTURY: AN INTRODUCTION TO INDUSTRIAL AND ORGANIZATIONAL PSYCHOLOGY
Published by McGraw-Hill, an imprint of The McGraw-Hill Companies, Inc. 1221 Avenue of the Americas, New York, NY, 10020. Copyright © 2004 by The McGraw-Hill Companies, Inc. All rights reserved. No part of this publication may be reproduced or distributed in any form or by any means, or stored in a database or retrieval system, without the prior written consent of The McGraw-Hill Companies, Inc., including, but not limited to, in any network or other electronic storage or transmission, or broadcast for distance learning.

Some ancillaries, including electronic and print components, may not be available to customers outside the United States.

This book is printed on acid-free paper.

domestic   1 2 3 4 5 6 7 8 9 0 DOW/DOW 0 9 8 7 6 5 4
international 1 2 3 4 5 6 7 8 9 0 DOW/DOW 0 9 8 7 6 5 4

ISBN 0-07-283022-0

Publisher: *Steve D. Rutter*
Sponsoring editors: *Ken King/John Wannemacher*
Developmental editor: *Elsa Peterson*
Marketing manager: *Melissa S. Caughlin*
Senior media producer: *Sean Crowley*
Senior project manager: *Christina Thornton-Villagomez*
Production supervisor: *Janean Utley*
Senior designer: *Gino Cieslik*
Lead supplement producer: *Marc Mattson*
Photo research coordinator: *Nora Agbayani*
Art editor: *Jennifer DeVere*
Photo researcher: *David A. Tietz*
Permissions: *Judi Kincaid*
Cover and interior design: *Kay Fulton*
Typeface: *10/12 Minion*
Compositor: *The GTS Companies/York, PA Campus*
Printer: *R.R. Donnelley and Sons Inc.*

Library of Congress Cataloging-in-Publication Data

Landy, Frank J.
    Work in the 21st century : an introduction to industrial and organizational psychology /
Frank J. Landy, Jeffrey M. Conte.
        p. cm.
    Includes index.
    ISBN 0-07-283022-0 (hc. : alk. paper)
    1. Psychology, Industrial. 2. Organization—Research. 3. Organizational behavior. 4.
Work. 5. Twenty-first century. I. Title: Work in the twenty first century. II. Conte, Jeffrey
M. III. Title.
HF5548.8.L254 2004
158.7—dc21

              2003054092

INTERNATIONAL EDITION ISBN 0-07-121480-1
Copyright © 2004. Exclusive rights by The McGraw-Hill Companies, Inc. for manufacture and export. This book cannot be re-exported from the country to which it is sold by McGraw-Hill. The International Edition is not available in North America.

www.mhhe.com

Landy

Frank Landy is a professor emeritus in Industrial and Organizational Psychology at Penn State University. He has also been a visiting lecturer or researcher at Stanford University, The University of California at Berkeley, Stockholm University, Gothenburg University, Cluj-Napoca University (Romania) and Ljubljana University (Slovenia). He received his Ph.D. in Industrial and Organizational Psychology at Bowling Green State University. He has served as an editor of various I-O journals as well as president of SIOP. His career has been divided among research, teaching, text and journal writing, and consulting. Frank's research has been funded by federal agencies including the Department of Justice, the Department of Labor, the Equal Employment Opportunity Commission (EEOC), the Nuclear Regulatory Commission, and the Department of Agriculture. He has received numerous awards and national recognition for his research on I-O topics. Frank is also a much-sought-after expert witness in state and federal cases that involve charges of race, gender and age discrimination as well as human factors issues such as product warning signs and labels, accidents, and product defects. He currently directs the Litigation Support Division of SHL, an international assessment and consulting firm. In his capacity as an expert witness, he has been retained by the Department of Justice, EEOC, and many private employers and has also been part of policy-level groups responsible for drafting, revising, and interpreting Federal statutes (Americans with Disabilities Act, Age Discrimination in Employment Act, Civil Rights Act of 1991) as well as professional guidelines on fair employment (SIOP Principles and APA Standards). He remains active in the employment and human factors litigation arena today.

In his spare time, Frank collects and plays acoustic guitars, performs in community theater, competes in high-mountain trail runs after a long career of marathon road-racing, and works at perfecting his fly fishing techniques. Frank lives with his wife Jeanne in the high mountains of Colorado.

Conte

Jeff Conte is an assistant professor in the Department of Psychology at San Diego State University. He received his B.A. from the University of Virginia and his Ph.D. in Industrial and Organizational Psychology from Penn State University. He teaches courses in introductory I-O psychology, advanced personnel psychology, and psychological testing and measurement. His research interests include personnel selection, personality predictors of job performance, time management, and the factors associated with health and stress in the workplace. Jeff also has interests in cross-cultural research and has conducted research in organizations across the United States as well as in Canada and France. Jeff's research has been funded by the National Institute of Mental Health. He has published in and provided reviews for many I-O psychology and management journals.

Jeff has worked with a variety of organizations addressing such issues as human resource selection, performance appraisal, stress, training evaluation, and organizational factors related to safety. His research and practice has included a wide variety of occupations including lawyers, engineers, firefighters, police officers, and public transportation drivers. In his spare time, Jeff enjoys running, tennis, and other outdoor sports in San Diego.

BRIEF CONTENTS

CONTENTS

PART 2   INDUSTRIAL PSYCHOLOGY

3 PART
ORGANIZATIONAL PSYCHOLOGY

4 PART   THE WORK ENVIRONMENT

The world of work in the 21st century is very different from what it was as recently as ten years ago. Today's workplace is technological and multicultural. Work is often accomplished by teams rather than by single individuals. The computer dominates the workplace. In any given company or department, we find greater diversity in terms of demographic characteristics, interests, and styles than in past decades. Although mental and physical abilities remain important attributes for predicting job success, personality and interpersonal skills are receiving increased attention. A satisfying life is now defined as striking a balance between work and non-work. In addition, the psychological "stability" of work may be at an all-time low. Mergers, acquisitions, downsizing, outsourcing, and radically changing technologies have all made the idea of "life-long employment" at one company, or even in one occupation, an elusive dream. All of these themes will appear in the text and will be tied together in a way that will acknowledge the rich and intriguing nature of the modern workplace.

Our motivation for writing this text flows directly from the changed nature of work described above. We set out to present a realistic, forward-looking view of modern work and the application of psychology to that view. One of us (Frank Landy) wrote several I-O texts between 1974 and 1989. Revisiting the nature of work in 2000 was a eye-opener for us both. We both believed there was a need to describe the sweeping changes, and found that none of the I-O psychology texts on the market addressed them adequately. We also wanted to show how I-O research, theory, and practice could be responsive to those changes. Although it took an extraordinary amount of research and almost 1,600 references to document the changed nature of work in the 21st century, we feel our effort is worth it and today's instructors will agree.

An important thing to keep in mind in studying I-O psychology is that work is complex and cannot be reduced to a set of equations or principles. In the real world, all of the components of work, the work environment and, most importantly, the people who populate the workplace, interact in complicated ways. For example, in considering organizational and individual effectiveness, we cannot think of hiring strategies in a vacuum. Hiring is preceded by recruiting and screening. It is followed by training and socialization. Once the individual joins the organization, there are issues of satisfaction, performance, rewards, and motivation. The way the organization is designed, both psychologically and physically, can limit or enhance productive efforts. This textbook necessarily treats these topics one at a time, but no topic covered in the text can really "stand alone." In the real world, the topics are interrelated, and we will show these interrelationships in the text.

STRUCTURE AND CONTENT OF THE TEXT

Because the full range of industrial and organizational psychology is so broad, we have broken the text into four sections. The first section addresses the fundamentals of the field by examining what I-O psychologists do and where they do it, as well as the methods we use to accomplish research and application. The second section considers topics in personnel psychology such as individual differences, assessment, performance evaluation, staffing, and training. The third section examines organizational topics such as motivation, attitudes, fairness, leadership, work teams, and organizational design. The fourth and last section cover stress, workplace health, and the design of work and workplaces, including safety issues.

The content of our text supports our observation that work in the 21st century has changed from what it was previously. In virtually every chapter, we include substantially modified treatments of topics, as well as entirely new topics that might not have appeared 10 years ago. Consider the following representative list:

- good work
- a theory of multicultural work
- validity and the law
- individual differences
- the content versus the process of assessment
- a model of job performance
- performance management
- rater error as motivated behavior
- the legal context of performance rating
- theories of employment discrimination
- team training, ethics training
- motivational metaphors
- action theory of motivation
- the emotion/mood/disposition interface
- fairness and justice in the workplace
- cross-cultural studies of leadership
- a model of team effectiveness
- episodic versus continuous organizational change
- culture versus climate
- stress and workplace violence
- bullying at the workplace
- culture and climate interpretations of safety

There is another parameter that sets our text apart from its competitors: range. The authors of this text have taught at institutions ranging from four year state to premier private research universities. We also have a domestic-international balance. Frank Landy has taught I-O topics in Slovenia, Germany, Romania, Australia, Sweden, Russia, South Africa, the United Kingdom, and Mexico. Jeff Conte is also interested in cross-cultural topics and has conducted research in organizations across the United States as well as in Canada and France. We *know* what cross-cultural means. Moreover, both authors have done extensive research in practical settings. We span the application continuum from tightly controlled laboratory experiments to real-world consulting at Fortune 100 companies. As a result, we can distinguish the applicable from the inapplicable. This is reflected in our determination to tell the reader what matters in the actual workplace and what doesn't. If you look at work through 20th century lenses, the gap between science and practice does not seem so large. When you try on 21st century lenses, the gap is considerably larger. That means we need stronger and wider and longer bridges to negotiate that gap. We have made every effort to build those bridges. We want to prepare the student to deal with the workplace as he or she will see it in the next few years, not as it was 10 or more years ago. Fortunately, the theory, research, and practice that constitute modern I-O psychology provide the materials for those bridges.

As you read through the book, you will notice that a given topic may appear in several different chapters. That is not a mistake or oversight. The fact is that some topics have relevance in many different chapters and to mention them only once presents too sterile a view of work dynamics. As an example, competencies are higher order forms of ability, personality, interests, and attitudes. Competency modeling is an enhanced form of job analysis. Competencies can be learned. And there are both leader competencies and team competencies. This means that you will see the term "competency" in several chapters. Even though you will see the term often, it will be treated from a different perspective each time it appears. You will see similar treatments of issues related to work/family balance. This balance is important in the attitudes that an individual holds toward work and organizations. Balance is also important in addressing work stress and work design. So "balance" will appear in at least three chapters. We hope that this method of treatment will provide a richer understanding of the effects of work on people and people on work.

STRUCTURE OF THE CHAPTERS

Within each chapter, we have further divided concepts and topics into stand-alone modules. A module consists of material that is relatively homogeneous within a particular chapter. As examples, one module might deal with the historical development of a concept, the second with modern approaches, the third with applications of the concept, and the fourth with related concepts. Some chapters have as few as three modules, while others have four or five modules depending on how much material is covered by the chapter. Each module ends with critical thinking questions designed to encourage students to apply the material covered in the module, summary points, and glossary terms.

Every module can be considered valuable in one way or another. Nevertheless, we realize that it may be difficult to cover every module in a semester. Thus, each module has been designed as a stand-alone unit, permitting the instructor to cover or skip any particular module. As an example, an instructor might cover the first 3 modules in a chapter, but may choose to skip the final module on "Specialized Topics." We believe this modular approach gives instructors maximum flexibility. In addition to covering or deleting a module within a chapter, or changing the order of modules within a chapter, an instructor can assign modules across chapters, in essence creating a new "chapter". For example, an instructor might assign a module on statistics from Chapter 2, a module on job analysis from Chapter 5, and a module on assessment from Chapter 4 to create a "validity" chapter. Although we believe that the modules within a chapter complement each other, instructors might prefer a different order of modules.

SUPPLEMENTS FOR STUDENTS AND INSTRUCTORS

Landy & Conte *Work in the 21st Century* offers several supplements to enhance learning processes and teaching activities.

Instructor's Manual

Here you will find learning objectives, chapter outlines, glossary terms, and suggestions for class discussions and activities.

PowerPoint Slides

This package of 10–15 slides per chapter includes lecture outlines in addition to figures and tables from the text. The slides can be used as is or customized to match your course design and goals.

Dual-Platform Computerized Test Bank

This array of 30–50 multiple choice items per chapter covers all the important concepts with factual and applied questions as well as questions of a more conceptual nature to facilitate critical thinking.

Online Learning Center for Instructors

The instructor side of the Landy & Conte *Work in the 21st Century* website at www.mhhe.com/landy1 contains all the material you need to design your course. Not only is it a convenient way to access the Instructor's Manual, PowerPoint slides, links and supplementary material, but it also includes the following course management systems. Ask your local McGraw-Hill representative for your password.

- **WebCT and Blackboard**—Populated **WebCT** and **Blackboard** course cartridges are available for free upon adoption of a McGraw-Hill textbook. Contact your McGraw-Hill sales representative for details.
- **PageOut**—Build your own course website in less than an hour. You don't have to be a computer whiz to create a website, especially with an exclusive McGraw-Hill product called PageOut. It requires no prior knowledge of HTML, no long hours of coding, and no design skills on your part. With PageOut, even the most inexperienced computer user can quickly and easily create a professional-looking course website. Simply fill in templates with your information and with content provided by McGraw-Hill, choose a design, and you've got a website specifically designed for your course. Best of all, it's free. Visit us at **www.pageout.net** to find out more.
- **Knowledge Gateway**—McGraw-Hill service is second to none. We offer a help desk that can be reached by phone, e-mail, or online with a special website called Knowledge Gateway. For larger adoptions, if hands-on training is necessary, we have a team of experts ready to train you on campus. This FREE service is available to support PageOut, WebCT, and BlackBoard users.

Instructor's Resource CD-ROM

This CD-ROM conveniently contains the Instructor's Manual, Test Bank and Brownstone testing system, and PowerPoint slides described above.

Student Study Guide and Workbook

Packaged in a CD-ROM included with each new copy of the textbook, this guide is a valuable tool for maximizing students' understanding of material and preparation for exams. The guide was developed in close conjunction with the textbook and facilitates the instructor's course design by providing students with the same learning objectives, chapter outlines, and glossary terms as the Instructor's Manual. In addition, it includes practice exam questions and exercises for each chapter. The workbook exercises, based on organizational issues that I-O psychologists are often asked to study and resolve, facilitate active learning and practical application of the ideas and concepts discussed in class and in the textbook.

Online Learning Center

The student side of the Landy & Conte *Work in the 21st Century* website at www.mhhe.com/landy1 contains links to a variety of Internet resources as well as supplementary material on many I-O topics.

   Also visit McGraw-Hill's Psychology Supersite at http://www.mhhe.com/psych This comprehensive Web resource provides a superstructure that organizes and houses all of our psychology text websites.

ACKNOWLEDGEMENTS

We are deeply grateful to our many colleagues who provided assistance, which came in several forms. We asked a number of I-O psychologists to examine the initial outline for the text as well as the internal structure of chapters relevant to their expertise. The following individuals were kind enough to provide such advice: Rich Klimoski, Wally Borman, Jim Farr, David Kravitz, Dave Harrison, Diane Catanzaro, Michael Harris, Irv Goldstein, Harold Goldstein, Shelly Zedeck, Ivan Roberston, Laura Koppes, Mark Griffin, Beryl Hesketh, Paul Thayer, Susan Mohammed, Neal Schmitt, and Dick Jeanneret.

Other colleagues were kind enough to send us "care packages" of their work on particular areas. These generous offers to share work that was in progress, awaiting publication, or in technical reports were instrumental in allowing us to incorporate updated material. These colleagues included Peter Warr, Howard Weiss, Ann Howard, Anat Rafaeli, Miriam Erez, Donna Chrobot-Mason, Paula Caligiuri, Kecia Thomas, Bruce Avolio, Cary Cooper, Dianne Maranto, Lee Hakel, Dan Cable, Karen Smola, Jim Farr, Patti Ambrose, Terry Mitchell, André Büssing, Wilmar Schaufeli, Heinz Schuler, Scott Highhouse, Randy Gordon, Sharon Parker, Tim Judge, Talya Bauer, Ruth Kanfer, Robert Tett, Bob Pritchard, Robert Roe, Steve Kozlowski, Susan Vanhemmel, Chris Hartel, Nigel Nicholson, Dirk Steiner, Jan Cleveland, Fritz Drasgow, Zeynep Aycan, Rupande Padaki, and Dov Eden.

Our colleagues at our respective institutions were a captive, but nevertheless enthusiastic, audience. At SHL, these included Rick Jacobs, Gary Schmidt, Jurgen Bank, Dave Bartram, Helen Baron, Brian Cawley, Laurence Karsh, Jone Papinchock, Barb Nett, Meredith Ramsey, Angie Olson, Heather Grab, Julene Gonzales, Eugene Burke, Danielle Pare, and Lauren Havighurst. At San Diego State, many colleagues within and outside the psychology department helped to provide a supportive environment in which to work. In particular, Keith Hattrup, Karen Ehrhart, and Mark Ehrhart represent a wonderful group of I-O psychologists at San Diego State University. Betsy Hnath read various chapters from the perspective of the student. Stephanie Howard was our main research assistant for most of the project and went well beyond what was expected in her efforts to track down obscure research studies. Heather Grab performed similar services later in the project and also did a great job helping to develop supplement materials.

In addition, several colleagues went well out of their way to help us by providing reviews of draft material, suggestions for additional research, and contacts with researchers whose excellent work might have gone unnoticed. These colleagues include Michael Frese, Kevin Murphy, Michelle Dean, Kurt Kraiger, Bernie Weiner, Ben Schneider, Bob Wood, David Day, and Bob Guion.

We also wish to acknowledge those who accepted McGraw-Hill's invitation to review our outline and critical content. These reviewers include

John F. Binning,
Illinois State University;

Lou Buffardi,
George Mason University;

Gary J. Greguras,
Louisiana State University;

Joseph A. Karafa,
Ferris State University;

Janet Kottke,
California State University, San Bernardino;

Debra A. Major,
Old Dominion University;

Corey E. Miller,
Wright State University;

Frederick L. Oswald,
Michigan State University;

Sylvia G. Roch,
Albany University—State University of New York at Albany.

Our editorial team at McGraw-Hill was headed by Ken King, publisher and sponsoring editor. Ken was the inspiration for the modular approach and provided us with the perfect balance of guidance and autonomy. Freelance developmental editor Elsa Peterson was as much a part of the final product as the authors. In addition to being a spectacular word goddess, Elsa is smart, funny, and sensitive to the idiosyncrasies of an author. Senior project manager Christina Thornton-Villagomez did a masterful job in overseeing the transformation of the manuscript into the book. Our marketing manager, Melissa Caughlin, has done a wonderful job of bringing our text to the attention of our target audience of instructors and students. To these individuals and the many other members of our McGraw-Hill team we express our heartfelt thanks.

A NOTE FROM FRANK LANDY

Writing this text has been a joy for me on many levels. On a personal level, it has provided me the opportunity to do several things that I really enjoy—principally read and write. I have been a behavioral scientist for over 35 years and I still get a thrill from making complex concepts comprehensible to a novice reader. This project has also provided me the opportunity to work with a wonderful coauthor, Jeff Conte. Jeff is smart, conscientious, and most importantly, has a wonderful sense of what will be good for the student. In the course of writing the text, I had close contact with many I-O psychology friends and colleagues in the United States and abroad and it was very pleasing to renew old acquaintances and make new ones through this communication. My wife Jeanne and my non-psychologist friends were wonderfully supportive and tolerant as I cancelled out of one after another non-work event to work on "the book." And when I talked about new "insights" that I had extracted from reading that I had done, they were kind enough not to leave the room as a group (although, eventually, they did all leave the room). Finally, I thank Bob Guion, as I have been doing for more than three decades now, for his guidance and support throughout this project. It was the publication of his 1998 text in *Assessment* (Guion, 1998) that moved me to consider this project in the first place.

A NOTE FROM JEFF CONTE

I want to express my deep appreciation to Frank Landy for offering me the opportunity to work with him on this book. My teaching and research have both been influenced by Frank's support and mentoring in graduate school and beyond, and it has been particularly gratifying to work with him so closely in writing this book. I thank Rick Jacobs, a friend and mentor who has greatly influenced my thinking about I-O psychology and who has been very supportive throughout my career. I greatly appreciate the unwavering support and encouragement that I have received from my parents (Anne and Tom) and siblings (T. J., Scott, and Deanna). I would also like to thank Michelle Dean, Paula Caligiuri, Kat Ringenbach, and Marcus Foster for their support and encouragement throughout the writing of this book.

Frank J. Landy
Jeffrey Conte

FUNDAMENTALS

WHAT IS INDUSTRIAL AND ORGANIZATIONAL PSYCHOLOGY?

1 CHAPTER

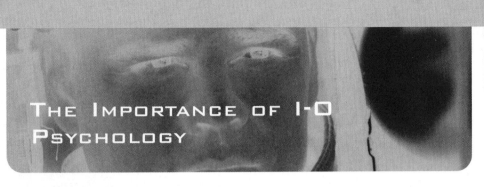
THE IMPORTANCE OF I-O PSYCHOLOGY

THE IMPORTANCE OF WORK IN PEOPLE'S LIVES

Most adults devote the majority of their waking weekday (and often weekends as well!) to work. Proportionally, this is a greater devotion of time and energy than to any other single waking human activity. For this reason alone, we can assume that work is important to people. Then there is the fact that most people need to earn money, and do so by working. But the experience of work goes well beyond the simple exchange of time for money. There have been some eloquent discussions of the meaning of work by non-psychologists. One of the best known is Studs Terkel, who chronicled the meaning of work in his classic book, *Working*. Terkel interviewed 120 people and asked them to describe what work meant to them (see Box 1.1).

Another nonpsychologist social observer, Barbara Garson, interviewed people who had what would generally be considered "boring" jobs for her book, *All the Livelong Day* (Box 1.2).

Consider the contrast between one of her interviews and the firefighter interviewed by Terkel. Both interviews were with individuals who actually had jobs. But there is another way to look at the experience of work. Talk to people who are about to lose or who have lost their jobs. Harry Maurer wrote a book called *Not Working* (1979), based on interviews with people who had lost their jobs (Box 1.3).

Note the common theme that appears in each of these interviews: Work is a defining characteristic of the way people gauge their value to society, their family, and themselves. The National Research Council, in a book about the changing nature of work (NRC, 1999), adds support to this observation. When asked the question, "If you were to get enough money to live as comfortably as you would like for the rest of your life, would you continue to work or would you stop working?" The percentage of people reporting that they would continue working has averaged approximately 70 percent since at least 1973. This is dramatic evidence of the centrality of work as a noneconomic experience.

Another interesting aspect of the three interview excerpts presented above is the nature of the interviewers. Even though none of the three was a psychologist, each took an experiential view of work. They were interested in how work "felt" to the workers. This is a current theme in the work of industrial and organizational (I-O) psychologists—trying to understand the *experience* of work.

The Concept of "Good Work"

Gardner (2002) notes that psychology has often ignored how workers actually "conceptualize their daily experiences—the goals and concerns they bring to the workplace." He goes on to characterize what he calls "good work" (Gardner, Csikszentmihalyi, & Damon, 2001). Good work is work that "exhibits a high level of expertise, and it entails regular concern with the implications and applications of an individual's work for the wider world" (Gardner, 2002).

BOX 1.1   GOOD WORK

I was in a fire one night, we had all-hands. An all-hands is you got a workin' fire and you're the first in there, and the first guy in there is gonna take the worst beatin'. You got the nozzle, the hose, you're takin' a beating. If another company comes up behind you, you don't give up that nozzle. It's pride. To put out the fire. We go over this with oxygen and tell the guy "Get out, get oxygen." They won't leave. I think guys want to be heroes. You can't be a hero on Wall Street.

There's guys with black shit comin' out of their ears. You got smoke in your hair. You take a shower, you put water in your hair, and you can still smell the smoke. It never leaves you. You're coughing up this black shit. But you go back, and you have coffee, maybe a couple of beers, you're psyched up.

SOURCE: Terkel, 1974, pp. 758–59.

In 2002 it is easy to think of examples of "good" work using Gardner's definition. The police officers and firefighters who used their skills to save and protect lives at the World Trade Center on September 11, 2001, were clearly engaged in "good" work and had prepared for that day all of their working lives. The same is true of United Nations soldiers sent abroad to protect innocent civilians from genocide, or the staff of food kitchens or homeless shelters. The interesting aspect of "good" and "bad" work is that the individual worker and the employer together have the power to define good work, or to transform

The opportunity for "good work" often arrives unannounced, as exemplified in the aftermath of the World Trade Center collapse.

Baptiste—A box assembler in a Ping Pong paddle factory

> What do you do to change it, to make it more interesting? Ah ha—he smiled again—I do it with my eyes closed.

Baptiste explained how he did dozens at a time with his eyes closed. If anyone passed behind him, they could not tell that he was working blind.

> Keypunching occupied the eyes, hands, feet, and enough of the brain to make it impossible to talk or daydream. It seemed totally confining. But there was one free sense.

"One thing Aida and I used to do," said a puncher who became a supervisor, "was to have races. On the old machines you had to hit harder and they made a louder noise. So we could hear each other, and when we were doing the same job, we could race. Sometimes, we'd synchronize—adjust so that you'd move into the next field exactly together."

Another puncher . . . was a syncopater. "I like to keep a certain rhythm going . . . I'd move forward when the woman next to me was halfway through another field, then she'd move forward when I was halfway through the next. So you'd get a constant like bum, bum, bum, zing; bum, bum, bum, ba-bum, zing."

SOURCE: Garson, 1975, 1984, pp. 19, 250–251.

---

good work into bad and vice versa. A disreputable accounting firm can cheat and mislead clients and the public, thus engaging in bad work; that same firm and its employees could be doing good work if they are helping people to manage their money and protect their retirement plans.

Martin Luther King, Jr., captured the distinction between good and bad work eloquently: "If a man is called to be a street sweeper, he should sweep streets even as Michelangelo painted, Beethoven composed music, or Shakespeare wrote poetry. He should sweep streets so well that all heaven and earth will pause to say, 'Here lived a great street sweeper who did his job well'" (King, 1956).

The point we are making is that the study of work by I-O psychologists and students (you!) is potentially "good work" because it enables you to develop and use skills, and to use them for the benefit of someone other than simply yourself. It is also encouraging to see that I-O psychology has actually anticipated Gardner's observation about missing the "experience" of work. In the last decade, there has been a rapid and substantial increase in research related to the feelings that workers bring to and take from the workplace. In addition, there has been a dramatic increase in research directed toward work-life balance issues. In other words, I-O psychology has recognized that the "experience" of work is more complex than simply tasks and productivity and accidents. You will see the results of this research in Chapter 10 on emotions in the workplace.

Gardner describes the depressing consequences of settling for "bad" work:

> We resign ourselves to our fate. It is difficult to quit one's job, let alone one's whole profession, and few in midlife, saddled with mortgage and, perhaps, tuition payments, have the fortitude to do so. As a result, we are left with a society in which profit motives reign supreme—and in which few feel in a position where they can perform good work (Gardner, 2002, p. B2).

It is important to keep in mind that "good" and "bad" work are not fixed quantities. It is up to each worker and employer to define the nature of the work they undertake. This means that there are often hidden opportunities available for "good" work. In later chapters, we will discuss the concept of contextual work or organizational citizenship behavior. These two concepts are related to a worker "going the extra mile," contributing more than is expected. These behaviors would also be expected to help define good work. The experience of work should be one of our primary goals in the study of work behavior and should be elevated to a position equal with concerns for productivity. All good work is productive work, but not all productive work is good work.

BOX 1.3

BEING OUT OF WORK

I was frightened. I didn't want to be laid off. And then there were these people with ten, fifteen, twenty years who were saying, "I wish they'd lay me off. I'm tired of working." Well, they don't really want that. I know it's a lie. Why come to work every day if you really want to be laid off that bad? Because a person with that much time can afford to take off. They can use up their casual days or anything. But when somebody reports to you and says, "You're going to be laid off indefinitely," then hey, you feel like you're out in the world all by yourself. You wonder what you're going to do. You've been out working, struggling, trying to get . . . and you can't get. And you think, "How am I gonna get it? What am I gonna do?" It really is something to think about, something to frighten you. So I always say don't ever let people tell you what they think when it never happened to them. Let it happen to them, and they'll realize. They say all those things—"I don't want to work"—well, quit your job, so I can get it! Because I want to work! I'm one of those determined people. I enjoy working. I mean, you've got to sweat a little, you got to give a little in order to receive. 'Cause these people ain't givin' away nothin'.

So one day—it was a Thursday; they usually inform you on a Thursday—here come the foreman and the steward. My steward had been telling me he didn't know exactly what they were gonna do. But that Thursday he came around and said, "We're gonna try and get you to work next week, but then you'll be laid off indefinitely." Oh, God.

I said, "All right." And the next week I only worked one day, and that was it. That was during the week in March when the real big layoff came. A lot of people got kicked out.

It wasn't so bad at first, especially after my sub pay came through. I was getting $122 a week unemployment, plus sub pay. It came to about $170. That was pretty good. When I was working, I was taking home about $15 more. So I felt pretty secure when I was getting sub. But I still didn't like it. It's just the idea of sitting down. I'd rather work for what I receive. It's all right receiving it, and it's my money true enough; but yet and still, why sit down when I can be putting my body to some other use? . . . And I started getting nervous. My doctor asked me about it. You can probably tell just sitting here. I am getting really fidgety, and I think it's because sitting around the house has started to get next to me. So I'd leave the house just to get some air.

It's like something is pulling me down. I can't understand it. I don't have any energy. Something just seems like it's taking over. As if my body was useless, and I can't do anything. Sometimes I don't even get up till about twelve. And I don't want to clean up, even though I can't stand to see things out of order. I have to make myself get up and do it. Sometimes I just sit around and look at the walls until they're caving in on me.

SOURCE: Maurer, 1979, pp. 103–104.

HOW DOES I-O PSYCHOLOGY CONTRIBUTE TO SOCIETY?
What Is I-O Psychology?

INDUSTRIAL-ORGANIZATIONAL (I-O) PSYCHOLOGY

The application of psychological principles, theory, and research to the work setting.

Throughout this book we will use the term **I-O psychology** as a synonym for **"industrial and organizational psychology."** The simplest definition of industrial and organizational psychology is "the application of psychological principles, theory, and research to the work setting." Don't be fooled, however, by the phrase "work setting." The domain of I-O psychology stretches well beyond the physical boundaries of the workplace because many of the factors that influence work behavior are not always found in the work setting. These factors include things like family responsibilities, cultural influences, employment-related legislation, and nonwork events (reflect, for example, on how the terrorist attacks of September 11, 2001, changed the working life of most people). Even more significant is the influence of personality on work behavior. While an individual's personality may actually influence work behavior, his or her personality is often influenced by events that occurred before he or she began full-time employment. In addition, I-O psychologists are concerned about the effect of work on nonwork behaviors. Spouses and children are well aware of the effect of a "bad day at work" on home life. I-O psychology concentrates on the reciprocal impact of work on life and life on work.

SOCIETY FOR INDUSTRIAL AND ORGANIZATIONAL PSYCHOLOGY (SIOP)

An association to which many I/O psychologists belong. Designated as Division 14 of the American Psychological Association (APA).

A more formal definition of I-O psychology, approached from the perspective of the I-O psychologist and what he or she does, has been adopted by the **Society for Industrial and Organizational Psychology** (an association to which many I-O psychologists, both practitioners and researchers, belong, and which we will refer to in this text by the acronym **SIOP**):

Industrial-Organizational (called I-O) Psychologists recognize the interdependence of individuals, organizations, and society, and they recognize the impact of factors such as increasing government influences, growing consumer awareness, skill shortages, and the changing nature of the workforce. I-O psychologists facilitate responses to issues and problems involving people at work by serving as advisors and catalysts for business, industry, labor, public, academic, community, and health organizations.

They are:

Scientists who derive principles of individual, group, and organizational behavior through research;

Consultants and staff psychologists who develop scientific knowledge and apply it to the solution of problems at work; and

Teachers who train in the research and application of Industrial-Organizational Psychology (www.siop.org).

Table 1.1 presents a more detailed description of the most common areas of concentration for I-O psychologists.

TABLE 1.1	Common Areas of Concentration for I-O Psychologists

Selection and placement

Developing tests.

Validating tests.

Analyzing job content.

Identifying management potential.

Defending tests against legal challenge.

Training and development

Identifying training and development needs.

Forming and implementing technical and managerial training programs.

Evaluating training effectiveness.

Career Planning.

Organizational development

Analyzing organizational structure.

Maximizing satisfaction and effectiveness of employees.

Facilitating organizational change.

Performance measurement

Developing measures of performance.

Measuring the economic benefit of performance.

Introducing performance evaluation systems.

Quality of worklife

Identifying factors associated with job satisfaction.

Reducing stress in the workplace.

Redesigning jobs to make them more meaningful.

Engineering psychology

Designing work environments.

Optimizing person–machine effectiveness.

Making workplaces safer.

SOURCE: Adapted from www.siop.org.

TABLE 1.2	Common Job Titles for I-O Psychologists

Staff member, Manager, Director, Vice President of:
  Personnel
  Human Resources
  Organizational Planning
  Personnel Development
  Organizational Development
  Management Development
  Personnel Research
  Employee Relations
  Training
  Affirmative Action
Assistant, Associate, Full Professor of:
  Psychology
  Management
  Organizational Behavior
  Industrial Relations
  Human Resources
Corporate Consultant
Private Consultant
Research Scientist: Private Sector
Research Scientist: Government
Research Scientist: Military
Research Scientist: Test Publisher

PERSONNEL
PSYCHOLOGY

Field of psychology that addresses issues such as recruitment, selection, training, performance appraisal, promotion, transfer, and termination.

HUMAN
RESOURCES
MANAGEMENT
(HRM)

Practices such as recruiting, selection, retention, training and development of people (human resources) in order to achieve individual and organizational goals.

ORGANIZATIONAL
PSYCHOLOGY

Field of psychology that combines research from social psychology and organizational behavior and addresses the emotional and motivational side of work.

Table 1.2 presents some common job titles for I-O Psychologists. As you can see, I-O psychologists can wear many different hats.

Traditionally, I-O psychology has been divided into three major concentrations: personnel psychology, organizational psychology, and human engineering. We will briefly consider each of these concentrations. Even though we will talk about them separately, they often overlap considerably, as we will see.

Personnel psychology (often seen as part of **human resources,** or **HR**) addresses issues such as recruitment, selection, training, performance appraisal, promotion, transfer, and termination. The approach assumes that people are consistently different in their attributes and work behaviors; and that information about these differences can be used to predict, maintain, and increase work performance and satisfaction.

Organizational psychology combines research and ideas from social psychology and organizational behavior. It addresses the emotional and motivational side of work. It includes topics such as attitudes, fairness, motivation, stress, leadership, teams, and the broader aspects of organizational and work design. In some senses, it concentrates on the reactions of people *to* work and the action plans that develop as a result of those reactions. Both work and people are variables of interest and the issue is the extent to which characteristics of the people match the characteristics or demands (Kristoff, 1996) of the work. Of course, organizational psychology has implications for performance, but they may not be as direct as is the case with personnel psychology.

Human engineering (also called **human factors psychology**) is the study of the capacities and limitations of humans with respect to a particular environment. The human engineering approach is almost the opposite of the personnel approach. Remember, in the personnel approach the goal is to find or fit the best person to the job. In the human engineering approach the task of the human engineer is to develop an environment that is compatible with the characteristics of the worker. The "environmental" aspects this may include are quite diverse; among them are tools, work spaces, information display, shift work, work pace, machine controls, and even the extent to which safety is valued in the organization or work group.

HUMAN
ENGINEERING OR
HUMAN FACTORS
PSYCHOLOGY

*Study of the capacities
and limitations of
humans with respect
to a particular
environment.*

The Demographics of I-O Psychologists

The major professional organization for psychologists of all kinds in the United States is the **American Psychological Association (APA).** Recently, the American Psychological Society (APS) was formed to serve the needs of the more basic areas of psychology. Clinical, Counseling, and School psychologists make up over 50 percent of the more than 155,000 APA members, while the remaining members are active in a wide range of specialties ranging from I-O psychology to media psychology, rehabilitation psychology, and adult development and aging. The APA has various divisions that represent various types of psychologists; the division for I-O psychologists is Division 14. Most I-O psychologists belong to Division 14 of APA, SIOP, or both. In the year 2000, I-O psychologists represented approximately 6 percent of all members of APA. In 2001, approximately 6,000 I-O psychologists (including approximately 2,600 students) were members of Division 14.

AMERICAN
PSYCHOLOGICAL
ASSOCIATION
(APA)

*The major professional
organization for
psychologists in the
United States.*

It is interesting to trace the changes in demographic characteristics of I-O psychologists who were members of APA between 1985 and 2000. The major shift was in gender. In 1985, 15 percent of I-O psychologists were women. By 2000, that percentage had doubled to 30 percent. The ethnic minority membership since SIOP was founded in 1982 has also doubled (O'Connor & Ryan, 1996). According to recent salary and employment surveys conducted by SIOP (Katkowski & Metsker, 2001), the average salary for a PhD in I-O psychology was $90,000; for a master's level I-O psychologist it was $67,000. The highest paid I-O psychologists in private industry worked in energy, information technology, banking, and telecommunications, averaging approximately $120,000 per year; while the lowest earners were found in state and local government positions, averaging approximately $70,000. I-O psychologists whose primary responsibility is teaching at private and public colleges and universities often earn additional income from consulting with government and industry (Katkowski & Metsker, 2001).

I-O psychologists work in a wide variety of employment settings. Figure 1.1 presents percentages for areas of primary employment.

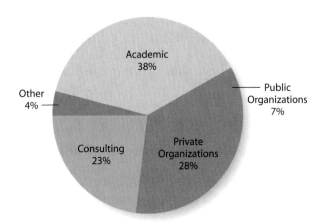

FIGURE 1.1

**Where I-O
Psychologists are
Employed.** SOURCE: SIOP
survey, 2002.

SIOP AS A RESOURCE

The Society for Industrial and Organizational Psychology is the single best resource for anyone interested in I-O psychology. The society accepts student members. Its website address is provided in the Online Learning Center for this book. The website is continually updated and includes the following types of information:

- The history of I-O psychology and SIOP.
- Membership information.
- An electronic version of the quarterly newsletter of SIOP called *TIP (The Industrial-Organizational Psychologist).*
- JobNet, a system that matches employers seeking I-O psychologists with applicants for I-O positions.
- A listing of educational institutions that offer graduate training programs in I-O psychology.
- A list of SIOP publications.

A BRIEF HISTORY OF I-O PSYCHOLOGY

Since we will present the historical context of various I-O topics when we cover them in subsequent chapters, here we will sketch the evolution of I-O psychology in broad and simple terms. In addition, we will present a description of the development of American I-O psychology since it is valuable for you to see how the science evolved in this country. Having said that, we also point out that there were parallel developments in other countries such as England (Shimmin & Wallace, 1994; Chmiel, 2000), Australia, Germany, the Netherlands (van Strien, 1998; Drunen & van Strien, 1999; Shimmin & van Strien, 1998) and eastern European countries such as Romania (Pitariu, 1992; Rosca & Voicu, 1982). Unfortunately, for many countries, there is no English version of the development of I-O psychology. For the interested reader, however, one of the first modern American I-O psychologists, Morris Viteles, did a wonderful job of describing the status of I-O psychology around the world during the period from 1922 and 1932 (Viteles, 1926; 1928; 1930; 1932). Arthur Kornhauser (1929) also provided a description of I-O psychology in England and Germany. One of the most comprehensive surveys of international applied psychology, particularly with respect to vocational counseling, as it was practiced in 1937, appears in a book by Keller and Viteles (1937). As we present the various topics, note that we make use of a wide variety of contemporary research and theory produced by non-American scholars. For further reading on the development of I-O psychology as a science and a practice in America, we recommend several excellent and detailed reviews (Baritz, 1960; Katzell & Austin, 1992; Landy, 1993, 1997; Koppes, 1997; Benjamin, 1997).

You may ask why we need *any* historical treatment. The answer is that to know where we are now and where we are going as a field, it helps to know how we got here. When we look at history from a broad perspective, it is possible to make some good guesses about the future. And knowing the discipline's history helps us understand the context in which research and application were conducted, which in turn helps us appreciate the value of that research today. Consider Table 1.3, which lists the titles of articles in the first year of publication of one of the major I-O journals, the *Journal of Applied Psychology* (JAP). Now look at Table 1.4. This is a list of articles which appeared in the last few years in the same journal. Quite a contrast! There are two reasons for the difference between what was important in 1917 and what is important today. The first reason is the change in the world of work. The second reason is the accumulation of knowledge about work-related behavior in the last 85 years. Figure 1.2 presents a broad time line for the development of our field from its inception to the present time.

TABLE 1.3	Titles of Research Articles in the *Journal of Applied Psychology*, 1917

Estimates of the military value of certain personal qualities

The legibility of the telephone directory

The psychology of a prodigious child

A test for memory of names and faces

Practical relations between psychology and the war

The moron as a war problem

Mental tests of unemployed men

A trial of mental and pedagogical tests in a civil service examination for policemen and firemen

The attitude and reaction of the businessman to psychology

A note on the German recruiting system

1876–1930

The roots of I-O psychology trace back nearly to the beginning of psychology as a science. Wilhelm Wundt founded one of the first psychological laboratories in 1876 in Leipzig, Germany. Within 10 years, he had established a thriving graduate training and research enterprise. He hoped to put scientific psychology on an even footing with the more established physical sciences of chemistry, physics, and biology. In the mid-1880s, he trained two psychologists who would have a major influence on the eventual emergence of I-O psychology: Hugo Munsterberg and James McKeen Cattell (Landy, 1992; 1993; 1997; Sokal, 1982). Munsterberg left Germany for America in 1892 and became the director of the psychological laboratories at Harvard University.

TABLE 1.4	Titles of Research Articles in the *Journal of Applied Psychology*, 2001

Effects of computer surveillance on perceptions of privacy and procedural justice

How employees respond to personal offense: The effects of blame, attribution, victim status and offender status on revenge and reconciliation in the workplace

Attributions of the "causes" of group performance as an alternative explanation of the relationship between organizational citizenship behavior and organizational performance

Influence of performance evaluation rating segmentation on motivation and fairness perceptions

The effect of item content overlap on organizational commitment questionnaire-turnover cognitions relationship

Organizational efforts to affirm sexual diversity: A cross-level examination

Justice at the millennium: A meta-analytic review of 25 years of organizational justice research

Minority dissent and team innovation: The importance of participation in decision making

Investigating the influence of social desirability on personality factor structure

Relationship of core self-evaluations to goal setting, motivation, and performance

What I think you think of me: Women's reactions to being viewed as beneficiaries of preferential selection

Pink triangles: Antecedents and consequences of perceived workplace discrimination against gay and lesbian employees

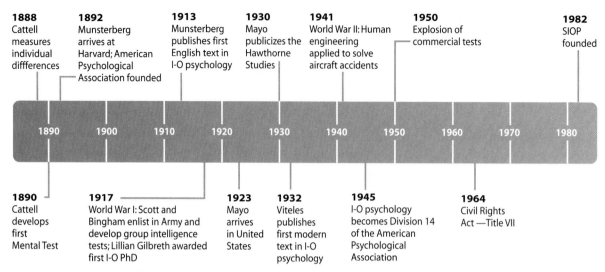

FIGURE 1.2 Important Dates in the Evolution of I-O Psychology

Munsterberg was one of the first to measure abilities in workers and tie those abilities to performance—something that may seem in hindsight like an obvious path to follow, but was innovative at the time. In another departure from the practice of his day, he applied rudimentary statistics to "analyze" the results of his studies. The world's first I-O psychology textbook, written in 1912 and translated from German to English in 1913, (Munsterberg, 1912; 1913) was another of Munsterberg's memorable contributions to the field. At the time of his death in 1916, Munsterberg was at the pinnacle of his career at Harvard. In conjunction with pursuing his research on industrial efficiency, he devoted considerable energy to persuading the leaders of American government and industry that I-O psychology was a key contributor to the nation's economic development. I-O psychology was really only "industrial" psychology in those days, devoted to the goal of increasing productivity. It was known by some as "economic" psychology.

Cattell was an American contemporary of Munsterberg and is recognized for being among the first to realize the importance of differences among individuals as a way of predicting their behavior. Wundt, under whose direction he studied, was interested in general laws of behavior and less interested in the differences among subjects in responding to his experimental stimuli. He and other experimental psychologists of the time considered those differences as "error" that served to complicate and muddy their results. Cattell observed instead that these differences were reliable properties of the subjects and could be used to understand behavior more fully. After a brief stay in England, Cattell joined the faculty of the University of Pennsylvania in 1888, and then of Columbia University in 1893, where he remained until his retirement in 1917.

Contemporaneously with Munsterberg and Cattell, two other leaders in I-O psychology, Walter Dill Scott and Walter Van Dyke Bingham, were working at the Carnegie Institute, developing methods for selecting and training sales personnel (Ferguson, 1965; Landy, 1993; 1997). When the United States entered World War I in 1917, Scott and Bingham volunteered to help with the testing and placement of more than a million army recruits. Together with other prominent psychologists, they adapted a well-known intelligence test (the **Stanford-Binet test,** designed for testing one individual at a time) to make it suitable for mass group testing. This new form of test was called the Army Alpha. (The Army Beta test was like the Army Alpha but was nonverbal and administered to recruits who were illiterate.) When the war ended, private industry set out to emulate the successful testing of army personnel, and mental ability testing soon became commonplace in the work setting.

STANFORD-BINET TEST

A well-known intelligence test designed for testing one individual at a time. Originally developed by Alfred Binet and Theodore Simon in 1905, the Binet-Simon test was updated starting in 1916 by Lewis Terman and colleagues at Stanford University, which determined the test's current name.

Prior to 1917, there had never been a graduate degree conferred in industrial psychology. Lillian Gilbreth was awarded the first PhD in industrial psychology by Brown University for her research applying the **Scientific Management** principles of Frederick W. Taylor to educational institutions. Scientific Management was based on the principles of **time and motion study.** She and her husband Frank Gilbreth became well-known human engineering practitioners and management consultants. As America entered World War II, the field of human engineering emerged. Until then, human engineering was little more than the study of time and motion. Time and motion specialists (like Frederick W. Taylor and the Gilbreths) broke every action down into its constituent parts, timed those movements with a stopwatch, and developed new and more efficient movements that would both reduce fatigue as well as increase productivity.

1930–1964

Until 1930 industrial psychology focused on the use of mental ability tests to select the most proficient workers. Elton Mayo, a psychologist from Australia, arrived in the United States in 1924 (Griffin, Landy, & Mayocchi, 2002) and immediately began studying not the efficiency of workers, but their emotions. He was particularly interested in the possibility that work "caused" workers to act in pathological ways. He proposed that there was a mental state known as **revery obsession** that resulted from the mind-numbing, repetitive, and difficult work that characterized the factories of the day. Mayo proposed that since workers were not required to use their intellect but only their physical effort, their minds would inevitably wander and in this wandering, various paranoid thoughts would arise. As a result, they would be unhappy, prone to resist management attempts to increase productivity, and sympathetic to labor unions. It is interesting to note that such a reaction to boring work today would be considered normal rather than pathological.

When Mayo was given a faculty appointment at Harvard in 1926 (Trahair, 1984), research was being done at the Hawthorne, Illinois, plant of the Western Electric Corporation. These studies are classics and are known collectively as the **Hawthorne studies.** The research had begun as simple attempts to increase productivity by manipulating lighting, rest breaks, and work hours (Roethlisberger & Dickson, 1939). But the results of the experiments were puzzling. Sometimes, when conditions were actually made worse (e.g., lighting was reduced), production improved; and when conditions were made better (e.g., lighting was enhanced), production sometimes dropped! Mayo suggested the workers be interviewed to see what was going on. This led to the rather dramatic discovery (for the time) that workers' attitudes actually played a role in productivity. In the context of the Hawthorne experiments, the very fact that someone was finally paying attention to the workers seemed to have affected behavior. This has become known as the "Hawthorne Effect"—the change in behavior that results from researchers paying attention to the workers. We will revisit this concept in the chapter on emotion in the workplace. Until that time, it had been generally accepted that the only significant motivator of effort was money and that the environment, rather than the person, was of primary importance. The results of the Hawthorne studies ushered in a radically new movement known as the **Human Relations Movement.** Researchers in this movement were interested in more complicated theories of motivation, as well as in the newly discovered emotional world of the worker. Studies of job satisfaction became more common.

World War II brought some interesting new problems, particularly in the Air Force. The aircraft that had been used in World War I were primitive and differed little from one model to another. They were biplanes (i.e., structured with two wings, one on top of the other) with simple controls for the throttle, the flaps, and the rudder. Some also had crudely mounted machine guns. Bombs were dropped over the side by hand. But in the two decades between the wars, tremendous advances had been made in aircraft and other tools of battle. There were many different types of aircraft: fighters, bombers, and transport planes, to name a few. And even *within* a type of aircraft, controls (flaps, landing gear, throttle) and displays (gauges and

---

SCIENTIFIC MANAGEMENT

A movement based on principles developed by Frederick W. Taylor; suggests there is one best and most efficient way to perform various jobs.

TIME AND MOTION STUDIES

Studies that broke every action down into its constituent parts, timed those movements with a stopwatch, and developed new and more efficient movements that would reduce fatigue and increase productivity.

REVERY OBSESSION

Australian psychologist Elton Mayo proposed that this mental state resulted from the mind-numbing, repetitive, and difficult work characterizing U.S. factories in the early 20th century, causing factory workers to be unhappy, prone to resist management attempts to increase productivity, and sympathetic to labor unions.

HAWTHORNE STUDIES

Research done at the Hawthorne, Illinois, plant of Western Electric that began as attempts to increase productivity by manipulating lighting, rest breaks, and work hours. Research showed the important role workers' attitudes played in productivity.

HUMAN RELATIONS MOVEMENT

The results of the Hawthorne studies ushered in this movement, which focused on work attitudes and the newly discovered emotional world of the worker.

dials that signaled airspeed or altitude) were located in different places. This meant that as pilots moved from one plane to another, they would encounter completely different cockpit configurations. This in turn led to an astounding number of crashes, many fatal, as pilots would mistakenly activate the landing gear instead of the flaps, or the flaps instead of the throttle. Applied psychologists suggested that cockpits be standardized with respect to the placement of displays and controls, and that controls be given unique shapes so that a pilot would know simply by grasping a control that it was the correct one. The landing gear control was to be shaped like a wheel or tire, and the flap control to feel like a flap would feel, and so forth. When these innovations were implemented, the resulting immediate reduction in accidents assured human engineering its place as a subarea of industrial psychology.

In the more traditional areas of I-O psychology, the war brought renewed interest in ability testing (to accurately place recruits in these new technologically advanced military jobs) as well as the introduction of the assessment center, a technique we will examine in the chapter on assessment. The Office of Strategic Services (OSS) was the department of the government charged with gathering and analyzing military intelligence. Part of its responsibility was to run a spy network to anticipate enemy strategies. Candidates for these spy positions were sent to a secluded farm near Washington, D.C.—hence the term, assessment "center" (Guion, 1998)—for extensive testing, which often took a week or longer. The testing consisted not only of interviews and paper and pencil tests, but "exercises" intended to determine which candidates could withstand the stress and rigors (often very physical) of working behind enemy lines. As it has been described, "To this end, they were sent over obstacle courses, attacked in stress interviews, and observed when they were falsely told that they had flunked out—the week was calculated to reveal every strength and weakness they might have" (Bray, Campbell, & Grant, 1974, p. 17). A well-known personality theorist, Henry Murray, was in charge of the assessment center for OSS; thus it is not surprising that personality attributes were central to the assessment exercises (Guion, 1998).

In both the United States and allied countries (e.g., England), the morale of war industry workers was a central concern, as well as the effects of fatigue on performance. In England, psychologists were particularly interested in munitions workers and conducted various studies to reduce fatigue and increase morale.

In contrast to the depression of the early 1930s, when employers were laying off workers rather than hiring them, and consequently had little interest in selection testing, the post–World War II years were a boom time for industry, with many jobs to be filled and applicants to be tested. Interestingly, however, when the war ended and the soldiers came back to work, there was an increasing trend toward labor unrest. Increasing numbers of authorized and unauthorized (sometimes called "wildcat" strikes) work stoppages were staged by unions and workers, and management was very concerned about the effect of these strikes on productivity. This was a period of unprecedented interest in worker attitude surveys. The results of these surveys were regularly published in business publications. There is no clear reason for this rapid increase in labor unrest. One might speculate that having faced death on the battlefields of Germany, France, Italy and the islands of the Pacific Ocean, workers were less likely to passively accept the decisions of organizations or their leaders.

By 1950, as employers realized that interests and attitudes and personality might be contributors to desirable outcomes such as productivity and workforce stability, a glut of tests had entered the market. The influx of new tests for selection continued unabated until the passage of the **Civil Rights Act of 1964.** The Civil Rights Act was written in sections, called "titles," with each title addressing a specific area of possible discrimination such as voting, education, or housing. The section dealing with employment discrimination was **Title VII** and it required employers to justify the use of tests for selection. If the test could not be shown to be related to job performance, and if a protected group (demographic groups specifically identified in the legislation, e.g., African Americans, Hispanics, women) tended to score lower on that test, on average, than the nonprotected group, resulting in fewer offers of employment, the test might be considered illegal. This

CIVIL RIGHTS
ACT OF 1964,
TITLE VII

Federal legislation that prohibits employment discrimination on the basis of race, color, religion, sex, or national origin, which define protected groups. Prohibits not only intentional discrimination, but also practices that have the unintentional effect of discriminating against individuals because of race, color, national origin, religion, or sex.

legislation revolutionized selection testing and led to the development of a broad base of technical knowledge about the characteristics of employment tests.

Defining a "historical" period is, to some extent, difficult and arbitrary. Nevertheless, the mid-1960s seems to mark a line of demarcation between "classic" and "modern" thinking. Because we will pick up on the continuing evolution of theory and practice in the chapters that follow, we will conclude our formal "history" section in this period of the mid-1960s. But we leave you with some generalizations that can be drawn from the early history of I-O psychology that point out important themes.

1. Mental ability tests have always played an important part in the practice of industrial psychology.
2. Most industrial psychologists were focused on improving productivity and reducing counterproductive behavior such as absenteeism and turnover.
3. There was a tendency to see the three different branches of I-O psychology as unrelated to, and possibly in competition with, one another to explain industrial behavior.
4. It was taken for granted that the unit of analysis was the individual worker rather than the work group, organization, or even culture.

We make these generalizations to highlight the difference between the I-O psychology of 1964 and the I-O psychology of today. Consider how those generalizations above would change to be applicable today.

1. Mental ability is only one of a number of important attributes that play a role in the practice of I-O psychology.
2. While many I-O psychologists continue to address issues of productivity and efficiency, others explore issues of worker well-being, work–family balance, and the experience of work by workers.
3. I-O psychologists see the three major branches of the discipline as complementary rather than independent or antagonistic. I-O psychologists take a systems view of work behavior and acknowledge that there are many individual, social, work environment, and organizational variables that interact to produce behavior at the workplace.
4. The worker is one level of analysis, but the work group, the organization, and even the culture represent additional and valuable levels of analysis.

In the chapters that follow, we will trace the evolution of I-O psychology from what it was in 1964 to what it is today. It is our hope that this will provide a foundation for understanding how the science of I-O psychology will continue to evolve over your lifetime.

THE CHALLENGES TO I-O PSYCHOLOGY IN THE 21ST CENTURY

As we have seen, there are many opportunities for I-O psychology to contribute to employers, workers, and the broader society in which we live. To make these contributions, I-O psychology needs to meet three challenges.

• *I-O psychology needs to be relevant.* This means that we need to study the problems of today, not those of yesterday. At this time, relevance means addressing problems of globalization of the economy, increasing technological evolution of the workplace, team and group contributions rather than exclusively individual contributions, and the balance of work and nonwork. That is not to say that earlier research was misguided or "wrong" but rather that older research gives us a foundation for newer research and application.

• *I-O psychology needs to be useful.* I-O psychology, like counseling, school/educational, and clinical psychology, is an applied subdiscipline. The value the discipline adds is in putting our theories and research findings into action. I-O psychologists must always be thinking of ways to put our research into practice.

- *I-O psychology needs to be grounded in the scientific method.* The confidence that society has in I-O psychology depends on this. Careful and systematic observation, the development of hypotheses that can be tested, the public collection and analysis of data, and a logical connection between the data and the interpretations of these data are the bases for our "reputation" in research and practice. Beginning in the early 1990s, the courts have become more exacting about what testimony will be accepted as "scientific." This is further evidence of the importance of science and the scientific method in the larger world.

MODULE 1.1 SUMMARY

- Work is important because it occupies much of our time, provides us with a livelihood, and defines how we feel about ourselves. "Good work" enables workers to develop and use skills to benefit others.
- I-O psychology applies psychological principles, theory, and research to the workplace and to all aspects of life that are touched by work. SIOP, APA, and APS are the primary professional membership organizations for I-O psychologists.

- I-O psychology began with studies of industrial efficiency and individual differences. The latter led to mental ability tests. The Hawthorne Studies prompted the study of workers' emotions. Human engineering came to prominence during World War II. Title VII of the Civil Rights Act of 1964 required employers to justify testing and other policies in terms of equal opportunity.
- I-O psychology in the 21st century needs to be relevant, useful, and grounded in the scientific method.

KEY TERMS

industrial-organizational (I-O) psychology

Society for Industrial and Organizational Psychology (SIOP)

personnel psychology

human resources management (HRM)

organizational psychology

human engineering or human factors psychology

American Psychological Association (APA)

TIP (The Industrial-Organizational Psychologist)

Stanford-Binet test

Scientific Management

time and motion studies

revery obsession

Hawthorne studies

Human Relations Movement

Civil Rights Act of 1964 Title VII

CRITICAL THINKING EXERCISES

1.1 Industrial safety is a great concern for auto assembly plants. Identify a method of improving safety from each of the three areas of I-O psychology.

Personnel Psychology:

Organizational Psychology:

Human Factors Psychology:

1.2 Consider the distinctions between I-O psychology of 1964 and I-O psychology of today, as summarized on p. 15. Now read the following multiple choice question, identify what you consider to be the correct answer, and explain that answer.

The major difference between the I-O psychology of 1964 and modern I-O psychology is:

a. Assessing mental ability is no longer important to I-O psychologists

b. The social nature of work is more important now than it was in 1964

c. Work was less central in the lives of workers in 1964; work is now a more central part of everyone's life

d. Productivity, absenteeism, and turnover are no longer important areas for research and practice in I-O psychology

HOW THIS COURSE CAN HELP YOU

KNOWLEDGE ABOUT THE 21ST-CENTURY WORKPLACE

Working is a part of almost everyone's life. Outside of the classroom, you will likely do what most other people do: spend 50 percent or more of your waking weekday hours at work. This means that a course in I-O should benefit you in several ways. First, it can help you understand what you are experiencing in the workplace. You will have a basis for knowing if the human resource (HR) policies your organization follows are new or old, tested or untested, likely to be effective or ineffective. Second, chances are that you will eventually be placed in the position of managing the work of others, and in that role either developing or at least implementing work-related policies. The material of this course and the text itself should provide you with a good foundation for developing and/or implementing effective policies. Third, you will hear secondhand about the joys and frustrations of friends and family with their organizations and work. Many of them will not have the understanding gained from a course like the one you are taking now. You will be able to act as a resource in helping them understand the policies that are affecting them.

You will see another benefit from this course that goes beyond the relationship of you or your friends and relatives to a particular organization or job. There are national debates that relate to work. As a result of having taken this course, you will be better informed about many of the issues that form these debates than your colleagues or relatives. As examples of the debates that are currently on the table, consider the following:

1. Is employment discrimination old news or is it still occurring? If it is occurring, who are its most common victims? To the extent that it is occurring, what steps can be taken to reduce it? What are the various steps that comprise an employment discrimination lawsuit?

2. How serious is the issue of stress in the workplace? How can workplace stress affect the rest of your life? Is stress a legitimate "disease"? Can it be considered as an occupational hazard? How can stress be reduced at work?

3. Are workplaces generally "safe"? What is the responsibility of the worker and what is the responsibility of the employer for creating and maintaining safety at the workplace? Is repetitive motion injury/syndrome real or just imagined? Can work ever be made safer?

4. How can the jobless be brought back into the workforce? How effective are **welfare-to-work programs,** which require work in return for government subsidies? What can be done to increase the probability that a welfare recipient of today will be the full-time employee of tomorrow? If the government proposes to pay welfare recipients less than

The need for work-family balance is a central concern for many of today's workers.

the minimum wage in return for their "work" requirement, will this help or hinder the passage from welfare to work?

5. To what extent should work and nonwork lives be kept separate? Should working parents expect their employing organizations to provide family-friendly workplaces? In households with two wage earners, how can both partners lead productive and satisfying work lives yet still maintain a productive and satisfying relationship with each other?

6. Do foreign-based companies actually have better methods of production, or are they more profitable simply because they pay their workers less? Is there any value to U.S. employers in adopting the work practices of other countries, or should we stick with what has made America great? Should everyone working for an American company, either in the United States or in another country, be expected to accept American culture as part of the work environment?

These are just some of the debates that you will see in any newspaper or on any television news program over the course of several months. When you have finished this course, you will have a knowledge base to discuss these and similar issues responsibly. That does not mean that you can solve these problems, but it does mean that you will have something sensible and unique to add to the discussion.

You may also have discussions with others who have taken a course like this, perhaps your parents, co-workers, or managers. If they have not taken this course in the last 5 to 10 years, they may be working from an outdated experience and knowledge base. Just consider how the world has changed since, say, the 1980s.

- Personal computers and the phenomenon of digitization (turning information into data coded as "1" or "0") now dominate the workplace.

TELECOMMUTING

Arrangement that allows employees to do their work from home or other locations.

VIRTUAL TEAM

Team that has widely dispersed members working together toward a common goal and linked through computers and other technology.

- Many workers do their work from home (**telecommute**), and many work groups and work teams are located in many different offices and work as **virtual teams,** seldom if ever meeting physically as a group.
- Client meetings, organizational meetings, and training are conducted through the videoconferencing mode.
- Work performance can be monitored electronically.
- Three out of every five jobs are now directly or indirectly providing a service rather than manufacturing "goods."
- Increasingly more work is done by teams as opposed to individuals.
- There is little stability in many business sectors. Downsizing, rightsizing, mergers, and acquisitions have radically altered the psychological contract between an organization and its employees.
- Workers are expecting greater recognition and support from their organizations with respect to creating and maintaining family-friendly workplaces.
- Workforces are becoming increasingly diverse, and not only in terms of age, gender, race, and disability. These demographic variables represent an increasing diversity of interests, values, attitudes, and cultures.
- The nature of work has become more fluid, where jobs may not be well defined, tasks may not be routine, and the groups assigned to tasks may vary in their type and number of people.
- Work is now international or global.

As the automobile ad proclaims, "This is not your father's Oldsmobile." The information you derive from this course will be substantially different from what your parents' generation learned in a similar course.

PREPARING FOR A CAREER IN I-O

We assume that most of the students who take this course are doing so to fulfill a requirement for their major or an elective. We also assume that a small percentage will decide to go to graduate school for further training in HR or I-O psychology. The following section is written for those who plan to pursue postgraduate training.

Education and Training

To call yourself an I-O psychologist, you will need to pursue either a master's degree or a PhD. If you expect to practice (as opposed to teach) I-O psychology, virtually all states also require that you possess a license to practice under the heading of a professional psychologist. Fewer I-O psychologists are licensed than clinical or counseling psychologists, in part because what is being licensed is the use of the term "psychologist" rather than what is actually done. Thus, an individual doing HR consulting may not need a professional license. The licensing requirements vary by state, and all require some form of advanced degree. In addition, many require a period of supervised practice. The SIOP website provides a good general description of these licensing requirements, as well as contact information for each state's licensing body. It is clear that licensing is necessary to protect the public from untrained or poorly prepared therapists in clinical and counseling psychology. It is not so clear in the area of I-O, since I-O psychologists are not really health care providers in the same way. I-O psychologists are almost always retained by organizations rather than by single individuals, and most organizations have professionals within their ranks who can distinguish between the trained and untrained I-O psychologist. Individual members of the public considering using the services of a therapist are less able to make such distinctions. Licensure is currently a "hot" topic among I-O psychologists and you can follow this debate on the SIOP website.

Advanced training in I-O psychology is widely available, both in the United States and abroad. The SIOP website provides a list of those programs as well as links to many of them. Some programs offer only a PhD, some offer either a PhD or a master's degree, and some offer only a master's degree (often called a "terminal" master's degree). We have listed all current I-O programs in *The Student Study Guide and Workbook*.

The SIOP website also provides an elaborate description of the type of curriculum you will encounter, as well as a list of the skills and competencies which would be expected of a master's or PhD candidate to qualify for graduation.

Getting into a Graduate Program

There is no "standard" process by which departments choose students, but it's generally the case that students are admitted only once a year, in the fall. All programs will examine both your overall grade point average (GPA) and the GPA you achieved in your major. Most programs will also examine your last two years independently of your overall GPA. They want to know how you did once you chose and became committed to a major. Most programs will place some emphasis on your Graduate Record Examination (GRE) scores (both general and advanced). They will also examine how many courses you took in I-O, statistics, tests and measurements, and possibly relevant courses in the business school, and other programs such as sociology and labor studies. There is usually an emphasis on a background in statistics, since you will need to be comfortable with a wide range of statistics to understand much of the published I-O research. At the very least, you will be expected to have done well in the basic descriptive and inferential statistics course offered at your school. Additional statistics and research methods courses will make you a more attractive candidate.

In many programs, there is no requirement that you be a psychology major. The emphasis is on exactly what courses you have taken (and, of course, your grades in those courses) rather than the major you chose. All programs will expect letters of reference from knowledgeable faculty. You may also solicit letters from nonfaculty sources, but they should address skills that you will need in an I-O graduate program (e.g., communication skills, research skills, statistical experience, relevant work experience).

There are some additional "credentials" which you can accumulate to improve your chances of admission. If you have had experience as a research assistant to one of your professors as an undergraduate, that will be noticed and considered favorably. If that experience was in an I-O or testing area, or involved statistical analysis or data gathering, it will be viewed even more favorably. A second valuable credential is an internship at a local management or I-O consulting firm, or in the HR department of a local business. These are experiences you may want to actively seek out if you plan to apply to graduate programs.

Since a critical ingredient for success in a graduate program is the "fit" between the program and the student, it is a good idea to make a personal visit to the universities you are considering, if possible. Although you may not be able to meet with all of the faculty members of the program, you can certainly meet some of their current students and get a sense for the fit between you and the program. If you are unable to visit, ask each program for the names and phone numbers of current students who can answer some of your questions and give you a feel for the program. In addition, most graduate programs have websites (many listed on the SIOP website) that will allow you to make a "virtual" visit to the campus. Some I-O grad programs (e.g., George Mason University, Bowling Green State University) also have newsletters. Ask for copies of any available newsletters to do further research on the program. If you visit a campus, it is a good idea to read the research articles and books written by the I-O faculty of that program before you go. See what their interests are and, if you can, set up a meeting with one or more of the faculty. This will enable you to get a better idea of their areas of interest, and give them a chance to get to know something about you.

One final piece of advice: If you choose to build up your credentials after graduation but before formally applying to a graduate program, consider taking classes as a nondegree student. At some universities, you can do this as long as you have a bachelor's degree. If you are permitted to take those graduate courses and do well in them, you will have a track record at the graduate level and can make a strong case for your subsequent admission based on your demonstrated competence to do graduate work. In addition, you will have the opportunity to work with the same faculty who make the admissions decisions, thus transforming yourself from an unknown to a known quantity. Even if you decide not to pursue a graduate degree in I-O psychology, you may find one or more graduate courses (taken as a nondegree student) valuable in your career.

MODULE 1.2 SUMMARY

- In this course you will gain knowledge about the workplace, work-related issues, and the ways that work has changed over recent decades.
- To call yourself an I-O psychologist you need to earn a graduate degree and, in many jurisdictions, obtain a license. SIOP provides information about licensing requirements.

- To be admitted to a graduate program, it is advantageous to do well in statistics and methods courses, obtain strong letters of recommendation, and gain experience as a research assistant or as an intern with a management or I-O consulting firm.

KEY TERMS

welfare-to-work program
telecommuting
virtual team

CRITICAL THINKING EXERCISE

1.3 A friend who received his undergraduate degree in political science last year is visiting you. He picks up your I-O textbook and becomes interested in the topics. He asks you what he has to do to become an I-O psychologist. What steps will you recommend?

MULTICULTURAL AND CROSS-CULTURAL ISSUES IN I-O PSYCHOLOGY

MULTICULTURALISM

There are some pretty dramatic differences between the world you know and the world your parents experienced when they were your age. You might immediately think of technological differences, but equally dramatic are the "people" differences. In the course of a day, you will encounter a wide range of nationalities—possibly East African, Israeli, Russian, Mexican, Pakistani, Japanese, Chinese, or Dutch, just to mention a few. In earlier years, you would have expected to encounter this diversity in New York City, or London. Now you are just as likely to see this diversity in almost any medium- to large-sized city in the United States and even more so in educational settings.

Nationalities can be thought of as boxcars. In and of itself, a nationality is simply a geographic reality. You claim a nation as your country of birth—you were born in the United States, or Russia, or Thailand, or India. Your nationality, like a boxcar, has importance only because it carries important psychological material. Geographers, economists, and political scientists may be interested in nationality per se, but psychologists are concerned with the behavioral implications of nationality. Perhaps the most important material for a psychologist is **culture.** A culture can be defined as a "system in which individuals share meanings and common ways of viewing events and objects" (Ronen, 1997). It is culture that distinguishes people more than nationality. For example, you might sit next to someone on a plane going from Denver to Chicago and strike up a conversation. If you were to ask your seatmate where she was from and she said, "the U.S.," you wouldn't know much more than before you asked. But if she said New Orleans, Detroit, or Austin, you might very well follow up with a question or comment about the food, music, or politics of her home city or state. When you do that, you have begun to address cultural similarities and differences between yourself and your seatmate.

In I-O psychology, some of the most obvious cultural differences we need to address are related to nationalities. As you saw above, the definition of culture emphasizes the *sharing* of meanings and interpretations. This highlights the opportunity for people to bring *different* meanings and interpretations to an event or an object. This is why a recognition of culture's influence is so important for I-O psychology. As the world of work brings together people of many different nationalities (and, more important, cultures), the opportunities for misunderstandings and ineffective or counterproductive human resource applications grow as a function of the number of different cultures grows.

A brief example of culture in the classroom might help to make the issue of culture more concrete (Aguinis & Roth, 2002). Imagine that instead of your current instructor, your instructor in this course was a well-known Taiwanese professor of I-O psychology.

CULTURE

A system in which individuals share meanings and common ways of viewing events and objects.

This psychologist had never taught in the United States before but spoke excellent English. Imagine that this instructor engaged in the following behaviors:

1. Changed the syllabus for the course frequently throughout the term without warning or explanation.
2. Read lectures directly from notes.
3. Would not accept any questions from students during the class period.
4. Expected unquestioning deference and respect both in and out of the classroom.

In most American classrooms, the Taiwanese scholar might not fare very well. He might be viewed as arbitrary, imperious, and poorly prepared. Yet in most traditional Taiwanese college classrooms, his behavior would be considered appropriate. Similarly, if you were an American student in a traditional Taiwanese college classroom, other students and the instructor might be horrified if you challenged the instructor on a point he or she had made, or expressed any personal feelings or emotions on a topic. These would be examples of the clash between the American and Taiwanese cultures. Without an understanding of the differences in culture, you might interpret the same actions very differently.

THE MULTICULTURAL NATURE OF WORK IN THE 21ST CENTURY

Consider the following facts:

- More than 100,000 U.S. companies are involved in worldwide ventures that are worth over $1 trillion; U.S. corporations have invested more than $400 billion abroad and employ more than 60 million overseas workers (Cascio, 1998).
- One in five American jobs is tied directly or indirectly to international trade; foreigners hold top management positions in one-third of large U.S. firms and Americans hold similar positions in one-fourth of European-based firms (Cascio, 1998).
- The demise of the former Soviet Union and the development of the European Union has led to mass movements of people across borders.
- Economic blocs have formed enabling easy movement of the goods and people of one nation to another. These blocs include the North American Free Trade Agreement (NAFTA), Southern Cone Common Market (MERCOSUR), the European Union (EU), the Association of Southeast Asian Nations (ASEAN), and the Economic Community of West African States (ECOWAS) (Aguinis & Henle, 2002).

The facts above define what has come to be called the global economy. It is no longer possible for any country, regardless of size, to exist without economic connections with other countries. To be sure, there have always been "connections" between countries, but they usually shared a border or a culture. Now, connections are much wider, more complex, and more intense.

For the I-O psychologist, the importance of this connectedness is that it brings many different cultures into contact with one another at the workplace. The challenge then becomes one of developing systems (e.g., training, motivation, or reward) that will be compatible with so many different ways of viewing objects or events, that is, compatible with so many different cultures. For example, American workers might expect individual rewards for outstanding performance, while Japanese or Swedish workers might consider them insulting. Conversely, group or team rewards would be compatible with Swedish or Japanese cultures, yet considered inappropriate for American workers (Fulkerson & Tucker, 1999). Consider that almost *half* of McDonald's restaurants are located outside the United

As more corporations employ workers in foreign countries, work in the 21st century is increasingly a global concept.

States (Cascio, 1998). Developing a uniform human resource system for such a diverse workforce is a challenge for the U.S.-based central management. The key to meeting this challenge is understanding culture.

Why Should Multiculturalism Be Important to You?

It seems clear that living and working in a multicultural environment is part of the definition of the 21st century. Not only are we exposed to multiple national cultures, but there are multiple domestic cultures to experience as well. These domestic cultures (or subcultures) are defined by age, gender, race, disability, geographic region, education, or even leisure pursuits (K. M. Thomas, 1998). And many of these cultures and subcultures overlap and interact with each other, resulting in even greater complexity (Brett, Tinsely, Janssens, Barsness, & Lytle, 1996). Consider the overlapping cultures represented by a 52-year-old Pakistani chemical engineer, who is also vegetarian, female, Christian, New York City resident, and a marathon runner; or a 27-year-old African-American male police officer who plays the cello in his spare time, is a Jehovah's Witness, and lives in Boise, Idaho.

In your working life, it is a virtual certainty that you will come in contact with co-workers, superiors, subordinates, clients, and vendors who have cultural values and beliefs different from your own. For that reason, you need to understand not only the fact that cultures *do* differ systematically, but also *how* they may differ.

As a student in I-O courses, it will also be useful for you to recognize the importance of cultural differences to what is examined in field and laboratory research. In many of the leading I-O psychology and human resource management (HRM) publications, the subjects are most commonly American, the context of the research is American, and the outcomes or results of the research are interpreted for application to the American context. There is nothing necessarily wrong with limiting research investigations to uniquely American situations and problems. But it is important to remember that these results may not always generalize to non-American cultures, particularly since many of those cultures are considerably more homogeneous than is true of the United States. And many, if not most, of those cultures have been around considerably longer than their younger American counterpart.

Why Is Multiculturalism Important for I-O Psychology?

Although I-O psychology is distinct from other areas of psychology, it does share some values with all areas. Multiculturalism is one of those. Consider the following reasons for valuing a multicultural psychology in general (Fowers & Richardson, 1996), and notice how they fit with the goals of I-O psychology in particular.

1.   Definitions of psychology usually include the phrase "the scientific study of human behavior," which implies that human behavior in all parts of the world must be investigated, not just those aspects of behavior conveniently available to investigators in highly industrialized nations (Triandis & Brislin, 1984). I-O psychology should be just as interested in theories of work motivation or personnel selection as they apply to cultures other than the United States as they are in U.S. applications.

2.   Psychology has tried hard to be color blind and in the process has "perpetuated racism in blinding us to the discrimination that is an everyday experience for members of minority groups . . . This color blind approach . . . does not recognize authentic differences that are defining features of identity" (Fowers & Richardson, 1996).

There is a continual attempt in the American workplace (and in other American settings, such as educational institutions) to deny that there are any cultural differences between (or even among) men and women, or whites, Hispanics, and blacks. Similarly, U.S.-based multinational corporations often attempt to apply a "one-size-fits-all" mentality to human resource practices in all of their locations throughout the world.

3.   Multiculturalism promotes diversity and diversity is enriching (Fowers & Richardson, 1996).

As we will see throughout the textbook, non-American scholars have proposed many excellent theories of work behavior based on research with non-American workers. These theories are valuable for application not only in the United States, but also by U.S. multinational corporations in foreign countries.

Although both the I-O psychology and HRM fields are beginning to recognize the importance of a multicultural foundation for understanding work behavior, the recognition has come mostly in the form of applications devoid of theory. A case in point has been the problem of **expatriates:** American managers and professionals assigned to work in locations outside the United States. A great deal of expense and effort is involved in getting an expatriate settled in a new location. If the expatriate is not successful in that new location, the parent organization has wasted a considerable financial investment, in addition to losing productivity and goodwill in the new location. Many expatriates fail because they cannot or will not adapt to the culture of the new location (including colleagues and subordinates). As a result, expatriate selection and training has become a booming area for practice and has inspired many effective programs.

It is only recently that the I-O literature has begun to include research of a theoretical nature concerning expatriate success. Some examples include applications of personality

EXPATRIATES

Managers or professionals assigned to work in a location outside their home country.

theory (Ones & Viswesvaran, 1999; Caligiuri, 2000), models of the adjustment of the expatriate's spouse to relocation (Shaffer & Harrison, 2001), and feelings of fairness held by the expatriate (Garonzik, Brockner, & Siegel, 2000). Several of these studies have demonstrated the value of using personality factors such as emotional stability and tolerance for novel experiences for the selection of expatriates. Interestingly, many of these theoretical developments may also serve the purpose of understanding the broader issues of relocation, even relocation within the United States.

American scholars and researchers have dominated many areas of psychology since the discipline began almost 125 years ago. Although these psychologists have contributed many genuine advances, a certain insularity has characterized American psychology as well. This has been particularly true in applied areas such as I-O psychology. In applied psychology, research and theory tends to flow *from* "problem" areas rather than anticipating them. As a result, researchers have tended to develop theories that are relevant to U.S. situations, with less concern about their applicability in other countries. Hermans and Kempen (1998) have dubbed this the **"West versus the Rest" mentality.** Not surprisingly, attempts to apply American theories to non-American situations are not always successful. It appears that culture may actually determine (or "moderate") the effectiveness of an HRM initiative (Earley & Erez, 1997). This is important information because it provides a road map for modifying a theory developed in one culture for application to a different culture.

"WEST VERSUS THE REST" MENTALITY

Tendency for researchers to develop theories relevant to U.S. situations, with less concern given to their applicability in other countries.

A THEORY OF CULTURAL INFLUENCE

It does not necessarily take a behavioral scientist to realize that principles or strategies that apply in one culture might not apply in another. But it does take a behavioral scientist to understand *why* they may not apply. By understanding the "why," we are actually understanding the meaning and importance of that cultural variable. To return to our example, a manager may realize that individual rewards seem ineffective in Japan but effective in the United States. But that manager may not understand the underlying principle: The Japanese culture is a **collectivist culture** that values the group more than the individual. The U.S. culture is an **individualist culture** that values the individual more than the group. By understanding the underlying cultural principle, and gaining the ability to place other cultures on the collectivist–individualist continuum, the manager might be able to design effective reward schemes for operations elsewhere, for example, in Germany, Thailand, or Egypt.

COLLECTIVIST CULTURE

A culture that values the group more than the individual.

INDIVIDUALIST CULTURE

A culture that values the individual more than the group.

Hofstede's Theory

As you might expect, culture is more complex than a single continuum like individualist–collectivist. As a result of some pioneering research by a Dutch researcher Geert Hofstede (1980, 2001), we know a good deal about the defining characteristics of culture, particularly culture at the workplace. Hofstede distributed questionnaires to IBM employees worldwide between 1968 and 1972, and more than 116,000 employees from 72 countries returned them. In his continuing analysis of those data, he has developed a theory that proposes five basic elements on which cultures can be distinguished. Think of each of these elements like a continuum stretching from one pole to another. As an example, think of the individualist–collectivist continuum discussed in the previous paragraph. Indeed, the *individualism/collectivism* continuum was one of the primary aspects of culture that Hofstede uncovered. The five elements are presented and defined in Table 1.5. These can almost be thought of as the "personality" of a nationality. This is the essence of what a culture is: a "collective psyche." The importance of Hofstede's

TABLE 1.5	**The Five Dimensions of Hofstede's Theory of Culture**

- **Individualism/collectivism:** the degree to which individuals are expected to look after themselves versus remaining integrated into groups (usually the family).
- **Power distance:** the degree to which less powerful members of an organization accept and expect an unequal distribution of power.
- **Uncertainty avoidance:** the extent to which members of a culture feel comfortable in unstructured situations.
- **Masculinity/femininity:** the distribution of emotional roles between the genders with the masculine role being seen as "tough" and the feminine role as being "tender"; masculine cultures tend to emphasize accomplishment and technical performance while feminine cultures tend to emphasize interpersonal relationships and communication.
- **Long-term versus short-term orientation:** the extent to which members of a culture expect immediate versus delayed gratification of their material, social, and emotional needs.

SOURCE: Adapted from *Culture's Consequences: International Differences in Work-Related Values,* by G. Hofstede, 2001, Thousand Oaks, CA: Sage.

theory for I-O psychology is substantial. In the last several decades, Hofstede has refined his theory to address specific aspects of the workplace. By examining each of the five dimensions of culture, he has been able to propose suggested characteristics of cultures that fall on one or the other end of his cultural continua and the relationship of these characteristics to work behavior. Table 1.6 presents Hofstede's characterizations. As you can see, each of the five dimensions has implications for the workplace. One can also take the dimensions of culture, as proposed by Hofstede, and compare and contrast various countries to see which are alike and which are different. Such a comparison appears in Figure 1.3. This means, for example, that if a particular HR strategy is relatively compatible with the American culture (high individualism, low power distance, high masculinity, low uncertainty avoidance, low long-term orientation), it might also be effective in the German culture (although Germany is somewhat higher in uncertainty avoidance and long-term orientation); but is less likely to be effective in a Chinese culture (high collectivism, high power distance, and so forth). It is equally important to realize that what might work in a German culture, might also work in an American culture. This provides an additional reason for being aware of non-American research and theory.

Noe et al. (2001) provide additional applications of the Hofstede theory in contrasting countries. They make the following observations:

- *Individualism/collectivism.* In countries such as the United States, Great Britain, and the Netherlands, individuals tend to show greater concern for themselves and their families than for the community; in Columbia, Pakistan, and Taiwan, greater concern is expressed for the community than for the individual.

- *Power distance.* Denmark and Israel seek to reduce inequalities in power, while India and the Philippines accept and maintain such power distances.

- *Uncertainty avoidance.* The cultures of Singapore and Jamaica accept uncertainty and take one day at a time, but Greek and Portuguese cultures seek certainty.

- *Masculinity/femininity.* In masculine cultures such as the United States, Japan, and Germany, performance, success, and accumulated wealth are important, but in feminine

INDIVIDUALISM/ COLLECTIVISM

The degree to which individuals are expected to look after themselves versus remaining integrated into groups.

POWER DISTANCE

The degree to which less powerful members of an organization accept and expect an unequal distribution of power.

UNCERTAINTY AVOIDANCE

The extent to which members of a culture feel comfortable in unpredictable situations.

MASCULINITY/ FEMININITY

The distribution of emotional roles between genders with the masculine role seen as "tough" and the feminine role seen as "tender."

LONG-TERM VERSUS SHORT-TERM ORIENTATION

The extent to which members of a culture expect immediate rather than delayed gratification of their material, social, and emotional needs.

| TABLE 1.6 | The Implications of Cultural Dimensions for Human Resource Management |

DIMENSION	HRM IMPLICATION
High power distance	Centralized decision making
	Many supervisors per employee
	Autocratic leadership
Low power distance	Decentralized decision making
	Few supervisors per employee
	Participative leadership
High uncertainty avoidance	Accepting of technical solutions
	Strong loyalty to employer
	Innovators constrained by rules
Low uncertainty avoidance	Skeptical of technical solutions
	Weak loyalty to employer
	Innovators not constrained by rules
High individualism	Employees act in their individual interest
	Poor performance a legitimate reason for dismissal
	Training focused at individual level
Low individualism	Employees act in the interest of their in-group
	Poor performance a legitimate reason for reassignment of tasks
	Training focused at group level
High masculine	Fewer women in professional/technical jobs
	Pressure toward traditional gender roles
	Men describe themselves as more competitive than women do
Low masculine	More women in professional/technical jobs
	Nontraditional gender roles more common
	Women describe themselves as more competitive than men do
High long-term orientation	Building relationships and market position valued
	Ordinary human relations source of satisfaction
	Deferred gratification of needs accepted
Low long-term orientation	Short-term results and bottom line valued
	Daily human relations not a source of satisfaction
	Immediate gratification of needs expected

SOURCE: Hofstede, 2001.

cultures such as Sweden, Norway, and the Netherlands, people, relationships, and the environment are more important than wealth and accomplishment.

• *Long-term versus Short-term Orientation.* Cultures with a short-term orientation, such as the United States and Russia, focus on the past and present and honor tradition. Conversely, countries like Japan and China tend to have a long-term orientation and are not nearly as concerned with immediate benefit as they are with thrift and persistence.

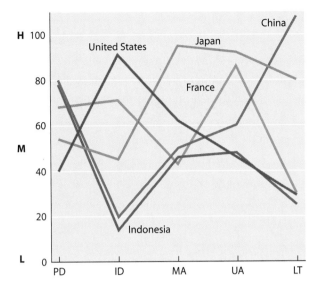

FIGURE 1.3

Cultural Differences among Countries
SOURCE: Hofstede, 1993, p. 91.

In applying Hofstede's theory of cultural determination to the workplace, Noe, Hollenbeck, Gerhart, and Wright (2001) identified several reasons why managers ought to be sensitive to culture.

- Cultures differ strongly on how subordinates expect leaders to lead and what motivates individuals; therefore the selection and training of managers should vary across cultures.
- Cultures influence human resource practices. For example, in the United States hiring decisions depend heavily on an applicant's technical skills, while in collectivist cultures such as Japan, much more emphasis is placed on how well the individual will fit into a group.
- Compensation policies vary greatly across cultures. In the United States, the highest paid individual in a company may earn 200 times more than the lowest paid individual. In collectivist cultures, the highest paid individual rarely earns more than 20 times the compensation of the lowest paid individual.
- In collectivist cultures, group decision making is more highly valued, but in individualist cultures, individual decision making is more the norm. This type of cultural discrepancy will inevitably lead to problems in communication and decision making when an individual who shares one culture is placed into work groups or work settings with individuals from another culture.

If diversity is to produce the anticipated economic and intellectual rewards, managers must be aware of the various cultures operating in the workplace and be prepared to provide the training and support necessary to join those cultures productively. We will consider the topic of workplace diversity in greater detail in a later chapter. The point to keep in mind here is that diversity comes with a cost. It may very well bring about cultural clashes and conflict. Nevertheless, the benefits are likely to outweigh the costs.

Some Thoughts on Theories of Cultural Influence

Hofstede's theory is not the only theory of cultural influence. Triandis (1995; Triandis & Bhawuk 1997) suggested a variation on Hofstede's dimension of individualism/collectivism—that is, a horizontal/vertical dimension interacts with individualism/collectivism yielding a 2 × 2 matrix (see Figure 1.4). **Horizontal cultures** are those which minimize distances between individuals (much like Hofstede's power distance dimension) while **vertical cultures** accept and depend on those distances.

HORIZONTAL CULTURE

A culture that minimizes distances between individuals.

VERTICAL CULTURE

A culture that accepts and depends upon distances between individuals.

FIGURE 1.4

**Triandis's View
of Cultural
Determinants in
the Workplace**

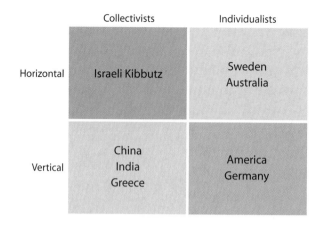

Most theories of cultural influence have incorporated the individualism/collectivism dimension of Hofstede in one way or another (e.g., Trompenaars & Hampden-Turner, 1998), and it appears that this dimension will be the backbone of any future theories. But Hofstede's analysis was conducted by averaging the responses of all respondents from a given country and assigning that average as the country value on the dimension. Thus, we really have a theory of countries, not individuals. It is vitally important to realize that within a country, not all individuals share the same culture. As we will see in Chapter 14 on organizations, the extent to which values are shared varies across work groups and has an effect on the behavior of each group. Thus, while Hofstede's theory may describe a country's average belief system, that belief system is not necessarily universal—or even prevalent—in that country. As an example, the Honda of America Corporation has four production plants in Ohio. Those plants have adopted a collectivist, low power distance, feminine, long-term orientation culture much as one might expect to see in Japan. Here is a Japanese culture embedded in the heartland of America. The entire Honda organization, regardless of where a plant may be, applies this culture and trains all of its employees in it with successful results.

Keep in mind that cultural variables represent only one of the many influences on work behavior. Other influences include individual skills and motivation, managerial skills, leadership behaviors, HRM practices, and other individual and group variables. Nevertheless, culture is a key factor in appreciating the complexity of the modern workplace. It is important to acknowledge that psychology is neither sociology nor anthropology. I-O psychology focuses on the *perception* of the culture by the individual worker, not necessarily any "objective" measure of culture. While mainstream I-O psychology has only recently acknowledged the importance of culture in work behavior (Earley & Erez, 1997; Kraut & Korman, 1999), we can predict that its role in the new global definition of work will become more obvious in the next decade. We will remind you of the issue of culture as it applies in the chapters that follow.

MODULE 1.3 SUMMARY

- Culture is a system of shared meanings and ways of viewing events and things.
- The global economy has made it important for all countries to foster economic connections with others.
- It is important for I-O psychologists to recognize and study the multiplicity of cultural factors that influence workplace behavior.

- Individualism/collectivism, power distance, uncertainty avoidance, masculinity/femininity, and long-term versus short-term orientation are key considerations in describing and characterizing various cultures.

KEY TERMS

culture

expatriates

"West versus the Rest" mentality

collectivist culture

individualist culture

individualism/collectivism

power distance

uncertainty avoidance

masculinity/femininity

long-term versus short-term orientation

horizontal culture

vertical culture

CRITICAL THINKING EXERCISES

1.4 Ben & Jerry's Homemade, Inc., the Vermont-based manufacturer of ice cream, frozen yogurt, and sorbet, is known for having a rule that the compensation for the highest paid employee (i.e., the CEO) could not be more than seven times the pay of the lowest paid employee. Applying Hofstede's model of cultural influence, which of the five dimensions was most closely related to this rule? Justify your answer.

1.5 Hofstede used five distinct dimensions to describe culture. For each of the following statements, agree or disagree and identify which of Hofstede's dimensions supports your answer.

- Greek workers will be more threatened by the possibility of downsizing than workers in Singapore.
- A kibbutz is just as likely to work in India as in Israel.
- American citizens are more likely than Swedish citizens to argue against applying an estate tax to the assets of someone who dies.

1.4 MODULE

THE ORGANIZATION OF THIS BOOK

Themes

Several themes run through the chapters of this book. They will be more apparent in some chapters than others. The first theme is one of a unified science of industrial and organizational psychology. Unified means several things in this context. First, to truly understand work behavior we must be willing to consider and acknowledge the interplay of many different approaches. For example, when we consider the issue of safety in the workplace, we could consider the individual strategies for creating a safe workplace embodied in the personnel, organizational, or human engineering approaches. The personnel approach would suggest selecting people who are likely to act in safe ways and then training them in those ways. The organizational approach might suggest rewarding people for safe behavior and reducing stress in the workplace. The engineering approach might endorse modifying the environment, equipment, and work procedures to eliminate the hazards associated with common accidents, as well as creating and maintaining a climate of safety in individual work groups. The unified approach means not preferring one or another of these approaches, but realizing that all approaches are useful and can be skillfully applied, either individually or in combination depending on the situation at hand. We will apply the same theme of unity to the many other topics you will encounter in the book.

"Unified" has another meaning in our treatment of I-O psychology. It means that research and theories from non-American researchers are just as valuable to understanding work behavior as the work by American researchers. We will freely discuss the work of our colleagues in other countries and combine it with what has been learned in the United States to develop a broader and deeper understanding of work behavior. As you read in Module 1.3, all workers and work have been globalized, whether or not they embraced the concept of globalization. As a result, in many instances the research of a single country will not be sufficient to understand the behavior of workers in that country or any other. So we will present you with the best thoughts of those who study work behavior, regardless of the country in which it is studied.

The second theme that will be apparent in our treatment is a holistic theme. By this we mean that we cannot and should not try to understand any work behavior by considering variables in isolation. There is a natural temptation to look for quick and simple answers. In some senses, the scientific method yields to that temptation by having the goal of parsimony, that is, choosing simple explanations and theories over complex ones. But in the real world, unlike the laboratory, we cannot control multiple forces that act on an individual. Your behavior is not simply a result of your mental ability or of your personality. The behavior of your instructors is not just the result of their knowledge or attitudes, or of the culture in which they were raised. These behaviors are influenced by all of those things, and to consider only one variable as *the* explanatory variable is an endeavor doomed to failure. We will remind you frequently that you must look at the person as a whole entity, not as a single variable. Human behavior in real-world situations is like a stew. We may know every ingredient that went into that stew, yet the actual experience of tasting the stew is much more than the single elements that made it up, and is certainly not described by any one of those elements.

Parts

The book is divided into four parts.

- The first part contains the descriptive information about I-O psychology, some historical background and principles, and the basic methods of data collection and analysis.
- The second part deals with material that has often been labeled "industrial" (as opposed to "organizational"). This includes material on individual differences, assessment, training, performance and its evaluation, and job analysis.
- The third part covers material that is usually referred to as "organizational" and includes topics such as emotion, motivation, leadership, groups and teams, fairness and justice, and organizational theory.
- The fourth and final part considers the work environment. It includes treatments of safety, workplace and organizational design, and stress.

Resources

As a student of I-O psychology, you will want to consult resources beyond those offered by your instructor, this text, and its supplements. The most important of these resources are knowledge bases. This knowledge can come in two forms: paper and electronic. The electronic resources are websites and search engines that will identify useful information for you. Because website addresses change frequently, we will use this book's Online Learning Center to list the most useful websites for the material covered in each chapter. The paper resources are the various journals and books that provide information about the topics covered in the text. Table 1.7 presents a list of the most

TABLE 1.7	Useful Scientific Journals in I-O Psychology
Journal of Applied Psychology	Journal of Occupational and Organizational Psychology
Personnel Psychology	Leadership Quarterly
Human Performance	Training and Development Journal
Administrative Science Quarterly	Applied Psychology: An International Review
Human Factors	International Journal of Selection and Assessment
Academy of Management Journal	Work and Stress
Academy of Management Review	Journal of Occupational Health Psychology
Annual Review of Psychology	Journal of Organizational Behavior
The Industrial-Organizational Psychologist (TIP)	Journal of Personality and Social Psychology
Organizational Behavior and Human Decision Processes	
International Review of I/O Psychology	
International Review of Applied Psychology	

common scientific journals that carry articles relevant to the text material. In the references at the end of the book, you will see these journals cited frequently. If you want to do additional reading on a topic or are preparing a course paper or project, you should go to these journals first. In addition to journals, SIOP publishes the most current thinking on various topics in two series: the "Frontier Series" for research and the "Practice Series" for practice. These volumes present the most recent work available from some of the world's best I-O psychologists. Table 1.8 provides the titles and publication year of each of these volumes.

These books represent another excellent information base for your further reading. One final published source is the Annual Review of Psychology series published by Annual Reviews, Inc. One volume is published each year with separate chapters covering all of the major areas of psychology, including I-O psychology. This is an excellent resource for higher level reading on topics of interest.

TABLE 1.8	Useful Scientific and Practical Texts in I-O Psychology
FRONTIERS SERIES	**PRACTICE SERIES**
Career Development in Organizations: Hall (1986)	*Compensation in Organizations:* Rynes and Gerhart (2000)
Productivity in Organizations: Campbell and Campbell (1988)	*Creating, Implementing and Managing Effective Training:* Kraiger (2001)
Training and Development in Organizations: Goldstein (1989)	*Diagnosis for Organizational Change:* Howard (1994)
Organizational Climate and Culture: Schneider (1990)	*Diversity in the Workplace:* Jackson (1992)
Work, Families, and Organizations: Zedeck (1992)	*Employees, Careers and Job Creation:* London (1995)
Personnel Selection in Organizations: Schmitt and Borman (1993)	*Evolving Practices in Human Resource Management:* Kraut and Korman (1999)
Team Effectiveness and Decision Making: Guzzo and Salas (1994)	*Individual Psychological Assessment:* Jeanneret and Silzer (1998)
The Changing Nature of Work: Howard (1995)	*Managing Selection in Changing Organizations:* Kehoe (1999)
Individual Differences and Behavior in Organizations: Murphy (1996)	*Organizational Development:* Waclawski and Church (2001)
Perspectives on International Industrial/Organizational Psychology: Earley and Erez (1997)	*Organizational Surveys:* Kraut (1996)
The Changing Nature of Performance: Ilgen and Pulakos (1999)	*Performance Appraisal:* Smither (1998)
Measuring and Analyzing Behavior in Organizations: Drasgow and Schmitt (2001)	*The 21st Century Executive:* Silzer (2001)
Multilevel Theory, Research and Methods in Organizations: Klein and Kozlowski (2000)	*The Nature of Organizational Leadership:* Zaccaro and Klimoski (2001)

MODULE 1.4 SUMMARY

- This book treats I-O psychology in a unified and holistic manner.
- The four parts of this book discuss the basics of I-O, industrial topics, organizational topics, and the work environment.

- You should use this book's supplements, I-O journals, websites, SIOP Frontiers Series and Practice Series, and the *Annual Review of Psychology* to find additional information for your course work, papers, and projects.

CRITICAL THINKING EXERCISE

1.6 We have proposed that I-O psychology must be unified and holistic in approach. Suppose it were not.

How would the value of I-O psychology be diminished if it were not unified? If it were not holistic?

Below is a realistic case for you to read that includes topics from every chapter in the book. After each paragraph, you will find the number of the chapter that contains information relevant to the case. We don't expect you to be able to "solve" the case or address the issues presented. Instead, we present the case as a vivid example of the complexity of work behavior and environments. After you complete each chapter in class, you will find it useful to come back to this case, identify the paragraphs relevant to the chapter you have read, and determine how the chapter material applies to the case. What we want you to do now is simply read and appreciate the experience of work in the 21st century.

CASE STUDY 1.1   **Police Officer, Milford, USA**

Welcome to Milford. We're a "rust belt" survivor: Unlike a lot of towns around here, we've actually grown in the last few decades. Our town, with a current population of 600,000, has a fairly good economic base, since we have an auto assembly plant and a glass factory as well as a state university campus and a regional airport. About 50,000 of our residents are Hispanic, mostly descended from Mexicans and Central Americans who came to the area decades ago as migrant farm workers and moved into town when agriculture declined. We have the kinds of problems with crime and drugs that you'd expect in any city of this size, but on the whole it's a pretty good place to live. *(Chapter 1)*

I'm 48 now and a captain of patrol with the Milford Police Department. I started working for the department when I was 26 years old, a little later than most of the other officers. Before that I spent five years in the navy maintaining sonar units, then used my military education benefit to get a college degree in law enforcement. At age 33 I was promoted from patrol officer to patrol sergeant. Five years after that I became a lieutenant, and in four more years I made my present grade. Except for two years behind a desk during my stint as a lieutenant, I've spent my entire career on the street. *(Chapter 3)*

I've seen lots of different "systems" in my 22 years on the force. Systems for hiring, systems for promotion, systems for discipline, systems for training. If you didn't like a particular system, all you had to do was wait a few years, and it would change because someone in power wanted a change. But now I'm a "person in power" and I have a say in these "systems." I remember reading once that the best performance evaluation system people ever saw was the one they had in their *last* job. Boy, is that on the money! You hear people's criticisms and you try to think of a way to make the system better, but no matter what you propose, they come back and complain that the old way was better. Sometimes it seems my work life was easier when I just had to *put* up with systems, not help *make* them up. *(Chapters 6, 7, and 11)*

I have four direct reports: patrol lieutenants, shift commanders. We work the evening watch, which is roughly from 3.00 P.M. to 11.00 P.M. I say "roughly" because some of the subordinates come in at 2:30 and others leave at 11:30 to cover shift changes. We tried a rotating shift schedule many years ago, but that was a disaster. Now we follow a fixed shift system in which officers work consistent hours weekdays and every third weekend. Shift assignment follows strict seniority rules—new hires and newly promoted officers work what we call "graveyard"—the night shift, from 11.00 P.M. to 7.00 A.M. They have to wait until someone else quits, is fired, or retires before they can move up to evening and day shifts. This is good and bad. It's good for the cops because building your seniority to move off the graveyard shift, and eventually making it to the day shift, is something to look forward to. But it's bad from a law enforcement standpoint because there's a natural tendency to have a lot more problems during graveyard hours than at other times. I mean, when John Q. Public decides to act stupid, it's usually between 11.00 P.M. and 7.00 A.M. And here we are with mostly green recruits right out of the police academy on that shift, being supervised by newly promoted officers. We don't even have any top echelon officers working: Lieutenants cover the captain's duty on the night shift. If you ask me, the department would have far fewer problems with patrol officer performance if only you could put the most experienced officers and supervisors where they were needed the most, on night watch. *(Chapters 12 and 16)*

There's a new breed of officer that I've been seeing in the last 5 to 10 years and I can't say I like it. These young guys don't really seem as committed to being a cop as I was when I started. They treat it like a "job," not like a profession. They use all their sick time, they're always looking to join "better" departments where the pay scale is higher. They seem to "expect" that they'll be respected by civilians and fellow officers. They don't seem to understand that respect is earned, not bestowed. Something funny happens to them after the academy. When they arrive for their first shift after graduation, they're like kids starting first grade. Big eyes, lots of questions, asking for "feedback," asking for responsibility. They think they can do it all. But in less than a year, it's a different story. You have to stay on their case to get anything done. They take longer meal breaks, find more excuses for not being able to respond to a call,

saunter in two minutes before roll call. Just another job to them. *(Chapters 8, 9, and 10)*

Maybe this is because of the way recruits are tested. When I started, only the best were hired. The person who got the highest score on the civil service test, and was the fastest and the strongest on the physical ability test, was the person who got hired. You filled out a questionnaire to see if you had emotional problems; this was reviewed by the department shrink. You took a medical and they ran a background check on you. But now it's different. Now, in addition to the civil service test, recruits are interviewed about things like "interests" and "values" and "ethics." They also take a personality test, whatever that is. And they fill out a form about what they like and don't like in a job. I don't understand why they changed the system. Bad guys are still bad guys and they still do bad things. What's so complicated about that? You want a cop who is stand-up, not afraid to do what it takes. You want a cop who is honest. You want a cop who is in for the long haul and who understands the chain of command. Why, all of a sudden, does the cop have to have a "personality"? *(Chapters 3 and 4)*

Another thing is the job is getting much more technical. The city council just approved funds for equipping every patrol car with a computer and they are even talking about giving every cop a "Personal Digital Assistant." They thought the police officers would love coming into the 21st century. According to them, we can use the computers and handheld gizmos to analyze various crime patterns in our sectors, run more sophisticated checks for wants and warrants, look at traffic patterns for selective enforcement of moving violations where they are most dangerous. What the city council geeks didn't think of is that the majority of cops are not "generation Xers." Some of us still have trouble using bank machines, let alone "surfing the Web." I don't even see where we're supposed to fit a computer into the patrol car. The front seat and dash are already clogged up with the radio, the light control board, and the console for the clipboard and the memo pad. Where's a computer going to go, on the roof? And of course all the new kids on the job will make the rest of us look bad. They probably grew up with a computer in their cribs. *(Chapters 3 and 16)*

Since I've been on the force I've seen various trends and fads come and go. The latest buzzwords seem to be "community policing" and "quality-of-life" issues. Not surprisingly, the new cops seem to take to these better than the veterans, and this is causing a certain amount of friction. The veterans call the new cops assigned to community policing units "Officer Lollipop." The new cops joke that the veterans are "storm troopers" and "Neanderthals." It doesn't help that some of the new cops score better on the promotional exams and get promoted faster. That means that the younger "bosses" don't always have the respect of the older subordinates. And the beat cops who aren't promoted just get older and more cynical. *(Chapters 4, 7, and 14)*

The force has changed in other ways as well. When I started, I could count the number of female police officers in the department on one hand and have a finger or two left over. Now, the department is almost 20 percent female. That makes it tougher for the supervisors, because even though the law says they have to treat females the same as males, in reality the women get treated with kid gloves because the bosses are afraid of being accused of bias. Given the Hispanic community in town, we've always had a small but steady percentage of Hispanic officers. In recent years more blacks have gotten on the force, and now black officers outnumber the Hispanics. This has led to rivalry and competition, particularly when it comes to promotion exams. Everybody counts to see how many white, black, and Hispanic officers are promoted. Since the Hispanics have more seniority, they expect to have more promotions, but the blacks figure since there are more of them there should be proportionately more black supervisors. To make matters worse, the female officers always seem to do better on the exams than the men. As a result, I actually report to a female assistant chief. And she's been in the department for only 13 years! But she's a great test taker. And everybody knows that we had to have a woman somewhere up there in the chain of command, whether she could do the job or not. The problem is that you don't get respect from being a good test taker, you get it for being a good cop. Most of the officers don't pay much attention to her. Her decisions are always second-guessed and checked out with the other two male assistant chiefs. *(Chapter 11)*

The chief of police is a good guy. He has been in the department for just 16 years, but he's a college grad and went nights to get a master's in public administration. He's sharp and is always trying out new stuff. Last year he hired an outside consulting firm to run the promotion exams. Some of the consultants are psychologists, which was a little strange since the department already has a shrink on retainer. For the last sergeant's exam, they had a bunch of the current sergeants complete some "job analysis" forms. That seemed like a pretty big waste of time. Why not just get the most experienced officers together for an hour's discussion and have the consultants take notes? This "job analysis" thing led to an unusual promotion examination. They did use a knowledge test that made sure the candidates knew the criminal code and department policies, but they also had the candidates play the role of a sergeant in front of a panel of judges. The judges were from other police departments, which didn't make sense. How could they know what would be the right way to behave in our department? But the good part was that everyone got a score for performance and this score was added to the written test score. It was objective. The time before that, the lieutenants and captains got together for a few hours and talked about all the candidates and just made up a list according to their experiences with the candidates, which everybody agreed was unfair. *(Chapters 1, 2, and 5)*

Over the last couple of years, there has been a new kind of tension in the department. It became really obvious after the 9/11 thing, but it was building up before that. In a nutshell, officers are more interested in having a life outside the department instead of making the department their whole life. I'm talking about the veterans, not just the young new guys. Their mind is not on their work the way it ought to be. It got a lot worse after 9/11 because we've been expected to do so much more but with the same number of officers. We've tripled our airport detachment and had to post officers at city court, the bus station, and the power plant. And we've been getting a lot more calls about suspicious people and activities, especially people from other countries. A lot of private citizens have gotten so distrustful of foreigners that they act as if they'd like nothing better than to have the police force arrest every illegal alien it could find. But when you talk to those same people at work, all of a sudden they'd just as soon we look the other way because they know their corporate profits depend on having a cheap labor pool of undocumented workers. You'd expect the immigration authorities to give us some guidelines about this, but when I think about them I get just as annoyed as I do thinking about the other federal law enforcement agencies we're supposed to "interface" with now. We get overlapping or conflicting information from the different agencies, or else the information is so general or outdated that it doesn't really help us do our jobs. All of this extra responsibility has meant lots of overtime. Overtime used to be a big reward; now it's a punishment. And it looks like sick leave is off the charts. Some of the officers are snapping at each other and civilians. And a week does not go by when we don't have at least one police cruiser in a wreck. The officers seem really distracted. *(Chapters 15 and 16)*

Citizens are not doing so well either. The economy headed south and unemployment went way up. Ever notice that people act funny when they lose their jobs? Men are the worst. They feel worthless and angry. They do things that they would never do otherwise. A traffic stop turns into World War III. All of a sudden, we cops are the enemy. A complete about-face from the first few months after 9/11 when we were the heroes. People couldn't thank us enough for keeping them safe. It made us feel really good. It sure helped recruiting, too. All of a sudden we had a big surge in applicants to take the test. It was nice while it lasted. But when the conventions canceled, and the orders for cars dropped, and the state had to start cutting back on services, we were not the good guys anymore. I know life is tough. I know people take hits when the economy sours, but how can we help them? It's not our fault. We just end up dealing with the consequences. *(Chapters 10 and 15)*

One of the other captains just came back from a seminar on new techniques in law enforcement where they talked about "teams." I don't know what is so new about that. We've always had squads of officers assigned to a beat or sector. But he says that is not what they were talking about. They were talking about putting teams together based not on seniority but on abilities and interests. They were talking about "competencies," whatever that means. I didn't think the officers would go for this. But he showed us a half-dozen studies that were done by people from top law enforcement schools. When I looked at the results, I had to agree that this team approach might actually work. What they found, when they gave it a chance, was that the officers were more involved in their jobs, felt more in control, and took pride in showing that they were more effective on patrol. Response times went down, more

problems were handled with summonses and bench warrants rather than arrests, and resisting arrest charges and claims of brutality went down. The studies showed that sick leave went down as well. Hard to understand, but the numbers don't lie. Maybe these experts are right, "team" policing would help us get out of this slump. *(Chapter 13)*

But the academics can have some pretty dumb ideas, too. One of the sergeants is taking a course at the community college on employee attitudes, so he asked some of us to fill out a form to determine our job satisfaction. It was pretty simple, just asking us to agree or disagree with some sentences. He took the forms away, analyzed them, and came back to tell us what we already knew. We like our work, we don't like our bosses, there are too many "rules" we have to follow in the department, our pay is OK, and we can get promoted if we are lucky and study hard. Why did we need to fill out a questionnaire to come to those conclusions? *(Chapter 10)*

The job satisfaction questionnaire did reveal one sore point that all of us can sense. We have a problem in the department with leadership. There are plenty of "bosses" but not many of them are leaders. Some of them play tough and threaten their officers with three-day suspensions for making mistakes. If the officer dares to speak back, it might go up to five days off without pay. Some of the other bosses try to be your friend, but that won't work either. What you want is someone to help you do your job, not somebody to have coffee with. I was lucky when I was a lieutenant. My captain was somebody I could look up to, and he showed me what it takes to be a good cop and a good leader at the same time. Not everybody gets that kind of training. It seems like there should be a training program for bosses, just like there's one for new officers—sort of an academy for supervisors. I mentioned that to one of the other captains, who said it would be money down the drain. You would take officers off the street and have nothing to show for it. I know there's an answer to his objection, but I can't think what it would be. *(Chapter 12)*

There is another problem that I see, but the questionnaire didn't ask any questions about it. We don't really trust anybody except other cops. The courts seem to bend over backward to give the perps a break. The lawyers are always picking away at details of the arrest. Are you sure you saw him on the corner *before* you heard the alarm? Did you ask for permission to search her purse? How could you see a license plate from 25 feet away when the sun was almost down? Even the DA, who is supposed to be on your side, is always telling you that you should have done something differently. The problem is that this makes the average cop just want to make up whatever details are necessary to get the perp off the street. On the one hand, I can't disagree with my officers that the system seems to be working against us and what we are trying to do. On the other hand, I don't think that this is the way a police department should think or behave. We should all be working together in the criminal justice system, not trying to "win." *(Chapter 14)*

But this is why the police force feels defensive against the rest of the city government. And why we were not pleased last week when the mayor announced that all city employees would have their performance evaluated once a year, and that includes the police department. Something to do with "accountability in government." He has asked each city department to develop its own system, but it has to be numerical. He also said that there have to be consequences for poor performance. The chief is thinking about preventing anyone from taking a promotion exam if his or her performance is "unacceptable," but he hasn't told us how he plans to determine what is acceptable. I think this is a disaster waiting to happen. *(Chapter 6)*

I'm proud of being a cop and I feel a lot of satisfaction with what I've achieved in my career. But to tell you the truth, the way things are going around here, retirement is starting to look more and more attractive to me. *(Chapter 10)*

STUDYING AND INTERPRETING WORKER BEHAVIOR

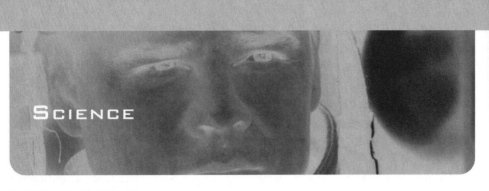

SCIENCE

WHAT IS SCIENCE?

For many of us, the term **"science"** evokes mental images of laboratories, test tubes, and computers. We may imagine people wearing white lab coats, walking around making notes on clipboards. Certainly laboratories are the homes for some scientific activity and some scientists do wear white lab coats, but the essence of science is not where it is done or how scientists are dressed. Science is defined by its goals and its procedures.

All sciences share common goals: the understanding, prediction, and control of some phenomenon of interest. Physics addresses physical matter, chemistry addresses elements of matter, biology deals with living things, and psychology is concerned with behavior. The I-O psychologist is particularly interested in understanding, predicting, and influencing behavior related to the workplace. All sciences also share certain common methods by which they study the object of interest, whether that object is a chemical on the periodic table of elements or a human being employed in a corporation. These common methods include:

1. A logical approach to investigation, usually based on a theory, a **hypothesis,** or simply a basic curiosity about an object of interest. In I-O psychology, this might be a theory about what motivates workers, a hypothesis that freedom to choose work methods will lead workers to be more involved with their work, or curiosity about whether people who work from their homes are more satisfied with their jobs than people who work in offices.

2. Science depends on data. These data can be gathered in a laboratory or in the real world (or, as it is sometimes referred to, the field). The data gathered are intended to be relevant to the theory, hypothesis, or curiosity that precipitated the investigation. For example, I-O psychologists gather data about job performance, abilities, job satisfaction, and attitudes toward safety.

3. Science must be communicable, open, and public. Scientific research is published in journals, reports, and books. Methods of data collection are described, data are reported, analyses are displayed for examination, and conclusions are presented. As a result, other scientists or nonscientists can draw their own conclusions about the confidence they have in the findings of the research or even replicate the research themselves. In I-O psychology, there is often debate—sometimes heated argument—about theories and hypotheses. The debate goes on at conferences, in journals, and in books. Anyone can join the debate by simply reading the relevant reports or publications and expressing opinions on them, or by conducting and publishing one's own research.

4. Science does not set out to prove theories or hypotheses. It sets out to *disprove* them. The goal of the scientist is to design a research project that will eliminate all plausible explanations for a phenomenon except one. The explanation that cannot be disproved

SCIENCE

Approach that involves the understanding, prediction, and control of some phenomenon of interest.

HYPOTHESIS

Prediction about relationship(s) among variables of interest.

or eliminated is the ultimate explanation of the phenomenon. For example, in lawsuits involving layoffs brought by older employees who have lost their jobs, the charge will be that the layoffs were caused by age discrimination on the part of the employer. A scientific approach to the question would consider that possibility, as well as the possibility that the layoffs were the result of:

- Differences in the past performance of the individuals who were laid off.
- Differences in the skills possessed by the individuals.
- Differences in projected work for the individuals.
- Differences in training, education, or credentials of the individuals.

5. One other characteristic of science that is frequently mentioned (MacCoun, 1998; Merton, 1973) is that of **disinterestedness**—the expectation that scientists will be objective and not influenced by biases or prejudices. Although most researchers are, and should be, passionately interested in their research efforts, they are expected to be *dispassionate* about the results they expect that research to yield—or, at the very least, to make public any biases or prejudices they may harbor.

It will become apparent as we move through the chapters of this book that I-O psychology is a science. I-O psychologists conduct research based on theories and hypotheses. They gather data, publish those data, and design their research in a way that eliminates alternative explanations for the research results. I-O psychologists (and scientists in general) are not very different from nonscientists in their curiosity or the way they form theories, hypotheses, or speculations. What sets them apart as scientists is the method they use (Klahr & Simon, 1999).

THE ROLE OF SCIENCE IN SOCIETY

We are often unaware of the impact that science has on our everyday lives. The water we drink, the air we breathe, even the levels of noise we experience have been influenced by decades of scientific research. Consider the challenge faced by a pharmaceutical company that wants to make a new drug available to the public. The Food and Drug Administration (FDA) requires the pharmaceutical company to conduct years of trials (experiments) in the laboratory and in the field. These trials must conform to the standards of acceptable science: They will be based on a theory, data will be gathered, compiled, and interpreted, and all alternative explanations for the effects of the drug will be considered. In addition, the data will be available for inspection by the FDA. Before the drug can be released to the public, the FDA must agree that the data show that the drug actually makes a contribution to medicine, and that it has no dangerous side effects.

The importance of the scientific method for the impact of human resource and I-O practices can also be seen in society, particularly in the courts. As we will see in several of the chapters that follow (most notably, Chapter 11), individuals often bring lawsuits against employers for particular practices, such as hiring, firing, pay increases, and harassment. In these lawsuits, I-O psychologists often testify as expert witnesses. An **expert witness,** unlike a fact witness, is permitted to voice opinions about practices. An I-O psychologist might be prepared to offer the opinion that an employer was justified in using a test, such as a test of mental ability, for hiring purposes. This opinion may be challenged by opposing lawyers as "junk science" that lacks foundation in legitimate scientific research.

Prior to the actual testimony of the expert in front of a jury, the opposing lawyers may ask the judge to prevent the expert from voicing this opinion in front of a jury, arguing that the jury will be swayed by the fact that an expert is testifying, even though the testimony may not be scientifically credible. The formal name for this challenge is a **Daubert challenge.** It derives its name from litigation surrounding the alleged cancer-causing

---

DISINTERES-TEDNESS

Characteristic of scientists who should be objective and uninfluenced by biases or prejudices when conducting research.

EXPERT WITNESS

Witness in a lawsuit who is permitted to voice opinions about organizational practices.

DAUBERT CHALLENGE

Challenge in which opposing lawyers may ask the judge to prevent the expert witness from voicing an opinion in front of a jury, arguing that the jury will be swayed by an expert testifying about a topic that cannot be considered a legitimate scientific topic.

properties of silicon breast implants (*Daubert v. Merrill-Dow,* 1993). Daubert was the name of one of the women suing an implant manufacturer. In this case, numerous experts testified about many different theories involving the development of cancers. Much of the testimony was speculative and represented the "theories" of each expert without any confirming data. As a result of this case, the federal court system introduced a method for distinguishing between "legitimate science" and "junk science." If an expert wants to present a theory in his or her testimony, the theory must meet several requirements. The most important of these are:

- The theory must be recognized by the particular scientific area as worthy of attention. This recognition comes through publication in scholarly journals.
- The theory must have been **peer reviewed,** or subjected to scientific scrutiny that considers plausible alternative explanations.
- The theory must have a known "error rate," meaning that its accuracy has been evaluated with data.
- The theory must be replicable, or testable, by another scientist. This means that all of the variables, methods of data collection, and so forth must be public and observable, and that the findings can be repeated by other scientists.

PEER REVIEWED

Process in which research is subjected to scientific scrutiny by peer researchers who evaluate the research and consider plausible alternative explanations.

As you will see when we examine the role of mental ability testing in employment decisions, in the hypothetical case described above, the expert would be permitted to present an opinion about the potential value of mental ability testing for the purposes of hiring. Mental ability has been included in the applied psychology literature for over 100 years. Research studies on mental abilities have appeared in dozens of psychological journals; to qualify for publication in those journals, they had to undergo critical evaluation by eminent scientists who are reviewers for those journals. Statistical analyses have been conducted which demonstrate a significant association between mental ability and job success. Finally, the journal articles and technical reports provide all of the information necessary to confirm or test this proposed or theoretical relationship.

The scientific method is not the only method for arriving at the "truth," but it is one of the most commonly accepted methods for protecting individuals from the consequences of policies based on uninformed speculation.

WHY DO I-O PSYCHOLOGISTS ENGAGE IN RESEARCH?

An old truism admonishes that those who do not study history are condemned to repeat it. A less elegant representation of the same thought was the movie *Groundhog Day,* in which Bill Murray gets to repeat the events of a particular day over and over again, never learning from his mistakes. Without access to scientific research, the individuals who make human resource (HR) decisions in organizations would be in Murray's position, unable to learn from mistakes (and successes) that are already documented. Each HR director would reinvent the wheel, sometimes with good and sometimes with poor results. By conducting research, we are able to develop a model of a system—a theory—and predict the consequences of introducing that system or of modifying a system already in place.

Consider the example of hiring. Imagine that an organization has always used a first-come, first-served model for hiring. When a job opening occurs, the organization advertises, reviews an application blank, does a short unstructured interview, and hires the first applicant who has the minimum credentials. Research in I-O psychology has demonstrated that this method does not give the employer the best chance of hiring successful employees. An employer that conducts a structured job-related interview, and that also includes explicit assessments of general mental ability and personality, will tend to make better hiring decisions. We can predict this because of decades of published research which form the foundation for our theory of successful hiring. When an organization decides on a course of action, it is predicting (or anticipating) the outcome of that course of action. The better the research base that employers depend on for that prediction, the more confident they can be in the likely outcome. Both science and business strategy are based on the same principle—predictability (Xiao & Vincente, 2000). Business leaders prefer to avoid unpleasant surprises; theory and research help them to do so.

MODULE 2.1 SUMMARY

- Like other scientists, I-O psychologists conduct research based on theories and hypotheses. They gather data, publish those data, and design their research to eliminate alternative explanations for the research results.
- The scientific method has important repercussions in society, particularly in the courts where I-O psychologists often testify as expert witnesses.

- I-O research is important to organizations because every course of action that an organization decides on is, in effect, a prediction or anticipation of a given outcome. The better the research base that supports that prediction, the more confident the organization can be of the outcome.

KEY TERMS

science

hypothesis

disinterestedness

expert witness

Daubert challenge

peer reviewed

CRITICAL THINKING EXERCISES

2.1 In many criminal cases, law enforcement agencies call in "profilers" to help in the identification of a suspect. Consider the five elements of a legitimate science identified in the first section of this module. Using those elements, would you consider "profiling" to be scientific? Explain your answer.

2.2 The Daubert Principles used to determine what might constitute the testimony of an expert witness—are assumed to distinguish between real science and junk science. Examine the Daubert principles in light of the five elements of a science. Do the Daubert challenge principles agree with these five elements? Explain your answer.

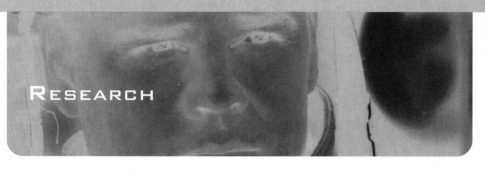

RESEARCH

RESEARCH DESIGN

In the introductory section, we have considered the scientific method and the role of research in I-O psychology. Now we will consider the operations that define research in greater detail. In carrying out research, a series of decisions need to be made before the research actually begins. These decisions include:

- Will the research be conducted in a laboratory under controlled conditions, or in the field?
- Who will the participants be?
- If there are different conditions in the research (e.g., some participants exposed to a condition, and other participants not exposed to the condition), how will participants be assigned to the various conditions?
- What will the variables of interest be?
- How will measurements on these variables be collected?

Collectively, the answers to these questions will determine the **research design,** the architecture for the research.

Spector (2001) has reviewed research designs in I-O psychology and devised a system of classification for distinguishing among the typical designs based on the earlier work of Schaubroeck and Kuehn (1992). He breaks designs down into three basic types: **experimental, quasi-experimental,** and **nonexperimental.** Experimental designs, whether the experiment is conducted in a laboratory or in the field, involve the assignment of participants to conditions. As an example, some participants may receive a piece rate payment for their work while others receive an hourly rate. These two different rates of pay would be two separate conditions, and participants might be assigned randomly to one condition or the other. The random assignment of participants is one of the characteristics that distinguishes an experiment from a quasi-experiment or nonexperiment. If participants are randomly assigned to conditions, then any differences that appear after the experimental treatment are more likely to conform to cause-effect relationships.

It is not always possible to assign participants randomly to a condition. For example, an organization might institute a new pay plan at one plant location, but not at another. Or the researcher would assess employee satisfaction with an existing pay plan, then the organization would change the pay plan, and the researcher would assess satisfaction again with the new plan. This would be called a quasi-experimental design.

In the experimental and quasi-experimental designs described above, the pay plan was a "treatment" or condition. Nonexperimental designs do not include any "treatment" or conditions. In a nonexperimental design, the researcher would simply gather information

a

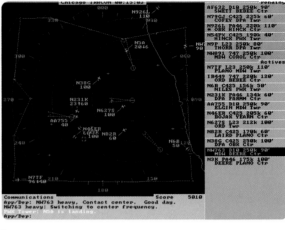

b

One way to enhance validity is to make experimental conditions as similar as possible to actual work situations. (a) Actual radar being used by an air traffic controller; (b) a simulated radar screen designed for an experiment.

OBSERVATIONAL DESIGN

The researcher observes employee behavior and systematically records what is observed.

SURVEY DESIGN

Research strategy in which participants are asked to complete a questionnaire or survey.

about the effects of a pay plan without introducing any condition or treatment. Researchers often use the term "independent variable" to describe the treatment or antecedent condition and the term "dependent variable" to describe the subsequent behavior of the research participant. Spector (2001) identifies two common nonexperimental designs as the **observational design** and the **survey design.** In the observational design, the researcher watches an employee's behavior and makes a record about what is observed. An observer might, for example, study communication patterns and worker efficiency by recording the number of times a worker communicates with a supervisor in a given time period. Alternatively, in the survey design, the worker is asked to complete a questionnaire describing typical interaction frequency with his or her supervisor. Table 2.1 presents an outline of the more common experimental designs in I-O psychology. We will discuss the strengths and weaknesses of various research designs in greater detail in Chapter 8 when we consider the evaluation of training programs.

These various designs are not used with equal frequency. Schaubroeck and Kuehn (1992) found that 67 percent of published studies conducted by I-O psychologists were done in the field and 33 percent in a laboratory. Laboratory-based studies were usually experimental in design and used students as participants. Most field studies were not

TABLE 2.1	Common Research Designs in I-O Psychology
DESIGN	**DESCRIPTION**
Experimental	Random assignment of participants to conditions
Laboratory	
Field	
Quasi-experimental	Nonrandom assignment of participants to conditions
Nonexperimental	No unique conditions for participants
Survey	
Observational	

SOURCE: Adapted from Spector (2001).

experimental and typically used employees as participants. In a follow-up study, Spector (2001) found very similar results. Austin, Scherbaum, and Mahlman (2002) found virtually identical results. There are several reasons for the prevalence of nonexperimental field research in I-O psychology. The first is the extent to which a laboratory experiment can reasonably simulate "work" as it is experienced by a worker. The essence of laboratory research is control over conditions. This means that the work environment tends to be artificial and sterile, and the research deals with narrow aspects of behavior. Experiments are difficult to do in the field because workers can seldom be randomly assigned to conditions or treatments. The goal of a real-life business organization is an economic one, not a scientific one. Finally, laboratory experiments often involve "samples of convenience" (i.e., students) and there is considerable doubt that the behavior of student participants engaging in simulated work reasonably represents the behavior of actual workers. Laboratory studies provide excellent methods of control and are more likely to lead to causal explanations. Field studies permit researchers to study behaviors difficult to simulate in a laboratory, but cause-effect relationships are more difficult to examine in such field studies.

METHODS OF DATA COLLECTION
Qualitative and Quantitative Research

Historically, I-O psychology, and particularly the "I" part of I-O, has used **quantitative methods** for measuring important variables or behavior. Quantitative methods rely heavily on tests, rating scales, questionnaires, and physiological measures (Stone-Romero, 2002). They yield results in terms of numbers. They can be contrasted with more **qualitative methods** of investigation, which generally produce flow diagrams and narrative descriptions of events or processes, rather than "numbers" as measures. Qualitative methods include procedures like observation, interview, case study, and analysis of diaries or written documents. The preference for quantitative over qualitative research can be attributed, at least in part, to the apparent preference of journal editors for quantitative research (Hemingway, 2001), possibly because numbers and statistical analyses conform to a traditional view of science (Symon, Cassell, & Dickson, 2000). It is interesting to note that in the early days of psychology, the "experimental method" was **introspection,** in which the participant was also the experimenter, who would record his or her experiences in completing an experimental task. This method would be considered hopelessly subjective by today's standards.

You will notice that we described the issue as qualitative *and* quantitative research, as opposed to qualitative *versus* quantitative research. The two are not mutually exclusive (Dachler, 2000; Rogelberg, 2002). Consider an extended observation of a worker which might include videotaped episodes of performance. That video record could easily be used to develop a frequency count of a particular behavior. The same could be done with an interview, or a diary kept by a worker. Much of the resistance to qualitative research is the result of seeing it as excessively subjective. This concern is misplaced. All methods of research ultimately require interpretation, regardless of whether they are quantitative or qualitative. The researcher is an explorer, trying to develop an understanding of the phenomenon he or she has chosen to investigate, and in so doing, should use all of the information available, regardless of its form. The key is in combining information from multiple sources to develop that theory. Rogelberg and Brooks-Laber (2002) refer to this as **triangulation**—looking for converging information from different sources. Detailed descriptions of qualitative research methods have been presented by Locke and Golden-Biddle (2002) and Bachiochi and Weiner (2002). Stone-Romero (2002) presents an excellent review of the variations of research designs in I-O psychology as well as their strengths and weaknesses.

QUANTITATIVE METHODS

Rely on tests, rating scales, questionnaires, and physiological measures, and yield numerical results.

QUALITATIVE METHODS

Rely on observation, interview, case study, and analysis of diaries or written documents and produce flow diagrams and narrative descriptions of events or processes.

INTROSPECTION

Early scientific method in which the participant was also the experimenter, recording his or her experiences in completing an experimental task; considered very subjective by modern standards.

TRIANGULATION

Approach in which researchers seek converging information from different sources.

CASE STUDY 2.1 Triangulation: The Financial Consultant

In Chapter 5, we will consider the topic of **job analysis.** Job analysis is a process used by I-O psychologists to gain understanding of a job. It includes an investigation of the tasks and duties that define the job, the human attributes necessary to perform the job, and the context in which that job is performed. Job analysis typically involves the combination of data from many different sources in coming to a complete understanding, or theory, of the job in question.

Consider the job of a financial consultant who advises individual private clients on how to invest their money. (These consultants are often called stockbrokers.) All of the large financial investment firms, such as Merrill Lynch, Morgan Stanley, and Salomon Smith Barney, have thousands of financial consultants. Suppose you were hired as an I-O psychologist to study and "understand" the job of a financial consultant with an eye toward developing a recruiting, selection, and training program for such individuals.

How might you achieve this understanding? First, you might examine what the organization has to say about the job on its Web page and in its recruiting materials. Then you might talk with senior executives of the organization about the role the financial consultant plays in the success of the organization. Next you might tour the country interviewing and observing a

sample of financial consultants as they do their work, in the office and outside the office. You might also ask them to show you their daily appointment calendars and answer questions about the entries in these calendars. As part of this experience, you might spend several days with a single financial consultant and observe the variety of tasks he or she performs. Next you might interview the immediate managers of financial consultants and explore their views of what strategies lead to success or failure for consultants.

You might also interview retired financial consultants, as well as financial consultants who left their consulting positions with the company to become managers. Finally, you might ask a sample of financial consultants and managers to complete a questionnaire in which they rate the relative importance and frequency of the tasks that consultants perform, as well as the abilities and personal characteristics necessary to perform those tasks successfully. By gathering and interpreting this wealth of information, you will gain an excellent understanding of the job. Each of the methods of investigation gave you additional information. No one method was more important than any other method. What is clear is that no method, alone, would have been sufficient to achieve an understanding of the position. This is the type of "triangulation" that Rogelberg and Brooks-Laber (2002) were advocating.

JOB ANALYSIS

Process used by I-O psychologists to develop an understanding of a job by identifying the duties of the job and the KSAOs required to perform them.

GENERALIZE

To apply the results from one study or sample to other participants or situations.

GENERALIZABILITY AND CONTROL IN RESEARCH

Generalizability

One of the most important issues in conducting research is how widely the results can be generalized. There is a relatively simple answer to that question. An investigator can **generalize** results to areas that have been sampled in the research study. Consider Figure 2.1, which is made up of concentric circles representing various factors or variables which might be sampled in a study. The first area for sampling might be participants or employees. If our research sample is representative of a larger population (e.g., all individuals who work for the organization who have the same job title), then we can feel more confident in generalizing to this larger population of participants who *might have been* in our study. The next circle represents job titles. If the job titles of the participants in our study are a representative sample of the population of job titles that exist in a particular company, then we can be more confident about generalizing to this larger population of jobs. The next circle represents time. If we have collected data at several different points in time, we can feel more confident in

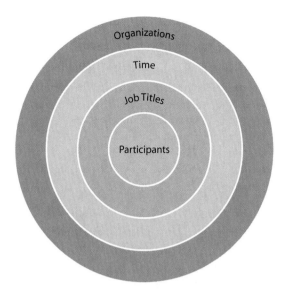

FIGURE 2.1

Sampling Domains for I-O Research

generalizing across time periods than if all the data came from one point in time. The final circle represents organizations. If we have collected our data from many different organizations, we can be more confident in extending our findings beyond a single organization. Let's take a concrete example. Suppose you conducted a research study to assess the extent to which recent college graduates would adapt to working overseas. How would you maximize the generalizability of your conclusions? You might take the following steps:

1. Sample graduates from many different educational institutions.
2. Sample graduates from several different graduating classes.
3. Sample graduates with degrees in a wide variety of majors.
4. Sample graduates who work for many different companies.
5. Sample graduates who work in many different departments within those companies.
6. Sample graduates assigned to many different countries outside the United States.

If you were able to achieve this wide-ranging sampling, your results would be quite generalizable. But, of course, sampling such as we have described above is time consuming and expensive, so compromises are often made. The important thing to keep in mind is that every time a compromise is made (e.g., data are gathered from graduates of only one institution, or from one graduating class, or from only one major, or from those who were assigned to only one country), the generalizability of the results is reduced. Sample size should not be confused with sample representativeness. A large but nonrepresentative sample is much less valuable for purposes of generalizability than a smaller but representative sample.

Control

When research is conducted in the field, events and variables often can obscure the results. The primary reason why psychologists do laboratory studies is to eliminate these distracting variables through **experimental control.** If you tried to study problem-solving behaviors among industrial workers at the workplace, you might find your study disrupted by telephone calls, machine breakdowns, missing team members, urgent requests from a supervisor. But if you conduct the same study in a laboratory, none of those distractions will be present. By using this form of control, you eliminate possible confounding influences which might make your results less reliable or harder to interpret.

There is another form of control that can be equally powerful. It is known as **statistical control.** As an example, suppose you wanted to study the relationship between job satisfaction

EXPERIMENTAL CONTROL

Characteristic of research in which possible confounding influences that might make results less reliable or harder to interpret are eliminated; often easier to establish in laboratory studies than in field studies.

STATISTICAL CONTROL

Using statistical techniques to control for the influence of certain variables. Such control allows researchers to concentrate exclusively on the primary relationships of interest.

and leadership styles in a company, and had a representative sample of employees from many different departments, of both genders, of varying age, and of varying educational backgrounds. Suppose that you were concerned that the relationship of interest (job satisfaction and leadership style) might be obscured by other influences such as the employees' age, gender, educational level, or home department. You could use statistical techniques to control for the influence of these other variables and allow you to concentrate exclusively on the relationship between satisfaction and leadership style. In I-O psychology, statistical control is much more common than experimental control.

ETHICS

Physicians swear to abide by the Hippocratic oath to "do no harm." This is the keystone of their promise to behave ethically. Most professions have ethical standards that educate their members regarding appropriate and inappropriate behavior, and psychology is no exception. Every member of the American Psychological Association agrees to follow the ethical standards published by that governing body (APA, 2002). If a member violates a standard, he or she can be dropped from membership in the organization. Although I-O psychologists do not have a separate code of ethics, SIOP has endorsed a collection of 61 cases that illustrate ethical issues likely to arise in situations that an I-O psychologist might encounter (Lowman, 1998). Lowman (1985a; 1985b; 1989; 1990; 1991a; 1991b) has also written extensively on the topic of ethical practice for I-O psychologists. In addition to the principles and case book for I-O psychologists, other societies (e.g., The Society for Human Resource Management, 1990; Academy of Management, 1990) publish ethical standards that are relevant for I-O psychologists.

Formulating ethical guidelines for I-O psychologists can be very challenging because the work of an I-O psychologist is incredibly varied. Issues include personnel decisions, safety, organizational commitment, training, and motivation, to name but a few. The issues may be addressed as part of a consulting engagement, in-house job duties, or research. Because every situation is different, there is no simple formula for behaving ethically (although the "do no harm" standard never ceases to apply). The case book described above addresses topics as varied as testing, validity studies, result reporting, layoffs, sexual harassment, employee assistance programs, data collection, confidentiality, and billing practices. Since this is your first course in I-O psychology, it is unlikely that you will be hired in the capacity of an I-O psychologist until you have completed a number of additional courses or received a graduate degree in I-O psychology. Nevertheless, if you are assisting an I-O psychologist in research or practice, or are simply interested in learning more about ethical guidelines of the profession, it would be prudent to review the APA Ethical Standards as well as the casebook on the ethical practice of I-O psychology (Lowman, 1998).

MODULE 2.2 SUMMARY

- Research designs may be experimental, quasi-experimental, or nonexperimental; two common nonexperimental designs are observation and survey. About two-thirds of I-O research uses non-experimental designs.

- Quantitative research yields results in terms of numbers, whereas qualitative research tends to produce flow diagrams and descriptions. The two are not mutually exclusive; however, the process of triangulation involves combining results from different sources, which may include both kinds of research.

- The results of research can be generalized to areas included in the study; thus, the more areas a study includes, the greater its generalizability. Researchers eliminate distracting variables by using experimental and statistical controls.

- Ethical standards for I-O psychologists are set forth by the APA, SIOP, and other organizations such as the Society for Human Resource Management and the Academy of Management. The overriding ethical principle is "do no harm."

KEY TERMS

research design

experimental design

quasi-experimental design

nonexperimental design

observational design

survey design

quantitative methods

qualitative methods

introspection

triangulation

job analysis

generalize

experimental control

statistical control

CRITICAL THINKING EXERCISES

2.3 Suppose you wanted to study the relationship between a worker's respect for his or her supervisor and that worker's honesty at the workplace. Would you choose an experimental, quasi-experimental, or nonexperimental design? Why?

2.4 In Case Study 2.1, we used the job of a financial analyst to demonstrate the concept of "triangulation" in data collection. If you were to use the method of triangulation for studying the job of a high school guidance counselor, what multiple sources of information might you use?

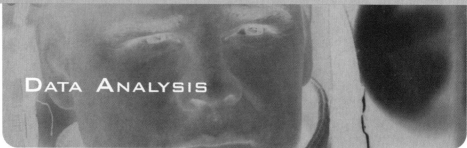

DATA ANALYSIS

DESCRIPTIVE AND INFERENTIAL STATISTICS

Descriptive Statistics

In our discussion of research, we have considered two issues thus far: how to design a study to collect data, and how to collect those data. Assuming we have been successful at both of those tasks, we now need to analyze those data to determine what they may tell us about our initial theory, hypothesis, or speculation. We can analyze the data we have gathered for two purposes. The first is simply to describe the distribution of scores or numbers we have collected. A distribution of numbers simply means that the numbers are arrayed along two axes. The horizontal axis is the score or number axis running from low to high scores. The vertical axis is usually the frequency axis, which indicates how many individuals achieved each score on the horizontal axis. The statistical methods to accomplish such a description are referred to as **descriptive statistics.** You have probably encountered this type of statistical analysis in other courses, so we will simply summarize the more important characteristics for you. Consider the two distributions of test scores in Figure 2.2. Look at the overall shapes of those distributions. One distribution is high and narrow; the other is lower and wider. In the left graph, the distribution's center (48) is easy to determine; in the right graph, the

> **DESCRIPTIVE STATISTICS**
>
> *Summarize, organize, and describe a sample of data.*

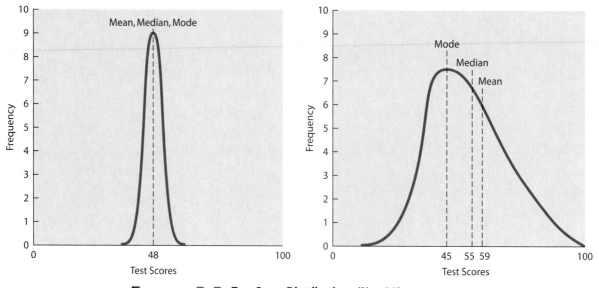

F I G U R E   2.2   Two Score Distributions (N = 30)

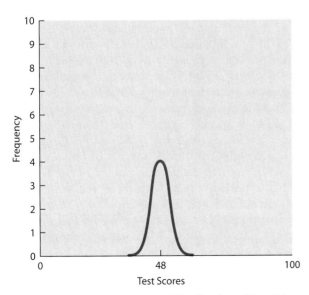

THE STAT FAMILY

distribution's center is not as clear unless we specify the central tendency measure of interest. One distribution is bell shaped or symmetric, while the other is lopsided. Three measures or characteristics can be used to describe any score distribution—**measures of central tendency, variability,** and lopsidedness (technically called **skew**).

Measures of central tendency include the **mean,** the **mode,** and the **median.** The mean is the arithmetic average of the scores, the mode is the most frequently occurring score, and the median is the middle score (the score which 50 percent of the remaining scores fall above, and the other 50 percent of the remaining scores fall below). As you can see, the two distributions have different means, modes, and medians. In addition, the two distributions vary on their lopsidedness or skewness. The left distribution has no skew; the right distribution is positively skewed, with some high scores pulling the mean to the positive (right) side.

Another common descriptive statistic is the standard deviation or the variance of a distribution. In Figure 2.3, you can see that one distribution covers a larger score range

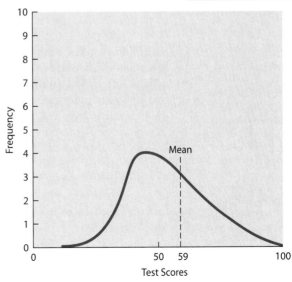

FIGURE 2.3 Two Score Distributions (N = 10)

and is wider than the other. We can characterize a distribution by looking at the extent to which the scores deviate from the mean score. The typical amount of deviation from a mean score is the standard deviation. Since distributions often vary from each other simply as a result of the units of measure (e.g., one distribution is a measure of inches, while another is a measure of loudness), sometimes it is desirable to standardize the distribution so that they all have means = .00 and standard (or average) deviations = 1.00. The variance of a distribution is simply the squared standard deviation.

Inferential Statistics

In the studies that you will encounter in the rest of this text, the types of analyses used are not descriptive, but inferential. When we conduct a research study, we do it for a reason. We have a theory or hypothesis to examine. It may be a hypothesis that accidents are related to personality characteristics, or that people with higher mental ability test scores perform their jobs better than those with lower scores, or that team members in small teams are happier with their work than team members in large teams. In each of these cases, we design a study and collect data in order to come to some conclusion, to draw an inference about a relationship. Once again, in other courses, you have likely been introduced to some basic **inferential statistics**. Statistical tests such as the t-test, analysis of variance or F-test, or chi-square test can be used to see if two or more groups of participants (e.g., an experimental and a control group) tend to differ on some variable of interest. For example, we can examine the means of the two groups of scores in Figure 2.3 to see if they are different beyond what we might expect as a result of chance. If I tell you that the group with the lower mean score represents high school graduates and the group with the higher mean score represents college graduates, and I further tell you that the means are statistically significantly different from what would be found with simple random or chance variation, you might draw the inference that education is associated with higher test scores. The statistical test used to support that conclusion (e.g., a t-test of mean differences) would be considered an inferential test.

Statistical Significance

Two scores, derived from two different groups, might be different, even at the third decimal place. How can we be sure that the difference is a "real" one—that it exceeds a difference we might expect as a function of chance alone? If we examined the mean scores of many different test groups, such as the two displayed in Figure 2.3, we would almost never find that the means were *exactly* the same. A convention has been adopted to define when a difference or an inferential statistic is significant. **Statistical significance** is defined in terms of a probability statement. To say that a finding of difference between two groups is significant at the 5 percent level, or a probability of .05, is to say that a difference that large would be expected to occur only 5 times out of 100 as a result of chance alone. If the difference between the means was even larger, we might conclude that a difference this large might be expected to occur only 1 time out of 100 as a result of chance alone. This latter result would be reported as a difference at the 1 percent level, or a probability of .01. As the probability goes down (e.g., from .05 to .01), we become more confident that the difference is a real difference. It is important to keep in mind that the significance level addresses only the confidence that we can have that a result is not due to chance. It says nothing about the strength of an association or the practical importance of the result. The standard, or threshold, for significance has been set at .05 or lower as a rule of thumb. Thus, unless a result would occur only five or fewer times out of a hundred as a result of chance alone, we do not label the difference as statistically significant.

In recent years I-O psychologists have vigorously debated the value of significance testing (Krueger, 2001; Murphy, 1997; Schmidt, 1992, 1996). Critics argue that the .05 level is arbitrary and that even higher levels—up to .10, for example—can still be practically important. This is a very complex statistical debate that we will not cover here, but it is important to remember that you are unlikely to encounter studies in scientific journals with probability values higher than .05. The critics argue that there are many interesting findings and theories that never see the scientific light of day because of this arbitrary criterion for statistical significance.

The Concept of Statistical Power

Many studies have a very small number of participants in them. This makes it very difficult to find statistical significance even when there is a "true" relationship among variables. In Figure 2.3 we have reduced our two samples in Figure 2.2 from 30 to 10 by randomly dropping 20 participants from each group. The differences are no longer statistically significant. But from our original study with 30 participants, we know that the differences between means are not due to chance. Nevertheless, the convention we have adopted for defining significance prevents us from considering the new difference to be significant, even though the mean values and the differences between those means are identical to what they were in Figure 2.2.

The concept of **statistical power** deals with the likelihood of finding a statistically significant difference when a true difference exists. The smaller the sample size, the lower the power to *detect* a true or real difference. In practice, this means that researchers may be drawing the wrong inferences (e.g., that there is no association) when sample sizes are too small. The issue of power is often used by the critics of significance testing to illustrate what is wrong with such conventions. Schmidt and Hunter (2002b) argued that the typical power of a psychological study is low enough that more than 50 percent of the studies in the literature do not detect a difference between groups or an effect of a treatment or independent variable on a dependent variable when one exists. Thus, adopting a convention that requires an effect to be "statistically significant" at the .05 level greatly distorts what we read in journals and how we interpret what we do read.

Power calculations can be done before a study is ever initiated, informing the researcher of the number of participants that should be included in the study in order to have a reasonable chance of detecting an association (Cohen, 1988, 1994; Murphy & Myors, 1998). Research studies can be time consuming and expensive. It would be silly to conduct a study that could not detect an association even if one were there. The power concept also provides a warning against casually dismissing studies that do not achieve "statistical significance" before looking at sample sizes. If the sample sizes are small, we may never know whether or not there is a real effect or difference between groups.

STATISTICAL POWER

The likelihood of finding a statistically significant difference when a true difference exists.

CORRELATION AND REGRESSION

As we saw in the discussion about research design, there are many situations in which experiments are not feasible. This is particularly true in I-O psychology. It would be unethical, for example, to manipulate a variable that would influence well-being at work, with some conditions expected to reduce well-being and others to enhance well-being. The most common form of research is to observe and measure natural variation in the variables of interest and look for associations among those variables. Through the process of **measurement,** we can assign numbers to individuals. These numbers represent the person's standing on a variable of interest. Examples of these numbers are a test score, an index of stress or job satisfaction, a performance rating, or a grade in a training program. We may wish to examine the relationship between two of these variables to predict one variable from the other. For example, if we are interested in the association between an individual's cognitive ability and training success, we can calculate the association between

MEASUREMENT

Assigning numbers to characteristics of individuals or objects according to rules.

FIGURE 2.4

**Correlation between
Test Scores and
Training Grades**

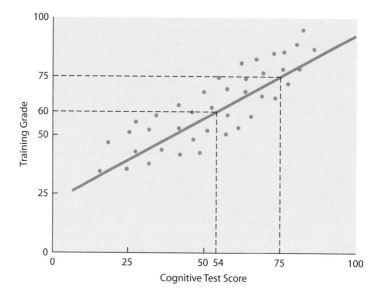

those two variables for a group of participants. If the association is statistically significant, then we can predict training success from cognitive ability. The stronger the association between the two variables, the better the prediction we are able to make from one variable to another. The statistic or measure of association most commonly used is the **correlation coefficient.**

**CORRELATION
COEFFICIENT**

*Statistic assessing
the bivariate, linear
association between
two variables. Provides
information about
both the magnitude
(numerical value) and
the direction (+ or −)
of the relationship
between two variables.*

SCATTERPLOT

*Graph used to plot the
scatter of scores on two
variables; used to
display the correlational
relationship between
two variables.*

**REGRESSION
LINE**

*Straight line that best
"fits" the scatterplot
and describes the
relationship between the
variables in the graph;
can also be presented
as an equation that
specifies where the line
intersects the vertical
axis and what the angle
or slope of the line is.*

The Concept of Correlation

The best way to appreciate the concept of correlation is graphically. Look at the hypothetical data in Figure 2.4. The vertical axis of that graph represents training grades. The horizontal axis represents a score on a test of cognitive ability. For both axes, higher numbers represent higher scores. This graph is called a **scatterplot** because it plots the scatter of the scores. Each dot represents the two scores achieved by an individual. The 40 dots represent 40 people. Notice the association between test scores and training grades. As test scores increase, training grades tend to increase as well. In high school algebra, this association would have been noted as the slope or "rise over run" meaning how much rise (increase on the vertical axis) is associated with one unit of run (increase on the horizontal axis). In statistics, the name for this form of association is correlation, and the index of correlation or association is called the correlation coefficient. You will also notice that we have drawn a solid straight line that goes through the scatterplot. This line (technically known as the **regression line**) is the straight line that best "fits" the scatterplot. The line can also be presented as an equation that specifies where the line intersects the vertical axis and what the angle or slope of the line is.

As you can see from Figure 2.4, the actual angle of the line that depicts the association is influenced by the units of measurement. If we plotted training grades against years of formal education, the angle or slope of the line might look quite different, as is depicted in Figure 2.5 where the slope of the line is much less steep or severe. For practical purposes, the regression line can be quite useful. It can be used to predict what value on the Y variable (in Figure 2.4, training grades) might be expected for someone with a particular score on the X variable (here, ability test scores). Using the scatterplot that appears in Figure 2.4, we might predict that an individual who achieved a test score of 75 could be expected to also get a training grade of 75 percent. We might use that prediction to make decisions about whom to enroll in a training program. Since we would not want to enroll someone who might be expected to fail the training

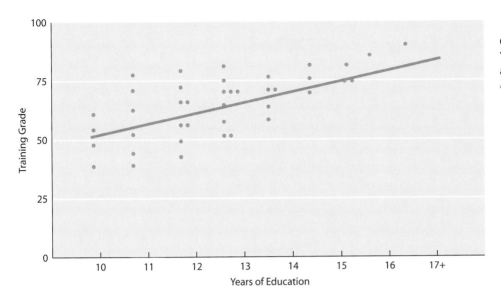

FIGURE 2.5

Correlation between Years of Education and Training Grades

program (in our case, receive a training grade of less than 60 percent), we might limit enrollment to only those applicants who achieve a score of 54 or better on the cognitive ability test.

The Correlation Coefficient

For ease of communication and for purposes of further analysis, the correlation coefficient is calculated in such a way that it always permits the same inference, regardless of the variables that are used. Its absolute value will always range between 0.00 and 1.00. A high value (e.g., .85) represents a strong association and a lower value (e.g., .15) represents a weaker association. A value of .00 means that there is no association between two variables.

Correlation coefficients have two distinct parts. The first part is the actual value or magnitude of the correlation (ranging from .00 to 1.00). The second part is the *sign* (+ or −) which precedes the numerical value. A positive (+) correlation means that there is a positive association between the variables. In our examples, as test scores and years of education go up, so do training grades. A negative (−) correlation means that as one variable goes up, the other variable tends to go down. An example of a negative correlation would be the association between age and visual acuity. As people get older, their uncorrected vision tends to get worse. In I-O psychology, we often find negative correlations between measures of commitment and absence from work. As commitment goes up, absence tends to go down, and vice versa. Figure 2.6 presents examples of the scatterplots that represent various degrees of positive and negative correlation. You will notice that we have again drawn straight lines to indicate the best fit straight line that represents the data points. By examining the scatterplots and the corresponding regression lines, you will notice something else about correlation. As the data points more closely approach the straight line, the correlation coefficients get higher. If all of the data points fell exactly on the line, the correlation coefficient would be 1.00 and there would be a "perfect" correlation between the two variables. We would be able to perfectly predict one variable from another. As the data points depart more from the straight line, the correlation coefficient gets lower until it reaches .00, indicating no relationship at all between the two variables.

Up to this point, we have been assuming that the relationship between two variables is **linear** (i.e., it can be depicted by a straight line). But the relationship might be **nonlinear**

LINEAR

Relationship between two variables that can be depicted by a straight line.

NONLINEAR

Relationship between two variables that cannot be depicted by a straight line; sometimes called "curvilinear" and most easily identified by examining a scatterplot.

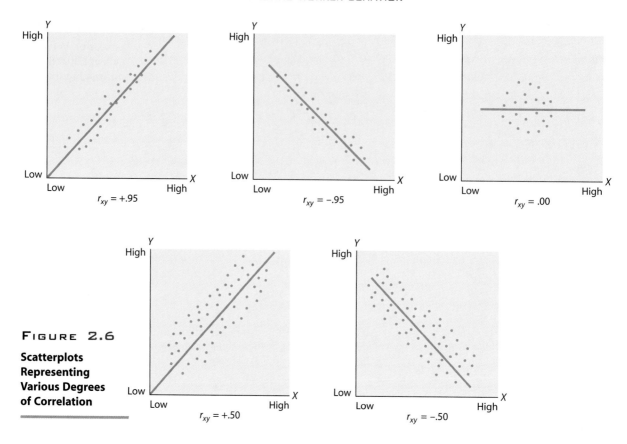

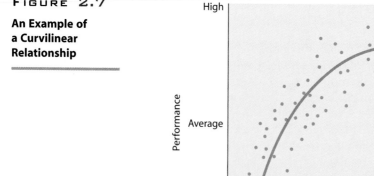

FIGURE 2.6

Scatterplots Representing Various Degrees of Correlation

(sometimes called "curvilinear"). Consider the scatterplot depicted in Figure 2.7. In this case a straight line does not represent the shape of the scatterplot at all. But a curved line does an excellent job. In this case, although the correlation coefficient might be .00, one cannot conclude that there is *no* association between the variables. We can conclude only that there is no *linear* association.

FIGURE 2.7

An Example of a Curvilinear Relationship

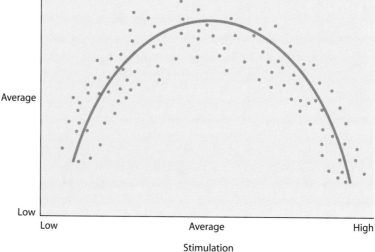

An officer directing traffic at a congested intersection is likely to experience information overload.

In this figure we have identified the two variables in question as "stimulation" and "performance." This scatterplot would tell us that stimulation and performance *are* related to each other, but in a unique way. Up to a point, stimulation aids in successful performance by keeping the employee alert, awake, and engaged. But beyond that point, stimulation makes performance more difficult by turning into information overload, which makes it difficult to keep track of relevant information and to choose appropriate actions. Most statistics texts that deal with correlation offer detailed descriptions of the methods for calculating the strength of a nonlinear correlation or association. But for the purposes of the present discussion, you merely need to know that one of the best ways to detect nonlinear relationships is to look at the scatterplots. As in Figure 2.7, this nonlinear trend will be very apparent if it is strong one. In I-O psychology, many if not most of the associations that interest us are linear.

Multiple Correlation

As we will see in later chapters, there are many situations in which more than one variable is associated with a particular aspect of behavior. For example, you will see that although cognitive ability is an important predictor of job performance, it is not the only predictor. Job performance is multiply determined. Other variables that might play a role are personality, experience, and motivation. If we were trying to predict job performance, we would want to examine the correlation between performance and all of those variables simultaneously, allowing for the fact that each variable might make an independent contribution to understanding job performance. Statistically, we could accomplish this through an analysis known as multiple correlation. The **multiple correlation coefficient** would represent the overall linear association between several variables (e.g., cognitive ability, personality, experience, motivation) on the one hand, and a single variable (e.g., job performance) on the other hand. As you can imagine, these calculations are so complex that their study is appropriate for an advanced course in prediction or statistics. For our purposes in this text, you will simply want to be aware that techniques are available for examining relationships involving multiple predictor variables.

MULTIPLE CORRELATION COEFFICIENT

Statistic that represents the overall linear association between several variables (e.g., cognitive ability, personality, experience) on the one hand, and a single variable (e.g., job performance) on the other hand.

BOX 2.1   EXPERIMENTAL DESIGN AND CAUSATION

It is not always easy to separate causes and effects. The experimental design that you use often determines what conclusions you can draw. A story is told of the researcher who interviewed the inhabitants of a particular neighborhood. He noted that the young people spoke fluent English. In speaking with the middle-aged people who would be the parent generation of the younger people, he found that they spoke English with a slight Italian accent. Finally, he spoke with older people (who would represent the grandparent generation of the youngest group) and heard a heavy Italian accent. The researcher concluded that as you grow older, you develop an Italian accent. It is a safe bet that had the researcher studied a group of people as they aged, he would have come to a very different conclusion, perhaps even an opposite one.

SOURCE: Adapted from N. Charness, ed., *Aging and Human Performance* (New York: John Wiley, 1985), p. xvii.

CORRELATION AND CAUSATION

Correlation coefficients simply represent the extent to which two variables are associated. They do not signal any cause-effect relationship. Consider the example of height and weight. They are positively correlated. The taller you are, the heavier you tend to be. But you would hardly conclude that weight *causes* height. If that were the case, we could all be as tall as we wish simply by gaining weight.

The question of correlation and causality has important bearing on many of the topics that we will consider in this book. For example, there are many studies that show a positive correlation between the extent to which a leader acts in a considerate manner and the satisfaction of the subordinates of that leader. Because of this correlation, we might be tempted to conclude that consideration *causes* satisfaction. But we might be wrong. Consider two possible alternative explanations for the positive correlation.

1.   Do we know that considerate behavior causes satisfaction rather than the other way around? It is possible that satisfied subordinates actually elicit considerate behavior on the part of a leader (and conversely, that a leader might "crack down" on dissatisfied work group members).

2.   Can we be sure that the positive correlation is not due to a third variable? What if work group productivity were high because of a particularly able and motivated group? High levels of productivity are likely to be associated with satisfaction in workers, and high levels of productivity are likely to allow a leader to concentrate on considerate behaviors instead of pressuring workers for higher production. Thus, a third variable might actually be responsible for the positive correlation between two other variables.

A key characteristic of leaders is that they influence followers.

META-ANALYSIS

Cancer researchers, clinicians, and patient advocates have recently engaged in a vigorous debate over whether women aged 40 to 70 can decrease their chances of dying from breast cancer by having an annual mammogram. One expert asserts that the earlier cancer can be detected, the greater the chance of a cure, and that an annual mammogram is the only reliable means of early detection. Another argues that this is not necessarily true and, furthermore, because mammograms deliver potentially harmful radiation, they should be used only every two or three years unless a patient has significant risk factors for the disease. Still another says that mammograms give a false sense of security and may discourage patients from monitoring their own health. Experts on all sides cite multiple studies to support their position. And women are left with an agonizing dilemma: Who is right? What is the "truth"?

As you will see when you wade into the I-O research literature, similar confusion exists over the interpretation of study results in psychology topics. You may find *hundreds* of studies on the same topic. Each study is done with a different sample, a different sample size, and a different observational or experimental environment. By 1976, for example, more than 3,000 studies of job satisfaction had been contributed to the literature (Locke, 1986), a number that now is likely to be closer to 5,000. It is not uncommon for individual studies to come to different conclusions. For example, one study of the relationship between age and job satisfaction may have administered a locally developed satisfaction questionnaire to 96 engineers employed by Company X between the ages of 45 and 57. The study might have found a very slight positive correlation (e.g., $+.12$) between age and satisfaction. Another study might have distributed a commercially available satisfaction questionnaire to 855 managerial level employees of Company Y between the ages of 27 and 64. The second study might have concluded that there was a strong positive correlation (e.g., $+.56$) between age and satisfaction. A third study of 44 outside sales representatives for Company Z between the ages of 22 and 37 using the same commercially available satisfaction questionnaire might have found a slight negative correlation between age and satisfaction (e.g., $-.15$). Which study is "right"? How can we choose among them?

Meta-analysis is a statistical method for combining results from many studies to draw a general conclusion (Glass, 1976; Hunter, Schmidt, & Jackson, 1982; Murphy, 2002b; Landy, 2002c; Schmidt & Hunter, 2002a). Meta-analysis is based on the premise that observed values (like the three correlations shown above) are influenced by **statistical artifacts** (characteristics of the particular study that distort the results). The most influential of these artifacts is sample size. Others include the spread of scores and the reliability of the measures used ("reliability" is a technical term that refers to the consistency or repeatability of a measurement; we will discuss it in the next section of this chapter). Consider the three hypothetical studies we presented above. One had a sample size of 96, the second of 855, and the third of 44. Consider also the range of scores on age for the three studies. The first had an age range from 45 to 57 (12 years). The second study had participants who ranged in age from 27 to 64 (37 years). The participants in the third study ranged from 22 to 37 years of age (15 years, with no "older" employees). Finally, two of the studies used commercially available satisfaction questionnaires, which very likely had high reliability, and the third study used a "locally developed" questionnaire which may have been less reliable. Using these three studies as examples, we would probably have greater confidence in the study with 855 participants, with an age range of 37 years, and which used a more reliable questionnaire. Nevertheless, the other studies tell us something. We're just not sure what that something is, because of the influences of the restricted age ranges, the sample sizes, and the reliabilities of the questionnaires.

In its most basic form, meta-analysis is a complex statistical procedure that includes information about these statistical artifacts (sample size, reliability, and range restriction) and corrects for their influences, producing an estimate of what the actual relationship is in the studies available. But it is possible to include variables beyond these statistical artifacts that might also influence results. A good example of such a variable is the nature of participants in the study. Some studies might conclude that racial or gender stereotypes influence performance ratings, while other studies conclude that there are no such effects. If we separate the studies into those done with student participants and those done with employees of companies, we might discover that stereotypes have a strong influence on student ratings of hypothetical subordinates, but that stereotypes have no influence on the ratings of real subordinates by real supervisors.

Meta-analysis can be a very powerful research tool. It combines individual studies that have already been completed and, by virtue of the number and diversity of these studies, has the potential to "liberate" conclusions that were obscure or confusing at the level of

META-ANALYSIS

Statistical method for combining and analyzing the results from many studies to draw a general conclusion about relationships among variables.

STATISTICAL ARTIFACTS

Characteristics (e.g., small sample size, unreliable measures) of a particular study that distort the observed results. Researchers can correct for artifacts to arrive at a statistic that represents the "true" relationship between the variables of interest.

the individual study. Meta-analyses are appearing with greater regularity in the I-O journals (Landy, 2002c) and represent a real step forward in I-O research (Murphy, 2002b). We will examine the application of meta-analysis to the relationship between tests and job performance in Chapter 4.

MODULE 2.3 SUMMARY

- Descriptive statistics are expressed in terms of absolute values without interpretation. Inferential statistics allow a researcher to identify a relationship between variables. The threshold for statistical significance is .05, or 5 occurrences out of 100. Statistical power comes from using a large enough sample to make results reliable.

- A statistical index that can be used to estimate the strength of a linear relationship between two variables is called a correlation coefficient. The relationship can also be described graphically, in which case a regression line can be drawn to illustrate the relationship. A multiple correlation coefficient indicates the strength of the relationship between one variable and the composite of several other variables.

- Correlation is a means of describing a relationship between two variables. When examining any observed relationship and before drawing any causal inferences, the researcher must consider whether the relationship is due to a third variable or whether the second variable is causing the first rather than vice versa.

- Meta-analysis, the statistical analysis of multiple studies, is a powerful means of estimating relationships in those studies. It is a complex statistical procedure that includes information about statistical artifacts and other variables, and corrects for their influences.

KEY TERMS

descriptive statistics	inferential statistics	linear
measure of central tendency	statistical significance	nonlinear
variability	statistical power	multiple correlation coefficient
skew	measurement	meta-analysis
mean	correlation coefficient	statistical artifacts
mode	scatterplot	
median	regression line	

CRITICAL THINKING EXERCISES

2.5 If you were to examine the correlation between age and stamina in a group of individuals who did not exercise, you would find a strong negative correlation—older individuals would demonstrate less stamina. In contrast, if you were to study the same relationship in a group of individuals who engaged in strenuous cardiovascular exercise (e.g., did track workouts four times per week), the relationship would be considerably weaker. Which of the following statistical principles would be demonstrated by such a study and why?

Regression	Significance
Multiple correlation	Statistical artifact
Statistical power	
Statistical control	

2.6 Correlation cannot be equated with causation. We presented the example of height and weight to illustrate that point. Give three additional examples of correlations that would be misleading if they were explained using a cause-effect logic.

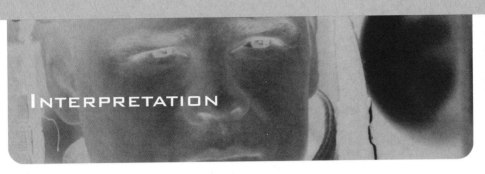

INTERPRETATION

So far, we have considered the scientific method, the design of research studies, the collection of data, and the statistical analyses of data. All of these procedures prepare us for the most important part of research and application: the interpretation of the data based on the statistical analyses. The job of the psychologist is to make sense out of what he or she sees. Data collection and analysis are certainly the foundations of making sense, but data do not make sense of themselves, they require someone to interpret them.

Any measurement that we take is a sample of some behavioral domain. A test of reasoning ability, a questionnaire related to satisfaction or stress, or a training grade are all samples of some larger behavioral domain. We hope that these samples are consistent, accurate, and representative of the domains of interest. If they are, then we can make accurate inferences based on these measurements. If they are not, our inferences, and ultimately our decisions, will be flawed, regardless of whether the decision is to hire someone, institute a new motivation program, or initiate a stress reduction program. We use measurement to assist in decision making. Because a sample of behavior is just that—an example of a type of behavior but not a complete assessment—all samples, by definition, are incomplete or imperfect. So we are always in a position of having to draw inferences or make decisions based on incomplete or imperfect measurements. The challenge is to make sure that the measurements are "complete enough" or "perfect enough" for our purposes.

The technical terms for these characteristics of measurement are **reliability** and **validity.** If a measure is unreliable, we would get different values each time we sampled the behavior. If a measure is not valid, we are gathering incomplete or inaccurate information. Although the terms "reliability" and "validity" are most often applied to test scores, they could be applied to any measure. We must expect reliability and validity from any measure that we will use to infer something about the behavior of an individual. This includes surveys or questionnaires, behavioral measures such as counts of production, interview responses, performance evaluation ratings, and test scores.

RELIABILITY

When we say that someone is "reliable," we mean that he or she is someone we can count on, someone predictable and consistent, someone we can depend on for help if we ask for it. The same is true of measures. We need to feel confident that if we took the measure again, at a different time, or if someone else took the measurement, the value would remain the same. Suppose you went for a physical and before you saw the doctor, the nurse took your temperature and found it to be 98.6. If the doctor came in five minutes later and retook your temperature and reported that it was 101.5, you would be surprised. You would have expected those readings to agree, given the short time span between measurements. With a discrepancy this large, you would wonder about the skill of the

RELIABILITY

Consistency or stability of a measure.

VALIDITY

The accurateness of inferences made based on test or performance data; also addresses whether a measure accurately and completely represents what was intended to be measured.

nurse, the skill of the doctor, or the adequacy of the thermometer. In technical terms, you would wonder about the reliability of that measure.

Test-Retest Reliability

There are several different aspects to measurement reliability. One aspect is simply the temporal consistency—the consistency over time—of a measure. Would we have gotten the same value had we taken the measurement next week as opposed to this week, or next month rather than this month? If we set out to measure someone's memory skills and this week find that they are quite good, but upon retesting the same person next week we find that they are quite poor, what do we conclude? Does the participant have a good memory or not? Generally speaking, we want our measures to produce the same value over a reasonable time period. This type of reliability, known as **test-retest reliability,** is often calculated as a correlation coefficient between measurements taken at time one and measurements taken at time two. Consider Figure 2.8. On the left side, you see high agreement between measures of the same people taken at two different points in time. On the right side, you find low levels of agreement between the two measurements. The measurements on the left would be considered reliable, while those on the right would be considered unreliable, at least from a temporal perspective.

TEST-RETEST RELIABILITY

Calculated by correlating measurements taken at time one with measurements taken at time two.

Equivalent Forms Reliability

Remember when you took the SAT®? The SAT has been administered to millions of high school students over the decades since its introduction. But the *same* SAT items have not been administered to those millions of students. If that were the case, the answers to those items would have long since been circulated among dishonest test takers. For many students, the test would simply be a test of the extent to which they could memorize the right answers. Instead, the test developers have devised many different *forms* of the examination that are assumed to cover the same general content, but with

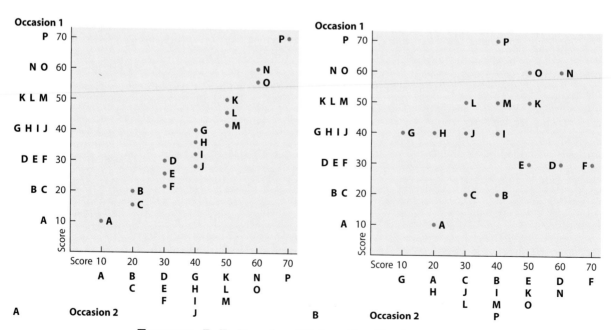

FIGURE 2.8 **Examples of High and Low Test-Retest Reliability: Score Distributions of Individuals Tested on Two Different Occasions**

items unique to each form. Assume you take the test in Ames, Iowa, and another student takes a different form of the test in Philadelphia. How do we know that these two forms reliably measure your knowledge and abilities; that you would have gotten roughly the same score had you switched seats (and tests) with the other student? Just as was the case in test-retest reliability, you can have many people take two different forms of the test and see if they get the same score. By correlating their two test scores, you would be calculating the **equivalent forms reliability** of that test. Look at Figure 2.8 again. Simply substitute the term "Form A" for "Occasion 1" and "Form B" for "Occasion 2" and you will see that the left part of the figure would describe a test with high equivalent forms reliability, while the test on the right would demonstrate low equivalent forms reliability.

Internal Consistency

As you can see from the examples above, to calculate either test-retest or equivalent forms reliability, you would need to have two separate testing sessions (either with the same form or different forms). Another way of estimating the reliability of a test is to pretend that instead of one test, you really have two or more. A simple example would be to take a 100-item test and break it into two 50-item tests by collecting all of the even-numbered items together and all of the odd-numbered items together. You could then correlate the total score for all even-numbered items that were answered correctly with the total score for all of the odd-numbered items answered correctly. If the subtest scores correlated highly, you would consider the test reliable from an **internal consistency** standpoint. If we are trying to measure a homogeneous attribute (e.g., memory, stress, or interpersonal skills), all of the items on the test should give us an equally good measure of that attribute. There are more sophisticated ways of estimating internal consistency reliability based on the average correlation between every pair of test items. A common statistic used to estimate internal consistency reliability using such averages is known as *Cronbach's Alpha*.

Inter-rater Reliability

Often several different individuals make judgments about a person. These judgments might be ratings of performance of a worker made by several different supervisors, assessments of the same candidate by multiple interviewers, or evaluations made by several incumbents about the relative importance of a task in a particular job. In each of these cases, we would expect the raters to agree regarding what they have observed. We can calculate various statistical indices to show the level of agreement among the raters. These statistics would be considered estimates of inter-rater reliability.

As you can see from our discussion of reliability, there are different ways to calculate the reliability index, and each may describe a different aspect of reliability. To the extent that any of the reliability coefficients are less than 1.00 (the ideal coefficient denoting perfect reliability), we assume there is some error in the observed score and that it is not a perfectly consistent measure. Nevertheless, measures are not expected to be perfectly reliable; they are simply expected to be *reasonably* reliable. The convention is that values in the range of .70 to .80 represent reasonable reliability. Although we have considered each of these methods of estimating reliability separately, they all address the same general issue that we covered earlier in the chapter: generalizability. The question is, to what extent can we generalize the meaning of a measure taken with one measuring device at one point in time? A more sophisticated approach to the question of reliability is based in **generalizability theory** (Cronbach, Gleser, Nanda, & Rajaratnam, 1972; Guion, 1998), which considers all different types of error (e.g., test-retest, equivalent forms, and internal consistency) simultaneously, but a description of this technique is beyond the scope of this text.

EQUIVALENT FORMS RELIABILITY

Calculated by correlating measurements from a sample of individuals who complete two different forms of the same test.

INTERNAL CONSISTENCY

Form of reliability that assesses how consistently the items of a test measure a single construct; affected by the number of items in the test and the correlations among the test items.

GENERALIZABILITY THEORY

A sophisticated approach to the question of reliability that simultaneously considers all types of error in reliability estimates (e.g., test-retest, equivalent forms, and internal consistency).

VALIDITY

The second characteristic of good measurement is validity. Reliability dealt with whether or not we had consistent information on which to base decisions. Validity addresses the issue of whether the measurements we have taken accurately and completely represent what we had hoped to measure. For example, consider the job of a physician in general practice. Suppose we wanted to develop a measure of the performance of general practitioners and that we decided to use malpractice insurance rates over the years as a measure of performance. We note that these rates have gone up every year for a particular physician, and we conclude that the physician must not be very good. If he or she were good, we would have expected such malpractice premiums to have gone down.

In the physician example, the measure we have chosen to represent performance would be neither accurate nor complete. Malpractice rates have much less to do with a particular doctor than they do with claims in general and with amounts awarded by juries in malpractice lawsuits. Both the number of malpractice suits and the jury awards for those suits have climbed steadily over the last few decades. As a result, you would note that malpractice premiums (like car insurance premiums) have climbed steadily *every year for almost every physician*. Further, a physician in general practice has a wide variety of duties, including diagnosis, treatment, follow-up, education, referral, record keeping, continuing education, and so forth. Even if malpractice premium rates were accurate representations of performance in certain areas such as diagnosis and treatment, many other areas of performance would have been ignored by this one measure.

In considering reliability, we examine the extent to which we can infer that the measure we have is a consistent one, one that is unlikely to change rapidly and unpredictably. We want to infer that what we are measuring is stable. In both reliability and validity, the question is whether what we have measured allows us to make predictions or decisions, or take actions, based on what we assume to be the content of those measures. In our physician example, if we were deciding whether to allow a physician to keep a medical license or to be added to the staff of a hospital, and we based that decision on our chosen "performance" measure (malpractice premiums), our decision (or inference that physicians with a history of increasing premiums were poor performers) would not be a valid decision or inference.

You will remember that we concluded our discussion of reliability by introducing the concept of generalizability. What we said was that reliability was really a unitary phenomenon and that the various estimates of reliability (e.g., test-retest) were really just different ways to get at a single issue: consistency of measurement. The important concept to keep in mind was generalizability. The same is true of validity. Like reliability, there are several different ways to gather information about the accuracy and completeness of a measure. Also like reliability, validity is a unitary concept; you should not think that one type of validity tells you anything different about the completeness and accuracy of a measure than any other type of validity (Binning & Barrett, 1989; Guion 1998; Landy, 1986). Like reliability, validity concerns the confidence with which you can make a prediction or draw an inference based on the measurements you have collected. There are three common ways of gathering validity evidence. We will describe each of these three ways below.

Although validity is relevant to discussions of any measurement, most validity studies address the issue of whether an assessment permits confident decisions about hiring or promotion. Although most validity studies revolve around tests (e.g., tests of personality or cognitive ability), other assessments (e.g., interviews, application blanks, or even tests of aerobic endurance) might form the basis of a validity study. For the purposes of this chapter, we will use hiring and promotion as the examples of the decisions that we have to make. For such purposes, we have a general hypothesis that people who score higher or better on a particular measure will be more productive and/or

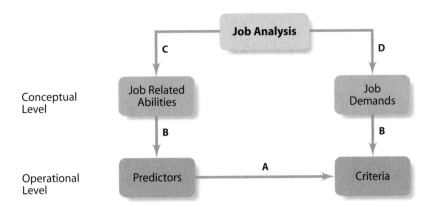

FIGURE 2.9

Validation Process from Conceptual and Operational Levels

satisfied employees (Landy, 1986). Our validity investigation will be focused on gathering information that will make us more confident that this hypothesis can be supported. If we are able to gather such confirming information, we can make decisions about individual applicants with confidence—our inference about a person from a test score will be valid. Remember, validity is not about tests, it is about decisions or inferences.

I-O psychologists usually gather validity evidence using one of three common designs. We will consider each of these designs in turn. All three fit into the same general framework (see Figure 2.9). The box on the top is labeled "Job Analysis." Job analysis is a complex and time-consuming process which we will describe in detail in Chapter 5. For purposes of the current discussion, you simply need to think of job analysis as a way of identifying the important demands (e.g., tasks, duties) of a job and the human attributes necessary to carry out those demands successfully. Once the attributes (e.g., abilities) are identified, the test that is chosen or developed to assess those abilities is called a **predictor,** which is used to forecast another variable. Similarly, when the demands of the job are identified, the definition of an individual's performance in meeting those demands is called a **criterion,** which is the variable that we want to predict. In Figure 2.9, you will see a line with an arrow connecting predictors and criteria. This line represents the hypothesis we outlined above. It is hypothesized that people who do better on the predictor will also do better on the criterion—people who score higher will be better employees. We gather validity evidence to test that hypothesis.

Criterion-Related Validity

The most direct way to support the hypothesis (i.e., to connect the predictor and criteria boxes) is to actually gather data and compute a correlation coefficient. In this design, technically referred to as a **criterion-related validity** design, you would correlate test scores with performance measures. If the correlation was positive and statistically significant, you would now have evidence improving your confidence in the inference that people with higher test scores have higher performance. By correlating these test scores with the performance data, you would be calculating what is known as a **validity coefficient.** The test might be a test of intelligence and the performance measure might be a supervisor's rating. Since we mentioned a "supervisor's rating," something becomes immediately obvious about this design: We are using the test scores of people who are employed by the organization. This can be done in two different ways.

Predictive Validity The first method of conducting a criterion-related study is to test all applicants, then hire applicants without using those test scores to make the hiring decision. You would then go back to the organization after some time period had passed (e.g., six or nine months) and collect performance data. This design, where there is a time lag

PREDICTOR

The test chosen or developed to assess attributes (e.g., abilities) identified as important for successful job performance.

CRITERION

An outcome variable that describes important aspects or demands of the job; the variable that we predict when evaluating the validity of a predictor.

CRITERION-RELATED VALIDITY

Validity approach that is demonstrated by correlating a test score with a performance measure; improves researcher's confidence in the inference that people with higher test scores have higher performance.

VALIDITY COEFFICIENT

Correlation coefficient between a test score (predictor) and a performance measure (criterion).

between the collection of the test data and the criterion data, is known as a **predictive validity design** because it enables you to predict what would have happened had you actually used the test scores to make the hiring decisions. If the test scores were related to performance scores, you may conclude that you should not have hired some people. Their performance was poor, as were their test scores. From the point at which the employer knows that the validity coefficient is positive and significant, test scores can be used for making future hiring decisions. The validity coefficient does not, by itself, tell you *what* score to designate as a passing score. We will deal with this issue in Chapter 7 where we consider the actual staffing process. The predictive validity design we have described above is only one of many different predictive designs you might employ. Some other predictive validity designs are presented in Table 2.2.

Concurrent Validity   In research on many diseases such as cancer and coronary heart disease, researchers carry out a process known as a clinical trial. The clinical trial design assigns some patients to a treatment group and others to a control group. The treatment group actually gets the treatment under study (e.g., a pill) while the control group does not. Instead, the control group gets a placebo (e.g., a pill with neutral ingredients). It is difficult to recruit patients for many clinical trials because they want to be in the treatment group and don't want to take the chance of being assigned to a control group (although they would not typically know to which group they had been assigned). If the treatment is actually effective, it will benefit the treatment group patients, but the control group patients will not experience the benefits. Many employers and I-O researchers are like the prospective patients for the control group—they don't want to wait months or even years to see if the "treatment" (e.g., an ability test) is effective. While they are waiting for the results, they may be hiring ineffective performers.

There is a criterion-related validity design that directly addresses that concern. It is called the **concurrent validity design.** This design has no lag between gathering the test scores and the performance data because the test in question is administered to current employees rather than applicants, and performance measures can be collected on

TABLE 2.2	Variations of Predictive Validity Designs

TYPE OF VALIDITY	PROCEDURE
1. Follow up—random	Test applicants; select randomly; collect criterion data later; correlate test scores and criterion data
2. Follow up—present system	Test applicants; select using procedures used in past; collect criterion data later; correlate test scores and criterion data
3. Select by test	Test applicants; select based on test scores; collect criterion data later; correlate test scores and criterion data
4. Hire, then test	Hire applicants; test during orientation or training; collect criterion data later; correlate test scores and criterion data
5. Shelf research	Hire applicants; collect criterion data later; examine personnel folders for potential predictors; correlate potential predictors and criterion data

Source: Based on R. M. Guion and C. J. Cranny (1982), pp. 239–44.

those employees simultaneously, or concurrently (thus the term, concurrent design). Since the employees are actually working for the organization, the assumption is made that they must be at least minimally effective, alleviating any concern about adding new employees who are not minimally effective. As in the case of the predictive design, test scores are correlated with performance scores to yield a validity coefficient. If it is positive and significant, the test is then made part of the process by which new employees are hired.

There is a potential disadvantage in using the concurrent design, however. We have no information about those who are *not* employed by the organization. This has both technical and practical implications. The technical implication is that you have range restriction—only the scores of those who scored highly on the predictor—so the correlation coefficient may be artificially depressed and may not be statistically significant. There are statistical corrections that can offset that problem. The practical problem is that there might have been applicants who did less well than the employees did on the test, yet might have been successful performers. Since they were never hired, the employer will never know. I-O psychologists have conducted a good deal of research comparing concurrent and predictive designs, and their general conclusion has been that, even though the concurrent design might underestimate validity coefficients, in practice this does not usually happen (Barrett, Phillips, & Alexander, 1981; Guion & Cranny, 1982; Schmidt, Gooding, Noe, & Kirsch, 1984). One final problem with concurrent designs is that the test-taking motivation may not be as high for those who are already employed. It is also useful to remember that both concurrent and predictive designs are only two variations on many different ways to assemble validity data (Guion, 1998; Landy, 1986). We will now consider two additional methods for collecting validity data.

Content-Related Validity

The SIOP Principles define **content-related validation** strategy as "a study that demonstrates that the content of the selection procedure represents an adequate sample of important work behaviors and activities, and/or worker knowledge, skills, abilities or other characteristics (KSAOs) defined by the analysis of work" (SIOP, in press). The job analysis in Figure 2.9 is an example of this strategy. As another example, assume you are the director of a temporary employment agency and want to hire applicants who can be assigned to word processing tasks for companies. You know that these companies typically use either WordPerfect or Microsoft Word and use either a MacIntosh or a PC system. So you ask the job applicants to demonstrate their proficiency with both of these word processing packages on both PCs and Macs. Since not all employers have the latest hardware or software, you also ask the applicants to perform sample word processing tasks on various versions of the software and different vintages of hardware. By doing this, you have taken the essence of the work for which you are hiring individuals—word processing on any of a number of hardware and software configurations—and turned it into a test.

There can be little argument that at least conceptually there is a clear link between test scores and probable performance in our example. Of course, you would also need to demonstrate that the test you had assembled fairly represented the types of word processing projects that the temporary employees would encounter. If you were using only the word processing test, you would also need to show that actual word processing (e.g., as opposed to developing financial spreadsheets with Excel) is the most important part of the work for which these temps are hired. If, for example, the temps were hired to answer phones or manually file records, the test of word processing would be largely irrelevant. But assuming that the job the temps will be asked to do is word processing, you can infer that applicants who do better on your test will tend to do better at the actual

CONTENT-
RELATED
VALIDATION
DESIGN

Demonstrates that the content of the selection procedure represents an adequate sample of important work behaviors and activities and/or worker KSAOs defined by the job analysis.

word processing tasks in the jobs to which they are assigned. The validity of the inference is based not on a correlation, but on a logical comparison of the test and the work. To return to Figure 2.9, although the focus of the study is the association between a predictor and a criterion (in this case the speed and accuracy of word processing), no criterion information from the work setting is collected.

The example of the word processing test was simple and straightforward. Many jobs are not quite as simple as that of a word processor. Consider the position of a manager of a cellular telephone store with 5 inside and 15 outside sales and technical representatives. Suppose the company were to open a companion store in the next town, and needed to hire a manager for that store. How could we employ a content-related design to gather data that would give us confidence in making the hiring decision? The job of manager is complex, involving many varied tasks, as well as a wide variety of knowledge, skills, abilities, and interpersonal attributes. Using Figure 2.9 as our model, we would analyze the job to determine the most important tasks or duties, as well as the abilities needed to perform those tasks. How would we do this? By asking experienced employees and supervisors in other cellular phone stores to give us the benefit of their observations and personal experience. We would ask them to complete one or more questionnaires that covered tasks and their importance and necessary abilities. Based on an analysis of their answers, we could then identify or develop possible predictors for testing manager candidates. We would then choose the set of predictors which measured abilities that had been judged to be most closely related to various performance demands for managers.

Through the use of knowledgeable incumbent employees and supervisors, we would have been able to make the logical connection between the predictors and anticipated performance. Although content-related validation designs for jobs can become rather complex, we have described the "basic" model so you can get a feel for how the content-related strategy differs from the criterion-related strategy. But remember, both strategies are addressing the same basic hypothesis: People who do better on our tests will do better on the job.

Construct-Related Validity

Calling **construct validity** a "type" of validity is a historical accident and not really correct (Landy, 1986). In the 1950s, a task force outlined several ways to gather validity evidence and labeled three of them: criterion, content, and construct (Cronbach & Meehl, 1955). The labels have stuck. Modern I-O psychology, however, does not recognize that distinction—referred to sarcastically by Guion (1980) as the "holy trinity." Instead, as we have described above, validity is considered "unitarian" rather than "trinitarian." There are literally hundreds of ways of gathering evidence that will increase the confidence of our decisions or inferences. Criterion-related designs and content-related designs are two of the many available approaches (Guion, 1998; Landy, 1986). Every study could have a different design, even though some may be more popular than others. The same is true with validity designs. Every validity study could have a different design, but criterion- and content-related designs are among the most popular, for reasons we will describe below.

A simple definition of construct validity is that it represents "the integration of evidence that bears on the interpretation or meaning of test scores—including content and criterion-related evidence—which are subsumed as part of construct validity" (Messick, 1995, p. 742). A **construct** can be defined as a "concept or characteristic that a predictor is intended to measure" (SIOP, in press). A construct is a broad representation of a human characteristic. Intelligence, personality, and leadership are all examples of constructs. Memory, assertiveness, or supportive leader behavior are all examples of these broader entities.

FIGURE 2.10

**A Model for
Construct Validity**

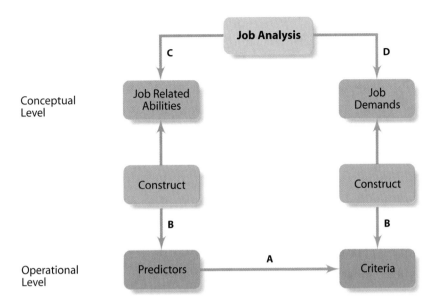

Examine Figure 2.10. As you can see by comparing this with Figure 2.9, we have simply added the term "construct" to our generic validation model. The modified figure demonstrates that constructs are related to both abilities and job demands. Let's return to the job of a financial consultant for an investment banking firm. As a result of a job analysis, we were able to determine that memory and reasoning were important parts of the job of a financial consultant since the job required the consultant to remember data about various stocks and bonds and to use that information to develop an investment strategy for an individual client. What is one of the broad and essential attributes necessary to do well on both a test of reasoning and memory, and to be effective in advising clients on how they should invest their money? It is intelligence, or cognitive ability. In this case, the construct is intelligence and we see it as underlying both performance on the test and performance on the job. In other words, doing well on the job requires the same construct as doing well on the test.

The contribution of the concept of construct validation is that it encourages the investigator to cast a broad net in gathering evidence to support decisions or inferences. In a criterion-related study, there was a tight focus on a test score and a performance score. In content-related validation, there was a tight focus on a job analysis. In our example of the financial consultant, construct validation would allow for evidence from studies that have been done previously on the topics of intelligence, reasoning, and memory; job analysis information on the financial consultants in many different forms and industries; well-developed theories of decision making and memory; and even observations of how memory and reasoning are used in a broad range of occupational groups. It could also include evidence from criterion- or content-related studies of the job in the firm that is considering using the memory and reasoning test. Arvey (1992) presents another example of a construct validation design in the area of physical ability testing for police officers. That example is shown in Figure 2.11. In this case, the constructs are strength and endurance rather than intelligence. In the case of strength, the hypothesis is that strength underlies the ability to perform bench dips, climb walls, wrestle with a dummy, and drag a dummy in a test environment, as well as the ability to climb real walls and restrain real suspects. Similarly, the endurance hypothesis is that individuals who can do well on a mile run can also do well in pursuing suspects in a foot chase. Endurance is the construct that underlies doing well both on the test and on the job. Evidence that bears on these two hypotheses could come from a literature review on

FIGURE 2.11

**Construct Validity
Model of Strength
and Endurance
Physical Factors**
SOURCE: Arvey (1992), Fig. 3,
p. 65.

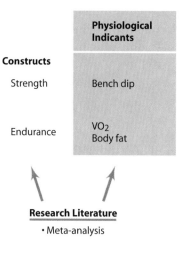

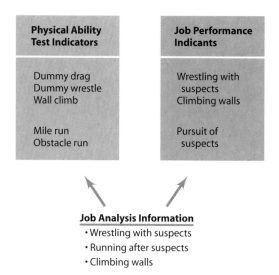

Constructs	Physiological Indicants	Physical Ability Test Indicators	Job Performance Indicants
Strength	Bench dip	Dummy drag Dummy wrestle Wall climb	Wrestling with suspects Climbing walls
Endurance	VO₂ Body fat	Mile run Obstacle run	Pursuit of suspects

Research Literature
• Meta-analysis

Job Analysis Information
• Wrestling with suspects
• Running after suspects
• Climbing walls

physical performance, laboratory studies, field studies, accepted theories of muscular strength and aerobic endurance, and observations or interviews of police officers (or even suspects). The key is in the integration of this evidence to strengthen our confidence that making hiring decisions based on strength or endurance measures will lead to more effective performance for police officers.

The more evidence we can gather, the more confident we can be in our decisions and inferences. As you will recall, we began this module by pointing out that we seldom have complete information on which to base decisions. We deal in samples of behavior. As a result, we must eventually make a decision that the information we have is sufficiently reliable, accurate, and comprehensive to make the necessary decisions or draw the necessary inferences. Sometimes the decisions are small and simple and we don't need a great deal of evidence, as in the example of hiring the word processing temps. In other situations, such as the development of a national recruiting and selection program for financial consultants, the decisions are big and complicated and we need a lot of evidence. The scope of the decisions and inferences will dictate how much evidence we need to be confident in those decisions. There is no clear bright line that says "collect this much evidence and no more." As a general principle, it is more effective to use several different designs and gather substantial evidence, regardless of what we call the evidence, than to depend on a single design, such as a criterion-related or content-related design. The greater the accumulation of evidence, the greater our confidence. Here we might think of the combination of the lab and field study. The lab study provides rigorous cause-effect analyses and the field study provides real-world relevance.

VALIDITY AND THE LAW: A MIXED BLESSING

Until the 1960s, discussions about validity and the validation process were of interest only to a relatively small community of I-O psychologists and psychometricians. The Civil Rights Act of 1964 and the resulting development of the Equal Employment Opportunity Commission changed all that. By 1972 the government was requiring employers to present validity evidence as a defense against employment discrimination claims. If, for example, a minority or female applicant complained of failing to receive a job offer because of unfair discrimination, the employer was required to show that the test or hiring practice in question was fair and job-related (in I-O terms, "valid"). Furthermore, the employer was told that the only convincing evidence would be in the form of a criterion-related study. By 1978 the government had grudgingly broadened its view a bit to permit content-related and construct-related evidence, but it was clear that the "gold standard" would still be criterion-related evidence (Landy, 1986).

For the last 30 years, in the context of employment discrimination lawsuits, judges have issued opinions on the adequacy of validity models and validity evidence, and, more importantly, on what they believe to be the necessary elements for those models. As a result, what had originally been three *examples* of designs for gathering evidence have become the *only* three acceptable models or designs, and the characteristics that constitute an "acceptable" study have become increasingly detailed. This is a good news–bad news situation. The good news is that the concept of validity is receiving the attention it deserves. The bad news is that the evolving view of validation is becoming more distant from the way it was originally conceived and from the way I-O psychologists think of the concept in the 21st century. Most judges are not particularly talented psychometricians (just as, we hasten to add, most psychometricians would not necessarily be talented judges). There is an increasing tension between I-O psychology and the courts on technical issues related to assessment and decision making (Landy, 2002a, 2002b). The current federal guidelines which are often relied upon in discrimination cases (Uniform Guidelines, 1978) are hopelessly out of date on issues such as validation strategies. As long as they remain an "authority" in discrimination cases, there will be a serious lack of agreement between I-O psychology and public (and employer) policy. We will revisit the issue of the interface of law and I-O psychology in Chapters 7 and 11.

MODULE 2.4 SUMMARY

- To interpret data, it is important to consider reliability, which is the extent to which the measures are consistent over time, in different equivalent forms, and from one rater to another.
- There are several traditional designs for demonstrating validity, including content, criterion-related, and construct. All designs are intended to answer the question of whether better performance on the test or predictor is associated with better performance on the job.

- The question of validity is significant in many court decisions affecting workplace issues, the advantage being that it gives recognition to the value of I-O research. Its drawback is that the courts and legislatures have narrowed the range of research designs that are considered acceptable, and have established guidelines that do not keep up with current work in the field.

KEY TERMS

reliability	generalizability theory	predictive validity design
validity	predictor	concurrent validity design
test-retest reliability	criterion	content-related validation design
equivalent forms reliability	criterion-related validity	construct validity
internal consistency	validity coefficient	construct

CRITICAL THINKING EXERCISES

2.7 Suppose that your instructor gave an examination by computer, and the electronic file containing your responses was inadvertently erased, requiring a second test. Assume further that the instructor administered this repeat test two weeks later. After readministering the test, a backup file of the first test result was discovered and your instructor correlated the first set of class scores with the second set and found a correlation of +.30. Would this mean that one or the other (or both) of the two tests was unreliable? Explain your answer.

2.8 Plant X of Company A creates a new job associated with a new manufacturing technology. In order to develop a strategy for hiring applicants for that job, they ask Plant Y of Company A, a plant that has been using the new technology for several months, to provide a sample of workers who hold the job title in question to complete a potential screening examination for the job. Plant X then correlates the test scores of these workers with performance ratings. What type of validity design has Plant X chosen? Name one alternative design they might have chosen and describe how it would have satisfied their need.

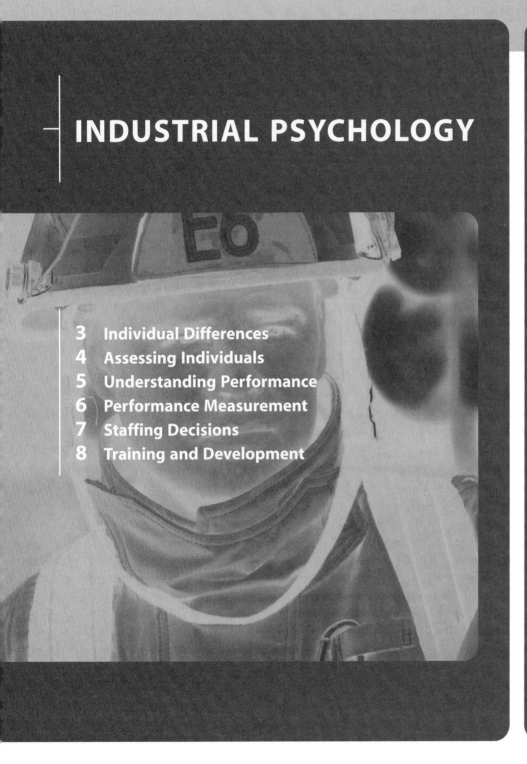

INDUSTRIAL PSYCHOLOGY

2 PART

INDIVIDUAL DIFFERENCES

AN INTRODUCTION TO INDIVIDUAL DIFFERENCES

What do Princess Diana, the Pope, Yo-Yo Ma, Stephen King, Michael Jordan, George W. Bush, your grandmother, and your instructor have in common? Not much. They are different in abilities, interests, experiences, personality, age, gender, race, and backgrounds. Indeed, the only thing we can say with certainty about these individuals is that they are substantially different from one another. We would not expect your grandmother to try out for an NBA team, or Stephen King to officiate at a religious service, or your instructor to meet with heads of state of foreign countries. Many psychologists, including I-O psychologists, believe that the differences among individuals can be used, at least in part, to understand and predict their behavior.

But it isn't good enough to say simply that people are different. You don't have to be a psychologist to recognize that. Some types of differences prove more useful than others in predicting and understanding behavior. The differences among people on various attributes like intelligence, and personality, and knowledge are important in understanding a wide variety of socially important outcomes (Lubinski, 2000), including:

- Academic achievement
- Intellectual development
- Crime and delinquency
- Vocational choice
- Income and poverty
- Occupational performance

This chapter will deal with the concept of **individual differences** related to occupational performance. In the next chapter, we will show you the scientific ways that I-O psychologists use to measure these differences.

INDIVIDUAL DIFFERENCES

Dissimilarities between or among two or more people.

SOME BACKGROUND

Psychology began in a laboratory in Germany in 1876. The father of the discipline, Wilhelm Wundt, was anxious to show that psychology was different from philosophy and medicine. Since this was a new science and the existing physical sciences like chemistry, biology, and physics had discovered many general principles that enhanced their importance, Wundt set out to uncover general principles of human behavior as well. He developed techniques for studying the sensations and reactions of people, examining the dimmest light that individuals could see, the faintest sound they could hear, and how quickly they could react to a signal. But those who assisted in conducting his experiments quickly discovered that not everyone had the same reaction time, or could see the same dim light, or hear the same soft tone. In other words, they discovered that there were *differences* among individuals.

MENTAL TEST

Instrument designed to measure a subject's ability to reason, plan, and solve problems; an intelligence test.

DIFFERENTIAL PSYCHOLOGY

Scientific study of differences between or among two or more people.

INTELLIGENCE

The ability to learn and adapt to an environment; often used to refer to general intellectual capacity, as opposed to cognitive ability or mental ability, which often refer to more specific abilities such as memory or reasoning.

MENTAL ABILITY

Capacity to reason, plan, and solve problems; cognitive ability.

METRIC

Standard of measurement; a scale.

PSYCHOMETRICS

Practice of measuring a characteristic such as mental ability, placing it on a scale or metric.

INTELLIGENCE TEST

Instrument designed to measure the ability to reason, learn, and solve problems.

These differences detracted from the precise results Wundt sought, but to one of his students they represented a fascinating discovery. James McKeen Cattell (1860–1944), an American who received a PhD in psychology under Wundt's direction, soon began measuring and charting the differences among people using "psychological" variables. In 1890 Cattell developed the concept of a **mental test** as a way of charting these differences. Since the subject matter of this research was differences, the study of differences became known as **differential psychology** (Landy, 1993; 1997).

After leaving Wundt's laboratory at the University of Leipzig, Cattell went to England and worked with another researcher very interested in individual differences, Francis Galton. Galton was gathering information that would support his cousin Charles Darwin's radical theory of evolution. In earlier years, Galton had measured inherited characteristics like height, weight, reach, and hair color. With his new mental test, Cattell was able to expand the number of inherited characteristics that he could examine. After working with Galton for several years in developing a comprehensive mental test, Cattell returned to America and used this test to measure the **intelligence** of incoming college students. He believed that he could use the resulting scores to help students choose curricula and to predict who would successfully complete college. Cattell had developed methods of measuring **mental ability,** placing it on a scale or **metric.** As a result, the actual measurement of abilities became known as **psychometrics.**

While other early psychologists began to focus on *pathological* aspects of mental function, the pioneers of differential psychology were primarily interested in the mental abilities of "normal" people. Several were aware of Cattell's work in measuring intelligence. In France, Alfred Binet was measuring mental abilities of French school children. Lewis Terman was conducting similar studies in California with a translation of Binet's test. Hugo Munsterberg was measuring the abilities of trolley drivers in order to predict the likelihood of accidents. When the United States entered World War I in 1917, the leading industrial psychologists of the time persuaded the Army to use an **intelligence test** to screen recruits and determine who should attend officer's candidate school. Two years after the war's end, Walter Dill Scott, one of the founding fathers of I-O psychology, proclaimed that "possibly the single greatest achievement of the American Psychological Association is the establishment of individual differences" (Lubinski, 2000).

In the postwar years, intelligence tests were adapted for use in selecting individuals for jobs with government and industry. By 1932 measuring the differences in intelligence among individuals in order to predict things like accidents and productivity was a well-established practice (Landy, 1997; Viteles, 1932).

DIFFERENTIAL PSYCHOLOGY, PSYCHOMETRICS, AND I-O PSYCHOLOGY

Nearly a century later, measuring the differences among individuals to predict later behavior ("psychometrics") remains one of the most common frameworks applied by I-O psychologists. It is different from the framework used by an experimental psychologist. The experimental psychologist usually designs an experiment that will show how all people are alike in their response to a stimulus, and looks outside the individual to the stimulus as a way to explain behavior. In contrast, the differential psychologist is person-centered, looking for qualities or characteristics within the person that will help us understand that person's behavior (Hattrup & Jackson, 1996). In the past, I-O psychology—particularly the applied aspect of it—depended on these differences to predict things like job success, job satisfaction, and counterproductive behavior. I-O psychology still makes great use of the individual differences approach, but as we will see later in this chapter and in succeeding chapters, there is more to behavior than simply individual differences.

The marriage of psychometrics and differential psychology was a good one. The differential psychologist identified what should be measured, and the **psychometrician** set

PSYCHOMETRICIAN

Psychologist trained in measuring characteristics such as mental ability.

about measuring it. As we saw from the work of Cattell and his contemporaries, the attribute most commonly measured was some form of intelligence. It was widely believed that **cognitive ability** was the single most important attribute that an individual possessed. We use cognitive abilities to acquire knowledge, solve problems, and apply reason to situations. Consequently, many studies were conducted to show that an individual's general intellectual capacity was closely associated with that individual's occupational and vocational success. The pioneers in theories of intelligence referred to this attribute as **"g,"** an abbreviation for **general mental ability** (Hull, 1928; Spearman, 1927). Today's psychologists still use that term, and we will use it in this book.

VARIETIES OF INDIVIDUAL DIFFERENCES

In the past decade, there has been a substantial shift in thinking about individual differences. Instead of simply examining "g" to understand and predict the behavior of workers—a tendency that Sternberg and Wagner (1993) called the **g-ocentric model,** researchers are moving toward broadening the field of examination. In addition to cognitive ability, I-O psychologists now consider individual differences in **physical abilities, personality, interests, knowledge,** and **emotion** in examining the behavior of people in work settings. This is the result of several forces. In the early years of testing, the only available tests were intelligence tests. Since that time, psychologists have developed many reliable methods for measuring personality, knowledge, interests, and emotional reactions to work. In addition, our understanding of the many facets of performance has become more sophisticated. Overall performance, like an overall GPA, has little meaning. Murphy (1996) proposes that there are many different attributes of people that serve many different demands of the job (see Figure 3.1).

Let's apply that view to a particular job. Some of the most important things that firefighters do are driving the fire truck to the fire, applying water to the fire, providing medical assistance, rescuing trapped citizens, and learning new procedures and how to use new equipment. To accomplish these tasks, firefighters work in teams. To provide medical

FIGURE 3.1 The Link between Attributes and Behavior in Organizations
Source: K. R. Murphy (1996a).

COGNITIVE ABILITY

Capacity to reason, plan, and solve problems; mental ability.

"g"

Abbreviation for general mental ability.

GENERAL MENTAL ABILITY

The nonspecific capacity to reason, learn, and solve problems in any of a wide variety of ways and circumstances.

g-OCENTRIC MODEL

Tendency to understand and predict the behavior of workers simply by examining "g".

PHYSICAL ABILITIES

Bodily powers such as muscular strength, flexibility, and stamina.

PERSONALITY

An individual's behavioral and emotional characteristics, generally found to be stable over time and in a variety of circumstances; an individual's habitual way of responding.

INTERESTS

Preferences or likings for broad ranges of activities.

KNOWLEDGE

A collection of specific and interrelated facts and information about a particular topical area.

EMOTION

An affect or feeling, often experienced and displayed in reaction to an event or thought and accompanied by physiological changes in various systems of the body.

assistance and learn new procedures, the firefighter needs cognitive ability. To rescue trapped citizens and apply water to the fire, the firefighter needs both physical ability and courage in addition to problem-solving skills. To accomplish teamwork with fellow firefighters and to deal with victims, the firefighter needs communication skills. To drive the truck to the fire accurately and safely, the firefighter needs good vision, coordination, and the knowledge or memory of how to get to the location of the fire. If we only bothered to examine the differences among individuals in cognitive ability (or "g"), we would only be able to predict and understand a limited portion of the firefighter's job performance. To understand the full range of performance, we need to consider attributes beyond "g."

There is a growing consensus (Murphy, 1996; Guion, 1998) that we can divide the individual differences useful in understanding work behavior into certain categories, including:

- Cognitive ability
- Physical ability
- Personality
- Interests

In the next section, we will consider these broad categories of attributes as well as the theories that further define them. Before we do so, we need to consider the fundamental assumptions that I-O psychologists make when they apply the individual differences model. They are listed as follows (adapted from Guion, 1998).

1. Adults have a variety of attributes (e.g., intelligence, personality, interests) and the levels of these attributes are relatively stable over a reasonable time period (several years).

The performance of most jobs requires multiple abilities. What are some of the abilities called for in the job of firefighter?

James McKeen Cattell began testing incoming students, first at the University of Pennsylvania in 1892, then at Columbia in 1900. He wanted to identify the characteristics of "individual differences" of the students so that he could eventually predict which applicants for college admission were likely to get a degree. The following is a list of some of information Cattell gathered on each student:

- Memory
- Reasoning
- Numerical skills
- Reaction time
- Hair color

- Weight
- Height
- Right or left handedness

Questions:

1. Which of the characteristics in the list above are not a part of one of the categories of individual differences in this module?
2. Which of the characteristics in the list would be unlikely to be associated with college success?
3. Which characteristics in the list do you think are still routinely gathered in the college admissions process?

---

2. People differ with respect to these attributes (i.e., there are "individual differences") and these differences are associated with job success.

3. The relative differences between people on these attributes remain even after training, job experience, or some other intervention. Thus, if individual A has less of an attribute than individual B before training or job experience, and if they both receive the same training or experience to increase that attribute, individual A will still have less of that attribute than individual B after the training or intervention, even though *both* may have higher levels of the attribute after training or experience.

4. Different jobs require different attributes.

5. These attributes can be measured.

With these assumptions in mind, we can now examine these attribute categories in the next modules.

MODULE 3.1 SUMMARY

- The *individual differences* among people on various attributes like intelligence, personality, and knowledge are important in understanding a wide variety of socially important outcomes.

- James McKeen Cattell developed the concept of a *mental test* as a way of charting the differences among people. Since the subject matter of this research was differences, the study of differences became known as *differential psychology.* The actual measurement of abilities became known as *psychometrics.*

- The differential psychologist is person-centered, looking for qualities or characteristics within the person that will help us understand that person's behavior. The differential psychologist identifies what should be measured, and the *psychometrician* set about measuring it.

- The attribute most commonly measured by early differential psychologists was some form of *intelligence.* It was widely believed that *cognitive ability* was the single most important attribute possessed by an individual. The pioneers in theories of intelligence referred to this attribute as "*g*," an abbreviation for *general mental ability.*

- In addition to cognitive ability, I-O psychologists consider individual differences in *physical abilities, personality, interests, knowledge,* and *emotion* in examining the behavior of people in work settings.

KEY TERMS

individual differences

mental test

differential psychology

intelligence

mental ability

metric

psychometrics

intelligence test

psychometrician

cognitive ability

"g"

general mental ability

g-ocentric model

physical abilities

personality

interests

knowledge

emotion

CRITICAL THINKING EXERCISES

3.1 How would differential psychology and psychometrics help to understand the academic achievement of students in grades K–12?

3.2 Why should I-O psychologists examine individual differences? Wouldn't it be better to identify how people are the same rather than how they are different?

MENTAL AND PHYSICAL ABILITIES

A TAXONOMY OF ABILITIES

In the 1950s, Edwin Fleishman began a program of research to determine the most common mental and physical abilities associated with human performance, including work performance. Through a combination of field and laboratory research, he and his associates developed a comprehensive list, or **taxonomy,** of 52 abilities (Fleishman & Reilly, 1992). These can be divided into the broad categories of cognitive, physical, and **perceptual-motor abilities** (see Table 3.1). As you can see, they cover an impressive variety—and this list does not cover personality, **affect,** or interest! Fleishman's work expanded the study of individual differences far beyond his predecessors' focus on differences in intelligence.

Fleishman's list of abilities can be used for many different applied purposes. It is an effective way to analyze the most important abilities in various occupations (Gael, 1988; Landy, 1989). It can also be used to determine training needs, recruiting needs, and even work design. Once we know the basic abilities that can be brought to the job, it is much easier to identify which of those abilities are truly important.

TAXONOMY

An orderly, scientific system of classification.

PERCEPTUAL-MOTOR ABILITIES

Physical attributes that combine the senses (e.g., seeing, hearing, smell) and motion (e.g., coordination, dexterity).

AFFECT

The conscious, subjective aspect of emotion.

TABLE 3.1   **Definitions of Abilities in the Taxonomy with Task Examples**

CONSTRUCT LABEL	OPERATIONAL DEFINITION	LEVEL SCALE	
		LEVEL RATING	EXAMPLE
Verbal abilities	**Cognitive abilities**		
1. Oral Comprehension	The ability to listen to and understand information and ideas presented through spoken words and sentences.	High—Understanding a lecture on advanced physics. Low—Understanding a television commercial.	
2. Written Comprehension	The ability to read and understand information and ideas presented in writing.	High—Understanding an instruction book on repairing a missile guidance system. Low—Understanding signs on the highway.	
3. Oral Expression	The ability to communicate information and ideas in speaking so others will understand.	High—Explaining advanced principles of genetics to college freshmen. Low—Canceling newspaper delivery by phone.	

(continued)

TABLE 3.1   *(continued)*

| | | LEVEL SCALE | |
CONSTRUCT LABEL	OPERATIONAL DEFINITION	LEVEL RATING	EXAMPLE
4. Written Expression	The ability to communicate information and ideas in writing so others will understand.	High—Writing an advanced economics textbook. Low—Writing a note to remind someone to take something out of the freezer to thaw.	
Idea Generation and Reasoning Abilities			
5. Fluency of Ideas	The ability to come up with a number of ideas about a given topic. It concerns the number of ideas produced and *not* the quality, correctness, or creativity of the ideas.	High—Naming all the possible strategies for a particular military battle. Low—Naming four different uses for a screwdriver.	
6. Originality	The ability to come up with unusual or clever ideas about a given topic or situation, or to develop creative ways to solve a problem.	High—Inventing a new type of human-made fiber. Low—Using a credit card to open a locked door.	
8. Problem Sensitivity	The ability to tell when something is wrong or is likely to go wrong. It does *not* involve solving the problem, only recognizing that there is a problem.	High—Recognizing an illness at an early stage of a disease when there are only a few symptoms. Low—Recognizing that an unplugged lamp does not work.	
11. Deductive Reasoning	The ability to apply general rules to specific problems to come up with logical answers. It involves deciding if an answer makes sense.	High—Designing an aircraft wing using the principles of aerodynamics. Low—Knowing that, because of the law of gravity, a stalled car can coast down the hill.	
12. Inductive Reasoning	The ability to combine separate pieces of information, or specific answers to problems, to form general rules or conclusions. It includes coming up with a logical explanation for why a series of seemingly unrelated events occur together.	High—Diagnosing a disease using the results of many different lab tests. Low—Determining clothing to wear on the basis of the weather report.	
13. Information Ordering	The ability to correctly follow a given rule or set of rules in order to arrange things or actions in a certain order. The things or actions can include numbers, letters, words, pictures, procedures, sentences, and mathematical or logical operations.	High—Assembling a nuclear warhead. Low—Putting things in numerical order.	
14. Category Flexibility	The ability to produce many rules so that each rule tells how to group (or combine) a set of things in a different way.	High—Classifying man-made fibers in terms of their strength, cost, flexibility, melting points, etc. Low—Sorting nails in a toolbox on the basis of length.	

(continued)

TABLE 3.1   *(continued)*

CONSTRUCT LABEL	OPERATIONAL DEFINITION	LEVEL SCALE	
		LEVEL RATING	EXAMPLE

Quantitative Abilities

CONSTRUCT LABEL	OPERATIONAL DEFINITION	LEVEL RATING / EXAMPLE
9. Mathematical Reasoning	The ability to understand and organize a problem and then to select a mathematical method or formula to solve the problem.	High—Determining the mathematics required to simulate a space craft landing on the moon. Low—Determining how much 10 oranges will cost when they are priced at 2 for 29 cents.
10. Number Facility	The ability to add, subtract, multiply, or divide quickly and correctly.	High—Manually calculating the flight path of an aircraft, taking into account speed, fuel, wind, and altitude. Low—Adding 2 and 7.

Memory

7. Memorization	The ability to remember information such as words, numbers, pictures, and procedures.	High—Reciting the Gettysburg Address after studying it for 15 minutes. Low—Remembering the number on your bus to be sure you get back on the right one.

Perceptual Abilities

15. Speed of Closure	The ability to quickly make sense of information that seems to be without meaning or organization. It involves quickly combining and organizing different pieces of information into a meaningful pattern.	High—Interpreting the patterns on a weather radarscope to decide if the weather is changing. Low—Recognizing a song after hearing only the first few notes.
16. Flexibility of Closure	The ability to identify or detect a known pattern (a figure, object, word, or sound) that is hidden in other distracting material.	High—Identifying camouflaged tanks while flying in a high speed airplane. Low—Tuning in a radio weather station in a noisy truck.
19. Perceptual Speed	The ability to quickly and accurately compare letters, numbers, objects, pictures, or patterns. The things to be compared may be presented at the same time or one after other. This ability also includes comparing a presented object with a remembered object.	High—Inspecting electrical parts for defects as they flow by on a fast-moving assembly line. Low—Sorting mail according to zip codes with no time pressure.

Spatial Abilities

17. Spatial Organization	The ability to know one's location in relation to the environment, or to know where other objects are in relation to one's self.	High—Navigating an ocean voyage using only the positions of the sun and stars. Low—Using the floor plan to locate a store in a shopping mall.

(continued)

TABLE 3.1   *(continued)*

| | | LEVEL SCALE | |
| | | LEVEL | |
CONSTRUCT LABEL	OPERATIONAL DEFINITION	RATING	EXAMPLE
18. Visualization	The ability to imagine how something will look after it is moved around or when its parts are moved or rearranged.	High—Anticipating your opponent's as well as your own future moves in a chess game. Low—Imagining how to put paper in the typewriter so the letterhead comes out at the top.	
Attentiveness			
20. Selective Attention	The ability to concentrate and not be distracted while performing a task over a period of time.	High—Studying a technical manual in a noisy boiler room. Low—Answering a business call with coworkers talking nearby.	
21. Time Sharing	The ability to efficiently shift back and forth between two or more activities or sources of information (such as speech, sound, touch, or other sources).	High—Monitoring radar and radio transmission to keep track of aircraft during periods of heavy traffic. Low—Listening to music while filing papers.	
	Psychomotor abilities		
Fine Manipulative Abilities			
27. Arm-Hand Steadiness	The ability to keep the hand and arm steady while making an arm movement or while holding the arm and hand in one position.	High—Cutting facets in diamonds. Low—Lighting a candle.	
28. Manual Dexterity	The ability to quickly make coordinated movements of one hand, a hand together with the arm, or two hands to grasp, manipulate, or assemble objects.	High—Performing open-heart surgery using surgical instruments. Low—Screwing a light bulb into a lamp socket.	
29. Finger Dexterity	The ability to make precisely coordinated movements of the fingers of one or both hands to grasp, manipulate, or assemble very small objects.	High—Putting together the inner workings of a small wrist watch. Low—Putting coins in a parking meter.	
Control Movement Abilities			
22. Control Precision	The ability to quickly and repeatedly make precise adjustments in moving the controls of a machine or vehicle to exact positions.	High—Drilling a tooth. Low—Adjusting a room light with a dimmer switch.	
23. Multilimb Coordination	The ability to coordinate movements of two or more limbs together (for example, two arms, two legs, or one leg and one arm) while sitting, standing, or lying down. It does not involve performing the activities while the body is in motion.	High—Playing the drum set in a jazz band. Low—Rowing a boat.	

(continued)

TABLE 3.1   *(continued)*

CONSTRUCT LABEL	OPERATIONAL DEFINITION	LEVEL SCALE	
		LEVEL RATING	**EXAMPLE**
24. Response Orientation	The ability to choose quickly and correctly between two or more movements in response to two or more different signals (lights, sounds, pictures, etc.). It includes the speed with which the correct response is started with the hand, foot, or other body parts.	High—In a spacecraft that is out of control, reacting quickly to each malfunction with the correct control movements. Low—When the doorbell and telephone ring at the same time, quickly selecting which to answer first.	
25. Rate Control	The ability to time the adjustments of a movement or equipment control in anticipation of changes in the speed and/or direction of a continuously moving object or scene.	High—Operating aircraft controls used to land a jet on an aircraft carrier in rough weather. Low—Riding a bicycle alongside a jogger.	
Reaction Time and Speed Abilities			
26. Reaction Time	The ability to quickly respond (with the hand, finger, or foot) to one signal (sound, light, picture, etc.) when it appears.	High—Hitting the brake when a pedestrian steps in front of the car. Low—Starting to slow down the car when a traffic light turns yellow.	
30. Wrist-Finger Speed	The ability to make fast, simple, repeated movements of the fingers, hands, and wrists.	High—Typing a document at the speed of 90 words per minute. Low—Using a manual pencil sharpener.	
31. Speed of Limb Movement	The ability to quickly move the arms or legs.	High—Throwing punches in a boxing match. Low—Sawing through a thin piece of wood.	
Physical abilities			
Physical Strength Abilities			
32. Static Strength	The ability to exert maximum muscle force to lift, push, pull, or carry objects.	High—Lifting 75-pound bags of cement onto a truck. Low—Pushing an empty shopping cart.	
33. Explosive Strength	The ability to use short bursts of muscle force to propel oneself (as in jumping or sprinting), or to throw an object.	High—Propelling (throwing) a shot-put in a track meet. Low—Hitting a nail with a hammer.	
34. Dynamic Strength	The ability to exert muscle force repeatedly or continuously over time. This involves muscular endurance and resistance to muscle fatigue.	High—Performing a gymnastics routine using the rings. Low—Using pruning shears to trim a bush.	
35. Trunk Strength	The ability to use one's abdominal and lower back muscles to support part of the body repeatedly or continuously over time without "giving out" or fatiguing.	High—Doing 100 sit-ups. Low—Sitting up in an office chair.	

(continued)

TABLE 3.1 *(continued)*

		LEVEL SCALE	
CONSTRUCT LABEL	OPERATIONAL DEFINITION	LEVEL RATING	EXAMPLE
Endurance			
40. Stamina	The ability to exert oneself physically over long periods of time without getting winded or out of breath.	High—Running a 10 mile race. Low—Walking a quarter of a mile to deliver a letter.	
Flexibility, Balance, and Coordination			
36. Extent Flexibility	The ability to bend, stretch, twist, or reach out with the body, arms, and/or legs.	High—Working under a car dashboard to repair the heater. Low—Reaching for a microphone in a patrol car.	
37. Dynamic Flexibility	The ability to quickly and repeatedly bend, stretch, twist, or reach out with the body, arms, and/or legs.	High—Maneuvering a kayak through swift rapids. Low—Hand picking a bushel of apples from a tree.	
38. Gross Body Coordination	The ability to coordinate the movement of the arms, legs, and torso together in activities where the whole body is in motion.	High—Performing a ballet dance. Low—Getting in and out of a truck.	
39. Gross Body Equilibrium	The ability to keep or regain one's body balance to stay upright when in an unstable position.	High—Walking on narrow beams in high-rise construction. Low—Standing on a ladder.	
Sensory abilities			
Visual Abilities			
41. Near Vision	The ability to see details of objects at a close range (within a few feet of the observer).	High—Detecting minor defects in a diamond. Low—Reading dials on the car dashboard.	
42. Far Vision	The ability to see details at a distance.	High—Detecting differences in ocean vessels on the horizon. Low—Reading a roadside billboard.	
43. Visual Color Discrimination	The ability to match or detect differences between colors, including shades of color and brightness.	High—Painting a color portrait from a living subject. Low—Separating laundry into colors and whites.	
44. Night Vision	The ability to see under low light conditions.	High—Finding one's way through the woods on a moonless night. Low—Reading street signs when driving at dusk (just after the sun sets).	
45. Peripheral Vision	The ability to see objects or movement of objects to one's side when the eyes are focused forward.	High—When piloting a plane in air combat, distinguishing friendly and enemy aircraft. Low—Keeping in step while marching in a military formation.	

(continued)

TABLE 3.1	(continued)		

		LEVEL SCALE	
CONSTRUCT LABEL	**OPERATIONAL DEFINITION**	**LEVEL RATING**	**EXAMPLE**
46. Depth Perception	The ability to judge which of several objects is closer or farther away from the observer, or to judge the distance between an object and the observer.	High—Throwing a long pass to a teammate who is surrounded by opponents. Low—Merging a car into traffic on a city street.	
47. Glare Sensitivity	The ability to see objects in the presence of glare or bright lighting.	High—Snow skiing in bright sunlight. Low—Driving on a familiar roadway on a cloudy day.	
Auditory and Speech Abilities			
48. Hearing Sensitivity	The ability to detect or tell the difference between sounds that vary over broad ranges of pitch and loudness.	High—Tuning an orchestra. Low—Noticing when the hourly watch alarm goes off.	
49. Auditory Attention	The ability to focus on a single source of auditory (hearing) information in the presence of other distracting sounds.	High—Listening to instructions from a coworker in a noisy saw mill. Low—Listening to a lecture while people are whispering nearby.	
50. Sound Localization	The ability to tell the direction from which a sound originated.	High—Determining the direction of an emergency vehicle from the sound of its siren. Low—Listening to a stereo to determine which speaker is working.	
51. Speech Recognition	The ability to identify and understand the speech of another person.	High—Understanding a speech presented by someone with a strong foreign accent. Low—Recognizing the voice of a coworker.	
52. Speech Clarity	The ability to speak clearly so that it is understandable to a listener.	High—Giving a lecture to a large audience. Low—Calling the numbers in a bingo game.	

Source: Adapted from Fleishman et al. (1999); Fleishman & Reilly (1992).

COGNITIVE ABILITIES

Intelligence as "g"

Many people consider the terms intelligence, IQ, cognitive ability, and mental ability to be synonyms for one another. We will make some distinctions. **IQ** is an historical term that stood for **Intelligence Quotient** and refers to the way early intelligence test scores were calculated. The term no longer has scientific meaning, although it is still often used by the general public. Mental ability and cognitive ability are current terms, which scientists often use interchangeably. Cognitive ability and mental ability often refer to specific abilities

IQ

Abbreviation for intelligence quotient.

INTELLIGENCE QUOTIENT

Measure of intelligence obtained by giving a subject a standardized "IQ" test. The score is obtained by multiplying by 100 the ratio of the subject's mental age to chronological age.

such as memory or reasoning; intelligence, on the other hand, most often refers to general intellectual capacity (often called "g" for general mental ability). Intelligence can be defined as the ability to learn and adapt to an environment. One or another variation of this definition has been used since at least 1921 (Sternberg & Kaufmann, 1998). A group of leading I-O psychologists recently defined it as follows: "Intelligence is a very general mental capability that, among other things, involves the ability to reason, plan, solve problems, think abstractly, comprehend complex ideas, learn quickly, and learn from experience" (Arvey et al., 1995).

Sternberg and Kaufmann (1998) pointed out that no matter how enduring this definition may be for Western cultures, other cultures have different views of who is "an intelligent person." Speed of learning, for example, is not always emphasized in non-Western cultures. In fact, "other cultures may be suspicious of work done quickly" (Sternberg & Kaufmann, 1998), and in some cultures, the word intelligence means "prudence" and "caution." Nevertheless, for our purposes, we will accept the meaning generally assigned by Western psychologists. Intelligence is required whenever people must manipulate information of any type (Murphy, 1996). Measures of "g" assess reasoning ability, knowledge acquisition, and problem-solving ability (Lubinski, 2000).

Is "g" Important at Work?

META-ANALYSIS

Statistical method of combining many small studies to reach a conclusion.

Yes. Almost every job requires some active manipulation of information. This means that your level of general mental ability can affect your performance on any job. The greater the amount of information that needs to be manipulated, the more important "g" becomes. **Meta-analyses** of the relationship between "g" and job performance (Hunter & Hunter, 1984; Schmidt & Hunter, 1998) demonstrated very clearly that as the complexity of the

Critical abilities for the job of emergency dispatcher include verbal comprehension, reaction time, and problem solving.

job increased, the predictive value (i.e., validity) of tests of general intelligence also increased. In practical terms, this means that if the information-processing demands of a job are high, a person with lower general mental ability is not as likely to be successful as a person of higher general mental ability. That does not mean, however, that high general mental ability guarantees success on that job. If the job also requires interpersonal skills, communication skills, and certain personality traits, even a person with high general mental ability (but lower levels of those noncognitive traits) might fail.

In 1965 Tanner showed that he could accurately predict which Olympic athletes were competing in which sports by looking at their body builds. But *within* each Olympic event, the same individual differences were useless as predictors of who would get a medal (Lubinski, 2000). In this example, think of body build as "g," and all the other attributes of the athletes as specific abilities and attributes; "g" may help a candidate get into the police academy, but it will not ensure that the person will become a successful police officer.

Some of today's psychologists continue to believe that nothing more than measures of "g" are needed to predict training, grades, and job performance (Ree & Earles, 1992). Another psychologist framed the issue somewhat differently.

> General mental ability (g) is a substantively significant determinant of individual differences for any job that includes information-processing tasks . . . The exact size of the relationship will be a function of . . . the degree to which the job requires information processing and verbal cognitive skills (Campbell, 1990).

From Campbell's statement we can infer that since "g" represents information-processing ability, then it should logically predict information-processing performance in the workplace. In addition, we can infer that jobs differ in terms of how much "information processing" they require. A backhoe operator certainly has to process some information, but not as much as a software help-desk operator. The backhoe operator will depend much more heavily on visual/spatial ability than on problem solving or reasoning ability.

Can Your Level of "g" Change?

Today's researchers observe a fascinating phenomenon: Intelligence continues to rise over time. Individuals appear to be getting smarter and smarter through the lifespan, and new generations appear to be smarter than their parents. The phenomenon is labeled the **Flynn effect** after a political scientist who has done extensive research on the topic (Flynn, 1984, 1987, 1999). It amounts to a gain of 15 points in average intelligence test scores per generation. This is a substantial increase, considering that the **mean** intelligence on most tests is pegged at 100 with a **standard deviation** of 15. Many psychologists have proposed theories as to why this is occurring, including better health care, better nutrition, increased schooling, and better-educated parents (Sternberg & Kaufmann, 1998). It could also be because we live in an increasingly complex environment both at work and at home (Neisser et al., 1996). The phenomenon of increasing intelligence is interesting for two reasons. First, it refutes the perception of many people that intelligence is fixed at an early age. Second, it suggests that the complexity of modern work settings may very well act as a stimulant for cognitive growth. It also raises a crucial question for I-O psychologists: Is the increase in intelligence keeping up with the increase in complexity of the environment?

Cognitive Abilities beyond "g"

The majority of today's psychologists agree that while "g" is important, more specific cognitive abilities also play a role in performance, with some specific abilities important for some jobs and other specific abilities important for other jobs. The example of the backhoe operator and the software help-desk operator points out the importance of specific cognitive abilities.

FLYNN EFFECT

Phenomenon in which new generations appear to be smarter than their parents by a gain of 15 points in average intelligence test score per generation; named after the political scientist who did extensive research on the topic.

MEAN

The arithmetic mean or average, computed by dividing the sum of all values in a set by the number of values comprising that set.

STANDARD DEVIATION

Measure of the extent of spread in a set of scores.

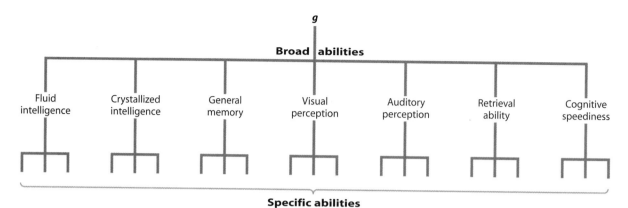

FIGURE 3.2 Carroll's Hierarchical Model SOURCE: Carroll (1993).

The question then becomes, How many specific abilities are there? There is no conclusive answer to that question, but we can say with great confidence that there is more than one (i.e., more than just "g"). As you saw in Table 3.1, Fleishman and his colleagues posited 52 abilities, 21 of which are in the cognitive category, but "g" is not one of them. The reason for this is that Fleishman was more concerned with identifying *specific* abilities than general mental ability. It is now generally accepted that cognitive ability is best conceptualized as having multiple layers of abilities.

Carroll (1993) proposed that there are three layers, or strata, to intelligence (see Figure 3.2). The highest layer is "g"; the next layer down consists of seven more specific abilities: fluid intelligence, crystallized intelligence, memory, visual perception, auditory perception, information retrieval, and cognitive speed (Murphy, 1996). The lowest and most specific level includes abilities that are tied to the seven broad abilities in the middle level. For example, information ordering (one of Fleishman's proposed abilities) would be connected to fluid intelligence, and spatial relations would be associated with visual perception.

There are many other theories of cognitive abilities, but all resemble Carroll's. The important thing to remember is that "g" will only get you so far in understanding work behavior. Different jobs will require additional specific cognitive abilities as well. It is fair to say that a person with a high level of "g" will probably be a successful performer at certain tasks of almost every job (Schmidt & Hunter, 1998), but that other abilities will vary in importance depending on the job in question. As we will see in the subsequent sections of this module, not only will cognitive abilities play a role in job success and satisfaction, but so also will personality, emotional reactions, and interests.

You might wonder if it is possible to have *too much* intelligence. This reminds us of a story that is often told about a well-known boxer. A radio interviewer was talking with a retired middleweight boxer who had fought for many years and had a relatively undistinguished career, finishing with approximately 60 wins and 30 losses. The interview went something like this, with the interviewer represented by "I" and the boxer by "B."

I You must have fought many interesting boxers in your career.

B Yeah, there were plenty of them.

I I noticed that you fought so-and-so four times and beat him all four times.

B Yeah, that surprised me because he had a lot better record than me.

I Why did it surprise you?

B   Because he was so smart. He was always thinking ahead, what combination he would set up, where he wanted to be in the ring, and things like that. He was really smart, always thinking.

I   Then let me ask the obvious question—why do you think you beat him so consistently?

B   I guess it was because when he was thinking, I was punching.

So it does appear that, occasionally, too much "g" can get you hurt!

PHYSICAL, SENSORY, AND PSYCHOMOTOR ABILITIES
Physical Abilities

In the introductory section to this module, we considered Fleishman's taxonomy of human abilities. That taxonomy remains one of the most detailed statements of the range of physical abilities found in humans. There are many jobs that are physically demanding and for which physical ability testing is appropriate. Some examples are firefighter, mine worker, and baggage handler. Each of these jobs requires strength, flexibility, and **stamina** or aerobic endurance. In Table 3.2, we "analyze" the job of firefighter using the Fleishman taxonomy.

Hogan (1991a; 1991b) suggested that seven physical abilities are sufficient for analyzing most jobs. Guion compared Hogan's seven abilities with similar abilities identified by Fleishman and Reilly (1992) and found a close match. As you can see in Figure 3.3, several of Hogan's dimensions are combinations of Fleishman's dimensions (e.g., Hogan combines extent flexibility and dynamic flexibility into a single dimension called "flexibility").

STAMINA

Physical ability to supply muscles with oxygenated blood through the cardiovascular system; also known as cardiovascular strength or aerobic strength or endurance.

TABLE 3.2	Fleishman Taxonomy with Firefighting Examples

Static Strength. This is the ability we generally think of when we hear the word *strength*. It is the amount of force that is exerted against a fairly immovable or heavy external object. Force is exerted continuously and might involve pushing, pulling, or lifting. Examples of this would include prying a door open, lifting a person, or holding hoses.

Explosive Strength. This is the ability to use energy in one or a series of explosive muscular acts. What is needed is a burst of muscular energy rather than a steady effort. Examples might be jumping over an obstacle, using an ax, or kicking open a door.

Dynamic Strength. This ability involves using your arms and trunk in moving your own body weight for some period of time or across some distance. An example would be climbing a rope or pulling yourself along using only your arms. Another important part of this ability is that you must use the same arm muscles repeatedly or continuously.

Stamina. This is the ability to maintain physical activity over a long period of time. This deals with the extent to which the cardiovascular system (heart and lungs) is exercised. A good example of the use of this ability would be climbing up 20 flights of stairs. Another example would be running a long distance.

Extent Flexibility. This ability involves stretching or extending arms and legs and their particular muscle groups. An example of this ability would be stretching a leg up above your waist to climb over a wall. A second example would be reaching with your arms at an extreme angle so that a ladder could be put in place.

Dynamic Flexibility. This is the ability to make repeated or continuous arm and leg flexing movements with some speed. An example would be pulling in a hose or rope, hand over hand, in a short time or quickly climbing up a ladder.

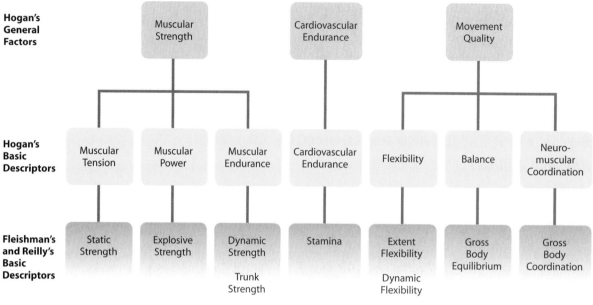

FIGURE 3.3 **A Model of Physical Abilities** SOURCE: Guion (1998).

In a manner reminiscent of Carroll's theory of intelligence, she then combines her seven measures to form three higher-order physical abilities: muscular strength, cardiovascular endurance, and movement quality. For most jobs, this three-ability taxonomy would likely be sufficient since most physically demanding jobs require **muscular tension, muscular power,** and **muscular endurance,** not just one of the three. Similarly, flexibility and balance usually go together in a physically demanding job.

Fairness of Physical Ability Tests   Because employers often use physical ability tests to screen applicants for physically demanding jobs, it is important to determine whether such tests are fair to female applicants and older applicants. Because we lose muscle, stamina, and flexibility as we age, the older an applicant is the less well he or she is likely to perform on physical ability tests. For women the situation has an additional consideration. On average, females have less muscle mass (which means diminished muscular strength) and lower levels of cardiovascular endurance (or stamina) than men (Hogan, 1991a). In contrast, on measures of flexibility (e.g., sit and reach tests) women tend to do better than men. However, most physically demanding jobs require—or are perceived by employers to require—more muscular strength and stamina than flexibility. This has meant that male candidates, who tend to excel on those physical tests, are predominantly hired for such jobs. As a result, women candidates for popular positions such as firefighter have filed employment discrimination suits (Brunet v. City of Columbus, 1995).

You have probably observed that women and men of all ages can increase their individual physical abilities with exercise and training. In addition, it is clear that many jobs require a fixed level of strength and endurance and that more is not always better. If your job requires you to lift 25-pound boxes from a conveyor belt and place them on a table, the fact that you are strong enough to move 100-pound boxes is irrelevant to the task at hand. In this case, more strength would not lead to higher performance. This means that it is not always necessary for individuals to compete *against* each other on physical ability tests; they merely need to demonstrate sufficient strength and endurance to perform the tasks that comprise the job. By training for several months prior to the administration of physical ability tests, women candidates are able to improve their performance significantly.

Thus, one way of helping women to do better on these tests is for employers to encourage them to train ahead of time (McArdle, Katch, & Katch, 2001). We can predict that this same strategy may help older job seekers as well.

Sensory Abilities

Sensory abilities are the physical functions of vision, hearing, touch, taste, smell, and kinesthetic feedback (e.g., noticing changes in body position). Hogan includes kinesthetic feedback in a dimension she called "movement quality." The sensory abilities of vision and hearing are particularly interesting for applied I-O psychologists because employers often test these abilities in would-be employees.

To prevent employers from using a disability as an excuse to reject an applicant who is capable of performing a job, the **Americans with Disabilities Act** of 1990 forbids them from asking about or testing areas such as sensory or physical abilities that may be considered "disabilities" until after they have made a job offer to the candidate.

Until recently, cognitive psychologists considered sensory abilities to be independent of cognitive abilities, but Carroll's (1993) model of intelligence calls that assumption into question. Remember that two of his mid-level abilities are visual perception and auditory perception. But in most real-life settings, sensation and perception are inextricably bound together. We usually infer from some kind of report (verbal or behavioral) that a person has sensed something. There has been little research on this question, but as the development of Carroll's model continues, the interplay between senses and intelligence will become more prominent.

Psychomotor Abilities

Psychomotor abilities, sometimes called **sensorimotor,** or just **motor abilities,** deal with issues of coordination, dexterity, and reaction time. Once again, Fleishman (Fleishman & Reilly, 1992) has done the most extensive work in identifying these abilities (see Table 3.3). A simple inspection of these abilities immediately brings to mind the jobs for which they may be important (e.g., crane operators, organists, watch repair technicians, surgeons, wait staff, and bartenders). Once again, from this discussion it should be clear that many of these abilities (e.g., rate control and aiming) may very well be associated with visual and/or auditory perception or cognitive speed, facets of Carroll's theory of intelligence.

TABLE 3.3	Psychomotor Abilities

1. Arm-hand steadiness
2. Manual dexterity
3. Finger dexterity
4. Control precision
5. Multilimb coordination
6. Response orientation
7. Rate control
8. Reaction time
9. Wrist-finger speed
10. Speed of limb movement

SOURCE: Adapted from Fleishman et al. (1999); Fleishman & Reilly (1992).

SENSORY ABILITIES

Physical functions of vision, hearing, touch, taste, smell, and kinesthetic feedback (e.g., noticing changes in body position).

AMERICANS WITH DISABILITIES ACT

Federal legislation in 1990 requiring employers to give applicants and employees with disabilities the same consideration as other applicants and employees, and to make certain adaptations in the work environment to accommodate disabilities.

PSYCHOMOTOR ABILITIES

Physical functions of movement, associated with coordination, dexterity, and reaction time; also called motor or sensorimotor abilities.

SENSORIMOTOR ABILITIES

Physical functions of movement, associated with coordination, dexterity, and reaction time; also called psychomotor or motor abilities.

MOTOR ABILITIES

Physical functions of movement, associated with coordination, dexterity, and reaction time; also called psychomotor or sensorimotor abilities.

The work of researchers like Carroll blurs the classical distinctions between cognitive and "noncognitive" abilities. In some senses, this is a good development. Until recently, psychologists tended to treat abilities in isolation when it is clear in real life (and—more importantly for us—in work) that all of these abilities interact within a single person to produce a response or action. Theories like Carroll's will require us to consider the individual in a more realistic way by looking at these interactions.

MODULE 3.2 SUMMARY

- Fleishman and his associates developed a taxonomy of 52 abilities, divided into the broad categories of cognitive, physical, and perceptual-motor abilities.
- "Intelligence [or "g"] is a very general mental capability that . . . describes a person's ability to learn from experience.
- Meta-analyses of the relationship between "g" and job performance demonstrated that the more complex the job, the stronger the predictive value of general intelligence tests.
- Carroll proposed that intelligence had three layers, or strata. The highest layer is "g"; the next layer down consists of seven more specific abilities: fluid intelligence, crystallized intelligence, memory, visual perception, auditory perception, information retrieval, and cognitive speed.

- Physically demanding jobs require strength, flexibility, and stamina or aerobic endurance. Hogan proposed a seven-measure taxonomy of physical abilities, and combined these seven measures to form three higher-order physical abilities: muscular strength, cardiovascular endurance, and movement quality.
- It is important to determine whether employers' physical ability tests are fair to female applicants and older applicants, since both of these groups tend to have less strength than young men do. One way of enhancing the performance of females and older applicants on these tests is to encourage applicants to train ahead of time.

KEY TERMS

taxonomy
perceptual-motor abilities
affect
IQ
meta-analysis
Intelligence Quotient

Flynn effect
mean
standard deviation
stamina
muscular tension
muscular power

muscular endurance
sensory abilities
Americans with Disabilities Act
psychomotor abilities
sensorimotor abilities
motor abilities

CRITICAL THINKING EXERCISES

3.3 Examine the Fleishman Taxonomy of Abilities which appears in Table 3.1. Using that list of abilities, identify what you feel are the five most important abilities for the following jobs:

Manager of a supermarket
Used car salesperson
Leader of a religious congregation

Civil engineer who specializes in highway construction
College-level teacher
Kindergarten teacher
Prison guard
Accountant
Coach of a professional tennis star

What Do a Major League Baseball Team and a Railroad Have in Common? Confusion about Reaction Time

During the eighth inning of a professional baseball game, a relief pitcher was warming up to come into the game. Unlike many ballparks, this stadium had the bullpens located along the first and third baselines. The catcher's back is toward home plate and as he warms up, the pitcher is throwing the ball to the catcher and toward the ground-level stands on the third base line. There was a net behind the catcher to protect the fans in the field-level seats from a wild pitch, but the net had been lowered somewhat because it interfered with the vision of some fans. The pitcher was almost finished with his warm-up and was throwing pitches at speeds between 90 and 96 miles per hour. One of these pitches sailed over the catcher's outstretched mitt and over the protective net, hitting a spectator in the cheek and breaking most of the bones on the left side of her face. She had been a successful financial consultant making a six-figure income before being hit by the pitch. After being hit, she lost vision in her left eye, had occasional seizures, and suffered memory and reasoning impairments. She sued the pitcher, the team owner, and the stadium owner. One of the "defenses" of the team and stadium owner was that the fan should have ducked before the pitch hit her.

A young man driving with his girlfriend along a four-lane highway inexplicably lost control of his car. The car went into a shallow ditch and emerged on the shoulder. The car was not badly damaged but the young man's girlfriend had hit her head on the dashboard and her shoulder on the passenger door and was in pain. They turned off the highway to take a more direct route to a nearby hospital. As they headed down a dirt road, they crossed a train track. As they crossed, their car was hit in the rear by a passenger train going 64 miles per hour. There was no visual obstruction at the railroad crossing and the young man said that he was aware that the train was coming but could not react quickly enough to stop. The engineer testified that he had seen the car coming down the road when the train was 800 yards away from the crossing and the car was at least 400 yards from the crossing. The only action the engineer could take was to blow the whistle continually and apply the emergency brakes of the train. Despite the braking, the train did not come to a stop until it was 600 yards past the crossing. Luckily, neither passenger in the car was killed or seriously injured. The passengers sued the railroad claiming, among other things, that the driver could not react in time to stop the car since the train was traveling too fast.

Both of these lawsuits involve reaction time. Both the baseball fan and the driver seem to be victims of reaction times slower than what was required to avoid injury. Both were expected to react quickly enough to save themselves. While it might have been possible for the driver to avoid the accident, it was impossible for the baseball fan to avoid the pitch (even assuming she was looking directly at the relief pitcher instead of the batter at home plate). The fastest recorded reaction time for a human being is between 25/100 and 30/100 of a second. An example of someone who can react that quickly is a spectacular fast-draw artist. It was possible to calculate how much time the baseball fan would have had to react once it was apparent that the catcher would not stop the ball. The ball reached her head in less than one-tenth of a second, almost three times faster than the fastest recorded reaction time. Based on calculations from the accident scene, the driver of the car had more than six seconds to react to the presence of the train, exceeding the time necessary to react (even for a normal person) by more than five seconds. He could have stopped but did not.

Think about reaction time as it has been defined by Fleishman in Table 3.1. What jobs are you familiar with where reaction time will be crucial to success (or may be implicated in injury or death)?

3.2   **A Level Playing Field**

It is common to test for physical abilities before choosing candidates for recruit positions in fire academies. Although physical abilities will be improved in the 16 weeks of the academy training program, you still require a minimum amount of ability to profit from the training. Most fire departments administer physical ability tests that simulate actual tasks performed by firefighters. As examples, candidates may be asked to carry heavy hose bundles up stairs, or open fire hydrants with wrenches or hang heavy exhaust fans in windows. Two tests, in particular, seem to be harder for female applicants than their male counterparts. The first is the "dummy drag" simulation. In this test, the candidate is asked to drag a 150-pound dummy through a 40-foot maze with several left and right turns in it. The second task is pulling 50 feet of a simulated fire hose through a 50-foot maze with two right turns. Since men tend to be larger and stronger, they simply pick up the dummy and carry it through the maze, while women are more likely to drag the dummy along the floor of the maze. Similarly, for the hose pull, men tend to simply loop the hose over their shoulder and pull it through the maze in one single movement. The test is not exactly the same as the actual task, however; in an actual fire situation the firefighter is usually pulling a person or a hose through a burning room and must stay close to the ground since the toxic fumes, smoke, and temperature (often as high as 2000 degrees) are more deadly in the upper part of a room.

If you wanted to make these test components more realistic, how would you redesign the test course? If you did redesign it, do you think that the performance of women would improve? Why or why not?

PERSONALITY AND INTERESTS

PERSONALITY

There is now a broad consensus that personality represents an important area of individual differences for examination by I-O psychologists (Murphy, 1996; Hough & Schneider, 1996; Mount & Barrick, 1995). There are clear connections between aspects of personality and various work behaviors, both productive (e.g., job performance) and counterproductive (e.g., dishonesty, absenteeism). This consensus is the result of concentrated work on developing a taxonomy of personality factors. This taxonomy is labeled the **Big 5** or the **Five Factor Model (FFM)** (Digman, 1990; McCrae & Costa, 1985, 1987). This model is the result of both statistical analyses of personality test information gathered over many decades, and a careful conceptual analysis of what most personality tests were trying to assess. Like most innovations, it has its critics, but for our purposes in this book it is a good basic model for describing the potential importance of personality variables in understanding job performance.

The Five Factor Model

As suggested by its title, the Five Factor Model (FFM) proposes that we can describe someone's "personality" by looking at five relatively independent factors. Personality can be defined in simplest terms as the typical way that an individual has of responding. It is considered a trait because it is fairly stable, even though situations and circumstances might lead a person to behave in a way that is out of character with his or her overall personality. The FFM identifies five different components which, when taken together, give a fair representation of how a person typically responds to events and people. These components and their definitions are presented in Table 3.4.

BIG 5

A taxonomy of five personality factors; the Five Factor Model (FFM).

FIVE FACTOR MODEL (FFM)

A taxonomy of five personality factors, comprised of conscientiousness, extraversion, agreeableness, emotional stability, and openness to experience.

TABLE 3.4 — The Five Factor Model

FACTOR	CHARACTERISTICS
1. Conscientiousness	Responsible, prudent, self-control, persistent, planful, achievement oriented
2. Extraversion	Sociable, assertive, talkative, ambitious, energetic
3. Agreeableness	Good natured, cooperative, trusting, likeable, friendly
4. Emotional stability	Secure, calm, low anxiety, low emotionality
5. Openness to experience	Curious, intelligent, imaginative, independent

Source: Based on Digman (1990); McCrae & Costa (1985, 1987).

It is important to keep in mind that the five factors are intended to measure normal personality, not to identify any evidence of psychopathology. We will make that distinction clearer in Chapter 4 when we discuss how personality is measured. Of the five factors, the first to have attracted most attention from I-O psychologists was **conscientiousness.** More recently, extraversion, openness to experience, and agreeableness are also attracting increased attention. In some early research, Barrick and Mount (1991) proposed, on the basis of a meta-analysis, that in all likelihood conscientiousness was positively related to success in all aspects of work for all occupations. That was a strong statement, but it was supported by their analyses. Naturally, there were disagreements with the five factor taxonomy and with the presumed overarching importance of conscientiousness. The first disagreement was that five factors are too few to capture the full range of aspects of personality (Hough, 1992; Tellegen, 1993; Tellegen, Grove & Waller, 1991; Tellegen & Waller, 2000). The second criticism was that although conscientiousness might be correlated with a wide range of work behaviors, it was not *highly* correlated with them. In addition, extraversion often correlated as highly with behavior as conscientiousness. A third criticism was that there were combinations of the five factors that led to greater predictive power than any one of the factors by itself (Dunn, 1993; Hogan & Hogan, 1989; Ones, Viswesvaran, & Schmidt, 1993). The first and third criticisms present an interesting dilemma, since one argues for *more* factors while the other seems to be arguing for *fewer* factors.

What seems to be true is that although each of the five factors does predict successful in contrast to unsuccessful performance of certain behaviors, some combinations of the factors may be stronger predictors than any single factor by itself. This introduces the idea of a **functional personality at work** (Barrick, Mount, & Judge, 2001; Mount & Barrick, 1995). This means that not just one factor predicts success, but a combination of factors. For example, Ones et al. (1993) found that individuals who were high on the conscientiousness, **agreeableness,** and **emotional stability** factors of the FFM tended to have higher **integrity.** Integrity in this context means honest, reliable, and ethical. Dunn (1993) found that managers believed that a combination of conscientiousness, agreeableness, and emotional stability made applicants more attractive to managers who had hiring responsibilities. Hogan and Hogan (1989) found that the same factors were related to employee reliability (Mount & Barrick, 1995).

Other meta-analyses also reveal relationships between the FFM and job performance, both in the United States (Hurtz & Donovan, 2000) and with European data (Salgado, 1997, 1998). The latter series of meta-analyses suggest that at least for many European countries, culture may not be a moderator variable for the personality/performance relationship. Nevertheless, remember from Chapter 1 that Hofstede's (1980, 2001) model of cultural influence showed that the biggest cultural differences seemed to be between Asian and Western nations, so the jury is still out on whether the personality/performance relationship holds true in countries like China and Japan. There is reason to expect that it will be different from its manifestation in the Europe or the United States since the collectivist cultures of China and Japan emphasize group outcomes over individual outcomes.

Implications of the Five Factor Model   It appears that as the aspect of work behavior we are trying to predict gets broader (e.g., overall job performance), large FFM factors like conscientiousness do as well as smaller and more discrete factors. There is some debate whether to use broad or narrow personality dimensions (Hogan & Roberts, 1996; Ones & Viswesvaran, 1996; Schneider, Hough, & Dunnette, 1996). It turns out that narrow traits seem to be useful for predicting very specific job behaviors and broader traits for predicting broader behaviors, so it is not necessary to choose between the two approaches. Each has its own use.

CONSCIENTIOUS-NESS

Quality of having positive intentions and carrying them out with care.

FUNCTIONAL PERSONALITY AT WORK

The way that an individual behaves, handles emotions, and accomplishes tasks in a work setting; a combination of Big 5 factors.

AGREEABLENESS

Likable, easy to get along with, friendly.

EMOTIONALLY STABILITY

Displaying little emotion; showing the same emotional response in various situations.

INTEGRITY

Quality of being honest, reliable, and ethical, as in an employee.

Hough suggested that the FFM factor of consciousness should be broken down into two discrete factors called **achievement** and **dependability.** Achievement consists of hard work, persistence, and the desire to do good work. Dependability represents being disciplined, well organized, respectful of laws and regulations, honest, trustworthy, and accepting of authority (Hough, 1992). When we break conscientiousness down into those two facets, it turns out that dependability is a better predictor of employee reliability than conscientiousness, and achievement is a better predictor of effort than conscientiousness. But if we try to predict ratings of overall job performance, then conscientiousness does as well as either achievement or dependability (Mount & Barrick, 1995). Another general finding is that as the behavior we are trying to predict (e.g., effort or reliability) becomes more specific, the correlations with both the FFM factors and the more refined factors go up. The more specific we are about the aspect of performance we are trying to predict, the more accurate the prediction is.

Tett (1995) made the point with a few concrete examples. He suggested that the "dependable" (or "rule-bound") aspect of conscientiousness might actually be counterproductive in professions such as musician, sculptor, painter, actor, choreographer, and even management positions in which the manager is expected to "think outside the box" (e.g., marketing manager). He referred to the problem of too much attention to detail and rules as "analysis-paralysis."

Problems can also arise when an individual has plenty of "g" but lacks other attributes. The recent movie *A Beautiful Mind* tells the story of John Nash, a Nobel Prize–winning mathematician who was brilliant (in a "g" sense) and high on achievement as defined above, but who was severely impaired in social and interpersonal skills. Nash was emotionally unstable, eventually disintegrating into paranoia and delusional states. Early in his career, he was favored because of his sheer brilliance ("g") and tenacity (conscientiousness), but his impairments in other dimensions eventually rendered him useless to the research facility where he was employed. Nash's story illustrates the point that to get a true understanding of behavior, we often need to decompose elements (like conscientiousness) or consider patterns or combinations of elements.

There is a final aspect of the research on the Five Factor Model that deserves discussion. Have you ever had a job in which you were closely supervised and required to follow very detailed work and organizational procedures? In that environment, you would have had little opportunity to let your "habitual way of responding" (i.e., your personality) appear in your behavior. Think of the opposite situation—a job where you had a good deal of control over your work habits. In the latter, you could really be "you"—and whether you performed well or poorly probably depended on how well your personality was suited to the job's demands. That is exactly what Barrick and Mount (1993) found with their research on the FFM. In jobs where the employee had a great deal of control (i.e., autonomy), personality was much more predictive of performance than in jobs where the employee had little or no control. You will remember that this is how we defined a "moderator" variable in Chapter 2. In this case, control moderated the relationship between personality and performance. It has been commonly found that if a situation allows for little discretion on the part of a person (referred to as a "strong" situation), personality will play a minor role in his or her behavior.

How can we summarize what we know about the relationship between personality and work behavior? And what can we say more specifically about the FFM compared to other theories, such as Hough's (1992)? We believe that the following conclusions can be drawn with confidence.

1.   Personality differences play a role in work behavior independent of the role played by cognitive ability (Borman, White, Pulakos, & Oppler, 1991; Mount & Barrick, 1995; Murphy, 1996).

ACHIEVEMENT

A facet of conscientiousness consisting of hard work, persistence, and the desire to do good work.

DEPENDABILITY

A facet of conscientiousness, consisting of being disciplined, well organized, respectful of laws and regulations, honest, trustworthy, and accepting of authority.

2. Personality is more closely related to motivation aspects of work (e.g., effort expenditure) than to technical aspects of work (e.g., knowledge components). Personality is more likely to predict what a person *will* do and ability measures are more likely to predict what a person *can* do (Campbell, 1990; Mount & Barrick, 1995).

3. The FFM is a good general framework for thinking about important aspects of personality (Digman, 1990; Guion, 1998; Lubinski, 2000).

4. The more relevant and specific the work behavior we are trying to predict, the stronger the association between personality and behavior (Mount & Barrick, 1995).

5. Conscientiousness is best considered a combination of achievement and dependability. Achievement will predict some behaviors (e.g., effort) and dependability will predict other behaviors (e.g., attendance) (Hough, 1992; Moon, 2001; Mount & Barrick, 1995; Stewart, 1999).

6. Conscientiousness (along with its constituent factors achievement and dependability) has widespread applicability in work settings. It is possibly the most important personality variable in the workplace and it may be the equivalent of "g" in the noncognitive domain (Schmidt & Hunter, 1992).

7. Conscientiousness and its constituent factors (achievement and dependability) have a greater impact on behavior in situations where the worker has substantial autonomy (Barrick & Mount, 1993).

8. Conscientiousness, achievement, and dependability are only a small collection of a number of interesting facets of personality. The single-minded pursuit of "g" slowed down advances in understanding intelligence for almost 80 years. We should not let the same thing happen with the single-minded focus on conscientiousness (Collins, 1998).

9. There is evidence that factors other than conscientiousness have applicability for specific job families and occupations. Extraversion appears related to sales performance; openness to experience predicts training and expatriate success; agreeableness is associated with performance in customer-service and team-oriented jobs; emotional stability contributes to a broad range of jobs including management positions as well as jobs in the safety/security sector (Barrick, Mount & Judge, 2001; Mount, Barrick, & Stewart, 1998; Vinchur, Schippmann, Switzer, & Roth, 1998).

Psychologists will continue to debate the number of elements of personality, the names of those elements, and the content of those elements, but we think that it is safe to say that personality is divided into no fewer than 5 basic elements and no more than 10 or 11. For the time being, we can use the Five Factor Model (McCrae & Costa, 1987) and the Nine Factor Model (Hough, 1992) as examples of the upper and lower limits. Neither of those models is "right" in any scientific sense. They are both plausible and they both have their applications. It is not uncommon to see some personality tests that measure more than the 10 or 11 elements we have proposed (e.g., the OPQ 32 or the 16PF tests), but these tests are addressing much more distinct facets of personality rather than its basic dimensions.

Tellegen (1993; Tellegen & Waller, 2000) has proposed an intriguing seven-factor model. His model includes the five dimensions of the FFM plus two other dimensions: positive and negative valence. **Positive valence** is represented by descriptions such as remarkable, extraordinary, excellent, and outstanding and appears to be a continuum running from normal to exceptional. **Negative valence,** on the other hand, is the dark side of personality and is represented by descriptions such as cruel, evil, wicked, and sickening. It represents a continuum from decent to awful (Lubinski, 2000). Although there needs to be much more research on Tellegen's view of personality, these two additional dimensions strike a chord. We have all known people who were extraordinary in every respect. We want to be like them and be around them. And we have probably known a despicable

POSITIVE
VALENCE

Continuum of favorable personality characteristics running from normal to exceptional.

NEGATIVE
VALENCE

Continuum of unfavorable personality characteristics running from normal to abominable.

BOX 3.2 PERSONALITY TESTING FAQ

Q: There are many personality tests and scales available. How do you choose among them?

A: Use valid and reliable tests that cover at least the Five Factor Model dimensions.

Q: Why should you use a test that measures more than one aspect of personality when you are interested in only one?

A: Because behavior usually is a function of many different influences, not just one.

Q: What do personality tests measure?

A: A person's typical "style."

Q: Why use personality tests to make employment decisions?

A: Because most workers and managers use terms like "being a team player," "remaining calm under pressure," "being persistent," and "taking initiative" as critical for success in almost any job.

Q: Do personality tests predict job performance?

A: Yes.

Q: Do personality tests predict performance in all jobs?

A: Probably, but they are less predictive for jobs with little autonomy.

Q: Weren't personality tests developed to measure psychopathology and for use in clinical settings?

A: Many years ago, that was true. The tests available today are designed to assess normal personality.

Q: People's behavior changes constantly. Doesn't this invalidate personality tests?

A: By definition, personality is relatively stable over time and from one set of circumstances to another and continues to affect our lives in important ways. Even though behavior changes occasionally, stable aspects of personality are still effective predictors.

Q: Do personality measures discriminate against ethnic minorities, women, older individuals, and the disabled?

A: There is no evidence of discrimination against these groups in well-developed personality tests. People over 40 tend to receive more positive scores than those under 40. There are some differences between males and females (men have higher scores on emotional stability and women have higher scores on conscientiousness) but these are not significant enough to result in different hiring decisions.

Q: Do personality tests invade privacy?

A: Some appear to. Choose tests with the highest validity and reliability, and the fewest number of offensive-appearing questions.

Q: What is the best way to use personality measures for pre-employment screening?

A: In combination with measures of technical skills, experience, and the ability to learn.

Q: Is it easy to fake on personality measures?

A: Some tests (e.g., integrity tests) are easier to fake than others, but it appears that the faking rate among applicants is low and faking does not appear to affect the validity of these measures substantially.

Source: Based on Hogan, Hogan & Roberts (1996).

person whom we avoid like the plague. Furthermore, both types of people might be high or low on conscientiousness, openness to experience, or even agreeableness!

Practical Issues Associated with Personality Measures

Up to this point, we have been dealing with the "science" of personality. But there are also practical questions that arise about the measurement of personality for making employment decisions. Hogan, Hogan, and Roberts (1996) addressed those larger practical questions as summarized in Box 3.2.

Faking The final question in Box 3.2 brings up a controversial point about personality tests. Some tests, particularly some commercially available integrity tests, are very transparent. It is obvious how one should answer the test questions in order to appear to have high integrity. A candidate might bear the following "script" in mind when answering the test questions:

> I have never stolen anything since I was a young child, and even then, I don't think I ever stole anything. I do not have any friends who steal, or would even *think* of stealing anything. If they did, they could not be my friends anymore and I would tell the appropriate

authorities that they had stolen something. I think that showing up for work late, not doing a complete job, leaving work early, and taking sick days when you are not sick is also stealing and I would not do any of those things or be friends with anyone who would. I would inform management if I ever found out that a co-worker was engaging in any of these behaviors.

This "script" is only partly facetious. It is amusing in its extremity, but it makes the point that it is possible to answer questions on a personality-like device in a way that gets the best result—that is, an offer of employment. But what about tests that are not so transparent? From a practical standpoint, there are actually three questions to answer: (1) How easy is it to fake personality tests? (2) How many people do it? and (3) How much does it matter whether people do or do not fake? Let's take these one at a time.

SELF-PRESENTATION

A person's public face or "game face."

SELF-EFFICACY

Feeling of capability; belief that one can overcome obstacles and accomplish difficult tasks.

SOCIAL DESIRABILITY

Desire to be appealing to others.

How easy is it to fake personality tests? Not difficult. As Hogan et al. (1996) pointed out, some are easier to fake than others. But you can answer any personality test in a way that makes you look "good." The real question is whether that is "faking." From some perspectives, personality is all about **self-presentation;** it is your public face, your "game face." So to the extent that the personality test is a paper-and-pencil form of self-presentation, it is not faking, nor is it distortion (Hogan et al., 1996; Mount & Barrick, 1995). People often view themselves in more positive terms than an outside observer might. When you consider faking from this vantage point, there is not much of a distinction between self-esteem or **self-efficacy** and "faking." Another way to think of how you might answer a personality inventory is that you are really answering as an "ideal candidate" for the position might answer the question (Schmit & Ryan, 1992; Schmit & Ryan, 1993). People responding simply to make themselves look good—**social desirability**—will not end up looking like the ideal candidate and thus may actually be doing themselves as much harm as good. As we will see in Chapter 14, it is increasingly obvious that for an individual to succeed within an organization, there should be a good match or "fit" between the culture of the organization and the personality of the individual. Distorting responses in order to "look good" will not make that match any better.

How many people fake personality measures? It is not clear what the prevalence of distortion is (Mount & Barrick, 1995) because the prevalence depends, as we've seen in the preceding paragraph, on how you define faking. The main line of evidence to suggest that faking may be occurring is that applicant groups often have significantly more positive scores on given personality measures than employed groups (Bass, 1957; Kirchner, Dunnette, & Mousely, 1960). In addition, sophisticated statistical analyses of responses to personality questionnaires (Michaelis & Eysenck, 1971; Schmit & Ryan, 1993) show that there are different patterns of responses from applicants than from employees or students. Not surprisingly, some studies say the rate of faking is substantial while others say it is minimal.

Which brings us to the third question: How much does it matter? The answer is that it does not appear to matter much. In studies where participants were instructed to distort their responses to make themselves look more favorable, the predictive validity of the personality measures remained the same (Hough et al., 1990). And if we return to the self-presentation view of personality, "distortion" could either increase or decrease the validity of the personality measures. If the job in question were a sales position, a desire to look "good" in the eyes of another might actually be a job-related attribute (Hogan et al., 1996). On the other hand, if an individual is having a performance counseling discussion with a supervisor, a more realistic presentation of strengths and weaknesses by the individual would be more effective than trying to look good. The issue of faking is not "settled" yet, but there does seem to be some agreement that it is not a fatal flaw in personality testing (Hough, 1998; Hough & Ones, 2001; Ones & Viswesvaran, 1998; Salgado, Viswesvaran, & Ones, 2001; Viswesvaran & Ones, 1999).

There is one additional cautionary note of some practical significance for test-takers inclined to intentionally distort their responses. Most personality tests have a "lie" scale which indicates if a person is trying to make themselves look "ideal" in some way. The test report for an individual will usually include a cautionary note indicating a lack of confidence in the resulting scores if the applicant scored too high on the lie scale.

VOCATIONAL INTERESTS

Measures of **vocational interest** have been around for almost 80 years, but they have received only passing attention from I-O psychologists. Two reasons explain this lack of attention. The first is the belief that vocational interests do not predict job performance. The second is that they were often thought to be in the domain of vocational counseling and only useful for advising students about vocations and occupations. As we will see below, there are reasons to reconsider these measures of individual differences.

In their simplest form, vocational interests are expressions of *liking* about environments (including social environments) and activities. When someone expresses a liking for "mechanical things" or "science" or "being around people," they are expressing an interest. An interest is less a behavior than a vision of oneself in a desired environment. You may like working with mechanical things but have a job as an accountant, or like working with people and have a job as a snow cat operator. If your interest (i.e., working with mechanical things or working with people) is strong and you find yourself in an environment that is not aligned with that interest, we would expect there to be some consequences. One of those consequences should be dissatisfaction with your occupation and probably with your job. We can see the prevalence of this dissatisfaction in the workforce when we consider how many people retire at the first opportunity in order to devote themselves to a second career that they "always wanted to do." A second, related consequence ought to be tenure in the occupation or job. People whose job and occupation are compatible with their interests should, all other things being equal, stay in that occupation (and possibly that job) for long periods of time. Finally, there ought to be some consequences for performance. If you are in a job or occupation that does not match a strong interest, it is more likely that your performance will be poorer than if you were in a job that matched your interests. This assumes, of course, that interests also reflect abilities to some extent.

It is important to remember that there are a myriad of other factors that can affect your job tenure, satisfaction, and performance. But that does not deny the possibility that interests add information that is not covered by ability or personality (Hogan & Blake, 1996; Lubinski, 2000). It is also intriguing that vocational interests appear in early adolescence (as early as age 13) and remain relatively stable over long periods of time (Lubinski, 2000). The reluctance of I-O psychologists to consider vocational interests in their decomposition of work behavior is unfortunate. To be sure, the associations with performance are not as high as one finds when considering mental ability or personality, but they are there and they are reliable (Barge & Hough, 1988). Since one of the primary activities for I-O psychologists, whether employed within organizations or as consultants, is maintaining or enhancing profitability, it is not hard to understand why they would be more interested in predictors (such as "g" or conscientiousness) that are more strongly associated with performance. Similarly, it is not surprising that they would be less interested in predictors of satisfaction or occupational tenure than of performance. But that is a narrow view of work

Parents are often an important influence on their children's choice of occupation.

VOCATIONAL INTEREST

Preference or liking for a particular activity or setting (as in a job or occupational setting).

TABLE 3.5	Holland's Adjectival Descriptions of Six Personality Types
Realistic	Asocial, conforming, frank, genuine, hard-headed, materialistic, natural, normal, persistent, practical, self-effacing, inflexible, thrifty, uninsightful, uninvolved
Investigative	Analytical, cautious, critical, complex, curious, independent, intellectual, introspective, pessimistic, precise, rational, reserved, retiring, unassuming, unpopular
Artistic	Complicated, disorderly, emotional, expressive, idealistic, imaginative, impractical, impulsive, independent, introspective, intuitive, nonconforming, original, sensitive, open
Social	Ascendant, cooperative, patient, friendly, generous, helpful, idealistic, empathic, kind, persuasive, responsible, sociable, tactful, understanding, warm
Enterprising	Acquisitive, adventurous, agreeable, ambitious, domineering, energetic, exhibitionistic, excitement-seeking, extroverted, flirtatious, optimistic, self-confident, sociable, talkative
Conventional	Careful, conforming, conscientious, defensive, efficient, inflexible, inhibited, methodical, obedient, orderly, persistent, practical, prudish, thrifty, unimaginative

SOURCE: Hogan & Blake (1996).

RIASEC

Acronym for Holland's model of vocational interests which proposes six interest types of people: realistic, investigative, artistic, social, enterprising, and conventional.

and workers. As we will see in Part III of this book, the investigation of satisfaction and organizational, occupational, and job tenure is beneficial not only to workers but also to employers.

As was the case with intelligence and personality, the area of vocational interests is dominated by one model. Developed and presented by Holland (1973; 1985), it is known by the acronym, **RIASEC** (see Table 3.5). The model proposes six interest types of people: Realistic, Investigative, Artistic, Social, Enterprising, and Conventional; the label RIASEC comes from the first initial of each interest type. An additional feature of the model is that the types are arranged hexagonally, with each type occupying a particular position (see Figure 3.4). As can be seen from that figure, some types are adjacent to each other and

FIGURE 3.4

Personality Dimensions Underlying the Hexagonal Representation of Holland's Vocational Typology SOURCE: Hogan & Blake (1996).

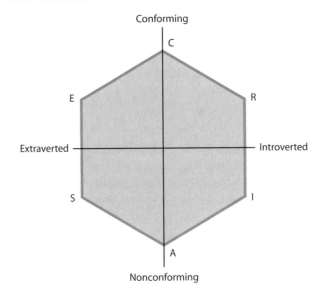

some types are directly opposite from each other. Thus, enterprising is opposite from investigative. Practically speaking, this means if you express interests that would be enterprising, it would be unlikely that you would express interests that are investigative. And when you look at the definitions in Table 3.5, that makes sense. Investigating interests include reserved, cautious, and retiring behavior. Enterprising interests, on the other hand, represent excitement-seeking, talkative, and adventurous behaviors. Types that are close to each other in the hexagon are more compatible. Thus, it would not be surprising to see someone who expresses social interests to express enterprising interests as well. The social type includes friendly and sociable interests while enterprising types include agreeable, extroverted, and social interests.

Like intelligence and the FFM theory of personality, it is likely that interests can be more specific than the RIASEC factors, but as a basic model this is a good one to use in developing more discrete measures of interests.

MODULE 3.3 SUMMARY

- There are clear connections between aspects of personality and various work behaviors, both productive (e.g., job performance) and counterproductive (e.g., dishonesty, absenteeism). I-O psychologists studying personality use a taxonomy labeled the Big 5 or the Five Factor Model (FFM).

- Of these five factors, the one that has attracted the most attention from I-O psychologists is conscientiousness. Barrick and Mount concluded, on the basis of a meta-analysis, that conscientiousness was positively related to success in all aspects of work for all occupations.

- Hough proposed nine basic personality factors rather than five; she suggested that the FFM factor of conscientiousness should be broken down into two discrete factors called achievement and dependability.

- Tett (1995) suggested that the "dependable" (or "rule-bound") aspect of conscientiousness might actually be counterproductive in professions where the employee is expected to "think outside the box." The same can be true of "g" when success in the job depends on action rather than thought. Problems can arise when

an individual has plenty of "g" but lacks other attributes.

- Barrick and Mount found through FFM research that in jobs where the employee had a great deal of control or autonomy, personality was much more predictive of performance than in jobs where the employee had little or no control.

- Tellegen (1993; Tellegen & Waller, 2000) has proposed an intriguing seven-factor model of personality which includes the five dimensions of the FFM plus two other dimensions: positive and negative valence.

- Hogan, Hogan, and Roberts addressed practical questions about using the measurement of personality for making employment decisions.

- Job applicants taking personality tests are likely to give the answers they believe are most likely to result in an offer of employment, which may be interpreted as "faking."

- The area of vocational interests is dominated by Holland's model, known by the acronym RIASEC. The model proposes six interest types of people: Realistic, Investigative, Artistic, Social, Enterprising, and Conventional.

KEY TERMS

Big 5
Five Factor Model (FFM)
conscientiousness
functional personality at work
agreeableness
emotionally stability

integrity
achievement
dependability
positive valence
negative valence

self-presentation
self-efficacy
social desirability
vocational interest
RIASEC

CRITICAL THINKING EXERCISES

3.4 Refer to Point #9 on p. 102. You will see the following general findings:

1. Extraversion is related to sales success.
2. Openness to experience is related to success of Americans who go to work in a different country.
3. Openness to experience is related to training success.
4. Agreeableness is related to success in customer service positions.
5. Emotional stability is associated with success in safety and security jobs.

For each of these general findings, explain *why* the particular Big Five Factor is associated with success in that job.

3.5 Consider each of the factors of the Five Factor Model. Identify a job in which *too much* of the factor would lead to failure in an important part of that job. Explain *why* too much of the factor is a problem.

Conscientiousness

Agreeableness

Extraversion

Emotional stability

Openness to experience

3.6 Imagine that you have just picked up from the airport a friend who will accompany you on a ski trip. Your friend tells you that she talked to the person who sat next to her for three hours and came to the conclusion that this person had "zero personality." Applying the Big 5 model to your friend's "analysis," which of the five dimensions do you think that your friend would have been able to assess in that three-hour plane ride?

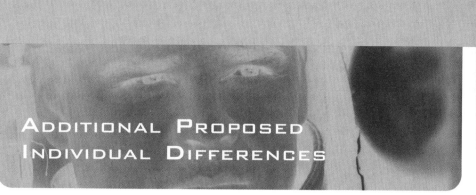

ADDITIONAL PROPOSED INDIVIDUAL DIFFERENCES

The collection of cognitive abilities, physical and motor abilities, personality, and interests covers the major categories of proposed individual differences. The patterns formed by their combinations describe much of the variation among individuals. Nevertheless, some scientists propose additional aspects of individual differences. Below we will briefly cover some of them.

SKILLS

Skills are practiced acts. Shooting a basketball, using a computer keyboard, and persuading someone to buy something are all examples of skills. They come with hours, days, and weeks of practice. It is unlikely that skills can be developed without certain abilities (eye-hand coordination, or memory, or reasoning) and personality characteristics (persistence or agreeableness), and knowledge (understanding the controls that activate a piece of equipment). Although the skills depend on these ability, personality, and knowledge factors, the reason we call them skills is that they develop through practice. Technical and job-related skills are as varied as jobs and job tasks. There are other nontechnical skills that are more widespread than any technical skill. Examples include negotiating skills, communication skills, and conflict-resolution skills. These three are often lumped together by nonpsychologists and called **people skills.** Since they come into play most commonly in situations involving leader-follower and team member interactions, we will discuss these skills in the chapters that deal with teams and leadership.

KNOWLEDGE

Knowledge can be defined as "a collection of discrete but related facts and information about a particular domain. It is acquired through formal education or training, or accumulated through specific experiences" (Peterson, Mumford, Borman, Jeanneret, & Fleishman, 1999, p. 71). Knowledge is closely connected to skill when we are considering job-related skills (as opposed to psychomotor skills like shooting a basketball). Knowledge supports skill development and it comes in many varieties. It can be very basic (knowledge of mathematical operations or of vocabulary), or it can be sophisticated (knowledge of the circuitry of a notebook computer). Table 3.6 presents some representative categories of knowledge as identified in the comprehensive occupational information network that has come to be known as

SKILLS

Practiced acts, such as shooting a basketball, using a computer keyboard, or persuading someone to buy something.

PEOPLE SKILLS

A nontechnical term that includes negotiating skills, communication skills, and conflict resolution skills.

Dealing cards is an example of a well-developed psychomotor skill.

TABLE 3.6	Descriptions and Definitions of Knowledges	
CONSTRUCT LABEL	**OPERATIONAL DEFINITION**	**LEVEL SCALE**
	Business and management	
1. Administration and Management	Knowledge of principles and processes involved in business and organizational planning, coordination, and execution. This includes strategic planning, resource allocation, manpower modeling, leadership techniques, and production methods.	High—Managing a $10 million company. Low—Signing a pay voucher.
2. Clerical	Knowledge of administrative and clerical procedures and systems, such as word processing systems, filing and records management systems, stenography and transcription, forms design principles, and other office procedures and terminology.	High—Organizing a storage system for company forms. Low—Filing letters alphabetically.
3. Economics and Accounting	Knowledge of economic and accounting principles and practices, the financial markets, banking, and the analysis and reporting of financial data.	High—Keeping a major corporation's financial records. Approving a multimillion dollar loan to a real estate developer. Low—Answering billing questions from credit card customers.
4. Sales and Marketing	Knowledge of principles and methods involved in showing, promoting, and selling products or services. This includes marketing strategies and tactics, product demonstration and sales techniques, and sales control systems.	High—Developing a marketing plan for a nationwide phone system. Low—Selling cakes at a bake sale.
5. Customer and Personal Service	Knowledge of principles and processes for providing customer and personal services, including needs assessment techniques, quality service standards, alternative delivery systems, and customer satisfaction evaluation techniques.	High—Responding to a citizen's request for assistance after a major natural disaster. Low—Processing customer dry-cleaning drop-off.
6. Personnel and Human Resources	Knowledge of policies and practices involved in personnel/human resources functions. This includes recruitment, selection, training, and promotion regulations and procedures; compensation and benefits packages; labor relations and negotiation strategies; and personnel information systems.	High—Designing a new personnel selection and promotion system for the Army. Low—Filling out a medical claim form.

(continued)

TABLE 3.6   *(continued)*

CONSTRUCT LABEL	OPERATIONAL DEFINITION	LEVEL SCALE
Manufacturing and production		
7. Production and Processing	Knowledge of inputs, outputs, raw materials, waste, quality control, costs, and techniques for maximizing the manufacture and distribution of goods.	High—Managing a food processing plant. Low—Putting a computer back into its packing materials.
8. Food Production	Knowledge of techniques and equipment for planting, growing, and harvesting of food for consumption, including crop rotation methods, animal husbandry, and food storage/handling, techniques.	High—Running a 100,000 acre farm. Low—Keeping an herb box in the kitchen.
Engineering and technology		
9. Computers and Electronics	Knowledge of electric, circuit boards, processors, chips, and computer hardware and software, including applications and programming.	High—Creating a program to scan computer disks for viruses. Low—Operating a VCR to watch a prerecorded training tape.
10. Engineering and Technology	Knowledge of equipment, tools, mechanical devices, and their uses to produce motion, light, power, technology, and other applications.	High—Designing an efficient and clean power plant. Low—Installing a door lock.
11. Design	Knowledge of design techniques, principles, tools and instruments involved in the production and use of precision technical plans, blueprints, drawings, and models.	High—Developing detailed design plans for a new high-rise office complex. Low—Drawing a straight line 4 3/16 inches long.
12. Building and Construction	Knowledge of materials, methods, and the appropriate tools to construct objects, structures, and buildings.	High—Building a high-rise office tower. Low—Sawing a board in half.
13. Mechanical	Knowledge of machines and tools, including their designs, uses, benefits, repair, and maintenance.	High—Overhauling an airplane jet engine. Low—Replacing the filters in a furnace.
Mathematics and science		
14. Mathematics	Knowledge of numbers, their operations, and interrelationships, including arithmetic, algebra, geometry, calculus, statistics, and their applications.	High—Deriving a complex mathematical equation. Low—Adding two numbers.
15. Physics	Knowledge and prediction of physical principles, laws, and applications, including air, water, material dynamics, light, atomic principles, heat, electric theory, earth formations, and meteorological and related natural phenomena.	High—Designing a cleaner burning gasoline engine. Low—Using a crowbar to pry open a box.

(continued)

TABLE 3.6 *(continued)*

CONSTRUCT LABEL	OPERATIONAL DEFINITION	LEVEL SCALE
16. Chemistry	Knowledge of the composition, structure, and properties of substances and of the chemical processes and transformations that they undergo. This includes uses of chemicals and their interactions, danger signs, production techniques, and disposal methods.	High—Developing a safe commercial cleaner. Low—Using a common household bug spray.
17. Biology	Knowledge of plant and animal living tissue, cells, organisms, and entities, including their functions, interdependencies, and interactions with each other and the environment.	High—Isolating and identifying a microscopic virus. Low—Feeding domestic animals.
18. Psychology	Knowledge of human behavior and performance, mental processes, psychological research methods, and the assessment and treatment of behavioral and affective disorders.	High—Treating a person with a severe mental illness. Low—Monitoring several children on a playground.
19. Sociology and Anthropology	Knowledge of group behavior and dynamics, societal trends and influences, cultures, their history, migrations, ethnicity, and origins.	High—Developing a new theory about the development of early civilizations. Low—Identifying two cultures in a story as being different.
20. Geography	Knowledge of various methods for describing the location and distribution of land, sea, and air masses, including their physical locations, relationships, and characteristics.	High—Developing a map of the world showing mountains, deserts, and rivers. Low—Knowing the capital of the United States.
Health services		
21. Medicine and Dentistry	Knowledge of the information and techniques needed to diagnose and treat injuries, diseases, and deformities. This includes symptoms, treatment alternatives, drug properties and interactions, and preventive health-care measures.	High—Performing open-heart surgery. Low—Using a small bandage.
22. Therapy and Counseling	Knowledge of information and techniques needed to rehabilitate physical and mental ailments and to provide career guidance, including alternative treatment, rehabilitation equipment and its proper use, and methods to evaluate treatment effects.	High—Counseling an abused child. Low—Putting ice on a sprained ankle.

(continued)

TABLE 3.6   *(continued)*

CONSTRUCT LABEL	OPERATIONAL DEFINITION	LEVEL SCALE
Education and training		
23. Education and Training	Knowledge of instructional methods and training techniques, including curriculum design principles, learning theory, group and individual teaching techniques, design of individual development plans, and test design principles.	High—Designing a training program for new employees. Low—Showing someone how to bowl.
Arts and humanities		
24. English Language	Knowledge of the structure and content of the English language, including the meaning and spelling of words, rules of composition, and grammar.	High—Teaching a college English class. Low—Writing a thank-you note.
25. Foreign Language	Knowledge of the structure and content of a foreign (non-English) language, including the meaning and spelling of words, rules of composition and grammar, and pronunciation.	High—Providing spoken translation of a political speech while listening to it at an international meeting. Low—Saying "please " and "thank-you" in a foreign language.
26. Fine Arts	Knowledge of theory and techniques required to produce, compose, and perform works of music, dance, visual arts, drama, and sculpture.	High—Composing a symphony. Low—Attending a popular music concert.
27. History and Archaeology	Knowledge of historical events and their causes, indicators, and impact on particular civilizations and cultures.	High—Determining the age of bones for placing them in the fossil history. Low—Taking a class in U.S. history.
28. Philosophy and Theology	Knowledge of different philosophical systems and religions, including their basic principles, values, ethics, ways of thinking, customs, and practices, and their impact on human culture.	High—Comparing the teachings of major philosophers. Low—Watching a TV program on family values.
Law and public safety		
29. Public Safety and Security	Knowledge of weaponry, public safety, and security operations, rules, regulations, precautions, prevention, and the protection of people, data, and property.	High—Commanding a military operation. Low—Using a seatbelt.
30. Law, Government, and Jurisprudence	Knowledge of law, legal codes, court procedures, precedents, government regulations, executive orders, agency rules, and the democratic political process.	High—Being a judge in a federal court. Low—Registering to vote in a national election.

(continued)

TABLE 3.6	*(continued)*	
CONSTRUCT LABEL	**OPERATIONAL DEFINITION**	**LEVEL SCALE**
Communications		
31. Telecommunications	Knowledge of transmission, broadcasting, switching, control, and operation of telecommunication systems.	High—Developing a new, worldwide telecommunication network. Low—Dialing a phone.
32. Communications and Media	Knowledge of media production, communication, and dissemination techniques and methods, including alternative ways to inform and entertain via written, oral, and visual media.	High—Producing a combined TV, radio, and newspaper campaign to inform the public about world hunger. Low—Writing a thank-you note.
Transportation		
33. Transportation	Knowledge of principles and methods for moving people or goods by air, sea, or road, including their relative costs, advantages, and limitations.	High—Controlling air traffic at a major airport. Low—Taking a train to work.

SOURCE: Adapted from Peterson et al. (1999).

O*NET

Collection of electronic databases, based on well-developed taxonomies, that has updated and replaced the Dictionary of Occupational Titles.

TACIT KNOWLEDGE

Action-oriented, goal-directed knowledge, acquired without direct help from others; colloquially called "street smarts."

PROCEDURAL KNOWLEDGE

Familiarity with a procedure or process; knowing "how."

DECLARATIVE KNOWLEDGE

Familiarity with facts or abstract concepts, often acquired through direct instruction; knowing "that."

O*NET (Peterson et al., 1999). This figure provides the name of the knowledge domain, the definition of the knowledge, and examples of what someone with a great deal or very little of the knowledge might be capable of doing. Perhaps the most immediate example of individual differences in knowledge is the distribution of test grades in your class. Although many variables may play a role in this grade distribution, one of those variables is certainly knowledge of the course material as presented in the text and lectures.

Another kind of knowledge that has been proposed is called **tacit knowledge,** studied by Sternberg and his colleagues (Sternberg & Wagner, 1986; Sternberg, Wagner, & Okagaki, 1993). They distinguish between "academic" and "tacit" knowledge, the latter described as "action oriented knowledge, acquired without direct help from others, that allows individuals to achieve goals they personally value" (Sternberg, Wagner, Williams, & Horvath, 1995). They describe tacit knowledge as "knowing how" rather than "knowing that." A more formal way of distinguishing these two types of knowledge is **procedural knowledge** (knowing how) in contrast with **declarative knowledge** (knowing that).

The researchers give an example of how tacit knowledge about getting along with your boss might affect your behavior: If you need to deliver bad news, and it is Monday morning, and you know the boss's golf game was rained out the day before, and the whole staff is nervous and walking on eggs, tacit knowledge would tell you that it would be best to deliver the bad news later. A common nonscientific term for tacit knowledge might be "street smarts." One of the important distinctions researchers make between formal or academic knowledge on the one hand and tacit knowledge on the other is that tacit knowledge is always goal-directed and useful, while academic knowledge may not be. People develop tacit knowledge about environments and processes that are personally valuable to them. Research seems to indicate that tacit knowledge is something above and beyond intelligence (Sternberg et al., 1995). Learning little tricks to perform better might be considered the light side of the tacit knowledge coin, and learning how to manipulate people might be the dark side.

EXPERIENCE

The concept of tacit knowledge leads directly to a consideration of **experience** as an aspect of individual difference. Although experience does not always lead to tacit knowledge, tacit knowledge depends on experience. Just as most people would agree that individuals often differ in knowledge, they would also agree that individuals often differ in experience. This experience can be with a task, a job, an organization, or an occupation. Experience is often confused with seniority, but doing the same thing 100 times (seniority) is not the same as doing 100 things one time (experience). Jacobs, Hofmann and Kriska (1990) suggested that experience on a given job is valuable up to a point, but then its value declines as the same work tasks and challenges begin to appear with greater frequency over time, making them less valuable "learning" experiences.

Two refined models of experience have been presented in the last few years. Quinones, Ford, and Teachout (1995) proposed that experience can be considered along two dimensions: **measurement modes** and **level of specificity.** Measurement modes refer to the unit of measurement we use to assess experience. They propose that there are three modes: "amount" or the number of times a person has actually performed the task; "time," which would represent the length of time an individual has been performing a task or job; and "type," which captures some qualitative aspects of the experience related to task difficulty or job complexity. The second dimension of experience in their model addresses the issue of how specific the experience was. There are three levels of specificity: task, job, and organizational. Using this model, we can now describe experience as falling into one of the nine cells formed by the combination of these two dimensions of mode and specificity (see Figure 3.5). These cells provide an understandable method for categorizing experience. With such a framework, it will be much easier to examine the relationship between experience and work performance.

EXPERIENCE

Direct participation in, or observation of, events and activities that serves as a basis for knowledge.

MEASUREMENT MODES

Unit of measurement used to assess experience.

LEVEL OF SPECIFICITY

Method used to gauge experience according to task, job, and organizational characteristics.

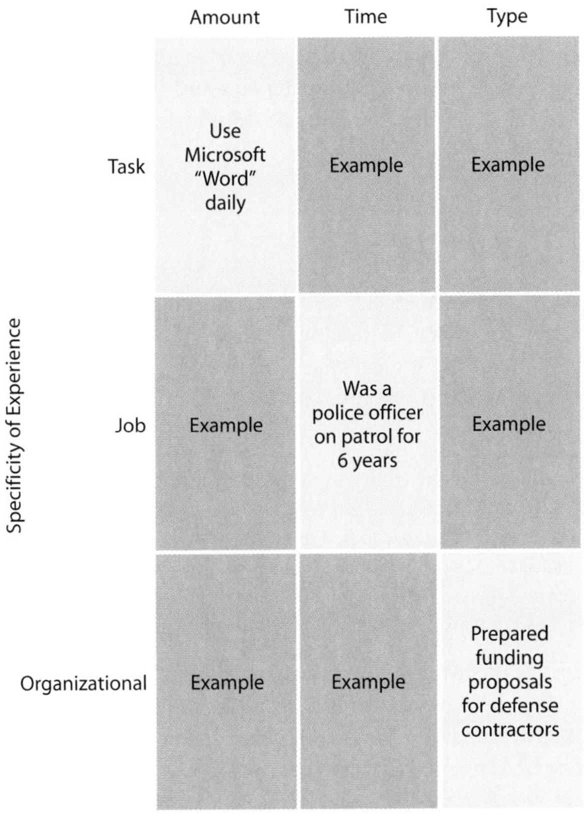

FIGURE 3.5

Modes of Experience

	Amount	Time	Type
Task	Use Microsoft "Word" daily	Example	Example
Job	Example	Was a police officer on patrol for 6 years	Example
Organizational	Example	Example	Prepared funding proposals for defense contractors

Specificity of Experience

Tesluk and Jacobs (1998) expanded on the Quinones et al. (1995) model and suggested ways of combining the alternative measures suggested by the latter (amount, time, and type) to get a more complete index of experience. They also suggested that experience has a direct impact on increased work knowledge and skills, motivation, values, and attitudes, as well as indirect effect on job performance. Much of the emphasis in the Tesluk and Jacobs work experience model is on shaping experiences to make them of maximal value. We will return to the issue of shaping work experience in Chapter 8.

COMPETENCIES

COMPETENCIES

Sets of behaviors, usually learned by experience, that are instrumental in the accomplishment of various activities.

In the past decade it has been common for I-O psychologists to talk about combinations of knowledge, skills, abilities, and personality characteristics (KSAOs) in terms of **competencies.** Many different definitions and sets of competencies have been suggested. Kurz and Bartram (2002) have defined competencies as "sets of behaviors that are instrumental in the delivery of desired results or outcomes." Following from that definition, it is reasonable to assume that people can differ in the extent to which they possess competencies. But competencies are different from knowledge, or a skill, ability, or personality characteristic, in that a competency is really a collection of all of these specific individual difference characteristics. The essence of a competency is the *combination* of these characteristics and is not dominated by any one (Harris, 1998).

Competencies are unique in another way as well. Abilities can be defined and measured in the abstract, as can personality characteristics. But competencies only have meaning in the context of organizational goals. For example, you could distinguish between two individuals based on their measured conscientiousness, their reasoning ability, or their skill with a word processing program. But a competency of organizing and executing a business plan would require a combination of these three individual elements, in addition to various aspects of technical and procedural knowledge (Kurz & Bartram, 2002), and would have relevance only to that series of actions. Thus, competencies are really collections and patterns of the individual difference attributes we have already covered, rather than separate characteristics. We will return to competencies and how they are identified (competency modeling) in Chapter 5, as a new way of thinking about analyzing jobs—a process called **job analysis**).

JOB ANALYSIS

Method for determining the important tasks of a job and the human attributes necessary to successfully perform those tasks.

EMOTIONAL INTELLIGENCE

In the 1980s Howard Gardner (1983, 1993) proposed a novel theory of intelligence. Rather than a unitary approach to intelligence such as "g," he posited seven different types of intelligence, including logical-mathematical, bodily-kinesthetic, linguistic, musical, spatial, interpersonal, and intrapersonal. He described the latter two intelligences as follows:

> Interpersonal intelligence is the ability to understand other people: what motivates them, how they work, how to work cooperatively with them. Successful sales people, politicians, teachers, clinicians, and religious leaders are all likely to be individuals with high degrees of interpersonal intelligence. Intrapersonal intelligence, a seventh kind of intelligence, is a correlative ability turned inward. It is a capacity to form an accurate veridical model of oneself and to be able to use that model to operate effectively in life. (1983, p. 9)

EMOTIONAL INTELLIGENCE (EI)

A proposed kind of intelligence focused on our awareness of our own and others' emotions.

Gardner's notion of inter- and intrapersonal intelligence was popularized by Goleman (1995) using the label **emotional intelligence (EI).** EI is a relatively new concept with little in the way of an empirical data base at this point, but two questions about it have emerged. The first and perhaps simpler question is whether this actually represents a kind of intelligence, a skill developed and honed with practice, or a personality characteristic (Barrett, 2001). In many respects, this becomes more a semantic battle than a theoretical one. Nevertheless, the studies which have been done on the **construct** have been disappointing, failing to identify EI as something different from attributes with which we are already familiar (Davies et al., 1998; Roberts, Zeidner, & Mathews, 2001). It is not uncommon for the imagination of nonscientists to run ahead of the scientific foundation for a concept. Emotional intelligence is an example of such a disconnect, at least at this point. The concept had intuitive appeal but still lacks an adequate scientific foundation. The lack of a substantial data base has not discouraged commercial test publishers from developing tests of EI. We will return to a discussion of EI measurement in Chapter 4.

> **CONSTRUCT**
>
> *A proposed variable capable of being examined through scientific methodology.*

IDENTIFYING INDIVIDUAL DIFFERENCES: SINKING SHAFTS

As we saw in the earlier section describing the history of individual differences, Francis Galton was one of the early advocates of studying such differences. In 1890, Galton wrote that "One of the most important objects of measurement is . . . to obtain a general knowledge . . . of capacities . . . by sinking shafts at a few critical points" (Lubinski, 2000). By this, Galton meant that we can use psychometric tests to explore individual abilities and other attributes the way miners use drilling to explore minerals in the earth. That is an excellent way to think of what we are doing when we study individual differences: We are sinking shafts to obtain more general knowledge about behavior at work. The concept of sinking shafts also provides a good framework for looking at how I-O psychologists envision individual differences today as opposed to 25 years ago. Before, we concentrated on only one shaft—intelligence. Today we are sinking many more shafts, as well as deeper ones (e.g., specific aspects of cognitive ability; the constituents of conscientiousness). Before we were content to stop at a more superficial level ("g"). Today we are sinking stronger shafts because the reliability and validity of our measuring devices are better.

We need to keep in mind that not all individual differences will tell us something important. As in drilling for oil, water, or gold, we don't always "strike it rich." This is one of the reasons we do research: to see which shafts provide encouragement. To continue with the drilling metaphor, we can distinguish between the differential psychologist, the psychometrician, and the applied I-O psychologist. The differential psychologist examines the psychological landscape and identifies some attractive areas for drilling. The psychometrician actually sinks the shaft. The applied I-O psychologist uses what comes out of that shaft, but instead of oil, water, or gold, what comes out are valuable predictors of performance. In this chapter, we have examined the areas that appear fruitful for exploration. In the next chapter, we will examine the methods by which these areas can be explored: the actual assessment methods for examining these individual differences.

However, you must continually remind yourself (and we will help remind you) that behavior is complex and people are whole. No single area of individual difference (e.g., intelligence) is likely to completely (or even substantially) explain any important aspect of work behavior (Murphy, 1996). The concept of a competency follows from that principle. In a similar vein, you cannot separate an individual's intelligence from his or her personality, knowledge, or experience (Hattrup & Jackson, 1996). When you look at the behavior of any individual, you need to remember that they are whole, intact entities. To acknowledge a person's individuality, we need to go beyond considering just one or another possible predictor of his or her behavior (Schneider, 1996; Schneider, Smith, & Sipe, 2000).

MODULE 3.4 SUMMARY

- Skills are practiced acts. Although skills depend on ability, personality, and knowledge factors, what makes us call them skills is that they develop through practice.

- Knowledge can be defined as "a collection of discrete but related facts and information about a particular domain. It is acquired through formal education or training, or accumulated through specific experiences." Another proposed kind of knowledge is tacit knowledge, described as "knowing how" rather than "knowing that." A more formal way of distinguishing these two types of knowledge is procedural knowledge (knowing how) compared with declarative knowledge (knowing that).

- Although experience does not always lead to tacit knowledge, tacit knowledge depends on experience. Experience is often confused with seniority, but doing the same thing 100 times (seniority) is not the same as doing 100 things one time (experience).

- Competencies are "sets of behaviors that are instrumental in the delivery of desired results or outcomes." Competencies are different from knowledge, or a skill, ability, or personality characteristic, in that they are really a collection of all of these specific individual difference characteristics.

- Those who invoke the concept of emotional intelligence suggest that there is a unique kind of intelligence that is focused on our awareness of our own and others' emotions.

- We can use psychometric tests to explore individual abilities and other attributes the way miners use drilling to explore minerals in the earth. Not all individual differences will tell us something important; behavior is complex and people are whole. No single area of individual difference (e.g., intelligence) is likely to completely (or even substantially) explain any important aspect of work behavior.

KEY TERMS

skills

people skills

O*NET

tacit knowledge

procedural knowledge

declarative knowledge

experience

measurement modes

level of specificity

competencies

job analysis

emotional intelligence (EI)

construct

CRITICAL THINKING EXERCISES

3.7 As the issue of security continues to assume more importance in our everyday lives, the role of the "security screener" (e.g., at airports, courthouses) becomes more central. Considering all of the categories of individual differences (e.g., abilities, personality, interests, and additional attributes) that you have encountered in this chapter, which categories, and which attributes within these categories, would you identify as critical for the success of security screeners?

3.8 Employers (and often parents!) lament that their employees (or children) lack "common sense." In this chapter we have covered many different human attributes, but common sense was not one of them. Nevertheless, to the nonpsychologist, common sense has some meaning. From what you have examined in this chapter, identify the attributes that you think define common sense.

3.9 The point of this chapter is that each individual is really a combination of abilities, personality, interests, and other attributes. In the following matrix, you will see that the rows represent areas on which individuals may differ—what we have been calling attributes. The columns represent different people with whom you are familiar, including a column for yourself, one for a family member, and one for a close friend or coworker. We want you to mark the columns, one at a time, placing an H (for high), M (for medium), or an L (for low) in each box to indicate the extent to which the person whose name appears at the top of the column possesses that attribute. When you have finished, look at the pattern of differences. These same differences appear with any collection of people—coworkers, classmates, relatives, and so on.

INDIVIDUAL DIFFERENCE CHARACTERISTIC	SELF	FAMILY MEMBER	CLOSE FRIEND OR CO-WORKER
Oral comprehension			
Written expression			
Memorization			
Mathematical reasoning			
Spatial organization			
Static strength			
Trunk strength			
Dynamic strength			
Stamina			
Conscientiousness			
Agreeableness			
Intellect			
Neuroticism			
Extraversion			
Realistic			
Artistic			
Investigative			
Social			
Enterprising			
Conventional			

H = high

M = medium

L = low

ASSESSING INDIVIDUALS

4 CHAPTER

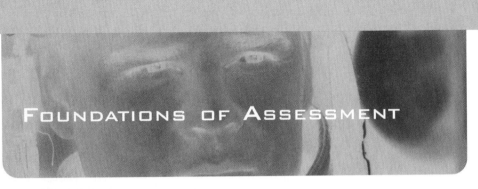

FOUNDATIONS OF ASSESSMENT

THE PAST AND THE PRESENT OF TESTING

Yvonne felt as if she had been preparing for this day forever. There had been similar days, sure—the SAT exam to get into college, and the civil service test she took to get her summer job in the State Personnel Department. But this was show time. A high GRE score would be the ticket she needed for getting into a good graduate program. And that was exactly the problem. Yvonne choked up on standardized tests—always had and probably always would. Even though her SAT score had been low, she would finish with a 3.26 overall GPA and a 3.5 in her major. But getting into graduate school was not going to be as easy as it had been to qualify for her undergraduate program. The thing that really annoyed her was that these tests measured such a narrow band of who she was and what her capabilities were that it was a joke. How would they know that Yvonne was funny, loyal, and friendly, and had learned to read music in a weekend? Did they even care that she took hard courses rather than "cruisers"? She understood that there had to be *some* standard way of selecting among applicants, she just wished that it was not a standardized test.

Society seems to have a love-hate relationship with psychological testing, a practice almost as old as psychology itself. The term **"mental test"** was introduced by Cattell in 1890. As we described in Chapter 1, in World War I over a million soldiers were tested for intelligence in order to determine which were best suited to be officers and which for infantry. Up to that point, intelligence testing had been done on an individual basis, and this first trial of group testing was considered a massive success for the testing enterprise.

But with this success came an embarrassment; soon after the war, psychological testing began to be used as the justification for limiting immigration. The army testing program discovered that immigrants and their offspring, who did not speak English as a first language, scored lower on these intelligence tests. Fearing that unchecked immigration would reduce the national intelligence level, Congress enacted immigration quotas. While social critics were quick to point out the potential unfairness of intelligence testing, advocates saw it as a way to avoid the class system that had characterized industry and education in the 19th century. In their view, a test was "objective" and thus freed decisions (about jobs or education) from the grasp of favoritism and nepotism.

Private industry, like the government, was impressed by the success of the army testing programs and moved to implement testing as a way of selecting the most promising candidates from a pool of job applicants. Soon, however, the Great Depression of the 1930s arrived, drastically reducing the need to select from an applicant pool. There were no jobs to be had. When America entered World War II, the country returned to a full employment mode and virtually every able-bodied and motivated worker, male or female, either had a job or was serving in a branch of the armed services. Ships and airplanes were being built in record numbers, requiring one of the first "24/7" industrial environments. Now there was no need for selection for the opposite reason: There were many more jobs than people.

MENTAL TEST

Term introduced by James McKeen Cattell to describe early intelligence tests.

On the military front, commanders quickly realized that war was now much more technologically advanced than it had been a generation earlier. Personnel needed to operate many different types of aircraft and ships with complex maintenance and repair demands. The task of the armed forces was no longer simply distinguishing between officers and infantry. The war effort needed pilots, bombardiers, artillery personnel, radar and sonar operators, and an enormous training and administrative staff. Psychological testing was once again pushed to the forefront as a tool in the war effort, this time with more sophisticated tests for the placement of recruits.

By the end of the World War II, developers of tests had virtually glutted the market, offering ability, personality, interest, and knowledge tests. Neither the government nor the psychological profession exercised much control over the quality of the tests or the meaning of the test scores. A thriving and competitive testing industry operated without constraint until the early 1960s, when two societal forces converged to rein in testing. The first was a new wave of criticism about the value of testing from social observers (Gross, 1962; Whyte, 1956). These critics pointed out that employers were expecting job applicants to submit to a range of tests that had little apparent relationship to the job for which they were applying. Many of the tests, particularly the interest and personality tests, asked questions of a personal nature—topics like religion, sex, and politics. The second force was the passage of the Civil Rights Act of 1964, which prohibited discrimination in employment, including testing. If a test had the effect of reducing the employment opportunities of protected subgroups (e.g., African Americans, women), then the employer would need to provide evidence of the validity of that test. Since many of the tests available at that time had little validity evidence, employers saw this as a difficult hurdle to overcome.

As a result of the questions about the invasion of privacy and the possible discriminatory effects of tests, there was a marked reduction in test use for selection purposes. Although this reduction was most marked for personality testing, there was a more general disaffection with standardized testing. The reticence lasted well into the 1970s, by which time more evidence of validity for tests had become available and the courts had clarified what was acceptable evidence for validity. By the mid-1980s, testing was back in full swing and personality testing, in particular, began to appear with greater frequency.

As we will see in the modules that follow, the content and process of employment testing is varied and encouraging. I-O psychologists have identified many different attributes that appear to contribute to work performance. Furthermore, I-O psychologists have identified many different methods for assessing these attributes.

But concerns about the "fairness" of testing continue to arise in many different settings. To mention just a few, some universities have decided to abandon standardized testing for applicants and introduce nonstandardized techniques that will permit motivation, interests, and values to play a greater role in student admissions. In both teacher and student testing in K-12 environments, there is a vigorous debate about the value of standardized tests for teacher certification and the awarding of high school diplomas. For example, many school districts require the successful completion of a series of content-specific tests (e.g., in mathematics or biology) as well as more general tests (e.g., knowledge of liberal arts) before granting teachers a permanent teaching certificate. These requirements occasionally result in lawsuits by unsuccessful teacher candidates (e.g., Gulino, 2002). In the wake of scandals such as the Enron and WorldCom accounting fraud cases, MBA programs are now considering the use of new "tests" of ethics, morality, and integrity to determine whom to admit to their MBA programs (Jackson, 2002).

Underlying all of these debates, the issue of fairness remains: Are standardized tests both effective and fair instruments for selecting among individuals? For every standardized test, there will be critics suggesting that the standardization prevents an illumination of the "essence" of the person. For every nonstandardized suggestion, there will be critics who will argue that the lack of standardization permits favoritism. Psychological testing will always have a values component to it in addition to the issues related to content and process.

WHAT IS A TEST?

Robert Guion (1998) defined a **test** as "an objective and standardized procedure for measuring a psychological construct using a sample of behavior" (p. 485). Seventy years earlier, Clark Hull (1928) had proposed a virtually identical definition. Few definitions in psychology have remained so constant for such a long time. One of the appealing characteristics of this definition is that it is broad enough to cover a wide variety of tests and testing procedures. It encompasses paper and pencil tests, interviews, actual attempts to perform a piece of work (a work sample test), and even an application blank. The definition is also broad enough to cover many different types of content, including cognitive ability, personality, values, communication skills, interpersonal skills, and technical knowledge. In the modules that follow, we will review various content categories, as well as various techniques for assessing that content. As an example, if we were interested in the technical knowledge of an applicant for a word processing position, we could give the applicant a paper and pencil test and an interview, check with previous employers, have the applicant complete an actual word processing task at a workstation, or examine the applicant's formal education credits. Each of these techniques could be used to assess the same attribute: technical knowledge. Similarly, we might be interested in a number of different attributes of the applicant beyond technical knowledge, including communication skills, personality characteristics, interests, integrity, and career plans. We might use one or more interviews to assess each of these additional attributes. As you can see from Figure 4.1, in most practical testing situations, we are looking at the combination of attributes to be assessed (content) and ways to assess those attributes (process). Most employers look at several attributes using several techniques. In Chapter 3, we introduced the acronym KSAO (knowledge, skill, ability, other characteristic) to summarize the attributes of a worker. In one way or another, every test is an assessment of one or more of these content areas.

TEST

An objective and standardized procedure for measuring a psychological construct using a sample of behavior.

What Is the Meaning of a Test Score?

As Guion (1998) suggested, the term "objective" in his definition of a test implies quantification. When someone takes a test, he or she expects to receive a score on that test. It may be a simple pass-fail score (e.g., you may pass or fail a driver's license examination) or a score on some graded continuum (such as an 88 percent on a midterm examination or a B+ on a term paper). But the simple process of assigning a score is quite different from interpreting the meaning of that score. For example, if your instructor curves exam scores, and the exam was a tough one, an 88 might very well be in the A range and signal excellent performance. If, on the other hand, the test was an easy one and virtually everyone got a 94 or above (except you), your 88 might be in the B range or lower.

Meaning is usually assigned to test scores through a process known as **norming.** Norming simply means comparing a score to other relevant test scores. In many employment settings, we compare individuals to one another, so the rules we use for making these

NORMING

Comparing a test score to other relevant test scores.

Attributes	Methods of Assessment	
	Paper and pencil test	Interview
Reasoning		
Social skills		

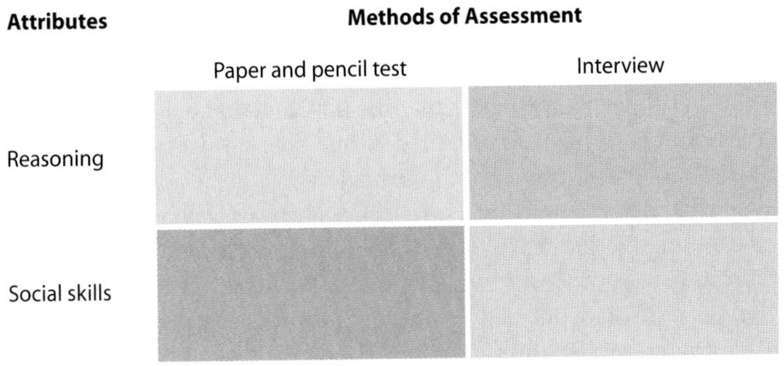

FIGURE 4.1

Two Attributes Measured Using Two Different Procedures

comparisons should be unambiguous and fair. Test scores are often interpreted relative to some set of norms. In the classroom example above, your score of 88 percent is given meaning, or interpreted, by comparing it to the grades of your fellow students (the **norm group**). Instead of being compared to others in your class who took the same test you did, the instructor could have compared your score (and the scores of your classmates) to those of earlier classes who took midterms in the same content area. Or the instructor may not have curved the test at all but held to some previously determined comparison scale (90 percent to 100 percent = A; 80 percent–89 percent = B, etc.). The development of test norms is very technical; excellent discussions of the process are presented in Guion (1998) and Cohen and Swerdlik (2002). For our purposes, it is simply important to be aware that while a test produces a "score," there is a need to interpret or give meaning to that score. As you will recall from our earlier discussion of validity in Chapter 2, validity is about inference: What can we infer from a test score about future performance? The meaning of a test score is a question of validity (Messick, 1995).

Test Users and Test Interpretation

The issue of validity and meaning of a test score brings us to the more practical issue of who will interpret the test. Suppose you had been in an auto accident and were concerned about possible long-term effects from a blow to the head that you experienced in that accident. You might go to a neurologist for sophisticated testing to look for any impairment. Suppose further that the results of that testing arrived in the mail filled with numbers, diagnostic categories, and technical descriptions of the results of that testing. After poring over the results for an hour, you still might not know if there was permanent damage or not. Anyone without formal training in neurology would have difficulty understanding the meaning of the numbers and narrative from a standard neurological test battery.

Similarly, an individual not formally trained in the area of psychological assessment will have a difficult time interpreting the results of many psychological tests. Furthermore, individuals who lack suitable training are prone to making erroneous interpretations and, consequently, inappropriate decisions and actions. Fortunately, several documents are available that spell out proper and ethical procedures for test score interpretation and use (e.g., American Educational Research Association et al., 1999; Eyde, Moreland, Robertson, Primoff, & Most, 1988; Moreland et al., 1995; Society for Industrial and Organizational Psychology, in press). Table 4.1 presents a list of the competencies that would be expected of those responsible for administering and interpreting psychological tests. As you can see, psychological testing, if it is to be done ethically and effectively, is no simple process.

What Is a Test Battery?

A **test battery** is a collection of tests rather than a single test. The tests in a battery are usually of different attributes. These attributes may be within a single area, such as a cognitive battery including subtests of reasoning, memory, and comprehension; or the attributes may be from conceptually different areas, such as a battery that includes a measure of cognitive ability, a personality test, a physical ability test, and a test of vocational interests. The term "battery" usually implies that all of the tests will be taken either in a single testing period or over a very short period of time. But whether the information being considered is from several different assessment devices administered at one time or over a lengthy period of time, the critical issue is how to combine that information. Will it be combined to yield a single score with weights assigned to individual tests using a statistical equation of some type, or will the evaluator combine the individual test scores using a logical or nonstatistical process to yield a final recommendation? We considered the issue of statistical combination in Chapter 2 in the section on regression, but we will consider the broader issue of how test information may be combined at greater length in Chapter 7 when we deal with staffing decisions.

NORM GROUP

Group whose tests scores are used to compare and understand an individual's test score.

TEST BATTERY

Collection of tests that usually assess a variety of different attributes.

TABLE 4.1	Twelve Minimum Competencies for Proper Use of Tests

ITEM NO.	COMPETENCY
1.	Avoiding errors in scoring and recording.
2.	Refraining from labeling people with personally derogatory terms like *dishonest* on the basis of a test score that lacks perfect validity.
3.	Keeping scoring keys and test materials secure.
4.	Seeing that every examinee follows directions so that test scores are accurate.
5.	Using settings for testing that allow for optimum performance by test takers (e.g., adequate room).
6.	Refraining from coaching or training individuals or groups on test items, which results in misrepresentation of the person's abilities and competencies.
7.	Willingness to give interpretation and guidance to test takers in counseling situations.
8.	Not making photocopies of copyrighted materials.
9.	Refraining from using homemade answer sheets that do not align properly with scoring keys.
10.	Establishing rapport with examinees to obtain accurate scores.
11.	Refraining from answering questions from test takers in greater detail than the test manual permits.
12.	Not assuming that a norm for one job applies to a different job (and not assuming that norms for one group automatically apply to other groups).

SOURCE: Moreland et al. (1995).

ADMINISTRATIVE TEST CATEGORIES

In descriptions of tests and testing, you may encounter several terms that require a brief explanation.

Speed versus Power Tests

Some tests have rigid and demanding time limits such that most test takers will be unable to finish the test in the allotted time. These are called **speed tests.** Your score on a speed test would be calculated by considering the number of items you were able to complete correctly in the time available. As Murphy and Davidshofer (2001) pointed out, if someone scores poorly on a speed test, it is not clear whether the person actually knew the answers but could not respond quickly enough, or if the person would have been unable to answer correctly no matter how much time was allotted. **Power tests** have no rigid time limits. While some test takers may still not finish, enough time is given for a majority of the test takers to complete all of the test items. The items on power tests tend to be answered correctly by a smaller percentage of test takers than those on speed tests.

Assessment professionals find that speed tests provide greater variability among candidates, allowing for more effective prediction, but they carry some vulnerabilities. The most obvious of these is whether the job actually requires such speed for successful performance. Few jobs have such demands. The second potential pitfall is the possibility of introducing unfairness to the testing process by emphasizing speed. One of the documented effects of the aging process is a decline in information processing speed. As we age, we take longer to complete cognitive operations. In many instances, this slowing process is irrelevant to the actual demands of a job; it won't matter that a worker took 10 or 20 seconds rather than three seconds to accomplish a task. Nevertheless, there are some professions (e.g., airline pilot, police officer, firefighter, bus driver) where speed of information processing or reaction might be critical. Disabled individuals, particularly those with learning disabilities, may also find themselves at a disadvantage on a speeded test. One of the most common requests for a testing accommodation made by individuals under the Americans with Disabilities Act (1990) is for additional time to complete a test. Thus, speed tests may increase the risk of legal challenge from many groups unless it can be shown that the type of speed required by the test is also required by the job.

The television show *Jeopardy* is an example of a speed test.

Group versus Individual Tests

Most standardized written tests, even if they are administered to single individuals, could be administered in group format. A cognitive ability test taken by applicants for a position in the police academy could be taken in a hall or a convention center with 20,000 other test takers, or the same test may be taken individually in a room on any army base where a candidate is stationed during a call-up of the reserves. **Group tests** are efficient because they allow for the testing of many candidates simultaneously, resulting in rapid screening compared to individually administered tests. Group testing is also often valuable in reducing the costs (both in time and money) of testing many applicants.

Certain tests, however, can be given only on an individual basis. Examples include an interview, a test of hand-eye coordination, or an elaborate assessment of candidates for a high-level executive position based on interviews, work samples, and individually administered personality tests. **Individual tests** are also often more appropriate when the employer wishes to assess a candidate's *style* of problem solving rather than the simple *products* of the problem-solving process. Individual testing formats are also appropriate when the examiner needs to establish an interpersonal rapport with the test taker, as is commonly the case in certain clinical tests such as the Rorschach Inkblot test. Even though tests such as the Rorschach are often used in individual assessment, there is little evidence that they represent added value (i.e., validity) beyond information gathered using more structured devices (Murphy & Davidshofer, 2001).

Paper and Pencil versus Performance Tests

Paper and pencil tests are one of the most common forms of industrial testing. The paper and pencil test requires no manipulation of any objects other than the instrument used to respond. By extension, the modern version of the paper and pencil test might be the computer keyboard test where the keys and mouse are used only to choose the correct response or produce a narrative response to a question. Given the increasing popularity of computer administered tests, it might be better to adopt a term other than "paper and pencil testing"; a distinction such as nonmanipulative versus manipulative might be more apt.

Performance tests require the individual to make a response by manipulating a particular physical object or piece of equipment. The score that the individual receives on the test is directly related to the quality or quantity of that manipulation. An example might be a test administered to a candidate for a dental hygienist position. The candidate might be asked to prepare a tray for cleaning or scaling teeth, to prepare a syringe of novocaine for administration by the dentist, or to prepare a mold for taking an impression of a row of teeth. In this case, the candidate's *skill* in performing these tasks may be as important as his or her knowledge of *how* to carry out the actions.

Where to Find Tests

At various points in the text, we mention some specific tests by name. There are literally thousands of psychological tests available on a broad range of topics. If you wanted to find a test, how would you do it? Textbooks on testing provide lists and examples of tests. For example, Anastasi and Urbina (1997) presented an extensive list of tests covering a range of topics, as well as a listing of test publishers. A more complete listing of tests, as well as reviews of those tests, can be found in two established sources. The first is known as the **Mental Measurements Yearbook (MMY).** This was first published in 1938 (Buros) and has been updated an additional 13 times. The 15th edition (Plake, Impara, & Spies, 2003) is scheduled for publication in 2003. The Buros Institute (named after the founder of the MMY, Oscar K. Buros) also publishes a companion volume without reviews called

GROUP TEST

Can be administered to large groups of individuals; often valuable in reducing the costs (both in time and money) of testing many applicants.

INDIVIDUAL TEST

Test given only on an individual basis.

PAPER AND PENCIL TEST

One of the most common forms of industrial testing that requires no manipulation of any objects other than the instrument used to respond.

PERFORMANCE TEST

Requires the individual to make a response by manipulating a particular physical object or piece of equipment.

MENTAL MEASUREMENTS YEARBOOK

Widely used source that includes an extensive listing of tests as well as reviews of those tests.

TABLE 4.2	Short Employment Tests, Second Edition

Purpose: "Measures verbal, numerical, and clerical skills."

Population: Adults.

Publication Dates: 1951–1993.

Acronym: SET.

Scores, 4: Verbal, Numerical, Clerical, Total.

Administration: Group or individual.

Forms, 4: 1, 2, 3, 4.

Price Data, 1994: $60 per 25 test booklets including manual ('93, 71 pages), test booklet, and key; $20 per keys; $22 per examination kit (Form 1); $28 per examination kit (Forms 2, 3, 4).

Time: 5(10) minutes.

Comments: Distribution of Form 1 restricted to banks which are members of the American Banking Association.

Author: George K. Bennett and Marjorie Gelink.

Publisher: The Psychological Corporation.

SOURCE: Impara & Plake (1998).

Tests In Print. The most recent edition of this companion text was published in 2002 (Murphy, Plake, Impara, & Spies, 2002). Table 4.2 presents a typical entry in the *Mental Measurements Yearbook.*

TESTING AND CULTURE

In the 1950s and 1960s, testing was largely lacking in controls, either legal or professional. As social critics pointed out, the quality of tests was therefore variable, and the potential for cultural influence and bias was substantial. An example would be a test that used a very high level of vocabulary to assess a relatively simple and straightforward skill. Instead of asking "How much is two plus two?" the item might have read, "If one were asked to calculate the arithmetic sum of the two integers which have been produced below, what would the resultant number be?" The second item would surely be more difficult for someone with a limited vocabulary or low reading comprehension to answer, even though both items are ostensibly assessing the same basic skill—arithmetic proficiency. Modern tests have eliminated most if not all of these reading level problems. What they may not have done, however, is to eliminate cultural influences.

Murphy and Davidshofer (2001) distinguished among three terms in discussing tests and testing: **bias, fairness,** and **culture.** They rightly pointed out that bias is a technical and statistical term that deals exclusively with the situation in which a given test results in errors of prediction for a subgroup. Thus, if a test underpredicts the job performance of women (i.e., predicts that they will score lower on some criterion than they actually do) and overpredicts the job performance of men (i.e., predicts that they will score higher on some criterion than they actually do), then the test would be said to be biased.

In contrast, fairness is a value judgment about actions or decisions based on test scores. Many employers base their decision to hire on a paper and pencil test of general mental ability. Many applicants believe that in addition to (or instead of) the cognitive ability test, dependability and motivation should play a role in a hiring decision. This was the view of

BIAS

Technical and statistical term that deals exclusively with a situation where a given test results in errors of prediction for a subgroup.

FAIRNESS

Value judgment about actions or decisions based on test scores.

CULTURE

System in which individuals share meanings and common ways of viewing events and objects.

Yvonne in the example at the beginning of this chapter. In the view of many applicants, the test and the method of hiring is unfair even though there may be no statistical bias in predictions of success. Murphy and Davidshofer (2001) considered fairness to be a philosophical or political term and not a scientific one. They gave an example to make their point: A test of physical strength might predict job success equally for male and female firefighter applicants, yet eliminate most of the female applicants because they have less upper body strength than males. Many individuals would consider such a test unfair even though it was unbiased, because it prevents women from becoming firefighters. In contrast, a biased test might be used to increase the number of minorities in a particular job or company, but still be considered fair because it corrects for a past underrepresentation of those minority group members.

Culture is a third concept, separate in many respects from either fairness or bias. Culture addresses the extent to which the test taker has had an opportunity to become familiar with the subject matter or processes required by a test item (Eelles, 1951; Murphy & Davidshofer, 2001). In many tests for teacher certification, there is a component that addresses the general cultural literacy of the candidate—for example, how well he or she knows works of art and music, variations of modern dance, and the deeper meaning of literary passages (National Evaluation Systems, 2002). Minority candidates often do poorly on these tests of cultural literacy and argue that they are at a disadvantage compared to candidates (particularly majority candidates) who have been exposed to this knowledge through home and school environments. In 1972 Williams proposed a test called the BITCH—the Black Intelligence Test of Cultural Homogeneity. The test was composed of items that utilized the black ghetto slang of the time. Williams was not actually suggesting that the BITCH be used to replace other tests of intelligence. Instead, he published it in an attempt to highlight the influence of culture and subculture on language, and therefore on test scores. One item asked for the meaning of the phrase "running a game." Which of the following was the correct interpretation?

a. Writing a bad check.
b. Looking at something.
c. Directing a contest.
d. Getting what one wants.

The correct answer in 1972 (and still today in many black neighborhoods) was "d." But how many white test takers would have known that? Most whites got that answer wrong. Herlihy (1977) made the same point with a test called the CRUST (Cultural/Regional Uppercrust Savvy Test) (Cohen & Swerdlik, 2002). Consider the following CRUST item:

The Blue Book is:

a. The income tax guidelines.
b. A guide to pricing used cars.
c. A booklet used for writing essay exams.
d. A social register listing 400 prominent families.

Again, the correct answer is "d" from the perspective of the person who constructed the test, but only those in the highest levels of society would be likely to know this.

Greenfield (1997) presented examples of difficulties in "transporting" North American cognitive ability tests to other cultures. In one example from Cole, Gay, Glick, and Sharpe (1971), Liberians were asked to engage in a cognitive sorting task. They were asked to sort 20 objects into categories. According to the test developers, the objects divided evenly into four categories: food, food containers, clothing, and implements. Rather than sorting the 20 objects into these four categories, however, the Liberian participants made functional pairings of the objects. For example, they paired a potato with a knife, reasoning that a knife is used to cut a potato. When they were asked why they did that, they would reply that this is how a "wise man" would complete the task. After repeated attempts to get them to use the four neat categories of items, and repeatedly getting the "wise man" response, the researchers asked the participants to sort the items as a "fool" would do it. The subjects promptly sorted the items into the four categories that the researchers preferred. As Greenfield noted "the researchers' criterion for *intelligent* behavior was the participants' criterion for *foolish;* the participants' criterion for *wise* behavior was the researchers' criterion for *stupid*" (p. 116). Greenfield concluded that to use a test developed in one culture for another culture, there must be agreement on the value of particular responses to particular questions, as well as agreement that the items mean the same thing in the different culture. Note that neither of these requirements has anything to do with the quality of the test's linguistic translation; instead, they relate to meaning in a deeper sense.

A recent study of East Indian and American workers underscored Greenfield's caution (Ghorpade, Hattrup, & Lackritz, 1999). Although the researchers found few differences between Indian and American men or women with respect to the measurement of the personality variable Locus of Control, there were substantial differences between Indian and American women in the meaning of a self-esteem measure. Indian women were much more likely to feel guilt over individual activities such as seeking opportunities to succeed and achieve that might be seen as evidence of self-esteem by American women. This was likely the result of differences between Indian and American women on Hofstede's collectivism–individualism dimension. In addition, it is likely that American women were more likely to identify with the masculine end of Hofstede's masculinity–femininity dimension, favoring accomplishment rather than interpersonal relations. Thus, if Indian and American women were compared on self-esteem, a researcher might see the Indian women as having "less" esteem when, indeed, what Americans view (and admire) as self-esteem had a far less positive connotation to the Indian women.

As Americans from different ethnic groups increasingly mingle in public schools, universities, other public institutions, and work settings, they are becoming more familiar with each other's subculture today than was the case 30 years ago. As a result, the concept of the cultural content in current tests is becoming less of an issue in explaining differences among ethnic groups. At the same time, cultural content is becoming an increasingly important issue in the workplace because of the growing multicultural nature of work and the increasing cultural diversity of applicant populations.

MODULE 4.1 SUMMARY

- Employment testing was first widely used after World War I and has been heavily influenced by the Civil Rights Act of 1964. I-O psychologists are interested in determining how effective various tests are in predicting work performance. They have identified many different attributes that appear to contribute to work performance and many different methods for assessing these attributes.

- The definition of a test encompasses paper and pencil tests, interviews, actual attempts to perform a piece of work (a work sample test), and even an application blank. The definition is also broad enough to cover many different types of content, including cognitive ability, personality, values, communication skills, interpersonal skills, and technical knowledge.

- In Chapter 3 we introduced the acronym KSAO (knowledge, skill, ability, other characteristic) to summarize the attributes of a worker. In one way or another, every test is an assessment of one or more of these content areas.

- Tests can be described or differentiated according to categories that include speed versus power tests, individual versus group tests, and paper and pencil versus performance tests.

- In discussing tests and testing, it is important to consider three factors: bias, or errors of prediction; fairness, a value judgment about decisions based on test scores; and culture, the extent to which a test taker has the opportunity to become familiar with the subject matter.

KEY TERMS

mental test

test

norming

norm group

test battery

speed test

power test

group test

individual test

paper and pencil test

performance test

Mental Measurements Yearbook

bias

fairness

culture

CRITICAL THINKING EXERCISES

4.1 Jennifer applied for a position as a receptionist in a local medical practice office. In addition to providing her résumé and references from former employers, she was invited to lunch with several of the physicians. Would this lunch constitute a "test" according to Guion's definition? Why or why not? In the lunch described above, what KSAOs would it be possible to assess?

4.2 An instructor of one of your classes indicated that he or she planned to assign letter grades after comparing test scores to a "norm" group and asked for suggestions about the proper "norm" group to choose, which norm group would you recommend and why?

TRADITIONAL ASSESSMENT PROCEDURES

PROCEDURES FOR ASSESSING ABILITIES

Cognitive Ability Tests

Guion (1998) defined **cognitive ability tests** as those which

> . . . allow a person to show what he or she knows, perceives, remembers, understands, or can work with mentally. They include problem identification, problem-solving tasks, perceptual (not sensory) skills, the development or evaluation of ideas, and remembering what one has learned through general experience or specific training (p. 486).

Even though Guion identified what seem to be a variety of cognitive abilities (e.g., remembering, problem identification) as we saw in Chapter 3, there is still a vigorous debate regarding whether there is only one overarching cognitive ability—"g" or "general mental ability"—or several distinct facets or abilities (Ackerman, 1992; Carroll, 1993; Olea & Ree, 1994; Ree, Earles, & Teachout, 1994).

In more than a century of cognitive ability testing, there have been tests that produce a single number intended to represent cognitive ability, tests of specific abilities, and test batteries that purport to measure several different facets of cognitive ability.

Tests That Produce a Single Score   An example of a test intended to produce a single score representing general mental ability is called the Wonderlic Personnel Test. It includes 50 items that assess verbal, numerical, and spatial abilities. Because its administration time is 12 minutes and most applicants cannot finish the test in the allotted time, the Wonderlic is considered a speed test. There are elaborate norms for the Wonderlic, making its interpretation relatively simple. Its ease of administration and scoring make it a popular device for many organizations. Murphy and Davidshofer (2001) endorsed the use of the Wonderlic, pointing to its high reliability and strong correlations with other, more elaborate, tests of intelligence.

Tests of Specific Abilities   As implied by Guion's defintion of a cognitive ability test, many tests concentrate on only one aspect of cognitive ability. An example of such a test is the Bennett Test of Mechanical Comprehension. Figure 4.2 presents an example from one form of the Bennett Test (1980). The item asks the test taker to examine the two different cutting instruments and to deduce, either from experience or logic, that the shears labeled B would be

Which would be the better shears for cutting metal?

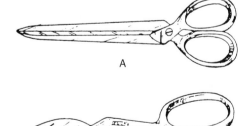

FIGURE 4.2 **Sample Item from Bennett Mechanical Comprehension Test**
SOURCE: Bennett Mechanical Comprehension Test, Form BB, Item Y.

more effective at cutting metal than A. One can imagine that such a test item might be well suited for choosing applicants for the trade position of sheet metal worker or plumber.

Another example of a specific mental ability is spatial relations. Consider the item in Figure 4.3. It requires the test taker to do some actual mental manipulation of the factory shown from the front by "turning" the factory in his or her mind and then choosing the response below that would most closely resemble how the factory would look from the back. This ability to manipulate objects in one's mind is particularly useful for many hardware repair or "trouble shooting" professions such as an auto mechanic or computer repair technician, where it is necessary to visualize a component buried deep under the hood of a car or in a hard drive. There are many other examples of specific cognitive abilities, such as clerical and perceptual accuracy, memory, and reasoning. Most testing texts (Anastasi & Urbina, 1997; Cohen & Swerdlik, 2002; Guion, 1998; Murphy & Davidshofer, 2001) provide detailed descriptions of these tests. Mumford, Baughman, Supinski and Anderson (1998) presented a sophisticated treatment of how to measure complex cognitive abilities such as reasoning and creative problem solving.

Cognitive Test Batteries   Multiple aptitude test batteries have a long history in psychological testing in industry. In part, this is a historical accident since some of the early batteries were developed before the move toward the construct of general mental ability. Thurstone (1938) introduced a test of Primary Mental Abilities (PMA) which assessed numerical ability, verbal ability, reasoning, spatial relations, perceptual speed, and memory.

FIGURE 4.3

Spatial Relations Item from a Test for Firefighters

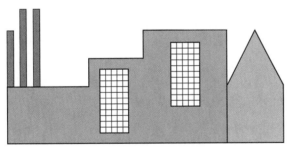

Above is a picture of a factory shown from the front.
From the back, it would look like:

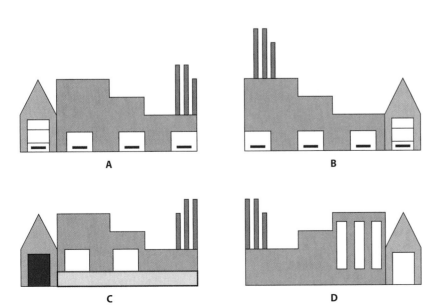

A   B

C   D

More recent examples of multiple aptitude test batteries include the Armed Services Vocational Aptitude Battery or ASVAB (Katz, 1987; Murphy & Davidshofer, 2001), the Differential Aptitude Test Battery or D.A.T. (Psychological Corporation, 1973, 1974), and the General Aptitude Test Battery or GATB (Hartigan & Wigdor, 1989). The ASVAB, as implied by its name, is used exclusively by the armed services for selection and placement. The GATB is used exclusively by the federal government to assist in the selection and placement of civilian workers. The D.A.T. is commercially available for employer use. Students are more likely to be more familiar with the Scholastic Aptitude Test (SAT) or Graduate Record Examination (GRE), both examples of cognitive test batteries. While each of these batteries is slightly different, in one way or another they all measure verbal, numerical, spatial, and reasoning abilities. Although **cognitive test batteries** take longer to administer than a "single score" test like the Wonderlic, or any test of an individual facet of cognitive ability, they do have the advantage of providing more detailed information about particular manifestations of cognitive ability that may be more important in one job than another.

Knowledge Tests

Tests you will take in this and other courses are **knowledge tests.** They assess the extent to which you know course material. These types of tests are typically tailored to course or training material. Knowledge tests are also administered for licensing and certification purposes, including teacher certification, nuclear power plant operator licensing, and licenses to practice law or medicine, or to sell investments. Knowledge tests are like any other type of test and require the same care in development, norming, and administration. We will discuss non-paper and pencil forms of knowledge tests in Module 4.3.

TESTS OF PHYSICAL ABILITIES

As we saw in Chapter 3, there are seven basic physical ability attributes (Hogan, 1991). These include static strength, explosive strength, coordination, and stamina or aerobic endurance. While it is possible to measure each of these physical abilities in isolation, most physically demanding jobs actually require combinations of these abilities. As a result, many physical ability testing procedures tend to use simulated pieces of work to assess the combined abilities. For example, consider a test frequently used to assess the physical abilities of firefighter candidates (see Table 4.3). As you can see, each event requires multiple abilities. An excellent review of physical abilities and their measurement appears in a study of age and physical abilities conducted for the Equal Employment Opportunity Commission (EEOC) and the Department of Labor (Landy, Bland, Buskirk, et al., 1992). There is substantial evidence that measures of physical abilities can improve the prediction of job success for many physically demanding jobs (Arnold, Rauschenberger, Soubel, & Guion, 1982; Campion, 1983; Hoffmann, 1999; Reilly, Zedeck, & Tenopyr, 1979). Arvey, Landon, Nutting, and Maxwell (1992) provide a good description of the development and validation of an entry-level physical ability examination for police officers.

Psychomotor Abilities

Tests of **psychomotor abilities** involve the coordinated movement of the limbs in response to situational factors. It may be a complex task in which the individual is required to move arms and legs in coordination, as in flying an airplane, driving a vehicle, or playing an organ; or it may be a simple or discrete action such as firing a weapon, pulling a lever, or administering an injection to a patient. For some jobs, psychomotor abilities represent characteristics of the individual that have some potential for contributing to successful

---

COGNITIVE TEST BATTERY

Collection of tests that assess a variety of cognitive aptitudes or abilities; often called Multiple Aptitude Test Batteries.

KNOWLEDGE TEST

Assesses the extent to which individuals understand course or training materials; also administered for licensing and certification purposes.

PSYCHOMOTOR ABILITIES

Associated with coordination, dexterity, and reaction time; also called motor or sensorimotor abilities.

TABLE 4.3	Physical Ability Tests for Firefighters

Stairway climb: Candidate wears fire protective clothing and air tank and carries seven pieces of equipment up three flights of stairs, one piece at a time. Each piece of equipment weighs between 25 and 55 pounds.

Hose pull: Candidate wears air tank, stands in one spot, and pulls 50 feet of fire hose filled with water using a hand-over-hand technique.

Ladder pull: Candidate wears air tank and pulls a16-foot ladder from the ladder bed of a fire truck, places it on the ground, picks it back up, and replaces it in the ladder bed.

Dummy drag: Candidate drags a 125-pound sandbag around a serpentine course of 40 feet. The candidate must keep one knee in contact with the ground and may not lift or carry the sandbag but must drag it.

Blind crawl: Candidate wears fire protective clothing and an air tank. After putting on a blackened face mask, the candidate must crawl through a plywood maze that has several turns in it. In addition, there are sandbags located strategically throughout the maze. The maze is approximately 40 feet in length.

Pike pole: Candidate wears an air tank and alternately pulls and pushes a 75-pound weight attached to a pole hanging from a frame. The candidate must complete as many repetitions as possible in a four-minute period. A repetition is defined as one push and two pulls.

Fan hang: Candidate wears fire protective clothing and an air tank and lifts a 50-pound fan from ground level, hanging it on a standard door frame.

job performance above and beyond cognitive abilities, physical abilities, or personality characteristics. Psychomotor abilities are usually assessed using a task that requires dexterity, such as placing pins in slots with tweezers, such as is depicted in Figure 4.4. Ackerman and his colleagues have developed some sophisticated computer-based psychomotor tests for the selection of applicants for jobs such as air traffic controllers (Ackerman & Cianciolo, 1999, 2002).

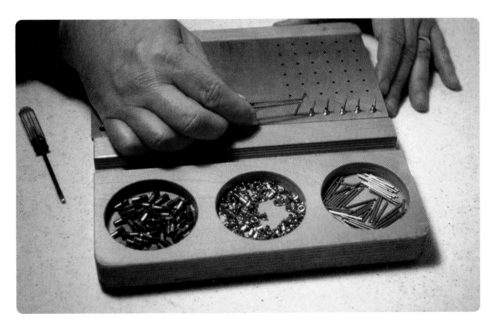

FIGURE 4.4

The Crawford Small Parts Dexterity Test

PERSONALITY

As we have seen in Chapter 3, personality attributes are now widely recognized as contributors to job success. There are many commercially available instruments for measuring personality characteristics, many based on the Big Five model described in Chapter 3. Table 4.4 lists some of the more commonly used personality instruments. The history of personality testing can be described in two general phases. The early foundation of personality testing was focused on the identification of the abnormal personality and evidence of possible psychopathology (i.e., mental illness). Using personality testing for that purpose might be thought of as an attempt to screen *out* potentially problematic employees. With the advent of instruments intended to provide quantitative descriptions of the normal (rather than abnormal) personality, personality testing in employment shifted to a screen *in* process whereby employers sought to identify applicants with positive personality characteristics (e.g., conscientiousness, emotional stability, or agreeableness) that would contribute to effective performance.

As you can see, Table 4.4 is separated into two sections. The upper section includes tests which have been frequently used for purposes of identifying signs of psychopathology—**screen out tests.** The tests listed in the lower section have been more frequently used to identify variations of normal personality—**screen in tests.** There is an important distinction between these two different categories of tests. Tests developed or intended to identify psychopathology, or used commonly for such purposes, are considered "Medical Tests" under the Americans with Disabilities Act (1990), particularly if the test is administered by a clinical or counseling psychologist or a psychiatrist. As such, they may not be administered until *after* an offer of employment has been made, as is the case with physical examinations, because emotional disorders are considered covered disabilities under the ADA. Applicants might be placed at a disadvantage in the selection process if their condition were revealed through preemployment testing. On the other hand, tests developed or intended to assess normal personality may be administered as preemployment tests and used for purposes of choosing among applicants prior to an offer of employment. If an employer administers a test such as the MMPI-II in order to choose among applicants prior to an offer of employment, that practice can be challenged in court and the applicant will likely win that challenge.

There are many positions of public trust (e.g., public safety officers, nuclear power plant operators, air traffic controllers, commercial airline pilots) that warrant testing for possible psychopathology to guard against catastrophic pathological actions by the incumbent. But most job titles in industry do not directly involve the health and welfare of

SCREEN OUT TEST

Used to eliminate candidates who are clearly unsuitable for employment; tests of psychopathology are examples of screen out tests in the employment setting.

SCREEN IN TEST

Used to add information about the positive attributes of a candidate that might predict outstanding performance; tests of normal personality are examples of screen in tests in the employment setting.

TABLE 4.4	Some Commonly Used Personality Instruments
Minnesota Multiphasic Personality Inventory II (MMPI-II)	
California Psychological Inventory (CPI)	
Personality Research Form (PRF)	
Edwards Personal Preference Schedule	
Jackson Personality Inventory-Revised (JPI-R)	
16 PF Select	
NEO-PI	
Hogan Personality Inventory	
OPQ 32	

This questionnaire is designed to provide information on your typical behavior within work and similar situations. You are asked to rate how strongly you agree with a number of statements. When you have decided, completely fill in the circle corresponding to your rating (1, 2, 3, 4 or 5), in the appropriate space on your answer sheet. Please try to avoid the middle answer (unsure).

EXAMPLE QUESTIONS:

1	**2**	**3**	**4**	**5**
STRONGLY DISAGREE	**DISAGREE**	**UNSURE**	**AGREE**	**STRONGLY AGREE**

ANSWER SHEET

1. I enjoy talking to new people

2. I usually keep things tidy

1 ① ② ③ ④ ⑤
2 ① ② ③ ④ ⑤

In the examples, the person has **agreed** with the statement "I enjoy talking to new people" and **strongly disagreed** with the statement "I usually keep things tidy."

FIGURE 4.5 What the OPQ32 Looks Like Source: Occupational Personality Questionnaire (OPQ32).

the public, and testing for the abnormal personality would be questionable in such jobs. Figure 4.5 presents some sample items from the Occupational Personality Questionnaire (OPQ32) test, which is frequently used to assess normal personality in job applicants.

Emotional Intelligence

As we saw in Chapter 3, the concept of **emotional intelligence (EI)** has achieved some notoriety with the public, if not widespread acceptance by psychologists. As there is no general agreement on the definition of EI, there can be no agreement on how to measure it. Recall also from Chapter 3 that Davies, Stankov and Roberts (1998) found little evidence for the reliability or validity of existing EI tests. That is not say that there are no instruments available which claim to measure EI. A score on a test of EI is often called an **emotional intelligence quotient,** or **EQ,** to parallel the notion of IQ. As an example, the MHS Corporation is marketing an array of products related to EI and EQ, including the MSC test of emotional intelligence, a scale for measuring organizational emotional intelligence, a 360-degree measure of emotional intelligence, an emotional intelligence interview protocol, a youth version of the emotional intelligence test to be used with children between the ages of 7 and 18, and a series of books and videotapes intended to help people more fully develop their emotional intelligence.

In the absence of any substantial data confirming the meaning of emotional intelligence, this array of products is disappointing, at least for scientists if not the public. In 1966 Marvin Dunnette wrote "Fads, Fashions, and Folderol," a sobering piece about research, theory, and practice in I-O. Fads were defined as "practices and concepts characterized by capriciousness and intense but short-lived interest" (p. 343). As data accumulate, emotional intelligence may very well prove to be a useful addition to the testing toolbox, but to avoid the graveyard of the "fads," more concerted efforts of assessing emotional intelligence will be required.

Interests and Values

It has been traditional to assess vocational interests as a way of guiding vocational choice. The three most popular instruments used for this type of assessment have been the Strong Vocational Interest Blank (SVIB), which began its development in 1921; the Kuder Occupational Interest Survey, developed and revised by G. F. Kuder (1966; Kuder & Diamond,

EMOTIONAL INTELLIGENCE (EI)

A proposed kind of intelligence focused on people's awareness of their own and others' emotions.

EMOTIONAL INTELLIGENCE QUOTIENT (EQ)

Parallels the notion of intelligence quotient (IQ); a score on a test of emotional intelligence.

TABLE 4.5	Personality Types and Their Associated Occupations

The Realistic type likes realistic jobs such as automobile mechanic, aircraft controller, surveyor, farmer, or electrician.

The Investigative type likes investigative jobs such as biologist, chemist, physicist, anthropologist, geologist, or medical technologist.

The Artistic type likes artistic jobs such as composer, musician, stage director, writer, interior decorator, or actor/actress.

The Social type likes social jobs such as teacher, religious worker, counselor, clinical psychologist, psychiatric caseworker, or speech therapist.

The Enterprising type likes enterprising jobs such as salesperson, manager, business executive, television producer, sports promoter, or buyer.

The Conventional type likes conventional jobs such as bookkeeper, stenographer, financial analyst, banker, cost estimator, or tax expert.

Source: Spector (2000).

1979); and the Self-Directed Search test based on Holland's (1985, 1994) theory of vocational choice, which we presented in Chapter 3. In more recent adaptations of the SVIB, connections have also been made with Holland's six occupational types or vocational themes. Table 4.5 presents the occupational groupings associated with various expressed interests.

The logic of vocational interest testing is simple. A candidate's score is compared to various occupational norm groups. The norm group with the closest match in terms of expressed interests is assumed to be the occupation for which the applicant is best suited. Interest tests are seldom used for selecting applicants for particular jobs. They are used more frequently to assist individuals in choosing or changing occupations. It is assumed that the norm group is composed of individuals with interests that support satisfaction and basic levels of success in that occupation. Thus, interest tests might be thought of as a form of motivational assessment.

In earlier years, values were sometimes also assessed. One of the most popular instruments was the Allport-Vernon-Lindzey Study of Values (Allport, Vernon, & Lindzey, 1960). Traditionally, values inventories were very similar to interest inventories. Values were thought to be broader and more stable than interests (Murphy & Davidshofer, 2001; Super, 1973). More recently, "values" have taken on a new meaning, closer to the concept of ethical or moral behavior. In the wake of the various accounting scandals (e.g., Enron, Arthur Andersen, WorldCom), there has been a renewed call for the assessment of the "values" of business leaders and MBA students who may become those leaders (Browning, 2002). At this point, however, there are no widely accepted or data based measures of these new values.

MODULE 4.2 SUMMARY

- A vigorous debate continues over whether there is only one overarching cognitive ability—"g" or "general mental ability"—or several distinct facets or abilities. Psychologists have developed tests that produce a single number intended to represent cognitive ability, tests of specific abilities, and test batteries designed to measure several different facets of cognitive ability.

- Because most physically demanding jobs require combinations of physical abilities, many physical ability assessment procedures use simulated pieces of work (e.g., carrying a load up a ladder) rather than individual physical tests (e.g., sit-ups or bench presses). There is substantial evidence that measures of physical abilities can improve the prediction of job success for many physically demanding jobs.

- Personality testing in employment has shifted from a screen *out* process to a screen *in* process whereby employers seek to identify applicants with positive personality characteristics (e.g., conscientiousness, emotional stability, or agreeableness). There are many commercially available instruments for measuring personality characteristics, many based on the Big Five model.

- Assessments of vocational interests are often used to assist individuals in choosing or changing occupations.

KEY TERMS

cognitive ability test

cognitive test battery

knowledge test

psychomotor abilities

screen out test

screen in test

emotional intelligence (EI)

emotional intelligence quotient (EQ)

CRITICAL THINKING EXERCISES

4.3 What abilities do video games such as Snood or Pac-Man involve? Give an example of a job for which a Snoodlike test might be appropriate for applicant screening.

4.4 The norms for most vocational interest forms are based on the responses of individuals currently employed in a particular occupation. What are the disadvantages of such a norming system?

ADDITIONAL ASSESSMENT METHODS

CONTENT VERSUS PROCESS

It is common for employers and applicants to confuse the content of testing with the process of testing. As we suggested earlier in this chapter, it is possible to distinguish between *what* attribute is being assessed and *how* it is being assessed. For example, after applying for a job with a local company, an applicant might describe the process as including a personality test, a cognitive test, an interview, and a background check. The terms "personality" and "cognitive" describe the content of the assessment and the terms "interview" and "background check" describe the process of the assessment. The reason that this content–process distinction is important is that you will often see claims for the "validity" of the interview, work sample, or biodata test. But the validity depends not so much on the process by which the information was gathered as on the content of that information. In the sections that follow, we will consider information gathered in ways other than a paper and pencil format. But as we discussed in Module 4.1, many of these methods can be used to gather many different kinds of information. For example, an interview could assess communication skills, knowledge, ability, or personality—or, as is most often the case, a combination of those "content" categories, depending on what questions are asked and how it is scored.

INDIVIDUAL ASSESSMENT

By their design, most paper and pencil tests are intended to be administered to large groups of individuals. For some situations, however, only one candidate (or a very few) will be assessed on many different attributes. This type of assessment process is often described as **individual assessment.** To select a CEO for a Fortune 500 company, for example, an executive recruiting firm may be retained to create a short list of three to five candidates who will then undergo intensive assessment. This assessment often includes paper and pencil tests, but they are administered and scored individually and may be used for creating a profile of a candidate rather than comparing one candidate with another. Because the target populations are usually upper-level executives in an organization, individual assessment is sometimes referred to as executive or senior leader assessment (Howard, 2001). Although frequently used for selection, individual assessment can also be used to identify training needs, provide career counseling, or to provide performance feedback to key organizational members. Because it is time intensive and requires skilled assessors, it is expensive and unlikely to be used for any other than key positions in the company.

Individual assessment is complex, involving a wide variety of content areas as well as a wide variety of assessment processes. The tools most frequently used include various interactive assessment tools rather than paper and pencil tests. A primary reason for this is that the nature of the position is usually so complex that no paper and pencil test would, by itself, provide sufficient information. Although more than one candidate may

INDIVIDUAL ASSESSMENT

Situation in which only one candidate (or a very few) is assessed on many different attributes.

TABLE 4.6	**Percentage of Assessors Using Different Assessment Methods**			
	I-O SIOP[1]	NON-I-O SIOP[2]	NON-I-O NON-SIOP[3]	TOTAL
Assessment methods				
Personal history form	81.5	83.0	81.1	81.9
Ability tests	77.8	78.8	66.4	74.3
Personality inventories	79.6	79.0	77.9	78.9
Projective tests	32.4	45.0	48.1	41.7
Simulation exercises	41.9	26.5	17.5	28.8
Interview	96.3	94.0	96.2	95.5

[1] SIOP members who are trained as I-O psychologists
[2] SIOP members who are not trained as I-O psychologists
[3] Non-SIOP members who are not trained as I-O psychologists

SOURCE: Ryan & Sackett (1992).

be undergoing assessment, each candidate is usually assessed in isolation from the others. This allows the organization to keep the identity of candidates a closely held secret for the protection of the reputation of both the company (should a chosen candidate reject an offer) and the candidate (should the organization ultimately reject a candidate).

As shown in Table 4.6, the "typical" individual assessment is likely to include ability tests, personality tests, a personal history statement, and interviews. It may also include simulation exercises or work samples, and less frequently, a clinically based personality test such as the Rorschach Inkblot Test or the Thematic Apperception (TAT) test. As we indicated earlier, there is not much scientific support for the use of these clinically oriented tests, but they are still occasionally used. Figure 4.6 presents a hypothetical framework for an individual assessment. The assessor might be directly involved in the interviews, the direct report simulation, the dimension rating, and the factor rating. Co-workers might be involved in the peer meeting and 360-degree profile. Tests and the in-basket simulation might provide quantitative scores for the candidate. All of this information would be combined by the assessor to make a recommendation, complete a comprehensive report on a candidate, and to provide feedback to that candidate. Figure 4.7 presents an example of a decision matrix that might be produced after assessing four candidates for an executive-level position. Candidate B appears to be strongest, and candidate C the weakest.

Individual assessment is not without criticisms. Guion (1998) listed the most common:

1. Individual assessment is not validated as rigorously as other traditional forms of assessment.

2. Assessment conclusions are often unreliable across assessors.

3. Assessment summaries are often influenced by only one or two parts of the process.

4. Heavy emphasis is placed on personality attributes without any clear link between these attributes and job success.

5. For some positions (e.g., managerial or sales), valid assessment cannot be done unless there are realistic interpersonal interaction components beyond an interview.

6. Many individual assessments invade the privacy of the candidate by asking for information unrelated to the work associated with the position in question.

These criticisms reduce to questions of validity, reliability, and ethics. The text by Silzer and Jeanneret (1998), which is an excellent primer on the process and content of individual

Competencies	Interview	Tests	In-Basket Simulation	Dir. Report Simulation	Peer Meeting	Dimension Rating	Factor Rating	360 Profile
Assessor Initials								
Thinking Skills								
1. Seasoned Judgment								
2. Visionary Thinking								
3. Global Perspective								
Strategic Management								
4. Strategic Business Planning								
5. Managing Execution								
Leadership								
6. Attracting and Developing Talent								
7. Empowering Others								
8. Leadership Versatility								
Interpersonal Skills								
9. Influencing and Negotiating								
10. Building and Sustaining Relationships								
Communication								
11. Fostering Open Dialogue								
12. High-Impact Delivery								
Motivation								
13. Drive for Stakeholder Success								
14. Entrepreneurial Risk Taking								
Adjustment								
15. Mature Confidence								
16. Adaptability								
17. Career and Self-direction								
Person/Job Fit or Overall Rating								

FIGURE 4.6 **A Blueprint for Individual Assessment** Source: Executive Success Profile.

Competency Factors

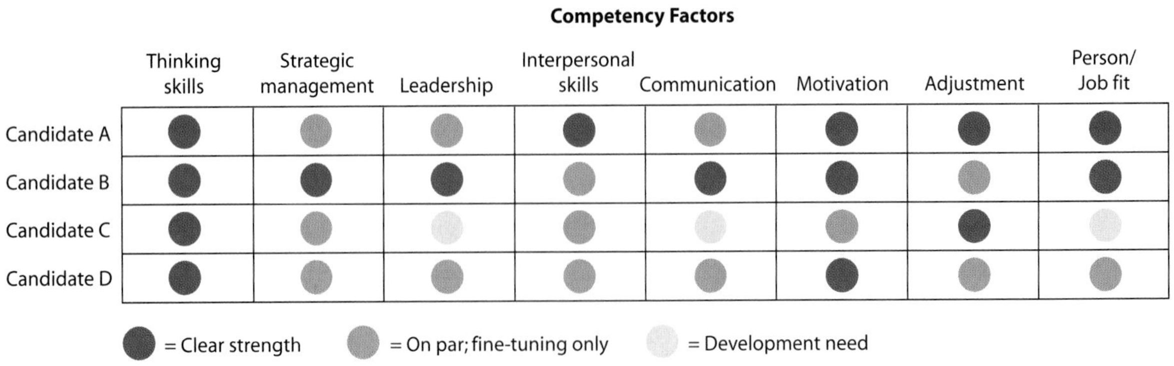

FIGURE 4.7 **Candidate Comparison Matrix** Source: Executive Success Profile.

assessment, points out that a well designed individual assessment program should have no difficulty avoiding these pitfalls.

INTERVIEWS

In one form or another, an interview plays a role in virtually every selection or promotion decision. This has been true for many decades; one of the first texts dealing with employment interviewing was written by Bingham and Moore in 1931. Over the years, there have been many fine texts (e.g., Webster, 1982) and reviews of the research on the interview (e.g., Guion, 1998; Landy, 1989; Huffcutt & Arthur, 1994; McDaniel, Whetzel, Schmidt, & Maurer, 1994; Posthuma, Morgeson, & Campion, 2002; Salgado, Viswesvaran, & Ones, 2001; Schmitt, 1976; Ulrich & Trumbo, 1965; Wagner, 1949).

Interview Content

Interview content is often dictated by the amount of structure in the interview. A structured interview consists of very specific questions asked of each candidate, often anchored in asking the interviewee to describe in specific and behavioral detail how he or she would respond to a hypothetical situation. This has been labeled the **situational interview,** a subcategory of the structured interview. In addition, **structured interviews** typically have tightly crafted scoring schemes with detailed outlines for the interviewer with respect to assigning ratings or scores based on interview performance. An **unstructured interview** has much broader questions that may vary by candidate and allow the candidate to answer in any form he or she may prefer. In addition, unstructured interviews are more likely to have less detailed scoring formats, allowing greater discretion by the interviewer for scoring (Huffcutt & Arthur, 1994). An example of structured interview questions is presented in Table 4.7. The questions were developed to elicit behavioral skills from candidates for 911 emergency dispatcher positions.

For the most part, interviews cover one or more of the following content areas: job knowledge, abilities, skills, personality, and person–organization fit (Harris, 1998; Huffcutt, Conway, Roth, & Stone, 2001). Salgado and Moscoso (2001) provided more detail on content. In a meta-analysis of the employment interview, they found interesting content differences between conventional interviews and tightly structured behavioral interviews. They discovered that the less structured or conventional interview seems to be more closely associated with personality and social/communication skills. On the other hand, the tightly structured behavioral interview was more closely associated with job knowledge and technical attributes, and, to a much lesser extent, personality characteristics. Similar results have been reported by Huffcutt et al. (2001).

These results take on more meaning when considered in the context of reviews of the validity of the interview. It has been generally found (McDaniel et al., 1994; Weisner & Cronshaw, 1988) that the highest validity coefficients are associated with structured and behavioral interviews (often in the range of +.60) compared to the more personality-based interviews, which have validity coefficients more often in the range of +.30. These results would seem to be a strong recommendation for tightly structured interviews based on task-based job demands over interviews intended to assess personality characteristics or personal style. But a note of caution should be sounded here. Many of the studies on which these meta-analyses were based were conducted in an earlier time, before the emergence of team environments and client-centered work. As a result, many of the criteria used in the validation studies were task based. It is not surprising, then, that lower validity coefficients would be observed for interviews centered on personality characteristics. These "personality based" interviews were also done in a time when few sound personality tests were available. In the context of the current state of the field, it might be reasonable to use psychometric devices (e.g., the NEO-PI, the Hogan Personality Inventory, or the OPQ32) to assess personality attributes and the structured behavioral interview to assess knowledge and skills. Guion (1998) concluded that the structured interview is a valuable tool in the assessment tool bag. We agree.

SITUATIONAL INTERVIEW

Asks the interviewee to describe in specific and behavioral detail how he or she would respond to a hypothetical situation.

STRUCTURED INTERVIEW

Consists of very specific questions asked of each candidate; includes tightly crafted scoring schemes with detailed outlines for the interviewer with respect to assigning ratings or scores based on interview performance.

UNSTRUCTURED INTERVIEW

Includes questions that may vary by candidate and that allow the candidate to answer in any form he or she may prefer.

TABLE 4.7	Examples of Structured Interview Questions and the Real-Life Incidents that Are the Foundation for These Questions

These questions were used to interview applicants for emergency telephone operator positions.

INTERVIEW QUESTION	CRITICAL INCIDENT
1. Imagine that you tried to help a stranger, for example, with traffic directions or to get up after a fall and that person blamed you for their misfortune or yelled at you. How would you respond?	1. Telephone operator tries to verify address information for an ambulance call. The caller yells at them for being stupid and slow. The operator quietly assures the caller an ambulance is on the way and that she is merely reaffirming the address.
2. Suppose a friend calls you and is extremely upset. Apparently, her child has been injured. She begins to tell you, in a hysterical manner, all about her difficulty in getting baby-sitters, what the child is wearing, what words the child can speak, and so on. What would you do?	2. A caller is hysterical because her infant is dead. She yells incoherently about the incident. The operator talks in a clear calm voice and manages to secure the woman's address, dispatches the call, and then tries to secure more information about the child's status.
3. How would you react if you were a salesclerk, waitress, or gas station attendant, and one of your customers talked back to you, indicated you should have known something you did not, or told you that you were not waiting on them fast enough?	3. A clearly angry caller calls for the third time in an hour complaining about the 911 service because no one has arrived to investigate a busted water pipe. The operator tells the caller to go to _____ and hangs up.

SOURCE: Schneider & Schmitt (1986).

Interview Process

Independent of the actual content of the interview, there are many relevant process issues. How should interviews be conducted? How should interviewers be trained? What are some potential sources of bias in interviews? Table 4.8 presents information on many of these practical issues. Recent studies (e.g., Huffcutt & Roth, 1998; Latham & Skarlicki, 1996) appear to confirm, at least on a preliminary basis, that little adverse impact is associated with the structured interview, particularly when compared with more traditional paper and pencil tests of cognitive ability. Nevertheless, these studies have examined traditional domestic demographic characteristics such as race and gender. As applicant populations become increasing multicultural, the issues of bias in the interview may reemerge due to the more dramatic cultural differences that may appear in applicant responses. For example, many Asian cultures value modesty in self-presentation. Thus, Asian applicants may be less comfortable than American applicants in extolling their virtues when asked by an interviewer to describe strengths and weaknesses (a common question in unstructured interviews).

ASSESSMENT CENTERS

ASSESSMENT CENTER

Collection of procedures for evaluation that is administered to groups of individuals; assessments are typically done by multiple assessors.

Even though the word "center" evokes an image of a physical place, **assessment centers** are collections of procedures for evaluation, no matter where these procedures are carried out.

TABLE 4.8	Potential Influences on Employment Interviews

Nature of the Information: negative vs. positive

Placement of Information: early or late in the interview

Presence of Interviewer Stereotypes (e.g., Ideal Candidate)

Interviewer Knowledge of the Job in Question

Method used by Interviewer to Combine Information

Nonverbal Behavior of Candidate: posture, gestures

Attitudinal or Racial Similarity of Candidate and Interviewer

Gender Similarity of Candidate and Interviewer

Quality of Competing Candidates

Interviewer Experience

Applicant Physical Appearance

Attention to Factual Detail by Interviewer

Extent to Which Interview Is Structured

Note Taking by Interviewer

Use of Same Interviewer(s) for All Candidates

SOURCES: Based on Landy (1989); Huffcutt & Woehr (1999).

Assessment centers are very much like the individual assessment procedure we described earlier, except they are administered to groups of individuals rather than single individuals, and the assessments are typically done by multiple assessors rather than a single assessor. Assessment centers have a long and successful history, and there are many good books and articles describing variations on the technique (Bray, Campbell, & Grant, 1974; Finkle, 1976; Guion, 1998; Spychalski, Quinones, Gaugler, & Pohley, 1997; Thornton & Byham, 1982). In earlier years, there were as many variations of assessment centers as there were users. For this reason, a task force published *Guidelines and Ethical Considerations for Assessment Center Operations* (Task Force on Assessment Center Guidelines, 1989). These guidelines have done much to standardize the assessment center process and protect the rights of those being assessed.

Most assessment centers share the following characteristics (Finkle, 1976):

1. Assessment is done in groups. A typical group size is 12 although smaller subgroups may be formed for specific exercises. The group format provides opportunity for peer evaluation.

2. Assessment is done by groups. Unlike the usual evaluators in individual assessment, assessment center evaluators are usually managers chosen from the organization but unfamiliar with the candidates.

3. Multiple methods of assessment are employed. Like individual assessment, these might include paper and pencil tests, group exercises, interviews, and clinical testing. A typical group exercise might be a leaderless group discussion that is observed and rated by the assessors. An individual exercise might be an in-basket exercise in which a candidate is presented with the contents of a typical in-basket and asked to deal with each element in the basket by making a phone call, sending an e-mail, writing a memo, or starting a file for information.

4. Assessment centers invariably have a "feel" of relevance to them, both for assessors and for those being assessed. They are seen as much more "real" than interviews, paper and pencil tests, or even isolated work simulations.

TABLE 4.9	Portion of a Report Based on Assessment Center Evaluation

There were several indications from his behavior that his strong desire to make a favorable impression promoted above average tenseness in the assessment situation. On several occasions, his behavior was characterized by nervousness and controlled quietness, as though he were reluctant to enter into a situation until he felt absolutely sure of himself.

The picture he created was that of a young man eager to cooperate, comply, and do his best in order to fulfill the expectations others had for him.

In most respects, the trainee's general abilities compare favorably with the total sample of men in the Management Progress study.

Most members of the staff anticipated a very successful career in the Bell System for the trainee.... There was a mild amount of disagreement concerning the speed with which he is likely to reach the district level of management. Everyone agreed that he presently displays the abilities and potential to perform effectively at the district level.

SOURCE: Bray, Campbell, & Grant (1974).

As in the individual assessment procedure, the results of the assessment center may include a report, recommendation, and feedback to the participants. An excerpt from a typical report appears in Table 4.9 On the basis of assessment center results, the organization may make one or more of the following decisions (Finkle, 1976):

1. An assessee may or may not qualify for a given job or job level.
2. Assessees may be ranked on a series of attributes and placed into different categories representing anticipated speed of promotion (e.g., fast track vs. normal progression groups).
3. Predictions of long-range potential may be made for one or more of the assessees.
4. Development and learning experiences for aiding the assessee in personal or professional growth might be recommended.

There is general agreement that assessment centers can be valuable procedures for selection, promotion and training needs analysis (Bartram, 2002; Borman, 1982; Gaugler, Rosenthal, Thornton, & Bentson, 1987; Hunter & Hunter, 1984; Schmitt, Gooding, Noe, & Kirch, 1984). There is less agreement with respect to why they work (Klimoski & Brickner, 1987; Lance, Newbolt, Gatewood, Foster, French, & Smith, 2000; Landy, 1989; Sackett & Tuzinski, 2001). Although the "why" question may be an interesting one for scientific and research purposes, it is less important from a practical perspective. Assessment centers include many different types of exercises and assess many different attributes. The information is eventually combined to yield a decision or recommendation that will be as good or as poor as the information that went into it. Decomposing the assessment center into its constituent elements and asking which part makes the greatest contribution is like decomposing a bouillabaisse and asking which ingredient made it taste so good.

One intriguing finding from a German study (Schuler, Moser, & Funke, 1994) was that assessment center results are much more predictive when the assessors have known the candidates for more than two years than when they have known them for less than two years. This suggests that assessors may be considering much more than the results of the assessment exercises in making evaluations, most likely past observations of the candidate's performance. At the very least, this study brings into question the practice of choosing assessors who are unfamiliar with the candidates.

Assessment centers can be expensive and time consuming. They are likely to be of greatest value to large organizations that favor internal movement and promotions and invest heavily in the learning and development of their members. Most other organizations can accomplish assessment more effectively with more traditional assessment procedures.

WORK SAMPLES AND SITUATIONAL TESTS

Work Sample Tests

As the name implies, **work sample tests** measure job skills by taking samples of behavior under realistic joblike conditions. One of the earliest applications of this technique was in the selection of trolley car operators in Boston in 1910. Trolley cars frequently came into contact with people, horses, bicycles, and the newly introduced automobile. Munsterberg (1913) set up a "work station" to simulate the controls of the trolley car and projected events onto a screen to see how potential operators would respond. Since this study was carried out a decade before the correlation coefficient became a common index of validity, Munsterberg's assertion that his workstation predicted operator success is anecdotal.

In today's work sample tests, the performance may or may not be assessed at an actual workstation, but the task assigned and the equipment used to complete the task are designed to be realistic simulations of the actual job. Consider the example of an individual applying for a position as an accounts payable clerk. The applicant might be given a checkbook in which to make entries, a work report from which to generate an invoice, a petty cash ledger to balance, and a payroll task. The results would then be compared against some standard and a score assigned representing the level of test performance. Table 4.10 illustrates some work sample elements.

Like assessment centers, work samples have a "real" feeling to them and usually elicit good reactions from candidates. Further, various studies have affirmed that work samples can be valid assessment devices (Hunter & Hunter, 1984). This is not surprising because work samples usually come directly from the tasks of the job in question, and it is easier to document their job relatedness. But like other formats, work samples are not intrinsically valid. Their job relatedness depends heavily on the attributes being assessed by the format. Using the example of the bookkeeping applicant, good performance may be the result of specific knowledge (the candidate is familiar with the software), general knowledge (the candidate is

A 1920s example of work sample testing: an apparatus to test the skills of prospective trolley drivers.

WORK SAMPLE TEST

Assessment procedure that measures job skills by taking samples of behavior under realistic joblike conditions.

TABLE 4.10	Some Examples of Work Sample Tests

MOTOR WORK SAMPLES	VERBAL WORK SAMPLES
Carving dexterity test for dental students	A test of common facts of law for law students
Blueprint reading test	Group discussion test for supervisor
Shorthand and stenography test	Judgment and decision-making test for administrators
Rudder control test for pilots	Speech interview for foreign student
Programming test for computer programmers	Test of basic information in chemistry
Map reading test for traffic control officers	Test of ability to follow oral directions

familiar with check registers, invoicing, and so forth), or cognitive ability (the candidate is able to solve the problem presented by the task through trial and error). When work sample tests make unique contributions to test performance (e.g., above and beyond what might be predicted by a simple test of cognitive ability), it is likely due to general or specific knowledge. Callinan and Robertson (2000) suggested that work samples are best suited for predicting success in blue-collar jobs that involve skilled motor performance rather than jobs which deal with people. As Guion (1998) pointed out, the value of a work sample can be evaluated just as one would evaluate any assessment device—job relatedness, perceived fairness, and cost effectiveness. In Chapter 6, we will describe various techniques used to elicit knowledge from nuclear power plant operators, such as the "walk-through" method. This might also be considered an example of a work sample (Hedge, Teachout, & Laue, 1990).

Situational Judgment Tests Recently, the notion of the work sample test has been expanded to cover white collar positions by creating what Motowidlo and colleagues (Motowidlo, Dunnette, & Carter, 1990; Motowidlo & Tippins, 1993) have referred to as low-fidelity simulations and others have referred to as **situational judgment tests (SJT)** (McDaniel, Morgeson, Finnegan, Campion, & Braverman, 2001). A situational judgment test is commonly a paper and pencil test that presents the candidate with a written scenario and then asks the candidate to choose the best response from a series of alternatives (see Figure 4.8).

McDaniel et al. (2001) have reviewed the research on situational judgment tests and noted that in one form or another, such tests have been part of the assessment practice of I-O psychologists since the 1920s. In a meta-analysis of 102 validity coefficients, they concluded that there is substantial evidence of validity or job relatedness in these types of

SITUATIONAL JUDGMENT TEST

Commonly a paper and pencil test that presents the candidate with a written scenario and asks the candidate to choose the best response from a series of alternatives.

FIGURE 4.8 An Example of a Situational Judgment Exercise

A man on a very urgent mission during a battle finds he must cross a stream about 40 feet wide. A blizzard has been blowing and the stream has frozen over. However, because of the snow, he does not know how thick the ice is. He sees two planks about 10 feet long near the point where he wishes to cross. He also knows where there is a bridge about 2 miles downstream. Under the circumstances he should:

A. Walk to the bridge and cross it.
B. Run rapidly across on the ice.
C. Break a hole in the ice near the edge of the stream to see how deep the stream is.
D. Cross with the aid of the planks, pushing one ahead of the other and walking on them.
E. Creep slowly across the ice.

SOURCE: Northrup (1989).

tests. They found that the single strongest component of these tests was general mental ability. Nevertheless, there appears to be more to SJTs than just "g".

Clevenger, Pereira, Weichmann, Schmitt, and Harvey (2001) evaluated the use of SJTs in hiring decisions for a government agency and a private sector transportation company. In addition to SJTs, they collected data on personality, cognitive ability, technical job knowledge, and job experience of the candidates. They found that SJTs were able to improve the prediction of performance even after the contributions of all of these other variables had been controlled, and even though the SJT scores were substantially correlated with the measure of cognitive ability. They suggested that SJTs are best used to measure procedural knowledge (what we referred to as tacit knowledge in Chapter 3). Another advantage of SJTs discovered in this study was that the differences in scores between whites and both African Americans and Hispanics was considerably less than typically found in standard tests of cognitive ability. This may be a case of having your cake and eating it too. Not only did the SJT give a good assessment of general mental ability with lower adverse impact, it also measured something in addition to "g" which was job related. In a recent follow-up study, Chan and Schmitt (2002) found once again that SJT scores contributed to the prediction of job performance for 160 civil service employees, beyond what could be predicted from cognitive ability, personality, and job experience. This study is particularly interesting because it was done in Singapore, suggesting that at least the format of the SJT can travel internationally.

SJTs have also been adapted for video presentation by using video vignettes, rather than a written description, to present the scenario. The results are encouraging. In two similar studies, Weekly and Jones (1997) and Chan and Schmitt (1997) found that black–white differences in SJT scores were smaller with a video than with a paper and pencil presentation, and that SJT produced more favorable attitudes toward the assessment process, particularly among African-American test takers.

The results of research on the SJT are very positive. They seem to possess three important characteristics for modern and practical assessment: They are job-related, they are well accepted by test takers, and they have reduced adverse impact compared to other traditional assessment devices. Further, the recent research on video presentations suggests that further advances are likely to occur in this area, particularly in terms of increasing the fidelity of the simulation from low to high and in further increasing the acceptance of the format by test takers.

BIOGRAPHICAL DATA

It is common for organizations to gather personal information from applicants for positions. The best example is the type of information collected on an application blank: information about previous jobs, education, and specialized training. This type of information can also be used to predict job performance; the collection of it can be thought of as a "test" if the method used to collect it is standardized, the scoring objective, and the sample of behavior examined reasonable. This type of information has been variously labeled personal history, life history, biographical information, or—the simplest label—**biodata.**

In the 1950s and 1960s, biodata predictors were based less on theory than statistics. If a particular piece of information (e.g., educational accomplishment) could be shown to predict success, it was included in an application blank. If no relationship could be found, it was not included. William Owens pioneered what has been called the rational approach to the use of life history data for the prediction of success (Owens & Schoenfeldt, 1979; Mumford & Owens, 1982; Mumford, Snell, & Reiter-Palmon, 1994; Mumford & Stokes, 1991). Instead of simply looking at statistical relationships between individual history information items and success, Owens identified broader life history factors as a way of arranging all of the hundreds of pieces of information that could be gathered about someone. The underlying model for this type of biodata instrument is the **ecology model** (Mumford, Uhlman, & Kilcullen, 1992). In its simplest form, this model proposes that the

BIODATA

Information collected on an application blank or in a standardized test that includes questions about previous jobs, education, specialized training, and personal history; also known as biographical data.

ECOLOGY MODEL

Underlying model for life history biodata instruments. Proposes that the events that make up a person's history represent choices made by the individual to interact with his or her environment. These choices can signal abilities, interests, and personality characteristics.

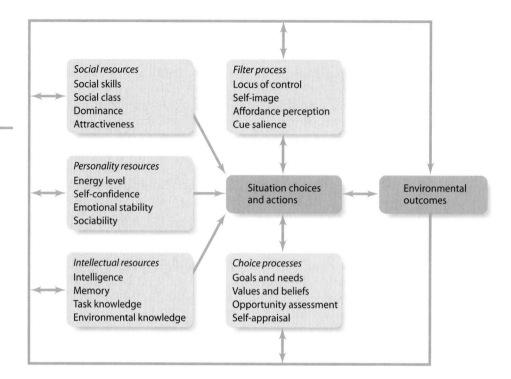

events that make up a person's history are neither accidental nor random. They represent choices made by the individual to interact with his or her environment. As a result, these choices can signal abilities, interests, and personality characteristics. Thus, personal history data can be used as a surrogate or as an addition to other assessment information. As Figure 4.9 shows, there are many potential influences on the situations and actions that individuals choose from all available situations and actions. These precursors of situational choice and actions are the focus of biodata instruments.

Mael (1991) has suggested some characteristics of biodata items that distinguish them from other types of assessment, such as personality tests. Guion (1998) has summarized these characteristics as follows:

1. *Historical.* The item refers to events which have already occurred or are occurring rather than future, hypothetical events. For example, "Do you intend to develop computer skills?" is not a biodata item, but "How many times did you access the Internet in the past week?" is.

2. *External.* The events are observable and may involve others. They are not events that occur solely in one's own head. This would exclude items of the "how did you feel . . ." variety. An example of an external item might be, "Have you ever been suspended from your job without pay for disciplinary reasons?"

3. *Objective.* The events are factual and do not involve interpretation. For example, "I think my last boss disliked me" would not qualify as a biodata item because it attributes attitudes to the supervisor that this person may not have had. An objective item might be, "How many training courses have you taken outside of your company in the past five years?"

4. *Discrete.* The event described is concrete, with a beginning and/or ending, rather than open ended. An example might be, "When did you receive your permanent teaching certificate?"

5. *Control.* The event describes an action over which the applicant had control. An example might be, "How many times have you applied for a promotional opportunity in your company in the last five years?"

6. *Relevant and noninvasive.* The event should have at least the appearance of job relatedness and avoid overly personal aspects of a person's past. An example would be historical familial issues such as relations or income. "How many public presentations have you made in the last year outside of your company?"

Using these guidelines, Mael (1991) presented an illustration of acceptable and unacceptable biodata items (see Table 4.11).

TABLE 4.11	Examples of Good and Poor Biodata Items

Historical	*Future or hypothetical*
How old were you when you got your first paying job?	What position do you think you will be holding in 10 years?
	What would you do if another person screamed at you in public?
External	*Internal*
Did you ever get fired from a job?	What is your attitude toward friends who smoke marijuana?
Objective	*Subjective*
How many hours did you study for your real estate license test?	Would you describe yourself as shy?
	How adventurous are you compared to your co-workers?
Firsthand	*Secondhand*
How punctual are you about coming to work?	How would your teachers describe your punctuality?
Discrete	*Summative*
At what age did you get your driver's license?	How many hours do you study during an average week?
Verifiable	*Nonverifiable*
What was your grade point average in college?	How many servings of fresh vegetables do you eat every day?
Were you ever suspended from your Little League team?	
Controllable	*Noncontrollable*
How many tries did it take you to pass the CPA exam?	How many brothers and sisters do you have?
Equal access	*Nonequal access*
Were you ever class president?	Were you captain of the football team?
Job relevant	*Not job relevant*
How many units of cereal did you sell during the last calendar year?	Are you proficient at crossword puzzles?
Noninvasive	*Invasive*
Were you on the tennis team in college?	How many young children do you have at home?

Source: Mael (1991).

In a later study, Mael, Connerly, and Morath (1996) identified four possible factors that determine whether a biodata item might be seen as invasive. Invasive items are those that might stigmatize someone, might remind the individual of traumatic events, were unduly intimate, or concerned religion.

Like other assessment instruments we have discussed, biodata instruments derive their job relatedness and value from the constructs they try to assess (e.g., cognitive ability, personality, experience, knowledge) and not from any magical properties of the format itself. Several studies have demonstrated that biodata items can improve prediction of success when added to other discrete assessment techniques such as the interview (Dalessio & Silverhart, 1994), personality tests (McManus & Kelly, 1999), and even general mental ability (Mount, Witt, & Barrick, 2000). But if one were to develop a comprehensive battery of devices including cognitive ability, personality, interest inventories, and job knowledge, it is not yet clear how biodata information would add to what is assessed by those other techniques. There are also some lingering concerns about the fairness of certain types of biodata items. For example, Whitney and Schmitt (1997) found that compared with Whites, Blacks were more likely to describe past experiences that emphasized "the maintenance or restoration of long-standing traditions" and activities that were group rather than individually oriented. Even though the research was performed with college students, it certainly suggests that more research needs to be done in the area of ethnic and cultural influences on biodata instruments. The good news is that current research on biodata is considerably more theory based than it has been in the past (Mitchell, 1994). Once biodata instruments become more standardized and there is some agreement regarding what they measure most effectively, biodata may represent an attractive alternative to other available assessment devices.

GRADES AND LETTERS OF RECOMMENDATION

Employment applications, especially those for entry-level positions, often solicit high school and college grade point averages. In spite of their popularity, there is little careful research to support the use of grade point averages (GPAs) as a predictor, independent of measures of general mental ability, personality, or interests. In addition, substantial adverse impact against minority applicants appears to be associated with the GPA (Roth, BeVier, Switzer, & Schippmann, 1996; Roth & Bobko, 2000). There is some evidence that GPA and positive letters of recommendation can predict who will be *offered* a job, but not who will be successful in that job (Marshall, 1985).

Similarly, even though employers almost always ask job applicants for references or letters of recommendation, there has been little serious research on the validity or fairness of these devices (Loher, Hazer, Tsai, Tilton, & James, 1997). Since the threat of litigation from disgruntled rejected applicants looms large in the minds of many recommenders and reference sources, they are unlikely to provide negative information. In addition, without a great deal of imposed structure, and a clear understanding of the information base of the reference source, the information provided is often irrelevant, uninterpretable, or both.

MODULE 4.3 SUMMARY

- It is important for employers and applicants to distinguish between the content of testing (*what* attribute is being assessed) and the process of testing (*how* it is being assessed). For example, the terms "personality" and "cognitive" describe the content of the assessment, and the terms

"interview" and "background check" describe the process of the assessment.

- Individual assessment is complex, involving a wide variety of content areas and assessment processes. The tools used most frequently include various interactive assessment tools rather than paper and pencil tests, as the nature of the position is usually so complex that no paper and pencil test would, by itself, provide sufficient information.

- An interview plays a role in virtually every selection or promotion decision. Interviews vary in their structure and content. They can range on a continuum from very unstructured to very structured, and can cover one or more of the following content areas: job knowledge, abilities, skills, personality, and person-organization fit.

- Assessment centers have a long and successful history. They are administered to groups of individuals rather than single individuals, and the assessments are typically performed by multiple assessors. There is general agreement that an assessment center can be a valuable procedure for selection, promotion, and training needs analysis.

- Other common assessment devices include work samples, situational judgment tests, and biographical data, as well as grades and letters of recommendation.

KEY TERMS

individual assessment

situational interview

structured interview

unstructured interview

assessment center

work sample test

situational judgment test

biodata

ecology model

CRITICAL THINKING EXERCISES

4.5 Recall a recent instance in which you were interviewed for a full-time or part-time position. Was the interview structured or unstructured? Name three ways that you could have improved this interview.

4.6 Many medical students are technically proficient but have variable "patient" skills. Describe a work sample test that could be used for assessing "bedside manner" as part of a physician licensing exam.

SPECIAL TOPICS IN ASSESSMENT

INCREMENTAL VALIDITY

In the preceding two modules, we have described quite a few tools that might go into the assessment toolbag. Until recently, assessment research often took on the flavor of a competition—which tool was better, a paper and pencil test of "g" or an interview? One study reported that "the validity" of a test of general mental ability was +.35 while another study reported that "the validity" of an interview was +.46, suggesting somehow that an interview is a more valid assessment device. Similarly, one might explore the differences in validity between a personality test and an interest test, or a work sample and a paper and pencil test. These are misleading questions for a number of reasons. First, we cannot answer these questions without answering another question: better for what? Predicting satisfaction, or performance, or tenure, or management potential? Another reason why the questions were misleading is their implication that one is forced to choose a single instrument rather than developing a battery of assessment devices. Finally, the questions were misleading because they mixed test content with test process (e.g., test of "g" versus interview).

In the past few years, dozens of studies have purported to demonstrate the value of one or another device or test. Many of these studies compared the device of interest to another device. In addition, studies examined the predictive validity of particular combinations to demonstrate the added, or incremental, value of combining two devices. Thus, a study might show that the validity of a paper and pencil test of general mental ability was found to be +.35 but when it was combined with an interview, the validity of the two measures combined was +.51. Thus, one might conclude that the value of the interview is incremental, that is, it added to the validity of the paper and pencil test. Examples of **incremental validity** studies include:

- Personality measures and biodata (McManus & Kelly, 1999).
- Biodata and general mental ability (Mount et al., 2000).
- Personality measures and assessment centers (Goffin, Rothstein, & Johnston, 1996).
- Cognitive ability, interviews, and biodata (Bobko, Roth, & Potosky, 1999).
- Personality measures and mental ability (Kanfer & Kantrowitz, 2002).

These studies point to an important principle: In assessment the issue is not *which* tool to use, but what *combination* of tools to use for the greatest predictive ability at the lowest cost.

As we saw in Chapter 3 on individual differences and will see in greater detail in the chapters covering performance theory and prediction, industrial behavior is very complicated. It involves technical tasks as well as social ones. Successful performance in virtually any job depends on many different KSAOs. As a result, it makes little sense to limit the toolbag to one and only one tool. As Maslow said many years ago (1971), when the only tool in your bag is a hammer, you tend to treat everything as if it were a nail. As we continue

INCREMENTAL
VALIDITY

The value in terms of increased validity of adding a particular predictor to an existing selection system.

to gather information about the incremental validity of various combinations of assessment tools, we will be better able to make practical recommendations about the most fair and effective assessment programs, as well as what tests and procedures might act as substitutes for other tests and procedures.

CONTROVERSIAL ASSESSMENT PRACTICES

Graphology

Handwriting analysis, or **graphology,** has been popular as a parlor game and carnival attraction for many decades. The principle behind graphology is that traits can be assessed from various characteristics of a person's handwriting. Since graphology is not widely used in the United States—although Gatewood and Field (2001) estimated that 2,500 U.S. firms use graphology as a screening device!—there would be little reason to even mention it if it were not for the increasing presence of other cultures in the American workplace and the appearance of Americans in the international workplace. Thus, Americans who emigrate to France or Israel may be surprised to be asked to provide a handwriting sample as part of a preemployment screening process. Similarly, a manager in an American workplace who formerly worked for a French or Israeli company may suggest that his or her HR department consider adding a graphology component to the screening of applicants.

Rafaeli and Klimoski (1983) studied the relationship between assessments of the handwriting of 104 real estate agents conducted by expert graphologists and measures of the performance of those agents. No relationship was found. Other studies have come to similar conclusions. When a study seems to support the validity of the graphological analysis, it is clear that the "validity" was produced by the content of what participants wrote, not the characteristics of their handwriting (Ben-Shakhar, Bar-Hillel, Bilu, Ben-Abba, & Flug, 1986). In a meta-analysis of graphology studies, Neter and Ben-Shakhar (1989) found that graphologists were no better than nongraphologists in predicting future performance by examining an applicant's handwriting.

The lack of value notwithstanding, it is interesting to speculate *why* graphology seems to have such a firm foothold in France and Israel. We asked two questions of a French (Steiner, 2002) and an Israeli (Eden, 2002) I-O colleague: Is it true that graphology is still practiced widely? If so, why? Both colleagues answered that it was correct that graphology was still practiced widely in their countries, much to their embarrassment. Indeed, our Israeli colleague reported that many employers prefer to receive résumés in handwritten form so that they can be subjected to graphological analysis. The "why" question was a bit more complicated. Our Israeli colleague speculated that the reason for the widespread use of graphology in Israel was that the procedure has been used in France for over 100 years, and there were very close ties between Israel and France until the mid-1950s. The Israelis generally adopted French business practices, including those related to HR, without much critical evaluation. The French colleague answered that graphology had been practiced in France since 1870, inspired by a book published in Italy in 1622. At the turn of the 20th century, graphology was popular in many European countries. By the late 1940s graphology had taken on the status of a vocational training program in France, complete with two-year diplomas. To this day graphologists in France exert a strong commercial lobbying effort. A French psychologist has written extensively about the history and futility of handwriting analysis (Bruchon-Schweitzer, 2002), but apparently to no avail.

The Polygraph

It is ironic that the first **polygraph** (often known as the "lie detector" test) was introduced into the United States by one of the fathers of I-O psychology, Hugo Munsterberg (Landy, 1992, 1997; Munsterberg, 1913). Like graphology, the polygraph relies on deceptively simple logic.

GRAPHOLOGY

Technique that presumes that traits can be assessed from various characteristics of a person's handwriting; also known as handwriting analysis.

POLYGRAPH

Machine that measures a person's physiological reactions. Approach assumes that when people are being dishonest, their physiological reactions will signal that they are being deceptive; often known as a "lie detector" test.

FIGURE 4.10

**Physiological
Responses Assessed
by the Polygraph**

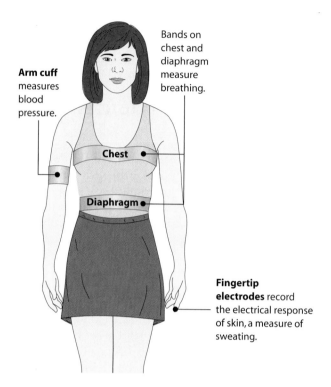

Arm cuff measures blood pressure.

Bands on chest and diaphragm measure breathing.

Chest

Diaphragm

Fingertip electrodes record the electrical response of skin, a measure of sweating.

The assumption is made that when people are being dishonest, their physiological reactions will signal that they are being deceptive. The measures that a polygraph takes are illustrated in Figure 4.10; several different pens record physiological activity (thus the term "polygraph").

Both the theory and technique of lie detection have been the subject of extensive critiques (Iacono & Lykken, 1997; Landy, 1989; Lykken, 1981; 1983; Sackett & Decker, 1979). The National Academy of Sciences recently completed an extensive review of the subject (National Academies, 2002) and concluded once again that there is little value in using the polygraph for employee selection purposes. They liken the polygraph community to a cult or priesthood with secret rituals and faith-based beliefs.

Virtually every review, report, and critique reaches the same conclusion: The polygraph has no value for preemployment screening. The U.S. Congress passed the Employee Polygraph Protection Act in 1988; since then, the polygraph has virtually disappeared from the applicant screening process in most private sector jobs. The law still permits the use of the device for security service firms and organizations that manufacture controlled substances. In addition, federal agencies (e.g., FBI, CIA, NRC, nuclear weapons labs) are permitted to use the polygraph for preemployment and incumbent screening (Maranto, 2001). These exceptions are disappointing, particularly in light of the most recent government report on the value of the polygraph for preemployment screening (National Academies, 2002). If there is no empirical support for the theory or the technique, it is hard to understand why it may be unacceptable for use with one group of applicants but acceptable for another. As was the case with emotional intelligence tests, there is often a chasm between science and practice. I-O psychologists are working to fill that chasm with data.

Interestingly, many employers who are permitted to use the polygraph as part of a screening process, such as police departments, are only mildly interested in the scientific and psychological debate. They point out that since the employee or applicant *believes* that the polygraph "works," he or she will make admissions on application blanks and during polygraph examination interviews that would not normally be made. Obviously, this dynamic is exactly the one that concerns the civil liberties community: the intimidating and possibly insidious power of the process, not just its results.

DRUG AND ALCOHOL TESTING

There are several issues to address with respect to drug and alcohol testing in the workplace. The first is how acceptable the practice is to employees and prospective employees. As we will see in Chapter 11 when we consider fairness issues related to assessment, this type of screening is considered more acceptable by the public at large and employees when the job in question involves the possible risk to the public (Murphy, Thornton, & Prue, 1991).

The second issue relates to the legality of this type of screening. The courts have not yet finished deciding which practices impinge too greatly on an individual's right to privacy. Courts have upheld the right of railroads to test for the presence of drugs following an accident. In addition, it has been judged acceptable to test for drugs when screening applicants for drug enforcement posts with the federal government (Cascio, 1998a; 1998b). In many areas of the private sector, drug screening is common for new hires. Harris (2000) reported that as many as two-thirds of large and medium companies screen new hires and as many as one-third of these companies screen current employees for drugs. With respect to alcohol use, current laws permit the random testing of individuals who work for commercial trucking companies, the aviation and rail industries, mass transit, as well as nonrandom testing after an accident. Cascio (1998b) suggested several steps that an employer might take to enhance the defensibility and acceptability of a drug-testing program (see Table 4.12). In addition to the courts, employees and the public in general are very concerned about maintaining procedural justice when implementing a drug-testing program. In 1988 the federal government passed the Drug Free Workplace Act (DFWA) as a more affirmative approach to the problem of drugs in the workplace. As a result of DFWA, all federal contractors with contracts worth more than $25,000 are required to establish a drug-free policy. For nongovernment contractors, the DWFA allows for reduced worker compensation insurance premiums for employers, as well as access to an information network regarding drug testing (Gutman, 2000).

Extensive literature exists on the effects of alcohol and drugs on various aspects of physical and mental performance. As examples, it is well known that alcohol will slow reaction time, impair reasoning ability, induce drowsiness and clumsiness, and have a generally dulling effect on various senses. The same is true with various drugs, both illegally

TABLE 4.12	Ways to Enhance the Defensibility of a Drug Testing Program

To avoid legal challenge, companies should consider instituting the following commonsense procedures:

1. Inform all employees and job applicants, in writing, of the company's policy regarding drug use.

2. Include the policy, and the possibility of testing, in all employment contracts.

3. Present the program in a medical and safety context—that is, state that drug screening will help improve the health of employees and will also help ensure a safer workplace.

4. Check the testing laboratory's experience, its analytical methods, and the way it protects the security and identity of each sample.

5. If drug testing will be used with employees as well as job applicants, tell employees in advance that it will be a routine part of their employment.

6. If drug testing is done, it should be uniform—that is, it should apply to managers as well as nonmanagers.

SOURCE: Adapted from Cascio (1998b).

obtained and prescribed. Thus, from the performance perspective it seems clear that such substances will lead to lowered performance in a wide range of physical and mental tasks. But that is a "here and now" issue. Few would disagree that if an individual can be classified as intoxicated due to alcohol or drugs, he or she should not be permitted to engage in any work activity that might bring harm to the person, a co-worker, or the public. But the more intriguing question is whether a past history of use predicts future behavior. There is some evidence that drug use affects absenteeism and involuntary turnover. Normand, Salyards, and Mahoney (1990) reported that 5,500 applicants for postal positions were given drug tests. After 15 months, the new employees who had tested positive for drugs at the time of hire had an absenteeism rate almost 60 percent higher than those who had tested negative. In addition, almost 50 percent more of employees who had tested positive were fired during the 15 months than those who had tested negative (many for excessive absenteeism). Harris and Heft (1993) reviewed the drug-testing programs of large American companies and concluded that the outcomes most commonly predicted were absenteeism and involuntary terminations.

The problem of drugs or alcohol at the workplace must be kept in perspective. Most estimates suggest that fewer than 4 percent of applicants, and only 2 percent of incumbents, will test positive for drugs. Nevertheless, if one of those employees happens to be an airline pilot, the drug use poses a serious public safety problem. At 10:30 A.M. on July 1, 2002, both the pilot and the copilot of an America West flight were stopped before they were able to take off in a jet bound for Phoenix from Miami with 124 passengers on board. Each had a blood alcohol level that indicated impairment.

Given these concerns, why not simply test all employees all the time? Isn't that the safest policy? Perhaps it would be, if we could have perfect confidence in the accuracy of those tests. But large numbers of false positive indications (a person who fails a drug screen urinalysis who then tests negative using a different and more sophisticated protocol) have undermined confidence in the results of most mass administered drug-screening programs. As Harris (2000) suggested, these false positives come from sloppy procedures, inaccurate tests, or both. There are alternative types of drug tests, particularly those called immunoassay tests, that are considerably more reliable (Harris, 2000), but they are often prohibitively expensive for the employer. Unfortunately, the tests and testing procedures are outside the expertise of the I-O psychologist. What we can do is identify the performance areas most likely to be affected by the use of drugs or alcohol, and suggest occupations or jobs where such testing makes most sense.

INTEGRITY TESTING

Until recently, integrity testing meant honesty testing. Employers have always been concerned with dishonest employees. We will consider counterproductive employee behavior in depth in Chapters 5 and 10, but for now, note that employee theft can make the difference between profitability and failure for an organization. Employers are often vigorous in investigating incidents of employee dishonesty after the fact. Money or product is disappearing—who is taking it? But honesty and integrity tests were developed to *predict* who might act dishonestly in the future rather than who is actually responsible for a counterproductive act.

Although honesty and integrity tests have been around for more than 50 years (Ash, 1976), there has been more enthusiasm for them in the past 15 to 20 years for several reasons. The first reason is economic: More and more employers are concerned about the high cost of dishonest employees, and integrity tests are relatively inexpensive. In addition, from the I-O perspective various meta-analyses demonstrated the predictive power of such tests. Finally, the polygraph legislation passed in 1988 radically reduced the use of the polygraph for preemployment honesty screening, making paper and pencil tests more attractive, particularly those shown to be valid for predicting important work behaviors such as

TABLE 4.13	Examples of Overt and Covert Integrity Test Items

Overt Items

There is nothing wrong with telling a lie if no one suffers any harm (True or False?)

How often have you arrived at work under the influence of alcohol?

Do your friends ever steal from their employers?

Covert or Personality-based Items

Do you like taking risks?

Would your friends describe you as impulsive?

Would you consider challenging an authority figure?

theft and absence. In jobs where polygraphs are permitted, integrity tests are considerably cheaper than extensive background checks or polygraph tests.

There are two different types of integrity tests: overt and personality based. The **overt integrity test** asks questions directly about past honesty behavior (stealing, etc.) as well as attitudes toward various behaviors such as employee theft. The **personality based integrity test** measures honesty and integrity with less direct questions dealing with broader constructs such as conscientiousness, reliability, and social responsibility and awareness. Examples of both types of items are presented in Table 4.13.

There have been many extensive and high-quality reviews of integrity test research, and these reviews have concluded that those who score poorly will be poorer employees for any number of different reasons. They may be more likely to lie or steal, be absent, or engage in other counterproductive behaviors (Murphy & Davidshofer, 2001; Ones, Viswesvaran, & Schmidt, 1993; Sackett & Decker, 1979; Sackett & Harris, 1984; Sackett & Wanek, 1996). In the abstract, this sounds promising, but in the concrete, there are some problems with integrity tests. Murphy and Davidshofer (2001) summarized these concerns as follows:

1. It is difficult to know exactly what any given test of integrity measures. For example, taking a long lunch hour may be considered an indication of "theft" (of time) on one test and not even mentioned in another test.

2. Unlike ability or even personality tests, applicants are seldom informed of their scores or the results of an integrity test. This is particularly disturbing if a candidate has been rejected for a position and can't find out why. Nor are applicants warned of the risks and consequences of even taking the test in the first place, raising an ethical issue of informed consent. Of course, any applicant who refused to take the test would be considered to have withdrawn his or her application for employment, so it is not clear what the practical value of informing applicants might be.

3. Often, integrity test scores are reported in a pass–fail or, more commonly, a recommended–not recommended format. As we will see in Chapter 7, the setting of pass–fail scores is very technical, and it is not clear that the test publishers take these technical issues into account. That raises the possibility of false negatives as we discussed with the polygraph—the possibility that an individual would be erroneously rejected as a "risk."

Cascio (1998b) made an additional point about integrity as a concept. Many employers and test publishers treat honesty as a trait, much like intelligence. But it is much easier for a person to "go straight," by behaving more honestly and morally, than it is for a person with lower general mental ability to "go smart." Yet an honesty or integrity score is treated like a cognitive ability score. If a person gives honest answers to overt questions about past

OVERT INTEGRITY TEST

Asks questions directly about past honesty behavior (stealing, etc.) as well as attitudes toward various behaviors such as employee theft.

PERSONALITY BASED INTEGRITY TEST

Test that infers honesty and integrity from questions dealing with broad constructs such as conscientiousness, reliability, and social responsibility and awareness.

indiscretions, he or she may be rejected even though he or she may have reformed. Ironically, the only way for the reformed individual to pass the test might be to lie!

You will recall that we discussed the concept of integrity in the section on personality in Chapter 3. The discussion was in the context of the "bandwidth" debate concerning the FFM of personality. Some argue for a "narrow" bandwidth (e.g., separate scores for separate dimensions such as conscientiousness or emotional stability), and others argue for a wider bandwidth which would involve developing a complex test to assess a complex trait. Integrity is a perfect example of this debate. One might approach the measurement of integrity by using a "broad bandwidth instrument" such as an integrity test, or inferring integrity from the combination of scores on conscientiousness, agreeableness, and emotional stability. Although this debate is largely theoretical, it also has practical implications. If an employer wants to assess the integrity of an applicant, what is the best way to do so? On the one hand, there is the ease of administration of an instrument to get right at integrity—the dedicated integrity test—rather than combining scores from three different dimensions of a broader personality test, such as the NEO-PI. On the other hand, much more is known about the meaning of any of the FFM dimensions than the typical score on an integrity test. In addition, the information gathered using a traditional FFM instrument can be used for predicting many behaviors beyond honesty. Thus, for the time being we see more practical advantages to using the "narrow bandwidth" approach of combining FFM scores than the broad bandwidth approach of using an integrity test.

COMPUTER-BASED ASSESSMENT

Virtually every commercial test available in paper form is also available on the computer. Many are also available on the Internet, allowing for direct transmission and scoring of the tests. This is a win–win situation for the employer and the applicant. It reduces time and effort for the applicant, and it permits the employer to process large amounts of data in very sophisticated ways in order to make selection decisions. It also cuts down on the time it takes to inform applicants of their status in the hiring sequence.

The variety of tests that can be presented on a computer platform is almost without limits. One might test for cognitive ability, personality, interests, and even psychomotor abilities. In addition, it is possible to present work samples, situational judgment tests, and very sophisticated and complex interactive cognitive tasks. The use of Web cameras also permits some limited interpersonal testing, although there are still some elements of one-on-one interaction that are impossible to simulate by means of the computer.

The topic of Web-based interaction brings up an often asked question regarding computer-based test presentation: Are we measuring the same thing as we are with a paper and pencil test or interview? The answer is, yes and no. For most measures of general mental ability and specific cognitive abilities, the answer is yes, unless the tests are speed tests rather than power tests. Because it requires the test taker to be dexterous with the mouse or keyboard, speed adds a different dimension to the assessment (Mazzeo & Harvey, 1988; Mead & Drasgow, 1993). In addition, the computer can be used to assess attributes that could never have been assessed by paper and pencil tests, such as reaction time and spatial and perceptual abilities (Murphy & Davidshofer, 2001). The following are some examples:

- Schmitt, Gilliland, Landis, and Devine (1993) described a computer-based system for assessing applicants for secretarial positions.
- We saw earlier that Ackerman and Cianciolo (1999, 2002) developed computer-based exercises for air traffic control positions.
- Olson-Buchanan, Drasgow, Moberg, Mead, Keenan, and Donovan (1998) developed a video-interactive test for assessing conflict resolution skills.
- Baron and Chaudry (1997) developed a computer-based interactive device for assessing customer relations skills.

There are many excellent reviews of the promise of computer based testing, as well as its potential problems (Drasgow & Olson-Buchanan, 1999; McBride, 1998; Olson-Buchanan, 2001). At this point in development, the elegance and excitement of this medium is tempered by its costs. Well-developed and engaging computer (and particularly video) assessment exercises are extremely expensive, which means that they are out of the reach to the small- to middle-sized organization. For large organizations that screen many applicants (e.g., federal and state agencies, large muncipal and state police and fire departments, large manufacturing organizations), such a testing format can be extremely powerful and cost effective because, among other advantages, it does not require applicants to actually come to a central location for assessment. This is an exciting area for psychological assessment and substantially more data should be available in the next few years.

Computer Adaptive Testing

An interesting innovation in computer testing is a "tailored" procedure known as **Computer Adaptive Testing (CAT)** (Anastasi, 1982; Murphy & Davidshofer, 2001). In this procedure, a candidate does not need to answer every item on a test for adequate assessment. By presenting a candidate with a few items (e.g., 10) that cover the range of difficulty of the test, it is possible to identify a candidate's approximate level of ability and then ask only questions that will further refine the applicant's position within that category. The preliminary test, which every candidate takes, is called a **routing test.** The subsequent tests are the actual measurement tests (see Figure 4.11).

The potential advantages of CAT are obvious. Testing can be done more quickly since each candidate takes fewer items than would appear on a paper and pencil test. There are some additional, less obvious, advantages (Anastasi, 1982). This type of test produces scores with equal or higher validity and reliability than conventional tests. Finally, CAT provides much finer discrimination among applicants at the high and low ends of the ability scale. The American Council on Education has published an informative set of guidelines related to the use of CAT in educational settings (Green et al., 1995), but these guidelines are also useful for industrial application. Because of the technical and empirical challenges of CAT, it is still out of the reach of most employers, but the armed services are currently using and refining such systems for recruit screening on the ASVAB (Murphy & Davidshofer, 2001). A CAT-based examination you may take if you consider pursuing a graduate career in I-O psychology is the Graduate Record Examination (GRE).

COMPUTER ADAPTIVE TESTING (CAT)

Presents a test taker with a few items that cover the range of difficulty of the test, identifies a test taker's approximate level of ability, and then asks only questions to further refine the test taker's position within that ability level.

ROUTING TEST

Preliminary test used in computer adaptive testing that identifies a test taker's approximate level of ability before providing additional questions to refine the test taker's position within that ability level.

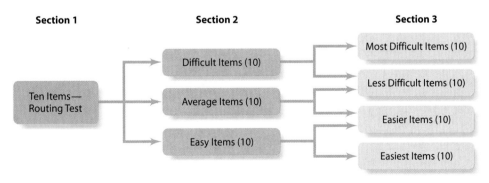

Section 1　　**Section 2**　　**Section 3**

Ten Items— Routing Test

Difficult Items (10)

Average Items (10)

Easy Items (10)

Most Difficult Items (10)

Less Difficult Items (10)

Easier Items (10)

Easiest Items (10)

FIGURE 4.11   **The Routing Test in Computer Adaptive Testing**
In computer adaptive testing, test items are arranged in terms of their difficulty. Every candidate takes the same routing test, then one test from Section 2 and one from Section 3, based on his or her performance on the earlier section test.
SOURCE: Murphy & Davidshofer (2001).

MODULE 4.4 SUMMARY

- An important issue in assessment is not *which* tool to use, but what *combination* of tools to use for the greatest predictive ability at the lowest cost. I-O psychologists have examined the predictive validity of particular combinations to demonstrate the added value of combining two or more assessment devices.

- Controversial assessment practices include graphology, the polygraph, drug and alcohol testing, and integrity testing. These assessment practices are evaluated by the same criteria as other tests: reliability and validity.

- Virtually every commercial test available in paper form is also available on the computer. The variety of tests that can be presented on a computer platform is almost without limits. At this point, however the elegance and excitement of the computer-based medium is tempered by this costs: Well-developed and engaging computer (and particularly video) assessment exercises are extremely expensive.

KEY TERMS

incremental validity

graphology

polygraph

overt integrity test

personality based integrity test

Computer Adaptive Testing (CAT)

routing test

CRITICAL THINKING EXERCISES

4.7 A consultant claims that a new interview protocol will show greater validity than a test of intelligence for hiring purposes. How would you challenge those claims?

4.8 Could an assessment of "sales skills" be developed for Internet or computer presentation? Would any additional face-to-face assessment be necessary? What information could face-to-face assessment provide that could not be provided by computer assessment?

UNDERSTANDING PERFORMANCE

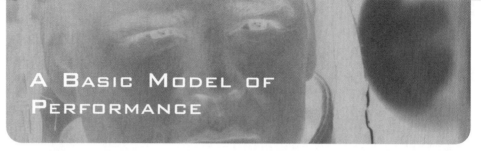

A BASIC MODEL OF PERFORMANCE

I-O psychologists have devoted a great deal of their research and practice to understanding and improving the performance of workers. All of us who have participated in a work group (or a classroom learning experience) have observed differences in the performance of group members. Some perform at a very high level while others perform a good deal lower. Research has shown that the ratio of the productivity of the highest performer to the lowest performer in jobs of low difficulty ranges from 2:1 to 4:1, while in jobs of high difficulty, this ratio can be as much as 10:1 (Campbell, Gasser, & Oswald, 1996). This represents a striking degree of variation, variation that is crucial to an employer struggling to survive in a competitive environment. Imagine having an employee who resolves an average of 5 customer complaints a day, compared to one who handles 15. Or a sales representative who closes on 5 contracts a month versus one who brings in 50. From this it is clear why I-O psychologists and employers are vitally interested in employee performance. But what do we mean when we say "performance"?

In earlier chapters this book presented fairly explicit descriptions of some common psychological variables. We have seen personality decomposed into various factors (e.g., Digman, 1990; Hough, 1992), intelligence parsed into levels or layers of cognitive abilities (e.g., Carroll, 1993), and examined a six-factor model of vocational interest (Holland's RIASEC model). We have presented evidence that these factors help us predict worker success or job performance. But when it comes to performance, we have not yet focused on the question of the *type* of performance being predicted.

CAMPBELL'S MODEL OF JOB PERFORMANCE

Remember that psychology deals with behavior. In the case of I-O psychology, that means the behavior of workers, or worker performance. Consider the following variables that I-O psychologists have used as measures of performance (Campbell, McCloy, Oppler, & Sager, 1993):

Time to complete a training course.

Number of pieces produced.

Total days absent.

Total value of sales.

Promotion rate within an organization.

An important question that is often overlooked is, to what extent does an individual worker have any of these measures of performance under his or her control? Let's examine each of the above performance measures from that standpoint.

- Time to complete a training course might be constrained by how much time the worker can be away from the workplace.
- Number of pieces produced is affected by the technology and equipment used by that worker.
- Total days absent does not distinguish between excused and unexcused, sick days, personal days, or vacation days.
- Total value of sales will be affected by discounts or territory or marketing promotions, or by the value of the products the employee is assigned to sell.
- Promotion rate within an organization will be affected by the turnover rate in that organization.

Thus, we can see that in each of these cases, the "performance" measure was not really (or at least not exclusively) an individual behavior.

A number of I-O psychologists (Campbell, 1990a, 1990b, 1999; Campbell et al., 1997; Campbell et al., 1993; McCloy, Campbell, & Cudeck, 1994) have argued persuasively that I-O psychology has spent a great deal of time describing the various worker attributes that "cause" or are related to performance, but little time describing actual performance at the individual worker level. Your authors agree. Campbell and his colleagues have proposed a model of work performance that provides a more detailed view of performance, and one that helps to separate the factors that are directly under the worker's control from those that aren't. Before presenting his model, some definitions are necessary (Campbell et al., 1993).

Performance is behavior. In its ideal form, it is something that people actually do and can be observed. In many jobs, of course, the "behavior" is thinking, planning, or problem solving and cannot be actually observed; instead, it can only described with the help of the individual worker. In the work setting, performance includes only those actions or behaviors that are relevant to the organization's goals and can be measured in terms of each individual's proficiency. Performance is what the organization hires an employee to do and to do well. Performance is *not* the consequence or result of action; it is the action itself.

As this 1920s photo indicates, work has changed considerably since the introduction of the factory system.

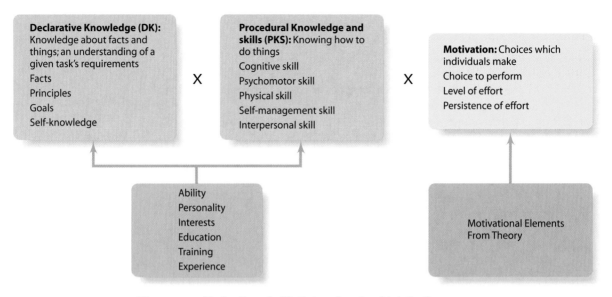

FIGURE 5.1 Campbell's Determinants of Job Performance SOURCE: Based on Campbell, McCloy, Oppler, & Sager (1993).

Effectiveness is the evaluation of the results of performance. The variation in a measure of effectiveness is often controlled by factors beyond the actions of an individual, as is evident from the example of total value of sales.

Productivity is the ratio of effectiveness (output) to the cost of achieving that level of effectiveness (input) (Mahoney, 1988). A profit margin for a unit or company is an index of productivity. For in-depth discussions of the relationship between performance and productivity, see Campbell and Campbell (1988) and Pritchard (1992).

Based on extensive research with army enlisted personnel, Campbell developed a hierarchical model of job performance (Campbell, 1990a; Campbell, McHenry, & Wise, 1990; Campbell & Zook, 1990). He postulated three and only three direct determinants of job performance: **declarative knowledge (DK), procedural knowledge and skill (PKS),** and **motivation (M)** (see Figure 5.1). By determinants, he means the basic building blocks or causes of performance.

Campbell's model also proposes that many of the variables we have examined in earlier chapters and will examine in later chapters (ability, personality, interest, training and experience, motivators) have an *indirect* effect on performance. These variables can affect performance only by changing the level of DK, PKS, or M. For example, increased training or experience will affect performance by increasing DK or PKS; incentives for performance will affect performance by increasing M (inducing the person to perform at a higher level, or to perform for a longer period of time).

There is one other important aspect to Campbell's model: actual performance components. DK, PKS, and M are **determinants of performance,** but they are not behaviors (i.e., they are not performance itself). Campbell's research identified at least eight basic performance components (Table 5.1), some or all of which can be found in every job. When we combine the eight performance components with the three direct determinants of performance and the various indirect determinants of performance, we get an expanded model such as the one depicted in Figure 5.2. Although the model specifies eight distinct **performance components,** not all components will appear in all jobs. Nevertheless, the model allows performance in any job to be parsed into all or some subsets of these components. Campbell asserted that three of the performance components—core task proficiency,

TABLE 5.1	Campbell's Eight Performance Components

Performance components and definitions

Job-specific task proficiency: An individual's capacity to perform the core substantive or technical tasks central to the job.

Non-job-specific task proficiency: An individual's capacity to perform tasks or execute performance behaviors that are not specific to their particular jobs.

Written and oral communication task proficiency: An individual's proficiency in writing and speaking, independent of the correctness of the subject matter.

Demonstrating effort: The consistency of an individual's effort; the frequency with which people will expend extra effort when required; the willingness to keep working under adverse conditions.

Maintaining personal discipline: The extent to which an individual avoids negative behavior such as excessive absenteeism, alcohol or substance abuse, and law or rules infractions.

Facilitating peer and team performance: The extent to which an individual supports peers, helps peers with problems, helps to keep a work group goal directed, and acts as a role model for peers and the work group.

Supervision/leadership: Proficiency at influencing the performance of subordinates through face-to-face interpersonal interaction and influence.

Management/administration: Behavior directed at articulating for the unit, organizing people and resources, monitoring progress, helping to solve problems that might prevent goal accomplishment, controlling expenses, obtaining additional resources, and dealing with other units.

SOURCE: Based on Campbell, McCloy, Oppler, & Sager (1993).

demonstrated effort, and maintenance of personal discipline—are essential at some level for *every* job.

Campbell's expanded model has a great deal of intuitive appeal as well as research support (McCloy et al., 1994). It occupies a valuable middle ground between a view of performance as some unitary entity or a single broad factor—a view that contradicts what we can observe at work every day—and an equally ineffectual view that says every job is different and there can be no general understanding of job performance beyond the particular job being considered. It also helps us as I-O psychologists to keep our psychological "eye on the ball"; to concentrate our attention on aspects of work behavior that are under the direct control of the worker.

PERFORMANCE COMPONENTS

May appear in different jobs and result from the determinants of performance; John Campbell and colleagues identified 8 performance components, some or all of which can be found in every job.

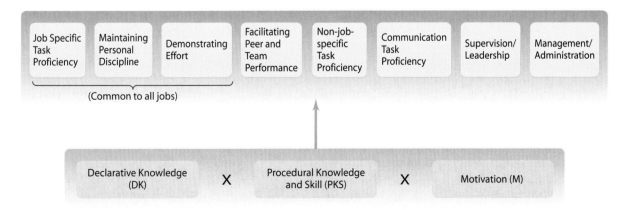

FIGURE 5.2 **The Full Campbell Model** SOURCE: Based on Campbell, McCloy, Oppler, & Sager (1993).

FIGURE 5.3

**Criterion
Contamination,
Deficiency, and
Relevance**

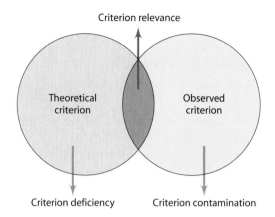

CRITERION DEFICIENCY AND CONTAMINATION

**CRITERION
DEFICIENCY**

*Occurs when an actual
criterion is missing
information that is part
of the behavior one is
trying to measure.*

**CRITERION
CONTAMINATION**

*Occurs when an actual
criterion includes
information unrelated
to the behavior one is
trying to measure.*

**ULTIMATE
CRITERION**

*Ideal measure of all of
the relevant aspects of
job performance.*

**ACTUAL
CRITERION**

*Actual measure of job
performance obtained.*

Campbell's approach to defining job performance introduces two concepts that are well established in I-O psychology: **criterion deficiency** and **criterion contamination.** As you will recognize from our treatment of validity in Chapter 2, in the validity context, performance would be referred to as a criterion. In an ideal world, we would be able to measure all relevant aspects of job performance perfectly. A collective measure of all of these aspects would be called the **ultimate criterion,** but since we can never reliably measure all aspects of performance, we settle for an **actual criterion.**

A classic validity study might test cognitive ability (the predictor) by correlating it with a measure of job performance (the actual criterion) to see if higher scores on the test are associated with higher levels of performance. The differences between the ultimate criterion and the actual criterion represent imperfections in measurement—contamination and deficiency. A contaminated actual criterion includes information unrelated to the behavior we are trying to measure. For example, if a production figure for an individual worker is affected by the technology or the condition of the particular machine that worker is using, then we would consider that production figure (i.e., criterion) contaminated. Similarly, if we consider the performance of a police officer to be defined exclusively by the number of criminals apprehended, ignoring many other important aspects of the police officer's job, then that statistic would be considered a deficient criterion. The relationships between criterion deficiency, criterion contamination, and criterion relevance are graphically presented in Figure 5.3.

Campbell's model of performance, by focusing on worker behaviors and the extent to which the worker has complete control over outcomes, protects against criterion contamination. Similarly, by providing eight of the most important and unique aspects of performance in most jobs, it also protects against criterion deficiency. It is important to keep in mind that probably not a single job has only *one* behavior that defines successful performance. Just as the predictor side of the basic work prediction equation is complex, requiring a consideration of many different combinations of human attributes, so is the criterion side, requiring a consideration of many different aspects of performance. Workers call on many attributes to perform their jobs, and each of these human attributes (predictors) is associated with certain aspects of performance.

MODULE 5.1 SUMMARY

- I-O psychologists have devoted a great deal of their research and practice to understanding and improving the performance of workers. They have also spent a great deal of time describing the various worker attributes that "cause" or are related to performance, but little time describing actual performance at the level of the individual worker.

- Campbell's performance model occupies a valuable middle ground between an unrealistic view of performance as a single broad factor and an equally ineffectual view that there can be no general understanding of job performance beyond the particular job being considered because every job is different. Campbell's model also helps I-O psychologists to concentrate on aspects of work behavior that are under the direct control of the worker.

- In nearly all jobs, performance is multidimensional; that is, just as the predictor side of the basic work prediction equation requires a consideration of many different combinations of human attributes, the criterion side requires a consideration of many different aspects of performance. Workers call on many attributes to perform their jobs, and each of these human attributes is associated with unique aspects of performance.

KEY TERMS

performance
effectiveness
productivity
determinants of performance
declarative knowledge (DK)

procedural knowledge and
  skills (PKS)
motivation (M)
performance components
criterion deficiency

criterion contamination
ultimate criterion
actual criterion

CRITICAL THINKING EXERCISES

5.1 A software company has decided to reward employees for performance by establishing a piece rate incentive. For the "help desk operator," they have proposed paying each operator for the number of problems solved successfully. They will monitor calls to identify successful resolutions and they will also ask the callers if they were satisfied with the help desk operator. Name a "criterion deficiency" and a "criterion contamination" problem with this plan.

5.2 Campbell's model of performance (see Figure 5.1) distinguishes between declarative knowledge (DK) and procedural knowledge and skills (PKS). Consider the following knowledges and classify them as predominantly declarative or predominantly procedural.

> The most direct driving route from Denver to Salt Lake City.
>
> The most effective way to get your car to a gas station when the fuel gauge is reading empty.
>
> Rebooting your computer.
>
> Extent of technical terms/language to use with a customer.
>
> Persuading your supervisor to allow you to take a personal day of vacation.

EXTENSIONS OF THE BASIC PERFORMANCE MODEL

TASK PERFORMANCE VERSUS CONTEXTUAL PERFORMANCE

ORGANIZATIONAL CITIZENSHIP BEHAVIOR (OCB)

Behavior that goes beyond what is expected.

ALTRUISM

Helpful behaviors directed toward individuals or groups within the organization, such as offering to help a co-worker who is up against a deadline.

GENERALIZED COMPLIANCE

Behavior that is helpful to the broader organization, such as upholding company rules.

CONTEXTUAL PERFORMANCE

Activities not typically part of job descriptions but support the organizational, social, and psychological environment in which the job tasks are performed; similar to organizational citizenship behavior.

TASK PERFORMANCE

Proficiency with which job incumbents perform activities that are formally recognized as a part of their job.

When performance is discussed, it is usually in the context of one or more tasks that define a job. These tasks can be found in job descriptions, work orders, and so forth. But there is more to work life than just assigned tasks. You have probably observed that, when it comes to job performance, there are two kinds of workers. The first does exactly what they are assigned, and no more. They are reluctant to put themselves out for co-workers or to expend any extra effort on behalf of the organization. The second type of worker is the exact opposite. These workers go out of their way to make life easier for their co-workers and supervisor. They can always be counted on to stay a little later or report a little earlier than expected. The term "expected" is the important concept here. It is not that the first type of employee is doing anything wrong. Why should you do anything beyond what you are paid for? But we can observe that some people do work more than what they are paid for.

A number of years ago, Organ and his colleagues (Smith, Organ, & Near, 1983) labeled this type of behavior—going beyond what is expected—**organizational citizenship behavior (OCB)** and developed questionnaires to assess that behavior in workers. The questionnaires seem to assess two separate aspects of OCB, one labeled **altruism**—helpful behaviors directed toward individuals or groups within the organization, such as offering to help a co-worker who is up against a deadline—and **generalized compliance**—behavior that is helpful to the broader organization, such as upholding company rules (Organ & Ryan, 1995).

Borman and Motowidlo (1993) have refined the concept of OCB further and labeled these extra-role behaviors **"contextual performance,"** which they contrast with **task performance.** Task performance is defined as "the proficiency with which job incumbents perform activities that are formally recognized as a part of their job" (p. 73). Contextual performance, in contrast, is more informal and can be characterized as follows:

- Supports the organizational, social, and psychological environment in which the job tasks are performed.

- Unlike task requirements, which vary from job to job, contextual performance is common to most jobs.

- Although differences among individuals in task performance tend to be tied to abilities and knowledge, differences in contextual performance are more clearly tied to personality.

- Task activities are part of a job description, contextual activities are not.

As a result of their own earlier research (Borman, Motowidlo, & Hanser, 1983; Brief & Motowidlo, 1986) as well as the research of others (Katz & Kahn, 1978; Smith et al., 1983;

Organ, 1988), Borman and Motowidlo (1993) identified five specific aspects of contextual performance:

1. Persisting with enthusiasm and extra effort as necessary to complete your own task activities successfully.
2. Volunteering to carry out task activities that are not formally part of your own job.
3. Helping and cooperating with others.
4. Following organizational rules and procedures.
5. Endorsing, supporting, and defending organizational objectives.

The first three of these dimensions correspond to the altruism aspect of OCB and the last two correspond to what the OCB model calls general compliance.

Peterson et al. (1990) demonstrated that while measures of cognitive ability are most closely associated with task performance, measures of personality do a better job of predicting contextual performance. Motowidlo, Borman, and Schmit (1997) provided a theoretical explanation of the personal attributes that appear to contribute to contextual and task performance. They proposed that technical task performance is determined by cognitive ability, predominantly through the effect of cognitive ability on knowledge, skills, and habits. Cognitive ability becomes particularly important in technically complex tasks and tasks requiring problem solving and reasoning. In contrast, contextual performance is best predicted by personality dimensions, particularly conscientiousness, because individuals high in conscientiousness are much more likely to persist with extra effort in completing their work and following organizational rules and procedures. They also proposed that learning experiences will influence both task and contextual performance. Van Scotter, Motowidlo, and Cross (2000) have demonstrated that both contextual performance and task performance contribute independently to career success, and Motowidlo and Van Scotter (1994) have shown that contextual performance and task performance contribute independently to ratings of overall performance. This latter point is particularly interesting because it shows that evaluations are influenced not only by what you are *assigned* to do, but also by what you *volunteer* to do.

Motowidlo et al. (1997) made a strong case for the increasing importance of contextual performance in today's workplace, citing the following factors:

1. Global competition will require more effort from employees.
2. Teams are more common now than solitary work.
3. Downsizing requires adaptability and extra effort.
4. Customer service is increasingly important.

The concept of contextual performance fits in nicely with Campbell's model, which we considered earlier in this chapter (Campbell et al., 1996). Figure 5.4 shows the relationship between the five contextual performance factors and Campbell's eight performance components. You will remember from Chapter 3 that the Big Five factor of conscientiousness could be broken down further into achievement and dependability (Hough, 1992). We see a similar structure here. Campbell's "demonstration of effort" component can be seen as having at least two distinct facets: "persisting" and "volunteering." Campbell's model and the theory of contextual performance actually complement each other. Note that all of the dimensions of contextual performance meet the standards that Campbell sets for what should be considered "performance"; they are observable actions and they are under the control of the individual. It seems clear both from research as well as from our own experience in jobs that contextual performance is an important part of success at any job.

FIGURE 5.4

Matrix with Contextual Factors and Campbell's Performance Components

SOURCE: Based on Campbell, Gasser, & Oswald (1996).

(Campbell Factors)	(Contextual factors)				
	Persisting	**Volunteering**	**Helping**	**Following Rules**	**Supporting**
Job specific task proficiency					
Non-job-specific task proficiency					
Communication task proficiency					
Demonstrating effort	XX	XX			
Maintaining personal discipline				XX	
Facilitating team and peer performance			XX		
Supervision/ leadership					XX
Management/ administration					XX

TYPES OF PERFORMANCE MEASURES

The I-O literature commonly distinguishes among different types of performance indicators. Three different categories have been suggested: objective measures, judgmental measures, and personnel measures (Guion, 1965).

Objective performance measures are usually a "count of the results of work" (Guion, 1965). This might mean the number of strokes it took a professional golfer to complete a round in the Masters tournament in Augusta, Georgia. It could also be the number of cases heard by a municipal judge, or the number of claims processed by an insurance claims adjuster.

Judgmental measures are evaluations made of the effectiveness of an individual's work behavior. The judgments are most often made by supervisors in the context of a yearly performance evaluation. Campbell et al. (1993) referred to evaluations as "expert" judgments. The supervisor is asked to consider the subordinate's performance on a number of discrete aspects of performance, and to assign a rating that represents the supervisor's assessment of that subordinate on each performance aspect. We will consider the process and elements of performance evaluation in greater detail in the following chapter.

Employers typically keep a record of **personnel measures** in a personnel folder; these include such data as absences, accidents, tardiness, rate of advancement (in salary or job title), disciplinary actions, and commendations or notes of meritorious behavior. These measures usually record an event rather than an outcome (e.g., production measure) or an evaluation (e.g., a performance rating).

In light of Campbell's model, we have reason to be concerned with most objective measures as well as many of the personnel measures. Many would fail as indicators of performance because they are not under the complete control of the individual (e.g., total dollars in sales) or are not actual behaviors (e.g., promotional history). To return to Campbell's point, as I-O psychologists, we should focus on individually controlled behavior when we

OBJECTIVE PERFORMANCE MEASURE

Usually a quantitative count of the results of work such as sales volume, complaint letters, and output.

JUDGMENTAL MEASURE

Evaluation made of the effectiveness of an individual's work behavior; judgment most often made by supervisors in the context of a performance evaluation.

PERSONNEL MEASURE

Measure typically kept in a personnel file including absences, accidents, tardiness, rate of advancement, disciplinary actions, and commendations of meritorious behavior.

examine performance (Campbell et al., 1993). In Campbell's view, the type of measure most likely to yield a reasonable estimate of individual behavior is the judgmental measure (e.g., performance rating) that permits the evaluator to account for influences out of the control of the individual worker. For example, if an employee is working a difficult sales territory, the manager is aware of that handicap and can adjust the judgment accordingly. If the manager were required to use an "objective" measure of sales success, the employee would be at a considerable disadvantage. It is not so much that objective measures are to be avoided or that ratings are to be preferred. They each have their advantages and disadvantages, as we will see in the next chapter. But we should be clear that objective measures are not performance from the psychological perspective—they are the results of performance.

Adaptive Performance

Campbell (1999) acknowledged that at least one performance component is not included in his model. That is an area known as **adaptive performance** (Pulakos, Arad, Donovan, & Plamondon, 2000). The changing nature of work would seem to require workers who are flexible and able to adapt to changing circumstances. Pulakos et al. (2000) cited the following circumstances of today's workplace that favor this adaptability:

ADAPTIVE
PERFORMANCE

Performance component that includes flexibility and the ability to adapt to changing circumstances.

- Changing technologies alter work tasks.
- Mergers, downsizing, and corporate restructuring require employees to learn new skills.
- Globalization requires individuals to work in different cultures.

Pulakos et al. (2000) proposed that adaptive performance is a valid performance component and that it can be further divided into eight types of adaptive behavior. As Table 5.2 shows, each aspect of adaptability requires flexibility, but in a different way. "Cultural adaptability" involves an appreciation of differences in values, customs and cultures, while "emergency or crisis situation" adaptability requires quick response, analysis, decision making, and action.

Pulakos et al. (2000) tested this taxonomy on a wide variety of jobs and the results provided support for their propositions. Consider the data excerpted from the results

Globalization emphasizes the importance of adaptive performance, as it requires individuals to work in different cultures.

TABLE 5.2	Eight Adaptive Performance Areas and Definitions

Handling emergencies or crisis situations: Reacting with appropriate urgency in life-threatening, dangerous, or emergency situations; quick analysis and decision making in emergency situations; maintaining emotional control and objectivity.

Handling work stress: Remaining calm in spite of demanding workload or schedule; managing frustration with constructive solutions instead of blaming others; acting as a calming and settling influence on others.

Solving problems creatively: Uses unique types of problem analysis; generates new and innovative ideas in complex areas; considers a wide range of possibilities; thinks outside of the box.

Dealing with uncertain and unpredictable work situations: Taking effective action without having all the facts or information; easily changes gears, adjust plans, goals, and schedules to match a changing situation; provides focus for self and others when situation is changing rapidly.

Learning work tasks, technologies, and procedures: Enthusiastic about learning new approaches and technologies; keeps knowledge and skill up to date; seeks out and participates in training that will prepare for changes in work demands.

Demonstrating interpersonal adaptability: Flexible and open-minded in dealing with others; considers others' viewpoints and opinions and alters own opinion when appropriate; works well with a wide diversity of people; accepts negative feedback without defensiveness.

Demonstrating cultural adaptability: Seeks to understand the culture of others; adapts easily to other cultures and behavior patterns; shows respect for others' values and customs; understands the implications of own behavior for maintaining positive relationships with other groups, organizations, or cultures.

Demonstrating physically oriented adaptability: Adjusts to challenging physical environments and extremes of temperature, noise, dirt, etc.; pushes self to complete physically demanding tasks; improves physical condition to meet job demands.

SOURCE: Adapted from Pulakos, Arad, Donovan, & Plamondon (2000).

that appear in Table 5.3. The rows represent job families and the columns represent the eight different types of adaptability. Incumbents in each of the jobs represented by the rows were asked to indicate the extent to which their jobs required the various types of adaptive performance. A value of 3.00 or higher means that the incumbents considered that particular aspect of adaptive performance critical for job success. An examination of the figure confirms what one might expect with respect to the unpredictability of certain jobs. Special Forces soldiers, combat noncommissioned officers, and military police experienced the highest need for adaptability. In contrast, equipment repair technicians (Craft A), accountants, and administrators required the least amount of adaptability. It is also informative to look across the occupations at the dimensions of adaptability most commonly required. By far the most important was handling work stress, followed by learning work tasks and technologies and dealing with unpredictable work situations.

Although this research is very new, it appears promising. We conclude from it that adaptive performance can be added to Campbell's performance components, and that occupations will vary not only in the *extent* to which adaptability is required, but also in terms of the *type* of adaptive performance that is most critical.

The Case of Expert Performance

EXPERT PERFORMANCE

Performance exhibited by those who have been practicing for at least 10 years and have spent an average of four hours per day in deliberate practice.

Most of us admire the performance of experts in various settings. We marvel at the intricacy of a world-class pianist or violinist, or the speed and ruthlessness of a master chess player. In our daily lives, we also appreciate **expert performance** when we encounter a software engineer who solves our computer problem in minutes after we have struggled

TABLE 5.3   **Means and Standard Deviations for Different Types of Adaptability Required by Different Jobs**

JOB	n	ADAPTIVE PERFORMANCE DIMENSIONS							
		A	B	C	D	E	F	G	H
Accounting	337	0.77 (1.22)*	2.92 (1.06)	1.63 (1.18)	2.52 (1.09)	1.84 (1.05)	2.12 (1.08)	0.91 (1.04)	0.58 (0.93)
Engineer support	345	0.81 (1.19)	+3.34 (0.85)	1.69 (1.13)	2.85 (1.03)	1.92 (1.06)	2.34 (0.99)	1.19 (1.08)	0.46 (0.74)
Sales/marketing	115	1.65 (1.32)	2.46 (1.15)	1.76 (1.28)	2.67 (1.02)	1.94 (1.05)	1.98 (1.06)	1.06 (1.23)	1.14 (1.11)
Craft A**	331	2.03 (1.42)	2.68 (0.96)	1.88 (1.18)	2.64 (0.98)	1.96 (1.01)	2.13 (1.05)	1.28 (1.16)	2.16 (1.14)
Special Forces	17	2.87 (1.02)	+3.52 (0.81)	+3.35 (0.95)	+3.25 (0.80)	+3.41 (0.76)	2.71 (0.80)	+3.34 (1.46)	2.72 (1.13)
Combat NCO***	99	+3.54 (1.13)	+3.72 (0.72)	+3.26 (0.99)	+3.59 (0.82)	+3.78 (0.78)	2.76 (0.89)	2.40 (1.16)	+3.47 (0.92)
Administrative specialist	22	1.22 (1.41)	2.76 (1.02)	1.91 (1.35)	2.67 (1.00)	2.45 (0.96)	2.03 (0.96)	1.14 (1.02)	2.26 (1.41)
Military police	29	+3.74 (0.77)	+3.65 (0.58)	2.81 (1.05)	+3.53 (1.01)	+3.61 (0.65)	+3.12 (0.79)	2.70 (1.07)	+3.45 (0.88)
Research scientist	13	0.30 (0.69)	+3.81 (0.92)	+3.65 (0.90)	+3.11 (0.71)	+3.45 (0.84)	+3.13 (0.67)	0.71 (0.85)	0.20 (0.28)

Note. A = Handling emergencies or crisis situations; B = handling work stress; C = solving problems creatively; D = dealing with uncertain and unpredictable work situations; E = learning work tasks, technologies, and procedures; F = demonstrating interpersonal adaptability; G = demonstrating cultural adaptability; H = demonstrating physically oriented adaptability;

*Values in parentheses are standard deviations.

**Craft A = higher level installation and repair of equipment.

***NCO = noncommissioned officer.

+indicates type of adaptability important for this job.

Source: Adapted from Pulakos, Arad, Donovan, & Plamondon (2000).

fruitlessly for hours, or the garage mechanic who listens to our car for 30 seconds and is able to diagnose with incredible accuracy a problem deep in the bowels of the engine.

We tend to assume that expertise of this level is a result of an innate ability, a talent bestowed on few mortals and, unfortunately, not on us (Ericsson & Charness, 1994; Ericsson & Lehman, 1996). This common assumption appears to be wrong. It is not that the experts are more intelligent or have faster reactions times. What separates the experts from you and me is depressingly simple: They practice. Of course, you may practice too and still not be at the level of the expert you admire. But the difference is in the *type* of practice and the *duration* of that practice. In virtually any area, including sports, music, chess, science, and work, people have become experts by following a demanding regimen. They have been practicing for at least 10 years, spend an average of four hours a day in practice, and their practice is deliberate (Ericsson & Charness, 1994).

In the world of work, you might wonder why there are not more experts, since many people perform their work duties for at least four hours a day and have been doing the same type of work for 10 years or more. The answer is that their activities do not constitute **deliberate practice.** In many, if not most, organizations, there is an acceptable level of performance and individuals are compensated for that level. There is no reason to become an expert, short of the intrinsic value of knowing you are an expert or the extrinsic value of being recognized by others as an expert. In addition, at work there is little opportunity for deliberate practice. Deliberate practice means "individualized training on tasks selected by a qualified teacher" (Ericsson, Krampe, & Tesch-Romer, 1993). To use a sports example, if you have trouble returning a tennis serve to your backhand, you may have an opportunity to practice that return 10 or 12 times in a set with no feedback other than the flight of the tennis ball. Deliberate practice would be done with a coach who delivers hundreds of serves per hour to your backhand and provides feedback on technique after each serve. How many workers have the luxury of going back over a poorly performed task hundreds of times with the assistance of a personal coach?

The fact is, however, that we will encounter some expert workers in our work lives. Instead of thinking of them as "gifted" (i.e., the fortunate recipients of an innate God-given ability), think of them as dedicated and focused on their areas of expertise. These are individuals who have spent thousands of hours honing their skills over 10 or more years, with at least some form of deliberate practice. Golfer Tiger Woods and tennis player Andre Agassi are often thought of as prodigies since they came to national prominence in their respective sports as adolescents. What we often overlook, however, is that both of these stars began their deliberate practice before the age of four—another piece of evidence that becoming an "overnight" success takes 10 or more years.

Consider what Campbell's performance model has to say about expert performance. Note particularly the importance of the three areas of DK, PKS, and M. The expert performer has increased declarative knowledge as well as procedural knowledge and skill through extensive and deliberate training (one of the precursors to DK and PKS), and has made the decision to persist in performing at high levels of effort. Not everyone has the time, energy, and desire to be a world-class performer at any activity. But whatever one's baseline level of performance is, one can improve upon it by increasing DK, PKS, and M. And these performance determinants can, in turn, be increased with sustained deliberate practice.

CONSTRAINTS ON PERFORMANCE

Above, we have considered the "sunny side" of performance and productivity: leveraging organizational goals through human attributes that lead to high levels of worker performance. But there is a cloudy side to the picture as well. There are constraints to this leveraging process, and they can be collected under the heading **counterproductive employee behavior.** Robinson and Bennett (1995) broke counterproductive behavior into

DELIBERATE PRACTICE

Individualized training on tasks selected by a qualified teacher.

COUNTER-PRODUCTIVE EMPLOYEE BEHAVIOR

Voluntary behavior that violates significant organizational norms and threatens the well-being of the organization, its members, or both.

FIGURE 5.5

Sackett and DeVore's Hierachical Model of Deviance
SOURCE: Based on Sackett & DeVore (2001).

two separate aspects: deviance directed toward the organization, and deviance directed toward other individuals. They defined counterproductive behavior as "voluntary behavior that violates significant organizational norms and in so doing, threatens the well-being of the organization, its members or both" (p. 556). Rather than contributing to the goals of the organization, these actions run directly counter to those goals. Although we deal with counterproductive behavior in detail when we discuss job dissatisfaction in Chapter 10, it is also worthwhile to consider it here so that we can fully understand performance from an organizational perspective. Sackett and DeVore (2001) provided a good description of the concept of counterproductive work behavior. They proposed a hierarchical explanation with a broad factor of counterproductive behavior at the top level, two less broad factors of organizational deviance and interpersonal deviance in the middle level, and individual counterproductive behaviors such as theft, absence, sabotage, and substance abuse at the lowest levels (Figure 5.5). We will consider three common counterproductive behaviors: dishonesty, absenteeism, and sabotage.

Dishonesty   Employee theft is a major issue in many organizations, particularly retail businesses. In 1993 Murphy estimated that annual losses to American corporations as a result of employee theft fell somewhere between $5 and $50 *billion* dollars. Greenberg and Scott (1996) stated that "theft among employees has reached epic proportions" (p. 112). And recorded theft is generally assumed to underestimate actual theft figures. Dishonesty involves more than employee theft of goods. It can also involve theft of time (arriving late, leaving early, taking unnecessary sick days) or dishonest communications with customers, co-workers, or management. Each of these behaviors lowers productivity by raising the cost of production, lowering output, or both. Typical approaches to controlling dishonesty are through the modification of attitudes toward the organization, as we discuss in Chapter 10, or the use of selection batteries that include integrity and/or conscientiousness assessments (Chapter 4). There is some research suggesting that theft, at least in part, may be precipitated by feelings of inequity and perceived violations of principles of justice (Cropanzano, 2001; Greenberg, 1990; Greenberg & Scott, 1996).

Absenteeism   Employers lose money with every employee absence, for an absent employee cannot be a productive employee. Although absence for reasons of illness or injury is, of course, recognized as legitimate, many employers strive to minimize these kinds of absences through stress reduction (Chapter 15) or increases in workplace safety (Chapter 16). The type of absenteeism that most attracts the interest of I-O psychologists, however, is "avoidable" absence; those occasions when an employee decides to stay away from work for reasons other than illness (excluding stress-related absences) or injury. Nicholson

DISHONESTY

Employee theft of goods and theft of time (arriving late, leaving early, taking unnecessary sick days) or dishonest communications with customers, co-workers, or management.

ABSENTEEISM

Type of counterproductive behavior that involves failure of an employee to report for or remain at work as scheduled.

and his colleagues (Chadwick-Jones, Nicholson, & Brown, 1982; Nicholson, Brown, & Chadwick-Jones, 1976) suggested that absenteeism is really a function of an informal agreement between a worker and a supervisor, or a worker's estimate of what is permitted by the organization. In Chapter 10, we will address the issue of absenteeism through the concepts of commitment and job dissatisfaction.

SABOTAGE

Acts that damage, disrupt, or subvert the organization's operations for personal purposes of the saboteur by creating unfavorable publicity, damage to property, destruction of working relationships, or harming of employees or customers.

LORDSTOWN SYNDROME

Act of sabotage named after a General Motors plant plagued with acts of sabotage.

Sabotage   Employee sabotage can be defined as "the intention to damage, disrupt, or subvert the organization's operations for personal purposes of the saboteur by creating unfavorable publicity, damage to property, destruction of working relationships, or harming of employees or customers" (Crino, 1994, p. 312). In the early 1970s, at the height of the microassembly movement in automobile production, line workers were often expected to complete their operation on a moving auto body in 30 seconds or less. As stress and frustration among the workers grew, acts of sabotage increased. Workers intentionally dropped nuts and bolts into the engine, or neglected to anchor parts to the car body appropriately. This became known as the **Lordstown Syndrome,** named after one General Motors plant particularly plagued with these acts of sabotage. Although Chen and Spector (1992) found that high levels of sabotage were associated with low levels of satisfaction, this type of acting out clearly includes other dynamics as well. There are many dissatisfied workers in some work environments, yet few of them resort to sabotage. There is likely to be some combination of personality factors (e.g., extremely low levels of conscientiousness and emotional stability bordering on the pathological) and high levels of dissatisfaction and alienation.

When we think of sabotage, we usually conjure up a picture of an employee engaging in some action that will harm rather than help the organization. But there are occasions when life is not so simple. On January 1, 2003, a Frontier Airlines mechanic working at Denver International Airport was so concerned about the condition of a 737 jet about to take off for Dallas that he tossed a wheel chock into one of the engines to prevent the pilot from leaving the gate area and departing (Leib, Morgan, & Hughes, 2003). The mechanic had brought his concern to the attention of his supervisor, who nonetheless had decided that the plane was safe to depart, so the mechanic took matters into his own hands. The mechanic was suspended from his job and was charged with a federal crime—destruction of an aircraft—which could result in a jail sentence of up to 20 years plus a $250,000 fine. Was this an act of sabotage, or an instance of contextual behavior driven by conscientiousness?

MODULE 5.2 SUMMARY

- I-O psychologists are increasingly interested in organizational citizenship behavior (OCB)—behavior that goes beyond what is expected on the job. This concept has been further developed to include extrarole behaviors that are part of *contextual* performance, which is contrasted with traditional views called *task* performance. Research indicates that measures of cognitive ability are most closely associated with task performance, whereas measures of personality do a better job of predicting contextual performance.

- I-O psychologists commonly distinguish among different types of performance indicators. Three categories commonly discussed are objective

measures, judgmental measures, and personnel measures.

- Adaptive performance is a new component that can be added to Campbell's performance model. Research suggests that occupations vary not only in the *extent* to which adaptability is required, but also in the *type* of adaptive performance that is most critical.

- I-O psychologists also study counterproductive work behaviors, including deviance directed toward the organization and toward other individuals. Three common counterproductive behaviors are dishonesty, absenteeism, and sabotage.

KEY TERMS

organizational citizenship behavior (OCB)

altruism

generalized compliance

contextual performance

task performance

objective performance measure

judgmental measure

personnel measure

adaptive performance

expert performance

deliberate practice

counterproductive employee behavior

dishonesty

absenteeism

sabotage

Lordstown Syndrome

CRITICAL THINKING EXERCISES

5.3 Consider the following multiple choice question that deals with contextual performance. Choose the correct alternative and explain why it is correct, and why each of the other alternatives is incorrect.

Contextual performance is most likely to contribute to organizational effectiveness:

1. In routine jobs with well-defined boundaries performed by single contributors.
2. For technical jobs but not for nontechnical jobs.
3. When performance expectations are made explicit for the job incumbent.
4. When the organization provides a service rather than produces goods and there are many competitors.

5.4 There are three types of performance measures: objective, personnel, and judgmental. Consider the job of a sales manager for an appliance store. Provide an example of an objective, a personnel, and a judgmental performance measure for this manager's performance.

5.3 MODULE

JOB ANALYSIS: FUNDAMENTAL PROPERTIES AND PRACTICES

JOB ANALYSIS

Process that determines the "essence" of a collection of tasks falling within the scope of a particular job title; involves an attempt to develop a theory of human behavior about the job in question.

In earlier chapters, we have used the term **job analysis** in a general sense to mean a process that determines the "essence" of a collection of tasks falling within the scope of a particular job title. We will now consider that process in much greater detail.

The purpose of a job analysis is simple. The analyst wants to understand what the important tasks of the job are, how they are carried out, and what human attributes are necessary to carry them out successfully. In short, job analysis is an attempt to develop a theory of human behavior about the job in question. This theory will include performance expectations (properties of the job in the context of the organization's expectations) as well as the required abilities, knowledge, experience, skill, and personal characteristics necessary to meet those expectations.

THE USES OF JOB ANALYSIS INFORMATION

The results of a job analysis can be used for many different purposes, including:

Job Description This is a description of the job in relatively simple terms, listing the type of tasks that are carried out, the required worker attributes, and training and experience requirements. Job descriptions are very useful for recruiting purposes.

Recruiting If we know what the job requires and we know which human attributes are necessary to fulfill those requirements, we can target our recruiting efforts to specific groups of potential candidates. For technical jobs, these groups might be defined by credentials (a bachelor's degree in engineering) or experience (five years programming in C++).

Selection Once we know the attributes most likely to predict success, we can identify and choose (or develop) the actual assessment tools. Based on the job analysis, we may choose a personality test that measures the Big Five, a commercially available test of general mental ability or reasoning, or develop an interview format intended to get at some subtle aspects of technical knowledge or experience.

Training A job analysis helps us to identify the areas of performance that create the greatest challenge for incumbents; based on this, we can provide preassignment or post-assignment training opportunities. We may discover that in automobile manufacturing subassembly, one of the most troublesome tasks is installing the dashboard console without pinching the bundled wiring that powers the displays on that dash. Newly hired assembly line workers who will be assigned to that subassembly task can receive specific training modules designed to help them perform this task better. Modules can also be prepared for the line supervisors who direct that subassembly operation so that they can follow up the initial training with online coaching.

Compensation   Since a job analysis identifies the major performance components and expectations for each job, management can place a monetary value to the organizational mission on each of those components. Management can also determine the level of performance expected on each of those components for each job in the organization as a way of identifying the comparative value of each job. These components and levels of performance can then help set the budget for the organization's human resources. An organization may decide, for example, that rapidly changing technology makes their market so unstable that they will place higher value on demonstrated individual adaptability (as defined above by Pulakos et al., 2000) and non-job-specific task proficiency (as defined above in Campbell's model), and less value on written and oral task communication proficiency or the maintenance of personal discipline (from the Campbell model). This means that jobs that depend heavily on the first two performance components will pay better than jobs with heavy concentrations of the latter components.

Promotion/Job Assignment   The concept of a **job ladder** or **job family** is based on the observation that a particular job may have closer connections to a subset of other jobs than to a job chosen at random. Accounting jobs are closer to budgeting and invoicing positions than they are to engineering or production positions. Job analysis permits the identification of clusters of positions that are similar, either in terms of the human attributes needed to be successful at them or in terms of the tasks carried out in those jobs. This in turn allows the organization to identify logical career paths as well as the possibility of transfer from one career ladder to another.

JOB LADDER OR JOB FAMILY
Cluster of positions that are similar in terms of the human attributes needed to be successful in those positions or in terms of the tasks that are carried out.

Workforce Reduction/Restructuring   Mergers, acquisitions, downsizing, and rightsizing are all terms that imply job changes—often involuntary ones on the part of the employees. Mergers and acquisitions call for identifying duplicative positions and centralizing functions. The challenge is to identify which positions are truly redundant and which provide a unique value added. In downsizing and rightsizing interventions, positions with somewhat related tasks are often consolidated into a single position. The job descriptions of those who stay with the organization are enlarged with the result that more responsibilities are assumed by fewer people. In both the merger/acquisition and the downsizing/rightsizing scenarios, management's key role is deciding which tasks to fold into which positions; detailed job analyses provide a template for making these decisions rationally.

Criterion Development   As you will recall from our discussion of validity in Chapter 2, the criterion is the behavior that constitutes or defines successful performance of a given task. It is the dependent variable in criterion-related validity studies. Independent variables such as scores on a test of mental ability are correlated with criterion measures to demonstrate that those scores are valid predictors of probable job success. In content-related validity studies, as we saw in Chapter 2, the I-O psychologist establishes logical links between important task-based characteristics of the job and the assessment used to choose among candidates. It is the job analysis that provides the raw material for criterion development. For example, in a criterion-related validity study of a problem-solving test for software consultants, a job analysis might tell us that one of the most common and important tasks of the consultant is to identify a flaw in a software program. As a result, we might then develop a measure of the extent to which the consultant does consistently identify the flaw without asking for assistance. This measure might be in the form of a rating scale of "troubleshooting" that would be completed by the consultant's supervisor. We would then have both the predictor score and a criterion score for the calculation of a validity coefficient.

Performance Assessment   An extension of the use of job analysis for criterion development is the development of performance assessment systems. Once the job analyst identifies

FIGURE 5.6

An Early Example of Job Analysis
SOURCE: Cades (1924); cited in Viteles (1932).

JOB SPECIFICATION NO.

Name of Job: QUILLER   *Department:* COTTON WINDING   *Number Employed:* 15

DUTIES:

1. Twist in the new warp to the old one.
2. Set the guides right.
3. Keep the warp straight and see that the ends are running on properly.
4. Doff, i.e., take off the bobbins.
5. Put on new bobbins.
6. Oil and clean machine.
7. Straighten out ends with a big lease.
8. Put on new bands whenever needed.
9. Take out tangles and twists of the warp.
10. Take out tangles of the yarn and smashes against the reeds.
11. Watch for double ends; remove and tie over if any occur.
12. Make sure that the machine is regulated properly.

NATURE AND CONDITIONS OF WORK:

Hours from 7 to 5:30, Saturday from 7 to 12. Overtime *None.*
Piece rate: Pay beginning at…per…raised after…to…and after…to…

Temporary	...	Permanent	x	Hot	...
Heavy	...			Steamy	...
Coarse	...	Fine	very	Wet	...
Dirty	...	Clean	x	Dusty	...
Standing	x	Sitting	...	Routine	...
Noisy	x	Quiet	...	Varied	...
Walking	x	Manual labor	...	Illumination	fair
Stooping	x	Clerical	...	Ventilation	fair
Lifting	...	Operative	x	Cement floor	x
Pulling	x	Mechanical	...	Wooden floor	x
Pushing	...	Counting	...	Wet floor	...
Jerking	...	*Tying knots*	x		

MACHINES USED:

Quilling machine
TIME TO LEARN AND NATURE OF TRAINING: Helper for 2 weeks.
Twisting in twisting chair, etc. Can learn in 3 months. May become a fair operator in 6 months.
PROMOTION from skein winding to ………… *no plan* …………
ALLIED JOBS: Skein winding.
ADVANTAGES: Good pay, clean work.
DISADVANTAGES: Mostly standing work; requires careful, constant application.
REMARKS: This quilling is on various colored yarns. Quilling in Mercerizing Department is all white and generally heavier yarn.

QUALIFICATIONS

GENERAL		*EDUCATIONAL*		*PHYSICAL*	
Sex—Female		*None*	...	*Height*—	
Age Limits—16 to 25		*Read*	x	Preferably medium height	
Preferred Age—18 to 22		*Write*	x	or over	
Race and Nationality—		*Add & Sub.*	...	*Weight*—	
White American born		*Fractions*	...	Medium	
				Preferably right handed	
COMPETENCY		*EXPERIENCE*		*Endurance*	x
Special Traits		*Required*—none		*Power*	...
Distribution	5	*Desirable*—		*Eyesight*	good
Persistence	5	Work with yarn		(Normal or corrected	
Observation	5			vision)	
Co-ordination A	4				
Vis. Disc.	4			*TEMPERAMENTAL*	
Alertness	4			*Patience*	
				Carefulness	

critical performance components of a job, it is possible to develop a system for evaluating the extent to which an individual worker has fallen short of, met, or exceeded the standards set by the organization for performance on those components. We will deal with the issue of performance evaluation in detail in Chapter 6.

A BRIEF HISTORY OF JOB ANALYSIS

One of the first I-O psychologists to introduce standardized job analysis was Morris Viteles. As early as 1922, he used job analysis to select employees for a trolley car company (Viteles, 1922). An example of his job analysis areas is presented in Figure 5.6, showing how the technique was applied to the job of Quiller in a knitting mill. As you can see, the analyst first described the duties of the incumbent, then the nature and conditions of work, and finally, some basic qualifications. Having done that, the analyst then completed a form called a **job psychograph** which displayed the mental requirements of the job (see Figure 5.7). The reason we present these artifacts is to show that the purpose of job analysis has not changed in over 70 years: it remains one of understanding the behavioral requirements of work. It was then and is now the analyst's best attempt at developing a theory of work performance.

Over the years, experts have presented many different systems to accomplish job analysis. There are many excellent reviews of these systems (Gael, 1979, 1988), but since many

JOB PSYCHOGRAPH

Early form used in a job analysis to display the mental requirements of the job.

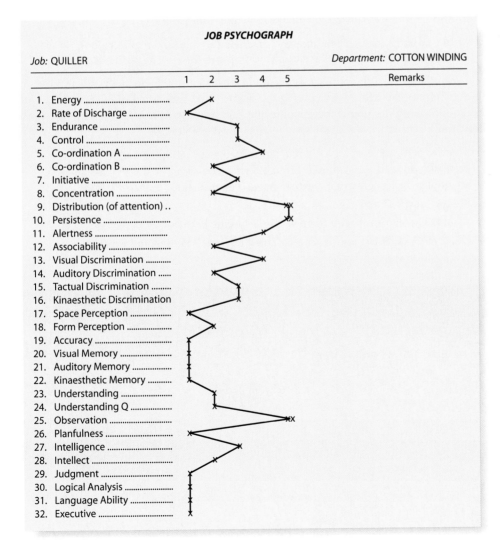

FIGURE 5.7

The Job Psychograph of Viteles SOURCE: Viteles (1932).

JOB PSYCHOGRAPH

Job: QUILLER

Department: COTTON WINDING

	1	2	3	4	5	Remarks
1. Energy						
2. Rate of Discharge						
3. Endurance						
4. Control						
5. Co-ordination A						
6. Co-ordination B						
7. Initiative						
8. Concentration						
9. Distribution (of attention)						
10. Persistence						
11. Alertness						
12. Associability						
13. Visual Discrimination						
14. Auditory Discrimination						
15. Tactual Discrimination						
16. Kinaesthetic Discrimination						
17. Space Perception						
18. Form Perception						
19. Accuracy						
20. Visual Memory						
21. Auditory Memory						
22. Kinaesthetic Memory						
23. Understanding						
24. Understanding Q						
25. Observation						
26. Planfulness						
27. Intelligence						
28. Intellect						
29. Judgment						
30. Logical Analysis						
31. Language Ability						
32. Executive						

are no longer in use, we will not describe them here. What we can say is that these systems became increasingly detailed over the decades, with greater concentration on tasks and lesser concentration on human attributes. Fortunately, that trend has been reversed in recent years, and we will present some newer systems that have brought I-O psychology back to an examination of the behavioral roots of work.

TYPES OF JOB ANALYSIS

As you saw from the examples above, the purpose of a job analysis is to combine the task demands of a job with our knowledge of human attributes and produce a theory of behavior for the job in question. There are two ways to approach building that theory. One is called the **task-oriented job analysis;** this approach begins with a statement of the actual tasks as well as what is accomplished by those tasks. A second method is called the **worker-oriented job analysis;** as a starting point, this approach focuses on the attributes of the worker necessary to accomplish the tasks. The following example might help to make the distinction clearer. For the job of a snow-cat operator at a ski slope, a task-oriented job analysis form might include the statement:

> Operates Bombardier Sno-Cat to smooth out snow rutted by skiers and snowboard riders, and new snow that has fallen.

In contrast, a worker-oriented job analysis statement might be:

> Evaluates terrain, snow depth, and snow condition and chooses the correct setting for the depth of the snow cut, as well as the number of passes necessary on a given ski slope.

Regardless of which approach is taken, the next step in the job analysis is to identify the attributes—the **KSAOs** we covered in Chapter 3 on individual differences—that an incumbent needs for either performing the tasks or executing the human behaviors described by the job analysis. KSAOs can be defined as follows:

- Knowledge: "A collection of discrete but related facts and information about a particular domain . . . acquired through formal education or training, or accumulated through specific experiences" (Peterson et al., 1999, p. 71).
- Skill: A practiced act.
- Ability: The stable capacity to engage in a specific behavior.
- Other characteristics: personality variables, interests, training and experience.

Sidebar definitions

TASK-ORIENTED JOB ANALYSIS

Approach that begins with a statement of the actual tasks as well as what is accomplished by those tasks.

WORKER-ORIENTED JOB ANALYSIS

Approach that focuses on the attributes of the worker necessary to accomplish the tasks.

KSAOs

Individual attributes of knowledge, skills, abilities, and other characteristics that are required to successfully perform job tasks.

Drivers lacking the required skills and abilities are likely to have accidents.

FIGURE 5.8

The Role of Job Analysis in Assessment

Finally, when the appropriate KSAOs are identified, tests and other assessment techniques can be chosen to measure those KSAOs (see Figure 5.8).

Job analysis methods have evolved using both task-oriented and worker-oriented systems (e.g., Fine, 1989; McCormick, Jeanneret, & Mecham, 1972). Since both approaches end up in the same place—a statement of KSAOs—neither can be considered the "right" way to conduct a job analysis. For practical purposes, since worker-oriented job analyses tend to be more generalized descriptions of human behavior and behavior patterns, and less tied to the technological aspects of a particular job, they produce data more useful for structuring training programs and giving feedback to employees in the form of performance appraisal information. In addition, as we have seen, the volatility that exists in today's typical workplace can make specific task statements less valuable in isolation. Tasks move from job to job, are made obsolete by technology changes, or are assumed by teams rather than individuals. For all of these reasons, employers are significantly more likely to use worker-oriented approaches to job analysis today than they did in the past.

Morgeson and Campion (1997) suggested a staggering number of potential distorting influences in job analysis data collection, and concluded that task-oriented job analysis is less vulnerable to those influences than is the worker-oriented approach. The potential distorting influences include such factors as a need on the part of the employee doing the reporting, commonly referred to as a **subject matter expert (SME),** to conform to what others report, the desire to make one's own job look more difficult, attempts to provide the answers that the SME thinks the job analyst wants, and mere carelessness. Although task-based analysis may be a good measuring tool, in the opinion of your authors it is hardly of value to measure the wrong thing (task-level analysis) well. To borrow a euphemism once applied to Cattell's brand of psychometrics, doing so would be like losing your wallet on a dark street and hunting for it on the next block where there are streetlights.

SUBJECT MATTER EXPERT (SME)

Employee (incumbent) who provides information about a job in a job analysis interview or survey.

HOW JOB ANALYSIS IS DONE

Regardless of the approach the job analyst decides to use, information about the job is the backbone of the analysis, and there are many ways to get it. The more information and the more ways the analyst can collect that information, the better the understanding of the job. Some common methods include:

1. *Observation*—This was perhaps the first method of job analysis I-O psychologists used. They simply watched incumbents perform their jobs and took notes. Sometimes they asked questions while watching, and not infrequently they even performed job tasks themselves. Near the end of World War II, Morris Viteles studied the job of navigator on a submarine. He attempted to steer the submarine toward the island of Bermuda. After five not-so-near-misses of 100 miles in one direction or another, one frustrated officer suggested that Viteles raise the periscope, look for clouds, and steer toward them (since clouds tend to form above or near land masses). The vessel "found" Bermuda shortly thereafter. One of your authors has observed or participated in jobs as diverse as police patrol, iron ore mining four miles beneath the surface north of the Arctic Circle, cookie packing, airport runway repair, packing baggage into the cargo hold of a Boeing 727 and 747, nuclear control room operation, and overhead crane operation. The more jobs one seriously observes, the better one's understanding of not only the jobs in question, but of work in general.

2. *Interviews*—it is important to supplement observation by talking with incumbents, either at the worksite or in a separate location. These interviews are most effective when structured with a specific set of questions based on observations, other analyses of

the types of jobs in questions, or prior discussions with HR reps, trainers, or managers knowledgeable about the jobs.

3. *Critical Incidents and Work Diaries*—I-O psychologists have used other techniques to capture important information about jobs. The **critical incident technique** asks SMEs to identify critical aspects of behavior or performance in a particular job that led to success or failure. The supervisor of a computer programmer might report, say, that in a very time-urgent project, the programmer decided to install a subroutine without taking the time to "debug" it; eventually, the entire system crashed because of a flaw in the logic of that one subroutine.

The second method—a **work diary**—asks workers and/or supervisors to keep a log of their activities over a prescribed period of time. They may be asked to simply jot down what they were doing at 15 minutes after the hour for each hour of their work day. Or they may list everything that they have done up to a lunch break.

4. *Questionnaires/Surveys*—Expert incumbents or supervisors (SMEs) often respond to questionnaires or surveys as part of a job analysis. These questionnaires include task statements in the form of worker behaviors. SMEs are asked to rate each statement from their experience on a number of dimensions such as frequency of performance, importance to overall job success, and whether the task or behavior must be performed on the first day of work or can be learned gradually on the job. Questionnaires also ask SMEs to rate the importance of various KSAOs for performing tasks or task groups, and may ask the SMEs to rate work context. Unlike the results of observations or interviews, the questionnaire responses can be statistically analyzed to provide a more objective record of the components of the job.

Over the years, several commercially available job analysis surveys have been popular. Perhaps the best known and most widely used of these instruments is the Position Analysis Questionnaire (PAQ) developed by McCormick et al. (1972). Jeanneret (1992) has expanded and revised the PAQ system and maintained a substantial database of job analysis information for many occupations over the 30 years of its use. Other survey-based systems include the Fleishman Job Analysis System (based on the Fleishman taxonomy that we examined in Chapter 3); the Occupational Analysis Inventory (Cunningham, Boese, Neeb, & Pass, 1983), best suited for occupational education and guidance work; the Common Metric Questionnaire (CMQ) developed by The Psychological Corporation (1993); and the Work Profiling System (WPS) developed by Saville & Holdsworth Limited (2001), which is an example of computer-based job analysis data collection augmented by an expert system that matches people and jobs. We will examine this system more deeply in a later section of this chapter. A book published by the National Research Council (1999) provides an excellent description of each of these commercially available systems.

CRITICAL INCIDENT TECHNIQUE

Approach in which subject matter experts are asked to identify critical aspects of behavior or performance in a particular job that led to success or failure.

WORK DIARY

Job analysis approach that requires workers and/or supervisors to keep a log of their activities over a prescribed period of time.

MODULE 5.3 SUMMARY

- Job analysis attempts to develop a theory of human behavior about the job in question. This theory includes performance expectations as well as the experience and KSAOs necessary to meet those expectations.
- The results of a job analysis can be used for many different purposes, including job description, recruiting, selection, training, compensation, criterion development, and performance assessment.
- Job analysis methods are often broken down into two different but related approaches: a

task-oriented approach and a worker-oriented approach. Whichever approach is initially selected, the next step in a job analysis is to identify the KSAOs that an incumbent needs for performing the tasks or executing the human behaviors described in the job analysis.

- There are many ways to obtain job analysis information, including observation, interviews, critical incidents, work diaries, and questionnaires or surveys. The more ways the analyst can collect information, the better the understanding of the job.

KEY TERMS

job analysis

job ladder or job family

job psychograph

task-oriented job analysis

worker-oriented job analysis

KSAOs

subject matter expert (SME)

critical incident technique

work diary

CRITICAL THINKING EXERCISES

5.5 Assume that you work in the human resources department of an organization that needs to reduce its overhead and has decided to accomplish this by consolidating two departments and eliminating redundant job titles. Assume further that no job analysis information was available, but you were authorized to take whatever steps were necessary to provide a justification for which jobs would be eliminated. You decide that a job analysis of some sort would be appropriate. Draw a flow diagram that shows each step you would take in providing that justification. The flow diagram should include the types of data you will gather, from whom you will gather it, and what you will do with those data in making your recommendations.

5.6 There are six methods identified for collecting job analysis information: observation, performing actual job tasks, interviews, critical incident identification, work diaries, and job analysis questionnaires. Consider each and list a shortcoming of each of those methods. Assuming that you would use three methods in a single project to collect job analysis information, which of the three methods listed above would you use? In what order would you arrange these methods (i.e., which type of data would you gather first, then second, then last)? Why would you use this order?

JOB ANALYSIS: NEWER DEVELOPMENTS

ELECTRONIC PERFORMANCE MONITORING AS PART OF A JOB ANALYSIS

The introduction of computers and other technology-based information networks into the workplace has clearly revolutionized planning, production, and distribution. But this new technology has introduced another, less obvious, opportunity: the opportunity to monitor work processes, both actively and passively. When a commercial airplane crashes, investigators scramble to find the two "black boxes" containing the voice recorder and the event recorder. The voice recorder may reveal certain information about the accident—what the cabin crew heard and saw—and the event recorder may reveal independent information—altitude, position of flaps and throttle, and so on. The flight can be "monitored" after the fact.

In many jobs, similar monitoring can occur during work as well as after the fact. Consider the phone calls you make to your local telephone company with a question about your bill, or the call you make to a ticket service to buy tickets to a theatrical performance. A recorded message will tell you that your "call may be monitored for quality control purposes." That means that the performance of the agent or representative with whom you are talking is being monitored and "critical incidents" in success and failure can be identified.

ELECTRONIC PERFORMANCE MONITORING

Monitoring work processes with electronic devices; can be cost effective and has the potential for providing detailed and accurate work logs.

The good news for employers about **electronic performance monitoring** is that many jobs lend themselves to producing job analysis information without any input at all from SMEs. Since the system records the actions of workers, it is a simple step to develop a frequency count of those actions, telling the analyst how often the action occurs in a day or week. Frequency is often highly correlated with the importance of a task. Electronic performance monitoring can be very cost effective and has the potential for providing detailed and accurate work logs. Indeed, the practice of monitoring without SME input is not unique to the digital age. Recall the excerpt in Chapter 1 about the Blue Shield claims adjuster in Barbara Garson's book on boring work (Garson, 1994). The claims adjuster's performance output was monitored regularly—and that was in 1970. In a more recent example, Sanchez and Levine (1999) described truck leasing companies that monitor driver performance by hooking an onboard computer to the truck engine and tracking speed, idle time, and other characteristics of driving behavior. The dark side, of course, is related to employee privacy rights and perceptions of fairness. If the new technology of the workplace is to provide raw material for job analysis, there will need to be checks and balances that will ease the concerns of workers regarding punitive actions by the employer. In Chapter 6 on performance measurement, we will cover electronic monitoring in more detail from the employee's perspective.

COGNITIVE TASK ANALYSIS

In line with the movement toward worker-oriented job analysis, experts have suggested that **cognitive task analysis** is a needed extension of traditional job analysis procedures (Vincente, 1999). Most job analyses concentrate on observable behavior—either task completion or action patterns. But cognitive behavior is not directly observable, so a new technique must be used. DuBois (2002) defined cognitive task analyses as "methods for decomposing job and task performance into discrete, measurable units, with special emphasis on eliciting mental processes and knowledge content" (p. 83).

A precursor of cognitive task analysis is a technique known as a **think-aloud protocol** (Ericsson & Simon, 1993), which cognitive psychologists have been using for many years to investigate the manner in which experts think in order to achieve high levels of performance (Goldstein & Ford, 2002). In a think-aloud-protocol, an expert performer actually describes in words the thought process that he or she uses to accomplish a task. An observer/interviewer takes notes and may ask some follow-up questions based on what the performer says. In this way, the unobservable becomes observable. As an example, Ericsson and Charness (1994) reproduced the think-aloud protocol of a person who was able to correctly multiply 24 by 36 mentally (i.e., without the use of a paper and pencil):

> 36 times 24
>
> 4
>
> carry the—no wait
>
> carry the 2
>
> 14
>
> 144
>
> 0
>
> 36 times 2 is
>
> 12
>
> 6
>
> 72
>
> 720 plus 144
>
> 4
>
> uh uh
>
> 6
>
> 8
>
> uh, 864

The focus is not on the KSAOs that the expert calls upon, but the cognitive operations employed. Put another way, cognitive task analysis concentrates on *how* behavior occurs rather than on *what* is accomplished. It is not that the old methods are replaced with cognitive task analysis. Instead, cognitive task analysis is added to the job analysis toolbag. Goldstein and Ford (2002) made the following distinction:

> Rather than looking at tasks and KSAOs as separate entities, a cognitive task analysis approach attempts to link tasks and KSAs based on the flow from the goals of the people completing a task to the various actions a person might take in performing the task. An examination of the differences between experts and novices in terms of goals and actions can help identify areas for training and development to transform novices toward expertise (p. 96).

As the workplace becomes more technologically complex and volatile, it is clear that the old methods of task-based observation and interview will be ineffective in describing

COGNITIVE TASK ANALYSIS

Consists of methods for decomposing job and task performance into discrete, measurable units, with special emphasis on eliciting mental processes and knowledge content.

THINK-ALOUD PROTOCOL

Approach used by cognitive psychologists to investigate the thought processes of experts who achieve high levels of performance; an expert performer describes in words the thought process that he or she uses to accomplish a task.

many of the more critical cognitive operations that lead to success. Much of the work done involves diagnosis, problem solving, and planning—activities that are not easy to observe.

Cognitive task analysis is time consuming and requires a good deal of expertise to do well. As a result, it may be a luxury for low-level jobs or jobs for which the cost of a mistake is small. But for critical positions where the consequence of an error is extremely high, cognitive task analysis may be a useful addition to the job analysis arsenal. DuBois (1999) suggested that employers consider the following indicators to determine whether a cognitive task analysis may be worthwhile:

· Persistent performance problems.
· Costly errors or accidents.
· Training is difficult to transfer to job behavior.
· Achieving high levels of performance takes a long time.

Cognitive task analysis can be accomplished using a number of methods, all quite new and relatively untested. Nevertheless, because cognitive task analysis is a genuine advance in the understanding of work, I-O psychologists are confident that this area will grow quickly. Your authors predict that by the year 2010 cognitive task analysis will become a common part of a job analysis and will likely extend down to lower-level jobs from upper-level jobs where it was first used.

THE CONTEXT OF WORK

CONTEXT OF
THE WORK

Conditions or characteristics of work that can change the demands on the incumbent; includes interpersonal relationships, physical work conditions, and structural job characteristics.

The "job" of a wide receiver on a professional football team is to run as far and as fast as he can and catch a football. That is the content of the work. The **context of the work** changes that job just a bit. The complete job description, including the context, might read as follows:

> Runs as fast as possible down a wet and slippery field, first avoiding the legal attempt by a defensive back to separate the wide receiver's head from his shoulders, at a point 15 yards past the line of scrimmage, cutting inches behind a crossing tight end teammate and defender who collectively weigh 500 pounds and are moving at the speed of light, in order to catch a pass with the velocity and girth of an artillery shell while another defender is pulling his jersey with one hand and reaching down his throat with the other, anticipating that within a second, an additional defender will attempt to embed his helmet several inches deep in the wide receiver's lower back and kidney area.

That is the "contextualized" job of a wide receiver. While the workplace is not usually as sensationalized as the football field, there are conditions of work or context which can change the demands on the incumbent. Communicating with a co-worker may seem like a simple task unless it is attempted in the midst of noise and dangerous moving equipment such as lifttrucks and overhead cranes. Explaining a procedure may seem like a simple task until the explanation is being given by a police officer to an irate motorist who has been given a ticket for speeding past a stopped school bus. Tasks are not performed in a void; instead, they are performed in a context which includes interpersonal, physical, and structural characteristics. Some (McCormick et al., 1972), but not all, systems of job analysis include a consideration of the work context. For some occupations (e.g., administrative work), the context may play a minor role in performance, but in others (e.g., public safety, the military, heavy industrial work), the work context may completely transform the job demands, requiring additional cognitive or physical abilities or higher levels of certain personality attributes.

Strong, Jeanneret, McPhail, Blakley, and D'Egidio (1999) developed a taxonomy for describing the work context (see Table 5.4). Their taxonomy suggests that context has three different aspects: interpersonal relationships, physical work conditions, and structural job

TABLE 5.4	Variables That Define Work Context

INTERPERSONAL RELATIONSHIPS

Communication

   Formality   —Formal vs. personal.

   Method   —Face to face, telephone, e-mail, etc.

   Objectivity   —Subjective vs. data-based information.

   Frequency   —Extent of interpersonal communication required.

   Privacy   —Extent to which communication can be monitored.

Types of role relationships required

   Supervisory role

   Sales role

   Service role

   Adversarial role

   Team participant role

Responsibility for others

   For safety

   For work outcomes and results

Conflictual contact with others

   Interpersonal conflict   —Nature of role places worker in conflict with others (e.g., police officer, labor relations manager).

   Strained interpersonal relations   —Worker required to deal with others who are unpleasant (e.g., customer service reps, food service workers).

PHYSICAL WORK CONDITIONS

Work setting

   Variety of work settings   —Indoors, outdoors, in a vehicle, etc.

   Privacy of work area

   Physical Proximity to other workers

Environmental conditions

   Extreme conditions   —Temperature, noise, confined space, pollution.

   Exposure to job hazards   —Radiation, heights, dangerous equipment.

   Possibility of injury

   Impact of injury   —Extent, duration, seriousness of potential injury.

Job demands

   Body positioning   —Extent of sitting, walking, standing, climbing.

   Work attire   —Requirement to wear special clothing or equipment.

STRUCTURAL JOB CHARACTERISTICS

Criticality of position

   Consequence of error.

   Impact of decisions.

(continued)

TABLE 5.4	(continued)

Responsibility/accountability.

Decision latitude.

Routine vs. challenging work

Frustrating circumstances.

Degree of automation.

Task clarity.

Required precision.

Required attention to detail.

Required vigilance.

Monotony.

Structured vs. unstructured work.

Level of competition.

Pace and scheduling

Frequency and stringency of deadlines.

Distraction and interruptions.

Machine-driven work pace.

SOURCE: Based on Peterson, Mumford, Borman, Jeanneret, & Fleishman (1999).

characteristics, each with its own unique facets. By using these facets, we can make reliable distinctions among various occupational groups such as managers, nurses, janitors, and maintenance repair personnel.

There are many potential advantages to including work context variables in job analysis. As mentioned above, context may help define the requisite KSAOs for a successful incumbent. In addition, it has been traditional to compensate workers with premium pay for unusually difficult, hazardous, or unappealing work, so context may play a role in compensation policies. Finally, knowledge of context may help an employer to portray more realistically to prospective employees the less attractive characteristics of the job (Strong et al., 1999). Incomplete knowledge of work context often leads to early turnover by new employees. This early turnover is expensive, given the time and energy that went into selection, orientation, and training. It is better to have a candidate decline an offer based on full knowledge of the job and the work context, than to have a candidate with incomplete knowledge accept the position and then leave after two weeks.

A popular technique for providing practical information about a prospective job is called the **realistic job preview (RJP).** RJPs include task information as well as information about the context of the work (Phillips, 1998). For the position of a bank teller, RJP information would include things like the nature of the training program, the importance of accuracy, the pressure of the work, the nature of customers (including rude ones), pay and promotion rates, and how to move into management. Wanous and Dean (1984) found that employees who did not receive RJPs for bank teller positions tended to leave after six months, while those receiving RJPs often withdrew before or during training. Expanding upon these findings, Phillips (1998) found that RJPs led to higher levels of performance for those who stayed, as well as lower levels of both voluntary resignations and involuntary terminations.

A NEW ADDITION TO JOB ANALYSIS INSTRUMENTS: THE PERSONALITY-RELATED POSITION REQUIREMENTS FORM (PPRF)

As you read in Chapters 3 and 4, personality measures have become very popular in industrial selection. But historically, job analysis instruments ignored personality attributes and concentrated on abilities, skills and, less frequently, knowledge. Guion and his colleagues (Guion, 1998; Raymark, Schmit, & Guion, 1997) developed a commercially available job analysis instrument, the **Personality-Related Position Requirements Form (PPRF),** devoted to identifying personality predictors of job performance. This instrument is not intended to replace other job analysis devices that identify knowledge, skills, or abilities, but to supplement job analysis by examining important personality attributes in jobs. Guion enlisted 145 experienced I-O psychologists to nominate and evaluate the relevance of 44 different aspects of personality for work performance. A subsequent statistical analysis revealed 12 basic work-related personality dimensions, listed and defined in Table 5.5. An example of a page from the actual PPRF job analysis booklet appears in Figure 5.9.

PERSONALITY-RELATED POSITION REQUIREMENTS FORM (PPRF) *Job analysis instrument devoted to identifying personality predictors of job performance.*

TABLE 5.5	Twelve Personality Dimensions Covered by the PPRF
DIMENSION	**DEFINITION**
I. SURGENCY	
I–A: General leadership	A pattern of visibility and dominance relative to others; the tendency to initiate action, to take charge of situations or groups, to influence or motivate behavior or thinking of other persons or groups of people to bring about or maintain work effectiveness.
I–B: Interest in negotiation	An interest in bringing together contesting parties through mediation or arbitration of disputes or differences in view or, as a contesting party, deal or bargain with others to reach agreement, synthesis, or compromise; a style of leadership characterized by an ability and willingness to see and understand differing points of view, and an interest in making peace and achieving workable levels of harmony.
I–C: Achievement striving	A strong ambition and desire to achieve; in competition with others, a desire to win and a continuing tendency to exert effort and energy to win or to do better than others; in competition with one's self, a desire to exert effort to advance, to do better than one's own prior achievement in specific activities; a tendency to excel relative to others or to a personal standard; to go beyond what is expected and required in an attempt to become the best; not to accept satisfactory or good enough but to strive for excellent.
II. AGREEABLENESS	
II–A: Friendly disposition	A tendency to be outgoing in association with other people, to seek and enjoy the company of others; to be gregarious, to interact easily and well with others, to be likable and warmly approachable.
II–B: Sensitivity to interests of others	A tendency to be a caring person in relation to other people, to be considerate, understanding, and even empathic and to have genuine concern for others and their well-being.
II–C: Cooperative or collaborative work tendency	A desire or willingness to work with others to achieve a common purpose and to be part of a group; a willingness and interest in assisting clients and customers as a regular function of the person's work, or assisting co-workers as needed to meet deadlines or achieve work goals.

(continued)

TABLE 5.5	*(continued)*

DIMENSION	DEFINITION
III. CONSCIENTIOUSNESS	
III–A: General trustworthiness	A pattern of behavior that leads one to be trusted by other people with property, money, or confidential information; a pattern of honoring the property rights of others and general concepts of honesty, truthfulness, and fairness; a deserved reputation for following through on promises, commitments, or other agreements—in short, a pattern of behavior that leads people to say approvingly. "This person can be counted on."
III–B: Adherence to a work ethic	A generalized tendency to work hard and to be loyal; to give a full day's work each day and to do one's best to perform well—following instructions and accepting company goals, policies, and rules—even with little or no supervision; an approach to work characterized by industriousness, purposiveness, persistence, consistency, and punctuality.
III–C: Thoroughness and attentiveness to details	A tendency to carry out tasks with attention to every aspect, including attention to details that others might overlook or perform perfunctorily; a meticulous approach to one's own task performance or the work of others, including careful inspection or analysis of objects, printed material, proposals, or plans.
IV. EMOTIONAL STABILITY	
IV: Emotional stability	A calm, relaxed approach to situations, events, or people; emotionally controlled responses to changes in the work environment or to emergency situations; an emotionally mature approach to potentially stressful situations with tolerance, optimism, and a general sense of challenge rather than of crisis; maturity in considering advice or criticism from others.
V. INTELLECTANCE	
V–A: Desire to generate ideas	A preference for situations in which one can develop new things, ideas, or solutions to problems through creativity or insight, or try new or innovative approaches to tasks or situations; to prefer original or unique ways of thinking about things.
V–B: Tendency to think things through	A habit of thinking, of mentally going through procedures or a sequence of probable events before actually taking actions; a tendency to seek information, to evaluate it, and to consider the consequences or effects of alternative courses of action.

Source: Guion (1998).

Each of the PPRF dimensions relates to one or more of the Big Five personality dimensions (Digman, 1990) described in Chapter 3. A follow-up study (Raymark et al., 1997) demonstrated that because the PPRF correlated different personality requirements with different jobs, it could be used to distinguish among 260 different job titles. A "friendly disposition," for example, was judged most valuable for sales clerk and cashier positions, and least valuable for janitorial occupations. For "thoroughness and attention to details," personnel administration, management, and accounting occupations had the highest scores. "General trustworthiness" scores were considered most valuable for cashier and teller occupations.

Like cognitive task analysis, the PPRF is still too new to have much published research on applications. Nevertheless, like cognitive analysis, we are confident that it will see considerable use and make a clear contribution to the job analyst's ability to understand the requirements of the job in question.

EFFECTIVE PERFORMANCE IN THIS POSITION REQUIRES THE PERSON TO:	Not Required	Helpful	Essential
Set 1			
1. lead group activities through exercise of power or authority.	☐	☐	☐
2. take control in group situations.	☐	☐	☐
3. initiate change within the person's work group or area to enhance productivity or performance.	☐	☐	☐
4. motivate people to accept change.	☐	☐	☐
5. motivate others to perform effectively.	☐	☐	☐
6. persuade co-workers or subordinates to take actions (that at first they may not want to take) to maintain work effectiveness.	☐	☐	☐
7. take charge in unusual or emergency situations.	☐	☐	☐
8. delegate to others the authority to get something done.	☐	☐	☐
9. make decisions when needed.	☐	☐	☐
Set 2			
10. negotiate on behalf of the work unit for a fair share of organizational resources.	☐	☐	☐
11. work with dissatisfied customers or clients to achieve a mutually agreeable solution.	☐	☐	☐
12. help people in work groups settle interpersonal conflicts that interface with group functioning.	☐	☐	☐
13. help settle work-related problems, complaints, or disputes among employees or organizational units.	☐	☐	☐
14. negotiate with people outside the organization to gain something of value to the organization.	☐	☐	☐
15. mediate and resolve disputes at individual, group, or organizational levels.	☐	☐	☐
16. negotiate with people within the organization to achieve a consensus on a proposed action.	☐	☐	☐
17. mediate conflict situations without taking sides.	☐	☐	☐

FIGURE 5.9

A Sample Page from the PPRF SOURCE: Guion (1998).

A SUMMARY OF THE JOB ANALYSIS PROCESS

It should be apparent from the preceding discussion that there is no one best way to perform a job analysis, but we can draw some conclusions about the process generally.

1. The more information you can gather from the greatest number of sources, the better your potential understanding of the job.
2. Molecular task-based analyses are often less useful for many purposes than worker- or behavior-based analyses.
3. Most job analyses should include considerations of personality demands and work context; some job analyses should include considerations of purely cognitive tasks.

AN EXAMPLE OF A PC-BASED JOB ANALYSIS INSTRUMENT

WORK PROFILING SYSTEM (WPS)

PC-based job analysis instrument used to streamline the job analysis process, reducing costs to the organization, minimizing distractions to the SMEs, and increasing the speed and accuracy of the process.

The **Work Profiling System (WPS)** (Saville & Holdsworth, 2001) is an example of how the data collection and interpretation process of job analysis can be streamlined, reducing costs to the organization, minimizing distractions to the subject matter experts (SMEs), and increasing the speed and accuracy of the process. Additional information about the system can be found on the website of SHL USA, the consulting firm that developed and administers the WPS (www.shlusa.com).

The WPS uses three databases that are interrelated through an expert computer system which uses sophisticated algorithms to weigh and integrate information from the databases. The first database is derived from responses to a structured questionnaire for assessing the actual work performed in the job in question. The second database is constructed from a comprehensive model of the human attributes necessary to perform those tasks. The third database includes relevant assessment methods to tap the human attributes identified as important for the job.

To use the WPS, each SME from whom information is sought fills out an on-screen job analysis questionnaire. Figure 5.10 presents the number of task categories and task statements for three broad employment sectors covered by the three WPS questionnaires as well as the content areas of task categories. SMEs respond using scales to indicate the typical percentage of their time spent on a task as well as the relative importance of the task. A separate "Work Context" section covers various aspects of the work situation similar to the context factors discussed above.

The WPS human attribute model (Figure 5.11) covers physical and perceptual abilities, cognitive abilities, and personality and behavioral style attributes.

Once the SMEs have entered their responses to the job analysis and work context questions, the WPS system uses a series of algorithms and equations to produce the following reports:

- Job Description Report specifies the important tasks and task categories of the job as well as the context in which the job is performed.
- Person Specification Report identifies the human attributes necessary for successful performance of the job.
- Performance Review Form is based on the required behaviors and activities of the job; it is a worksheet and rating form which can be used to structure performance evaluation and feedback for the job in question.
- Individual Development Planner is a series of worksheets used by the incumbent and manager for jointly identifying key tasks to target for employee improvement.
- Interview Questions Report contains a series of suggested questions to include in a preselection interview of a candidate.
- Caveats Report suggests behaviors that might be expected for someone who scores high or low on a particular personality dimension.

FIGURE 5.10

Structure of the WPS Questionnaires
SOURCE: Saville & Holdsworth Limited (2001).

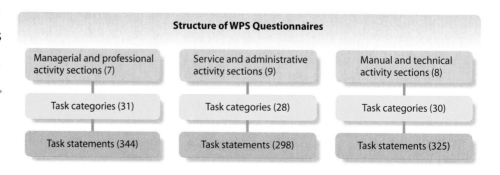

Structure of WPS Questionnaires

Managerial and professional activity sections (7)	Service and administrative activity sections (9)	Manual and technical activity sections (8)
Task categories (31)	Task categories (28)	Task categories (30)
Task statements (344)	Task statements (298)	Task statements (325)

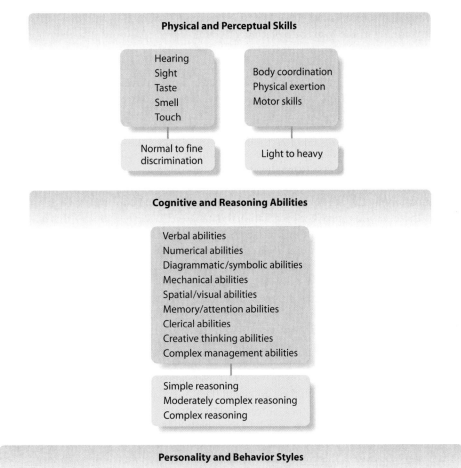

FIGURE 5.11

Human Attribute Model of the WPS
SOURCE: Saville & Holdsworth Limited (2001).

- Recommended Assessment Methods Report suggests job-relevant assessment methods such as ability tests, personality questionnaires, and assessment exercises to use in constructing a selection battery for the job in question.
- Technical Report contains all of the basic data, tables, and calculations that were used in the development of the other reports. This is the report that might be required were a job analysis challenged in an employment discrimination lawsuit.

Computer-based job analysis systems provide a number of advantages. The first is time and convenience to the employer. SMEs need not be assembled in one spot at one time as is often the case with traditional job analysis; they can work from their desks at their own pace and submit their responses electronically. A second advantage is the efficiency with which the expert system can create reports. The reports can serve a wide range of purposes, from individual goal-setting and performance feedback to elaborate person–job matches to support selection and placement strategies. Finally, since systems like this use the same taxonomies and processes across jobs, they make it easier to understand job similarities and career paths, thus facilitating vocational counseling and long-term strategic HR planning in the form of replacement charts for key positions. Possible shortcomings of such systems, of course, are the same shortcomings that would be apparent with more traditional paper and pencil based systems. If the data being collected are poor, or the task or human attribute taxonomies are flawed or irrelevant, then the results, reports, and decisions made on the basis of that system will also be flawed or irrelevant.

O*NET

In the early 1930s, the federal government introduced a program to match applicants with job openings (Droege, 1988; Dunnette, 1999). It was up to each local office to develop its own occupational information base; since these bases were local, there could be little collaboration among the network of offices. Accordingly, in 1934 efforts were begun to standardize these services and develop a national database. The cornerstone of this effort was a program of job analysis and by 1939, 54,000 job analyses had been completed and the first ***Dictionary of Occupational Titles (D.O.T.)*** was published. One of the major purposes of the *D.O.T* was, and still is, for use in occupational counseling.

In 1991, the last year of its publication, the *D.O.T.'s* fifth edition contained information on more than 13,000 occupations (Dunnette, 1999). By this time it was apparent that the *D.O.T.*, at least in the form of its fifth edition, had become less useful. The primary reason for this was its heavy dependence on task-based information relevant to a particular job title, with no direct link to human abilities or attributes. As we have seen, task-based descriptions of occupations provide limited value in work environments with shifting job boundaries. Further, each revision of the *D.O.T.* was expensive and time consuming. A decision was made to change both the format and the content of the *D.O.T.* (Dunnette, 1999).

In 1995 the federal government introduced the concept of an electronic database to replace the *D.O.T.* The database was called the **Occupational Information Network** or **O*NET** (Dye & Silver, 1999). O*NET is actually a collection of databases, several of which you have already seen. Figure 5.12 highlights those sections that are mentioned earlier in this chapter as well as in Chapter 3 on individual differences. All of O*NET's six major databases are still being developed and completed. In addition, expert computer systems have been developed to allow the databases to be combined in ways that will facilitate person–job matches, the same goal set for the original *D.O.T.* in 1939. When O*NET is completed, information describing each job in the system will be available for each of the six databases. Thus, if you were interested in pursuing a career as a jet engine mechanic, you could enter O*NET with the job code for jet engine mechanic, and get information on variables such as experience requirements, work context, typical tasks and duties, wage expectations, requisite abilities, and basic skills. And you could get all of this information in seconds while sitting at your own computer. Furthermore, unlike the old printed *D.O.T*, O*NET can be updated instantaneously as changes occur in the labor market, technology, or training and experience requirements.

In addition to the transformation from a print medium (*D.O.T*) to an electronic medium (O*NET), an even greater change occurred in content. Each of the O*NET databases is now based on well-developed taxonomies, such as the Fleishman taxonomy for abilities we examined in Chapter 3. O*NET was not designed as a job analysis system, but it will have the capability to compare a new job to its current job base and identify jobs most similar to that new job. This matching process will, in turn, permit instantaneous access to a description of the new job's probable requisite abilities, knowledge, and other human attributes. It would also make it possible to fit the job into other labor market databases, including estimates of the probable worth or initial wage estimate for that job.

Not all jobs and job families have yet been entered into the O*NET databases, but when the system is complete, it is expected to meet at least the following needs:

- Identifying occupational skill standards common to clusters of occupations, or job families.

DICTIONARY OF OCCUPATIONAL TITLES (D.O.T.)

Document that includes job analysis and occupational information used to match applicants with job openings; a major purpose of the D.O.T was, and still is, for use in occupational counseling.

OCCUPATIONAL INFORMATION NETWORK (O*NET)

Collection of electronic databases, based on well-developed taxonomies, that has updated and replaced the D.O.T.

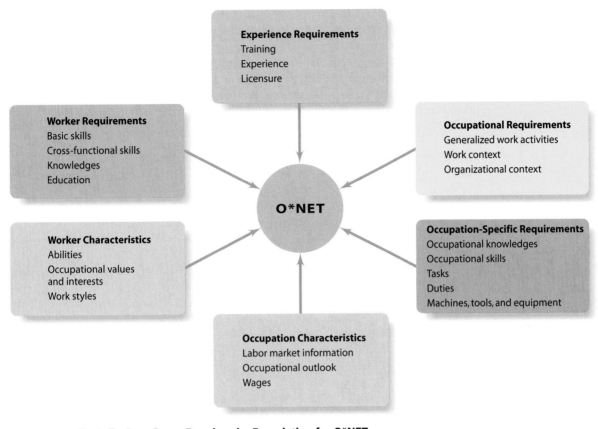

FIGURE 5.12 Data Bases Forming the Foundation for O*NET
SOURCE: Mumford & Peterson (1999).

- Facilitating school-to-work transitions by linking educational programs to occupational standards.
- Assisting laid-off workers in finding re-employment through job search assistance, labor market information, and training.
- Assisting employers in building high-performance workplaces by providing information about the business practices associated with existing high-performance workplaces. (Adapted from Peterson, Borman, Hansen, & Kubisiak, 1999)

O*NET is a broad public policy initiative that embodies all of the best characteristics of defining performance in the modern workplace. It is accessible to many different user groups, including both employees and applicants. In addition, since it is in electronic form, it lends itself to quick updating of changes in existing jobs as well as the appearance of new jobs. Much work remains to be done before the database is complete, but when that is done, the content and format will guarantee its value and relevance for many decades. This system is likely to be in place over your active work life. Because it is developed primarily by I-O psychologists doing "good work," those interested in I-O psychology will be interested in it.

COMPETENCY MODELING

We introduced the concept of competencies in the discussion of individual differences (see Chapter 3). In this section we will deal with competencies from a different perspective: the process of **competency modeling.** You will recall that we defined competencies as "sets of behavior that are instrumental in the delivery of desired results or outcomes" (Kurz &

COMPETENCY MODELING

Process that identifies the characteristics desired across all individuals and jobs within an organization; these characteristics should predict behavior across a wide variety of tasks and settings, and provide the organization with a set of core characteristics that distinguish it from other organizations.

Bartram, 2002). We further described competencies as being rooted in a context of organizational goals rather than in an abstract taxonomy of human attributes.

Just as job analysis seeks to define jobs and work in terms of the match between required tasks and human attributes, competency modeling seeks to define organizational units (larger entities than simply jobs or even job families) in terms of the match between the goals and missions of those units and the competencies required to meet those goals and accomplish those missions. Thus, competency modeling is a natural extension of the job analysis logic rather than a replacement for job analysis. It is competency modeling that has the power to connect individual behavior with organizational viability and profitability. The competency modeling approach "emphasizes the characteristics desired across all individuals and jobs within an organization. . . these more global competencies are expected to not only predict behavior across a wide variety of tasks and settings but also provide the organization with a set of core characteristics that distinguish the company from others in terms of how it operates it business and treats its employees" (Goldstein & Ford, 2002, p. 272).

Like cognitive task analysis, the Personality-Related Position Requirements Form, and the Work Profiling System, competency modeling goes beyond traditional job analysis by recognizing that work and the workplace are in a state of rapid evolution. Sanchez and Levine (1999) provided an example: In considering the job title "quality auditor," a traditional job analysis might suggest that the "ability to perform accurate numerical calculations involving unit transformations" and "knowledge of relevant standard operating procedures" would be important KSAOs. Competency modeling, in contrast, might identify the need for "constructive communication involving nontechnical aspects of the job like the management of trust and the effective delivery of potentially threatening information" (Sanchez & Levine, 1999, p. 58).

Goldstein and Ford (2002) presented examples of two different approaches to competency modeling. One approach is to identify outstanding performers and analyze their performance and competencies. The employer could then take that home-grown taxonomy of performance components and competencies and use it as a model for the match between individuals and organizationally relevant work. This might be accomplished through a combination of traditional job analysis techniques, such as observation and critical incident interviews, with the addition of newer techniques such as cognitive task analysis and think-aloud protocols. In contrast to this process, a second approach is that of using mission statements and corporate goals as the foundation for competency modeling. This approach was in fact adopted by Intel Corporation, which tied it to identifying employee competencies compatible with the corporation's core values. These values were (1) taking risks and challenging the status quo, (2) emphasizing quality by setting high goals, (3) demonstrating discipline in project planning, meeting commitments, and conducting business with a high level of integrity, (4) serving customers by delivering innovative and competitive products as well as communicating expectations in a clear and timely fashion, (5) being results oriented, and (6) working as a team that has mutual respect for its members (Goldstein & Ford, 2002; Meister, 1994).

Competency modeling represents the evolution of work analysis along the lines suggested by Campbell's (1990a) study of performance components; it addresses the issue of what organizations pay people to do. In the past, traditional task-oriented job analysis often stopped short of considering the strategic goals of the organization. There was a link missing that connected human behavior and organizational goals. In some senses, motivation theories attempted to fill that gap, as we will see in Chapter 9. But as we suggested in Chapter 1, I-O practice and theory needs to be unified rather than fragmented. It is not enough to place the burden for the link between behavior and organizational success on the shoulders of one process (e.g., motivation of employees or methods of selection). Instead, the link should be apparent in many different approaches, including job and work analysis. By directly addressing the needs and the goals of the organization, competency modeling helps to reinforce that link.

MODULE 5.4 SUMMARY

- Electronic performance monitoring facilitates the gathering of job analysis information independent of what might be collected from subject matter experts (SMEs). Although electronic performance monitoring can be very cost effective and has the potential for providing detailed and accurate work logs, it is often unpopular with workers.

- Cognitive task analysis can provide a valuable addition to traditional job analysis procedures. Most job analyses concentrate on observable behavior, but special data collection techniques must be used for cognitive behavior because it is not directly observable. Because cognitive task analysis concentrates on *how* behavior occurs rather than on *what* is accomplished, it is a useful addition to the job analysis toolbag.

- Historically, job analysis instruments ignored personality attributes, concentrating on abilities, skills, and, less frequently, knowledge. A recently developed job analysis instrument (the Personality-Related Position Requirements Form) identifies personality predictors of job performance.

- The *Dictionary of Occupational Titles (D.O.T.)* was developed to provide a national database of jobs and job analysis information. In 1995 the federal government supplanted the *D.O.T.* with the Occupational Information Network, or O*NET, which is a collection of databases that contains information on experience requirements, work context, typical tasks and duties, wage expectations, requisite abilities, and basic skills.

- Just as job analysis seeks to define jobs and work in terms of the match between required tasks and human attributes, competency modeling seeks to define organizational units in terms of the match between the goals and missions of those units and the competencies required to meet those goals and accomplish those missions. Thus, competency modeling is a natural extension of the job analysis logic rather than a replacement for job analysis.

KEY TERMS

electronic performance
  monitoring
cognitive task analysis
think-aloud protocol
context of the work
realistic job preview (RJP)

Personality-Related Position
  Requirements Form (PPRF)
Work Profiling System (WPS)
*Dictionary of Occupational
  Titles (D.O.T.)*

Occupational Information
  Network (O*NET)
competency modeling

CRITICAL THINKING EXERCISES

5.7 Pick a friend or a classmate and create a think-aloud protocol for one of the following operations:

Tie a shoelace.

Decide on which channel to stop on while flipping channels with the channel changer.

Executing a left-hand turn across three lanes of oncoming traffic at an intersection with no traffic signals or signs.

Make sure you list each mental operation in detail, as if you would use the resulting protocol to train someone else to perform the action.

5.8 In the text we described three examples of electronic performance monitoring: monitoring of telephone service provided by customer service representatives, monitoring keystrokes and use of program menus by data processors, and the monitoring of truck driver performance with onboard computers. Identify three other jobs or occupations in which performance could be electronically monitored and describe how this would be carried out.

JOB EVALUATION, COMPARABLE WORTH, AND THE LAW

JOB EVALUATION

In determining how to pay individuals within an organization, employers must consider at least two perspectives. The first is the external perspective, that is, what is the marketplace paying for people who hold particular job titles: What pay rate would be considered "equitable" by an applicant or incumbent compared to the going market rate? All other things being equal, an incumbent or candidate is more likely to be attracted to a higher-paying than a lower-paying position. The second perspective is an internal one. The organization has a fixed amount of money to distribute to its employees. How will that fixed amount be divided? When individuals compare themselves to other employees of the same organization, will they consider themselves "equitably paid"? **Job evaluation** is a method for making these internal decisions by comparing job titles to one another and determining their relative merit by way of these comparisons. In most systems, there are pay ranges within a job title or category, allowing managers to make adjustments for the market, or for a particular incumbent with a special skill or knowledge.

Like traditional task-oriented job analysis, job evaluation represents more a view of the past than of the future, and for many of the same reasons. The procedures and principles are well described in many traditional personnel administration guides, such as *Elements of Sound Base Pay Administration* published jointly by the Society for Personnel Administration and the American Compensation Association (1981). In the past, compensation was viewed in terms of tasks and jobs. Most job evaluation systems identify what they call **compensable factors.** These factors usually include skills, responsibility, effort, and working conditions. With the changing theories of work as well as the structural and technological changes that are occurring in the workplace, it is becoming more common to think of work roles, competencies, human attributes, and team responsibilities than tasks or the traditional compensable factors such as responsibility or effort. Like traditional job analysis, job evaluation can play a worthwhile role. What is needed is to replace the old anchors used for comparison with new anchors. Before suggesting how that might be done, let's consider what job evaluation has been up to this point.

An Example of a Job Evaluation

Consider the typical output of a job evaluation for the position of forklift operator as presented in Table 5.6. In this figure, we see a number of discrete factors (e.g., experience, education, resourcefulness, monotony, hazards). Each of these factors represents an opportunity for a job to be assigned "points" representing how much of each factor is represented in the job. More points mean more of the factor. Thus, since the forklift job is not monotonous, it receives only 10 points. If the job was subassembly work on a production line with a 45-second cycle time for installing a motor, the monotony score might

JOB EVALUATION

Method for making internal pay decisions by comparing job titles to one another and determining their relative merit by way of these comparisons.

COMPENSABLE FACTORS

Factors in a job evaluation system that are given points that are later linked to compensation for various jobs within the organization; factors usually include skills, responsibility, effort, and working conditions.

TABLE 5.6	Job Evaluation Form for Forklift Operator	

	POINTS
Experience	
Must learn to operate fork truck and hand truck if he does not have this skill. Two to three weeks on-the-job training.	48
Education	
Requires ability to speak, read, and write English and understand simple written instructions. Should have knowledge of simple mathematics in order to complete certain daily reports. Grammar school education desirable.	32
Responsibility for equipment, tools, product, or material	
Could damage products if not stacked properly in freezer. Cost would vary from $100 to $500.	94
Resourcefulness	
Some variety in the job. Exercises some discretion in keeping freezer in order.	52
Responsibility for work of others	
None.	35
Monotony	
Has a number of tasks to perform. Works in several places and moves around.	10
Pressure of work	
Occasionally has problems keeping up with work pace.	46
Physical effort	
On feet most of day when not driving lift truck. Pushes and/or pulls stack of empty pallets with truck or moves full pallet with hand truck. Lifting involved in carrying boxes of damaged packages.	30
Surroundings	
In freezer (0°) for approximate total of 1½ to 2 hours daily. Occasionally on dock. Noisy in Cartoning Department.	38
Hazards	
Operates fork truck. Often ice on freezer floor; could skid. When driving fork truck on dock must be cautious—ice and water. Pallets of cases incorrectly stacked in freezer could topple on him.	30
Concentration	
Duties require close attention most of the time.	75
Total	490

be 40 points. Similarly, the opportunity for damage to the equipment or product is high, so the forklift job gets 94 points. For an accounting position, only 10 points might be assigned for this "responsibility" category.

Once points are assigned to each category, they are totaled to provide a summary point value for the job, and jobs are compared to each other for purposes of assigning hourly wage or salary rates. In the current example, there are 11 factors to be considered. These factors may be weighted differentially; an organization may value experience more than education, or resourcefulness more than concentration. This differential value concept is easily handled by allowing different categories to use different point scales. Experience may vary from a low of 0 (for a job that requires no experience) to a high of 60, while education may vary from a low of 0 (no formal education required) to a high of 50 for a high school diploma requirement.

In some respects, the job evaluation report in Table 5.6 resembles the job specification done in 1922 which we presented in Figure 5.6. The only real difference is that points have been added to categories in the job evaluation example. That is not to say that something is "wrong" or "old" about the notion of using internal work comparisons as a way of allocating money. What we are saying is that many job evaluation systems are using increasingly irrelevant comparison factors. Consider Table 5.7. Here we replace the "old" factors with new factors adapted from Campbell's performance model (Campbell et al., 1993). We also add adaptability, as suggested by the work of Pulakos et al. (2000), and the work context factors suggested by Strong et al. (1999). Heneman, Ledford, and Gresham (2000) presented a thoughtful treatment of the challenges of modern compensation systems. Their conclusions match the themes we have been following throughout this chapter: Modern employers need to link their compensation systems more closely to the strategic goals of their organization.

TABLE 5.7	Forklift Operator Job Evaluation Using Campbell's Eight Performance Factors, Adaptability Factors, and Work Context

FORKLIFT OPERATOR	POINTS
Task proficiency: Routine tasks	30
Nonspecific task proficiency: All tasks job specific.	10
Written and oral communication: Simple oral demand.	10
Facilitating peer and team performance: Works alone.	10
Supervision/leadership: No subordinates.	10
Management/administration: No administrative tasks.	10
Handling emergencies: Occasional loading dock emergencies.	20
Creative problem solving: Often must rearrange orders.	40
Unpredictable work situations: Usually routine situations.	20
Learning new technologies: No new technologies.	10
Interpersonal adaptability: Occasionally deals with demanding department managers.	40
Physically oriented adaptability: Extremes of heat and cold from freezer facilities to loading dock in winter and summer; dirt, noise, other forklifts operating in close proximity.	70
Interpersonal conflict: Occasional competing demands from different department managers.	20
Job demands: On and off lift truck continually, moves empty pallets by hand; repacks load by hand.	60
Consequence of error: Moves full pallets of expensive product; each pallet has a value in excess of $10,000.	50
Vigilance demands: Must be aware of the movement of workers and other forklifts in confined, visually confusing, poorly lit, and dirty storage areas.	80
Work Pace	20
Total	510

Note: Each compensable factor is worth a maximum of 100 points.

SOURCE: Based on Campbell, McCloy, Oppler, & Sager (1993).

THE CONCEPT OF COMPARABLE WORTH

Comparable worth is a phrase that contains practical, philosophical, social, emotional, and legal implications. In its simplest form, it means that people who are performing comparable work should receive comparable pay, so that their worth to the organization in terms of compensation is "comparable." That is the practical implication of the term. Various experts have suggested the use of internal controls (e.g., job evaluation) and external controls (e.g., salary surveys) to assure this comparability, or that job evaluation techniques be used to calibrate the pay levels of various jobs in an organization and thus assure at least some internal comparability.

> **COMPARABLE WORTH**
>
> *Notion that people who are performing jobs of comparable worth to the organization should receive comparable pay.*

The problem with this concept is arriving at a definition of "comparable work." Should this be defined based on skills and abilities required for the work, tasks assigned to the job title, experience and education required, competencies required, or roles filled? If it were simply based on abilities and skills utilized in the job, one might expect a loading dock supervisor and a librarian to be paid similarly since they both check things in and out of their respective work locations, use inventory lists, and record the movements of material. If it were based on tasks assigned, one would expect a librarian in town A to be paid comparably to a librarian in town B, but you would not necessarily expect any comparability between the job of a loading dock supervisor and the job of a librarian.

There has been a great deal of debate regarding the relative pay levels of men and women. The question is whether or not women are paid less than men for the "same" work (Michael, Hartmann, & O'Farrell, 1989). Thus, the phrase "comparable worth" has taken on legal and social policy meanings well beyond the process of calibrating pay scales within an organization. The **Equal Pay Act of 1963** requires "equal pay for equal work." Equal work has usually been defined in terms of similar or identical job titles. Consider the example of an accounting department in a retail business. One subsection is devoted to billing (accounts receivable), while the other subsection is responsible for paying vendors or suppliers (accounts payable). Let's assume that the accounts receivable subsection is composed of predominantly male employees, and that they are paid at a higher scale than the accounts payable employees, who are predominantly female. The female employees in accounts payable might justifiably argue that their work is comparable to that of the males in accounts receivable, and therefore they are entitled to comparable compensation. The company might respond that the value of the work of the accounts receivable subsection is considerably greater than the value of the work of the accounts payable department and use a job evaluation analysis to support its position. But the job evaluation process itself might be criticized, either for using the mechanics of the process to prop up long-standing patterns of discrimination (Trieman & Hartmann, 1981) or for being subject to various biasing influences that might creep into each stage of the job evaluation process (Arvey, 1986).

> **EQUAL PAY ACT OF 1963**
>
> *Prohibits discrimination on the basis of sex in the payment of wages or benefits, where men and women perform work of similar skill, effort, and responsibility for the same employer under similar working conditions.*

In the end, the comparable worth issue is about the social value of fairness, not just about the mechanics of a process such as job evaluation. It is about the motives and potential biases of decision makers and, as such, is more likely to be resolved on a case by case basis by judges or juries than by science. Rynes and Gerhart (2001) and Michael et al. (1989), among others, provide excellent treatment of general compensation issues as well as the more specific issues associated with comparable worth arguments.

JOB ANALYSIS AND EMPLOYMENT LITIGATION

In the decades since the passage of Title VII of the Civil Rights Act of 1964, job analysis has occupied a central role in employment discrimination lawsuits for several reasons. In all trials, criminal or civil, there is a heavy dependence on the chain of evidence. In employment litigation, this chain means a series of links or connections between a test score and a predicted level of performance. We examined these links in some detail in Chapter 2 when we discussed models of validation. Traditional task-oriented job analysis has often been accepted as a necessary, although not sufficient, condition for establishing the validity of selection tests. In other words, while a competent job analysis would not guarantee that a test would be found valid, the *absence* of a credible job analysis might be enough to doom any claim of job-relatedness. How could a test be job related if the testing agent did not know what the critical tasks of the job were? This is the logic of the *Uniform Guidelines on Employee Selection Procedures* (1978), and these guidelines are the only formal statement of the government's position on job-relatedness. As such, they are often cited as the standard for the consideration of the adequacy of a job analysis.

Despite the fact that acceptable methods of job analysis have been recognized for decades, court cases dealing with employment discrimination even today often dissolve into arcane and mind-numbing arguments about the adequacy of SMEs or the missing link between a test question and a job task. Landy (1986) has likened the arguments to those of the scribes in biblical times who sat outside the temple doors, interpreting scripture to determine whether or not a sin had been committed. The *Uniform Guidelines* were published in 1978, long before the advent of globalization, digitization, teamwork, validity generalization, performance models such as Campbell's, cognitive task analysis, and competency modeling. As a result, the gap between the evolution of I-O psychology and the *Uniform Guidelines* continues to grow. This creates a problem of interpretation or extrapolation if only the guidelines are used for evaluation of a validity design. Since employers must still recognize the controlling power of the *Uniform Guidelines,* it is important to show how these guidelines can be interpreted as consistent with current needs and practice. This is the joint responsibility of the I-O psychologist and the employer. Fortunately, SIOP continues to update HR scientific knowledge and principles for test validation. A revision of the SIOP Principles will be published in 2003. Thus, the best suggestion for an employer is to be aware of the *Uniform Guidelines* as well as the 2003 revision of the SIOP Principles and to use both documents to evaluate the adequacy of a validity design. It is likely that there will always be a role for some traditional form of job analysis such as a task or human attributes-based analysis; the addition of the newer and more vibrant extensions such as competency modeling, cognitive task analysis, and performance components to facilitate strategic planning will enhance the results of a job analysis even more.

MODULE 5.5 SUMMARY

- In determining how to pay individuals within an organization, employers must consider two perspectives. The first is the external perspective: How does the pay rate compare to the going market rate? The second perspective is internal, one which can be addressed by job evaluation or by comparing job titles to one another and determining their relative merit by way of these comparisons.

- Most job evaluation systems identify compensable factors, which usually include skills, responsibility, effort, and working conditions. With the changing theories of work and the structural and technological changes occurring in the workplace,

organizational decision makers are increasingly thinking of work roles, competencies, human attributes, and team responsibilities rather than tasks or the traditional compensable factors such as responsibility or effort.

- The phrase "comparable worth" has taken on legal and social policy meanings beyond the process of calibrating pay scales within an organization. The comparable worth issue is about the social value of fairness, not just the mechanics of a process such as job evaluation. It is about the motives and potential biases of decision makers and, as such, is more likely to be resolved on a case-by-case basis by judges or juries than by science.

• Since the passage of Title VII of the Civil Rights Act of 1964, job analysis has occupied a central role in employment discrimination lawsuits. Traditional task-oriented job analysis has often been accepted as a necessary, although not sufficient, condition for establishing the validity of selection tests. Thus, although a competent job analysis would not guarantee that a test would be found valid, the absence of a credible job analysis might be enough to doom any claim of job-relatedness.

KEY TERMS

job evaluation

compensable factors

comparable worth

Equal Pay Act of 1963

CRITICAL THINKING EXERCISES

5.9 Historically, the compensable factors included in a job evaluation have been skills, responsibility, effort, and working conditions. Based on what you have encountered in this chapter, what compensable factors would you add to this list?

5.10 In supermarkets you are more likely to find women as cashiers than behind the meat counter. Further, cashiers are usually paid less than employees of the meat department. Cashiers have complained that women are being paid less than men in this store and cited the wage differential between the mostly male meat cutter job title and the mostly female cashier job title as evidence that supports their complaint. Management argues that the profit in the meat department largely determines the profit of the store, thus the wage differential is fair to employees.

Consider this situation from the two opposite perspectives, management and cashiers.

If you were hired in the capacity of an I-O psychologist by store management to use job evaluation to provide data in support of management's position, what type of evaluation data would you gather?

PERFORMANCE MEASUREMENT

6 CHAPTER

BASIC CONCEPTS IN PERFORMANCE MEASUREMENT

USES FOR PERFORMANCE INFORMATION

Performance measurement is universal. Your instructor will measure your performance in this class by assigning a grade. You, in turn, may measure your instructor's performance by completing an instructor evaluation rating form at the end of the course. Fans measure the performance of their favorite baseball team by looking at their win-loss record and current standing in the league. Parents often use performance measurement devices such as homemade charts to track their children's accomplishment of household chores. In the world of work, supervisors evaluate their subordinates' performance by means of an annual review. Performance evaluation is prevalent in many facets of our lives.

In many work settings, performance measurement goes beyond the annual review and can be used for many purposes. Some of the most common are:

- *Criterion data*—In a criterion-related validation study of a selection device or battery, the I-O psychologist can correlate an individual's performance data with test data to determine if the test predicts successful performance.

- *Employee development*—A worker is given information about strengths and weaknesses, and works with a supervisor to develop a plan to strengthen weaknesses and build upon strengths; based on the profile of performance strengths and weaknesses, employers may design a series of training modules or experiences for an employee.

- *Motivation/satisfaction*—By setting appropriate performance standards, evaluating employees' success in meeting those standards, and giving employees feedback regarding the extent to which they are meeting or exceeding those standards, an organization can increase the motivation and satisfaction of those employees (Bobko & Colella, 1994).

- *Rewards*—Employers compare workers to one another to determine how to distribute rewards such as salary increases and bonuses.

- *Transfer*—Employers can use a profile of performance capabilities to determine which employees are best suited for a transfer from one job family or job title to another.

- *Promotion*—To the extent that documented performance capabilities are part of a higher-level job, employers can use performance information as part of the assessment procedure that determines promotions.

- *Layoff*—If an organization finds it necessary to downsize, one factor that might be used to guide the selection of those to be laid off could be performance; employees with the fewest performance strengths would be the most likely candidates for layoff.

Types of Performance Data

As you learned in Chapter 5, three different types of data can be used to represent performance: objective, personnel, and judgmental data. You also were introduced to the concept of criterion contamination and deficiency, underscoring the point that quality control issues figure in the choice of a performance measure.

Relationships among Performance Measures

We introduced the three classes of performance data independently, but it might be reasonable to assume that they are not independent. For example, we might assume that there should be a relationship between the objective indicators of an employee's performance and the ratings a supervisor assigns to that employee. But as reasonable as this might seem, research indicates that the relationships among the different types of performance measures are very weak. Heneman (1986) analyzed the results of 23 independent studies and, even after adjusting the correlations for the effects of unreliability in the measures, found very low correlations between supervisory ratings and **objective performance measures** such as sales volume, complaint letters, and output. Specifically, the correlation was approximately +.20. Although such a value may be statistically significant, we would expect the value to be much higher if we are really just looking at different measures of the same thing, that is, performance. A later study by Bommer, Johnson, Rich, Podsakoff, and McKenzie (1995) examined a larger number of studies and found a slightly higher average correlation (about +.39) between ratings and objective measures of performance after correcting for sample size and range restriction as well as rater unreliability. The point to be understood here is that performance measures do not seem to be interchangeable.

These studies lead us to several conclusions. The first is that each type of performance measure gives us a different perspective on performance. As Campbell (1990) pointed out, there is no "general" or unitary performance factor. A second conclusion that follows from the first is that we cannot simply substitute an objective measure for a rating, or vice versa. Bommer et al. (1995) suggested that the traditional distinction between "objective" and "subjective" or "judgmental" measures is a false one, since even so-called objective measures entail many judgments (e.g., in looking at the number of production defects attributed to a certain employee, what do you decide to call a "defect"?). A third conclusion to be drawn from these studies is that despite the intuitive appeal of objective measures, they are not necessarily more reliable. Further, objective measures tend to be more narrow in scope than judgmental measures. As Campbell (1990) argued, **judgmental performance measures** (such as supervisory ratings) are more likely to capture the nuances and complexity of work performance than objective measures.

Hands-on Performance Measures

As we saw in Chapter 4, work samples measure job skills by taking a sample of behavior in standardized conditions. Although we discussed work samples as a form of preemployment assessment, they can also be used for assessing the current skills of an employee. To assess computer skills, for example, we could present a spreadsheet problem or a memo to be edited, or ask for the production of a PowerPoint slide show, and score according to how well (or quickly) the individual accomplished the task. Since the performance measure requires the employee to engage in work-related tasks, this procedure is often called **"hands-on-performance measurement"** (Harris, 1987; Wigdor & Green, 1991). Hands-on measures are usually carefully constructed simulations of central or critical pieces of work that involve single workers, thus eliminating the effects of inadequate equipment, production demands, or day-to-day work environment differences—some of the contaminating influences in objective measures. It also permits the observation of infrequent but important work activities, such as a firefighter's use of hydraulic cutters to extract an accident victim from a vehicle, or a nuclear power plant operator's reducing the temperature of superheated reactor water.

OBJECTIVE PERFORMANCE MEASURE

Usually a quantitative count of the results of work such as sales volume, complaint letters, and output.

JUDGMENTAL PERFORMANCE MEASURE

Evaluation made of the effectiveness of an individual's work behavior, most often by supervisors in the context of a yearly performance evaluation.

HANDS-ON PERFORMANCE MEASUREMENT

Requires an employee to engage in work-related tasks; usually includes carefully constructed simulations of central or critical pieces of work that involve single workers.

As part of a large-scale project for studying the performance of military personnel, the U.S. Army developed a hands-on measure of the proficiency of the position of tank crewman (Wigdor & Green, 1987). The parts of the hands-on assessment included some of the most important aspects of tank crewman performance as determined through a job analysis. The hands-on measure required the crewman to climb into a tank and:

- Operate the radio system used to communicate with friendly ground forces outside the tank.
- Operate the internal communication system used to speak with other crew personnel in the tank when it is in operation.
- Position the tank cannon for firing.
- Disassemble and reassemble an automatic handheld weapon.

Each crewman was asked to complete the tasks one at a time while a trained observer scored the actions on a checklist. The resulting performance measures were reliable. In addition, since they came directly from a job analysis, they were also valid. Since hands-on measures are based directly on the job in question, employees trust them as measures of performance (Hedge & Borman, 1995). Trust is a major issue in performance measurement, one we will discuss at some length later in the chapter.

An extension of the hands-on methodology is known as **"walk-through testing"** (Hedge & Teachout, 1992). This method requires an employee to actually describe to an interviewer in detail how to complete a task or job-related behavior. The interviewer then scores the employee on the basis of the correct and incorrect aspects of the description. In some applications of this method, the employee actually "walks through" the facility (e.g., a nuclear power plant) answering questions as he or she actually sees the displays or controls in question. The advantage to this extension of the hands-on method is that it permits the assessment of actions that are not feasible for hands-on assessment (Hedge & Borman, 1995). As an example, instead of actually manipulating controls, as in the hands-on measure, a nuclear power plant operator might be asked to simply describe the procedure for correcting a low-water alarm for a cooling system or reacting to an unexpected release of radioactive water.

The disadvantages of hands-on measures are that they can be expensive to develop, they cover only a portion or sample of the work performance of an individual, and they measure what an individual "can do" rather than what that individual "will do" (Hedge & Borman, 1995; Landy, 1989).

The "road test" to qualify for a driver's license is an example of a hands-on performance test.

WALK-THROUGH TESTING

Requires an employee to describe to an interviewer in detail how to complete a task or job-related behavior; employee may literally walk through the facility (e.g., a nuclear power plant) answering questions as he or she actually sees the displays or controls in question.

Electronic Performance Monitoring

As you saw in the last chapter, the modern workplace provides many opportunities to gather performance information through the electronic medium. In the year 2000, an estimated 40 million workers were being monitored by computer, videotape, and audio devices (Botan, 1996). On the positive side, the claim is made that since such measures are clearly objective and job-related, they are more "fair" than other measures. Those opposed to **electronic performance monitoring** argue that it is "an invasion of privacy and disregards human rights, undermines trust, reduces autonomy and emphasizes quantity at the exclusion of quality . . . causes stress . . . and leads to declines in employee morale and productivity" (Hedge & Borman, 1995). An example of this critical view is presented by a case study of an airline's monitoring of its reservations agents. Agents were allowed 11 seconds between calls, and a total of 12 minutes in a workday to get a drink of water, use

ELECTRONIC PERFORMANCE MONITORING

Monitoring work processes with electronic devices; can be very cost effective and has the potential for providing detailed and accurate work logs.

Electronic performance monitoring is often used in customer service call centers and other telephone-based work situations.

the bathroom, and so on. If an agent was unplugged from the electronic system more than two times a week without authorization, the airline instituted disciplinary measures (Piller, 1993).

The research data on electronic performance monitoring from actual work situations is sparse and is usually related to attitudes rather than performance. For example, Botan (1996) found that 465 information workers (telephone operators and installers) reported that the more they were monitored, the more likely they were to feel that their privacy had been invaded, their role in the workplace was uncertain, their self-esteem was lowered, and workplace communication suffered. On the other hand, a good deal of laboratory research has been done, and the results seem to support both the advocates and the critics of electronic performance monitoring (Aiello & Kolb, 1995; Alge, 2001; Douthitt & Aiello, 2001; Larson & Callahan, 1990; Stanton & Barnes-Farrell, 1996). These studies usually involve monitoring the performance of students who are assigned computer-based tasks, in general concluding that employees are more likely to be positive toward performance monitoring if:

- They believe the activities monitored are job relevant.
- They are able to participate in the design or implementation of the monitoring system (in Chapter 11, where we deal with fairness, we will see that participation is seen as "voice," an opportunity to be heard). In addition, the possibility of exerting an influence can reduce stress.
- They are able to delay or prevent monitoring at particular times.

These studies also indicated that improved performance resulted when:

- Highly skilled students/workers were monitored.
- The student/worker was able to delay or prevent monitoring at particular times.
- Lower-skilled students/workers were not monitored.

Certainly, there is a difference between actual workers and students playing a role as workers. It is unfortunate that more field research has not been conducted, but as monitoring continues to increase, more field research is likely to emerge.

It appears that electronic performance monitoring must be used carefully to avoid reducing motivation and satisfaction while improving performance. Hedge and Borman (1995) suggested that the most effective use might be for employee development, as a way of providing feedback concerning effective and ineffective work behaviors. This is suggested by an interviewing study (Laabs, 1992) conducted with managers and employees at companies like Duke Power, AT&T, Toyota, Avis, and Charles Schwab. Turnage (1990) suggested that if the results of monitoring provide accurate, meaningful, and nonevaluative feedback, then goal setting and feelings of personal control will be enhanced, which in turn will enhance worker motivation.

Performance Management

Twenty years ago, I-O and HR texts had extensive sections on "performance appraisal" or "performance evaluation." Now you are just as likely to encounter the term "performance management" along with the other two because most people who have been evaluated are unhappy with their evaluation, unless of course they receive the highest marks available (Bernardin et al., 1998). The cynic might suggest that by choosing the term "performance management," we have simply put old wine in new bottles and that there is really no difference. The cynic would be wrong.

As we saw in Chapter 5, the term "performance" derives its meaning from the organizational context in which it occurs. As Campbell (1993) observed, performance is determined by what is valuable to the organization. It is the behavior for which the employee is compensated. In the past, performance appraisal and evaluation systems were based exclusively on task-oriented job analysis systems and were only accidentally related to organizational goals or profitability. **Performance management** systems emphasize the link between individual behavior and organizational strategies and goals by defining performance in the context of those goals (Banks & May, 1999). They combine traditional task analysis with strategic job analysis, thus including goals and organizational strategies in the process.

Performance management also differs from performance appraisal in several other important ways. Banks and May (1999) have noted the following differences:

• Performance appraisal occurs once a year and is initiated by a request from HR; performance management occurs at much more frequent intervals and can be initiated by a supervisor or by a subordinate.

• Performance appraisal systems are developed by HR and handed to managers to use in the evaluation of subordinates; performance management systems are jointly developed by managers and the employees who report to them.

• Performance appraisal feedback occurs once each year and follows the appraisal process; performance management feedback occurs whenever a supervisor or subordinate feels the need for a discussion about expectations and performance.

• In performance appraisal, the appraiser's role is to reach agreement with the employee appraised about the level of effectiveness displayed and to identify areas for improvement; in performance management, the appraiser's role is to understand the performance criteria and help the employee understand how his or her behavior fits with those criteria, as well as to look for areas of potential improvement. Thus, in performance management, the supervisor and the employee are attempting to come to some shared meaning about expectations and the strategic value of those expectations, rather than simply clarifying the meaning of a nonstrategic performance area and definitions of effectiveness in that area.

• In performance appraisal, the appraisee's role is to accept or reject the evaluation and acknowledge areas that need improvement; in performance management, the role of the appraisee is identical to the role of the appraiser: to understand the performance criteria and understand how his or her behavior fits with those criteria.

Performance management has three distinct components. The first component consists of the definition of performance, which includes organizational objectives and strategies. The second component is the actual measurement process itself. The third component is the communication between supervisor and subordinate about the extent to which individual behavior fits with organizational expectations (Banks & May, 1999). When seen in this light, it becomes clear that performance *appraisal* is most closely related to the second component of the performance management system, the measurement component. But because it lacks the additional components entailed in performance *management* (i.e., active involvement of the appraisee in developing and understanding the measurement system, and follow-up and ongoing communication regarding expectations and accomplishments of the organization and individual), performance appraisal is a one-dimensional process in a multidimensional world.

Many of the components of performance management have been recommended for years as valuable to performance assessment. The importance of performance management is that the process combines most of these suggestions and adds the overlay of the strategic importance of various performance areas, a concept seldom adopted in more traditional performance assessment initiatives.

Perceptions of Fairness in Performance Measurement

Both Bernardin et al. (1998) and Banks and May (1999) emphasized that traditional performance appraisal systems often engender anger and hostility among those appraised. In Chapter 11 on fairness, you will see that performance appraisal is one of the most common sources of feelings of unfairness and injustice among workers. A lengthy research trail confirms that the process of being appraised can upset people. Landy and his colleagues (Landy, Barnes, & Murphy, 1978; Landy, Barnes-Farrell, & Cleveland, 1980) identified four factors associated with fairness perceptions in performance measurement:

1. The frequency of appraisal was positively related to perceptions of fairness.
2. Joint planning with a supervisor to eliminate weaknesses enhanced fairness perceptions.
3. The supervisor's knowledge of the duties of the person being rated resulted in greater feelings of fairness.
4. The supervisor's knowledge of the actual performance of the person being rated was also associated with perceptions of fairness.

Interestingly, the actual rating the employees received was not related to feelings of fairness, as long as the four conditions described above were met. The employees may not have been happy with their rating, but at least they felt that they were treated fairly.

As we will see in Chapters 9, 10, and 11, feelings of fairness are important; they have implications for motivation, satisfaction, performance, turnover, absence, and other counterproductive behaviors such as theft and sabotage. Recently, fairness perceptions in performance measurement have been framed as "justice" issues. We will consider procedural, distributive, and interpersonal justice in great detail in Chapter 11. In the case of performance measurement, these justice issues take on a specific form. **Distributive justice** is related to whether the rewards (or punishments) match the performance; **procedural justice** is related to the actual process by which ratings were assigned; and **interpersonal justice** is related to the respectfulness and personal tone of the communications surrounding the evaluation, particularly the feedback and performance planning that follows the evaluation (Gilliland & Langdon, 1998).

Gilliland and Langdon (1998) suggested that procedural and interpersonal fairness become particularly important when evaluations and decisions are negative. A good example of this phenomenon is the case of downsizing and accompanying layoffs. When layoffs occur, they frequently involve middle-level managers. The majority of middle-level managers are age 40 or older, since it usually takes substantial experience and seniority to rise to that level. Many of these individuals have been with the organization for 20 years or more and feel betrayed when they are laid off. Most layoff decisions are based, at least in part, on evaluations of past performance. Sometimes this involves averaging performance scores from the past few years, whereas in other cases it involves a new performance appraisal used solely for the purpose of providing information for the layoff decisions. Until the layoff, many of the middle-level managers had never paid close attention to the performance evaluation process. Many report that they had not been evaluated for many years and had never received any negative information about their performance from their manager. As a result, when they file a lawsuit against the organization for their layoff, nominally on the basis of age discrimination, the underlying reason is their belief that the employer acted unfairly. They cite the performance evaluation system as flawed, and allege that they were treated unfairly in the evaluation process. To put their arguments in a "justice" perspective, they claim that their performance was acceptable and that the layoff was not warranted (distributive justice); that the evaluation process

DISTRIBUTIVE JUSTICE

Focuses on the fairness of outcomes related to decisions made in the organization.

PROCEDURAL JUSTICE

Focuses on the fairness of the process by which ratings were assigned or decisions were made.

INTERPERSONAL JUSTICE

Focuses on the respectfulness and personal tone of the communications surrounding the evaluation, particularly the feedback and performance planning that follows the evaluation.

was arbitrary, slipshod, and inconsistent (procedural justice); and that no one ever took the time or showed the courtesy to explain the process or provide feedback about their performance over the years (interpersonal justice). These "justice" claims are the foundation for their belief that they were treated unfairly. When we consider the role of performance measurement in employment litigation later in this chapter, we will see that judges and juries are also influenced by the procedural fairness of the performance measurement process.

Gilliland and Langdon (1998) listed actions an employer can take to enhance feelings of fairness surrounding performance measurement:

- Make sure that employees have the opportunity to participate in all phases of the performance management process, including the development of the process, the evaluation itself, and the feedback process. The value of this suggestion has been confirmed in a meta-analysis of 27 separate studies of the relationship between participation and satisfaction. Cawley, Keeping, and Levy (1998) found that participation in the development and implementation of the performance measurement system was highly correlated (+.61) with employee satisfaction with and acceptance of the performance measurement system.
- Ensure consistency in all steps and phases of the process.
- Ensure that evaluations are based on job-related factors and free from biases.
- Provide an avenue for employees to challenge and discuss the accuracy of the evaluation.
- Communicate with employees about all aspects of the process.
- Provide timely and informative feedback.
- Treat employees with courtesy and respect.
- Make sure that employees are not surprised by outcomes (positive or negative).

Each of these recommendations addresses some issue of perceived justice, as we have described these concepts above. We will deal with these issues again in Chapter 11 when we consider perceptions of fairness in the workplace.

MODULE 6.1 SUMMARY

- In many work settings, performance measurement goes beyond the annual review and is used for many purposes, such as employee development, motivation, rewards, transfer, promotion, and layoffs.
- Hands-on performance measures are usually carefully constructed simulations of critical pieces of work that involve single workers. Hands-on performance measurement also permits the assessment of infrequent but important work activities. An extension of the hands-on methodology is known as "walk-through testing," which requires an employee to describe to an interviewer in detail how to complete a task or job-related behavior, usually at the workplace in question.
- Electronic performance monitoring can be a cost-effective way to gather performance information. The research data on electronic performance monitoring from actual work situations is sparse and is usually related to attitudes rather than performance. However, it appears that organizations must use electronic performance monitoring carefully to avoid reducing worker motivation and satisfaction while improving performance.
- Since the 1980s many organizations have replaced the terms "performance appraisal" and "performance evaluation" with the term "performance management." Performance management systems emphasize the link between individual behavior and organizational strategies and goals by defining performance in the context of those goals.
- Traditional performance appraisal systems often engender anger and hostility among those appraised. Recently, fairness perceptions in performance measurement have been framed as "justice" issues that include distributive justice, procedural justice, and interpersonal justice.

KEY TERMS

objective performance measure

judgmental performance
measure

hands-on performance
measurement

walk-through testing

electronic performance
monitoring

performance management

distributive justice

procedural justice

interpersonal justice

CRITICAL THINKING EXERCISES

6.1 Many individuals think that "objective" measures are the preferred way to assess performance since they would seem to be less subject to interpretation than subjective measures. Do you agree? Identify one objective measure of performance and describe the different ways it might be subject to interpretation.

6.2 Performance assessments are often seen as unfair to the person being assessed. List three reasons why a company or manager should care about whether or not performance assessments are perceived as fair by employees.

PERFORMANCE RATING— SUBSTANCE

CLOSE-UP ON A RATING SYSTEM

In many of the courses you take, you will be asked to rate the instructor's effectiveness at the end of the term. An example of a typical rating form appears in Table 6.1. As you can see, there are seven rating questions and one open-ended question. This rating form has four distinct parts. The first part consists of instructions (e.g., how to enter the responses).

TABLE 6.1	Hypothetical Instructor Evaluation Form

Preliminary questions

1. What Grade do you expect to receive in this course?____

   For the remaining questions, use the following response scale:

   1 = Very poor

   2 = poor

   3 = Satisfactory

   4 = Good

   5 = Outstanding

   6 = Irrelevant to this course

2. The degree to which your knowledge and understanding of subject matter was enhanced by this course

3. Your overall summary evaluation of this course

Instructor-related questions

4. Degree to which the instructor is clear and well organized

5. Degree to which exams and assignments contribute to learning

6. Degree to which instructor is helpful to students in and out of class

7. Degree to which this instructor has made you want to take additional courses in this area

8. Your overall summary evaluation of the instructor

9. Any additional comments you would like to make:

   _____

   _____

   _____

The second part consists of the actual areas of instruction to be rated. For example, question 4 deals with how well organized the instructor is, question 5 deals with testing techniques, and question 6 deals with interpersonal factors. The third part of the form contains the actual numbers or ratings that will be assigned (1–6), and the fourth part deals with the definition of those numbers (e.g., 1 = very poor, 3 = satisfactory, 5 = outstanding). If you were the instructor, how would you feel about being evaluated on this form? Suppose that your evaluation determined whether or not you would get a salary increase for the coming year. Suppose further that your evaluation was poor. Would you feel "fairly" treated in this evaluation process? You might not, and you might single out the rating form and process as the source of your feelings of unfairness. You might raise the following objections:

1. You have high standards and gave few A's; students punished you for those standards.

2. The form ignores many classroom behaviors that add to the value of your teaching, such as your creative ability to devise easy-to-understand examples, or your habit of arriving early and staying after class to chat with students.

3. There are no definitions of what is meant by "poor" or "satisfactory" or "outstanding"; the standard of each student is used in deciding what rating correctly conveys his or her evaluation.

4. Students in your course are mostly nonmajors who lack a firm base in the major area and struggled with the material because it was unfamiliar. The nonmajors would probably not take another course in this area because this course simply fulfilled an elective slot.

5. Many of the written comments indicated that the students wanted more humor in the lectures, but you are simply not a humorous lecturer.

6. You have been assigned the most popular class time, 11:00 A.M.; as a result, your section had three times more students than any other section.

Many I-O psychologists have studied student ratings of instructors (Centra, 1993; d'Appolonia & Abrami, 1997; Greenwald, 1997; Greenwald & Gillmore, 1997; Marsh, 1984; Marsh & Roche, 1997). Their general conclusions are that the departments that create these

Students are often asked to rate their instructors.

rating forms are unsophisticated with respect to the theory of rating and to the best practices in the development of performance rating forms (McKeachie, 1997). Like any performance rating forms, instructor rating forms can be valuable adjuncts to the instructional process if they are well developed.

THEORIES OF PERFORMANCE RATING

Since performance rating is one of the most common techniques for performance measurement, it has received a great deal of attention (Landy & Farr, 1980; Landy & Farr, 1983; Landy, Zedeck, & Cleveland, 1983; Murphy & Cleveland, 1995). This attention has led to increasingly sophisticated models of the performance rating process. One of the early theories was presented by Landy and Farr (1980), who addressed the various factors that comprise the process of rating. Figure 6.1 presents that model and the descriptions of the factors in that model. This is a dizzying array of possible influences, but it does point out the complexity of the performance rating process. In the years since that model was proposed, other researchers have presented additional models, often emphasizing the cognitive factors in rating rather than the situational factors. These models have emphasized things like memory, reasoning, and information processing (Feldman, 1981; Murphy & Balzer, 1986; Srull & Wyer, 1989; Woehr & Feldman, 1993).

Borman, White, Pulakos, and Oppler (1991) proposed a model that addresses the content input to supervisory ratings (see Figure 6.2). As you can see, they identified five direct contributors and two indirect contributors to supervisory ratings. Ability and job knowledge, the indirect contributors, influence supervisory ratings through their effects on task proficiency.

A recent trend in the examination of the phenomenon of supervisory rating has been to emphasize the **context** of the rating. Context includes both the announced purpose and other, nonannounced agendas. Note that in the original Landy and Farr (1980) model, context was represented by "Purpose for Rating" and "Organization Characteristics." Context variables have been greatly expanded since then, and we will discuss them in detail later in this chapter.

CONTEXT

Includes both the announced purpose and other, nonannounced agendas of the circumstances surrounding performance ratings.

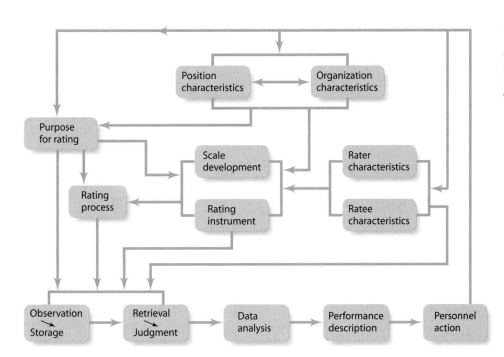

FIGURE 6.1

A Process Model of Performance Rating
SOURCE: Landy & Farr (1980).

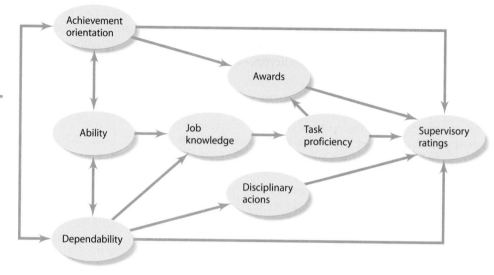

FIGURE 6.2

A Content Model of Performance Rating
SOURCE: Adapted from Borman, White, Pulakos, & Oppler (1991).

FOCUS ON PERFORMANCE RATINGS
Overall Performance Ratings

Performance rating forms often have different levels of magnification. Some are very broad and culminate with overall ratings of performance, such as you saw in questions 3 and 8 of Table 6.1. This high-level focus is usually driven by a desire for simplicity, and usually for administrative purposes. For example, monetary rewards may be distributed to people who have been rated above some predetermined level. But, for all practical purposes, overall performance has no "real" or conceptual meaning. It is like a grade point average. It is a simple administrative index. Studies have demonstrated that these overall ratings are differentially affected by various factors, including some that have not been explicitly presented to raters for consideration. For example, Ganzach (1995) demonstrated that negative performance information has a stronger influence on overall ratings than positive performance when the overall level of performance is not high. As the old saying goes, one "Aw, darn!" incident neutralizes a thousand "Way to go!" incidents.

Johnson (2001) showed that both contextual performance factors (Borman & Motowidlo, 1993, 1997) and adaptability factors (Pulakos et al., 2000), which we described in the last chapter, influenced overall performance ratings. In the Johnson study, supervisors made explicit ratings on contextual and adaptive performance, but many performance rating forms include neither of these performance aspects. It is likely that even though they are not included, they still influence overall ratings, in part, because they seem to be universal performance requirements of the modern workplace. Rotundo and Sackett (2002) found that overall ratings of performance were influenced by three factors: **task performance, contextual performance,** and **counterproductive performance.** The relative importance of these factors did not vary by job, even though the jobs included accountant, administrative assistant, cashier, machine operator, and nurse. This is surprising. For example, we might think of contextual performance as more important for evaluating the overall performance of an administrative assistant than an accountant.

What we can conclude from this research on the value of "overall performance ratings" is that they are not very valuable, at least from the psychological perspective. This overall rating is a box car, carrying a mix of "freight." As Campbell (1990) pointed out, there is no "unitary" performance factor, so from a conceptual standpoint there is nothing to represent. Further, the research described above shows not only that many different factors influence overall ratings, but also that these factors may *differ* from rater to

TASK PERFORMANCE

Proficiency with which job incumbents perform activities formally recognized as a part of their job.

CONTEXTUAL PERFORMANCE

Performance that supports the organizational, social, and psychological environment in which the job tasks are performed; behaviors or activities that are not typically part of job descriptions.

COUNTER-PRODUCTIVE PERFORMANCE

Voluntary behavior that violates significant organizational norms and in so doing, threatens the well-being of the organization, its members, or both; also called counterproductive employee behavior.

rater, making it impossible to draw valid comparisons *between* workers who are rated by different supervisors. Instead of obtaining overall performance ratings, it is advisable to obtain ratings of specific aspects of performance. If necessary, these individual ratings can be summed or averaged (with or without specific weights) to yield an overall estimate of performance.

Trait Ratings

The only reason we introduce the notion of trait ratings is to warn you against them. Performance ratings were introduced by Patterson in 1923 and at that time, it was common to have supervisors evaluate subordinates on traits such as "persistence," "concentration," or "alertness." Look back at the job description from 1922 that was presented in Figure 5.6 in Chapter 5. The modern view of performance evaluation is that the rater should be describing actions or behaviors (Campbell, 1990) rather than broad and amorphous "traits" that may or may not be of value in a job. Well-defined traits, such as the Big Five personality characteristics, may very well support effective performance, but they are not actions or behaviors. Traits are habits or tendencies that can be used as predictors of performance but not as measures of performance. In addition, as we will see in Module 6.4, performance measurement systems based on behaviors are much more legally defensible than those based on traits.

Task-Based Ratings

Task-based performance rating systems are usually a direct extension of job analysis (Harvey, 1991). The rater is asked to indicate the effectiveness of an employee on individual critical tasks or on groups of similar tasks, often called **"duties,"** to distinguish task groups from individual tasks. Table 6.2 presents examples of task groups for the position of patrol officer. As you can see from those examples, the tasks actually help the rater to better understand what they are rating in that duty (group) area. These types of ratings tend to be the most easily defended in court, and most easily accepted by incumbents, because of the clear and direct relationship between the duties rated and the job in question.

DUTIES

Groups of similar tasks; each duty involves a segment of work directed at one of the general goals of a job.

CRITICAL INCIDENTS

Examples of behavior that appear "critical" in determining whether performance would be good, average, or poor in specific performance areas.

Critical Incidents Methods

Critical incidents (Flanagan, 1954) are examples of behavior that appeared "critical" in determining whether performance would be good, average, or poor in specific performance areas (Landy, 1989). As an example, consider the duty area of "written communication"

TABLE 6.2	Duty Areas for a Patrol Officer

1. Apprehension/intervention
2. Providing information to citizens
3. Traffic control
4. Report writing
5. Testifying
6. First aid
7. Research
8. Training

TABLE 6.3	Effective and Ineffective Behaviors in the Duty Area of Written Communication

	WRITTEN COMMUNICATIONS
Effective	Concise and well written; includes relevant exhibits and references to earlier communication on same topic
	Communicates all basic information without complete reference to earlier communications
Average	All of the basic information is there but it is necessary to wade through excessive verbiage to get to it
	Important pieces of information missing in order to achieve full understanding
Ineffective	Borders on the incomprehensible. Facts are confused with each other, sequences are out of order, and frequent references to events or documents with which the reader would be unfamiliar

for a middle-level managerial position as it appears in Table 6.3. As you can see, the examples (i.e., critical incidents) are arranged along a scale from "effective" to "ineffective." By using these incidents, it is possible to develop rating scales that can serve as defining points or benchmarks along the length of that scale. In practice, one identifies a duty area through job analysis, interview, or workshop, and then asks incumbents or supervisors to describe particularly effective and ineffective instances of behavior in this duty area. In examining the rating scale, the rater gets a sense of both what is being rated and the levels of performance. We will examine one of these rating methods, known as behaviorally anchored rating scales (or BARS), in a later section of this chapter.

Contextual and Adaptive Performance Ratings

Although the rating of contextual performance is still relatively new by psychological standards, it has accumulated an impressive research base. The research on the identification of contextual dimensions suggests that these are valuable additions to task-based performance rating (Borman & Motowidlo, 1993, 1997; Conway, 1999; Motowidlo & Van Scotter, 1994; Hattrup, O'Connell, & Wingate, 1998; Kiker & Motowidlo, 1999; Van Scotter & Motowidlo, 1996; Van Scotter, Motowidlo, & Cross, 2000). As we described above, it seems like a natural evolution, since at least some contextual factors appear to play a role in virtually all jobs. The same appears to be true of adaptive performance dimensions (Pulakos, Arad, Donovan, & Plamandon, 2000). You will recall that we discussed adaptive performance at some length in Chapter 5. Some jobs simply require more adaptability than others, regardless of the person who occupies the particular position. From a defensibility perspective, however, it would be prudent to include questions about the value of these dimensions in a job analysis to show that they are important for the performance of a particular job. Judges and juries tend to be very literal and are reluctant to simply take a psychologist's word that these are important "for every job." They would prefer that this association be confirmed by SMEs (incumbents or supervisors).

Structural Characteristics of a Performance Rating Scale

Regardless of which technique you use to gather performance information (e.g., behaviorally anchored scales), the characteristics of the scale you use can also affect the validity of the resulting ratings. Consider Figure 6.3, which presents an array of rating scales that

FIGURE 6.3

A Variety of Rating Formats Source: Guion (1965).

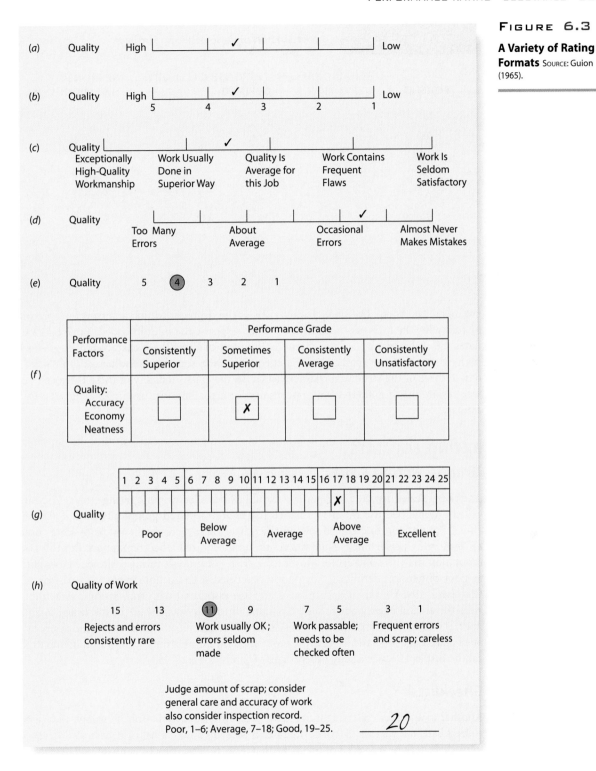

differ in certain respects. There are actually three fundamental characteristics of rating scales, and they are displayed in that figure. The first characteristic is the extent to which the duty or characteristic being rated is behaviorally defined. The second characteristic is the extent to which the meaning of the response categories is defined (what does a rating of "satisfactory" or "4" mean). The benchmarks on the scale that define the scale points

	TABLE 6.4	An Evaluation of Various Rating Formats

FORMAT	BEHAVIORAL DEFINITION	RESPONSE CATEGORY DEFINED	RESPONSE UNAMBIGUOUS
(a)			
(b)			
(c)	x	x	
(d)	x	x	
(e)			x
(f)	x	x	x
(g)			x
(h)	x	x	

are called "anchors." The final characteristic is the degree to which a person interpreting or reviewing the ratings can understand what response the rater intended. Table 6.4 evaluates the scales that appear in Figure 6.3 on each of these three characteristics. A check mark means that the characteristic is adequate in the scale being evaluated. Only scale *f* has all three of the structural characteristics. To the extent that any of these three characteristics are missing, there is an opportunity for error in either assigning or interpreting ratings.

RATING FORMATS

Graphic Rating Scales

The rating scales depicted in Figure 6.3 would all be called **graphic rating scales.** They are called graphic because the performance scores are displayed graphically on a scale that runs from high on one end to low on the other. These were the first type of scales used for evaluating performance and, as a result, have acquired a bad reputation. But this bad reputation may be undeserved. Most of the critics of graphic rating scales cite flaws such as poor dimension definitions, or poorly described scale anchor points (e.g., Murphy & Cleveland, 1995). Graphic rating scales are also associated with trait ratings, since those were the attributes originally rated. But none of these criticisms are of the rating format itself. If a graphic rating scale has well-defined dimensions, understandable and appropriately placed anchors, and an unambiguous method for assigning ratings to individuals, it can be just as effective as any other format (Landy & Farr, 1983).

Checklists

Another method for collecting judgmental performance information is through the use of a **checklist.** In a checklist format, the rater is presented with a list of behaviors and asked to place a check next to each of the items that best (or least) describe the ratee. These items may have been taken directly from a job analysis or a critical incident analysis. Usually, the items have values assigned to them (although the rater does not know what these values are) that correspond to the level of performance represented by those items. These weights are derived from the expert judgments of incumbents and supervisors of the position in question. This form of checklist is called a **weighted checklist.** The final rating for an individual is the sum or average of all items checked. Table 6.5 presents an example of a checklist for a college instructor.

TABLE 6.5	A Performance Checklist for a College Instructor

_____ The instructor creates a classroom environment that encourages questions and discussion (4.2).

_____ The instructor presents material clearly (2.2).

_____ Lectures were adequately organized (1.7).

_____ The instructor was enthusiastic and friendly (2.7).

_____ The instructor used examples from his/her experience or research (3.8).

Note: Effectiveness values range from 1.00 (minor contribution to effectiveness) to 5.00 (major contribution to effectiveness). The instructor's score is the average of the items checked.

One variation of the checklist is known as the "forced choice" format. In the generic checklist approach, the number of statements checked is left to the rater. One rater might check eight statements and another rater only four. One rater might check only positive statements while another might choose positive and negative. The rater who checked only positive items might be said to be influenced by social desirability, the desire to say nice things rather than true things about a ratee. The **forced choice format** requires the rater to pick two statements out of four that could describe the ratee. These statements have already been chosen based on their social desirability values, as well as their value in distinguishing between effective and ineffective performance. Let's consider the college instructor again. Look at the four statements in Table 6.6. Statements (a) and (c) have been shown to be associated with effective (c) and ineffective (a) instructor classroom behavior. Statements (b) and (d) are unrelated to classroom effectiveness, but do represent desirable (b) and undesirable (d) things to say about classroom behavior. If required to choose two statements, it is unlikely that a rater will choose both a desirable and an undesirable statement, for example, both (b) and (d). Nevertheless, raters are permitted to choose a desirable statement _and_ a statement associated with effective classroom behavior. Managers do not like forced choice methods because it is difficult for them to see exactly what will yield a high or low performance score for the person they are rating. Of course, that was exactly the rationale behind the development of this type of measurement method in the first place!

Both checklists and forced choice formats represent easy ways to generate a performance score for an individual, but they are not particularly conducive to providing feedback to the employee. In that sense, they represent the "old" view of performance _assessment_ rather than the newer view of performance _management_ (Banks & May, 1999; Bernardin, Hagan, Kane, & Villanova, 1998).

FORCED CHOICE FORMAT

Requires the rater to choose two statements out of four that could describe the ratee.

TABLE 6.6	An Example of a Forced Choice Format

Choose the two items which best describe your instructor:

_____ (a) Will only answer questions after class or during office hours but not during lecture.

_____ (b) Is friendly toward students when he/she meets them outside of class.

_____ (c) Creates a classroom environment that is conducive to discussion and questioning.

_____ (d) Often comes to class wearing wrinkled clothing.

Behavioral Rating

BEHAVIORALLY
ANCHORED
RATING SCALES
(BARS)

Rating format that includes behavioral anchors describing what a worker has done, or might be expected to do, in a particular duty area.

We introduced you to **behaviorally anchored rating scales (BARS)** earlier, in our discussion of critical incidents. BARS ratings are only one of a class of rating formats that include behavioral anchors. These anchors describe what a worker has done, or might be expected to do, in a particular duty area. Although all include behavioral anchors, they vary somewhat in the way that the behavior is considered.

Behaviorally Anchored Rating Scales (BARS)   These rating scales are sometimes called "behavioral expectation scales" since they occasionally ask the rater to describe what a worker might be expected to do (i.e., behave) in a hypothetical situation. An example of a BARS format appears in Figure 6.4. The traditional method for constructing BARS scales is very time consuming and involves a great deal of SME interaction (Landy & Farr, 1983; Landy & Guion, 1970; Smith & Kendall, 1963). This is good news and bad news. The good news is that through such involvement, fairness perceptions are enhanced and we achieve the strategic focus that Banks and May (1999) described as a goal of performance management. The bad news is that it might take months to develop an effective set of scales. But if we accept the performance management position, this time is well invested because it is spent developing an administrative tool and trying to understand the nature of work.

MIXED
STANDARD
SCALE (MSS)

Method of performance rating that is like a checklist, except that it includes behavioral expectation statements like those found in BARS scales; includes three statements for each dimension that describe good, average, and poor performance.

Mixed Standard Scale (MSS)   This method of performance rating is like a checklist format, except that it includes behavioral expectation statements like those found in BARS scales (Blanz & Ghiselli, 1972; Saal, 1979). There are two unique characteristics about the **mixed standard scale (MSS)**. First, it is not apparent to the rater what dimensions are being measured. The rater is simply presented with a series of statements randomly ordered. In addition, there are three statements for each dimension. One statement describes good performance, a second average performance, and a third poor performance. Consider the

FIGURE 6.4

Behaviorally Anchored Rating Scale for Firefighters

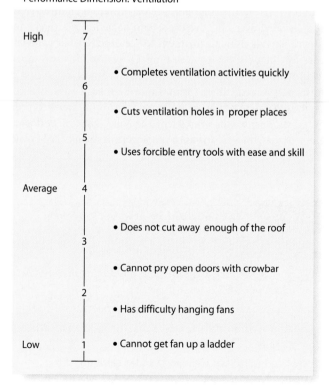

Performance Dimension: Ventilation

High — 7

6 — • Completes ventilation activities quickly

• Cuts ventilation holes in proper places

5 — • Uses forcible entry tools with ease and skill

Average — 4

3 — • Does not cut away enough of the roof

• Cannot pry open doors with crowbar

2 — • Has difficulty hanging fans

Low — 1 • Cannot get fan up a ladder

TABLE 6.7	Mixed Standards Rating Scale (MSS)

Listed below are a number of descriptions of behavior relevant to the job of patrol officer. Your task is to examine each example carefully and then to determine in your own mind the answer to the following question: Is the patrol officer to be rated "better than this statement," "worse than this statement," or "does this statement fit this patrol officer?"

If you believe that the person you are rating is "better than the statement," put a + in the space to the right of the statement. If you believe that the person is "worse than the statement," put a − in that space. If you believe that the statement "fits" the patrol officer, put a 0 in that space.

Be sure that you write either a +, a −, or a 0 after each of the statements listed below.

		RATING
(B)	1. The officer could be expected to misinform the public on legal matters through lack of knowledge. (P)	+
(C)	2. The officer could be expected to take the time to answer a rookie's question carefully. (G)	0
(B)	3. This patrol officer never has to ask others about points of law. (G)	−
(A)	4. The officer could be expected to refrain from writing tickets for traffic violations that occur at a particular intersection that is unusually confusing to motorists. (G)	+
(A)	5. The patrol officer could be expected to call for assistance and clear the area of bystanders before confronting a barricaded, heavily armed suspect. (A)	+
(C)	6. The officer could be expected to use racially toned language in front of minority group members. (P)	+
(B)	7. This officer follows correct procedures for evidence preservation at the scene of a crime. (A)	0
(A)	8. The patrol officer could be expected to continue to write a traffic violation in spite of hearing a report of a nearby robbery in progress. (P)	+
(C)	9. This officer is considered friendly by the other officers on the shift. (A)	+

Note: The letters G, A, and P immediately following the statements indicate whether the item describes good, average, or poor performance. In practice, the rater is not told which item relates to which scale or the level of performance represented by each item.

statements in Table 6.7. Three dimensions of patrol officer performance are being rated: Dimension A is "judgment," dimension B is "knowledge," and dimension C is "relations with others." Raters are instructed to examine each statement and decide if the person they are rating is "better than" the statement, "equal to" the statement, or "worse than" the statement. The raters use the symbols +, 0, or −, respectively to indicate their judgments. In Table 6.7 the letters that precede each statement indicate to which of the three dimensions it belongs. The letters G, A, or P at the end of each statement indicate whether the statement was intended to describe good, average or poor performance. The rating column indicates simulated judgments that a rater might have provided.

Mixed standard scales have both advantages and disadvantages. The advantage, like that of the checklist, is simplicity. The disadvantage is the scoring. The major scoring difficulty is in dealing with "inconsistencies" in the judgments, which are frequent (Barnes-Farrell & Weiss, 1984). For example, how would you score a scale in which the rater indicated that on a particular dimension, such as "judgment," the employee was better than the good statement, but worse than the average statement? In other rating formats, such as the BARS technique, this error could not occur because you would assign only one "score" or rating per dimension. Philosophically, the mixed standard method runs counter to current thinking, which includes the rater and the ratee as partners in the measurement process (Banks & May, 1999), because it hides the true definition of performance from the rater. Perhaps fortunately, mixed standard scales have not been the subject of any employment discrimination suits. It would be challenging to explain such a system to a jury. Murphy and Cleveland (1995) also noted that the mixed standard format is not conducive to providing feedback, since even the rater does not know how to put the performance statements together in any coherent way.

Behavioral Observation Scales (BOS)   In BARS evaluation, the rater picks a point on the rating scale that describes either how the individual has behaved in the past or, absent any direct observation of relevant behavior by the rater, how the individual *might be expected* to behave. The **behavioral observation scale (BOS)** method grew out of the idea that it would be more accurate to have raters evaluate what someone actually *did* rather than what he or she *might* do. Murphy and Constans (1987) conducted research on BARS scales by using videotape depictions of performance and asking raters to evaluate the people they saw on the videotapes. If a rater saw a behavior that was exactly described by an anchor on the rating scale, the rater assigned a rating close to the value of that anchor. The problem in this study was that even if the videotape showed many other instances of poor behavior on the same dimension, a good rating was assigned because the rater saw an exact (although unrepresentative) duplication of a scale anchor.

Unlike the BARS method, the BOS asks the rater to consider how frequently an employee has been seen to act in a particular way (Latham & Wexley, 1981). Consider the example of a dimension called "overcoming resistance to change," which is depicted in Table 6.8. As you can see, the rater assigns ratings that range from "almost never" to "almost always." The score for an individual is calculated by the number of times each anchor is chosen. The BOS method does support feedback and is considerably easier to develop than either the BARS or mixed standard format. Because it is often developed directly from a job analysis, it is also somewhat easier to defend than some other techniques (Guion, 1998).

> **BEHAVIORAL OBSERVATION SCALE (BOS)**
>
> *Asks the rater to consider how frequently an employee has been seen to act in a particular way.*

TABLE 6.8	**An Example of a Behavioral Observation Scale**

Overcoming Resistance to Change*

1. Describes the details of the change to subordinates

Almost Never	1	2	3	4	5	Almost Always

2. Explains why the change is necessary

Almost Never	1	2	3	4	5	Almost Always

3. Discusses how the change will affect the employee

Almost Never	1	2	3	4	5	Almost Always

4. Listens to the employee's concerns

Almost Never	1	2	3	4	5	Almost Always

5. Asks the employee for help in making the change work

Almost Never	1	2	3	4	5	Almost Always

6. If necessary, specifies the date for a follow-up meeting to respond to the employee's concerns

Almost Never	1	2	3	4	5	Almost Always

Total = _____

Below Adequate	*Adequate*	*Full*	*Excellent*	*Superior**
6–10	11–15	16–20	21–25	26–30

*Scores are set by management.

SOURCE: Latham & Wexley (1981).

EMPLOYEE COMPARISON METHODS

In rating methods, an individual employee is evaluated with respect to a standard of some sort. These standards are embodied in the anchors of the rating scale and the definition of the dimension to be considered. There are other forms of evaluation that involve the direct comparison of one person to another; these are called **employee comparison methods.** The most obvious of these methods is a **simple ranking** of employees on some dimension, duty area, or standard. Employees are ranked from top to bottom according to their assessed proficiency. If multiple dimensions are considered, the individual can be assigned a score equal to the sum of their ranks or the average of those ranks. Recalling our earlier discussion of "overall performance," it would be better to get individual ranks on independent aspects of performance and average or sum them than to ask for an "overall rank" of an individual.

A variation of ranking is the **"paired comparison"** method, in which each employee (typically in a work group or a collection of individuals with the same job title) is compared with each other individual in the group on the various dimensions being considered. If there are three individuals in the group, person A is compared with person B and C on one dimension; then person B is compared with person C on that dimension. The individual's "score" is the number of times he or she was chosen over the other members. The same comparison is then made on a second and a third dimension until each individual is compared with every other individual on each of the relevant dimensions. Paired comparison ranking can become extremely time consuming as the number of people to be compared increases. In a group with 10 members (a common work group size), the evaluator would have to make 45 comparisons for each dimension considered. If the group has 20 individuals, the number of comparisons grows to 190, so if each individual is considered on 10 dimensions, that becomes 1,900 comparisons! The formula for calculating the number of pairings of objects is

$$n(n - 1)/2$$

where n is the number of objects.

Employee comparisons can be useful in certain situations. One common problem that confronts organizations is whom to lay off when downsizing is required. The context is usually a loss of work. In the defense industry, for example, the closure of military bases and the end of the cold war resulted in the cancelation of many defense-related contracts to build submarines, tanks, planes, and weapon systems. This meant that in a department where 50 design or software engineers might have been needed to satisfy the military contracts in 1980, only 10 were needed in 2000. The challenge would be in deciding which 10 would stay. The issue is not performance management or feedback. It is a simple issue of deselection. In these situations, organizations typically rank individuals on dimensions including technical performance, new or anticipated work to be completed, knowledge and skills necessary for new or anticipated work, and so forth. Overall rankings are then calculated based on the rankings achieved in the individual dimensions, the engineers are ordered from the most to least valuable, and the least valuable employees are laid off. Such downsizing is a harsh reality, but it can be a fair one and can be accomplished relatively quickly.

A clear disadvantage of employee comparison methods for purposes other than layoffs is the absence of any clear standard of performance, other than an employee's rank among colleagues. This makes feedback difficult. The obvious goal for an employee is to get a better rank, but little guidance is provided on how to do that. There is also the difficulty of comparing individuals in different groups. The problem becomes even more obvious when we consider the situation when layoffs are required. Assume that a defense contractor had to lay off 40 software engineers from a group of 50, but they were spread across seven departments and three plant locations. There would be no way to compare

EMPLOYEE COMPARISON METHODS

Form of evaluation that involves the direct comparison of one person with another.

SIMPLE RANKING

Employees are ranked from top to bottom according to their assessed proficiency on some dimension, duty area, or standard.

PAIRED COMPARISON

Technique in which each employee in a work group or a collection of individuals with the same job title is compared with each other individual in the group on the various dimensions being considered.

the 50 engineers directly to one another. Instead, the comparisons might have to be done within a department, within a location, or even within departments in each separate location. Then, in order to end up with one layoff list, it would be necessary to assume that the ranks in each group were comparable, that is, 1 in department A was equal to 1 in department B. As the number of groups grows, this assumption becomes increasingly difficult to accept.

Concluding Thoughts on Performance Rating Formats

There are many performance rating formats from which to choose, each with its own advantages and disadvantages. One distinction among them seems to be that some are better suited to providing feedback, goal setting, and supervisor/subordinate communication than others. This is a major issue in performance management, and the research we've cited indicates that those methods that make communication difficult are less attractive. In addition, some methods seem to be more defensible than others, which is another important consideration in today's increasingly litigious workplace. Beyond those distinctions, however, any of the methods can work as long as the dimensions to be considered are well defined and job related; the anchors are behavioral, appropriate, and accurately placed; and the method used to assign ratings or rankings and interpret them is unequivocal. Added to those characteristics, of course, are the motivation and training of the rater, topics we will cover shortly.

MODULE 6.2 SUMMARY

- Since performance rating is one of the most common techniques for performance measurement, it has received a great deal of attention which has led to increasingly sophisticated models of the performance rating process. Research suggests that it is better to obtain ratings of specific aspects of performance than of overall performance.

- Although the rating of contextual performance is still relatively new, it has accumulated an impressive research base. Research on contextual performance dimensions suggests that these are valuable additions to task-based performance rating.

- Rating formats for performance evaluation instruments include graphic rating scales, checklists, behaviorally anchored rating scales (BARS), mixed standard scales (MSS), and behavioral observation scales (BOS).

- Regardless of which rating format is used, the characteristics of the performance scale can affect the validity of the resulting ratings. Three fundamental characteristics of rating scales are (1) the extent to which the rated dimension is behaviorally defined, (2) the extent to which the meaning of the response categories is defined, and (3) the extent to which a person interpreting the ratings can understand what response the rater intended.

- Performance evaluation methods that involve direct comparison of one person to another are called employee comparison methods. These methods include simple ranking and the paired comparison method.

KEY TERMS

context	graphic rating scale	mixed standard scale (MSS)
task performance	checklist	behavioral observation scale (BOS)
contextual performance	weighted checklist	
counterproductive performance	forced choice format	employee comparison methods
duties	behaviorally anchored rating scales (BARS)	simple ranking
critical incidents		paired comparison

6.3 Consider the rating of the instructor described in the first part of Module 6.2 that accompanies Table 6.1. If you were the head of the department in which this instructor taught, how would you revise the performance rating form to deal with the instructor's feeling of unfairness?

6.4 Apply the performance rating scale in Table 6.1 to the best and worst instructor you have encountered in your educational career. Rate these instructors on their overall performance. Now go back over those two ratings and apply a "think aloud" protocol (such as we described in Chapter 5) to understand why you assigned the overall score to each. List the factors that influenced your ratings.

PERFORMANCE RATING—PROCESS

RATING SOURCES

Up to this point, we have been using the generic term "the rater," or specifying supervisory ratings in our discussion. But there are many different sources of rating information. These include not only the supervisor, but also peers, the incumbents, subordinates of the incumbent, clients, suppliers, and others. A relatively new development in performance measurement is called the 360 degree assessment, which includes many and sometimes all of these sources. We will discuss **360 degree feedback** systems in the section on performance feedback. For now, we will consider each of these sources independently.

Supervisors

First- and second-level managers and supervisors are by far the most common source of performance information. Supervisors can closely observe the behavior of the incumbent, and they are in a good position to evaluate the extent to which that behavior contributes to unit and organizational success. It is also the supervisor who is expected to provide feedback to the individual worker, both informally on a frequent basis and formally in periodic structured performance evaluations.

In spite of the supervisor being the logical choice for at least one important perspective on employee performance, many supervisors actively avoid evaluation and feedback. Why? Fried, Tiegs, and Bellamy (1992) found a number of factors that explained why supervisors avoided evaluating subordinates. The most important of these was the length of time that the subordinate had reported to the superior (less time led to more reluctance), the amount of experience the subordinate had (less experience, resulting in more corrective feedback, led to more reluctance), and the amount of trust between the supervisor and subordinate (lower levels of trust on the part of the subordinate led to more challenges of the evaluations, and more reluctance on the part of the supervisor to evaluate). The study also suggested that the subordinate's confidence in the operation of the performance evaluation system (i.e., procedural, distributive, and interpersonal justice perceptions) might influence the behavior of the subordinate and, in turn, the level of reluctance on the part of the supervisor. In other words, the less confident the subordinate is in the system, the more he or she is likely to feel unfairly evaluated and to challenge the evaluation.

Fried, Tiegs, and Bellamy (1992) emphasized the substantive reasons why supervisors might avoid evaluating subordinates. But there are logistic and procedural reasons as well. The most obvious reason is that it takes time—time the manager would prefer to be spending on other "work" related tasks. When you consider the supervisor's responsibility in an idealized performance management system, there would seem to be little time left for doing anything but "managing" the performance of subordinates. But when a supervisor complains that it takes too much time to provide performance goals and feedback to subordinates, the supervisor may be misconstruing his or her job. In the performance management arena, defining and communicating about subordinate performance with the subordinate is seen as one of *the* major duties of a supervisor, not as a distraction from more important tasks. It is important to help supervisors understand that the more effective their performance evaluation and feedback, the easier their job becomes and the more effective their work groups and departments become.

The more subtle reasons for supervisors' avoidance of the evaluation process include the desire to avoid giving negative feedback for fear of creating hostility in the workplace, fear of experiencing the dissatisfaction the process can cause incumbents, fear that they may be challenged on their evaluations, and even the fear that they may be become a party to a lawsuit brought by an incumbent charging unfairness. This is how some supervisors see performance evaluation: a recipe for trouble.

As the nature of work changes, the emphasis on supervisory ratings will also change. An increasing number of workers will have fewer opportunities for regular face-to-face communication with supervisors. Downsizing has resulted in more direct reports to fewer managers. Team and group work has recast the supervisor/manager as a resource to the team rather than a director of activity. The virtual nature of work may mean that a supervisor and a subordinate are in physically different locations. All of these influences suggest that supervisors may be less central to the performance evaluation process than was previously the case. It is not that supervisors will have no information to add, but that collecting information from a supervisor may not be sufficient for a complete assessment of a worker's performance.

Peers

Peers are more likely than supervisors to interact with a worker on a daily basis; thus, peers may be more likely to know more about typical performance. In contrast, supervisors are more likely to be familiar with maximum performance. Thus, in theory, peers should be a good source for performance information. Latham (1986) suggested that peers are an excellent source not only because of their immediate interactions, but also because the peer sees how the worker interacts with others, including supervisors, subordinates, and (in a service-oriented business) customers. Hedge and Borman (1995) noted some downsides to peer evaluation. One obvious obstacle is the same one facing supervisors—many "peers" may be geographically separated from each other, particularly in cases where an individual may work from home. Another problem arises when the peer ratings are used for administrative purposes, including compensation changes, promotions, or layoffs. A conflict of interest is likely when peers are competing for fixed resources. Nevertheless, peers as a source of performance information may be valuable for nonadministrative purposes such as performance improvement or new skills development, as well as in the context of work group or team performance.

Self-Ratings

Self-ratings have often been part of the traditional performance appraisal system. An individual is told to complete a rating form on him- or herself and bring it to a meeting with the supervisor, who has filled out the identical form on the subordinate. The supervisor and subordinate then discuss agreements and disagreements in the ratings they have assigned. As a result of the discussion, the "final" rating form which the supervisor places into the employee's personnel file is a consensus form, one that evolves from the discussion. The supervisor may change a rating after the discussion, or the employee may agree that the supervisor's rating was more accurate than his or her own rating. The very act of soliciting information from the worker is likely to increase perceptions of procedural justice on the part of that worker (Greenberg, 1986). The potential for distortion and inaccuracy in self-ratings obviously exists since it is common for individuals to have higher opinions of their own work than their supervisors do (Atwater, 1998). This disortion is minimized, however, when the employee knows that the self-ratings will be discussed with the supervisor. Further, if ratings are to be used for administrative purposes (e.g., salary increases, promotions), we have a conflict of interest, much as we had for peer ratings. Once again, however, for nonadministrative purposes and in the context of a performance management system, self-ratings may play an important role in understanding performance.

Subordinate Ratings

Increasing numbers of organizations are looking at the value of a subordinate's evaluation of a boss. Bernardin, Dahmus, and Redmon (1993) found that supervisors were supportive of this source of information, as long as it was not used for administrative decisions. This parallels our cautions above about peer and self-ratings. It appears that there is a valuable role for information from a wide variety of sources, as long as it is used for feedback and employee development. As you will see when we cover leadership in Chapter 12, subordinates may be in the best position to evaluate leadership behaviors (or the lack thereof) and the effect of those behaviors on subordinates. Hedge and Borman (1995) suggested another positive outcome from the use of subordinate performance evaluations: They encourage the subordinate to consider the challenges and performance demands of that supervisor, thus gaining a better appreciation of the duties of a supervisor. This in turn might act as a modest form of realistic job preview for those subordinates who seek to advance up the management ladder. Hedge and Borman also cautioned that it is critical that subordinate feedback be kept anonymous to prevent retaliation from a less-than-enthusiastic supervisor.

Customer and Supplier Ratings

Many job titles require interaction with individuals outside the organization. The most obvious of these is the customer, but employees may also have important interactions with suppliers and vendors who provide materials and services to the organization. The perspective of these outside parties is likely to be unique and provides the opportunity to fill out the employee's performance profile. The "outsider" perspective should be particularly important from a business strategy vantage point (Bowen & Waldman, 1998). You will remember that Campbell (1990) anchored performance in business goals and strategies. Very few organizations would say that they have *not* adopted a customer-driven focus. Thus, in our new view of how performance should be defined, we should pay particular attention to customer-oriented behavior. We must be cautious, however, to limit our inquiries to those areas of performance that a customer sees. This will represent a subset of all of the duties of the employee and may be limited to interpersonal, communication, and motivational issues. While the ratings of suppliers might be less salient than those of customers to the issue of customer service, suppliers also have an opportunity to see the interpersonal and communication aspects of an employee's performance. In addition, suppliers may provide valuable information about some of the more technical aspects of performance, since they are likely to be involved in discussions about product specifications, costs, and delivery schedules.

360 Degree Systems

The collection of information sources we have reviewed represent a wide variety of perspectives. By using these sources, we are looking at the behavior of an employee from many possible angles (Dalessio, 1998). Thus, the use of the varied sources has become known as

FIGURE 6.5

**Potential Sources
for 360 Degree
Feedback**

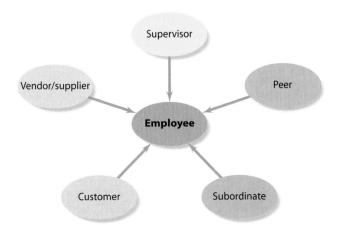

the "360 degree" evaluation. Because of the sensitivity of information from some of these sources and because of the potential conflicts that arise when administrative issues are involved, 360 degree systems are often used for feedback and employee development. See Figure 6.5 for potential sources of 360 degree feedback. We will examine the mechanics of, and research on, 360 degree systems when we consider performance feedback in Module 6.4.

RATING DISTORTIONS

Even though the intent of a rating system is to collect accurate estimations of an individual's performance, and we build in structural characteristics to assist in the gathering of those accurate estimations, raters don't always provide those accurate estimates. In Module 6.4, we will explore the motivational reasons for this inaccuracy, but here we will identify some of the most common inaccuracies that creep into ratings. Traditionally, these have been labeled **rating errors** but they may not really be "errors" as much as intentional or systematic distortions. From a psychometric point of view, they do represent "systematic error," meaning that they do not represent completely "true" estimates of performance. However, this is a technical use of the term "error," rather than the more general

RATING ERRORS

*Inaccuracies in ratings
that may be actual
errors or intentional or
systematic distortions.*

meaning of the term (e.g., "the rater made an error"). Although many different types of errors have been proposed, we will consider only the most common of them.

Central Tendency Error

It is often the case that raters choose a middle point on the scale as a way of describing performance, even though a more extreme point might better describe the employee. They are being "safe" by not picking a more extreme score, and thus are committing a **central tendency error.** Some rating systems may encourage a central tendency bias by requiring any rater who chooses an extreme score to provide a written justification for that choice, thus making it more difficult to choose any rating other than an average one.

Leniency–Severity Error

This type of distortion is the result of raters who are unusually easy (**leniency error**) or unusually harsh (**severity error**) in their assignment of ratings. The easy rater gives ratings higher than an employee deserves, while the harsh rater gives ratings lower than the employee deserves. In part, these errors are usually the result of anchors that permit the rater to impose idiosyncratic meanings on words like "average," "outstanding," and "below average." The problem is that the rater can feel free to use a *personal* average rather than one that would be shared with other raters. Many supervisors are well known for being "demanding" and requiring extraordinary accomplishment for any rating other than "average." Other supervisors give everyone good marks, either to avoid friction or to be seen favorably by their subordinates. One safeguard against this type of distortion is to use well-defined behavioral anchors for the rating scales.

Halo Error

Often, when a rater has a series of dimensions to rate, he or she assigns the same rating to the employee on each of those dimensions. In other words, there is a *halo* or aura that surrounds all of the ratings, causing them to be similar. This might be the result of simple laziness on the part of the rater, or because the rater believes that one particular dimension is key and all the other dimensions or performance areas flow from that one important area. The rater might also subscribe to a "unitary view" of performance (Campbell, 1990). In this view, raters assume that there is really one general performance factor and that people are either good or poor performers; they further assume that this level of performance appears in every aspect of the job. It might also be that the rater considers a performance area not included in the rating form (e.g., adaptability or contextual performance) as the key to successful performance, and therefore allows that "invisible" area to influence all of the other ratings. One other downside to **halo error** is that it can have the effect of not identifying strengths and weaknesses that the employee may have, thus defeating one of the purposes of feedback. It should be noted, however, that not all rating dimensions are completely independent. Thus, a rating on one dimension that is close to the rating on another may not be distortion but a reflection of *the fact* that certain behaviors go together. We might expect, for example, an association among dimensions like customer service, communication, and interpersonal skills. Not all halo is distortion.

RATER TRAINING

It has generally been assumed that rater distortions are unintentional, that raters are unaware of influences that distort their ratings. As we will see in the next module, that assumption may not be correct. Raters may know exactly what they are doing and why they are doing it. In other words, the distinct possibility exists that these distortions are

CENTRAL TENDENCY ERROR

Error in which raters choose a middle point on the scale to describe performance, even though a more extreme point might better describe the employee.

LENIENCY ERROR

Occurs with raters who are unusually easy in their ratings.

SEVERITY ERROR

Occurs with raters who are unusually harsh in their ratings.

HALO ERROR

Occurs when a rater assigns the same rating to an employee on a series of dimensions, creating a halo or aura that surrounds all of the ratings, causing them to be similar.

motivated. Nevertheless, some distortions may be corrected through training. We will consider three types of training: administrative, traditional psychometric approaches, and frame-of-reference training.

Administrative Training

Most evaluation systems are straightforward and easy to understand, such as the traditional graphic rating systems. Experienced managers have been doing performance ratings for their entire managerial careers. They themselves have also been evaluated in management and nonmanagement positions. So for simple, straightforward, and well-designed graphic rating systems, little administrative training is required. On the other hand, if the system is an uncommon one (e.g., mixed standard, BARS, or BOS), the raters will need some orientation, if for no other reason than to understand how this system differs from others they may have seen in the past. If one or more of the structural characteristics (e.g., dimension definition, anchors, method for assigning or interpreting a rating) is deficient, administrative training becomes more important. The training would be directed to developing a consensus among raters about the meaning of dimension headings or anchor meanings. Of course, the more direct solution would be to make the scale better, not to "train away" its deficiency.

Psychometric Training

Psychometric training involves making the raters aware of the common rating distortions described earlier (central tendency, leniency/severity, and halo) in the hope that making these distortions more salient will reduce the likelihood of distortions. While that makes some sense, assuming that the distortions are not motivated, the actual effect of this type of training is questionable. In a classic study, Bernardin and Pence (1980) demonstrated that when raters are instructed to avoid leniency and halo distortions, they do, but the resulting performance ratings are less accurate than if they had not received this training. Bernardin and Pence suggested that the reason for this surprising result was that the trained raters were concentrating on producing a distribution of ratings that had no leniency/severity or halo, which they were able to do. But the raters were less concerned about accurately describing performance than about avoiding "distortions." The battle was won, but the war was lost. These findings have been replicated by Woehr and Huffcutt (1994).

> **PSYCHOMETRIC TRAINING**
>
> *Training that makes raters aware of common rating errors (central tendency, leniency/severity, and halo) in the hope that this will reduce the likelihood of errors.*

Frame-of-Reference Training

As you saw in the description of process models of performance rating (Feldman, 1981; Landy & Farr, 1980; Woehr & Feldman, 1993), there has been an increasing interest in the cognitive aspects of performance rating. Researchers (e.g., Guion, 1998; Murphy, Garcia, Kerkar, Martin, & Balzer, 1982; Murphy & Cleveland, 1995) have concentrated on factors like the observational skills of the rater and the dynamics of memory. **Frame-of-reference training** (Day & Sulsky, 1995; McIntyre, Smith, & Hassett, 1984; Pulakos, 1984) is based on the assumption that a rater needs a context for providing his or her rating—a "frame." This type of training includes the following steps: (1) providing information about the multidimensional nature of performance, (2) making sure that the raters understand the meaning of the anchors on the scale, (3) engaging in practice rating exercises of a standard performance presented by means of videotape, and (4) providing feedback on that practice exercise. This technique has been shown to be more effective than the traditional psychometric approach (Athey & McIntyre, 1987; Bernardin & Beatty, 1984; Guion, 1998; Hauenstein, 1998; Woehr, 1994). It has been suggested that as a result of the practice exercise and feedback, the information storage and retrieval in memory is more effective.

> **FRAME-OF-REFERENCE (FOR) TRAINING**
>
> *Training based on the assumption that a rater needs a context or "frame" for providing a rating; includes (1) providing information on the multidimensional nature of performance, (2) ensuring that raters understand the meaning of anchors on the scale, (3) engaging in practice rating exercises, and (4) providing feedback on practice exercises.*

THE RELIABILITY AND VALIDITY OF RATINGS
Reliability

A lively debate about the reliability of performance ratings has been raging in recent years (Hanges, Schneider, & Niles, 1990; Murphy & DeShon, 2000a, 2000b; Schmidt, Viswesvaran, & Ones, 2000; Viswesvaran, Ones, & Schmidt, 1996). Some researchers (Rothstein, 1990) have demonstrated that the inter-rater reliability of performance ratings (i.e., degree of agreement between two raters of the same person) may be in the range of $+.50$ to $+.60$, values usually considered to represent "poor" reliability. Those values should not be surprising, however. When we examined sources of performance information, we saw that each of these sources (e.g., supervisors, subordinates, peers, self) brought a *different* perspective to the process. That being the case, why should we expect high agreement among them? If agreement were high among these many sources, it would most likely mean that we were getting redundant information and wasting the time of at least some of the raters. Even when we compare ratings from the same level of the organization (e.g., two supervisors of an employee or two peers), these raters still probably see or concentrate on different behaviors. Supervisors are not, nor are they intended to be, redundant. Usually, the inter-rater reliabilities are calculated between a first- and a second-level supervisor. It is the first-level supervisor who has the most frequent interaction with the ratee and the most awareness of day-to-day *behavior*. The second-level supervisor is more likely aware of the *results* of behavior or of *extreme* behavior (either good or bad) on the part of the employee. It is likely that each information source is describing behavior reliably, but each is describing different behavior. The challenge is to combine those sources to get the full performance picture. The more information gathered, the more comprehensive and accurate the complete performance estimate will be.

Validity

The validity of performance ratings depends foremost on the manner by which the rating scales were conceived and developed. The first step in developing effective scales is a consideration of the meaning of performance in the organization; this can be based on a job or work analysis. The scales should represent important aspects of work behavior. If these aspects of work behavior are truly important, and if these rating scales fairly represent these aspects, they support valid inferences about performance level. Another step in supporting valid inferences is to make sure that the scales have appropriate structural characteristics (i.e., dimension definitions, anchors, and scoring schemes). Finally, because valid inferences are further supported by knowledgeable raters, rater training is a recommended way of assuring this knowledge base.

MODULE 6.3 SUMMARY

- Sources of performance rating information include supervisors, peers, the incumbent being rated, subordinates of the incumbent, clients, and suppliers. A relatively new development in performance measurement called 360 degree assessment includes many and sometimes all of these sources.
- I-O psychologists have identified some common inaccuracies or errors that affect performance ratings, including central tendency error, leniency error, severity error, and halo error.
- Some performance rating distortions may be corrected through rater training, which can include

administrative training, traditional psychometric approaches, and frame-of-reference training.

- I-O psychologists continue to be concerned about the reliability and validity of performance ratings. The relatively low interrater reliability of performance ratings likely results from the different behavior described by each information source. The challenge is to combine those sources to get the full performance picture. The more information gathered, the more comprehensive and accurate the complete performance estimate will be.

KEY TERMS

360 degree feedback

rating errors

central tendency error

leniency error

severity error

halo error

psychometric training

frame-of-reference (FOR) training

CRITICAL THINKING EXERCISES

6.5 Suppose you are a fourth grade elementary school teacher and the school district has decided to use 360 degree feedback with its teachers. Further assume that they intend to ask the following groups to comment on your effectiveness as a teacher: your students, parents of those students, fellow fourth grade teachers, teacher aides who work or have worked in your classroom, student teachers who have taught in your classroom and observed you, and your principal. Which of these sources would be most effective? Least effective? Explain why.

6.6 Imagine you are a department manager and you receive from supervisors in your department a set of performance ratings that they have completed on their direct reports. Imagine further that on a 5 point rating scale (where 5 is the highest rating) over 90 percent of the ratings were 5's. How would you go about determining if these were really outstanding performers or whether the ratings were influenced by leniency bias?

THE SOCIAL AND LEGAL CONTEXT OF PERFORMANCE EVALUATION

THE MOTIVATION TO RATE

As we discussed above, most attempts to improve performance evaluation systems make the assumption that raters desire to provide accurate ratings, but for various reasons (e.g., the rating format, training, unintentional tendencies to distort), they find it difficult to do. Some researchers take a very different view of the performance evaluation process. They suggest that many raters have no intention of being accurate. Instead, they use the process as a means toward an end of some kind, either personal or organizational (Banks & Murphy, 1985; Cleveland & Murphy, 1992; Kozlowski, Chao, & Morrison, 1998; Longnecker, Sims, & Gioia, 1987; Murphy & Cleveland, 1995).

Longnecker, Sims, and Gioia (1987) interviewed 60 managers from seven large organizations who, collectively, had performance appraisal experience in 197 organizations. Consider some quotes from those managers as presented in Box 6.1. They provide vivid examples of managers who are less concerned about the accuracy of ratings than they are about the effect of ratings on themselves, their subordinates, and the organization. These quotes ring true to anyone who has had an in-depth discussion with a manager about performance evaluations. Frank Landy was once gathering performance ratings in a police department as part of a test validation project. Just as the rating session was to begin, one of the raters (a police sergeant) announced that he would be happy to help the city with the test validation project, but that the researcher should be aware that he had no intention of telling the truth about his subordinates. He further explained that there was a bond of faith, trust, and interdependence between him and his subordinates, and that he was not about to weaken that bond by possibly saying something negative about one of his reports.

Longnecker et al. (1987) described the theme of their interviews as the "Politics of Performance Appraisal"; politics was "the deliberate attempts by individuals to enhance or protect their self-interests when conflicting courses of action are possible" (p. 184). Cleveland and Murphy (1992) described the same phenomenon from a more psychological perspective. They recast performance appraisal as a goal-directed activity and identified three different stakeholders in the process, each with different goals. The first stakeholder was the rater, the second was the ratee, and the third was the organization. They delineated the goals of each stakeholder as follows:

Rater Goals

Task performance: using appraisal to maintain or enhance ratee's performance goals or levels.

Interpersonal: using appraisal to maintain or improve interpersonal relations with the ratee.

Strategic: using appraisal to enhance the standing of the supervisor or work group in the organization.

Internalized: using appraisal to confirm the rater's view of him- or herself as a person of high standards.

Ratee Goals

Information gathering: to determine the ratee's relative standing in the work group; to determine future performance directions; to determine organizational performance standards or expectations.

Information dissemination: to convey information to the rater regarding constraints on performance; to convey to the rater a willingness to improve performance.

Organizational Goals

Between-person uses: salary administration, promotion, retention/termination, layoffs, identification of poor performers.

Within-person uses: identification of training needs, performance feedback, transfers/assignments, identifying individual strengths and weaknesses.

Systems-maintenance uses: manpower planning, organizational development, evaluating the personnel system, identifying organizational training needs.

GOAL CONFLICT

The problem with having multiple stakeholders with differing goals is that they often conflict when a single system is used for performance evaluation. Consider some typical conflicts:

• A rater wants to make his or her group look good, a ratee wants to learn what the organizational performance standards are, and an organization wants to make salary decisions.

• A rater wants to motivate a ratee to perform at a higher level, a ratee wants to explain why his or her performance was constrained by work conditions, and an organization wants to make layoff decisions.

When a single system is used to satisfy multiple goals from different stakeholders, the rater must choose which goal to satisfy before assigning a rating. The rater may wish, for example, to "send a message" to the employee by giving an inappropriately low rating, but at the same time does not want the individual to be laid off. The rater must make a choice between these conflicting goals.

There are no easy solutions to these problems. One solution is to have multiple performance evaluation systems, each used for a different purpose. For example, one system might be used for performance planning and feedback (a within-person use) while another, completely different system might be used to make salary or promotion decisions (a between-person use). Another solution might be to obtain heavy involvement of the stakeholders (raters, ratees, and human resource reps) in the development of the system (Cleveland & Murphy, 1992). This is exactly what performance management advocates recommend (Banks & May, 1999). Finally, Cleveland and Murphy suggested rewarding supervisors for accurate ratings. The problem, of course, is that it is virtually impossible to determine which ratings (or raters) are accurate and which are not.

This line of theory and research is sobering. It calls into question the assumption that rating distortions are unintentional rather than intentional. Banks and Murphy (1985) found that, even though raters may be *capable* of producing accurate performance evaluations, they may be *unwilling* to do so.

PERFORMANCE FEEDBACK

Throughout the chapter, we have been addressing the issue of performance feedback to an incumbent. We have dealt with the types of information to be presented, the formats most conducive to feedback, and the possible sources of feedback. Now we will consider the actual feedback process.

Individual workers seek feedback because it reduces uncertainty and provides external information about levels of performance to balance internal (self) perceptions (Murphy & Cleveland, 1995). Most workers prefer to receive positive feedback and most supervisors prefer to give positive feedback. But there is always room for improvement, so most workers get mixed feedback, some positive and some directed toward improving skills or eliminating weaknesses. This becomes particularly problematic when the same information

Feedback, especially when negative, is not always welcome or accepted.

is used for multiple purposes. When the purpose of evaluation is performance improvement, it is best to keep administrative issues off the table, and the best way to do that is to have a separate system for making administrative decisions. Some organizations use a schedule that separates administrative discussions (e.g., promotions, raises, bonuses) from feedback and planning discussions by as many as six months, and use different "metrics" for discussing salary adjustments (e.g., individual accomplishments, profitability of the company, past salary history).

Even when feedback discussions are kept separate from administrative discussions, individuals may have a "ceiling" for absorbing negative comments. Kay, Meyer, and French (1965) examined the relationship between the number of negative comments in a feedback session and the reactions of the recipient to the feedback. They found that as the number of negative comments increased, so did the defensive comments and reactions of the recipient. This suggests that if there are several different areas in which performance improvements are required, the feedback should be stretched over several sessions rather than presented all at once. They also found that many supervisors tend to use positive comments to "cushion" negative feedback. The supervisor makes a positive comment, then delivers the negative information, and follows it with another positive comment. This is referred to as the "praise-criticism-praise sandwich": The positive information is the bread and the negative information is the meat. Subordinates quickly learn the supervisor's strategy and tend to focus on the bad news, paying little attention to the positive comments, which may be dismissed as "trying to stay on my good side." When the supervisor makes a positive comment after the negative feedback, this is a signal that the "punishment" is over (Landy, 1989).

Remember our earlier discussion about perceptions of fairness of appraisal. The same principles hold true for perceptions of fairness of feedback. The employee is more likely to accept negative feedback if he or she believes that:

- The supervisor has a sufficient "sample" of the subordinate's actual behavior.
- The supervisor and subordinate agree on the subordinate's job duties.
- The supervisor and subordinate agree on the definition of good and poor performance.
- The supervisor focuses on ways to improve performance, rather than simply documenting poor performance.

"Destructive" Criticism

One often hears the term "constructive criticism" used to describe negative feedback. But there is a dark side to negative feedback as well. It has been described as "destructive" criticism. Baron (1990) defined **destructive criticism** as negative feedback that is cruel, sarcastic, and offensive. It is usually general rather than specific, and often directed toward personal characteristics of the employee rather than job-relevant behaviors. Not surprisingly, Baron (1988, 1990) discovered that such criticism leads to anger, tension, and resentment on the part of the employee. Although no research has established direct connections between destructive criticism and violence, it is tempting to see the link in publicized cases of violent behavior of employees toward supervisors. Box 6.2 describes an incident that might very well have been linked to the nature of the negative feedback that the employee received. Baron observed that destructive criticism usually occurs after a period in which the supervisor has allowed incidents of poor performance on the part of the subordinate to pile up. By then, the supervisor inevitably has strong emotions attached to the poor performance, and the feedback consequently comes out as destructive. Unfortunately, most of us have experienced this buildup or its effects—we have acted destructively in giving feedback, and we have been the recipients of destructive feedback. We may have become increasingly, and silently, annoyed with a roommate or office colleague for his or her sloppiness, until we finally asked if they were raised in a barn or a pigsty— not the most effective way to begin the conversation.

DESTRUCTIVE
CRITICISM

Negative feedback that is cruel, sarcastic, and offensive; usually general rather than specific and often directed toward personal characteristics of the employee rather than job-relevant behaviors.

A University of Michigan administrator has been charged by police with shooting a colleague to death in a dispute over a job-performance evaluation.

Police said Donald Koos's uncomplimentary evaluation of William Aparicio's work apparently motivated Mr. Aparicio to kill the assistant director of the university's Neuro-Psychiatric Institute last week.

University officials said Mr. Koos, 30, and Mr. Aparicio, 46, had worked together for more than a year and seemed to get along well. Mr. Aparicio has been serving as the institute's administrative manager.

Police believe Mr. Aparicio learned recently that he had been turned down in his bid to become the institute's top administrator and that he blamed his rejection on an assessment of his performance by Mr. Koos, also a candidate for the job.

SOURCE: *Chronicle of Higher Education*, 1978.

Once destructive criticism has been delivered, is there any way to repair the damage? Baron suggested a way. He studied the effects of destructive criticism in both the laboratory and the field, and discovered that the most direct way to counteract the damaging effect was with an apology. If the apology included an explanation that the supervisor did not intend to be cruel, but instead was trying to set high standards because the work was difficult, it was even better. What did not work, and indeed made the situation worse, was to provide the recipient of the destructive criticism an opportunity to "vent" his or her anger to a third party. This often served to increase the anger and hostility (Baron, 1990).

The implications are clear. If you delivered destructive feedback, apologize as quickly as possible and make it clear that you didn't mean to humiliate the recipient, although you could imagine that it might appear that way. The longer the period of time between the destructive criticism and the apology, the stronger will be the anger and hostility that builds up in the recipient. The recipient may retaliate by delivering his or her own destructive criticism, and your relationship will spiral downward until and unless both parties apologize.

360 Degree Feedback

As we have seen in earlier sections of this chapter, an organization has a wide array of possible information sources for performance evaluation. It is also true, as a general principle, that the greater the number of independent sources, the more complete the performance picture. It also follows logically that the more credible information is available, the more effective the feedback can be. To implement 360 degree feedback effectively, Harris (2000) offered the following guidelines:

1. Ensure the anonymity of the sources. The best way to do this is to have multiple raters for each source. For example, if a supervisor is being evaluated, all subordinates can provide feedback and their ratings and comments can be aggregated, so that no one subordinate can be identified.

2. Rather than allowing the ratee to choose the evaluators, the evaluators should be jointly identified by the supervisor and the employee being rated.

3. Use 360 feedback exclusively for developmental and growth purposes, not for administrative decisions.

4. Train those who will be information sources as well as those who will deliver the feedback.

5. Follow up the feedback session with regular opportunities for the supervisor to assess progress and provide positive feedback.

In assembling the information for the feedback meeting, it is important to look for common themes. It is not essential for various sources to agree with each other on details (or even on ratings assigned). It is assumed that each information source is providing reliable and unique descriptions; each evaluator has been exposed to different performance incidents. Nevertheless, there will be themes that run through the ratings and comments (e.g., this manager reacts well in crisis situations; this manager does not solicit the opinions of others before making a decision). The final "report" that will be used for providing feedback is more art than science. It requires a good narrative that identifies consistent themes and highlights both strengths and weaknesses. It is best to shape the report around behaviorally oriented statements since this makes the feedback more specific and tends to guard against the appearance of an overly personalized evaluation. The effect of the feedback will be more profound if general themes can be identified from converging sources of information. The most significant discrepancy is usually between self-assessments and the assessments of others. Kenny and DePaulo (1993) found that individuals tend to be inaccurate about the effect they have on other people. They tend to impose their own perceptions of their behavior on other people. One of the most significant effects of the 360 feedback system is that it helps employees see how others view them.

Not everyone agrees that 360 degree feedback accomplishes the goal of increasing self-awareness. Brett and Atwater (2001) conducted a study with employed or recently employed managers who were enrolled in an MBA program. They found that even with multiple sources of feedback, ratees perceived negative feedback as inaccurate and not very useful and responded with anger and discouragement. This was despite the clear understanding by the recipient that the feedback was to be developmental, with no implications for administrative decisions. This was a unique study in several respects. Since the feedback was not solicited or used by an employer, it may have appeared less credible to the ratees. In addition, as Brett and Atwater pointed out, since many of the employers knew that the ratees had left or would not return to the employing organization, they may have been more negative in their comments than was warranted by the behavior of the ratee. Currently, there is more theory and practice surrounding 360 degree feedback than solid research evidence. Nevertheless, 360 degree feedback does seem to fit well with the newer conceptions of performance management.

PERFORMANCE EVALUATION AND CULTURE

The 360 degree feedback process is a good way to introduce a discussion of the effect of culture on performance appraisal. You will recall Hofstede's theory of culture from the introductory chapter. In 360 degree feedback, subordinates are expected to evaluate supervisors. But consider a culture in which power distance is high, a culture in which workers expect supervisors to have and exercise considerable power over subordinates. In such a culture 360 degree feedback systems might threaten both the subordinate and supervisor. As another example of cultural aspects of performance evaluation, consider the issue of self-appraisal. Compared to U.S. workers, workers in China are very modest in describing their skills and accomplishments. Fahr, Dobbins, and Cheng (1991) compared self and supervisory ratings of 982 supervisor-subordinate teams in Taiwan. American workers gave themselves higher ratings than their supervisors gave them. Chinese workers gave themselves lower ratings than those assigned by supervisors, which Fahr et al. referred to as **modesty bias.** American managers viewing Chinese worker self-ratings in the context of their American experience would be very concerned about these self-ratings and might be inclined to think that the performance of Chinese workers was substandard. Interestingly, the same phenomenon was found with young and well-educated Chinese workers, indicating the strength of this cultural phenomenon.

While published research on the relationship between culture and performance evaluations is quite limited, there is a good theoretical basis for expecting such a relationship. Further, as the globalization of work continues and multicultural environments become

MODESTY BIAS

Occurs when raters give themselves lower ratings than are warranted.

increasingly common, cultural issues will assume even greater importance. Davis (1998) provided another example of cultural influences. Singapore Airlines has offices in Thailand. When asked to complete performance evaluations on their subordinates, the Thai managers were very reluctant to say anything negative about their employees, fearing that this would be considered a negative deed, causing them to have bad karma and resulting in a reincarnation at a lower level in the next life (Chee, 1994). Davis examined Hofstede's theory of culture, and suggested that Hofstede's five dimensions of culture might affect performance evaluations as follows:

- Individualist cultures will be more amenable to traditional performance evaluation; collectivist cultures will be more amenable to the evaluations of groups or teams.
- Cultures characterized as high in power distance will be more resistant to 360 degree systems than those low in power distance.
- Cultures with low tolerance for uncertainty will tend to be characterized by blunt and direct performance feedback.
- Masculine cultures will emphasize achievement and accomplishments while feminine cultures will emphasize relationships.
- Short-term orientation cultures will emphasize relationships rather than performance; long-term orientation cultures will emphasize behavioral change based on performance feedback.

These predictions represent knowledgeable speculation about the "clash" of evaluation and feedback systems with culture, but they are plausible given what we know about culture and about the social content of performance evaluation. The conclusion is that organizations need to be sensitive to cultural issues when introducing performance evaluation systems into multinational environments.

We need to caution you, however, that whenever we talk about culture, it should be recognized that there are differences *within* cultures as well. Not everyone in a culture necessarily shares the values of that culture.

PERFORMANCE EVALUATION AND THE LAW

Easy approval is expected Thursday when a judge reviews Ford Motor Company's proposed $10.5 million settlement of two class actions stemming from the automaker's controversial and now-abandoned manager evaluation system (Gallagher, 2002).

Up to this point in our discussion, we have been considering issues related to perceptions of fairness, as well as the technical, psychometric, and procedural characteristics of performance evaluation systems. The quote above from the *Detroit Free Press* March 13, 2002, adds another dimension to performance measurement: the legal dimension.

When people feel unfairly treated by an HR system, they often allow lawyers to express their feelings by bringing lawsuits against their employers. In January 2000, the Ford Motor Company introduced a new evaluation system for its 18,000 senior managers. It was a **forced distribution rating system,** requiring evaluators to place managers into one of three categories—A, B, or C (with A being the highest performance category). The company mandated that 10 percent of the managers be placed in category A, 80 percent in category B, and 10 percent in category C. Any manager who was rated a C would receive no salary increase in that year, and if a manager received a C for two years running, he or she would be subject to demotion or termination.

As you might imagine, at least 1,800 managers were very unhappy. Their concerns were basic. Most obvious was their anger about being denied salary increases. In addition, it was clear that their jobs might be in jeopardy if they were placed in the C category for

FORCED DISTRIBUTION RATING SYSTEM

Requires evaluators to place employees into performance categories based on a predetermined percentage of employees in different categories (low, moderate, high).

a second year. At the heart of their discontent was the idea that *forcing* a performance distribution was arbitrary. How could the company simply categorize 10 percent of its employees as poor performers, regardless of their skills, accomplishments, or job-related behaviors? They saw this as the HR equivalent of the child's game of musical chairs. Students at the low end of a score distribution may see the same phenomenon when the instructor grades on a curve, predetermining that some students will receive lower grades because of the superior performance of other students, rather than because of the quality of their own performance.

Ford was not alone in adopting this type of forced distribution system. Similar systems had been adopted by other large employers such as General Electric, Hewlett-Packard, Sun Microsystems, Intel, and Cisco. Before its fall from grace, the Enron energy system had also adopted a forced distribution system which was nicknamed "rank and yank" since the lower-ranked employees were often terminated (Amalfe & Adelman, 2001). In a letter to GE shareholders, the guru of corporate strategic thinking and GE chairman, Jack Welch, summed the philosophy up as follows:

> [N]ot removing the bottom 10 percent early in their careers is . . . a form of cruelty because inevitably a new leader will come along and take out that bottom 10 percent right away, leaving them, sometimes midway through their careers, stranded . . . A company that bets its future on its people must remove that lower 10 percent and keep removing it every year—always raising the bar of performance and increasing the quality of its leadership (cited in Amalfe & Adelman, 2001).

The Ford program seemed to offend almost every group of managers. The company was hit with lawsuits claiming age, gender, and race (both black and white) discrimination. In an attempt to mollify the managers, Ford changed the policy to require that only 5 percent of its managers be placed in category C. This change had no effect on the anger of the managers, and the suits remained in place. Ford eventually eliminated the forced distribution system and paid over $10 million to the litigants. It is not hard to understand why organizations may find a forced distribution system attractive. HR managers have observed that, left on their own, many managers will produce overly lenient performance score distributions. Garrison Keillor pokes fun at this phenomenon in his description of Lake Wobegon, where "all the children are above average." When every employee occupies a position at or near the top of the scale, it makes it that much more difficult for managers to justify a number of decisions such as promotion, compensation, or layoffs.

While the Ford case may be the most recent and public of lawsuits involving performance evaluation, it is hardly unique. A recent review of court cases between 1980 and 1995 involving performance evaluation uncovered no fewer than 1,870 federal court decisions (Werner & Bolino, 1997). This number does not include lawsuits brought in state or county court, or lawsuits that were settled or dismissed before a decision was rendered. This represents a striking amount of unhappiness. Using an analytic technique called **policy capturing,** Werner and Bolino analyzed 295 cases that were heard by a U.S. Circuit Court of Appeals to determine how judges look at performance evaluation. This technique allows researchers to code various characteristics of the case (e.g., was a job analysis used to develop the system, were the raters trained) and see which characteristics the judges mentioned in rendering their decision. Of the 295 cases, 35 percent were age discrimination, 33 percent alleged race discrimination, 16 percent gender discrimination complaints, and 11 percent were multiple categories (e.g., age and race, gender and age), disability, or national origin cases.

The results of the analysis showed that judges were primarily concerned with issues of fairness rather than the technical characteristics of the system (e.g., validity, traits vs. behaviors as anchors). The characteristics most commonly cited in the decisions were (1) whether or not a job analysis was used to develop the system, (2) whether the raters were given written instructions, (3) whether the organization provided a mechanism for

POLICY CAPTURING

Technique that allows researchers to code various characteristics and determine which weighed most heavily in raters' decision making.

employees to appeal their ratings, and (4) whether multiple raters agreed on the ratings. There was some evidence that rater training (an extension of the second characteristic listed above) might also be important to judges. The issue of the validity of the system was mentioned in only 9 of the 295 cases, an indication of the lack of interest by the judges in the technical side of the system. From the traditional I-O perspective, this result was surprising. It was, however, consistent with other reviews of judicial decisions (e.g., Barrett & Kernan, 1987; Field & Holley, 1982). We have emphasized throughout this text that we need to have a "theory" of performance. The courts do not agree. They care more about fairness than theory. Robert Guion, a well-known I-O psychologist, commented that employers "can be fairly stupid as long as they are stupid *fairly*" (2002). By this Guion meant that the law does not require a business to use best practices as long as every employee is subject to the *worst practices* without regard to demographic characteristics like race or gender or age. In another respect, this finding should not surprise us. Plaintiffs come to court seeking justice and fairness, not theoretical explanations. Courts provide a stage for fairness discussions. Even though the courts may be more interested in fairness than theory, good theory will usually produce fair measures.

Malos (1998) examined court decisions as well as the research literature on performance measurement systems, and suggested various safeguards that an employer can put in place to reduce the probability of a lawsuit and increase the defensibility of a performance measurement system if a lawsuit is filed. Table 6.9 presents suggestions regarding the substance of performance appraisals while Table 6.10 addresses procedures. As you can see, the suggestions in Table 6.9 are largely ignored by the courts in rendering decisions. That does not mean that they are unimportant. It may very well be that these "substance" factors are some of the elements that influence whether a lawsuit is filed in the first place. The "procedural factors" in Table 6.10 are what seem to be important in determining whether it will be the employee or the company who wins if a lawsuit is actually filed.

One troublesome aspect of the Werner and Bolino (1997) analysis of court decisions suggested a possible conflict between the courts and I-O psychology. They found that judges are very concerned about agreement among raters. Yet it is widely accepted among I-O psychologists that different raters bring different perspectives and observations to the evaluation. This is the underlying philosophy of 360 degree systems. It will be important for I-O psychologists to educate judges and juries about these issues of "agreement" as performance evaluation systems include more raters from different levels in (and outside) the organization. This will become particularly important when a performance evaluation system serves multiple purposes (e.g., employee development as well as salary decisions).

TABLE 6.9	The Relationship between Court Decisions and the Substance of Rating

Appraisal criteria

- Should be objective rather than subjective.
- Should be job related or based on job analysis.
- Should be based on behaviors rather than traits.
- Should be within the control of the ratee.
- Should relate to specific functions, not global assessments.
- Should be communicated to the employee.

SOURCE: Malos (1998).

TABLE 6.10	The Relationships between Court Decisions and Rating Procedures

Appraisal procedures

- Should be standardized and uniform for all employees within a job group.
- Should be formally communicated to employees.
- Should provide notice of performance deficiencies and of opportunities to correct them.
- Should provide access for employees to review appraisal results.
- Should provide formal appeal mechanisms that allow for employee input.
- Should use multiple, diverse, and unbiased raters.
- Should provide written instructions and training for raters.
- Should require thorough and consistent documentation across raters that includes specific examples of performance based on personal knowledge.
- Should establish a system to detect potentially discriminatory effects or abuses of the system overall.

SOURCE: Malos (1998).

Performance Evaluation and Protected Groups

As you saw in the Ford Motor Company case, several different demographic groups contended that they were systematically disadvantaged by the forced distribution ranking system. Lawsuits were brought by women, African Americans, and older managers. These complaints are not unique to forced distribution systems. The same arguments have been made by the same demographic groups in other lawsuits involving performance ratings that do not result in forced distributions. They are most often brought against trait-based systems, but unfairness has been alleged against behavior-based systems as well. The argument is that ratings are unduly subjective, implying that the decisions based on those ratings are not reliable or valid. It is further argued that, because the ratings are subjective and have no basis in actual behavior, supervisors are free to interpret the scales any way they like. Consequently, they may use unfair negative stereotypes about women, African Americans, older employees, or disabled employees, resulting in lower ratings for those individuals.

Since the late 1970s, researchers have been studying the possibility of systematic unfairness in performance ratings. Their results have found little evidence of such unfairness. Landy and Farr (1980, 1983) examined literature from the 1950s to the 1980s and failed to find any striking evidence of discrimination in ratings. Subsequent studies and meta-analyses have drawn the same conclusions (Arvey & Murphy, 1998; Landy, Shankster, & Kohler, 1994; McEvoy & Cascio, 1989; Oppler, Campbell, Pulakos, & Borman, 1992; Pulakos, White, Oppler, & Borman, 1989; Sackett & DuBois, 1991). Arvey and Murphy concluded that "the notion that performance evaluations and particularly supervisory ratings of performance are biased against racial and gender groups is simply not supported by empirical data" (p. 163). They further suggested that when differences between men and women, or whites and African Americans are found, these differences are small and most likely due to true differences in performance rather than bias. Some critics make the more refined argument that it is really the more "subjective" systems that permit the greatest amount of bias. Bernardin, Hennessey, and Peyfritte (1995) examined that question and found no evidence of systematic discrimination in any of the common formats, graphic or behaviorally anchored. This is consistent with the conclusions of the Landy and Farr (1980, 1983) review of the performance rating literature. They found that as long as the scales were well developed, the actual rating format had little influence on the statistical characteristics of the resulting ratings.

As a result of over two decades of research and review, we can safely conclude that performance evaluations do not systematically discriminate against protected subgroups (age, gender, race, disability) as is often alleged. That is not to say that a particular supervisor may not harbor prejudiced feelings toward a particular subordinate based on a demographic characteristic of that subordinate, and rate that subordinate more harshly than he or she deserves as a result of that prejudice. It is difficult for any HR system, including a performance evaluation system, to prevent an individual intending to discriminate unfairly from doing so. But there is nothing inherent in the performance evaluation system per se that leads to systematic discrimination against protected groups. Indeed, many of the structural characteristics and issues we have discussed in this chapter explicitly focus raters on evaluating job-relevant behavior. For example, a performance evaluation system that assesses behaviors rather than traits and that uses multiple raters increases the likelihood that evaluations will be reliable, valid, and based on actual performance.

MODULE 6.4 SUMMARY

- Some research suggests that many raters have no intention of providing accurate performance ratings, but instead are using the process as a means toward an end, either personal or organizational. As such, performance appraisal ratings can be affected by organizational politics and the perspectives of different stakeholders involved in the process.

- Individual workers seek performance feedback because it reduces uncertainty and provides external information about levels of performance to balance internal perceptions. Most workers prefer to receive positive feedback, and most supervisors prefer to give it. Because there is always room for improvement, most workers get some positive feedback and some directed toward improving skills or eliminating weaknesses.

- As a general principle, the greater the number of independent sources of information, the more complete the performance picture. It follows logically that the more credible information is available, the more effective the feedback can be. One

of the most significant effects of the 360 feedback system is that it helps employees see how others view them.

- Although published research on the relationship between culture and performance evaluations is limited, there is a good theoretical basis for expecting such a relationship. As the globalization of work continues and multicultural environments become increasingly common, cultural issues in performance evaluation and other human resource practices will assume even greater importance. Organizations will need to be sensitive to cultural issues when introducing performance evaluation systems into multicultural environments.

- When people feel unfairly treated by the performance evaluation system, they often bring lawsuits against their employers. In performance evaluation cases brought to court, judges appear to be primarily concerned with issues of fairness rather than the technical characteristics of the system (e.g., validity, traits versus behaviors as anchors).

KEY TERMS

destructive criticism

modesty bias

forced distribution rating system

policy capturing

CRITICAL THINKING
EXERCISES

6.7 As we have seen in considering the various motivational influences on a supervisor's ratings, the actual ratings may need to be evaluated in some context to be of any value. Does this mean that performance rating should be abandoned? Why or why not?

6.8 We discussed a "modesty bias" that is common to some Asian cultures. In many Latin cultures, it is considered inappropriate to openly criticize a peer or subordinate. For example, Latin managers might be more reluctant than non-Latin managers to record negative instances of subordinate performance. How might you reconcile this cultural tendency with the need to collect accurate performance information in a Latin culture? How would this tendency of Latin managers affect the comparison of workers in a multinational organization in which some workers report to Latin managers, and others to non-Latin managers?

STAFFING DECISIONS

7 CHAPTER

CONCEPTUAL ISSUES IN STAFFING

AN OVERVIEW OF THE STAFFING PROCESS

The day had started out fine for the vice president of HR. He met the CEO for breakfast to talk about the new performance management system that was being considered. At 9:30 he would interview a candidate for the HR compensation specialist position in the Seattle plant. But at 9:15, the administrative assistant rushed in and said, "Look out the window." On the spacious lawn outside, several dozen people were carrying signs protesting the underrepresentation of people of color in the company's management ranks. The signs also announced a boycott of the company until their staffing policies become "more responsible and sensitive to the makeup of the community." Seconds later, the phone rang and the receptionist said that reporters from two newspapers and a local TV station wanted interviews about the $30 million lawsuit that had just been announced by a national employment law firm, charging systemic discrimination against people of color. The VP felt as if he might faint. The thought that kept going through his mind was, I've been so careful to comply with all the regulations, to make sure our policies are fair!

In other chapters of this book, we have discussed the value of a diverse workforce, individual attributes and their value in job success, and assessment devices such as tests. For the organization, these serve as tools that are used to make decisions about whom to hire, whom to promote, or even whom to lay off. These decisions are called staffing decisions because they determine and define the staff or workforce of the organization. For the purposes of this chapter, we will define **staffing decisions** as those associated with recruiting, selecting, promoting, and separating employees. It is important to note that from practical, scientific, and legal perspectives the decision to separate an individual from an organization (layoff or termination, sometimes called "deselection"), involves many if not all of the same issues that are in play in hiring or promoting an individual.

Guion (1998) presented a sequential view of the staffing process (see Figure 7.1). As Guion's model shows, the organization uses a job or needs analysis to identify the characteristics of individuals they would like to hire (or, in the layoff situation, those they would like to retain). This information guides the selection process. In subsequent steps, the candidate pool is gradually narrowed through rejection decisions until a selection is made and an individual is placed in a position.

> **STAFFING DECISIONS**
>
> *Associated with recruiting, selecting, promoting, and separating employees.*

STAFFING FROM THE STRATEGIC PERSPECTIVE

You will notice that the top right-hand box in Figure 7.1 portrays both a job and a needs analysis for identifying desired traits. Until recently, a typical staffing situation would begin

FIGURE 7.1

**Sequential View of
the Staffing Process**
SOURCE: Guion (1998).

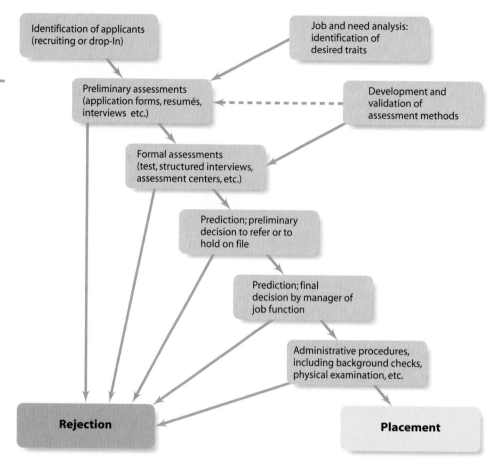

with a vacant job title, either because someone has left the organization or a new job title has been created. But as we have seen in other chapters, today's workplace is much more volatile. Jobs change, reporting relationships change, and organizational strategy changes. Figure 7.2 illustrates the types of changes that complicate today's staffing. This means that the staffing challenge is more complex than simply looking up the KSAOs for a job as identified by a job analysis.

Snow and Snell (1993) have used historical trends to identify three different models of staffing. Model 1 assumes well-defined jobs in a stable industry. They considered this the earliest staffing model chronologically and associate it with the emerging factory system of the 1920s. Model 2, more characteristic of the 1980s, views staffing as a support mechanism to implement a predetermined strategy. For example, in the late 1970s watch manufacturers decided to develop lines of digital watches in addition to conventional analog watches. The staffing process, consequently, was redirected toward a different type of design and production engineer, one more familiar with the emerging digital technology. Watch manufacturers made a strategic decision to enter a new market, and that decision directed the recruiting and selection (i.e., staffing) process. In Snow and Snell's Model 3, which the researchers consider to be the most advanced view of what a modern idealized staffing process would accomplish, the staffing process seeks to identify individuals with core attributes, both cognitive and personality, who will ultimately develop the strategy of the organization rather than implement a strategy chosen by someone else.

Table 7.1 presents these three models and their characteristics. Although we have described these models as being tied to an "era," they are most appropriately applied

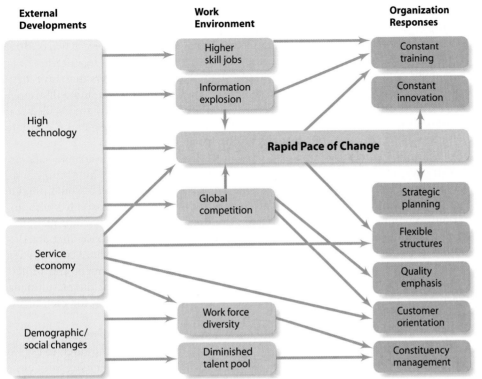

External
Developments

Work
Environment

Organization
Responses

FIGURE 7.2

Current Influences on the Staffing Process
SOURCE: Howard (1991).

| | TABLE 7.1 | **Alternative Views of the Staffing Process** |

	MODEL 1: STAFFING AS PERSON-JOB MATCH	MODEL 2: STAFFING AS STRATEGY IMPLEMENTATION	MODEL 3: STAFFING AS STRATEGY FORMATION
Characteristics	Staffing based on job analysis	Staffing based on competitive strategy (part of implementation)	Staffing based on strategy formation
	Many candidates available per job	Role descriptions	Broad skill base
	Tests to measure individual differences	Interdepartmental team synergies	Rapid deployment of resources
	Validation studies	Open-system perspective	Open-system perspective
	Closed-system perspective		
Assumptions	Organizations and jobs can be separated into individual components	Deductive logic	Inductive logic
		Reactive staffing	Proactive staffing
	People and jobs are stable	Tight fit between strategy and staffing	Loose fit between strategy and staffing (slack)
	Job performance can be measured validly and reliably		
Applications	Organizations with stable, definable jobs	Organizations with clear strategies and known competencies	Organizations that need the ability to develop or change strategy quickly

SOURCE: Snow & Snell (1993).

to a type of industry or competitive environment. In today's business world, there are still organizations that have well-defined jobs and operate in a relatively stable environment. Auto manufacturers, for example, may change models only every two or three years. The steel and mining industries change even more slowly. Organizations like these might follow staffing Model 1. Similarly, there are organizations that have identified a "niche" or a clear strategy for succeeding in a certain market and will arrange their HR processes around that strategy. A watch manufacturer may have decided that the wave of the future is the incorporation of a Global Positioning System (GPS) into the wristwatch. This type of organization might adopt staffing Model 2. Finally, we might have the rapidly changing environment of the computer hardware and software industry, an environment that is globally competitive and driven by innovation more than stability. For that type of organization, the application of Model 3 would provide the types of people who will help create strategy "on the fly," if necessary. It is also important to point out that the same organization (e.g., a computer keyboard manufacturer) might use all three models for different staffing needs. In the basic manufacturing processes, they might use Model 1. In the service, troubleshooting, and redesign area, they might use Model 2. And for mid- to upper-level management and professional staff, they might use Model 3. Table 7.2 illustrates the goals of the recruitment, selection, promotion, and deselection elements of the staffing process for each of the three models.

This three-phase model of Snow and Snell paints an exciting and dynamic picture of the "evolved" staffing philosophy of the 21st century. Murphy (1999), however, suggested that such a staffing model, while seemingly in tune with the rapidly changing work environment, is ultimately self-defeating. The problem is absence of stability. Murphy argued that workers need time to become socialized into the organization, and to develop expertise and knowledge of technology and performance systems. While Murphy's concerns may be realistic, they are not so much about staffing systems as about organizational

TABLE 7.2 **Goals of the Staffing Process Associated with Various Staffing Models**

	MODEL 1: STAFFING AS PERSON-JOB MATCH	MODEL 2: STAFFING AS STRATEGY IMPLEMENTATION	MODEL 3: STAFFING AS STRATEGY FORMATION
Recruitment	Expand pool of job applicants	Attract targeted individuals to enhance core competencies	Build relationships with potentially useful human resources
Selection	Achieve person-job fit by rejecting less desirable applicants	Develop a configuration of individuals that meets synergistic needs of strategy	Enhance strategic capability by choosing individuals who bring new skills to the company
Appraisal	Based on job performance	Based on strategy implementation	Based on strategy formation
Promotion	Reward is upward movement within a hierarchy	Reward is increased centrality to current strategy	Reward is greater inclusion in strategy-formation process
Deselection	Keep key people based on current job requirements	Keep people with core competencies	Keep people who have unique skills

SOURCE: Adapted from Snow & Snell (1993).

designs: The staffing model is simply supporting an organizational model. His conclusion suggests, as we have above, that an organization may need to have several staffing models operating simultaneously.

THE IMPACT OF STAFFING PRACTICES ON FIRM PERFORMANCE

In some respects, we have begged a question in discussing staffing practices. We have simply asked you to assume that staffing practices will have a positive bottom-line effect; that firms that follow certain staffing practices will be better performers than firms that don't. This assumption has been the subject of research, and the conclusion is that staffing practices (and HR practices more generally as well) do have a positive association with firm performance. Huselid (1995) identified a number of "high performance work practices" based on theory and research, and examined the relationship between those practices and outcomes such as turnover, firm productivity, and corporate financial performance (i.e., share value and percentage return on investment). **High performance work practices** included the use of formal job analyses, selection from within for key positions, the amount of training received by employees, merit-based promotions, and the use of formal assessment devices for selection.

By arranging almost 1,000 companies according to the extent to which each followed high performance practices, Huselid was able to calculate the association between high performance practices and concrete outcomes. Thus, for every increase of one standard deviation in high performance practices, he found that firms might expect a decrease of 7 percent in turnover, an increase of $27,044 in sales per employee, and increased profitability of $3,814 per employee. These are impressive numbers. Cascio (1998b) estimated that the effects of high performance work practices on the market value of a firm appear to fall between $15,000 and $45,000 per employee, and will also affect whether the firm even survives in a competitive environment (Davidson et al., 1996; Welbourne & Andrews, 1996).

It is tempting to view staffing as a logistical problem, with cost/benefit ratios, job demands, and applicant attributes. But there is another view that must be added for a complete consideration of the staffing process—a consideration of the various stakeholders in staffing.

> HIGH PERFORMANCE WORK PRACTICES
>
> *Include the use of formal job analyses, selection from within for key positions, merit-based promotions, and the use of formal assessment devices for selection.*

STAKEHOLDERS IN THE STAFFING PROCESS

In making staffing decisions, the usual focus is on the organization itself. Does the decision enhance the position of the organization by increasing productivity, maintaining quality, increasing a customer base, or other benefits? That was the key question addressed by Huselid's (1995) research as described above. But the organization as a whole is not the only customer or stakeholder in the staffing decision. Other stakeholders include the line managers, co-workers, and, as we will see in Chapter 11, the candidate (Gilliland & Cherry, 2000).

Line Managers

In many if not most organizations, line managers are actively involved in the selection decision, both in terms of gathering information from applicants, usually in the form of one or more interviews, and of sharing in the ultimate decision regarding whom to hire, promote, or lay off. As a result, the line manager seeks an accurate, easy-to-administer, and easy-to-defend staffing process (Gilliland & Cherry, 2000). Once a decision is made, it is the line manager who will be expected to supervise the new addition (whether a hire or promotion) to the work group. Or, if a department or work group is being downsized, it will be the manager's responsibility to maintain group effectiveness with a reconfigured work group. For all these reasons, it is in the best interest of the manager to see that the staffing decision is an effective one.

Co-workers

Like the manager, the co-worker has a stake in the staffing decision. If the decision is a hiring or promotion decision, the co-worker will be either a peer or a subordinate. In a layoff, the decision may have both practical and emotional consequences. In many instances, after a layoff occurs, fewer people are expected to complete a broader range of tasks. In addition, the perceived fairness of the layoff decision may have direct effects on how committed to the organization the remaining co-workers feel. In addition to its direct effects upon co-workers, the quality of the staffing decision may also affect the reputation of the work group or department (Gilliland & Cherry, 2000).

Applicants

Applicants can have very strong feelings about the staffing process, including communications about the staffing process (e.g., schedule for a hiring decision), the actual assessment devices themselves, and the process by which the decisions are made. Naturally, when applicants are rejected by the staffing system, they are more likely to think poorly of the organization and view the staffing process as biased or impersonal. Even if they are selected, the manner by which the staffing decision is carried out will have an influence on how they perceive the culture and climate of the organization.

Table 7.3 summarizes the goals of the various stakeholders beyond the formal organization or the HR department. Gilliland and Cherry (2000) suggested that the staffing practice of an organization will have direct consequences on outcomes as diverse as legal challenges (e.g., charges of discrimination in selection), likelihood of desirable applicants

TABLE 7.3	Stakeholder Goals in the Staffing Process
CUSTOMER	**NEEDS, DESIRES, AND GOALS FOR SELECTION**
Line managers	• Accurate and informative indicators of applicant potential
	• Quick and easy-to-use selection process
	• Flexibility and accommodation of selection procedures
	• Perceived validity of selection process
Co-workers	• Accurate and informative indicators of applicant potential
	• Input into the selection decision-making process
	• Perceived validity of selection process
Applicants	• Appropriate hiring decision
	• Unbiased, job-related selection process that gives them a chance to demonstrate their potential
	• Honest and sensitive interpersonal treatment
	• Timely and informative feedback

Source: Gilliland & Cherry (2000).

accepting offers, satisfaction of individuals hired or promoted, quality of the relationship between the line manager and the selected individual, and even the possibility of keeping unsuccessful candidates as customers of the organization.

There are additional potential stakeholders in the staffing process. These might include society at large in the example of high reliability (e.g., nuclear power industry) and public safety (e.g., police, fire, and corrections) environments. In organizations whose workers are represented by collective bargaining agreements, unions may have (or seek) a voice in decisions such as promotions and layoffs. Finally, minority groups have a stake in staffing practices, particularly with respect to the potential impact of affirmative action programs (AAPs). We will consider issues associated with AAPs in considerable detail in Chapter 11 when we discuss perceptions of fairness and justice in the workplace.

STAFFING FROM THE INTERNATIONAL PERSPECTIVE

Most of what we will discuss in this chapter is directed toward staffing in U.S. companies within the context of Equal Employment Opportunity laws and assessment systems commonly found here. But what about other countries? Do they make staffing decisions differently? Nyfield and Baron (2000) surveyed employers in 14 different countries around the world. Their analysis revealed the following:

- Job descriptions are used universally.
- Educational qualifications and application forms are also widely used for initial screening.
- The most common postscreening techniques include interviews and references.
- Unlike the common practice in the United States, cognitive ability tests are used less frequently and personality tests more frequently.
- Only 50 percent of the countries sampled used statistical/actuarial approaches to decision making.

Stakeholders in corporate performance may include customers, area residents, and others outside the structure of the organization.

Nyfield and Baron (2000) suggested that differences in staffing techniques and strategies flow from cultural differences among nations such as those suggested by Hofstede (1980, 1991). They hypothesized that collectivist cultures prefer objective methods and are more likely to try to verify all candidate information, while individualist cultures prefer to take a more personal approach, examining the unique characteristics of the applicant, including such things as economic need and personal ties to the applicant. They concluded by pointing out the substantial differences that organizations may encounter when attempting to apply a staffing strategy from one country to another country. As one example, they point to the different meanings of a high school diploma. In many countries, a student must take a demanding examination to complete high school, whereas this is less common in the United States. Another example of cultural differences is a cognitive test that included numerical reasoning questions based on a table of life expectancies; such a test would be unremarkable in the United States, Germany, or the United Kingdom, but it would evoke a very negative reaction in Italy because the example dealt with the taboo topic of death.

Ryan, McFarland, Baron, and Page (1999) examined the broader issue of the connection between staffing practices and culture and found some modest relations between the

POWER DISTANCE

The degree to which less powerful members of an organization accept and expect an unequal distribution of power.

UNCERTAINTY AVOIDANCE

The extent to which members of a culture feel comfortable in unstructured situations.

MULTINATIONAL STAFFING

Procedures that involve staffing for organizations in more than one country.

Hofstede dimensions of **power distance** and **uncertainty avoidance** on the one hand, and selection strategies on the other. For example, they found that countries characterized as high in the desire to avoid uncertainty used a wider variety of tests, conducted more interviews, and verified their selection data more frequently. Although these cultural investigations are still fragmentary and more descriptive than explanatory, they are much more promising than simply noting that countries are similar or different in selection or staffing strategies. Multicultural research will continue to expand and make contributions to our understanding of the effectiveness and acceptability of various staffing strategies.

Love, Bishop, Heinisch, and Montei (1994) presented a case study in the challenges to **multinational staffing.** They studied a motor assembly plant which was predominantly Japanese owned and directed, but located in the United States and staffed with American workers. Thus, there was the potential for a clash between Japanese management principles (based in part on cultural variables such as collectivism) and American staffing principles. Just such a clash did occur. The Japanese executives were opposed to traditional job analysis techniques for several reasons. The primary reason was that—contrary to the principles of Japanese management systems in which the individual is less important than the group—job analysis tended to isolate the subject matter experts (SMEs) from the work group. Another objection was that, even though Japanese incumbent assemblers in a plant in Japan might have been used as SMEs, they would have resisted questionnaires and individual discussions without being able to discuss their responses with their fellow workers. Finally, since the collectivist culture in Japanese companies rejects individual performance measures, there were no performance measures to correlate with test scores in a criterion-related design that the American lawyers recommended for the company. This case study is an interesting example of the practical problems of multinational staffing. But in addition to the particular differences in applying a staffing method common in country A to an organization dominated by managers from country B, an equally interesting question is the broader dimensions on which countries may differ.

MODULE 7.1 SUMMARY

- In the staffing process, managers may use a job or needs analysis to identify the characteristics of individuals they would like to hire. Often the candidate pool is narrowed through sequential rejection decisions until a selection is made.

- Research indicates that staffing practices (and HR practices more generally) have a positive association with organizational performance. Several studies have indicated that "high performance work practices" have a positive impact on the organization's productivity, share value, and percentage return on investment.

- In making staffing decisions, the usual focus is on the organization itself. However, several other important stakeholders participate in the staffing decision, including the line managers, co-workers, and the candidate.

- Studies indicate that international differences in staffing techniques and strategies are associated with cultural differences among nations. Collectivist cultures prefer objective staffing methods and are more likely to try to verify all candidate information, while individualist cultures prefer to take a more personal approach to staffing by examining the unique characteristics of the applicant, including such things as economic need and personal ties to the applicant.

KEY TERMS

staffing decisions

high performance work practices

power distance

uncertainty avoidance

multinational staffing

CRITICAL THINKING EXERCISES

7.1 Consider the three models that have been proposed by Snow and Snell. The U.S. Department of Defense is faced with continuing challenges from potential adversaries with respect to human rights and aggression from rogue nations. Which of the three models would be most appropriate for staffing senior leadership positions in the armed forces for the foreseeable future? Why?

7.2 As we have seen, there are many different stakeholders in the staffing process. From the perspective of firm profitability, which three stakeholder groups would you nominate as the most important? Why?

7.2 MODULE

EVALUATION OF STAFFING OUTCOMES

S taffing outcomes might be evaluated in a number of different ways. The three major aspects of evaluation are validity, utility, and fairness. We will consider each of these separately.

VALIDITY

Staffing decisions are intended to serve a business-related purpose. The outcomes of staffing decisions are expected to populate an organization with workers who possess the knowledge, skills, abilities, and personality characteristics that will enable the organization to succeed. Staffing decisions involve inferences about the match between a person and a job; the decision maker would like to infer or predict something about the probable success of various candidates, and choose those candidates with the highest probability of success. Thus staffing decisions are, or ought to be, valid decisions.

As we have seen in Chapter 2, there are many different methods for assessing the **validity** of a selection device or test. We can apply these methods to testing the validity of staffing decisions. The most common of the validity designs are the criterion-related, content-related, and construct-related. The **criterion-related validity** design provides perhaps the easiest way to illustrate the role of validity in staffing decisions. Consider the three scatterplots in Figure 7.3. These scatterplots depict various levels of association between a test or test battery being used for selection and some criterion of interest (e.g., level of performance). Consider the bottom case (c) where the validity coefficient = .00. No matter what predictor (test) score a candidate obtains, there is no useful predictive information in that test score. Regardless of whether the candidate obtains a test score of 10 or of 70, there is no way to predict what that candidate's performance will be. We only know it will be somewhere between 60 and 100.

Now look at the middle case (b) where the validity coefficient = +.50. While prediction is not perfect, an individual's test score at least narrows the range of probable performance or criterion scores. For example, if the candidate receives a test score of 50, we can predict that the performance score will fall somewhere between 70 and 90.

Finally, consider the case of perfect prediction, as illustrated in the top case (a). Here, the validity coefficient = +1.00. This means that each and every test score has one and only one performance score associated with it. If a candidate scores a 50 on the test, we can predict with great precision that the candidate will achieve a performance score of 80. Although such precision is never achieved with typical assessment devices, it gives us a graphic idea of the power of accurate staffing decisions.

Selection Ratios

The relationship between the number of individuals assessed and the number actually hired is called the **selection ratio (SR).** Although this may seem counterintuitive, low selection

VALIDITY

The accurateness of inferences made based on test or performance data; also addresses whether a measure accurately and completely represents what was intended to be measured.

CRITERION-RELATED VALIDITY

Approach demonstrated by correlating a test score with a performance measure; improves researcher's confidence in the inference that people with higher test scores have higher performance.

SELECTION RATIO (SR)

Index ranging from 0 to 1 that reflects the ratio of positions to applicants; calculated by dividing the number of positions available by the number of applicants.

262

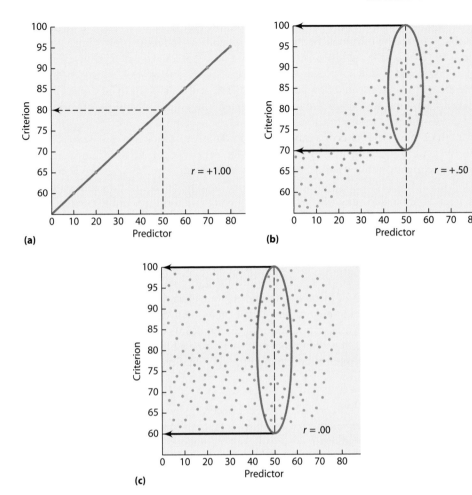

FIGURE 7.3

Scatterplots Depicting Various Levels of Relationship between a Test and a Criterion

ratios are actually better than high selection ratios because the more people we assess, the greater the likelihood that we will find individuals who score high on the test. If the test is a valid one, this translates into a higher likelihood that we will be able to hire a good performer. The formula for calculating the selection ratio is SR = $n/$N where n represents the number of jobs available (the number of hires to be made) and N represents the number of people assessed. For example, if we have 100 applicants for 10 positions, the SR would be .10 (10/100). If there were 200 applicants instead of 100, the selection ratio would be .05 (10/200). Thus, by assessing 200 applicants instead of 100, we are much more likely to find high scorers (and better performers). Of course, this comes with a cost—the cost of assessing 100 more applicants. We will discuss the issue of cost/benefit, or utility, later in this chapter.

Prediction Errors and Cut Scores

As you can see from the three cases illustrated above, the level of validity is associated with prediction errors. In the case of a validity coefficient = .00, we are virtually assured of making a prediction error. Our best "prediction" about the eventual performance level of *any* applicant, regardless of his or her test score, would be average performance. In contrast, when the validity coefficient = +1.00, there will be no error in our prediction of eventual performance. When validity coefficients are less than 1.00, there will be some error in our predictions (and staffing decisions).

FALSE POSITIVE

Decision in which an applicant was accepted but performed poorly; decision is false because of the incorrect prediction that the applicant would have performed successfully and positive because the applicant was hired.

FALSE NEGATIVE

Decision in which an applicant was rejected but would have performed adequately or successfully; decision is false because of the incorrect prediction that the applicant would not have performed successfully and negative because the applicant was not hired.

TRUE POSITIVE

Decision in which an applicant was accepted and performed successfully; decision is true because of the correct prediction that the applicant would be a good performer and positive because the applicant was hired.

TRUE NEGATIVE

Decision in which an applicant was rejected and would have performed poorly if he or she were hired; decision is true because of the correct prediction that the applicant would not be a good performer and negative because the applicant was not hired.

CUT SCORE

Specified point in a distribution of scores below which candidates are rejected; also known as a "cutoff score."

In making a staffing decision, we might commit two types of errors. We might predict that a person will be a successful performer and the individual turns out to be unsuccessful. That is called a **false positive** error; we falsely predicted that a positive outcome would occur and it did not—the person failed. The second type of error occurs when someone we predicted would be a poor performer actually turns out to be successful. This is called a **false negative** error; we falsely predicted a negative outcome would occur and it did not—the person succeeded.

Both of these types of errors can be costly for an organization. If we make a false negative error, we will decide not to hire an individual who might have contributed substantially to the organization. If we make a false positive error, we will hire someone who will detract from the effectiveness of the organization. To complete the picture, a **true positive** is a prediction that someone will be a good performer and this turns out to be true; a **true negative** is an accurate prediction that someone will be a poor performer. In Figure 7.4 we have graphically presented the two types of true and false decisions. But consider the effect of *moving* the score we use to hire individuals, known as the **cut score,** up or down, as we have shown in Figure 7.4. Instead of hiring all individuals with cut scores equal to or greater than 50, suppose we only hired individuals who had scores equal to or greater than 75. The consequence of increasing our cut score will be that we will make fewer false positive errors—almost everyone we hire will be an above average performer. But we will make many more false negative errors. Many of the applicants we rejected would have been above average performers. If we want to hire large numbers of individuals, this also means that we will have to assess many more candidates to get the small percentage who will score above 75.

What would happen if we were to lower our cut score instead of raising it? It would change the type of prediction errors that would occur. By lowering the cut score from 50 to 25, we will reduce the number of candidates that we incorrectly reject, but we will also substantially increase the percentage of poor performers among the candidates that we hire.

As you can see from the illustration below, having a "valid" selection device is only one of the factors in determining whether or not our staffing decisions will be effective. Even with a valid selection device, the decision about where to set the cut score in conjunction

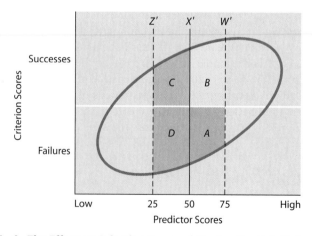

FIGURE 7.4 The Effect on Selection Errors of Moving the Cutoff Score The cutoff, *X'*, equates false positive (lower right) and false negative (upper left) errors, resulting in a minimum of decision errors. Raising the cutoff to *W'* results in a decrease of false positives *(A)* but an even greater increase in false negatives *(B)*. Similarly, lowering the cutoff to *Z'* yields a decrease in false negatives *(C)* but a larger increase in false positives *(D)*.

with a given selection ratio can detract from the predictive value of that device. In many situations, the best staffing strategy is to choose a cut score that minimizes both types of errors. In some situations, however, where the cost of a performance mistake can be catastrophic (e.g., a nuclear power plant operator or a commercial airline pilot), a better strategy might be to be very selective and accept a higher false negative error rate to reduce the frequency of false positive errors. The technology of actually setting the "best" cut score is complex and beyond the scope of this discussion. Detailed discussions of these various tables and graphs can be found in books devoted to psychometric testing (Anastasi & Urbina, 1997; Guion, 1965, 1998; Murphy & Davidshofer, 2001). We will discuss various types of cut scores later in this chapter.

Using a criterion-related design, it is relatively easy to grasp the issue of false positive and false negative prediction errors because we have a criterion score distribution on which we can designate the differentiating line between success and failure. By doing that, we can then designate a cut score on the test or predictor and actually see the extent to which errors are occurring. The same types of errors will occur regardless of which validity design we use, but in content- and construct-related designs they cannot be as easily quantified. Nevertheless, it remains true that the greater the number of unwanted errors (false positives or false negatives), the poorer will be the staffing decisions.

The concept of true negative and false negative errors may seem a bit too hypothetical, since we can never *know* for sure that an individual whom we rejected would have been a poor performer: We never had a chance to see him or her work. To some extent, that is true. But we can collect data on another group of individuals who are similar to the applicants—current employees. This was the concurrent validity design we studied in Chapter 2. Granted, most of the workers currently employed will be at least satisfactory. But unless prediction is perfect (which it never is), some small number will be less than satisfactory, perhaps 10 percent to 15 percent (Hull, 1928; Hunter, Schmidt & Pearlman, 1979; Landy, 1989). These are the false positive errors made in selection. In addition, a company might use a true predictive validity design, collect assessment data for a period of years on a new assessment battery, put those data away and not use them to make actual decisions, then return to those data several years later and create the scatterplot showing the relationship between the assessment data and performance. This would tell them how many errors and correct decisions they would have made with any cut score. In this case, a true negative occurs if the organization used this true predictive validity design and later found that someone who would have been rejected (based on a hypothetical or predetermined cut score) had below average performance. A false negative occurs if the organization used this true predictive validity design and later found that someone would have been rejected (based on a hypothetical or predetermined cut score) who had an above average performance. At that point, the organization would choose a cut score to minimize prediction errors and reject any subsequent applicants with predictor scores below that cut point.

Establishing Cut Scores

There are two different ways of establishing cut scores: the criterion-referenced method and the norm-referenced method. **Criterion-referenced cut scores** (sometimes called "domain-referenced" cut scores) are established by actually considering the desired level of performance for a new hire, and finding the test score that corresponds to that desired level of performance. Remember that in Figure 7.3 we presented the scatterplot of test and performance scores for candidates. In that case, we were discussing how one might determine the expected performance level from a test score. A cut score could be set by just reversing that process. We could have a sample of employees take the test, measure their job performance (e.g., through supervisory ratings), and then see what test score corresponds to acceptable performance as rated by the supervisor.

CRITERION-
REFERENCED
CUT SCORE

Established by considering the desired level of performance for a new hire and finding the test score that corresponds to the desired level of performance; sometimes called "domain-referenced" cut score.

An alternative method of setting criterion-referenced cut scores would be to ask a group of subject matter experts (SMEs) to examine the test in question, consider the performance demands of the job, then pick a test score that they think a candidate would need to attain to be a successful performer. These techniques tend to be complex for SMEs to accomplish, and have been the subject of a great deal of debate with respect to their accuracy (Jaeger, 1989; Maurer & Alexander, 1992; Maurer, Alexander, Callahan, Bailey, & Dambrot, 1991; Shephard, 1978).

Norm-referenced cut scores are not tied to any expected level of performance on the job. The term "norm" is a shortened version of the word "normal" or average. Thus, norm-referenced cut scores are based on the average of the test takers' scores rather than any notion of job performance. In educational settings, passing scores are typically pegged at 60. Any score below 60 is assigned a letter grade of F (for "failing") and a student gets no accumulated credit for work in that course. Many civil service commissions use a similar method for determining who "passes" a test for a city or state government job. There is no connection between that score and any aspect of anticipated performance (other than the simple notion that people with scores below the cut score are likely to do less well on the job than people with scores higher than the cut score). Frequently, when there are many candidates for a few openings, a "cut" score will be chosen that will reduce the applicant population by a specific percentage (e.g., the test will "pass" the candidates who are in the top 25 percent of the score distribution). Naturally, if the applicant population turned out to be very talented, then the staffing strategy would commit many false negative errors, because many who were rejected might have been good performers. On the other hand, the utility of the staffing strategy might be high because the expense of processing those additional candidates in later assessment steps might have been substantial.

When a test ends up in court and there are discussions of how cut scores were set, norm-referenced cut scores fare poorly compared with criterion-referenced scores (Lanning v. SEPTA, 1998, 1999, 2000) because the **Uniform Guidelines on Employee Selection Procedures** (*Uniform Guidelines*, 1978), the official government administrative guidelines, instruct that cut scores should be set to be compatible with expected levels of job performance. Lacking this clear tie to expected job performance, norm-referenced cut scores are vulnerable to charges of unfairness.

UTILITY

In the previous section on validity, we introduced two variables that interact with validity to determine the effectiveness of a staffing strategy. These variables were the number of people we would need to test to identify a sufficient number of high-quality candidates, and the cost of hiring a candidate who turned out to be unsuccessful. Validity is one, but not the only, statistical indicator of a successful staffing strategy.

In general, the concept of utility addresses the cost/benefit ratio of one staffing strategy versus another. For that reason, the term "utility gain" is synonymous with utility. Consider the following possibilities:

1. The cost of testing a candidate for an entry level job would be $10,000 per candidate.
2. There are 15 candidates for 10 jobs.
3. The cost of ineffective performance for the job in question is negligible.
4. The previous staffing strategy had identified large numbers of candidates who turned out to be successful on the job in question.

In each of those circumstances, we might be considering a demonstrably valid staffing strategy, yet reject it. In the first scenario above, the cost of testing exceeds the outcome of testing. In the second scenario, there is little selection to be done. As long as the

15 candidates meet minimal requirements, then elaborate testing is unnecessary. This is related to the selection ratio (SR) which we discussed earlier. In this example, the SR would be very high (10/15 = .67). In the case of the third scenario, there is little downside to a false positive error, so there is little to protect against. In the fourth scenario, unless the cost of testing for the new strategy is less than the cost for the old strategy, and/or unless the validity of the new strategy is considerably better than the validity of the old system, there is little advantage to changing systems. This last scenario introduces the concept of the **base rate,** or the percentage of the current workforce that is performing successfully. If performance is very high (i.e., the base rate of success is high), then any new system is likely to add very little to the productivity of the organization.

    Utility analysis calculations can be very complex, including estimated dollar values of various performance levels, administrative and material costs for the systems being compared, the number of candidates applying for the positions in question, current base rate, and the validity coefficients for the two systems being compared. In addition, there are even more exotic accounting principles which can be applied to any savings, such as the opportunity value of the money saved, changes in tax rates, and so forth (Boudreau, 1991; Cascio & Morris, 1990; Cronshaw & Alexander, 1985). Russell, Collela, and Bobko (1993) took utility calculations ever further, looking at the relative effectiveness of strategies for companies in different circumstances. They suggested, for example, that a company that has little capital available for investment in state-of-the-art assessment systems and is currently doing well might make different decisions about a selection strategy than a company that has plenty of capital but not much time because they are fighting for survival against a competitor who is turning out a superior product or service.

    Under some circumstances, it is possible to show dramatic dollar values for certain staffing strategies. The greatest utility gain will be shown when there are many candidates for a small number of positions, the dollar value (in terms of contribution to the organization) of the jobs in question is high, the cost of testing for the old system is higher than the cost of the new system, and the validity of the new system is substantially higher than that of the old system. Hunter, Schmidt, and Pearlman (1979) illustrated this point by examining the projected gain for using a test called the Programmer Aptitude Test (PAT) to select programmers for the federal government. The PAT had a validity estimated to be approximately +.76. If no other test had been used prior to the introduction of the PAT, the validity of the "previous" strategy would be .00. If there were 20 applicants for each programmer position (a selection ratio of 1/20 or .05), the use of the PAT would have increased the productivity of programmers by *$97 million per year!* Even if there had been a test in place with a validity = +.50 and the selection ratio was 1/10 instead of 1/20, the estimated productivity gain would still have been $28 million.

    Latham and Whyte (1994; Whyte & Latham, 1997) have done some interesting research on how utility results affect the decision by experienced managers to adopt or not adopt a selection strategy. Surprisingly, they found that a presentation of the positive utility (i.e., the utility to be gained) aspects of a selection strategy actually resulted in a *lower* likelihood that a manager would adopt the selection strategy, which is exactly the opposite of what we would expect. Latham and Whyte concluded that utility analyses may be of little value to managers in deciding whether or not to adopt a selection strategy. But this may be a bit misleading. While it may be true that there is little value in presenting utility calculations to decision makers (e.g., line managers or the VP of HR), that does not mean that the I-O psychologist should abandon the utility calculations. He or she can still decide, based on utility calculations, *which* alternatives to present to managers. The I-O psychologist can then present relevant data (e.g., the cost of implementing the new system) in a more familiar cost/benefit framework. Virtually every line manager and HR representative will eventually ask cost/benefit questions.

BASE RATE

Percentage of the current workforce that is performing successfully.

UTILITY ANALYSIS

Technique that assesses the economic return on investment of human resource interventions such as staffing or training.

Cronshaw (1997) came up with an interesting rejoinder to the Latham and Whyte research findings. He suggested that the utility presentation tended to make the managers reject the recommended selection strategy because they saw it as an attempt to persuade rather than simply inform them; they were reacting negatively to the "hard sell." Cronshaw's explanation is appealing. It is difficult to imagine that a manager would not only ignore, but actually decide *against* using a system that demonstrated a positive bottom-line impact. Few managers would work against their own self-interests and those of their organization in such a way. Cronshaw suggested that if there is a moral here, it is that I-O psychologists should present utility analysis information simply as information, and not use it as a sales and marketing tool.

The concept of economic utility, or utility gain, is a good one to keep in mind when evaluating the effectiveness of a staffing strategy. Often the calculations become so arcane that the point of the exercise is lost. In addition, some of the estimations of productivity gain and cost reduction (such as those for the PAT) can be staggering and result in arousing considerable skepticism on the part of managers about the procedures used to calculate them. Nevertheless, when evaluating a staffing strategy, the I-O psychologist needs to consider the anticipated costs and benefits to the organization.

FAIRNESS

There are many different ways of defining a "fair" staffing strategy. Feelings of unfairness often lead to some negative action on the part of an employee or applicant. These actions include the initiation of lawsuits, filing of formal grievances with company representatives, and counterproductive behavior. As we saw above, there are also stakeholders beyond the applicant (e.g., line managers, co-workers, or union representatives) in whom feelings of unfairness might arise. When acted upon, these feelings of unfairness almost always cost the organization time and money and detract from the overall value of the staffing strategy. In Chapter 11, we will consider fairness from the perspectives of applicants and the law in much greater detail.

CASE STUDY 7.1 A Large Staffing Project

Metropolitan Motor Company (MMC) decided to open a new assembly plant in southwest Tennessee for their new compact passenger car line. The plant would require a workforce of approximately 1,700 production workers, 370 supervisors and managers, 125 engineers and engineering technicians, and 110 administrative and office personnel. The cafeteria and security functions would be outsourced to independent contractors. Below we describe the sequence that was used to staff the hourly production positions in this new facility.

Before announcing the location of the facility, MMC did some investigation of the educational characteristics of the labor force in Tennessee, as well as a review of the secondary school system in a five-county area surrounding the plant site. It decided to give first priority in employment for entry-level and skilled positions to residents in the five-county area, then to Tennessee residents, and finally to anyone, regardless of place of residence.

The vice president of corporate HR took several trips to talk to state and local officials about locating the facility in the area. Department of Labor officials in Tennessee agreed that the state employment offices would accept and screen applications for entry-level positions, using criteria developed by MMC. To ensure an adequate pool of applicants, MMC posted job openings on the Internet and developed an advertising campaign for Tennessee to make applicants aware of the website. The website, which directed interested individuals to visit their nearest state employment office to apply, included a virtual tour of the new plant with 360-degree photos and a chat line for communications between company representatives and interested applicants.

Job analysis of the positions at other MMC assembly plants had determined that specific physical abilities, specific personality characteristics, and general mental ability were required in all production positions. MMC used the following procedures to screen applicants for these qualifications.

Hourly applicants who passed the screening at the state offices for minimum requirements (e.g., education, experience) were given a phone number to call to schedule a visit to a central placement office in the new plant. There they used computer terminals to take a basic mental ability test and a personality test. MMC had hired an outside consulting company to receive the answers and score these tests by means of online data transfer. The results were returned within six hours.

Applicants who scored well enough to continue were asked to call and schedule a physical fitness test to determine their stamina and agility, since the basic production job required the employee to stand continuously, handle boxes of parts, and occasionally assume awkward positions for assembly operations. The physical fitness screening was done at the local YMCA and two health clinics associated with hospitals in the area. Those who passed the fitness test were then asked to schedule an interview with a selection team at the new plant.

The selection team consisted of experienced employees from another MMC assembly plant: a first- and second-level supervisor and two production workers. Prior to the interview, one of the production workers gave groups of applicants a short walking tour of the new plant, followed by a short video that showed the assembly operations as they were performed at another plant similar to the new facility. The applicants were given an opportunity to ask questions of the experienced production worker, and then were each interviewed by the four-member selection team according to a structured set of questions developed by the MMC human resources department.

After the structured interviews, the outside consulting firm that had scored the earlier, online tests evaluated each candidate according to the interview dimensions. Those who were considered eligible for hiring were asked to complete an information form indicating preferences for tasks, days of work, and shift assignment. These preference sheets were input for making initial assignments for the successful applicants. In addition to handling the applicant's preference sheets, the outside consulting firm also made recommendations regarding initial assignments based on the results of the online testing and the interviews.

Applicants who received job offers were told that although some adjustments might be possible, they would be expected to keep their assigned job and work schedule for at least six months. At the end of that time, individuals could apply for shift or job changes. After the initial six-month change request, individuals could bid on new shifts and new positions on a yearly basis. If the employee had no disciplinary actions and had arrived on time for 98 percent of the scheduled workdays, he or she would be eligible for a change in work. Such changes would be determined among eligible employees strictly by seniority. After considering the initial offer of employment and assignment, applicants decided whether to accept or reject the offer. A medical examination was administered to those applicants who accepted an offer of employment and they received an employee handbook that outlined expectations and benefits.

This case study is a realistic description of the steps or phases in a large-scale staffing effort. From initial planning to a completely staffed production force, it might have taken 18 months to complete, and cost in excess of $1.5 million. And that only encompassed the production workers. Other systems would be used to recruit and select professional, administrative, and managerial staff members. Many of the individuals who would fill these nonproduction slots would be recruited internally from other MMC facilities, thus providing opportunities for upward mobility in those facilities as well.

MODULE 7.2 SUMMARY

- Staffing outcomes can be evaluated in terms of various considerations, including validity, utility, and fairness.

- In making a staffing decision, false positive and false negative errors may be committed. Both of these types of errors can be costly for an organization. Alternatively, correct decisions in a staffing context are called true positives and true negatives.

- The concept of economic utility, or utility gain, is a good one to keep in mind when evaluating the effectiveness of a staffing strategy. I-O psychologists need to consider both the anticipated costs and benefits to the organization of the staffing strategy.

- Feelings of unfairness about a staffing strategy often lead to negative actions on the part of an employee or applicant. These actions include the initiation of lawsuits, filing of formal grievances with company representatives, and counterproductive behavior. Feelings of unfairness, when acted upon, almost always cost the organization time and money and detract from the overall value of the staffing strategy.

KEY TERMS

validity
criterion-related validity
selection ratio (SR)
false positive
false negative

true positive
true negative
cut score
criterion-referenced cut score
norm-referenced cut score

Uniform Guidelines on Employee Selection Procedures
base rate
utility analysis

CRITICAL THINKING EXERCISES

7.3 A consulting company approaches an organization and suggests that it can improve productivity substantially by administering a battery of tests. These tests will include three different tests of mental ability. In examining the technical manual for this battery, you discover than one of the three tests typically produces very high scores, the second typically produces very low scores, and the third has just as many high as low test scores. What would be your response to the suggestion that all three tests be used in the battery? Why?

7.4 A school district has developed a certification test for teacher candidates that assesses basic skills (i.e., reading, writing, communication, and content area). To set a cut score on that test, the school district has assembled a group of current teachers to provide judgments of how many items a candidate should answer correctly on each test in order to function effectively in the school district. The current teachers are given the correct answers to each item and told how previous groups of candidates have done on these tests. Would you consider this method of score setting criterion-referenced or norm-referenced? Why?

PRACTICAL ISSUES IN STAFFING

A STAFFING MODEL

Modern jobs are complex. They consist of personal, interpersonal, and technical demands. To succeed in them, individuals must have attributes like conscientiousness, general mental ability, communication skills, and specialized knowledge. Consider Table 7.4. On the left side of the figure is a list of the attributes necessary to meet the job demands on the right side of the figure. High-quality staffing decisions are made based on a number of different pieces of information, not just one. This means that information about candidates must be combined in order to make a good staffing decision. Before we examine ways to combine information, we want to introduce two concepts. These concepts are ways that staffing strategies vary.

Comprehensiveness

A staffing model needs to be comprehensive. A **comprehensive staffing model** should gather enough high-quality information about candidates to predict the likelihood of their success on the varied demands of the job. This does not mean we need to predict *every* aspect of job performance accurately, but it does mean that we should at least be trying to predict the important aspects of performance. Broadly, this might mean that we should be able to predict both technical performance and contextual

COMPREHENSIVE STAFFING MODEL

Model that gathers enough high quality information about candidates to predict the likelihood of their success on the varied demands of the job.

TABLE 7.4	The Challenge of Matching Applicant Attributes and Job Demands
APPLICANT ATTRIBUTES	**JOB DEMANDS**
Physical ability	Checking invoices
General mental ability	Processing customer orders
Problem solving	Reducing shipping costs
Oral communication	Attending staff meetings
Written communication	Developing price structure
Personality	Supervising assistants
Interests	Developing spreadsheets
Interpersonal skills	
Knowledge	

performance. Within each of those domains, we should be trying to predict more specific important behaviors as well. These behaviors are usually identified through some form of job analysis.

Compensatory

Given that we have decided that we need to have multiple pieces of information in order to make good staffing decisions, we now need to decide how to combine the information. Generally speaking, most KSAOs interact to yield successful performance. This means that we can average them together, much as we would average individual course grades to get a GPA. By averaging your grades, you see that one good grade can compensate for a poorer grade. Your A in industrial psychology will offset the B− you got in organic chemistry. The same is true with staffing decisions. A good score in an interview or work sample test might compensate for a slightly lower score on a cognitive ability test. If one attribute (e.g., communication skill) turns out to be much more important than another (e.g., stamina), there are ways to weight the individual scores to give one score greater influence on the final total score. We will review some of those methods below. The point here is that in most instances, humans are able to compensate for a relative weakness in one attribute through a strength in another one, assuming both attributes are required by the job. Most exceptions to this rule relate to physical (e.g., muscular strength) or sensory (e.g., vision) abilities. A legally blind applicant for the position of bus driver would be an example of such an exception. This example reflects a noncompensatory or multiple hurdle model, which will be discussed shortly.

In our discussions to this point, we have alluded to multiple pieces of information about a candidate, each of which may help to predict eventual job performance. But we have not dealt with the issue of how such multiple pieces of information might be combined. In the following section, we will consider this issue of information combination.

An example of compensatory skills: a physically small woman uses social skills to succeed in the job of police officer.

COMBINING INFORMATION

Statistical versus Clinical Decision Making

There are two basic ways to combine information in making a staffing decision: clinical and statistical. In **clinical decision making,** or the intuitive method, the decision maker examines multiple pieces of information, weights them in his or her head, and makes a decision about the relative value of one candidate over another—or simply makes a select/reject decision about an individual candidate. Clinical decisions tend to be unreliable and idiosyncratic (Meehl, 1954, 1957, 1965).

In **statistical decision making** (or, as it is often called, actuarial decision making), information is combined according to a mathematical formula. In Table 7.5, we present the test scores for five candidates for the job of customer service representative for a telephone company. As you can see, candidate B had the highest total score even though her score was not the highest on cognitive ability. In Chapter 4 we discussed online assessment and scoring provided by consulting companies. These systems employ statistical combinations of assessment data for making hiring recommendations.

The Hurdle System of Combining Scores

In the example from Table 7.5, we considered each of the five candidates, regardless of how low a score he or she obtained on any of the assessment dimensions. But sometimes a score can be so low as to suggest there is little hope of compensation. For example, a firefighter must have a minimum amount of aerobic endurance or stamina to fight a fire using a self-contained breathing apparatus (Sothmann et al., 1990). If a candidate for a firefighter position lacks the necessary minimum of stamina, no amount of cognitive ability or motivation can make up for that. As a result, the fire department might want to set a minimum or cut score on the stamina measure and disqualify a candidate from further consideration unless he or she achieves that minimum. If the candidate does exceed that minimum, then all the scores, including the stamina score, can be combined in a **compensatory system.** In this case, the test of stamina would be called a "hurdle" because the candidate could not continue unless the hurdle were cleared. The **hurdle system** is a noncompensatory strategy since an individual knocked out of the assessment process has no opportunity to compensate at a later assessment stage for the low score that knocked him or her out of the process. In essence, the hurdle system establishes a series of cut scores rather than a single one.

If there are several dimensions that warrant such minimum scores, a **multiple hurdle system** might be constructed which would exclude from further consideration; all candidates who did not exceed each of the minimum dimension scores. No compensation from high

CLINICAL DECISION MAKING

Uses judgment to combine information and to make a decision about the relative value of different candidates or applicants.

STATISTICAL DECISION MAKING

Combines information according to a mathematical formula.

COMPENSATORY SYSTEM

Model in which a good score on one test can compensate for a lower score on another test.

HURDLE SYSTEM

Noncompensatory strategy in which an individual has no opportunity to compensate at a later assessment stage for a low score in an earlier stage of the assessment process.

MULTIPLE HURDLE SYSTEM

Constructed from multiple hurdles so that candidates who do not exceed each of the minimum dimension scores are excluded from further consideration.

TABLE 7.5	Using Multiple Predictors to Choose a Candidate*					
CANDIDATE	**ORAL COMMUNI- CATION**	**WRITTEN COMMUNI- CATION**	**COGNITIVE ABILITY**	**EXPERIENCE**	**CONSCIEN- TIOUSNESS**	**TOTAL SCORE**
A	5	7	8	4	5	29
B	9	8	6	5	9	37
C	9	9	4	3	6	31
D	6	6	9	7	5	33
E	5	5	7	6	7	30

*All attribute scores were transformed such that the highest possible score on any single attribute is 10 and the lowest score is 0.

scores on other dimensions would be permitted. It would also be possible to set relatively high hurdles on each dimension and only consider candidates who successfully passed every hurdle. If there were more successful candidates than positions, however, it would still be necessary to somehow order the candidates, possibly by a sum of their actual scores.

Often an employer will set up the hurdles so that they are sequential. For example, the first hurdle might be a test of cognitive ability. If the individual exceeds the minimum score, the next hurdle might be a work sample test. If the individual exceeds the cut score for the work sample test, he or she is scheduled for an interview. Generally, the more expensive and time consuming the step or hurdle, the later it is placed in the sequence. That way the costs are reduced since smaller and smaller numbers of candidates move on to the later hurdles. For individuals who pass all the hurdles, scores can then be combined in a compensatory system to allow for relative strengths and weaknesses to offset each other.

Hurdle systems are often employed with large numbers of candidates and few openings. This is a way to cut down on cost and processing time, as well as to make sure that only the best candidates are being considered. In years past, when the New York City Police Department tested for new police officers, it was not unusual to receive 60,000 applications for 5,000 openings. The written cognitive ability test was used as a first hurdle to bring that number down to fewer than 20,000 for further consideration. In various years, the written examination was administered in Madison Square Garden (an arena that holds 20,000 spectators for a sports event) or in more than 300 different high schools in the five boroughs of New York City. To get a more personal feel for the size of this undertaking, imagine taking a test with 20,000 other individuals in any large football stadium where you have watched a game.

Although multiple hurdle systems can be effective in reducing large applicant pools to a more manageable size, there should be a rationale for how the hurdles are arranged and how the cut scores are chosen. A good rationale will not only help in defending the system if it is legally challenged, but it will also be more likely to lead to perceptions of fairness by those who fail to clear a hurdle.

Combination Scores by Regression (The Compensatory Approach)

MULTIPLE
REGRESSION
ANALYSIS

Results in an equation for combining test scores into a composite based on the correlations among the test scores and the correlations of each test score with the performance score.

In Chapter 2 we presented the concept of multiple correlation as a way of examining the association between a number of test scores and a single performance score. A complementary analysis, known as **multiple regression analysis,** develops an equation for combining test scores into a composite based on the individual correlations of each test score dimension with the performance score and the intercorrelations between the test scores. The regression analysis uses a compensatory model where scoring higher on one predictor can make up for scoring low on another predictor.

Consider the three diagrams presented in Figure 7.5 In part (a), you can see that there is little overlap or intercorrelation between the two predictor variables but both are correlated with the criterion. In part (b), although there is some overlap or intercorrelation between the two predictor variables, each still captures some unique variance in the criterion variable. In part (c), there is substantial overlap and intercorrelation between the predictor variables; you predict about the same amount of criterion variance no matter which predictor you use. These figures graphically illustrate the concept of multiple regression. In the situation depicted in part (a), each variable contributes substantially to predicting a unique aspect of the criterion. As an example, predictor 1 might be a personality test and predictor 2 a test of cognitive ability. If the job considered was a sales representative for a medical company, predictor 1 might predict customer interaction satisfaction and predictor 2 might predict troubleshooting the piece of equipment that is being sold. Thus, it makes intuitive sense that each predictor would add some unique value to the prediction situation.

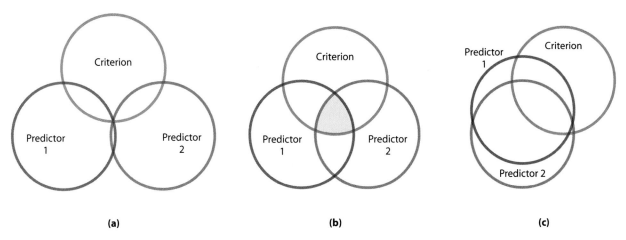

FIGURE 7.5 The Relationship between Predictor Overlap and Criterion Prediction

In contrast, consider part (b). Assume that the two predictors were variations of a cognitive test with predictor 1 a test of general mental ability and predictor 2 a test of technical knowledge. Predictor 1 might correlate with the capacity of the sales representative to learn about new products and predictor 2 might correlate with troubleshooting success. But as you can see, the two predictors themselves are correlated with each other, so we already cover some of the predictive value of predictor 2 when we use data on predictor 1. This means that we get some added or incremental value from the second predictor but not as much as we realized in part (a).

Finally, as in part (c), assume that predictor 1 is a test of general mental ability marketed by consulting company ABC and predictor 2 is a test of general mental ability marketed by company XYZ. Both essentially measure the same attribute and there is little value in the second test, regardless of which test is administered first.

Combining scores using the multiple regression technique is a complex mathematical process that weights the individual predictor scores in terms of their individual correlations with the criterion and their intercorrelation with each other. The multiple regression technique requires both predictor data and criterion data, so it can be used only if some measures of performance are available. This method takes advantage of the characteristics of the sample of people actually used for the calculation of the prediction equation (e.g., current employees). Consequently, while the equation may perfectly fit this sample, it may provide a less than perfect fit for another sample (e.g., the applicants). As a result, when using multiple regression techniques, it is common to try out the resulting equation on a second sample to see if it still fits well. This process is known as **cross-validation.** Cross-validation is usually carried out with an incumbent sample. The results are then used to weight the predictor scores of an applicant sample.

Score Banding

Recently, a new method known as **score banding** has been suggested for identifying successful candidates. Unlike the situation where there is a discrete pass–fail or cut score, score banding creates categories of scores, with the categories arranged from high to low. As a student, you are familiar with score bands as they relate to letter grades. For example, the "A band" might range from 100 to 90, the "B band" from 89 to 80, and so on. Psychometricians and statisticians universally accept that every observed score (whether a test score or a performance score) has a certain amount of error in it; the amount of error is associated with the reliability of the test. The less reliable the test, the greater the error.

CROSS-VALIDATION

Process used with multiple regression techniques in which a regression equation developed on a first sample is tested on a second sample to determine if it still fits well; usually carried out with an incumbent sample, and the cross-validated results are used to weight the predictor scores of an applicant sample.

SCORE BANDING

Approach in which individuals with similar test scores are grouped together in a category or score band, and selection within the band is then made based on other considerations.

In practical terms, this means that when you take a test, the score you obtain might have been different had you taken the test yesterday or tomorrow or next week. If the test is very unreliable, then your score could be wildly different on a new administration. If the test is very reliable, there may be only a slight change in your test score.

Often, candidates obtain scores that are within one point of each other; sometimes they even differ by only $\frac{1}{10}$ of a point. Is a candidate with an observed test score of 92.1 *really* better than another candidate with a score of 92.0 or 91.6? One way to answer the question is to look at a statistic called the **standard error of measurement (SEM)**, a measure of the amount of error in a test score distribution. If the difference between two candidates is less than the standard error of measurement, then one can conclude that the candidates are not really different. In our example above, if the standard error of measurement turned out to be two full test score points, then to be really different, two candidates would need to be separated by at least two score points—and we would conclude that 92.1, 92.0, and 91.6 were not substantially different from one another.

Using the principle of the standard error of measurement, a method has been proposed for establishing bands of scores to replace individual scores (Cascio, Outtz, Zedeck, & Goldstein, 1991; Guion, 1998). Using this approach, all candidate scores within a band are considered "equal" with respect to the attribute being measured if they fall with some specified number of SEMs of each other (usually two SEMs). It is assumed that any within-band differences are really just differences due to the unreliability of the measure. Using the banding approach, all candidates in the highest band would be considered before any candidates in the next lower band. Since candidates within a given band are equal, a supplementary strategy must be used to decide which candidates within that band to select, that is, if the number of people within a band exceeds the number of openings or selections to be made. For example, where applicants for an expatriate manager position were placed in bands based on a combined personality and cognitive ability test battery, candidates within the highest band might be further ordered by the number of relevant foreign languages they speak, or the number of overseas assignments they have had.

Once a higher band has been depleted, then the decision maker moves to the next lower band until it is depleted, and so on, until all positions have been filled or the candidate list exhausted. Using this system, candidates in lower bands are not considered until the next higher band has been completely exhausted. This is known as a **fixed band** system. An alternative, known as a **sliding band system,** permits the band to be moved down a score point (or to slide) as the highest score in a band is exhausted (Zedeck, Cascio, Goldstein, & Outtz, 1996). Suppose the top score band went from 95 (the highest obtained score) to 90. Once everyone with a score of 95 was offered a position, and either accepted or declined, then the score band could be shifted down one point and would now be 94 to 89.

Banding is controversial (Campion et al., 2001; Schmidt, 1991). Critics claim that banding is used to further social goals, particularly to ensure that more minority candidates are "competitive" in selection situations. Advocates of banding argue that while one effect of banding might be to place minority applicants in a better competitive position, these candidates may have been lower in the original score distribution only because of measurement error. In other words, if one simply rank-ordered candidates based on observed test scores, allowing individuals to be separated by only fractions of a point, then these lower-ranking candidates would be subject to many more false negative errors by decision makers.

Indeed, if candidates are selected randomly from within a band, banding does not make any major differences in who is selected and can be considered one of a number of staffing strategies that might make sense in some circumstances (Guion, 1998). As Guion concluded, it is not as effective as advocates claim, nor as damaging as critics claim. It does appear, however, that applicants for entry-level and promotional positions vary in their beliefs about the reason for and value of score banding. In a study of banding strategies

STANDARD ERROR OF MEASUREMENT (SEM)

Statistic that provides a measure of the amount of error in a test score distribution; function of the reliability of the test and the variability in test scores.

FIXED BAND SYSTEM

Candidates in lower bands are not considered until higher bands have been completely exhausted.

SLIDING BAND SYSTEM

Permits the band to be moved down a score point (or to slide) when the highest score in a band is exhausted.

in police department hiring and promotional testing practices, Truxillo and Bauer (1999) found that African American candidates considered banding fairer than did their white counterparts. Whites believed that banding was being used to achieve affirmative action goals. In contrast, blacks believed that banding was used to offset test unreliability. These results make it clear that the credibility of staffing decisions may depend on the system used to make those decisions, at least with employee subgroups. But in the case of race, this may be a lose–lose proposition. If score banding is used, whites may distrust the resulting decisions; if straight rank-ordering is used, minority candidates may be the ones to distrust the results. It is probably fair to say that in organizations where tension exists between demographic subgroups, novel staffing strategies may exacerbate that tension, whereas in organizations where there is little tension, a novel staffing strategy will be liked or disliked equally by the subgroups.

Subgroup Norming

As we have seen in Chapters 3 and 4, African Americans typically score lower than whites on cognitive ability tests and, as a result, often get fewer job offers than their white counterparts. This difference may or may not eventually be found to represent unfair discrimination. If the test is job related, then the result may be unfortunate, but it is not necessarily illegal. Many organizations, however, have adopted affirmative action plans whereby they agree to work toward a goal of greater representation of minority workers in the organization. These goals can be difficult to meet if the employer uses a cognitive ability test and ranks candidates based on their scores. Many African Americans are likely to be out of selection range because of their relatively lower test scores on cognitive ability tests.

Prior to 1991, one way of dealing with this disparity was to develop separate lists for white and black candidates, then rank the candidates *within* their respective demographic group. For the purposes of selection, the employer could then simply start at the top of both lists and choose the best candidates in each group until the available openings were filled. Using this top-down selection process, the lowest score of a selected black candidate would likely be lower than the lowest score among the selected white applicants. In a hurdle system, the cut score would actually be set lower for the African American candidates than their white counterparts. In either case, the "passing score" would actually be different for white and black candidates. The proportion of minority candidates hired would then satisfy the employer's demographic hiring goals (e.g., 15 percent minority selection rate). Critics of affirmative action and race-conscious hiring labeled this procedure a "quota" system and argued that it was inappropriate since employers were using it not to hire "the best" applicants but to meet affirmative action goals or to avoid a lawsuit. Even the U.S. Employment Service (USES), a branch of the U.S. Department of Labor, adopted the practice of separate norms for majority and minority job applicants who took the General Aptitude Test Battery (GATB), a cognitive ability test commonly administered by that agency. Unfortunately, the USES was not completely open about this practice, knowing that it might be controversial. When this practice came to light, it sparked a heated public policy debate about this use of separate norms (Hartigan & Wigdor, 1989).

In 1990, Congress drafted an amendment to Title VII (the employment section) of the Civil Rights Act of 1964. After a bitter battle between conservatives and liberals, it was passed and then vetoed by the first President Bush. A new version was drafted in 1991 and, after much negotiation, was passed and Bush did not veto it. One concession that the liberals made to the conservatives in order to get the bill passed was that quotas would be made illegal. The USES GATB race norming controversy was still fresh in everyone's mind. It followed, then, that **subgroup norming** (i.e., developing separate appointment lists for white and black candidates or for male and female candidates) would also be illegal. Thus, norming by subgroup (i.e., race, color, religion, sex, or national origin) is

SUBGROUP NORMING

Approach that develops separate lists for individuals within different demographic groups, then ranks the candidates within their respective demographic group.

impermissible as a staffing strategy. In 2002 the City of Chicago was ordered to pay $5.2 million to 19 Chicago firefighters after a jury concluded that the city had selected candidates for a promotional position using a scoring scheme that assisted African American candidates (*National Law Journal,* 2002). Unless the Civil Rights Act of 1991 is amended once again to permit race norming, I-O psychologists will have little opportunity to study this issue.

There is one exception to the prohibition against race norming. If an employer was already under a court order that required setting separate pass scores for whites and blacks when the Civil Rights Act of 1991 was passed, that employer would still be permitted to race norm test scores to meet the requirements of the court order for minority hiring.

One form of special-group norming for which there is no explicit prohibition is age norming (i.e., developing separate appointment lists or cut scores for age groupings). Age norming can be particularly important when using physical ability tests since young people tend to do better on these tests than older applicants. The issue of the relative value of using separate cut scores or appointment lists for different demographic groups is far from settled and is likely to remain an unanswered question for some time in the future (Brown, 1994; Gottfredson, 1994; Sackett & Wilk, 1994).

SELECTION VERSUS PLACEMENT

In our discussion of staffing strategies, we have assumed that there was only one position (or job title) for which staffing decisions might be made. But if you recall from Case Study 7.1 on the Metropolitan Motor Company, many different production jobs were being filled. Instead of a situation in which 20 people were applying for one job, or for three openings with the same job title, MMC had openings in several job titles simultaneously. This happens frequently and when it does the staffing decision becomes considerably more complex. It becomes a process of matching or optimizing the fit between an applicant and a job opening. The challenge is to *place* an individual rather than simply *select* an individual. We can think of selection as choosing one individual from among many applicants to fill a given opening. In contrast, placement is a process of matching multiple applicants and multiple job openings.

The tricky question is how to achieve the match. Cascio (1998a) offered three different strategies:

1. Vocational guidance: Place candidates according to their best talents.
2. Pure selection: Fill each job with the most qualified person.
3. Cut and fit: Place workers so that all jobs are filled with adequate talent.

Consider the three candidates for three jobs as illustrated in Table 7.6. Assume that the "tests" in question for jobs 1, 2, and 3 are work sample tests in which the candidate is actually asked to perform an important job task. As you can see, using the vocational guidance strategy, candidate A would be placed in Job 3, candidate B in job 1, and candidate C in job 2. In contrast, using the pure selection strategy, candidate A would be selected for all three jobs—a practical impossibility. The cut and fit strategy places candidate A in Job 1, candidate B in Job 2, and candidate C in Job 3.

Elaborate placement strategies have been the exception in the past. Staffing decisions have tended to be more selection than placement. That situation may well change in the future. In their models for strategic staffing Snow and Snell (1993) argued that flexibility would be an important characteristic of the successful organization of the future. To the extent that is the case, placement strategies will likely be more effective than pure selection strategies. In addition, the increasing use of work teams also suggests that the rigid selection model might be less effective than a placement model that can also take into account the KSAOs of existing team members in deciding where to place a new hire or promotion.

TABLE 7.6	The Challenge of Placing Multiple Candidates

PREDICTED CRITERION SCORES (IN Z-SCORE UNITS) FOR THREE APPLICANTS TO EACH OF THREE JOB AND ASSIGNMENTS MADE UNDER THREE ALTERNATIVE CLASSIFICATION STRATEGIES

	JOB 1	JOB 2	JOB 3	NUMBER OF JOBS ADEQUATELY FILLED	NUMBER OF WORKERS PLACED ACCORDING TO THEIR HIGHEST TALENT
Worker A	1.0	0.8	1.5		
Worker B	0.7	0.5	−0.2		
Worker C	−0.4	−0.3	−1.6		
Minimum qualification score (in Zscore units)	0.9	0.0	−2.0		
Classification strategies: Place each according to his best talent (vocational guidance)	B	C	A	1	1
Fill each job with the most qualified person (pure selection)	A	A	A	1	1
Place workers so that all jobs are filled by those with adequate talent (cut and fit)	A	B	C	3	0

SOURCE: Cascio (1982).

DESELECTION

There are two typical situations in which an individual is selected to leave rather than join an organization. The first is **termination for cause,** and the second is a layoff or downsizing situation. In a termination for cause, the individual has usually been warned one or more times about a problem, and either cannot or will not correct it. The individual is usually well aware that his or her behavior has fallen below some standard, and that the consequences for failing to correct the deficiency may be termination. The worker may or may not believe the decision to terminate is fair, but it does not come unexpectedly.

Layoffs are different. They often come without warning, or with a generic warning that the workforce is going to be reduced. But a given individual is often unaware that he or she may be the one losing a job. As a result, there is a great deal of emotion surrounding the layoff. Many employees become angry and feel that an implicit agreement has been violated. They agreed to do good work and the employer agreed to maintain their employment. But in downsizing situations, it is often a matter of distinguishing between the outstanding employee and the adequate employee, not between the adequate and the inadequate employee. Thus, adequate employees often believe that they have been unfairly chosen for layoff because their work was "fine."

TERMINATION FOR CAUSE

An individual is fired from an organization for a particular reason; the individual has usually been warned one or more times about a problem, and either cannot or will not correct it.

LAYOFF

Job loss due to employer downsizing or reductions in force; often comes without warning or with a generic warning that the workforce will be reduced.

In layoff situations, the staffing strategy must be very clear (since the employer may very well end up defending it in a lawsuit). It is much better to have an actuarial or statistical decision rule than a clinical or intuitive one. The statistical rule makes it more difficult to argue that the decision was biased or inaccurate. It is also better to make the decision by combining multiple criteria rather than relying on a single dimension. So instead of deciding who will be laid off based on the average of the last two years of performance ratings, the employer may use four criteria, equally weighted: years with the company, number of skills the individual possesses, the past two years of performance ratings, and the foreseeable pieces of work for the particular person over the following 18 months. Seniority is a surrogate for dependability and corporate memory; skills possessed signals flexibility for future assignments; performance ratings represent a foundation of success; and foreseeable pieces of work represent value added for keeping the person. Just as applicants seeking to be hired for a position sometimes question the fairness of both the procedure and the outcome, employees chosen for deselection may have feelings of perceived unfairness. But the feelings are likely to be more intense and lead to more dramatic actions. For that reason, the deselection staffing strategy needs to be coherent, consistent, and balanced. The best way to achieve consistency is to use a statistical approach for combining information rather than a clinical approach.

NUMBER OF DECISIONS TO BE MADE
Large Staffing Projects

Although we have been discussing staffing in relatively large and complex organizations in this chapter, the actual number of decisions that needed to be made might have been small (e.g., to choose 3 new hires from a group of 30 applicants). There are, however, occasions when the applicant pool is massive and the number of selection hires equally massive. Earlier we gave an example of the New York City Police Department. In 1984 the NYPD had 65,000 applicants for appointment to the police academy. The eventual eligibility list from which recruits would be chosen was to last for three years, at which time a new open application period would begin. During that three-year period, as many as four recruit classes would graduate each year. Each recruit class had 500 officers in it. Thus, the number of academy appointments would be 6,000 over the life of the list. Research by the NYPD had shown that it was necessary to look at four candidates to get one who would pass all of the screens—psychological, background, and medical. Thus, to appoint 6,000 recruits, they would need to have at least 24,000 on the eligibility list. Making matters worse, the NYPD knew that as time passed, some individuals would lose interest and take other jobs; others would move out of state; and some would become ineligible because of felony convictions, emerging medical conditions, or other circumstances. Thus, the NYPD actually needed an initial list of about 30,000 candidates.

In staffing projects this large, concessions must be made. Clearly, labor intensive assessment procedures such as interviews, assessment centers, or work samples are not feasible. In the NYPD staffing scheme, physical ability testing was also ruled out since there would be a rigorous fitness training program in the 16-week academy course. Although the only test used at the time was a cognitive ability test, the selection ratio of 50 percent (i.e., the NYPD would place one of every two applicants on the eligibility list) eliminated what would have been lower hiring rates for minority applicants had the selection ratio been smaller. In all likelihood, this would have led to a lawsuit. If the same project were undertaken today, there would be good reason to add personality tests and possibly a biodata form to the assessment battery. These three devices could be used in a hurdle or complete compensatory decision scheme.

The sheer size of the decision process requires an actuarial rather than a clinical decision strategy. But some compromise is necessary, since it would be economically and logically

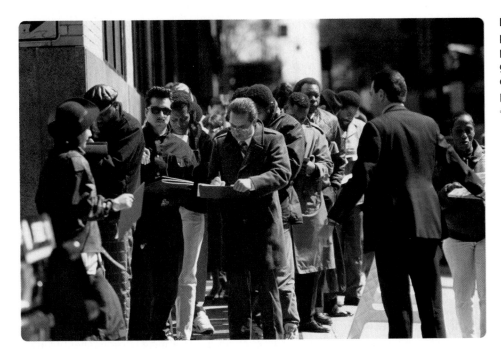

Large staffing projects entail careful planning to make good selection decisions from a large pool of applicants.

difficult to get measures in any medium other than the paper and pencil one. This means that the posthire training program would need to emphasize the KSAOs that were important parts of the job but which were not initially assessed. Since the missing attribute information also represents potential inaccuracy in predictions, and the obtained paper and pencil scores might not fairly represent the complete set of skills brought to the job by the candidate, it might be wise to use a banding approach to appointment as well. If banding is used, make sure that race or gender is not used as a method for selecting from within a band. Although there may be some special circumstances in which race or gender might be considered a relevant factor in hiring, the use of these variables for selecting from within a band might be interpreted as subgroup norming (Sackett & Wilk, 1994).

In large-scale projects, utility can be a big issue. The cost of testing large numbers of candidates can be expensive. But if the validity of the proposed procedure is higher than the validity of the current procedure, these increased costs will be offset by the productivity gains realized from this increased validity. Fairness is also a critical issue. If a device is used to make decisions that will cut down on the size of the applicant pool, but this device has adverse impact against protected subgroups, then the likelihood of a lawsuit increases which also increases the eventual cost of the strategy and reduces utility. Even if the device is eventually shown to have high validity, the economic benefit of using the test will have been reduced by the cost of defending it.

In summary, large-scale projects would seem to suggest standard, well-established, and feasible selection strategies. A good core strategy in this example would be cognitive ability and personality testing. In addition, the size of the applicant pool and the availability of SMEs and incumbents to actually complete assessment devices suggests a place for scored biodata questionnaires.

Small Staffing Projects

Suppose that in contrast to the large-scale staffing challenges we've been discussing, we wanted to help our local coffee house to choose a new shift manager. Instead of 60,000 applicants, there were 5. Would the decision process be different? Yes and no. Yes, the decision maker would have the luxury of using a wider range of assessment tools. For example, the candidates might be asked to take part in a structured interview which would provide information about skills (e.g., communication), abilities (e.g., personnel problem solving), knowledge (e.g., of retail sales) and personality (e.g., conscientiousness and integrity). In addition, each candidate might be asked to complete a personality inventory and a test of math and reading skills.

The actual assessment devices and procedures, then, might be different when the project is a small one. But the decision-making process might not change. Even with a small number of candidates and decisions, it would still be wise to use an actuarial rather than clinical decision scheme. Adverse impact would be much less of an issue, though perceptions of psychological fairness would be just as important. Sackett and Arvey (1993) considered many of the issues related to selection in small settings and made the following recommendations:

- Develop a job relatedness justification based on judgment and rationality rather than on numbers and data analysis.
- Consider the utility gain of the proposed staffing strategy; because of the small number of applicants and selections, there may be only slight payoff in using expensive assessment programs.
- Make sure that every candidate is exposed to the same assessment procedures; because the number of candidates is small, it might be tempting to "wing it," but this would expose the organization to charges of adverse treatment despite the difficulty of demonstrating adverse impact.

Sackett and Arvey (1993) observed that many managers feel that if they "can't do it by the book, don't do it at all." But the alternative to doing it by the (staffing) book is not random, capricious, or intuitive selection—the alternative is simply choosing a selection and decision-making strategy that is rational, job-related, and feasible, given the constraints of the situation. Sackett and Arvey concluded, "We believe that I-O psychology can contribute to better selection in any setting, regardless of the size" (p. 445). We agree.

MODULE 7.3 SUMMARY

- High-quality staffing decisions are based on combining a number of different pieces of information about candidates. Staffing strategies vary in their comprehensiveness and in whether they are compensatory or noncompensatory.
- There are two basic ways to combine information in making a staffing decision: clinical and statistical. Clinical decisions tend to be more variable and reflect the strategies of the decision maker, whereas statistical decisions tend to be more reliable and consistent across decision makers.
- Score banding is a relatively new method that has been used to identify successful candidates. Fixed band and sliding band systems have been developed. However, banding is controversial and in organizations where tension exists between demographic subgroups, novel staffing strategies such as banding may exacerbate that tension.
- Prior to 1991, one way of dealing with racial subgroup differences on selection tests was to develop separate lists for these subgroups and then to rank the candidates within their respective demographic group. However, the 1991 Civil Rights Act made race norming illegal. Notably, one form of special-group norming for which there is no explicit prohibition is age norming.
- Two typical situations in which an individual is selected to leave rather than join an organization are termination for cause and layoffs. In layoff situations, the staffing strategy must be very clear since the employer may end up defending it in a lawsuit.
- Large-scale staffing projects will often require standard and well-established selection strategies. In small staffing projects, managers are encouraged to choose a selection and decision-making strategy that is rational, job-related, and feasible, given the constraints of the situation.

KEY TERMS

comprehensive staffing model

clinical decision making

statistical decision making

compensatory system

hurdle system

multiple hurdle system

multiple regression analysis

cross-validation

score banding

standard error of measurement (SEM)

fixed band system

sliding band system

subgroup norming

termination for cause

layoff

CRITICAL THINKING EXERCISES

7.5 Admissions to medical school are typically made on a hybrid model involving clinical and statistical components. MCAT scores and grades are examined to determine which candidates will be interviewed, then candidates who make that cut visit the medical school for interviews with staff and faculty. An admissions committee then combines the information clinically and decides whom to admit. If you were asked to make the process "more statistical," what recommendations would you make? Do you think the current model is an effective one? Why or why not?

7.6 Beginning in November 2001, the newly created federal Transportation Security Administration (TSA) was faced with the task of replacing private contractor airport security screeners with government employees. Well over 10,000 replacements had to be made and well over 100,000 applicants sought the new government positions. Consulting companies bid on this federal contract. Suppose company A suggested that the project could be accomplished more quickly if a job analysis were not conducted. Suppose company B suggested that "selection panels" be formed to interview and screen applicants. Suppose company C proposed to administer mental ability tests using local colleges to give tests at computer workstations. Which of these proposals would appear most promising and which least promising? Why?

LEGAL ISSUES IN STAFFING DECISIONS

CHARGES OF EMPLOYMENT DISCRIMINATION

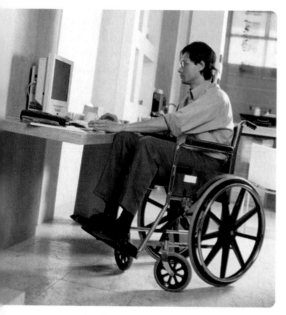

Individuals with disabilities are a protected class for equal opportunity in employment.

EXPERT WITNESS

Witness in a lawsuit who is permitted to voice opinions about organizational practices.

Although discussions of employment litigation often revolve around a practice (e.g., performance appraisal) or an assessment device (e.g., a test or an interview), employment discrimination charges result not from practices or devices, but from decisions. And although it is common to think of applicants who were denied a job bringing lawsuits, it is seven times more likely that a company will be sued by an employee or a former employee than by an applicant (Sharf & Jones, 2000).

There are many bases for bringing charges against an employer, including not only employment discrimination but also the Equal Pay Act, the Fourteenth Amendment of the Constitution promising "due process," or the Family and Medical Leave Act of 1993. Cases can be filed in state as well as federal courts. A fuller explanation of all relevant federal laws and a description of important or defining cases can be found in Gutman (2000). For our discussion, however, we will concentrate on employment discrimination cases filed in federal courts, usually by groups of individuals, claiming violations of Title VII of the Civil Rights Act of 1964, the Americans with Disabilities Act, or the Age Discrimination in Employment Act. These are the types of cases in which I-O psychologists are most commonly involved as **expert witnesses.**

Regardless of who sues a company, the consequences can be substantial. Consider the settlements of employment discrimination suits brought by the Equal Employment Opportunity Commission (EEOC) in the past 10 or 15 years (Sharf & Jones, 2000). The *lowest* settlement in a discrimination case was in an age discrimination suit brought against Maytag—that settlement was $16 million and covered hundreds of individual plaintiffs. These figures only cover suits in which the EEOC was involved. Most suits are filed by single individuals without any involvement of the EEOC. The largest was a race discrimination case brought against Texaco, a case that settled for almost $180 million, covering several thousand individual plaintiffs. If we look at jury verdicts, we see the same expensive picture. The average winning plaintiff in a gender discrimination case was awarded $264,000; in race cases, plaintiffs were awarded $242,000 each, on average. In age cases the average award jumps to $300,000 (Sharf & Jones, 2000). Since lawyers for plaintiffs typically receive anywhere from 25 percent to 40 percent of the award, it is easy to see why employment discrimination cases are brought against employers. For a large corporation, the costs of defending the case may run into the millions of dollars. If the defendant company loses, it may be required to pay awards like those mentioned above, adding up to many more millions of dollars when there are numerous plaintiffs. In addition, the company may lose customers and stock value as a result of the bad publicity surrounding the charges of discrimination.

Of the federal employment discrimination cases filed, approximately 10 percent are gender cases, 9 percent race cases, 18 percent age cases, and 6 percent disability cases (Sharf & Jones, 2000). The large number of age cases results, in part, from the relentless downsizing trend that began in the early 1980s. When downsizing occurs, it often hits middle-level managers the hardest; typically, they are over the age of 40, the age at which protection begins under the Age Discrimination in Employment Act. The lion's share of employment lawsuits, however, remains the suit brought by a single individual claiming that a termination was unfair.

THEORIES OF DISCRIMINATION

Intentional Discrimination or Adverse Treatment

The law and the courts recognize two different theories of discrimination. The first theory charges an employer with intentional discrimination and is also referred to as **adverse (or disparate) treatment.** Under this theory, the plaintiff attempts to show that the employer actually treated the group to which the plaintiff belongs (e.g., women, African Americans) differently than majority applicants or employees. For example, if a female applicant is asked if she has any domestic responsibilities that might interfere with her work, but a male applicant is not asked that question, that would be considered an adverse treatment of the female applicant. Since the employer intentionally asked that question only of females, this falls under the intentional discrimination theory. Similarly, older employees or African American employees might charge that the employer intentionally gave developmental assignments to younger or white employees but not to them. This would also justify a charge of intentional discrimination. Intentional discrimination charges are attractive to plaintiff lawyers because under an intentional theory, they can request a jury trial, and juries tend to be more favorable toward plaintiffs than judges.

Unintentional Discrimination or Adverse Impact

The second theory that can be used to file discrimination charges acknowledges that the employer may not have *intended* to discriminate against a plaintiff, but a practice implemented by the employer had the *effect* of disadvantaging (i.e., had an adverse or disparate impact on) the group to which the plaintiff belongs (e.g., African Americans, women, individuals 40 years of age or older). With the exception of age discrimination charges, an **adverse impact** case is made by showing statistical disparities between a majority and a minority group in terms of outcomes. Thus, a woman plaintiff might charge that men in a company get promoted at a greater rate than women, or a Hispanic employee might allege that whites are paid, on average, $8,300 more a year than Hispanics. Because statistics are so heavily involved in demonstrating a violation of the law in adverse impact cases, these are sometimes called "statistical discrimination" cases.

Adverse Impact Determination   In an adverse impact case, the burden is on the plaintiff to show that (1) he or she belongs to a protected group, and (2) members of the protected group were statistically disadvantaged compared to majority employees or applicants. There are several ways of demonstrating this disadvantage. The *Uniform Guidelines* suggest using an **"80 percent" or "4/5ths" rule.** If it can be shown that a protected group received only 80 percent of the desirable outcomes (e.g., promotions) received by a majority group, the plaintiffs can claim that they have met their burden of demonstrating adverse impact.

ADVERSE (OR DISPARATE) TREATMENT

Type of discrimination in which the plaintiff attempts to show that the employer actually treated the plaintiff differently than majority applicants or employees; intentional discrimination.

ADVERSE IMPACT

Type of discrimination that acknowledges the employer may not have intended to discriminate against a plaintiff, but an employer practice did have an adverse impact on the group to which the plaintiff belongs.

"80 PERCENT" OR "4/5THS" RULE

Guideline for assessing whether there is evidence of adverse impact; if it can be shown that a protected group received less than 80 percent of the desirable outcomes (e.g., job offers, promotions) received by a majority group, the plaintiffs can claim to have met the burden of demonstrating adverse impact.

ADVERSE IMPACT RATIO

Obtained by dividing the selection ratio of the protected group by the selection ratio of the majority group; if this ratio is lower than 80 percent, there is evidence of adverse impact.

For example, suppose 50 whites and 25 blacks applied for a promotion in an organization. Further, suppose that eight whites and one black were promoted. That would mean that 16 percent of the whites (8/50) and only 4 percent of the blacks (1/25) were promoted. One could then calculate an **adverse impact ratio** by dividing the black promotion rate (4 percent) by the white promotion rate (16 percent), resulting in a ratio of 25 percent. This would mean that the black promotion rate was only 25 percent of the white promotion rate. This value is far lower than the 80 percent threshold dictated by the Uniform Guidelines.

The 80 percent rule is crude and can be affected substantially by sample sizes. With small sample sizes, the difference of one or two people might swing the conclusion from one of adverse impact to one of no adverse impact, or vice versa. As a result, most cases include a determination of whether the challenged practice had a *statistically significant* impact on the plaintiff group. If the difference between the majority and minority groups is likely to occur only 5 times out of 100 as a result of chance alone (remember our discussion of statistical significance in Chapter 2), then one could claim that adverse impact had been demonstrated. If adverse impact is demonstrated, then the burden of the case shifts to the employer to demonstrate that the challenged practice was job related and therefore valid.

There are many steps to an employment discrimination suit. Although I-O psychologists who have served as expert witnesses in such suits are aware of the various phases of this type of litigation, many other psychologists would not be unless they were a party to the suit. Nevertheless, many readers may have a relative or friend involved in an employment discrimination suit and may be asked about the various phases when it is known that this type of material is covered in class. For these reasons, we have presented a detailed view of the phases of employment discrimination litigation in the Online Learning Center that accompanies this book. Case Study 7.2 considers an employment discrimination suit from the perspective of the I-O psychologist. Refer to the Online Learning Center for additional detail about the meaning of phases referred to in the case study.

7.2 An Employment Discrimination Suit

The Mortgage Company of America (MCA) had started as a small local mortgage broker in California. Over a period of 10 years, it had grown from 5 brokers and 2 administrative assistants in a small office in downtown Sacramento to a firm with 37 offices in 14 states, 260 brokers, 58 managers and executives, and an administrative staff of 112. MCA had expanded by acquiring small mortgage companies in urban environments and by opening branch offices.

Early in the expansion of MCA, an I-O psychologist had been retained to develop a hiring system.

She was on the faculty of a college near the corporate headquarters and a speaker at an area conference on human resources for small companies that MCA's CEO had attended. MCA had not had the time or expertise to develop an in-house support system, so many staff functions such as HR and accounting had been outsourced. Although an accounting department was eventually created, HR remained an outsourced function. Since the major staffing need was going to be brokers, the I-O psychologist developed a structured interview and work sample test for screening. She also recommended a personality test. She had spent several days in one of the firm's larger offices and had concluded that two of the most important functions of the broker were the ability to actually find lenders (usually banks) to match the home buyer's situation, and to negotiate with those lenders to close the deal. The biggest problem in the "negotiation" was dealing with the underwriter for the lender. Underwriters tend to be overly cautious and demanding in terms of background information about the prospective borrower and are continually asking for additional bits of information, often as late as 72 hours before a loan is to be closed (i.e., agreed upon).

As a result of the I-O psychologist's observations, the work sample test involved the use of the Web to track down potential lending institutions for a hypothetical "client." The structured interview included questions about methods of negotiation, conflict resolution, and past experiences with demanding colleagues. The personality test was based on the Big Five model. She recommended that particular attention be paid to the scales of conscientiousness and agreeableness.

Two years previously, a complaint had been filed with the EEOC charging MCA with race discrimination in hiring with respect to African American applicants for broker positions. The initial complaint came from a single African American employee who had been denied a broker's position. When the charge was filed with the EEOC, the media covered it, and it received both local and national news attention. As a result, a rash of similar complaints surfaced in other cities in which MCA had done hiring. Among other allegations, the plaintiff charged that the work sample was biased against African Americans who were less familiar with the use of the Internet for getting information quickly. He further argued that Web-based skills could be easily picked up in a one- or two-day orientation/training program and were inappropriate for entry-level screening. He also alleged that all the interviewers who administered the structured interview were white males and that their interview scores were influenced by negative stereotypes which they had concerning African Americans. Finally, the plaintiff contended that the personality measures were scored using predominantly white norms; as a result, black candidates were adversely treated.

The employee handbook and company policy clearly stated that MCA was an equal opportunity employer and would not tolerate any form of discrimination. EEOC sent several letters to company lawyers asking for information relevant to the charge: data about the number of applicants in the past three years, the race of those applicants, the decision about each applicant, and a description of the procedure used to make hiring decisions. Company screening and hiring data were culled from the files and the I-O psychologist provided a narrative description of the screening devices and process.

After providing the information to EEOC, the local EEOC office issued a right-to-sue letter to the employee. The EEOC had applied the 80 percent rule and concluded that there was evidence of adverse impact against African American applicants. The employee took the letter to a local lawyer who proceeded with the case. In the meantime, the EEOC regional office also entered the suit on behalf of not only the single African American employee, but also other African American employees who worked in other MCA offices and had filed similar individual charges. After further information requests and analyses, the EEOC concluded that evidence of adverse impact against African Americans in hiring occurred in 16 of the 37 offices of MCA.

The EEOC had initiated mediation discussions between the plaintiffs and the company, but not much progress had been made. Then MCA was informed by a large employment law firm that they would ask the court to certify a class of African American applicants and employees who would charge the company with systematically discriminating against African Americans in virtually all aspects of employment—recruiting, hiring, pay, training, performance evaluation, promotions, and discipline. The class was expected to include not only the 43 black employees, but also 26 black former employees and 322 black applicants for positions with the company over the past three years. Company lawyers estimated that if the company lost at trial, the award might be in excess of $10 million. Since the plaintiffs were now represented by an experienced and effective private law firm, the EEOC dropped out of the suit for budgetary reasons. The new law firm filed suit in federal district court and asked for the certification of a class.

This was the first time that Mortgage company of America had faced such a threat. As a result, the in-house company lawyer suggested that they retain an outside law firm to handle the case. The outside law firm recommended that the I-O psychologist who had developed the screening system be retained as an expert in the case. She was contacted and agreed to serve in that role.

Over the course of **discovery,** the company produced papers that filled approximately 17 cardboard boxes. These included personnel records, applicant flow data, company policy, and various administrative memos. In addition, the CEO, vice presidents of human resources and operations, two regional managers, and six office managers were deposed by lawyers for the plaintiffs. Lawyers for the company deposed 16 plaintiffs. In a hearing following this phase of discovery, the judge considered **class certification** and ultimately granted the designation of two classes: one class that included applicants and a second class that included past and present employees. Class certification is a process that allows the different plaintiffs to present a common complaint. The judge also set a date for trial and a schedule for additional discovery, including reports from and sworn testimony (called **depositions**) of expert witnesses. The plaintiffs also retained a statistician and an I-O psychologist, as well as an economist who would testify about monetary issues such as lost wages.

Although the I-O psychologist had been involved in the development of the screening system, she had not been consulted on issues related to compensation, training, performance evaluation, discipline, or promotion. She discovered that the policies regarding these practices had not yet been fully established and that each office had developed its own methods for making these decisions. In contrast, the screening system she had developed was being used consistently in each office, and hiring decisions were ultimately made by the vice president of HR using an equation she had developed when creating the screening system.

The plaintiff's expert reports were filed, and 30 days later the defendant's expert replied with a rebuttal report. The I-O psychologist for the plaintiffs had made a number of criticisms of the hiring policies of the defendant company. His major points were that there had been no formal job analysis, that the structured interview was subjective and influenced by stereotypes, that the interviewers were not adequately trained, that the work sample was inappropriately influenced by speed factors, and that no criterion-related validity study had been performed to justify the use of the personality test.

In the rebuttal report submitted in response to these criticisms, the company I-O psychologist answered that even though she had not administered and scored questionnaires, a job analysis had been done. She further contended that since she had developed the interview questions along with the scoring scheme for answers to those questions, the interview was not subjective. She pointed out that speed *was* a factor in the job and that brokers needed to get preliminary information to a potential client about the availability of loans within hours. Finally, she identified several meta-analyses that concluded that conscientiousness and agreeableness were valuable predictors in sales positions, and the broker job was a type of sales position. In the midst of the expert discovery process, the original African-American employee was fired for refusing to accept an assignment, and the lawsuit was amended to include charges of retaliation for having filed the original suit.

As the trial date approached, the judge required the company to have **settlement discussions** with the plaintiffs. Settlement discussions are attempts to reach a mutually acceptable resolution rather than have a trial. The company offered to settle the case for $1 million without any admission of wrongdoing. The plaintiffs' lawyers countered with a request for $13 million and agreements to replace the current hiring system and to provide opportunities for training and development for current African American employees. The company I-O psychologist argued strongly that the current hiring system was defensible and effective. It had identified successful brokers, was fast and efficient, and had never been the source of complaints prior to this recent charge.

Three days before trial, the company lawyers and the plaintiff lawyers reached a settlement agreement. The plaintiff class would be given a total of $4 million, of which $1.3 million would go to the plaintiff law firm. In addition, the HR department would modify the screening program as follows:

- The work sample test time limit would be increased from 30 minutes to one hour.
- A criterion-related validity study of the personality test would be initiated (although the current test and cut scores would continue to be used until that study had been completed).
- Interviewers would be brought to corporate HR for training.
- The I-O psychologist for the plaintiffs would collaborate with the I-O psychologist for the company in developing the validity study and the interviewer training.
- The company would establish a budget of $100,000 for this work and would pay the fees of the plaintiffs' psychologist as well as the fees of their own expert from this fund.

The agreement was presented to the judge who approved it without comment. The litigation process from initial complaint to approved settlement lasted 27 months.

The cost to the company for outside counsel, expert witnesses, and administrative expenses was approximately $1.7 million. This figure did not include the salaries of company staff members who worked in various phases of the defense. Although the company had been considering going public at the time the initial complaint was filed with the EEOC, they postponed the public offering until after the settlement was approved. The initial public offering was well received by the investment community and the company continues to grow. The cost of the settlement as well as the direct costs for defense (excluding salary costs) were paid by an insurance policy held by the company. The company recognized its vulnerability in areas related to promotional systems, compensation, training, and discipline. With the help of the I-O expert, the company recruited and hired a full-time I-O psychologist to assist in the development of those additional HR systems.

MODULE 7.4 SUMMARY

- Although discussions of employment litigation often revolve around a practice (e.g., performance appraisal) or an assessment device (e.g., a test or an interview), employment discrimination charges result not from practices or devices, but from decisions about whom to hire, promote, or lay off.
- I-O psychologists commonly serve as expert witnesses in employment discrimination cases filed in federal courts. These cases are most often filed by groups of individuals claiming violations of Title VII of the Civil Rights Act of 1964, the Americans with Disabilities Act, or the Age Discrimination in Employment Act.
- The law and the courts recognize two different theories of discrimination. The adverse treatment theory charges an employer with intentional discrimination. The adverse impact theory acknowledges that the employer may not have *intended* to discriminate against a plaintiff, but a practice implemented by the employer had the *effect* of disadvantaging the group to which the plaintiff belongs.
- In an adverse impact case, the burden is on the plaintiff to show that (1) he or she belongs to a protected group, and (2) members of the protected group were statistically disadvantaged compared to majority employees or applicants. The *Uniform Guidelines* suggest using an "80 percent" or "4/5ths" rule to demonstrate evidence of adverse impact.

KEY TERMS

expert witness	"80 percent" or "4/5ths rule"	class certification
adverse (or disparate) treatment	adverse impact ratio	deposition
adverse impact	discovery	settlement discussions

CRITICAL THINKING EXERCISES

7.7 For each of the following discrimination charges, indicate which is likely to be a charge of intentional discrimination, and which a charge of adverse impact.

1. A female applicant for a position of baggage handler for an airline. A supervisor who interviews her rejects her, indicating that most of the women who succeeded in the job were physically larger than she is.

2. An African American applicant for a position as a reservation clerk for a major hotel chain is told that he has been rejected because his score on a test of clerical accuracy falls below a specific cut point.

3. A Somali applicant for a position as a claims adjuster for a major insurance company is rejected because of a concern that Somalis are sympathetic toward Arab terrorists and might engage, directly or indirectly, in terrorist activities.

7.8 Review Case Study 7.2 on the employment discrimination suit. Note that the I-O psychologist retained by the company felt strongly that the company should not settle but should instead proceed with the trial. If the company had proceeded instead of settling, what major obstacles would the company have to overcome in establishing the validity and fairness of its hiring process?

TRAINING AND DEVELOPMENT

8 CHAPTER

FOUNDATIONS OF TRAINING AND LEARNING

Jackie slid into the driver's seat and checked the map one more time before turning the key. It was Monday, and for the duration of the week she would be commuting not to her office but to an off-site center where she and other new managers from various departments and locations in her company would receive training to develop their supervisory skills. Backing out of her driveway, Jackie realized that she was more nervous than she had anticipated. She didn't know what to expect from the training program, either in terms of what would be required of her or of what she would be learning. She also wondered how her fellow engineers, who had become her subordinates when she was promoted, would react when she returned to work. Would they be on the lookout for her to "act like a manager" instead of like a colleague? She wasn't even sure how supportive her own boss was of this training program or of any changes in her supervisory style that might result from it. As we will describe in this chapter, Jackie's apprehension about the purpose and effects of the training program is legitimate. I-O psychologists have done a great deal of research on training relevant to Jackie's concerns and questions. Research on training has also provided guidelines to training practitioners about the best ways to identify training needs, design and implement training programs, and evaluate the effectiveness of training.

Training is big business, particularly in the United States, Japan, and western Europe. A survey by researchers at the American Society for Training and Development (Van Buren & King, 2000) indicated that training expenditures as a percentage of payroll averaged 3.2 percent in European companies, 2 percent in U.S. organizations, and 1.2 percent in Japanese companies. Organizations in the United States spend more than $60 billion annually on training. Evidence indicates that these training expenditures are paying off in terms of higher net sales and gross profitability per employee (Bartel, 1994; Bassi & McMurrer, 1998). In addition, many organizations are using training and development as a way to attract and retain their most successful employees.

Given how expensive and important training is, it is important for I-O psychologists to use a systematic approach to training that includes an assessment of training needs, incorporation of principles of learning, consideration of transfer of the training, and an evaluation of training programs. In this chapter, we will discuss this scientific approach, which has resulted in great strides in our understanding of training and development.

In an assessment of training research over the preceding decade, Salas and Cannon-Bowers (2001) expressed optimism about the fact that there are more theories, models, empirical studies, and meta-analyses on training than ever before. They concluded that "there has been nothing less than an explosion in training-related research in the past 10 years" (p. 472). Although the science of training has progressed greatly in recent years, many challenges lie ahead. We will describe these encouraging advances as well as the hurdles facing today's training researchers and practitioners.

In Chapter 3 we discussed individual differences and how they relate to a variety of work outcomes. For selection purposes, I-O psychologists assume that individual difference characteristics on which hiring decisions are based are relatively stable over time. This assumption is supported by research evidence for certain individual difference characteristics (e.g., general mental ability, personality) that are used in selection (Costa & McCrae, 1997; Murphy & Davidshofer, 2001). In contrast, researchers and practitioners in the training field assume that knowledge and skills can be changed and enhanced. For example, effective training programs can enhance knowledge about sexual harassment and safety procedures. Training can also develop interpersonal and computer skills, which in turn can be applied back on the job. Skills and knowledge, then, are generally more "trainable" than abilities or personality characteristics, which are considered more stable. In sum, although training cannot change or enhance all individual difference characteristics, it can be used in combination with selection and other human resource systems to assemble a strong workforce.

TRAINING, LEARNING, AND PERFORMANCE

Training is the systematic acquisition of skills, concepts, or attitudes that results in improved performance in another environment (Goldstein & Ford, 2002). The basic foundation for training programs is **learning,** a relatively permanent change in behavior and human capabilities that is produced by experience and practice. Learning outcomes can be organized into three broad categories: cognitive, skill-based, and affective outcomes (Kraiger, Ford, & Salas, 1993). An example of a **cognitive outcome** is declarative knowledge: knowledge of rules, facts, and principles. In training programs, for example, police officers acquire declarative knowledge about laws and court procedures. Declarative knowledge is an important component of Campbell, McCloy, Oppler, and Sager's (1993) theory of performance, which we discussed in Chapter 5. **Skill-based outcomes,** which are similar to Campbell et al.'s procedural knowledge, concern the development of motor or technical skills. For example, motor skills might involve the coordination of physical movements such as using a specialized tool or flying a certain aircraft, while technical skills might include understanding a certain software program or exhibiting effective customer relations behaviors. **Affective outcomes** include attitudes or beliefs that predispose a person to behave in a certain way. Attitudes may be developed or changed through training programs, which can be powerful sources of socialization for new and existing employees (Feldman, 1989). Examples of attitudes that can be acquired or modified through training are organizational commitment and tolerance for diversity.

It is important to note that training, learning, and performance are distinct concepts. First, training is a planned experience that is expected to lead to learning, which may occur through informal experiences as well. How much is learned in training, however, is influenced by several factors (characteristics of trainees and training design) that will be described in greater detail below. Second, learning is expected to increase performance on the job. As we discussed in Chapter 5, **performance** is something that people actually do and, in many cases, performance can be directly observed. In contrast, learning cannot be observed, so we often assume that learning takes place from observing performance such as in a test that follows a class or a training session. Thus, in many cases learning results in higher performance in training and back on the job. However, this desirable situation is not necessarily the case, particularly if the work environment is not supportive of employees demonstrating newly learned knowledge and skills. Although all learning does not result in higher performance, careful attention to training design, principles of learning, and work environment characteristics can greatly increase the likelihood that learning will result in improved job performance. The point is that training increases the probability of learning, and learning increases the probability of better job performance (Landy, 1989).

TRAINING

Systematic acquisition of skills, concepts, or attitudes that results in improved performance in another environment.

LEARNING

A relatively permanent change in behavior and human capabilities produced by experience and practice.

COGNITIVE OUTCOME

Type of learning outcome that includes declarative knowledge, or knowledge of rules, facts, and principles.

SKILL-BASED OUTCOME

Type of learning outcome that concerns the development of motor or technical skills.

AFFECTIVE OUTCOME

Type of learning outcome that includes attitudes or beliefs that predispose a person to behave in a certain way.

PERFORMANCE

Actions or behaviors relevant to an organization's goals and can be measured in terms of each individual's proficiency.

FIGURE 8.1

Goldstein and Ford's Training Model
SOURCE: Adapted from Goldstein & Ford (2002).

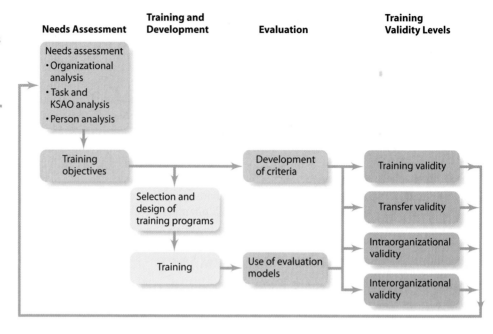

By understanding the factors that affect learning, training researchers and practitioners can enhance the performance of individuals, teams, and organizations.

The types of training programs offered by organizations vary greatly and include new employee orientation, team training, sexual harassment awareness, and the development of cross-cultural, management, and leadership skills. Although the specific requirements of these training programs vary greatly, training researchers and practitioners benefit from using a consistent framework or model when designing, implementing, and evaluating all training programs. In this chapter we follow Goldstein and Ford's (2002) training model, which is shown in Figure 8.1. This model begins with needs assessment and then moves to training and development, followed by training evaluation, and then to a consideration of training validity levels. Following that, we consider special issues in training and development, including leadership and management development, sexual harassment awareness training, and cross-cultural training.

TRAINING NEEDS ANALYSIS

A three-step process of organizational, task, and person analysis; required to develop a systematic understanding of where training is needed, what needs to be taught or trained, and who will be trained.

TRAINING NEEDS ANALYSIS

Before training design issues are considered, a careful needs analysis is required to develop a systematic understanding of where training is needed, what needs to be taught or trained, and who will be trained (Goldstein & Ford, 2002). **Training needs analysis** (Table 8.1) typically involves a three-step process that includes organizational, task, and person analysis.

TABLE 8.1	Training Needs Analysis
A. Organizational analysis	Examines companywide goals and problems to determine where training is needed.
B. Task analysis	Examines tasks performed and KSAOs required to determine what employees must do to perform successfully.
C. Person analysis	Examines knowledge, skills, and current performance to determine who needs training.

Organizational analysis examines organizational goals, available resources, and the organizational environment to determine where training should be directed. This analysis identifies the training needs of different departments or subunits. Organizational analysis also involves systematically assessing manager, peer, and technological support for transfer of training, a topic that is discussed in more detail later in the chapter. Similarly, organizational analysis takes into account the climate of the organization and its subunits. For example, if a climate for safety is emphasized throughout the organization or in particular parts of the organization (e.g., production), then training needs will likely reflect this emphasis (Zohar, 2002).

Research also indicates that several organizational characteristics can affect whether training has an impact back on the job. For example, supervisor and peer support for training helps to motivate employees entering training and increases the likelihood that they will transfer newly acquired KSAOs to the job (Colquitt, LePine, & Noe, 2000; Tracey, Tannenbaum, & Kavanagh, 1995). For example, if an employee is welcomed back after a training program by a manager who says, "Now that you've got that out of your system, I hope you're ready to get back to work," the employee is not likely to be highly motivated to utilize the newly learned skills back on the job. Thus, it is critical to conduct an organizational analysis before developing a training program so that appropriate support for training exists.

Task analysis examines what employees must do to perform the job properly. As we discussed in Chapter 5, a job analysis identifies and describes the tasks performed by employees and the KSAOs needed for successful job performance. If available, the results of a job analysis are very helpful in determining training needs. Task analysis, which examines what the content of training should be, can consist of (1) developing task statements, (2) determining homogeneous task clusters (which are more usable and manageable than individual task statements), and (3) identifying KSAOs required for the job. The links between task clusters and KSAOs can be used to develop training programs that are directed toward enhancing critical KSAOs. Table 8.2 shows task clusters derived from a task analysis conducted on the job of a train operator. The results of the task analysis would be used to design training that ensured that train operators would, for example, obtain knowledge of the steps they must take in emergency situations.

Task analysis can also include an assessment of competencies, which are broader than knowledge, skills, or abilities. As we discussed in Chapter 5, **competencies** are "sets of behaviors that are instrumental in the delivery of desired results or outcomes" (Kurz & Bartram, 2002). Organizations are increasingly trying to identify "core competencies" that are required for all jobs (Shippmann et al., 2000), and training needs analysis is an important part of the process of identifying and developing such competencies. For example, if a training needs analysis indicates that innovativeness is important to the success of a particular company, a training program may be designed to help employees become more innovative and creative. Given the increased emphasis on competencies in organizations, competency training might be included as a supplement to existing training on more specific technical skills (Kraiger, 2002a).

Recall the cognitive task analysis procedure that we discussed in the job analysis section in Chapter 5. Cognitive task analysis can also be useful in conducting a needs analysis in advance of a training program. Traditionally, task analysis has focused on identifying knowledge, skills, and abilities required for successful task and job performance. Cognitive task analysis can supplement traditional task analysis by providing a detailed description of the cognitive skills and mental demands needed to perform a task proficiently (Militello & Hutton, 1998; Salas & Cannon-Bowers, 2001).

Person analysis identifies which individuals within an organization should receive training and what kind of instruction they need. Employee needs can be assessed using a variety of methods that identify weaknesses that training and development can address. Many of the issues we discussed in Chapter 4 on assessment and Chapter 6 on

---

ORGANIZATIONAL ANALYSIS

Component of training needs analysis that examines organizational goals, available resources, and the organizational environment; helps to determine where training should be directed.

TASK ANALYSIS

Component of training needs analysis that examines what employees must do to perform the job properly.

COMPETENCIES

Sets of behaviors instrumental in the delivery of desired organizational results or outcomes.

PERSON ANALYSIS

Component of training needs analysis that identifies which individuals within an organization should receive training and what kind of instruction they need.

TABLE 8.2	Task Clusters for Train Operators
1. Preoperation responsibilities	Preparing for operating the train for a given shift. This includes reporting for duty in a state of preparedness with proper equipment, and getting information from the bulletin board and/or dispatcher.
2. Preoperation equipment inspection	Checking the train for defects and safety, including checking brake system, gauges, and track under the train.
3. Train operations	The actual operation of the train in a safe and timely manner. This includes controlling the train in the yard or on the road, consideration of conditions such as weather, curves and grades, speed restrictions, and interpretation of warnings/signals.
4. Maintaining schedule	Activities associated with timely operations, including adhering to the timetable and communicating with personnel to prevent disruption of service.
5. Emergency situation activities	Identifying and reacting to emergency situations, keeping customers safe, communicating with the control center, and troubleshooting mechanical difficulties.

performance evaluation are relevant when training specialists are conducting a person analysis. For example, assessments of KSAOs can be obtained from the performance evaluation system or from a 360 degree feedback system that provides input for training and development activities. Objective data on accidents and job performance are often examined as part of the needs analysis, and written tests are used to assess employees' current job knowledge. Organizations are increasingly using person analysis to determine how prepared employees are for a particular training program. Specifically, assessments of trainee personality, ability, and experience are increasingly being used as part of the needs assessment process. We will further discuss trainee characteristics below.

To summarize, assessing training needs is a three-part process that includes: (1) organizational analysis, which identifies companywide goals and problems; (2) task analysis, which identifies the tasks to be performed, how work should be done, and the KSAOs needed to complete those tasks; and (3) person analysis, which focuses on identifying individuals who need training. Careful needs assessment sets the stage for specifying the objectives of the training program. Training objectives are needed to design the training program, to use as goals to motivate trainees to learn, and to evaluate the effectiveness of the training program. On the basis of the needs analysis, it is possible to specify objectives or goals for the training program (Landy, 1989). Objectives are important for several reasons. First, they represent information for both the trainer and the trainee about what is to be learned. Second, training objectives help to motivate trainees by providing clear goals for them. Third, training objectives are necessary to evaluate a training program properly. We will discuss training evaluation in more detail later in the chapter.

THE LEARNING PROCESS IN TRAINING

After training needs have been determined and used to develop training objectives, training design begins with an understanding of how learning occurs. As shown in Figure 8.2, several trainee characteristics (e.g., readiness to learn, motivation to learn) and training design characteristics (e.g., principles of learning, objectives) affect the learning process and learning outcomes.

Trainee Characteristics

Trainee readiness refers to whether employees have the personal characteristics necessary to acquire knowledge from a training program and apply it to the job (Noe, 2002). These characteristics include general mental ability, goal orientation, and experience level. Several studies involving a variety of occupations (e.g., pilots, technicians, enlisted army and air force recruits, and computer programmers) indicate that general mental ability ("g") is predictive of performance in training (Ree & Carretta, 2002; Ree & Earles, 1991). In a meta-analysis spanning 85 years, Schmidt and Hunter (1998) found that "g" had a validity of +.56 in predicting training outcomes. Overall, research indicates that "g" is important for predicting performance in training, which in turn is related to performance on the job. Assessing cognitive ability before training can be useful in grouping individuals based on their readiness to learn the material. For example, with a group of trainees of widely varying cognitive ability, high-ability trainees will be bored, while low-ability trainees will have trouble keeping pace with their peers. With a group of trainees of similar ability, training facilitators can proceed through material at a pace appropriate to the backgrounds of the participants (Fleishman & Mumford, 1989).

Another indicator of trainee readiness is goal orientation. Individuals with a **performance orientation** are concerned about doing well in training and being evaluated positively. They perceive their abilities as somewhat fixed, and they are generally not open to learning environments in which errors and mistakes are encouraged. They direct their energy toward performing well on tasks, often at the expense of learning. Performance-oriented learners are often sensitive to feedback, which can lead them to

TRAINEE READINESS

Refers to whether employees have the personal characteristics necessary to acquire knowledge from a training program and apply it to the job.

PERFORMANCE ORIENTATION

Orientation in which individuals are concerned about doing well in training and being evaluated positively.

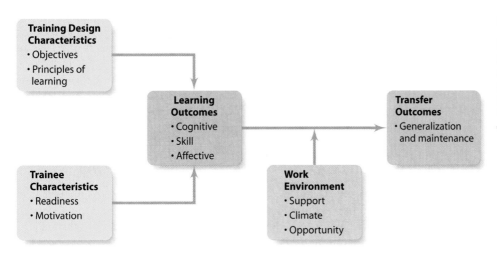

FIGURE 8.2

Characteristics Affecting Learning and Transfer Outcomes
SOURCE: Adapted from Baldwin & Ford (1988).

reduce their efforts and goals in challenging situations (Farr, Hofmann, & Ringenbach, 1993). In contrast, individuals with a **mastery orientation** are concerned with increasing their competence for the task at hand, and they view errors and mistakes as part of the learning process. Mastery-oriented individuals are flexible and adaptable in learning situations, which is particularly critical for learning dynamic tasks and complex decision making (Ford, Smith, Weissbein, Gully, & Salas, 1998; Phillips & Gully, 1997). Kanfer and her colleagues (Kanfer & Ackerman, 2000; Kanfer & Heggestad, 1997) have identified mastery orientation as a basic dimension of general motivation. Compared to performance-oriented learners, individuals with a mastery orientation are more motivated to learn, more actively engaged in the training task, more prepared to acquire new skills in training, and more effective at transferring their new skills to the job (Brett & VandeWalle, 1999; Towler & Dipboye, 2001). Because it is beneficial for all trainees to have a mastery orientation, Noe and Colquitt (2002) suggested several ways to induce a mastery orientation: Goals should be set around learning and experimenting with new ways of performing trained tasks, competition with other trainees should be de-emphasized, and trainees should be encouraged to make errors and experiment with new knowledge or skills during training.

An additional indicator of readiness is the trainee's experience level. Inexperienced trainees with lower ability generally benefit more from longer and more structured training programs (Fleishman & Mumford, 1989; Gully, Payne, Koles, & Whiteman, 2002). In contrast, experienced trainees with high ability thrive in shorter, less structured training programs. Even prior negative experiences can be useful in heightening motivation to learn before training begins. For example, pilots often receive assertiveness training because some air accidents have been caused by a lack of communication and hesitancy to express concerns in the cockpit. In 1982 an Air Florida jet taking off from Reagan National Airport in Washington, D.C., crashed into the 14th Street bridge. Among the elements responsible for this accident was the unwillingness of a copilot to disagree with the pilot and abort the take-off to return for additional deicing. Smith-Jentsch, Jentsch, Payne, and Salas, (1996) found that pilots who had experienced accidents or near-accidents benefited more from assertiveness training and subsequently performed better after training than those who had no negative experiences. The authors suggested that the negative experiences motivated the pilots to learn how to avoid aviation mishaps and that an opportune time to provide training is after a negative experience such as an accident, injury, or production problem. The negative experience provides a window of opportunity for the organization to offer immediate training rather than merely make a note of the incident for a later training effort.

Trainee Motivation is the extent to which trainees are interested in attending training, learning from training, and transferring the skills and knowledge acquired in training back to the job (Ford et al., 1998; Mathieu & Martineau, 1997). Researchers often use an **expectancy framework** to study and understand training motivation (Baldwin & Ford, 1988). That is, if trainees believe the work environment is favorable before they begin the training program, they will be more motivated to learn. Thus, managers and trainers should develop an environment that facilitates training motivation, which can be enhanced by using principles from several learning and motivation theories.

Learning and Motivational Theories Applied to Training

Reinforcement Theory   B. F. Skinner's (1954) work on reinforcement was important in early theories of motivation. Skinner also applied principles of reinforcement theory to the educational and learning process. He proposed that learning results from the association between behaviors and rewards. **Positive reinforcement** occurs when behavior is followed by a reward, which increases the probability that the behavior will be repeated. As a learning mechanism, positive reinforcement is useful in pointing out when the correct behaviors and skills are demonstrated in training and on the job. Reinforcement is generally most effective when it occurs immediately after a task has been completed or performed. Rewards that positively reinforce desired behaviors can range from praise from a supervisor, peer, or trainer to gifts, cash bonuses, attention, recognition, and career opportunities. For example, a trainer can praise trainees who effectively demonstrate the skill they were just taught. Employers can provide positive reinforcement by offering career opportunities to employees who engage in training and development programs. Reinforcement theory suggests that trainers and supervisors can best enhance learning and transfer of knowledge and skills by identifying what rewards or outcomes the learner finds most positive (Goldstein & Ford, 2002; Noe, 2002).

An example of a training and motivational method that is based primarily on reinforcement theory is **behavior modification.** This approach involves identifying, measuring, rewarding, and evaluating employee behaviors aimed at performance improvement. In a field experiment of employees working in an operations division that was responsible for processing and mailing credit card bills, Stajkovic and Luthans (2001) compared the effects of money administered using a behavior modification approach to three other reinforcers that were implemented in three different groups: a routine pay for performance approach, recognition, and feedback. The behavior modification approach included the following steps:

1. Supervisors identified critical, observable, and measurable behaviors that had a high potential for improving worker performance.
2. Supervisors were trained in how to identify the antecedents and consequences of the identified behaviors.
3. Supervisors provided workers with ongoing help and coaching about the specifics of the program.
4. Supervisors continually reminded workers that monetary rewards were contingent on the workers being engaged in the critical performance behaviors.

The behavior modification intervention had stronger effects on performance (37 percent increase) than routine pay for performance (11 percent increase), recognition (24 percent), or feedback (20 percent). The results of this study demonstrate two important points. First, simple recognition and feedback can be effective in increasing performance. Second, a systematic behavior modification program provides further increases in performance. A meta-analysis that covered the past 20 years of empirical research on behavior modification also indicated that behavior modification consistently results in increased task performance (Stajkovic & Luthans, 1997). Collectively, these studies indicate that principles of reinforcement can be used as part of training and motivational programs to improve and sustain performance.

Cognitive and Social Learning Theories Cognitive theories focus on how individuals process and interpret information, while acknowledging that humans do not always learn by performing a task and receiving direct reinforcement. Instead, humans can use memory, judgment, and reasoning to make connections between what they observe and how they should behave or perform in work and nonwork situations. **Social learning theory** is a cognitive theory that proposes that there are many ways to learn. For example, humans can learn indirectly by observing others (Bandura, 1997). Observational learning occurs when people watch someone (in person or via a videotape) perform a task and then rehearse those activities mentally until they have an opportunity to try them out. Social learning theory is at work when trainees are being mentored and when they are "learning the ropes" by watching more experienced colleagues perform certain tasks. Trainees can also learn by asking more experienced employees questions and by listening to them describe the critical behaviors that lead to successful performance (Landy, 1989).

BEHAVIOR MODIFICATION

A training and motivational method based primarily on reinforcement theory; involves identifying, measuring, rewarding, and evaluating employee behaviors aimed at performance improvement.

SOCIAL LEARNING THEORY

Cognitive theory that proposes that there are many ways to learn including observational learning, which occurs when people watch someone perform a task and then rehearse those activities mentally until they have an opportunity to try them out.

BEHAVIORAL MODELING

Learning approach that consists of observing actual job incumbents (or videos of job incumbents) who demonstrate positive modeling behaviors, rehearsing the behavior using a role-playing technique, receiving feedback on the rehearsal, and trying out the behavior on the job.

Given the increasing number of jobs in the service industry and the increasing use of teams in organizations, interpersonal skills training has become increasingly important. A technique called **behavioral modeling** is often used to apply principles of social learning theory to the development of interpersonal skills in managers and supervisors. Behavioral modeling consists of observing actual job incumbents or videos of job incumbents that demonstrate positive modeling behaviors, rehearsing the behavior using a role-playing technique, receiving feedback on the rehearsal, and finally trying out the behavior on the job. For example, behavioral modeling occurs when telemarketing trainees listen in while an experienced telemarketer talks with a customer. Baldwin (1992) studied the effects of alternate modeling strategies on interpersonal skills training. He found that showing trainees a video of a person using correct behaviors and a video of a person using incorrect behaviors was more effective than showing only the video of positive modeling behaviors. May and Kahnwieler (2000) used behavioral modeling to improve interpersonal skills using role-play practice exercises. They found that practice sessions that broke down tasks into manageable parts led to high retention rates and high scores on a simulated interpersonal skills case study.

Applications of behavioral modeling are also being utilized in technical and computer skills training programs. In a field experiment examining different approaches to computer training for novice computer users in the navy, Simon and Werner (1996) compared the behavioral modeling approach to a self-study course and a traditional classroom approach. Behavioral modeling included observing the trainer, practicing the tasks, receiving feedback, and experimenting with new ways to carry out the tasks. Results indicated that behavioral modeling was superior to the other approaches at time 1 (immediately after training) and time 2 (one month later) across evaluation measures that included attitudes about the training, knowledge gained from the training, and demonstration of skills learned. Another study found that managerial trainees performed better when exposed to behavioral modeling for computer training than to computer-assisted instruction (Gist, Schwoerer, & Rosen, 1989). These studies indicate that both managerial and nonmanagerial employees can benefit from behavioral modeling in terms of computer skill development and demonstration.

Social learning theory is a broad-based approach that includes self-efficacy, goal setting, and feedback, which are important aspects of the learning process that occur in training. As we will discuss further in Chapter 9, these three concepts are also important parts of motivational theory and practice. **Self-efficacy,** the belief in one's capability to perform a specific task or reach a specific goal (Bandura, 1997), enhances trainees' motivation, learning, and subsequent performance on the job (Colquitt et al., 2000). Trainees high in self-efficacy are likely to attempt difficult tasks both in training and back on the job. Researchers have found that self-efficacy plays an important role in a variety of training programs including negotiation skills training, computer software training, and training in innovative problem solving. Training specialists can increase trainees' self-efficacy by using behavioral modeling and by providing words of encouragement. Machin (2002) and Noe (2002) noted that trainees' self-efficacy levels can also be increased by:

SELF-EFFICACY

Belief in one's capability to perform a specific task or reach a specific goal.

1. Providing as much information as possible before training about the training program and the purpose of training.
2. Reducing perceived threats to trainees by initially emphasizing learning outcomes and de-emphasizing performance outcomes, which become more important after training.
3. Showing employees the training success of peers in similar jobs.
4. Helping trainees develop better learning strategies to use during training, such as summarizing main points and using memory aids to help retention.

GOAL SETTING

Motivational approach in which specific, difficult goals direct attention and improve performance in training and on the job.

Goal setting can strengthen trainee motivation and self-efficacy, which in turn are helpful in enhancing learning and skill acquisition in training. A great deal of research indicates that specific, difficult goals improve performance in training and on the job (Austin & Vancouver, 1996; Locke & Latham, 1990). Thus, trainers should encourage trainees to set specific, difficult goals, which help to direct and focus their attention on the most important tasks. Machin (2002) emphasized the importance of goal setting and suggested that trainers ensure that all trainees have the following:

1. Clear short-term goals for the training program (e.g., "I will complete all of the required modules in the allocated time").

2. Short-term goals for the immediate transfer of their training (e.g., "I will begin to use my new knowledge and skills in the first opportunity I have").

3. Long-term goals that focus on continued mastery and use of training content (e.g., "I will seek feedback from my supervisor and peers after one month and continue to review my progress each month").

In a study of air force trainees who used an air traffic control simulation task, Kanfer and Ackerman (1989) examined whether goal setting is more helpful for skill acquisition if it occurs early or late in the learning process. The task in this study required trainees to accept and land planes on correct runways based on information they were provided on weather conditions and the amount of fuel remaining in the planes. Trainees performed the task over 10 trials. They were randomly assigned either an early goal (during trials 2, 3, and 4) or a late goal (during trials 5, 6, and 7), both of which indicated that trainees should achieve a certain score during those particular trials. Kanfer and Ackerman found that only goals assigned late in the learning process had a positive influence on skill acquisition and task performance. The results indicate that goal setting is unlikely to have an impact early in the skill acquisition process when attentional demands are high. Instead, goal setting enhances skill acquisition later in the learning process when learners have had a chance to practice the task.

Feedback is also important in enhancing learning and performance in training and on the job. Feedback enhances motivation and keeps goal-directed behavior on target. Feedback about performance in training and on the job is most effective when it is accurate, timely, and constructive (Goldstein & Ford, 2002). Managers should use a clear and nonthreatening manner when they deliver feedback, which should deal specifically with job-relevant behaviors (Kluger & DeNisi, 1996).

Principles of Learning

Practice and Overlearning   The old saying "practice makes perfect" is applicable to training, particularly because practice is critical to retaining newly learned skills. The Greek philosopher Aristotle stated that "What we have to do we learn by doing," which indicates that **active practice** has been emphasized for many centuries. The principle of active practice is still used today in many training programs. For example, military recruits actively practice assembling and disassembling guns, which is preferable to passively watching someone else, such as a drill sergeant, do so.

Training researchers and practitioners often ask, "How much practice is enough?" Some suggest that it is sufficient to practice until the task can be performed once without errors. However, as many concert musicians can attest, this approach is unlikely to lead to adequate, long-term task performance (Driskell, Willis, & Copper, 1992). If you have ever taken piano lessons, you have probably observed that playing a piece without errors in one practice session does not in any way guarantee that you will be able to play it flawlessly a week later, or even the next day. Instead, you need to continue practicing it to the point of overlearning. Similarly, training programs should emphasize overlearning by presenting trainees with several extra learning opportunities even after they have demonstrated mastery of a task. Overlearning results in **automaticity,** which occurs when tasks can be performed with limited attention. An example of automaticity is when experienced drivers

FEEDBACK

Knowledge of the results of one's actions; enhances learning and performance in training and on the job.

ACTIVE PRACTICE

Involves actively participating in a training or work task rather than passively observing someone else performing the task.

AUTOMATICITY

Occurs when tasks can be performed with limited attention; likely to develop when learners are given extra learning opportunities after they have demonstrated mastery of a task.

In an example of overlearning, military trainees continue to practice assembling and disassembling their weapons even after they have demonstrated initial mastery of this task.

pay little attention to steering while driving. People often refer to automaticity by saying they can do the task "on auto-pilot" or "in my sleep."

Overlearning is critical in jobs in which the task is not likely to be performed on the job very often and where performance on the first attempt is critical (e.g., emergency procedures, military endeavors, avoiding accidents while driving). The military has demonstrated positive benefits from overlearning with the assembly and disassembly of weapons, which personnel must do under time pressure and with precision (Schendel & Hagman, 1982). In a meta-analysis of over 50 studies on overlearning, Driskell et al. (1992) found that overlearning had a significant and positive effect on long-term retention for both physical and cognitive tasks. In sum, overlearning increases the length of time training material is retained; thus, if training involves learning a skill, then employees should be asked to demonstrate the skill even after they have shown some initial mastery level.

The extent to which the task trained is similar to the task required on the job is referred to as **fidelity.** It is important that training tasks have fidelity so that the extra time and expense of overlearning in training can directly benefit performance on the job. Training tasks should have both physical and psychological fidelity. **Physical fidelity** refers to the extent to which the training task mirrors the physical features of the actual task. For example, airplane simulator tasks possess physical fidelity when they accurately represent the layout of the cockpit as well as the motion that occurs in actual aircraft (Goldstein & Ford, 2002). **Psychological fidelity** refers to the extent to which the training task helps trainees to develop the knowledge, skills, abilities, and other characteristics (KSAOs) that are necessary to perform the job. A training program that emphasizes the development of critical KSAOs identified in a task analysis would possess high psychological fidelity. For example, if lieutenant candidates in a fire department are trained (and tested) in a simulated setting where they have to respond to a fire by actually speaking the directions and orders they would give, this setting would call forth their communication and decision-making skills and would possess psychological fidelity (Goldstein, Zedeck, & Schneider, 1993).

FIDELITY

Extent to which the task trained is similar to the task required on the job.

PHYSICAL FIDELITY

Extent to which the training task mirrors the physical features of the task performed on the job.

PSYCHOLOGICAL FIDELITY

Extent to which the training task helps trainees to develop the knowledge, skills, abilities, and other characteristics (KSAOs) necessary to perform the job.

Trainee pilots use simulators with high physical and psychological fidelity.

High-fidelity simulators are often very expensive. Research has investigated whether low-fidelity simulators are effective in training required KSAOs. For example, Jentsch and Bowers (1998) found that flight simulators with low physical fidelity do elicit behaviors that are important for on-the-job performance. Nevertheless, pilots often prefer to receive training on the more expensive, high-fidelity simulators. Overall, training specialists must consider the trade-offs among fidelity, cost, trainee preferences, and transfer of training to the job.

Whole versus Part Learning   Another important consideration in training is the size of the tasks practiced. **Whole learning** occurs when the entire task is practiced at once. **Part learning** occurs when subtasks are practiced separately and later combined. Trainers and training designers should consider the task's difficulty level (task complexity) and the extent to which the subtasks are interrelated (task organization) in determining the usefulness of whole and part learning. Whole learning is more effective when a complex task has relatively high organization. When a complex task has low organization, part learning is more efficient. For example, developing skills to land airplanes involves complex tasks that can be decomposed; thus, it is often beneficial to use a part learning approach, which is less intimidating and frustrating to novice pilot trainees than a whole learning approach. Once some of the difficult parts of the task have been automatized, trainees can gradually be moved to performing the whole task (Rogers, Maurer, Salas, & Fisk, 1997). Part learning also occurs when surgeons practice individual tasks such as making incisions, tying sutures, and clamping blood vessels many times separately before they combine these tasks in performing an operation (Machin, 2002). Another example of part learning is the way that actors rehearse various parts of a play (e.g., dance steps, fight scenes, pieces of dialogue) without the other actors. Gradually, the pieces are brought together until the actors are ready for a run-through of the entire play, which they then do intact for the rest of rehearsals. When using part learning approaches, it is important for trainers to determine the correct sequence for learning the subtasks and how they should be combined so that trainees can eventually perform the overall task effectively and efficiently (Goldstein & Ford, 2002).

WHOLE LEARNING

Training approach in which the entire task is practiced at once.

PART LEARNING

Training approach in which subtasks are practiced separately and later combined.

Massed versus Distributed Practice   Trainers and training researchers have also considered how to set up practice sessions. **Massed practice** conditions are those in which individuals practice a task continuously and without rest. **Distributed practice** gives individuals rest intervals between practice sessions, which are spaced over a longer period of time. In general, distributed practice results in more efficient learning and retention than massed practice because the rest periods reduce fatigue and allow time for strengthening of learned associations (Cascio, 1998; Kanfer, Ackerman, Murtha, & Dugdale, 1994). For simple motor tasks (e.g., computer keyboard skills), brief rest periods between practice sessions are helpful. For tasks of high complexity (e.g., air traffic control simulation, airplane flight simulation), longer rest periods between practice sessions are more beneficial for learning and skill acquisition. In terms of implications for training design, these findings suggest that we can expect a significant increase in learning from training programs that present distributed as opposed to massed material (Donovan & Radosevich, 1999).

College students preparing for a test often wonder whether weeks of inattention to a course can be remedied by pulling an "all-nighter," which involves cramming information into their memory just before an exam (Landy, 1987). Cramming is the equivalent of massed practice and, in general, is an ineffective learning strategy. The problem with cramming is that the information learned is not retained for very long. Although cramming may improve performance marginally if the exam comes within hours of the massed practice, the material will not be retained as part of the body of knowledge students accumulate in school. The research described above suggests that students can benefit from studying that is distributed over time, which will lead to better exam performance and higher retention of the material.

LEARNING ORGANIZATIONS

Peter Senge's (1990) book, *The Fifth Discipline: The Art and Practice of Learning Organizations,* popularized the concept of the learning organization, which is a useful extension of the principles of learning described above. **Learning organizations** are companies that emphasize continuous learning, knowledge sharing, and personal mastery (Jeppensen, 2002). Several additional features include:

1. Emphasizing problem solving and innovation.
2. Developing systems that enhance knowledge generation and sharing.
3. Encouraging flexibility and experimentation.
4. Valuing the well-being and development of all employees.
5. Encouraging employees to find or make opportunities to learn from whatever situation is presented (Confessore & Kops, 1998; London & Mone, 1999).

Tannenbaum (1997) developed a Learning Environment Survey that assesses many of the characteristics of learning organizations. Table 8.3 shows examples from the survey, which included scales assessing tolerance for mistakes as part of learning, openness to new ideas, and the supportiveness of supervisors for training. In a study of more than 500 employees across seven organizations, Tannenbaum found evidence that organizations with stronger learning environments demonstrated greater levels of organizational effectiveness.

Some organizations that have made lifelong learning an important part of their mission have established corporate universities. For example, Motorola University was developed in 1980 as a separate program outside of the Human Resources department of Motorola Corporation. Motorola University focuses on addressing special business needs such as retraining and updating workers, and it requires employees worldwide to complete a certain number of training hours focusing specifically on Motorola products and services (Baldwin, Danielson, & Wiggenhorn, 1997; Goldstein & Ford, 2002). Consistent with cutting-edge trends in training practice, Motorola University is branching out from

TABLE 8.3	Learning Environment Survey

Learning Environment Survey: All scales used a 7-point response format

1	2	3	4	5	6	7
Strongly disagree	Somewhat disagree		Neither agree or disagree		Somewhat agree		Strongly agree

My organization typically:

1. Provides people with opportunities to learn new things.

2. Assigns people to positions to stretch them.

3. Tolerates mistakes when someone is first learning a new task or skill.

4. Views new problems and work challenges as opportunities to develop people's skills.

5. Monitors to see that people continue to develop and learn throughout their career.

6. Expects everyone, not just management, to solve problems and offer solutions.

7. Rewards employees for using what they have learned in training on the job.

In my organization:

8. Supervisors and co-workers help reschedule work so that employees can attend training.

9. Supervisors provide constructive feedback when someone tries something new on the job.

10. Supervisors offer people opportunities to use new skills they learned in training.

11. Training is considered an important part of career development.

12. The successful people go to training.

13. It is acceptable to question others about why things are done a certain way.

SOURCE: Tannenbaum (1997).

its fixed campuses to include computer-based training programs that provide enhanced individual flexibility.

Other well-known corporate universities include General Motors University, Xerox's Document University, and McDonald's Hamburger University, which is based in Oakbrook, Illinois. Hamburger University has granted more than 65,000 "Bachelors of Hamburgerology" degrees since the program began in 1961 in the basement of a McDonald's restaurant. At Hamburger University, McDonald's managers learn about supervisory skills, employee motivation, and company values such as quality, service, cleanliness, and pride (Wexley & Latham, 2002). With the use of electronic and computer-based technology, training courses are provided in 22 languages at Hamburger University, which now operates in Japan, Germany, England, and Australia.

Tolbert, McLean, and Myers (2002) emphasized that global changes and challenges facing corporations require an emphasis on global learning organizations. They argued that many organizations are ethnocentric, and that successful organizations will instead need to be globally inclusive. Figure 8.3 shows the shift they advocated. Organizations aiming to become truly global will need to plan and structure management development that includes international and cross-cultural experiences. They will also need to train their employees to work in cross-cultural teams. To help employees be prepared to think and work with a global perspective, organizations can use features of learning organizations (e.g., continuous learning and improvement) in combination with recruitment and selection

FIGURE 8.3

Global Learning Organizations

SOURCE: Tolbert, McLean, & Myers (2002).

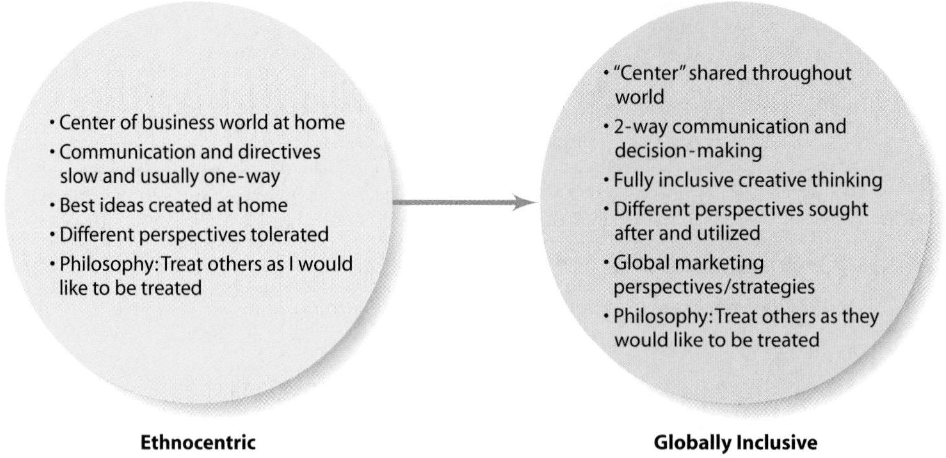

Ethnocentric circle:
- Center of business world at home
- Communication and directives slow and usually one-way
- Best ideas created at home
- Different perspectives tolerated
- Philosophy: Treat others as I would like to be treated

Globally Inclusive circle:
- "Center" shared throughout world
- 2-way communication and decision-making
- Fully inclusive creative thinking
- Different perspectives sought after and utilized
- Global marketing perspectives/strategies
- Philosophy: Treat others as they would like to be treated

Ethnocentric   **Globally Inclusive**

procedures. Overall, training researchers and practitioners are optimistic about these systematic, integrated approaches to learning. Additional research is needed that evaluates the conditions under which learning organizations thrive and the barriers to changing an organization's culture in this way.

MODULE 8.1 SUMMARY

- Training is a major expenditure for many companies, and evidence suggests that it pays off in higher sales and profitability. Many organizations also use training to attract and retain their most successful employees.

- I-O psychologists often use a training model that begins with needs assessment, then training and development, followed by training evaluation, and finally a consideration of training validity levels.

- Needs analysis is a systematic means of understanding where training is needed, what needs to be taught or trained, and who will be trained.

Training needs analysis typically involves organizational, task, and person analysis.

- After determining training needs and training objectives, training design begins with an understanding of how learning occurs. Trainee characteristics (readiness to learn, motivation to learn) and training design characteristics (principles of learning, objectives) affect the learning process and learning outcomes.

- I-O psychologists use principles from reinforcement theory and social learning theory to design training programs and to enhance learning processes during training.

KEY TERMS

training
learning
cognitive outcome
skill-based outcome
affective outcome
performance
training needs analysis
organizational analysis
task analysis
competencies
person analysis

trainee readiness
performance orientation
mastery orientation
trainee motivation
expectancy framework
positive reinforcement
behavior modification
social learning theory
behavioral modeling
self-efficacy
goal setting

feedback
active practice
automaticity
fidelity
physical fidelity
psychological fidelity
whole learning
part learning
massed practice
distributed practice
learning organization

CRITICAL THINKING EXERCISES

8.1 Describe how learning to drive involves part learning. Next, describe whether you think that the learning sequence is likely to be different if one is learning to drive a car with an automatic transmission compared to one with a standard transmission.

8.2 When learning new information in school or on the job, do you tend to have a mastery orientation or a performance orientation? Does the orientation that you typically use help or hinder what you learn and how you later apply that information when you take a test or perform on the job?

CONTENT AND METHODS OF TRAINING

TRAINING METHODS

Training methods are generally categorized into on-site and off-site programs, and each of these categories can be divided into several types. The following discussion is meant to be a representative, rather than an exhaustive, description of commonly used methods. Later in the chapter, we will discuss additional types of training (e.g., cross-cultural, management development, and sexual harassment awareness training). It is important to note that while these methods differ in their specific applications, all have in common the learning principles discussed earlier in the chapter. Salas and Cannon-Bowers (2001) echoed this idea by noting that most effective training methods are created around four basic principles:

1. They present relevant information and content to be learned.
2. They demonstrate KSAOs (knowledge, skills, abilities, and other characteristics) to be learned.
3. They create opportunities for trainees to practice the required skills.
4. They provide feedback to trainees during and after practice.

On-Site Training Methods

On-the-job training involves assigning trainees to jobs and encouraging them to observe and learn from more experienced employees. Nearly all employees receive some on-the-job training following initial formal training. Although on-the-job training is necessary and can be very beneficial, it is often done in an unsystematic way that is at odds with many of the ideas discussed earlier in the chapter. Alternatively, if on-the-job training includes training objectives, behavioral modeling, and regular feedback, then it is likely to be an effective training method (Goldstein & Ford, 2002).

Apprenticeship A particular form of on-the-job training is an **apprenticeship,** which is a formal program used to teach a skilled trade (Goldstein & Ford, 2002). The apprenticeship approach is used for many (primarily "blue-collar") jobs including bricklayers, electricians, plumbers, carpenters, sheet metal workers, roofers, cement masons, and pipefitters. Approximately 61 percent of organizations employing individuals in such jobs have apprenticeship training programs which last from two to five years (McMurrer, Van Buren, & Woodwell, 2000). Apprenticeship programs combine on-the-job instruction with a minimum of 144 hours a year of classroom instruction. An apprentice becomes a journeyman after a specified training period. With further experience, the journeyman goes on to become a certified skill tradesperson.

A successful apprenticeship program includes modeling, practice, feedback, and evaluation. Apprentices should begin their training by gaining the prerequisite knowledge.

Next, behavioral modeling is used as journeymen and certified tradespersons model the correct behaviors for apprentices to observe. The apprentice then has an opportunity to perform and practice the tasks. Finally, the apprentice receives feedback and additional practice opportunities until the task is performed adequately and safely (Noe, 2002).

Apprenticeship programs are a more important part of education and training in several European countries, such as Germany and Denmark, than in the United States. The German apprenticeship program is often highlighted as a model for providing young workforce entrants with the skills and credentials needed for an occupation (Noe, 2002). Many Germans who do not go on to college (approximately two-thirds) participate in apprenticeship programs, which are supported by leaders from government, labor, business, and education. One concern about apprenticeship systems, however, is that they provide workers with very specific skills that are not always adaptable to other jobs. The changing nature of work in the United States and abroad may create difficulties for apprentices whose skills are very narrowly focused. Although apprenticeship systems in Germany, the United States, and other countries successfully train individuals in developing specialized skills, retraining may be needed to enable employees to move to related jobs when economic conditions change. Personal characteristics such as adaptability, flexibility, and openness will allow all employees, including apprentices, to remain valuable assets in changing times (Cascio, 1998; Ilgen & Pulakos, 1999).

Job rotation   Another common training method is **job rotation,** which involves moving employees to various departments or areas of a company, or to various jobs in a single department (Noe, 2002). Employees who participate in job rotation develop a wider range of skills than they would by remaining in a single job, area, or level of the organization. For example, an entry-level employee in a large human resources (HR) department might be rotated through the staffing, compensation, benefits, and training areas in order to learn about these different HR functions. This rotation might involve three to six months in each specialty area. Job rotation can also be used to prepare high-potential employees for future management responsibilities. New college graduates and MBAs may participate in job rotation as a way to determine where they would be most effective in the organization (Wexley & Latham, 2002). For example, a newly hired executive or manager might be rotated through the HR, operations, accounting, and finance departments in order to develop firsthand knowledge of the departments and functions within the organization. On the interpersonal level, employees who have been rotated through a series of jobs often develop an important network of contacts across the organization. Job rotation also promotes the development of decision-making and problem-solving skills, and provides employees with experiences that will help them qualify for future promotions. Research indicates a positive association between job rotation and both job promotions and salary increases (Campion, Cheraskin, & Stevens, 1994). As with other training techniques, job rotation is most successful if it is part of an overall career development system that offers employees a variety of job-relevant experiences and opportunities.

The PricewaterhouseCoopers (PwC) consulting company provides an example of a successful job rotation program. Its "Tours of Duty" program typically lasts one to two years and allows consultants to rotate among different PwC consulting teams from around the world. Consultants who are "on tour" are able to enhance the host team's ability to meet its business needs by sharing their knowledge and skills with team members. In the process, consultants develop language skills, experience a foreign culture, and enhance their technical and interpersonal skill sets (Barbian, 2002).

Off-Site Training Methods

Classroom lectures are one of the most common training methods. Lectures are an efficient way to present a large amount of information to a large number of trainees.

JOB ROTATION
Approach that involves moving employees to various departments or areas of a company, or to various jobs within a single department.

CLASSROOM LECTURE
Training method in which the trainer communicates through spoken words and audiovisual materials what trainees are supposed to learn; also commonly used to efficiently present a large amount of information to a large number of trainees.

They are often supplemented with class discussion, case studies, and audiovisual materials. The lecture method is relatively inexpensive compared to other training methods, and it works well when the goal is for trainees to obtain knowledge. In a meta-analysis of managerial training techniques, Burke and Day (1986) found that the lecture method fared well in comparison to other training methods. However, the lecture method does not work well in situations in which skill acquisition is critical. The lecture format has often been criticized because it fosters a passive environment that does not require trainees to become involved in learning the material (Goldstein & Ford, 2002). Thus, trainers should encourage active participation from trainees in lectures by including job-related examples and exercises that promote learning and transfer to the job (Noe, 2002).

Programmed instruction presents information to learners using principles of reinforcement (Goldstein & Ford, 2002). In this approach, trainees are given instructional materials in written or computer-based forms that reinforce them positively as they move through the material. This self-paced approach works most effectively if it provides immediate feedback and reinforcement regarding correct and incorrect responses. The culture assimilator, a collection of scenarios describing challenging, cross-cultural incidents that is used in preparing employees to work in another culture, is one programmed instruction approach currently receiving a lot of attention. We will discuss the culture assimilator further in the cross-cultural training section below.

Programmed instruction can involve **linear programming,** in which all trainees proceed through the same material, or **branching programming,** a customized approach that enables each learner to practice material he or she had difficulty with when it was first presented. Compared with linear programming, branching models are more adaptive and responsive to the needs of individual trainees. Reviews of programmed instruction, lecture, and discussion training methods found no significant differences in immediate learning and retention across the three methods, but trainees using programmed instruction learn material in approximately 30 percent less time (Goldstein & Ford, 2002). With rapid increases in computer and multimedia technology, a great deal of programmed instruction is moving from written formats to computer-assisted instruction. Recent advances in multimedia technology, which can simultaneously present text, graphics, animation, and videos, are making computer-assisted programmed instruction more interesting and appealing, but researchers have yet to examine the effects of these advances empirically. Nevertheless, computer-based training holds vast potential as a way to improve the delivery and cost-effectiveness of programmed instruction.

Simulators are designed to reproduce the critical characteristics of the real world in a training setting that produces learning and transfer to the job. If you have taken a course in CPR (cardiopulmonary resuscitation), you have probably used a simulator: a dummy designed to resemble a stroke or heart attack victim. Simulators are virtually the only safe way to train pilots to fly airplanes and to prepare nuclear power plant operators to work in and respond to crises in their facilities. Simulators are very useful for developing motor skills. They are also useful in developing management and decision-making skills as they allow trainees to see the impact of their decisions in a risk-free environment (Noe, 2002). Goldstein and Ford (2002) provided four reasons for using simulators:

1. *Controlled reproducibility*—simulators effectively reproduce the real-world environment in the training setting.
2. *Safety considerations*—required real-world behavior is often too complex to be handled safely by the trainee.
3. *Learning considerations*—most simulators effectively utilize learning principles such as active practice and feedback, and are designed to support transfer of training.

4. *Cost*—simulators provide a low-cost method for trainees to practice and acquire skills. Although simulators are expensive, they are a better use of organization money than the cost of trainee mistakes on the job when high-priced equipment and even human lives are at stake.

The concept of fidelity, which we discussed earlier in the chapter, is particularly important in simulators, which must be as similar to the actual task as possible in terms of physical layout (physical fidelity) and in mirroring the KSAOs required for performing the task on the job (psychological fidelity). Flight schools use high-fidelity flight simulators to train and evaluate pilots and their coordination with copilots. Flight simulators provide physical fidelity by replicating the cockpit as well as the motion that a pilot would feel in a real aircraft (Goldstein & Ford, 2002). For example, helicopter simulators have a screen on which images are projected as well as a tilt platform that is used to simulate balance in the ear. Such simulators can induce motion sickness in seconds! Flight simulators provide psychological fidelity by requiring trainees to utilize relevant KSAOs while performing all technical aspects of flight including altitude control, navigation, and the use of safety checklists (Smith-Jentsch, Salas, & Brannick, 2001). Greater fidelity in the simulator task leads to higher job-relevant learning and subsequent transfer to the job. Given the many benefits simulators provide, they will continue to be used in a variety of industries, and I-O psychologists will continue to explore ways to maximize the transfer of skills learned while using simulators.

Distance Learning and Computer-Based Training

Distance learning allows trainees to interact and communicate with an instructor by using audio and video (television, computer, or radio) links that allow for learning from a distant location (Goldstein & Ford, 2002). Distance learning can occur across multiple sites at one time, and it provides a more affordable, learning-tailored alternative to live instruction (Hannafin & Hannafin, 1995). Although distance learning by radio and television has long been used for elementary schooling, especially in sparsely populated areas such as rural Alaska and the Australian outback, advances in technology since the 1980s have expanded the available media to videoconferencing and online collaboration. The added benefits of these interactive media have made computer-based distance learning increasingly popular in the workplace. Many U.S. businesses (including Kodak and IBM), as well as colleges and universities, offer extensive distance learning programs. In addition, many countries including the United Kingdom, the Netherlands, Germany, and Spain have widely recognized open universities that use distance learning (Hawkridge, 1999).

Distance learning has great promise, but I-O research in this area is just beginning. Threlkeld and Brozoska (1994) studied achievement levels in distance and traditional learners, and found no significant differences between the two groups. Two later studies indicated that higher levels of interaction and feedback enhance attitudes about distance learning (Webster & Hackley, 1997; Zhang & Fulford, 1994). Not surprisingly, distance learning works best when it is free of technical problems. Specifically, audio and video transmissions should be fast, clear, and consistent so that equipment concerns do not detract from the advantages of this new learning platform (Goldstein & Ford, 2002).

Like distance learning, computer-based training has expanded greatly in recent years. Many organizations are moving a growing proportion of their training from traditional classroom settings to computer-based training because of its reduced costs and increased flexibility. For example, Merrill Lynch uses computer-based training with its

DISTANCE LEARNING

Approach that allows trainees to interact and communicate with an instructor by using audio and video (television, computer, or radio) links that allow for learning from a distant location.

Distance learning has become an efficient and popular method of training workers.

financial planners and consultants, who have responded positively to the increased individualization and accessibility that this form of training provides (Guernsey, 2000). **Computer-based training** is defined as "text, graphics, and/or animation presented via computer for the express purpose of teaching job-relevant knowledge and skills" (Brown & Ford, 2002, p. 194). This definition includes Web-based training, corporate intranets, multimedia environments, and e-learning; thus, computer-based training may involve distance learning or the participants may be physically in one location. From a learning perspective, the differences among these specific types of computer-based training are often negligible. What is important is that they all allow trainees to individualize their learning experience (Filipczak, 1996). Successful computer-based training will need to incorporate learning principles derived from the more general training literature such as specific learning objectives, active practice, and feedback.

Compared to traditional instructor-led training, computer-based training offers trainees more control over their instruction. Trainees can choose how many practice opportunities they take and how much time they spend on the different tasks provided in computer-based training. This individualized aspect of computer-based training provides an advantage for trainees, but it is up to them to utilize this increased flexibility to their advantage. In a study of technical employees in a Fortune 500 company, Brown (2001) examined the effects of computer-based training on the development of problem-solving skills. He found that trainees who invested effort and time into computer-based training successfully learned the computer-based material. However, many trainees elected to skip practice opportunities and to stay for half the time allotted for the training session. This study indicated that employers should not assume that providing access to computer-based training will automatically result in practice and learning. This study reinforces the point that using new technology in training programs or other interventions does not always guarantee success. Training designers and managers who use computer-based materials will need to explore ways to encourage learners to practice and to stay on task, such as increasing the accountability of trainees with follow-up meetings (Brown, 2001). Although there is much promise to computer-based training, overall many unanswered questions also remain regarding how effective this approach will be in terms of learning and transfer back to the job.

TRAINING "CRITICAL THINKING"

Above we described different modes or types of training. In this section we will focus on training in a specific content area, critical thinking, that is receiving increased attention in colleges and universities as well as in some organizations. What distinguishes critical thinking from ordinary thought is that it requires active involvement in applying the principles under discussion, rather than simple memorization of facts or principles. The increased emphasis on critical thinking in today's society is evident in the recent announcement that the College Board is undertaking a major overhaul of the SAT I, the standardized test required for admissions at most colleges and universities in the United States. In particular, the verbal section of the revised SAT I is being renamed "critical reading" as it focuses on critical thinking and analysis of long and short reading passages (Lewin, 2002). It is safe to say that critical thinking skills will continue to be important in preparing for tests, making decisions, and adapting to challenges in the changing workplace. Training approaches and teaching philosophies that encourage students to develop transferable critical thinking skills will better prepare them for the unknown challenges in their future endeavors (Halpern, 1998).

Advances in technology and changes in necessary skills have made the ability to think critically in the workplace more important than ever before. Whenever workers grapple with complex issues, difficult decisions, and ill-defined problems, they will benefit from using **critical thinking skills** (Halpern, 1998). The importance of critical thinking can be seen in the U.S. Navy's Tactical Decision Making Under Stress (TADMUS) program. This program focuses on the development of naval officers' critical thinking skills in novel or unexpected situations (Cohen, Freeman, & Thompson, 1998). Critical thinking skills training in the TADMUS program uses instruction, demonstration, and practice to teach naval officers methods for identifying and handling different kinds of uncertainty. The training program provides practice with realistic problems and exercises that naval officers are likely to encounter on the job. For example, one exercise involves a time-pressured situation in which a navy ship needs to be defended against an approaching aircraft whose intent is unclear. Officers are asked to think through the difficult situation and make a decision about how they would respond. Next, they receive feedback about the likely result of their decisions and information regarding the correct way to approach and resolve the situation, which helps to further develop their critical thinking skills. Independent tests of the critical thinking skills training with naval officers indicated positive effects on decision-making processes, accuracy of situation assessment, and the appropriateness of actions suggested (Cohen et al., 1998).

One of the goals of this book is to show how many of the broad principles of I-O psychology can be applied in situations encountered in the workplace. We believe the best way to achieve this is to encourage you to utilize critical thinking. We are confident you will be able to retain and apply these I-O principles beyond this course if you think critically about how they may apply to practical problems, and follow up by discussing alternative solutions or applications with your instructor and peers.

TRANSFER OF TRAINING

Throughout this chapter, we have emphasized the importance of the extent to which material learned in training transfers back to the job. **Transfer of training** is the degree to which trainees apply the knowledge, skills, and attitudes gained in training to their jobs (Machin, 2002; Wexley & Latham, 2002). An organization's **transfer of training climate** refers to workplace characteristics that either inhibit or facilitate the transfer to the job of what has been learned in training. A positive transfer climate is one in which adequate resources are present, opportunities for using skills learned in training exist, and positive reinforcement for using training content is given (Colquitt et al., 2000). Table 8.4 provides a summary of characteristics of a positive transfer of training climate. A positive transfer climate is particularly important because research indicates that new employees learn about the way training is viewed in the organization early in the socialization process and continue gathering information with each training course they attend (Feldman, 1989). For example, new employees whose co-workers grin sarcastically and ask, "When do you go for training?" are likely to conclude that the less time spent in training, the better impression they will make on peers. Thus, organizations

TRANSFER OF TRAINING

Degree to which trainees apply the knowledge, skills, and attitudes gained in training to their jobs.

TRANSFER OF TRAINING CLIMATE

Workplace characteristics that either inhibit or facilitate the transfer to the job of what has been learned in training.

TABLE 8.4	Characteristics of a Positive Transfer of Training Climate

Early socialization indicating that training is important.

Continuous learning culture.

Adequate peer and supervisor support.

Opportunities to use learned capabilities.

Access to equipment or resources that are essential for transfer of training.

Adequate working conditions.

Regular feedback and positive reinforcement for improved performance.

should pay careful attention to messages employees hear about training within and across departments.

Several studies indicate that a positive transfer of training climate has a significant impact on the extent to which course material is applied back on the job (Warr, Allan, & Birdi, 1999). For example, Rouillier and Goldstein (1993) studied management trainees in fast food companies who were trained on topics such as employee relations, food preparation and handling, shift management, and customer service. They found that transfer climate had a positive impact on transfer of training to the job. Tracey, Tannenbaum, and Kavanagh (1995) investigated the effects of the work environment on the transfer of newly trained supervisory skills in a sample of 505 supermarket managers from 52 different stores. They found that supermarket managers who received social support from peers and their bosses were more effective in utilizing the skills learned in training. A recent meta-analysis by Colquitt et al. (2000) indicated that the transfer of training climate also influences reactions to training, motivation to learn, and skill acquisition.

A work environment that supports what is learned in training and co-workers/supervisors who reinforce those new skills, abilities, and attitudes are necessary supplements to training programs. In particular, off-site training programs will be effective only if management supports and reinforces the efforts of training facilitators. Off-site training programs sometimes use elaborate and expensive methods like paintball wars, fighter-pilot simulations, and a course at the BMW Performance Center that features driving a car while blindfolded. Ellin (2000) noted that although it may be fun to pelt one's boss with paint or to drive a BMW blindfolded with the help of a colleague, most of these off-site programs create an artificial, almost vacationlike atmosphere that does not easily transfer back to the workplace. Some employees report that such off-site training programs increase morale for a day or so, and then everyone returns to their high workload and forgets about such team-building exercises (Ellin, 2000). Thus, it is important for managers to consider transfer issues when adopting training programs, and to take steps to ensure the supportiveness of the post-training work environment. For example, managers might carefully consider what knowledge and skills were learned in training and then ensure that trainees are provided with opportunities to use the new skills and knowledge soon after they return to the job.

In what ways might an offsite training program featuring paintball wars provide learning that will transfer well to the workplace?

MODULE 8.2 SUMMARY

- Most effective training methods are created around four basic principles: presenting relevant information and content to be learned; demonstrating KSAOs to be learned; creating opportunities for trainees to practice the required skills; and providing feedback to trainees during and after practice.
- Training methods are generally categorized into on-site and off-site programs. On-site training methods include on-the-job training, apprenticeships, and job rotation. Off-site programs include classroom lectures, programmed instruction, and simulators.

- Distance learning and computer-based training have both expanded greatly in recent years. They provide opportunities for reduced costs and for increased flexibility for both trainers and trainees.
- An important consideration for I-O psychologists, trainers, and trainees is the extent to which material learned in training transfers back to the job. A positive transfer of training climate has a significant impact on the extent to which course material is applied back on the job.

KEY TERMS

on-the-job training
apprenticeship
job rotation
classroom lecture
programmed instruction

linear programming
branching programming
simulator
distance learning
computer-based training

critical thinking skills
transfer of training
transfer of training climate

CRITICAL THINKING EXERCISES

8.3 Do you think that classroom lectures are an effective training method? What are the advantages and disadvantages of the lecture as a training method?

8.4 Do you think the revised SAT I that places a greater emphasis on an analysis of short and long reading passages does a better job of assessing critical

thinking skills than the older version of the SAT that required students to recognize antonyms and complete sentences with missing words? Why? Do you think that the SAT I does a better job of assessing preparedness for college than the previous version of the SAT?

EVALUATING TRAINING PROGRAMS

TRAINING EVALUATION

Training evaluation involves the systematic collection of descriptive and judgmental information that can be used to make effective training decisions. Such decisions include the selection, adoption, modification, and financial evaluation of various training activities (Goldstein & Ford, 2002). Implicit in this definition are several purposes of training evaluation (Sackett & Mullen, 1993):

1. To determine whether trainees have achieved the objectives of the training program.
2. To provide feedback that can improve training programs for future participants, ultimately increasing their job performance and productivity.
3. To justify the costs of training programs, which can be expensive. Evaluation can demonstrate the worth of training to top management by indicating whether the accomplishment of key business objectives improved after training.

As you can see, the goal of training evaluation is not simply to label a training program as good or bad. This is important to keep in mind; some trainers avoid evaluations that might identify minor problems or errors for fear that top management may try to "pull the plug" on such a program. Instead, the focus should be on how making minor modifications based on training evaluation can make a training program more effective in meeting its objectives (Goldstein & Ford, 2002). Training objectives are critical in identifying the criteria by which the training program is judged. For training evaluation to be done well, it has to be planned in advance based on the overall training objectives, rather than simply being considered at the end of the program. Often, multiple criteria or outcomes are used to assess the success of a training program. The approaches discussed below provide various frameworks with which to think about criteria in the context of training evaluation.

TRAINING CRITERIA

Kirkpatrick's (1959, 1998) four-level model is the most common and well-known framework with which to categorize training criteria. **Reaction criteria** (Level 1) are measures of trainee impressions of the training program. Measures of reaction criteria are sometimes called "smile sheets" as they simply assess trainees' enjoyment of and satisfaction with the training program. **Learning criteria** (Level 2) assess how much trainees learned in the training program. Learning criteria are often assessed with a written test, which might evaluate knowledge acquired in a training program. **Behavioral criteria** (Level 3) measure how well the behaviors learned in training transfer to the job. Behavioral criteria might include ratings of on-the-job performance of behaviors taught in the training program. **Results criteria** (Level 4) provide measures of how well the training can be related to organizational outcomes. For example, results criteria might assess whether a training program resulted in productivity gains, cost savings, error reductions, or increased customer satisfaction. Results criteria are often considered most important to organizational decision makers because they have direct implications for organizational objectives and outcomes.

Reaction and learning criteria are considered **internal criteria** because they focus on what occurred within the training program. Behavioral and results criteria are considered **external criteria** because they assess changes that occur back on the job. Surveys of companies' evaluation practices indicate that organizations frequently use reaction criteria, but they use learning, behavioral, and results criteria much less frequently. Specifically, a recent survey indicated that organizations were using the four evaluation levels at the following percentages: reaction: 84 percent; learning: 39 percent; behavior: 15 percent; and results: 7 percent (McMurrer et al., 2000).

For many years, Kirkpatrick's framework was considered to be a hierarchical approach to evaluation that included reaction criteria at the lowest level and results criteria at the highest level. This approach assumed that lower-level measures were correlated with higher measures and that positive trainee reactions were critical in achieving favorable outcomes for learning, behavioral, and results criteria. Because reaction criteria are the easiest to collect, researchers have investigated whether they are truly correlated with the other levels of training criteria. If so, then there would be little need to collect the other criteria because one could make the inference that positive trainee reactions would have beneficial effects on learning, transfer, and results criteria.

A meta-analysis by Alliger, Tannenbaum, Bennett, Traver, and Shotland (1997) indicated that there were only modest correlations among the various levels of training criteria. Their results suggested that Kirkpatrick's taxonomy should be augmented to include multiple criteria at Levels 1 and 2 (see Table 8.5). Specifically, their framework divided Level 1 criteria into affective reactions ("I found this training program to be enjoyable") and utility reactions ("This training program had practical value" or "This training program was job relevant"). They concluded that affective reactions can be important, particularly when unfavorable reactions to training have negative effects on perceptions of the training department and future training efforts. However, utility reactions were more closely linked with learning and behavioral criteria than were affective reactions. Accordingly, if the purpose of collecting reaction criteria is to predict transfer of training, then evaluators should ask utility-oriented questions.

INTERNAL CRITERIA

Assess trainee reactions to and learning in the training program; generally assessed before trainees leave the training program.

EXTERNAL CRITERIA

Assess whether changes as a result of training occur when trainees are back on the job.

TABLE **8.5**	**Training Criteria Taxonomies**
KIRKPATRICK'S TAXONOMY	**AUGMENTED FRAMEWORK**

Reaction	Reaction
	    Affective reactions
	    Utility judgments

Learning	Learning
	    Immediate knowledge
	    Knowledge retention
	    Behavior/skill demonstration

Behavior	Transfer
Results	Results

Source: Alliger, Tannenbaum, Bennett, Traver, & Shotland (1997).

Alliger and colleagues (1997) suggested that learning outcomes should be divided into immediate knowledge, knowledge retention, and behavior/skill demonstration. This is consistent with Kraiger et al.'s (1993) expanded framework of learning outcomes that we discussed earlier in the chapter. Recall that Kraiger et al. described learning as a multidimensional process that includes three types of outcomes (cognitive, skill-based, and affective). Alliger et al. did not revise Kirkpatrick's Level 3 criteria except to use the term "transfer" instead of "behavioral" to emphasize that these measures assessed on-the-job performance. Consistent with other studies and organizational reports, Alliger and colleagues found that assessors rarely examined Level 4, results criteria.

UTILITY ANALYSIS

Although organizations do not often collect Level 4, results criteria, training evaluators and specialists continue to be interested in ways to assess the financial return for training investments. As we discussed in Chapter 7, **utility analysis** is a technique that assesses the return on investment of training and other human resource interventions (Landy, Farr, & Jacobs, 1982). Utility analysis employs accounting procedures to measure the costs and benefits of training programs. Costs generally include the equipment, facilities, materials, and personnel expenditures across different stages of the training process. The benefits of the training program are based on several factors including:

- The number of individuals trained.
- Estimates of the difference in job performance between trained and untrained employees.
- The length of time a training program is expected to influence performance.
- The variability in job performance in the untrained group of employees (Noe, 2002).

A utility analysis can provide training evaluators and organizational decision makers with an overall dollar value of the training program. For example, Mathieu and Leonard (1987) examined the effects of a training program in supervisory skills for bank supervisors. After taking into account the costs of the program, they found that the utility of training a group of 15 bank supervisors was more than $13,000 for the first year after training. Although a utility of less than $1,000 per trainee might not seem like a lot, the net utility of the training program in the third year was estimated to be more than $100,000 owing to the increased effectiveness of the supervisors. Utility analysis can also compare the return on investment of different training programs. In their examination of the utility of managerial, sales, and technical training programs, Morrow, Jarrett, and Rupinski (1997) found that sales and technical training programs had greater effects on job performance and greater returns on investment than managerial training programs. To perform utility analysis, training evaluators use complex formulas that are beyond the scope of this book, but are covered in detail in other sources (Cascio, 2000; Wexley & Latham, 2002).

VALIDITY OF TRAINING PROGRAMS

Goldstein and Ford (2002) suggested that training evaluation really deals with the basic issue of validity; specifically, training evaluation attempts to collect different types of validity evidence for training programs. They discussed four ways to examine the validity of training programs:

1. Training validity is the extent to which trainees meet the criteria established for the training program.
2. Transfer validity is the extent to which trainees match the criteria established for success when they are back on the job.

3. Intraorganizational validity is the extent to which the training program will be effective with different groups of trainees within the same company.
4. Interorganizational validity is the extent to which the training program will be effective with different trainees in companies other than the one that developed the training program.

This validity perspective emphasizes that trainers and training managers should carefully think through the inferences they would like to make about their training programs. Training validity and transfer validity overlap with training criteria from other evaluation models, whereas intraorganizational and interorganizational validity are more unique to Goldstein and Ford's (2002) approach. Whether trainers use this evaluation framework or another depends on the objectives of the training program, which are developed by means of a needs analysis. When trainers clearly specify training objectives, training outcomes can be easily evaluated in relation to those objectives. For example, using multiple criteria when the objective of a training program is to improve morale (for which reaction criteria are appropriate) will be costly and will likely meet resistance from upper management. In particular, if a training program is to be used with several other groups of employees within and outside the organization, Goldstein and Ford's (2002) validity approach provides a valuable perspective for evaluating the training program. In summary, the criteria for training effectiveness have been outlined for many years, although expanded frameworks have been suggested recently (Alliger et al., 1997; Kraiger, 2002b; Kraiger et al., 1993). These approaches provide trainers with a variety of ways to conceptualize and measure training criteria.

TRAINING EVALUATION DESIGNS

The purpose of training is to bring about systematic changes in knowledge, skills, and attitudes. Evaluation designs are used to determine whether training objectives have been met and whether post-training changes in knowledge, skills, and attitudes are a result of training. Training evaluators attempt to infer that such changes are a result of the training program. However, a variety of factors can make these inferences difficult. Developing a good evaluation design can help to reduce concerns about such factors, which are called threats to validity.

The characteristics of strong experimental designs that we discussed in Chapter 2 are the same as those required for strong training evaluation designs. Why? Because these designs assess whether training or other organizational interventions caused changes in job performance or other outcomes. Since training is so expensive, particularly when one considers the time trainees spend away from work, it is important for training managers to provide evidence that training brought about desired changes in knowledge, skills, or attitudes.

The strongest training evaluation designs include random assignment of participants to conditions, a control group, and measures that are obtained both before and after training has occurred. An example of a design that includes these characteristics is the **pretest posttest control group design** (shown in Table 8.6). In this design, participants are randomly assigned to either the experimental group (training) or the control group, which does not receive training. Both groups are measured prior to training on knowledge or

PRETEST POSTTEST CONTROL GROUP DESIGN

Generally includes random assignment of participants to conditions, a control group, and measures obtained both before and after training has occurred.

TABLE 8.6	Pretest Posttest Control Group Design		
GROUP	**PRETEST**	**TRAINING**	**POSTTEST**
Trained (experimental)	Yes	Yes	Yes
Not trained (control)	Yes	No	Yes

TABLE 8.7	Pretest Posttest Control Group Design Used by Simon and Werner		
GROUP	**PRETEST**	**TRAINING**	**POSTTEST**
Lecture	Yes	Yes	Yes
Self-paced	Yes	Yes	Yes
Behavior modeling	Yes	Yes	Yes
Control group	Yes	No	Yes

SOURCE: Simon & Werner (1996).

skills to be trained (e.g., computer skills). The experimental group receives training, whereas the control group does not. After the training, the trained and control groups are assessed on the knowledge or skills trained. After controlling for any preexisting differences—which may occur, but are unlikely with the use of random assignment—a statistical test is conducted to determine if the trained group changed significantly more than the control group.

In a training program that we discussed earlier, Simon and Werner (1996) used a variation of the pretest posttest control group design that included random assignment to conditions, three experimental groups, and a control group. Their design, which is shown in Table 8.7, included three types of computer skills training: lecture, self-paced, and behavior modeling. Each of the three training groups received pretests and posttests, as did the control group. This design allowed the researchers to compare the training programs to each other and to a control group. The results indicated that participants in all experimental conditions performed significantly better than participants in the control group. Among the experimental groups, the behavioral modeling program resulted in the highest learning, retention, and demonstration of computer skills.

The **Solomon four-group design** is perhaps the most rigorous and elegant evaluation design (Braver & Braver, 1988; Solomon, 1949). Table 8.8 shows the original design, which includes random assignment to groups, pretests for a training and a control group, and posttests for all four groups. Bretz and Thompsett (1992) used a variant of this design to compare the effects of an integrative-learning training program with traditional, lecture-based learning and a control group. The training programs were focused on developing participants' knowledge of manufacturing resource planning, which is a method for effectively using and integrating the resources in a manufacturing company. Integrative learning sessions involved active participation from trainees in group discussions, games, and stories related to manufacturing processes. A knowledge test and reaction criteria were

TABLE 8.8	Solomon's Four-Group Design		
GROUP	**PRETEST**	**TRAINING**	**POSTTEST**
Trained (A)	Yes	Yes	Yes
Trained (B)	No	Yes	Yes
Control (A)	Yes	No	Yes
Control (B)	No	No	Yes

used in the evaluation design. Participants in both experimental groups learned significantly more than those in the control group. No significant differences in learning were found between the groups that used the integrative and traditional approaches. However, participants in the integrative-learning program had much more positive reactions than those in the lecture-based training program. These results show the importance of using a rigorous design and multiple criteria to gain a fuller understanding of the impact of training programs.

The studies described above are examples of rigorous training evaluation designs conducted and implemented by I-O psychologists. These evaluation designs are often difficult to implement in organizations. For example, evaluation is difficult when a training program that has already begun gets shortened or interrupted because of events in the organization or the economy. Another difficulty in evaluation occurs when changes in training materials are made during the course of the training program. From a training design perspective, rigorous training evaluation will be difficult when managers insist on sending all employees from a particular department to training at the same time; thus, random assignment of trainees to conditions would not be possible. In other cases, a control group may not be possible. In such situations, modified versions of the training evaluation designs described above may be used to lessen concerns that arise when either random assignment or the use of a control group is not possible (e.g., Haccoun & Hamtiaux, 1994). Thus, it is critical for training specialists to be aware of a variety of training evaluation designs and to understand the strengths and weaknesses of each. Thorough discussions of more complex training evaluation designs can be found in several sources (Cook, Campbell, & Peracchio, 1990; Goldstein & Ford, 2002; Wexley & Latham, 2002).

SPECIAL TOPICS IN TRAINING EVALUATION
Equal Employment Opportunity Issues in Training

Training programs can also be evaluated in terms of whether decisions associated with training opportunities unfairly discriminate against members of protected groups (e.g., women, minorities, disabled individuals). First, applicants cannot be eliminated from consideration for hiring if they lack a skill or knowledge that can be learned in a brief training session (*Uniform Guidelines,* 1978). Second, protected group members who are current employees should have the same access to training experiences and challenging work assignments that majority group members have. Organizations should also be concerned if protected group members fail training programs at higher rates than majority group members. To defend against charges of unfair discrimination in training, organizations should document their training practices and programs thoroughly. This should include monitoring each employee's progress in training and development programs (Schuler & Jackson, 1996).

A more recent concern about unfair discrimination in training concerns age discrimination. Given the aging population and workforce, organizations will employ an increasing number of individuals 40 years of age and over (Thayer, 1997). The Age Discrimination in Employment Act (ADEA) prohibits discrimination on the basis of age in human resource decisions such as hiring, firing, and pay as well as employer-provided training and development. If older workers are not given equal access to training and development, the Equal Employment Opportunity Commission (EEOC) may take on the case on their behalf. For example, four employees from the University of Wisconsin Press, who were ages 46 through 54 and who were the oldest employees at the time, were discharged and replaced by four younger employees. The employer's rationale for this decision was that the older employees lacked updated computer skills. The EEOC successfully argued that the older workers were ready, willing, and able to receive training for these computer skills and were illegally denied the opportunity. The jury returned a verdict of intentional age discrimination and awarded $430,427 in pay and damages to be shared by the four plaintiffs (Gutman, 2001).

Maurer and Rafuse (2001, p. 117) noted that "although most employees are very sensitive to sexism and racism, somehow the ageist idea that you can't teach an old dog new tricks does not seem to carry the same taboo in society and the workplace." They provided suggestions for managing employee development and avoiding claims of age discrimination, including:

1. Developmental opportunities such as training classes, job assignments, job rotations, and tuition-assistance should be allocated on an age-neutral basis.

2. All employees should be encouraged to participate in training, development, and learning opportunities.

3. Personnel decisions should be monitored to ensure that older employees have equal opportunities.

4. Workshops or training interventions should be offered to teach managers about age-related stereotypes and the potential effects they can have on decisions and behavior. Managers should also be trained specifically on the ADEA.

5. As with other HR procedures, job-relevant criteria should be used for all decisions about training and development opportunities.

There is a significant body of research indicating that job performance does not decline with age (Arthur, Fuentes, & Doverspike, 1990; McEvoy & Cascio, 1989). Thus, with predicted skill shortages in the labor market, organizations are increasingly likely to rely on experienced workers in utilizing their existing skills and expanding their skill base through developmental opportunities (Thayer, 1997). Overall, organizational efforts to avoid age and other types of discrimination in training and development opportunities will result in a reduced likelihood of lawsuits, an increased skill base, and an increased return on investment in their employees (Walker, 1999).

Training/Coaching for Tests

Student performance on tests such as the GRE, GMAT, and LSAT is critical to gaining entrance to graduate school. Similarly, employee scores on promotion, credentialing, or assessment tests involve "high stakes" that can affect the salaries and careers of test takers (Sackett, Schmitt, Elsington, & Kabin, 2001). To improve their scores, many individuals attend coaching or test-preparation programs, which are designed to inform them about test content, provide study materials, and recommend test-taking strategies. Test-preparation programs, which can cost up to $2,000, are offered by a variety of companies, such as Stanley Kaplan and The Princeton Review. The major test-preparation companies provide testimonials from students whose scores increased substantially and often guarantee that program participants will be satisfied with their results. Here is an example:

> Guaranteed Satisfaction: A GRE prep course is a big investment in terms of both time and money. With our course, your investment will pay off. Our GRE students boast an average score improvement of 200+ points.

Do these programs actually improve test performance? In general, research in educational and psychological testing indicates that score gains from coaching programs are small. Rigorous studies that randomly assign participants to training and control groups generally find an expected score gain of approximately .15 standard deviations (Powers, 1993; Powers & Rock, 1999). This score gain equates to an improvement of about 15 points on the verbal or math portion of the SAT or GRE. Certainly, claims by coaching programs of average score increases of 200 points are unwarranted (Allalouf & Ben-Shakar, 1998; Kaplan & Saccuzzo, 2001).

Messick and Jungeblut (1981) investigated expected test score gains as a function of length of the coaching program. They found that score gains increased modestly with the length of the program, but at a certain point there were diminishing returns even in these modest gains as large increases in training time were necessary for successive increases in score gains. An increase in effect size from .1 to .2 standard deviations (10–20 points on the SAT) is to be expected from an increase in training time of 45 hours. However, an additional 203 hours of training time is necessary to produce the next .1 standard deviation gain in test scores. Messick and Jungeblut observed that the time required to realize score gains in excess of .3 standard deviations (30 points on the SAT) rapidly approaches that of full-time schooling.

Researchers have also considered whether scores on promotion or other tests in work settings can be improved with the help of coaching or training programs. A study by Ryan, Ployhart, Greguras, and Schmit (1998) conducted with firefighter job applicants found no significant difference in performance on an ability test between those who received training (program participants) and those who did not (control group members). The program participants received training consisting of several hours of practice and feedback on items similar to those on the ability test. The program also included a session with hints on preparing for and taking the test, such as developing a study schedule, taking practice exams, and reading all directions. Participants were also assisted in forming study groups to continue preparation following the training program. The control group members were not presented with any of this information. Even after this type of intervention, there was no significant difference in test performance between those who received training and those who did not.

We should note, however, that promotional candidates for police officer and firefighter tests have for decades been using the techniques presented to the program participants in the above study. We suspect that even though not instructed to, control group members may have done many or all of the things that the program participants did. For example, control group members usually can get test-preparation booklets at book stores, and they very often form "eating clubs," which are really study groups that meet at mealtime. Thus, this tradition may be one reason why no significant difference was found in test performance between the groups in the Ryan et al. (1998) study. Perhaps using an occupation other than police officer or firefighter would provide a fairer test of whether scores on promotion tests can be improved as a result of a coaching program.

In sum, the effects of training or coaching on performance on ability tests appear to be small. Although these programs are often well received by program participants, research indicates that a practical effect can only be realized by hundreds of hours of instruction. Thus, employers and individuals need to think carefully about the time and money they invest in these programs.

MODULE 8.3 SUMMARY

- Training evaluation involves the systematic collection of descriptive and judgmental information that can be used to make effective training decisions such as the selection, adoption, modification, and financial evaluation of various training activities.

- Kirkpatrick's four-level model is the most common and well-known framework with which to categorize training criteria. This model includes reaction, learning, behavioral, and results criteria.

- Training evaluation can include a utility analysis that employs accounting procedures to measure the costs and benefits and assess the return on investment of training.

- Training evaluation designs determine whether training objectives have been met and whether post-training changes in knowledge, skills, and attitudes are a result of training. I-O psychologists use a variety of different training evaluation designs including the pretest posttest control group design and the Solomon four-group design.

KEY TERMS

training evaluation

reaction criteria

learning criteria

behavioral criteria

results criteria

internal criteria

external criteria

utility analysis

pretest posttest control group design

Solomon four-group design

CRITICAL THINKING EXERCISES

8.5 What would you tell training specialists who suggested that they don't have the time or the support for conducting training evaluation? What arguments can be made to those skeptical of the need for training evaluation?

8.6 Match these four criteria with Kirkpatrick's four levels (reaction, learning, behavior, results):

1. Trainees all receive above 90 percent correct on a knowledge test given immediately after training.

2. Trainees report that they learned a lot during the training program.

3. Employees who have gone through training have higher sales revenues compared to those who have not gone through training.

4. Supervisor ratings indicate trainees demonstrate increased knowledge on the job about sales products.

SPECIALIZED TRAINING PROGRAMS

Training and development are lifelong processes for executives, managers, and their employees, all of whom are increasingly finding that learning is necessary for job security and career opportunities. Whereas training is most often focused on the employee's current job, development involves learning that prepares the employee for future challenges, opportunities, and jobs. **Development** generally refers to formal education, job experiences, relationships, and assessments of personality and abilities that help employees prepare for the future (Noe, 2002). In this module, we focus on management and leadership development as well as specific training applications including sexual harassment awareness training and cross-cultural training.

MANAGEMENT AND LEADERSHIP DEVELOPMENT

As we will describe further in Chapter 12, effective leaders and managers are critical to organizational success. Leaders provide structure to work activities and help a diverse workforce be productive in increasingly complex and unpredictable times. The increased use of teams and the globalization of the economy require leaders to have broad skills that help to enhance individual, team, and organizational effectiveness. Trainers have met these challenges with an increased focus on management and leadership development that includes both formal and informal experiences (Goldstein & Ford, 2002). Such development strives to develop critical competencies in leaders, such as the capacity to solve business problems and to transmit the organization's strategy and values (Hollenbeck & McCall, 1999).

Day (2001) distinguished between leader development and leadership development. He noted that leader development concentrates on developing or enhancing individual KSAOs. In contrast, leadership development is focused on building leaders' social skills and social competence so that they can reduce team conflict and help team members work cooperatively. We will address the distinction between leader development and leadership development further in Chapter 12 as we consider the essence of leadership itself. In this chapter we will focus on several training methods that are increasingly being used in the field of management and leadership development, including assessment centers, 360 degree feedback, coaching, and informal training experiences (McCauley, 2001).

Assessment Centers

As we saw in Chapter 4, **assessment centers** are being used in corporations in the United States and abroad. An assessment center is not a particular place in an organization. Instead, it is a method that has traditionally been used as a selection procedure to assess

DEVELOPMENT

Formal education, job experiences, mentoring relationships, and assessments of personality and abilities that help employees prepare for the future.

ASSESSMENT CENTER

Collection of procedures for evaluation that is administered to groups of individuals; assessments are typically performed by multiple assessors.

"managerial potential" (Bray, Campbell, & Grant, 1974). More specifically, assessment centers evaluate organizational, leadership, and communication skills by having candidates participate in numerous exercises (e.g., role play, leaderless group discussion, in-basket) and complete many paper and pencil tests. An increasing number of organizations are using assessment centers as a part of leadership and management development programs. In the late 1990s, approximately 69 percent of companies using assessment centers were using them for developmental purposes (Kudish et al., 1998). In these companies, managers deemed to have high potential are invited to participate in an assessment center that assesses their strengths and weaknesses. Feedback obtained from the assessment center is used to create a developmental plan based on the skills and competencies required for successful performance as a manager or executive.

Jones and Whitmore (1995) conducted a 10-year follow-up evaluation of a developmental assessment center in a large insurance company. They found no differences in terms of career advancement between a group of 113 participants who went through the assessment center and a control group of 167 who did not. Nevertheless, among those who participated in the assessment center, those who followed the developmental recommendations they received based on the assessment center were more likely to be promoted than those who did not. Because the results indicated that assessment center ratings of career motivation were the best predictors of participation in development and subsequent promotions, the authors concluded that the overall effectiveness of their developmental assessment center was limited. In contrast, Englebrecht and Fischer (1995) found that participation in a developmental assessment center led to superior performance among supervisors compared to participants in a control group. This study also showed that the positive effects of the developmental assessment center did not diminish over a three-month period, indicating that assessment centers can have lasting effects as developmental experiences (Gist & McDonald-Mann, 2000). Researchers and practitioners in I-O psychology will continue to examine the short- and long-term outcomes associated with developmental assessment centers.

360 Degree Feedback

Feedback is critical in motivating change and providing direction for development (Hollenbeck & McCall, 1999). As we discussed in Chapter 6, the term **360 degree feedback** (also called multisource feedback) describes the process of collecting and providing a manager or executive with feedback that comes from many sources, including supervisors, peers, subordinates, customers, and suppliers. To help with development, such feedback should be anonymous, confidential, and timely. Raters who provide feedback anonymously are likely to be more open and honest. If the feedback is provided confidentially (only to the recipient for his or her use), the recipient is likely to be more open to receiving such feedback. Computers and technology make it easier to collect multisource feedback and provide it to the executive or manager in a timely manner. Such feedback provides a rich source of information that can be used to generate a specific developmental plan (Markos, 2001).

Several studies indicate that 360 feedback is received positively and that it is effective at improving performance (Smither et al., 1995; Walker & Smither, 1999). For example, Walker and Smither (1999) found that managers initially rated poor or moderate showed significant improvements in feedback ratings from subordinates over a five-year period. They also found that managers who met with subordinates to discuss their upward feedback improved more than other managers. However, a study by Brett and Atwater (2001) found that managers did not see negative feedback from a multirater system as accurate or useful, and that they responded with negative reactions such as anger and discouragement. Notably, a facilitator perceived participants who found feedback less useful to be less focused on development. These findings suggest that it is critical for facilitators to emphasize the developmental aspects of 360 degree feedback in order to reduce negative reactions. Research is needed that examines how to increase participants' openness to negative, developmental feedback. Coaching, which is frequently a follow-up to 360 degree feedback, may be used to emphasize the developmental nature of the feedback and to help managers deal with any negative reactions they might have.

As we discussed in Chapter 1, in cultures in which power distance is high, workers expect supervisors to have and exercise considerable power over them. Upward feedback may be seen as offensive in cultures with high power distance as it might threaten both the subordinate and the supervisor. Not only would managers be offended in getting the feedback from subordinates, but subordinates would be offended by being asked to give it. Alternatively, 360 feedback might actually go over better in low power distance and collectivist cultures, where any feedback that helps the team succeed is likely to be received positively. Indeed, in the United States and abroad 360 degree feedback for teams is increasingly being used for team development, a topic that we will discuss in Chapter 13 (Brutus, Leslie, & McDonald-Mann, 2001; Hallam, 2001).

Coaching

Like 360 degree feedback, **coaching** has become an important part of leadership development. Coaching is a practical, goal-focused form of personal, one-on-one learning for busy employees that may be used to improve performance, enhance a career, or to work through organizational issues or change initiatives (Hall, Otazo, & Hollenbeck, 1999; London, 2002). Thus, a coach works individually with an employee to help develop his or her skills and to provide reinforcement and feedback. Coaching provides a practical, flexible, targeted form of individualized learning for managers and executives. Coaching has grown rapidly because it meets the need for a leadership development tool that responds to changes in the business environment (Hollenbeck, 2001). It may be used "to improve performance, to improve or develop executive behaviors, to work through organizational issues, to enhance a career, or to prevent derailment" (Hall et al., 1999, p. 39). Before 1990, coaching was considered to be a remedial technique that was used for managers with flaws or weaknesses. Peterson (2002) noted that by the late 1990s coaching had taken on a positive, proactive tone. He described the old and new assumptions about coaching, which are summarized in Table 8.9.

Although coaches may come from within the organization, external consultants are increasingly being used as coaches. Coaches are generally chosen based on their credibility, trustworthiness, and expertise in coaching and business (Hollenbeck, 2001). Initial studies indicate that executive coaches tend to achieve significant results (Edelstein & Armstrong, 1993; Hall et al., 1999). However, given the high cost of coaching, rigorous research is needed to evaluate its impact on learning and on-the-job behaviors as well as its overall cost effectiveness.

Informal Training

Informal training, which can include specific job assignments, experiences, and activities outside work, has received increased attention as an important part of leadership and management development. The notion is that challenges in the job itself can stimulate learning. McCall, Lombardo, and Morrison (1988) described the "Lessons of Experience" that help propel some managers to the top of their organizations. They noted that learning from experience is a continuous process that often entails dealing with hardship or failure. For example, executives who learn from business mistakes often recognize the importance of being persistent and correcting or compensating for weaknesses. This work suggested that employees must be adaptable and resilient in the face of change and career barriers (London & Mone, 1999).

COACHING

A practical, goal-focused form of personal, one-on-one learning for busy employees that may be used to improve performance, enhance a career, or work through organizational issues or change initiatives.

INFORMAL TRAINING

Training experiences that occur outside of formal training programs. Can include specific job assignments, experiences, and activities outside of work.

TABLE 8.9	Old and New Assumptions about Coaching

ASSUMPTIONS IN REMEDIAL APPROACHES TO COACHING	ASSUMPTIONS FOR POSITIVE PROACTIVE COACHING
People resist change and the coach's task is to motivate them to develop.	People are motivated to learn and grow; the coach's task is to tap into motivation to develop.
Coaching needs to start with a through assessment or needs analysis so people have an accurate picture of themselves and their development needs.	Insight is a never-ending discovery process that is nurtured throughout the entire coaching process; all that is necessary to begin is a good starting point.
Coaches need to provide feedback to the people they coach.	Although feedback from the coach may be helpful, the coach's primary role is to help people improve their ability to nurture deeper insights by gathering their own feedback.
Coaches have a more objective understanding than the participant.	Both coaches and participants have important insights and information. By working together, they can put together a more useful picture of what is happening.
Coaches need to be experts in a given topic in order to teach it to people.	Coaches need to be experts in how people learn so they can help people actually change behaviors and become more effective. One of the most valuable things a coach can do is help people learn how to learn for themselves.
Coaching takes a great deal of time and effort.	Coaching is about finding leverage so that people focus on the one or two things that will have the greatest payoff.
Coaching is about fixing problem behaviors. This assumption often leads to a focus on the past.	Coaching is about improving future performance; it works best when the focus is on understanding what works for the person, what does not work, and what the person will do the next time he or she is in that situation.

SOURCE: Peterson (2002).

On-the-job experiences and informal training can be an important part of the learning and development of managers. For example, work transitions (e.g., taking on a new assignment), task-related job demands (e.g., implementing changes), and job demands from obstacles (e.g., lack of adequate resources) are three important types of work experiences that provide the challenge that promotes learning and development (McCauley, Ruderman, Ohlott, & Morrow, 1994). Job assignments that require high levels of responsibility and critical decision making help managers develop the knowledge, skills, and insights that are critical to effective performance (Tesluk & Jacobs, 1998). In sum, relevant experiences on the job provide informal training that can lead to both short-term (KSAO development) and long-term (job performance, career development) outcomes. Although much training occurs in formal organizational settings, informal training and development can also be a critical component of individual (managerial) and organizational success.

SPECIALIZED TRAINING PROGRAMS
Sexual Harassment Awareness Training

Prohibition against sex discrimination in Title VII of the Civil Rights Act of 1964 includes coverage for **sexual harassment,** which includes direct requests for sexual favors (**quid pro quo sexual harassment**) and workplace conditions that constitute a **hostile working environment.** Sexual harassment claims in the United States have almost tripled in the period from 1991 to 2000, from 7,906 to 21,613, respectively. Sexual harassment has negative consequences for employee health, job satisfaction, organizational commitment, attendance, and productivity (Glomb, Munson, Hulin, Bergman, & Drosgow, 1999). In addition, sexual harassment lawsuits against companies can be extremely costly. Mitsubishi's $34 million settlement in 1998 is the largest ever for a sexual harassment claim. Ford Motor Company recently settled a $7.75 million sexual harassment lawsuit that involved as many as 900 women in Ford plants across the nation (Robinson, 1999).

The Equal Employment Opportunity Commission (EEOC) encourages employers to take steps to prevent sexual harassment, including the following:

- Clearly communicate to employees that the organization has a zero tolerance policy toward sexual harassment.
- Establish an effective complaint or grievance process.
- Take immediate and appropriate action when an employee complains.

In two important cases in 1998, the Supreme Court ruled that an employer's liability can be reduced if it has training programs and other procedures in place to reduce sexual harassment (*Faragher v. City of Boca Raton*, 1998; *Burlington Industries v. Ellerth*, 1998).

Sexual harassment awareness training programs are currently being conducted by many organizations including Sony, Chase Manhattan Bank, CompUSA, and the U.S. Office of Personnel Management (Wexley & Latham, 2002). This awareness training attempts to reduce the incidence of sexual harassment by increasing employee knowledge about the law and about inappropriate behaviors and situations. For example, employees may evaluate various hypothetical scenarios, determining whether they represent a hostile environment and/or quid pro quo. Employees also learn how to access the company's procedure for reporting sexual harassment.

Sexual harassment awareness training for supervisors and employees should have similar content, but supervisors should be given additional training because of their specific duties under the law and because of the formal power inherent in their position (Johnson, 1999). Supervisors and human resource representatives need to know how to implement a response to a sexual harassment charge, from communication of the initial complaint to managing sexual harassment investigations, resolving ongoing harassment situations, executing corrective actions against the perpetrator, and supporting the victim's healing process.

Several studies indicate that sexual harassment awareness training is effective in increasing knowledge about sexual harassment and the ability to identify inappropriate behaviors (Blakely, Blakely, & Moorman, 1998; Moyer & Nath, 1998). Wilkerson (1999) found that frontline supervisors, managers, and executives who had attended awareness training were able to identify harassment more effectively than a similar sample that had not attended training. Unfortunately, this study did not examine whether participants in sexual harassment awareness training were actually less likely to engage in sexual harassment or were more likely to intervene when they saw it happening. Perry, Kulik, and Schmidtke (1998) found that sexual harassment awareness training using videos showing appropriate and inappropriate behaviors increased knowledge acquisition and reduced the inappropriate behavior of those who had a high propensity to harass. However, this training program did not influence participants' long-term attitudes about sexual harassment. Overall, more field research is needed on the short- and long-term effects of sexual harassment

SEXUAL HARASSMENT

Unwelcome sexual advances, requests for sexual favors, and other conduct of a sexual nature constitute sexual harassment when submission to or rejection of this conduct explicitly or implicitly affects an individual's employment, unreasonably interferes with an individual's work performance, or creates a hostile work environment.

QUID PRO QUO SEXUAL HARASSMENT

Involves direct requests for sexual favors, for example, when sexual compliance is mandatory for promotions or retaining one's job.

HOSTILE WORKING ENVIRONMENT SEXUAL HARASSMENT

Occurs when a pattern of conduct, which is perceived as offensive and is related to sex or gender, unreasonably interferes with work performance.

BOX 8.1

A QUESTION OF SEXUAL HARASSMENT

Brenda works in a school office and reports to the principal, Ms. White. Ms. White's husband is a teacher in the school, and Brenda has frequently observed Ms. White criticizing him or being rude to him in front of others. Brenda's impression is that their marriage is unhappy. On several occasions, Mr. White has tried to engage Brenda in conversation and suggested that they have lunch together sometime. Brenda, who is married, did not want to be impolite, so she gave him noncommittal responses. Then one day he came up from behind and kissed Brenda, who pushed him away. Mr. White quickly apologized and asked Brenda not to tell anyone, especially his wife, about the incident.

Would Mr. White's behaviors fit the sexual harassment definition of hostile working environment, quid pro quo, or both? Why?

awareness training, which will remain an important component of training for executives, managers, and their employees.

Ethics Training

An increasingly important consideration for educators and training specialists is whether training can improve ethics or integrity. The highly publicized Enron, Arthur Andersen LLP, and WorldCom accounting scandals in 2002 prompted calls for ethics training in business schools and organizations with the presumption that such courses will improve participants' ethical decision making in the short and long term. Although many companies have ethics training programs, they typically last for only a few hours; moreover, in some cases the behaviors of upper management do not support the principles taught in these programs. An ironic example of this point is the flurry of activity on the Internet auction site eBay by people eagerly attempting to buy items from an ethics training program that Enron once offered for its employees (Hubbard, 2002).

Given how important integrity and ethics are for organizational decision making, an appropriate approach would be to use both selection and training to increase the likelihood that employees will perform their jobs ethically. For example, organizations could select individuals who are high on integrity and conscientiousness, and then provide ethics training and other learning opportunities that supplement an overall Human Resource system that supports ethical behaviors (Wells & Schminke, 2001). As we have discussed throughout this chapter, all types of training benefit from a work environment that supports and further develops the knowledge, skills, and attitudes learned in training.

Cross-Cultural Training

We tend to assume that other cultures exist in other countries, but not here at home. In fact, we all interact daily with people from a variety of cultures, including corporate or work cultures, gender cultures, sports-fan cultures, and politically based cultures. Many employers encounter the greatest cross-cultural challenge when they send employees to work abroad. Such employers are increasingly finding that training is critical in helping **expatriates**—managers and employees who are working abroad—adapt to the new environment. Serious and expensive problems occur when expatriates return from their assignments early because of poor performance or, more commonly, lack of adjustment to the new culture. Expatriate turnover is often attributed to the culture shock that typically occurs four to six months after arrival in the foreign country. Symptoms of **culture shock** include homesickness, irritability, hostility toward host nationals, and loss of ability to work effectively (Cascio, 2003).

To facilitate adjustment to the host country, companies often offer language training programs for expatriates. Many organizations offer additional forms of **cross-cultural training** designed to prepare persons of one culture to interact more effectively with persons

EXPATRIATE

Manager or professional assigned to work in a location outside of his or her home country.

CULTURE SHOCK

Condition typically experienced four to six months after expatriates arrive in a foreign country; symptoms include homesickness, irritability, hostility toward host nationals, and inability to work effectively.

CROSS-CULTURAL TRAINING

Designed to prepare individuals from one culture to interact more effectively with individuals from different cultures; goal is to develop understanding of basic differences in values and communication styles.

EXAMPLE INCIDENT FROM A CULTURAL ASSIMILATOR

A professor was 20 minutes late for an appointment that he had made with two of his graduate students. The students were looking at their watches when the professor finally came into the room. The professor said, "I am terribly sorry I am late."

Which one of the following is most likely in East Asia?

1. The students might jokingly say, "Better late than never."
2. The students might be very aggressive toward the professor in the subsequent discussion.
3. The students would say, "That's OK. We don't mind."
4. The students would be very surprised at the professor's saying that he is sorry.

Alternative Responses

1. The students might jokingly say, "Better late than never." This is not the correct answer. It is not very likely that Asian students would joke with a professor in the classroom.

2. The students might be very aggressive toward the professor in the subsequent discussion. This is very unlikely. It is unlikely for an East Asian student to be aggressive toward a professor. In general, a person in a subordinate position rarely becomes aggressive toward a person in a superordinate position.

3. The students would say, "That's OK. We don't mind." This is the correct answer. Even when students are angry at a professor, they usually do not express their feelings. However, if the students were late for their appointment, then the professor would be angry and would express his impatience.

4. The students would be very surprised at the professor's saying that he is sorry. This is a wrong answer. Being late is certainly thought of negatively in East Asia, and even the professor would apologize to students for his delay.

SOURCE: Harrison (1992).

from different cultures (Bhawuk & Brislin, 2000). The goal of cross-cultural training is to develop trainees' understanding of basic differences in values and communication styles. Because cultural values are usually subconscious, cross-cultural training strives to enhance awareness of these values by using written scenarios as well as behavioral and experiential components that involve active participation by the trainees. Cross-cultural training also attempts to reduce the potential for misunderstandings in cross-cultural interactions. An example of a common misunderstanding that can result from cross-cultural interactions is as follows. A German couple bought an inn in rural Nova Scotia and hired local carpenters to make improvements. The husband then left for a two-week business trip, and the wife found that the carpenters failed to arrive for work. When she made phone calls to find out why they were absent, she learned that, in the local culture, it is unacceptable for a woman to have men working in her house when she is there alone.

A variety of different cross-cultural training approaches have been developed including videos, brief orientation sessions led by consultants, and fully developed cross-cultural training programs. One of the most researched and valid methods of cross-cultural training is the **cultural assimilator,** a written or computer-based tool for individual use which presents a collection of scenarios describing challenging, cross-cultural critical incidents (Triandis, 1995). In this programmed instruction technique, trainees are asked to review the critical incidents and select one of several behavioral alternatives. Next they receive feedback on the cultural implications of their choice and the desired response. Box 8.2 provides an example incident and alternative responses from a cultural assimilator developed by Harrison (1992).

When trainees use a cultural assimilator, they learn about behaviors that are appropriate in their own culture but not appropriate in another culture, and they learn to make attributions that are similar to those made by people in the new culture (Kraiger, 2002a). An assimilator developed for a particular culture is called a **culture-specific assimilator.** Researchers and cross-cultural trainers have developed such assimilators for several countries including Venezuela, China, Greece, Thailand, and Honduras (e.g., Tolbert & McLean, 1995).

CULTURAL ASSIMILATOR

Written or computer-based tool for individual use which presents a collection of scenarios describing challenging, cross-cultural critical incidents.

CULTURE-SPECIFIC ASSIMILATOR

Assimilator developed for a particular culture.

Culture-specific assimilators have been criticized for focusing narrowly on one culture. This criticism is becoming increasingly relevant given that the global workplace often involves interactions with individuals from several cultures. In response to this criticism, a **culture-general assimilator** has been developed that is used to sensitize people to cross-cultural differences that they may encounter across a wide variety of cultures (Cushner & Brislin, 1996). This assimilator consists of 100 critical incidents based on a model of competencies that are valuable in cultural and business interactions in any culture. Bhawuk (1998) extended this work by incorporating Hofstede's (1980) individualism–collectivism construct to develop a theory-based culture assimilator that prepares people for successful interactions in a number of different countries. Bhawuk found that individuals trained using the theory-based assimilator compared favorably to a control group and those trained using a culture-specific assimilator for Japan in terms of satisfaction with the training program, intercultural sensitivity, and the appropriateness of attributions made in difficult critical incidents. Future work will likely continue developing theory-based, cross-cultural training approaches that prepare expatriates for interactions in any culture.

There is also increased interest in cross-cultural training that includes behavior modeling approaches based on social learning theory. Harrison (1992) examined the individual and combined effects of behavior modeling and a cultural assimilator in the cross-cultural training of 65 U.S. government employees. He compared four groups: a control group and three groups that received, respectively, a culture-specific assimilator (based on the Japanese culture), behavioral modeling training, and combined training that included the culture-specific assimilator and behavior modeling. Participants received training in the Japanese culture because it was more likely that they would be assigned there than to some other foreign location. Recall that Box 8.2 provides an example incident and alternative responses from a cultural assimilator developed by Harrison (1992). Compared to those in the control group and those receiving either individual method, participants receiving both methods had significantly higher gains in learning and displayed significantly higher performance on a role-play task. Despite the longer time and effort required by the combined approach, participants viewed it as favorably as each individual method. Thus, the results supported the effectiveness of using the combined approach in terms of reaction, learning, and behavioral criteria.

Three reviews have summarized and evaluated the benefits of cross-cultural training across the wide variety of methods that have been developed. In a review of 29 studies, Black and Mendenhall (1990) found that cross-cultural training had a positive impact on the individual's skill development, situational adjustment, and job performance. Deshpande and Viswesvaran (1992) conducted a meta-analysis of 21 studies and found positive effects of cross-cultural training on adjustment to the host country and job performance of expatriate managers. A recent meta-analysis by Morris and Robie (2001) provided additional support for the finding that cross-cultural training has significant, positive effects on performance. The effects of cross-cultural training on adjustment to the host country were lower than for performance, but were still positive. All three reviews found that evaluation studies of cross-cultural training rarely included an assessment of actual turnover rates and cultural competence, which indicates that future research in this area should focus on examining these important outcomes. Nevertheless, the existing data indicate that cross-cultural training methods are effective in increasing job performance and cross-cultural adjustment.

Recent research has indicated that the cross-cultural adjustment of expatriates is influenced by how well their family adjusts to the new culture (Caligiuri, Hyland, Joshi, & Bross, 1998; Shaffer & Harrison, 2001). If the expatriate's spouse and children are able to establish themselves and fit into the new culture, the expatriate is more likely to perform well in the new job and remain in the international assignment. These studies suggest that organizations that take steps to ensure that spouses and other family members receive cross-cultural training are likely to increase the odds of expatriate success.

From a more general perspective, all employees will increasingly interact with individuals who come from a variety of different cultural and ethnic backgrounds. As we will discuss in more detail in Chapter 11, diversity training is a valuable way to prepare employees for intercultural relations. In this sense, cross-cultural and diversity training have similar goals. In the increasingly global workplace, effective employees will benefit from possessing **intercultural sensitivity,** which is the ability to interpret events in the same way as those from other cultures (Dunbar, 1996). Intercultural sensitivity consists of the following eight dimensions:

1. Comfort with other cultures.
2. Positive evaluation of other cultures.
3. Understanding cultural differences.
4. Empathy for people in other cultures.
5. Open-mindedness.
6. Sharing cultural differences with others.
7. Seeking feedback about how one is received in other cultures.
8. Adaptability.

Intercultural sensitivity can be enhanced through the use of cross-cultural and diversity training techniques that provide opportunities to hear about and discuss similarities and differences across individuals and cultures. K. M. Thomas (1998) suggested that interventions and training programs geared toward improving intercultural relationships should focus on developing multicultural awareness in all employees. Developing multicultural awareness (through cross-cultural training, diversity training, and other methods) should allow employees to make appropriate attributions about diverse colleagues both at home and abroad, which is consistent with the general notion of the culture-general and theory-based assimilators that have been recently developed.

Overall, there are a variety of new developments in cross-cultural training, including an increase in theory-based cognitive and behavioral approaches. Given the global concerns of cross-cultural training, the field will also benefit from increased use of computer-based and multimedia approaches. In addition, cross-cultural training in countries other than the United States is likely to receive increased consideration. Alexander Thomas (1998) and his colleagues in Germany have developed cultural assimilators for German managers going to China and Indonesia, and we expect that researchers from other countries will increasingly develop and use cross-cultural training approaches as well.

> **INTERCULTURAL SENSITIVITY**
>
> *Ability to interpret events in the same way as those from other cultures.*

MODULE 8.4 SUMMARY

- Specialized training programs that are receiving increased attention in organizations include management and leadership development programs, sexual harassment awareness training, and cross-cultural training.

- The increased use of teams and the globalization of the economy require leaders to have broad skills that enhance individual, team, and organizational effectiveness. Trainers have met these challenges with an increased focus on management and leadership development programs that include approaches such as developmental assessment centers, 360 degree feedback, and coaching.

- Sexual harassment awareness training programs attempt to reduce the incidence of sexual harassment by having employees evaluate various hypothetical scenarios to determine if they represent sexual harassment, and by explaining how to access the company's procedure for reporting sexual harassment.

- Cross-cultural training is designed to prepare individuals from one culture to interact more effectively with individuals from different cultures. Employers are increasingly finding cross-cultural training critical in helping expatriate employees adapt to the new environment.

KEY TERMS

development
assessment center
360 degree feedback
coaching
informal training
sexual harassment

quid pro quo sexual harassment
hostile working environment
  sexual harassment
expatriate
culture shock

cross-cultural training
cultural assimilator
culture-specific assimilator
culture-general assimilator
intercultural sensitivity

CRITICAL THINKING EXERCISES

8.7 Some studies have found differences in the way men and women perceive work situations that may be considered inappropriate under sexual harassment laws. How would sexual harassment training be able to address the differing perceptions of men and women?

8.8 Because your boss knows you have taken an I-O psychology course, she asks you to provide a report of the advantages and disadvantages of using 360 degree feedback as part of the management development program. What advantages and disadvantages will you include in your report? Overall, are you optimistic or pessimistic about the use of 360 degree feedback as part of the management development program?

ORGANIZATIONAL PSYCHOLOGY

3 PART

THE MOTIVATION TO WORK

AN INTRODUCTION TO MOTIVATION

THE CENTRAL POSITION OF MOTIVATION IN PSYCHOLOGY

It was a Friday afternoon in November, and Ted was tired. A cold wind was blowing, the sun was going down, and he felt as if the semester had been dragging on forever. As he walked across campus, posters reminded him that the football team had an important game on Saturday, and that one of his favorite groups would be giving a free concert on Sunday. He had promised his parents he'd come home for dinner tonight, and his friends were planning a party after tomorrow's football game. It could be a really fun weekend—but he had two midterms on Monday. Thinking about how great it would be to unwind for a couple of days, Ted considered how well prepared he was for the exams. He knew he didn't stand a chance to ace either one of them without some serious studying over the weekend, but he didn't feel motivated in that direction. He was doing pretty well so far in those classes, one of which was an elective. Maybe he could spend a few hours cramming on Sunday night after the concert. Or he could simply enjoy himself all weekend and go to the exams refreshed and revitalized on Monday. Then again, if he did poorly on the exams, his grades could suffer, which in turn could jeopardize his financial aid package. Ted's dilemma centers around motivation. Motivation is, among other things, about choices. It is about prioritizing goals, choosing where to expend your energy. By the end of this chapter, you will have a better idea of how Ted might find the motivation to study this weekend.

We can see how important the concept of motivation is to psychology by examining the number of research articles and books that incorporate the word "motivation" in the title. From 1950 to 2002, the term "motivation" has appeared in the titles of more than 40,000 publications. Furthermore, we can observe that the importance of motivation seems to be increasing when we consider that, prior to 1980, "motivation" appeared approximately 5,000 times each decade, whereas in the 1980s and 1990s it appeared more than 12,000 times each decade.

Motivation concerns the conditions responsible for variations in intensity, quality, and direction of ongoing behavior (Vinacke, 1962). The motivation of workers has been a key interest for I-O psychologists for almost 100 years (Munsterberg, 1913). In the early 20th century, an I-O psychologist, Hugo Munsterberg, defined a motivation problem among employees of knitting mills. The employees, who worked 12-hour shifts, six days a week, needed to be constantly alert for spools of yarn that were about to run out, so that they could immediately replace them with full spools. To help the employees stay alert, Munsterberg suggested a low-tech form of amusement: allowing kittens to play with balls of wool and yarn on the factory floor. This modification did result in greater worker satisfaction and alertness.

MOTIVATION

Concerns the conditions responsible for variations in intensity, quality, and direction of ongoing behavior.

Historically, factory and millwork has been a popular target for the application of motivational theories. Consider the auto plant of the 1970s described by Barbara Garson (1972):

> The underlying assumption in an auto plant is that no worker wants to work. The plant is arranged so that employees can be controlled, checked, and supervised at every point. The efficiency of an assembly line is not only in its speed but in the fact that the workers are easily replaced. This allows the employer to cope with high turnover. But it's a vicious cycle. The job is so unpleasantly subdivided that men are constantly quitting and absenteeism is common. Even an accident is a welcome diversion. Because of the high turnover, management further simplifies the job and more men quit. But the company has learned to cope with high turnover. So they don't have to worry if men quit or go crazy before they're forty. (p. 73)

The tedium of factory work has been captured in song as well. James Taylor's 1978 song "Millwork" portrays the mind-numbing character of repetitive jobs.

> Millwork ain't easy, millwork ain't hard
> Millwork it ain't nothin' but an awful boring job
> I'm waitin' for my daydream to take me through the morning
> And put me in my coffee break
> Where I can have a sandwich and remember.
> Then it's me and my machine
> For the rest of the morning
> And the rest of the afternoon
> And the rest of my life.

Today's auto plants and textile mills are very different, with substantial automation and liberal use of robots to free the human operator from much of the boredom and danger of factory work. In addition, our understanding of motivation has progressed from kittens on the factory floor to elaborate models involving worker expectancies, goals, feelings of competence, and vastly more interesting tasks for the worker to perform. In this chapter we will consider many of the modern models of work motivation as well as earlier research and theories that brought us to this point.

Motivating workers is a greater challenge in a machine-controlled work environment.

A BRIEF HISTORY OF MOTIVATION THEORY IN I-O PSYCHOLOGY

The earliest I-O theories of motivation were anchored in the notions of **instincts,** principally driven by psychodynamic theories of personality, most notably Sigmund Freud's approach. Instincts were thought to be inborn tendencies that directed behavior. An individual was said to engage in some activity (e.g., work) because of an economic instinct, but the existence of that instinct was inferred from the engagement of that individual in work. This approach eventually proved useless because of its circular nature. In addition to the problem of circularity, since instinct theory emphasized internal causes of behavior, it largely ignored the interaction between an individual and an environment.

The term "instinct" was gradually replaced with terms such as need, motive, and drive (Viteles, 1953). Maslow (1943) proposed a need theory that replaced an infinite number of "instincts" with a specific set of needs. Like instincts, **needs** were thought to be inborn and universally present in humans. Since a great deal of motivational research was being conducted on animals (studying hunger and thirst), **drives** were the nonhuman equivalent of motives and needs. Maslow's need theory allowed for the environment to play a role in motivated behavior by suggesting that when one set of needs was satisfied by environmental forces, the next higher set of needs became activated. He proposed five basic needs ranging from the physical to the aesthetic. We will cover his theory in some detail in the next module.

At about the time that Maslow's need theory was becoming widely known, the behaviorism of B.F. Skinner (1938) was also becoming a powerful force. The **behaviorist approach** placed the emphasis for behavior and directed activity directly on the environment rather than on any "internal needs" or instincts. The disagreements between the behaviorists and nonbehaviorists became known as the "nature versus nurture" controversy. Other, broader approaches also allowed for the influence of the environment, but in a much less mechanical way than suggested by the behaviorists. An example of this broader approach was Lewin's **Field Theory** which proposed that various forces in the psychological environment interacted and combined to yield a final course of action (Lewin, 1935, 1938). Each force was thought to have a "valence" (much like the valences of chemical elements) that attracted or repelled the individual. The application of Lewin's approach in industry became known as **group dynamics.**

Between 1940 and 1960, the struggle for preeminence in motivation theory was between the behaviorists and the need theorists. By 1960 the emergence of cognitive psychology resulted in a radical shift in the battle for "motivational superiority." New motivational theories emerged that emphasized the thought and decision processes of the individual. Today's theories of motivation are largely cognitive at their foundation. The differences among them are more a matter of *what* people think about in choosing courses of action, rather than any dispute regarding *whether* thought enters into motivation.

METAPHORS FOR MOTIVATION

Given the number of citations for the term motivation in the literature, it should not surprise you to learn that hundreds of motivational theories have been proposed in the last 100 years. These theories can be collected into groups such as behaviorist theories, need theories, or cognitive theories, and we will present representative theories in later sections of the chapter. Various theories have appeared as research has clarified various motivational dynamics. To show how motivational thinking has changed over time, we will consider the theories in the order in which they appeared.

Weiner (1991, 1992) suggested that the best way to gain an understanding of the wide variation in motivational theories, as well as of the evolution of motivational thinking, was

INSTINCT
Inborn tendency thought to direct behavior.

NEED
Internal motivation thought to be inborn and universally present in humans.

DRIVE
Nonhuman equivalent of motives and needs.

BEHAVIORIST APPROACH
B. F. Skinner's approach that placed the emphasis for behavior and directed activity directly on the environment rather than on any internal needs or instincts.

FIELD THEORY
Kurt Lewin's approach proposing that various forces in the psychological environment interact and combine to yield a final course of action.

GROUP DYNAMICS
Approach that grew from the application of Kurt Lewin's field theory to industry.

TABLE 9.1	Motivational Metaphors
METAPHOR	**CHARACTERISTIC**
Person as machine	Automatic response by individual
Pushed by internal needs	Responds to needs and drives
Pulled by environmental stimuli	Responds to external stimuli and reinforcement
Person as godlike	Voluntary response by individual
Person as scientist	Analyzes internal and external information
Person as judge	Hypothesizes about the foundation for events and actions of others
Person as intentional	Develops goals and action plans

through the use of metaphors. A metaphor is intended to illuminate an obscure or difficult concept by example. When we say that a supervisor has a "steel-trap mind," we don't expect to open the person's skull and find a steel trap. Instead, we are trying to convey some sense of the supervisor through the use of the metaphor. We may mean that the supervisor has an excellent memory, or is relentlessly logical, or very goal directed. The point is that once a topic or event is on the supervisor's radar screen (another metaphor!), it will not disappear by accident.

Weiner suggested that all motivational theories can be described by one of two metaphors: the person as a machine, and the person as godlike. In his reference to God, Weiner is not invoking any particular religious meaning, but the notion of some entity more capable than most humans. Further, within these two metaphors, certain submetaphors have emerged as motivational theory has matured. We will examine these metaphors in some detail in the following section, but it might help to have a road map (see Table 9.1) before beginning this consideration.

Person as Machine

Machines have the following properties: They have parts that interact, they have a function, their behaviors/actions are reflexive and involuntary and performed without conscious awareness; instead, their actions and reactions are controlled by activating stimuli. Freudian psychoanalytic theory, drive theory proposed by animal learning theorists, behaviorism, and some versions of the Lewin's field theory all support the **"person as machine"** metaphor, as do most motivational theories developed between 1930 and 1960. In the 1950s, learning theorists were forced to incorporate higher order mental processes into their theories (Weiner, 1991), thus making the machine metaphor less applicable. Learning experiments demonstrated that subjects developed expectancies about the connections between actions and rewards and set or accepted goals related to performance.

Person as Godlike

In contrast to machines, godlike entities are thought to be intentional rather than automatic or reflexive, and to be perfectly rational. The early cognitive theories of motivation also assumed that humans were perfectly rational. As one cognitive psychologist wrote, "they are aware of all possible alternative goal-related actions, they know the likelihood

"PERSON AS MACHINE"

Metaphor suggesting that people's behaviors and actions are reflexive and involuntary and are performed without conscious awareness.

that each action will result in goal attainment, and the value of each goal has been determined. Then, all of the available choices are compared regarding their expectancies of resulting in goal attainment and the value of the goals" (Weiner, 1991, p. 925). Many, if not all, modern motivational theories incorporate the notion of expectancies and the role of those expectancies in directing behavior. Thus, we can see that a dramatic shift occurred in motivational thinking in the late 1950s and early 1960s.

The past several decades have also seen a shift in the manifestation of the **"person as godlike"** metaphor. It is a small step from the individual as perfectly rational to the person as an active information gatherer and analyst. This led to a refinement of the godlike metaphor to the "person as scientist" metaphor. As we will see, this metaphor was emphasized in most of the work motivation theories proposed between 1960 and 1990. The **"person as scientist"** metaphor suggested that people sought knowledge and understanding as a way of mastering their environment (Kelley, 1967), indeed that the "ultimate aim of the individual is the accurate prediction of his or her environment" (Weiner, 1991, p. 926). The assumption is that people "want to know." *What* they want to know varies from theory to theory, but not the desire to know.

There is one problem with the person as scientist metaphor, which assumes that individuals are perfectly rational: They aren't. As Dawes (1988) noted:

> Psychologists and behavioral economists studying the decision making of individuals tend to reach the conclusion that individuals do not make decisions based on rational and normative principles. Not only do [they] tend to violate the principle of maximizing expected utility, they are often patently irrational (p. 13).

This inability to reason in perfectly rational ways was recognized by two Nobel prize winners, the psychologist and economist Herbert Simon (1960) and, more recently, the psychologist Daniel Kahneman. Simon described this phenomenon as the **"limited rationality"** of the human decision maker. Kahneman and his research collaborator Amos Tversky have demonstrated the limits of that rationality through both laboratory and field research (Kahneman, Slovic, & Tversky, 1982).

Because of the growing recognition that individuals are not perfectly rational, newer theories of motivation have been emerging, theories that allow for the influence of emotionality on decision making. This in turn has led to a greater emphasis on the social world—the world outside the individual—as opposed to a focus on a completely internal process by which an individual calculates probabilities. Weiner has labeled this new submetaphor the **"person as judge."** Within the context of this metaphor, an individual seeks information about the extent to which the self and others are perceived as responsible for positive and negative events. The person looks for evidence of intention in the actions of others and considers those intentions in choosing a personal course of action. Thus, the I-O view of motivation has become much more socially oriented, and the evaluation of the actions of others has become more central to explaining motivated behavior.

In summary, modern motivational theory tends to view the individual as an active information gatherer (the godlike metaphor) rather than a passive respondent to either internal or external stimuli (the machine metaphor). Further, it is increasingly obvious that the individual is not perfectly rational (the scientist metaphor) in gathering and using information. Instead, the individual is influenced by social information in the form of attributions involving the intentions of others (the person-as-judge metaphor). This evolution of motivational theory has not been accidental or capricious. It has resulted from decades of careful research and theorizing both in the laboratory and in the field. We will use these metaphors to provide a more detailed consideration of motivational theories in Modules 2 and 3 of this chapter. First, however, we need to deal with some other basic issues in work motivation.

"PERSON AS GODLIKE"

Metaphor suggesting that people are perfectly rational and intentional rather than automatic or reflexive.

"PERSON AS SCIENTIST"

Metaphor suggesting that people are active information gatherers and analysts who seek knowledge and understanding as a way to master their environment.

LIMITED RATIONALITY

Inability of humans to reason and make decisions in perfectly rational ways.

"PERSON AS JUDGE"

Metaphor in which an individual seeks information about the extent the person and others are perceived as responsible for positive and negative events; looks for evidence of intent in the actions of others and considers those intentions in choosing a personal course of action.

THE MEANING AND IMPORTANCE OF MOTIVATION IN THE WORKPLACE

Motivation and Performance

In Viteles's (1953) pioneering book on motivation in the workplace, *Motivation and Morale in Industry,* it was clear that he equated motivation with productivity. He saw motivation as the method by which an employer "aroused the cooperation of individual workers" (p. ix). He titled the first section of his book, "Mobilizing the Will-to-Work." He noted that in a survey of employers conducted in 1946, 73 percent identified the "general indifference in workers" as the major reason for a decline in postwar productivity. In the half century since Viteles's book appeared, I-O psychologists have not appreciably changed their general acceptance of the connections among the constructs of motivation, performance, and productivity. Indeed, Pritchard (1990, 1992, 1995) has developed an intricate performance and productivity measurement system called ProMES (Productivity Measurement and Enhancement System) based on the premise that increasing the amount of time and effort that an individual devotes to a task (i.e., increasing the task motivation for a person) will result in high levels of personal performance and increased productivity for the organization. We will examine the ProMES system in some detail in Module 9.4.

A very basic model for considering the role of motivation in performance is the following: Performance = (Motivation × Ability) − Situational Constraints. It is important to take note of the multiplication sign in this conception. This sign means that if motivation is equal to zero, then ability will not matter since anything times zero equals zero. Similarly, it means that even modest increases in motivation can be magnified by ability. In other chapters in the book, we consider ability (e.g., intelligence), performance (e.g., performance on demanding technical tasks), and situational constraints (e.g., stress or difficult working conditions). Although performance can require very complex behavior, you can be certain that motivation plays a role in both successful and unsuccessful performance. It is important to recognize that motivation is not simply about productivity—sabotage and absence are motivated behaviors as well.

Motivation and Work–Life Balance

All of us probably know at least one person we would consider a workaholic: an individual who is addicted to work and pays the cost for that addiction in reduced physical health and mental well-being. In some senses, the workaholic might be described as being *too* motivated because the overemphasis on work has led to an underemphasis on other aspects of life; the workaholic lacks **work–life balance.** We might think of motivation as a resource, with only so much to spread around. If too much is "spent" in one area, there is little left for other areas.

In the early days of motivation theorizing, a great deal of attention was devoted to the concept of "energizing" an individual. It was assumed that unless incentives were available, an individual would remain passive and inert. There is not much support for that view of motivation today. Current motivational discussions revolve around the concept of direction more than simple energy enhancement. All people, unless ill or impaired, will expend energy in one way or another. The same principles that apply to work motivation will apply to the motivation to do things other than work. In some senses, the employer is always competing with other forces for the time and attention of the employee. Some employers might consider a workaholic to be a "win" because the person devotes inordinate energy to work.

The nonworkaholic employee feels tension between competing forces: work on the one hand, and family, leisure, and healthful activities on the other. A consideration of work motivation in a vacuum is a meaningless exercise. Work motivation can only have

WORK–LIFE BALANCE

Area of research that investigates whether the satisfaction one experiences at work is affected by the satisfaction one experiences in nonwork and vice versa, particularly to the extent that one environment has demands that conflict with the other.

meaning within the context of a rich and complex life in which there are forces competing with the workplace for time and effort. We will consider the challenge of this work–life balance in detail in Chapter 10.

Motivation and Attitudes

As we noted in the last section, Viteles's (1953) book was titled *Motivation and Morale in Industry*. "Morale" was the term commonly used to include work-related attitudes and the concept of job satisfaction. It was believed that a happy worker was a productive worker and that somewhere in the mix, we would also find work motivation. The foundation for that belief is not clear. Perhaps the notion was that if you make a worker happy, he or she will reward the organization with productivity, or that unhappiness is distracting. Most motivational models are hedonistic at some level. They assume that individuals seek conditions of pleasure rather than conditions of pain. A typical motivational analysis would attempt to identify what work characteristics were capable of making a worker happy or unhappy. This would be done by means of an attitude survey. **Attitudes** are the relatively stable feelings or beliefs that are directed toward specific persons, groups, ideas, jobs, or other objects. If the respondents to the survey indicated that their current work was boring and made them unhappy, then the employer was advised to use work of a higher interest level as an incentive for higher levels of productivity. Offering or exposing a worker to more interesting work was assumed to increase his or her motivation to work. Attitudes and attitude measurement were seen as pathways to uncovering the motivational key.

Attitudes have become less important in the study of work motivation over the last several decades. In 1950 the general belief was that different things motivated different people. As a result, it was critical to assess the level of satisfaction with various motivators to know how to increase or maintain work motivation for any individual. But beginning with the cognitive theories that began to appear in the early 1960s, the "conditions" for motivation became more explicit and universal, and less individually based. For example, goal-setting theory proposed that setting hard and explicit goals for individuals was motivating. We didn't need to ask the worker to express his or her attitude about the goal-setting process or the goals that had been set. It was assumed that goals were important for all individuals. Attitudes and their measurement remain important in many areas of I-O psychology, and we will cover those topics in great detail in Chapter 10.

Motivation and Personality

As we have seen in Chapter 3, I-O psychologists generally agree that personality can be divided into dimensions such as agreeableness, conscientiousness, and so forth. We have also

ATTITUDES
Relatively stable feelings or beliefs directed toward specific persons, groups, ideas, jobs, or other objects.

"What do you think . . . should we get started on that motivation research or not?"

seen that personality can be a predictor of work performance. Since we know that motivation can also affect work performance, it is reasonable to consider what, if any, connections may exist between personality and work motivation. Judge and Ilies (2002) recently completed a meta-analysis on exactly that topic. They examined the relationship between measures of the Big Five personality traits and various indicators of motivation from several current motivational theories. These indicators included the number and difficulty of goals set by an individual, belief on the part of the individual that hard work would lead to rewards, and belief on the part of the individual in his or her ability to perform a task or job. Judge and Ilies found 65 studies and 105 correlation coefficients that could be included in the meta-analysis.

The results showed that strong and consistent relationships do exist between personality characteristics and performance motivation. Neuroticism was consistently negatively related to performance motivation (recall that the positive end of the neuroticism scale is emotional stability). In contrast, conscientiousness was positively related to all indicators of performance motivation. Put another way, conscientious and emotionally stable individuals set more challenging goals, were more likely to believe that hard work would lead to rewards, and were more confident in their ability to accomplish a task or job.

The personality-motivation connection is an important one, since past theories of work motivation give little emphasis to individual difference measures such as personality traits. They tend to take a one-size-fits-all approach. Nor have work motivation theories paid much attention to individual differences in cognitive ability, assuming instead that everyone is "smart enough" to set and remember goals and calculate expectancies. Perhaps one of the reasons why the person-as-scientist theories have lost their appeal is that not everyone is as intelligent or emotion-free as the scientist assumed by the theory. As motivation theory evolves into the person-as-judge metaphor, it should be increasingly valuable to look at personality traits in our attempts to understand work motivation.

MODULE 9.1 SUMMARY

- Worker motivation has been a key interest for I-O psychologists for almost 100 years. The earliest I-O theories of motivation were anchored in the notions of instincts. The term "instinct" was gradually replaced with terms such as need, motive, and drive.

- Weiner suggested that the best way to understand the wide variation in motivational theories, as well as of the evolution of motivational thinking, is through one of two metaphors: the person as a machine, and the person as godlike. Within these two metaphors, certain submetaphors have emerged as motivational theory has matured.

- Modern motivational theory views the individual as an active information gatherer (the godlike metaphor), rather than a passive respondent, to either internal or external stimuli (the person-as-machine metaphor). Further, it is increasingly obvious that the individual is not perfectly rational (the person-as-scientist metaphor) in gathering and using information. Instead, the individual is influenced by social information in the form of attributions involving the intentions of others (the person-as-judge metaphor).

- Early and modern approaches to motivation are based on the premise that increasing the amount of time and effort that an individual devotes to a task (i.e., task motivation) will result in higher levels of individual performance and increased productivity for the organization. A basic model for considering the role of motivation in performance is: Performance = (Motivation × Ability) − Situational constraints.

- In recent decades, attitudes have become less important in the study of work motivation, whereas personality characteristics have become more important.

KEY TERMS

motivation

instinct

need

drive

behaviorist approach

Field Theory

group dynamics

person-as-machine

person-as-godlike

person-as-scientist

limited rationality

person-as-judge

work–life balance

attitudes

CRITICAL THINKING EXERCISES

9.1 People engage in many dangerous behaviors, including smoking, substance abuse, driving without seatbelts, and so on. How can these behaviors be accounted for using the person-as-machine metaphor?

9.2 Competitive individuals are often described as having a "fire burning inside." Would this explanation be more compatible with instinct theory, the person-as-machine metaphor, or the person-as-godlike metaphor? Why?

MOTIVATIONAL THEORIES—CLASSIC APPROACHES

PERSON-AS-MACHINE THEORIES

Earlier in this chapter, we presented an overview of motivational theories in the form of two metaphors: person-as-machine and person-as-godlike. We will use those metaphors as organizing devices for a consideration of some representative theories of work motivation.

As you will recall, the machine metaphor is based on the premise that motivation is a largely unconscious process, in which the individual responds to internal conditions (e.g., needs or drives) or external stimuli (e.g., rewards) in a reflexive or automatic way. We will consider two classic examples of these two mechanical approaches, an internal theory and an external theory.

An Internal Mechanical Theory: Maslow's Need Theory

Maslow (1943) proposed that all humans have a basic set of needs and that these needs express themselves over the life span of the individual as internal "pushes" or drives. As such, it was more a theory of human development than a theory of work motivation. Generally, the theory proposed that when we are young, we are more concerned with our physical well-being. As we become more secure in our physical world, we then begin to emphasize social needs. Finally, when our social foundation seems secure, we then concentrate on developing our abilities and capacities to their fullest.

I-O psychology found **Maslow's need theory** (See Figure 9.1) attractive for considering the specialized issue of work motivation and adapted it to the work setting. Before examining its application to work, let's examine the critical elements of the theory. Maslow suggested that every person has five basic need sets. He further proposed that these need sets were arranged hierarchically; one need set would have to be fulfilled before the next higher need set was activated. These need sets, arranged from the lowest or most basic to the highest or most advanced, are described as follows:

1. *Physiological needs:* Learning theories generally refer to these as basic needs or drives which are satisfied by such things as food, water, and sleep.

2. *Security needs:* This category refers to the need of an individual to produce a secure environment—one free of threats to continued existence.

3. *Love or social needs:* These needs are associated with interpersonal factors. They refer to an individual's desire to be accepted by others.

4. *Esteem needs:* These needs are associated with being respected for accomplishments or capabilities.

5. *Self-actualization needs:* These needs refer to an individual's desire to develop his or her capacities to the fullest. In Maslow's theory, few people would ever completely

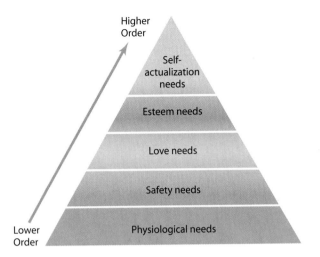

FIGURE 9.1
**Maslow's Hierarchy
of Needs**

satisfy this need. Instead, the individual would always be seeking to grow and develop. Some exceptions might be Martin Luther King, Jr., Gandhi, or Mother Teresa (although even they might have claimed that they were not finished "growing").

In Maslow's theory, individuals would be motivated to fulfill the most basic set of unfulfilled needs. If an individual's physiological and security needs were fulfilled, then the individual would expend energy attempting to fulfill the love needs. When the love needs were met, the individual would be "motivated" by circumstances that would satisfy the esteem needs, and so on. Should a lower-level need that had once been satisfied reemerge (e.g., a life threatening illness occurs to a formerly healthy person), the person would immediately revert to actions that might satisfy that now-unsatisfied lower-level need.

When we apply Maslow's approach to the work setting, some interesting implications arise. The first, and most important, implication is that to influence motivation, the employer needs to know at what need level the individual worker is operating. If the employer is offering opportunities for esteem as an incentive for hard work when the worker is concerned about making enough money to feed a family, the employer's incentives will have little effect. The second implication, equally important, is that a group of workers may all be functioning at different needs levels, requiring a motivational scheme tailored to each individual.

As you can see, Maslow's model fits the person-as-machine metaphor quite well. The behavior of the individual is unconscious and automatic. The individual will respond to whatever satisfies the lowest level of unfulfilled need. In addition, as Maslow proposed that all individuals operate in the same manner, the theory is universal. Even though Maslow's theory is seldom explicitly invoked by organizations today, the existence of the benefits/rewards menu or smorgasbord in many organizations indicates that Maslow's theory has had some influence on modern organizational practices. For example, workers are allowed to choose among alternative rewards and benefits packages, which can address multiple needs.

Maslow's theory has been a popular way to think about work motivation, even though there has been relatively little research directly testing his propositions, and the research that has been carried out has not been particularly supportive. For example, Hall and Nougaim (1968) found that the more a need was met or satisfied, the more important it became. This is a direct contradiction of Maslow's idea about how the hierarchy functions. Several other studies (Lawler & Suttle, 1972; Wahba & Bridwell, 1976) also failed to find support for the model, in part because the theory was somewhat

BOX 9.1

EMPLOYEE HIERARCHY OF NEEDS

Although Scott Adams's cartoon character, Dilbert, is hardly a "scientific reference," even Dilbert seems to acknowledge Maslow's hierarchy. As you can see in the pyramid, Dilbert identifies six need levels rather than the five proposed by Maslow. As Adams explains:

> Before you can hope to motivate employees you must understand their hierarchy of needs. Employees will not develop a need for things at the higher levels of the pyramid until they have totally satisfied their needs at lower levels. Make sure they get plenty of the stuff on the lower levels, but not so much that they develop a need for more money.

SOURCE: Adams (1996).

More money

False hope of advancement

Recognition

Thrill of empowerment

Artificial challenge created by poor planning and inadequate resources

Coffee, donuts, caffeinated soft drinks

simplistic, not directly acknowledging that most of us have many different needs that operate simultaneously rather than one at a time. Why, then, has it proven so popular? In part, the answer is historical. It was the first theory to acknowledge that different people might have different needs in the workplace. If there was a theory of work motivation prior to Maslow's, it was a simple economic one: Money motivated all people. The individual differences perspective made more sense (and still makes some sense) to both workers and managers. Maslow's was also a simple theory to understand, and took an attractively optimistic view of *Homo sapiens* as a self-actualizing organism. As you will see in later theories, many elements of Maslow's thinking have endured, particularly the notion of needs. What has not stood the test of time is the idea of a hierarchy for these particular need categories.

In addition, of course, the nature of work has changed dramatically since 1943. The country was in the midst of World War II and had just come out of a damaging depression that had left many lower-level needs unfulfilled. The fear of unemployment would continue to stalk all who experienced the Great Depression of the 1930s. Social Security was a rudimentary program, and other social safety nets such as unemployment insurance or medicare did not exist then. In addition, most work was fairly uncomplicated, non-technological factory work. As we have seen, work has changed and motivation theory has changed with it.

Variations on Maslow's Theory Since Maslow's five factor need theory was introduced, psychologists have suggested a number of modifications. (For a lighter variation of need theory, see Box 9.1.) The first, proposed by Herzberg, was called the **two-factor theory.** Herzberg (1966) suggested that there were really two basic needs, not five, and that they were not so much hierarchically arranged as independent of one another. These two needs were called **hygiene needs** (Maslow's physical and security needs) and **motivator needs** (Maslow's social, esteem and actualization needs). Herzberg believed that meeting hygiene needs would eliminate dissatisfaction, but would not result in motivated behavior or a state of positive satisfaction. In contrast, meeting motivator needs would result in the expenditure of effort as well as positive satisfaction. Although Herzberg's theory generated considerably more research than the "parent" theory of Maslow, the support for his theory was as disappointing as it had been for Maslow. As with Maslow's

TWO-FACTOR THEORY

Herzberg suggested two basic needs, not five, and they were independent of one another.

HYGIENE NEEDS

Lower-level needs described in Herzberg's two-factor theory; meeting these needs would eliminate dissatisfaction, but would not result in motivated behavior or a state of positive satisfaction.

MOTIVATOR NEEDS

Higher-level needs described in Herzberg's two-factor theory; meeting such needs resulted in the expenditure of effort as well as satisfaction.

theory, it was also difficult to determine exactly what Herzberg's theory might predict (King, 1970).

Alderfer (1969, 1972) suggested that, instead of the five factor structure of Maslow or the two factor structure of Herzberg, human needs are best thought of as arranged in three levels. He labeled these levels "existence" (the physiological and security levels of Maslow), "relatedness" (combining parts of Maslow's love and esteem need categories), and "growth" (combining the remaining aspects of Maslow's esteem level with his self-actualization category). Alderfer adopted the hierarchical dynamic of the Maslow approach, suggesting that the lowest-level unmet need category would dominate an individual's behavior and interests. He also suggested that if a need were frustrated, then an individual might "regress" or activate a lower-level need that had been met previously. While I-O psychologists have not found much support for the hierarchical elements of **ERG theory,** they have found modest support for the notion that three need categories seem more likely than the two of Herzberg or the five of Maslow, at least in the work setting (Rauschenberger, Schmitt, & Hunter, 1980; Wanous & Zwany, 1977).

These needs theories are mainly of historical rather than functional value. Today's theorists and practitioners have little enthusiasm for an approach that does not allow for the concepts of expectancy, evaluation, or judgment on the part of the individual.

An External Mechanical Theory: Reinforcement Theory

Approximately 60 years ago, a young psychologist working on problems of animal learning discovered that the manner by which rewards were connected to behavior could have a dramatic effect on animal performance. The psychologist was B. F. Skinner, now considered the father of modern behaviorism. In its simplest form, behaviorism (or **reinforcement theory**) proposes that behavior depends on three simple elements: stimulus, response, and reward. It would not matter if the behavior being observed were that of a white rat in an experimental cage, a child learning how to use a knife and fork, or a worker faced with a production challenge. The mechanical proposition of behaviorism is that if a response in the presence of a particular stimulus is rewarded (i.e., reinforced), that response it likely to occur again in the presence of that stimulus. Consider, for example, a monetary bonus as a reward in a work setting. If a worker produces at a particular level, and receives a bonus for that performance, reinforcement theory predicts that the worker is more likely to achieve that level of performance again in the future.

When a reward depends on a response, it is called a **contingent reward** (i.e., the reward is contingent on the response). Contingent reward or reinforcement is a central proposition of the behaviorist approach. A second important proposition has to do with the schedule of reward or reinforcement. Rewards can be given continuously (every time a correct response occurs, a reward is presented) or intermittently (only a portion of correct responses are rewarded). Skinner (Ferster & Skinner, 1957) discovered that **intermittent rewards** actually produced higher levels of performance than **continuous rewards.**

These two principles—contingent reinforcement and differing schedules of reinforcement—have been applied frequently in the industrial context; examples include piece work payment in manufacturing, year-end performance bonuses, sales commissions, and the like. We will present an example of this application in the last module of this

Pulling a lever is not an intrinsically interesting task, but people will do it repeatedly if they believe it yields generous rewards on an unpredictable timetable.

INTERMITTENT REWARD

System in which only a portion of correct responses are rewarded.

CONTINUOUS REWARD

System in which a reward is presented every time a correct response occurs.

chapter. In Chapter 16, you will find another example of the application of reinforcement theory, in this case to the driving behavior of pizza delivery drivers.

Although the results of experiments using contingent reinforcement—whether in the classroom, the nuclear family, or the workplace—can be impressive, many problems are associated with this approach to the concept of motivation. First, the approach is impractical. There are few jobs or tasks that can be so neatly compartmentalized as the job of a pizza delivery driver. Single contributor jobs are rapidly giving way to team and group work. In addition, we cannot observe some of the most important behaviors that occur in the workplace, because they are not simple physical actions but complex cognitive processes. If we observed a technician troubleshooting a piece of electronic equipment, the behavior we observed would be looking at the equipment, referring to a manual, and occasionally activating the equipment, but when the equipment was finally fixed, we would recognize that it was fixed as a result of some behavior we could *not* observe: gathering information, thinking, and hypothesis testing. Finally, the principle of contingent reinforcement requires careful observation of the behavior of the worker, an additional and time-consuming task for a supervisor. More importantly, however, the approach had no role for any cognitive activity. As we indicated in the introduction, behaviorism, like other person-as-machine theories, could not account for expectancies, the effects of goals, or even the simplest of intentions on the part of the worker. Locke (1980) presented an excellent critical review of the strengths and shortcomings of behaviorism in the role of a theory of motivation. We are not arguing that reinforcement theory is "wrong" or ineffective; nevertheless, as a complete theory of work motivation, behaviorism falls short, as do other person-as-machine approaches that fail to acknowledge higher mental activities such as reasoning and judgment, and thus, it represents more of a historical artifact in the evolution of motivation theory than a viable approach.

PERSON-AS-GODLIKE THEORIES: THE SCIENTIST MODEL

By 1970 most areas of psychology were caught up in the so-called cognitive revolution. Motivation theory, and work motivation theory in particular, were no exception. The key ingredient in this approach was the capacity of an individual to learn from the past and anticipate the future. This allowed for the possibility of intentional behavior, planning, goal acceptance, and, most importantly, choice. The mechanical theories did not include the concept of choice in any formal way. To use Weiner's "godlike" metaphor, workers were now seen as rational beings capable of gathering and analyzing information, and making decisions based on that information.

PATH-GOAL THEORY

First formal work motivation theory to suggest that people weighed options before choosing among them; if a worker saw high productivity as a path to the goal of desired rewards or personal goals (e.g., a pay increase or increased responsibility), that worker would likely be a high producer.

VIE THEORY

Motivation theory that assumes individuals will rationally estimate the relative attractiveness and unattractiveness of different rewards or outcomes (valence), performance will lead to particular outcomes or rewards (instrumentality), and effort will lead to performance (expectancy).

VALENCE

Strength of a person's preference for a particular outcome.

Vroom's VIE Theory

The first formal work motivation theory to suggest that people weighed options before choosing among them was the **path-goal theory** of Georgopolus, Mahoney, and Jones (1957). They reasoned that if a worker saw high productivity as a path to the goal of desired rewards or personal goals (e.g., a pay increase or promotion, or increased power, prestige, or responsibility), that worker would likely be a high producer. Conversely, if low productivity was seen as a path to desired rewards (e.g., less stress, more time with family, approval of co-workers), that worker would likely be a low producer.

This theory was a simple one in conception, but it marked a dramatic shift in thinking about motivation: a shift from the person-as-machine to the person-as-scientist. The new approach was presented in a considerably more elegant way by Vroom (1964) in the **VIE theory** (valence, instrumentality, expectancy). In chemistry, a valence refers to the attracting or repelling force of an element. Vroom reasoned that psychological objects in an environment also have attracting and repelling forces; **valence** is the strength of a person's preference for a particular outcome. Most people would find that money is attracting while uninteresting work is repelling. For the most part, this element of Vroom's theory was not much different from the earlier person-as-machine approaches. It was a simple recognition that people have needs or desires.

The second element in Vroom's theory, instrumentality, represented the answer to the question, If I am able to perform as expected, will I receive what has been promised? **Instrumentality** deals with the relationship between performance and the attainment of a certain outcome. Consider a promotion. A promotion usually means a higher salary as well as increased prestige. But it may also include increased responsibility, longer hours, and even lower total annual compensation (since most managers and supervisors are not eligible for overtime pay). So you can see that there may be many instrumentalities in a given situation, each one related to the valued or nonvalued circumstances of a particular outcome, such as the promotion. This is where the person-as-scientist comes in. Vroom proposed that once an individual became aware of these various instrumentalities, he or she could combine that information in such a way as to decide whether, on balance, the outcome would be more positive than negative (i.e., there were more positive valences than negative valences associated with the outcome). This analysis would then lead to some choice of action.

The third element of the theory, **expectancy,** had to do with an individual's belief that a particular behavior (e.g., hard work) will lead to a particular outcome (e.g., a promotion). When we put the three elements (V, I, E) together, we can see the complete theory. The theory proposes that individuals ask themselves the following questions:

1. *Valence:* To what extent do I value those other outcomes and how will they combine into a bottom-line result that I would characterize as either "good" or "bad"?
2. *Instrumentality:* Is the outcome I am anticipating (e.g., a promotion) likely to yield other outcomes (e.g., longer working hours thus increased work-family conflict, a change in compensation, resentment from former co-workers who are now subordinates, different tasks)?
3. *Expectancy:* Is the action I am considering (e.g., working hard, staying late, volunteering for a difficult task) likely to lead to a desired outcome (e.g., a promotion)?

As you can see, the theory assumed that the individual was a "calculator." He or she was expected to estimate the probability that a behavior (e.g., hard work) would lead to an outcome (e.g., a promotion), the probability that a primary outcome (e.g., a promotion) would lead to secondary outcomes (e.g., compensation changes, working hour changes), and the relative attractiveness and unattractiveness of those secondary outcomes. A manager who wanted to apply Vroom's theory would concentrate on three things:

1. Connect positively valent benefits to outcomes.
2. Clarify instrumentalities by letting employees know what benefits might accrue from an outcome.
3. Clarify expectancies by letting employees know that an action would lead to an outcome.

As was true of the need theories described earlier, there have been many variations of Vroom's VIE theory (Graen, 1969; Lawler, 1971; 1973; Porter & Lawler, 1968). Research on the model seemed to support the notion that effort was related, to some extent, to cognitions (i.e., perceived expectancies and instrumentalities). Nevertheless, research also indicated that in making behavioral choices, individuals considered things other than instrumentalities and expectancies. The VIE model was elegant and uplifting. It elevated the status of the individual to one of a rational being. Nevertheless, it may have pushed the notion of rationality beyond reasonable limits by assuming that people could and would go through the somewhat tortured calculations necessary for all but the simplest

INSTRUMENTALITY

Perceived relationship between performance and the attainment of a certain outcome.

EXPECTANCY

An individual's belief that a particular behavior (e.g., hard work) will lead to a particular outcome (e.g., a promotion).

of decisions. Not surprisingly, humans have been found to fall short of the cognitive capabilities of godlike entities.

In addition, VIE theory ignored many noncognitive elements in choice, such as personality and emotion. A more recent meta-analysis has raised an additional point (Van Eerde & Thierry, 1996). The original theory, as proposed by Vroom, was a within-individuals theory (i.e., which of Y choices would be most attractive to a single individual) rather than a between-individuals theory (i.e., which of X people would be more motivated). Unfortunately, Van Eerde and Thierry found that most of the research was done on the *between*-individuals version of the theory. In many respects, the job of a manager is to motivate each individual. Thus, the between-person results are largely irrelevant to the challenge of increasing motivation within a single individual.

Dissonance Theory

In 1957 Festinger proposed **dissonance theory** which suggested that tension exists when individuals hold "dissonant cognitions" (incompatible thoughts). For example, consider an individual who purchases a new sports-utility vehicle and later discovers that this SUV is prone to rollover accidents. The individual now has two incompatible thoughts: "I am a smart person who made a wise purchase of a neat car" versus "I am not a very smart person; I just bought an expensive new car that may result in my death or injury." This individual will then expend energy to reduce the tension caused by these dissonant cognitions. The energy may be directed toward the manufacturer of the car, and the new owner may try to return the SUV for a refund. Alternatively, the new owner may convince him- or herself that the rollover tests were inaccurate, or that it is really driver behavior rather than vehicle characteristics that are responsible for rollovers. One way or another, energy will be expended to reduce the tension resulting from dissonant cognitions. This approach assumes that individuals always seek some sense of "balance" (i.e., absence of tension) and will direct their behavior toward seeking and maintaining that balance.

Equity Theory

Adams (1965) transplanted Festinger's ideas to the workplace and developed a theory that has come to be known as **equity theory.** He suggested that individuals look at their world in terms of comparative **inputs** and **outcomes.** Like Vroom's VIE theory, Adams proposed that people are calculators, but in a somewhat different way than Vroom proposed. They calculate what they are investing in their work (e.g., training, effort, abilities) and what they get out of it (e.g., compensation, co-workers, interest level of the work itself). They then compare their inputs and outcomes to those of **"comparison others"** (e.g., peers, co-workers) by developing a ratio. If their own **input/outcome ratio** was identical to the input/output ratio of their comparison other, then there would be no tension, and no subsequent action to relieve that tension. Consider the example of a sales representative for a medical company who discovers that even though she is receiving a 5 percent commission on gross sales, a representative for the same company in a neighboring state is receiving a 7 percent commission. According to equity theory (and common sense), something is bound to happen. This "something" might be a call to the sales manager requesting an increase in commission rate, a call to a recruiter to look for a new job, an attempt to sabotage the efforts of the fellow sales representative, or a reduction in postsales contacts with customers (activities that, while expected, generate no direct income in the short term).

The mathematical description of equity theory appears as Figure 9.2. In this formulation, O stands for outcomes and I stands for inputs. The subscripts p and o stand for "person" and "other" (i.e., comparison person or comparison other). As you can see,

---

DISSONANCE THEORY

Festinger's theory that tension exists when individuals hold "dissonant cognitions" (incompatible thoughts); assumes that individuals always seek the absence of tension and will direct their behavior toward reducing it.

EQUITY THEORY

Adams's motivational theory that individuals look at their world in terms of comparative inputs and outcomes; individuals compare their inputs and outcomes with peers or co-workers by developing an input/outcome ratio.

INPUTS

Training, effort, skills, and abilities that employees bring to or invest in their work.

OUTCOMES

Compensation, satisfaction, and other benefits employees derive from their work.

COMPARISON OTHERS

Co-workers or other idealized persons to whom the individual compares him or herself in determining perceived equity.

INPUT/OUTCOME RATIO

Results when employees compare their inputs and outcomes to those of peers and co-workers to determine if they are being treated equitably.

$$\frac{O_p}{I_p} = \frac{O_o}{I_o}$$

Equity

$$\frac{O_p}{I_p} > \frac{O_o}{I_o} \qquad \frac{O_p}{I_p} < \frac{O_o}{I_o}$$

Inequity

FIGURE 9.2   **Mathematical Description of Equity Theory**

when the ratio of input to outcome is the same for p and o, a condition of equity exists. However, if either the $O–I$ ratio for "person" is higher or lower than the ratio for "other," inequity exists, creating a state of tension.

The early laboratory studies of equity theory used method of payment as a way of manipulating outcomes. Participants were assigned to either an hourly payment or piece rate payment, and they were either intentionally overpaid or underpaid. Overpayment participants were told that more money was available than had been originally anticipated and, as a result, they would get $2.25 per hour instead of the agreed upon $1.50 per hour (remember, these studies were done in the 1960s!) or 10 cents a piece instead of 7 cents a piece. Conversely, in the underpayment condition, participants were told that less money was available than originally anticipated and, as a result, they would be paid $1.50 per hour (or 4 cents a piece) instead of the $1.75 per hour (or 7 cents a piece) originally promised. Table 9.2 presents the predicted reactions of the participants. Generally, results supported the underpayment predictions but not the overpayment ones. Evidently, being paid more than you expected is neither painful nor tension producing for most people.

Most of the research on equity theory was definitional. What was an "outcome"? What was an "input"? Who was a "comparison other"? Can outcomes (e.g., access to a training program) become inputs (i.e., increased ability level)? Do outcomes (e.g., salary or praise) diminish in value over time? Are individuals capable of or willing to conduct the often intricate calculations implied by the theory (Birnbaum, 1983; Landy, 1989; Mellers, 1982)? Is a moral maturity dimension involved in equity considerations (Vecchio, 1981)? As was the case with VIE theory, many researchers and practitioners questioned whether workers were as "rational" as the theory suggested. The only difference between them is that equity theory proposes a socially based rationality and VIE theory makes no explicit mention of any "comparison other."

TABLE 9.2	Equity Theory Predictions of Employee Reactions to Inequitable Payment	
	UNDERPAYMENT	**OVERPAYMENT**
Hourly payment	Subjects underpaid by the hour produce less or poorer-quality output than equitably paid subjects.	Subjects overpaid by the hour produce more or higher-quality output than equitably paid subjects.
Piece-rate payment	Subjects underpaid by piece rate will produce a large number of low-quality units in comparison with equitably paid subjects.	Subjects overpaid by piece rate will produce fewer units of higher quality than equitably paid subjects.

SOURCE: Steers, Porter, & Bigley (1979).

MODULE 9.2 SUMMARY

- Maslow proposed that all humans have a basic set of needs which express themselves over the life span as internal drives. He further proposed a hierarchical arrangement of these needs: One need set must be fulfilled before the next higher need set is activated. Maslow's theory has been a popular way to think about work motivation, even though there has been relatively little research supporting it.

- Two principles from behaviorist reinforcement theory—contingent reinforcement and differing schedules of reinforcement—are often applied in the work context. Nevertheless, as a complete theory of work motivation, behaviorism falls short because it fails to acknowledge higher mental activities such as reasoning and judgement.

- Person-as-godlike theories include Vroom's VIE theory and equity theory, both of which assume that individuals are intentional and rational in their behavior. The primary difference between them is that equity theory proposes a socially based rationality, whereas VIE theory makes no explicit mention of any "comparison other."

KEY TERMS

Maslow's need theory

two-factor theory

hygiene needs

motivator needs

ERG theory

reinforcement theory

contingent reward

intermittent reward

continuous reward

path-goal theory

VIE theory

valence

instrumentality

expectancy

dissonance theory

equity theory

inputs

outcomes

comparison others

input/outcome ratio

CRITICAL THINKING EXERCISES

9.3 During the summer of 2002, a drought in the Southwest led to many forest fires. Several of these fires were set intentionally by a part-time firefighter anxious to make additional money. Apply two classic theories of motivation to this behavior.

9.4 The stars of TV shows often threaten to leave the show unless they are paid more money for each episode, even though they are already making a substantial salary. For example, the stars of "Friends" make more than $1 million per episode. Using either equity theory or Vroom's VIE theory, explain the tendency among these stars to ask for more money.

MODERN APPROACHES TO
WORK MOTIVATION

PERSON-AS-INTENTIONAL

VIE theory and equity theory seem cumbersome because of their heavy reliance on the person-as-scientist model and, in particular, the concept of perfect rationality. But they share another characteristic as well. Both assume that individuals' behavior is intentional. Other motivation theories arose at the same time as equity and VIE theory with less emphasis on the "person-as-scientist" and more emphasis on the notion of intentional behavior.

Goal-Setting Theory

The most representative of the **person-as-intentional** approach is **goal-setting theory** as proposed by Locke and his colleagues. Unlike need, equity, and VIE theory, goal-setting theory has endured and evolved into a mature and comprehensive approach to work motivation. Thus, even though it arose in the "classic" period for motivational theories, it has become a distinctly modern theory.

The notion of a goal as a motivational force has been well established (Baldamus, 1951; Locke, Shaw, Saari, & Latham, 1981; Ryan, 1970). Austin and Vancouver (1996) presented a detailed history of the concept and a framework that suggests that, one way or another, any coherent description of motivated behavior must include goals. Locke (1968) was one of the first to adapt the general concept of goals to work motivation; one of the most comprehensive descriptions of the theory appears in a book by Locke and Latham (1990). In a subsequent paper, Locke and Latham (1996) pointed out that it does not require much investigation to establish the centrality of goals in everyday life. Without prodding, people will readily express their actions in terms of a purpose: You take a course to prepare for a career; you take a job to explore an occupation; you go to the gym to improve your general fitness or a specific muscle group. These purposes can also be thought of as intentions or goals. It is this notion of purposefulness and intentionality that is peculiar to goal setting theory.

A simple representation of goal setting theory appears in Figure 9.3. Research on this basic theory has been supportive. Most studies show that specific, difficult goals lead to higher levels of performance, assuming that the individual has accepted the goals. For a student with a cumulative GPA of 2.5, a goal of achieving a GPA of 3.4 in the next semester would likely be a specific, difficult goal. This is true both within subjects (i.e., you will perform better if you set a harder goal than an easier one) and between subjects (individuals who set hard goals perform better than individuals who set easy goals). It also appears to be true that individuals who set specific, difficult goals perform better than individuals who simply adopt a "do your best" goal or no goal at all.

This model makes a distinction between goal acceptance and goal commitment. Goal acceptance implies that a goal has been assigned. Goal commitment is broader and can include not only assigned goals but self-set goals as well. As we will see shortly, when individuals are

PERSON-AS-
INTENTIONAL
APPROACH

Motivational approach that assumes individuals are intentional in their behavior.

GOAL-SETTING
THEORY

Approach in which the general concept of a goal is adapted to work motivation; a goal is seen as a motivational force, and individuals who set specific, difficult goals perform better than individuals who simply adopt a "do your best" goal or no goal at all.

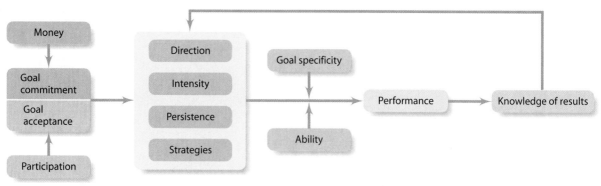

<figure>**FIGURE 9.3** **A Diagram of Goal Theory**</figure>

FEEDBACK LOOP

Connection between knowledge of results and the intermediate states that occur between goal commitment and performance.

free to revise assigned and accepted goals, these goals can become self-set, thereby transforming what was acceptance into commitment. Most recent versions of goal-setting theory have concentrated on the concept of commitment (Mitchell, Thompson, & George-Falvy, 2000).

The model identifies the mechanisms, or intermediate states, by which goals affect performance. Locke et al. (1981) proposed that goals have the effect of "directing attention and action (direction), mobilizing energy expenditure or effort (effort), prolonging effort over time (persistence) and motivating the individual to develop relevant strategies for goal attainment (strategy)" (p. 145). Another important factor is the **feedback loop** between knowledge of results and the intermediate states between goal commitment and performance. This feedback connection makes the theory much more dynamic by showing that as the individual evaluates his or her performance, intermediate states may be changed. For example, if an individual falls short of a specific hard goal (e.g., to get an A on a term paper), he or she may concentrate harder on library research to the exclusion of other leisure activities (direction),

An important element in the goal setting theory of motivation is feedback. Production charts are used to motivate workers on a production floor.

increase the number of hours spent reading course material each a week (effort), start the term paper sooner next time (persistence), or take advantage of the instructor's office hours for guidance on the paper (strategy). If the individual does one or all of these things, then he or she is eventually more likely to meet the hard goal of completing the term paper in time to polish it and make sure it qualifies for a high grade. This feedback loop broadens goal-setting theory from a "snapshot" theory of a single action or sequence of actions into a richer consideration of not only present, but past and future as well.

This feedback loop is associated with what has come to be known as **control theory.** Control theories assume that an individual compares a standard (in this case the goal) to an actual outcome and adjusts behavior to bring the outcome into agreement with the standard. A more recent and detailed presentation of control theory appears in Figure 9.4. As you can see, the researchers recognized additional factors that might influence ultimate goal accomplishment. These include task complexity, situational constraints, level of goal commitment, affect or emotion, and level of organizational commitment. In addition, note that rewards (and punishments) that have nothing to do with goal accomplishment can also affect the level of commitment of the individual to the organization and the subsequent willingness to accept continued or new goals.

Having accepted the contribution of goal setting theory, Mitchell et al. (2000) identified a number of practical issues that remain to be addressed.

- Should goals be related to quantity or quality of performance? The answer seems to be that quantity and quality are related such that when high quantity goals are set, the quality of performance declines. To prevent such slippage, it seems best to set both quality and quantity goals rather than one or the other.
- Should goals be related to process or outcomes? Process goals refer to *how* work is done. Outcome goals are related to the actual level of production. The conclusion is that process goals may be more appropriate for complex tasks, as these may require a great deal of learning. If the task is relatively simple, outcome goals will lead more quickly to higher performance.
- How should goals be set? The three major methods for setting goals are to assign them, to ask individuals who will receive the goals to participate in setting them, and to ask individuals to set their own goals. The emerging consensus is that participative goal setting is most effective, although assigned goals can also be effective if they are "sold"

CONTROL THEORY

Based on the principle of a feedback loop, which assumes that an individual compares a standard to an actual outcome and adjusts behavior to bring the outcome into agreement with the standard.

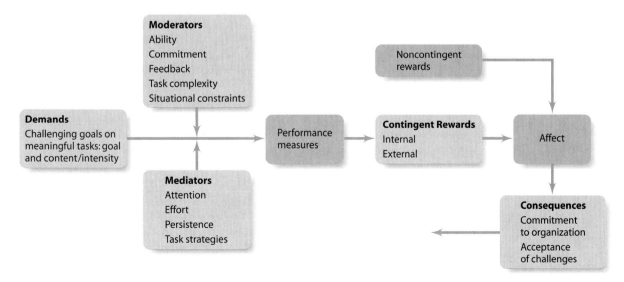

FIGURE 9.4 Control Theory View of Goal Setting Source: Austin and Klein (1996).

rather than simply dictated. In a later section of this chapter, however, we will see that cultural issues may come into play as well. In high power distance cultures, individuals may prefer assigned goals over participatively set goals.

• How many goals should be set? The answer to this question is that multiple goals are acceptable, but they should be examined closely to make sure they are compatible (e.g., a goal of increasing production by 10 percent would be incompatible with a goal of decreasing overtime by 10 percent). It may also be wise to assign weights or priorities to multiple goals, since some are likely to be more important than others. As mentioned earlier in this chapter, Pritchard (1995) developed a method for increasing motivation and performance (ProMES) that incorporates such a weighting scheme. We will examine ProMES in Module 9.4.

• How difficult is a difficult goal? There is no good answer to this question. Difficulty can be determined by comparison to an individual's typical performance or by comparison to the performance of others. Generally, a difficult goal would be one that could be achieved by no more than 10 percent to 20 percent of the people attempting it, or by individuals only 10 percent to 20 percent of the time that they attempt it. The critical issue is that individuals need to view a goal as possible, otherwise they will not accept it.

• Should rewards be contingent on goal accomplishment? The conclusion is that when goals are of medium difficulty, rewards are appropriate for goal accomplishment. If the goals are very difficult, the individual should be rewarded for partial goal attainment, otherwise the goals themselves may become unattractive over time. It might also be appropriate to increase the bonus or reward as the individual gets closer to the difficult goal. It appears that if rewards are given on an all-or-nothing basis (i.e., no rewards unless complete goal accomplishment occurs), easy goals result in underperformance and difficult goals result in quitting. The best result seems to come from incremental rewards linked to increments of achievement, much like piece rate systems.

• When should individual goals be used and when should group goals be used? Mitchell et al. (2000) suggested that the answer depends on the nature of the task. If the task requires interdependence and cooperation, group goals might be appropriate, whereas if the work is independent and workers are sole contributors, individual goals may be more appropriate. Once again, however, we need to introduce the concept of culture. In collectivist cultures, it may be difficult to work within an individual goal setting program; to do so may even be viewed as offensive.

Challenges for Goal-Setting Theory   The changing nature of work will present new challenges for the continuing development and relevance of goal-setting theory. Locke and Latham have depended heavily on laboratory and field research for the development of their theory (Locke, 2001; Locke & Latham, 1996). Historically, a great deal of that research involved single contributors working on relatively simple tasks. Today's workplace, however, is increasingly complex and team-based, so the research design needs to include more complex cognitive work in order to adapt the theory to the new work environment. In addition, Locke acknowledged (2001) that current research efforts should be directed toward integrating variables such as knowledge and skill into the model.

Recently, some researchers have begun an ambitious program of looking at the effect of goal setting on complex cognitive tasks (Atkins, Wood, & Rutgers, 2002; Wood, Atkins, & Tabernero, 2001; Wood, Falvy, & Debowsky, 2001). These research designs include some relevant cognitive tasks, such as conducting automated literature searches on the Internet and examining the effect of the form of feedback on decision making. This is exactly the type of research that can help goal-setting theory to remain relevant.

Levels of Explanation in Goal Setting   When Locke introduced goal-setting theory, he presented it as a relatively simple way to increase performance by recognizing a very human characteristic that seemed to be missing in other theories: intention. But Locke and Latham

FIGURE 9.5 The Relationships among Needs, Motives, Goals, and Performance
SOURCE: Locke & Latham (1996).

(1996) wisely made the point that simply identifying a goal to which a person may be committed does not fully explain the individual's behavior. They suggested that goal-setting theory is just a first-level explanation of behavior. Goals are seen as the most immediate antecedents to behavior. But the question of where goals come from remains. Locke and Latham hypothesized that goals may very well derive from higher-order concepts such as values or motives. These would be second-level explanations of goal-setting theory. They gave the example of a person who has a goal to become CEO within 15 years of joining the company, and that this goal derives from a motive of ambition. They also invoked the notion of the Type A personality. (We will see in Chapter 15 that a Type A personality, among other characteristics, seeks to accomplish more and more.) The Type A person is likely to set multiple and difficult goals obsessively, particularly when competing with others. Still a higher order, or third level, of explanation would investigate where motives or values originate. As you will recall, Maslow suggested that motives were inborn. All three levels describe an influence on action or behavior, but at increasingly higher levels. As you can see in Figure 9.5, needs influence motives, motives influence goals, and goals influence performance. As Locke and Latham (1996) pointed out, the closer the level of explanation is to the behavior in question, the stronger the connections.

The notion of levels of explanation leads us to examine other current theories of work motivation. As you will see, goals and goal setting play an important role in these theories. In some senses, the theories we will now consider are actually second-level explanations of behavior in the context of goals and goal setting. One way or another, they all include goals.

Control Theories and the Concept of Self-Regulation

In the goal-setting model presented above, we pointed out the feedback loop between the actual results of behavior (i.e., performance and goal achievement) and the intermediate states. Control theory is based on the principle of a feedback loop. A simple example of a feedback loop is the thermostat in your home. When the temperature increases, the thermostat rises, and when it reaches a set point, it signals the heating system to turn off. When the temperature drops below a certain level, the thermostat once again signals the heating system to bring the heat back on until the set temperature is achieved. The essence of a thermostat, or any control system, is the feedback loop. The system revolves around discrepancies; in the case of room temperature, the discrepancy is between the actual temperature of the room and the thermostat setting. Figure 9.6 presents a simplified view of a control model.

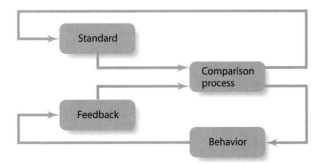

FIGURE 9.6   Simple Control Systems Model SOURCE: Taylor, Fisher & Ilgen (1984).

The feedback loop in goal-setting theory deals with the discrepancy between actual goal accomplishment and the goal to which the individual was committed. Locke and Latham (1996) suggested that if the individual falls short of the goal, intermediate states will be influenced. It is also possible that an individual might replace the goal with an easier one (or negotiate with a supervisor or manager to make the goal easier). But this is just the tip of the iceberg with respect to work behavior in its richest form. Individuals have multiple goals, some assigned and some unassigned. In addition, the priority of these goals can change overnight based on shifting organizational priorities. Individuals can make more progress on some goals than others, and feel more or less confident about the likelihood of achieving some goals rather than others. All of these complications introduce another concept into the motivational mix: the concept of self-regulation.

SELF-REGULATION

Process by which individuals take in information about behavior and make adjustments or changes based on that information; these changes affect subsequent behavior (e.g., strategies, goal commitment).

Self-regulation is compatible with control theory. In its simplest form, **self-regulation** means that individuals take in information about behavior and make adjustments based on that information, just as the heating system takes in information and makes adjustments. The only difference is that the heating system doesn't feel bad or depressed when the temperature in the room drops. It never asks the question, Is the temperature perhaps set too high? Should I adjust the setting? It simply makes an adjustment. But humans have bad days when they lose confidence in themselves and question the goals they have accepted or set for themselves. The complexity of the workplace suggests that instead of a simple feedback loop, there are many feedback loops which are arranged in hierarchies. The person receives information about performance, abilities, and organizational expectations and, as a result, makes changes in behavior, experiences differing emotions, and may even change his or her self-image (i.e., becoming more or less confident in his or her abilities, or the likelihood of accomplishing a goal). These changes in turn affect subsequent behavior (e.g., strategies, goal commitment).

We are not trying to bewilder you with the complexity of understanding why individuals expend effort in a particular direction. Instead, we are trying to impress on you the concept that people are active self-regulators who depend on multiple feedback loops for adjusting to changes in their internal and external environments. To make matters even more complicated, some theorists (Gollwitzer, 1990; Kuhl, 1992) proposed that differences exist among individuals with respect to their focus on external or internal cues. It has been suggested that those who focus on external or environmental cues are more likely to engage in self-regulation than those who focus inward (Austin & Klein, 1996). Cognitive abilities may also play a major role in an individual's capacity to engage in self-regulation (Kanfer, 1992; Kanfer & Ackerman, 1989; Kuhl & Kraska, 1989). It is safe to say that individuals need to depend on cognitive abilities such as memory, reasoning, and comprehension (verbal and oral) for processing feedback and changing behavior.

THE CONCEPT OF SELF-EFFICACY IN MODERN MOTIVATION THEORY

You can probably recall occasions when you were not feeling very confident about accomplishing a goal (e.g., getting a good grade on a midterm examination). This feeling of confidence (or lack thereof) was labeled "self-efficacy" by Bandura (1986), and it has come to play an increasingly important role in most modern theories of work motivation. **Self-efficacy** is defined as the belief in one's capacity to perform a specific task or reach a specific goal (Bandura, 1997). This is different from the broader notion of self-esteem, which is the pride someone feels from having accomplished a difficult task. The social aspect of esteem is that we experience it when we gain the respect of others. Efficacy relates more specifically to our confidence in our ability or the likelihood that we will be able to successfully complete a difficult task. According to Bandura, individuals arrange goals from the most immediate to the most distant. Immediate (or proximal) goals provide

SELF-EFFICACY

Belief in one's capability to perform a specific task or reach a specific goal.

opportunities for satisfaction and increased feelings of self-efficacy, while maintaining interest in the task. Since proximal goals are also correlated with distant goals, they facilitate progress toward those less immediate goals. To revisit our earlier example, taking and passing a course in calculus (proximal goal) is related to eventually getting a job in engineering (distant goal). If you successfully complete the course, you will increase your confidence in successfully completing other courses, as well as in your eventual ability to succeed in a career related to that course. Thus, after passing the calculus course, you would be more likely to sign up for additional courses, and possibly take other steps leading to a particular career (e.g., schedule a summer internship).

Bandura's model incorporates elements of control theory in the following way. According to Bandura (1991), individuals are constantly monitoring their behavior and accomplishments to see whether their behavior is moving them closer to or farther away from important goals. The evaluation leads to both emotional and cognitive reactions. If a person is making progress toward goals, or meeting or even exceeding goals (a "positive discrepancy"), the result is satisfaction and an increase in feelings of efficacy. This in turn leads the person to set higher goals within the limits of his or her ability. In contrast, if a person is not making progress toward goal accomplishment or fails to meet a goal (a "negative discrepancy"), the result is dissatisfaction and a reduction in feelings of efficacy. Possible reactions to this negative evaluation include changing strategies, lowering or abandoning one's goal, or increasing effort (Donovan, 2001). Bandura proposed that motivated behavior involves a cycle of setting challenging goals, monitoring success at meet-

According to efficacy theory, coming close to winning will motivate some people to try harder next time.

ing these goals, taking actions to reduce any discrepancies (positive or negative) between the goal and the outcome, then setting new and more challenging goals, starting the cycle all over again (Bandura, 1986).

Some researchers are skeptical of the effect of overshooting a goal, which Bandura suggests should lead to the establishment of higher goals. Klein (1991a; 1991b) suggested that when goals are met or exceeded, people "say 'good enough,' and focus their attention on other concerns" (p. 35). This is similar to the observation in equity theory that people have no problem dealing with overpayment. No tension is created and there are few behavioral consequences. There is too little research on the issue of positive discrepancies to draw any conclusions from these criticisms at this point.

Since efficacy is so central to goal-directed behavior and performance, it is reasonable to ask how efficacy is developed and increased. Wood and Bandura (1989) suggested four separate avenues:

- *Mastery experiences:* Successful performance of challenging tasks strengthens beliefs in one's capabilities, while failures decrease those beliefs.
- *Modeling:* People have a tendency to compare their capabilities with those of others. When an individual sees someone similar (in terms of abilities, knowledge, and so forth) succeed at a difficult task, the individual's own beliefs in efficacy can be strengthened. If, on the other hand, this comparison person fails, then the individual's efficacy beliefs will be reduced.
- *Social persuasion:* Individuals can be encouraged by others who express confidence in their ability to accomplish a difficult task.
- *Physiological states:* When people experience the symptoms of stress or fatigue, they tend to interpret this as an indication that the task exceeds their capabilities, thus reducing their feelings of efficacy. Techniques that reduce stress or fatigue will increase one's feelings of efficacy while completing a difficult task.

How can we put these approaches to work in increasing our own self-efficacy or the self-efficacy of a friend or co-worker? Consider the following possibilities:

1. Provide guidance or technical or logistic support to the individual, increasing the likelihood that he or she will experience success on a challenging task (i.e., a mastery experience).
2. Provide successful role models, perhaps by pairing an individual with a fellow worker of similar experience who has mastered a difficult task.
3. Be a targeted "cheerleader" emphasizing the individual's knowledge and ability (as opposed to simply expressing confidence that he or she will succeed).
4. Take steps to reduce stress in the individual's environment that is unrelated to the challenging task.

There is an enormous amount of research activity surrounding goal-setting theory, feedback loops, and efficacy. The very concept of efficacy is becoming increasingly refined. For example, Wood and his colleagues distinguished between search efficacy and processing efficacy in complex cognitive tasks (Wood, Atkins, & Tabernero, 2000). Search efficacy dictates the breadth and depth of the search for information. In a literature search, this might mean how many key words are used and how they are connected. Individuals with low search efficacy would choose fewer key words and would seldom link them. Processing efficacy, in contrast, describes the confidence that an individual has in whether he or she, once having acquired the information, can transform it into something useful. They suggested that individuals low in one or both of these efficacies will perform very differently from individuals high on these two separate efficacies. With the increase in the extent that the modern worker does more cognitive than strictly physical work, research such as this will become increasingly important.

It is much too early to draw any firm conclusions about a complete and credible explanation of motivated behavior. Nevertheless, it is not too early to be confident that any ultimate explanation will involve the concept of efficacy.

ACTION THEORY

ACTION THEORY (RUBICON THEORY)

Includes broad consideration of the role of intention in motivated behavior as well as the connection between intention and action.

Perhaps the broadest consideration of the role of intention in motivated behavior appears in the form of what has become known as **action theory.** This approach is most popular among German applied psychologists (Frese & Sabini, 1985; Frese & Zapf, 1994; Gollwitzer, 1993; 1999; Gollwitzer, Heckhausen, & Ratajczak, 1990; Heckhausen, 1977) and is also known as the **Rubicon theory,** based on a famous incident involving Julius Caesar's civil war on Rome and the Roman Senate. Prior to crossing the Rubicon River with his legions on the way to Rome in 49 B.C., Caesar asked his advisors if this was a wise plan. Having concluded that it was reasonable, Caesar did cross the river, thereupon opening himself to the charge of high treason. One of his advisors then revisited the wisdom of the decision to wage war in Rome. Caesar is reported to have said that he would not talk about *whether* to wage war, but only how to win it (Heckhausen, Gollwitzer, & Weinert, 1987). Caesar had moved on from the decision to wage war to developing a plan to win the war. His advisors had not yet made that transition. Their minds were still on the other side of the Rubicon.

Gollwitzer (1993) has written extensively on the connection between intention and action, distinguishing between goal intentions ("I intend to achieve X") and implementation intentions ("I intend to initiate the goal-directed behavior X when I encounter situation Y"). He is particularly interested in how people turn intention into action. He identified four consecutive action phases in active goal pursuit:

1. *Predecisional*—examining one's desires in order to determine which desire is the strongest and most feasible to attain.
2. *Postdecisional*—planning and developing strategies for successful action.

3. *Actional*—expending effort to achieve the desired outcome.

4. *Evaluative*—comparing what was achieved with what was desired.

Gollwitzer believed that intentions are particularly important for overcoming any obstacles that may arise in phases 1 or 2. Also, people are far more likely to accomplish goals when both goal intention and implementation intention are present.

When we have competing wishes and desires, we can remind ourselves of our intentions, and it is the intentions that help us establish priorities so that we can eliminate conflicts between our wishes and desires. This is closely related to Locke and Latham's concept of commitment: Once an intention is formed as a result of establishing priorities, there is no longer any need to deliberate contrasting alternatives. Once Caesar crossed the Rubicon, it was no longer necessary to debate the wisdom of that course of action. In addition, implementation intentions help us to articulate when, where, and how we intend to achieve our goals (Gollwitzer, 1993). You decide that you will complete your term paper by the middle of the semester. You buy some new software for your computer, set up a schedule for a period of research each week and post that schedule on your door, apply for a study carrel in the library, cancel plans for a trip with friends, and ask a professor if you can sit in on some lectures in another class that relate to your term paper. Because you have both a goal intention and an implementation intention, the chances are greatly enhanced that you will have your term paper completed by the middle of the semester.

Frese and Zapf (1994) published the most accessible description of action theory. An action (e.g., performing a work task) has two elements: the **action process** and the **action structure.** The action process is displayed in Figure 9.7. An action starts with a goal (or choice among goals), and proceeds to a consideration of events that may occur in the future, then to the development of several alternative plans, the selection of one of those alternative plans, the execution and monitoring of the chosen plan, and, finally, the processing of information resulting from the execution of the plan. The last step, feedback, then influences the goal development process once again.

The action structure includes two aspects. The first is the notion that no observable action occurs in a vacuum. It is the result of a number of prior events and plans, hierarchically arranged. The second is that the feedback and resulting regulation of actions occur at different levels. Some are at the conscious level (e.g., was my performance up to the standard I expected?) and others are at an unconscious or automatic level (e.g., adjusting the swing of a hammer to hit a nail more solidly).

In some senses, action theory is proposed as an alternative to motivation theory. Hacker (1992) notes that often, the highest performers in a job are those with the best understanding of the job rather than those who are most motivated. Action theorists are, by definition,

ACTION PROCESS

Starts with a goal, proceeds to a consideration of possible future events, then to the development of alternative plans, the selection of a plan, the execution and monitoring of the chosen plan, and the processing of information resulting from the execution of the plan; the last step, feedback, influences goal development once again.

ACTION STRUCTURE

Includes the notion that (1) observable action is the result of a number of prior events and plans, hierarchically arranged and (2) the feedback and resulting regulation of actions occur at different levels.

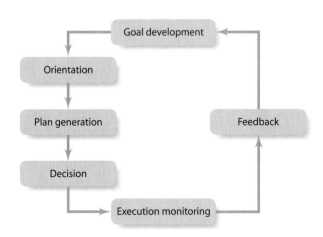

FIGURE 9.7

The Action Process
SOURCE: Frese & Zapf (1994).

more concerned with action than motivation. Nevertheless, this may ultimately be a semantic exercise. The goal-setting advocates would claim that there is little difference between the various hierarchical levels of the action structure and the notion of goal specificity. Further, they would claim that the action process is virtually identical to the elaborated goal-setting and feedback model presented in Figure 9.4 (the newer version of goal-setting theory).

The action theorists are strongly cognitive in their orientation. The goal-setting theorists are cognitive as well, but also see a role for emotions and beliefs. It would not be difficult to graft these emotion and belief components onto action theory, and we might predict that such a combination will occur in the next few years. Certainly, the goal-setting theorists acknowledge that their model needs to be more fully developed. In addition, they realize that the model must be expanded to deal with multiple and occasionally conflicting goals. An action theory framework might help with this development.

COMMON THEMES IN MODERN APPROACHES

After examining the modern approaches to motivation theory, can we find any common themes? Yes, there are several. First, intention plays a key role in motivated behavior. The most common form of that intention is a goal. Any viable theory of motivated behavior will need to have a goal-like element. These goals will be associated with anticipated happiness or unhappiness. Second, the concept of feedback is critical if we are to consider any but the simplest act at one point in time. Third, the theory needs to include some element of the person-as-scientist. The person need not be a completely rational or accurate scientist, but must be considered an information gatherer and analyst. Fourth, the theory should include some concept of self-assessment. It is clear that individuals commonly take stock of where they are compared to where they want to be. Finally, there will be some noncognitive element in the "ultimate" motivation theory. This element may be personality, or values, or even the feeling that arises from the efficacy belief. What is becoming clearer from motivational research is that individuals are not just primitive scientists, they are critical scientists as well. They do not merely use information, they evaluate and judge it. As a result, the person-as-scientist metaphor is giving way to that of the person-as-judge.

From a practical standpoint, then, I-O psychologists know a great deal about motivation, even without a complete and comprehensive theory. The challenge to motivation theory now is more theoretical and research-based than practical. We have many of the pieces to the puzzle, we simply need to figure out how to assemble them. But another problem may emerge while we are assembling the puzzle. The nature of work will not stand still. It has changed radically and will continue to change. The real challenge will be to craft a theory that can deal with work as it exists in the 21st century: work that is team based, technological, multicultural, rapidly changing, and done for organizations with limited loyalty to their members.

MODULE 9.3 SUMMARY

- The most representative of the person-as-intentional approach is goal-setting theory, which has evolved into a mature and comprehensive approach to work motivation. The notion of a goal as a motivational force is well established. Most studies indicate that specific, difficult goals lead to higher performance, assuming that the individual has accepted the goals.

- Additional motivational theories use the concept of goals and goal setting. Control theory is based on the principle of a feedback loop, which deals with the discrepancy between the set goal and the actual goal. Control theory suggests that people are active self-regulators who depend on feedback for adjusting to changes in their environment.

- Self-efficacy, which is playing an increasingly important role in most modern theories of work motivation, can be developed through mastery experiences, modeling, social persuasion, or physiological states. There is an enormous amount of research on the relationships between goal setting, feedback, and self-efficacy.

KEY TERMS

person-as-intentional approach

goal-setting theory

feedback loop

control theory

self-regulation

self-efficacy

action theory (Rubicon theory)

action process

action structure

CRITICAL THINKING EXERCISES

9.5 Many top-level executives have pay packages tied to the value of their company's stock. As the stock price goes up, an executive's bonus goes up. This has been identified as one possible reason for the recent scandals derived from the overstatement of corporate earnings to drive stock prices higher. How could goal-setting theory be used to alter this method of compensation?

9.6 Recall the last time you did less well than you had expected in an examination. Using the feedback loop concept of control theory, describe how you altered your behavior to prepare for the next examination in that subject.

PRACTICAL ISSUES IN MOTIVATION

CAN MOTIVATION BE MEASURED?

The short answer is yes. As we saw above, there are motivational indicators like the number and difficulty of goals accepted by an individual, or the strength of a person's belief that hard work will yield rewards. Thus, we can estimate the motivation of a person in a particular context. But what about the broader issue of whether some people are simply more motivated, generally, than others? As we saw earlier in the chapter, Judge and Ilies (2002) seem to suggest that conscientiousness and emotional stability may be surrogates for a general level of motivation. It is more likely that their results mean that certain trait requirements may be needed for motivational interventions to work, rather than simply assuming that certain personality types are "naturally" motivated.

MOTIVATIONAL TRAIT QUESTIONNAIRE (MTQ)

Provides a standardized method of assessing six distinct aspects of general performance motivation.

Kanfer and her colleagues (Heggestad & Kanfer, 2001; Kanfer & Ackerman, 2000; Kanfer & Heggestad, 1997) have developed an instrument known as the **motivational trait questionnaire (MTQ)**. The MTQ measures six distinct aspects of what might be called "general" motivation. These aspects are assessed by a 48-item questionnaire. The general areas and some sample items assessing them appear in Table 9.3. Some of the areas (e.g., emotionality) are quite close to other well-known personality dimensions, such as emotional stability, that form the Big Five theory. But Kanfer and Ackerman have focused more

TABLE 9.3	Sample Items from the Motivational Trait Questionnaire

Desire to learn—the need to achieve by learning new skills or acquiring knowledge ("I prefer activities that provide me with an opportunity to learn something new").

Mastery—personal goal setting and continued task improvement even when not required ("I set high standards for myself and work toward achieving them").

Other referenced goals—tendency to compare performance to the performance of others ("Whether I feel good or not about my performance depends on how it compares to the performance of others").

Competitiveness—a focus on competition and wanting to do better than co-workers or peers ("I would rather compete than cooperate").

Worry—concerns about having one's performance evaluated ("Before beginning an important project, I think of the consequences of failing").

Emotionality—focus on the emotions of being evaluated in a performance context ("I am able to remain calm and relaxed before I take a test").

Source: Kanfer & Ackerman (2000).

directly on personality in the performance context. The MTQ has been carefully constructed and is the basis for a good deal of ongoing research. It does appear that the MTQ is one standardized method for measuring general performance motivation.

CROSS-CULTURAL ISSUES IN MOTIVATION

As you have seen in many earlier sections of the book, the changing nature of work has made the issue of culture a critical one in many areas of I-O psychology. Motivation is no exception. Kanfer's model of motivation, presented above, can be used to highlight some of these cultural issues. For the purposes of this discussion, recall the cultural theory of Hofstede (2001). He proposed that cultures differed on the basis of five dimensions: (1) collectivism–individualism, (2) uncertainty avoidance, (3) masculinity–femininity, (4) power distance, and (5) long-term versus short-term orientation. Consider the theory and the MTQ questionnaire broadly. The first thing you notice is that it is directed toward the individual. Each sample question revolves around "I." It would appear that the questionnaire is more suitable for an individualist culture than a collectivist one.

The MTQ dimensions themselves raise the same question. In a collectivist culture, would an individual who is not interested in competition, mastery, or comparing his or her performance to that of a peer or coworker be considered unmotivated? As another example, recall Hofstede's view of masculinity and femininity as a cultural continuum. Masculine cultures tend to value success while feminine cultures tend to value interpersonal relations. Hofstede's masculinity–femininity dimension predicts that women in low masculine cultures will describe themselves as more competitive than men, while the opposite would be true in high masculine cultures. Would a woman from a high masculine culture (e.g., Japan) be considered less motivated when compared to her male counterparts? What about the woman from the high masculine culture being compared to her female counterpart from a low masculine culture (e.g., Sweden)? Would the woman from the high masculine culture be considered less motivated? Finally, the Hofstede dimension of uncertainty avoidance suggests cultural interpretations of the MTQ. Hofstede (2001) speculated that in low uncertainty avoidance cultures, "achievement" can be recast as "hope for success," while in high uncertainty avoidance cultures, "achievement" is more appropriately thought of as "fear of failure."

We are not criticizing the work of Kanfer and her colleagues in these examples. On the contrary, we commend them for exploring individual differences in performance motivation and developing an instrument to assist in that exploration. Their research is quite new, and it is reasonable to pursue the theory and questionnaire within one culture before looking at its applicability across cultures. There is reason, however, to suspect that cultural differences will appear. Kanfer and Ackerman (2000) have already uncovered differences in response patterns to the MTQ as functions of age and gender. There is every reason to suspect that similar differences will emerge when the instrument and theory are examined from the cross-cultural perspective.

Erez (1997) noted that across all cultures, managers tend to employ four types of motivational practices:

1. Differential distribution of rewards—rewarding high performers.
2. Participation in goal setting and decision making—allowing subordinates to help make decisions.
3. Design and redesign of jobs and organizations—modifying task assignments and reporting relationships.
4. Quality improvement interventions such as total quality management (TQM) or quality circles—focusing subordinates on strategic objectives.

She then demonstrated how these motivational interventions need to be modified to fit the culture in which they are applied. As an example, in an individualist culture with low power distance (e.g., the United States), profit- and gain-sharing programs might work well as a way to distribute rewards. In contrast, in a collectivist culture with high power distance (e.g., Japan), it might be more suitable to distribute rewards unequally to organizational units or divisions, but equally within those units. Similarly, if we look at goal setting, in individualist cultures characterized by high power distance, it might be more appropriate to assign goals to the worker rather than involve the worker in setting those goals. In contrast, in collectivist cultures characterized by low power distance, the work group might be responsible for goal setting, while in a high power distance culture, group goals might simply be assigned to the group.

The practical implications of culture for work motivation are substantial. As Erez and Eden (2001) noted, in the past it might have been unusual for workers from one culture to work alongside those from another culture, that is, to work with "foreigners." Now the practice is so common now that the word "foreigner" is rarely used, and it is generally considered insulting rather than descriptive. Not only do new workers come from different cultures with different expectations, but it is also increasingly likely that a supervisor or manager may bring a new culture into the workplace. While I-O psychologists within a given culture may have the research and theory to support a particular motivational intervention within that culture, the value of that intervention will decrease in direct proportion to the multicultural nature of the company and workforce. We have barely scratched the surface of understanding the implications of culture for work motivation.

GENERATIONAL DIFFERENCES AND WORK MOTIVATION

In most families, the behaviors and interests of children—in music, dress, food, and attitudes toward work—differ substantially from the behaviors and interests of their parents. Given that culture is defined as a circumstance of shared values, generational differences could be construed as differences between cultures, much like the differences between nationalities as discussed by Hofstede (2001). In much the same way, there often seem to be differences in work values between workers (and managers) who are from one generation and those from a different generation. A generation (sometimes called a "cohort") is defined by group members who share birth years and significant life events (Kupperschmidt, 2000). The implication of this definition is that the accident of the birth years places individuals in the same "life experience" pool, and, as a result, is likely to have an influence on the values of the members.

Generation Xers are generally defined as those born between 1961 and 1980 (Waclawski, 1999). The term "Gen X" has often been used in a stereotypical way, ascribing various characteristics to the "younger" generation in a universal fashion. There has been a continuing debate about the extent to which Gen Xers, who may now be in their early 40s and working as middle managers, subscribe to the same motivational techniques and theories as managers who were already in the workplace when earlier studies were conducted.

Consider the following debate between a critic of the "new" values and a member of the "new" generation:

THE CRITIC: [They] grow up painfully, commercialized even in their school days, they cannot spell, flimsy, shallow, amusement seeking creatures, their English is slipshod and commonplace, veteran teachers are saying that never in their experience were young people so thirstily avid of pleasure as now—selfish, and so hard!

THE 25-YEAR-OLD RESPONDENT: [Our behaviors] are a logical reaction to the "helplessness" of parents and other adults. The modern child from the age of 10 is almost his/her own boss. The complexity of the world we face makes only more necessary our bracing up for the fray, we have to work out this problem all alone. I doubt if any generation was ever thrown quite so completely on its own resources as ours is. We have a very real feeling of coming straight up against a wall of diminishing opportunity. I do not see how it can be denied that practical opportunity is less for this generation than it has been for those preceding it.

Consider how well this exchange reflects today's prevailing attitudes. Then consider that it was written in 1911 and you will realize that the generation gap is nothing new (Waclawski, 1999).

For many reasons the question of the values and motivation of members of younger generations is an important one. The most obvious of these is demographic reality. With the passage of time, members of a new generation will predictably continue to increase in representation in the workforce. Thus, it is important to understand their motivational scheme. In addition, they are the cohort that will be most influenced over the long term by the "new" workplace (e.g., teams, technology, globalization, multicultural environments, and downsizing). As such, they represent the trial cohort for new methods of work organization (including motivational frameworks).

Although there has been a great deal of speculation and opinion regarding the motivation of the Gen X worker, there has been relatively little formal research. One recent study, however, provides some interesting data to add to the debate. Smola and Sutton (2002) contrasted the work values of the baby boom generation (workers born between 1946 and 1964) with those of Generation X workers. They chose these groups because, together, they represent the majority of the current workforce.*

Smola and Sutton analyzed 362 responses to a work values questionnaire from employed individuals in a wide variety of occupations and organizational levels. Although the respondents represented a wide range of ages and generations, they compared the responses of those who fell into the "boomer" generation with those who were members of Gen X. They were also able to compare their questionnaire results with those collected in a similar study done in 1974 (Cherrington, 1980). The analyses were intended to answer three questions:

1. Are there generational differences between baby boomers and Gen Xers? The data seemed to indicate that the answer to this question is yes. The younger employees appeared to be less loyal to the company and more "me" oriented, wanted to be promoted more quickly, and were less likely to consider work as the centerpiece of their lives. Surprisingly, the Gen Xers also appeared to feel more strongly than the boomers that working hard made one a better person and that one should work hard even if a supervisor is not around.

2. Are the work values of today's workers different from those of 1974? Again, the data suggested that the answer is yes. Today's workers, regardless of age, value "pride in work" less than the workers of 1974. Today's workers were also less likely to believe that work success should be equated with life success, that work should be a central part of life, and that hard work makes one a better person. In general, it appears that work is simply less important now than it was 25 years ago.

3. Do work values change as workers grow older? Values do appear to change with age. In general, work becomes less idealized. As workers age, they appear to be less convinced that work is a central part of life, that hard work makes you a better person, or that a worker needs to feel a sense of pride in his or her work.

The authors concluded that the work experience of the Gen Xers has influenced their work values and, to a lesser extent, the values of their boomer co-workers. Since the 1980s downsizing initiatives have become a way of life. Downsizing sends the message that workers are disposable and that loyalty to an organization—and possibly to an occupation—is futile. As world events such as 9/11 remind individuals of their vulnerability, we predict that the ties between individuals and work will become even weaker. There are several motivational implications of these results. The first, and most obvious, is that employers of the 21st century need to be concerned with the values and motivation of all employees,

---

*People born between 1979 and 1994 are called variously, the Millennial generation, Generation Yers, or the Next Generation (Smola & Sutton, 2002).

not just those born in a particular era. In addition, these results suggest that many traditional approaches to motivation—those that ignore issues such as a work–life balance or consider work to be in *competition* with nonwork activities—are doomed to fail. Finally, if organizations expect commitment and loyalty *from* employees, they will need to demonstrate their commitment and loyalty *to* employees. Layoffs, downsizing, and temporary workers run contrary to any meaningful psychological contract between employers and employees. We realize, of course, that global competition is a reality and that cutting and controlling costs, including payroll costs, may be central to an organization's survival. Nevertheless, if that is to be the new work environment, then radically different models of motivation may be called for.

MOTIVATIONAL INTERVENTIONS

Although we have considered the application of motivation theory at various points in the chapter, it might be helpful to describe three specific techniques of interventions that have been popular in applied settings: contingent rewards (behaviorism), job enrichment, and a feedback program.

Contingent Rewards

Luthans, Paul, and Baker (1981) provided an example of the application of behaviorism in work behavior. They focused on the behavior of sales personnel in a department store. They were concerned with three specific behaviors (i.e., responses) of the sales personnel: responding quickly to potential buyers (defined as within five seconds of the customer's arrival), keeping merchandise shelves stocked to within 70 percent of capacity, and remaining within three yards of the assigned sales position in the store. Rewards for these behaviors included time off and cash bonuses. A total of 16 departments from a large store were chosen for the study. Eight of the departments were control departments where no rewards were given (although employees were informed of the new performance expectations). Sales personnel in the other eight departments received contingent rewards for the target behaviors. The contingent reinforcement had immediate and dramatic results. On every target behavior, the experimental (reward) departments exceeded the performance level of the control departments. The results of the experiment are graphically displayed in Figures 9.8 and 9.9.

Reinforcement is a key factor in sales behavior.

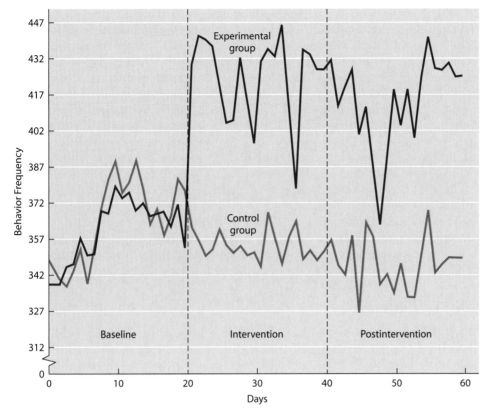

FIGURE 9.8

Aggregate Retailing Behavior Source: Luthans, Paul, & Baker (1981).

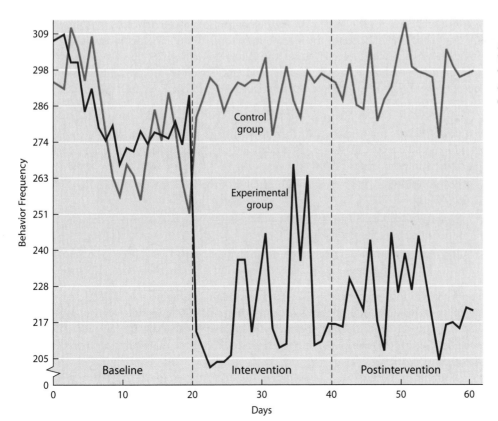

FIGURE 9.9

Absence from the Workstation and Idle Time Source: Luthans, Paul, & Baker (1981).

These figures show an interesting phenomenon in the postintervention period. Traditional reinforcement theory would suggest that after the reinforcement is withdrawn, behavior should return to prereinforcement levels. This did not occur. In this case, the experimental sales personnel may have experienced the positive effect of good retail and attendance behavior. Scolding and threatening by supervisors stopped, customers were more courteous and rewarding because the sales personnel were more attentive and the merchandise was better displayed, and skills in retail sales might have improved, resulting in higher sales and *self-image*. Notice that even the behaviorists grudgingly accepted the possible influence of self-efficacy and emotions. Nor could they deny that something *cognitive* happened, whether it was learning new sales techniques, expectation of future rewards, or the positive discrepancy between the goals set and results.

It seems clear that as a technology for changing behavior, reinforcement theory can be helpful. Nevertheless, the ultimate explanation of why long-term change might have occurred will require a more complex model than stimulus-response-reinforcement. In addition, even as a technology, behaviorism is most likely to be effective in developing simple individual behaviors (e.g., improving attendance, increasing individual sales) rather than complex group behaviors (e.g., developing a team-based marketing plan for a new product).

Job Enrichment

Based in part on Maslow's theory, researchers have proposed that jobs that satisfy higher order needs (love, esteem, and self-actualization) are capable of motivating individuals. Such jobs are considered more "enriched" and interesting than jobs that are tedious and simply represent a way to make money. This concept can be broadened to include the notion of "enriching" any job. The implication is that a job that has been enriched (i.e., given an increased capacity to satisfy higher-level needs) will be more motivating after it has been enriched than it was before. The application, then, is to enrich a job as a way of increasing motivation.

We will consider the issue of how the concept of **job enrichment** was developed in the next chapter. For current purposes, simply think of an enriched job as more interesting than an unenriched job. Hackman and Oldham (1975, 1976) developed a way to score jobs on their potential to motivate an individual. This motivation potential (assessed by a questionnaire) is tied to five job characteristics.

- *Skill variety*—the number of skills required to perform a task or job successfully.
- *Task identity*—the extent to which a task or job is self-contained, with a clear beginning, middle, and end; the extent to which a task can be meaningfully understood in relation to other tasks.
- *Task significance*—the perceived importance of the job for the organization or society as a whole.
- *Autonomy*—the extent to which the individual worker can control schedules, procedures, and so forth.
- *Task feedback*—the extent to which the individual worker gets direct information from the task itself (as opposed to a supervisor) about his or her level of performance.

A job high in motivating potential would be one that is high on each of these five characteristics. Hackman and Oldham also proposed that the individual worker must be focused on higher order need strength for these job characteristics to have any effect. For the purposes of this example of application, we will assume that our hypothetical workers have this property.

Using the example (sales personnel in the department store) from the application of reinforcement theory, we can see the differences in applied approaches. Consider the task of the sales personnel in that example. The job enrichment approach would not depend

JOB ENRICHMENT

A motivational approach that involves increasing the responsibility and interest level of jobs in order to increase the motivation and job satisfaction of the employees performing those jobs.

on cash bonuses and days off to motivate the employees. Instead, the manager might engage in the following actions for the sales position:

1. Provide sales personnel with computers to track customer patterns; involve them in planning promotions and special sales. (Skill variety)

2. Clarify exactly what the tasks and subtasks of retail selling are in the organization, identifying sales cycles (weekly, monthly, quarterly, annual) and distinctions between sales and marketing. (Task identity)

3. Show the effect of the retail sales of one person on (*a*) department and store profitability and (*b*) organizational stability; point out the importance of the job to customers (e.g., how the community might suffer if the job did not exist). (Task significance)

4. Provide sales personnel the opportunity to have a say in scheduling and, particularly, in identifying which of several alternative procedures or sales techniques might be used to make a sale. (Autonomy)

5. Provide computer-based feedback on a daily and weekly schedule regarding individual "profitability," sales volume, and so forth; provide simple "satisfaction with service" forms for customers to complete, or encourage sales personnel to ask the customer at the end of the transaction if he or she was satisfied with the transaction. (Feedback)

In practice, most applications of this job enrichment approach have also involved changing pay schedules, methods of supervision, planning and decision-making strategies, and work group interaction patterns. Nevertheless, a job enrichment approach might act as a vehicle for facilitating these changes, and have a value added effect beyond the enriching of the task and job.

ProMES

As we mentioned briefly earlier in this chapter, Pritchard and his colleagues have been developing a productivity improvement plan labeled **ProMES,** which stands for productivity measurement and enhancement system (Pritchard, 1990, 1995; Pritchard, Jones, Roth, Steubing, & Ekeberg, 1988; Pritchard, Paquin, DeCuir, McCormick, & Bly, 2001).

Pritchard (1992) defined productivity as "how well a system uses its resources to achieve its goals." ProMES is intended to maximize motivation primarily through cognitive means. ProMES assumes that the real issue in productivity is knowing how to allocate time and energy across possible actions or tasks (Pritchard et al., 2001). Like the German action theorists, Pritchard concentrated on the "act," which he defined as the "doing of something, like writing, running, talking or repairing a machine" (p. 5). Every act has associated with it amplitude, direction, and persistence. The theory attempts to explain why certain acts are chosen over others (direction) and how much energy is devoted to the task once it has been chosen (amplitude and persistence).

Pritchard and his colleagues used the example of an electronics factory to describe ProMES in concrete terms (Pritchard et al., 2001). In this company, one group depended on the output of another group for their productivity. The overall task of the group was to produce batches of circuit boards. When they had completed a batch, the boards were sent on to quality control for inspection. The team was also expected to maintain their equipment and keep their workplace clean. The steps in implementing a ProMES system include the following:

1. *Forming a design team.* This team consists of people who will actually do the work and their supervisors, as well as facilitators who will assist the design team in subsequent steps.

2. *Identifying objectives.* The design team comes to some agreement on the objectives of their work unit. In this example, the team identified the following objectives:

a. Maintain high production.

b. Make optimal quality boards.

PROMES

Productivity Measurement and Enhancement System: utilizes goal setting, rewards, and feedback to increase motivation and performance.

c.   Maintain high attendance.

d.   Follow cleanup and maintenance procedures correctly.

3.   *Identifying indicators.* **Indicators** are quantitative measures of how well each objective is being met. It is important that the indicators chosen be under the control of team members. For the objectives above, the team chose the following indicators, respectively:

a.   Percent of boards completed, defined as the number of boards completed divided by the expected number of boards to be completed.

b.   Inspections passed, defined as the percentage of boards passing inspection.

c.   Percent attendance, defined as the total hours worked divided by the maximum hours possible.

d.   Audit violations, defined as the number of violations on a regularly occurring audit of cleanup and maintenance procedures.

Table 9.4 gives some examples of objectives and indicators used in a variety of work settings.

TABLE 9.4   **Examples of Objectives and Indicators for Professional and Service Jobs**

ORGANIZATIONAL CONSULTANTS

Setting: This unit worked with clients doing individual assessments of various types ranging from one-day assessment to multiple-day assessment centers.

Objective 1.   Profitability

Indicator 1.   Cost Recovery. Average amount invoiced per assessment divided by cost for that assessment.

Indicator 2.   Billable Time. Percent monthly billable time on days when any assessment function is done.

Indicator 3.   Billing Cycle Time. Average number of days between billing trigger and invoice submission.

Objective 2.   Quality of Service

Indicator 4.   Validity of Selection Assessments. Percentage of hits: people assessed predicted to be high performers who turn out to be high performers and those predicted to be marginal who are marginal. Index is based on a 6-month follow up.

Indicator 5.   Cycle Time. Percentage of assessment reports going out that went out on time.

Indicator 6.   High Quality Experience of Participant. Percentage of participants giving "Satisfied" and "Very Satisfied" ratings at the time of assessment.

Indicator 7.   Customer Satisfaction. Percentage of participants responding "Satisfied" and "Very Satisfied" to customer satisfaction measure.

Indicator 8.   Consultant Qualifications. Percent licensable consultants who are licensed within two years of joining the firm.

Indicator 9.   Ethics/Judgment Training. Percent staff with a minimum of 4 hours ethics/judgment training in the last 12 months.

Objective 3.   Business Growth

Indicator 10.   Assessment Revenue. Average revenues for the last three months from the assessment function.

Objective 4.   Personnel Development and Satisfaction

Indicator 11.   Personnel Skill Development. Number of actual tasks the person had been trained on divided by the number of possible tasks that person could be trained on.

Indicator 12.   Personnel Satisfaction. Average number of "OK" and "Good" days per person per month based on data entered when each person entered his/her weekly time card.

(continued)

TABLE 9.4 *(continued)*

PHOTOCOPIER REPAIR PERSONNEL

Setting: Technicians go out on service calls to repair customers' photocopiers.

Objective 1. **Quality:** Repair and maintain photocopiers as effectively as possible.

Indicator 1. Mean copies made between service calls.

Indicator 2. Percentage repeat calls.

Indicator 3. Percentage of preventive maintenance procedures correctly followed.

Objective 2. **Cost:** Repair and maintain photocopiers as efficiently as possible.

Indicator 4. Parts cost per service call.

Indicator 5. Labor time per service call.

Indicator 6. Percentage of repeat service call caused by a lack of spare parts.

Objective 3. **Administration:** Keep accurate records of repair and maintenance.

Indicator 7. Percentage of required repair history information filled in correctly.

Indicator 8. Percentage of parts warranty claims correctly submitted.

Objective 4. **Attendance:** Spend the available work time on work related activities.

Indicator 9. Percentage of labor contract hours actually spent on the job.

Objective 5. **Ambassadorship:** Behave as correctly as possible on the job.

Indicator 10. Percentage of important social behaviors shown on the job as measured by customers' ratings.

SOURCE: Pritchard, Paquin, De Cuir, McCormick, & Bly (2001).

4. *Defining contingencies.* In this step, the team makes an expert judgment about the extent to which improvements on each objective (defined by the indicator) will contribute to overall success. Each objective is given its own contingency, a very formal process involving the gathering and analysis of each contingency. In the current example, the team judged that little additional gain took place from exceeding a 99 percent passing rate on boards. It was also clear that while there was little gain in productivity in moving from 88 percent to 94 percent attendance, there was considerable gain in moving from 94 percent to 98 percent attendance.

5. *Designing the feedback system.* A feedback system is developed that provides information, through managers and supervisors, to team members on each of the indicators. The data usually cover a one-month period and include historical data from the preceding month as well. The system also includes an effectiveness score for each indicator, an overall effectiveness score, and changes in the effectiveness score from one month to another. The actual calculation of these scores is complex and beyond the scope of this example. Team members are trained in the meaning and calculation of these scores. An example of a feedback sheet appears in Table 9.5.

6. *Giving and responding to feedback.* Within a few days of the end of the reporting period, the report is completed and distributed by supervisors at a team meeting. The team discusses the areas of accomplishment and the areas that need improvement in the next month.

7. *Monitoring the system.* It is important to revisit the adequacy of the system that was developed (e.g., objectives, indicators, feedback report) to see if any "tweaking" is necessary.

TABLE 9.5	Example Feedback Report

BASIC PRODUCTIVITY DATA

OBJECTIVES AND INDICATORS	INDICATOR VALUE	EFFECTIVENESS SCORE
I. PRODUCTION Percent Boards Completed	97%	+30
II. QUALITY Percent Passing Inspection	99.8%	+67
III. ATTENDANCE Percent of Max Attendance	96%	0
IV. HOUSEKEEPING AND MAINTENANCE Number of Housekeeping and Maintenance Violations	10	−5
	OVERALL EFFECTIVENESS SCORE =	+92

CHANGE DATA: FROM LAST MONTH TO CURRENT MONTH

INDICATOR	INDICATOR VALUE FOR LAST MONTH	INDICATOR VALUE FOR CURRENT MONTH	EFFECTIVENESS CHANGE FROM LAST MONTH
Percent Boards Completed	98%	97%	−15
Percent Boards Passing Inspection	99.6%	99.8%	+27
Percent of Maximum Attendance	95%	96%	+40
Number of Housekeeping & Maintenance Violations	12	10	+2

IMPROVEMENT PRIORITIES FOR NEXT MONTH

INDICATOR	INDICATOR VALUE FOR CURRENT MONTH	INDICATOR VALUE FOR NEXT MONTH	GAIN IN EFFECTIVENESS
Percent Boards Completed	97%	102%	+84
Percent Boards Passing Inspection	99.8%	100%	+4
Percent of Maximum Attendance	96%	98%	+30
Number of Housekeeping and Maintenance Violations	10	5	+5

SOURCE: Pritchard, Paquin, De Cuir, McCormick, & Bly (2001).

The ProMES system has been used by many organizations and in many different countries. The cumulative evidence shows very significant gains in productivity following the introduction of ProMES. As you can see, the primary element of the ProMES system is information, particularly as it is fed back to workers. This is most clearly a person-as-scientist approach. But worker participation in the design and development of the system gives it a less sterile and calculating tenor. It also assumes that individual workers will accept and commit to the system. It seems clear that when productivity increases, other good things are likely to happen as well (e.g., increased job security, compensation, and feelings of efficacy). Like the action theorists, Pritchard has some ideas about why ProMES works so well, but he is less interested in parsing the process than simply in improving productivity. Like the action theorists, he believes that the key to productivity is not in "motivating" workers with traditional approaches, but in helping them gain a better understanding of the job.

SOME SAMPLE APPLICATIONS

As you can see, each of these three motivational interventions—contingent rewards, job enrichment, and ProMES—is unique, and each has been shown to produce good results. This reinforces the point that it is not necessary to have a complete and accurate theory of human motivation to increase worker motivation. Even though we may not yet have a complete and accurate theory of work motivation, managers can nevertheless influence subordinate motivation through the various mechanisms we have covered in this chapter.

MODULE 9.4 SUMMARY

- Motivation can be measured by indicators such as the difficulty of goals accepted by an individual or the strength of a person's belief that hard work will yield rewards. Recent research suggests that conscientiousness and emotional stability may be surrogate measures for general motivation levels. An instrument called the Motivational Trait Questionnaire provides a standardized method for measuring general performance motivation.

- Culture has significant practical implications for work motivation. Although I-O psychologists within a given culture may have the research and theory to support a particular motivational intervention within that culture, the value of that intervention will decrease in direct proportion to the multicultural nature of the company and workforce.

- Debate continues on the extent to which Gen Xers are motivated by the same values and processes as earlier generations. There has been a great deal of speculation and opinion, but relatively little formal research, regarding the motivation of the Gen X worker. However, recent research has identified some differences in values and preferences between generations.

- Specific motivational interventions that have been popular in applied settings include contingent rewards, job enrichment, and feedback programs such as the ProMES system.

KEY TERMS

motivational trait questionnaire (MTQ)

job enrichment
ProMES

indicators

CRITICAL THINKING EXERCISES

9.7 Assume that as a manager of a fast-food restaurant, you want to increase the cleanliness of the seating area by having your staff be more attentive to that area. Using a program of contingent rewards, how would you do that? Is there any research evidence to support your plan?

9.8 ProMES has been used successfully as a method of motivation in more than a dozen countries. What characteristics makes ProMES suitable for crossing cultural boundaries? In which country/culture do you think ProMES would work particularly well? Why? In which country/culture do you think ProMES would not work particularly well? Why?

ATTITUDES, EMOTIONS, AND WORK

JOB SATISFACTION

THE EXPERIENCE OF EMOTION AT WORK

October 3, 2002 began like any other work day at the Fitzgerald Auto Mall in Kensington, Maryland. Shortly after seven o'clock that morning, two men chatted outside; one was Gary Huss, the body shop manager, and the other was Sonny Buchanan, who was preparing to mow the grass at the dealership. They each went about their business, but 20 minutes later the unthinkable happened: Mr. Buchanan was shot and killed by an unknown assailant—the "Washington area sniper" (later determined to be two gunmen, who terrorized the Maryland and Virginia suburbs for several weeks, eventually killing 10 people and seriously wounding 3 others before their arrest). In the hours and days after the killing, the employees of the car dealership expressed a wide range of emotions. Some were irritable. One of the managers reported, "I was ticked, I was grouchy. Everything bothered me." Kay Varner, a receptionist, was feeling guilt because she had continued answering calls

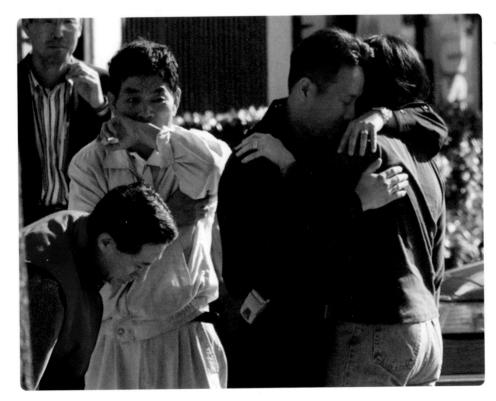

Workplace violence is emotionally traumatic to workers and disruptive to an organization.

at the switchboard rather than running to Buchanan to help stop the bleeding. Gary Huss said that he felt it was his responsibility to be strong for his employees and not let his emotions show. Even customers were affected. If their repairs were not completed on time, they told employees, "It's OK. I know what you're going through." Many employees were diagnosed as suffering from post-traumatic stress disorder (Zaslow, 2002).

A violent death at the workplace is bound to arouse extreme emotions, but less dramatic events, such as a layoff, can also be emotionally charged. A worker who was laid off from a frozen foods plant described his last day at work like this:

> The job wasn't really that great. I washed big pans that were used to cook the short ribs. They were about five feet long and two feet wide. They were covered with grease and I would push this cart along the line and collect all the dirty pans and bring them over to the washer. I would stack them on these racks and then wheel the racks into the big washer. Then I would start the pulley and open the wash valve and wait for them to come out the other end. This would take a minute, maybe two. I don't really remember. When they came out, I would wheel them back to the other end of the line, unload them and pick up some more dirty pans . . .
>
> I used to joke at lunch. I'd say, "If anybody hears that layoffs are comin', do me a favor. Send in my name." Then a funny thing happened. I got laid off. I couldn't believe it. First, I thought it was one of the guys pulling a joke. But then I heard other people got notices too, and I knew it wasn't a joke. I felt like a kid who wet his pants. I was afraid to go home and tell my wife. The rest of the day, nobody talked to me. They looked at me like I had cancer. I tried to smile, but I wanted to puke. The end of the day, I didn't want to leave. I even thought about just working through the next shift. It was crazy, like I thought if I didn't leave the pan washer, they couldn't lay me off. But the afternoon shift guy came and I had to leave.

Life is full of strong emotions. Consider the elation you experienced when you received an A on a term paper and the anger you experienced when you took a test that you felt was grossly unfair. Similar emotions occur at the workplace. In the course of a day at work, you may be angry with a co-worker, stressed by your boss, amused by another colleague, intimidated by the security people, and proud from the praise given by a manager. You may have come to work in a foul mood because of an encounter with another driver on the commute. This foul mood might have put a damper on the first few hours at work. You might leave work in such a great mood that you decide to take your children and spouse out to dinner and a movie. The school experience is not much different; roommates are all too often aware of the effects of good and bad days in class on each other.

Emotions experienced at work affect both work behavior and nonwork behavior. Similarly, nonwork-related emotions affect both work and nonwork behavior. Understanding emotions at work is no simple task. Not only do we have the complexity of work and nonwork stimuli, but also we have a range of different reactions, ranging from attitudes to emotions to moods. In this chapter we will deal with these complex relationships of work and nonwork emotions and attitudes, and their effects on behavior.

JOB SATISFACTION: SOME HISTORY
The Early Period of Job Satisfaction Research

In the mid-1920s, Elton Mayo, an Australian psychologist, introduced the concept of emotions into mainstream American I-O psychology (Griffin, Landy, & Mayocchi, 2003). He argued that factory work resulted in various negative emotions such as anger, fear, and suspicion (Mayo, 1923a, 1923b, 1923c). This in turn led to the development of labor unions and worker unrest, including lowered performance and increased illness. This was a novel suggestion. Until this point, there had been little interest among psychologists or managers in the happiness of workers. It was assumed that workers cared only about wages and that as long as they were paid adequately, they would be happy. There were occasional surveys of worker satisfaction—but the surveys asked managers about the happiness of the workers, rather than asking the workers themselves (Houser, 1927).

In the early 1930s, two very different research projects breathed life into the concept of **job satisfaction.** The first was a survey of all the working adults in a small town in Pennsylvania. Robert Hoppock (1935) was interested in the answer to two questions: How happy were workers, and were workers in some occupations happier than workers in other occupations? He discovered that only 12 percent of the workers could be classified as dissatisfied. He also found wide variations among individuals within occupational groupings; nevertheless, workers in some occupational groups (e.g., professionals and managers) were, on the whole, happier than those in other categories (e.g., unskilled manual laborers). These findings suggested that *both* job-related *and* individual differences variables might influence job satisfaction.

The second research project was begun at the Hawthorne plant of the Western Electric Company in Cicero, Illinois, in the late 1920s (Roethlisberger & Dickson, 1939). The purpose of the research was to examine the relationship between various physical aspects of work and the work environment, such as lighting, workday length, the timing of rest breaks, and their influence on productivity. The studies showed that the *perceptions* of workers had a greater effect on productivity than the physical working conditions. More surprisingly, the results showed that with almost all of the experimental conditions the researchers introduced, production improved. When illumination was reduced virtually to the level of candlelight, production improved. When the length of the workday was increased, production improved. When rest pauses were eliminated, production improved. These results were so unexpected that the researchers followed up the experiments with extensive interviews and an examination of workers' diaries in an attempt to determine why the reduced illumination and longer work periods did not have the hypothesized effect of reducing productivity. The researchers discovered that because of the experiment, the workers received considerably more attention from their supervisors and managers than they had previously. This increased attention was viewed positively and explains why attitudes toward supervision improved. Thus, the improved attitudes of workers toward supervisors as a result of the increased attention appeared to be responsible for the increase in productivity. This actually led to the introduction of a new term into the literature of social psychology—the **Hawthorne effect,** meaning a change in behavior or attitudes that was the simple result of increased attention.

At the time this research was reported, the general conclusion drawn by I-O psychologists was that morale and production seemed to be closely linked. As we will see later in the chapter, this conclusion was wrong. Nevertheless, both researchers and managers were quick to embrace this conclusion and it has been hard to dispel. The Hawthorne study results have been analyzed and reanalyzed, interpreted and reinterpreted, and many different theories have been proposed to account for the surprising results (Landsberger, 1958). But one thing is beyond dispute: Following closely on the heels of Mayo's early research on the effect of factory work on emotions, and the discovery of individual differences in satisfaction by Hoppock, the Hawthorne studies galvanized social scientists and gave impetus for the study of worker attitudes and the new construct of job satisfaction. In 1932 job satisfaction was not even listed in the subject index of the leading textbook in I-O psychology (Viteles, 1932). Four decades later, in 1976, more than 3,000 research articles had been published on the topic (Locke, 1976). By 2002 the total ran to almost 10,000 studies.

The years between 1935 and 1955 were very active for job satisfaction research, largely because satisfaction was thought to be closely linked to two outcomes very important to industry: the prevention of labor unrest in the form of strikes, and productivity. The notion was that if an employer could keep worker morale high, the company would

JOB SATISFACTION

Positive attitude or emotional state resulting from the appraisal of one's job or job experience.

HAWTHORNE EFFECT

A change in behavior or attitudes that was the simple result of increased attention.

The Western Electric "Hawthorne" plant in Cicero, Illinois was the site of early work in I-O psychology.

be strike free and profitable. Most attempts to measure satisfaction asked workers about their most important needs and the extent to which those needs were being met. It was believed that the greater the extent to which important needs were met, the greater would be worker satisfaction (Schaffer, 1953). In addition, social psychology was emerging during this period in the development of psychology. Social psychologists became very interested in attitudes of all sorts, and attitudes toward work represented a good integration of the theories of social psychologists with the interests of industrial psychologists.

In the late 1950s, two reviews of the research conducted to that point came to very different conclusions. Brayfield and Crockett (1955) concluded that there was little evidence of any substantial connection between satisfaction and performance. In contrast, Herzberg, Mausner, Peterson, and Capwell (1957) concluded that there was a connection between satisfaction and at least some work behaviors, particularly absenteeism and turnover. This led to the introduction of one of the first modern theories of job satisfaction, the "two factor" theory (Herzberg, Mausner, & Snyderman, 1959). You will recall from Chapter 9 that Herzberg proposed that job satisfaction was the result of intrinsic characteristics of the job (e.g., interesting work, challenge) while job dissatisfaction was the result of extrinsic characteristics (e.g., pay, working conditions). Herzberg proposed that extrinsic factors satisfied "hygiene" needs and intrinsic factors satisfied "motivator" needs. This theory resulted in a flurry of activity, but eventually the theory was rejected on both logical (King, 1970) and empirical grounds (Ewen, Smith, Hulin & Locke, 1966; Hinrichs & Mischkind, 1967).

An Evolution

You will recall that we introduced Weiner's (1991) metaphors for motivation theory in Chapter 9. These metaphors are also useful for illustrating the evolution of job satisfaction. This is not surprising, since the concepts of work motivation and job satisfaction have always been closely linked (Landy, 1989; Viteles, 1953). It has generally been assumed that motivation has connections to hedonistic states (i.e., feelings of pleasure or pain will lead to action to increase pleasure or reduce pain), and since satisfaction and dissatisfaction statements are similar to expressions of pleasure or pain, it would seem to follow that expressions of satisfaction would hold some meaning for motivational states. The person-as-machine metaphor of motivation theory fits the early period of job satisfaction research very well. The assumption was made that certain needs within the individual impelled action. These same needs were thought to form the basis of satisfaction. If an individual's important needs were met, he or she would be satisfied (and productive). Although early researchers (Schaffer, 1953) did not specify what these needs might be, Herzberg did. Herzberg's motivator needs fell rather clearly into the higher order needs described by Maslow (e.g., esteem and self-actualization), while his hygiene needs were more closely aligned to Maslow's lower order needs (e.g., safety and social needs). But even though Herzberg was more specific about categories of needs, the two factor theory was clearly a person-as-machine theory as we described in Chapter 9.

In the late 1960s and early 1970s, the cognitive revolution in psychology led to a shift in the motivation metaphor. The person as scientist became the guiding metaphor. One of the hallmarks of this metaphor was the data-gathering and analysis process of the individual. This shift can also be seen in satisfaction theory. Two theories in particular illustrate this point. Porter and Lawler (1968) proposed that overall job satisfaction was the result of various calculations that individuals made with respect to what they believed they deserved from a job. Their theory had elements of both VIE theory and equity theory. Lawler (1973) later expanded that theory and we have presented it in graphic form in Figure 10.1. Similarly, Locke (1976) introduced what he called the **value theory** of job satisfaction. He proposed that the relative importance of a particular job aspect to a given worker influenced the range of that worker's responses to it. For example, if you valued pay highly, then actual pay would have a substantial effect on your overall job satisfaction. Similarly, if you did not place much

VALUE THEORY

Job satisfaction theory proposed by Locke, in which the relative importance of a particular job aspect to a given worker influenced the range of that worker's responses to it.

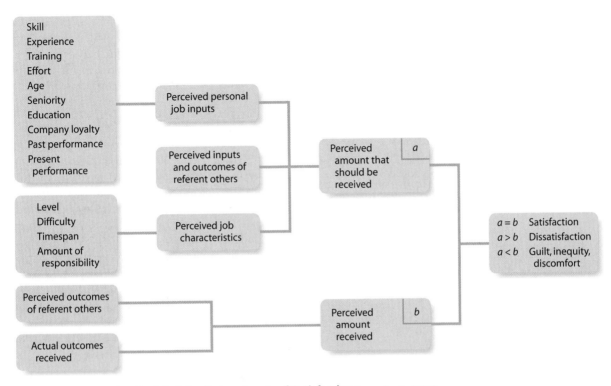

FIGURE 1 O . 1 **Model of the Determinants of Satisfaction** SOURCE: Lawler (1973).

value on promotional opportunities, then your actual opportunity to get a promotion would not have a strong influence on your overall satisfaction. To extend this logic to the educational setting, if you value the praise of an instructor over the admiration of your classmates, your overall satisfaction with school would be more heavily influenced by your interactions with your instructor than with your classmates. Locke added a twist to the Lawler model by specifying differential importance for various aspects of work.

Although the theories of both Lawler and Locke generated research, neither emerged as a comprehensive explanation of the phenomenon of job satisfaction (Landy, 1989). Other theories were proposed, such as Landy's (1978) **opponent process theory** of job satisfaction, based largely on theories of emotion rather than cognition. This theory hypothesized that every emotional reaction was accompanied by an opposing emotional reaction. Thus, if you experienced happiness when you interacted with a supervisor, there was also an underlying negative emotional reaction that would not be apparent as long as the interaction continued. But if the interaction stopped (e.g., you were transferred or your supervisor quit), the negative emotional state would appear since there would be no positive emotional state to oppose it (thus the term "opponent process" theory). The anguish you experience when a romantic relationship ends is a familiar example of this process. Warr (1987) proposed a theory based on nine specific job factors (e.g., money, variety, skill use) and suggested that too much of some factors (e.g., control, interpersonal contact) actually caused *dis*satisfaction. This was a novel proposition since most theories predicted that more of something might be associated with satisfaction and less of something with dissatisfaction. None had suggested that more of something would be associated with dissatisfaction.

Although conceptually interesting, neither Landy's nor Warr's theories ever generated much research. These theories are of interest because both were much more "emotional" than existing theories of satisfaction. Instead of focusing on the objective aspects of work

OPPONENT PROCESS THEORY

Job satisfaction theory in which every emotional reaction is accompanied by an opposing emotional reaction.

or attitudes of workers, they concentrated on the experience of emotions by workers. In addition, both theories were much more concerned with understanding the experience of emotion than in the possible relationship between emotions and productivity or turnover. As you will see in later modules of this chapter, current thinking and research is similarly concerned with the experience of emotions rather than the prediction of performance.

Antecedents and Consequences of Job Satisfaction

Job satisfaction research between 1935 and 1990 has been characterized as atheoretical (Brief & Weiss, 2002; Judge, Parker, Colbert, Heller, & Ilies, 2001). This criticism has been leveled in part because researchers depended on statistical analyses as a surrogate for theory. They looked for correlations between reports of job satisfaction and observable aspects of work. The best example is pay. Studies would examine the relationships among desired levels of pay, observed levels of pay, and reported job satisfaction (Graham & Welbourne, 1999; Igalens & Roussel, 1999; Judge & Welbourne, 1994; Law & Wong, 1998). Similar analyses were made for virtually every aspect of work imaginable—work challenge, quality of supervision, company policies, and various aspects of the physical work environment, even including the use of stereo headsets by workers (Oldham, Cummings, Mischel, Schmidtke, & Jhou, 1995). Locke (1976; Locke & Henne, 1986) presented an exhaustive review of many of the precursors of job satisfaction that have been examined. Table 10.1 provides a summary of a sample of these investigations. In addition to looking

TABLE 10.1 **A Sample of the Effects of Events and Agents on Job Satisfaction**

SOURCE	EFFECT
Events or conditions	
Work itself: challenge	Mentally challenging work that the individual can successfully accomplish is satisfying.
Work itself: physical demand	Tiring work is dissatisfying.
Work itself: personal interest	Personally interesting work is satisfying.
Reward structure	Just and informative rewards for performance are satisfying.
Working conditions: physical	Satisfaction depends on the match between working conditions and physical needs.
Working conditions: goal attainment	Working conditions that facilitate goal attainment are satisfying.
Agents	
Self	High self-esteem is conducive to job satisfaction.
Supervisors, co-workers, subordinates	Individuals will be satisfied with colleagues who help them attain rewards.
	Individuals will be satisfied with colleagues who see things the same way they do.
Company and management	Individuals will be satisfied with companies that have policies and procedures designed to help the individual attain rewards.
	Individuals will be dissatisfied with conflicting roles or ambiguous roles imposed by company, management, or both.
Fringe benefits	Benefits do not have a strong influence on job satisfaction for most workers.

Note: The interested reader is directed to Locke's (1976) review for a more detailed presentation of these conclusions.

at aspects of workers as precursors of satisfaction, investigators have also examined demographic variables such as age (Farr & Ringseis, 2002), gender (Konrad, Ritchie, Lieb, & Corrigal, 2000; Witt & Nye, 1992), and even inherited genetic disposition (Arvey, Bouchard, Segal, & Abraham, 1989; Lykken, McGue, Tellegen, & Bouchard, 1992). We will examine some data on inherited disposition later in the chapter. Unfortunately, without a comprehensive and cohesive theory of job satisfaction to explain the findings of individual studies, this type of data-driven research is not particularly helpful.

Just as there has been wide variation in the investigation of the precursors of job satisfaction, there has also been a wide variation in the variables examined as possible consequences of job satisfaction. These variables have included such behaviors as productivity/performance (Judge, Thoreson, Bono, & Patton, 2001; Katzell & Thompson, 1990; Katzell, Thompson, & Guzzo, 1992; Koys, 2001; Ostroff, 1992; Ryan, Schmit, & Johnson, 1996), lateness, absenteeism, turnover, physical health, mental health, and the experience of well-being in general (Warr, 1990, 1999; Wright & Cropanzano, 2000). We will consider withdrawal behavior, such as lateness, absence, and turnover, in some detail in Module 10.2. Within the broad area of performance, recent investigations have examined the link between satisfaction and customer service behaviors (Schmit & Alscheid, 1995; Schneider, Ashworth, Higgs, & Carr, 1996) and aspects of organizational citizenship behavior. Organizational citizenship, which we introduced in Chapters 5 and 6, represents extra effort on the part of a worker in such prosocial behaviors as volunteering to help coworkers, persisting in difficult tasks, and working faster to meet a deadline. Taking into consideration all of the possible precursors of job satisfaction with all of the possible consequences—and all of the enthusiastic researchers—you can understand why 10,000 studies of job satisfaction have been produced. Figure 10.2 provides a graphic illustration of the range of possible studies. Unfortunately, 50 years of enthusiastic research without the guidance of a compelling theory led to a large number of publications but not much genuine understanding. We will return to the issues of antecedents and consequences in subsequent modules.

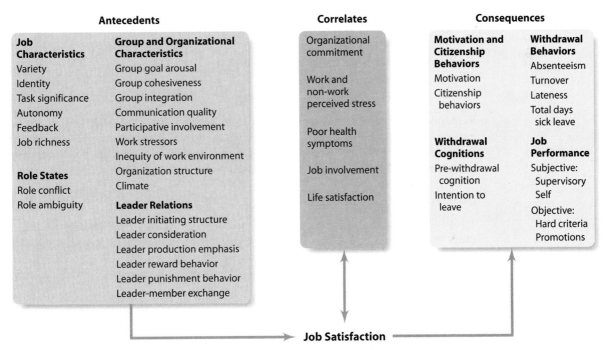

FIGURE 10.2 Classification of Presumed Antecedents, Correlates, and Consequences of Job Satisfaction Source: Kinicki, McKee-Ryan, Schriesheim, & Carson (2002).

THE MEASUREMENT OF JOB SATISFACTION

There are two different measurement issues that we will discuss concerning job satisfaction. The first is the distinction between satisfaction with specific aspects of work (often called facet satisfaction) versus a measure of overall satisfaction. The second is the use of actual questionnaires to measure satisfaction.

Overall versus Facet Satisfaction

OVERALL SATISFACTION

Overall assessment of job satisfaction that results either from mathematically combining scores based on satisfaction with specific important aspects of work or a single overall evaluative rating of the job.

Various researchers and practitioners have taken different positions on both the value of **overall satisfaction** and how it might be calculated (Rice, Gentile, & McFarlin, 1991). As we saw above, many researchers took the position that overall satisfaction is the result of combining satisfaction with specific important aspects of work. Thus, they would advocate using a mathematical formula for weighting and combining satisfaction with specific aspects. Others pointed out the frequent high intercorrelations between measures of satisfaction and various facets of work, so it seems useless to bother computing individual facet scores (Judge & Hulin, 1993). Indeed, there are some instances in which an overall score will work just fine (e.g., comparing one plant or division of an organization to another) and other instances in which facet information might be more useful (e.g., trying to identify which aspects of the work environment might play a central role in recruiting new employees). Wanous, Reichers, and Hudy (1997) demonstrated that even single-item measures of job satisfaction (e.g., Overall, how satisfied are you with your current job?) may work well in many situations. As an example of this type of measure, consider the now-famous "faces" scale. Almost 60 years ago, the faces scale (see Figure 10.3) was developed as a single-item measure of job satisfaction (Kunin, 1955, 1998). This format has been used to elicit overall satisfaction from workers with their jobs, satisfaction of customers with food or service, and even to help patients describe their current level of experienced pain or discomfort. It appears to be both a simple and an elegant way to get right to the core of an emotional reaction.

Judge and colleagues (2001) described a simple five-item scale that appears to work well as a measure of overall satisfaction:

> I feel fairly satisfied with my present job.
> Most days I am enthusiastic about my work.
> Each day at work seems like it will never end.
> I find real enjoyment in my work.
> I consider my job to be rather unpleasant.

FACET SATISFACTION

Information related to specific facets or elements of job satisfaction.

JOB DESCRIPTIVE INDEX (JDI)

One of the most extensively researched and documented job satisfaction instruments; assesses satisfaction with five distinct areas: the work itself, supervision, people, pay, and promotion.

Respondents use an agree–disagree format to reflect their attitude. As we will see in the next module, the greatest concern in current discussions of job satisfaction is not whether overall or **facet satisfaction** should be measured, but whether there is any value in measuring satisfaction (at least as an attitude) at all (Judge et al., 2001; Weiss, 2002).

Satisfaction Questionnaires

Table 10.2 displays some of the items from a questionnaire called the **Job Descriptive Index (JDI)** (Smith, Kendall, & Hulin, 1969). It is one of the most extensively researched and documented instruments to be used to measure job satisfaction (Kinicki, McKee-Ryan, Schriesheim, & Carson, 2002). It assesses satisfaction with five distinct areas of work: the work

FIGURE 10.3

Faces 1, 4, 6, 8, and 10 of the Circular Face Series SOURCE: Kunin (1955).

TABLE 10.2	Sample Items From the JDI

Think of the work you do at present. How well does each of the following words or phrases describe your job? In the blank beside each word or phrase below, write:

____Y____ for "Yes" if it describes your work

____N____ for "No" if it does NOT describe it

____?____ for "?" if you can not decide

WORK ON PRESENT JOB

_____ Fascinating

_____ Pleasant

_____ Can see results

PRESENT PAY

_____ Barely live on income

_____ Bad

_____ Well paid

OPPORTUNITIES FOR PROMOTION

_____ Opportunities somewhat limited

_____ Promotion on ability

_____ Regular promotions

SUPERVISION

_____ Doesn't supervise enough

_____ Around when needed

_____ Knows job well

CO-WORKERS

_____ Stimulating

_____ Unpleasant

_____ Smart

JOB IN GENERAL

_____ Pleasant

_____ Worse than most

_____ Worthwhile

Source: Balzer, Smith, Kravitz, Lovell, Paul, Reilly, & Reilly (1990).

itself, supervision, people, pay, and promotion. It also includes a separate overall satisfaction measure called Job In General (Balzer et al., 1990). A recent review and meta-analysis (Kinicki et al., 2002) confirmed the construct validity and reliability of the instrument. The disadvantages of the JDI are that the actual questionnaire tends to be lengthy (it has 72 questions) and that the broad category of "work" does not provide much information about issues such as creativity, independence, variety, or other aspects of the work itself. It is also interesting to note that the "?" response is scored as slightly more negative than positive. The "?" response is intended to indicate that the respondent is unsure whether the characteristic describes the job. The scoring scheme assumes that a response that is not positive is, by default, negative rather than neutral. In other words, if I am asked if my job is stimulating and I respond with a "?", I am saying that it is *not* stimulating. Hanisch (1992) demonstrated that such a scoring scheme was appropriate. She found that individuals who were classified as "dissatisfied" were more likely to choose the "?" alternative than those who were classified as "satisfied."

An alternative to the JDI is the **Minnesota Satisfaction Questionnaire** (MSQ) (Weiss, Dawis, England, & Lofquist, 1967). While the JDI uses 72 items to assess five areas of satisfaction, the MSQ assesses more refined aspects of work (e.g., achievement, ability utilization) with only five items per area (Kinicki et al., 2002). The MSQ also allows one to calculate an "extrinsic" and an "intrinsic" satisfaction score. **Intrinsic satisfaction** is related to the work that individuals do—aspects that are central or intrinsic to their job; **extrinsic satisfaction** concerns whether employees are satisfied with aspects that are extrinsic, or external, to job tasks, such as pay or benefits. There is as much research data available for the MSQ as for the JDI, so either one might be suitable for the assessment of specific areas of satisfaction. As Kinicki et al. (2002) pointed out, both are acceptable. One question that remains, however, is whether there is any practical value in obtaining anything other than an overall measure of satisfaction.

MINNESOTA SATISFACTION QUESTIONNAIRE (MSQ)

A commonly used job satisfaction instrument that assesses particular aspects of work (e.g., achievement, ability utilization) as well as scores for extrinsic satisfaction and intrinsic satisfaction.

INTRINSIC SATISFACTION

Concerns aspects central, or intrinsic, to the job itself, such as responsibility.

EXTRINSIC SATISFACTION

Concerns aspects extrinsic, or external, to job tasks, such as pay or benefits.

Up to this point, we have been considering the traditional method of collecting attitude data—the completion of a paper and pencil attitude survey—but researchers are turning with increased frequency to the Internet to collect such data because of the increased efficiency of this medium. Some preliminary findings about this medium are encouraging. It does not appear to matter whether attitude surveys are administered in paper and pencil format or over the Internet. Regardless of the medium, the same attributes appear to be assessed with little distortion (Booth-Kewley, Edwards, & Rosenfeld, 1992; Stanton, 1998). Donovan, Drasgow and Probst (2000) studied the JDI specifically and found that computerized administration worked well. The increased efficiency of computer and Internet administration make this a finding of considerable practical significance. One caution needs to be made, however, which is the concern for representativeness. Not everyone has equal access to or equal facility with the Internet medium. Thus, the data may be describing a distinct subset of individuals rather than the broader sample often addressed by the more traditional paper and pencil measurement medium.

We have been considering the issue of job satisfaction from the scientific perspective, but it is good to remember that a job is embedded in the larger context of life. Major life events have a way of focusing one's attention. The events of September 11, 2001, the sniper shootings described in the introduction to this chapter, even the unexpected death of a close friend at work, tend to make us reevaluate our priorities. After an event of this nature, you may find yourself asking if the level of physical and emotional effort devoted to work is worthwhile—Am I getting as much out of work as I am putting in, and are the rewards of work equal to the rewards I might get from some other form of work, or from nonwork activities? We will return to these questions in the other modules of this chapter.

MODULE 10.1 SUMMARY

- The emotions we experience, whether at work or elsewhere, affect both our work behavior and our nonwork behavior. To understand emotions at work, psychologists consider the complexity of work and nonwork stimuli as well as the range of people's reactions, ranging from attitudes to emotions to moods.

- Research at Western Electric's Hawthorne plant showed that the perceptions of workers had as great an affect on productivity as the physical working conditions. Following closely on the heels of Mayo's research on the effect of factory work on emotions, and the discovery of individual differences in satisfaction by Hoppock, the Hawthorne studies gave impetus for the study of worker attitudes and the new construct of job satisfaction.

- Herzberg and colleagues found a connection between satisfaction and other work behaviors, which led them to introduce one of the first modern theories of job satisfaction, the "two factor" theory. They proposed that extrinsic factors satisfied "hygiene" needs and intrinsic factors satisfied "motivator" needs.

- Two reliable, valid, and commonly used job satisfaction instruments are the Job Descriptive Index and the Minnesota Satisfaction Questionnaire. Recent research indicates that job satisfaction instruments have similar meaning and validity whether they are administered in paper and pencil format or over the Internet.

KEY TERMS

job satisfaction

Hawthorne effect

value theory

opponent process theory

overall satisfaction

facet satisfaction

Job Descriptive Index (JDI)

Minnesota Satisfaction
   Questionnaire (MSQ)

intrinsic satisfaction

extrinsic satisfaction

CRITICAL THINKING EXERCISES

10.1 Use the questions in Table 10.2 to describe the best job and the worst job you have ever had. What are the differences between them?

10.2 Sometimes job satisfaction is defined as a cognition (attitude), sometimes as an emotion, and sometimes as both. Consider a time when you were satisfied with your job and a time you were dissatisfied with your job (these can be two different jobs) and list the cognitions (thoughts) you had and the emotions you had below:

	SATISFIED	DISSATISFIED
Cognition		
Emotion		

10.2
MODULE

MOODS, EMOTIONS, ATTITUDES, AND BEHAVIOR

IS EVERYBODY HAPPY? DOES IT MATTER IF THEY ARE?

Over the years, two phenomena have puzzled researchers of job satisfaction. The first is the enduring finding that very few people report dissatisfaction with their jobs. Hoppock (1935) estimated the number of dissatisfied workers at about 12 percent. This percentage has not changed appreciably in over 70 years. In addition, the percentage seems to be about the same in most countries (Büssing, 1992). The second phenomenon is the relatively low level of correlation between overall satisfaction and almost every work behavior, including performance and withdrawal. This is particularly noteworthy with respect to the low level of correlation between satisfaction and performance. Managers continue to believe that this relationship is stronger than the data show. This highlights one of the important differences between science and commonsense beliefs: Science is characterized not by assumption but by data collection. These two findings—the robust reports of high satisfaction and the low correlation between satisfaction and performance—have led to an increased effort to develop both theories of satisfaction and ways of thinking about it. These theoretical efforts have taken two very different directions, as we shall discuss next.

Work that is well done provides intrinsic satisfaction, even if—as in the case of a Buddhist sand painting—the tangible result may not last long.

ALTERNATIVE FORMS OF WORK SATISFACTION

In 1974 Bruggemann and her colleagues (Bruggemann, Groskurth, & Ulich, 1975) proposed a theory of work satisfaction that addresses both of the puzzling phenomena described above. They suggested that there were multiple forms of work satisfaction and dissatisfaction. Only certain forms would be expected to correlate to particular work behaviors. As a result, simply measuring aggregate satisfaction (whether by a single overall measure or by a faceted questionnaire), without any consideration of its type, would yield low positive correlations. Further, with multiple types of satisfaction, there are many opportunities to report the experience of satisfaction, which accounts for the high levels of reported satisfaction typically found. Unfortunately, Bruggemann abandoned this research

TABLE 10.3	**Different Forms of Work Satisfaction**

Progressive work satisfaction: A person feels satisfied with the work. By increasing the level of aspiration, a person tries to achieve an even higher level of satisfaction. Therefore, a "creative dissatisfaction" with respect to some aspects of the work situation can be an integral part of this form.

Stabilized work satisfaction: A person feels satisfied with the job, but is motivated to maintain the level of aspiration and the pleasurable state of satisfaction. An increase of the level of aspiration is concentrated on other areas of life because of few work incentives.

Resigned work satisfaction: A person feels indistinct work satisfaction and decreases the level of aspiration in order to adapt to negative aspects of the work situation on a lower level. By decreasing the level of aspiration, a person is able to achieve a positive state of satisfaction again.

Constructive work dissatisfaction: A person feels dissatisfied with the job. While maintaining the level of aspiration, a person tries to master the situation by problem-solving attempts on the basis of sufficient frustration tolerance. Moreover, available action concepts supply goal orientation and motivation for altering the work situation.

Fixated work dissatisfaction: A person feels dissatisfied with the job. Maintaining the level of aspiration, a person does not try to master the situation by problem-solving attempts. Frustration tolerance makes defense mechanisms necessary, efforts at problem solving seem beyond any possibility. Therefore, the individual gets stuck with his or her problems and pathological developments cannot be excluded.

Pseudo-work satisfaction: A person feels dissatisfied with the job. Facing unsolvable problems or frustating conditions at work and maintaining one's level of aspiration, for example, because of a specific achievement motivation or because of strong social norms, a distorted perception or a denial of the negative work situation may result in pseudo-work satisfaction.

SOURCE: Büssing (2002).

area in 1981 before translating the work into English. Recently, André Büssing has taken up Bruggemann's model, completed its conceptual development, and begun gathering data that appear to support her theory.

Based on Bruggemann's initial theory, Büssing and his colleagues (Büssing, 2002; Büssing & Bissels, 1998; Büssing, Bissels, Herbig, & Krusken, 1998) have proposed four different forms of work satisfaction and two forms of work dissatisfaction (see Table 10.3). These six forms are the result of the interaction of three basic variables: (1) the discrepancy between what a person desires from work and what he or she actually gets, (2) changes in goal or aspiration levels as a result of work experience, and (3) the extent to which a person engages in coping or problem-solving behavior. The theory is presented graphically in Figure 10.4. The top section describes the discrepancy between what is desired and what is received. The middle section describes various changes in levels of aspiration. In the right-hand section, which addresses dissatisfaction, the role of problem solving or coping becomes apparent. On the bottom, we see the results in terms of the forms of satisfaction.

This theory is of considerable practical significance. Büssing identified the forms of **resigned work satisfaction** and **constructive work dissatisfaction** as most salient for organizations. Individuals characterized as constructively dissatisfied are identified as aroused or energized; they are the most appropriate audience for joining in any attempts at organizational change. By harnessing this dissatisfaction and its associated energy and problem-solving character, the organization can be improved while the individual develops personally. On the other hand, resigned work satisfaction is associated with reduced effort and willingness to change or adapt, both of which create serious problems for organizations faced with the challenge of doing more work with fewer people while adapting to external pressures from customers and competitors to innovate. Resigned work satisfaction will make change

RESIGNED WORK SATISFACTION

Associated with reduced work effort and a reduced willingness to change or adapt.

CONSTRUCTIVE WORK DISSATISFACTION

A type of dissatisfaction that energizes individuals and is beneficial for motivating them to join attempts at organizational change.

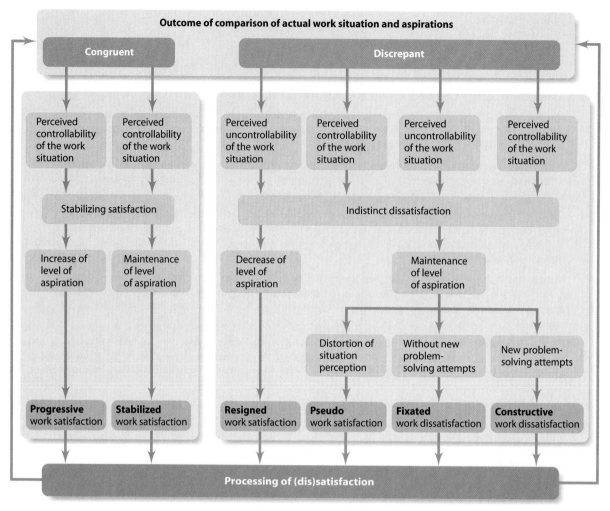

FIGURE 10.4 Different Forms of Work Satisfaction and Dissatisfaction
SOURCE: Adapted from Bruggeman, Groskurth, & Ulich (1975); and from Büssing (1992).

more difficult. Büssing suggested that the most effective way to address resigned satisfaction is to prevent it. This might be accomplished by asking a "complainer" to join a group appointed to study the issue associated with the complaint—in other words, intervene before constructive dissatisfaction turns into resigned satisfaction. He reasoned that since resigned work satisfaction develops over long periods of time, once developed it is resistant to change. For the constructively dissatisfied employee, on the other hand, increasing opportunities for input in problem solving as well as increasing extrinsic rewards (e.g., flexible working hours, increased pay, and enhanced promotional opportunities) will be effective.

Büssing proposed that rather than treating dissatisfaction and satisfaction as simply two ends of a single continuum, we think of various forms of each. And each form requires a different approach. Since there are four different ways of being satisfied, it is not surprising that 80 percent of all employees are "satisfied," but that does not necessarily mean the organization is healthy. Indeed, in the case of constructive dissatisfaction, a little bit of unhappiness of the right variety is good. Büssing provided no detailed explanation of why some people increase, others maintain, and still others decrease aspirations; however, it is likely that these aspirations change as a result of changes in feelings of esteem or efficacy, as we described these variables in Chapter 9 when discussing work motivation. Büssing's theory of work satisfaction is a refreshing approach and one worth following.

SATISFACTION VERSUS MOOD VERSUS EMOTION

Using Bruggemann's model, Büssing suggested that the problem with satisfaction research is that there are many different forms of satisfaction. Others, however, have taken a very different approach to solving the riddle of job satisfaction. Weiss argued that the problem is that satisfaction is conceptualized as a feeling or an emotion, but measured as a cognition. Virtually all devices to measure job satisfaction deal with it as an attitude, as a cognitive evaluation of the discrepancy between "what I want" and "what I get" from a job. But the two examples that we used to introduce this chapter (the sniper killing and the layoff) were not descriptions of how people calculated discrepancies. They described how people felt.

Weiss and his colleagues believe that most of the research on job satisfaction between 1930 and the present has missed the point by not explicitly recognizing the distinctions among moods, emotions, and attitudes (Brief & Weiss, 2002; Weiss, in press; Weiss & Cropanzano, 1996). Even though attitudes are thought to be composed of cognitions, affect, and behavioral intentions, most satisfaction researchers have tended to acknowledge only the cognitive aspects of attitudes. So when Weiss and his colleagues argued that one should study emotions rather than attitudes, they are really suggesting that research needs to be redirected to look at moods and emotions at work, rather than focusing exclusively on cognitions. Weiss and his colleagues further suggested that we should focus on things like stressful events, interactions with supervisors and co-workers, and the effect of physical settings for evidence of the influence of moods and emotions on behavior.

Substantial evidence is accumulating that moods and emotions are associated with work behaviors, including organizational citizenship behavior (George, 1990, 1991; George & Brief, 1992), performance judgments (Fried, 1991; Judge & Ferris, 1993; Robbins & DeNisi, 1998), creative problem solving (Estrada, Isen, & Young, 1997; Isen, 1999), and withdrawal behaviors such as absenteeism and turnover (Cropanzano, James, & Konovosky, 1993; George, 1989).

Brief and Weiss (2002) defined **moods** as "generalized feeling states not . . . identified with a particular stimulus and not sufficiently intense to interrupt ongoing thought processes; alternatively, **'emotions'** are normally associated with specific events or occurrences and are intense enough to disrupt thought processes" (p. 282). Moods are usually described as positive or negative while emotions are described more specifically (e.g., anger, fear, or joy). We may come to work feeling generally "down" but still get our work done. This would be a negative mood. We tell co-workers, "It's not my day." On the other hand, we may have a disagreement with a co-worker that ends in a shouting match. For the next few hours, our work is disrupted, we can't concentrate, and we go over the argument in our head. This is an emotion—a strong one.

In general psychology, there has been a great deal of work done on the identification of specific emotions. Weiss (2002) presented a useful scheme for distinguishing emotions from other related constructs (see Figure 10.5). In this scheme, specific emotions are affective states, but conceptually different from moods and stress. It is generally accepted that discrete emotions can be positioned around a circle. The technical term for this

MOOD

Generalized state of feeling not identified with a particular stimulus and not sufficiently intense to interrupt ongoing thought processes.

EMOTION

Feeling normally associated with specific events or occurrences which is intense enough to disrupt thought processes.

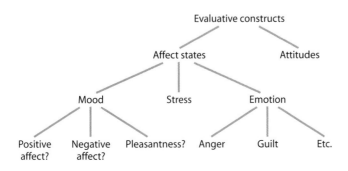

FIGURE 10.5

Distinctions Among Emotional Constructs SOURCE: Adapted from Weiss (2002).

FIGURE 10.6

Affect Circumplex

SOURCE: Adapted from Weiss (2002).

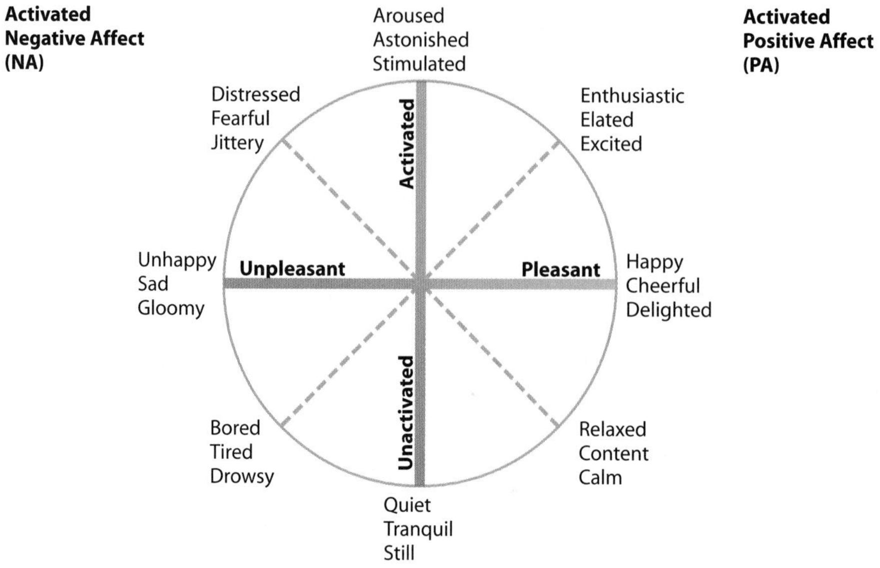

AFFECT CIRCUMPLEX

Figure in which opposite emotions appear directly across from each other in the circle.

PROCESS EMOTION

Reaction that results from consideration of the tasks one is currently doing.

PROSPECTIVE EMOTION

Reaction that results from a consideration of the tasks one anticipates doing.

RETROSPECTIVE EMOTION

Reaction that results from a consideration of the tasks one has already completed.

arrangement is the **affect circumplex** (Weiss, 2002). As shown in Figure 10.6, opposite emotions appear directly across from each other in the circle. Bored is the opposite of excited; unhappy is the opposite of delighted. In addition, there are two more basic dimensions on which emotions differ: degree of activation and degree of pleasantness.

The emotional labels in Figure 10.6 are general and could be used to describe either work or nonwork feelings. Pekrun and Frese (1992) suggested a structure for considering emotions specific to work. They proposed that emotional reactions can result from consideration of the tasks you are doing right now, which they labeled **process emotions** (e.g., you might experience boredom from reading this chapter), from a consideration of the tasks you anticipate doing, labeled **prospective emotions** (e.g., you are eagerly anticipating seeing a movie this evening), or from a consideration of the tasks you have already completed, labeled **retrospective emotions** (e.g., you feel pride in receiving a high grade on a class assignment). Further, they proposed that emotions arise from social interactions that are independent of those that arise from task-related activities. Table 10.4, which presents the

TABLE 10.4 Taxonomy of Work-Related Emotions

		POSITIVE	NEGATIVE
	Process	Enjoyment	Boredom/satiation
Task-related	Prospective	Hope Anticipatory joy	Anxiety Hopelessness (Resignation/despair)
	Retrospective	Relief Outcome-related joy Pride	Sadness Disappointment Shame/guilt
Social		Gratitude Empathy Admiration Sympathy/love	Anger Jealousy/envy Contempt Antipathy/hate

SOURCE: Pekrun & Frese (1992).

view of Pekrun and Frese, is not intended to be a definitive listing of all possible work-related emotions. Instead, it is an attempt to apply the construct of emotion more specifically to the work setting. They also suggested that emotions can only result when barriers of some sort are present. We will return to this notion at the end of this chapter.

Dispositions and Affectivity

Brief and Weiss (2002) were enthusiastic about recent research on the role of dispositions on job satisfaction. Dispositions are most often thought of as personality traits. Two traits receive most of the attention in examining the concept of disposition: neuroticism and extraversion from the five factor model of personality. Neuroticism is often referred to as **"negative affectivity" (NA)** while extraversion is referred to as **"positive affectivity" (PA)**.

> Individuals high in (neuroticism) are prone to experience a diverse array of negative mood states (e.g., anxiety, depression, hostility, and guilt) and individuals high in (extraversion) are prone to describe themselves as cheerful, enthusiastic, confident, active, and energetic (Brief & Weiss, 2002, p. 284).

Job satisfaction and affectivity have reciprocal influences on each other to the extent that positive people tend to be more satisfied with their jobs, and this satisfaction in turn helps maintain a positive level of general life satisfaction, further enhancing their positive affectivity (Isen & Baron, 1991). It is also likely that one's disposition might make negative information about work more salient to the high NA person, while positive information is more salient to the high PA person—the proverbial difference between the person who sees the glass as half full and the person who sees it as half empty.

But the dispositional explanation of moods and emotions is only one of many alternative explanations. A range of external events might also exert influence on mood and emotion. Moreover, the things that happen outside work can influence emotions and moods that are brought to the workplace, and vice versa. Most of us can remember the effect of a failed romantic relationship on studying or working. Similarly, the threat of a layoff can spill over into nonwork settings, leading to generalized anxiety and depression which make it difficult to derive pleasure from previously pleasurable activities and relationships.

There seems to be an emerging consensus that personality characteristics are likely to influence moods, but not necessarily discrete emotions. But moods might very well create circumstances that lead to discrete emotions. A person who is habitually "down" is not much fun to be with. As a result, co-workers may avoid interactions with the person, leading him or her to experience discrete emotions of anger or unworthiness. In contrast, a person who is habitually "up" might be sought out by co-workers and supervisors, leading that person to experience emotions of happiness and acceptance.

Genetics and Job Satisfaction

This brings us to one final and intriguing research hypothesis regarding job satisfaction and work-related emotional experiences: that emotional experience may be influenced by genetics. In 1986 Staw, Bell, and Clausen reported that the positive affectivity (e.g., individuals described as cheerful) or negative affectivity (e.g., individuals described as irritable or depressed) as measured in adolescence predicted job satisfaction as long as 50 years later! Thus, dispositions might be considerably more stable than implied by the term "mood." Irritable adolescents were dissatisfied workers in adulthood, and happy adolescents were happy workers in adulthood. Although this prediction was far from perfect (i.e., the correlation coefficient was of the magnitude of +.30), it was intriguing to find such stability over a 50-year period.

Genetic researchers studying twin data (identical/monozygotic and fraternal/dizygotic twins) have presented additional data suggesting that identical twins tend to experience

---

NEGATIVE AFFECTIVITY (NA)

Characteristic in which individuals are prone to experience a diverse array of negative mood states (e.g., anxiety, depression, hostility, and guilt).

POSITIVE AFFECTIVITY (PA)

Characteristic in which individuals are prone to describe themselves as cheerful, enthusiastic, confident, active, and energetic.

work more similarly than fraternal twins (Arvey et al., 1989; Bouchard, Arvey, Keller, & Segal, 1992; Lykken, Bouchard, McGue, & Tellegen, 1993). In an analysis of data from a Swedish twin database, Hershberger, Lichenstein, and Knox (1994) found evidence of genetic influences on the way that individuals perceive their work organizations (a concept known as organizational climate, which we will cover in detail in Chapter 14). This genetic hypothesis is not without its critics (e.g., Cropanzano & James, 1990), but it remains an intriguing possibility. Given the complexity of the hypothesis and the need to gather a great deal of additional data to truly test the hypothesis, no conclusion can be drawn at this stage.

Consider the following illustrative example of the possible links between genetic variables and mood or disposition. Cortisol is a hormone often associated with the experience of stress. Cortisol levels are unique to individuals, that is, they represent an individual differences variable that is stable like intelligence or personality (Roy, Kirschbaum, & Steptoe, 2001). Research has also shown that identical twins are more alike in characteristic cortisol levels than fraternal twins or nontwin siblings (Walker, Bosnall, & Walder, 2002). This means that cortisol has some association with genetic makeup and is stable. Thus, a child who has high levels of cortisol in adolescence, and is stressed by schoolwork, may very well experience the same levels of stress as an adult at work because of the same characteristically high cortisol levels. This stress would likely appear as negative affectivity in mood/disposition questionnaires or as dissatisfaction in job satisfaction questionnaires. In this instance, the reported negative affectivity or dissatisfaction would be, at least in part, due to a genetic individual differences variable. The individual did not "inherit" job dissatisfaction but a type of physiological reactivity induced by high levels of cortisol, resulting in stress at work. Of course the phenomena of reported negative moods or dissatisfaction are much more complex than a simple genetic predisposition, but we cannot rule out at least some role for genetics in the explanation of emotions at work. For our present purposes, we will simply conclude that there is good reason to suspect that at least dispositions (if not more specific job attitudes) have a genetic element to them, but considerably more research will be required before anyone can speak with confidence on the possible connection.

The Concept of Core Evaluations

A number of I-O researchers have proposed that individuals make **core evaluations** of their circumstances and that these core evaluations affect both job and life satisfaction (Judge, Locke, & Durham 1997; Judge & Bono, 2001; Judge, Bono, & Locke, 2000; Judge, Locke, Durham, & Kluger, 1998). The elements of core evaluations include self-esteem, self-efficacy, locus of control, and the absence of neuroticism (see Figure 10.7). Judge, Bono, and Locke (2000) found that the self-evaluations have effects on both job and life satisfaction, independent of the actual attributes of the job itself. They have also demonstrated that self-evaluation measures taken in childhood and young adulthood predict an individual's job satisfaction as measured in middle adulthood years. These results are important for three reasons. First, they confirm once again that objective reality (i.e., actual job characteristics) may be a great deal less important than subjective reality (i.e., perceptions) in understanding how individuals adjust to work. Another important aspect of their model and findings is that they have moved job satisfaction theory and research from the person-as-scientist metaphor to the person-as-judge metaphor. This is important because it permits a clearer integration of motivational theories and satisfaction theories. Finally, the longitudinal aspect of their research shows that these characteristics (i.e., self-evaluation dimensions) are stable over time and predictably influence how a given individual perceives a circumstance (work or nonwork).

Viewing job satisfaction through the lens of emotions and moods is very promising, but there is an enormous amount of research to do in this area. We do not yet know what

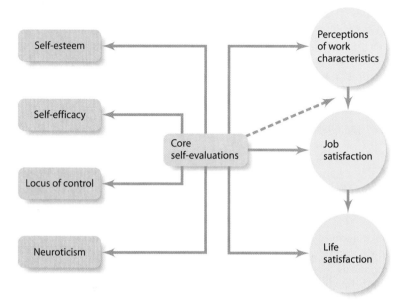

FIGURE **1 0.7 Elements of Core Evaluations** Hypothesized model relating dispositional characteristics to perceptions of intrinsic work characteristics, job satisfaction, and life satisfaction. Dashed line depicts a moderating effect of core self-evaluations on the relationship between perceived work characteristics and job satisfaction. With the exception of the loading of neuroticism on the core self-evaluations factor, all hypothesized linkages were hypothesized to be positive. Source: Judge, Locke, Durham, & Kluger (1998).

the relative contributions are of discrete emotions, compared with more general moods, to work behavior. Moods may contribute to some behaviors (e.g., turnover) and emotions to other behaviors (e.g., problem solving). Nor do we know how long moods or emotions last and exert an influence. An hour? A day? A week? Do emotions that arise at work have a greater effect on work or nonwork behavior? What about emotions that arise outside of work?

Grandey (2000) emphasized another concept in emotions: that for many jobs, the *regulation* of emotional expression may be critical. This has been labeled **emotional labor** (Hochschild, 1983; Morris & Feldman, 1996), which we will discuss at length in Chapter 15 when we consider stressors in the workplace. Employers (and customers) expect workers in customer service positions to display positive emotions and suppress negative emotions. For Emergency Medical Services (EMS) professionals, it is critical to display a calm and confident demeanor, regardless of how dire the circumstances. Research into the role of emotions at work is exciting and promising. It is likely that more progress will be made in understanding job satisfaction in the next decade than has been realized in the previous seven decades.

EMOTIONAL LABOR

The regulation of emotional expression that may include displaying positive emotions and suppressing negative emotions.

THE CONCEPT OF COMMITMENT

The concept of **commitment** is often associated with both attitudes and emotions. Commitment to a relationship, an organization, a goal, or even an occupation involves emotional attachments, as well as evaluations of whether current circumstances are what one expected or might expect in the future. Porter, Steers, Mowday and Boulian (1974) proposed that organizational commitment includes three elements: (1) acceptance and belief in an organization's values, (2) a willingness to exert effort on behalf of the organization to help meet the goals of that organization, and (3) a strong desire to remain in the

COMMITMENT

Psychological and emotional attachment an individual feels to a relationship, an organization, a goal, or an occupation.

organization. We will address the issue of the match between the values of an individual and the values of the organization in Chapter 14. We have already touched on effort expenditure in the discussions of job performance in Chapters 5 and 6 and motivation in Chapter 9. In this chapter, we will address the third aspect of commitment—the desire to remain in an organization. In particular, we will concentrate on the issue of organizational withdrawal in the form of lateness, absenteeism, and turnover.

Forms of Commitment

AFFECTIVE COMMITMENT

An emotional attachment to an organization.

CONTINUANCE COMMITMENT

Perceived cost of leaving an organization.

NORMATIVE COMMITMENT

An obligation to remain in an organization.

Meyer and Allen (1991) suggested that organizational commitment could be based on any one of three elements: (1) an emotional attachment to an organization, or **affective commitment,** (2) an element representing the perceived cost of leaving the organization, or **continuance commitment,** and (3) an element representing an obligation to remain in the organization, or **normative commitment.** Thus, some people stayed with an organization because they wanted to (attachment), others because they needed to (continuance), and others because they felt they ought to (normative). These three different foundations for commitment would have differential relationships with various work-related behaviors. Thus, they expected affective commitment and normative commitment to be related to job performance but not continuance-based commitment. Some research also suggests that affective commitment is a better predictor of absenteeism and turnover than either continuance or normatively based commitment (Eby, Freeman, Rush, & Lance, 1999).

In an extension of this three-component model of commitment, Meyer, Allen, and Smith (1993) suggested that one can be committed to entities or objects other than an organization. Traditionally, commitment had been associated with organizations and was studied in relation to turnover (Buchanan, 1974; Porter, Steers, Mowday, & Boulian, 1974). The notion was that an individual committed to an organization was less likely to leave than someone not so committed. Meyer et al. introduced the concept of commitment to an *occupation* as an adjunct to organizational commitment. They found that the three foundations for organizational commitment could also be applied to the notion of **occupational commitment.** They further discovered, as with organizational commitment, that various types of commitment led to different predictions about behaviors such as performance and turnover intention. They also found that these two forms of commitment— organizational and occupational—had independent influences on performance and turnover intention. Supporting research by Lee, Carswell, and Allen (2000) confirmed the importance of considering both organizational and occupational commitment when studying work-related behavior.

OCCUPATIONAL COMMITMENT

Commitment to a particular occupational field; includes affective, continuance, and normative commitment.

Individual Difference Variables and Commitment

Further explorations of the dimensionality of commitment have been made by Morrow (1993) and Randall and Cote (1991). Cohen (1999) has suggested an even simpler model in which a particular personality variable, the "Protestant work ethic," influences job involvement, which in turn influences various commitment foundations. He contrasted Morrow's model with Randall and Cote's model (see Figure 10.8). As you can see, the major difference between the two is that in Morrow's model, job involvement is a result of career commitment and the Protestant work ethic, while in Randall and Cote's model, job involvement follows a Protestant work ethic but precedes career commitment. Cohen collected data from nurses in two Canadian hospitals and found much stronger support for the Randall and Cote model of commitment than for Morrow's. The value of this type of research is in suggesting that behaviors such as absenteeism and turnover can only be understood when considered in light of multiple forms of commitment (e.g., organizational

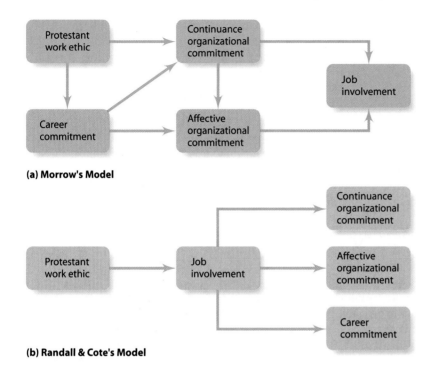

FIGURE 10.8

Two Models of Commitment
SOURCE: Cohen (1999).

(a) Morrow's Model

(b) Randall & Cote's Model

and occupational) and multiple foundations for those commitments (affective, continuance, and normative).

Ellemers, de Gilder, and van den Heuvel (1998) have suggested that one may also develop commitment to a work team in addition to organizations and occupations. Presumably, this form of commitment would also influence decisions regarding absence and turnover. As you will see in Chapter 14 when we examine organization theory, interventions such as Total Quality Management, lean manufacturing methods, and just-in-time production methods depend very heavily on the concept of team commitment. The study by Ellemers and colleagues is particularly encouraging because it was done with Dutch and Belgian workers, suggesting that the construct of commitment may apply to other cultures, not just American culture. Mitchell, Holtom, Lee, Sablynski, and Erez (2001) recently introduced the term **job imbeddedness** to represent the many and varied types of commitment between individuals and co-workers, teams, organizations, and careers.

Some data suggest that the longer an individual continues with an organization, the stronger his or her commitments become (Cohen, 1999; Judge & Watanabe, 1995). This makes sense. In terms of organizational policies, many benefits increase with greater seniority, leading to stronger continuance commitment. In addition, the number of individual friendships and positive organizational experiences increase affective commitment. Finally, individuals feel more responsible for various aspects of organizational functioning, leading to increased normative commitment. In 1974 Ghiselli suggested that some workers are simply more "prone" to change jobs than others. He called this the **hobo syndrome.** Judge and Watanabe (1995) found that one of the best predictors of turnover was the number of times an individual had previously changed jobs. One interpretation of this result is that something in the personality of certain people (e.g., negative affectivity, which we discussed earlier) makes them chronically unhappy and forever looking for greener pastures. An equally plausible explanation, however, might be based on commitment. Individuals who have been with an organization for a short period of time have a weaker commitment foundation. This would suggest that, rather than looking for people

JOB
IMBEDDEDNESS

The many and varied types of commitment that individuals feel toward co-workers, teams, organizations, and careers.

HOBO
SYNDROME

Some workers are simply more prone to change jobs than others.

**WITHDRAWAL
BEHAVIORS**

*Absenteeism, turnover,
tardiness, and
retirement may be
different manifestations
of a larger construct
called withdrawal.*

**WORK
WITHDRAWAL**

*Represents an attempt
by the individual to
withdraw from work
but maintain ties to the
organization and the
work role; includes
lateness and
absenteeism.*

**JOB
WITHDRAWAL**

*Represents an
individual's willingness
to sever ties to an
organization and the
work role; includes
intentions to quit or
retire.*

**PROGRESSION
HYPOTHESIS**

*A progression of
withdrawal behaviors
that start with
tardiness, increase to
absenteeism, and
eventually result in a
decision to quit or retire.*

who are not "hobos," organizations might concentrate on the early socialization process for their new employees, keeping them with the organization until commitment foundations are established and strengthened (Cable & Judge, 1996; Cable & Parsons, 2001; Wanberg & Kammeyer-Mueller, 2000).

WITHDRAWAL BEHAVIORS

One of the earliest and most enduring research questions related to job satisfaction has been the hypothesis that dissatisfaction would lead to withdrawal from the workplace. In earlier years, behaviors such as absenteeism, turnover, and tardiness have been treated as separate variables. Hundreds of studies have searched for statistically significant predictors of absence (Nicholson, Brown, & Chadwick-Jones, 1976, 1977; Nicholson & Johns, 1985), turnover (Hom & Griffeth, 1995; Mobley, 1977), or tardiness (Blau, 1994). More recently, however, there has been a growing tendency to see each of these behaviors as simply a different manifestation of a larger construct called withdrawal (Johns, 2001). Hulin (1991; Hanish & Hulin, 1990, 1991) has suggested that these various behaviors are all attempts to adapt to unfavorable job conditions and attitudes. He added retirement to this list as well (Hanish & Hulin, 1990).

Hulin (e.g., Hanish & Hulin, 1990) further suggests that there are really two different types of **withdrawal behaviors:** work withdrawal and job withdrawal. **Work withdrawal** includes lateness and absenteeism and represents an attempt by the individual to withdraw from work but still maintain ties to the organization and the work role. **Job withdrawal,** on the other hand, includes intentions to quit or retire, and represents an individual's willingness to sever ties to the organization and the work role. Viewed from that perspective—although turnover, absenteeism, and tardiness all represent withdrawal in one form or another—each represents substantially different courses of action. It is tempting to see these behaviors arranged as a progression (Johns, 2001), with a gradual escalation of withdrawal behaviors, starting with tardiness, increasing to absenteeism, and eventually resulting in a decision to quit or retire. Some studies have found evidence of this proposed progression. In a study of hospital workers, Rosse (1988) found a progression from lateness to absence and from multiple absences to quitting. Koslowsky, Sagie, Krausz, and Singer (1997) conducted meta-analyses of studies examining withdrawal behaviors and found some support for the lateness-to-absence progression. The **progression hypothesis** is an intriguing one and deserves additional consideration. If it is true, it provides employers with an "early warning" system for turnover and absence.

MODULE 10.2 SUMMARY

- Bruggemann and her colleagues suggested the presence of multiple forms of work satisfaction and dissatisfaction, but only certain forms could be expected to correlate with certain work behaviors. Büssing and his colleagues updated this research and identified *resigned work satisfaction* and *constructive work dissatisfaction* as most salient for organizations.

- Substantial evidence indicates that moods and emotions are associated with work behaviors, including organizational citizenship behavior, performance, creative problem solving, and withdrawl behavior.

- Researchers have considered the intriguing hypothesis that genetics may influence emotional experience. A study of twin data suggested that identical twins tend to experience work more similarly than fraternal twins.

- The elements of *core evaluations* include self-esteem, self-efficacy, locus of control, and the absence of neuroticism. Individuals make core evaluations of their circumstances and these evaluations affect both job and life satisfaction.

- Commitment to a relationship, an organization, a goal, or an occupation involves emotional attachments. Some people stay with an organization because they want to (affective commitment), others because they need to (continuance commitment), and others because they feel they ought to (normative commitment). It is important to consider both organizational and occupational commitment when studying work behavior.

- There has been a growing tendency to view lateness, absence, and turnover as different manifestations of a larger construct called withdrawal. Some studies have found evidence that these behaviors can be arranged as a progression, with a gradual escalation of withdrawal behaviors, starting with tardiness, increasing to absenteeism, and eventually resulting in a decision to quit or retire.

KEY TERMS

resigned work satisfaction	negative affectivity (NA)	occupational commitment
constructive work dissatisfaction	positive affectivity (PA)	job imbeddedness
mood	core evaluations	hobo syndrome
emotion	emotional labor	withdrawal behaviors
affect circumplex	commitment	work withdrawal
process emotion	affective commitment	job withdrawal
prospective emotion	continuance commitment	progression hypothesis
retrospective emotion	normative commitment	

CRITICAL THINKING EXERCISES

10.3 Consider two professional athletes who have been traded from one team to another. One athlete had been with the same team for seven years before being traded, while the other athlete had been with a team for two years before the trade. Analyze the commitment levels of each athlete using the three elements suggested by Meyer and Allen.

10.4 The progression approach to withdrawal behaviors proposes that little withdrawals (tardiness) eventually escalate into larger withdrawals (absence). Assuming this proposition is true, how would it affect your behavior as a manager?

RELATED TOPICS

With a research base of 10,000 studies to choose from, dozens of special and interesting topics might be covered in greater detail. We have chosen four topics that parallel a major theme of this book—the changing nature of work. Work is becoming less stable, there is a greater tendency toward working in a "virtual" workplace, work is more multicultural, and work–life balance is becoming more important to workers. We will consider the issues of involuntary job loss (typically through layoff), the special challenges that the virtual workplace and telecommuting bring to the experience of work, cross-cultural issues in attitudes and emotions, and issues of work–family balance. After considering these four special topics, we will present a theoretical bridge between the concepts of motivation and emotion.

JOB LOSS

The true and most basic meaning of work appears when someone loses a job. At the beginning of this chapter, we presented the reactions of the pan washer when he was laid off. Maurer (1979) has written a compelling book about job loss constructed from interviews with individuals who have lost their jobs. In some senses, losing one's job is comparable to the event of quitting one's job. The difference—and it is a crucial one—is that with job loss, the concept of commitment is a great deal less relevant. In many, if not most, instances, the worker may have a strong affective, continuance, or normative foundation for remaining with the organization. This may be exactly why job loss, like an unwanted divorce or romantic breakup, can be so devastating. It represents an involuntary separation from an entity (job, organization, or work group) to which the individual remains committed.

Warr has systematically studied the effect of job loss on the well-being of individuals (Warr, 1983; 1987; 1990; 1999). He argued that "paid employment is central to the functioning of societies and to the mental health of individuals" (1999, p. 392). Warr has reached certain conclusions about the effects of unemployment:

1. The psychological health of unemployed workers is poorer than that of employed workers.
2. This poorer health is the result of (not the *cause* of) unemployment, since a return to paid employment is usually followed by an improvement in psychological well-being.
3. Losing one's job often results in depression, insomnia, irritability, lack of confidence, inability to concentrate, and general anxiety.

Warr concluded that the reasons for these effects are complex. First, the loss of work reduces income and daily variety. There is a suspension of the typical goal setting that guides day-to-day activity. There are fewer decisions to make since there is little to decide about. The decisions that are made border on the trivial—when to get up, when to shop,

10.3

when to look for a job. New skills are not developed and current skills begin to atrophy. And social relations are changed radically. Remember the comment of the pot scrubber that people avoided him. Jahoda (1981) concisely described of the effects of employment on well-being:

> First, employment imposes a time structure on the waking day; second, employment implies regularly shared experiences and contacts with people outside the nuclear family; third, employment links individuals to goals and purposes that transcend their own; fourth, employment defines aspects of personal status and identity; and finally, employment enforces activity (p. 188).

Recent meta-analyses (Murphy & Athanasou, 1999) confirmed the negative effects of unemployment on mental health and well-being, as well as the positive effects of employment on these facets of life.

In earlier decades, research tended to focus on the plight of the unemployed male, since the male participation rate in the workforce, at least after the age of 35, was considerably higher than female participation. For example, Warr chose to study *paid* employment and excluded housework and volunteer nonpaid work from consideration. Recent surveys show that over 60 percent of U.S. women in the employable age ranges are members of the paid workforce (Fullerton, 1995). In many European countries, (e.g., Sweden), women have been members of the full-time paid workforce at higher percentages for decades. Thus, there is reason to enhance and expand job loss research so that it will compare and contrast the emotional experiences of men and women. There may be interesting differences in how the two genders cope with the experience. A related hypothesis has to do with the presence of children. It is reasonable to expect that when parents are supporting children, job loss can be devastating, particularly for single-parent families. Important research needs to be performed on the effect of job loss on different family configurations, including dual-earning parents, single-earning parents, and single-parent families (examining male and female care givers separately).

Unemployment comes in many different forms. Chronologically, the first opportunity for unemployment comes when an individual finishes school and seeks paid employment for the first time. Interestingly, it appears that there are differences between the experience of unemployment for individuals who have never had full-time employment and the experience of losing a full-time paid job. In a longitudinal study of students making the transition from school to paid employment, Winefield and Tiggemann (1990; Winefield, Winefield, Tiggemann, & Godney, 1991) discovered that the employed were higher on measures of self-esteem, optimism, and internal locus of control than the unemployed. But an unexpected finding was that the unemployed did not really *deteriorate* on these measures as unemployment stretched out for several years. While the experience of employment enhanced these measures, unemployment had little effect. Winfield and Tiggemann suggested that the effect of unemployment may not be as devastating to younger workers as it is to older workers. This makes sense from many perspectives. First, many younger individuals can continue to depend on parents and the extended family to provide moral and economic support until a job arrives. In addition, their commitment foundations (i.e., affective, continuance, and normative) are considerably weaker. The practical and scientific lesson from this research is that the experience of unemployment is likely to be qualitatively different for younger workers than for older workers, just as it is likely to be different for men and women. Thus, any research that studies the "effects" of unemployment but does not distinguish among respondents by age, work experience, or gender is likely to produce confusing or misleading results.

A relevant issue concerning the concept of job loss is the experience of psychological insecurity, in addition to the more obvious and associated economic insecurity. Are all individuals equally plagued with insecure feelings as a result of the increasing phenomena of downsizing, mergers, and acquisitions? The answer seems to be no. The individuals most likely to be negatively affected by feelings of insecurity are those most invested and involved in their jobs and organizations (Probst, 2000). It is ironic that in many instances, those who have the least to fear, because of their high levels of performance and motivation, are those who are most fearful. This may be the result of having more at stake than those uninvolved with their work or organization. By extension, the effects of insecurity may actually diminish performance and motivation over time, resulting in a self-fulfilling prophecy: The most motivated and effective employees end up performing more poorly, thus confirming their fears by increasing the possibility that they might be laid off as a result of diminished performance. Parker, Chmiel, and Wall (1997) studied the employees of a chemical plant in the United Kingdom that was embarking on a strategic downsizing initiative. They found that the debilitating effects of insecurity in organizations undergoing downsizing can be counteracted by establishing clear roles and responsibilities for those workers who are not downsized, as well as increasing their participation in work-related decision making. Both of these measures reduce uncertainty and enhance feelings of control. In Chapter 15 we will see that uncertainty and lack of control are major determinants of stress.

Modern work is a great deal less secure, both actually and psychologically, than has been the case previously. For moral as well as pragmatic reasons, we need to know more about the experience and the threat of unemployment. It is likely that research and theory building in this area will grow substantially in the next decade. As we will see in the last section of this module, these feelings of insecurity have far-reaching effects, including effects on the behavior of children of insecure workers.

TELECOMMUTING

TELECOMMUTING

Accomplishing work tasks from a distant location using electronic communication media.

Virtually all of the research on job satisfaction and work-related emotion has been done with participants who have traditional jobs in a particular workplace to which they are expected to report on a regular basis, usually 40 hours a week. But, as we have seen, the nature of work is changing. In 1990 roughly 4 million workers were engaged in **telecommuting,** which is defined as accomplishing work tasks from a distant location using electronic communication media. By 1997 that number had risen to 11 million (Holland & Hogan, 1998). There is every indication that the number of telecommuters will continue to increase in the foreseeable future. Even though the phenomenon of telecommuting is with us to stay, I-O psychologists know very little about any emotional or attitudinal experiences associated with the practice.

A lack of data has not prevented a heated debate about the advantages and disadvantages of telecommuting. Cascio (1998) suggested a number of advantages to telecommuting, including psychological and economic ones. While acknowledging that some circumstances do not lend themselves to telecommuting (e.g., poor quality electronic communications connections, lack of office space in the home or on the road, supervisors not committed to the concept), Cascio suggested that for many telecommuting workers, strategic planning skills and self-reported productivity went up. Further, telecommuters reported higher satisfaction than in their former traditional work arrangements, as well as higher levels of life and family satisfaction. Although some isolated scientific studies have investigated telecommuting (Hill, Miller, Weiner, & Colihan, 1998) as well as some texts that provide predictions and theoretical considerations of the phenomenon (Donaldson & Weiss, 1998; Duxbury, Higgins, & Neufeld, 1998; Igbaria & Tan, 1998; McCloskey & Igbaria, 1998), most "reports" of the advantages of telecommuting are anecdotal.

Holland and Hogan (1998) took strong exception to Cascio's implied endorsement of telecommuting. They contended that telecommuting, like most other management initiatives, is a strategy intended to cut organizational costs by reducing the cost of office space, support personnel, and so forth. They argued that the possible negative effects of telecommuting are daunting. These include:

1. Worker alienation will increase due to lack of face-to-face social interaction.

2. Nonparticipation at the actual work site will rob individuals of the important sense of identity that is derived from the work experience.

3. Telecommuters will be less likely to be promoted because, since they are out of sight, they will also be out of mind.

4. Telecommuting will require a particular type of person, the individual who is ambitious and conscientious. But the very characteristic that makes them good at telecommuting—ambition—will also lead to rapid disillusionment with the lack of promotional opportunities.

Cascio (1999) conceded that there is little hard evidence from which conclusions about the effect of telecommuting can be drawn; nevertheless, there are circumstances (e.g., the right job, the right person, the right boss, and the right reason) where telecommuting can be effective for the organization and satisfying and enriching for the individual. The best balance is for the worker to spend three days of work at home and the other two at the physical work location. He also cited data (Duxbury, Higgins, & Neufeld, 1998) indicating that telecommuting can appreciably improve the satisfaction derived from home and family experiences, allowing employed parents greater freedom in juggling work and nonwork demands. Hill et al. (1998) gathered data from IBM employees that appear to contradict this presumed advantage. Telecommuters reported that work–family balance had been negatively affected by telecommuting because they worked longer hours and there was an unpleasant blurring of the boundary between work and family. They noted, "it may be that teleworkers must find new cues to let them know when it is time to quit" (p. 679).

It is clear that telecommuting is here to stay and that it will become increasingly common. Both proponents and opponents of telecommuting make reasonable points. There is simply too little data to form any firm conclusions about the emotional, attitudinal, and behavioral correlates of telecommuting. The only thing we can say with confidence is that there will be consequences. Many telecommuters have experienced that they are not perceived as "working" by friends and acquaintances when they are working from home. This has both emotional (e.g., "my work is being devalued by my friends") and practical consequences (e.g., "people expect to be able to call me up to 'play hooky' whenever they feel like it"). We will learn much more about these phenomena in coming years as telecommuting becomes more prevalent.

WORK–FAMILY BALANCE

People obviously have both work and nonwork lives. For many individuals, particularly those in the 30–50 age range, nonwork life is dominated by the family. Data (and common sense) suggest that both physical and psychological well-being are affected whenever an individual's life is out of balance, when too much time and energy are invested in one sphere (Zedeck, 1992). A criticism commonly leveled at someone who seems overly obsessed with an activity or cause is, "Get a life!" What this really means is, in effect, get more *balance* in your life. Many elite athletes look back on periods of their life with melancholy, recognizing that their devotion to their training program brought them fame and fortune, but regretting having lost out on other important experiences. Many working adults have the same experience, but without the fame and fortune. Few tombstones display the epitaph, "I wish I had spent more time at the office."

Most research and theory related to **work–family balance** actually concentrates on the effects of a *lack* of balance. These effects are often discussed in terms of the stress created by conflicting demands between work and nonwork activities. Another way to

WORK–FAMILY
BALANCE

Area of research that investigates whether the satisfaction that one experiences at work is in part affected by the satisfaction that one experiences in nonwork and vice versa.

say this is that the satisfaction that one experiences at work is in part affected by the satisfaction that one experiences in nonwork and vice versa, particularly to the extent that one environment has demands that conflict with the other. We will discuss these stresses and their consequences in Chapter 15. In the remainder of this chapter, we will deal more broadly with the concept of balance and some of the factors that play a role in achieving balance.

One of the most substantial influences on achieving a work–family balance is an organizational culture that specifically endorses family values. As May (1998) pointed out, "many traditional (workplace) cultures still value 'face time' and reinforce the message that working in nontraditional arrangements (such as telecommuting) means that you are not serious about work" (p. 81). Wentworth (2002) took this a step further, noting the irony between the employer provision of various on-site services (e.g., child care, dry cleaning, auto maintenance) which appear to elevate family issues to equal status with work issues, and the steady increase in the number of working hours. Interestingly, Goff, Mount, and Jamison (1990) found that supportive supervision was closely related to work–life balance. Workers cared less about whether the company provided on-site child care services than they did about the organization's realization that child care was an important value for its workers. Bluestone and Rose (1997) estimated that by the end of the 1980s, "the typical dual earner couple . . . was spending an additional day and a half on the job every week" than they had in the decade of the 1970s (p. 12). American workers worked 36 hours more per year in 2000 than they did in 1990 (Wentworth, 2002). Although it is tempting to simply identify the number of hours worked as the culprit (Lewis & Cooper, 1999), Friedman and Greenhaus (2000) suggested that the real problem is not hours, but the interference and distraction that work poses for nonwork enjoyment.

Wentworth (2002) pointed to the electronically enhanced communications environment in which most people work, which includes fax machines, beepers, cell phones, and e-mail. One is never out of touch—which may be a boon to sales representatives eager to strike while the client is hot, and to medical professionals whose timely advice may save a life, but a burden to many other workers who find no opportunity to "turn off" their thoughts about the job. As Wentworth noted, the idea that a job is "24/7" does not even raise an eyebrow today; on the contrary, it is seen as a positive value indicating commitment to a job, organization, and career. It suggests that a worker who needs to be constantly reachable must be important to the organization. But it also suggests that work is more important than nonwork.

In assessing work–life imbalance, it has also been popular to point to multiple roles—particularly for employed women who are traditionally care givers in the home environment—as culprits (Burke & Greenglass, 1987; Williams, Suls, Alliger, Learner, &

SOURCE: DILBERT reprinted by permission of United Feature Syndicate, Inc.

The pervasiveness of electronic communications in today's careers can contribute to work-family conflict.

Wan, 1991). The theory was that more roles meant more responsibility, fewer degrees of freedom and flexibility, and greater stress. Recently, Barnett and Hyde (2001) advanced a nontraditional approach by suggesting that instead of a negative influence, multiple roles for both men and women enhance feelings of well-being through the following mechanisms:

1. Success in one role can buffer the effects of failure in another role.
2. The added income of dual-earning couples contributes to familial well-being.
3. Multiple roles increase the opportunity for social support, which in turn enhances well-being.
4. Multiple roles increase opportunities for success and the development of feelings of esteem and efficacy.
5. Multiple roles, with accompanying successes and failures, give individuals a better opportunity for achieving long-term emotional balance.
6. Multiple roles increase an individual's cognitive complexity and provide enhanced social/cognitive skills, in turn protecting against stress.
7. When spouses share work and nonwork experiences, they build a joint experience base that enhances communication and marital quality.

As far back as the 1960s, I-O psychologists recognized that the work schedule of a father had an effect on the emotional and cognitive development of his children, independent of the behavior and characteristics of his wife (Landy, Rosenberg, & Sutton-Smith, 1969;

Sutton-Smith, Rosenberg, & Landy, 1968). Although the focus of that research was on child development rather than work settings, it was clear that work affected important nonwork variables and relationships. Barling and his colleagues demonstrated that a parent's insecurity about continued employment has a predictable effect on the academic performance of college students (Barling, Dupre, & Hepburn, 1998; Barling & Mendelson, 1999; Barling, Zacharatos, & Hepburn, 1999). When parents feel secure about employment, children earn better grades than they do when their parents are worried about layoffs. The feelings of parents about work also affected the developing attitudes of children and adolescents toward work. Schmitt, Sacco, Ramey, Ramey, and Chan (1999) reported similar results with much younger children enrolled in Head Start programs.

The point we are making in this section is that one can only really understand the emotional experience of work by considering it in the larger context of life and nonwork roles. One can imagine a continuum with an exclusive nonwork focus on one end, an exclusive work focus on the other end, and a balance between work and nonwork in the middle. The challenge for any individual is to design both work and nonwork environments in a way that will increase the likelihood of a balance. And this balance will be disturbed at various times on both sides of the equation. The birth of a child, an illness or death, even the purchase of a new home, will alter the nonwork side; a promotion, a layoff, even a major work-related project or deadline will alter the work side. Catastrophic events like the terrorist attacks of September 11, 2001, will create seismic imbalances for both sides. The challenge, for organizations and individuals, is to restore balance.

The design of work is jointly shared by a worker and an organization. The design of nonwork is jointly shared by a worker and others with whom the worker interacts in the nonwork environment. Balance will be jointly determined by those two forces. Perhaps the most important element in achieving that balance, however, is for all parties—in both work and nonwork environments—to acknowledge the legitimacy and importance of the other parties.

WORK-RELATED ATTITUDES AND EMOTIONS FROM THE CROSS-CULTURAL PERSPECTIVE

For most of its history, research on job satisfaction has been carried out by American researchers with U.S. participants (Judge et al., 2001). Further, the studies that have been researched in other countries tend to be unique, often yielding results that are not replicated in subsequent studies. Thus, the powerful research tool of meta-analysis is difficult to apply to these non-U.S. studies.

In contrast, recent work with a multicultural focus seems to be producing some interesting and logical results. You will recall that Hofstede's model of culture and its consequences identified the individualism–collectivism dimension as an important aspect of culture. Preliminary research findings indicate that individualism and job satisfaction are positively correlated in some countries, while collectivism and job satisfaction are correlated in other countries (Judge, Parker, 2001). Hui and Yee (1999) found that in environments where work groups are "warm" and co-workers are enthusiastic about helping each other, the correlation between collectivism and satisfaction was more positive than that found in environments where the work group atmosphere was "cold" (i.e., mutual support was the exception rather than the rule). This in turn suggests that in individualist countries such as the United States there would be a positive correlation between individualist values and job satisfaction, while in collectivist countries such as Japan, South Korea, or China, there would be a stronger positive correlation between satisfaction and collectivist values.

As we will see in Chapter 14, a key concept in organizational psychology is "fit." The degree of fit seems to be related to both emotional reactions to work and subsequent work behaviors. In another example of the concept of fit, Robert, Probst, Martocchio,

Drasgow, and Lawler (2000) found that while worker empowerment was associated with higher levels of satisfaction in the United States, Mexico, and Poland, it was associated with dissatisfaction in India. In part, they explained this finding in terms of the desire for greater hierarchical structure in India, a country that values high power distance between levels of the organization. Here, we are talking about the fit between the design of work and cultural values as a possible determinant of job satisfaction. The practical implication is that multinational organizations must be sensitive to this fit between values and work if they are concerned about the satisfaction of their employees in differing cultural environments. This is particularly true in the case of expatriates transplanted into a new culture (Caligiuri, Hyland, Bross, & Joshi, 1998).

It is also clear that the instruments most commonly used to assess satisfaction (e.g., the Job Descriptive Index and the Minnesota Satisfaction Questionnaire) may not travel well across national borders. Hulin and Meyer (1986) found that approximately one-third of the JDI items did not appear to have the same meaning in non-U.S. samples as in U.S. samples. Other studies also questioned the value of using U.S developed instruments for assessing satisfaction (Ryan, Chan, Ployhart, & Slade, 1999; Simonetti & Weitz, 1972). For example, Ko, Price, and Mueller (1997) were unable to reproduce the Meyer and Allen three-component commitment model in South Korea. Although there is even less research on the issue of emotion and affectivity, the evidence that does exist suggests substantial differences in the emotional architecture of various cultures (Russell, 1991). In practical terms, this means that the greater the distance between a particular location and the United States with respect to basic cultural values such as individualism or power distance, the less relevant are the results of American studies of satisfaction and emotion. Like many other areas we cover in this text, we conclude that as the nature of work becomes more multicultural and global, it will be increasingly important to include cultural variables in our research designs.

A POSSIBLE CONNECTION BETWEEN MOTIVATION AND EMOTION

In the general psychological literature, motivation and emotion have always been paired (Weiner, 1992). The logic is straightforward. People are thought to engage in activities that are likely to produce pleasure, avoid pain, or both. In the work setting, the feeling of accomplishment for meeting a difficult goal would be considered pleasurable, and the criticism from a manager or co-worker for slacking off would be considered a type of pain. But a simple principle such as pleasure/pain does not do justice to the complexity of the emotion/motivation connection. Recall the work of Pekrun and Frese (1992) that we reviewed in discussing workplace emotions. They proposed that the only time an emotion is experienced in the workplace is when there is a barrier between the individual and the goal. If the barrier is overcome and the goal attained, the person experiences a pleasurable emotion (e.g., pride, enjoyment, relief, gratitude), and when the person fails to achieve the goal, a negative emotion is experienced (e.g., shame, anger, disappointment, resentment).

If these researchers are right, then little or no emotion is experienced if there is no barrier to success or goal attainment. It is interesting to observe individuals who are unchallenged by their work. They often create artificial challenges for themselves. A stocker in a supermarket stacks boxes of toilet paper on top of each other, higher and higher, until the tower collapses. The stocker brags to another stocker that she made a tower 15 boxes high, surpassing the old "record" by 4 boxes! An assembly worker closes his eyes while assembling parts to see if he can do it without looking. After four minutes he opens his eyes to discover that he has assembled the part perfectly, and he feels pride in that accomplishment. Had he assembled the part with his eyes open, he would have experienced no emotion at all. In virtually every workplace, similar examples exist. In both of these instances, the workers created an artificial barrier to relieve boredom and create an emotion of some type. A barrier is really a surrogate for the concept of unpredictability. The barrier means that there is the possibility that we will not succeed in achieving our goal, that success is not completely predictable. Thus, the Pekrun-Frese proposition can be transformed into a hypothesis that emotions stem from unpredictability.

One of the unique characteristics of humans is that we experience and are aware of emotions. There have been many theories that humans engage in activity for the purpose of arousal and that arousal is pleasurable (Schachter, 1964; Schachter & Singer, 1962; Weiner, 1992). Physiological arousal is thought to be one of the cornerstones of the emotional experience (Weiner, 1992). Given these propositions, it is then possible to tie the Pekrun-Frese notion of a barrier (or unpredictability) to arousal and propose that individuals will be motivated to engage in activities that have some modest level of unpredictability in order to have some sort of emotional experience. They will, of course, seek to have positive rather than negative emotional experiences and will set goals that are reasonably difficult (as Locke [2001] suggested) but more likely than not achievable. In addition, there will be individual differences in what level of unpredictability represents a "modest" level. What is modest for you may be "scary" for me. It is also likely that individuals will vary in their beliefs about their ability to achieve a goal (i.e., they will vary in their levels of efficacy). This will also affect the definition of what each individual considers a "difficult" goal. Individuals will not knowingly choose to experience a negative emotion. Rather, they will underestimate or overestimate the difficulty of the goal or their own capabilities and choose accordingly. Nevertheless, at some basic level, they are choosing a course of action that they believe will lead to the experience of an emotion.

This suggests that individuals can be motivated by challenge and the opportunity to experience positive emotions, but there must be a barrier or unpredictability of some kind involved. "Same old, same old" is not motivating since it is not likely to yield an emotional experience. Thus, the connection between emotion and motivation is that people will expend energy to experience emotions and that emotions will only be experienced in environments with some reasonable barriers to success or unpredictability. Considered from this perspective, the novelty and challenge suggested by many motivational interventions (e.g., ProMES, job redesign, participative decision making, or goal setting) make good sense since they provide the opportunity for an emotional experience, an opportunity to feel uniquely "human." We are not suggesting a "theory" of motivation but simply one plausible way of thinking about the connections between emotion and motivation. There are many equally plausible ways to pursue this connection. We have chosen this path because it is compatible with the intriguing notion of the role of barriers in work-related emotions as suggested by Pekrun and Frese (1992).

MODULE 1O.3 SUMMARY

- A major theme of this book is the changing nature of work. Four topics related to job satisfaction parallel this theme: (1) work is becoming less stable, (2) there is a greater tendency toward working in a "virtual" workplace, (3) work is more multicultural, and (4) work–life balance is becoming more important to workers.

- Job loss can be devastating because it represents an involuntary separation from an organization to which the individual remains committed. Recent meta-analyses confirm that unemployment has negative effects on mental health and the

experience of well-being. The experience of unemployment is likely to be qualitatively different for younger workers than for older workers, just as it is likely to be different for men and women.

- Telecommuting is a relatively new work arrangement that is becoming increasingly common. The advantages and disadvantages of telecommuting are hotly debated, but too little data exist to form any firm conclusions about the emotional, attitudinal, and behavioral correlates of telecommuting.

- Both physical and psychological well-being are affected by the extent to which an individual's life is in balance. Most research and theory related to work–family balance concentrates on the effects of a *lack* of balance. One can only really understand the emotional experience of work by considering work in the larger context of life and nonwork roles.

- Multinational organizations must be sensitive to the preferences and values of employees from

different cultural environments. This is particularly true for expatriates who are transplanted into a new culture. As the nature of work becomes more multicultural and global, it will be increasingly important to include cultural variables when examining attitudes and emotions at work.

KEY TERMS

work–family balance

telecommuting

CRITICAL THINKING EXERCISES

10.5 If an organization announces a downsizing, would the emotional impact be greatest on (a) a worker who joined the organization directly from school five years ago, (b) one who joined the organization directly from school a year ago, or (c) one who graduated from school three years ago, but was laid off by a previous employer and employed by the current organization for one year? Explain your answer.

10.6 American workers are more likely to confront a supervisor or manager if they are unhappy with some aspect of their work. Asian workers are less likely to engage in such confrontation. Does this mean that the Asian workers will experience more job dissatisfaction or negative emotions than their American counterparts? Explain your answer.

FAIRNESS AND DIVERSITY IN THE WORKPLACE

11 CHAPTER

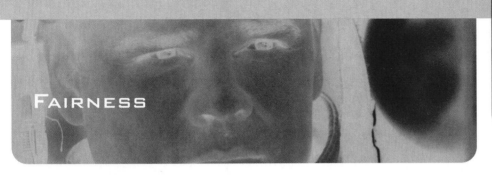

FAIRNESS

THE CONCEPT OF JUSTICE

Russell Cropanzano is an I-O psychologist who has done a great deal of research on the topic of fairness in the workplace. He begins a recent book with a true story about a small town in southern Colorado (Cropanzano, 2001). It is worth summarizing because it vividly captures the concept we will be discussing in this chapter. It makes the point that justice and the perception of fairness arouse such strong emotions that people are willing to die for them.

Ludlow, Colorado is a ghost town today, with a small cemetery and plaque commemorating an event that took place nearly 90 years ago, in 1915. The Colorado Fuel and Iron Company was a major employer in that part of the state. It was owned by John D. Rockefeller and was typical of companies in the mining industry of the time. Colorado Fuel and Iron dominated the lives of the 9,000 miners and their families. In the decade preceding the event of 1915, miners had protested against mine owners in many parts of the country. The Irish miners in the anthracite region of Pennsylvania banded together to form a group called the Molly McGuires. This group was responsible for the destruction of mines and the death and injury of mine owners and foremen. In Idaho, miners were accused of killing the former governor of the state, Frank Steunenberg, for siding with mine owners. He died when he opened a booby-trapped mailbox as his daughter watched. An interesting sidelight of the trial held for those accused of his murder was the attendance of Hugo Munsterberg, one of the first I-O psychologists, who was asked by a magazine to use his new lie detection technique to determine which side was telling the truth (Landy, 1992). He concluded that a prosecution witness was telling the truth and the defendant was not.

But back to Ludlow. The miners moved their families out of the company-owned housing and set up a tent city on the outskirts of town. This was the opening act that would signal a strike against the mining company. The working conditions and pay of a miner at that time were terrible. Cropanzano described the issues that led to the strike:

> [This was] an era when being a miner was little better than a paid death sentence . . . workers wanted better pay and working conditions. The Ludlow demands included a 10 percent pay increase, an eight-hour workday, and enforcement of state mining laws. But there were also concerns with personal dignity. The miners wanted to choose where they lived, select their own doctors, and spend their money in stores of their choosing. And perhaps, most fundamentally, they wanted the recognition of their union, the United Mine Workers, as a vehicle for ensuring that miners had a place at the decision-making table." (p. xi)

The strike had stretched out for 15 months and the Colorado National Guard was brought in to restore "order." As the soldiers faced off against the miners, an inadvertent shot was fired, setting off a battle that lasted an entire day. The soldiers killed miners, women and children, then looted and burned the tents. It became known as the Ludlow massacre.

As the Ludlow Massacre demonstrated, people are often willing to place themselves in harm's way for the sake of "justice."

Cropanzano believes that the miners were motivated to endure hardships, and even the possibility of death, by a desire for justice. Not money, not power—simply justice. The miners were denied three types of justice. First, they were denied a fair outcome. The mine owners got rich while the miners starved. Second, they were denied the opportunity to influence any important outcomes through joint decision making. The owners decided everything. Finally, the miners were treated as if they were beneath contempt, not even worth thinking about. These three types of justice have been labeled, respectively, *distributive, procedural,* and *interactional* justice (Colquitt, Conlon, Wesson, Porter & Ng, 2001). These three types of justice play as significant a role at the workplace today as they did at Ludlow in 1915.

An individual's view of the extent to which he or she is being treated fairly will influence the emotional (Martin & Bennett, 1996) and behavioral (Greenberg, 1990) reactions of that individual to the work environment. Perceptions of justice have been found to affect organizational citizenship, trust in the organization, respect for leaders, thoughts of quitting, and job performance (Colquitt et al., 2001). In its most extreme form and with a small number of people, a perception of injustice can lead to violence in the workplace (Sackett & DeVore, 2001). Kabanoff (1991) suggested that justice is a framework for looking at an organization. It is "an ever present, deep, and slowly moving current that shapes people's relations with other organizational members and the nature and strength of people's attachments to organizations in general" (Kabanoff, 1991, p. 436). Miller (2001) went further and suggested that justice is a central concept because it affects the way people think of themselves. People have certain beliefs about what they are "worth" as individuals. When a situation arises that challenges those beliefs (e.g., they do not receive the expected reward), they are forced to choose between a change in their belief about themselves (I am not worth what I thought I was) or in belief about their organization (my company is not honorable because it will not reward me as promised). Because perceptions of fairness and justice affect so much of what goes on at the workplace, we believe it is important enough to devote considerable space to the topic.

Justice, Fairness, and Trust

The terms "justice," "fairness," and "trust" are often used interchangeably, and although they are closely related, they are still worth differentiating from one another. Justice and fairness are used to characterize an event or an exchange relationship. A worker will describe a pay increase as unfair, a company policy as unjust, or a supervisor as a fair person. **Trust,** on the other hand, is more an expectation than a reality. It is a belief about how a person or an organization *will* act on some future occasion. One need look no further than the Enron scandal to realize how quickly trust among employees can erode when organizational members discover that leaders have acted irresponsibly. Kramer (1999) characterized trust as a psychological state, a state that becomes increasingly powerful as uncertainty and risk increase. Thus, in a time of low unemployment and a good economy, there is little discussion of the trust that an individual has in an employer. But when unemployment is high or the threat of downsizing, mergers, or acquisitions looms, trust becomes a more potent influence on behavior and emotions.

> **TRUST**
>
> *Belief in how a person or an organization will act on some future occasion.*

Kramer (1999) identified several aspects of organizations and institutions that undermine trust. He wrote that trust can be a scarce resource that is difficult to build and easy to lose. Distrust has been defined as a "lack of confidence in the other, a concern that the other may act as to harm one, that he does not care about one's welfare or intends to act harmfully, or is hostile" (Grovier, 1994). As we have seen in Chapter 9 on motivation, one compelling view of a person is that of an organism seeking meaning from events, even when these events seem meaningless. In this view, the person is a scientist gathering data or a judge evaluating that data and drawing a conclusion. It seems clear that trust in organizations and institutions—public and private—has eroded over recent decades. In 1964, 75 percent of Americans expressed trust in the government; by 1997 that number had shrunk to 25 percent. During that same period, the trust placed in medical institutions diminished from 73 percent to 29 percent, in universities from 61 percent to 30 percent, and in private companies from 55 percent to 21 percent (Kramer, 1999). Therefore, it is not surprising that employees may not trust their employers. The effect of this distrust is to question the fairness of any action taken by that employer, in particular, actions that have an adverse effect on the employee. Such actions would include failure to receive a promotion or satisfactory pay increase, performance evaluations, and layoffs resulting from downsizing, to mention a few.

How is trust undermined? Kramer suggested three possible mechanisms: unmet expectations, behavior of leaders, and technology.

Unmet Expectations A gap that often appears between what an organization promises and what it achieves can result in unmet expectations. A software company may have a strategic plan, shared with all employees, to achieve market dominance in less than two years, to double profitability, to avoid downsizing, and to introduce a new line of products. Two years later, when the company is still fifth place in the market—with unchanged profitability levels, having experienced one small and one large downsizing, and introduced no new product line—its employees are suspicious of most company pronouncements. The organization leaders were wrong before; why would they be right this time?

Leader Behavior Trustworthiness in organizations is often inferred from the behavior of their visible leaders. Leaders are taken to represent the core values of an organization. If a leader is seen to cheat and lie, the trustworthiness of not only that leader, but also the institution for which he or she stands, is perceived as lacking in trustworthiness (Zimmer, 1972). The impact of untrustworthy behavior on the part of the leader is particularly powerful on those who most believed in his or her integrity. Jack Welch, the CEO of General Electric for many years, preached a "lean and mean" business environment, urging cost cutting and downsizing at every opportunity. It was recently revealed that during his period at the helm of GE and in his retirement package, he had been given thousands of dollars monthly for jets, wine, clothes, and multiple residences. This took the nation by surprise: that a leader who preached austerity enjoyed such luxuries. Had these perks been revealed while he was still CEO, his "vision" for a lean and mean organization would have been less compelling to the organization's members. Kramer (1999) suggested that a certain level of distrust of institutions and organizations may be valuable as a check and balance. As we saw in Chapter 10 in the discussion of job satisfaction, one view holds that dissatisfaction, like distrust, can be energizing and used as a foundation for change and development.

Technology   Technologies can also undermine trust. The best example is surveillance and employee monitoring systems. Such systems send the message that the employee is not to be trusted. It is ironic that these systems are introduced to *increase* employee trustworthiness, but instead send the message that employees are not trustworthy (Kramer, 1999). Consider the monitoring plans of many retail operations (e.g., supermarkets, restaurants) which introduce the concept of a "secret shopper" or "secret patron" in which a company representative poses as a customer and reports back to management about the level of service, food quality, and so on. Employees then begin to see every customer as a potential secret shopper and themselves as surrounded by spies. Hochschild (1983) described a Delta Airlines program encouraging passengers to complain directly to the company about any aspect of flight attendant service with which they were unhappy. The flight attendants began to doubt that "passengers" were passengers at all, instead suspecting that they were company spies (Kramer, 1999). Instead of improving reliability of service, the program created fear and resentment, and a radical reduction in trust among employees.

As in friendships and romantic relationships, once trust in an organization has been lost, it is extremely hard to rebuild. There are several reasons for this. First, we tend to remember and dwell on negative events as opposed to positive ones (Slovic, 1993). Negative events are simply more visible and memorable. In addition, when making decisions of any kind, most people tend to give greater weight to negative events in the past than positive ones. Finally, it seems that negative gossip in an organization is more likely to be transmitted than positive gossip (Burt & Knez, 1995). Thus, once an event occurs that damages or destroys trust, that event looms larger in the organizational environment. There is an old saying that captures this dynamic: Fool me once, shame on you; fool me twice, shame on me. People do not like to be fooled and, once they feel they have been fooled, they will take steps to prevent it from happening a second time. People who have lost trust begin to seek out information that will confirm their distrust, and they are less open to information that challenges that distrust. For organizations, the moral is a simple one: If you have the trust of your employees, protect that trust as a scarce resource.

APPROACHES TO ORGANIZATIONAL JUSTICE

ORGANIZATIONAL JUSTICE

Type of justice that is composed of organizational procedures, outcomes, and interpersonal interactions.

Although the concept of **organizational justice** has been around for almost 30 years, there is still no generally accepted framework for studying justice in the workplace (Gilliland & Chan, 2001). Most research and theory have concentrated on the various ways justice and injustice might arise in organizational settings. There is some consensus on various types of organizational justice. As we mentioned earlier, three have been suggested: distributive, procedural, and interactional (Colquitt et al., 2001). We will consider each of these in turn.

Distributive Justice

In most organizational settings, there is either an implicit or explicit agreement or contract about the exchange relationship between the employer and employee (Schalk & Rousseau, 2001). The employee invests something in the organization (e.g., effort, skill, loyalty), and the organization rewards the employee for that investment. Another way to say this is that an organization distributes rewards to employees based on some scheme or equation. Employees will form an opinion regarding whether or not this distribution scheme is fair. **Distributive justice** concerns the perceived fairness of the allocation of outcomes or rewards to organizational members. You will recall that several of the motivation theories we reviewed in Chapter 9 include the concept of expectations, implying perceptions of fairness in rewards. Others, like equity theory, explicitly include fairness perceptions.

There are many different definitions of what is "fair" in the distribution of rewards. One definition is based on merit. The people who work hardest or produce the most should get the greatest rewards. This is called the **merit or equity norm.** Another definition is based on the notion of equality: Every member gets the same share of rewards, regardless of effort. Finally, the definition of fairness can be based on the **need norm:** People receive rewards in proportion to their needs (Gilliland & Chan, 2001). In the United States, the equity norm is the most common foundation for defining fairness (Greenberg, 1982). Nevertheless, in many countries the **equality norm** is stronger. For example, the Scandinavian countries have a long tradition of distributing rewards based on the equality norm. This is also true of Asian countries such as Japan and China. Both of these cultures would be classified as collectivist using the Hofstede (2001) model we presented in Chapter 1.

Regardless of how you define distributive justice, there seems to be a mechanism of comparison that leads to justice perceptions. Individuals compare what they get to what they expect to get. There is a subtle difference between what one expects and what one deserves. For example, if your company has a bad year, you might *expect* a modest salary increase, if any, but you may still feel that you *deserve* a substantial increase. It is not completely clear if your feelings of fairness or unfairness spring from expectations or from feelings of deservedness. In addition, it is not clear how strongly the simple favorability or unfavorability of an outcome influences perceptions of fairness. For example, you might not get a reward but grudgingly concede that another person who did get the reward deserved it. You would classify this as unfavorable but fair. Alternatively, you might get a reward that you don't believe you deserve. This would be favorable but unfair. In many cultures (again, primarily collectivist cultures), there is a strong modesty bias in which individuals are reluctant to claim credit for positive outcomes. In these cultures (in contrast to the United States), "fairness" will take on a very different meaning.

Procedural Justice

Distributive justice is about outcomes—who gets what. **Procedural justice** is about the process (or procedure) by which rewards are distributed. The U.S. Constitution supports the concept of "due process," meaning that individuals have the right to a fair process under the law as well as a fair outcome. An important aspect of fair treatment is the ability to register objections. In labor-management contracts, this is covered by the concept of the "grievance," or the right of an individual worker or group of workers to challenge an unfavorable action taken by the organization. In I-O psychology, this ability to challenge a process or outcome has been labeled **"voice"** (Folger, 1977; Folger & Cropanzano, 1998). The concept of voice means that the individual has the possibility of influencing a process or outcome. Avery and Quinones (2002) suggested that although voice has many different aspects, the most important is the perception that workers actually have an opportunity to express an objection. Thus, an organization may have many potential channels available for registering objections about policies or events, but unless employees know what these channels are and how to use them, and believe that their objections will actually be considered, these channels are useless in producing feelings of justice and fairness. Schminke, Ambrose, and Cropanzano (2000) suggested that organizations with high

DISTRIBUTIVE JUSTICE
Perceived fairness of the allocation of outcomes or rewards to organizational members.

MERIT OR EQUITY NORM
Definition of fairness based on the view that those who work hardest or produce the most should get the greatest rewards; most common foundation for defining fairness in the United States.

NEED NORM
Definition of fairness based on the view that people should receive rewards in proportion to their needs.

EQUALITY NORM
Definition of fairness based on the view that people should receive approximately equal rewards; most common foundation for defining fairness in Scandinavian and Asian countries.

PROCEDURAL JUSTICE
Perceived fairness of the process (or procedure) by which rewards are distributed.

VOICE
Having the possibility of challenging, influencing, or expressing an objection to a process or outcome.

degrees of centralization (i.e., procedures that every division or department must follow, centralized HR functions) are more likely to be seen as procedurally unfair than decentralized organizations.

Kernan and Hanges (2002) examined the effect of justice perceptions in a pharmaceutical company following a reorganization. They collected perceived fairness data from the "survivors" of the reorganization, that is, those who were not terminated. Interestingly, they found that survivors' job satisfaction, organizational commitment, intentions to quit, and trust in management were all affected by perceptions of the procedural fairness with which layoffs were carried out. Further, they found that the single most important determinant of procedural justice in this situation was the opportunity for employees to have input into the reorganization procedures (i.e., voice). This is an important finding. The conventional wisdom has been that survivors are happy to have kept their jobs; if they experience any emotion, it is one of relief. The results of this study show, on the contrary, that the experience of downsizing and reorganization has a negative impact on survivors as well as victims when principles of procedural justice appear to have been violated.

Schroth and Shah (2000) examined the effect of experiences of procedural fairness on self-esteem. This is an important issue because several theories of work motivation depend on the concept of self-esteem. Thus, it is useful to know which events may enhance or diminish self-esteem. Their study looked at the effect of fair and unfair procedures combined with positive and negative outcomes. These researchers discovered that when an interaction was considered procedurally fair and resulted in a positive outcome for the study participant, esteem was enhanced. Conversely, when procedures were considered procedurally fair, but the outcome was negative, esteem was reduced. In the case of negative outcomes, fair procedures led to lower self-esteem than was the case with the unfair condition. Ironically, this result suggests that unfair procedures can insulate an individual from having to consider the possibility that he or she is unqualified or performed poorly. This is similar to the common complaint of sports fans, "we wuz' robbed," when their team loses; if the outcome is in their favor, they scorn the complaints of the opposing fans as "sour grapes." When an applicant fails to obtain a job or appointment, he or she will often seek any opportunity to explain the result as one of unfairness. This is an effective way of protecting self-esteem.

Injustice—actual or perceived—often leads to outrage and violence.

Interactional Justice

A third type of organizational justice is **interactional justice,** the sensitivity with which employees are treated (Bies & Moag, 1986). This concept deals with the extent to which an employee feels respected by the employer. In an organizational layoff, for example, were employees informed as soon as possible, and in a complete and accurate way, why layoffs were necessary and how they would be accomplished? Were layoff announcements made in a sensitive way (in private with an opportunity for discussion) or in an insensitive way (the employees found out in a news release or in an impersonal e-mail memo)? Recently, Colquitt et al. (2001) completed a meta-analysis of justice studies and made a compelling argument that interactional justice has two separate facets: interpersonal and informational justice. Figure 11.1 illustrates their proposed typology of justice. In this typology, interpersonal justice deals with the extent to which people are treated with respect, politeness, and dignity. Informational justice addresses the explanations provided to people about procedures and outcomes (Colquitt et al., 2001). Informational justice is defined in terms of the fairness of communication systems and channels, particularly with respect to the person charged with communication responsibilities. It is defined by items such as:

- Has he/she been candid in his/her communications with you?
- Has he/she explained the procedures thoroughly?
- Has he/she communicated details in a timely manner?

In layoff situations, it is precisely the absence of such characteristics that often forms the core of feelings of unfairness (and serves as the foundation for litigation). The differences between interpersonal and informational justice are subtle since providing information can be seen as evidence of respect for the employee (Schminke et al., 2000). Nevertheless, as Colquitt et al. (2001) have shown, these do represent two different types of justice.

The distinction between procedural justice and interactional justice is also a subtle one. Cropanzano, Byrne, and Prehar (1999) suggested that these two different "types" of justice are simply distinctions between formal and informal procedures. Procedural justice studies tend to look at company policies, whereas interactional justice studies look at communications between employees and supervisors, including the supervisor's "style" of communication—cold and impersonal or warm and supportive. Donovan, Drasgow, and Munson (1998) developed a method to measure feelings of interpersonal justice which they labeled the PFIT (*p*erceptions of *f*air *i*nterpersonal *t*reatment) scale. The scale concentrates on relationships between employees, co-workers, and supervisors, including items such as:

- Supervisors play favorites.
- Employees are treated fairly.
- Employees are trusted.
- Co-workers put each other down.
- Employees' hard work is appreciated.

> **INTERACTIONAL JUSTICE**
>
> *Concerned with the sensitivity with which employees are treated and linked to the extent that an employee feels respected by the employer.*

FIGURE 11.1

Types of Justice

Justice versus Injustice

Gilliland, Benson, and Schepers (1998) proposed that injustice has a much greater impact than justice on subsequent attitudes, emotions, and behavior. Once an injustice threshold has been exceeded, there is no way to counteract the feelings of injustice. Even when employers try to make up for an injustice with fairer subsequent treatment they cannot undo the harm caused by the perceived injustice. Gilliland and Chan (2001) suggested that injustice, once experienced, leads to retaliation or reduced effort or motivation, while perceptions of justice lead to extra effort and feelings of inclusion and contribution. Currently, justice and injustice are considered two ends of a single continuum, with equal and opposite reactions. But many individuals experience justice quite differently from the way they experience injustice. The experience of injustice has a tendency to linger for a long time, sometimes over decades. Many of us remember for years an instance in which we were "screwed" by an employer, yet we tend to take just treatment for granted. We are also sensitive to incidents where valued co-workers are "screwed." We wonder if the same thing could happen to us, thus experiencing injustice vicariously.

The definition and measurement of justice perceptions is a relatively new area for I-O psychology. As a result, a great deal of basic work must still be done in determining how many different types of justice there are, how each type should be measured, how long lasting and powerful the emotions created by each type are, and how each type is related to various work behaviors. This is a very exciting area of research and application and is likely to receive continued attention.

MODULE 11.1 SUMMARY

- The extent to which workers feel that they are being treated fairly will influence their emotional and behavioral reactions to the work environment. Perceptions of justice have been found to affect organizational citizenship, trust in the organization, respect for leaders, thoughts of quitting, tendency to file lawsuits, and job performance.

- Employee trust in the organization and its leaders can be undermined in three ways: (1) the appearance of a gap between what an organization promises and what it achieves, resulting in unmet expectations; (2) untrustworthy behavior on the part of leaders; and (3) the use of surveillance or employee monitoring systems sending the message that the organization does not trust its employees.

- Although the concept of organizational justice has existed since the 1970s, there is still no generally accepted framework for studying justice in the workplace. Most research and theory has concentrated on the various ways that justice and injustice might arise in organizational settings. Three approaches to justice have received the most attention: distributive, procedural, and interactional justice.

- Some researchers have proposed that injustice has a much greater impact than justice on subsequent attitudes, emotions, and behavior. Even when employers try to make up for the injustice with fairer subsequent treatment, they cannot undo the harm caused by the perceived injustice.

- Defining and measuring justice perceptions is a relatively new area for I-O psychology. As a result, there is still much work to be done in determining how many different types of justice there are, how each type should be measured, how each type relates to various work behaviors, and how justice and injustice relate to each other.

KEY TERMS

organizational justice

trust

distributive justice

merit or equity norm

need norm

equality norm

procedural justice

voice

interactional justice

CRITICAL THINKING EXERCISES

11.1 Jennifer goes into a state employment office to apply for a job advertised in the local newspaper. A sign directs her to take a number and wait for an employment counselor to interview her. Other people are already waiting. Several people come in after her. During a two-hour wait she notices that other applicants are taken into interview rooms, including some who came to the office after her. She believes this is unfair. Which principle(s) of fairness would best describe Jennifer's reaction?

11.2 Mergers and acquisitions often result in the elimination of jobs in order to avoid unnecessary duplication of duties. Identify two justice principles that might become important in determining the feeling of fairness or unfairness on the part of those individuals who may lose their jobs.

11.2

MODULE

THE PRACTICAL IMPLICATIONS OF JUSTICE PERCEPTIONS

A substantial body of research suggests clear connections between perceptions of fairness and employee attitudes. As examples, Alexander and Ruderman (1987) found connections between fairness experiences and job satisfaction, feelings of organizational trust, and thoughts of quitting. McFarlin and Sweeney (1992) discovered that distributive and procedural justice were both important predictors of employee attitudes. Notably, distributive justice was a stronger predictor of pay satisfaction and overall job satisfaction than procedural justice, whereas procedural justice was a stronger predictor of organizational commitment that distributive justice.

McFarlin and Sweeney (1992) also found some evidence that distributive and procedural justice work jointly to influence behavior and attitudes. If distributive justice was low, procedural justice had a strong influence on the attachment that an individual had to an organization; similarly, if procedural justice was low, distributive justice had a substantial influence on attachment. Skarlicki and Folger (1997) determined that when procedural justice was low, perceptions of distributive injustice resulted in the inappropriate use of sick time, the damaging of equipment, and the spreading of rumors about fellow employees. If this interactive relationship turns out to be true, employers may take some solace in knowing that they can recover from one type of injustice by promoting perceptions of justice in another form.

As you read in Chapter 10, there has been an increasing interest in the emotional experience of work. Much of the research cited above addressed the cognitive aspects of attitudes, rather than emotions. But remember the last time you were treated unfairly by an employer. Your experience was not a cold and impersonal cognitive evaluation (i.e., there is great likelihood you were just "screwed"), but an affective reaction in the form of anger, disgust, or wide-eyed disbelief. Mikula, Scherer, and Athenstaedt (1998) studied the emotional consequences of perceived injustice in participants from 37 countries. They identified the most likely resulting emotions as anger, disgust, and sadness. Weiss, Suckow, and Cropanzano (1999) found that happiness is associated with the experience of distributive justice, and sadness with the experience of distributive injustice. They also found that if an individual did not receive a valued reward and, in addition, had perceptions of procedural unfairness, then the individual experienced anger. This line of research is quite new, so no firm conclusions can be drawn. Nevertheless, it seems a promising avenue for understanding violence at work. We will cover the issue of workplace violence in Chapters 15 and 16.

Although virtually any practice of an organization or behavior of a supervisor or coworker can lead to feelings of unfairness, two particular aspects have received considerable attention: performance evaluation and applicant reactions to selection techniques. We will consider each of these issues next.

PERFORMANCE EVALUATION

In Chapters 5 and 6 we considered the issues of performance and its measurement in some detail. Here we will deal specifically with the perception of fairness or unfairness associated with performance evaluation. When recounting experiences of unfair treatment, employees often include the performance evaluation process—the formal procedure by which a supervisor rates the performance of a subordinate. For example, Landy, Barnes-Farrell, and Cleveland (1980) discovered that an individual's reaction to a performance review was related less to whether the evaluation was positive and more to how the evaluation was carried out. Thus, the issue was a matter of procedural justice more than distributive justice. The conditions that led to the experience of fairness were (1) the supervisor was familiar with the duties and responsibilities of the subordinate, (2) the supervisor had an adequate opportunity to actually observe the subordinate at the workplace, and (3) the supervisor provided suggestions on how to improve performance. This was a surprise because the conventional wisdom held that people felt fairly treated if their evaluations were good and unfairly treated if their evaluations were poor (i.e., feelings were based on perceptions of distributive justice). It is also instructive to remember that many of these issues arise in litigation following layoffs, as we indicated in Chapter 6.

Landy et al. (1980) did not tie their results to any considerations of justice, but Greenberg (1986) did. He suggested that a person would feel justly treated when:

1. The supervisor gathered information in a careful manner.
2. The employee had an opportunity to discuss the evaluation with the supervisor after it had been completed.
3. The employee had the opportunity to disagree formally with the evaluation.
4. The supervisor was familiar with the work of the subordinate.
5. The supervisor was consistent in his or her judgment standards across subordinates and across time periods for the same subordinate.

As you can see, conditions 2 and 3 were associated with the concept of voice which we discussed earlier.

The concept of voice is common to the experience of fairness in virtually all decisions made about an individual. Employees want to be heard. If a procedure appears arbitrary or unfair, the opportunity to point out that unfairness can reverse the perception of unfairness. In many instances, what *appears* to the employee to be unfair is often simply a misunderstanding of the process or procedure. But if the employee never has the opportunity to object and have the procedure clarified, he or she will always believe that the process was unfair. Folger and Konovsky (1989) found that the feedback process was the most important determinant of feelings of fairness; once again, the concept of voice is key. Cawley, Keeping, and Levy (1998) completed a meta-analysis of 27 studies on the impact of employee participation in the evaluation process on feelings of fairness. They concluded that participation (e.g., discussing the evaluation before it was finalized) had a substantial effect on feelings of fairness by the person being evaluated.

As we described in Chapter 6, there has been a shift in today's workplace from performance measurement—documenting a given performance level of an employee—to performance management—a dialogue between a supervisor and subordinate about how to maximize performance (Banks & May, 1999). This shift clearly increases perceptions of fairness by the employee. Gilliland and Chan (2001) went even further in suggesting that the way managers are treated affects the way they treat their own subordinates. They hypothesized that managers who feel unfairly treated by their bosses might be more sensitive to the issue of fairness when they evaluate their subordinates. They also speculated that an employee who is sensitized to the possibility of unfairness may become overly sensitive to the possibility of unfair treatment and will be more likely to feel unfairly treated. As you can see, there are plenty of hypotheses concerning performance evaluation, but little conclusive evidence. Although much work remains to be done, everyone agrees that performance evaluation will inevitably result in feelings of fairness or unfairness. This makes it a productive area in which to examine the concept of justice.

APPLICANT PERCEPTIONS OF SELECTION FAIRNESS

Industrial and organizational psychologists have been involved in research on selection for over 90 years (Landy, 1993), but only in the last 10 years has serious attention been given to understanding the reactions that applicants have to selection devices and selection decisions (Anderson, Born, & Cunningham-Snell, 2001; Ryan & Greguras, 1998). Research on applicant reactions to selection procedures is important for several reasons. First, if applicants are unhappy about the selection process and believe they have been treated unfairly, they may reject the offer of employment. Second, because applicants talk to other applicants, selection procedures that are considered unfair affect the reputation of the selecting organizations. Finally and increasingly, applicants who believe they have been treated unfairly may end up suing an employer for discrimination. Applicant perceptions of recruiting and selection procedures are closely connected to perceptions of fairness, so this is an excellent opportunity to study the concept of organizational justice. There are also practical implications for studying applicant perceptions. From an applicant's perspective, understanding and building principles of fairness into the selection process can turn a potentially unpleasant experience into a more pleasant one. From an organization's perspective, assuring perceived fairness may result in a positive reaction by the applicant to an offer of employment. Even if the applicant is not offered a position, or does not accept one that has been offered, that applicant will still have positive or negative feelings about the organization which are likely to be communicated to friends and relatives.

Before reviewing this area of research, we must issue a note of caution. A great deal of this research is based on the use of student participants (e.g., Chan, Schmitt, Sacco, & DeShon, 1998; Elkins & Phillips, 2000; Kravitz, Stinson, & Chavez, 1996; Ployhart, Bennett, & Ryan, 1999). The students are asked to role-play the position of an applicant or give a more generalized response about the acceptability and perceived fairness of various selection techniques. In some cases these students are actually being considered for part-time positions at their schools. The use of student participants in this line of research may be a problem from several perspectives. First, attitudinal and emotional reactions to various devices are likely to develop over time. The first time you take a personality test or complete a biodata form and are rejected for a position, you may be annoyed but convinced that another job will come along. The 10th time you are rejected, you may be enraged and convinced that you are being treated unfairly. In addition, there is a difference between *pretending* you have been rejected and actually being rejected. The first experience is interesting, the second is punishing. Finally, there is a strong likelihood that college students, on average, have a higher intellectual ability than noncollege students. This means that they are likely to have more complex reasoning strategies than their nonstudent cohorts. We are not suggesting that the use of students invalidates findings, but our confidence in the research findings will increase as results from nonstudent applicants accumulate. Fortunately, even at this early stage of research, there is some convergence between findings with student and nonstudent populations (e.g., Bauer, Maertz, Dolen, & Campion, 1998; Macan, Avedon, Paese, & Smith, 1994; Rosse, Miller, & Stecher, 1994; Smither, Reilly, Millsap, Pearlman, & Stoffey, 1993).

Anderson et al. (2001) have reviewed the available research on applicant reactions. They came to several conclusions, which we have summarized.

Recruiting: Applicants see recruiters as the personification of the organization doing the recruiting; applicants prefer application blanks that state that the firm is an equal opportunity employer.

Biographical data: Applicants have doubts about the validity and fairness of forms that ask for biographical information as part of a selection process; they are less concerned when such forms are used for developmental or training purposes.

Mental ability tests: Candidates are more favorable toward cognitive ability tests with concrete items that appear to be related to the job.

Computer-based testing: Candidates are generally favorable toward computer-based testing because it is usually quicker, provides immediate feedback, and results in more timely employment decisions (*see also* Richman-Hirsch, Olson-Buchanan, & Drasgow, 2000).

Test-taking motivation: Candidates who are more favorably disposed to a selection procedure have higher test-taking motivation and, consequently, do better on the particular test.

Assessment centers: Assessment centers are viewed more favorably than standardized tests because to the candidates they appear to be related more to the job; in addition, applicants also view the face-to-face interaction with assessors favorably.

Personality tests: Applicants react less favorably to personality tests than other types of paper and pencil tests; this may be because they are less clearly related to job behavior, because they are longer, or because, unlike ability or knowledge tests, personality tests have no "correct" answers (*see also* Rafaeli, 1999).

Interviews: Candidates are more favorable to interviews that appear to be related to the job under consideration; they are not greatly influenced by the characteristics of the interviewer; candidates tend to dislike telephone interviews compared with face-to-face or teleconference interviews; "first" interviews lead an applicant to form initial impressions of an organization's attractiveness; reactions to subsequent interviews are more likely to be based on unfolding information about job attributes.

Work samples: Applicants express favorable opinions of work samples, which they view as fair and job-related.

Drug testing: As we saw in Chapter 4 on assessment, applicants who use drugs are less enthusiastic about drug testing; without any controls for applicant drug use, it also appears that favorability toward testing for substance abuse is influenced by how safety-sensitive the job is (Murphy, Thornton, & Prue, 1991; Murphy, Thornton, & Reynolds, 1990).

In a comparative evaluation of various selection techniques, Kravitz, Stinson, and Chavez (1996) found that respondents were positive toward techniques that had face validity (e.g., work samples, interviews) but less positive toward personality and integrity testing, and negative toward graphology, astrology, and polygraphs. Similar results have been found in cross-cultural studies (Steiner & Gilliland, 1996)

Based on the propositions of organizational justice that we reviewed earlier in this chapter, Anderson et al. (2001) suggested that the positive and negative reactions of applicants to selection procedures can be understood by applying justice principles (see Table 11.1). As you can see, there are aspects of procedural justice, informational justice, and interpersonal justice, as we have described them.

A Model of Applicant Decision Making

Anderson et al. (2001) presented five alternative models to account for how people choose jobs. The **rational economic model** sees the individual as an accountant, summing potential economic losses and gains and making the best economic choice. The **rational psychological model** also infers a "bookkeeper" mentality on the part of the applicant, but rather than simply tallying economic profits and losses, the "attractiveness of the job" depends on factors other than money, so the calculation is more of psychological gains and

RATIONAL ECONOMIC MODEL

Accounts for the way people choose jobs in which the individual is viewed as an accountant who sums potential economic losses and gains in making the best choice.

RATIONAL PSYCHOLOGICAL MODEL

Accounts for the way people choose jobs that infer a bookkeeper mentality on the part of the applicant, but also includes calculations that depend on psychological factors.

TABLE 11.1 Procedural Justice Implications for Selection

RULE	DEFINITION	EXAMPLES OF SUPPORTING SELECTION RESEARCH
Formal characteristics		
Job relatedness	The measurement of constructs relevant to the job	Chan et al. (1998a); Cunningham-Snell (1999); Gilliland (1994, 1995); Gilliland & Honig (1994a); Kluger & Rothstein (1991); Kravitz et al. (1996); Smither et al. (1993)
Opportunity to perform	The opportunity to display knowledge, skills and abilities	Bies & Shapiro (1988); Cunningham-Snell (1999); Gilliland (1995); Gilliland & Honig (1994a); Kluger & Rothstein (1991)
Consistency of administration	The standardization of administrative procedures across people and techniques	Gilliland (1995); Gilliland & Honig (1994a); Ployhart & Ryan (1998)
Information offered		
Performance feedback	The provision of timely and informative feedback regarding selection performance and the outcome	Gilliland (1995); Lounsbury et al. (1989); Gilliland & Honig (1994a)
Selection process information	The adequacy of information provided to applicants regarding the selection process	Cunningham-Snell (1999); Gilliland & Honig (1994a)
Honesty in treatment	The organization's integrity during selection	Gilliland (1995); Gilliland & Honig (1994a)
Interpersonal treatment		
Recruiter effectiveness	The interpersonal effectiveness and interest of the recruiter	Cunningham-Snell (1999); Gilliland (1995); Gilliland & Honig (1994a)
Two-way communication	The extent to which conversation flows in a normal pattern and applicants are given opportunities to ask questions	Cunningham-Snell (1999); Gilliland (1995); Gilliland & Honig (1994a)
Propriety of questions	The appropriateness of the questions asked	Bies & Moag (1986); Gilliland (1995); Gilliland & Honig (1994a)
Additional		
Ease of faking	The extent to which applicants believe information can be distorted in a socially desirable way	Gilliland (1995); Gilliland & Honig (1994a)

Source: Anderson, Born, & Cunningham-Snell (2001).

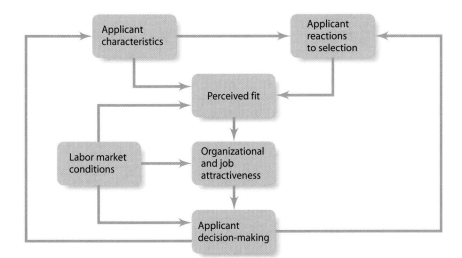

FIGURE 11.2

The Role of Applicant Reactions in Selection SOURCE: Anderson, Born, & Cunningham-Snell (2001).

losses. An **organizational fit model** is based on the match between the personality and values of the individual and the organization. A fourth model, the individual differences model, has individuals making selection decisions based on their particular personality or style, with less emphasis on the person–organization fit. In the fifth model, the negotiation process model, organizations and individuals behave as negotiators and, through the dynamics of the selection process, jointly decide whether to execute an employment contract.

Applying the discussion of metaphors for motivation from Chapter 9, the first two models adopt the person-as-scientist metaphor. The fourth model assumes the person-as-machine metaphor. The third and fifth models allow for the operation of the person-as-judge metaphor. As we have seen, fairness and justice affect emotions as well as attitudes. It is the emotional part that seems to defy the principal of complete rationality (economic or psychological). Further, it seems clear that people make decisions based, at least in part, on these emotions. This makes the person-as-machine view (model 4) less attractive.

Anderson et al. (2001) proposed a model (see Figure 11.2) that permits the emotional reactions of the applicant, particularly with respect to perceptions of justice and fairness regarding selection practices, to influence ultimate decisions about accepting a job offer. Emotions can enter into the model in terms of applicant characteristics (e.g., positive or negative affect) or applicant reactions to selection (i.e., attitudes and emotions associated with fairness and justice perceptions).

The Rejected Applicant

Gilliland et al. (2001) examined the wording of various types of rejection letters to determine if one or another was more likely to result in feelings of justice or fairness. They contrasted four different types of letters. The core of these letters appears in Box 11.1. Applicants who received either letter 1 (better qualified applicant) or letter 2 (hiring freeze) perceived the rejection more positively. Those who were told there was a hiring freeze as an explanation for the rejection were most likely to reapply for a later opening. Interestingly, any *combination* of the three nonstandard rejection explanations resulted in the most positive effects.

The implications of these findings are that if a candidate is to be rejected, a plausible reason should be supplied in the rejection letter; if more than one reason exists, all of those reasons should be presented. Gilliland et al. (2001) suggested that the wording of the letter can enhance feelings of justice and this serves as the foundation for the positive effects. Using the framework presented above about types of fairness, each nonstandard letter has the appearance of interpersonal fairness because each takes the opportunity to personalize the decision. Each represents indications of respect for the candidacy of the applicant

ORGANIZATIONAL
FIT MODEL

Accounts for the way people choose jobs by examining the match between the personality and values of the individual and the organization.

BOX 11.1   **DIFFERENT FORMS OF REJECTION LETTERS**

Standard Rejection Explanation

Dear Applicant:

Thank you for your interest in the ... position at ... company. I am sorry to inform you that we will be unable to pursue your application at this time. We wish you success in your future plans.

Sincerely yours, ...

Letter 1: Better Qualified Applicant

We received over 250 applications in response to our announcement and were very impressed by the extraordinary quality of many of the applicants. We interviewed a number of excellent candidates, including yourself, for the Senior Marketing Manager position. So that you could understand the quality of the applicant pool that we had to choose from, our top candidates had at least 15 years of experience in the sales and marketing field. In addition, they brought senior management and industry-related experience to the position.

Letter 2: Hiring Freeze

Unfortunately, in the end, we were unable to complete our hiring process. Here is how the process unfolded. We pro-

ceeded to the point of interviewing a couple of candidates, including you, but were unable to extend an offer. Rising short-term interest rates and reluctant consumer spending led to sharp declines in sales. The financial situation resulted in a freeze in hiring in our department.

Letter 3: Reputation of the Process

Over the years, we have received many questions about our application and interview process. The process was developed by the research firm of Johnson, Myers, and Associates and is similar to the process used by a number of Fortune 100 companies. The tests you completed are designed to provide an unbiased assessment of management ability and marketing personality. They have been demonstrated to be accurate indicators of success for our marketing manager positions. The interview questions were structured and job related and have been found to predict job performance. They also ensure that all candidates are treated consistently and appropriately. Overall, this selection process has proven to be highly effective for identifying successful candidates.

SOURCE: Based on Gilliland, Groth, Baker, Dew, Polly, & Langdon (2001).

and would be expected to result in enhanced feelings of fairness. Moreover, the "better qualified applicant" letter and the "hiring freeze" letter indicate additional principles of justice. The "better qualified applicant" and the "hiring freeze" letters suggest that the principles of distributive justice are being followed. In the hiring freeze letter, no one got the job so there was no outcome with which to be unhappy. In the "better qualified applicant" letter, the merit definition of distributive justice is being followed.

THE SPECIAL CASE OF AFFIRMATIVE ACTION

Since many, if not most, of the studies on perceived selection system justice have been made in the United States, and since this country tends to adopt the equity or merit principle for decisions about fairness, we don't know much about non-U.S. selection systems (particularly those that do not follow the U.S. model). It may very well be that the clash between a merit-based, equality-based, and need-based definition of distributive justice would be much more potent when justice principles are applied on a multinational level. Even within the U.S. system, the concept of affirmative action generates a great deal of emotion. Some individuals, particularly those who might be classified as racist or sexist, see affirmative action hiring programs as violating both equality and equity rules (Gilliland, 1993).

As you will recall from the earlier section on distributive and procedural justice, these two concepts appear to interact (Brockner & Weisenfeld, 1996; Gilliland, 1994). In the context of selection, this means that a negative hiring decision (potentially seen as low on distributive justice) might be perceived as less unfair if procedural justice principles (like those portrayed in Table 11.1) are maintained. It is common for an individual to consider the fairness of procedures when he or she is denied a desired outcome. In contrast, if an outcome is positive (i.e., a job is offered), violations of procedural justice principles will be less salient.

The United States has taken a particularly strong stand on equal employment opportunity. Through laws and policies, American employers promise applicants and employees equal opportunities for employment and job success. That is not to say that individuals are promised equal outcomes—simply equal opportunities. It is assumed that if all individuals have the same opportunity, then success will be dictated by merit—the skills and abilities of the applicant or the performance and motivation of the employee. This philosophy fits in well with the equity definition of distributive justice.

Unlike the equal opportunity philosophy, which stipulates that here and now, all individuals have an equal opportunity, there is another philosophy that also appears frequently in the American workplace: **affirmative action.** Affirmative action programs (AAP) acknowledge that particular demographic groups (e.g., women, African Americans, Hispanics, disabled) may be underrepresented in the work environment, and provide specific mechanisms for reducing this underrepresentation. This creates a potential problem. In the United States, the equity definition for distributive justice is the most commonly adopted definition. But AAPs provide enhanced opportunities for subgroups based on a principle of equality or need. White men often feel that they are treated unfairly or unjustly because of specific hiring preferences for women or African Americans. Women and African Americans, for their part, often feel that past discrimination has already robbed them of an equal opportunity to succeed, so they believe that they have been treated unfairly under the equity based definition of distributive justice. Thus, unhappily, both favored (e.g., African-American and women beneficiaries of AAPs) and nonfavored employees (e.g., white men) see themselves as "victims." Under these circumstances, it is easy to understand why AAPs are surrounded by so much emotion.

Underrepresented individuals often feel unjustly treated.

It is common for people to assume that affirmative action programs are simply hiring quotas, guaranteeing underrepresented employees a percentage of all available jobs. This is incorrect. Quotas are explicitly outlawed by the Civil Rights Act of 1991. Affirmative action programs can take many forms, including the following:

AFFIRMATIVE
ACTION

*Program that
acknowledges that
particular demographic
groups may be
underrepresented in
the work environment;
provides specific
mechanisms for
reducing this
underrepresentation.*

- Specialized recruiting programs intended to reach underrepresented groups in the workforce.
- Specialized pre- or posthire training to develop job-related KSAOs.
- Mentoring programs for underrepresented groups.
- Planned developmental opportunities such as assignment to particular teams and departments.
- Specialized performance feedback programs.

If individuals continue to see affirmative action programs as simple mechanical "quota" mechanisms, there will always be negative reactions. Majority applicants and workers will feel unjustly treated, and underrepresented beneficiaries of AAP will feel unjustly stigmatized and devalued.

AAPs represent one of the clearest examples of organizational actions that permit I-O psychologists to examine the perceptions of workplace justice. In the last 10 years there has been an increasing interest in studying the reactions of employees and applicants to AAPs.

The work of two researchers in particular can be used to describe research in this area. Heilman and her colleagues have concentrated on the issue of gender (Heilman & Alcot, 2001; Heilman, Battle, Keller, & Lee, 1998; Heilman & Blader, 2001; Heilman, Block, & Lucas, 1992; Heilman, McCullough, & Gilbert, 1996). Kravitz and his colleagues have examined the issue of race (Harrison, Kravitz, & Lev-Arey, 2001; Kravitz et al., 1997; Kravitz et al. 2000). As you can imagine, the dozens of studies conducted by these researchers and others on AAPs and their effects on applicants and employees have generated a considerable body of results. Some of the most salient findings are summarized in Table 11.2, which is based on the respective reviews and research of Kravitz and Heilman described above. You are encouraged to refer to these reviews for more detailed information about the specific studies. Once again we must express a note of caution about samples. Many of the studies use student participants, usually college students. As study participants, students may not be comparable to real-world employees, particularly when asked to imagine an employment setting. To draw any firm conclusions regarding the effects of AAPs on workplace behavior, we will need to develop a broader database with actual applicants and employees of organizations that have implemented AAPs.

Kravitz et al. (1997) found that there was slightly more support for AAPs directed toward women and the disabled than toward racial subgroups. However, the stronger the role that demographic status played in the AAP, the stronger the attitudes and often the active behavioral resistance by employees opposed to the program. Kravitz et al. suggested that if an AAP is to be successful, at the very least information must be provided that justifies it (other than simple underrepresentation), and the information must stress the importance of merit and qualification as one of the criteria for a decision as well as the past history of the organization in not pursuing workforce diversity. Unfortunately, in today's workplace many whites believe that discrimination is no longer a problem, so they are less willing to accept the possibility that present discriminatory environments represent evidence of the need for AAPs. This belief is inaccurate. There are still many instances of

---

TABLE 11.2   **Reactions to Affirmative Action Programs**

1. Attitudes toward AAPs are strongly associated with perceptions of fairness.

2. Blacks and women have substantially more positive attitudes toward AAPs than white males.

3. Political conservatives hold more negative attitudes toward AAPs than political liberals.

4. Individuals tend to make assumptions about the AAP that suit their underlying attitudes toward AAPs.

5. Justifications for AAPs that acknowledge the presence of past injustices at the organization are seen more positively than justifications based simply on issues of underrepresentation.

6. AAPs vary in "strength," with the mildest versions simply affirming equal opportunity or providing enhanced training opportunities for target groups and stronger versions explicitly expressing preferences in hiring for target groups, independent of abilities. The stronger the form of the AAP, the stronger the positive and negative attitudes associated with it.

7. Nonbeneficiaries of AAPs (e.g., white males) have a tendency to see beneficiaries (e.g., women and blacks) as less qualified and poorer performers in the organization.

8. When nonbeneficiaries of an AAP are informed that decisions were based on merit and not group membership, beliefs about the qualifications and performance of the beneficiary or target group member become more positive.

9. Beneficiaries of AAPs often feel stigmatized by being labeled an "AAP" hire and their performance may be affected by the perceived stigmatization.

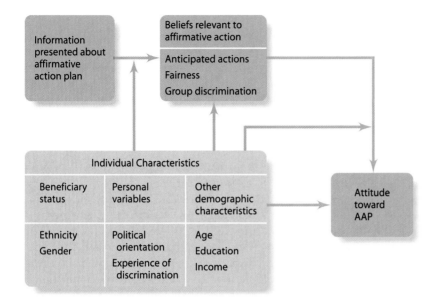

FIGURE 11.3

Conceptual Model of Determinants of Attitudes toward an Affirmative Action Plan SOURCE: Kravitz, Klineberg, Avery, Nguyen, Lund, & Fu (2000).

unfair discrimination, and as the workforce becomes more multicultural, these instances are more likely to increase than decrease. Kravitz and Klineberg (2000) presented a basic model that lays out the various influences on attitudes toward AAPs. As Figure 11.3 illustrates, attitudes about AAPs will be the result of both individual characteristics and organizational actions. Regardless of the complexities of these attitudes, however, feelings of justice and fairness are at the core of peoples' reactions.

Culture and Affirmative Action Programs

As we indicated earlier, affirmative action programs (AAPs) are peculiarly American. As such, they represent a disparity between an organizational policy and the commonly accepted equity definition of distributive justice. AAPs would likely generate considerably less tension in cultures where need and equality are seen as reasonable foundations for distributive justice. Indeed, many countries have a difficult time understanding why AAPs are so controversial in the United States. This provides a cautionary note for the practice of international and multicultural human resources. American expatriate managers should understand that managers and employees in other countries are not likely to be as concerned about AAPs as Americans. Further, foreign nationals who come to work in the United States in either a managerial or nonmanagerial role (particularly if they come from collectivist cultures), may have a difficult time understanding American worker resistance to AAPs or the lowered sense of self-esteem in beneficiaries of those programs. Steiner and Gilliland (2001) suggested that the cultural dimensions proposed by Hofstede (e.g., collectivism, power distance, uncertainty avoidance) may help us to understand why the perceived fairness of HR procedures may vary from country to country.

MODULE 11.2 SUMMARY

• Although almost any practice of an organization or behavior of a supervisor or co-workers can lead to feelings of unfairness, two particular aspects have received considerable attention: performance evaluation and applicant reactions to selection techniques.

• The concept of voice, or worker input, is common to the experience of fairness in most situations. If a procedure appears arbitrary or unfair, the opportunity to point out the unfairness can reverse that perception. In contrast, if employees lack an opportunity to object or have the procedure clarified, they will always believe that the process was unfair.

- I-O psychologists' study of applicant reactions to selection devices and selection decisions began relatively recently. Applicant perceptions of recruiting and selection procedures often lead to perceptions of fairness, so this area is important for the study of organizational justice.

- The model of Anderson and colleagues proposed that the emotional reactions of an applicant, particularly with respect to selection practices, influence ultimate decisions about whether to accept a job offer. Emotions can enter into the model in terms of applicant characteristics (e.g., positive or negative affect) and applicant reactions to selection (i.e., attitudes and emotions associated with fairness and justice perceptions).

- The United States has taken a particularly strong stand on equal employment opportunity. Through laws and policies, American employers promise applicants and employees equal opportunities for employment and job success. It is assumed that if all individuals have the same opportunity, then success will be dictated by merit. This philosophy fits in well with the equity definition of distributive justice.

- Affirmative action programs (AAPs) acknowledge that particular demographic groups (e.g., women, African Americans, Hispanics, disabled) may be underrepresented in the work environment, and provide specific mechanisms for reducing this underrepresentation. AAPs represent one of the clearest examples of organizational actions that permit I-O psychologists to examine the perceptions of workplace justice.

KEY TERMS

rational economic model
rational psychological model

organizational fit model

affirmative action

CRITICAL THINKING EXERCISES

11.3 Since performance evaluations seem to be related to feelings of injustice and unfairness, would it be better for organizations simply to forgo performance evaluations? Explain your answer.

11.4 For many government jobs, affirmative action programs have long been available to veterans in a form called "veterans preference," meaning that veterans get special consideration for job openings. There has been little tension surrounding the veterans preference form of affirmative action. Why do you suppose veterans preference is less controversial than affirmative action programs directed toward women or minorities?

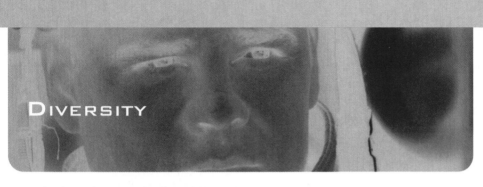

DIVERSITY

WHAT DOES DIVERSITY MEAN?

When the word **diversity** is used in the United States, it most often refers to the demographic characteristics of employees. A diverse workforce is thought to include both old and young, male and female, black, white, Hispanic, and Asian workers and managers. The term "multinational" also appears frequently to describe a diversity of nationalities (as opposed to skin color, gender, or age). As we will see, diversity is more than demographics. It means diversity in values, abilities, interests, and experiences. Of course, demographic differences often carry those psychological differences with them, but the demographic characteristics are like boxcars, simply transporting the more important variables. Unfortunately, like affirmative action, the term "diversity" has often taken on sociopolitical meaning. People are asked if they are "for" it or "against" it. As we will see below, it is largely beside the point to be for or against diversity. A diverse workforce is now a reality, not a goal or vision. In this module, we will address the issue of diversity not from the sociopolitical perspective but from the organizational perspective. One final term to keep in mind in our discussion is "multicultural." This is quite different from the terms diversity or multinational. A diverse or multinational workforce is a fact. An employer has or seeks to have a diverse or multinational employee base. A multicultural workforce, on the other hand, is a goal. As Cleveland, Stockdale, and Murphy (2000) explained, "Truly multicultural organizations are characterized by full structural and formal integration, minimal prejudice or discrimination, minimal subgroup differences in organizational attachment, and low levels of conflict." Thomas (1992) described the multicultural environment as "*one* culture reflecting the mixture of diversity in an organization rather than *several* minicultures reflecting the different elements in the mixture."

Jackson, May, and Whitney (1995) proposed that diversity can be considered from several perspectives. First, diversity can be predicated on attributes that are easy to detect, or on attributes that are less detectable. In addition, diversity can be distinguished on the basis of attributes that are related to tasks compared with those that are more relationship oriented. Table 11.3 presents the various ways in which diversity can be considered. Managers and workers tend to define diversity in terms of the readily detected attributes and demographic characteristics listed the table. For psychologists, however, there is more value in defining diversity in terms of the underlying attributes in that table. You will recognize those attributes from our earlier considerations of individual differences. These are the KSAOs that were described in Chapter 3 and Chapter 4.

THE DYNAMICS OF DIVERSITY

Pfeffer (1983) coined the term **relational demography** to describe the method by which work groups—and, by extension, organizations—are composed and changed. If an organization attempts to populate itself according to some formal or informal plan (e.g.,

DIVERSITY

Differences in demographic characteristics; also includes differences in values, abilities, interests, and experiences.

RELATIONAL DEMOGRAPHY

The relative makeup of various demographic characteristics in particular work groups.

TABLE 11.3	A Taxonomy for Describing the Content of Diversity	
	ATTRIBUTES MORE LIKELY TO BE TASK RELATED	**ATTRIBUTES MORE LIKELY TO BE RELATIONSHIP ORIENTED**
Readily detected attributes	Department/unit membership	Sex
	Organizational tenure	Socioeconomic status
		Age
	Formal credentials and titles	Race
	Education level	Ethnicity
	Memberships in professional associations	Religion
		Political memberships
		Nationality
Underlying attributes	Knowledge and expertise	Sexual orientation
	Cognitive skills and abilities	Gender
	Physical skills and abilities	Class identity
		Attitudes
		Values
		Personality
		Sexual identity
		Racial identity
		Ethnic identity
		Other social identities

Note: The examples shown are illustrative, not exhaustive.

SOURCE: Adapted from Jackson, May, & Whitney (1995).

creative, flexible, or conscientious people), these attempts will influence such things as recruiting, hiring, leadership, motivation, satisfaction, productivity, communication, and turnover (Landy, 2001). For example, Tsui and colleagues found that as work groups increased in racial and gender diversity, absenteeism and turnover increased (Tsui, Egan, & O'Reilly, 1991; Tsui & O'Reilly, 1989). The simplest way to interpret such findings is that as demographic diversity increases, so do variations in values, abilities, and motivations. Since individuals might prefer homogeneity to diversity, they may stay away from work more often (see Hulin's work withdrawal mechanism that we reviewed in Chapter 10) or even change jobs (Hulin's job withdrawal mechanism) as a way to avoid the conflicting values and interests that characterize a diverse workplace. As we will see in Chapter 14 on organizations, there is a tendency for work groups to seek homogeneity rather than diversity. Individuals prefer to associate with others who share their interests and values (Schneider et al., 1995). Both Pfeffer (1983) and Schneider (1987) proposed that work group homogeneity creates trust and enhances communication which, in turn, increase satisfaction, commitment, and effectiveness. Jackson (1991) found support for these propositions in the banking industry.

Herriot and Pemberton (1995) explained why group members appear to value homogeneity over diversity. They suggested that in diverse groups:

1. Others do not agree with your vision or goals.
2. Differences in visions and goals are the result of differences in values. When values are threatened, the result is defensive behavior.
3. When there are differences in vision and goals, there are disagreements about which projects to undertake and how to spend time and money.

4. Different visions are often associated with different analyses of the situation, leading to unproductive communication.

5. Differences in expertise and knowledge will lead to disagreement about methods and procedures.

With all of these difficulties, it is not surprising that group members may put up resistance to increased workplace diversity.

Diversity from the Work Group Perspective

The findings described above create a dilemma for the organization. It appears that workers are happier, more committed, and more effective when they work with others who are "like" them. In the past, even if there was some diversity at the work site, the solitary nature of most work allowed workers to largely ignore the differences in values and interests between themselves and other co-workers. But that is no longer possible for two reasons. First, work is no longer solitary. One way or another, many if not most workers will be in group or team environments for at least part of the workweek. Second, whether or not an employer finds this desirable, a demographic revolution is occurring at the workplace. Virtually every country has an "aging" workforce, which is a function of a much greater number of older individuals in the workforce than was the case 20 years ago. Thus, whether an organization has chosen to increase age diversity or not, it is happening. In addition, various social, political, and economic shifts precipitated by agreements like the European Union and the North American Free Trade Agreement (NAFTA), and the dissolution of the Warsaw Pact alliance in the former Soviet bloc, are breaking down national borders and resulting in more diverse work environments. Finally, the very existence of multinational corporations and a global economy suggests that work relationships will become increasingly diverse.

Jackson and Joshi (2001) addressed the issue of multicultural diversity from a training perspective. They reasoned that since multicultural environments will be associated with workforce diversity, the prudent employer will prepare employees to work in these diverse contexts. They noted the need for various types of training, depending on whether only two cultures are involved (e.g., an American-Japanese joint venture) or multiple cultures (e.g., a European Union team assembled from nine member countries). In addition, training for individuals would be different than training for teams. The training architecture they suggested is reproduced in Table 11.4. The issues of cross-cultural training and team training are covered in greater detail in Chapters 8 and 13, respectively.

Although diversity might have been a goal 15 years ago, it is now more of a challenge. As we will see, the problem is not simply fostering diversity, but managing it and fostering adaptation by diverse organizational members (Landy, 2001). There is an old saying that "everyone wants to get to heaven, but no one wants to die." The truth is that diversity does not come without costs. Nor is it a force that can be avoided.

But diversity also seems to have its advantages. Jackson et al. (1995) concluded that group heterogeneity (not only demographic heterogeneity but also background, experience, and personality) often enhances the creative efforts of work groups by widening the variety of approaches taken to problem solving. Watson, Kumar, and Michaelsen (1993) found that although culturally homogeneous work groups initially performed at higher levels, after 15 weeks the heterogeneous work groups became more effective. Landy (2001) offered the following tentative conclusions from the available data:

1. Initially, there will be some tension and lowered effectiveness in demographically heterogeneous work groups.

2. If work groups remain intact, effectiveness will increase.

3. The fewer the number of "out group" members (i.e., those unlike the majority in the group), the greater will be the initial tension and efforts to drive these dissimilar members out of the group.

TABLE 11.4	Approaches to Training Employees for Work in International Contexts	
DIVERSITY IN ORGANIZATIONS		
	INDIVIDUAL TRAINING	**TEAM TRAINING**
Single culture	Training regarding host country's culture, laws, and language geared for specific overseas assignment	Training modules that involve both parent country and host country nationals in mutual exploration of each other's culture, laws and language
Multiple cultures	Training programs aimed at developing global manager's generic intercultural competencies (e.g., interpersonal communication skills, ability to tolerate stress, emphasis on personal growth, sense of humor)	Training global, dispersed teams to develop common protocol for communication across distances using electronic mail, videoconferencing, and voice messaging facilities
		Team-based training modules designed to facilitate face-to-face interaction among team members
		Socialization of new team members to multicultural context
		Long-term training aimed at developing team identity
		Leadership training designed specifically for multicultural context

SOURCE: Jackson & Joshi (2001).

We will cover the issues of team composition and in-group and out-group status in Chapters 12 and 13.

Managing Diversity from the Organizational Perspective

The actual management of diversity will involve virtually all of the tools in the I-O psychologist's toolkit—recruiting, selecting, training, motivating, leading, and so forth. The most effective approach will likely differ for each organization and each situation. Nevertheless, Cleveland, Stockdale, and Murphy (2000) have identified the characteristics of organizations most likely to manage diversity successfully. A successful organization will:

1. Exhibit diversity at every level, not just at entry levels.
2. Foster diversity not only in formal levels of the organization, but also in less formal social networks.
3. Uncover and root out bias and discriminatory practices.
4. Build commitment and attachment to the organization among all members, not only in-group members.
5. Take steps to reduce interpersonal conflict.
6. Acknowledge and accommodate cultural differences rather than pretend they do not exist.

But just as diversity can be managed effectively, it can be mismanaged as well. Herriot and Pemberton (1995) identified two ineffective models for addressing diversity.

1. **Assimilation model:** Recruit, select, train, and motivate employees so that all share the same values and culture. This model assumes there are no advantages to a diverse workforce, an assumption that has been challenged (Jackson et al., 1995).

ASSIMILATION MODEL

Model for addressing diversity that recruits, selects, trains, and motivates employees so that they share the same values and culture.

2. **Protection model:** Identify disadvantaged and underrepresented groups and provide special protections for them. In the last section, we saw that this model often leads to justice and fairness debates, with resulting increases in dissatisfaction and anger and decreases in commitment and effectiveness.

They recommended a third model as the ideal for conceptualizing diversity.

3. **Value model:** Each diverse element of the organization is valued for what it uniquely brings to the organization.

The value model captures the concept of multiculturalism as we described it earlier in this module (Cleveland et al., 2000; Thomas, 1992). Herriot and Pemberton (1995) also identified several HR initiatives that support the value model (multicultural) of diversity.

Demographic diversity implies psychological diversity.

1. Recruit specifically with diversity in mind.
2. Ensure that career development is available for every member of the organization and hold managers accountable for that universal development.
3. Provide diversity training for all employees and managers.
4. Seek input from diverse group members, not just their managers.
5. Provide support and networks for diverse group members.
6. Develop connections to broader cultural groups in the community.

The recommendations provided for developing and managing a diverse workplace might be distilled into the principles of distributive justice (i.e., fairness in the distribution of outcomes) and procedural justice (particularly in providing an outlet for "voice") with which we began this chapter. In other words, diversity will thrive if the environment is open, inclusive, and just. Diversity will flounder when the environment is closed, exclusive, and unjust.

Leadership and Diversity

Organizations will need to pay close attention to the dynamics of work groups. Regardless of the values of the upper levels of the organization, work groups may very well strive for the comfort of homogeneity. This will place the major burden for managing diversity on the shoulders of the group or team leader (Lord & Gradwohl-Smith, 1999). From the leader's perspective, managing diversity requires an understanding of any stereotypes that might exist among group members and challenges them with a view toward changing those beliefs. But managing diversity also requires the leader to bear in mind that each member of the group is an individual, regardless of the attributes (demographic or psychological) he or she might share with other group members. Each worker, in a sense, has three identities. First, he or she is a member of the organization and should be treated in a manner consistent with the treatment of every other member of the organization. In addition, each worker belongs to a cultural group whose members share values. Finally, each worker is an individual with a unique past and future. Managers have always had to deal with the principles of consistency of treatment and uniqueness of individuals. But the challenge of diversity adds a level of culture that is becoming increasingly important in the workplace.

PROTECTION MODEL

Model for addressing diversity that identifies disadvantaged and underrepresented groups and provides special protections for them.

VALUE MODEL

Model for addressing diversity in which each element of an organization is valued for what it uniquely brings to the organization.

MODULE 11.3 SUMMARY

- Diversity can refer to demographic attributes that are easy to detect or psychological attributes that are more difficult to detect. Managers and workers tend to define diversity in terms of readily detected attributes such as demographic characteristics. For psychologists, there is more value in defining diversity in terms of the underlying psychological attributes or KSAOs that were described in Chapters 3 and 4.

- Diversity has both costs and benefits. Although initially there will be some tension and lowered effectiveness in demographically and culturally heterogeneous work groups, effectiveness will increase if work groups remain intact. Group heterogeneity often enhances the creative efforts of work groups by widening the variety of approaches taken to problem solving.

- Managing diversity involves the I-O psychologist's entire toolkit—recruiting, selecting, training, motivating, and leading. The most effective approach will probably differ for each organization and each situation. However, successful organizations will be more likely to exhibit diversity at every level, foster diversity in formal and informal ways throughout the organization, and uncover and root out bias and discriminatory practices.

- Two ineffective models for addressing diversity are the assimilation model and the protection model. The assimilation model involves recruiting, selecting, training, and motivating employees so that they share the same values and culture, whereas the protection model identifies disadvantaged and underrepresented groups and provides special protections for them. An alternative model for addressing diversity is the value model, in which each diverse element of the organization is valued for what it uniquely brings to the organization. Overall, diversity will thrive if the work environment is open, inclusive, and just.

KEY TERMS

diversity
relational demography

assimilation model
protection model

value model

CRITICAL THINKING EXERCISES

11.5 Psychologists think of diversity in terms of KSAOs, but nonpsychologists define diversity in terms of demographics. If one were to assemble a diverse group based on demographics, would there be psychological diversity as well? Explain your answer.

11.6 The assimilation model identified by Herriot and Pemberton (1995) attempts to create a homogeneous workforce through training and motivation. What are the advantages and disadvantages of such an approach?

LEADERSHIP

12 CHAPTER

THE CONCEPT OF LEADERSHIP

SOME CONCEPTUAL DISTINCTIONS

Take a moment and list all the leaders of whom you are a follower. The first leaders to come into mind may be your instructors, department chair, dean, and other school administrators all the way up to the president. Or you may think of your mayor, city council members, state representatives and senators, and U.S. representatives and senators. Or perhaps your sports coach, your cleric, or your supervisor at work. You may not have thought of all these individuals as leaders before—and you may or may not feel that their leadership is effective. Does the simple act of recognizing various leaders provide many insights *about* leadership? Not really. In this chapter we will examine leadership and studies that endeavor to identify what makes an effective leader.

Many treatments of leadership concentrate on "high impact" leaders: the corporate CEO, the chairman of the board, the president, the chairman of the Joint Chiefs of Staff. These top-echelon individuals operate in rarefied air. The problem in deriving our leadership principles from the study of that elite group is that there are not many of them, and each of them is in a dramatically different situation. For these reasons, we will concentrate less on executives than on middle- and lower-level leaders in organizations. For those interested in the particular issues related to executive leadership, Silzer's book (2002) will prove useful.

Leader Emergence versus Leader Effectiveness

It is important to distinguish between the concepts of **leader emergence** and **leadership effectiveness.** It is tempting to confuse the concepts by assuming that all who emerge as leaders will be effective. While that is sometimes the case, it is not always true. If we are interested in leadership emergence, we might study the characteristics of individuals who *become* leaders. On what basis were they elected or appointed, or simply accepted? If, on the other hand, we are interested in leader effectiveness, we might study what behaviors on the part of a designated leader (regardless of how he or she achieved that position) led to an outcome valued by the work group or organization.

Leader Emergence

Research on the relationship between leader emergence and the Big Five personality factors was recently examined in a meta-analysis by Judge, Bono, Ilies, and Gerhardt (2002). They found that several of the Big Five factors were associated with leader emergence. Leader emergence was defined as "whether (or to what degree) an individual is viewed as a leader by others" (p. 767). Emotional stability, extraversion, openness to experience, and conscientiousness were all positively associated with individuals who emerged as leaders.

LEADER EMERGENCE

Study of the characteristics of individuals who become leaders, examining the basis on which they were elected, appointed, or simply accepted.

LEADERSHIP EFFECTIVENESS

Study of which behaviors on the part of a designated leader (regardless of how that position was achieved) led to an outcome valued by the work group or organization.

Surprisingly, agreeableness was unrelated to leader emergence. The researchers also separated the studies into those conducted in business settings, military/government settings, and with students. They found that the most consistent correlate of both leader emergence and leader effectiveness was extraversion.

THE PROBLEM OF DEFINING LEADERSHIP OUTCOMES

In other chapters of this book, we have examined various approaches to improving individual performance and, as a result, organizational productivity. In many senses we knew what we were after: decreased absence, increased commitment, more persistence, creativity, and so forth. The situation is not so clear with leadership. Leadership has been variously credited with achieving technological breakthroughs, settling labor problems, bringing an organization back from bankruptcy, increasing share value, increasing consumer confidence, or simply creating a fun place to work. Which of these is the "right" outcome to examine? If we want to develop a theory of leadership impact, which criterion variable should we choose to "validate" the theory? Day (2001a) pointed out some of the difficulties in assessing leadership outcomes. It is assumed that leaders affect the structure and performance of an organization. But which aspects of structure? Which indicators of performance?

Leaders, particularly at top of an organization, are assumed to be visionary, not bound to the here and now. On what time frame should we measure or evaluate the outcomes of visionary behavior? A year? Five years? A decade? If we are going to evaluate the outcomes of leadership, when should we start and when should we stop counting? In the late 1970s, the Social Democratic Party, a party that had ruled Sweden for more than 40 years, was voted out of office. The departing prime minister, the late Olaf Palme, observed that the new ruling party and prime minister could do little since they came to "a set table." By this, Palme meant that change is slow and, in this case, it would be time for a new election before the new ruling party could accomplish anything of significance. He was right. Within six years, Palme's Social Democratic Party was back in power, the interim government having accomplished very little.

As Day (2001a) pointed out, the effects of a leader's behavior are not always immediately obvious or detectable. Consider the oriental game of Go, an elaborate form of checkers on a much larger board. The object of the game, which may take two to five hours to complete, is to surround all of your opponent's pieces, leaving no escape. You do this by playing on different parts of the board simultaneously with a "connection plan" in mind that your opponent will not see. Then, at a crucial time, you connect all of your pieces and win the game. There is a "lag" time between action and result. You may have positioned one of your pieces in a far corner of the board at the beginning of the game and that piece may be the key to winning the game. In the same way, a leader may put strategic plans into place and their effects may not be seen for months or even years.

LEADER VERSUS MANAGER OR SUPERVISOR

Let's start by specifying what we mean by a **leader.** Fiedler (1967) defined a leader as "the individual in the group given the task of directing and coordinating task relevant group activities, or who, in the absence of a designated leader, carries the primary responsibility for performing these functions in the group" (p. 8). With such a neutral definition, "leader" could be replaced with the words "director," "manager," "supervisor," or even "coordinator." But the term "leader" usually evokes a much more visceral reaction. A first lieutenant leading a squad of rangers into a cave complex in Afghanistan is a leader; a politician leading a grassroots effort to restore a wilderness area is a leader; a trauma surgeon directing the efforts of a team of medical specialists to save the life of a child hit by a car is a leader.

LEADER

The individual in a group given the task of directing task-relevant group activities or, in the absence of a designated leader, carries the primary responsibility for performing these functions in the group.

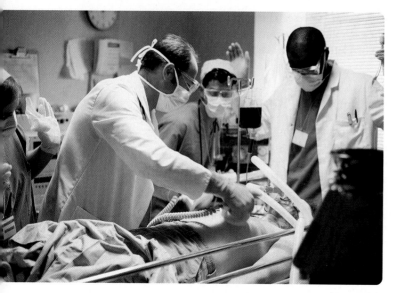

A surgeon assisted by a team is an example of a group with a clear designated leader.

In these instances, a leader is someone who influences, or attempts to influence, other people. The behaviors involved in exerting this influence can be called leadership, and those who exert such influence can be called leaders. But attempts at leadership are not always successful. Bass (1960) made the following distinctions:

Attempted leadership: Person A accepts the goal of changing person B, and can be observed attempting to change person B.

Successful leadership: Person B changes his or her behavior as a function of person A's effort.

Effective leadership: As a function of person B's behavioral change resulting from person A's efforts, person B will be more satisfied, will be better rewarded, and will have attained a goal of mutual importance to person A and person B.

Effective leadership is a win–win situation for the leader, the follower, and the organization. That is not necessarily true of either attempted or successful leadership. A manager may try unsuccessfully to persuade a work group to improve timeliness. The leadership was attempted. The manager might threaten the work group with punishment of some sort, and timeliness may actually improve, but three key group members may ask for a transfer to another department. The leadership was successful but not effective. As a third example, a manager might take his or her work group off-site for a discussion of obstacles to timeliness, agree to changes in work process, and praise workers in subsequent weeks for their newfound timeliness. In this case, the leadership was effective; the manager did not act merely as a supervisor.

The terms "manager" and "supervisor" are job titles. They imply the tasks or duties of the person who holds the title. They describes *what* is to be done. Leadership deals with *how* these tasks or duties are carried out with respect to members of the work group. "Leader" refers to a social-psychological aspect of the role of supervisor or manager. The manager seeks to bring order and consistency to work; the leader seeks change (Day, 2001a).

ATTEMPTED LEADERSHIP

Leader accepts the goal of changing a follower, and can be observed attempting to change the follower.

SUCCESSFUL LEADERSHIP

Follower changes his or her behavior as a function of the leader's effort.

EFFECTIVE LEADERSHIP

Leader changes follower's behavior, resulting in both leader and follower feeling satisfied and effective.

The Blending of Managerial and Leadership Roles

Until a few decades ago, many organizations would have been delighted with an effective leader but satisfied with a successful one. Effective leadership was thought to be the icing on the managerial or supervisory cake. Since effective leaders were uncommon, it was considered a stroke of luck for an organization to end up with one, in part, because of the belief that leaders were "born" rather than "made." Employers assumed that there were certain traits that made a good leader, and they selected people for managerial positions based on these traits. Unfortunately, the trait approach generally turned out to be useless in choosing managers who would also be effective leaders. So the employer settled for managers regardless of leadership ability.

As we will see later in this chapter, trait theory is making a comeback in the form of studies examining the relationship of Big Five factors and leader effectiveness. This more modern approach defines personality traits behaviorally, has a general consensus on the meaning of these traits, and considers them in the context of organizational and situational variables. This modern approach is turning out to be considerably more successful than traditional trait theory.

A man in a hot air balloon realized that he was lost. He reduced altitude and spotted a woman below. He descended a bit more and shouted, "Excuse me, can you help me? I promised a friend I would meet him an hour ago, but I don't know where I am!"

The woman below replied, "You are in a hot air balloon hovering approximately 30 feet above the ground. You are between 40 and 41 degrees north latitude. You are between 59 and 60 degrees west longitude."

"You must be an engineer," replied the balloonist.

"I am," replied the woman. "How did you know?"

"Well," answered the balloonist, "everything you've told me is technically correct, but I have no idea what to make

of your information. The fact is that I am still lost. Frankly, you've not been much help so far."

The woman below responded, "You must be in management."

"I am," replied the balloonist. "But how did you know?"

"Well, you don't know where you are, or where you are going. You have risen to where you are due to a large quantity of hot air. You made a promise you have no idea how to keep. You expect people beneath you to solve your problems. The fact is that you are in exactly the same position you were in before we met. But now, somehow, it's my fault."

In the last 40 years, we have learned an enormous amount about effective leadership. We have learned that many, if not most, people can become effective leaders given the right circumstances. We have also learned that leadership is not solely about the possession of certain traits. It is also about behaving in particular ways that facilitate the enthusiastic expenditure of energy by followers. I-O psychologists do not always agree exactly what those particular modes of behavior are, but they do agree that leadership is much more than the possession of key traits.

Modern approaches to defining the roles of managers and the required competencies have blended many of the duties of the manager with the expectations of what represents effective leadership (Tett, Guterman, Bleir, & Murphy, 2000). Among the many proposed taxonomies of managerial performance requirements (e.g., Hemphill, 1959; Mitchell, 1978; Tornow & Pinto, 1976; Williams, 1956; Yukl, 1987), perhaps the most recent and comprehensive was suggested by Borman and Brush (1993), who identified 246 potential dimensions of managerial performance from published and unpublished research. One of the most impressive aspects of their collection of dimensions was its derivation from a wide range of occupational settings, including hospitals, universities, police departments, manufacturing companies, the armed services, and high-tech firms. Using the judgments of more than 100 experienced I-O psychologists, Borman and Brush compressed the 246 managerial dimensions into 187, then subjected judgments to a statistical analysis that identified 18 broad areas of managerial responsibility, which we have presented in Table 12.1. In that table, we have indicated in bold face the dimensions that would seem most closely connected to leadership behavior.

Borman and Brush's (1993) taxonomy made the connection between leadership and management very clear: no fewer than 6 of the 18 dimensions are related to leadership. Their statistical analysis also confirmed that these leadership-related dimensions accounted for a little more than one-third of the tasks of a manager. It appears that modern conceptions of management include a large helping of leadership. Other, earlier attempts to map managerial behaviors suggested a similar relationship, but Borman and Brush were more comprehensive, identifying dimensions that do not appear in one or more of the earlier studies. In contrast, none of the dimensions mentioned in earlier taxonomies fails to appear in the Borman and Brush taxonomy.

Tett et al. (2000) argued that Borman and Brush identified managerial dimensions at too broad a level, and proposed 53 dimensions rather than 18. This is reminiscent of the debate we described in Chapter 3 over the Big Five personality factors: How many are sufficient? The answer to the debate about the number of managerial dimensions is the same

TABLE 12.1	Areas of Managerial Responsibility

Planning and Organizing

Guiding, Directing, and Motivating Subordinates

Training, Coaching, and Developing Subordinates

Communicating Effectively and Keeping Others Informed

Representing the Organization to Customers and the Public

Technical Proficiency

Administration and Paperwork

Maintaining Good Working Relationships

Coordinating Subordinates and Other Resources to Get the Job Done

Decision Making and Problem Solving

Staffing

Persisting to Reach Goals

Handling Crises

Organizational Commitment

Monitoring and Controlling Resources

Delegating

Selling/Influencing

Collecting and Interpreting Data

SOURCE: Based on Borman & Brush (1993).

as that for the number of personality dimensions: Some uses will call for finer distinctions (i.e., some subset of the 53 dimensions described in Tett et al.) and some uses will be better served by 18 broader dimensions. As is often the case, neither Borman and Brush nor Tett et al. are "right." The results of either study may prove useful in certain situations.

LEADER DEVELOPMENT VERSUS LEADERSHIP DEVELOPMENT

Day (2001b) made an important distinction between "leader development" and "leadership development" that strikes at the heart of the meaning of leadership. Most leadership training programs concentrate on developing, maintaining, or enhancing individual attributes such as knowledge, skills, and abilities. Thus, those who appoint or elect leaders expect them to be "self-aware, self-regulating, and self-motivating." Notice the emphasis on the word "self"; they assume that the leader will then bring these attributes to bear on followers, resulting in changes in the way people think or act. While Day did not dismiss these individual attributes, he proposed that training that focuses on them is not "leadership" development; instead, this is **leader development.** A training program with effective **leadership development** will concentrate not on the attributes of the leader, but on the nature of the leader-follower relationship.

Thus, Day (2001b) viewed the essence of leadership as one of social exchange. To him, leadership is "building networked relationships among individuals that enhance cooperation and resource exchange in creating organizational value" (p. 585). As long ago as 1975, Pfeffer and Salancik (1978; Salancik & Pfeffer, 1977) introduced this perspective, and it has become increasingly popular in recent years. They suggested, as Day (2001b) had proposed, that leadership grew out of interactions among individuals in the organization rather than being an entity independent of those interactions. For Day the single most important "ability" for creating leadership opportunities is the **interpersonal competence** of the person designated as the leader. Interpersonal competence includes social awareness (a concern for others similar to certain aspects of contextual performance that we reviewed in Chapters 5 and 6) and social skills such as the ability to resolve conflict and foster a spirit of cooperation. Citing the key to organizational success as the ability of the organization and all of its members to adapt to and create change, Day saw the task of the leader as one of preparing the group not only to embrace change, but to create and implement it. In Day's view, every work group member can and should be part of the leadership team. Leadership development is focused on integration (as opposed to differentiation) of the attributes of each member of the group. The leader leads by helping work group members relate to one another, engage in cooperative rather than independent action, and become more aware of the social nature of productive effort and change. By extension, this means that an effective leader will create an environment in which leadership emerges from and is carried out by the group, not the leader.

Thus, Day's (2001b) propositions are not so much about training and development as they are about the essence of leadership. He simply approached the concept by using training and development as a backdrop. Most leadership theories we will review, old and new, will focus on the individual attributes and behavior of the person designated as the leader. Thus, they are consistent with Day's view of leader—as opposed to leadership— development; they focus on sorting out or differentiating unique attributes of the individual leader, and making the leader aware of his or her own strengths and weaknesses. Even Day admitted that these individual attributes are important. Without recognizing them, the leader would be unlikely or unable to develop leadership in the group. Nevertheless, Day suggested that if the study of leadership stops with the individual, it will not contribute to the ultimate success of an organization. If one were to adopt Day's approach, individuals—regardless of their job title or formal position in the group—would not ask, "How can I be an effective leader?" Instead they would ask, "How can I participate productively in the leadership process?" (Day, 2001b; Drath & Palus, 1994).

THE MOTIVATION TO LEAD

When asked, "What made you want to become a CEO/president/coach/plant manager?" the respondent will often reply with a comment like: "I don't know, I guess they caught me in a weak moment." The implication (one shared by many nonleaders) is that no one in his or her right mind would actively seek out the headaches of leading or managing. But we know that people *do* aspire to positions of leadership, and often compete vigorously with others for those positions. Why do they do this? Leadership emergence studies tell us something about the characteristics of those who eventually become leaders, but these studies do not tell us *why* the individual wanted to become a leader.

House and Singh (1987) took an uncomplicated view of the process. Depending heavily on the psychodynamic work of McClelland (1975, 1979, 1982, 1985), they concluded that people who aspire to positions of leadership have a high power motive coupled with high activity inhibition and low affiliation needs. According to McClelland (1985), people learn that the exercise of power, or control, over others or the environment is pleasing: the **power motive.** To reproduce that pleasant feeling (what we called "affect" in Chapter 10), people look for additional opportunities to exercise control. Indeed, former Secretary of State Henry Kissinger is often quoted as having said, "Power is the ultimate aphrodisiac" (Bartlett's *Familiar Quotations,* 1998, p. 752). High **activity inhibition** is the psychological term used to describe a person who is not impulsive. A low **affiliation need** means that people do not have a great desire for approval or connections with others. According to House and Singh, the low affiliation motive permits an individual "to remain socially distant from subordinates and therefore to be more objective with respect to resource allocation, delegation, and discipline" (1987, p. 675).

INTERPERSONAL COMPETENCE

Includes social awareness and social skills such as the ability to resolve conflict and foster a spirit of cooperation.

POWER MOTIVE

Attaining control or power that results from people learning that the exercise of control over others or the environment is pleasing.

ACTIVITY INHIBITION

Psychological term used to describe a person who is not impulsive.

AFFILIATION NEED

Need for approval or connections with others.

Although most of us have known individual leaders who appeared to be driven by a desire for power, were deliberate rather than impulsive, and maintained a certain distance from their followers, we have also seen other leaders who seem less motivated by power than by duty, or the need to help others. Thus, the experience of power or control is a reward for many people, but there are clearly other motivational bases for the desire to lead.

Chan and Drasgow (2001) proposed a more complicated model, one that appears to account for greater variation in the motive to lead. They concluded that there was not one motivation to lead (i.e., a power motive) but three. These three motives and the characteristics that define them are shown in Table 12.2. The first motive, affective-identity, might be interpreted as a power motive characterized by a desire for control. The second motive, instrumental, emphasizes the personal benefits that come with being a leader. The third motive, social-normative, is more unselfish, emphasizing the duty to lead when called upon, and the honor and privilege of leading. Chan and Drasgow suggested that these three motives develop from a combination of personality characteristics, beliefs about leadership capability, and past leadership experiences. They also demonstrated that these motives are independent of general mental ability in predicting leadership potential ratings for military school cadets. Although cadets are a far cry from business leaders, leadership is taken quite seriously in military settings so research participants such as these are more relevant than, say, an undergraduate student pretending to be a leader for the purposes of an experiment.

What these results tell us is that there are several different motives for leading. They do not tell us that an individual can only be influenced by one motive at a time. For example, it is reasonable to assume that some individuals might be motivated by both the affective-identity and the instrumental dimensions (e.g., they like to lead and they also like the concrete benefits that come from leading). The Chan and Drasgow research is preliminary and dealt with a narrow range of participants (17- to 21-year-old students and military cadets). Nevertheless, the notion of multiple motivations to lead is more plausible than the proposition that all leaders are driven by a need for control and power.

TABLE 12.2	Motives to Lead
MOTIVE	**ITEM**
Affective-Identity	I prefer being a leader.
	I want to be the leader.
	I have a tendency to take charge in groups.
	I am seldom reluctant to be the leader of a group.
Instrumental	I am interested in leading if there are advantages to me.
	I will agree to lead if I can see personal benefits.
	Leading others is more of a dirty job than an honorable one.
Social-Normative	I feel I have a duty to lead when asked.
	I have been taught to volunteer to lead others when I can.
	I was taught to believe in the value of leading others.
	People should volunteer to lead rather than wait to be asked.

SOURCE: Based on Chan & Drasgow (2001).

MODULE 12.1 SUMMARY

- It is important to distinguish between the concepts of leader emergence, which examines the characteristics of individuals who become leaders, and leadership effectiveness, which examines the behaviors on the part of a leader that result in valued group or organizational outcomes.

- The terms "manager" and "supervisor" are job titles that imply the tasks or duties of the person who holds the title. They describe *what* is to be done. Leadership deals with *how* these tasks or duties are carried out with respect to members of the work group. Modern approaches to defining the roles of managers and the required competencies have blended many of the duties of the manager with expectations embodied in effective leadership.

- It has been argued that training that focuses on individual attributes is not "leadership" development, but "leader" development. In contrast, an effective leadership development training program concentrates on the nature of the leader-follower relationship.

- Research indicates that people who aspire to positions of leadership have a high power motive coupled with high activity inhibition and low affiliation needs. Additional research suggests that motives for leadership may develop from a combination of personality characteristics, beliefs about leadership capability, and past leadership experiences.

KEY TERMS

leader emergence
leadership effectiveness
leader
attempted leadership

successful leadership
effective leadership
leader development
leadership development

interpersonal competence
power motive
activity inhibition
affiliation need

CRITICAL THINKING EXERCISES

12.1 Every four years, the United States chooses a president. The campaign for the presidency often lasts for two years or more. Would you characterize the enventual election of a president as an example of leader effectiveness or leader emergence? Why?

12.2 We have seen that there may be many different, and sometimes competing, motives to lead. Using the Chan and Drasgow (2001) trichotomy of motives to lead, would a university be better served with a president who is driven predominantly by an affective-identity motive, an instrumental motive, or a social-normative motive? Why?

TRADITIONAL THEORIES OF LEADERSHIP

GREAT
MAN/GREAT
WOMAN THEORY

Developed by historians who examined the life of a respected leader for clues leading to his or her greatness; often focused on a galvanizing experience or an admirable trait (persistence, optimism, or intelligence) that a leader possesses to a singular degree.

THE GREAT MAN AND GREAT WOMAN THEORIES

As long as there have been leaders, there have been leadership "theories." Many of these are what might be called **"great man/great woman" theories,** which are developed by historians who pore over the life of a respected leader for clues of what led to his or her greatness. This hunt for clues is made easier by the penchant of leaders to write books about their experiences. Recent examples include books by political leaders such as Margaret Thatcher, Colin Powell, and Bill Clinton; championship NFL and NBA coaches such as Mike Shanahan and Pat Riley; and industry leaders such as cosmetics executive Estée Lauder and former General Electric chairman Jack Welch.

Two kinds of clues about leader greatness are popular: a galvanizing experience, such as overcoming a near-fatal illness; or an admirable trait such as persistence, optimism, or intelligence, which the leader possesses to a singular degree. If these theories are accurate, we might be able to predict that every child who has the strength to recover from rheumatic fever or the brilliance to graduate first in his or her class will go on to become the CEO of a major corporation or be elected head of state.

From the perspective of I-O psychology, great man/great woman theories are of little value. However, by examining the biographies of leaders, we can surmise that every successful leadership career is a combination of individual attributes and circumstances in which the leaders found themselves. For example, Harry Truman won admiration for leading the United States to victory in World War II. But Truman was thrust into the presidency as a result of the sudden death of Franklin D. Roosevelt. Truman's leadership success, therefore, may be attributed to a combination of factors: the circumstance of Roosevelt's death and its occurrence at a crucial phase of the war, and Truman's personal experiences and qualities that went into shaping him as an individual and a leader.

THE TRAIT APPROACH

When I-O psychologists set out to understand the leadership phenomenon in the 1920s and 1930s, the first approach they utilized was known as the **trait approach.** It was, in simple terms, an attempt to show that leaders possessed certain characteristics that nonleaders did not (see Table 12.3). It is not surprising that they favored this approach. As you will recall from our discussions about the history of I-O psychology, there was a single-minded devotion to individual differences like general mental ability ("g"), so it makes sense that every attempt to understand a phenomenon would begin with a search for relevant individual difference variables.

The "Great Man/Great Woman" theory of leadership is attractive but has not been supported by scientific research.

TABLE 12.3	**Some Characteristics of Leaders That Have Been Studied**	
Adjustment	Height	Psychoticism
Age	Intelligence	Responsibility
Altruism	Introversion	Scholarship
Ambition	Judgment	Self-confidence
Authoritarianism	Kindness	Sensitivity
Compatibility	Lability	Sociability
Conservatism	Masculinity	Stature
Deference	Maturity	Supportiveness
Dominance	Motivation	Surgency
Empathy	Neuroticism	Verbal facility
Esteem	Originality	Vocabulary usage
Extroversion	Perceptiveness	Weight
Fear of failure	Persistence	
Gender	Popularity	

The trait approach proved to be a dead end. No consistent relationships were found between traits and leader effectiveness, in part because there was little agreement about what these traits even meant. One researcher studied "empathy," while a second studied "kindness," and a third studied "supportiveness." Each defined the trait differently and used different methods of measuring it. But the larger reason for the failure of the approach might have been an unwillingness to accept leadership in a larger context which would include the organization, the situation, and the followers (Hollander & Julian, 1969). One final problem with the early trait approach was its obsession with productivity as a criterion. Every study attempted to show a positive correlation between a leader trait and a measure of subordinate productivity. In more recent years, it has become clear that leadership has to do with much more than productivity; factors like commitment, motivation, and satisfaction also play key roles. It is also clear that when the leader does affect productivity, he or she does it indirectly by influencing other variables.

TRAIT APPROACH

Attempts to show that leaders possessed certain characteristics that nonleaders did not.

THE "POWER" APPROACH TO LEADERSHIP

One of the most obvious characteristics of managers is that they have power that subordinates do not have. An organization gives a manager the power to make decisions about people, expenses, methods of production, and so forth. The higher the manager is in the organization, the more power, or authority, he or she tends to have. Thus, one approach to leadership might be to examine the types of power wielded by leaders. This is the **power approach** to leadership. French and Raven (1959) proposed that formal authority was only one kind of power. They suggested at least five different types of power, including:

- *Reward power*—the potential of a supervisor to mediate or dispense valued rewards.
- *Coercive power*—the potential of a supervisor to mediate or dispense punishments.
- *Legitimate power*—the "right" of a supervisor to influence a subordinate and the obligation of the subordinate to accept that influence.

POWER APPROACH

Examines the types of power wielded by leaders.

- *Referent power*—the identification of the subordinate with the supervisor; the desire of the subordinate to be like and act like the supervisor; the power of example.
- *Expert power*—the knowledge or expertise that a supervisor has in a special area.

The studies of how and when leaders used different power bases and combinations of them were very practical in orientation. Even though they were not necessarily guided by a clear "theory" of leadership, they did provide some direction for the exercise of leadership. Yukl (1998) suggested ways that various bases of power can be increased or maintained, as well as the most effective ways to use each power base (see Table 12.4). Pfeffer (1981; Salancik & Pfeffer, 1977) has characterized the modern organization as a political entity. Managers use their formal power or authority to increase other power bases (Yukl, 1998). They use methods such as:

- Forming coalitions (e.g., managers from different departments joining forces; a marketing manager forming an alliance with a supplier).
- Controlling important decisions (e.g., attempting to get sympathetic representatives appointed to decision-making groups).
- Co-opting the opposition (e.g., inviting a strong opponent to join a committee or decision-making body).
- Controlling information flow (e.g., limiting the distribution of information about bad decisions that the manager made, and maximizing the distribution of information about good decisions).

We will discuss the distribution and use of power in greater detail in Chapter 14 on organizational design. Issues of individual leader power are also important considerations in the functioning of teams, a topic we turn to in Chapter 13. In sum, we can conclude that the more power bases a leader has, the greater the potential to influence group members. But it is also true that whichever bases are used in any given situation, and how they are used, will ultimately determine their effects.

THE BEHAVIORAL APPROACH
The Ohio State University Studies

By the early 1950s, it was clear that the trait approach would not unlock the secrets of leadership. A group of leadership researchers at the Ohio State University decided to pursue a **behavioral approach.** Edwin Fleishman was one of these researchers; he described the process as follows:

> Focusing on the kinds of behavior engaged in by people in leadership roles, these investigators developed over 1,800 items (for example, "He calls the group together to talk things over"; "He knows about it when something goes wrong") descriptive of what supervisors do in their leadership roles. These items were then classified into ten broad categories of leader behavior (for example, initiation, domination, evaluation, communication). Questionnaires were then developed by means of which leader behavior could be described and scored on these ten dimensions. Each supervisor was described in terms of how frequently (for, example, always, often, . . . never) he did what each item stated. Repeated use of these questionnaires in a variety of leader-group situations (foreman-worker, executive-subordinate, school principal–teacher, university department head–professor, aircraft commander–crew, submarine officer–crew) showed that these ten categories overlapped with one another and that the items could be grouped into two more basic dimensions of leader behavior. These were labeled *consideration* and *initiating structure* (Fleishman, 1967, p. 362).

These two dimensions were defined as follows:

> **Consideration:** Includes behavior indicating mutual trust, respect, and a certain warmth and rapport between the supervisor and his group . . . This dimension seems to

BEHAVIORAL APPROACH

Begun by researchers at Ohio State University; focused on the kinds of behavior engaged in by people in leadership roles and identified two major types: consideration and initiating structure.

CONSIDERATION

Type of behavior identified in the Ohio State studies; included behavior indicating mutual trust, respect, and a certain warmth and rapport between the supervisor and group.

TABLE 12.4	Guidelines on Building and Using Power

HOW TO INCREASE AND MAINTAIN POWER	HOW TO USE POWER EFFECTIVELY
Legitimate power • Gain more formal authority. • Use symbols of authority. • Get people to acknowledge authority. • Exercise authority regularly. • Follow proper channels in giving orders. • Back up authority with reward and coercive power.	• Make polite, clear requests. • Explain the reasons for a request. • Don't exceed your scope of authority. • Verify authority if necessary. • Be sensitive to target concerns. • Follow up to verify compliance. • Insist on compliance if appropriate.
Reward power • Discover what people need and want. • Gain more control over rewards. • Ensure people know you control rewards. • Don't promise more than you can deliver. • Don't use rewards in a manipulative way. • Avoid complex, mechanical incentives. • Don't use rewards for personal benefit.	• Offer desirable rewards. • Offer fair and ethical rewards. • Explain criteria for giving rewards. • Provide rewards as promised. • Use rewards symbolically to reinforce desirable behavior.
Expert power • Gain more relevant knowledge. • Keep informed about technical matters. • Develop exclusive sources of information. • Use symbols to verify expertise. • Demonstrate competence by solving difficult problems. • Don't make rash, careless statements. • Don't lie or misrepresent the facts. • Don't keep changing positions.	• Explain the reasons for a request or proposal. • Explain why a request is important. • Provide evidence that a proposal will be successful. • Listen seriously to target concerns. • Show respect for target (don't be arrogant). • Act confident and decisive in a crisis.
Referent power • Show acceptance and positive regard. • Act supportive and helpful. • Don't manipulate and exploit people for personal advantage. • Defend someone's interests and back them up when appropriate. • Keep promises. • Make self-sacrifices to show concern. • Use sincere forms of ingratiation.	• Use personal appeals when necessary. • Indicate that a request is important to you. • Don't ask for a personal favor that is excessive given the relationship. • Provide an example of proper behavior (role modeling).
Coercive power • Identify credible penalties to deter unacceptable behavior. • Gain authority to use punishments. • Don't make rash threats. • Don't use coercion in a manipulative way. • Use only punishments that are legitimate. • Fit punishments to the infraction. • Don't use coercion for personal benefit.	• Inform target of rules and penalties. • Give ample prior warnings. • Understand situation before punishing. • Remain calm and helpful, not hostile. • Encourage improvement to avoid the need for punishment. • Ask target to suggest ways to improve. • Administer discipline in private.

SOURCE: Yukl (1998).

emphasize a . . . concern for group members' needs and includes such behavior as allowing subordinates more participation in decision making and encouraging more two-way communication.

Initiating structure: Includes behavior in which the supervisor organizes and defines group activities and his relation to the group. Thus, he defines the role he expects each member to assume, assigns tasks, plans ahead, establishes ways of getting things done, and pushes for production. This dimension seems to emphasize overt attempts to achieve organizational goals (Fleishman & Harris, 1962).

One interesting aspect of Fleishman and Harris's (1962) definitions is that, by consistently using the pronoun "he," they implied that leaders are males. As we will see later in this chapter, it is ironic that these two dimensions parallel the behavior patterns that have been studied in male and female leaders—interpersonal orientation (consideration) and task orientation (structure)—even while failing to acknowledge that leaders may also be female. Although the Ohio State University approach and this new behavioral approach generated hundreds of studies and represented a leap forward in the study of leadership, it did not solve the leadership riddle. As Yukl (1998) pointed out:

- The results were inconsistent from study to study.
- Because the studies depended on questionnaires, the measurement was subject to bias and error (e.g., the questionnaires asked respondents to recall incidents from earlier years and how many times each incident occurred).
- Responses might have been influenced by respondents' stereotypes, describing what they had been led to believe were the characteristics of successful leaders.
- Respondents might have attributed desirable behavior to leaders who were perceived as effective.

The University of Michigan Studies

Simultaneous with the Ohio State leadership studies, researchers at the University of Michigan also became interested in leadership behavior, but they concentrated more on the dynamics of how leaders and groups interacted (Yukl, 1998). Like the Ohio State studies, the Michigan group identified **task-oriented behavior** (initiating structure) as an important part of a leader's activities. They also found that **relations-oriented behavior** (similar to consideration in the Ohio State model) was important. What was different about the Michigan results was that **participative behavior** on the part of a leader was a key to group effectiveness. They suggested that leadership was not exclusively, or even predominantly, about individual leader-follower interactions. Instead, effective leaders expended considerable energy in interacting with the work group as a whole (Likert, 1961, 1967). We will revisit the issue of participation later in this module. The emphasis on participation by the Michigan researchers represented another step forward in the study of leadership.

Up to this point, all of the theories we have considered concentrated on the traits or behaviors of leaders, with little regard for the effect of situational or environmental variables. In the following section, we will consider theories that include situational variables in the explanation of leader behavior and effectiveness.

THE CONTINGENCY APPROACH

One general finding from both the power and the behavioral approaches has been that the success of any given tactic (e.g., the use of reward power, the initiating structure approach) depends or is contingent upon multiple factors or situations. As a result, a number of **contingency approach** theories were proposed to take into account the role of the situation in the exercise of leadership. Historically, Fiedler (1967) made the first comprehensive

---

INITIATING STRUCTURE

Type of behavior identified in the Ohio State studies; included behavior in which the supervisor organizes and defines group activities and his relation to the group.

TASK-ORIENTED BEHAVIOR

Identified by University of Michigan researchers as an important part of a leader's activities; similar to initiating structure from the Ohio State studies.

RELATIONS-ORIENTED BEHAVIOR

Identified by University of Michigan researchers as an important part of a leader's activities; similar to consideration in the Ohio State model.

PARTICIPATIVE BEHAVIOR

Identified in the Michigan studies; allows subordinates more participation in decision making and encourages more two-way communication.

CONTINGENCY APPROACH

Proposed to take into account the role of the situation in the exercise of leadership.

attempt to explain leader behavior from the contingency perspective. In essence the style adopted by a leader interacted with characteristics of the situation to determine effectiveness. Although the theory generated a good deal of debate and research (Landy, 1989), the accumulated evidence is not very supportive of Fiedler's propositions, particularly with his view of leadership style. Below, we will briefly describe two contingency theories that have been better accepted and supported.

Hersey and Blanchard's Situational Theory

Hersey and Blanchard (1977) proposed that the success of various leadership approaches depended in part on the maturity of the subordinate. Maturity had two different facets to it. **Job maturity** was defined by the subordinate's job-related ability, skills, and knowledge. **Psychological maturity** was defined as the self-confidence and self-respect of the subordinate (Yukl, 1998). A subordinate characterized as high in maturity would have both ability and confidence. A subordinate low in maturity would have neither. Hersey and Blanchard proposed that for subordinates with low maturity, structuring styles would work best. As the individual increased in maturity to a medium or moderate level, the leader should decrease his or her structuring behavior and increase considerate behavior. As subordinate maturity increased, both structuring and considerate behavior would diminish, allowing the fully mature subordinate to be self-directed. The theory is presented graphically in Figure 12.1. You can look at this figure either as a template for dealing with subordinates of varying levels of maturity, or for dealing with a subordinate whose maturity increases as a result of experiences such as job success, gaining increased skill levels, and building self-confidence.

In spite of its intuitive appeal, Hersey and Blanchard's theory received little direct support. Nevertheless, it served to emphasize the idea that leadership is not a "one-size-fits-all" process, as Yukl (1998) pointed out. Different styles may be warranted by different situations. Further, it makes one think twice about whether a manager is dealing with a "problem" subordinate or a "problematic" leadership style.

House's Path-Goal Theory

House and his colleagues proposed a leadership model that includes not only the characteristics of the subordinate, but also the characteristics of the situation (House, 1971; House & Mitchell, 1974). According to this model, the particular style of the leader will affect subordinate satisfaction, motivation, and ultimately performance. The effect will be either positive or negative depending on the situational and subordinate characteristics. The

> **JOB MATURITY**
>
> *A subordinate's job-related ability, skills, and knowledge.*
>
> **PSYCHOLOGICAL MATURITY**
>
> *The self-confidence and self-respect of the subordinate.*

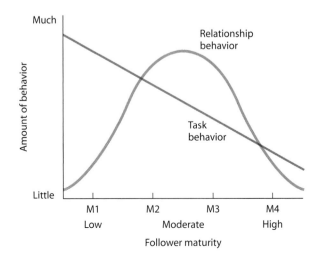

FIGURE 12.1

Behavior Prescriptions in Hersey and Blanchard's Situational Leadership Theory
SOURCE: Yukl (1998).

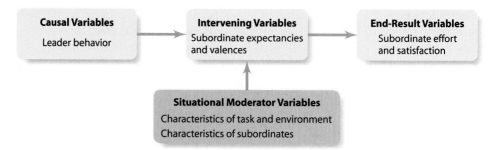

FIGURE 12.2 Causal Relationships in Path-Goal Theory of Leadership SOURCE: Yukl (1998).

PATH-GOAL THEORY

Leadership theory proposed by House et al.; includes both the characteristics of the subordinate and the characteristics of the situation; assumes that the leader's responsibility is to show the subordinate the path to valued goals.

model (see Figure 12.2) has been called the **path-goal theory** because it assumes that the leader's responsibility is to show the subordinate the path to valued subordinate goals. As House and Dessler described the theory, ". . . leader behavior will be viewed as acceptable to subordinates to the extent that the subordinates see such behavior as either an immediate source of satisfaction or as instrumental to future satisfaction" (1974, p. 13).

House and Mitchell (1974) described four distinct leadership styles, each of which we have seen in earlier theories (e.g., Ohio State, Michigan).

- Supportive leadership: creating a friendly, supportive environment.
- Directive leadership: specific task-relevant scheduling of the activities of subordinates as well as informing them of expectations.
- Participative leadership: inviting subordinates to share in discussions and decision making.
- Achievement-oriented leadership: providing subordinates with realistic, hard goals and the feedback and support to achieve those goals.

Figure 12.3 shows how directive leadership is thought to influence subordinate effort, or motivation, while Figure 12.4 shows the effect of a supportive leadership style. The boxes on the left of each figure illustrate the situational facets of the theory. Directive leadership is most effective when the job is not clearly defined (i.e., role ambiguity is high) or the relationship between performance and valued rewards is not obvious to the subordinate (Figure 12.3). Supportive leadership is best when the job is boring or the subordinate lacks self-confidence (Figure 12.4).

As was the case with the theory of Hersey and Blanchard, research support for House's model is sparse and often inconclusive, but the model has pointed out some possible situational variables not previously considered such as role ambiguity and

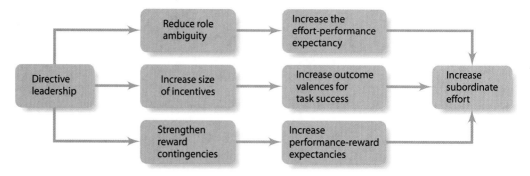

FIGURE 12.3 Causal Relationships for Effects of Directive Leadership Behavior on Subordinate Effort SOURCE: Yukl (1998).

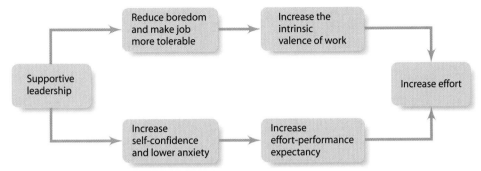

FIGURE 12.4

Causal Relationships for Effects of Supportive Leadership on Subordinate Effort
SOURCE: Yukl (1998).

boredom (Yukl, 1998). Although neither of these theories seems to have adequately captured all of the contingent or situational factors in leadership, both built on the earlier work of the Ohio State and Michigan groups and identified variables that will probably end up as integral parts of any comprehensive theory of leadership behavior that may emerge in the future.

The Case of Social Undermining: What about the "Fickle" Leader?

The contingency approach implies that leaders need to be flexible and consider the value of changing their style or behavior when the situation changes. But is it possible for a leader to be *too* situational? Recent research suggests this possibility. Vinokur and van Ryn (1993) examined behavior they called **social undermining,** in which a leader's criticism indicated a dislike for another individual, or leaders took actions that presented an obstacle to an individual's goal-directed behavior. The opposite of social undermining is **social support** by a leader. This type of behavior includes praise and respect for the individual, as well as efforts to increase the probability that the individual will achieve a desired personal goal. As we have seen, consideration and social support were key elements of both the Michigan and Ohio State models of leadership.

What happens when the leader engages in both undermining and support with the same subordinate? Duffy, Ganster, and Pagon (2002) studied 685 police officers in the former Yugoslav republic of Slovenia. They hypothesized that when these conflicting styles are seen in the same leader by a subordinate, the effect will be more damaging and stressful than simple social undermining alone. They reasoned that such conflicting responses would create aversive feelings of insecurity and lack of control. Also, it takes more emotional energy for a subordinate to deal with inconsistent leaders than with consistent ones, regardless of whether the consistency was positive (support) or negative (undermining). They found support for their hypothesis. Subordinates whose leaders demonstrated both supportive and undermining behavior were more counterproductive (e.g., took excessive work breaks, stole things from work), less confident about their skills, less committed to the organization, and showed higher stress levels (e.g., complaints of headaches, dry mouth, clammy hands) than subordinates whose leaders were consistently supportive or consistently undermining.

Admittedly, this research was carried out in a novel setting (Slovene police officers may differ significantly from typical U.S. workers in a number of ways) and represents the results of only one study. Nevertheless, it suggests an intriguing possibility: that subordinates also have a need for *consistency* in their interactions with a leader. Humans are "sense-making" organisms (Lord & Smith, 1999), and inconsistency is an obstacle to making sense. Consider a more benign version of the situation described above. Rather than adopting an extremely inconsistent "Dr. Jekyll and Mr. Hyde" approach to interactions, what if the leader were simply exquisitely in tune with all the nuances of the situation, including the subordinates, and cycled among styles (e.g., task oriented,

SOCIAL UNDERMINING

Behavior that includes a leader's criticism indicating a dislike for another individual, and actions that tend to present an obstacle to the individual's goal-directed behavior.

SOCIAL SUPPORT

Behavior that includes praise and respect for the individual, as well as efforts to increase the probability that the individual will achieve a desired personal goal.

supportive, achievement oriented) both within the same subordinates and between subordinates? How would the subordinates react? The leader may believe that he or she is being responsive by changing strategies rapidly. But to the follower, this may be nothing more than inconsistent behavior, as was the case in the social undermining research (Duffy et al., 2002).

THE CONSEQUENCES OF PARTICIPATION: THE VROOM-YETTON MODEL

You will recall that both the Michigan and the path-goal models identified a participative leadership style. Participative behaviors on the part of the leader were also implied in the Ohio State and Hersey and Blanchard models. Yukl (1981) identified the following advantages of a participative leader style:

- It helps subordinates understand the circumstances requiring a decision.
- Individuals are more likely to identify with the decision and work hard to make it succeed.
- Participation requires that objectives and plans necessary to meet those objectives be made clear to the participants.
- It makes potential rewards and punishments clearer, thus increasing motivation.
- Participation is a normal, mature, and satisfying experience.
- Participation results in social pressures on group members to accept the decision.
- It results in improved communications and more effective conflict resolution between leader and subordinate.
- It results in better decisions to the extent that the talent and skills of the group are tapped.

With so many advantages, it would seem that participative leadership styles should be universal. But a note of caution is sounded by the last advantage. Note the phrase "to the extent that the talent and skills of the group are tapped." It is possible that group members lack the abilities or knowledge to make difficult decisions. Furthermore, group members may be at odds with each other or with the leader about the decision. Then what? How will participation work under those circumstances?

There is the distinct possibility that in some situations the quality of the ultimate decision might suffer using a participative style. Vroom and his colleagues developed a model to address just this issue (Vroom & Jago, 1988; Vroom & Yetton, 1973). Yukl (1998) has summarized the decision rules regarding participation that have emerged from almost two decades of research on the Vroom-Yetton model:

1. When the decision is important and subordinates possess relevant information lacked by the leader, an autocratic decision is not appropriate because an important decision would be made without all of the available information.

2. When the decision quality is important and subordinates do not share the leader's concern for task goals, group decision making is inappropriate because it would give too much influence over an important decision to uncooperative and even hostile people.

3. When decision quality is important, the decision problem is unstructured, and the leader does not possess the necessary information and expertise to make a good decision, then the decision should be made by interaction among the people who have relevant information.

4. When decision acceptance is important and subordinates are unlikely to accept an autocratic decision, then an autocratic decision is inappropriate because it may not be implemented effectively.

5. When decision acceptance is important and subordinates are likely to disagree among themselves about the best solution to an important problem, autocratic procedures

and individual consultation are inappropriate because they do not provide the opportunity to resolve differences through discussion and negotiation among subordinates and between subordinates and the leader.

6.   When decision quality is not important but acceptance is critical and unlikely to result from an autocratic decision, the only appropriate procedure is a group decision because acceptance is maximized without risking quality.

7.   When decision acceptance is important and not likely to result from an autocratic decision, and subordinates share the leader's task objectives, subordinates should be given equal partnership in the decision process because acceptance is maximized without risking quality (pp. 130–31).

Table 12.5 and Figure 12.5 present the theory graphically.

TABLE 12.5   **Decision Procedures for Group and Individual Problems**

GROUP PROBLEM	INDIVIDUAL PROBLEM
AI.* You solve the problem or make the decision yourself, using information available to you at the time.	AI. You solve the problem or make the decision by yourself, using information available to you at the time.
AII. You obtain the necessary information form your subordinates, then decide the solution to the problem yourself. You may or may not tell your subordinates what the problem is in getting the information from them. The role played by your subordinates in making the decision is clearly one of providing the necessary information to you rather than generating or evaluating alternative solutions.	AII. You obtain the necessary information from your subordinate, then decide on the solution to the problem yourself. You may or may not tell the subordinate what the problem is in getting the information from him or her. The subordinate's role in making the decision is clearly one of providing the necessary information to you, rather than generating or evaluating alternative solutions.
CI. You share the problem with the relevant subordinates individually, getting their ideas and suggestions without bringing them together as a group. Then, *you* make the decision, which may or may not reflect your subordinates' influences.	CI. You share the problem with your subordinate, getting his or her ideas and suggestions. Then you make a decision, which may or may not reflect the subordinate's influence.
CII. You share the problem with your subordinates as a group, obtaining their collective ideas and suggestions. Then you make the decision, which may or may not reflect your subordinates' influence.	GI. You share the problem with your subordinate, and together you analyze the problem and arrive at a mutually agreeable solution.
GII. You share the problem with your subordinates as a group. Together you generate and evaluate alternatives and attempt to reach agreement (consenses) on a solution. Your role is much like that of chairman. You do not try to influence the group to adopt your solution, and you are willing to accept and implement any solution which has the support of the group.	DI. You delegate the problem to your subordinate, providing him or her with any relevant information that you possess but giving the subordinate responsibility for solving the problem alone. You may or may not request the subordinate to tell you what solution he or she has reached.

*Abbreviations are as follows:
A = Autocratic, C = Consultative, G = Group, D = Delegative.

Source: Vroom & Yetton (1973).

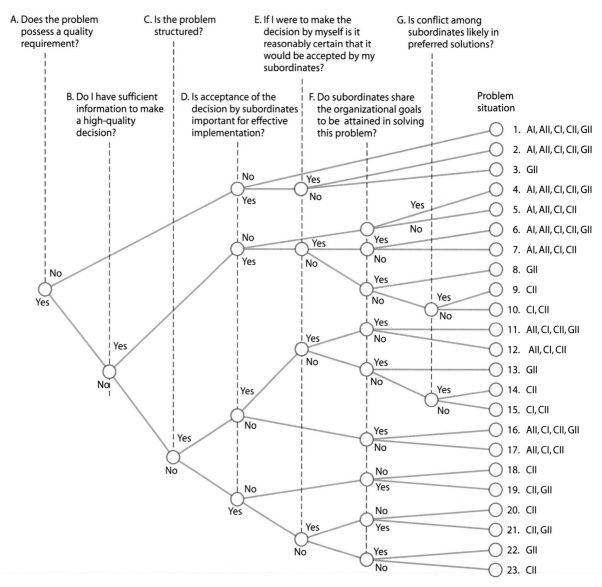

F I G U R E   1 2.5   The Vroom-Yetton Contingency Model of Leadership Behavior
Source: Vroom & Yetton (1973).

Research on the model seems to provide support for its value. Vroom and Jago (1988) found that when decision makers adopted a decision strategy suggested by the model (as opposed to an alternative decision process), the success rate for the decisions was 62 percent, in contrast with a 37 percent success rate for a nonrecommended strategy.

This model makes a practical contribution to leadership. The Vroom-Yetton model assumes that one of the most important duties of a leader is to make decisions, and it suggests a way to choose a decision-making strategy. Equally important, however, is the implication that group decision making or a completely participative style is not always appropriate. Although a participative style might contribute to the satisfaction of group members, it might lead to a poorer decision.

MODULE 12.2 SUMMARY

- From the perspective of I-O psychology, great man/great woman theories of leadership are of little value. However, by examining the biographies of leaders, we can surmise that every successful leadership career is a combination of individual attributes and of the circumstances in which the leaders found themselves.

- One of the most obvious characteristics of managers and leaders is their possession of power that subordinates do not have. French and Raven suggested five different types of power, including reward, coercive, legitimate, referent, and expert power. The more power bases a leader has, the greater the potential to influence group members.

- The Ohio State University studies identified consideration and initiating structure as important dimensions of leadership behavior. Researchers at the University of Michigan identified similar behavioral dimensions and proposed that participative (considerate) behavior on the part of the leader is a key to group effectiveness.

- Some leadership theories include situational variables in the explanation of leader behavior and effectiveness. Because the success of any given leadership tactic is contingent upon multiple factors or situations, a number of contingency theories take into account the role of the situation in the exercise of leadership.

- The Vroom-Yetton model suggested that although a participative style might contribute to the satisfaction of group members, under certain circumstances, it could lead to a poor decision.

KEY TERMS

great man/great woman theory

trait approach

power approach

behavioral approach

consideration

initiating structure

task-oriented behavior

relations-oriented behavior

participative behavior

contingency approach

job maturity

psychological maturity

path-goal theory

social undermining

social support

CRITICAL THINKING EXERCISES

12.3 In the new world of the global economy and the multinational organization, which of the following methods of exercising formal power or authority might be the most effective for a CEO of a multinational software company? Why?

1. Forming coalitions
2. Controlling important decisions
3. Co-opting the opposition
4. Controlling information flow

12.4 Facing bankruptcy, an international airline is considering radically altering the nature of its service in order to increase revenues. The airline proposes transforming itself from one catering to elite travelers to one with no frills. The CEO is considering asking all employees, including flight attendants, mechanics, pilots, and administrative staff, to join in the ultimate decision. Using flight attendants as your example, which decision model would you recommend to the CEO for including this group of employees in the decision? Why? Consider the Vroom-Yetton model and the decision tree that appears in Table 12.5 and Figure 12.5 in choosing a solution.

12.3

MODULE

NEW APPROACHES TO LEADERSHIP

LEADER-MEMBER EXCHANGE (LMX)

Most leadership theories, implicitly if not explicitly, assume that leaders treat all followers similarly. Dansereau, Graen, and Haga (1975) suggested that this approach was overly simplistic. In their **leader-member exchange (LMX) theory,** they hypothesized that leaders adopt different behaviors with individual subordinates and that the particular behavior pattern of the leader develops over time and depends, to a large extent, on the quality of the leader-subordinate relationship. Based on research conducted in manufacturing organizations, they proposed that subordinates fall into two distinct groups. **In-group members** have high-quality relationships with their leader and high latitude for negotiating their work roles; the leader tends to deal with in-group members without resorting to the use of formal power or authority. In contrast, **out-group members** have low-quality relationships with their leader and little latitude for negotiating their work roles; the leader is more likely to rely on formal power and authority to influence their behavior.

Graen, Liden, and Hoel (1982) examined the characteristics of high-quality relationships experienced by in-group members. Compared with out-group members, in-group members were more likely to remain with an organization. They also tended to see themselves as involved in a valuable exchange of knowledge, logistic and emotional support, and extra effort with their leaders. In high-quality relationship exchanges, leaders discussed performance with subordinates, initiated discussions about personal matters and problems, and appeared genuinely interested in work-related difficulties. Low-quality relationships of out-group members were characterized by higher turnover and the tendency to view the exchange with their leader as nothing more than a contractual agreement in which the worker contributes "eight hours work for eight hours pay." In low-quality relationships, leaders seldom talked to subordinates about effectiveness or helped them with difficult assignments.

Recent revisions of leader-member exchange (LMX) theory are more dynamic and describe a **"life-cycle" of a leader-follower relationship,** which begins tentatively, and then either evolves into a more trusting and committed relationship or remains fixed at the initial stage (Graen & Scandura, 1987; Graen & Uhl-Bein, 1991, 1995). The subordinates who experience the evolved relationship become in-group members while those who remain stuck at the first phase become out-group members. Unlike earlier versions of LMX theory which simply acknowledged that different relationships emerge or evolve, more current versions suggest that the task of the leader is to "drive" the relationship from the tentative first-stage relationship to a deeper, more meaningful one. In essence, all relationships begin as low quality and should be driven to high-quality levels by the leader. In some senses, a measure of leader success might be the percentage of "high-quality" subordinate relationships that a leader has.

LEADER-MEMBER EXCHANGE (LMX) THEORY

Proposed that leaders adopt different behaviors with individual subordinates; the particular behavior pattern of the leader develops over time and depends to a large extent on the quality of the leader-subordinate relationship.

IN-GROUP MEMBERS

People who have high-quality relationships with their leader and high latitude for negotiating their work roles.

OUT-GROUP MEMBERS

People who have low-quality relationships with their leader and little latitude for negotiating their work roles.

LIFE-CYCLE OF A LEADER-FOLLOWER RELATIONSHIP

Describes recent versions of leader-member exchange (LMX) theory that include a dynamic process in which the task of the leader is to drive the relationship from a tentative first-stage relationship to a deeper, more meaningful one.

An important facet of leadership is the ability to motivate followers in initiating goal-directed activity.

In a meta-analysis of LMX research, Gerstner and Day (1997) were enthusiastic about the contribution of the approach. They concluded that high-quality relationships are positively associated with subordinate job performance and with satisfaction (both overall and with the leader), and negatively associated with intentions to quit. Tierney, Farmer, and Graen (1999) discovered that when leaders build a high-quality relationship with innovative employees, the result is enhanced creative production from those employees. In contrast, creative employees appeared stifled in their creative efforts by low-quality leader relationships.

In spite of their general enthusiasm, Gerstner and Day (1997) were troubled that leaders and members often disagreed in describing the quality of the relationship. While a leader might have characterized a relationship as high quality, the subordinate often disagreed and considered it low quality. They were also troubled by the lack of knowledge about *how* relationships develop between leaders and members. They were more enthusiastic about evidence that relationships do indeed evolve over time (i.e., the life-cycle concept). They conclude by proposing that "the relationship with one's supervisor [is] a lens through which the entire work experience is viewed" (p. 840).

LMX theory is an appealing approach to leadership because it acknowledges that differential relationships exist between leaders and followers, and this conforms to what most of us have experienced in work settings. Nevertheless, it remains an intriguing addition to the leadership menu rather than a fully articulated and practical theory. Again, much more research remains to be done on this leadership approach.

TRANSFORMATIONAL LEADERSHIP

In the movie *As Good as It Gets,* Jack Nicholson plays a neurotic bachelor who becomes infatuated with a waitress played by Helen Hunt. Nicholson's character is sarcastic and punitive to most people with whom he comes in contact. Nevertheless, he is drawn to the waitress and, strangely, she is drawn to him. At a turning point in the movie, Hunt demands that Nicholson pay her a compliment or she will leave and not see him again. He struggles for a moment and then says, "You make me want to be a better man."

Nicholson's description of his relationship with Hunt is the essence of a theory of leadership called **transformational leadership,** which Burns (1978) introduced to describe the behavior of inspirational political leaders. Transformational leadership is the interplay between leaders and followers in which each raises the other to higher levels of morality and motivation. The leader transforms the followers by appealing to their nobler motives such as justice, morality, and peace. We have seen this capacity to transform followers in great leaders such as Martin Luther King, Jr., Mahatma Gandhi, and Archbishop Desmond Tutu. By articulating a vision of a better world and demonstrating through their own actions how to achieve that better world, leaders of this caliber persuade followers to believe that they as individuals *can* make a difference, to forget about pursuing their own concrete rewards, and to join in the effort to achieve that better world—in short, the leader makes them want to be better than they are.

Burns (1978) contrasted transformational leadership with **transactional leadership,** the more traditional process by which leaders show followers how they can meet their personal goals by adopting a particular behavior pattern. The leader makes it clear to the followers what behavior will be rewarded. Followers can then adopt that behavior pattern if they wish to achieve the promised rewards. A leader who develops an incentive program in which employees are rewarded for increased production is acting as a transactional leader. Bass and his colleagues have used Burns's notion of transformational leadership to describe the behavior of industrial leaders rather than political leaders (Avolio & Bass, 1991; Bass, 1985, 1997; Bass & Avolio 1997). Bass viewed the transformational leader as one who uses the following behaviors to motivate followers:

- Impressing on followers the importance and implications of the tasks they are performing.
- Persuading followers to ignore self-centered strategies and concentrate on the goals of the work group or organization.
- Appealing to higher order needs such as making a contribution, having an impact, improving society through their efforts (Yukl, 1998).

Bass and Avolio (1997) proposed that transformational leaders typically use one of four general strategies. The four are listed below along with a description of the critical characteristics of each (Bass, 1997, p. 133).

1. **Idealized influence:** Leaders display conviction, emphasize trust, take stands on difficult issues, emphasize the importance of commitment and purpose, and are aware of the ethical consequences of their decisions.
2. **Inspirational motivation:** Leaders articulate an appealing vision of the future, challenge followers with high standards, talk optimistically with enthusiasm, and provide encouragement and meaning for what needs to be done.
3. **Intellectual stimulation:** Leaders question old assumptions, values, and beliefs; stimulate new ways of doing things, and encourage expression of ideas and reasons.
4. **Individualized consideration:** Leaders deal with others as individuals; consider individual needs, abilities, and aspirations; listen attentively; and advise, coach, and teach.

These can be contrasted with the strategies of a transactional leader, which also appear in Figure 12.6.

In Burns's (1978) view, there was a single continuum running from transactional at one end to transformational at the other. Thus, if a leader were high on transformational strategies, that same leader would be expected to be low on transactional behaviors. Bass's view is somewhat different (Avolio et al., 1999; Bass, 1997). Instead of the styles being mutually exclusive, Bass perceived transformational leadership as building upon

FIGURE 12.6

Hierarchical Nature of Transformational Leadership SOURCE: Based on Bass (1997).

transactional leadership in a hierarchy with respect to their effectiveness (see Figure 12.6). As you can see, the lowest level is identified as **laissez-faire leadership.** Although some managers might mistakenly consider this a "leadership style," Bass did not agree. He included it in the hierarchy to contrast it with legitimate leadership styles—transactional and transformational. The three levels of transactional leadership are arranged in order of effectiveness; the transformational style (at the top) is the most effective, but it includes and builds upon transactional behaviors, in particular, contingent rewards. Avolio and Bass (1991; Bass & Avolio, 1997; Antonakis & Avolio, 2003) refer to this hierarchical model as the **"full-range" theory of leadership** since it ranges from no leadership (laissez-faire) through the transactional levels to the transformational level. Although Bass's full-range theory did not place particular emphasis on moral or ethical leadership as was true of Burns's (1978) original formulation of the concept, a recent study found that leaders described by their subordinates as exhibiting transformational leadership behaviors were high on moral reasoning scores (Turner, Barling, Epitropaki, Butcher, & Milner, 2002). In contrast, transactional behavior patterns were unrelated to moral reasoning.

Yukl (1998) summarized the research on transformational leadership and suggested guidelines for leaders wishing to adopt a transformational style (see Table 12.6). The development and validation of the theory of transformational leadership has been hampered to some extent by the fact that it depends heavily on a single self-report instrument called the **Multifactor Leadership Questionnaire (MLQ).** This has led to two major criticisms. First, there is a need for converging information from several approaches to identify the various transactional and transformational styles. As you will recall from Chapter 2,

INDIVIDUALIZED CONSIDERATION

Leaders deal with others as individuals; consider individual needs, abilities, and aspirations; listen attentively; and advise, coach, and teach.

LAISSEZ-FAIRE LEADERSHIP

Lowest level of leadership identified by Bass who contrasted it with transactional leadership and transformational leadership.

FULL-RANGE THEORY OF LEADERSHIP

Hierarchical model that ranges from laissez-faire leadership through transactional leadership to transformational leadership.

MULTIFACTOR LEADERSHIP QUESTIONNAIRE (MLQ)

Self-report instrument used in the development and validation of the theory of transformational leadership.

TABLE 12.6	Guidelines for Transformational Leadership

- Articulate a clear and appealing vision.
- Explain how the vision can be attained.
- Act confident and optimistic.
- Express confidence in followers.
- Provide opportunities for early successes.
- Celebrate successes.
- Use dramatic, symbolic actions to emphasize key values.
- Lead by example.
- Empower people to achieve the vision.

SOURCE: Yukl (1998).

inferences about behavior become stronger when there is "triangulation," or converging evidence from several methods of measuring a phenomenon (Yukl, 1998). The second criticism has to do with exactly how many different transactional and transformational strategies there are (Avolio & Sivasubramaniam, 2002; Bycio, Hackett, & Allen, 1995). Researchers have analyzed data from the MLQ and come up with alternative interpretations of its structure.

It will take some time to resolve these criticisms. The first is more serious than the second. If the transformational style exists only in the eye of the beholder, then attempts to structure or train transformational "behavior" are useless, since the behavior does not really exist. The issue of exactly how many strategies really exist is of lesser importance. The answer to that debate—like the answer to the debate about whether there is a Big Five or a Big Nine structure for personality (Digman, 1990; Hough, 1992)—is likely to be that for some purposes (e.g., training), more strategies are better, and for other purposes (e.g., articulating the transformational theory), a theory with fewer factors might be better (Avolio et al., 1999). We feel confident that by the time the next edition of this book appears, many of these issues will be resolved. What is clear, however, is that something like a transformational style has existed as long as there have been leaders, and that followers have been persuaded by particular leaders to put aside personal gain for the sake of some larger goal. Thus, the theory coincides with observation and experience.

THE CHARISMATIC LEADER

CHARISMA

A personal attribute of a leader that hypnotizes followers and compels them to identify with and attempt to emulate the leader.

CHARISMATIC LEADER

Followers are emotionally attached to this leader, never question the leader's beliefs or actions, and see themselves as integral to the accomplishment of the leader's goals.

One of the transformational strategies identified by Bass was labeled "idealized influence," which he also called **"charisma."** Charisma is most often associated with a personal attribute of a leader that almost hypnotizes followers and compels them to identify with and emulate the leader (Den Hartog & Koopman, 2001). But charisma would appear to have a shelf life as well, and can be diminished by situational factors. Bill Clinton was seen as charismatic until the Whitewater and Lewinsky scandals brought him down to the level of the "common man." This means that charisma really is a combination of personal characteristics and behaviors of the leader and beliefs of the followers.

House (1977) proposed a theory of leadership based on the concept of charisma. The followers of **charismatic leaders** are emotionally attached to the leader, never question the leader's beliefs or actions, and see themselves as integral to the accomplishment of the leader's goals. When carried to an extreme, this devotion can have disastrous consequences (e.g., Hitler and, more recently, Osama bin Laden). Yukl (1998) characterized charismatic leaders as follows:

- They have a strong need for power.
- They are supremely confident.
- They engage in behaviors designed to impress followers (e.g., talk about prior accomplishments).
- They articulate an appealing vision of some future state of affairs.
- They set an example for their followers through their own behavior (and may very well lose their appeal when less than attractive behavior surfaces, as was the case with Bill Clinton).
- They set high goals for followers and express confidence that the followers will achieve those goals.
- They attempt to appeal to fundamental motives of followers such as a need for power, affiliation, or achievement; they often make this appeal through inspirational speeches and writings.

House also suggested that charismatic leaders acquire some power from the situation; times of crisis are ripe for the emergence of a charismatic leader. Such was the case with Winston

Churchill during World War II and General Norman Schwartzkopf during Operation Desert Storm.

There are many different versions of **charismatic leadership theory** (Den Hartog & Koopman, 2001). Meindl (1990) proposed that the particular leader was largely irrelevant: In a crisis situation, followers will "perceive" charismatic characteristics in an individual and look to that person as a leader. Conger and Kanungo (1987) noted that certain behaviors on the part of the leader contribute to a charismatic aura, such as awareness of the realities of a situation, describing an idealized vision of some end state, and the use of innovative strategies for achieving that vision. Nevertheless, charisma is thought be as much a desire to *see* charisma on the part of the followers as it is charismatic *behavior* on the part of the leader. Many people have believed that Bill Clinton's charisma was due, in part, to the contrast with his predecessor as president, the less charismatic George H.W. Bush.

Finally, Shamir, House and Arthur (1993) suggested that the effectiveness of charismatic leadership is the result of followers reconceptualizing the importance of what they are doing rather than of any direct motivational characteristics of the leader. To be sure, the charismatic leader helps followers to recast their efforts to have a more enduring or moral purpose, but it is the change in how the followers see their efforts rather than any desire to emulate or "follow" the leader that is the active element of charismatic leadership.

Transformational and charismatic leadership seem to be closely related, at least on the surface. But there are some important differences. Although the transformational leader will often increase the esteem and effectiveness of followers, making them stronger than they had been, the charismatic style also emphasizes personal loyalty to the leader and thus may actually work to keep the followers weak (Yukl, 1998).

Transformational and charismatic leadership theories are "conceptually charismatic" themselves. They currently attract a great deal of attention, "shine" compared to other, less flashy theories (e.g., leader-member exchange or path-goal theory), have committed followers, and result in a substantial addition to the research data on leadership. Nevertheless, a great amount of work needs to be done before we declare that these theories explain the effect of leader behavior on followers. It has often been noted that life is a trail, not a campsite (Pyle, 1991). The same might be said of leadership theory: It is about paths, not end states.

> **CHARISMATIC LEADERSHIP THEORY**
>
> *Approach with many different versions of the notion that charisma is related to leadership; (1) in a crisis situation, followers perceive charismatic characteristics in an individual and accept that person as a leader; (2) certain leader behaviors (use of innovative strategies) contribute to a charismatic aura.*

MODULE 12.3 SUMMARY

- Leader-member exchange (LMX) theory proposes that leaders adopt different behaviors with individual subordinates. The advocates of this approach argue that subordinates fall into an in-group, in which members have high-quality relationships with their leader, or an out-group, whose members have low-quality relationships with their leader. A recent meta-analysis of LMX research concluded that high-quality relationships are positively associated with subordinate job performance and with satisfaction, and negatively associated with intentions to quit.

- Transformational leadership describes the behavior of inspirational leaders and involves an interaction between leaders and followers in which each raises the other to higher levels of morality and motivation. This type of leadership is often contrasted with transactional leadership, the process by which leaders simply show followers how they can meet their personal goals by adopting a particular behavior pattern. The transformational style is perceived as more effective.

- Charisma is most often associated with a personal attribute of a leader that compels followers to identify with and attempt to emulate the leader. The followers of charismatic leaders are emotionally attached to the leader, do not question the leader's beliefs or actions, and see themselves as integral to the accomplishment of the leader's goals.

KEY TERMS

leader-member exchange (LMX) theory

in-group members

out-group members

life-cycle of a leader-follower relationship

transformational leadership

transactional leadership

idealized influence

inspirational motivation

intellectual stimulation

individualized consideration

laissez-faire leadership

full-range theory of leadership

Multifactor Leadership Questionnaire (MLQ)

charisma

charismatic leader

charismatic leadership theory

CRITICAL THINKING EXERCISES

12.5 In some organizations, closeness to a supervisor or leader is ridiculed by fellow workers. This presents a dilemma for the leader intent on developing high-quality LMX relationships. If you were that leader, how would you go about creating a high-quality LMX work environment?

12.6 The plant manager of an electronics manufacturing company is fiercely loyal to his employees. The workers know that if there is ever any problem with payroll or benefits, they can come to him and he will fight for them against the human resources department. When the training department presented on-site workshops on the use of spreadsheets and quality assurance software, the manager arranged to get waivers for his managers so they would not have to waste their time in classes. Would you classify this plant manager as a transformational leader, a charismatic leader, or neither? Explain your answer.

EMERGING TOPICS AND CHALLENGES IN LEADERSHIP RESEARCH

LEADERSHIP IN A CHANGING WORKPLACE

As we have seen in virtually every chapter, the changes in the workplace in the past two decades have been substantial. One consequence of these changes is a very different work environment for leaders. We will review a few of the more salient changes with respect to the challenge of leadership.

Teams/Groups   Groups and teams are increasingly populating today's workplace. There are fewer and fewer single contributors. As we have seen in earlier sections of this chapter, many of the traditional leadership models are focused on the relationship between a single leader and a single follower. Things are a bit more complicated now. Certainly, individual interactions between a worker and a manager still take place, but there are also interactions between managers and teams/groups. It is no longer sufficient for a leader to concentrate on influencing individual work group members one by one. The team or group is a separate entity and must be considered independent of its members.

As if teams were not challenging enough, there is also the issue of virtual teams. A **virtual team** consists of geographically or organizationally dispersed members brought together through "a combination of telecommunications and information technologies to accomplish an organizational task" (Townsend, DeMarie, & Hendrickson, 1998, p. 17). As Bell and Kozlowski (2002) pointed out, this presents novel challenges for a leader, including the socialization of new team members and monitoring of the progress of the teams as they go about their work. They hypothesized that as the work of a virtual team becomes more complex, the communications will need to be more frequent and intense. By definition, much of this increased communication will not take place in a face-to-face scenario. This will make the monitoring function of the leader increasingly difficult and will also require virtual teams to become more self-managing than leader directed. These are just a few examples of the challenges that virtual teams will represent to leaders.

Telecommuting   The discussion of virtual teams anticipates a related issue. An increasing number of employees work from home part or all of the workweek. This is referred to as **telecommuting** or dispersed work (Adams, 2001). As with virtual teams, telecommuting will present monitoring and communication challenges for a leader. When Lyndon Johnson was majority leader in the Senate and then President, he used his imposing physical presence as a way to influence individuals (Caro, 2002). Johnson would not have been able to use that advantage had he been communicating by telephone, e-mail, or fax.

VIRTUAL TEAM
Widely dispersed members work together toward a common goal and are linked through computers and other technology.

TELECOMMUTING
Arrangement that allows employees to work from home or other locations.

Virtual teams may be more challenging to lead than real ones.

Dispersed work comes in many different forms (Adams, 2001). We have already alluded to the home office. In addition, there are drop-in work centers located close to employees' homes. Many offices now have "unassigned" work spaces for use by employees who travel a great deal and use regional or branch facilities to do their work. Thus, a manager may be faced with a very basic issue: tracking an employee down on a given day. Adams suggested that effective leaders in a dispersed work environment will need to be much more proactive about communications in both directions. They should not "sit and wait" for problems to resolve themselves, nor should they allow dispersed employees to be surprised by an action. With a sit-and-wait style, things could easily get out of control before the leader can exert any influence. With a "surprise" style, stress will become a significant obstacle to employee performance.

Temporary Workers   As organizations become "leaner" they are more likely to make use of temporary workers. Often an organization uncertain of long-term business prospects will fill vacant positions with consultants or contract workers. The advantage of hiring temporary workers is that it allows an organization to respond to market changes by quickly increasing or decreasing the workforce. From a leader's perspective, however, temporary workers represent a challenge. As temps are unlikely to have the same commitment or share the same values as full-time employees, they may be more difficult to motivate. In addition, these workers may be expected to support work groups and teams without being a member of any particular team. Some organizations develop an internal pool of "floating" employees and use this pool for dealing with unexpected terminations, illness, or resignations (Cascio, 1998). Although these in-house temporary workers may share the same values and have same level of commitment as full-time employees, they still move from assignment to assignment rapidly, and are not likely to be part of a team or to establish a relationship with a manager. There is also the possibility that the temporary workers may affect the behavior of the permanent employees. Harris (2000) suggested that the job satisfaction of permanent employees may decrease owing to feelings of insecurity, including their replacement with temporary or part-time workers.

Fuzzy Boundaries of Jobs   As we have seen, the meaning of a "job" is changing. The concept of a team changes the notion of individual contributions. In addition, rapid changes in technology and work processes also make a "job title" a moving target. This places increasing pressure on leaders to anticipate how work is evolving, and how the work roles of various team members are integrated. There is, however, one stable behavior emerging from the new work environment: contextual performance. Regardless of how rapidly work changes, it is likely that the contextual performance of individual workers will always represent a value added (Motowidlo & Van Scotter, 1994). Thus, one task of the modern leader may be to encourage and facilitate contextual behavior among followers.

MALE AND FEMALE LEADERS: ARE THEY DIFFERENT?

The demographics of the workforce are changing so there is every reason to believe that the demographics of the leaders will change as well (Lord & Gradwohl Smith, 1999). More women will assume leadership roles. An important question for both research and practice is the generalizability of our current leadership theories. There is the possibility that what we know about leadership is really only what we know about male leadership. Are there fundamental differences between the leadership behaviors of men and women?

We considered the issue of the historical lack of representation of women in positions of leadership, particularly at the top of the organizational ladder in the context of the glass ceiling phenomenon, in Chapter 11. Our concern here is not with issue of who *becomes* a leader, but whether leadership is exercised differently by women (compared to men) when they assume positions of leadership.

BOX

12.2   A SAMPLING OF WOMEN'S THOUGHTS ON LEADERSHIP

Whatever women must do they must do twice as well as men to be thought half as good. Luckily, this is not difficult.—*Charlotte Whitton*

If high heels were so wonderful, men would still be wearing them.—*Sue Grafton*

When women are depressed, they either eat or go shopping. Men invade another country.—*Elayne Boosler*

In politics, if you want anything said, ask a man; if you want anything done, ask a woman.—*Margaret Thatcher*

If men can run the world, why can't they stop wearing neckties? How intelligent is it to start the day by tying a noose around your neck?—*Linda Ellerbee*

There is considerable disagreement among researchers concerning the extent to which men and women differ on characteristics associated with leadership. Eagly and her colleagues argued that the differences are real and substantial (Eagly, 1995; Eagly & Johnson, 1990; Eagly, Karau, & Makhijani, 1995; Eagly, Makhijani, & Klonsky, 1992). Others are less convinced that such differences exist, and if they do, the researchers question the magnitude of those differences (Bass, 1981; Hyde & Plant, 1995; Lefkowitz, 1994; Nieve & Gutek, 1981). A number of studies showed statistically significant differences on attributes of men and women but many of these differences are too small to be of any practical significance (Feingold, 1994).

Eagly and Johnson (1990) conducted a meta-analysis of studies examining leadership style and gender, with interesting results. The stereotypical view is that women lead by emphasizing interpersonal interactions and men lead by emphasizing task completion. No such differences were found in field studies, but they did appear in laboratory studies. This suggests that stereotypes might have been operating in lab studies but not in real organizations. In field studies, however, Eagly and Johnson determined that women tended to prefer democratic and participative styles rather than the autocratic styles favored by men.

Feingold (1994) conducted a meta-analysis of personality differences between men and women in the general psychological literature. Although he did not focus on leadership, some of his findings are relevant to that topic. He found that men tended to be slightly more assertive than women and that women tended to be slightly more extraverted than men. But he also found a large and stable difference between the genders on the attribute of tender-mindedness, with women being substantially more tender-minded. Tender-mindedness includes nurturing behaviors and empathy. When the Feingold results are combined with those of Eagly and Johnson (1990), they suggest a potentially different "style" for male and female leaders, with females tending to favor more participative and democratic interactions with subordinates and to be more aware of interpersonal issues than their male counterparts.

But the question arises whether these differences matter in terms of the ultimate effectiveness of the leader. Little data are available to answer this question directly. Nevertheless, there is some theoretical basis for speculating that such differences may have an increasingly important impact on leader effectiveness. It is clear that the workplace is being transformed from one characterized by single contributors to one dominated by teams and interacting work groups. This in turn suggests that people skills (e.g., communication, negotiation, conflict resolution) will become increasingly important. This would seem to favor women as leaders. We hasten to add two qualifiers, however. First, statistical studies such as the meta-analyses described above present us with mean or average differences. But there is also variation within each gender. In all of the studies reviewed, there were male leaders who were nurturant, democratic, empathic, and participatory in style; there were also female leaders who were autocratic, task-oriented, nonempathic, and nonparticipatory. So we should not be misled by assuming *all* male leaders behave differently from *all* female leaders. Another thing to keep in mind is that behavior can be changed. The autocratic leader of today may be the democratic leader of tomorrow, regardless of gender. After being diagnosed and treated for prostate cancer in 2001, Rudolf Giuliani adopted a much softer demeanor as Mayor of N.Y.C. The real issue remains one of identifying effective leadership styles and communicating these styles to all leaders.

One additional phenomenon to consider when examining gender and leadership has to do with the extent to which the particular industry is a male- or female-dominated industry. Some research suggests that this variable has an effect on the leadership style adopted by female leaders. Gardiner and Tiggemann (1999) studied 60 male and 60 female Australian managers in male-dominated (e.g., academia, automotive, information technology, consulting, and timber) and female-dominated (e.g., childhood education, nursing, hairdressing) industries. They found that women in male-dominated industries were less likely to adopt a style that emphasized interpersonal orientations (as opposed to task orientations). Furthermore, they found that while the mental health of female managers was worse if they adopted an interpersonal style in a male-dominated industry, the mental health of male managers in male-dominated industries was better if they adopted an interpersonally oriented style. This intriguing finding suggests the possibility that if women behaved in an expected (interpersonal) way, they encountered resistance. In contrast, when men behaved in an unexpected (interpersonal) way, they encountered no such resistance. Since this last set of findings was peculiar to male-dominated industries, it suggests the potential influence of stereotypes that men hold about women. Thus, a subtle but important issue in considering the issue of men and women as leaders is the extent to which the industry in question is male or female dominated.

Yukl (1998) raised serious questions about the extent to which any conclusions about the interaction of gender and leadership can be drawn. For one thing, many leadership studies in the literature do not report the gender of leaders, making meta-analyses of the gender/leadership interaction difficult to conduct. In addition, any meta-analyses that were performed run the risk of being unrepresentative, since those studies that did not report leader gender would ordinarily be excluded from the analysis. Further, many of the studies that report gender differences do not seek explanations beyond the simple biological fact of gender. For example, a study might find that female leaders engage in significantly more one-on-one communication with followers than male leaders. But what if the work group size of the female leaders was substantially smaller than that of their male counterparts? Or what if the male leaders were overseeing the work of virtual teams and the female leaders were managing more traditional collections of single contributors? There is simply not enough good research available to draw any firm conclusions about leadership differences as a result of gender. The topic of gender and leadership will receive increasing attention. There are already many thoughtful theoretical treatments of the question (e.g., Cleveland, Stockdale, & Murphy, 2000). What I-O psychology needs now are some better designed studies to investigate this question.

PERSONALITY AND LEADERSHIP

As you saw in an earlier section of this chapter, the "trait" approach to leadership that characterized the research of the early investigators has been largely discredited. In large measure this has happened because the traits investigated were poorly defined and measured—traits like popularity, maturity, and creativity. It was not so much that these traits didn't make any sense; they did. The problem was that they meant something different and were measured differently by every researcher. They had no scientific credibility.

As we have seen in almost every chapter (but specifically in Chapter 3), the role of personality traits has become more prominent in I-O psychology as a result of the introduction of the Big Five and its derivatives. I-O psychologists now know what they are measuring and how they are measuring it when they examine personality traits. Using our examples from above, popularity might now be identified as agreeableness and extraversion; maturity might be equated with emotional stability and conscientiousness; and creativity would be considered similar to openness to experience. As we saw in Chapter 3, personality traits are considered "habitual ways of responding"; thus they are concrete behaviors. The classical leadership models identified leader traits by having subordinates describe the extent to which a leader behaved in a considerate, structuring, or participative manner. As the Big Five structure of personality has emerged, it is now possible to go beyond the work setting and ask how an individual such as a leader behaves in a much wider array of situations.

Virtually every classical and modern leadership theory implicates personality traits. Not every model incorporates every one of the Big Five, but in the aggregate, every one of the Big Five factors appears in one or another leadership theory, either directly or by implication. One interesting aspect of the role of personality in leader effectiveness is that the influence of personality is more apparent to the leader's followers than to his or her managers. Harris and Hogan (1992) found that the manager of a leader made judgments about the effectiveness of that leader based primarily on factors related to technical competence and knowledge. In contrast, the subordinates of the leader made effectiveness judgments based on personality characteristics, particularly trustworthiness.

Hogan, Curphy, and Hogan (1994) reviewed the research literature on the personality/leader effectiveness relationship and concluded that there was a strong foundation for believing that each of the Big Five factors contributed to leader effectiveness. They also pointed out that the Big Five factors emphasize the "bright side" of leadership: effectiveness. But some leaders fail despite having above average ability and the "right" personality characteristics. While some of these failures are the result of situational factors (e.g., the competition, the market, the unavailability of talented subordinates), for others the reasons for failure are more personal. They include arrogance, selfishness, insensitivity, excessive ambition, and compulsivity. Hogan et al. (1994) suggested that the predictors for this type of leader failure are more likely to be found in measures of psychopathology than in measures of the Big Five.

Judge, Bono, Ilies, and Gerhardt (2002) have conducted a meta-analysis on the relationship between personality and leader effectiveness and confirmed what Hogan et al. (1994) hypothesized. They examined leader effectiveness (as measured by ratings of the manager and/or subordinate of the leader) in three different settings: industry, government/military, and student (laboratory experiments where subjects were designated as "leaders" for short-duration projects). In an analysis of 222 correlations from 73 different samples, they demonstrated that emotional stability, extraversion, and openness to experience were positively associated with judged leader effectiveness in industry settings. In government/military settings, openness was not a predictor of leader effectiveness but conscientiousness was. In industry settings, conscientiousness was not a predictor of leader effectiveness, most likely because of the discretion used in the application of rules in the business setting, whereas in the government/military settings importance is attached to following rules and procedures. In student settings, all of the Big Five factors predicted leader effectiveness. Judge and Bono (2000) also looked more specifically at the contribution of Big Five dimensions to transformational leadership behaviors, and found that extraversion and agreeableness were predictive of transformational behaviors on the part of the leader. Given the nature of transformational leadership as we have discussed above, this should come as no surprise to you. For example, one would expect an inspirational leader to be very active, sociable, and assertive (i.e., extraverted) as well as sympathetic and cooperative (i.e., agreeable). As a result of these emerging relationships between personality and leadership, it is likely that future theories of leadership effectiveness will be more specific in their inclusion of leader personality characteristics.

CROSS-CULTURAL STUDIES OF LEADERSHIP

The Dutch place emphasis on egalitarianism and are skeptical of the value of leadership. Terms like leader and manager carry a stigma. If a father is employed as a manager, Dutch children will not admit it to their schoolmates.

Arabs worship their leaders—*as long as they are in power!*

Iranians seek power and strength in their leaders.

The Malaysian leader is expected to behave in a manner that is humble, modest, and dignified.

Americans appreciate two kinds of leaders. They seek empowerment from leaders who grant autonomy and delegate authority to subordinates. They also respect the bold, forceful, confident, and risk-taking leader as personified by John Wayne. (House, Wright, & Aditya, 1997, pp. 535–36).

These quotes came from managers in various countries who were asked to describe accepted leadership styles in their respective countries. They were describing their local leadership *culture.*

You will recall from our discussion of Hofstede's model of culture (see Chapter 1) that we would expect culture to affect the manner in which leadership is expressed, as well as the relative effectiveness of various leadership strategies. For example, the extent to which a culture could be characterized as collectivist or individualist, or high in power distance compared with low in power distance, would be expected to influence the effectiveness of participative versus autocratic, or individually directed versus team directed leadership strategies.

In 1991, House and his colleagues began the planning of a massive cross-cultural study of leadership (Den Hartog & Koopman, 2001; House, Javidan, & Dorfman, 2001; House, Wright, & Aditiya, 1997). The following are some of the questions they hoped to answer:

1. Are there universally (i.e., across all cultures) endorsed and rejected leader attributes and behaviors?

2. Are there some leader attributes and behaviors that are accepted in some cultures but rejected in others?

3. How does culture influence the acceptance and rejection of leader attributes and behaviors?

4. What is the effect of the presence of a rejected leadership attribute or behavior within a particular culture?

GLOBAL LEADERSHIP AND ORGANIZATIONAL BEHAVIOR EFFECTIVENESS (GLOBE)

Large-scale cross-cultural study of leadership by 170 social scientists and management researchers in over 60 countries.

The project was labeled **GLOBE,** an acronym for **global leadership and organizational behavior effectiveness.** It is now in its 12th year of operation and involves the efforts of 170 researchers (social scientists and management researchers) in over 60 countries ranging from Albania to Qatar to Zambia. To date, data have been gathered from over 18,000 middle managers in the cooperating countries. The initial stages of the project included the development of the questionnaires that would be used and the collection of data that would permit an analysis of the relationships between culture and leadership practices. Data are just beginning to emerge relative to the culture-leadership questions (questions 1 and 2 above), the results of which we will consider below. In future stages, the relationship between particular leadership styles and subordinate attitudes and performance will be examined within and between cultures. A final phase will involve laboratory and field experiments and studies to test some propositions and hypotheses that emerge from the data collected.

The answers to questions 1 and 2 are both yes. There are both universals and culture-specific accepted leader behaviors. In an analysis of the first wave of GLOBE data, Den Hartog (in press) identified a number of leader traits that were universally accepted and rejected, and certain attributes that were more acceptable in some cultures than

TABLE 12.7	Universal and Culture-Specific Aspects of Leadership		
UNIVERSALLY ACCEPTED	**UNIVERSALLY REJECTED**	**CULTURE SPECIFIC**	
Integrity—trustworthy, just, honest	Loner Noncooperative	Cunning Sensitive	
Charismatic, visionary, inspirational—encouraging, positive, motivational, confidence builder, dynamic	Ruthless Nonexplicit Irritable Dictatorial	Ambitious Status conscious	
Team oriented—team building, communicating, coordinating			
Excellence oriented, decisive, intelligent, win–win problem solver			

SOURCE: Adapted from Brodbeck et al. (2000).

in others (see Table 12.7). The list of universally accepted attributes fits neatly with the concepts of transformational and charismatic leadership. In contrast, the universally rejected leadership attributes would never be mistaken for the attributes of a transformational or charismatic leader. The attributes and behaviors that seem to be endorsed or rejected depending on the culture are hard to label, although the traits of ambition and status consciousness might fit into Hofstede's cultural concepts of power distance or individualism/collectivism.

Recently, Brodbeck et al. (2000) confirmed these findings in a smaller subset of those 60 cooperating nations. They examined GLOBE data from 22 European countries that were either members of the European Union (EU) or had applied for membership. As was the case with the larger data set analyzed by Den Hartog, Brodbeck et al. found universally accepted and rejected leader attributes and behaviors within the European culture, as well as leader characteristics that were more acceptable in some countries than others. These universals and **culture-specific characteristics** appear in Table 12.8. As an example of a culture-specific characteristics, autonomous leaders were perceived as more effective in Germany and Russia, but less effective in Great Britain and France. Similarly, while leaders who avoid conflict were seen as effective in Sweden and Italy, they were regarded as less effective in the Czech Republic and Poland. It is tempting to explain this difference in terms of the recent political histories of the Czech Republic and Poland; we might not be surprised that these countries value leaders who do not shy away from conflict, considering that they chafed under Soviet domination for decades, agitated for independence, and achieved it with the fall of the Berlin Wall.

Many of the universals appear to be traits similar to Big Five traits. Unfortunately, the GLOBE analyses did not adopt the Big Five structure so it is difficult to match the universals directly to Big Five factors. Nevertheless, the GLOBE studies seem to point, once again, to the possible role of personality in the exercise of leadership. In later phases of the GLOBE research, it would be useful if actual leaders were asked to complete Big Five–type instruments in order to reconcile the current GLOBE traits with a more standard taxonomy.

Although the GLOBE analyses and results will be appearing for the next decade, the implications of these early analyses seem clear. Transformational and charismatic leader behaviors travel well. This is good news for the multinational company and the global manager. It means that selection and training can emphasize these leader behaviors, which appear relevant regardless of the culture. In essence, these are "core" attributes and behaviors that are not specific to any culture. It is also cautionary news in the sense that it appears

CULTURE-SPECIFIC CHARACTERISTICS

Leader characteristics that are more acceptable in some countries than others.

TABLE 12.8 **Leadership Attributes by Region and Country Cluster**

Leadership prototypicality	NORTH/WEST EUROPEAN REGION					SOUTH/EAST EUROPEAN REGION				
	ANGLO	NORDIC	GERMANIC			LATIN	CENTRAL	NEAR EAST		
	(GB, IRL)	(SWE, NL FIN, DEN)	(CH, GER/w, GER/e, AUS)	(CSR)	(FRA)	(ITA, SPA, POR, HUN)	(POL, SLO)	(TUR, GRE)	(RUS)	(GEO)
High positive (facilitates outstanding leadership)	Performance Inspirational Visionary Team integrator Integrity Decisive Participative	Integrity Inspirational Visionary Team integrator Performance Decisive Nonautocratic Participative	Integrity Inspirational Performance Nonautocratic Visionary Decisive Participative Administrative Team integrator	Integrity Performance Administrative Inspirational Nonautocratic Visionary Participative Self-sacrificial Team integrator Diplomatic	Participative Nonautocratic	Team integrator Performance Inspirational Integrity Visionary Decisive Administrative Diplomatic Collaborative	Team integrator Visionary Administrative Diplomatic Decisive Integrity Performance Inspirational	Team integrator Decisive Visionary Integrity Inspirational Administrative Diplomatic Collaborative Performance	Visionary Administrative Performance Inspirational Decisive Integrity Team integrator	Administrative Decisive Performance Visionary Integrity Team integrator Humane Diplomatic Collaborative Modesty
Low positive (slightly facilitates)	Nonautocratic Administrative Diplomatic Collaborative Modesty Self-sacrificial Humane Conflict avoider	Collaborative Diplomatic Administrative Conflict avoider Self-sacrificial Humane Modesty	Diplomatic Collaborative Self-sacrificial Modesty Humane Conflict avoider Autonomous	Collaborative Decisive Modesty Autonomous Humane	Inspirational Integrity Team integrator Performance Visionary Decisive Diplomatic Collaborative Conflict avoider Administrative Modesty	Nonautocratic Participative Self-sacrificial Modesty Humane Status conscious Conflict avoider	Collaborative Participative Nonautocratic Modesty Self-sacrificial Status conscious Autonomous Humane Procedural	Participative Nonautocratic Self-sacrificial Modesty Humane Status conscious Conflict avoider	Participative Collaborative Diplomatic Status conscious Self-sacrificial Modesty Conflict avoider Autonomous	Inspirational Nonautocratic Self-sacrificial Status conscious Autonomous Participative Procedural
Low negative (slightly impedes)	Autonomous Status conscious Procedural	Autonomous Status conscious Procedural	Status conscious Procedural	Procedural Conflict avoider Face saver	Self-sacrificial Status conscious Autonomous Humane Procedural	Procedural Autonomous	Conflict avoider Face saver	Autonomous Procedural Face saver	Humane Nonautocratic Procedural Face saver	Conflict avoider Face saver Self-centered
High negative (impedes)	Face saver Self-centered Malevolent	Face saver Self-centered Malevolent	Face saver Self-centered Malevolent	Status conscious Self-centered Malevolent	Face saver Malevolent Self-centered	Face saver Self-centered Malevolent	Self-centered Malevolent	Self-centered Malevolent	Self-centered Malevolent	Malevolent

Key. AUS = Austria, CH = Switzerland, CSR = Czech Republic, DEN = Denmark, FIN = Finland, FRA = France, GB = United Kingdom, GER/w = Germany, GER/e = former East Germany, GEO = Georgia, GRE = Greece, HUN = Hungary, ITA = Italy, IRL = Ireland, NL = Netherlands, POL = Poland, POR = Portugal, RUS = Russia, SLO = Slovenia, SPA = Spain, SWE = Sweden, TUR = Turkey.

Source: Adapted from Brodbeck et al. (2000).

that there are some culture-specific leadership do's and don'ts. Before GLOBE, we knew that these do's and don'ts were bound to exist, but we did not know what they were for a specific culture. We are now beginning to get a road map from the GLOBE efforts and this will also make the leadership process considerably more effective within specific countries and cultures, particularly as the GLOBE results begin to find their way into managerial and leadership training programs.

LEADERSHIP IN A DIVERSE ENVIRONMENT

The workplace is becoming less white, less native born, less male, and less young. In addition, disabled workers are becoming more common in the workforce. Each of these changes requires a substantial shift in the thinking and the behavior of a leader. The most substantial challenge might be for the expatriate manager learning the customs and values of a completely different culture. Singling out an individual for praise might be wise in an individualist culture and ill-advised in a collectivist culture. Cultural issues are not limited to nationality, however; they also come into play when men and women work together. While managers a generation ago might have assumed that a pair of hockey tickets would make an ideal prize in a monthly sales contest, doing so today with a sales force comprised of a significant number of women will likely draw complaints. Another culturally sensitive matter that leaders must face is the commemoration of holidays. How does a leader reconcile Christmas, Hannukah, Kwanza, and Ramadan? What about workers who are Jehovah's Witnesses and celebrate only wedding anniversaries? I-O psychology will need to identify the ways that the leaders of today and tomorrow solve these dilemmas. Perhaps the answer can be found in cross-cultural research.

The GLOBE project illustrates the complexity of culture for a leader. On the one hand, there are certain universals (both good and bad) and, on the other hand, there are culture specific issues that present themselves to a leader. The multinational environment can be used both as a model and as a metaphor for any domestic workforce. As we have indicated at various points in this book, domestic workforces are becoming more culturally diverse (K. M. Thomas, 1998). A typical U.S. workforce will include Asian, African, Hispanic, former Soviet bloc, and Indian workers. As a result of the formation of the EU and the demise of the Warsaw Pact alliances, the workforces of many European countries are becoming similarly diverse. But country of birth is only one level of culture and diversity. Within native-born worker populations, whether in Sweden, Romania, or the United States, there may be subcultures defined by variables other than country of birth. Every country has its disadvantaged work groups. In Sweden, it might be those whose parents emigrated from Middle Eastern countries. In Romania, it might be people with Hungarian surnames. In the United States, it might be African Americans, Asian Americans, Hispanic Americans, or women.

Chrobot-Mason and Ruderman (2003) used the LMX model of leadership to suggest that it has been common in the past for leaders to use a simple heuristic to decide who is an in-group and who is an out-group member. If you look like the leader (e.g., white male), you may or may not become an in-group member. If you don't look like the leader, it is unlikely that you will become an in-group member. One way to take advantage of all the benefits that a diverse workforce can bring is for a leader to work hard on developing high-quality relationships with members who are not like themselves. This makes perfect sense and is compatible with the latest thinking of those advocating the LMX theory of leadership, that is, leaders should develop high-quality relationships with *all* work group members (Graen & Uhl-Bein, 1991, 1995).

An additional implication of the preliminary GLOBE results for domestic diversity issues resides in the "universals." It appears that transformational and charismatic leadership is universally valued. Thus, if a leader were to adopt a transformational or charismatic style with a work group, we would expect positive results (in terms of performance) and positive reactions (in terms of the attitudes of group members). This should be true regardless of the diversity of the work group. Transformational leaders are just as likely to enhance the work experience of men and women, African Americans and whites, abled and disabled, young and old.

To be sure, there is a knowledge component involved. Even the transformational leader can stub a toe without specific cultural and subcultural awareness. The Brodbeck et al. (2000) and Den Hartog (in press) studies identified attributes and behaviors that were not universal. Domestic transformational leaders need to be aware of the same nonuniversality in leading a work group. Chrobot-Mason and Ruderman (2003) suggested ways that the domestic leader can take these cultural and subcultural differences into account in work group interactions. K. M. Thomas (1998) pointed out that traditional leadership training has emphasized the preparation of a leader for carrying out business strategy. Day (2001b) called this *leader* training, not *leadership* training. Thomas argued that the multicultural leader, domestic or international, needs to understand and appreciate the differences that exist among work group members. The only way to achieve this appreciation is through reflection on one's own culture and the culture of others who populate the workplace.

We would like to end this section on workplace diversity by revisiting Day's (2001b) notion of shared leadership described earlier in this chapter. Both Chrobot-Mason and Ruderman (2003) and K. M. Thomas (1998) placed substantial emphasis on the behavior of the leader. Since the leader is the "lens" through which much of organizational culture and climate are seen, this emphasis is well placed. In addition, however, there is some logic for considering the attitudes and behavior of work group members. If leadership is a shared phenomenon, or a process that belongs to the work group and not solely to the leader, then the entire group must ultimately be involved in the development of "leadership." Of course, at the end of the day, it is the leader's responsibility to develop the environment that helps leadership to emerge as a group concept.

Thus, if there is a "formula" for advising leaders about how to deal with an increasingly diverse workforce, it would be to embrace transformational leadership styles, devote considerable effort to developing high-quality relationships, and do some thinking, reading, and talking about the cultures and subcultures they are likely to encounter among work group members. Simultaneously, the leader must develop an environment that brings all of the group members into the leadership circle. Mentoring, challenging job assignments, frequent supportive and individual discussions about organizational and individual member goals and performance are some of ways this environment might be created (Chrobot-Mason & Ruderman, 2003).

MODULE 12.4 SUMMARY

- Changes in the workplace since the 1980s have been substantial, resulting in a very different work environment for leaders. New challenges include leading virtual teams, telecommuters, and temporary workers.
- Some studies suggest a potentially different "style" for male and female leaders, with females tending to favor more participative and democratic interactions with subordinates and to be more aware of interpersonal issues than their male counterparts. Research is needed regarding whether these

differences actually matter in terms of the ultimate effectiveness of the leader.

- Trait theory is making a comeback in the form of studies examining the relationship of Big Five personality traits and leader effectiveness. This modern approach defines personality traits behaviorally, has a general consensus on the meaning of these personality traits, and considers them in the context of organizational and situational variables. This modern approach is considerably more attractive than traditional trait theory.

- House and his colleagues are conducting a large cross-cultural study of leadership called global leadership and organizational behavior effectiveness (GLOBE). To date, they have found that the list of universally accepted leader attributes fits neatly with the concepts of transformational and charismatic leadership. They also have identified some culture-specific leader characteristics that are more acceptable in some countries than in others.

KEY TERMS

virtual team

telecommuting

global leadership and organizational behavior effectiveness (GLOBE)

culture-specific characteristics

CRITICAL THINKING EXERCISES

12.7 In the new virtual work environment characterized by dispersed work teams and telecommuting, which of the following leadership approaches would be most difficult to implement? Why? Which would be easiest? Why?

1. LMX
2. Transactional
3. Transformational
4. Path-goal

12.8 A woman friend of yours who has never filled a formal management role before tells you that she had just been chosen to replace a departing manager. She asks you if, as a female leader, she should adopt a style different from her departing male counterpart. What would you advise her?

TEAMS IN ORGANIZATIONS

TYPES OF TEAMS

K urt recently completed a graduate program in I-O psychology and was hired by a consulting firm as an entry-level organizational consultant. He has been on the job for one week and has just been assigned to a project team consisting of fellow consultants from different international offices of the consulting firm. The project team's goal is to develop a new software product for a long-time client. Kurt's boss tells him not to worry because these global virtual teams are used all the time, and technology can reduce the geographical boundaries among team members. Kurt is about to "meet" his teammates over e-mail and then in a videoconference. He is uneasy about working on this project team because none of his teammates live in the United States and, for many of his team-mates, English is not their first language. Kurt is wondering how well this virtual team will work together and whether the geographical, cultural, and language barriers will prevent the team from achieving its objectives. He also has some reservations about the need for using a team for this project instead of simply having individuals provide separate inputs to a project leader.

Kurt's concerns are legitimate, and such concerns are becoming more common as many different kinds of teams are increasingly being used in the workplace. I-O psychology researchers and practitioners have studied a variety of team-related issues (e.g., team composition, selection, training, communication) that we will discuss in this chapter. With the predicted increase in the use of teams in organizations, these issues will continue to be of interest to I-O psychologists, managers, and employees working in teams.

Mohrman, Cohen, and Mohrman (1995) suggested several reasons for the increasing use of teams in organizations:

- Time is saved if work usually performed sequentially by individuals can be performed concurrently by people working in teams.
- Innovation and creativity are promoted because of cross-fertilization of ideas.
- Teams can integrate information in ways that an individual cannot.
- Teams enable organizations to quickly and effectively develop and deliver products and services, while retaining high quality.
- Teams enable organizations to learn and retain learning more effectively.

The use of teams in organizations presents both opportunities and challenges to managers and I-O psychologists. For example, the increase in team-based work provides I-O psychologists with opportunities to explore whether personality measures are beneficial for selecting employees who will work well in teams. The increased use of teams presents challenges having to do with team composition, training for teams, the motivation of teams, and the evaluation of team performance. We will discuss each of these topics in this chapter.

GROUPS AND TEAMS: DEFINITIONS

Before describing different types of groups and teams, it is important to consider some definitional issues in this area. Historically, groups have been distinguished from teams. Research on groups has traditionally been conducted by social psychologists who studied group processes in laboratory settings. In research on groups, for example, undergraduate students are often brought together to complete some group problem-solving or decision-making task. A problem with such research is that groups in laboratory settings do not have a chance to develop their own history and they often disband after a very brief time, limiting generalizability to work teams. In contrast, research on teams has generally been conducted by organizational psychologists and management researchers and in organizational settings that include many variables that make controlled experimentation difficult. Another distinction is that groups include members who may work together or may just share some resources, but teams always include members whose tasks are interdependent.

In recent years, I-O psychologists have given less recognition to distinctions between groups and teams than they previously did (Ilgen, 1999; Sundstrom, McIntyre, Halfhill, & Richards, 2000). For example, Guzzo (1995) noted that groups and teams have too much in common to make any grand distinction between them. Thus, the terms "group" and "team" are increasingly being used interchangeably. In this chapter, we will refer primarily to teams, as they are more relevant to the organizational framework that I-O psychologists use. Except for studies in which previous research has explicitly used groups, we will focus on research on teams, which have greater generalizability and applicability to the work teams that I-O psychologists study.

A **team** is defined as an interdependent collection of individuals who work together toward a common goal and who share responsibility for specific outcomes for their organizations (Sundstrom, DeMeuse, & Futrell, 1990). An additional requirement is that the team is identified as such by those within and outside of the team (West, Borrill, & Unsworth, 1998). No doubt you have been a team member, perhaps in sports or in the cast or crew of a stage production. Other examples of teams include assembly teams, management teams, emergency medical service and rescue teams, firefighter teams, surgery teams, military teams, symphony orchestras, string quartets, and rock groups.

TEAM

Interdependent collection of individuals who work together toward a common goal and who share responsibility for specific outcomes for their organizations.

TYPES OF TEAMS

Many different kinds of teams are used in the workplace. Below we discuss the types of teams that have recently received the most attention in organizations.

Quality Circles

Quality circles typically involve 6 to 12 employees who meet regularly to identify work-related problems and to generate ideas that can increase productivity or product quality (Guzzo & Dickson, 1996). **Quality circles** are often initiated by management, with meeting times allotted during work hours. Although quality circle membership is often voluntary, a supervisor may suggest that certain employees participate. Quality circles have their origin in participative management techniques that were developed in Japan and exported to the rest of the world (Cordery, 1996). Members of quality circles, however, are not given formal authority. Instead, they seek to have their ideas and solutions adopted and implemented by management.

Research evidence has been mixed for quality circles. Some research indicates that quality circles result in positive outcomes in the short term, but these gains are not sustained over time (Lawler, Mohrman, & Ledford, 1992). For example, Griffin (1988) conducted a longitudinal evaluation of quality circles in two comparable manufacturing plants, one that adopted quality circles and one that did not. He collected four waves of data, including one

QUALITY CIRCLE

Work group arrangement that typically involves 6 to 12 employees who meet regularly to identify work-related problems and generate ideas to increase productivity or product quality.

before implementation of the quality circles and three follow-up measurements. The results indicated that individual work attitudes, turnover intentions, and performance initially improved for the quality circles relative to the control group, but then declined to their original levels within 18 months after implementation of the quality circles.

Similarly, other research has found that many quality circles are initially successful in increasing quality or decreasing costs, but they do not appear to have further benefits after these early gains (Cannon-Bowers, Oser, & Flanagon, 1992; Guzzo & Dickson, 1996). This phenomenon has been called the "honeymoon effect" in quality circles. The honeymoon effect has been attributed to the fact that initial suggestions for improvements are often fairly easy and clear, and have a favorable impact on the bottom line if they are adopted. Over time, however, it becomes increasingly difficult for quality circle members to make additional suggestions that can increase quality or decrease costs. This lower success rate over time leads to a decrease in the positive attitudes that accompanied initial gains resulting from quality circle suggestions. This honeymoon effect may account for the decreasing popularity of quality circles in many U.S. organizations (Gibson & Tesone, 2001). Quality circles were most popular in the United States in the 1970s and early 1980s. By the late 1980s, however, many U.S. organizations that had tried quality circles had abandoned them. Nevertheless, the emphasis that many quality circles had on quality and participation has become the foundation for other techniques, including Total Quality Management and self-managing teams, which have remained popular in the United States (Worren, 1996).

Despite the decline in popularity of quality circles in the United States, they remain popular in Japan, where there is more support for and reinforcement of quality circle principles (Juran, 1992). Indeed, Japanese companies (e.g., Honda, Toyota) that have production plants in the United States developed quality circles in the 1990s and have had unique success with them. For example, Honda Corporation uses a quality circle approach called "The New Honda Circle." This approach has resulted in improved design and production processes for Honda's cars. As a result, quality circles at Honda have won several nationally recognized awards. Quality circles at Honda include production workers as well as coworkers from engineering, sales, and research and development. In these quality circles, no one is called an employee. Instead, everyone is an associate, and the first-level supervisor is called a team leader. These titles are not just for show; instead, they are indicative of a team culture that encourages participation and reduces the gap between leaders and production workers. In recognition of their suggestions, quality circle members at Honda accumulate points, which may lead to a new car or a vacation. In addition, associates are required to participate in some quality circle activity to be eligible for promotion. Overall, quality circles and similar participative programs emphasize continuous work improvement, and they serve as an important framework in the achievement of productivity and efficiency at Honda. The contrast between such success stories for Japanese firms in the United States and the overall decline in American quality circles may be due to the cultural clash between a collectivist activity (quality circle participation) in an individualist (American) culture.

Project Teams

Project teams are created to solve a particular problem or set of problems (Guzzo & Dickson, 1996). Project teams differ from other teams because they are disbanded after the project is completed or the problem is solved. Hackman (1990) noted that project teams have an unusual mix of autonomy and dependence. On the one hand, they are typically free, within broad limits, to proceed with the project work that members determine. On the other hand, they work for some client group and thus are dependent upon client preferences. Project teams are also called ad hoc committees, task forces, or cross-functional teams. The term "cross-functional" refers to the different departments or functions from which team members come. For example, a new product development team might include

PROJECT TEAM

Created to solve a particular problem or set of problems and is disbanded after the project is completed or the problem is solved; also called an ad hoc committee, a task force, or a cross-functional team.

employees from sales, engineering, marketing, production, and research and development units. New product development teams are commonly used to develop innovative products or to identify new solutions to existing problems.

Project teams often have clear deadlines, but members are often uncertain about how to accomplish the task (Gersick & Davis-Sacks, 1990). Thus, team members must work together quickly and creatively to come up with solutions. For example, Gersick (1990) examined a project team of four bankers brought together to design money market accounts for a large East Coast bank. Congress had just passed a law that allowed banks, for the first time since the early 1930s, to determine the interest rate they would pay. Banks could begin offering the product precisely 60 days after the bill was enacted. The project team members in Gersick's study met four times over a two-month period. Between meetings, team members communicated extensively with other employees in the bank so that they could determine the best way to install their product in all of the bank's systems. The team was able to implement the new money market account within the 60-day deadline and was able to teach bank employees about the new account in time for opening day. Gersick attributed the success of the team first to its members, who had enough expertise and influence to conceive a plan and implement a solution; and then to upper management, who gave the team support and enough latitude to make its own decisions. Gersick noted that the bank's Chairman called about the new account during a meeting and said, "It had better be good," but did not interfere with the team's decision-making process. The team members also communicated regularly and coordinated their work well, which ultimately resulted in a successful conclusion to the project. Later in the chapter, we will discuss the importance of team inputs and team processes as they relate to team effectiveness.

Project teams raise some organizational challenges because, although team members still belong to their functional units where they have certain roles to fulfill and their managers decide on rewards and promotions, they must fulfill other roles and expectations on the team. Some employees dislike being assigned to project teams because they feel they are losing out in terms of departmental power, advancement, and rewards. Nevertheless, organizations are increasingly using project teams in matrix organizations, in which individuals work on multiple teams, reporting at the same time to a project manager for a team project and a functional manager in a particular department. Such matrix arrangements help organizations to make the most out of limited human resources. We will describe matrix organizations in further detail in Chapter 14.

Production Teams

PRODUCTION TEAM

Consists of front-line employees who produce tangible output.

AUTONOMOUS WORK GROUP

Specific kind of production team that has control over a variety of functions, including planning shift operations, allocating work, determining work priorities, performing a variety of work tasks, and recommending new hires as work group members.

Production teams consist of front-line employees who produce tangible output such as cars, televisions, cell phones, or the mining of coal (Guzzo & Dickson, 1996). A common example is a team working on an assembly line in a manufacturing plant that produces Saturn automobiles. Compared to other automobile manufacturers whose employees work at single stations, Saturn is known for using interdependent teams to design and produce their cars, which are known for their high quality. Other types of production teams include maintenance crews, candy production crews, automotive parts manufacturing teams, coal mining crews, electronic assembly teams, and wood harvesting teams (Forsyth, 1999; Sundstrom et al., 2000). Many production teams have a meeting each morning to ensure that members are communicating and working interdependently to reach their production goals. In many production teams, members have direct access to other team members, allowing them to bypass supervisors in making and implementing certain decisions. It is often easy to measure the output of production teams in terms of quantity and quality and, therefore, also relatively easy to evaluate the team's performance and provide feedback (Reilly & McGourty, 1998).

An **autonomous work group** is a specific kind of production team that has control over a variety of its functions, including planning shift operations, allocating work, determining work priorities, performing a variety of actual work tasks, and making recommendations regarding the hiring of new work group members. Autonomous work groups, which are also known as self-managing or self-directed teams, are used by such industry leaders as AT&T, Coca-Cola, Federal Express, General Electric, Motorola, Texas Instruments, and Xerox (Ivancevich & Matteson, 2002). They were developed in Europe using sociotechnical system approaches to work design that give detailed attention to the social (human) and technical (technological) components of work (Trist & Bamforth, 1951).

The intent of autonomous work groups is to improve the integration of social and technical systems by allowing groups of employees to manage themselves. Management provides the autonomous work groups with the authority, materials, and equipment to perform their jobs (Pearce & Ravlin, 1987). Work is arranged so that cooperation and communication are encouraged among group members, and autonomous work group members have the opportunity to learn all of the jobs the group is expected to perform. Thus, autonomous work group members often have an enriched work environment because of the opportunity for developing and/or using multiple skills at work.

The senior author of this book observed autonomous work groups in a Saab plant in Trollhatten, Sweden. In this plant, autonomous work groups assembled car bodies, which would come from a central holding area on a large line shaped like a racetrack. Multiple autonomous work groups were located in the center of that "racetrack" and had the authority to pull a car off the central loop and into their area whenever they saw fit. In the finishing area, their general "quota" was 11 car bodies a day, but they often worked on as few as 7 and as many as 15 cars a day. In the group area, autonomous work group members had tables and chairs to sit and talk and plan. The group would decide when to bring a car body into the work area and which members would work on sanding, reassembling, and other tasks. The autonomous work group would then send the car back to the racetrack when they were finished working on it. This form of redesign worked well in Sweden because it was compatible with the collectivist, low power distance culture.

The differences between autonomous work groups and traditional work arrangements may even be observed in the same organization. For example, the same automobile company might have two assembly plants, one that uses traditional work groups with a production supervisor who makes all of the management decisions, and one that uses autonomous work groups. This often occurs in organizations that have developed a new manufacturing plant and senior management decides to implement autonomous work groups in the new location. New manufacturing plants that utilize an innovative work arrangement (e.g., autonomous work groups) are sometimes called greenfield sites (Cordery, 1996; Wall, Kemp, Jackson, & Clegg, 1986).

Conventional wisdom proposes that autonomous work groups have a favorable impact upon team member attitudes and behaviors, but research evidence supporting these claims is mixed (Guzzo & Dickson, 1996). Some research has indicated that autonomous work group members are more satisfied with their jobs than members of traditional work groups (Cohen & Ledford, 1994; Cordery, Mueller, & Smith, 1991). However, some studies have found that members of autonomous work groups are more likely to be absent and to leave their jobs than members of traditional work groups (Cordery et al., 1991; Wall et al., 1986). The findings of the Cordery et al. (1991) study are particularly difficult to explain because, compared with members of traditional work groups, members of autonomous work groups had higher job satisfaction, but also higher absenteeism and turnover. In our experience, one of the common consequences of autonomous work arrangements is that the team decides who will do what, and each member ends up doing what they are best at or have always done. Thus, the promised enrichment never occurs, which might explain the lack of positive findings in some autonomous work groups. Given the conflicting findings on the outcomes associated with the use of autonomous work groups, we expect that research will continue on this important type of work group arrangement.

Virtual Teams

On the popular television show *Star Trek,* being geographically separated by a vast distance was no problem for Captain Kirk and other members of the Star Trek Enterprise. They simply said, "Beam me up, Scotty" and, with the push of a button, face-to-face encounters were accomplished fairly easily (Robb, 2002). Although conducting meetings in the corporate world with geographically dispersed members has not reached that level of sophistication, much progress has been made in reducing the inconvenience of geographic separation among team members.

A **virtual team** has widely dispersed members working together toward a common goal and linked through computers and other technology such as the telephone, videoconferencing, and team support software (Joinson, 2002). Some virtual teams may meet in person on a regular basis, but in many virtual teams, members rarely, if ever, meet in person. Nevertheless, Cascio (2000) noted several advantages for organizations that use virtual teams: (1) saving time and travel expenses, (2) providing increased access to experts, (3) expanding labor markets by allowing firms to recruit and retain the best employees regardless of their physical location, and (4) having the opportunity to assign employees to multiple teams at the same time.

Members of virtual teams may be in different geographic locations within a single country, but given the global economy, the emergence of e-commerce, and the growth in mergers and acquisitions, virtual teams are increasingly likely to include members from various parts of the world (Avolio, Kahai, Dumdum, & Sivasubramaniam, 2001). Not surprisingly, the challenges to global virtual teams include time differences, cultural differences, and language barriers. Web-based language training and cross-cultural training are among the technological tools used to help global virtual team members work together. For example, Royal Dutch Shell Corporation, the oil giant based in the Netherlands, is a large user of virtual team software that provides global project teams with real-time online meeting tools, Web-based knowledge management programs, Internet-based team workspaces, and videoconferencing that help to compensate for team members' geographic separation (Robb, 2002).

Trust is also a critical concern in virtual teams. Because of the absence of face-to-face interactions, virtual teams must develop a "gel" or sense of belonging that provides the basis for information exchange and collaborative work (Avolio et al., 2001). Cascio (2000) noted that increased trust and a shared sense of belonging result when virtual team members exhibit virtual-collaboration behaviors, virtual-socialization skills, and virtual-communication skills. **Virtual-collaboration behaviors** include exchanging ideas without criticism, agreeing on responsibilities, and meeting deadlines. **Virtual-socialization skills** include soliciting team members' feedback on the process the team is using to accomplish its goals, expressing appreciation for ideas and completed tasks, and apologizing for mistakes. **Virtual-communication skills** include rephrasing unclear sentences or expressions so that all team members understand what is being said, acknowledging the receipt of messages, and responding within one business day. Although similar skills are needed to enhance communication in non-virtual (i.e., traditional) team or work environments, these virtual skills are particularly important because of the increased likelihood of miscommunication when team members are geographically separated, unfamiliar with each other, and lack face-to-face interactions.

More generally, an understanding of the problems that are relevant to all teams is helpful in managing virtual teams (Cascio, 2000). For example, team leaders should provide clear roles and responsibilities, clarify how decisions will be made, and explain the extent to which team members will share responsibility for implementing the team's decisions. Virtual team leadership is also critical in ensuring that regular communication and interaction among team members is maintained despite the geographic separation (Bell & Kozlowski, 2002). Because virtual teams are fairly new, research in this area is just

---

VIRTUAL TEAM

Composed of widely dispersed members working together toward a common goal and linked through computers and other technology such as the telephone, videoconferencing, and team support software.

VIRTUAL-COLLABORATION BEHAVIORS

Used in virtual team interactions that include exchanging ideas without criticism, agreeing on responsibilities, and meeting deadlines.

VIRTUAL-SOCIALIZATION SKILLS

Used in virtual team interactions that include soliciting team members' feedback on the work process used to accomplish team goals, expressing appreciation for ideas and completed tasks, and apologizing for mistakes.

VIRTUAL-COMMUNICATION SKILLS

Used in virtual team interactions that include rephrasing unclear sentences or expressions so that all team members understand what is being said, acknowledging the receipt of messages, and responding within one business day.

beginning. We expect research attention on virtual teams to increase as they are used more commonly in the advancing technological and global workplace.

As we discussed in Chapter 10 on work attitudes and emotions, there is little empirical data to support the use of telecommuting and other electronic work arrangements (Holland & Hogan, 1998). Nevertheless, it is clear that telecommuting and virtual teams are here to stay, and we look forward to additional research that examines the circumstances in which these work arrangements are most successful. It is also interesting to consider whether the individual difference characteristics we discussed in Chapter 3 are related to performance for individuals working in virtual teams or telecommuting. For example, we predict that personality characteristics such as agreeableness and openness to experience are likely to be associated with successful virtual team performance, but no studies to our knowledge have examined this relationship.

The authors of this book, the editors, and the production team worked as a virtual team while writing, editing, and publishing this book. Team members were geographically dispersed across several locations in the United States, including Colorado, Northern and Southern California, Connecticut, Illinois, and New York. Much of the collaborative work that went into the writing of this textbook was done by means of e-mail, fax, conference calls, and phone calls. Our virtual team benefited from team members exhibiting positive virtual-collaboration behaviors, virtual-socialization skills, and virtual-communication skills, as well as from clear roles and responsibilities identified by team leaders at the beginning of the project. For example, the authors would be busy writing the chapters, but would stop to help the developmental editor answer questions about proceeding with the production process. The developmental editor was also instrumental in noting when the authors' writing had glossed over important issues or needed clarification of particular ideas. Our virtual team members exhibited virtual-collaboration behaviors such as exchanging ideas between authors and the developmental editor without criticism, agreeing on responsibilities, and meeting deadlines. We also exhibited virtual-socialization skills in expressing appreciation for ideas and completed tasks and continually soliciting team members' feedback on important decisions. These positive and spirited discussions ensured that communication, cooperation, and interdependence were high in the virtual team, despite the geographic separation among team members.

A SPECIALIZED TEAM: AIRLINE COCKPIT CREW

Almost 100 years after the Wright brothers worked as a team to achieve the first recorded flight, teamwork in aviation is still a major concern (Prince, Chidester, Bowers, & Cannon-Bowers, 1992; Salas, Burke, Bowers, & Wilson, 2001). Airline cockpit crews perform highly interdependent tasks, some that occur routinely in all flights and others that may occur only in rare but well-practiced emergency situations (Ginnett, 1990). Cockpit crews are unique in that they work together for a brief time, and they must effectively perform critical tasks soon after the crew is formed. Newly formed crews are able to perform effectively soon after they meet because crew members receive extensive training that precedes their work on a particular crew.

Airline cockpit crews rarely run into problems, but the real requirements for effective teamwork occur when they encounter unusual situations. According to Ginnett (1990), crews benefit from an organizational context that provides:

1. Challenging objectives for safety, on-time performance, and fuel efficiency.
2. An education system that provides training and consultation to supplement members' task expertise.
3. An information system that provides the data needed to assess situations and evaluate alternative strategies for handling them.

The importance of teamwork: An airplane's cockpit crew must communicate and collaborate.

The selection system for airline cockpit crews is also important. Selection focuses on identifying crew members who have task-relevant skills and who can coordinate and communicate well with other team members. The captain of the crew plays a key role. According to Ginnett's case study (1990), key behaviors that a captain displays in leading a cockpit crew include:

1. Explicitly discussing tasks that require coordination between the cockpit and the cabin.
2. Explicitly setting norms or rules for appropriate crew behavior.
3. Appropriately managing the dynamics surrounding authority inherent in the captain's role.

Although some aspects of team performance are unique to airline cockpit crews, these teams also deal with many of the same issues that other teams in organizations must address, including team selection, coordination, communication, setting norms, and decision making. In addition, much like other teams, airline cockpit crews are strongly influenced by organizational context factors that can enhance or detract from their performance. These team inputs and processes are discussed in detail in the other modules of this chapter.

MODULE 13.1 SUMMARY

- The increased use of teams in organizations presents opportunities and challenges to managers and I-O psychologists. There are opportunities to increase organizational performance and to explore the role of personality measures in selecting employees who work well in teams. The challenges are in areas such as team composition, training for teams, the motivation of teams, and the evaluation of team performance.

- A team is an interdependent collection of individuals who work together toward a common goal and who share responsibility for specific outcomes for their organizations. Many different kinds of teams are used in the workplace including quality circles, project teams, production teams, and virtual teams.

- Production teams consist of front-line employees who produce tangible output. An autonomous work group is a specific kind of production team that has control over a variety of its functions. Autonomous work groups are intended to improve the integration of social and technical systems by allowing groups of employees to manage themselves.

- Organizations that use virtual teams benefit in a variety of ways, including saving time and travel expenses and providing increased access to experts. However, virtual teams, particularly those that rarely meet in person, face a variety of challenges.

KEY TERMS

team	production team	virtual-collaboration behaviors
quality circle	autonomous work group	virtual-socialization skills
project team	virtual team	virtual-communication skills

CRITICAL THINKING EXERCISES

13.1 In the time you spend on the computer or the Internet, do you interact as part of a group or team in any way? For example, have you worked interactively with team members on projects through e-mail or the Internet? If so, what virtual team skills and behaviors were important in enhancing team interactions and performance?

13.2 If you could choose your favorite team (whether it is in a sports, music, or business setting), what would it be? Describe why you chose this particular team and describe the ways in which it fits (or does not fit) the definition of a team provided in this chapter.

A MODEL OF TEAM EFFECTIVENESS

INPUT-PROCESS-OUTPUT MODEL OF TEAM EFFECTIVENESS

The **input-process-output model of team effectiveness** provides a way to understand how teams perform and how to maximize their performance (Gladstein, 1984; Hackman, 1987). Almost every recently developed team effectiveness model uses the input-process-output model (Cohen & Bailey, 1997; Guzzo & Shea, 1992). Inputs include the organizational context, the team task, and team composition. Team processes include norms, communication, coordination, cohesiveness, and decision making. Team outputs include productivity, innovativeness, and team member well-being. Figure 13.1 shows this model in which inputs affect team processes, which in turn affect team outputs. This model, which has been supported by a variety of research studies, proposes that inputs affect team outputs *indirectly* through team processes. Research has also indicated that inputs can have a *direct* effect on team outputs (Campion, Medsker, & Higgs, 1993). As you can see in Figure 13.1, there are direct links from team inputs to team outputs as well as indirect links between team inputs and outputs through team processes.

Team Inputs

Organizational Context   The organizational context—which includes the rewards system, the training system, the physical environment, managerial support, and technology—is important to team performance. These contextual influences enhance team interactions and increase team effectiveness by providing resources needed for performance and continued functioning of the work team. Gladstein (1984) found, for example, that external organizational variables such as market growth were positively related to team sales revenues. Research by Goodman and colleagues in coal mines found that technology and other contextual variables directly affect team processes and performance, and they should be

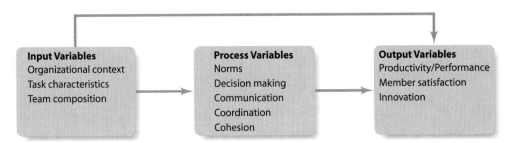

Input Variables
Organizational context
Task characteristics
Team composition

Process Variables
Norms
Decision making
Communication
Coordination
Cohesion

Output Variables
Productivity/Performance
Member satisfaction
Innovation

FIGURE 13.1   The Input-Process-Output Model of Team Effectiveness SOURCE: Adapted from Gladstein (1984).

included in models of team effectiveness (Goodman, 1986; Goodman, Ravlin, & Schminke, 1987). Further, the organizational reward system is a contextual influence on team performance. For example, teams are more successful if rewards and objectives are focused on team, not individual, behavior (Hackman, 1987). Pritchard's (1995) work on enhancing team motivation with the use of team goals, rewards, and feedback is consistent with this view. We will discuss team appraisal and feedback, as well as Pritchard's work in particular, later in the chapter.

Team Task   Team performance depends on the task that the team is required to perform. A widely cited way to categorize or classify tasks is the job characteristics approach, which we discussed in Chapter 9 (Hackman & Oldham, 1980). Job characteristics theory was developed as a way to understand how jobs motivate individuals, but it can be applied to teams as well. Viewed from the team perspective, job characteristics theory suggests that team members are motivated by tasks that require a variety of skills, provide considerable autonomy, are meaningful and important, and provide performance feedback (Fleishman & Zaccaro, 1992; Hackman, 1987). Research has indicated that the job characteristics approach successfully predicts performance in a variety of teams including management teams, clerical and administrative support teams, and in teams of professionals (Campion, Papper, & Medsker, 1996; Cohen & Bailey, 1997). For example, Campion et al. (1993) found that job design characteristics, in particular team autonomy, were predictive of team productivity and satisfaction. This research indicated support for the important role that task characteristics play in team performance. As such, teams should be given meaningful and interesting tasks that provide some degree of autonomy.

Team Composition   refers to the attributes of team members, including skills, abilities, experiences, and personality characteristics (Guzzo & Dickson, 1996). As every fan of professional sports teams can observe from the importance attached to the drafting and trading of players, one important strategy for enhancing team effectiveness is to select the individuals who can make the best contributions to the team. Stevens and Campion (1994) sought to determine the knowledge, skill, and ability (KSA) requirements for teamwork. Their focus was on team KSAs rather than technical KSAs and on selecting individuals who would work well in a team rather than individuals who would complement an existing team. They identified 14 specific team KSAs (Table 13.1), dividing them into interpersonal KSAs and self-management KSAs.

> **TEAM COMPOSITION**
>
> *The attributes of team members, including skills, abilities, experiences, and personality characteristics.*

Stevens and Campion (1993, 1999) also developed and validated a selection test for teamwork; sample items from this test are shown in Table 13.2. In two samples of production employees, the Teamwork Test was positively correlated with supervisor and peer ratings of teamwork and overall performance. An unexpected finding was that the Teamwork Test had a high correlation with cognitive ability tests. Stevens and Campion suggested that the high correlation may have resulted in part because the Teamwork Test is in a paper and pencil format that required some problem-solving, reading ability, and verbal skills, all of which overlap with the abilities required in traditional cognitive ability tests. Nevertheless, across the two samples, they found that the Teamwork Test significantly predicted teamwork performance and overall performance even after controlling for the influence of cognitive ability. Thus, the findings in this study indicate that the individual-level KSAs identified by Stevens and Campion can have practical value in the staffing of work teams.

Some recent studies have indicated that the cognitive ability and personality traits of team members are important predictors of team performance. For example, Barry and Stewart (1997) investigated whether extraversion and conscientiousness were related to team outcomes. Graduate students assigned to four-person and five-person teams engaged in a series of creative problem-solving tasks over a period of several weeks. First, contrary to hypotheses, the researchers found no correlation between conscientiousness and team

TABLE 13.1	Dimensions Comprising the Stevens and Campion (1999) Teamwork Test

I. Interpersonal KSAs

  A. Conflict Resolution KSAs

    1. The KSA to recognize and encourage desirable, but discourage undesirable team conflict.

    2. The KSA to recognize the type and source of conflict confronting the team and implement and appropriate resolution strategy.

    3. The KSA to implement an integrative (win–win) negotiation strategy, rather than the traditional distributive (win–lose) strategy.

  B. Collaborative Problems Solving KSAs

    4. The KSA to identify situations requiring participative problem solving and to utilize the proper degree and type of participation.

    5. The KSA to recognize the obstacles to collaborative group problem solving and implement proper corrective actions.

  C. Communication KSAs

    6. The KSA to understand communication networks, and to utilize decentralized networks to enhance communication where possible.

    7. The KSA to communicate openly and supportively; that is, to send messages that are

      a. behavior- or event-oriented.

      b. congruent,

      c. validating,

      d. conjunctive, and

      e. owned.

    8. The KSA to listen nonevaluatively and to appropriately use active listening techniques.

    9. The KSA to maximize the consonance between nonverbal and verbal messages and to recognize and interpret the nonverbal messages of others.

    10. The KSA to engage in small talk and ritual greetings as a recognition of their importance.

II. Self-Management KSAs

  D. Goal-Setting and Performance Management KSAs

    11. The KSA to establish specific, challenging, and accepted team goals.

    12. The KSA to monitor, evaluate, and provide feedback on both overall team performance and individual team-member performance.

  E. Planning and Task Coordination KSAs

    13. The KSA to coordinate and synchronize activities, information, and tasks among team members.

    14. The KSA to help establish task and role assignments for individual team members and ensure proper balancing of workload.

SOURCE: Stevens & Campion (1999).

performance. This is surprising because of the strong relationship of conscientiousness to performance in measures of individual, as opposed to team, performance. Second, the proportion of team members who were high on extraversion was related to team performance in a curvilinear manner. That is, teams having 20 percent to 40 percent of their members who were high on extraversion outperformed teams with either a lower or higher percentage of such members. In explaining this finding, the authors noted that extraversion increases the quantity of verbal communication within the team and thus is especially

TABLE 13.2	**Sample Items from Stevens and Campion's (1993) Teamwork Test**

1. Suppose you find yourself in an argument with several co-workers about who should do a very disagreeable, but routine task. Which of the following would likely be the most effective way to resolve this situation?

    A. Have your supervisor decide because this would avoid any personal bias.
    B. Arrange for a rotating schedule so everyone shares the chore.
    C. Let the workers who show up earliest choose on a first-come, first-served basis.
    D. Randomly assign a person to do the task and don't change it.

2. Your team wants to improve the quality and flow of the conversations among its members. Your team should:

    A. Use comments that build upon and connect to what others have already said.
    B. Set up a specific order for everyone to speak and then follow it.
    C. Let team members with more to say determine the direction and topic of conversation.
    D. Do all of the above.

3. Suppose you are presented with the following types of goals. You are asked to pick one for your team to work on. Which would you choose?

    A. An easy goal to ensure the team reaches it, thus creating a feeling of success.
    B. A goal of average difficulty so the team will be somewhat challenged, but successful without too much effort.
    C. A difficult and challenging goal that will stretch the team to perform at a high level but attainable so that effort will not be seen as futile.
    D. A very difficult, or even impossible goal so that even if the team falls short, it will at least have a very high target to aim for.

Note. Correct answers are in italics.

SOURCE: Stevens & Campion (1993).

important in work settings where there is social interaction (Barry & Stewart, 1997). The inclusion of too few extraverts results in a lack of communicative and assertive individuals needed for team success. However, since extraversion increases the quantity, but not necessarily the quality, of communication, teams with a high percentage of extraverts may be dysfunctional because of conflict and power struggles among these outspoken members. The drawbacks of having too many extraverts on the team were evident in the lower performance on the complex problem-solving tasks that the teams were given. Overall, the authors concluded that although extraversion is related to team performance, managers should be aware that team performance may suffer if team selection decisions overemphasize the importance of extraversion.

Barrick, Stewart, Neubert, and Mount (1998) studied 652 employees comprising 51 work teams and examined whether team composition variables (ability and personality) were related to team performance. They found that teams composed of members higher in cognitive ability, conscientiousness, agreeableness, extraversion, and emotional stability received higher supervisor ratings of team performance. Neuman and Wright (1999) used measures of cognitive ability and personality traits at the team level to predict the performance of 79 four-person teams. After controlling for cognitive ability, teams composed of members higher in conscientiousness and agreeableness had higher supervisor ratings of work team performance, higher objective measures of work team accuracy, and a greater amount of work completed. Collectively, these studies indicate that cognitive ability and certain personality traits are beneficial in predicting the performance of work teams. Across the studies, there has been relatively less emphasis on openness to experience, which has proven important in the training area and which should receive further consideration in research on team composition.

Cannon-Bowers, Tannenbaum, Salas, and Volpe (1995) identified a shared mental model as a knowledge-based team competency that is critical to team effectiveness. Mental models are organized ways of thinking that allow people to describe, explain, and predict the behavior of others (Mathieu, Heffner, Goodwin, Salas, & Cannon-Bowers, 2000). **Shared mental models** are organized ways for team members to think about how the team will work. Shared mental models provide team members with a common understanding of task requirements, and they improve coordination processes, which in turn improve team performance (Marks, Mathieu, & Zaccaro, 2001).

Many successful basketball teams have a shared understanding of how the offense will operate under various game situations. Teammates with a shared mental model know when to "run the fast break" or "slow things down" if one of their players gets a rebound from an opponent's missed shot. As another example, emergency medical service (EMS) teams benefit from using shared mental models of the situations they encounter. EMS team members have to make quick decisions in unexpected situations, all geared to the survival of the patient. Team members must determine how fast the driver should go and whether the siren should be on or not. They also need to determine what the patient needs most urgently and which emergency medical technician is best able to provide it. In both the basketball and EMS examples, when team members have a shared mental model, they are able to predict what their teammates are going to do in different situations, which leads to more effective team performance.

In summary, recent research has provided evidence that certain KSAOs and personality characteristics are positively related to team performance. We expect that research examining individual difference predictors of team performance will increase as organizations continue to use team-based approaches to achieve their goals. Although systematic research on such personality predictors of team performance is relatively new, research on the broadly defined area of team diversity is not, so we turn to that topic next.

Team Diversity   As we discussed in Chapter 11, the issue of diversity in teams and organizations is an interesting and controversial one. Milliken and Martins (1996) noted that although it often provokes intense emotional reactions because of its association with affirmative action and hiring quotas, the term "diversity" simply refers to differences or variety. Such differences among team members come in a variety of forms. Researchers studying diversity in teams often distinguish between demographic diversity and psychological diversity. **Demographic diversity** refers to differences in observable attributes or demographic characteristics such as age, gender, and ethnicity. **Psychological diversity** refers to differences in underlying attributes such as skills, abilities, personality characteristics, attitudes, beliefs, and values. Psychological diversity may also include functional, occupational, and educational backgrounds.

As we also discussed in Chapter 11, several studies have examined the effects of demographic diversity on individual and team outcomes at work. Research has indicated that individuals who are different from their work team in demographic characteristics (e.g., ethnicity, gender, age) are less psychologically committed to their organizations, less likely to remain with their organizations, and more likely to be absent from work (Tsui, Egain, & O'Reilly, 1992). Similarly, Jackson et al. (1991) suggested that such diversity may lead to discomfort among team members, who may react to this discomfort by withdrawing from the team or organization. However, researchers have also identified some benefits of demographic diversity. Examining gender and ethnic diversity, Watson, Kumar, and Michaelsen (1993) studied demographically similar and diverse groups that were asked to solve complex problems. They found that homogeneous groups initially worked together more effectively and performed better than diverse groups. Over time, however, the

SHARED MENTAL MODEL

Organized way for team members to think about how the team will work; helps team members understand and predict the behavior of their teammates.

DEMOGRAPHIC DIVERSITY

Differences in observable attributes or demographic characteristics such as age, gender, and ethnicity.

PSYCHOLOGICAL DIVERSITY

Differences in underlying attributes such as skills, abilities, personality characteristics, attitudes, beliefs, and values; may also include functional, occupational, and educational backgrounds.

demographically diverse groups became more effective than the homogenous groups at identifying problems and generating alternative solutions to the complex problems they were given. These findings suggest that heterogeneity based on demographic diversity may be a detriment to newly formed groups, but that heterogeneity can provide advantages if groups are given some time to interact.

Researchers have also investigated the effects of psychological diversity on individual and team outcomes. Psychological diversity among team members increases the pool of knowledge and skills available for completing team tasks. Thus, for idea-generation and decision-making tasks, heterogeneous teams outperform homogenous teams, which is likely due to the team members bringing a greater variety of perspectives to bear on the tasks (Magjuka & Baldwin, 1991; McGrath, 1984). In essence, the diversity helps the team develop more innovative and creative solutions. Not surprisingly, however, teams with diverse functional backgrounds and skills appear to have greater difficulty coordinating their efforts than teams with members who have homogenous functional backgrounds and skills. In addition, a great deal of heterogeneity in skills and values may make it difficult for adequate communication and coordination among team members, particularly when teams are newly formed (Ilgen, 1999).

Harrison and his colleagues conducted a series of studies that examined the effects of both demographic and psychological diversity over time. Harrison, Price, and Bell (1998) found that the length of time team members worked together weakened the (negative) effects of demographic diversity on team performance, but strengthened the (positive) effects of psychological diversity as team members had opportunities to engage in meaningful interactions. In a follow-up study, Harrison, Price, Gavin, and Florey (2002) found that over time, increasing collaboration among team members weakened the effects of demographic diversity on team outcomes, but once again strengthened the effects of psychological diversity. These findings are consistent with those of Watson et al. (1993) who found that psychological diversity hinders team performance only in the early stages of the group's development.

Overall, the research in this area indicates that diversity is a double-edged sword that provides both great challenges and great opportunities for teams and organizations (Milliken & Martens, 1996). The challenges stem partly from the fact that diversity comes in many forms. As we discussed in Chapter 11, there is much more value in examining the effects of diversity based on meaningful human attributes than on demographic differences. The opportunities provided by diverse teams stem from their ability to develop more innovative and creative solutions than homogeneous teams. These team diversity issues will continue to challenge managers, I-O psychologists, and team members who work in an increasingly multicultural and global workforce.

Team Processes

Norms   In contrast to organizational policies that specify formal rules and regulations, **norms** are the informal and sometimes unspoken rules that teams adopt to regulate member behavior (Feldman, 1984; Greenberg, 2002). Norms may regulate a variety of behaviors and customs, including unethical behavior, dress code, and the punctuality with which meetings and the workday begin and end. However, the most common norm relates to the productivity of team members. Some work teams have norms for high productivity, whereas other teams provide normative pressure on members to limit their productivity. Violation of productivity norms, which is likely to raise justice and fairness concerns, is often considered more seriously than violation of other norms—although dressing up in a business suit on Casual Friday is also an important faux pas to avoid. Indeed, companies such as Morgan Stanley and PaineWebber, traditionally known for formal dress codes, are even helping with the transition to casual attire by arranging for employee discounts at casual clothing retailers (Daniels, 2000).

NORMS

Informal and sometimes unspoken rules that teams adopt to regulate members' behavior.

Norms are more likely to be enforced if they facilitate team survival, if they simplify the behavior expected of members, and if they clarify what is distinctive about the team's identity (Feldman, 1984). Norms are likely to develop in several different ways: through explicit statements by team members, as carryover behaviors from past situations, or from the first behavior pattern that emerges in the team. A great deal of research has shown that norms have an important impact on conformity, team decision making, and team performance (Forsyth, 1999).

Communication and Coordination   Team performance depends heavily on effective communication, including proper information exchange (Suezey & Salas, 1992). Communication involves the transmission of information from one team member to another in a common language. Good communication across team members is important in nearly all teams, but it is particularly necessary with teams whose tasks are highly interdependent and dynamic. For example, flight crew members who are dependent on each other must communicate by providing information, listening actively, and being assertive in making quick decisions if unusual and often time-pressured circumstances arise (Prince et al., 1992).

Coordination is important in teams because of the interactive work that they conduct. Well-coordinated team members can obtain information from other team members when needed and move easily from one task to another (Swezey & Salas, 1992). Effective groups are able to minimize **coordination losses,** which occur when team members expend their energies in different directions, or fail to synchronize their work on time-critical tasks. Coordination or process losses were first observed in rope-pulling exercises in the early days of group research. Ringlemann (1913) found that when multiple people were asked to pull simultaneously on a rope, some were pulling while others were resting; thus, the force pulled by the group was always lower than the sum of force exerted by group members when they pulled individually. Later studies proposed that another phenomenon called *social loafing,* in which team members assume that other members will bear the burden, may have also been a factor in Ringlemann's findings. One or both of these phenomena may be involved in research results showing that team performance declines with the addition of extra members beyond the required minimum (Gladstein, 1984).

Social loafing occurs when reduced feelings of individual accountability result in reduced motivation and performance in groups (Latané, Williams, & Harkins, 1979). Workers are also motivated to engage in social loafing when they believe their behavior is not being monitored, which occurs more frequently in large work groups (Jones, 1984). Considerable research has examined social loafing, which has been documented in groups working on such tasks as maze performance, creativity problems, brainstorming, and vigilance exercises.

Social loafing is not inevitable when people work together. Shepperd's (1993) review of productivity loss in groups indicated that one way to remedy low productivity is to make individual contributions indispensable in achieving desired group outcomes. Shepperd suggested at least four ways to do this: (1) increase the difficulty of the task, (2) increase the uniqueness of individual contributions, (3) lead individuals to infer that attaining the collective good depends on their personal contributions, and (4) instruct individuals directly that their contributions are necessary. Based on extensive research on social loafing, these approaches are likely to improve group members' motivation and to increase overall group performance.

Cohesion   As teams mature, they often develop **cohesion,** which is the degree to which team members desire to remain in the team and are committed to the team goal (Forsyth, 1999). Highly cohesive teams are characterized by stability, pride in the team, feelings of unity and satisfaction that hold the team together, strong norms, and pressure for conformity. Cohesive team members are deeply involved in the team's activities, respond

---

COORDINATION LOSS

Reduced group performance that occurs when team members expend their energies in different directions or fail to synchronize or coordinate their work.

SOCIAL LOAFING

Reduced motivation and performance in groups that occurs when there is a reduced feeling of individual accountability or a reduced opportunity for evaluation of individual performance.

COHESION

Degree to which team members desire to remain in the team and are committed to team goals.

positively to each other, and communicate well. Thus, highly cohesive teams have more power over their members than teams with low cohesion (Goodman, Ravlin, & Schminke, 1987). A good example of a cohesive team is a successful hockey team whose members have pride in the team, feelings of unity, and strong norms for hard work during practices and games.

A meta-analysis by Mullen and Cooper (1994) found that cohesion is associated with successful team performance. Their study produced a few other notable findings as well. First, the relationship between cohesion and team performance occurs most consistently in project teams, which are truly interdependent; it occurs least consistently in service or sales teams, which are often not very interdependent. Second, the relationship from team performance to cohesion was stronger than the relationship from cohesion to team performance, suggesting that, contrary to the assumptions of many researchers, team performance affects cohesion more than the other way around. Practically, this finding suggested that teams that perform well are likely to become increasingly cohesive.

Teams occasionally have conflicting goals, as exemplified by the hostility between police and firefighters over how the World Trade Center site work should proceed.

Conflict may result between highly cohesive teams that appear to have tasks or goals that are at odds with each other (Thomas, 1992). An example is the work performed in clearing the site of the World Trade Center after its destruction by terrorists on September 11, 2001. As described in the book *American Ground: Unbuilding the World Trade Center,* the recovery and cleanup effort gave rise to substantial friction among fire department teams, police teams, and civilian teams (Langewiesche, 2002). The lack of cohesion among civilian volunteers was a factor in their dismissal from the site after the first few weeks. Employees of private organizations, various departments of the city, and other government departments disagreed on responsibilities and priorities. Most notably, firefighters saw their task as bringing out the remains of the approximately 300 fellow firefighters who lost their lives trying to save others; the police were dedicated to finding the bodies of their 35 fallen comrades. The bodies of the police officers were more likely to be found in the periphery of the buildings, since these officers were directing the building occupants to safety when the towers collapsed. In contrast, firefighters' remains were more likely to be found in the collapsed stairwells since many of them were still ascending the towers when they collapsed. There was also an image struggle. Firefighters were seen by the press and public as more "heroic" than the police, since so many firefighters died inside the buildings. As New York City and Port Authority police forces at the cleanup site watched the image of the firefighters grow, the long-standing jealousies between the two uniformed forces became increasingly strained. At one point firefighters, who were determined to suspend cleanup work until all possible remains of their comrades were found, actually came to blows with police officers, who were equally determined to prevent the firefighters from delaying the cleanup. Civilian workers, in contrast, were chiefly concerned with cleaning up the site and protecting against further collapse of any buildings. In addition, considering the enormous number of civilians (well over 2,000) who were killed or missing, they felt that non-uniformed remains in the rubble were not being accorded adequate respect. This tragic and traumatic event illustrates the point that as teams become more cohesive, there are increasing conflicts and tensions with other teams who may have different goals.

Decision Making   Decision making in teams is crucial to their success. Team decision making occurs through defining the problem, gathering information, discussing and evaluating alternatives, and deciding collaboratively on the appropriate course of action. A great deal of research on team decision making has examined the circumstances under which teams make poor decisions. Many faulty group decisions may be attributed to a phenomenon called groupthink, which was first identified by social psychologist Irving Janis. **Groupthink** is a mode of thinking that people engage in when they are deeply involved in a cohesive group and when group members' desire for agreement overrides their motivation to appraise alternative courses of action realistically (Janis, 1982). Groupthink is a specific example of **group polarization,** which is the tendency for groups to make decisions that are more extreme (i.e., more polarized) than those made by individuals. Researchers originally found that groups tended to make more risky decisions than individuals and called this the **risky-shift phenomenon.** Researchers later discovered that some groups made more cautious decisions than did individuals in the group. Thus, group polarization can involve either more cautious or more risky shifts in judgment following group discussion when compared to the average of individual judgments made prior to discussion (Bettenhausen, 1991; Myers & Lamm, 1976). Group polarization occurs because people working in groups tend to shift their opinions in the direction they think is consistent with the values of the group (Forsyth, 1999). In this way, group decisions are often more extreme than the decision that any individual in the group would make.

The faulty decision by President John F. Kennedy and his advisors to send commandos into Cuba to capture the area known as the Bay of Pigs has been partly attributed to groupthink (Janis, 1982). In April 1961, President Kennedy and his committee of advisors, which included members of the Central Intelligence Agency, the Joint Chiefs of Staff, and experts on foreign affairs, were contemplating an invasion of Cuba. The plan involved a squad of well-trained commandos who were to capture and defend the Bay of Pigs on the southern coast of Cuba. Once in control there, the commandos were to launch raids against Fidel Castro's army and encourage civilian revolt in the capital, Havana. The Bay of Pigs invasion took place on April 17 and was a disaster. The entire squad of commandos was killed or captured within days, and the U.S. government had to send food and supplies to Cuba to provide ransom in return for the surviving commandos (Forsyth, 1999). Janis (1982) described the Bay of Pigs invasion plan as a case of bad group decision making resulting from groupthink and labeled it as one of the "worst fiascos ever perpetrated by a responsible government" (p. 14).

The ill-fated decision by NASA officials to launch the *Challenger* space shuttle in January, 1986 has also been attributed to groupthink (Morehead, Ference, & Neck, 1991). Despite warnings by some engineers that the cold weather could make the solid rocket boosters on the shuttle too brittle, NASA officials decided to move forward with the launch, which resulted in the explosion of the *Challenger* 73 seconds after liftoff. Similar questions have been asked about decisions made during different parts of the construction and flight of the space shuttle *Columbia,* which disintegrated during reentry into the earth's atmosphere in February 2003.

Janis suggested that groupthink is a disease that infects healthy groups; he identified several symptoms that signal the existence of groupthink, including interpersonal pressure resulting from a highly cohesive group, illusions of invulnerability, and lack of open discussion. Groupthink is also more likely when groups use defective decision-making strategies such as considering only extreme alternatives, failing to develop contingency plans, and losing sight of overall objectives (Forsyth, 1999).

To prevent groupthink, it is helpful for group members to solicit many different views and to consider a wide diversity of perspectives and alternative courses of action. Group members should also be encouraged to express any doubts they have in a solution that is reached too quickly. Some research has shown that groupthink can be avoided if individuals are assigned to play a devil's advocate role that criticizes proposed courses of action

---

GROUPTHINK

Mode of thinking engaged in by people deeply involved in a cohesive group and when group members' desire for agreement overrides their motivation to appraise alternative courses of action realistically.

GROUP POLARIZATION

Tendency for groups to make more extreme decisions than those made by individuals.

RISKY-SHIFT PHENOMENON

Tendency for groups to make more risky decisions than individuals; related to the more general phenomenon of group polarization.

"All those in favor say 'Aye.'"
"Aye."   "Aye."   "Aye."
        "Aye."   "Aye."   "Aye."

and questions the assumptions underlying the popular choice among the group members. For example, Priem, Harrison, and Muir (1995) found that breaking the group into subgroups is helpful in reducing groupthink. They suggested that one subgroup should propose solutions and another subgroup should propose solutions opposite to those developed by the first group. The subgroups then interact and devise solutions that are acceptable to both. The researchers found that this approach helped to avoid the premature consensus that often leads to groupthink and led to strong agreement on the final decisions that were made. Because this study was conducted with students who had limited business and managerial experience, the subgroup method of reducing early consensus needs to be tested with more experienced participants in organizational settings before its validity can be fully assessed.

Team Outputs

Team outputs can be divided into several important areas, including team performance, team innovation, and team member well-being (Brodbeck, 1996). Team performance is often reflected in objective measures such as sales revenues, units produced, customers served, and patients treated. In determining what accounts for high team performance, we described team inputs and team processes earlier in this module. Important inputs are the organizational context, the team task, and team composition. For example, we have seen that teams composed of members with high cognitive ability and certain personality characteristics have high team performance. Team processes that are critical for high team performance include communication, coordination, and cohesiveness.

It is important to note that although team performance is often better than individual performance, research has indicated that team outputs are not always superior to individual outputs. For some cognitive and decision-making tasks, specifically, the best individual often outperforms an interacting group (Gigone & Hastie, 1997). So, using the output of a team will in some cases result in less optimal outcomes than using the output of the most qualified individual in the team. This cautionary note indicates that although teamwork is indeed appropriate for many situations, managers and I-O psychologists should carefully consider the task or situation before deciding that a team is best suited for a particular project.

A primary reason for implementing teams is to increase innovation in the organization (West et al., 1998). Several studies have demonstrated that team member heterogeneity leads to more creative team decision making (e.g., Jackson, 1996). In addition, teams and organizations whose goals or objectives relate to innovation are likely to produce more novel and creative ideas and products than teams without clear innovation goals. In a study of 418 project teams, for example, Pinto and Prescott (1988) found that a clearly stated mission, which clarifies team goals, was the only factor that consistently predicted team success at all stages of the innovation process. Further, West and Anderson (1996) found that team processes such as support for innovation were predictive of innovativeness in top management teams. They also found that the proportion of innovative team members was predictive of the innovativeness of new ideas made by the team. Thus, it appears that both team inputs and team processes are beneficial in increasing team innovativeness.

Another team output that I-O psychologists have studied is team member well-being and satisfaction. First, some evidence indicates that the implementation of autonomous work groups has a positive effect on group members' job satisfaction. These positive effects are considered to be a result of the increased participation, autonomy, and task variety available in such groups (Cordery, 1996). Similarly, Campion et al. (1993) found that three team task characteristics—participation, task variety, and task significance—were positively related to team member job satisfaction in service teams in the insurance industry. Second, working in a team can positively influence an individual's self-esteem (Hackman, 1992). Finally, team process variables (e.g., communication, cohesion) have been shown to positively influence individual member well-being and job satisfaction (West et al., 1998). As we might have expected, research to date indicates that positive interactions in teams contribute to higher team member satisfaction and well-being. As we discussed in Chapter 10, satisfaction has traditionally been conceptualized as a feeling or an emotion but measured as a cognition (Weiss, 2002). Accordingly, we look forward to the redirection of some of the research in this area toward examining the effects of working in a team on moods and emotions at work.

MODULE 13.2 SUMMARY

- The input-process-output model of team effectiveness provides a way to understand how teams perform and how to maximize their performance. This model, which has been supported by a variety of research studies, proposes that inputs affect team outputs indirectly through team processes. Research has also indicated that inputs can have a direct effect on team outputs.

- Inputs include the organizational context, the team task, and team composition. The organizational context can enhance team interactions and increase team effectiveness by providing resources needed for performance and continued functioning of the work team.

- Team performance also depends on the task the team is required to perform and the team's composition. Teams should be given meaningful and

interesting tasks that provide some degree of autonomy. In addition, recent research indicates that certain KSAOs are positively related to team performance.

- Diversity is a double-edged sword that provides challenges and opportunities for teams and organizations. The challenges stem partly from the difficulty that diverse teams often have in coordinating their efforts when they first form. The opportunities stem from their ability to develop more innovative solutions than homogeneous teams.

- Team processes include norms, communication, coordination, cohesiveness, and decision making. Teams that effectively manage these processes have higher performance, make better decisions, and have more satisfactory work experiences.

KEY TERMS

input-process-output model of
    team effectiveness

team composition

shared mental model

demographic diversity

psychological diversity

norms

coordination loss

social loafing

cohesion

groupthink

group polarization

risky-shift phenomenon

CRITICAL THINKING EXERCISES

13.3 Describe a team in which you have been a member. Discuss whether the team performed successfully. Would you attribute the team's successful or unsuccessful performance to team inputs or team processes? Be specific about which inputs (e.g., context, team composition) or processes (e.g., communication, coordination, cohesiveness) affected whether your team's performance was successful or unsuccessful.

13.4 When given a choice about how to work on a class project, some students decide to work alone, while others decide to work in a team. Taking into account the discussion about the relationships among team inputs, processes, and outputs, what are some of the reasons that students might decide to work on a team? Alternatively, what are some of the challenges of working on a team that might lead students to decide to work alone?

SPECIAL ISSUES IN TEAMS

TEAM APPRAISAL AND FEEDBACK

As organizational and managerial objectives are increasingly being tied to team goals, managers have been increasingly interested in evaluating team performance (Hedge & Borman, 1995). Waldman (1997) found that most employees working in teams tend to favor team-based performance appraisal, the one exception being that individuals with a high need for achievement still preferred individual performance appraisals. Nevertheless, if an organization wants to send a message that team performance is important to organizational success, it is important to appraise team performance (Reilly & McGourty, 1998).

Scott and Einstein (2001) suggested that performance appraisal systems that assess team-level outcomes should provide the team with the information it needs to identify team problems and further develop team capabilities. Xerox uses a team performance measurement system that was developed jointly by team members, managers, and customers to be aligned with organizational and team goals (Jones & Moffett, 1999). Allstate Insurance and Hewlett-Packard are among several other organizations to use strategic team-based performance appraisal systems that increase the likelihood of teams contributing positively to organizational effectiveness. In cases where both individual and team performance are important, team-level feedback helps to emphasize that the interaction among individual team members is what leads to the overall success. An example of this type of team-level feedback is a review of a theatrical play; cast members often see reviews as an indicator of team output, even though the critic may comment on the performances of particular actors.

Conducting team performance evaluations and providing feedback to teams, rather than to individuals, presents new challenges to managers in organizations. First, team-level evaluation and feedback are new to most organizations. Second, teams differ in their roles and responsibilities, and developing appraisal systems that assess performance over a wide variety of teams may be difficult. The move to team-based organizations raises old controversies about performance appraisal systems—for example, who should evaluate team performance: the team manager, team members, or customers of the team (Scott & Einstein, 2001)? Recent discussions of 360 degree feedback in team-based organizations suggest that all of these sources can provide important feedback to the team (Hallam, 2001).

In evaluating team performance, managers need to consider the extent to which behaviors and outputs of the team are measurable. This should be fairly easy for production teams, but may be more difficult for other types of teams in which outputs are less clear. In this case, it is important to exercise care in specifying team objectives, which should be linked to an organization's mission and strategy. For example, a cross-functional product development team might be assessed on the number of products brought to market in a particular time period. More generally, assessment of team performance may come from direct measures of team output, measures of the quality of team products, and 360 degree assessment of the team's performance from the team manager and both internal and external customers (Reilly & McGourty, 1998).

When conducting team evaluations, both judgmental and objective measures should be utilized wherever possible. Several studies have found differing results depending on the particular evaluation measure used. For example, Gladstein (1984) found that team ratings of process variables such as communication and supportiveness were positively associated with group ratings of satisfaction and performance (judgmental measures), but were unrelated to actual sales revenue (objective measures). Thus, it is best to use multiple indicators to develop the most complete understanding of which team inputs and processes relate to team outcomes.

ProMES

The ProMES (productivity measurement and enhancement system) approach provides opportunities for managers to evaluate and provide feedback to teams. As we discussed in Chapter 9, **ProMES** is a motivational approach that has resulted in significant gains in productivity in a variety of organizations (Pritchard, 1995). ProMES has been successfully implemented in several organizations in the United States, the Netherlands, Germany, and Australia. Much of the research on ProMES focuses on team goal setting, team evaluation, and team feedback. ProMES has been used with many different kinds of teams, including assembly-line work teams, manufacturing teams, maintenance teams, bank employees, painters, and customer service technicians. For example, Pritchard, Jones, Roth, Stuebing, and Ekeberg (1988) found increased performance and satisfaction in aviation maintenance teams after introducing team feedback and team goal setting. They suggested that teams that have clear goals and receive goal-relevant feedback will have higher motivation and performance.

When moving to team-based work, it is important for organizations to create conditions that foster efficient collective action (Hackman, 1992). A potential problem is that many employees in the United States and other individualistic countries are accustomed to thinking in terms of individual goals and outcomes. To counteract this tendency, there is a strong need to use a combination of team goals, team feedback, and team rewards to facilitate the development of team values and goals (Pritchard et al., 1988). Indeed, effective teams seek a great deal of feedback about their productivity and quality goals. This feedback helps them to develop strategies for attaining goals (Earley, Connolly, & Ekegren, 1989). With the increasing emphasis on teams in organizations, Pritchard's approach and others like it should become more common in implementing team goal setting, team appraisal, and team feedback (Hedge & Borman, 1995).

> **PROMES**
>
> *The productivity measurement and enhancement system. A motivational approach that utilizes goal setting, rewards, and feedback to increase motivation and performance.*

TEAM ROLES

Belbin's (1981, 1993) **team-role theory** is used by organizations and management consultants in Europe and Australia to assess and develop teams. Belbin proposed that effective teams contain a combination of individuals capable of working in the nine team roles that he identified. Table 13.3 identifies the strengths and weaknesses associated with each team role (Belbin, 1993). An individual may work in more than one team role, so that effective teams may include fewer than nine members. Belbin's team-role theory suggests that teams that are balanced in terms of the roles represented among their members will have the highest performance.

Several studies have tested Belbin's hypotheses regarding team-role balance and team performance. Senior (1997) examined 11 teams from a mixture of private and public organizations. She found a positive correlation between team-role balance and team performance, indicating support for the link Belbin made between team-role balance and team performance. A study by Prichard and Stanton (1999) tested Belbin's proposal that teams in which a wide range of team roles are represented perform better than those in which certain roles are overrepresented, which results in an imbalance of roles. The task performance of six teams of four individuals identified as Shapers by the Team-Role Self-Perception

> **TEAM-ROLE THEORY**
>
> *Belbin proposed that effective teams contain a combination of individuals capable of working in nine team roles; used by organizations and management consultants in Europe and Australia to assess and develop teams.*

TABLE 13.3	The Nine Team Roles

ROLES AND DESCRIPTIONS- TEAM-ROLE CONTRIBUTION	ALLOWABLE WEAKNESSES
Plant: Creative, imaginative, unorthodox. Solves difficult problems.	Ignores details. Too preoccupied to communicate effectively.
Resource Investigator: Extrovert, enthusiastic, communicative. Explores opportunities. Develops contacts.	Overoptimistic. Loses interest once initial enthusiasm has passed.
Coordinator: Mature, confident, a good chairperson. Clarifies goals, promotes decision making, delegates well.	Can be seen as manipulative. Delegates personal work.
Shaper: Challenging, dynamic, thrives on pressure. Has the drive and courage to overcome obstacles.	Can provoke others. Hurts people's feelings.
Monitor evaluator: Sober, strategic, and discerning. Sees all options. Judges accurately.	Lacks drive and ability to inspire others. Overly critical.
Teamworker: Cooperative, mild, perceptive, diplomatic. Listens, builds, averts friction, calms the waters.	Indecisive in crunch situations. Can be easily influenced.
Implementer: Disciplined, reliable, conservative, efficient. Turns ideas into practical actions.	Somewhat inflexible. Slow to respond to new possibilities.
Completer: Painstaking, conscientious, anxious. Searches out errors and omissions. Delivers on time.	Inclined to worry unduly. Reluctant to delegate. Can be a nit-picker.
Specialist: Single-minded, self-starting, dedicated. Provides knowledge and skills in rare supply.	Contributes on only a narrow front. Dwells on technicalities. Overlooks the "big picture."

SOURCE: Adapted from Belbin (1993).

Inventory (Belbin, 1981) was compared with that of six mixed teams of four individuals that filled the following roles: one Coordinator, one Plant, one Completer, and one Team Worker. Consistent with Belbin's proposal, the mixed teams performed better at planning proposals and reaching consensus than teams consisting of Shapers alone.

In studying team roles, Fisher, Hunter, and Macrosson (2001) examined 338 individuals working in 55 teams. Their results were not supportive of Belbin's nine team roles, but the data did fit easily into a Big Five personality framework. The authors suggested that it may well be possible to create a team-role theory based upon the Big Five model of personality, a suggestion consistent with the findings that a team's average scores on Big Five personality dimensions are positively related to team performance (Barrick et al., 1998; Barry & Stewart, 1997). Notice also that some of these team roles overlap with the managerial roles that we discussed in Chapter 12 on leadership (Borman & Brush, 1993; Yukl, 1998). The overlap between Belbin's team roles and the other taxonomies is worth considering in future research, particularly since Belbin's team-role theory remains popular in Europe and Australia.

TEAM DEVELOPMENT

Team development refers to changes in teams as they develop over time. Research and theory on team development offers general ideas about the progression of teams, but no definitive answers on the development of all teams. First, nearly all team development literature assumes that teams are not ready to perform effectively when they are formed (Guzzo & Shea, 1992). Thus, most teams must progress through a series of stages before they are able to perform effectively. Most models of group development include five stages, which are shown in Table 13.4 along with their major processes and characteristics. The five stages are known as forming, storming, norming, performing, and adjourning (Forsyth, 1999; Tuckman & Jensen, 1977).

Some research suggests that developmental stages occur in the same order for all groups. However, much of this work has been done in the laboratory and may not necessarily generalize to work teams. Some studies of teams in organizational settings indicate that some teams do not proceed through each of the five developmental stages. For example, in a case study of an airline cockpit crew, Ginnett (1990) provided evidence that a strong organizational context such as an airline cockpit can change the order of stages or remove the need for particular early stages. In essence, airline cockpit crews must perform effectively in a very short period of time and do not ordinarily go through the early developmental stages. In addition, research by Gersick (1988, 1989) indicated that deadlines can influence the appearance of stages of development. She found that initial periods of inertia and stability last approximately half the allotted time for many project teams. When

TABLE 13.4	Five Stages of Group Development	
STAGE	**MAJOR PROCESSES**	**CHARACTERISTICS**
1. Orientation (forming)	Members becoming familiar with one another and the group; dependency and inclusion issues; acceptance of leader and group consensus	Tentative, polite communications; concern over ambiguity, group's goals; active leader; compliant members
2. Conflict (storming)	Disagreement over procedures; expression of dissatisfaction; tension among members; antagonism toward leader	Criticism of ideas; poor attendance; hostility; polarization and coalition formation
3. Structure (norming)	Growth of cohesiveness and unity; establishment of roles, standards, and relationships; increased trust, communication	Agreement on procedures; reduction in role ambiguity
4. Work (performing)	Goal achievement; high task orientation; emphasis on performance and production	Decision making; problem solving; mutual cooperation
5. Dissolution (adjourning)	Termination of roles; completion of tasks; reduction of dependency	Disintegration and withdrawal; increased independence and emotionality; regret

SOURCE: Forsyth (1999).

half the time allotted for completion of the project had elapsed, project teams reached midpoint transitions in which they made dramatic progress; like many college students, team members get very motivated by an approaching deadline! Considering the differing findings of the research by Tuckman and Jensen (1977), Ginnett (1990), and Gersick (1989) on team developmental issues together, it appears that all teams have to deal with developmental issues, but the order and necessity of each stage depends on the type of team and the organizational context (McGrath & O'Connor, 1996).

TEAM TRAINING

CROSS-TRAINING

Involves rotating team members through different positions on the team so that they can acquire an understanding of the duties of their teammates and an overview of the team's task.

TEAM LEADER TRAINING

Training the team's leader in conflict resolution and team coordination.

TEAM COORDINATION TRAINING

Involves teaching team members about sharing information, managing conflict, solving problems, clarifying roles, and making decisions; used to help team members learn to employ the resources of the entire team effectively.

Team training, which involves coordinating the performance of individuals who work together to achieve a common goal, is often critical to team effectiveness (Noe, 2002). Three strategies are often used in team training: cross-training, team coordination training, and team leader training (Salas & Cannon-Bowers, 1997). **Cross-training** occurs when each team member is rotated through different positions on the team in order to acquire an understanding of the duties of his or her teammates. Cross-training provides team members with an overview of the team task and how each individual job contributes to team effectiveness (Marks, Sahella, Burke, & Zaccaro, 2002). Team members also develop shared mental models of the team's purpose, which help increase team coordination and performance. Through cross-training, team members develop knowledge and skills that can be used across multiple jobs. General Motors Corporation provides cross-training to its automotive team members, better enabling them to coordinate their work and to continue work when a team member is absent (Kaeter, 1993).

Team leader training involves training the team's leader in conflict resolution and team coordination. Team leader training is effective in increasing the amount of feedback the leader seeks from the team, which improves communication within the team. Team leaders who receive training can help team members to interact more effectively, which in turn increases team performance and effectiveness. Successful team performance also depends on the coordination of individual efforts. **Team coordination training** involves teaching team members about sharing information, managing conflict, solving problems, clarifying roles, and making decisions. Team coordination training helps team members learn to employ the resources of the entire team effectively, particularly in stressful situations (Salas, Burke, & Cannon-Bowers, 2002). For example, naval aviation teams commonly receive team coordination training that helps them to conduct missions in a safe and effective manner (Oser, Salas, Merket, & Bowers, 2001). Like individual training, team training should be sequenced according to task complexity. In addition, team training should be provided to the team as an entire unit and should include systematic procedures for providing feedback to trainees while they are learning team skills. Together, these three strategies enhance the likelihood that teams will work effectively to achieve their goals.

A particular type of team training is crew resource management training, which is the most widely used strategy to enhance teamwork skills within the aviation industry. Specifically, crew resource management involves training pilots and copilots to work more effectively as a team. The training helps develop critical competencies, such as coordination, communication, and decision making, in the team rather than in individuals. For example, crew members are trained to communicate with each other and with air traffic controllers about how to accomplish their technical objectives (e.g., flight control, navigation) and their procedural objectives (e.g., completing checklists) in routine situations as well as in emergency situations. Salas et al. (2001) reviewed 58 studies of crew resource management training to determine its effectiveness within the aviation industry. They found that this training produced positive reactions, enhanced learning, and brought about the desired behavioral changes. This meta-analysis indicated that team training can be effective and that focused, collaborative efforts to design, implement, and evaluate team training (as in the aviation industry) can be particularly effective.

Although there is much promise to team training approaches (e.g., crew management training), they tend to be developed and evaluated by a small set of researchers who study different kinds of military teams. These approaches, which typically include an investigation of the abilities needed for successful team performance, would benefit from the inclusion of research on cognitive and perceptual-motor abilities that we discussed in Chapter 3. Specifically, such team training approaches might more explicitly incorporate Fleishman's individual ability and performance taxonomies (Fleishman & Reilly, 1992; Fleishman, Quaintance, & Broedling, 1984). A great deal of work has gone into those taxonomies, which can be adapted for use with teams and team training.

CULTURAL ISSUES IN TEAMS

Hofstede's (1984, 2001) work on culture and values has direct implications for teams composed of members from different cultures. Recall that he discussed five primary dimensions on which countries differed: individualism-collectivism, power distance, uncertainty avoidance, masculinity-femininity, and long-term versus short-term orientation. Differences among team members in these cultural values can influence team interactions and performance (Unsworth & West, 2000). For example, organizations in individualistic cultures such as the United States and Great Britain may have a difficult time using or moving to team-based work arrangements because employees from these countries are most comfortable thinking in terms of individual accomplishments and individual accountability. In addition, according to Hofstede's (1984) results, the United States is the most individualist country of the 53 that were assessed. Given this and the fact that most research on teams has been conducted in the United States, it is likely that team processes will be different in countries that are less individualistic than the United States (Smith & Noakes, 1996). For example, individualism is an alien notion to Japanese workers, who are known for their devotion and loyalty to the team and whose personal success is measured by the success of their team and organization (Levine, 1997). According to Levine, a favorite saying in Japanese organizations is "your team can win even if you cannot." Many employees in Japan begin each workday by singing their company songs, and many show their lifelong identification with their employers by regularly wearing company colors (Levine, 1997). As we discussed earlier in the chapter, quality circles have been more successful and have remained more popular in Japan than in the United States, another indication that the nature of such teamwork differs across these cultures.

Teams tend to be extremely well accepted in collectivist cultures.

Hofstede's (2001) long-term vs. short-term orientation is another cultural variable that likely has an impact on team interactions. This dimension is very similar to a cultural dimension called **time horizon** by Trompenaars and Hampden (1998). Countries such as Japan and China have a long time horizon, which results in long-term planning; countries such as the United States and Russia have a short time horizon, which leads managers in these countries to focus on meeting short-term goals such as quarterly earnings reports. Trompenaars and Hampden (1998) give a vivid example of how the contrast in time horizons can cause interesting business dealings:

> [T]he Japanese were trying to buy the operations of Yosemite National Park in California. The first thing they submitted was a 250-year business plan. Imagine the reactions of the California authorities: "Gee, that is 1,000 quarterly reports." (p. 132).

TIME HORIZON

Cultural dimension that affects whether managers and employees focus on short-term or long-term goals.

Teams composed of members from different cultures are likely to have members whose time horizons differ, making team communication and decision making more challenging. Differences in time horizon may lead team members to perceive scheduling, goal setting, and deadlines very differently (Waller, Conte, Gibson, & Carpenter, 2001). These differences are likely to become sources of miscommunication and conflict for team members trying to develop timelines and meet deadlines. Individuals with long-term time horizons may perceive the behaviors of team members with short-term time horizons as shortsighted and bottom-line oriented. Conversely, individuals with short-term time horizons may find the attitudes and behaviors of team members with future time perspectives to be demanding, uptight, and misplaced (Hall, 1983; Jones, 1988).

Other evidence relating to how people from different cultures view time has suggested that team interactions will be affected by the cultural and national backgrounds of team members (Bluedorn, 2002; Waller et al., 2001). Research investigating differences in the pace of life across cities in the United States and other countries (Levine, 1997) has indicated that the pace of life is fastest in the United States, Japan, and countries in Western Europe (e.g., Switzerland, Germany) and slowest in relatively undeveloped countries (e.g., Mexico, Indonesia, Brazil). In the global workplace, teams will increasingly be composed of individuals from cultures with different perspectives on time, which are likely to influence team interactions and performance; for example, Levine, West and Reis (1980) found that latecomers to a team meeting were perceived positively in Brazil, but negatively in the United States.

Smith and Noakes (1996) discussed other effects that the cultural context has on team interactions in organizations. For example, the social loafing effect identified in Western cultures has not been found in some other countries; in fact, some research indicates that the effect is reversed in collectivistic cultures. Earley (1989) examined the effect of individualism versus collectivism on social loafing among 48 managers from the United States (individualists) and 48 managers from the People's Republic of China (collectivists). He found that social loafing occurred among individualists but not collectivists. In a follow-up study, Earley (1993) examined the effects of individualism versus collectivism in Chinese, Israeli, and American managers. As in the previous study, managers from the United States were considered to have an individualistic orientation whereas managers from China were considered to be collectivistic. Because Israeli society focuses on shared responsibility and group interests, Israeli managers also were considered to have a collectivistic orientation. Data from the individualism-collectivism scale supported these assumptions: The performance of American managers (individualists) working in a group was lower than the performance of individualists working alone. Moreover, the performance of collectivists was actually higher in a group context than in an individualist context. These findings support the idea that social loafing does not occur under the same circumstances across cultural settings. Managers will need to keep these cultural differences in mind when leading or working with team members from different cultures.

Norms for teamwork and communication among team members are also likely to differ across cultures (Smith & Noakes, 1996). For example, Merritt and Helmreich (1996) examined separate samples of U.S., Taiwanese, and Filipino aircraft carrier flight deck crews. They found that Taiwanese and Filipino crew members favored greater harmony, loyalty, and deference to authority, whereas the U.S. crew members gave more emphasis to personal responsibility and self-reliance. Because each of the crews examined in this study had members from only one culture, the effects of culture on team communication and interactions were minimized. We can predict, however, that cultural differences among multinational team members in the increasingly global workplace are likely to create added challenges to those that teams typically face.

It should be clear that members of multinational teams are likely to differ in terms of both culture and their preferred language, which can lead to communication and coordination problems. Accordingly, cross-cultural training and team training are needed to maximize the effectiveness of multinational teams. Overall, cultural issues in teams will continue to present both challenges and opportunities. An understanding of cultural differences and value preferences can provide I-O psychologists, managers, and team members opportunities to capitalize on cultural diversity rather than be impeded by it (Smith & Noakes, 1996).

MODULE 13.3 SUMMARY

- As organizational and managerial objectives are increasingly being linked to team goals, managers have become more interested in evaluating team performance. However, conducting team performance evaluations and providing feedback to teams, rather than individuals, presents several new challenges to managers.

- ProMES (productivity measurement and enhancement system) is a motivational approach that focuses on team goal setting, evaluation, and feedback. This approach provides opportunities for managers to motivate, evaluate, and reward teams.

- Belbin's team-role theory is used by organizations and management consultants in Europe and Australia to assess and develop teams. This theory proposes that teams that are balanced in terms of

the roles represented among their members will have the highest performance.

- Research and theory on team development offers general ideas about the progression of teams, but no definitive answers on the development of all teams. All teams have to deal with developmental issues, but the order and necessity of each stage depends on the type of team and the organizational context.

- The cultural and national backgrounds of team members affect team interactions. For example, norms for teamwork and communication among team members have been shown to differ across cultures. Thus, cross-cultural training and team training are needed to maximize the effectiveness of culturally diverse teams.

KEY TERMS

ProMES
team-role theory

cross-training
team leader training

team coordination training
time horizon

CRITICAL THINKING EXERCISES

13.5 Think of a team in which you are or have been a member. Did members of the team fill each of Belbin's nine roles (see Table 13.3)? If yes, discuss whether having each of the roles represented helped the team to perform well. If not, discuss which roles were not represented by team members and if those missing roles had a negative impact on team performance.

13.6 Major League baseball teams are increasingly composed of players who come from a variety of different countries and cultures. What challenges are culturally diverse baseball teams likely to face? Can you predict any problems that might occur in team processes or team performance in such culturally diverse teams?

THE ORGANIZATION OF WORK BEHAVIOR

14 CHAPTER

THE CONCEPTUAL AND THEORETICAL FOUNDATIONS OF ORGANIZATIONS

ORGANIZATIONS AND PEOPLE

Imagine that you have just obtained your degree and are fortunate enough to receive job offers from three potential employers. Imagine further that the first potential employer is Honda Motor Company, the second the Internal Revenue Service (IRS), and the third the ice cream enterprise Ben & Jerry's Homemade Holdings, Inc. These three possibilities might evoke very different reactions. Honda might evoke feelings of a team environment, one characterized by streamlined production methods and procedures and by a collective (as opposed to individualistic) culture. In contrast, the IRS job might evoke feelings of a stable organization with clearly defined duties and the absence of a profit motive. The third possibility, Ben & Jerry's, might imply a socially conscious, egalitarian, fun place to work—and the opportunity to sample lots of delicious ice cream. The reactions you have to these organizations—to their personalities—represent the "psychological" part of organizational psychology. We will discuss these reactions in Module 14.2 under the climate and culture of an organization. Before we do that, however, we need to consider the concept of organization, and why it is important to the understanding of work behavior.

When people join forces to accomplish a common goal and follow a set of operating procedures to develop products and services, they have formed an **organization.** Regardless of whether the organization is a small neighborhood pizza restaurant or a large multinational communications corporation, things need to be organized. These things include not only the people, but also equipment, processes, capital, and future planning. If a company is *dis*organized, disaster is likely. In earlier chapters, we have considered topics like selection, training, motivation, and leadership. But to some extent, we have ignored the larger context in which these processes play themselves out. That context is the particular organization in which the processes occur.

Organizations represent concrete examples of strategic thinking and planning. It has been said that the definition of strategic planning is buying from the unorganized and selling to the unorganized. For example, picture two new mothers who are exchanging stories about their pre- and postdelivery experiences. One mentions that even though she received lots of neat gifts for the baby and the new "family," what she really wanted more than anything during her first few days at home was a gourmet meal cooked by someone else. The other mother agrees instantly, and they decide to form a company that will buy and prepare food for meals from a "gourmet menu" and market these meals as gifts for new mothers (Hnath, 2002). They will begin locally and, if the idea catches on, expand and open locations in other cities. The markets where they will purchase the food are not organized to prepare and deliver the gourmet meals. The friends and relatives to whom they will sell the meal vouchers are, similarly, unorganized. They pick a name—"Postpartum Expressions"—and they have now formed an organization for the purpose of buying from, and selling to, the unorganized.

> **ORGANIZATION**
>
> *A group of people who have common goals and who follow a set of operating procedures to develop products and services.*

An enterprise made up of two young women has a simple structure, but in most organizations the structure can be quite complex. Let's explore this concept by looking at several enterprises, all having to do with the "business" of domestic and international crime. The HBO television program "The Sopranos" is intended to illuminate the organization of a crime family. The Soprano family is organized through a clear chain of command (e.g., the head of the family, supervisors called capos, and soldiers who do the enforcing). There are departments such as loan-sharking, prostitution, drugs, and gambling. There are rules (e.g., silence, life style that does not attract attention, respect for members of other crime families). All members of the organization (as well as most local and federal agencies) know the identity, status, and responsibilities of the other members.

Contrast the Soprano organization with the organization of the international terrorist organization known as al-Qaeda. Al-Qaeda is organized around cells, whose members are largely unaware of other cells. There is no clear reporting relationship or chain of command. Membership and operations change frequently, and often with little notice. Unlike the Soprano organization, al-Qaeda depends for its success on the lack of information that one cell might have of another, which makes it more difficult for an outsider to "put the pieces together."

Finally, we have the organization of any large municipal detective squad. Although the squad has a focus (e.g., homicide, robbery, assault, vice), within the squad, teams are formed and dissolved as a function of the case that comes in. For most squads, the detective who directs an investigation is often determined by who happens to pick up the phone when a complaint is called in. (This is called "catching" a case, and the squad often has a fixed rotation that determines who picks up the phone.) The detective in charge of the case may ask other detectives to assist, and has the discretion to reach out to other detectives in other precincts or even in other cities. The detective may also use support services such as a forensics lab, the district attorney's office, or even citizen groups. It is interesting to note that most large municipal police departments also have a division known as the organized crime unit. Any crime (e.g., drugs, murder, arson, assault) that may have been committed by a stable group of individuals, such as a crime family, is usually not given to an individual detective but assigned to this unit. This procedure supports the belief that organized crime is more complex and potentially dangerous to society than unorganized (i.e., individual) crime. Once again, we see the power of organization as opposed to disorganization.

Organizations are a way of life—in virtually all sectors of life.

Now consider three noncriminal enterprises: a typical university, an investment banking firm, and a marketing/advertising firm. Like the Sopranos, the university is organized along traditional lines with clear lines of authority (the president, deans, department heads, and faculty members). Different departments (e.g., English, biochemistry, psychology, nutrition) specialize in different areas. The entire university benefits from centralized support services such as accounting, libraries, physical plant, and maintenance. While beside the point, it is fascinating to contemplate any "cultural" differences that would emerge if a university president and an organized crime family head were to trade places for six months. Imagine the new president telling a dean to "fuhgedd aboud it" when the dean asks for an increase in the budget, or the new crime family head sending an e-mail to capos asking if it would be convenient to meet next week to discuss recruiting and training of new members.

In contrast, a large investment banking firm may employ 10,000 financial analysts or brokers and 10,000 research and administrative assistants paired with them, each with a desk and a focus on gathering assets for the organization by selling various investment instruments (e.g., stocks, bonds, annuities, 401k plans, estate plans). In essence, the firm is really a franchise operation for 10,000 separate businesses. Finally, the marketing/advertising company may consist of 20 professionals who may be asked to form small groups to "own" a campaign for a client. Like the detective teams, they may form to develop a campaign and dissolve when the campaign ends.

As the above examples show, there are many different ways of organizing the efforts of members of an organization to achieve the ends of that organization. In addition to each of the different methods of organizing, there are different organizational "personalities" (or cultures) that characterize each of these enterprises.

ORGANIZATION AS INTEGRATION

Hosking (1988) proposed that within the walls of an organization, many different organizing forces are at work. Successful organizations are those that are able to integrate these different forces. One force might be the human resources department which has a strategy for hiring and training. A second force might be the financial end of the business which has a strategy for workforce size and compensation. A third force could be the production department which has a strategy for turning out high-quality product at the lowest cost. A final force might be the sales and marketing department which has a strategy for new product development and distribution. From Hosking's perspective, success or failure depended on how well these various forces were integrated and a single pathway negotiated.

In the past, theories of organization have emphasized relatively static characteristics such as size, chain of command, compensation policies, or the specialization of duties. Each of these characteristics is an attempt to organize the effort of a single individual, to ensure that the person would behave within certain boundaries. These organizing efforts invariably create tensions between the individual and the organization, as the individual wants to do it one way, the organization another. Expense policies are a good example of this tension. The organization imposes a ceiling of $20, including tax and tip, for any single meal on its sales force. Sales reps in major metropolitan areas complain that $20 will barely cover dinner at a fast-food restaurant. Eventually, the organization and its sales reps negotiate a workable policy, one that recognizes geographic differences in the cost of food. The accounting function of the organization wants to protect against excessive costs and maintain a reasonable profit margin, while the sales reps want to maintain control over local decisions, including choosing where and what to eat.

At its most basic level, this is a dialogue about control: Who will ultimately control the behavior of the organization's members? As such, the dialogue contains elements of motivation, leadership, and satisfaction, to mention just a few. But at a deeper level, the dialogue also addresses the fit between the organization and the person. The sales rep says to himself, Why do I work for an organization that is so shortsighted? The manager of accounting says to herself, Who do these sales reps think they are? Do they think the organization exists just to make them happy? As you will see in the sections that follow, the concept of "fit" between the individual and the organization is a critical one for the organizational psychologist.

Organizational theory is very complex and multidisciplinary, involving specialists in policy, economics, production, strategic planning, psychology, anthropology, and sociology. We will concentrate on the psychology part of the puzzle. Nevertheless, there are many excellent resources for the student who wants to go deeper into the complexity of the modern organization. A text by Miner (2002) borders on being an encyclopedia of organizational theory. An outstanding reference source, it traces the evolution of organizational theory and the historical development of particular theories, evaluates alternative approaches, gives personal histories of the theorists, and speculates on the future of organizational theory. In the next section, we will consider the various formal ways that theorists and researchers have grappled with the description of an organization from the behavioral perspective.

THEORIES OF ORGANIZATION

Classic Organizational Theory

The modern view of the organization is a dynamic, interpersonal, and strategic one. It emphasizes process rather than formal organizational characteristics. In contrast, early theories of organization emphasized the architecture of the organization rather than the processes by which it operated. The best known of the early theorists was Max Weber, who proposed the **bureaucracy** as the ideal form of organization. This may seem ironic since the term "bureaucracy" today evokes images of inefficiency, ineffectiveness, and impersonality to most people. But Weber (1947) developed his theory as a form of social protest against the excesses of favoritism and nepotism that had characterized most organizations of the early 20th century, whether these organizations were fiefdoms of politicians or industrial giants.

Weber devised a method of describing an organization according to multiple dimensions; these are principally:

- **Division of labor,** which refers to dividing the performance of tasks in an organization into specialized jobs and departmental functions.
- **Delegation of authority,** which refers to information about which lower-level employees report to higher-level employees in an organization.
- **Structure,** which refers to the formal way an organization is designed in terms of division of labor, delegation of authority, and span of control; the number of levels—or height—of the organization.
- **Span of control,** which refers to the number of positions or people who report to a single individual, that is, the width of the organization.

Figure 14.1 illustrates the classic **organizational chart,** which is a diagram of an organization's structure.

This chart contains evidence of each of Weber's four dimensions. Division of labor is represented by boxes for the various departments and or titles; delegation of authority can be seen in vertical lines connecting departments or positions; structure is represented by the number of levels, or height of the organization; span of control is indicated by part A, small span, with few employees reporting to a single individual, and part B, large span, where several positions or people report to a single person—the width.

Embedded in this **classic organizational theory** were several assumptions about motivation, satisfaction, performance, and leadership, including the following:

- Leadership depends on clear lines of authority and delegation.
- Members find it satisfying and motivating to specialize in a particular content area, thus the division of labor and specialization.

BUREAUCRACY

Proposed by Max Weber in the 1940s to be the ideal form of organization; included a formal hierarchy, division of labor, and clear set of operating procedures.

DIVISION OF LABOR

The tasks performed in an organization can be divided into specialized jobs and departmental functions.

DELEGATION OF AUTHORITY

Information about which lower-level employees report to employees above them in an organization.

STRUCTURE

The formal way that an organization is designed in terms of division of labor, delegation of authority, and span of control; represented by the number of levels— or height—in an organization.

SPAN OF CONTROL

The number of positions or people reporting to a single individual— the width—in an organization.

ORGANIZATIONAL CHART

Diagram of an organization's structure.

CLASSIC ORGANIZATIONAL THEORY

Assumes there is one best configuration for an organization, regardless of its circumstances; places a premium on control of individual behavior by the organization.

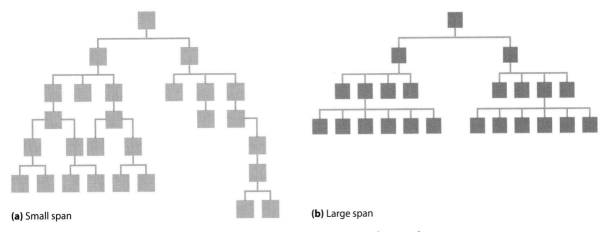

(a) Small span
(b) Large span

FIGURE 14.1 **Organization Charts for Large and Small Span of Control**

- Organizations can maximize performance and motivation by finding the optimal number of subordinates that a leader can manage, thus span of control and structure.

In sum, it was assumed that the "right" organization would induce effective behavior among its members. There was little concern for concepts such as participation, personality, efficacy, or leader style. In some senses, the early organizational theorists were large-scale behaviorists not much different from B.F. Skinner (discussed in Chapter 9 on motivation). They believed that the organizational environment represented the stimulus for behavior and that the success of the organization would represent the contingent reward for adapting to the environment. Between 1950 and 1970, I-O psychologists conducted a great deal of research on the effects of variations on these four basic dimensions of an organization. They debated whether "tall" or "flat" organizations were more effective and satisfying, or whether large or small spans of control were conducive to innovation.

Classic organizational theory was constrained in two ways. First, it assumed that there was *one best configuration* for an organization, regardless of its circumstances.

Attempts by an organization to control employee behavior are not always successfull. Source: L. J. Kopf, used by permission. © 2003.

Second, it assumed that organizations affected the behavior of their members, but ignored the possibility that the behavior of members affects the configuration of the organization. In later modules of this chapter, we will illustrate how both of these constraints diminished this approach to organizations; for the moment, we will consider only a few examples.

Classic organizational theory assumes that the individual who makes a decision will not be the individual who implements the decision. Yet many organizational interventions depend on vesting the power to make and the responsibility to implement a work-related decision to an individual or team that is closest to the actual work process—the production worker rather than the engineer. The classic organizational model places no value on participative decision making; in newer models, participation is essential for ensuring ownership and accountability at the lowest levels of the organization. The classic organizational model places a premium on control *by* the organization *of* individual behavior.

Human Relations Theory

As we saw above, classic organizational theory represented a disembodied view of organizational life. It did not consider the interrelationship between an organization's requirements and the characteristics of its members. **Human relations theory** added a personal or human element to the study of organizations.

McGregor's Theory X and Theory Y   Just as Weber's classic organizational theory of bureaucracy was a protest against the ills of the earlier organizational model of favoritism, Douglas McGregor's theory was a protest against the impersonal propositions of classic organizational theory. In his influential book *The Human Side of Enterprise,* McGregor (1960) proposed that the beliefs that managers hold about their subordinates influence their behavior toward those subordinates. As a way of making his theory more understandable, McGregor constructed two contrasting beliefs systems, which he labeled Theory X and Theory Y. **Theory X** managers believed that subordinate behavior had to be controlled in order to meet organizational ends—one of the basic propositions of classic organizational theory—and that a lack of focus would lead to apathy and resistance. Theory X managers were likely to use punishments and rewards as mechanisms of control. In contrast, **Theory Y** managers believed that subordinates were active and responsible and would be more motivated to meet organizational goals without unduly constraining organizational or managerial controls. Instead of a rigid use of concrete punishments and rewards, Theory Y managers were more likely to provide expanded responsibilities and challenges to subordinates. Although McGregor proposed these two systems merely as examples of alternative beliefs that managers might hold, many managers saw them as representing an either/or dichotomy, with no other alternatives. Since McGregor's death in 1964, others have proposed alternatives to the TheoryX/Y dichotomy (Ouchi, 1981; Schein, 1981).

As we described in Chapter 9 on work motivation, the 1960s was a time of cognitive revolution in all of psychology, including I/O psychology. McGregor's theory was a recognition that cognitive functions—thoughts and beliefs—might influence behavior. As such, it has historical significance. What was not widely recognized at the time was that the beliefs of the workers in the equation were as important as the beliefs of the managers despite the famous Hawthorne studies conducted by Mayo and his colleagues (Chapter 10). In those studies, they discovered that the beliefs of workers about managers had substantial effects on behavior and emotions.

The Growth Perspective of Argyris   Chris Argyris has been an influential organizational theorist for several decades. About the same time that McGregor's propositions were gaining favor among managers and practitioners, Argyris (1972) proposed a natural developmental sequence in humans that could either be enhanced or stunted by the organization. Like Maslow with his earlier (1943) motivational theory, Argyris proposed that growth was a

---

HUMAN RELATIONS THEORY

Adds a personal or human element to the study of organizations; considers the interrelationship between an organization's requirements and the characteristics of its members.

THEORY X

Developed by McGregor to describe the contrasting beliefs that managers hold about their subordinates; Theory X managers believe subordinates must be controlled to meet organizational ends.

THEORY Y

Theory Y managers believe subordinates would be motivated to meet goals in the absence of organizational controls.

natural and healthy experience for an individual. Further, organizations that acknowledged and aided this growth would be more likely to prosper than those that ignored or actively inhibited this growth. Argyris suggested that individuals developed in the following manner:

1. From passive to active organisms.
2. From dependent to independent organisms.
3. From organisms requiring immediate gratification to those capable of delaying gratification.
4. From organisms able to deal only with concrete operations to those able to deal in abstractions.
5. From organisms with few abilities to those with many abilities.

If we accept these assumptions (which seem quite reasonable and compatible with what we observe in the world around us), then it follows that certain forms of organization are counterproductive, including highly routine, assembly-line work and organizational structures that emphasize control. Argyris proposed that when individual workers encounter these inhibitions, they will react to them in predictable ways, including absenteeism, turnover, labor actions, and apathy. The organization following the classic model will react to negative worker behavior by exerting even more control, therefore exaggerating the behavior they are attempting to extinguish. The scenario suggested by Korman (1971) in Figure 14.2 provides a perfect example of this tension between the characteristics of the worker and the attempts to control by the organization.

For both McGregor and Argyris, the solution to the organizational puzzle was to integrate the goals of the organization with the goals of the individual. It is interesting to examine current organizational initiatives (e.g., TQM, Six Sigma, lean manufacturing) in that light. Many of these initiatives emphasize the importance of participation as a member of a team and the critical role of product and process quality. While it is probably true that most workers value the social rewards of teamwork, it is not clear that those same workers value quality to the same extent as the managers and strategic planners. Nor is it clear that the statistical analyses that form the foundation of many of these systems are as important to workers as the more generalized goal-setting and feedback process. Nevertheless, today's organizations have implemented much of the philosophy and theorizing of both McGregor and Argyris.

Contingency Theories

You will recall from our discussion of leadership theories in Chapter 12 that some theories were labeled **contingency** (or "it depends") **theories.** The word "contingency" in the leadership context and structure/process in the organizational context implies that behavior must be selected to fit the particular circumstance. Several theorists have departed from the one-best-way approach of the classic theories and suggested that the best way actually depends on the circumstances of the organization.

Woodward   British industrial sociologist Joan Woodward (1958) recognized that the technology employed in a particular company or industry could influence the most effective design for the organization. She contrasted three types of organizations:

- **Small batch organization**—produces specialty products one at a time.
- **Large batch and mass production organization**—produces large numbers of discrete units—assembly-line operations.
- **Continuous process organization**—depends on a continuous process for output or product, including organizations such as refineries, chemical plants, and distilleries.

In observing these three types of organizations, Woodward discovered that the span of control varied systematically by type of organization. The largest span of control was observed

CONTINGENCY THEORIES OF ORGANIZATION

Propose that the best way to structure an organization depends on the circumstances of the organization.

SMALL BATCH ORGANIZATION

Produces specialty products one at a time.

LARGE BATCH AND MASS PRODUCTION ORGANIZATION

Produces large numbers of discrete units, often using assembly-line operations.

CONTINUOUS PROCESS ORGANIZATION

Depends on a continuous process for output or product.

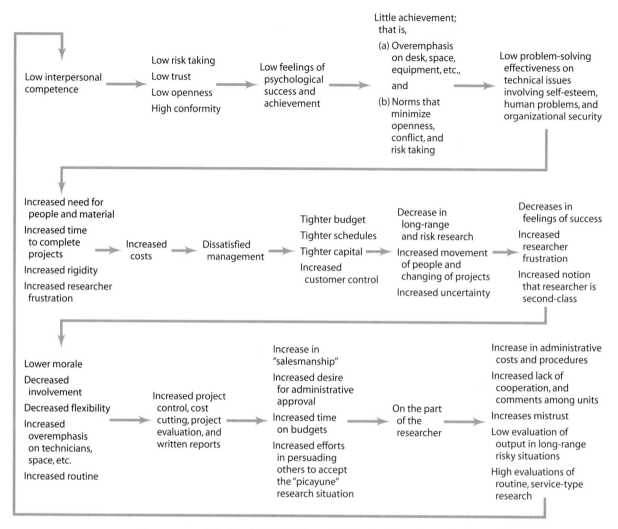

FIGURE 14.2 A Critical View of Behavior in an Organization Built upon Classic Organization Theory SOURCE: Adapted in Korman (1971) from Argyris (1965).

in mass production organizations and the smallest in continuous process environments, with small batch organizations falling in between. From this observation, she reasoned that different technologies are better served with different structural characteristics.

Woodward's approach was primitive by today's standards, but it did represent a departure from the classic approach. More importantly, she introduced the concept of technology into organizational thinking. This led to the development of more elaborate contingency theories, including the work of Lawrence and Lorsch (1967).

Lawrence and Lorsch   One of the most complete and detailed descriptions of the approach of Lawrence and Lorsch, as well as contingency theories generally, appears in the recent text of Miner (2002). The basic premise of this approach was that the stability of the environment dictates the most effective form of organization. Based on their own work as well as the research of Burns and Stalker (1961), Lawrence and Lorsch (1967) discovered that organizations in stable environments tended to be more "mechanistic" than those in unstable environments. A **mechanistic organization** depended on formal rules and regulations, made decisions at higher levels of the organization, and had smaller spans of control. In contrast, unstable or rapidly changing environments or industries seemed to spawn "organic" forms

MECHANISTIC
ORGANIZATION

Depends on formal rules and regulations, makes decisions at higher levels of the organization, and has small spans of control.

of organization. An **organic organization** had larger spans of control, less formalization of procedure, and decision making at middle levels of the organization.

Lawrence and Lorsch suggested that mechanistic and organic differences exist not only between companies and industries, but also within organizations. They proposed that managers who reside in different departments would have very different worldviews based on their environments. Thus, a research and development (R&D) manager would be in an organic environment and therefore less likely to depend on formal rules, would have larger spans of control, and would be more likely to delegate decisions to lower levels of the department. In contrast, a plant or shift manager might be in a mechanistic environment and use more formal rules, retain decision-making authority, and maintain more direct control of activities through smaller spans of control.

The challenge for the organization, then, is to develop an architecture that accommodates both the R&D manager and the plant manager. The former is operating in a rapidly changing environment and the latter in a relatively stable environment. Without intervention, these differences could easily lead to mutual suspicion and disrespect, as well as tension surrounding strategic planning, budgeting, and so forth. Unlike Woodward, who concentrated on differences among industries and companies, Lawrence and Lorsch identified the department as the important level for understanding how organizations operated. They proposed that if departments can adapt and integrate to changing external environments, the organization will prosper. In a broader sense, the same would be true for larger units within the corporation such as multinational locations, regions, or divisions.

The Sociotechnical Approach of the Tavistock Institute The **sociotechnical approach** began at the Tavistock Institute of Human Relations in England in the late 1940s. By examining the effects of technological change, Trist and Bamforth (1951) uncovered a number of dramatic changes in the social patterns of work that accompanied technological change. The change in technology had the effect of disrupting stable and satisfying social patterns, leading to various dysfunctional results such as rivalry, absenteeism, and dissatisfaction. One of the industries they studied was coal mining. In the early 1950s coal mining was transformed from a job accomplished by the collective sweat and muscle of individual miners to one accomplished by large machines that gouged coal out of the ground. The tight-knit miner work groups were replaced by single machine operators. Cohesive work groups were gone; old social interdependencies were swept away and new ones put in their place: Who would notify a worker's family if a miner were injured, or help accomplish a job when a worker was not feeling up to par? Rice (1958) found similar disruptions in the weaving mills of India when technology changed.

The sociotechnical approach includes a joint consideration of technology and social patterns. A more recent example is the transformation of the typical office. Until the 1970s, a secretary took dictation, typed the dictated material at a desk adjacent to many other secretaries, and filed documents in steel cabinets. There was ample opportunity for work- and nonwork-related communication in the filing and desk area. Today the secretary is a word processor, sitting in a cubicle, with a dedicated printer and an electronic filing system. Although younger workers take the new environment for granted and workers of all ages have developed other social patterns around that new environment, those who made the transition from the traditional office to the new office did not do so without psychological discomfort.

In many industries of the 21st century, technology is changing at a frantic pace. These changes are often billed as technological advances that permit greater efficiencies, lower costs, and greater profitability. Organizations often assume their employees will recognize that change is to be equated with survival and profitability. Nevertheless, change also has an emotional cost for many workers. Consider the social environment of the "virtual team." Although this may be an essential advance in the work process, it has the potential to generate dysfunctional results as in the British coal mines 50 years ago. When virtual discussions replace face-to-face interaction, the likelihood of misunderstandings and resentments

ORGANIC
ORGANIZATION

Organization with a large span of control, less formal procedures, and decision making at middle levels.

SOCIOTECHNICAL
APPROACH

Uncovered a number of dramatic changes in social patterns of work that accompanied technological change; developed at the Tavistock Institute of Human Relations in England in the late 1940s.

may increase. The impersonal nature of e-mail may turn what would have been a discussion into a battle. Fortunately, as we saw in Chapter 13, recent research in the composition and interactions of virtual teams can help the organization to avoid such pitfalls. The goal of the sociotechnical approach is not to impede progress in order to maintain social patterns, but to recognize the social changes that accompany many technological changes and equip those in charge of the technological change to anticipate and plan for the changes in social patterns.

Two Recent Approaches

Resource Theory: Pfeffer   In the late 1970s Pfeffer and Salancik (1978; Pfeffer, 1990) produced **resource theory** in which an organization must be viewed not as if it were in a vacuum, but in the context of its connections to other organizations. These connections are seen as critical to survival (Miner, 2002):

> Organizations survive to the extent that they are effective. Their effectiveness derives from the management of demands, particularly the demands of interest groups upon which the organizations depend for resources and support. . . . The key to organizational survival is the ability to acquire and maintain resources. . . . Organizations must transact with other elements in their environment to acquire needed resources. (Pfeffer & Salancik, 1978 as quoted by Miner, 2002)

According to Pfeffer, successful organizations are more likely than unsuccessful ones to form coalitions with other organizations. The more a coalition member can contribute to the collaboration, the more powerful that member is. Organizations are considered efficient to the extent to which they can accomplish their objectives, given the resources used (Miner, 2002). Once again, the image of the lean manufacturing organization comes to mind with its emphasis on the reduction of waste and the collaboration with suppliers and customers.

The Ecological/Evolutionary Approach   A very different view of organizations is embodied in the evolutionary (Aldrich, 1999) and ecological (Hannan & Freeman, 1977; Hannan & Carroll, 1992) approaches. The **ecological/evolutionary approach** adopts a biological model, much like the Darwinian model of evolution, and concentrates on explaining why some types of organizations thrive and diversify while others atrophy and disappear. As such, it is more a sociological approach to organizations than a psychological one. Like Darwinian evolutionary theory, it focuses on two basic mechanisms: random variation (i.e., many different types of emerging organizations) and natural selection (i.e., an economic and social environment that tends to favor one type of organization over another). Rather than assuming that organizations change and mature and grow in strength and stability, the evolutionary approach proposes that organizations change very slowly, but that environments change rapidly. The variety of organizations comes from the continual formation of new organizations and merged organizations as they take the place of less successful organizations that cease to exist.

These theories further suggest that many of the actions of individuals within an organization, assumed to be adaptive to a changing environment, are not. Instead, they are almost random responses to an environment changing at a rate and in a way that the members of the organization cannot contemplate. The argument is that organizations will change too slowly because of four factors:

1. Organization forms (e.g., structure, span of control, reporting relationships) do not change easily or quickly.
2. Resources are scarce and few organizations have the luxury of using these resources for the purpose of change.
3. Competitive pressures are unpredictable and uncontrollable.
4. Humans have limited rationality and often make poor decisions when effecting change.

RESOURCE THEORY

An organization must be viewed in the context of its connections to other organizations; the key to organizational survival is the ability to acquire and maintain resources.

EVOLUTIONARY/ ECOLOGICAL APPROACH

Adopts a biological model and concentrates on explaining why some types of organizations thrive and diversify, while others atrophy and disappear.

There is good news and bad news about this approach. The good news is, at least in theory, that it is possible to anticipate what forms of organization might be best suited to a particular environment (e.g., customer service compared to high technology). The bad news is that ecological/evolutionary theorists are pessimistic about the possibility of changing an existing organization from a less adaptive to a more adaptive form. Further, they have little regard for the powers of individual managers to effect change in a reasonable period of time. As Miner (2002) concluded, "there is little that can actually be put to use by a practitioner simply because the theory deals primarily with causal processes that are beyond the control of those who occupy positions within the organization" (p. 781).

Since our text takes exactly the opposite position by assuming that individual members of the organization are able to control many processes (e.g., selection, training, motivation, leadership), you might wonder why we bother to even present this evolutionary approach. We present it for two reasons. First, it is so unconventional that it provokes thought. Second, it suggests that events and circumstances outside of individual and group behavior can nonetheless influence that behavior. That does not mean that we should throw up our hands because larger forces are at work; instead, it means that we need to recognize that many nonbehavioral factors influence individual behavior.

Conclusions about Theories of Organization

Since organizations are often compared to individuals with respect to "personalities," it is tempting to compare the theories of organizations with theories of human motivation. You will recall that we used the metaphors of Weiner (1992) to describe motivation theory in Chapter 9. What happens if we apply the same metaphors to organization theory? Starting with the person-as-machine metaphor, the classic organization theories assume that people are machines, responding to the characteristics of an organization in an automatic and reflexive manner. The humanist theories of McGregor and Argyris parallel the more personal and benevolent theories of Maslow, but they are no less mechanical, assuming that people respond to how they are perceived (McGregor's Theories X and Y), or compatible with their stage of development (Argyris).

The contingency theories of Woodward, Lawrence and Lorsch, and the sociotechnical school are similarly mechanistic, attributing most of the influence on the behavior of individuals to the interaction between the environment and organizational structure or process. Resource theory rises to the level of person-as-scientist or at least it considers some of the key strategic people as scientists. Evolutionary and ecological theory falls somewhere below the person-as-machine model because it attributes little influence to individuals regardless of how they behave.

What is interesting is the discrepancy between many of the theories of organization and the current organizational interventions. Management by objectives (MBO), lean production, Six Sigma, and TQM systems all predicate a person-as-scientist model of one form or another, and most assume unlimited rationality of that scientist. Few of these interventions recognize the elements of the person-as-judge model that have become so prevalent in current theories of individual motivation. Most assume that efficacy will be enhanced and that individuals will seek challenge, but none of them directly recognize the role of efficacy in the judgments or decisions that organizational members make. There is a vigorous debate about whether interventions like Six Sigma or lean production will endure the test of time, or whether they will be rejected by cynical employees who do not accept the values or motivational schemes of their leaders. To the extent that these interventions do not recognize the person-as-judge, but instead assume the person-as-scientist model of motivation, they may very well ultimately fail. What we can say, however, is that there is a gap between organizational theory and motivational theory that will need a bridge for a complete understanding of the effects of people on organizations and organizations on people.

MODULE 14.1 SUMMARY

- Early theories of organization emphasized relatively static characteristics such as size, chain of command, or the specialization of duties. The best known of the early organizational theorists was Max Weber, who proposed the bureaucracy as the ideal form of organization. Weber described an organization according to multiple dimensions, principally division of labor, delegation of authority, structure, and span of control.

- The human relations approach added a personal element to the study of organizations. McGregor proposed that the beliefs that managers hold about their subordinates influence their behavior toward those subordinates. He constructed two contrasting beliefs systems, labeled Theory X and Theory Y, which reflected the degree to which managers believe employees are self-directed or need to be controlled.

- Several theorists have departed from the one-best-way approach of the classic theories, suggesting that the best way depends on the circumstances of the organization. Woodward recognized that the technology employed in a particular company or industry influenced the most effective design for the organization. Lawrence and Lorsch suggested that the stability of the environment dictated the most effective form of organization.

- The sociotechnical approach uncovered a number of dramatic changes in social patterns of work that accompained technological change. The goal of the sociotechnical approach is to recognize the social changes that often accompany technological changes and equip managers in charge of these technological changes to anticipate and plan for the changes in social patterns.

- Pfeffer and Salancik suggested that an organization must be viewed in the context of its connections to other organizations; the key to organizational survival is its ability to acquire and maintain resources by fostering such connections.

KEY TERMS

organization

bureaucracy

division of labor

delegation of authority

structure

span of control

organizational chart

classic organizational theory

human relations theory

Theory X

Theory Y

contingency theories of organization

small batch organization

large batch and mass production organization

continuous process organization

mechanistic organization

organic organization

sociotechnical approach

resource theory

evolutionary/ecological approach

CRITICAL THINKING EXERCISES

14.1 Using the taxonomy of Woodward, classify the following organizations in terms of small batch, large batch, or continuous processing entities:

Your college or university.

The local quickstop gas station.

The local YMCA.

The studio of a glassblower.

A TV-screen manufacturing facility.

A utility company.

14.2 Applying the sociotechnical approach, anticipate the effects of requiring travel agents to work from their homes three days a week rather than at the office.

SOME SOCIAL DYNAMICS OF ORGANIZATIONS

O rganizations by definition are social entities. They represent a collection of individuals who work for a common purpose. As such, they exhibit the characteristics of any social entity, including a climate, a culture, and role expectations. These characteristics can work either to support the goals of the organization, or to thwart them. In this module, we will consider the issues of climate and culture, as well as some unique challenges to organizations operating in a multicultural environment. Roles, in particular role conflict and ambiguity, are also part of the organizational landscape, but we will defer a discussion of these two concepts to Chapter 15, where we deal with stress in the workplace.

CLIMATE AND CULTURE

You will recall from our introduction to this chapter that we asked you to consider a wide variety of organizations—the IRS, Ben and Jerry's, an organized crime family, and two new mothers forming a meal service company. Each of these organizations probably evoked a somewhat different feeling in you. The IRS may have evoked a sense of predictability and standardization; Ben and Jerry's, a social and societal feeling; the organized crime family, fear and fascination; and the company formed by the two new mothers, warmth and admiration. Organizations do bring to mind feelings and beliefs—either intentionally or unintentionally. Although both the IRS and the organized crime family would claim that a positive feeling of "family" pervades their operations, you may have doubts about the reality of the IRS claim and the tone of the crime family claim. Discussions of culture and climate involve concepts such as beliefs, values, perceptions, and feelings. Culture is often associated with the more cognitive variables such as beliefs and values, while climate is more commonly associated with more affective states such as feelings.

Discussions of and research about organizational climate and culture have been with us for over 50 years (Schneider, 2000; Schneider et al., 2000) and have resulted in dozens of competing definitions and measurement devices. Based on this rich research tradition, we can draw at least one general conclusion: There is little agreement about what the concepts mean or how they affect the behavior of organizations or individuals in those organizations. In particular, the terms "climate" and "culture" are often used interchangeably which lead to conflicting results, interpretations, and recommendations. Nevertheless, it is clear that the psychological center of the consideration of organizations and organizational psychology includes these concepts.

As authors, we are in the curious and enviable position of being liberated by this wealth of divergent research and theory. We can review it and tell you what we think it all means and where the research is leading (or where we think it *should* lead). If this area interests you, you are in luck because there are many recent, outstanding treatments of the topic. Ashkanasy and his colleagues (Ashkanasy & Jackson, 2001; Ashkanasy, Wilderom &

Peterson, 2000) reviewed the history of the concepts as well as the implications for human resource practices domestically and internationally. James and McIntyre (1996) provided a detailed and compelling description of climate from the perspective of the individual worker. Rentsch (1990) presented a comprehensive review of the various meanings assigned to culture and climate by organizational researchers. We will use these and other publications as a foundation for presenting our view of the concepts and their value. We will begin with a consideration of climate, since it predates the concept of organizational culture by several decades (Ashkanasy & Jackson, 2001). Reichers and Schneider (1990) have presented an excellent chronology of the development of both concepts.

A Brief History of Climate

In 1939 Lewin, Lippit, and White (1939) described various types of organizations in terms of the "climate" that pervaded them. **Climate** is the shared perception of employees about their work entity: an organization, division, department, or work group. Based on their examinations of three different "types" of organizations, Lewin et al. proposed three different "types" of climates: autocratic, democratic, and laissez faire. Based in part on this work, Litwin and Stringer (1966) further decomposed climate into six dimensions: structure, individual responsibility, rewards, risk and risk taking, warmth and support, and tolerance and conflict. Campbell, Dunnette, Lawler, and Weick (1970) suggested that these factors actually described the way an organization treated its members. Lewin's **autocratic climate** in an organization might be expected to be highly structured, with little opportunity for individual responsibility or risk taking at the lowest levels. In contrast, the **democratic climate** in an organization would be characterized as less structured, with greater opportunity for individual responsibility and risk taking. Locke (1976) reviewed the available literature on climate and concluded that when employees "perceived" an organization, they looked at four basic dimensions (James & McIntyre, 1996):

1. Clarity, harmony and justice.
2. Challenge, independence and responsibility.
3. Work facilitation, support, and recognition.
4. Warm and friendly social relations.

Independently, James and McIntyre (1996) conducted statistical analyses of existing climate research and suggested four very similar dimensions, which they labeled:

1. Role stress and lack of harmony.
2. Job challenge and autonomy.
3. Leadership facilitation and support.
4. Work group cooperation, friendliness, and warmth.

James and James (1989) further decomposed these four factors (see Figure 14.3). Table 14.1 presents some examples of typical climate questionnaire items.

As you can see, the emerging model of climate implied that it could be thought of as a structural concept; it could be applied to any organization (or division, department, or even work group) and a score or series of scores could be obtained that described "the" climate of the entity. Recently, I-O psychologists have suggested that multiple climates exist within any organization and that these climates are defined less by structural components (e.g., degree of autonomy) than by the goal of the group (Schneider, Bowen, Ehrhart, & Holcombe, 2001). Thus, Schneider, Salvaggio, and Subirats (2002) identified a "service climate" that relates to customer satisfaction, Kraiger and Smith-Jentsch (2002) identified climates peculiar to air traffic controllers, Baer and Frese (2002) identified climates for initiative and innovation, and Hofmann and his colleagues (Hofmann & Stetzer, 1996, 1998;

CLIMATE

A shared perception among employees regarding their work entity: a particular organization, division, department, or work group.

AUTOCRATIC CLIMATE

Organization described by Lewin as highly structured organization with little opportunity for individual responsibility or risk taking at the lowest levels.

DEMOCRATIC CLIMATE

Organization described by Lewin as less structured, with greater opportunity for individual responsibility and risk taking.

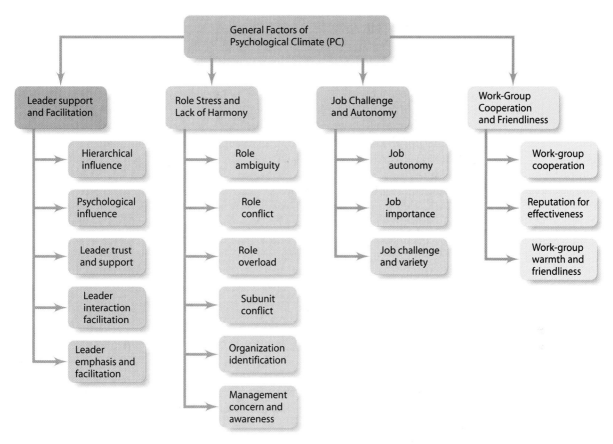

FIGURE 14.3 A Decomposition of Climate Factors Source: James & James (1989).

Hofmann & Morgeson, 1999) identified safety climates. (We will review the work by Hofmann and others in Chapter 16 in the module on safety in the workplace.)

It is not necessary to choose between these two sets of dimensions. Both have appeal and potential value. On the one hand, it may be valuable when contrasting organizations or qualitatively different groups within an organization (e.g., R&D versus customer service) to use the dimensions suggested by James and James (1989) to understand those differences. On the other hand, when considering differences between similar departments (e.g., customer service in one geographical region of a company against customer service in a different region), or differences within the same department at different times (e.g., 1996 versus 1999), it might be more useful to examine in some detail the "service climate."

TABLE 14.1	Some Typical Questions about Organizational Climate

Employees are encouraged to develop their skills and abilities.

This is not the type of organization that likes to take risks.

I feel personally close to my co-workers.

If I make a strategic decision related to my work, I feel that my boss will back me up.

I feel that I have a good measure of control in my work.

I am not given much responsibility in my work.

An Even Briefer History of Culture

Organizations are of interest to a much broader range of scholars than simply psychologists. Anthropologists, sociologists, and political scientists, to name but a few, are also interested in the way that organizations (whether the organization is IBM or a village in the mountains of Romania) develop, persist, and change. By the 1970s there was an increasing awareness that climate was not a large enough concept to capture many of the broader aspects of an organization. It was felt that climate dealt with the constraints on the actions of managers and leaders of the organization, but did not address issues of the value and meaning of those actions (Ashkanasy & Jackson, 2001). Therefore, the term **culture** was introduced to refer to the shared beliefs and values created and communicated by the managers and leaders of an organization to employees.

Because the concept of culture came from the anthropological tradition rather than the psychological tradition, many of the early discussions about the differences between the concepts were confusing. Traditionally, the measurement of climate was accomplished with questionnaires, and the measurement of culture was performed through observation and case study. Despite this inconsistency, culture did seem to be getting at something different from climate. As a result, attempts to use common measurement procedures and questionnaires for measuring culture were developed. One of the best known is the Organizational Culture Inventory (Cooke & Rousseau, 1988; Cooke & Szumal, 2000; Rousseau, 1988). Table 14.2 presents some examples of items from that questionnaire.

CULTURE

Shared beliefs and values created and communicated by the managers and leaders of an organization to employees.

TABLE 14.2 **Descriptions of the Twelve Styles Measured by the Organizational Culture Inventory™ (and Sample Items)**

Instructions: Please think about what it takes for you and people like yourself (e.g. your co-workers, people in similar positions) to "fit in" and meet expectations in your organization. Selecting from the response options below, indicate *the extent to which each of the following behaviors is expected.*

Response options:

1. Not at all
2. To a slight extent
3. To a moderate extent

4. To a great extent
5. To a very great extent

To what extent are people expected or implicitly required to . . .

CONSTRUCTIVE NORMS
[Cultural Styles Promoting Satisfaction Behaviors]

Achievement

An Achievement culture characterizes organizations that do things well and value members who set and accomplish their own goals. Members are expected to set challenging but realistic goals, establish plans to reach these goals, and pursue them with enthusiasm. *(Pursue a standard of excellence; openly show enthusiasm)*

Self-Actualizing

A Self-Actualizing culture characterizes organizations that value creativity, quality over quantity, and both task accomplishment and individual growth. Members are encouraged to gain enjoyment from their work, develop themselves, and take on new and interesting activities. *(Think in unique an independent ways; do even simple tasks well)*

Humanistic/Encouraging

A Humanistic-Encouraging culture characterizes organizations that are managed in a participative and person-centered way. Members are expected to be supportive, constructive, and open to influence in their dealings with one another. *(Help others to grow and develop; take time with people)*

(continued)

TABLE 14.2 *(continued)*

Affiliative

An Affiliative culture characterizes organizations that place a high priority on constructive interpersonal relationships. Members are expected to be friendly, open, and sensitive to the satisfaction of their work group. *(Deal with others in a friendly, pleasant way; share feelings and thoughts)*

PASSIVE/DEFENSIVE NORMS
[Cultural Styles Promoting People/Security Behaviors]

Approval

An Approval culture describes organizations in which conflicts are avoided and interpersonal relationships are pleasant—at least superficially. Members feel that they should agree with, gain the approval of, and be liked by others. *("Go along" with others; be liked by everyone)*

Conventional

A Conventional culture describes organizations that are conservative, traditional, and bureaucratically controlled. Members are expected to conform, follow the rules, and make a good impression. *(Always follow policies and practices; fit into the "mold")*

Dependent

A Dependent culture describes organizations that are hierarchically controlled and do not empower their members. Centralized decision making in such organizations leads members to do only what they are told and to clear all decisions with superiors. *(Please those in positions of authority; do what is expected)*

Avoidance

An Avoidance culture characterizes organizations that fail to reward success but nevertheless punish mistakes. This negative reward system leads members to shift responsibilities to others and avoid any possibility of being blamed for a mistake. *(Wait for others to act first; take few chances)*

AGGRESSIVE/DEFENSIVE NORMS
[Cultural Styles Promoting Task/Security Behaviors]

Oppositional

An Oppositional culture describes organizations that reward confrontation and negativism. Members gain status and influence by being critical and thus are reinforced to oppose the ideas of others. *(Point out flaws; be hard to impress)*

Power

A Power culture describes nonparticipative organizations structured on the basis of the authority inherent in members' positions. Members believe they will be rewarded for taking charge, controlling subordinates and, at the same time, being responsive to the demands of superiors. *(Build up one's power base; demand loyalty)*

Competitive

A Competitive culture describes organizations that value winning and reward members for outperforming one another. Members operate in a "win–lose" framework and believe they must work against (rather than with) their peers to be noticed. *(Turn the job into a contest; never appear to lose)*

Perfectionistic

A Perfectionistic culture characterizes organizations that value perfectionism, persistence, and hard work. Members feel they must avoid any mistakes, keep track of everything, and work long hours to attain narrowly defined objectives. *(Do things perfectly; Keep on top of everything)*

SOURCE: Adapted from Cooke & Lafferty (1989).

In recent discussions of the failures of various organizations as evidenced by dissolution, downsizing, and so forth, the organizational culture rather than a climate is often identified as a causal factor (Ashkanasy & Jackson, 2001). One hears talk of a "culture of failure," or a "culture of conformity." Weber (2000) identified the "clash" of cultures as the most likely reason for the failure of mergers and acquisitions, when two different cultures often come face-to-face. The duration and severity of this clash also appear to be related to the financial performance and stock value of the acquiring company (Ashkanasy & Holmes, 1995; Weber, 2000).

An Integration of Concepts

In an earlier publication, Landy (1989) wondered if culture was really just old wine in new bottles. That speculation appears to have been wrong. Now our opinion, based on the accumulation of research and theory, is that culture and climate are two different, yet overlapping concepts (Ashkanasy, Wilderom, & Peterson, 2000). In 1990 Reichers and Schneider lamented the histories and methods that stood in the way of the integration of the two concepts. After more than a decade of additional research and discussion, these obstacles are less dramatic than they once were. It seems to us that climate is about the context in which action occurs—reminiscent of Campbell et al.'s (1970) description of how an organization treats its members—and culture is about the meaning intended by and inferred from those actions.

This meaning dimension applies to both senior leaders of the organization and those in lower levels. Senior leaders are expected to articulate and represent the culture. Managers are expected to help translate that culture through leadership initiatives. Employees at all levels below the senior leaders are expected to attribute meaning to various actions. The senior leaders hope that the meaning attributed to various actions by employees is the meaning they intended. But employees may attribute very different meanings (and thus infer a very different culture) than the executives expect. Thus, when a company like GE preaches "lean and mean" as a culture, or a company like Enron preaches honesty as a value, employees are likely to see a very different meaning when they discover that the CEO was paid lavishly or the senior executive staff was dumping stock while urging employees to buy more.

Schneider (2000; Schneider et al., 2000) likened the dual histories of culture and climate to a case of sibling rivalry and suggested ways for the protagonists in the "climate versus culture debate" to learn from each other. Perhaps one way to integrate the concepts is to think of culture as being created and communicated from higher levels of the organization (e.g., senior executives) and climate being created at lower levels of the organization (managers and supervisors). This may be a somewhat idealized view since it is unlikely that either culture or climate can be so carefully constructed or controlled. Organizational cultures and group climates can emerge without the conscious efforts of senior leaders or managers. A commercial construction company might develop a reputation as "dangerous" among craft workers because of the high incidence of accidents, even though the senior leaders believe they have created a culture of safety. In addition, one might acknowledge many different climates within an organization that is attempting to articulate only one culture. For example, the electricians in our construction company may see themselves as safety-conscious, while the structural steelworkers may see themselves as brave and fearless (often a prescription for accidents). The unique translation of organizational values by different workgroups might be thought of as a "subculture."

It is worth remembering, however, that individuals may very well assign meaning to two different cultures: a work or organizational culture and a personal or nonwork culture. This is the essence of the tension between work and family which we have discussed throughout the text. It is a culture clash in which the organization is communicating one set of values and the family another. The forward-looking organization needs to acknowledge and address this potential clash of values and develop methods of "merging" them in a way that simultaneously meets the goals of the organization and the goals of the individual.

A NEW AVENUE FOR EXPLORATION: CLIMATE AND CULTURE STRENGTH

A relevant issue for both the concepts of climate and culture is the extent to which members of an organization *share* a perception (in the case of climate) or a value/belief pattern (in the case of culture). This sharing has been called **climate/culture strength.** Imagine a work group in which some members perceive a warm and supportive climate, others a neutral climate neither warm nor forbidding, and still others who experience the same climate as punitive and punishing. Schneider et al. (2002) addressed exactly that issue: the implications of a lack of consensus among organization members regarding the presence of a climate, in this case a customer service climate. They analyzed the responses of several thousand bank employees to a service climate questionnaire (Schneider et al., 2000) and related these measures of climate to the satisfaction expressed by several thousand bank customers in 118 branches with the service they had received from their bank branch. Schneider and colleagues hypothesized that the extent to which branch employees agreed on the service climate of the branch should play a role in the delivery of that service to customers. If all branch employees were consistent in their description of the service climate, one should see a clearer relationship between that climate and reported customer satisfaction with service than if there was widespread disagreement among employees about the climate.

The researchers labeled agreement among employees as the "strength" of the climate (which should not be interpreted as the *judged importance* of the climate) and calculated it as the standard deviation of the climate measure within a branch. If the standard deviation was high, that signaled a lack of consensus about the climate. They examined four different aspects of the service climate: (1) the extent to which the bank made an effort to meet customer needs, (2) the behaviors of the branch manager to support and reward the delivery of service, (3) the degree to which the branch sought feedback from customers about service, and (4) a global measure of the service climate. The results showed that when the employees agreed that their manager supported and rewarded the delivery of service, there was a positive relationship between various aspects of the service climate and customers' reports of satisfaction.

These results made sense to Schneider et al. because it is the manager who has the most influence on the employees, and the employees who have the most direct influence on the customers. The other aspects of climate (e.g., the customer orientation of the manager and the desire for customer feedback) are actually results of what the manager encourages in his or her employees. But, given that they all had the same manager, why would the employees of each branch not agree about the extent of managerial support for a service climate at their branch? The researchers suggested several possibilities: (1) some managers are better at communicating service expectations than others, (2) some employees may be better able to comprehend the manager's emphasis on service than other employees, and (3) managers may communicate with some branch employees and not with others, as suggested in the leader-member exchange theory of leadership that we reviewed in Chapter 12. It is not yet clear why the results were obtained, but they are interesting and the study took a very different approach to climate than had been taken before. It suggested that the extent of agreement among group members may be very important in translating perceptions into action.

Similar investigations of the strength of corporate cultures have also been conducted (Meglino, Ravlin, & Adkins, 1989, 1991). Since mergers and acquisitions often involve the clash of cultures, as we discussed earlier, the level of agreement among organizational members can actually represent a serious obstacle to integration. If the two parties in the merger have strongly held beliefs (i.e., cultures) that are divergent, the merger should prove to be much more difficult than if there was a lack of agreement within each party to the merger. The concept of member agreement is a fascinating one and is likely to generate a good deal of attention in the coming years.

CLIMATE/CULTURE STRENGTH

Extent to which members of the organization share a perception (in the case of climate) or a value/belief pattern (in the case of culture).

ORGANIZATIONAL CLIMATE AND CULTURE FROM THE MULTICULTURAL PERSPECTIVE

When Cultures Clash

In the early years of the 17th century, Dutch immigrants developed sections of the west coast of Sweden, including the port city of Gothenburg. Unlike a typical Dutch coastal city, Gothenburg had no canals, so to make it look and feel more like "home," the Dutch dug canals throughout the city. When they left many years later, the Swedes filled in the canals.

An American manager moves her family to Tokyo on an assignment from the U.S. company for which she has worked for many years. The U.S. company acquired a much smaller Japanese company and asked some key employees to move to Tokyo to ease the integration of the two companies. The manager reports to an upper-level executive of the acquired Japanese firm. In her first week, she is handed a schedule of weekend retreats that she will be expected to attend with her Japanese colleagues. These retreats are intense off-site events requiring overnight stays. No family members are permitted to accompany her. She is dumbfounded that her new boss would be so inconsiderate as to expect her to abandon her family during nonwork hours.

The anecdotes above are examples of a clash of cultures. Since there seems to be no recent effort to unearth the canals dug by the Dutch in Gothenburg, we will focus on the clash of organizational cultures demonstrated in the U.S.-acquired company in Japan. The increasing multicultural workplace and the rise of the multinational corporation makes these clashes increasingly common. Ashkanasy and Jackson (2001) identified four different models under which multinational companies can operate when confronted with differences in organizational culture.

ETHNOCENTRISM

Multinational model in which the values of the parent company predominate.

POLYCENTRISM

Multinational model in which the values of the local company are accepted.

REGIOCENTRISM

Multinational model which has a blending of the values of the parent organization and the local company.

GEOCENTRISM

Multinational model in which a new corporatewide policy handles an issue in a way that creates a global perspective.

- **Ethnocentrism**—the values of the parent company predominate; our American expatriate in Japan would simply refuse to take part in the retreats.
- **Polycentrism**—the values of the local company are accepted; our expatriate would agree to attend the retreats.
- **Regiocentrism**—a blending of the values of the parent organization and the local company; our American expatriate would suggest that the retreats be held during working hours or that family members be permitted to accompany participants if they would like, although they would be expected to entertain themselves.
- **Geocentrism**—a new corporatewide policy is developed to handle an issue in a way that would create a global perspective; our expatriate would join a team of individuals from the local and parent company with the goal of developing a workable global policy on retreats.

There is no "right" choice from the four alternatives presented above. The choice needs to be negotiated by representatives of the two different organizational cultures. The key point is that multinational corporations must acknowledge the existence of different cultures represented in different geographic locations. House et al. (1999) have suggested the use of Hofstede's dimensions of the culture of nations (e.g., power distance, collectivism) to describe the cultures of organizations. These organizational cultures (e.g., of the parent company) can then be compared to the national culture. Thus, the Hofstede dimensions could be used to contrast the culture of the larger U.S. company in our expatriate example, with that of the smaller Japanese acquisition. Instead of concentrating on one event at a time (e.g., the off-site retreat), the organizations could deal more directly with larger discrepancies in cultures or shared beliefs.

Aycan et al. (2000) collected data that confirm the presence and effect of country-specific cultures on organizational HR practices. They collected data from managers in 10 different countries and discovered, for example, that a paternalistic attitude among managers was much more likely to be found in India, Turkey, Pakistan, and China, where paternalism was valued. A paternalistic manager is one who provides "guidance, protection, nurturance, and care to the subordinate, and the role of the subordinate, in return, is to be loyal and deferent to the manager" (p. 197). Positive attitudes toward paternalism were much less likely to be found in Russia, Romania, the United States, Canada, Germany, and Israel. Similarly, Indian, Pakistani, Chinese, Turkish, and Russian managers were much more likely to consider loyalty to their communities as a desired value while Canadian and U.S. managers were much less likely to endorse it. Finally, they examined the concept of "fatalism" in various cultures. Fatalism was defined as the belief that whatever happens will happen and events are largely out of the control of the individual. Beliefs in fatalism were higher in India and Russia, and lower in most of the other eight countries. These various belief systems in turn affected the extent to which employees were exposed to job enrichment (job redesign), participation in decision making (leadership and motivation), and performance-contingent rewards (motivation and compensation).

The issue of multinational companies and culture is very complex because of the overlap between national cultures and organizational cultures. Nevertheless, we can be fairly certain that the insensitive multinational corporation—and more important, its employees—is more likely to encounter difficulties than one aware of and prepared to negotiate cultural differences.

SOCIALIZATION AND THE CONCEPT OF PERSON-ORGANIZATION (P-O) FIT

Organizational Socialization

Organizational fit is a key concept in organizational change. It is directed at improving the fit between an organization (or an idealized representation of that organization) and its employees by changing the nature of the organization. The premise of organizational change models is that people and organizations can be changed jointly through various interventions. Some of these interventions are aimed directly at changes in organizational structure or process with little more expected of the individual except technical or procedural learning. Other interventions expect considerably more of the employee in terms of changed beliefs, values, and attitudes, as well as increased commitment and motivation.

But the "change" in the match between the individual and the organization can come much earlier, at the point at which a new employee enters the organization. The process by which a new employee becomes aware of the values and procedures of the organization is called **socialization.** It starts at the recruiting stage, when the company provides information to the candidate about its values. It continues as the individual is evaluated, with the individual inferring characteristics of the organization based on the assessment procedures it uses. We have addressed the issue of the perceived fairness of screening and selection in Chapter 11. An applicant might turn down an offer of employment if he or she perceives the organizational culture implied by the selection process to be an unfair one. Worse, an applicant may accept a job in spite of perceived disagreements with an organization's culture. When a candidate is hired, socialization is present in the interactions between the newcomer and his or her manager, or in interactions with support departments such as HR or finance.

SOCIALIZATION

Process by which a new employee becomes aware of the values and procedures of an organization.

Recruitment as Socialization   The first stage at which socialization might occur is in recruitment and selection. Cable and his colleagues have studied the role of attraction and fit in the socialization process in some detail. Among other things, they have found that:

1. Applicants are attracted to organizations that have cultural characteristics compatible with the applicant's personality (Judge & Cable, 1997).
2. Organizations invest considerable effort in attracting and selecting applicants who appear to have values compatible with the culture of the organization (Cable & Judge, 1996, 1997; Cable & Parsons, 2001).

3. Organizations often attempt to lure attractive applicants by presenting favorable but inaccurate information about their culture, information intended to signal to the applicant a good fit (Cable, Aiman-Smith, Mulvey, & Edwards, 2000).

4. Interviewers make initial estimates of applicants with respect to the person-organization fit and make recommendations for hiring or further assessment based on those initial estimates (Cable & Judge, 1997).

5. Applicants are more interested in the fit between their own values and the culture of the recruiting organization than they are between their own demographic characteristics (e.g., age, gender, race) and the characteristics of the representatives of the organization (Cable & Judge, 1996).

Findings like these are compelling and important. They suggest that long before an individual is involved in an organizational change program or organizational development intervention, steps should be taken to assure a cultural-attitudinal match between that person and the organization.

Orientation as Socialization   Although the recruitment function of an organization can be considered as the start of the the socialization process, it is hardly the conclusion. When an individual joins the organization, additional formal and informal steps are taken to further the socialization and fit between the individual and the organization. Some formal steps include employee orientation through employee manuals, meetings with HR representatives to discuss benefits and conditions of employment, and meetings with line supervisors and managers to discuss duties, responsibilities, and expectations. Van Mannen and Schein (1979) defined organizational socialization as "the process by which an individual acquires the social knowledge and skills necessary to assume an organizational role"(p. 211). Recall our discussion in Chapter 3 about tacit knowledge. From that perspective, the socialization process is intended to develop that tacit knowledge base covering both technical and nontechnical aspects of the new organization and position.

Greenberg (2002) suggested that there are three stages of socialization. The first stage is the recruitment stage which we discussed earlier and Greenberg labeled "anticipatory socialization." But there are at least two subsequent stages: the encounter stage and the metamorphsis stage. These stages are presented graphically in Figure 14.4.

Realistic job previews (see Chapter 5) provide excellent opportunities for anticipatory socialization. Such previews lessen the possibility that the organization has been inaccurately

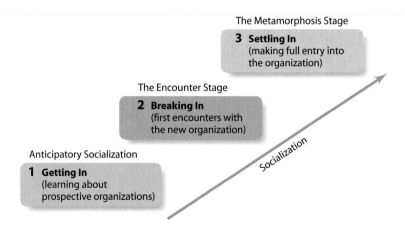

FIGURE 14.4 **The Three Stages of Socialization** Organizational socialization generally follows the three stages summarized here: *anticipatory socialization,* which involves getting in; the *encounter stage,* which involves breaking in; and the *metamorphosis stage,* which involves settling in. Source: Greenberg (2002).

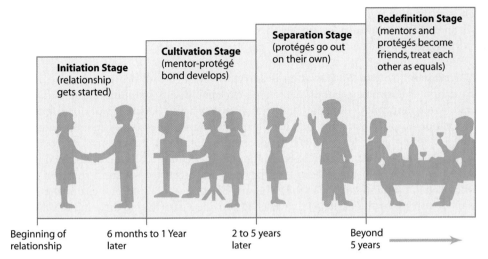

FIGURE 14.5

Mentoring: A Four-Stage Process
Relationships between mentors and their protégés tend to develop following the four stages summarized here.
SOURCE: Greenberg (2002).

described by a recruiter or inaccurately perceived by an applicant. In the encounter stage, new employees learn work procedures as well as the network of social relations in which the position is embedded. This means that the employee needs to know both the job and the people who populate the work group. Finally, in the metamorphosis stage, the individual is accepted as a fully functioning work group member. Often this metamorphosis is formal, as in the graduation from a training program or the successful completion of a probationary period. Equally often, however, the metamorphosis is more subtle, as is the case when someone is invited for a drink after work or to join a car pool.

One effective method for guiding the new employee through the socialization process is mentoring. Greenberg (2002) has suggested that like the broader concept of socialization, mentoring also proceeds in stages (see Figure 14.5). As you might expect, there is effective and ineffective mentoring. Some tips for effective mentoring are shown in Table 14.3.

TABLE 14.3   Ten Tips for Successful Mentoring

The long-term success of mentoring can be enhanced by adhering to the suggestions identified here. Both mentors and protégés should familiarize themselves with these guidelines before entering into a relationship.

Mentors should . . .

1. Be responsible *to* protégés, not *for* them.
2. Make the mentoring relationship fun and enjoyable.
3. Recognize that their involvement with their protégé extends beyond the workday.
4. Listen carefully to their protégés.
5. Openly acknowledge their failures as well as their successes.
6. Protect their protégés and expect their protégés to protect them.
7. Give their protégés not only directions but also options.
8. Recognize and encourage their protégés' small successes and accomplishments.
9. Encourage independent thinking among their protégés.
10. Focus not only on job skills but also on ethical values.

SOURCE: Greenberg (2002).

The socialization process requires effort, but effective socialization more than pays for itself in employee and work group well-being and stability, and in organizational productivity and commitment.

A Cautionary Note on Socialization Research Designs   Most of the work done on socialization of newcomers gathers data in waves, starting with attitudinal and cultural values of college students before they graduate, after they have been in the workforce for three to six months, and then after they have been in the workforce for 18 months (Bauer & Green, 1998; Cable & Parsons, 2001; Vandenberg & Self, 1993). Because many participants were either unavailable or failed to return questionnaires, the researchers explained in the description of their methodologies that they have only reported data on a subset of those who filled out a questionnaire. In the Cable and Parsons (2001) study, for example, slightly over 25 percent of the participants who had provided data during their initial stages of employment (i.e., six months after graduation) had left their organization by the time the third wave of data (i.e., 18 months after graduation) was gathered (Cable, 2002). Thus, the data analyzed pertained to those who remained at the firm 18 months after graduation: the survivors. For these individuals, a relationship was shown between the subjective feelings of fit expressed by the employees and various tactics used by the organization to accomplish this socialization. But we can speculate that those who did not share the values of the organization may have already departed, either through termination or resignation. It is possible, therefore, that the socialization was really just a final "polishing" of an already compatible employee (Schneider et al., 2002).

Socialization and Person-Organization (P-O) Fit Models   I-O psychology has a long history of supporting the notion that **person-job (P-J) fit**—the fit between individuals and the jobs they fill—is important both for the individual and for the organization. Vocational counseling was built on that premise, suggesting first that the fit between the intellectual demands of the job and the intelligence of the person would affect the physical and psychological well-being of the person, as well as his or her productivity (Fryer, 1931; Viteles, 1932). This was later broadened to include the match of interests and values of the person and the occupation which he or she chose (Holland, 1973, 1985; Super, 1973). It was widely accepted that unless there was a "fit" between the person and the job, as well as the person and the occupation, the result would be an unhappy worker and an unhappy organization. In the 1970s these notions were formalized in the model of work adjustment (Dawis & Lofquist, 1984). A good "fit" requires a match between not only the abilities of the person and demands of the job (satisfactoriness), but also the rewards desired by the individual and the rewards offered by the organization (satisfaction) (see Figure 14.6). In the last several decades, the notion of fit has evolved even further to include **person-organization (P-O) fit,** the fit between the person and the organization, not just the person and the job. In Chapter 15, which deals with stress and workplace health, we will discuss how P-O fit and P-J fit are related to the experience of stress, job dissatisfaction, commitment, and turnover.

Schneider's Attraction-Selection-Attrition (ASA) Model: The Dark Side of Socialization
Schneider (1987) proposed that organizations and individuals go through a process of jointly assessing probable fit based primarily on personality characteristics. His view of organizations was that "people make the place," rather than the organization (i.e., place) molding or shaping the people. He called his model the **attraction-selection-attrition (ASA) model;** simply put, organizations attempt to attract particular types of people. These types have personalities most like those of the founder or highest leaders of the organization. This is accomplished first through recruiting efforts: the attraction phase.

PERSON-JOB (P-J) FIT

Extent to which the skills, abilities, and interests of an individual are compatible with the demands of the job.

PERSON-ORGANIZATION (P-O) FIT

An employee feels that his or her values are consistent with the values held by the organization.

ATTRACTION-SELECTION-ATTRITION (ASA) MODEL

Proposes that organizations and individuals undergo a process of jointly assessing probable fit based primarily on personality characteristics; through attraction, selection, and attrition, the goal is to make the workforce homogeneous with respect to personality characteristics.

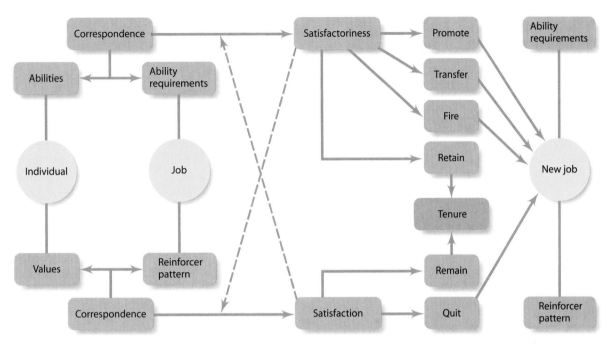

FIGURE 14.6 Prediction of Work Adjustment SOURCE: Dawis & Lofquist (1984).

After a promising candidate has been attracted and assumes the status of an applicant, the selection phase of the model begins. Through various assessment and selection mechanisms (e.g., testing, interviews, recommendations), offers are made to those candidates who still look promising.

But mistakes can be made, and individuals who have personalities unlike those of the founder or senior executives may still be hired. That is when the attrition phase kicks in. As the poor fit becomes obvious, the new employee, the organization, or both, engage in actions that result in the individual leaving. Some of these actions are direct: The employee simply resigns to take another job or the organization terminates the individual. Others are indirect: The employee may be marginalized and given trivial tasks, or left out of important meetings or excluded from key teams, until he or she gets the message and leaves. Or the individual may be given increasingly difficult and conflicting tasks until his or her performance appears below average.

Recall the discussion in Chapter 12 of leader-member exchange (LMX) theory, which posits that leaders inadvertently, or through some unintentional process of which they are unaware, favor one group of employees (the "in-group") over another group (the "out-group"). The attrition phase of Schneider's theory suggests there may be nothing inadvertent or unconscious about the creation of an out-group, in part because the manager of the new hire has been attracted and selected to fit the personality of his or her manager. Thus, it is a simple matter for this manager to recognize a poor fit between a new employee and the organization's leadership, and to take actions to eliminate the individual from the organization. One of these actions is treating the new employee as an out-group member. These are the attraction-selection errors addressed in the attrition phase. The flow chart in Figure 14.7 presents an idealized version of the ASA model. As you can see, the attraction, selection, and attrition process, by virtue of actions taken by the employer and by the applicant or employee, works to make the final workforce homogeneous with respect to personality characteristics. Schneider, Smith, Taylor, and

FIGURE 14.7

Simplified Version of ASA Model

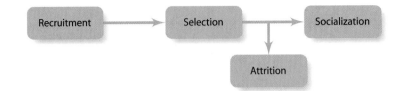

Fleenor (1998) presented preliminary data that seems to support this prediction of homogeneity.

Schneider's model is intuitively appealing and has attracted a good deal of attention and research (Anderson & Ostroff, 1997). Schneider, Goldstein, and Smith (1995) reviewed direct and indirect support for the model. There are still many conditions and variables to work out before the model is complete, but it presents clear implications even in its incomplete state. The most dramatic of these implications is that most attempts to "change the culture" of an organization are more likely to be accomplished by replacing people rather than by changing people in the organization. In many "turnaround" scenarios, a new CEO is brought in with a new vision. The CEO brings many upper level managers from his or her old company. They introduce the new culture, which was actually the culture they brought with them from their previous organization. In response, some people leave the organization, while others stay and adapt to the new culture. In some settings, the new CEO is explicit about introducing a new culture. For example, Los Angeles chose a new police chief to address a decade of scandal and ineffectiveness. The new chief, William Bratton, announced:

> This is an underperforming department. They know it. If you aren't prepared to embrace it (an agreement between the U.S. Department of Justice and the LAPD), put your retirement papers in, because you won't be part of my command staff driving change in this department. The department needs to clearly understand there's a new sheriff in town (Associated Press, 2002).

It might be argued that if Schneider's model correctly describes how organizations change, then the organization should take explicit steps to match the personalities of new hires to the personality of the leader or founder. While this might be effective in the short term, it could be less effective in the long run since the organization would have selected out any diversity in ways of thinking, values, attitudes, and maybe even abilities and skills. What is required is a balanced approach with a diversity in personalities among senior leaders, allowing for diversity among followers. In other words, a "perfect" match between the values and personality of employees and senior leaders may lead to a more cohesive workplace, but a less vibrant one. Schneider has not suggested *how* an organization should be staffed. Instead, he has described a process that commonly influences staffing. Schneider's model is exciting and presents an innovation over the traditional way of looking at the concept of organizational change and development as well as socialization.

SOCIALIZATION FROM THE INTERNATIONAL PERSPECTIVE

Like many other topics covered in this text, socialization research is heavily dominated by American and western European researchers (Bauer & Taylor, 2001). Nevertheless, it is likely that cultural influences weigh heavily on the socialization process. To return to Hofstede's model, one might expect the whole notion of socialization to be more prominent in collectivist rather than individualist cultures. Similarly, it is likely that socialization in masculine cultures would emphasize technical performance and task-related knowledge in contrast to a feminine culture where knowledge of group and interpersonal interactions would assume greater importance. One might also expect a very different—and formal—role for the manager in socialization in a high power distance culture and a less formal and more interactive role in low power distance cultures. These issues become particularly important for expatriate employees who may have become accustomed to one type of socialization process in their home culture and encounter a very different one in the host country. In such circumstances, the expatriate is particularly vulnerable to misinterpretations of the socialization process. For example, an expatriate from a low power distance culture might interpret the aloofness of a new manager as an indication of disapproval or dislike rather than a simple expression of a dominant culture. This places increased emphasis on an understanding of cultural diversity on both the host manager and the expatriate employee. For the expatriate experience, the roots of success or failure are closely entwined with the socialization process (Bauer & Taylor, 2001)

MODULE 14.2 SUMMARY

- Organizations are social entities. As such, they exhibit the characteristics of any social entity, including a climate, a culture, and role expectations. These characteristics can work to support the organization's goals or to hinder them.

- The emerging model of climate is a structural concept that can be applied to any organization (or division, department, or even work group). Recently, I-O psychologists have suggested that multiple climates, defined by the goals of various work groups, can exist within any organization.

- Culture and climate are two different, yet overlapping concepts. Climate is about the context in which action occurs, and culture is about the meaning that is intended by and inferred from those actions.

- A relevant issue for both climate and culture is the extent to which members of the organization share a perception (climate) or a value/belief pattern (culture). This sharing has been called climate/culture strength. Studies in this area suggest that the extent of agreement among group members may be very important in translating perceptions and values into actions and behaviors.

- The process by which a new employee becomes aware of the values and procedures of the organization is called socialization. It starts at the recruiting stage, when the company informs the candidate about its values. It continues as the individual is evaluated, with the individual inferring characteristics of the organization based on the assessment procedures it uses.

- I-O psychology has long supported the notion that person-job fit is important for both the individual and the organization. In the last several decades, the notion of fit has evolved even further to include the fit between the person and the organization.

- Schneider proposed that organizations and individuals go through a process of jointly assessing fit by means of a model he called attraction-selection-attrition. His view of organizations is that "people make the place" rather than the organization molding or shaping the people.

KEY TERMS

autocratic climate

democratic climate

climate

culture

climate/culture strength

ethnocentrism

polycentrism

regiocentrism

geocentrism

socialization

person-job (P-J) fit

person-organization (P-O) fit

attraction-selection-attrition
   (ASA) model

CRITICAL THINKING EXERCISES

14.3 Recall an organization for which you worked that left you feeling good. Then recall one that left you feeling bad. Contrast these two organizations using the four factors of climate identified by James and McIntyre:

1. Role stress and lack of harmony.
2. Job challenge and autonomy.
3. Leadership facilitation and support.
4. Work group cooperation, friendliness, and warmth.

After making this analysis, what can you conclude about the effect of climate on your work experience?

14.4 Schneider's ASA model suggests that efforts of organizational change are likely to be difficult. Organizational members whose values are not compatible with those of senior management may eventually leave the organization. What steps might an organization take, accepting the propositions of Schneider's model, to enhance Person-Organization fit?

ORGANIZATIONAL DEVELOPMENT AND CHANGE

rganizational development (commonly referred to as simply OD) and organizational change are closely related topics. Organizational change is a process, a goal, or both. OD is a toolbox of various methods for affecting that change. There is a great deal more theory and substance to the concept of organizational change than to the techniques of OD. Indeed, OD might be thought of more as a consulting venue for organizational psychologists than a substantive area. Many texts describe OD techniques in detail, so we will discuss the area of organizational change in some detail and spend less time on OD.

ORGANIZATIONAL CHANGE

Organizational change theory has used the same anchor for over 50 years. Kurt Lewin (1951) proposed the unfreeze-change-refreeze model, involving three stages in the process of changing an organization.

1. **Unfreezing,** in which individuals become aware of values and beliefs they hold.
2. **Changing,** in which individuals adopt new values, beliefs, and attitudes.
3. **Refreezing,** which is the stabilization of the new attitudes and values.

Various OD techniques are directed at facilitating one or more of those stages. Lewin believed that one could not really understand an organization until one tried to change it (Schein, 1996). In the early decades of the process of organizational change, this belief often led organizations to initiate a change program for the purpose of understanding the nature of their organization. Today, most organizational change initiatives are driven by a problem of some kind, rather than by a need for organizational self-examination—for example, a merger or acquisition is not going well, there is a loss of market share or consumer confidence, or a new competitor threatens. As a result, most people now think of organizational change as event-driven, prompted by an external circumstance that requires a revolution or transformation in culture, process, or vision.

Weick and Quinn (1999) acknowledged that some events require immediate attention (and abrupt change), but they are pessimistic about the success of attempts at such "episodic" change. Instead, they have suggested that the most successful program of change is likely to be one of continuous rather than episodic change. They make a compelling argument, and we will base our discussion of the concept of change on their thoughts.

Episodic Change

Episodic change can be characterized as infrequent, discontinuous, and intentional. We often hear that an organization has embarked on a plan to "reinvent" itself. This would be

SOURCE: DILBERT Reprinted by Permission of United Feature Syndicate, Inc.

an intentional plan to replace what they have with something new. Like a military campaign, the change would be launched with fanfare, have a planned end time, and involve clearly articulated pathways to change, with senior leaders disseminating information about the process and desired end state.

Weick and Quinn described the type of organization that most commonly embraces episodic change as follows:

- Tight interconnections between subunits.
- Efficiency as a core value.
- Concern with adapting to current events in the environment.
- Strong organizational cultures and subcultures.
- Involved more in imitation than innovation as a motivation for change.

Episodic change is embraced because it is focused, time urgent, and minimizes the feeling of uncertainty. Organizations that choose the episodic model aspire to a state of equilibrium. When it is reached, they tighten connections between departments even further, establish procedures that will ensure stability, and ignore signals in the environment that suggest further change and adaptation. The result is decreased effectiveness, increasing pressures for change, and entry into the next "revolutionary" period.

Beginning in the 1980s, many organizations found themselves struggling to remain profitable in a changing economy. As a result, they tried to increase their quality and quantity of production, diversify their product line, and introduce innovations to their production process—with fewer people. A typical organization would announce a one-time layoff that would be expected to "solve" the problem. The layoff required a transformation (a revolution) of structure and process. Once the transformation was under way, the goal was to get the layoff "over with" and return to a state of equilibrium as quickly as possible. However, most organizations found that increased competition, reduced confidence of consumers and investors, and other challenges made a new revolution necessary in the next fiscal year. So they embarked on another "episodic" change.

Episodic change is usually slow because it is so large in scope. In addition, it is seldom completed before another revolution is required, which organizations tend to shy away from until things get "bad." Most employees who have been through an episodic change remember it vividly because it was very stressful and disruptive. Such changes tend to be centered on, and driven by, upper levels of the organization because they are strategic and have an end state as a goal. This means that the organization most likely to adopt episodic change is in a state of inertia, sometimes just catching its organizational breath from the last episodic change. For this type of change, Lewin's basic unfreeze-change-refreeze process makes some sense. Ironically, Miller (1993, 1994) suggested that inertia is the unintended consequence of success. Weick and Quinn (1999) summarized Miller's research:

> Successful organizations discard practices, people, and structures regarded as peripheral to success and grow more inattentive to signals that suggest the need for change, more insular and sluggish in adaptation, and more immoderate in their processes, tending toward extremes of risk taking or conservatism. These changes simplify the organization, sacrifice adaptability, and increase inertia (p. 369).

In spite of the unattractiveness of this picture, many organizations continue to think of change in revolutionary/transformational/episodic ways. They think of "transforming" the old organization into a new one. But the old organization does not *become* the new organization, it is *replaced by* it (Ford & Ford, 1994). However, this replacement goal is seldom successful since it results in either-or thinking (Beer, Eisenstat, & Spector, 1990). As Weick and Quinn (1999) pointed out, the either-or logic maintains that the only way to circumvent "A" (the "bad" form of organization) is to replace it with the opposite, or "not-A." In fact, both A and not-A might be equally problematic. The following example illustrates what happens when authoritarian decision making is replaced with an edict that requires every decision to be made at a lower level of the organization.

> [T]his change is simple authoritarian decision-abdication, which means that authoritarian control from the top persists. As lower level managers try harder to guess what the right decisions are (i.e., those decisions that top management would have made), and err in doing so, the mandate is reaffirmed more forcefully, which worsens performance even more and creates a vicious circle. What was really intended was the creation of expectations of individual autonomy that allowed decisions to be made at the level where the expertise and information were lodged (Weick & Quinn, 1999, p. 370).

Weick and Quinn acknowledged that episodic change is likely to remain a popular choice among organizations as a model for change. But if episodic change is the model, some modifications of common OD techniques are needed (see Table 14.4).

Continuous Change

Unlike episodic change, **continuous change** describes a process that is "ongoing, evolving, and cumulative." It is much less likely to be intentional and more likely to be improvised.

CONTINUOUS CHANGE

Ongoing, evolving, and cumulative organizational change characterized by small, continuous adjustments, created simultaneously across units, that add up to substantial change.

TABLE 14.4	Suggested Modifications of Common OD Techniques If Episodic Change Is the Model
LESS EMPHASIS ON:	**MORE EMPHASIS ON:**
Closely held internal data generation	Data gathered from the environment and shared widely
Slow downward communication	Rapid data analysis to support rapid decision making
Individual unit learning	Learning about the whole organization
Direction from senior management	Shared direction including senior managers and other levels of the organization
Consultant as expert	Client as expert
Leaders who argue well	Leaders who speak differently

SOURCE: Based on Rorty (1989).

It is characterized as "small continuous adjustments, created simultaneously across units, [that] cumulate and create substantial change" (Weick & Quinn, 1999, p. 375).

Organizations most likely to be engaged in continuous change attach authority to tasks rather than to positions, and shift that authority as tasks change. In such organizations, job descriptions are in a continuous state of flux, and the organization accepts change as a constant (Weick & Quinn, 1999; Wheatley, 1992). Another characteristic of the continuous change environment is the short time gap between the identification of a needed change and the execution of that change (Moorman & Miner, 1998). Another feature of the continuous change model is that instead of altering a particular action on the part of one or more individuals, the range of skills and knowledge is altered.

Because continuous change appears to result in smaller changes than the more revolutionary episodic change model, it is tempting to conclude that continuous changes are less important or have less impact. But the cumulative effect of these changes produces results. As Weick and Quinn pointed out, successful revolutionary or episodic changes seldom acknowledge the earlier, smaller changes that made the revolution possible. Simply put, this means that lurking behind most successful episodic changes is a supporting cast of earlier and smaller continuous changes.

Lewin's (1951) unfreeze-change-refreeze model does not hold up well for the process of continuous change. Instead, the model needs to be freeze-rebalance-unfreeze, almost the opposite of the episodic sequence. Weick and Quinn employed the metaphor of Newtonian physics to contrast episodic and continuous change. Bodies in motion tend to remain in motion. Thus, the first step in the continuous change model is freezing to stop the motion—to stop changing and examine patterns of change to understand what is happening (Argyris, 1990; Weick & Quinn, 1999). The **rebalance** phase reframes what has happened and produces a cognitive framework that gives change deeper meaning. In the unfreezing phase, the organization goes back into the continuous change mode, but now with a revised cognitive architecture with which to make sense of what is going on and thus provide enhanced guidance for additional change. For example, a software company might hold a weekend retreat to review all of the product and process changes that had occurred in the last calendar year. As part of this review, they would conduct a "lessons learned" session that distinguishes between changes that had added value to the organization and those that had not. As a result, they would formally acknowledge and incorporate certain changes and eliminate others. They would then go back to the workplace with an altered organizational architecture, and dive back into the continuous change process.

A question commonly asked is whether change is managed or led (Kotter, 1995). Using the episodic/continuous distinction, it appears that episodic change is most commonly managed, while continuous change is most commonly led. When we manage change, we tell people what to do. When we lead change, we show people what to do and how to be. Weick and Quinn (1999) concluded that most large bureaucracies are like icebergs; they have rigid structures that change slowly, if ever, on their own. They need to be unfrozen, changed, and refrozen. But embedded within those bureaucracies are pockets of innovation. The challenge for the organization stuck in episodic change is to uncover these pockets and use them as a model to spread a more continuous culture through the organization. One way to do this would simply be to look for the best examples of self-initiated change among the organization's various work groups and departments—groups that are successful at "thinking out of the box"—and put them in the spotlight.

Weick and Quinn suggested that effective change is neither an on-again, off-again phenomenon, nor is it very closely related to planning. They urged researchers and practitioners to concentrate on "changing" rather than "change." Although they did not address the requisite attributes of the people who would engage in this continuous change, it seems clear that certain personality characteristics such as flexibility, willingness to take risks, and a tolerance for ambiguity would be central to the process. Judge, Thoreson, Pucik, and Welbourne (1999), conducting research with six different organizations headquartered on

REBALANCE

Stage in the freeze-rebalance-unfreeze continuous change process intended to reframe what has happened and produce a cognitive framework that gives change deeper meaning.

four different continents, discovered that an individual with a personality characterized by a positive self-concept and a willingness to tolerate risk was much better able to cope with organizational change. Although they acknowledged that an organization made up entirely of individuals willing to tolerate risk might be in a precarious position, the positive self-concept personality has also been associated with higher levels of performance.

In addition to the review article by Weick and Quinn, other excellent reviews of organizational change have been written by Hartley (2002), Noer (1999), Howard et al. (1991), Waclawski and Church (2002), Porras and Silvers (1991), and Beer and Walton (1987).

Resistance to Change

The barriers to organizational change are substantial and reside in both individuals and organizations. From the perspective of the individual, these barriers would include (Greenberg, 2002):

- Economic fear: Change may threaten job security.
- Fear of the unknown: having to make changes in established patterns of organizational and task behavior.
- Fear of altered social relationships: the possibility of changed co-workers.

Organizational barriers are equally formidable and would include:

- Structural inertia: Jobs are created with stability in mind; thus it takes considerable effort to change job descriptions, duties, reporting relationships, and so forth.
- Work group inertia: Strong norms exist for performing jobs in certain ways. These norms are often codified in written work procedures and labor management agreements.
- Threats to power balance: If the centrality of certain work units changes, power over scarce resources is likely to shift as well.
- Prior unsuccessful change efforts: Organizations that have experienced past failures at change will encounter greater caution among organizational members with respect to new initiatives for change.

So, with all of these barriers, is it possible to overcome resistance to change? The answer is yes, but it requires some planning. Nadler (1987) suggested the following steps:

1. Gain the support of the most powerful individuals in the organization.
2. Educate the workforce with an eye toward reducing their individual fears.
3. Get employees meaningfully involved in the change initiative.
4. Provide feedback for change efforts and rewards for successful change at regular intervals.
5. After a successful change, shift the focus from episodic to continual change, thus reducing future barriers to change.

Given the barriers to change as well as the steps necessary to reduce those barriers, it is not surprising that most attempts at change fail. This is less a reason to avoid change than a blueprint for how to be one of the organizations successful at it.

EXAMPLES OF LARGE-SCALE ORGANIZATIONAL CHANGE INITIATIVES

Explicit and implicit theories of organization are the foundation for many attempts at organizational change and development. Although these attempts at change are often viewed as purposefully targeted and directed to only one aspect of the organization, they carry with them some assumptions about "preferred" organizational structure or process. As a result, these interventions may be packaged and presented as motivational interventions. But the underlying assumption is that a change in some aspect of the organization will result in enhanced employee motivation.

Below we will present examples of several different development and change initiatives that have been introduced in the past few decades. These initiatives are intended to replace one form of organization considered ineffective with a more effective one.

Management By Objectives (MBO)

MANAGEMENT BY OBJECTIVES (MBO)

A concept to define and measure employee performance; proposed a plan to direct the efforts of workers and managers through objectives and methods to meet performance objectives.

The **management by objectives (MBO)** concept was introduced in the mid-1950s and served as a precursor to what we now refer to as goal-setting theory (Drucker, 1954; McGregor, 1960). MBO was intended to be a more objective way of defining and measuring employee performance. One way of directing the efforts of workers and managers is to have them develop a plan that includes performance objectives and methods to meet those objectives. This plan becomes the architecture for discussions between managers and subordinates. If the plan is effective, the organization will thrive and the workers and managers will be satisfied. A major shortcoming of this method of organizing work was that there might have been hundreds or even thousands of worker-manager plans, each requiring attention and effort, and not necessarily integrated into a "master plan." Thus, an attempt to organize at the lower, individual levels served to increase the possibility of disorganization at higher levels. MBO was the precursor to the team-based quality improvement programs such as quality circles which we discussed in Chapter 13 (Gibson & Tesone, 2001).

Matrix Organizations

MATRIX ORGANIZATION

Individuals have dual reporting relationships: reporting to a project (product) manager and to a home department (functional) manager.

Logically, the task of producing a good or a service can be divided into traditional departments such as purchasing, receiving, materials handling, production, quality control, and shipping. While this may appear to be efficient from the administrative perspective, it is a luxury that can seldom be afforded by small- to medium-sized organizations where individuals often must fill multiple roles. This is particularly true when the focus of the work is a project (e.g., developing or producing an improved model of the product, or offering a new customer service such as online checking of order status). As a result, many organizations form project teams with a life expectancy tied to the project timeline. When the project has been completed, team members return to their "home" departments. This has been called a **matrix organization** (Davis & Lawrence, 1977, 1978). In a matrix organization, individuals have dual reporting relationships: They report to a project (product) manager and to a home department (functional) manager. This type of organization can be very effective in making the most of limited human resources (see Figure 14.8). Because of the concentrated nature of project work, communication is often enhanced in matrix arrangements (Greenberg, 2002). But unless the efforts of the functional and project leaders are integrated, problems will arise. On the one hand, a condition of ambiguity, disorganization, or even anarchy might arise because there is no clear leader; on the other hand, a conflict or power struggle might emerge between product and functional leaders.

Total Quality Management (TQM)

TOTAL QUALITY MANAGEMENT (TQM)

A unique way of organizing productive effort by emphasizing team-based behavior directed toward improving quality and meeting customer demands.

W. E. Deming (1986) challenged modern organizations to focus on the customer as an indicator of organizational effectiveness and introduced the concept of total quality management to meet that challenge. **Total quality management (TQM)** is a "cooperative form of doing business that relies on the talents and capabilities of both labor and management to continually improve quality and productivity using work teams" (Jablonski, 1991). Rather than concentrating on the volume of production, TQM focuses on quality and customer demands and expectations. Note the phrase "using work teams" in the definition

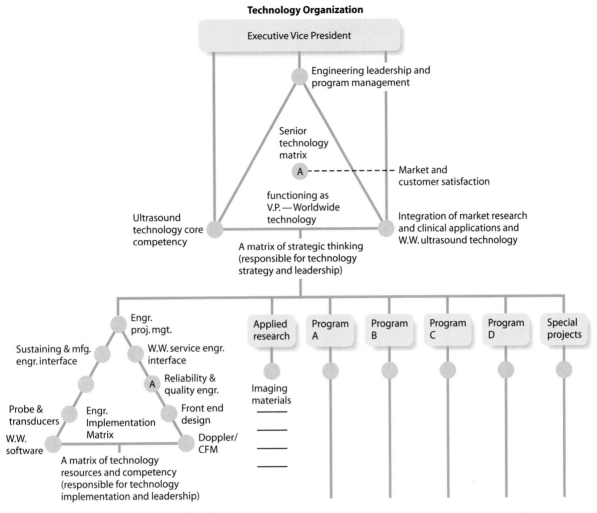

Technology Organization

FIGURE 14.8 Matrix Organization Source: Gene Larson, Advanced Technology Laboratories.

above. The emphasis is on creating an environment that will "support innovation, creativity, and risk taking to meet customer demands [using] participative problem solving, involving managers, employees, and customers" (Noe, Hollenbeck, Gerhart, & Wright, 2000). To achieve the ideal proposed by TQM, an organization must have certain properties. Blackburn and Rosen (1993) contrasted the properties of organizations that have successfully implemented a TQM model with organizations that have been less successful (see Table 14.5). The growing acceptance of the centrality of the "quality" concept is recognized by a series of annual awards created in 1987 during the Reagan administration, known as the Malcolm Baldrige National Quality Awards, which are bestowed on organizations that have made substantial improvements in quality.

As was the case with the other organizational initiatives, the TQM approach proposes a unique way to organize productive effort by emphasizing team-based behavior directed toward improving quality. It should come as no surprise that TQM systems are more easily implemented in collective rather than individualistic cultures. Cooney and Sohal (2003) have completed a detailed review of the effect of TQM on work design and redesign, with a particular emphasis on the probable consequences—positive and negative—for the workers in such a system. In theory, for example, the heavy emphasis on worker participation

TABLE 14.5	Differences Between Traditional & TQM Model from an HR Perspective	
HUMAN RESOURCE MANAGEMENT CHARACTERISTICS	**TRADITIONAL MODEL**	**TOTAL QUALITY MODEL**
Communications	Top-down	Top-down Horizontal, lateral Multidirectional
Voice and involvement	Employment at will Suggestion systems	Due process Quality circles Attitude surveys
Job design	Efficiency Productivity Standard procedures Narrow span of control Specific job descriptions	Quality Customization Innovation Wide span of control Autonomous work teams Empowerment
Training	Job-related skills Functional, technical	Broad range of skills Cross-functional Diagnostic, problem solving
Performance measurement and evaluation	Productivity Individual goals Supervisory review Emphasize financial performance	Productivity and quality Team goals Customer, peer, and supervisory review Emphasize quality and service
Rewards	Competition for individual merit increases and benefits	Team and group-based rewards Financial rewards, financial and nonfinancial recognition
Health and safety	Treat problems	Prevent problems Safety programs Wellness programs Employee assistance programs
Selection and promotion	Selection by manager	Selection by peers
Career development	Narrow jobs skills Promotion based on individual accomplishment Linear career path	Problem-solving skills Promotion based on group facilitation Horizontal career path

Source: Blackburn & Rosen (1993).

should enhance the satisfaction, motivation, and commitment of employees. In practice, however, the "decision" opportunities are really just elaborate opportunities for suggesting improvements, with no real opportunity for making decisions. As a result, employees become disenchanted with the promise of participation.

Six Sigma Systems

In 1986 the electronics giant Motorola was having quality problems. The CEO at the time formed a project group whose mission was to reduce the defect rate to less than 3.4 defects per 1 million opportunities. The statistical symbol for a standard deviation (the statistic we reviewed in Chapter 2) is the Greek letter sigma σ. A defect rate of 3.4 per million equates to more than six standard deviations from the number of units or products generated or transactions completed, thus the label **Six Sigma.** Companies that adopt Six Sigma systems train their employees and managers in methods of statistical analysis, project management, and design and problem solving (Barney, 2002). Managers who have mastered the various statistical and procedural aspects of Six Sigma management are known as "black belts" and are the tutors for less advanced managers who are known as "green belts."

Although Six Sigma systems were initially developed to monitor quantifiable defect rates, the philosophy has expanded to encompass the use of scientific and statistical methods to develop and test alternative approaches not only for production, but also for service and process outcomes. Whatever the "unit" of effort is—a product, customer invoice, statement in a computer program, response to a customer complaint—the number of defects can be calculated and compared to the total number of units. In addition to demanding near perfection from employees, Six Sigma requirements are often imposed on suppliers and subcontractors. The Six Sigma philosophy has clear implications for the way that workers and managers interact. Since the workers are closest to the problems and issues of quality, managers are asked to give more authority, power, and responsibility to those workers (Velocci, 1998). Most organizations that have adopted Six Sigma systems claim to see enhanced profitability because of the dual contributions of lower rejection and rework rates, and lower production costs that result from "doing it right the first time." Like TQM methods, Six Sigma systems emphasize the value of making changes before defects or errors occur rather than depending on postproduction or process inspections to uncover defects. As is the case with the power transfer from manager to employee, Six Sigma systems also require a substantial shift in power from senior-level executives to lower-level managers. There has been no serious evaluation research on Six Sigma programs; most articles are written like testimonials. Nevertheless, these programs represent dramatic organizational interventions.

Lean Production Manufacturing

In the 1980s Japanese auto manufacturers made significant inroads in virtually every Western market. It appeared that the Japanese cars were of higher quality, were priced more competitively, and were more readily available than their American and European counterparts. As a result, Japanese methods of production came under close inspection and were widely imitated. In recent years the "Japanese" method has been called **lean production.** Key to this method is the reduction of waste in every form: overproduction, lengthy waiting times for materials, excessive transportation costs, unnecessary stock, and defective product that must be reworked or scrapped. Central to the reduction of this waste is a process known as **just-in-time (JIT) production,** which depends on the detailed tracking of materials and production so that the materials and human resources necessary for production arrive just in time (Ohno, 1988).

One of the interesting implications of the lean production system was that for JIT to be successful, both suppliers and customers were drawn into the organizational circle. Customers were expected to provide reliable scheduling information while suppliers were expected to deliver high-quality materials in a reliable and timely fashion (Delbridge, 2003). In addition, the lean production system depended upon a minimum workforce with little or no unexcused absenteeism. For example, the U.S. plants operated by the Honda Motor Company expect no less than 98 percent attendance from every employee (although sick days are not counted as unexcused absences). From a psychological perspective, the lean

SIX SIGMA SYSTEMS

Approach to quality management providing training for employees and managers in statistical analysis, project management, and problem-solving methods to reduce the defect rate of products.

LEAN PRODUCTION

Method that focuses on reducing waste in every form, including overproduction, lengthy waiting times for materials, excessive transportation costs, unnecessary stock, and defective products.

JUST-IN-TIME (JIT) PRODUCTION

System that depends on the detailed tracking of materials and production so that the materials and human resources necessary for production arrive just in time; central to the reduction of waste in lean production processes.

"Lean production" depends on continual data analysis and behavior change.

organization depended on trust—trust that suppliers would provide timely high-quality material, trust that employees would be where they were supposed to be when they were supposed to be, and trust that customers would communicate in a timely and accurate manner.

Lean manufacturing also depends on the elimination of defects and waste in a manner similar to TQM. This is accomplished by urging (and sometimes requiring) production workers to be actively engaged in procedures to identify process improvements. Because the lean organization has a very narrow safety net, various disruptions (e.g., organized resistance by workers, an unreliable supplier, increased absenteeism or turnover) can place substantial stress on the system and its people. In addition, because priorities may change rapidly based on customer needs and market changes, many, if not all, workers are expected to be multiskilled so that they can switch activities and minimize wasted time (Delbridge, 2003).Without high levels of worker commitment and loyalty, lean organizations are likely to fail. Thurley (1982) suggested that for lean production methods to be successful, the following personnel mechanisms must provide support:

- Performance appraisal
- Motivation
- Self-appraisal and feedback
- Bonuses on the organizational and group/team level
- Job rotation
- Training and self-education
- Organizational redesign

That is a daunting list of supporting mechanisms and it paints a very demanding picture for the worker. Some observers have criticized lean manufacturing for making "workers feel obliged to contribute to the performance of the organization and to identify with its competitive success" (Delbridge, 2003). Delbridge and Turnbull (1992) went so far as to propose that any success that lean manufacturing enjoys is because "teamwork represents management by compliance, quality consciousness results in management through blame, and flexibility leads to management by stress" (Delbridge, 2003, p. 39). It is interesting to consider lean manufacturing in light of the concept of contextual performance that we described in Chapter 5 (Borman & Motowidlo, 1993). You will recall that contextual performance was distinguished from task performance and was characterized by behaviors such as helping co-workers, devoting extra effort to tasks, and volunteering to carry out tasks not formally assigned. The essence of contextual performance is that it is *voluntary;* the individual worker goes beyond what is expected. In many new organizational schemes such as TQM, Six Sigma, and lean production, manufacturing, contextual behaviors are now part of the job description, transforming the voluntary into the expected.

From the stress perspective, it is easy to see how the demands of these new schemes might easily overwhelm resources, particularly when the employee is at the mercy of suppliers, customers, and even fellow workers. Lean manufacturing, like the initiatives and philosophies described earlier, makes assumptions about the capacities and limitations of the humans who populate the organization. It assumes that, at best, this lean philosophy is compatible with how people construe work. At worst, it assumes that workers can tolerate a high degree of stress and pressure to perform. In either case, however, lean manufacturing requires a human resource management system distinct from one implied by MBO, TQM, or any of the other initiatives. Organizational initiatives such as lean manufacturing often require a radical redesign of HRM systems in order to be successful.

EMERGING COMMONALITIES AMONG ORGANIZATIONAL INTERVENTIONS

Most of the more recent organizational interventions such as TQM, Six Sigma programs, and lean production share some common elements.

1. *They are strategic.* They focus on the mission of the business and place great emphasis on client and customer satisfaction.
2. *They are team centered.* They concentrate on the efforts of individuals working in concert rather than single contributors.
3. *They are statistical.* They make use of sophisticated methods of data collection and analysis and feed those data back to members as a way of guiding behavior.
4. *They are participatory.* They engage members in the process of improving the quality of products.
5. *They are quality focused.* They concentrate on improving the quality of product and process as a way of increasing market share and decreasing costs.

As you can see, organizational interventions are more complex and far reaching than individual motivational interventions. However, interventions at the organizational level do include many of the components we find at the individual level, including goal setting and feedback, job enrichment and redesign, and participation in decision making. Recall from Chapter 9 the system called ProMES, which was developed by Pritchard (1990, 1992, 1995). Due to its reliance on multiple processes like statistical analysis, participation in strategic decision making, and goal setting, ProMES appears to be a promising way to bridge the gap between individual and organizational interventions.

ORGANIZATIONAL DEVELOPMENT

As we indicated earlier, **organizational development (OD)** is action oriented rather than theory or research oriented. As testimony to this point, the term "organizational development" has appeared in the article titles of the major industrial psychology journals less than 30 times in the past 50 years. Just as the practicing clinical psychologist is more interested in what works rather than in the research about what might work, so the OD specialist is most interested in techniques that actually work to help the client organization grow or change.

Based on our earlier discussion of organizational change, there might be three different settings for the effective use of OD. The first is in an episodic encounter in which an organization seeks to reinvent itself through revolution or imitation. The second circumstance would be in assisting an organization in its process of continuous change. The third scenario would be assisting an organization in evolving from an episodic to a continuously changing organization. The first scenario might require an unfreezing-change-refreezing process. The second would be appropriate for a freezing-rebalancing-unfreezing sequence. And the third might involve a hybrid sequence of unfreezing-change-rebalance.

A variety of techniques have been suggested for the unfreezing process. These include survey feedback, process consultation, team building, traditional management training,

ORGANIZATIONAL DEVELOPMENT (OD)

Action-oriented approach providing techniques that work to help a client organization grow or change.

and job redesign. Certainly many of the participative aspects of TQM, lean manufacturing, and Six Sigma systems aim at increasing the awareness of organization members about their current processes and behaviors. Increasing awareness is perhaps the most important goal of the OD process (Friedlander, 1980). The OD consultant might increase awareness by posing one or more of the following questions to individuals or groups:

- What methods does your department use to uncover production/service delivery problems?
- What methods does your department use to take full advantage of resources such as a technical department, design engineering department, or sales staff?
- What are the relationships within and between work groups that help or hinder problem solving?
- Will change occur more rapidly and effectively with autocratic or participative techniques?
- Does your current job or organizational design enhance or detract from the social environment of the department or work group?

Consultants often go to extremes to make their point. Consider what a group of office workers might gain from skydiving as part of an organizational development retreat.

Unlike the structured interview or situational judgment test, these questions have no correct answers, nor are there any standard circumstances or formats in which they might be posed. They are simply used as a device to bring to the surface consensus and disagreement among members of the organization about issues that may range from specific work procedures to the broader issue of organizational culture. The consultant will deem effective anything that gets the discussion and dialogue started; in many situations, multiple techniques might be used until something works. These techniques might include group discussions, individual presentations to the group, and surveys in which the respondents are asked to respond first in terms of the situation that currently exists, then in terms of the situation that *should* exist. The consultant might even suggest an Outward Bound type of experience and use that as the raw material to begin a discussion about communication, trust, or risk taking. Human Dynamics Associates (2002), a consulting firm in New Hampshire, offers a skydiving program called Jumpstart designed to foster group cohesion as well as improved morale and productivity. The program combines skydiving with seminars in team building. Although there have been no reports of the impact of this skydiving intervention on group cohesion or morale, we would be skeptical. Individual stress would be likely to cancel any positive effects. Further, the notion that people who are terrified together will feel closer or be happier as a result of that terror is questionable.

More frequently today than 10 years ago, OD consultants concentrate on the climate or subculture of a work group or department, or the culture of the organization. This trend is likely to continue since the opportunities for cultures to "clash" or impede change will only increase with the new multicultural, team-based, and technologically driven workplace.

Beckhard (1969) described OD as an approach that is planned and intentional, applied to an entire organization (which may be a department, division, or corporation), and managed from the top down. As Hartley (2002) pointed out, OD historically was directed toward issues of what an organization thought it should look like, emphasizing concepts such as trust, openness, and sharing without any direct consideration of context, power, or politics. Newer approaches take the more "real" view of organizational behavior as it plays out in the trenches. Nevertheless, whether the traditional or newer approach is taken, OD consultants tend to be used most frequently for effecting episodic change rather than continual change.

Examples of OD Techniques

Since organizational development is best thought of as a class of techniques, it is not surprising that there are literally hundreds of techniques. It would be inappropriate to catalog these techniques because the detail would be overwhelming and unnecessary for an introductory text, and because others have described the techniques in some detail. Two widely recognized and admired sources for reviewing OD techniques are Kanter, Stein and Jick (1992) and Cummings and Worley (2001). Nevertheless, it might be useful to present a sampling of the more commonly used techniques.

Survey Feedback   This consists of gathering data (e.g., climate perceptions) from different sources in the work organization (e.g., supervisors and incumbents) and using discrepancies in these perceptions as the background for discussion between the two groups in order to illuminate beliefs, values, and attitudes. It is hoped that through these initial discussions, barriers and facilitators to change can be identified. Another example is a survey that asks individuals to describe the climate or culture as they see it, and then as they think their senior leaders see it. Again, discrepancies would provide the foundation for discussion and change.

Team Building   Groups of individuals are given a specific task to accomplish or problem to solve. This may be done in the context of a training session or corporate retreat. In the process of solving the problem, team members are asked to observe the behavior of fellow team members and provide feedback to them about the effectiveness of that behavior. The goal of the exercise is to create a social environment that will permit an individual to try out and practice new behaviors or attitudes with relative impunity. In the early days of OD, the "problems" were artificial, such as deciding what supplies to take on a voyage to the dark side of the moon. More recently, local work-related problems have been chosen. Team building emphasizes issues such as task specification, role development, and consensus building.

Process Consultation   In this approach, an intact team or work group is asked to discuss a work-related issue while being observed by consultants or managers. They are then presented with feedback and asked to try alternative strategies for accomplishing their goal. The premise of process consultation is that behavior must change before attitudes. In many other OD interventions, it is assumed that attitudes must change before behavior.

We must sound a note of caution regarding organizational development. While there are many well-thought-out and systematic approaches to the practice of OD (Howard & Associates, 1991; Waclawski & Church, 2002), there are countless faddish and undocumented techniques as well, and just as many gullible organizations and managers willing to endorse these fads. In a book titled *The Witch Doctors,* Micklethwait and Wooldridge (1996) cynically observed that "the reason American businessmen talk about gurus is because they can't spell the word charlatan" (quoted in Weick & Quinn, 1999). This may be one reason why so many episodic change initiatives fail. The OD technique might have been one of the "fads" and not based on research, theory, or even accumulated experience. This may help account for the fact that Binney (1992) estimated that fewer than 30 percent of attempts to effect change through OD techniques are successful.

MODULE 14.3 SUMMARY

- Organizational Development (OD) and organizational change are closely related topics. Organizational change is a process, a goal, or both. OD is a toolbox of various methods for affecting that change.

- The theory of organizational change is strongly influenced by Lewin's three-stage process: unfreezing, changing, and refreezing. Various OD techniques are directed at facilitating one or more of those stages.

- Some organizational events seem to require immediate attention and abrupt change, but the success of such "episodic" change is questionable. Instead, the most successful program of change is likely to be one of continuous change, a process that is ongoing and evolving.

- The barriers to organizational change are substantial and reside in both individuals and organizations. Nevertheless, careful advance planning can overcome resistance to change.

- Examples of organizational development and change initiatives introduced in the past few decades include management by objectives (MBO), matrix organizations, total quality management (TQM), Six Sigma systems, and lean production. These initiatives are intended to replace an ineffective form of organization with a more effective one.

- Organizational development (OD) is action oriented rather than theory or research oriented. Some of the more commonly used OD techniques include survey feedback, team building, and process consultation.

KEY TERMS

unfreezing
changing
refreezing
episodic change
continuous change

rebalance
management by objectives (MBO)
matrix organization
total quality management (TQM)

Six Sigma systems
lean production
just-in-time (JIT) production
organizational development (OD)

CRITICAL THINKING EXERCISES

14.5 In the fall of 2002, there was a contract dispute between the longshoreman's union and the dock owners in California regarding wages. In the early stages of the dispute, the dock owners used a lockout to prevent the longshoremen from working. When the longshoremen were allowed to work, they proceeded at a much slower pace than they had before. How would these actions affect companies that have adopted lean production methods?

14.6 Would your university be better suited to episodic or continuous change? Why?

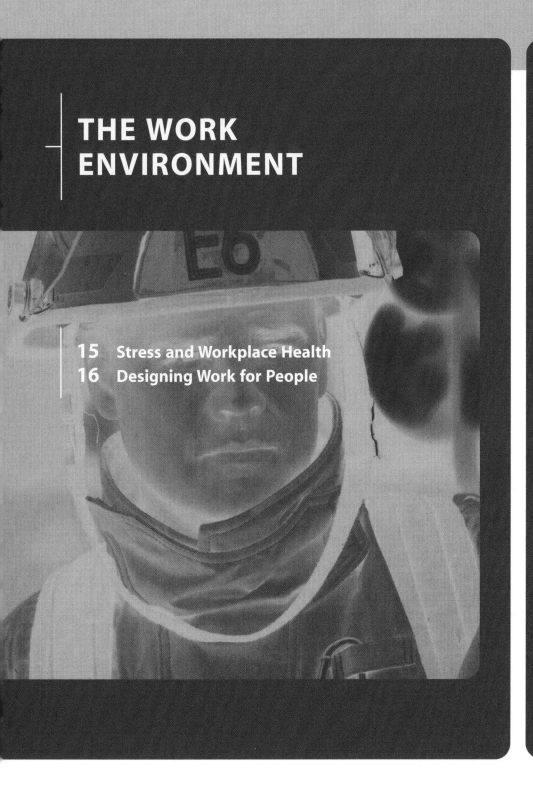

THE WORK ENVIRONMENT

4 PART

STRESS AND WORKPLACE HEALTH

THE PROBLEM OF STRESS

A t age 60, John Herbert (not his real name) was a successful executive with a Texas
paper company, looking forward to several more years of work before moving on
to a comfortable retirement. Imagine his distress when he was informed that his services
in the executive offices were no longer needed, and that he was being transferred to a warehouse position. In the warehouse, Herbert found himself reporting to a supervisor more
than 30 years his junior. Assigned to a variety of low-level janitorial tasks, Herbert suffered
abuse related to his age. Meanwhile, he observed that the company was moving younger
workers into executive positions like the one he had vacated.

Herbert sued for both emotional distress and age discrimination and was awarded
$800,000 for emotional distress and $2,250,000 in punitive damages, as well as a lesser sum
for age discrimination (DeFrank & Ivancevich, 1998). Herbert is not alone; since the early
1990s an increasing number of employees have sued their employers for damages resulting
from job-related stress (Keita & Hurrell, 1994; Moran, Wolff, & Green, 1995).

Lawsuits are just one among many major costs associated with work stress. American
employers spend more than $700 million annually to replace the 200,000 individuals aged
45 to 65 who die or are incapacitated by heart disease, a major cause of which is stress. In
2002 Americans paid about $330 billion for medical and disability-related costs of heart
disease (American Heart Association, 2002; Cartwright & Cooper, 1997). Stress is also a
known contributor to colds and flu, digestive difficulties, headaches, insomnia, stroke, and
other physiological problems as well as to impaired psychological well-being (e.g., anxiety,
depression, burnout) and counterproductive behaviors such as absenteeism and drug abuse
(Cooper, Dewe, & O'Driscoll, 2001; Krantz & McCeney, 2002).

It is no wonder, then, that I-O psychologists devote a great deal of effort to identifying
the causes of work stress, to understanding how it relates to health, and to developing
strategies for reducing or managing it. In this chapter we will describe these approaches
with a focus on understanding the variables that contribute to and reduce stress at work
and in other domains.

STUDYING WORKPLACE STRESS

A comprehensive framework for studying work stress was developed by Kahn and
Byosiere (1992). Their model presents several important factors in the stress process,
including (1) work stressors—task and role stressors, (2) moderators of the stress process—
individual differences, social support, and (3) consequences of stress—burnout, heart
disease (see Figure 15.1).

Two of the first "stress pioneers" were Walter Cannon and Hans Selye. Cannon was
a physiologist who studied animal and human reactions to dangerous situations. He
noted that animals and humans had an adaptive response to stressful situations in which

FIGURE 15.1

Theoretical Framework for the Study of Stress in Organizations
SOURCE: Adapted from Kahn & Byosiere (1992).

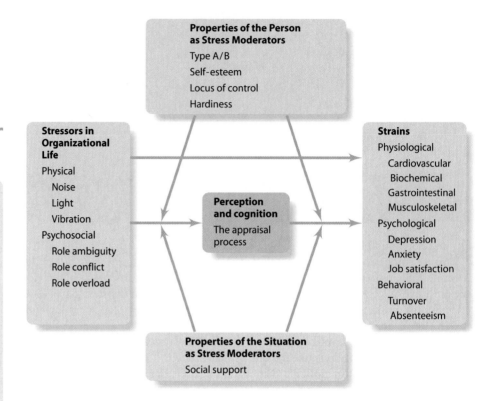

FIGHT-OR-FLIGHT REACTION

Adaptive response to stressful situations exhibited by animals and humans in which they choose to either fight or attempt to escape.

EUSTRESS

Type of stress that provides challenges that motivate individuals to work hard and meet their goals.

DISTRESS

Type of stress resulting from chronically demanding situations that produce negative health outcomes.

GENERAL ADAPTATION SYNDROME (GAS)

A nearly identical response sequence to almost any disease or trauma (poisoning, injury, psychological stress); identified by Hans Seyle.

ALARM REACTION

Stage of the General Adaptation Syndrome in which the body mobilizes resources to cope with added stress.

STRESS HORMONE

Chemical (e.g., adrenalin, noradrenalin, epinephrine, or cortisol) released in the body when a person encounters stressful or demanding situations.

they choose to either fight or attempt to escape. Cannon (1929) called this response the **fight-or-flight reaction,** and he is often credited with being the first to use the term "stress."

Often referred to as the "father of stress," University of Montreal physician and endocrinologist Hans Selye (1956) defined stress as "the non-specific response of the human body to any demand made on it." He was the first to distinguish between good stress (**eustress**) and bad stress (**distress**). Selye noted that eustress provides challenges that motivate individuals to work hard and meet their goals. Alternatively, distress results from stressful situations that persist over time and produces negative health outcomes.

Selye observed that the response sequence to almost any disease or trauma (e.g., poisoning, injury, psychological stress) is nearly identical. He named the progression the **General Adaptation Syndrome (GAS)** and divided it into three stages. First, in the **alarm reaction** stage, the body mobilizes resources to cope with added stress. In this stage, the heart rate increases and **stress hormones,** such as adrenalin, noradrenalin, epinephrine, and cortisol, are released. Second, in the **resistance** stage, the body copes with the original source of stress, but resistance to other stressors is lowered. Third, in the **exhaustion** stage, overall resistance drops and adverse consequences, including burnout, severe illness, and even death can result unless stress is reduced. The General Adaptation Syndrome suggests that psychological factors associated with stress play an important role in many of our worst afflictions, including heart disease.

Note that Cannon's (1929) fight-or-flight reaction comes in response to the type of stress that occurs suddenly and is likely to last only a short time—episodic, or acute, stress—whereas Selye's (1956) General Adaptation Syndrome tracks the body's response to stress over a longer period of time. We will examine this longer-lasting, or chronic, stress in this chapter. Although workplace stress can be episodic, as in the case of an on-the-job accident or a confrontation with an irate customer, it is chronic stress that is more common in work settings and more damaging to the body and mind. For these reasons, chronic stress has been and continues to be of most interest to I-O psychologists.

Recent studies of stress show that it involves, in addition to a physiological response consistent with Selye's findings, a cognitive appraisal of the situation and of the resources available to handle the stressors. Lazarus (1991) viewed stress as an ongoing process in which individuals make an appraisal of the environment and attempt to cope with the stressors that arise. This appraisal often triggers a set of coping responses by the body. In some circumstances, such as during exercise, the process can be healthy. However, when exposure to stress is chronic or persistent, the body responds negatively. It is important to note that most of these reactions are automatic. They happen whether we want them to or not, almost as if we have an allergic reaction to a psychologically threatening or stressful environment. In fact, some of these physiological reactions to stress (e.g., high blood pressure) have no obvious physical symptoms.

Individuals appraise, experience, and cope with stressful situations in different ways. We will consider different ways to prevent and cope with stress in detail later in the chapter, but it is helpful at this point to note that coping styles are typically divided into problem-focused and emotion-focused coping. **Problem-focused coping** is directed at managing or altering the problem that is causing the stress. Such coping may include defining the problem, generating different solutions and weighing their costs and benefits, and acting to solve the problem (Lazarus, 2000). For example, problem-focused coping might involve developing and utilizing time management skills and designing a specific plan of action for handling a job with many demands. **Emotion-focused coping** involves reducing the emotional response to the problem, which can mean avoiding, minimizing, and distancing oneself from the problem. For example, emotion-focused coping might involve obtaining social support from one's family and friends to help minimize the effects of a stressful job. We will discuss social support in more detail in Module 15.3.

WHAT IS A STRESSOR?

While we can talk about stress and the experience of stress, when it comes to research studies, it is often easier to get actual measurements of "stressors." **Stressors** (see Table 15.1) are physical or psychological demands to which an individual responds (Quick, Quick, Nelson, & Hurrell, 1997). Examples of physical stressors include excessive heat, noise, light, or even the incessantly ringing phone or the "ding" from your computer telling

RESISTANCE

Stage of the General Adaptation Syndrome in which the body copes with the original source of stress, but resistance to other stressors is lowered.

EXHAUSTION

Stage of the General Adaptation Syndrome in which overall resistance drops and adverse consequences (e.g., burnout, severe illness, and even death) can result unless stress is reduced.

PROBLEM-FOCUSED COPING

Directed at managing or altering a problem causing the stress.

EMOTION-FOCUSED COPING

Directed at reducing the emotional response to a problem by avoiding, minimizing, or distancing oneself from the problem.

STRESSORS

Physical or psychological demands to which an individual responds.

TABLE 15.1	Common Stressors in the Workplace

Heat, cold, noise

Role stressors

Workload

Work pace, time pressure

Work schedule (e.g., shift work)

Interpersonal demands and conflict

Situational constraints

Perceived control

Emotional labor

Traumatic job stressors (e.g., workplace violence)

you that you've got yet another incoming e-mail. Examples of psychological stressors are role ambiguity, interpersonal conflict, and lack of control. Reactions or responses to these stressors are commonly called **strains** (Cooper et al., 2001). Examples of strains that can result from chronic or persistent stress are burnout, anxiety, and physiological consequences such as high blood pressure and heart disease. These stressors and strains will be described in more detail in the next section.

STRAINS

Reaction or response to stressors.

COMMON STRESSORS AT WORK

Work stressors fall into two major categories: physical/task stressors such as noise, light, heat, and cold; and psychological stressors, which involve a multitude of subtle and not-so-subtle factors that an individual may find demanding.

Physical/Task Stressors

In their early studies of work stress, I-O psychologists focused on physical stressors and their effects on the experience of stress and subsequent strains. According to many experimental and field studies, uncontrollable noise is particularly stressful and leads to lower task performance and diminished motivation (Cohen, Evans, Stokols, & Krantz, 1986). Although we may associate noise with factories where loud machinery is in operation, the effects of physical stressors are not limited to manufacturing environments. In a recent study in an open office setting, Evans and Johnson (2000) found that exposure to low-level noise is associated with elevated levels of stress hormones and lower task performance. The importance of the increased hormone levels is that stressors may exist even when the worker is not aware of the stressor. For example, it is common for industrial psychologists to interview workers on noisy factory floors about their work. When asked, the workers commonly report that their environments are not noisy, despite the fact that they usually have to shout their responses. Interestingly, the same is true of workers in gambling casinos.

The demands of a given job (e.g., pace of work, workload, the number of hours worked) can also contribute to the experience of stress and to subsequent strains. For example, Hurrell (1985) studied several thousand postal workers and found that those working in machine-paced jobs experienced greater stress, anxiety, fatigue, and tension than those working in jobs where the pace was set by the employees (e.g., hand sorting, helping customers, delivering mail). In current times, postal workers must worry about an additional stressor—exposure to agents of bioterrorism such as anthrax. Such stress is particularly high because of the difficulty in identifying who instigated the anthrax attacks that occurred in October 2001 (Sun, 2002).

Although it may be clear that physical and task stressors have negative effects on employee health, more recent research in work stress has focused on psychological stressors that may not be as intuitively linked to health outcomes. As we will see in the following section, there is clear evidence that such psychological stressors play an equally important role in employee health and well-being. Keep in mind, however, that one type of stressor (e.g., physical or task) is not made less important by the presence of another stressor; thus, the effects of multiple stressors can be cumulative.

Psychological Stressors

Lack of Control/Predictability　Control is a major theme in the literature on stress (Ganster & Murphy, 2000; Landy, Quick, & Kasl, 1994). Varying levels of personal control and predictability have clear effects on job performance and work stress (Rastegary & Landy, 1993; Spector, 1986). As with any stressor, the individual's *perception* of control or predictability determines his or her response to the situation, and such perceptions

Employees in physically stressful workplaces are often not consciously aware of the stressful effects of noise, poor ventilation, or other adverse conditions.

are affected by characteristics of the job and work environment. The scheduling and pace of work can influence feelings of control. For example, flexible time schedules enhance feelings of control over one's schedule, even though the average arrival and departure times may differ only by minutes after a flexible time schedule has been introduced (Baltes, Briggs, Huff, Wright, & Neuman, 1999). Flextime also increases perceptions of control by helping employees to balance work and family commitments (Ralston, 1989). Perceptions of control in the workplace are also related to **autonomy,** the extent to which employees can control how and when they perform the tasks of their job (Hackman & Oldham, 1980). Overall, interventions that enhance perceptions of control on the job, such as participative decision making or flexible time schedules, are likely to reduce stress and subsequent strains. Below, we further discuss the importance of control, which is a major component of the Demand-Control model of stress developed by Karasek (1979).

Interpersonal Conflict   Negative interactions with co-workers, supervisors, or clients, or **interpersonal conflict,** can range from heated arguments to subtle incidents of unfriendly behavior (Jex, 1998). Interpersonal conflict can occur when resources at work are scarce (e.g., who gets to use the color copy machine first), when employees have incompatible interests (e.g., one member of a team is a stickler for detail, while another likes to complete the project as quickly as possible), or when employees feel they are not being treated fairly (e.g., bosses get big bonuses, but workers are told no funds are available for salary increases for the rest of the workforce). Interpersonal conflict can distract workers from important job tasks, and it can have physical health consequences. In a

AUTONOMY

Extent to which employees can control how and when they perform the tasks of their job.

INTERPERSONAL CONFLICT

Negative interactions with co-workers, supervisors, or clients which can range from heated arguments to subtle incidents of unfriendly behavior.

longitudinal study of more than 15,000 Finnish employees, the link between interpersonal conflict at work and subsequent health problems was significant—even when social class, marital status, conflict with spouse, and high alcohol consumption were taken into account (Romanov, Appelberg, Honkasalo, & Koskenvuo, 1996). Other negative work outcomes of interpersonal conflict range from depression and job dissatisfaction to aggression, theft, and sabotage (Chen & Spector, 1992; Frone, 2000a). Interpersonal conflict may also play a part in workplace violence (Jex, 1998), which is discussed later in this chapter.

Role Stressors Role ambiguity, role conflict, and role overload are collectively referred to as **role stressors.** The basic notion behind role stressors is that most jobs have multiple task requirements and responsibilities, or **roles** (Rizzo, House, & Lirtzman, 1970), and that a job is likely to be particularly stressful if these roles conflict with one another or are unclear. **Role ambiguity** occurs when employees lack clear knowledge of what behavior is expected in their job. In such cases, individuals experience uncertainty about which actions they should take in performing their job most effectively. **Role conflict** occurs when demands from different sources are incompatible. Students are well aware of this form of conflict, particularly toward the end of the term when they complain, "I have four papers due and all my professors act like I'm not taking any courses but theirs!" In addition to conflict between different tasks or projects, role conflict may also involve conflict between organizational demands and one's own values, or conflict among obligations to several different co-workers.

A more specific form of conflict is **role overload,** a stressor that occurs when an individual is expected to fulfill too many roles at the same time. Role overload can cause people to work very long hours, increasing stress and subsequent strains. Some workers complain that they are stressed from working "24/7"—that is, 24 hours a day, seven days a week. On the television show "Saturday Night Live," cast members joked that some people have a different 24/7 plan for avoiding stress: a work schedule of 24 hours a week, seven months a year. Most of us would agree that such a schedule (with full-time pay) would be a great way to reduce stress! Indeed, research shows a positive correlation between role stressors and a variety of work and health problems, including tension, anxiety, and a propensity to leave the organization (Day & Livingstone, 2001; Jackson & Schuler, 1985; Netemeyer, Johnston, & Burton, 1990).

Work-Family Conflict A different type of role stressor is **work-family conflict,** which occurs when workers experience conflict between the roles they fulfill at work and the roles they fulfill in their personal lives. Because working women and dual-career families have become the norm rather than the exception, work-family conflict has become a common source of work stress. Given that working women continue to take on most of the responsibilities within the home, women often fill more numerous roles than men (Cleveland, Stockdale, & Murphy, 2000). In a study of men and women working in high-ranking positions, women were more stressed by their greater responsibility for household and family duties. In addition, women with children at home had significantly higher levels of stress hormones after work than women without children at home or any of the men in the study (Lundberg & Frankenhaeuser, 1999).

However, these findings do not necessarily mean that the effect of work on women is exclusively negative. In fact, there is little evidence to indicate that a woman's employment harms her marriage or her children (Cleveland et al., 2000). One study concluded that, compared to men, women appear to have better coping strategies to handle stress (Korabik & McDonald, 1991). In particular, women are more likely than men to have access to social support, which we discuss later as a critical factor in reducing stress and its harmful effects.

Nevertheless, several recent studies have indicated that work-family conflict has a significant impact on health and well-being of both men and women. Thus, this type of

---

ROLE STRESSORS

Collective term for stressors resulting from the multiple task requirements or roles of employees.

ROLE

The expectations regarding the responsibilities and requirements of a particular job.

ROLE AMBIGUITY

Stressor that occurs when employees lack clear knowledge of what behavior is expected in their job.

ROLE CONFLICT

Stressor that occurs when demands from different sources are incompatible.

ROLE OVERLOAD

Stressor that occurs when an individual is expected to fulfill too many roles at the same time.

WORK-FAMILY CONFLICT

Occurs when workers experience conflict between the roles they fulfill at work and in their personal lives.

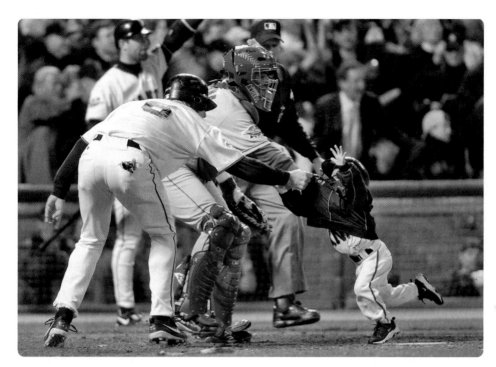

A sometimes risky approach to work-family balance is to bring one's child to work. Here three-year-old Darren Baker, son of San Francisco Giants manager Dusty Baker, is dragged out of harm's way by Giants first baseman J. T. Snow during a 2002 World Series game.

conflict seems to be an "equal-opportunity stressor" (Allen, Herst, Bruck, & Sutton, 2000). A study of 2,700 employed adults found that individuals who reported experiencing work-family conflict were as much as 30 times more likely to experience a significant mental health problem, such as depression or anxiety, than employees who reported no work-family conflict (Frone, 2000b).

Flexible time schedules and child care are becoming increasingly important to working men and women in many different careers. For example, although one might not think that child care would be important to professional athletes, it is provided to members of several sports organizations, including professional race car drivers (NASCAR) and the men's and women's professional golf associations. Players in the Ladies Professional Golf Association reported that the child care program reduces their concerns about balancing work and family, thereby letting them concentrate on their work (Stewart, 2002). Unfortunately, the average working parent is more likely than these athletes to experience work-family stress related to the lack of good child care. A recent study by the human resources firm Hewitt Associates found that only 1 in 10 U.S. companies offered on-site or off-site child care; another 10 percent arranged for employee discounts at local child care providers (Finnigan, 2001). Thus, 80 percent of the workers polled were on their own in terms of child care. It is reasonable to assume that a majority of them experienced work-family conflict at some time. The precipitating event is often an unexpected one, such as an illness or injury that prevents a child from attending school or day care. When that happens in a dual-income family, husband and wife are prone to experience a good deal of tension at the breakfast table as they decide who will stay home that day and assume the caregiver role.

Emotional Labor Interest in the role of emotions in the workplace has increased rapidly over the past decade (Fisher & Ashkanasy, 2000). Emotions are important to consider because stress is, first and foremost, an emotional reaction. **Emotional labor** is the regulation of one's emotions to meet job or organizational demands. The study of emotional labor addresses the stress of managing emotions when jobs require that workers display only certain expressions to clients or customers (Adelmann, 1995). Workers can regulate their

EMOTIONAL LABOR

Regulation of one's emotions to meet job or organizational demands; can be achieved through surface acting and deep acting.

Service occupations often involve masking one's emotions to keep customers happy.

emotions through surface acting and deep acting (Morris & Feldman, 1996). **Surface acting** consists of managing or "faking" one's expressions or emotions. **Deep acting** consists of managing one's feelings, including trying to feel the emotions required by the job. Imagine the telemarketer who learns during a lunch break that a parent has been diagnosed with a life-threatening disease. The struggle to maintain a cheery demeanor with customers would require considerable acting.

Hochschild (1983) estimated that at least one-third of American workers engage in emotional labor, which has been studied in several occupations including police officers, waiters and waitresses, bill collectors, salesclerks, bank tellers, and flight attendants. For example, waiters in fine restaurants report that they commonly display pleasant emotions while simultaneously hiding feelings of anger and frustration toward rude customers. Similarly, bill collectors are encouraged to ignore their feelings of irritation and hostility toward uncooperative debtors, and instead display neutrality or calmness—the emotions that their employers have found lead to a greater likelihood that debtors will pay their bills (Sutton, 1991).

Stress and discomfort are likely to occur when the required emotions differ from employees' actual emotions. Suppressing emotions or showing false emotions requires cognitive and physiological effort, which is likely to be stressful over the long term. Initial research has indicated that the stress of emotional labor can lead to job dissatisfaction, burnout, and turnover intentions (Brotheridge & Grandey, 2002; Grandey, 2000; Pugliesi, 1999). To reduce the stress of emotional labor, I-O psychologists recommend using humor, obtaining social support from co-workers, and depersonalizing the encounter with customers or clients. It is clear that additional consideration of emotional labor as a stressor is needed, particularly as the service sector continues to grow and more employees are required to provide "service with a smile" (Pugh, 2001). It also makes sense that a worker who is upset over a non-work interaction (e.g., a fight with a family member) would have difficulty expressing a calm, pleasant emotion that is required on the job. Given our earlier discussion about work-family conflict, research on the potential stress resulting from such conflicting emotions seems like a logical extension of current research on emotional labor.

SURFACE ACTING

Emotional labor that consists of managing or faking one's expressions or emotions.

DEEP ACTING

Emotional labor that consists of managing one's feelings, including emotions required by the job.

CONSEQUENCES OF STRESS

The link between occupational stress and adverse health outcomes among employees is clear (Cooper et al., 2001). The negative consequences of chronic stress can be divided into three categories: behavioral, psychological, and physiological (see Table 15.2).

Behavioral Consequences of Stress

Among the behavioral consequences of stress are absenteeism, accidents, alcohol and drug abuse, poor job performance, and counterproductive behaviors including workplace violence (Kahn & Boysiere, 1992). We will focus on the effects of stressors on two particularly important behavioral outcomes: (1) information processing, which affects a variety of other

TABLE 15.2	Consequences of Stress

Physical/Medical/Physiological

Heart disease and stroke

Ulcers

Back pain and arthritis

Headaches

Increased blood pressure and heart rate

Hormones (adrenaline, noradrenaline, cortisol)

Psychological

Burnout

Depression

Anxiety

Family problems

Sleep problems

Job dissatisfaction

Behavioral

Absence

Lateness

Drug, alcohol, and tobacco abuse

Accidents

Sabotage/violence

Poor decision making/information processing

Job performance

Turnover

SOURCE: Adapted from Quick, Quick, Nelson, & Hurrell (1997).

critical work outcomes, and (2) job performance, which can include information processing, but often involves a global measure of effectiveness.

Information Processing The influence of stress on information processing has been widely investigated. Chronic stress has detrimental effects on memory, reaction times, accuracy, and performance of a variety of tasks (Smith, 1990). In addition, individuals under stress often have difficulty focusing their attention. Stress leads to premature reactions to stimuli, restricted use of relevant cues, and increased errors on cognitive tasks (Svenson & Maule, 1993).

Because each of us has limited cognitive resources, stressful situations that restrict such resources will impair our ability to cope with the task at hand. Stress also correlates with lower creativity and poorer decision making, particularly under time pressure (Rastegary & Landy, 1993; Shanteau & Dino, 1993). For example, fast-food delivery drivers commonly have accidents during the rush period for deliveries (usually Friday nights between 5:00 P.M. and 9:00 P.M.). They often report never seeing the object (e.g., car, truck, jogger, motorcycle) whose path they turned across. They simply did not "process" that information when they turned left across traffic because they were looking for a street sign or a street number

FIGURE 15.2

Stress and Performance: Inverted U Relationship Source: Jex (1998).

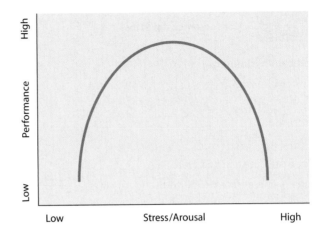

During the hectic evening hours. This is just one example of how the effects of high levels of stress on information processing can lead to a variety of negative work outcomes.

Performance   For nearly a century, I-O psychologists have investigated the hypothesis that arousal and performance have an inverted "U" relationship, as shown in Figure 15.2 (Yerkes & Dodson, 1908). The hypothesis is that as arousal increases, performance increases, but only up to a certain point, and then performance begins to decline. Thus, compared to situations with moderate arousal, both low levels of arousal (boredom) and high levels of arousal (extreme danger) result in lower performance. Alternatively, moderate arousal can lead to high motivation, energy, and attentiveness; this outcome is consistent with Selye's concept of eustress, which we discussed earlier in this chapter. Research on task performance in the laboratory supports predictions from the inverted U hypothesis (Jex, 1998).

Research in organizational settings indicates that work stress at any level, including moderate levels, has a direct, negative relationship with job performance. For example, in a sample of nurses Motowidlo, Packard, and Manning (1986) found that stress was negatively correlated with several job performance dimensions. Specifically, stress led to lower sensitivity, warmth, and tolerance toward patients, which were described as interpersonal aspects of job performance. A recent meta-analysis indicated that a widespread stressor, role ambiguity, has consistent, negative relationships with job performance (Tubre & Collins, 2000). The best explanation of these results has to do with the nature of the task. For the simple tasks performed in laboratory experiments, moderate arousal results in the highest performance. However, for complex tasks performed on the job, moderate to high levels of stress are detrimental to performance. When the complexity of the task is considered, the overall results seem to fit the inverted U hypothesis.

It is important to acknowledge that stress represents only one of many factors that may impact job performance (Jex, 1998). This is consistent with one of the themes of this book: that multiple influences affect behavior at work. The effects of stress on performance depend on several factors, including the complexity of the task performed and the personality characteristics of the individual performing the task. Nevertheless, it is clear that chronic stress commonly has negative effects on work performance.

Psychological Consequences of Stress

BURNOUT

Extreme state of psychological strain resulting from a prolonged response to chronic job stressors that exceed an individual's resources to cope with them.

The psychological consequences of stress include anxiety, depression, burnout, fatigue, job tension, and dissatisfaction with one's job and life (Kahn & Byosiere, 1992). **Burnout** is a particularly important and well-researched consequence of stress. It is an extreme state of psychological strain that results from a prolonged response to chronic job stressors that exceed an individual's resources to cope with them (Maslach, Schaufeli, & Leiter, 2001). Burnout was first observed in the "caring professions": nursing, social work, and teaching.

Intensive care nurses, for example, have heavy workloads and demanding caregiving responsibilities that often lead to burnout. Researchers have identified three components of burnout in these health care and human service settings: emotional exhaustion, feelings of depersonalization, and feelings of low personal accomplishment.

Emotional exhaustion occurs when individuals feel emotionally drained by work. Individuals who suffer from feelings of **depersonalization** have become hardened by their job and tend to treat clients or patients like objects. For example, a stock character in many movies about teenagers is a "hard-boiled" school administrator who seems to have completely forgotten what it is like to be a student. Individuals who have feelings of **low personal accomplishment** cannot deal with problems effectively and cannot understand or identify with the problems of others. They feel powerless to have any actual impact on problems, and thus are unlikely to implement effective solutions.

Burnout is typically measured with the Maslach Burnout Inventory (MBI) (Maslach, Jackson, & Leiter, 1996), a self-report measure that includes scales for the three burnout dimensions. Table 15.3 shows examples of burnout items. Extensive research indicates that chronic stressors (e.g., role ambiguity and role conflict) often lead to burnout (Jackson & Schuler, 1985; Lee & Ashforth, 1996).

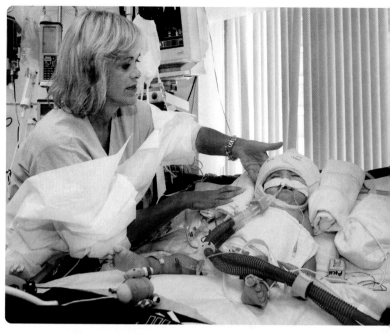

Working in a high-stakes job, where a mistake can be a matter of life or death, can lead to emotional burnout.

Recent research on burnout has expanded to occupations beyond the "caring professions" including managers, air traffic controllers, and military professionals (e.g., Demerouti, Bakker, Nachreiner, & Schaufeli, 2001). As a result, researchers have broadened the three burnout dimensions so that they are relevant beyond the human service and health care professions. Recent work on burnout (Maslach, Schaufeli,& Leiter, 2001) refers to the dimensions as (1) exhaustion, (2) depersonalization and cynicism on the job, and (3) a sense of ineffectiveness and lack of accomplishment on the job. The MBI-General Survey assesses these three dimensions with items parallel to those in the original MBI, with the modification that they do not explicitly refer to working with people.

Using samples from both the United States and the Netherlands, Schaufeli and Enzmann (1998) examined burnout across a variety of different occupations. This work indicated that police officers and security guards in both countries have relatively high levels of cynicism and feelings of ineffectiveness, but low levels of exhaustion. In contrast, teachers had the highest levels of exhaustion in both countries, but average levels of cynicism and feelings of ineffectiveness. Employees in the medical field had high levels of

EMOTIONAL EXHAUSTION

Burnout that occurs when individuals feel emotionally drained by work.

DEPERSONALIZATION

Burnout that occurs when individuals become hardened by their job and tend to treat clients or patients like objects.

LOW PERSONAL ACCOMPLISHMENT

Burnout in which individuals feel they cannot deal with problems effectively and understand or identify with others' problems.

TABLE 15.3	Examples of Burnout Items

1. I doubt the significance of my work.
2. I feel I am making an effective contribution to what this organization does.
3. I feel used up at the end of the workday.

SOURCE: Maslach, Jackson, & Leiter (1996).

personal inefficacy, but lower cynicism and exhaustion in both countries. Considering these findings, we might ask whether individuals exhibiting only one or two of the three burnout characteristics should be considered to have burnout. Indeed, there is a thriving research debate over that question, as well as whether one dimension of burnout precedes the others. Overall, however, research indicates that the basic patterns of burnout seem to be fairly similar across different occupations and countries (Maslach et al., 2001).

Some clear findings have emerged about who experiences burnout (Maslach et al., 2001). First, burnout is higher among younger employees who, compared to older employees, may be overwhelmed by new job demands. As mentioned above, burnout was first studied in the helping professions, which are dominated by women. Thus, conventional wisdom among burnout researchers was that women had higher burnout than men. However, this assumption has not been confirmed, although some studies have found that men are slightly higher on feelings of cynicism while women are slightly higher on exhaustion. Married individuals seem to be less prone than the unmarried to burnout, possibly because of the social support a spouse provides. In addition, individuals with personality characteristics such as low self-esteem and Type A behavior pattern (discussed below) are more prone to burnout (Semmer, 1996).

In sum, it is clear that work settings with chronic, overwhelming demands and time pressures put workers at high risk for burnout. As such, interventions intended to reduce burnout should be focused on both the individual and the job. A combination of stress management, skills training, and job design seems to be the most promising avenue to prevent or reduce the development of burnout (Van Dierendonck, Schaufeli, & Buunk, 2001). More will be said about job design in Chapter 16. The future of research and practice on burnout will focus on several issues. First, most burnout research uses cross-sectional designs in which stressors and burnout measures are collected at the same time. Future burnout research should link burnout to objective health and work outcomes in longitudinal designs in which burnout and baseline outcome measures are assessed at one point in time, followed by objective outcome measures (e.g., absence, lateness, physiological health indexes) at a later time. Second, researchers need to consider relationships among the three burnout dimensions. The evidence is unclear regarding whether exhaustion leads to depersonalization and low personal accomplishment, or whether the burnout process works in the opposite direction. Again, longitudinal designs will be most effective in clarifying these issues.

Physiological Consequences of Stress

Physiological changes in the body occur when stressful situations cause overactivation of the sympathetic nervous system, which produces several different kinds of stress hormones. These stress hormones cause an increase in heart rate and cardiac output in preparation for increased physical and cognitive activity (Krantz & Manuck, 1984). Initially, these changes can improve decision making, judgment, and physical performance. However, chronic activation of the sympathetic nervous system leads to excess amounts of stress hormones circulating in the blood supply and the brain.

Stress also causes the blood vessels to shrink in the peripheral areas of the body (Eliot & Buell, 1983). The combination of shrinking blood vessels and more blood moving through them causes "wear and tear" on the coronary arteries and the heart. This leads to thickening of plaque in the arteries (atherosclerosis) and heart disease (Krantz & McCeney, 2002). In addition, because the heart has to work harder to pump under these conditions, it requires more oxygen, which in turn often leads to elevated blood pressure. Greater oxygen consumption by the heart under these aroused conditions explains the increased heart attacks in persons who are under stress (Krantz & Manuck, 1984).

Although many of the physiological outcomes of stress are interrelated—that is, one outcome can affect another to start a vicious circle or snowball effect—they are often categorized according to three types. Cardiovascular outcomes of stress include changes in blood pressure, heart rate, and cholesterol. Gastrointestinal outcomes include digestive problems of various kinds. Biochemical outcomes of stress include increases in cortisol and catecholamines (stress hormones). Stressful work situations are linked to increased levels of cortisol, norepinephrine, and adrenalin in the bloodstream (Fox, Dwyer, & Ganster, 1993). Long-lasting, elevated stress hormone levels contribute to decreased functioning of the immune system and the development of coronary heart disease (Cohen & Hebert, 1996; Krantz & McCeney, 2002). In the United States, coronary heart disease is the leading cause of death among both men and women (American Heart Association, 2002). In sum, there is clear evidence of the negative physiological consequences that result from chronic exposure to stressors.

MODULE 15.1 SUMMARY

- Although workplace stress can be episodic, chronic stress is more common in work settings and more damaging to the body. For this reason, chronic stress is of most interest to I-O psychologists.
- Stress involves a cognitive appraisal of the situation and the resources available to handle the stressors. This appraisal often triggers a set of coping responses by the body.
- Stressors are physical or psychological demands to which an individual responds. Examples of physical stressors include excessive heat, noise, and light. Examples of psychological stressors are role ambiguity, interpersonal conflict, and lack of control.
- Reactions to stressors are called strains, which are often divided into three categories: behavioral, psychological, and physiological. Specific examples of strains that can result from chronic stress include burnout, anxiety, and physiological ailments such as high blood pressure and heart disease.

KEY TERMS

fight-or-flight reaction

eustress

distress

General Adaptation Syndrome (GAS)

alarm reaction

stress hormone

resistance

exhaustion

problem-focused coping

emotion-focused coping

stressors

strains

autonomy

interpersonal conflict

role stressors

role

role ambiguity

role conflict

role overload

work-family conflict

emotional labor

surface acting

deep acting

burnout

emotional exhaustion

depersonalization

low personal accomplishment

CRITICAL THINKING EXERCISES

15.1 Why are emotional labor and its effects of much greater concern today than 30 years ago? Identify three jobs that require emotional labor and explain why they do so.

15.2 Identify a time when you experienced psychological burnout in your job or at school. Which of the three burnout dimensions (emotional exhaustion, depersonalization, and low personal accomplishment) did you experience? Do you think that people generally experience one type of burnout at a time or all three types simultaneously?

THEORIES OF STRESS

everal theories of stress have been developed to organize the relationships among stressors, strains, and potential moderators of those relationships. Two theories that have received a great deal of attention are Karasek's Demand-Control Model and French's Person-Environment Fit Model. In addition, stress models have considered individual difference variables that influence the relationship between stressors and strains. We discuss several of these characteristics and then focus on one of the most intensively studied individual difference characteristics, the Type A Behavior Pattern, which is included in many models of the stress process.

DEMAND-CONTROL MODEL

DEMAND-
CONTROL MODEL

Suggests that two factors are prominent in producing job stress: job demands and individual control; developed by Robert Karasek.

JOB DEMAND

Component of demand-control model that refers to the workload or intellectual requirements of the job.

JOB CONTROL

Component of Demand-Control model that refers to a combination of autonomy in the job and discretion for using different skills.

Karasek's (1979) **Demand-Control Model** suggests that two factors are prominent in producing job stress: job demands and control (also known as decision latitude). In this model, **job demands** are defined as the workload or intellectual requirements of the job. **Job control** is defined as a combination of autonomy in the job and discretion for using different skills. Karasek proposed that the combination of high work demands with low control results in "high strain" jobs that result in a variety of health problems. Food service worker, waitperson, nurse's aide, and assembly-line worker are considered high strain jobs. Machine-paced jobs, in particular, were highlighted as having high demands and low control. In contrast, jobs characterized by high demands that also provide sufficient control create an "active" job situation that is stimulating and health promoting. Active jobs include lawyer, engineer, manager, and physician. Jobs with low control and low demands (e.g., janitor, night watchmen) were labeled as "passive" jobs. Finally, jobs with high control and low demands (e.g., architect, dentist) were considered as particularly low strain jobs (see Figure 15.3).

Tests of the Demand-Control model are often conducted using the Job Content Questionnaire (JCQ), designed to measure the "content" of a respondent's work (Karasek, 1985). The JCQ includes the following subscales:

- Role overload and role conflict (demands).
- Skill utilization and job decision latitude (control).
- Depression, job dissatisfaction, and sleep problems (health consequences).

The scales have been used extensively to investigate job-related stress and coronary heart disease in the United States and Sweden. For example, in a series of surveys involving U.S. and Swedish male workers, Karasek (1979) found that the combination of low control and heavy job demands correlated positively with mental strain (i.e., depression and exhaustion) and job dissatisfaction.

More recently, Karasek and Theorell (1990) found an increased risk of illness (two to four times more likely) for individuals whose lives or jobs make high demands on them

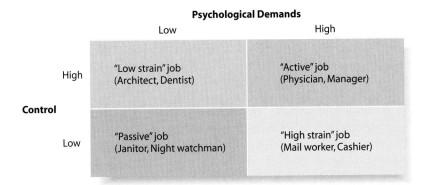

FIGURE 15.3

Demand-Control Model SOURCE: Adapted from Karasek (1979).

but allow little control. Thus, an individual who has a demanding work schedule or environment and does not have much decision latitude or control will have an increased risk for stress-related illnesses, both physiological and psychological. In contrast, individuals in active jobs that have high demands but high control maintained good health and had high job satisfaction. Karasek and Theorell (1990) noted that individuals in active jobs appear to participate actively in a variety of leisure activities as well, despite their high work demands. This finding is another example of the benefits of developing or designing jobs that allow workers to have control over decisions, resources, or the skills that they can use.

Ganster, Fox, and Dwyer (2001) tested the Demand-Control model in a sample of 105 full-time nurses. They found that nurses with the lowest perceptions of personal control and highest workload demands were ill more often and incurred the highest cumulative health care costs over the ensuing five-year period. Thus, jobs that have high demands and low control are costly to both individuals and the organizations for which they work. Nearly all studies on this stress model have been conducted in Europe and the United States. However, the Demand-Control model was also tested in a sample in the People's Republic of China (Xie, 1996). The results of this study were consistent with findings obtained in Western cultures, suggesting that this model applies well across various countries.

PERSON-ENVIRONMENT FIT MODEL

The Person-Environment (P-E) Fit model (French, Caplan, & Harrison, 1982) hypothesizes that the fit between a person and the environment determines the amount of stress that person perceives. A good person-environment fit occurs when a person's skills and abilities match the requirements of the job and work environment. For example, an introvert with a PhD in literature would be likely to have a good P-E fit with the job of university librarian, while an extraverted MBA might have a good P-E fit with the job of sales manager. The amount of stress a worker feels is influenced by perceptions of the demands made by the environment, and by perceptions of his or her capability to deal with those demands. Using this model, French et al. found that a poor fit between a person and the environment was frequently associated with increased strains. Alternatively, employees whose skills and abilities fit well with the work environment reported less stress and fewer strains (Edwards, 1996; French et al., 1982).

Karasek (1979) did not formally emphasize perception in the Demand-Control model. In contrast, the P-E fit approach focuses explicitly on the perceptions of individuals concerning their skills and abilities relative to the demands of the work environment. In addition, unlike the Demand-Control model, the P-E fit approach considers external influences such as social support from family and work sources. For example, Edwards and Rothbard (1999) found that the well-being of employees varied according to their perceptions of work and family experiences. The results of this study indicate that interventions to manage stress should consider the fit between employees and both their work and family environments, which is consistent with the research we discussed above on work-family conflict. In particular, if fit is bad in both the family and the work environment, the cumulative stress is likely to lead to low job performance and high health problems.

Early work did not always specify what "environment" was referred to in the P-E fit model. Recent work has more clearly differentiated between person-job fit and person-organization fit (Lauver & Kristof-Brown, 2001). **Person-job fit** refers to the extent to which the skills, abilities, and interests of an individual are compatible with the demands of the particular job. Alternatively, **person-organization fit** refers to whether the values of an employee are consistent with the values held by most others in the organization. In a diverse sample of managers, Lovelace and Rosen (1996) found that perceptions of poor person-organization fit were associated with greater levels of stress, job dissatisfaction, and intentions to quit one's job. Similarly, Saks and Ashforth (1997) found that favorable employee perceptions of person-organization fit correlated positively with intentions to remain with the organization and actual turnover. In addition, favorable employee perceptions of person-job fit correlated positively with job satisfaction and organizational commitment, and negatively with stress.

It is clear that different types of fit have an influence on a variety of problems, including stress, job dissatisfaction, and intentions to leave the organization. Organizations should strive to ensure that employees fit well in their jobs and have the skills necessary to complete their job tasks. In fact, fit is often increased through recruitment and selection processes that help applicants and those doing the hiring assess the likelihood that candidates will fit well in the job and in the organization (Schneider, 1987).

The P-E fit model suggests mechanisms by which individuals can protect themselves from the stress that accompanies a mismatch between the person and the environment. One of these protective mechanisms is social support. For example, employees who have seemingly impossible deadlines might seek informational and emotional support from co-workers. By reducing their experience of stress in this way, employees might be able to focus better and come closer to meeting their deadlines than if they were overwhelmed and suffering from strains. Overall, the P-E fit model allows us to examine work stress by looking at the interaction between the person and stressors in the work environment. This approach specifically acknowledges that stress can influence individuals differently depending on their preferences, values, and abilities (Edwards, 1996).

INDIVIDUAL DIFFERENCES IN RESISTANCE TO STRESS

As you have probably observed when you have been part of a group in a stressful situation, not everyone responds to stress in the same way. I-O psychologists have studied several individual characteristics as potential moderators of stressor-strain relationships. A moderator is a variable that affects the direction or strength of the association between two other variables. For example, if stressors led to strains for individuals with low self-esteem but not for those with high self-esteem, then self-esteem would be a moderator of the stressor-strain relationship (see Figure 15.4). If moderators reduce strains for only certain types of individuals, they are said to have an indirect effect on the reduction of strains. Individual difference characteristics that have received the most attention as moderators of the stressor-strain relationship are locus of control, hardiness, self-esteem, and the Type A behavior pattern.

Locus of control (LOC) is a construct that refers to whether individuals believe that what happens to them is under their control or beyond it (Rotter, 1966). Individuals characterized as internals believe that outcomes are a result of their own personal effort and ability, whereas persons classified as externals believe that outcomes are determined largely by other people, luck, or fate. Many elite professional athletes are confident—sometimes overconfident—that success lies completely in their hands (i.e., they have an internal LOC). In team sports, they like to be thought of as the "go to" person. Several studies have indicated

---

PERSON-JOB FIT

Extent to which the skills, abilities, and interests of an individual are compatible with the demands of the particular job.

PERSON-ORGANIZATION FIT

Extent to which the values of an employee are consistent with the values held by most others in the organization.

LOCUS OF CONTROL (LOC)

Construct that refers to the belief of individuals that what happens to them is under their control (internal LOC) or beyond their control (external LOC).

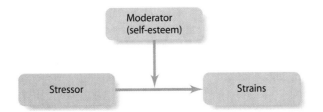

FIGURE 15.4

Example of a Moderator of the Stressor-Strain Relationship

that internals experience lower strains than do externals. Researchers have proposed that because internals believe they can control a stressful situation to achieve their goals, they experience fewer strains than externals exposed to the same stressors. Overall, evidence indicates that having an internal locus of control moderates the relationship between stressors and strains (Horner, 1996; Kahn & Byosiere, 1992).

Hardiness is a set of personality characteristics that provide resistance to stress (Kobasa, 1979). Specifically, individuals described as having a "hardy personality" possess three characteristics:

1. They feel they are in *control* of their lives.
2. They feel a sense of *commitment* to their family and their work goals and values.
3. They see unexpected change as a *challenge* rather than as an obstacle.

Cohen and Edwards (1989) observed that hardy individuals actively adopt problem-focused and support-seeking strategies. Kobasa, Maddi, and Kahn (1982) found that hardy individuals had fewer physiological reactions to stressors, reported fewer illnesses, and had higher levels of general well-being than those who were not hardy. Among executives and lawyers who were under a great deal of stress, those with hardy personalities were found to have significantly fewer strains than those who were not characterized as hardy (Maddi & Kobasa, 1984). Overall, evidence indicates that hardiness moderates the relationship between stressors and strains (Cohen & Edwards, 1989). A key component of hardiness is transformational coping, which involves actively changing perceptions of a stressful event by viewing it as a challenge that can be overcome. For example, hardy students facing an important and stressful exam might cope by interpreting their exam as an opportunity to show their knowledge, thereby exerting control through preparation and good study habits (Quick et al., 1997).

Self-esteem, or positive self-worth or self-concept, is considered an important resource for coping. Individuals with high self-esteem are more likely to adopt more effective coping strategies in the face of stress than individuals with low self-esteem (Ganster & Schaubroeck, 1995). Thus, when faced with the same environmental stressors, individuals with low self-esteem will experience more strains compared to those with high self-esteem. Overall, research generally indicates that self-esteem is a moderator of the stress-strain relationship (Cooper et al., 2001). Although high self-esteem is clearly important in reducing the effects of stress at work, there is some evidence that the effects of high self-esteem are not always positive. Although many people assume that low self-esteem is related to workplace violence, Baumeister, Smart, and Boden (1996) conducted an extensive literature review that indicated that aggression and workplace violence were most characteristic of individuals with high-self esteem. Later in the chapter, we will discuss more specifically the links among high self-esteem, stress, and violence in the workplace.

The Type A Behavior Pattern

The potential moderator of the stress-strain relationship that has been most intensively studied is the **Type A behavior pattern (TABP),** which was first identified in the late 1950s by two cardiologists, Meyer Friedman and Ray Rosenman (1959). Fifteen years later,

HARDINESS

A set of personality characteristics that provide resistance to stress; hardy individuals feel in control of their lives, have a sense of commitment to their family and their work goals and values, and see unexpected change as a challenge.

SELF-ESTEEM

A positive self-worth or self-concept that is considered to be an important resource for coping.

TYPE A BEHAVIOR PATTERN (TABP)

Set of characteristics exhibited by individuals who are engaged in a chronic struggle to obtain an unlimited number of poorly defined things from their environment in the shortest period of time; subcomponents include hostility, achievement strivings, impatience/irritability and time urgency.

Friedman and Rosenman wrote *Type A Behavior and Your Heart* (1974), in which they described the Type A behavior pattern as a set of characteristics exhibited by "individuals who are engaged in a relatively chronic struggle to obtain an unlimited number of poorly defined things from their environment in the shortest period of time and, if necessary, against the opposing effects of other things or persons in this same environment" (p. 67).

The Type A behavior pattern is also known as the **coronary-prone personality** because of its proposed links to coronary heart disease and heart attacks. Individuals who exhibit this behavior pattern (known as Type As) are characterized by ambitiousness, impatience, easily aroused hostility, and time urgency. Friedman and Rosenman (1974) suggested that the core characteristic of TABP is an incessant struggle to achieve more and more in less and less time. In fact, descriptions of Type As who are overly obsessed with saving time are common. For example, Type A men have been known to use two electric razors (one for each side of the face) at the same time to shave as quickly as possible (Bluedorn, 2002; Gilbreth & Carey, 1948). Generally, Type As seem to thrive on "life in the fast lane" as they focus on quickly doing things that result in occupational and material success. In contrast, Type Bs are often described as relaxed, patient, and easygoing.

Sapolsky (1998) described the history of how Friedman and Rosenman missed an opportunity to identify some of the typical characteristics of Type As in the early 1950s. In the waiting room outside Friedman and Rosenman's cardiology office, the lining of the chairs was worn down so much that the upholstery needed to be replaced frequently. The upholsterer noticed this first and asked, "What is wrong with your patients? People don't wear chairs out this way!" Only years later did Friedman and Rosenman begin their formal work on the Type A behavior pattern and thus realize that their heart patients had a consistent pattern of behavior, including nervous energy and fidgeting, that was related to heart disease.

In trying to understand the mechanisms behind the TABP, some researchers have suggested that perceptions of control may be important for Type As (e.g., Glass, 1977). Research has indicated that Type As do tend to desire control and responsibility, and they prefer to work alone (Clark & Miller, 1990; Strube, Lott, Heilizer, & Gregg, 1986). Many studies have also examined the outcomes associated with Type A behavior pattern. Compared to Type Bs, Type As are more punctual, work at faster rates, and are high achievers in college and in their professional careers (Gastorf, 1980; Taylor, Locke, Lee, & Gist, 1984; Yarnold & Grimm, 1982). So, although the Type A behavior pattern was initially studied because of its association with health problems, it also appears to be associated with positive outcomes such as high work performance and career success.

An important question is whether there is clear evidence that these positive outcomes come at the cost of higher strains and subsequent health problems. Specifically, researchers were interested in whether Types As respond to stressful situations with greater physiological arousal and thus suffer greater strains than Type Bs. Accordingly, many studies have attempted to link the TABP to increased physiological arousal and to the development of coronary heart disease. However, these efforts were slowed by the use of imprecise, global TABP measures that attempted to assess several different TABP subcomponents (Booth-Kewley & Friedman, 1987). This led researchers to focus on identifying specific subcomponents of the TABP that were most predictive of coronary heart disease. Subsequent studies indicated that **hostility** is the primary TABP subcomponent associated with increased secretion of stress hormones as well as increased risk of coronary heart disease and other long-term, harmful health outcomes (Krantz & McCeney, 2002; Miller, Smith, Turner, Guijarro, & Hallet, 1996). Thus, Type As who exhibit hostility pay a price for their accomplishments in terms of increasing their likelihood of suffering from a variety of long-term health problems.

Achievement Strivings and Impatience/Irritability   Although researchers identified hostility as the TABP subcomponent that is related to long-term health outcomes,

CORONARY-PRONE PERSONALITY

Alternative name given to Type A behavior pattern (TABP) because of its links to coronary heart disease and heart attacks.

HOSTILITY

Type A behavior pattern subcomponent associated with increased secretion of stress hormones and increased risk of coronary heart disease and other long-term, harmful health outcomes.

BOX 15.1

PACE OF LIFE ACROSS THE UNITED STATES AND OTHER COUNTRIES

Levine, Lynch, Miyake, and Lucia (1989) examined the relationship between the pace of life and coronary heart disease in 36 metropolitan areas across the United States. Four indicators of pace were assessed and then averaged to form an overall pace of life:

1. Walking speed of a sample of pedestrians over 60-foot distances in downtown locations.
2. Talking speed of postal clerks in answering a standard question about the difference between regular mail, certified mail, and insured mail.
3. Speed of a bank teller in giving change for two $20 bills.
4. The proportion of individuals wearing watches (concern with clock time).

As predicted, cities in the Northeast (e.g., Boston, New York) had the fastest pace of life, and cities in California (e.g., Los Angeles, San Diego) and the Southeast (e.g., Shreveport, Memphis) had the slowest pace of life. Notably, pace of life was strongly related to death rates from coronary heart disease across cities. Levine et al. explained that fast-paced cities (which they named "Type A" cities) appear to attract and create a large concentration of hard-driving Type A individuals. They also suggested that the stress of Type A cities leads to unhealthy behaviors (e.g., cigarette smoking, alcohol use, unhealthy diet) that increase the risk of coronary heart disease.

In a follow-up study, Levine and Norenzayan (1999) compared the pace of life in large cities from 31 countries around the world. They used three indicators of pace of life: walking speed in downtown locations, the speed with which postal clerks completed the simple task of providing change after the purchase of a single stamp, and the accuracy of public clocks. The pace of life was fastest in Japan and countries in Western Europe (e.g., Switzerland, Germany) and slowest in developing countries (e.g., Mexico, Indonesia, Brazil). Overall, the pace of life was significantly faster in economically productive countries and in individualist cultures. Fast-paced countries also tended to have higher rates of death from coronary heart disease and higher smoking rates.

Interestingly, Switzerland was first in clock accuracy (no surprise for the country known for precise watches) and New York City was one of only two cities (the other was Budapest) in which the postal clerk insulted the researcher. In summarizing his research, Levine (1997) described Japan as a paradox because, although it has a fast pace of life and workaholism is rampant, the incidence of coronary heart disease is relatively low. Levine attributed the low heart disease in Japan to a diet low in saturated fats, strong social support at work, and a collectivist culture that divides stress and work pressures equally among co-workers. Alternatively, typical fast-paced cities in the United States attract competitive Type As (Smith & Anderson, 1986) who work in an individualist culture that does not emphasize social support or shared goals. In combination with unhealthy behaviors (e.g., high-fat diet, smoking, alcohol use, lack of exercise), these characteristics contribute to the high rate of coronary heart disease in fast-paced cities in the United States. Overall, these studies indicate that the pace of life indeed differs across cities and countries and that it is associated with important economic and health outcomes.

Based on these findings, what can managers and executives in organizations in the United States learn from their Japanese counterparts?

investigators continued to examine other TABP subcomponents in their attempts to predict work and short-term health outcomes in Type As. Two TABP subcomponents that have received attention are achievement striving and impatience/irritability (Spence, Helmreich, & Pred, 1987). **Achievement striving (AS)** is the tendency to be active and to work hard in achieving one's goals, whereas **impatience/irritability (II)** reflects the intolerance and frustration that results from being slowed down.

The AS dimension, which overlaps with the Big Five dimension of conscientiousness, is positively correlated with academic performance, sales performance, and job satisfaction (Bluen, Barling, & Burns, 1990; Spence et al., 1987). The II dimension is associated with health problems such as insomnia, headaches, poor digestion, and respiratory difficulties (Barling & Boswell, 1995; Bluen et al., 1990). These studies indicate that AS and II are independent from each other and that these TABP subcomponents can be used to differentially predict performance and health outcomes.

Time Urgency   An additional TABP subcomponent that appears to be related to important work and health problems is **time urgency,** which refers to the feeling of being pressured

ACHIEVEMENT STRIVING (AS)

Type A behavior pattern subcomponent that involves the tendency to be active and to work hard in achieving one's goals.

IMPATIENCE/ IRRITABILITY (II)

Type A behavior pattern subcomponent that reflect intolerance and frustration resulting from being slowed down.

TIME URGENCY

Type A behavior pattern subcomponent that refers to the feeling of being pressured by inadequate time.

by inadequate time. Time-urgent individuals check their watches repeatedly, even when they are not under the pressure of deadlines, and they are concerned with saving relatively small amounts of time (often measured in minutes or seconds). Time-urgent individuals always seem to know what time it is, even when they are not wearing a watch. Increasing evidence indicates that individuals differ widely from one another in the degree to which they concern themselves with the passage of time and how to cope with it in accomplishing work-related and personal goals (Conte, Mathieu, & Landy, 1998). For example, some individuals are constantly making schedules, lists, and deadlines for themselves, whereas others do not pay attention to such temporal concerns.

Recent evidence suggests that time urgency has multiple dimensions including time awareness, eating behavior, nervous energy, list making, scheduling, speech patterns, and deadline control. Landy, Rastegary, Thayer, and Colvin (1991) developed Behaviorally Anchored Rating Scales (BARS) for these dimensions of time urgency. Definitions of some dimensions are shown in Table 15.4. One of the authors of this book used to do a little study in class that was a good "quick and dirty measure" of time urgency. He asked students if they had ever read the small print on theater tickets while waiting for the movie or play to start. Time-urgent students had read the tickets. This was closely associated with the nervous energy scale.

Research indicates that these time urgency dimensions are relatively independent, which means that individuals can be high on some dimensions, but relatively lower on others (Conte, Landy, & Mathieu, 1995; Landy et al., 1991). For example, workers may eat very quickly during a brief lunch break, but they may not focus much on making lists or following schedules very closely. Alternatively, some task-oriented individuals may work quickly and focus closely on schedules and deadlines, but they may not speak quickly or exhibit nervous energy.

Research also indicates that certain time urgency dimensions (e.g., list making, scheduling) are related to work outcomes, whereas other time urgency dimensions (e.g., eating behavior, nervous energy, speech patterns) are related to health outcomes. Menon, Narayanan, and Spector (1996) related time urgency to occupational stress and health outcomes in a sample of nurses and physicians. They found that rapid talking and eating behaviors were positively correlated with arguments on the job and with lowered resistance to physical illness. In contrast, scheduling, list-making, and time-awareness behaviors were

TABLE 15.4	Examples of Time Urgency Dimensions and Their Definitions
DIMENSION	**DEFINITION**
Time awareness	Extent to which an individual is aware of the time of day regardless of environment or circumstances.
Scheduling	Extent to which an individual schedules activities and keeps to that schedule, which might include leisure, personal, and/or work activities.
List making	Extent to which an individual engages in actions directed toward saving time through efficient planning.
Speech patterns	Extent to which an individual exhibits rushed speech patterns, including talking fast, interrupting others, and finishing the sentences of others.
Deadline control	Extent to which an individual creates or appears to be controlled by deadlines.

SOURCE: Adapted from Landy, Rastegary, Thayer, & Colvin (1991).

| BOX | 15.2 | THE INCREASINGLY TIME URGENT NATURE OF WORK AND LIFE |

The importance of utilizing time efficiently is certainly not a new one. In 1757 Benjamin Franklin wrote that "time is money." In 1877 the English journalist W. R. Greg echoed the sentiment: "Beyond doubt, the most salient characteristic of life in this latter half of the 19th century is its speed." A more contemporary view of how many people think of time is given by comedian Stephen Wright, who boasts, "I have a microwave fireplace. You can lie in front of it all night in only eight minutes."

At the beginning of the 21st century, life revolves increasingly around the clock, particularly in Western cultures. In our culture, businesses cater to the time-conscious cravings of individuals. We have instant burgers, instant breakfasts, instant coffee, instant photos, and instant replays, to name a few (Gleick, 1999). Time-saving devices such as computers, faxes, e-mail, and cell phones are increasingly becoming indispensable parts of our work and personal lives. Most of us probably know people who would love a microwave fireplace—people who are so obsessed with saving time that they rush through leisure activities that are supposed to be enjoyed at a relaxed pace. The popularity of instant products and time-saving devices indicates that people today, like Ben Franklin, view their time as a scarce and valuable commodity.

Researchers have attempted to determine how people became so obsessed with time. For example, Wright (1988) identified critical experiences that were related to the obsession with time in his Type A heart patients. These early experiences involved: (1) a high need to achieve, (2) success and therefore reinforcement for such efforts, and (3) exposure to timed activities that provided a personal blueprint for achieving by more efficient use of time and by being constantly active. According to Wright, these critical experiences result in people developing a "shotgun-like" effort to achieve as much as possible in as little time as possible. Many individuals utilize this approach in their jobs as they consider speed and efficiency to be signs of success. This approach is often carried over to personal activities as well.

Questions

1. In which jobs or occupations is the rapid completion of work a particularly high priority?
2. Can you identify jobs in which there are no time pressures? Is identifying such jobs more or less difficult than it was 10 years ago? Why?

positively related to job satisfaction, indicating that some time urgency dimensions can result in positive work outcomes.

Conte, Schwenneker, Dew, and Romano (2001) found that the deadline control time urgency dimension was significantly related to work pace—that is, individuals who were focused on deadlines worked faster than those who were not controlled by them. This finding is likely to be useful in organizations and industries in which a fast work pace is crucial. For example, there are immense pressures for efficient and timely development of new products in the computer industry. Time-urgent individuals who have experience working under time constraints may be able to withstand a higher level of time pressure when the work situation requires it (Freedman & Edwards, 1988). However, differences in the way team members approach and utilize time may be a source of tension and may make it difficult for teams to function well under deadline pressures (Waller, Conte, Gibson, & Carpenter, 2001).

Overall, specific TABP subcomponents do a better job of predicting particular criteria than a global Type A measure that combines a variety of different subcomponents. Thus, researchers and practitioners concerned about health and performance will have more success using TABP subcomponents to predict health and performance outcomes. In summary, research on TABP subcomponents indicates that:

- Achievement striving is positively related to desirable work outcomes.
- Impatience/irritability is related to short-term health problems.
- Hostility is most predictive of long-term health outcomes (e.g., coronary heart disease).
- The multiple dimensions of time urgency are related to a variety of work and health outcomes.

MODULE 15.2 SUMMARY

- Several theories of stress have been developed to organize the relationships among stressors, strains, and potential moderators of those relationships. Two theories of stress that have received a great deal of attention are Karasek's Demand-Control Model and French's Person-Environment Fit Model.

- Karasek's Demand-Control Model suggests that two factors are prominent in producing job stress: job demands and job control (also known as decision latitude). Karasek proposed that the combination of high work demands with low control results in "high strain" jobs that result in a variety of health problems.

- French's Person-Environment (P-E) fit model proposes that the fit between a person and the environment determines the amount of stress that a person perceives. A poor fit between the person and the environment is frequently associated with increased strains, but employees whose skills and abilities fit well with the work environment report less stress and fewer strains.

- I-O psychologists have studied several individual difference characteristics as potential moderators of stressor-strain relationships. Individual difference characteristics that have received the most attention as moderators of the stressor-strain relationship are locus of control, hardiness, self-esteem, and the Type A behavior pattern.

KEY TERMS

Demand-Control model
job demand
job control
person-job fit
person-organization fit

locus of control (LOC)
hardiness
transformational coping
self-esteem
Type A behavior pattern (TABP)

coronary-prone personality
hostility
achievement striving (AS)
impatience/irritability (II)
time urgency

CRITICAL THINKING EXERCISES

15.3 Hardiness is an individual difference characteristic that provides resistance to stress. Some studies have found that executives and lawyers benefit from having "hardy personalities" that protect them from these stressful jobs. What are two other inherently stressful occupations in which it is beneficial for incumbents to have hardy personalities? Why?

15.4 Besides the jobs listed in Figure 15.3 for the Demand-Control model, identify one job that should be in each of the four quadrants and explain why that job is characterized by high/low demands and high/low control.

REDUCING AND MANAGING STRESS

I n 1990 stress was listed for the first time as one of the top 10 occupational health risks in the United States. As a result, concerns about stress at work became much more prominent in public and government discussions of health (Sauter, Murphy, & Hurrell, 1990). These concerns led to the development of the field of **Occupational Health Psychology**, which involves the application of psychology to improving the quality of work life, and to protecting and promoting the safety, health, and well-being of workers.

Occupational health psychologists often divide their approaches to stress reduction and management into three major categories: primary, secondary, and tertiary interventions (Cooper et al., 2001; Quick et al., 1997). Table 15.5 provides a framework for stress management interventions. We will discuss these three types of strategies as well as recent reviews of their effectiveness.

PRIMARY PREVENTION STRATEGIES

Primary prevention strategies are concerned with modifying or eliminating stressors in the work environment and therefore said to be "stressor-directed" (Cooper & Cartwright, 2001). Primary interventions are the most proactive and preventative approaches to stress management (Cooper et al., 2001). Many primary intervention strategies give workers increased control over their job and work environment, which directly lowers stressors and increases employee satisfaction and well-being.

Primary prevention approaches include redesigning the task or work environment, encouraging participative management, developing clearer role descriptions, and modifying or changing Type A thought patterns. Another primary prevention strategy involves providing

OCCUPATIONAL HEALTH PSYCHOLOGY

Involves the application of psychology to improving the quality of work life, and to protecting and promoting the safety, health, and well-being of workers.

PRIMARY PREVENTION STRATEGY

Stress prevention strategy concerned with modifying or eliminating stressors in the work environment.

"Is there anyone here who specializes in stress management?"

TABLE 15.5	A Framework for Stress Management Interventions

Primary Prevention: Stressor-Directed

Scope: Preventative—Reduce the number and/or intensity of stressors.

Target: Alter work environments, technologies, or organizational structures.

Underlying assumption: Most effective approach to stress management is to remove stressors.

Examples: Job redesign; cognitive restructuring.

Secondary Interventions: Response-Directed

Scope: Preventative/reactive—modify individuals' responses to stressors.

Target: Individual.

Underlying assumption: May not be able to remove or reduce stressors, so best to focus on individuals' reactions to these stressors.

Examples: Relaxation training, biofeedback, stress management training, physical fitness, nutrition.

Tertiary Interventions: Symptom-Directed

Scope: Treatment—minimize the damaging consequences of stressors by helping individuals cope more effectively with these consequences.

Target: Individual.

Underlying assumption: Focus is on "treatment" of problems once they have occurred.

Examples: Employee assistance programs; medical care.

SOURCE: Adapted from Cooper, Dewe, & O'Driscoll (2001).

flexible work schedules, which can be seen in recent trends toward flextime, shorter work weeks, and job sharing. Earlier in the chapter, we discussed different coping styles or strategies. Primary prevention approaches are aligned with problem-focused coping strategies, which are directed at managing or altering the source of stress (Lazarus, 2000). We next discuss several examples of primary prevention approaches commonly used in organizations.

Work and Job Design

Work and jobs can be designed or redesigned to reduce such stressors as noise, interruptions, time pressure, role ambiguity, and the number of hours worked (Sparks, Cooper, Fried, & Shirom, 1997). In addition, jobs can be redesigned to increase worker participation in decision making and to increase autonomy on the job. Decades ago, restaurant owners decided to reduce the stress on short-order cooks by requiring waitpersons to clip their orders to a small, circular, revolving order stand. The cooks could then spin the stand around, see what orders were pending, and decide which ones to pull off first. This principle was extended to auto manufacturing by Saab and Volvo. Automobile bodies circled work teams on an oval track, and the teams decided when to pull a body off the track into a workstation for assembly and paint operations. Another example of redesigning work is the common "queuing" process that is found at many service centers. Customers stand in one line and are not permitted to approach a service desk until their number is flashed or an available agent is identified by electronic screen. This process increases the customer service agent's control over how quickly customers are served and thereby reduces the agent's stress. Such changes can help workers feel that their work is more meaningful and that they have control over work outcomes. This in turn leads to higher motivation and satisfaction as well as lower stress at work (Hackman & Oldham, 1980).

A study by Jackson (1983) provides a good example of the benefit of participative decision making. Jackson found that nursing and clerical employees who participated in decision making at staff meetings had increased perceptions of control and reduced role conflict and role ambiguity. With stressors reduced by this relatively simple change in the way meetings were conducted, employees had higher job satisfaction and lower emotional strain at work, which over time led to fewer absences and lower intentions to leave the job.

Cognitive Restructuring

Several of the approaches that we have discussed, including the Person-Environment fit model and the Type A behavior pattern, highlight the role of perceptions in the stress process. **Cognitive restructuring** interventions focus on changing perceptions and thought processes that lead to stress. These approaches reduce stress by changing an individual's perception of the work environment or one's capacities to meet the demands of the environment. Cognitive restructuring approaches encourage individuals to change negative thoughts to more positive ones (Quick et al., 1997). For example, a worker who thinks, "I can't handle this heavy workload," might be encouraged to think instead: "This workload is a challenge that I can handle if I break it down into manageable parts," or "I won't be considered a complete failure if I don't push very hard to finish this task today." Box 15.3 provides an example of how cognitive restructuring can be combined with other approaches to reduce stress and heart problems in Type A individuals.

SECONDARY PREVENTION STRATEGIES

Secondary prevention strategies involve modifying responses to inevitable demands or stressors; thus, they are said to be "response-directed." Because secondary prevention addresses the experience of stress rather than the stress or stressors, its role is often one of damage control. Thus, this type of intervention is often described as the "Band-Aid" approach (Cooper & Cartwright, 2001). Secondary prevention approaches are aligned with emotion-focused coping strategies, which seek to reduce the emotional response to the stressor and can involve avoiding, minimizing, and distancing oneself from the stressor (Lazarus, 2000). For example, emotion-focused coping might be used to reduce the stress experienced in a job that requires emotional labor.

Secondary prevention strategies that require no special training (but might be formally encouraged through an employer-sponsored program) include lifestyle choices such as physical fitness, healthy eating, and weight control, as well as a reduction in smoking and caffeine. Skills-training programs such as negotiation and conflict resolution are another form of secondary intervention. In addition, secondary stress management methods include relaxation techniques, biofeedback, and providing or encouraging social support at work. Many approaches use combinations of the above methods.

It is important to note that secondary prevention can be proactive or reactive. For example, Cooper et al. (2001) noted that training in conflict resolution skills can be used to reduce interpersonal conflict and its effects after it has occurred. Alternatively, such training can be used proactively to prevent interpersonal conflict from developing. Similarly, individuals can be proactive in exercising and maintaining a healthy diet, which can reduce or moderate future stress.

Stress Management Training

Programs involving stress management training are very popular with employers and employees. Cooper and Cartwright (2001) noted that the continued demand for stress management programs and the increasing stress levels reported in the literature are indicative of the acceptance by organizations that stress is an inherent and enduring feature of the work environment. **Stress management training** programs are useful for helping

COGNITIVE RESTRUCTURING

Type of stress intervention that focuses on changing perceptions and thought processes that lead to stress; reduces stress by changing the individual's perception of, or capacity to meet the demands of, the work environment.

SECONDARY PREVENTION STRATEGY

Stress prevention strategy that involves modifying responses to inevitable demands or stressors.

STRESS MANAGEMENT TRAINING

A program useful for helping employees deal with workplace stressors that are difficult to remove or change.

BOX 15.3

CARDIAC PSYCHOLOGY AND THE REDUCTION OF TIME PATHOLOGIES

A relatively new field called **cardiac psychology** combines the expertise of medical doctors (i.e., cardiologists) and psychologists in an attempt to reduce heart disease by changing the thought processes of Type A heart patients (Allan & Scheidt, 1996). Cardiac psychologists recommend a variety of approaches to reduce the "hurry sickness" observed in some extreme Type As. **Hurry sickness** involves severe and chronic feelings of time urgency that negatively affect one's lifestyle. A frequent symptom of hurry sickness is "racing mind syndrome," which is characterized by insomnia and rapid, shifting thoughts.

This new approach goes back to the pioneering work of Friedman and Rosenman, who noted that their Type A patients felt frustrated and hostile when they were prevented from finishing tasks or meeting their goals. In their attempts to change Type A thought patterns, Friedman and Rosenman reminded their Type A patients (most of whom had already had a heart attack) that a successful life is always unfinished. They drove their point home by reminding their patients that only a corpse is completely "finished" (Friedman & Rosenman, 1974).

Cardiac psychologists find that Type As can decrease their stress and strains if they let go of (1) their obsessive focus on time and (2) the anger and hostility that occurs when they are slowed down (Ulmer & Schwartzburd, 1996). Cognitive restructuring is an important part of reducing the stress that Type As commonly felt. For example, Type A patients are encouraged to think, "Perhaps I shouldn't get so angry because the driver who just cut me off may not have seen me."

Another critical part of the program involves behavioral drills designed to help those suffering from hurry sickness to slow down and see that rushing does not necessarily have to be a part of completing one's work or daily tasks. Here are some drills to reduce hurry sickness (Ulmer & Schwartzburd, 1996):

1. Walk and talk more slowly.
2. Linger at the table after eating; avoid rushing through lunch while working at your desk.
3. Practice doing or thinking about one thing at a time.
4. Practice listening without interrupting.
5. Drive in one of the slow lanes.
6. Stand in a long line and use your mind creatively to take advantage of the wait.
7. Don't wear your watch.
8. Practice meditation or relaxation exercises.
9. Listen to soothing music for 30 minutes and do nothing else.

As you may have guessed, these drills are difficult for Type As (and perhaps everyone—who likes to stand in a long line?). The first time a confirmed Type A tries driving five miles in the slow lane might not be a time we would enjoy riding along! Nevertheless, heart attacks have a funny way of changing preferences and behavior patterns. People who have had, or are told they are at great risk for, heart attacks make dramatic changes in their lifestyle. They lose weight, change their diet, take up exercise, and slow down. It is unfortunate that it takes a catastrophic event to motivate that change. Combined with cognitive restructuring and group therapy sessions, the behavioral drills are effective in reducing stress and heart problems in Type As (Ulmer & Schwartzburd, 1996).

CARDIAC PSYCHOLOGY

Combines the expertise of medical doctors (cardiologists) and psychologists in an effort to reduce heart disease by changing the thought processes of Type A heart patients.

HURRY SICKNESS

Severe and chronic feelings of time urgency that negatively affect one's lifestyle.

employees deal with those stressors that are difficult to remove or change. They often include a variety of secondary prevention techniques and may even include some primary techniques. For example, many stress management programs are described as cognitive-behavioral skills training programs.

Cognitive-Behavioral Skills Training   A variety of techniques are designed to help workers modify the appraisal processes that determine how stressful they perceive a situation to be, and to develop behavioral skills for managing stressors (Murphy, 1996). The most common type of cognitive-behavioral skills training is **stress inoculation,** which usually consists of an educational component—learning about how a person has responded to past stressful experiences; rehearsal—learning various coping skills such as problem solving, time management, relaxation, and cognitive coping; and application—practicing those skills under simulated conditions (Murphy, 1996). Thus, in many cases these approaches are a combination of primary (i.e., to reduce stressors by means of cognitive restructuring) and secondary (i.e., to manage or cope with symptoms of stress through behavioral skills training) prevention strategies.

Jones et al. (1988) developed an organizationwide stress management program that was used with employees of several hospitals. The program included video modules that enhanced the understanding of stress and provided information regarding how to develop and improve coping skills, health behaviors, and relaxation routines. In a longitudinal investigation that evaluated the impact of this stress management program, Jones et al. found that one result was a significant drop in the average number of monthly medication errors by doctors and nurses. In an additional two-year longitudinal investigation, they found that 22 hospitals that implemented the same organizationwide stress management program had significantly fewer medical malpractice claims compared with a similar, matched sample of 22 hospitals that did not participate. This study showed that well-conducted, psychological research efforts can decrease malpractice claims through stress management interventions.

Relaxation and Biofeedback Techniques

Relaxation techniques include progressive muscle relaxation and deep breathing exercises. **Progressive muscle relaxation** involves starting at the top or bottom on one's body, tightening one set of muscles at a time for five to seven seconds, and then letting those muscles relax. Individuals can work through each major muscle group and thus help to progressively relax the entire body. These relaxation techniques are effective in reducing arousal and anxiety (Murphy, 1996).

Biofeedback is a stress management technique that involves teaching individuals to control certain body functions such as heart rate, blood pressure, and even skin temperature by responding to feedback about their body from an electronic instrument (Quick et al., 1997). One simple and inexpensive biofeedback device is a skin-sensitive "biodot" that monitors stress levels and physiological changes according to color changes. The dot darkens after individuals discuss a stressful event and lightens when they feel more relaxed (Ulmer & Schwartzburd, 1996). Thus, this device shows individuals that stress—and relaxation, for that matter—leads to measurable changes in the body and that careful monitoring of the body can reduce anxiety and arousal.

Social Support

Social support is the comfort, assistance, or information an individual receives through formal or informal contacts with individuals or groups. Social support has been widely investigated as a way to reduce stress and strain at work. House (1981) identified four different kinds of social support.

1. *Instrumental support*—direct help, often of a practical nature; for example, a friend encourages a co-worker to slow down by suggesting joint walks during the lunch hour.

2. *Emotional support*—interest in, understanding of, caring for, and sympathy with a person's difficulties; this type of support is often provided by a therapist or a family member.

3. *Informational support*—information to help a person solve a problem; this type of support is often supplied by a health care professional. In addition, an increasing number of websites are popping up with useful information.

4. *Appraisal support*—feedback about a person's functioning that enhances his or her self-esteem; this often comes from a close friend, a therapist, family members, or other members of a support group.

Researchers have given considerable attention to the possibility that social support moderates or reduces health problems by protecting individuals from the negative effects of work stressors. Studying such effects is called the **buffer or moderator hypothesis** because it seeks to determine whether the negative effects of work stressors can be buffered or moderated by social support (Cohen & Wills, 1985). Evidence is mixed on the buffering

STRESS INOCULATION

Common type of stress management training that usually combines primary prevention and secondary prevention strategies.

PROGRESSIVE MUSCLE RELAXATION

Stress management technique to relax the, muscles, thereby helping to progressively relax the entire body.

BIOFEEDBACK

Stress management technique that teaches individuals to control certain body functions such as heart rate, blood pressure, and even skin temperature by responding to feedback from an electronic instrument.

SOCIAL SUPPORT

The comfort, assistance, or information an individual receives through formal or informal contacts with individuals or groups.

BUFFER OR MODERATOR HYPOTHESIS

Hypothesis that social support moderates or reduces health problems by protecting individuals from the negative effects of work stressors.

hypothesis, which could be due to the failure of researchers to emphasize the match between stressors and support. That is, buffering should work when there is a reasonable match between the stressors and the available social support. A longitudinal study of 90 blue-collar metalworkers found evidence for the buffering hypothesis in reducing anxiety and other strains when social support was matched directly to a social stressor such as conflict with one's supervisor (Frese, 1999). Social support at work may be particularly important as a moderator of the stress-strain relationship in the present day when traditional societal structures such as the extended family are smaller than they once were (Quick et al., 1997). For example, in 21st-century American society, many adult children no longer live close to their parents or siblings. They may see family members infrequently, usually over holiday periods that carry their own stress and strain. At the nuclear family level, parents and teenage children may eat two meals together during an entire week.

Employers can help build effective social support systems at work. For example, formal mentoring programs, reward and recognition systems, and newcomer socialization programs can make work environments more supportive. Allen, McManus, and Russell (1999) found evidence for the important role that more experienced peers can serve in mentoring newcomers and in enhancing socialization. In turn, they found a negative correlation between socialization and work stress, indicating that formal peer relationships can be critical in reducing stress and subsequent strains. Finally, the supportive relationships formed in team building have been shown to improve performance and reduce stress (Svyantek, Goodman, Benz, & Gard, 1999).

TERTIARY PREVENTION STRATEGIES

TERTIARY PREVENTION STRATEGY

Stress prevention strategy focused on healing the negative effects of stressors.

EMPLOYEE ASSISTANCE PROGRAM (EAP)

Counseling provided by an organization to deal with workplace stress, alcohol or drug difficulties, and problems stemming from outside the job.

Tertiary prevention strategies are "symptom-directed" and thus they are focused on healing the negative effects of stressors. Tertiary interventions include employee assistance programs and the use of medical care, individual psychotherapy, and career counseling (Quick et al., 1997).

Employee assistance programs (EAPs) were originally developed by organizations to address alcohol and drug problems, and they were subsequently broadened to include stress management interventions. In most organizations, EAPs involve some form of counseling to deal with work stress, alcohol or drug difficulties, and problems outside the job (e.g., family problems, behavioral and emotional difficulties). Employee assistance programs can be provided by the human resources department within an organization, or they may be provided by external consultants or vendors. If an organization is to have a successful EAP, its management must express support for the program, educate employees about it, provide the necessary training on its use, and make the program accessible to employees (Milne, Blum, & Roman, 1994). Organizations must ensure that confidentiality is maintained and that use of an EAP program does not harm job security or advancement. These suggestions are particularly important because unhealthy work climates and distrust in EAPs often prevent employees from seeking help for alcohol or drug abuse problems. For example, police officers often avoid in-house EAPs because they are uncertain of the confidentiality assurances and fear that they will be stigmatized by commanding officers and colleagues. Even to be seen talking with an EAP coordinator is "dangerous." Integrating positive messages about the EAP into different types of training programs may be effective in improving the use of EAPs by skeptical employees (Bennett & Lehmann, 2001).

Although EAPs are not often systematically evaluated by the organizations using them, the few evaluations that have been done indicate that EAPs are successful. Cooper and Saderi (1991) found improvements in the mental health and self-esteem of employees participating in EAPs. In addition, Cooper and Cartwright (1994) found that EAP programs can be very cost effective for organizations in terms of reducing absences, accidents, and health care costs. Nevertheless, even though focusing on the treatment of strains may be an effective short-term strategy, the approach is essentially reactive and recuperative rather than proactive and preventative (Cooper et al., 2001). Because EAPs focus on dealing with the long-term outcomes of stress, they should certainly not be the only approach that organizations utilize in the stress prevention and management process.

SUMMARY OF STRESS INTERVENTION STRATEGIES

Several recent studies have evaluated a variety of stress management interventions. In a study by Bellarosa and Chen (1997), 96 stress management experts evaluated occupational stress management interventions (e.g., relaxation, physical fitness, cognitive restructuring, stress inoculation, meditation, and assertiveness training) on the basis of practicality and effectiveness. The stress management experts evaluated relaxation as the most practical and easily implemented intervention, and they rated physical fitness as the most effective intervention. Evaluations by stress management experts are useful, but I-O psychologists and occupational health psychologists are also interested in more quantitative assessments of stress management interventions (Murphy, 1996; van der Klink, Blonk, Schene, & van Dijk, 2001).

Murphy (1996) conducted a comprehensive review of the effects of worksite stress management interventions on a variety of health and work outcomes (e.g., blood pressure, anxiety, headaches, and job satisfaction). The stress management programs included in this review were progressive muscle relaxation, meditation, biofeedback, cognitive-behavioral skills, and combinations of these techniques. Meditation produced the most consistent results across outcome measures, but it was infrequently used in organizations. Relaxation and cognitive-behavioral techniques were found to be quite successful. Overall, the study indicated that using a combination of techniques (e.g., muscle relaxation and cognitive-behavioral skills) was more effective across outcome measures than using any single technique. In another review of stress management interventions, Bunce (1997) also concluded that combining various stress management interventions is more effective than using any single approach. A recent meta-analysis found general support for the benefits of interventions for work-related stress (van der Klink et al., 2001). This study found that cognitive-behavioral approaches worked best in reducing stress, but relaxation techniques were also successful. Overall, these studies show reason for optimism about stress management interventions, particularly when a combination of techniques is used. In addition, successful stress management interventions must accurately identify the stressors causing strains, and then actively determine ways to reduce those stressors (Briner & Reynolds, 1999). Employees should also participate in the process of identifying stressors and implementing the various interventions designed to reduce stress and strains.

Primary stress prevention strategies are generally preferred over other interventions because they take an active approach to removing and reducing stressors (Quick et al., 1997). Secondary and tertiary interventions can play a useful role in stress management, but their effectiveness is limited because they fail to address the sources of stress itself. Thus, identifying and recognizing stressors and taking steps to remove or reduce them through job redesign, flexible work schedules, or other primary prevention strategies should receive the highest attention in organizations. Indeed, the limited research that has examined primary-level interventions has shown that they yield consistently positive and beneficial long-term effects (Cooper & Cartwright, 2001). Similarly, the National Institute for Occupational Safety and Health (NIOSH) urges occupational health psychology professionals to give special attention to the primary prevention of organizational risk factors for stress, illness, and injury at work.

STRESS AND WORKPLACE VIOLENCE

In this section we turn to a topic that has been receiving increased attention by I-O psychologists and others who are concerned about the violence that can occur in the workplace when stress prevention and management strategies fail.

Homicide is among the leading causes of death in the workplace, and the workplace is the site of one of every six violent crimes reported in the United States (Kennish, 1995, LeBlanc & Kelloway, 2002). Although many of the incidents comprising these statistics are perpetrated by nonemployees (e.g., cash register robberies), the risk of violence instigated by employees and former employees is real in today's workplace. In addition to critical concerns about on-the-job safety, workplace violence costs organizations and society billions of dollars (Flannery, 1995). Understanding why certain individuals engage in workplace violence requires consideration of both their personal characteristics and stressful aspects of their work environment. Kinney (1995) noted that stressful factors correlated with workplace violence include being passed over for an expected promotion, financial problems, estranged or strained relationships with co-workers, and a perception of being targeted by management.

Some clear characteristics of perpetrators of workplace violence have emerged, and many of these characteristics relate to issues discussed in this chapter. First, 97 percent of workplace violence perpetrators are male. More specifically, the perpetrator is typically a Caucasian male with very little (if any) social support—a "loner" (Hurrell, Worthington, & Driscoll, 1996). Violent individuals often have a fascination with guns and tend to have an external locus of control, hostile/impulsive personalities, and a pattern of drug and alcohol abuse (Martinko & Zellars, 1998).

Contrary to the common perception that low self-esteem correlates with workplace violence, Baumeister, Smart, & Boden (1996) found workplace violence is most commonly a result of a *high* self-esteem that is disputed by some person or circumstance (e.g., negative feedback or derogatory remarks). Stressors such as interpersonal conflict can lead to workplace violence when they result in wounded pride or "ego threats" to those with high self-esteem. Thus, managers and supervisors should be particularly careful to avoid disrespect or verbal abuse during stressful times (e.g., downsizing, performance reviews) that might interact with subordinates' high self-esteem and lead to workplace violence. Many perpetrators of workplace violence have just been passed over for a promotion, have received a negative evaluation, or have been fired. In fact, the last words spoken to three employees of an insurance company in Florida by a disgruntled former co-worker before he killed them were, "This is what you get for firing me" (Duncan, 1995).

Feldman and Johnson (1994) analyzed data from 60 incidents of workplace violence. They found that 68 percent of the perpetrators of violent acts had some type of psychiatric diagnosis before the incident. About one-third were diagnosed with depression, and about half were diagnosed with either a personality disorder or substance abuse. Overall, they concluded that most perpetrators of workplace violence had (1) personality disorders that made them respond poorly to stress, (2) conflicted relationships at work, and (3) inappropriate and angry reactions to perceived threats to their self-esteem.

Stress is clearly considered to be one of the causes of workplace violence. To compound the problem, recent work also suggests that workplace violence is a cause of stress. In particular, individuals who are victims of or witnesses to workplace violence report high job stress and subsequent strains (Mack, Shannon, Quick, & Quick, 1998). For all of the above reasons, it is advisable that every organization have policies and plans in place to reduce work stress and workplace violence. Workplace violence is certainly an area that I-O psychologists interested in work stress will continue to study. We will discuss workplace violence further in Chapter 16, which addresses work design and safety issues.

FUTURE WORK TRENDS AND CHALLENGES TO STRESS AND STRESS MANAGEMENT

The workforce of tomorrow will be more culturally and ethnically diverse, and will include larger numbers of older workers and women, than the workforce of previous decades. For this reason, it is important for I-O psychologists to determine whether the stress factors that predict coronary heart disease in male Caucasians (by far the most commonly studied group) are the same as in other populations (Keita & Hurrell, 1994; Quick et al., 1997). For example, coronary heart disease is the leading killer of African Americans and Mexican Americans as well as Caucasians, and there is evidence that genetics and nutrition play a role in the development of coronary heart disease for these ethnic groups (American Heart Association, 2002). However, the large body of research that indicates that work stress also plays a role in coronary heart disease has largely ignored the potential influence of ethnicity on the re-

An on-the-job confrontation or stressful event is often a precursor of workplace violence.

lationship between stressors and strains (Ford, 1985; Kahn & Byosiere, 1992). Gutierres, Saenz, and Green (1994) suggested that one underlying assumption in stress research is that employees of different ethnic backgrounds and genders respond similarly to work stressors. However, little data are available to support this assumption, and few researchers have investigated the moderators (e.g., individual differences, social support) of the stress-strain relationship in minority populations.

Similarly, the globalization of the economy presents new challenges in understanding and preventing stress in the workplace. Peterson et al. (1995) found that Western countries had significantly higher role ambiguity than non-Western countries. This raises the possibility that individuals from higher-stress Western countries may "inject" stress into non-Western cultures at great cost to individual employees and the organization.

Modifications intended to reduce stress, such as increases in flexible employment (e.g., flextime, part-time work), as well as changing organizational structures and work processes, are likely to lead to new stressors that are not yet well understood. For example, more organizations are using electronic performance monitoring (Hedge & Borman, 1995); as we discussed in Chapter 6, this new technique can often be stressful to employees. Several additional influences in the new millennium are predicted to be stressful, including technological change, global competition, downsizing, elder and child care, and increased teamwork (DeFrank & Ivancevich, 1998). There is little doubt that opportunities for the experience of stress at work are increasing rapidly. It is important to study and understand how these changes in the nature of work will influence the health and well-being of workers and their families. These new influences will clearly present challenges to I-O psychologists and occupational health psychologists in the years to come.

MODULE 15.3 SUMMARY

- The field of occupational health psychology involves the application of psychology to the protection and promotion of the safety, health, and well-being of workers. Occupational health psychologists often divide their approaches to stress prevention into three major categories: primary, secondary, and tertiary interventions.

- Primary prevention strategies aim to modify or eliminate stressors at work, and they are generally preferred over other interventions because they take an active approach. Primary prevention strategies include redesigning the work environment, modifying Type A thought patterns, and providing flexible work schedules.

- Secondary prevention strategies involve modifying responses to inevitable stressors. They include physical fitness, healthy eating, weight control, smoking and caffeine reduction, skills training programs, relaxation techniques, biofeedback, and providing or encouraging social support at work.
- Tertiary prevention strategies focus on healing the negative effects of stressors. They include employee assistance programs and the use of medical care, individual psychotherapy, and career counseling.
- Stress is recognized as a cause of workplace violence. Recent research also suggests that workplace violence is a cause of stress. It is advisable that every organization have policies and plans in place to reduce work stress and workplace violence.

KEY TERMS

occupational health psychology
primary prevention strategy
cognitive restructuring
secondary prevention strategy
stress management training

cardiac psychology
hurry sickness
stress inoculation
progressive muscle relaxation
biofeedback

social support
buffer or moderator hypothesis
tertiary prevention strategy
employee assistance program
 (EAP)

CRITICAL THINKING EXERCISES

15.5 For most students, the end of the semester or quarter is a stressful time. As you approach the end of the current term, if you had to choose one stress reduction approach from each of the three types of intervention strategies (primary, secondary, tertiary), which approaches would you choose? Why?

15.6 Identify the sources of social support in your life. Then provide two examples of occasions when these sources provided social support when you were under stress. What specific kinds of social support (e.g., emotional, informational, instrumental, appraisal) did these sources provide?

DESIGNING WORK FOR PEOPLE

16 CHAPTER

HUMAN FACTORS ENGINEERING (HFE)

THE IMPORTANCE AND MEANING OF HUMAN FACTORS

Human factors concerns are unique to industrial-organization (I-O) psychology because they typically involve many other areas of psychology including, in particular, physiological and cognitive psychology. As a result, courses in human factors are less common than courses in work motivation, training, or stress. Nevertheless, to give complete appreciation to the complexity of modern work, and particularly to issues related to work safety, we present this chapter as a primer or perhaps a sampler of human factors issues.

Workers are exposed to a wide variety of work "conditions." We covered many of those conditions in Chapters 5 and 15. They included physical conditions such as heat, light, and noise. They also included psychological conditions such as work pace, conflict, and responsibility. We also introduced the notion of compensation for working conditions in our discussion of job evaluation. In each of these discussions, working "conditions" were taken as a given. The individual worker was expected to either adapt, or at least put up with, these conditions.

The **human factors** approach uses the "knowledge of human [capabilities] to design systems, organizations, jobs, machines, tools, and consumer products for safe, efficient, and comfortable human use" (Helander, 1997, p. 4). The term "human factors" is synonymous with *human factors engineering* or *human factors psychology*. Human factors overlaps with related disciplines such as **ergonomics,** the study of the physical demands of work, such as reaching, stretching, lifting, and carrying; applied experimental psychology; occupational medicine; and exercise physiology. We will not deal directly with these latter areas, but you should understand that since human factors is related to these other disciplines, human factors research and practice may be the most interdisciplinary area of I-O psychology.

The human factors approach assumes that workers are a constant, and that the work needs to adapt to the worker. Human capacities and limitations include physical and cognitive abilities, knowledge, personality, and even physiology. The goal of the human factors psychologist is to develop a physical and psychological environment that is optimally compatible with the capacities and limitations of humans. Rather than accepting the environment as a constant, and selecting those few individuals who may be most compatible with it, the human factors psychologist catalogs human capacities and limitations, and develops an environment that is as ideally suited as possible to them.

This was not always the case. In the early days of the factory system, machines were designed by mechanical engineers who had little concern for the capacities and limitations of humans. An example of this can be seen in the design of a popular machine for working on metal parts called a lathe. The purpose of a lathe is to create a shape in a piece of steel or aluminum by spinning that piece at a high speed and applying a sharp bit to its surface while it is spinning. Before computers were introduced to the factory floor, lathes were operated by hand with lots of manual controls, usually in the form of wheels, levers, and buttons which were used to bring the bit into contact with the piece to be shaped.

HUMAN FACTORS

Approach that uses knowledge of human capabilities and limitations to design systems, organizations, jobs, machines, tools, and consumer products for safe, efficient, and comfortable human use. Synonymous with human factors engineering and human factors psychology.

ERGONOMICS

Study of the physical demands of work such as reaching, stretching, lifting, and carrying.

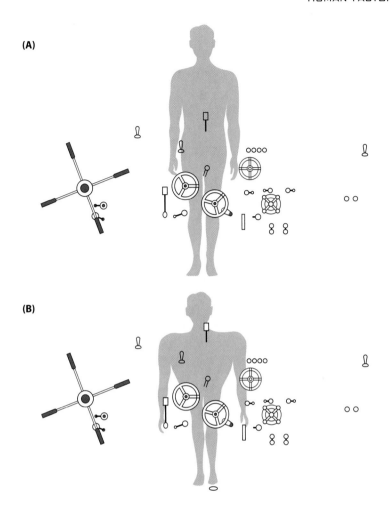

FIGURE 16.1

Two Views of the "Ideal" Lathe Operator The controls of a lathe in current use are not within easy reach of the average man but are so placed that the ideal operator should be $4\frac{1}{2}$ feet tall, 12 feet across the shoulders, and have an 8-foot arm span. SOURCE: Applied Ergonomics (1974).

(A)

(B)

Consider the two individuals depicted in Figure 16.1. The person in the top portion of the figure (A) represents a typical lathe operator (height, reach, build, and so on). But the "ideal" operator of a lathe designed by mechanical engineers in the 1920s, as sketched in the lower portion (B), would look much different. The ideal operator would be slightly over $4\frac{1}{2}$ feet tall and 12 feet across the shoulders, and would have an 8-foot arm span. This ideal operator was determined by the way the mechanical engineers designed the lathe, and we can be fairly certain that few real-life lathe operators resembled the ideal. The engineers most likely began their design with standard measurements of the components from which the machine would be built. From the human factors perspective, this was foolish. The mechanical engineers should have begun their design with an appreciation of the range of likely characteristics, capacities, and limitations of the operators of the lathe. The implications are clear. If the equipment and environment are not compatible with the humans who will use that equipment and populate that environment, we can expect problems in the form of lowered production, injuries, and accidents. We also can expect to see unhappy workers who are continually "taxed" by their work.

Figure 16.2 is a whimsical reminder of the fact that we often take human factors for granted. Imagine an elevator with such a control panel. Think of the extra time you might need to locate the button corresponding to the floor you wanted to visit. Worse than that, imagine the chaos of a telephone keypad with randomly arranged numbers. There are literally hundreds of devices you use every day that have been designed or modified by human factors specialists: the configuration of an automobile dashboard, the height and tilt of a

FIGURE 16.2

Before the Uniform Elevator Button Code of 1923

SOURCE: Based on *Esquire*, January 2002

USER FRIENDLINESS

Positive characteristic of machines, tools, and consumer products that are designed to be comfortable, easy to use, and compatible with human capacities and limitations.

chair, the keyboard and screen at a computer workstation, the arrangement of knobs and burners on a stove top, the positioning of the brakes on a mountain bike, even the way a radio dial or a TV remote control works. All of these are examples of products or objects designed to achieve **user friendliness**—that is, to be comfortable, easy to use, and compatible with human capacities and limitations. In this chapter, we will consider the concept and discipline of human factors engineering as it applies to work.

HUMAN FACTORS MODELS

Howell (1993) identified human factors as a dynamic force in both technology design and society. We have adapted his view in Table 16.1. In the left-hand column is the "need" or driving

TABLE 16.1	A Summary of Major System Design Issues and the Forces Driving Them
DRIVING FORCE	**APPLIED ISSUES**
Technology	
Computerization	Human-Computer Interaction (interface, software)
Automation	Skill maintenance, workload transition monitoring, troubleshooting function allocation, task design
Task complexity/speed	Cognitive demands, scheduling, workload, stress
Information display	Coding, design, quality distribution
General	"Technostress" organizational consequences
Society	
Demography	Special populations, system requirements
Skill/education trends	Talent shortfall (training, aiding, selection implications)
Geopolitical change	Military requirements, simulation, logistics support (e.g., maintenance)
	Technology transfer
Litigation/consumerism	Human error, safety (workplace, environment, consumer products)

SOURCE: Howell (1993).

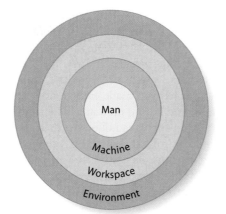

FIGURE 16.3

The Human Factors View of the Workplace
SOURCE: Applied Ergonomics (1974).

force. In the right-hand column is the human factor, or applied, issue or area of concentration. This table provides a good overview of the substance of human factors. Two very simple models can be used to position human factors in the broader perspective of the study of work behavior. Consider Figure 16.3. In a series of concentric circles, we see that the worker is embedded in a series of increasingly larger environments which include, respectively, equipment (e.g., computers), physical workspace (e.g., work cubicle or office), social work space (e.g., teams), and organizational workspace (e.g., climate or culture). Each of these environments has an influence on the performance of the individual. Traditionally, the human factors approach has concentrated on the interface between the worker and the equipment—and in the last several decades, the "equipment of choice" has been the computer. Figure 16.4 illustrates a very basic model of the interaction of the worker and equipment.

As you can see, there are several components to this model. There is the worker, the equipment, the way that the worker receives information from the equipment, and the way the worker controls the equipment. Both the equipment and the worker have an **input component** and an **output component.** An everyday example of this model may help you to understand it more clearly. Suppose you had a paper due in one of your classes and you were preparing it on your personal computer. As you sit in front of that computer, you see a screen and a keyboard. What appears on the screen represents output from the computer and input to you. What you type on the keyboard represents output from you, but input to the computer. You and the computer are connected through this information flow loop. You ask the computer to access information in a literature base related to industrial safety by first activating a search engine, then typing in a website, and finally inputting some key

INPUT COMPONENT

Provides information to a human or computer.

OUTPUT COMPONENT

Receives information from a human or computer and converts that information to action.

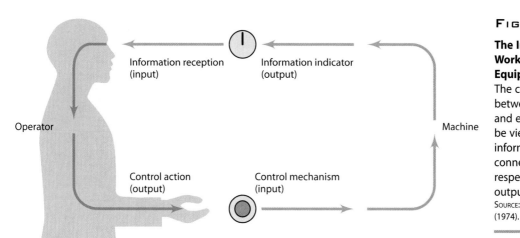

FIGURE 16.4

The Interaction of Worker and Equipment
The communication between a worker and equipment can be viewed as an information flow loop connecting their respective inputs and outputs.
SOURCE: Applied Ergonomics (1974).

Information reception (input)

Information indicator (output)

Operator

Machine

Control action (output)

Control mechanism (input)

words for the search. With that instruction, the computer accomplishes the search and provides you with the relevant journal articles. There have been a string of interactions between you and the computer. You turned it on, you activated its operating system, you started the search engine, you identified the website, and you listed the key words. At each point in this process, the computer asked you to make choices. You made these choices with the mouse or the keyboard, and when you made each choice, the computer "did its thing." There was considerable input and output on both sides of the keyboard.

This simple example introduces two additional technical terms that are important in human factors: displays and controls. **Displays** (e.g., computer screen) provide an individual with information, while **controls** (e.g., keyboard or mouse) permit an individual to take actions. There is a rich history as well as an active current research interest in the design of the most effective methods for display and control (Salvendy, 1997; Wickens, Gordon, & Liu, 1998). But displays and controls are only two components of a more elaborate model of work from the human factors perspective. Figure 16.5 presents a more complete systems view of the human factors approach to work. As you can see, virtually every topic covered in this book is represented in one or more of the blocks of the model in Figure 16.5. The environment, the operator, and the machine all form an integrated system and interact to yield productivity on the positive side, and accidents, injuries, and even violence on the negative side.

DISPLAY

Device such as a computer screen that provides an individual with information.

CONTROL

Device such as a keyboard or mouse that permits an individual to take actions.

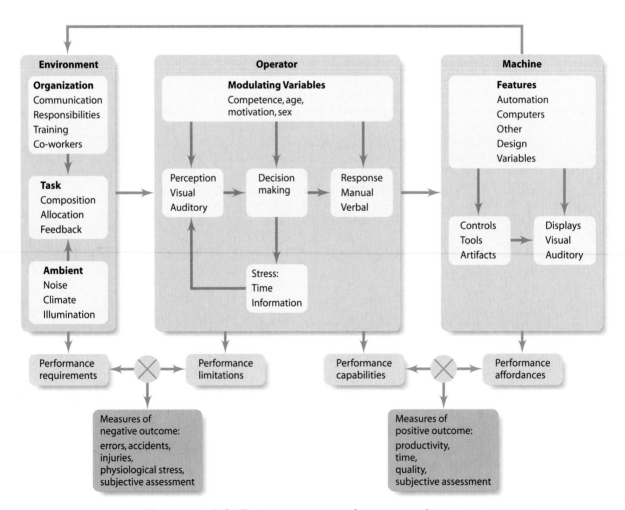

FIGURE 16.5 A systems approach to ergonomics SOURCE: Helander (1997).

Human factors is a global discipline. The same human factors issues affect virtually any industrialized country. Helander (1997) identified a number of human factors challenges that characterize work in 25 different countries. These include the change of work organization and design, work-related musculoskeletal disorders, and human-computer interface. **Musculoskeletal disorders** of the lower back and upper extremities are the most commonly studied injuries related to workplace safety. **Human-computer interface (HCI)** is the interaction between a human and a computer. Other factors that Helander identified are the change in social systems of work environments, high technology system design (particularly nuclear power plant control rooms), mental workload, and human reliability.

A MODERN HUMAN FACTORS CHALLENGE: CELL PHONES AND DRIVING

The next time you are driving or riding in a car, take a minute and gather some data. Observe how many drivers you see who have a cellular telephone to their ear; you will probably be astonished by the number. You might have thought you were the only one on the road who used a cell phone while commuting. Your astonishment can help to make our point. While you were driving and using your cell phone, you never *noticed* how many of your fellow drivers were doing the same thing. If you have a little extra time, don't just count them, watch them drive. They are clearly involved in their conversations. They may look distracted, happy, sad, or angry depending on the substance of the conversation. They are often driving more slowly than other drivers, who may be backed up behind them and annoyed. Drivers behind them may need to beep their horns to prompt them to step on the accelerator when a light turns green. They may pull into other lanes and into the path of other drivers without signaling. They may breeze through yellow or even red lights without touching the brakes. Since they are often holding the phone to their ear with one hand and controlling their vehicles with the other, or cradling the phone between their shoulder and ear, their maneuvers are often jerky and clumsy. In short, the highways are full of accidents waiting to happen.

Citizens in many areas have mounted a growing backlash against the use of cell phones while driving. Consider the following two examples. An elderly passenger was seriously injured in a collision between the car she was riding in and the car driven by a lumber sales representative who was talking on his cell phone when the collision occurred. Although the sales representative denied he was on the phone, his cell phone records demonstrated that he was 74 seconds into a call at the time of the collision. Observers reported that the sales representative accelerated through an intersection and never touched his brakes before the collision. The jury awarded the victim $21 million (Heller, 2002). In another incident, a driver on the Capital Beltway in Washington, D.C., was talking on her cell phone when her car went over a guardrail and into oncoming traffic, resulting in the death of five people ("Driver in Crash," 2002).

As a result of incidents like these, as well as scores of "near misses," states and local jurisdictions are passing laws banning the use of handheld cell phones while driving. A law passed by New York State in 2001 is representative of this new legislation (Perotta, 2002). Drivers can be fined $100 for a first violation, $200 for a second violation, and $500 for additional violations. Interestingly, the law forbids the use of handheld phones but permits the use of hands-free systems that use speakers or headsets. To be sure, accidents can occur when drivers are fumbling to dial a number or receive a call, or trying to continue a

Cellular phones and other electronic devices are bound to distract drivers from focusing their attention on traffic and road conditions.

conversation with a phone held to their ear while simultaneously trying to avoid an obstacle, change lanes, turn a corner, or shift gears. But holding the phone is only part, and possibly only a small part, of the problem. An equally important issue is the attention of the driver. A hands-free systems is not a mind-free system. The critical issue is whether the driver is paying attention to the control of the vehicle in the dynamic, often confusing, and dangerous environment of the road—or to the "stimuli" presented over the cell phone.

A growing body of research confirms the danger of driving and cell phone use. Hancock, Lesch, and Simmons (2003) studied the driving behavior of 36 drivers on a test track in Massachusetts. The study was intended to distinguish between the structural problems of cell phone use (i.e., the challenge of holding the phone while driving) and the functional problems (i.e., the cognitive challenge of performing two demanding tasks at once). An automobile was designed with a touch screen on the dashboard to simulate a hands-free cell phone system. The test track was arranged to have several critical demands (e.g., a signal to stop). The experiment looked at the performance of the drivers who were engaged in the use of the cell phone at a "demanding" moment. The drivers who were using the simulated cell phone failed to stop for a red light significantly more often than those who were not. In addition, even when the drivers did notice the red light and stopped, they braked much harder and stopped much more abruptly than those not using the cell phone. Abrupt stopping often leads to rear-end collisions.

The effect of this cell phone distraction was considerably more pronounced in older drivers than younger ones. Younger drivers in the study were between the ages of 25 and 36 while older drivers were between 55 and 65. We suspect that the effect on drivers younger than 25 would be more pronounced, particularly among young drivers who have just begun to drive. These inexperienced drivers must devote greater mental energy to routine driving operations. Since they are inexperienced, every operation requires attention. Thus, the demands of the cell phone impair not only unexpected actions, such as stopping for a light that turns red, but also routine actions such as maintaining a constant speed, which require more attention for the new driver than the experienced driver. Although the same distracting effects are likely to be seen in any inexperienced driver regardless of age, it will be most clearly seen in very young drivers.

The Hancock et al. study is very appealing because it is a field study using a real vehicle on a real road with a variety of subjects. Nevertheless, laboratory studies find much the same result. Strayer and Johnston (2001) used a simulated driving task and found that while cell phones were distracting and affected driving performance, neither music nor books-on-tape had the same distracting effect. In the case of cell phones, laboratory research, field research, observation, and personal experience point to the same conclusion: The active use of cell phones and driving don't mix. From a human factors standpoint, there is no easy "fix" to the problem. The hands-free fix solves the structural part of the problem, but not the functional part. The problem as a whole resides in the way that humans process information. They pay attention to the most salient information channel when choosing between information sources. For all practical purposes, the selection is automatic—it is not under our conscious control. The only effective way we can choose driving over cell phone conversation is to turn our cell phones off. In this case, the contribution of human factors psychology is to provide a scientific foundation for a shift in public policy: a shift toward limiting the use of cell phones while driving.

Another example of the same phenomenon is the pairing of global navigation systems (GPS) and video screens in cars to provide directions to destinations. The drivers will be required somehow to input information and view or listen to output while simultaneously driving. Consider that you most often look for directions when you are lost and you already have a condition of stress/arousal. The competing demands for cognitive attention presented by the interactive directions device will most certainly degrade performance.

MODULE 16.1 SUMMARY

- Human factors psychology is the study of the capacity and limitations of human beings in various environments; these capacities and limitations include abilities, skills, physiology, and knowledge.
- The goal of the human factors psychologist is to improve effectiveness and safety through the design of tools, machines, processes, and environments.

- The "machine," the operator, and the environment are among the key components in a human factors model. Displays provide information to the operator about the machine, and controls allows those operators to initiate or respond to environmental changes.
- A recent challenge to the human factors psychologist is a determination of the potential dangers and inefficiencies of using cell phones while engaged in other complex actions, such as driving.

KEY TERMS

human factors
ergonomics
user friendliness

input component
output component
display

control
musculoskeletal disorders
human-computer interface

CRITICAL THINKING EXERCISES

16.1 When a person driving a rental car stops for the first time to buy gasoline for the vehicle, he or she often spends considerable time trying to figure out how to open the lid that covers the gas cap. From a human factors perspective, how might this problem be resolved?

16.2 Car manufacturers are experimenting with the incorporation of a "mouse" (like a computer mouse) into the steering wheel of cars. The thumb-operated mouse can provide the driver with information about weather, driving directions, traffic, videos, and e-mail on a dashboard screen. From a human factors perspective, can we anticipate that this will lead to more or less effective driving performance? Why?

CONTEMPORARY WORK DESIGN CHALLENGES

TECHNOLOGY

As we have pointed out in earlier chapters, and as any observer of today's workplace would agree, the nature of work is changing rapidly. This adds to the challenge of designing work and organizations. Although it is impossible to anticipate exactly what changes will occur in technology or process in the next decade, we can look at some current technologies and examine how human factors research has studied and modified these technologies. The two most obvious and pervasive of these technologies are automation and computer use.

Automation

Automation describes a way of completing work through the use of mechanical or electrical devices rather than through direct human action (Wickens & Hollands, 2000). Robotics is a good example of automation. In an auto assembly plant, robots can be used to weld, to turn car bodies at angles, to distribute materials, or to carry out tests of stability of assembled parts. At one time, all of these activities were performed by humans. From the human factors perspective, automation poses a challenge. Because the human operator invariably interacts with the automated process, the challenge is to design an interface that is effective, safe, and comfortable for the human operator.

One common motivation for automating is to eliminate humans from a system. The term **human error** is often used to explain a catastrophic accident. The logic is that if we can get the human out of the system, the threat of accidents will be greatly reduced. Examples of completely or partially automated systems include refineries, space ships, engine block plants, nuclear power plants, and even the lowly automatic teller machine (ATM). What is not so obvious, however, is that these automated systems have not really eliminated the person from the system. People are still required to monitor, maintain, and troubleshoot the system, often from remote locations. This is a good news–bad news situation. The good news is that automated systems, on average, are more reliable than human systems. The bad news is that when automated systems go out control, they can go *wildly* out of control. An oil refinery shuts down automatically, creating dangerous toxic and flammable fumes. An engine block assembly operation drills holes where they shouldn't be for 700 engine blocks processed during a four-hour period. An ATM dispenses $100 bills instead of $10 bills for several hours. While you may wonder why the last example would be a problem for you, it is certainly a problem for the bank.

Perhaps one of the most dramatic examples of failed automation was the incident at the Three Mile Island nuclear power plant in Pennsylvania on March 28, 1979. This potential catastrophe was the result of a flawed interaction between an automated control system and human control room operators. As part of a routine maintenance program, the secondary or backup system for cooling the superheated water from the nuclear reactor was shut down. Plant personnel forgot to turn this backup system back on when the maintenance was completed. Two weeks later, a pump in the *primary* cooling system failed, and because the secondary cooling system had not been turned back on, the temperature in the reactor chamber began to climb. Then a valve stuck. Simultaneously, an automatic emergency system was activated to address the rising temperature. This automatic system was unrelated to the stuck valve, but as a result of that stuck valve, the action of the emergency system was exaggerated. Finally, the control room operators, confronted with massive amounts of information, some of it inconsistent, misinterpreted what was happening. The situation came close to becoming a genuine disaster in which thousands of people might have died. Of course, we can't blame the accident on one person or event, but it is clear nevertheless that human decisions played a major role in the accident, in spite of (or possibly even because of) automated systems or subsystems. Similarly, military and commercial pilots have been known to fly past a coordinate when the aircraft was on autopilot and the pilot was daydreaming or even dozing.

On the positive side, it is clear that automation has taken a great deal of the drudgery, inhumanity, and danger out of work, thus representing a tremendous contribution to organizations, workers, and society in general. As Wickens and Hollands (2000) suggested, automation can play several valuable roles by:

1. Carrying out functions that humans can't do (e.g., using robots to handle dangerous materials).
2. Carrying out functions that humans can do but do poorly (e.g., warning pilots when they are too close to the ground).
3. Assisting humans in areas where they have limitations (e.g., using a voice recognition system to allow a pilot to input completed elements of a preflight checklist and alert the pilot if he or she forgets a step).
4. Freeing humans to do more satisfying and valuable work (e.g., using robots to spot-weld auto bodies).

Nevertheless, automation has not taken the person out of the system. It has simply changed the role of the person in the system. Human factors addresses this interaction between worker and machine or process, particularly in terms of costs or problems. Wickens and Hollands (2000) identified some of these costs.

1. *Complexity:* Automated systems typically replace the functions of many different individuals and, as a result, represent a "job" that is much more complex than the work done by any one individual. This increases the potential for system failure. The greater the number of components to the automated system, the greater the opportunity for a failure of the system owing to a failure of one of the components. In addition, these new and complex systems "do" the work in a very different way from what the human operator might have done. As a result, individuals may have difficulty in understanding the system (or even distrust the automated system) because it does things differently.

2. *Reliability:* Operators may either undertrust the reliability of an automated system (e.g., because they don't understand it) or overtrust its reliability. In an undertrust situation, the operator may ignore an alarm from the system, or possibly even turn off the alarm component. In an overtrust situation, the operator depends on the system to provide more information than it is designed to provide. For example, the operator ignores various information about the automated system until a signal of some kind (e.g., an audible alarm) indicates a malfunction. But if the operator has not been monitoring various sources of information all along, by the time an alarm sounds, there may be too much complex information for the operator to process in a short period of time.

3. *Communications:* Although automated systems are not human, they still need to communicate with human monitors, operators, or users. Consider the following example of a "dialogue" between a customer calling with a question about a telephone service and a phone menu. The customer learned from a friend that the phone company would provide one-touch local weather updates and wants to get one.

Automated System (AS): Please listen carefully to the following options:

- To report a problem with your service, press 1.
- To question a recent bill, press 2.
- To terminate service, press 3.
- To apply for a job with the company, press 4.
- To inquire about new service, press 5.

The customer presses 5.

AS: please choose from the following options:

- To add a phone line, press 1.
- To change a phone number, press 2.
- To convert a number to "unlisted," press 3.
- To convert a number from unlisted to "listed," press 4.
- To transfer a number from one location to another, press 5.
- To repeat these choices, press 6.
- For all other questions about service, press 7.

The customer is confused and can't remember all the choices, so presses 6. After listening to the choices again, the customer presses 7.

AS: please choose from the following options:

- To add a phone line, press 1.
- To change a phone number, press 2.
- To convert a number to "unlisted," press 3.
- To convert a number from unlisted to "listed," press 4.
- To transfer a number from one location to another, press 5.
- To repeat these choices, press 6.
- For all other questions about service, press 7.

This is a silly, but not unusual, example of a communications problem between a human and an automated system. What the customer might not have known, but would have discovered if he or she chose none of the options and simply waited, was that a service representative would come on the line. Instead, the customer hangs up, looks up another number, and calls it in hopes of being able to talk with a real person. (The chances are good that the customer will instead get a different, even less helpful, phone menu.) The automated system has failed because of a communications flaw. In designing automated systems, it is critical to consider the nature of the "conversation" that will transpire between a user and the system.

Wickens and Hollands (2000) suggested five principles for making sure that automated systems are compatible with human operators.

1. Make sure that the displays and controls are effective.
2. Keep the human operator informed about the nature of the automated process and its status.
3. Make sure that the operator is trained in the process.
4. Make the transition to automation "gracefully" by introducing the automation as an aid to human performance, not a replacement.
5. Make the automation flexible so that an operator can decide when to use it, or to decide how much or what level of automation to use.

Computers

Computers are so pervasive in our culture that a general discussion of the design of computer systems at the workplace would fill a book, not a mere section of a chapter. Even the word "computer" can be misleading. For example, electric musical keyboards, drum sets, and guitars are computers, although we don't apply that term; we don't say we are going to the garage to play the computer. In contrast, a personal computer is neither personal, nor do we use it to compute much anymore (Craiger & Weiss, 1998). In this discussion, we will limit ourselves to a central aspect of computer use in the workplace: some characteristics of human-computer interaction (HCI).

Human-Computer Interaction (HCI):   An Example of Human-Computer Interaction
Buchanan and Boddy (1983) described the introduction of a computer into the process of cookie making. The computer standardized the mixing of dough as well as the monitoring of the weight and size of cookies after baking. Both of these operations are critical for successful mass production of cookies. Before the computer was introduced, dough was mixed by master bakers who directed a group of subordinates. Like a chef, the master baker approached the job almost as an art, adding a pinch here, a dash of water there, and personally directing the mixing of every batch of dough. The master baker was universally admired by others in the plant because of the high degree of skill and experience required. After computerization, the job was greatly simplified. It took only one person who needed no special skill other than to respond to the computer when it requested ingredients. After taking a sample of the completed dough, this person simply moved the dough on to the person who operated the oven, called the "ovensman."

The effect of computerization on the ovensman was very different. Prior to the introduction of the computer, the ovensman had to check the size, weight, and thickness of a sample of cookies in order to tell the wrapping department whether they needed to make any adjustments in their equipment. The ovensman would also direct the cookie makers to adjust their rollers if the cookies were too thick or too thin, but only after hundreds and sometimes thousands of cookies had already been made. Because this was all done by hand, it was very inefficient. When the computerized weighing system was introduced, the ovensman could get information much more quickly and, as a result, instruct the cookie makers to adjust their rollers much sooner. The cookie wrappers also got much more useful information, and in a more timely manner. As a result of computerization, the ovensman's position was viewed as much more responsible, one that was the kingpin to the entire quality control process.

From this example, we can see that no general statement can be made about the effect of computerization on any particular job, job family, or sector of the economy. Computerization may make some jobs more important and others less so. In addition, the stature of some jobs may increase while the stature of others decreases, leading to corresponding changes in employee status, satisfaction, and motivation.

User-Centered Design   Human-computer interaction research has evolved into a **user-centered design** of system development that is heavily influenced by applied psychology (Carroll, 1997). In the 1970s there was little concern or appreciation for the preferences, capabilities, or limitations of the computer user. Remember the idealized lathe operator we examined in Figure 16-1. The same situation would have been true of the idealized computer user in the 1970s. This user would not have resembled any human being we had ever seen. The keyboard would have been flat, the screen would have had glare and colors that made reading tiring. Various disk drives would have been tucked away under desks. Screens and keyboards would not have been adjustable for height. The development of modern computer systems is dominated by issues of usability, not technology. If a system cannot be used effectively by the intended end-user group, it has a bad design.

USER-CENTERED DESIGN

Approach to human-computer interaction research that focuses on the user during system development.

User-centered design is accomplished through **usability engineering,** an iterative process in which a basic system is designed and then redesigned with input from users. (Carroll, 1997; Craiger, 2000). An example of usability engineering is a word-processing system in which actual secretaries are involved in both the initial and redesign teams (Carroll, 1997). This design has been referred to as a **participatory design,** and is reminiscent of the behaviorally anchored scale development (BARS) for performance evaluation and management. In addition, the goal of the design would be stated in user-directed terms, such as "two thirds of the users will be able to prepare a two-page business letter in less than 10 minutes with fewer that three errors after 30 minutes of training" (Carroll, 1997, p. 69). The design and pilot testing of the system would also include procedures like cognitive task analysis and think-aloud protocols, much as we discussed in Chapter 5 on job analysis. The simplest way to contrast the "old" method of system design with the modern approach is to say that design came out of the laboratory and into the field. There is even a branch of user-center design known as **ethnographically informed design** (Bentley, Hughes, Randall, Rodden, & Sawyer, 1992) which takes into account power relationships, tacit knowledge of the organization and its procedures, and organizational climate and culture. The research of Buchanan and Boddy (1983) involving the production of cookies anticipated this move toward a greater recognition of the importance of social-organizational issues in systems design.

In summary, the new model of systems development is user oriented and heavily dependent on users as subject matter experts. The concentration on usability signals a shift from a technological focus to a strategic focus. It is equally, if not more, important to the organization that the end user of the system feel comfortable with it than that the system employs the full potential of available technology. If this comfort level is missing, the most sophisticated and powerful system is nothing but a method to collect dust. It is tempting for engineers to construct a technical masterpiece to impress other engineers, but the user is often not impressed. The moral: Just because you *can* do something from a technical standpoint doesn't mean that you *should.*

It is the job of I-O psychologists to address these issues of usability by means of the same tools that they would employ to develop any system intended to enhance human performance. These tools were discussed in the chapters on performance measurement (Chapter 6), training (Chapter 8), motivation (Chapter 9), leadership (Chapter 12), and organizational design (Chapter 14). They include methods like cognitive job analysis (e.g., think-aloud protocols), critical incidents interviewing, and statistical analysis of the relative effectiveness of different designs.

WORK SCHEDULES

The scheduling of work is under the control of the organization, and thus can be considered an issue of work design. As we have seen in Chapter 10 on job satisfaction and Chapter 15 on stress, work schedules are playing an increasingly important role in managing work–life balance in two ways: Individuals desire the freedom to pursue leisure activities outside of work, and they often have obligations to fulfill multiple roles as spouse, caregiver, and parent. This suggests that the scheduling of work can have substantial effects on worker well-being. There are three different scheduling formats that bear discussion: Shift work, flextime, and compressed workweeks. We will consider them separately.

Shift Work

The scheduling of work according to a particular time period is called **shift work.** The study of shift work and its effects on workers has a long and rich research history. This history is well presented in a number of sources (e.g., Johnson, Tepas, Colquhoun, & Colligan, 1981; Landy, 1989; Tepas, Paley, & Popkin, 1997; Wedderburn, 1981). Much of this work has centered on the 24-hour or **circadian cycle** of humans, whose physiology tends to make them active during hours of light and inactive (e.g., sleeping or resting) during hours of darkness. Thus, workers assigned to shifts during daylight hours are following the circadian cycle, while those whose shift includes hours of darkness are working against the cycle. Psychologists have found that, in general, disturbance of the circadian cycle has adverse consequences for health, performance, and general satisfaction. Shift work is categorized into two different types: fixed shifts and rotating shifts. If workers are permanently assigned to a particular shift, the shift is called a **fixed shift.** Typical shifts include the day shift (e.g., 7:00 A.M. to 3:30 P.M.), the afternoon or evening shift—often called the "swing" shift (e.g., 3:00 P.M. to 11:30 P.M.), and the night shift—often called the "midnight" or "graveyard" shift (e.g., 11:30 P.M. to 7:00 A.M.). Workers who move from shift to shift are said to be working a **rotating shift** schedule. Shifts can rotate rapidly (e.g., move to a different shift every week) or slowly (e.g., a worker may change shifts every three months). In union environments, workers can often bid on shifts based on seniority, resulting in more frequent shift changes for workers with less seniority.

Generally speaking, rotating shifts are more likely to be associated with problems than fixed shifts (Parkes, 1999). This is particularly true if the direction of the rotation is from day to night to evening (as opposed to day to evening to night). Rotating shifts, and particularly rapidly rotating shifts, lead to sleep disturbances, which in turn are associated with medical (e.g., gastrointestinal) and psychological (e.g., anxiety and depression) difficulties. Rotating shifts also seem to be particularly hard on older workers (Landy, 1989).

Shift work is more common in some occupational groups than others. Nurses, blue-collar workers, and public safety personnel have higher concentrations of shift workers than professional, managerial, or white-collar groups (Smith et al., 1999). The most frequently studied of those occupations is the nursing profession. Barton (1994) examined the differences between nurses who chose to work the night shift on a permanent basis and nurses who were assigned to rotating night shifts. Permanent night shift nurses reported significantly fewer problems with health, sleep, and social or domestic activities. This was particularly true for individual nurses who chose to work on the permanent night shift compared with nurses who chose to work on a rotating shift schedule. The most important reasons the nurses in this study gave for choosing the permanent night shift were

CIRCADIAN CYCLE

The 24-hour physiological cycle in which humans tend to be active during hours of light and inactive during hours of darkness.

FIXED SHIFT

Workers permanently assigned to a particular shift.

ROTATING SHIFT

Workers moved from shift to shift over a certain period of time.

Shift work is a necessity in essential services that need to be fully functional 24 hours a day, seven days a week.

that night shift work permitted them to more easily fulfill domestic responsibilities, and it paid better. Thus, for those who chose permanent night work, it actually improved control and scheduling of work-nonwork roles. But the nurses on a rotating shift schedule felt that their lives were disrupted every time they had to work afternoon or night shifts (Barton, 1994). It appears that night shift work provides a significant opportunity for establishing a work–life balance that is not possible with rotating shifts or, in some circumstances, day or afternoon shifts. This seems to be particularly true of dual wage earning families with young children. In another study of nurses, Bohle and Tilley (1998) found that work-nonwork conflict was one of the strongest predictors of satisfaction with shift work.

These balancing advantages notwithstanding, some research has shown that permanent day shift work tends to be more intrinsically satisfying than afternoon, night, or rotating shift work. Blau and Lunz (1999) analyzed the effect of various shift schedules on 705 medical technicians (MTs) and found that MTs who worked a permanent day shift reported that their jobs were considerably less routine than the jobs of MTs on any other shift. To some extent, this perception conforms to the reality of this job across shifts. Night shift MTs tend to perform standardized tests on samples gathered during the day. In addition, since many medical procedures are performed during the day and vary substantially from patient to patient, it makes sense that the work of the day shift MT would be less routine. The day shift MTs were also more satisfied with supervision, mainly because supervisors were available on the day shift, as opposed to the night shift, which often functioned without any direct supervision.

While the results of the Blau and Lunz (1999) study of MTs might seem to conflict with those of Barton's (1994) studies of nurses, we need to recognize that these studies are really looking at different things. Barton's nurses were choosing to emphasize nonwork outcomes such as domestic responsibilities, while the Blau and Lunz MTs were responding to questions about their satisfaction with their work roles. Furthermore, the median age of the MTs was 25, compared to an average age of 39 for the permanent night shift nurses. This suggests that the MTs were likely to have had little of the domestic strain that the nurses experienced; thus, night shift work was not particularly useful as a coping mechanism. Indeed, given their ages, it is likely that the MTs valued free time in the evening and nighttime hours more highly than did the nurses. Taken together, these studies point to the advantages of allowing workers to have some control over their shift choice. It would also appear that there may be a natural clustering of workers by age or nonwork responsibility that represents a win–win situation. The workers choose the shift that best satisfies their need for a work–life balance. Both studies are in agreement that rotating shifts are less attractive than permanent shifts.

Flexible and Compressed Workweek Schedules

Shift work, regardless of whether it is fixed or rotating, defines the work schedule rigidly. In general, shift workers are expected to work eight hours per day, five days per week. But there are other scheduling variations that are not so rigid.

Flextime Individual workers who are given discretion over the time they report to work and the time they leave work on a given day are working a **flextime** schedule. Such schedules are uncommon in manufacturing organizations, since the interdependence among workers in assembly-line and continuous process operations makes the absence of a particular worker particularly problematic (Baltes, Briggs, Huff, Wright, & Neuman, 1999). A survey of a diverse sample of more than 1,000 organizations in 1995 revealed that 66 percent of them permitted some form of a flexible workday (Hewitt Associates, 1995). That percentage has probably increased since 1995. In a typical flexible work schedule, every worker is expected to be at work during a "core" period (e.g., 10:00 A.M.–3:00 P.M.) but is permitted to arrive as early as 7:00 A.M. or leave as late as 9:00 P.M. (Baltes et al., 1999). Regardless of when they arrive and leave, they are expected to be at the workplace for

40 hours a week. In some organizations, the individual is also required to be at work 8 hours each day, whereas in other organizations, the individual is still expected to be at work for 40 hours a week but is permitted to balance those hours across days. For example, the employee may be at the workplace from 7:00 A.M. until 5:00 P.M. on Monday and Tuesday, from 9:00 A.M. to 3:00 P.M. on Wednesday and Thursday, and from 10:00 A.M. until 6:00 P.M. on Friday. Even though workers have the *option* of varying the time at which they arrive and depart, some research has suggested that the reality is less dramatic than the possibilities. Ronen (1981) found that after the introduction of flextime the average arrival time for workers was 8 minutes later than it had been before, and that the average departure time was 22 minutes later after the introduction of flextime.

The benefits of flextime to the individual worker are obvious. In addition to the psychological advantages of perceiving some control over the work schedule, there is the practical advantage of achieving a better balance between work and nonwork. Most workers express satisfaction with flextime schedules.

Compressed Workweek   Another nontraditional work schedule is the **compressed workweek,** which permits an employee to work for longer than eight hours a day and fewer than five days a week. A common plan is the 4/10 plan, which permits a worker to accumulate the 40 hours of the workweek in four days. For some workers, this affords the opportunity to enjoy an ongoing series of three-day weekends. For others, it permits them to take second jobs or pursue further education on a more regular basis while still working. A 1995 survey of 1,000 companies found that 21 percent offered workers the possibility of a compressed workweek. This type of schedule is found most commonly in manufacturing organizations (Baltes et al., 1999). As with flextime, workers tend to express satisfaction with the compressed workweek (Landy, 1989).

Consequences of Flextime and Compressed Workweek Schedules   Worker satisfaction with flextime and compressed workweek schedules is well documented (Baltes et al., 1999; Landy, 1989). But are these work schedules associated with organizational outcomes such as productivity, performance, and absenteeism? The activity of creating and maintaining nontraditional work schedules inevitably incurs some administrative costs, so organizations may well ask, What's in it for us? Baltes et al. (1999) conducted a meta-analysis of 39 studies on the effects of flextime (27 studies) and compressed workweeks (12 studies). The results of the analysis are useful and encouraging for both of these scheduling variations. They found that flextime was associated with higher productivity and lower absenteeism, although the impact on absenteeism was considerably greater than the effect on productivity. For the compressed workweek, they found that while absenteeism was unaffected, supervisors' ratings of performance were higher (though productivity was not).

Baltes et al. (1999) did some further analyses of their data and found that flextime had little effect on productivity, performance ratings, or absenteeism for professionals and managers such as accountants or sales managers. In addition, they found that, for non-professional and non-sales managerial workers, programs with extremely flexible hours were less effective than more conservative programs. They concluded that this was probably the result of the inability of employees in the workplace to communicate with absent employees. This would, of course, be particularly troublesome in organizations that depend heavily on teams and groups as opposed to single contributors. They also found that the effects of flextime tended to diminish after the initial period of adjustment (typically a few months); as workers became accustomed to the new scheduling, it became the norm. Remember also that one study demonstrated that *actual* arrival and departures schedules remained very much the same (Ronen, 1981).

In general, the research suggests that both compressed workweeks and flextime offer advantages, particularly in terms of worker satisfaction, without any systematic disadvantages. But the results also demonstrate that these two schedules are not similar in their organizational effects. Flextime is associated with reduced absenteeism and compressed workweeks are not. This makes sense. With a flextime schedule, the definition of being "late" for work changes dramatically, so that a worker can show up two hours late and still be counted present. In a compressed work schedule, late is still late. Many individuals in manufacturing environments will choose to be absent (perhaps take a sick day) rather than show up late. As a result, absences are unlikely to change in this environment. In addition, flextime is associated with increased productivity, but a compressed schedule is not.

Telecommuting   Technology has made it possible for some organizations to implement another way of giving workers more control over their daily schedule. Telecommuting, or working from home, is a reality for some millions of workers in the United States today this number is expected to grow substantially in the coming years. Telecommuting is a broad label that includes not only the obvious connection by means of a telephone, but also includes the dependence on computers, faxes, and handheld computers such as Palm Pilots (PDAs) and dedicated e-mail communication devices. The definition and parameters of the work-at-home arrangement, however, are nearly as varied as the participating organizations. Some workers are required to be at their home desks during the company's regular business hours, or to return phone calls and e-mails within a specified time limit even outside business hours, while others may set their own schedules. Some work at home all or most of the time, while others telecommute only one or two days a week.

We predict that the growing trend toward telecommuting will have an impact on the study of workplace scheduling, particularly of flextime and compressed workweeks. This is just one of several reasons why it is not clear whether the research results we have examined above will hold up as the nature of work changes. As organizations move toward more team-based work, flextime may become more of a problem for issues of performance and productivity. If team members are unable to move ahead with their work because they must wait for another member to arrive for a meeting or furnish a key component of a project, productivity is likely to suffer. To the extent that telecommuting becomes more common, it may be more difficult to isolate the effects of flextime and compressed workweeks on productivity or absenteeism. Flextime and compressed workweek schedules will still provide benefits to some organizations, but the number of organizations that benefit from these approaches may possibly diminish.

APPROACHES TO WORK DESIGN AND REDESIGN

We have examined a number of different work design issues. These have included technological variables (computers and automation) and social variables (work scheduling). Campion and Thayer (1985, 1987; Campion, 1988, 1989) have proposed that one might take many different approaches to designing or redesigning work, and since each approach has different goals, we might expect different outcomes. Campion and Thayer (1985) examined 700 different "rules" that have been suggested for designing work and reduced them to four different approaches, or models, which are presented in Table 16.2. As you can see, each model is based on a different theoretical approach, has a different goal, and seeks to affect a different outcome. In Table 16.3, you will see the specific questions that might be asked in designing or redesigning a job. If we use this framework to reconsider the design issues discussed thus far in the chapter, you can see that any given design change includes several different approaches, not just one. Our example of the introduction of the computer into cookie making, as well as the process of usability engineering, included elements of the motivational, mechanistic, and perceptual-motor approaches. The **motivational approach** to work design and redesign is used to increase worker satisfaction and reduce turnover through modification of motivational levels. The **mechanistic approach** to work design and redesign is used to increase productive efficiency through the modification of tasks or equipment. The **perceptual-motor approach** is used to reduce

MOTIVATIONAL APPROACH

Used in work design and redesign to increase worker satisfaction and reduce turnover through modification of motivational levels.

MECHANISTIC APPROACH

Used in work design and redesign to increase productive efficiency through the modification of tasks or equipment.

PERCEPTUAL-MOTOR APPROACH

Used in work design and redesign to reduce errors or accidents through knowledge of perceptual-motor skills and abilities.

TABLE 16.2	Models for Redesigning Work	
MODEL	**RELEVANT CONCEPTS**	**DISCIPLINE BASE**
Motivational	Job enrichment/enlargement Job satisfaction, Involvement	Organizational psychology Sociotechnical systems
Mechanistic	Task specialization/simplification Repetition	Industrial engineering Scientific management
Biological	Stress, Strain, Strength, Endurance, Noise, Climate Fatigue	Biomechanics Exercise physiology Erogonomics
Perceptual- Motor	Mental abilities and limitations Attention, Concentration	Cognitive psychology Information processing

SOURCE: Based on Campion (1989); Edwards et al. (2000).

errors or accidents through knowledge of perceptual-motor skills and abilities. Finally, the **biological approach** is used to reduce injuries and increase the physical comfort of workers through the reduction of fatigue and discomfort. Automation included elements of the mechanistic, biological, and perceptual-motor approaches. Work scheduling is related to the motivational and biological approaches. When we discuss accidents and

BIOLOGICAL APPROACH

Used in work design and redesign to reduce injuries and increase the physical comfort of workers through a reduction of fatigue and discomfort.

TABLE 16.3	Examples of Preliminary Questions for Implementing Job Design Based on Model Chosen
MODEL	**SAMPLE QUESTIONS**
Motivational	Does the job allow freedom and independence? Do the work activities provide clear information as to effectiveness? Does the job allow for learning opportunities? Does the job provide for feelings of achievement? Is the job important compared to others in the organization?
Mechanistic	Are the tools and equipment highly specialized? Does the job require performing the same action repeatedly? Is there spare time between activities? Does the job require extensive training time? Are the tasks simple and uncomplicated?
Biological	Does the job require substantial muscular strength? Does the job require extensive lifting? Does the job require substantial muscular endurance? Is the workplace free from excessive noise? Is there a comfortable temperature at the workplace?
Perceptual- Motor	Are gauges and meters easy to read? Are required computer programs easy to learn? Is the information you must process fairly minimal? Are printed materials used on this job easy to read? Is memory an important part of this job?

SOURCE: Based on Campion (1988).

accident-reduction techniques in a later section of this chapter, you will recognize elements of all four approaches.

Campion's (1988, 1989) models have several implications. First, we need to be clear about what outcomes we expect or desire in the design or redesign of work. If we are redesigning work to increase worker satisfaction and reduce turnover, we may want to choose the motivational approach. If, instead, we are trying to reduce injuries and increase the physical comfort of workers, we would rely on the biological model. To reduce errors or accidents, we would choose the perceptual motor approach. A second implication is that conflict may occur between the approaches, resulting in both anticipated and unanticipated outcomes. If you were to use the mechanistic approach to increase productive efficiency, you would simplify work. But by doing that, you would also make the work less interesting and motivating for the worker.

For example, consider the job of a receptionist. Initially, he or she may have diverse duties such as answering the telephone, greeting visitors, maintaining office supplies, and scheduling various in-house conference rooms. When the receptionist was busy attending to other duties, assume that callers got a voice mail menu instead of the live receptionist. Assume further that the CEO, feeling that voice menus were too impersonal, suggested that all other duties except answering the phone and greeting visitors be eliminated from the receptionist's duties. Although it might be true that the instances of a caller encountering a voice mail menu would be reduced, it is also likely that the interest value of the job for the receptionist would be degraded.

Thus, work design and redesign are complex undertakings; organizations need to be aware of the anticipated outcomes—and on the lookout for unplanned outcomes—resulting from a design change. Campion's work design models would be a good architecture to use for planning design changes. Campion's models, like any model or theory, are not necessarily a statement of "truth." Theories and models are not true or false, they are useful or useless. Campion's theory of design approaches is a useful one, one that has been replicated several times as well (Campion, 1989; Edwards, Scully, & Brtek, 2000).

WORK DESIGN AND DISABILITIES

AMERICANS WITH DISABILITIES ACT

Federal civil rights law designed to prevent discrimination and enable individuals with disabilities to participate fully in all aspects of society including the workplace; applies to a person with a physical or mental impairment that substantially limits major life activities (e.g., sitting, standing, or sleeping).

ACCOMMODATION

Adjustments or modifications to the work environment provided by an employer to enable people with disabilities to have equal employment opportunities.

As you will recall from Chapters 7 and 11, the **Americans with Disabilities Act** is a federal law designed to prevent discrimination and protect the rights of workers with covered disabilities. In addition to addressing hiring issues, the act covers aspects of work design and redesign. Caplan (1992) defined a disability as "an inability to accommodate the world as it is currently designed" (p. 88). If a disabled worker can perform an essential function with an **accommodation** such as a job design change, and the accommodation is reasonable and feasible, then the employer is required to make that accommodation. Some accommodations are relatively simple, such as enhanced lighting for workers with a visual impairment, or ramps for workers in wheelchairs. Other accommodations are more challenging. Noe, Hollenbeck, Gerhart, and Wright (2000) presented examples of the types of accommodations that might be implemented:

- Eliminating marginal tasks that pose challenges for the disabled worker, or shifting them to other workers.
- Redesigning work procedures.
- Altering work schedules.
- Reassigning a disabled worker to a job with essential functions that he or she can perform.
- Providing technology or support in the form of readers or interpreters for employees with reading or visual disabilities.
- Allowing an employee with visual difficulties to bring a guide dog to work.

Noe et al. (2000) described the innovative design efforts of a company that specializes in training the disabled (Ricklefs, 1997). One problem they addressed is the shaking that workers with cerebral palsy have in their hands, which makes it difficult for them to use a computer keyboard because they often strike keys inadvertently. The accommodation that the company introduced was a clear plastic shield over the keyboard which requires the user to put a finger through the hole above the particular key chosen. Similarly, the company designed a compact keyboard for a worker with muscular dystrophy, who would have difficulty moving his or her arms, so that the worker could strike every key without any arm movement.

Vanderheiden (1997) has provided a detailed treatment of the design and redesign approaches for accommodating various disabilities. He suggested three basic approaches:

The right workplace design can make work accessible for individuals with special needs. Carol Smith, who has cerebral palsy, uses a computer controlled by an infrared beam transmitter attached to her hat.

1. Change the individual (e.g., teach him or her "tricks" or "secrets" for doing things more easily).

2. Provide the individual with tools (e.g., telecommunication devices for the hearing impaired).

3. Change the way the work is designed (e.g., rearrange the essential functions of jobs).

The most common forms of accommodation involve what are known as "assistive technologies." Examples of these technologies are presented in Table 16.4. You will recall that earlier in this chapter we introduced the terms "display" (output to the worker) and "control" (input from the worker). Vanderheiden suggested a "maximization" principle to follow in designing work environments for the disabled. The designer should maximize the number of people who can receive output, and maximize the number of people who can provide input. Remember the figure that showed the "idealized" lathe operator? Old-time

TABLE 16.4	Examples of Assistive Technologies
TYPE OF LIMITATION	**ASSISTIVE TECHNOLOGY**
Hearing	Hearing aids, amplifiers, cochlear implants, headphones, text telephone sign language, lip reading
Vision	Magnifiers, Braille, raised line drawings, synthetic speech, tape recorders, talking clocks/signs/calculators, voice output computer screen readers
Physical impairment	Wheelchairs, mouthsticks/headsticks, computer keyboard guards, artificial limbs, hand and armrests
Cognitive impairments	Memory aids, cuing systems, calculators, text-to-speech aids
Speech impairment	Voice amplifiers, voice synthesizers, artificial larynxes

SOURCE: Adapted from Vanderheiden (1997).

TABLE 16.5	Examples of the Maximization Principle

Maximize the number of people who can hear auditory output clearly enough.

Maximize the number of people who will receive important information if they cannot hear (at the moment or at all).

Maximize the number of people who can see visual output clearly enough.

Maximize the number of people who will not miss important information if they cannot see.

Maximize the number of people who can understand output (visual, auditory, other).

Maximize the number of people who can reach the controls.

Maximize the number of people who can physically insert and/or remove objects as required for the operation of a device.

Maximize the number of people who can perceive hazard warnings.

Source: Based on Vanderheiden (1997).

lathes were not designed for maximizing input—except for those workers who were 12 feet across the shoulders! Examples of how the maximization principle would be applied appear in Table 16.5. It is important to note that by following maximization principles, designers may make the work better suited not only to disabled workers, but also to the nondisabled.

A Cross-Cultural Issue in Disability and Design

Integrating disabled workers into the workforce raises interesting cross-cultural issues. You will recall from Hofstede's model of culture that countries vary on the individualism–collectivism dimension. The United States is seen as predominantly individualistic, while China is characterized as collectivist. Because individuals in collectivist cultures are more concerned about what others think, there is a tendency to "hide" disabled family members to avoid shame and feelings of guilt (Aycan & Kanungo, 2001). In the United States, individuals with disabilities are not hidden or ignored, and are more likely to be present in the workplace. For multinational organizations, it is important to examine the extent to which the spirit and the letter of the "accommodations" requirement is met in non-U.S. facilities.

MODULE 16.2 SUMMARY

- Technological changes and advances create an increasingly complex and dynamic work environment. Two of these changes include the increased role of automation and computers in the workplace.

- User-centered research studies and equipment designs help to make the human-computer interaction more effective.

- Shift work can be either fixed or rotating. Modifications of the human circadian cycle suggest that shift work has an important influence on

worker happiness, effectiveness, and safety. The same is true for flextime and compressed workweek schedules.

- Work design and redesign can be planned around one of four distinct approaches or models: motivational, perceptual-motor, mechanistic, or biological. The purpose of the design or redesign determines which model is most appropriate.

- Sophisticated technologies currently exist for redesigning work to make it more compatible with the limitations of disabled workers.

KEY TERMS

automation

human error

user-centered design

usability engineering

participatory design

ethnographically informed
    design

shift work

circadian cycle

fixed shift

rotating shift

flextime

compressed workweek

motivational approach

mechanistic approach

perceptual-motor approach

biological approach

Americans with Disabilities Act

accommodation

CRITICAL THINKING EXERCISES

16.3 The Internet has become an avenue for banking, retail sales, and information access. Some Internet sites are more user-friendly than others. From the user's perspective, what characteristics distinguish a friendly from a nonfriendly site? How would you design a research project to make a nonfriendly site more friendly?

16.4 Many companies have rotating shift schedules that are planned more than a year in advance. An employee on a rotating shift will know months in advance which shift he or she will be assigned to on a given day. Assume that the shift rotation is rapid, that is, shifts change each week. Does foreknowledge of a shift assignment reduce any of the negative effects of rotating shifts? Why or why not?

SAFETY IN THE WORKPLACE

By any standard, accidents are a major factor in the workplace. Consider the following statistics relative to U.S. worksites:

- Every working day, there are 17 deaths at the workplace (National Safety Council, 1996).
- Although no one can put a monetary value on a life, each workplace death results in a cost of $780,000 to U.S. society in general (Kohn, Friend, & Winterberger, 1996).
- Workplace deaths and injuries result in costs of over $48 billion annually (Goetsch, 1996).
- Thirty-five million workdays are lost each year as a result of accidents and injuries, resulting in the loss of $40 billion in wages, as well as medical, administrative, and other costs (Cascio, 1998).

Table 16.6 lists the most common causes of deaths and injuries at the workplace.

TABLE 16.6	Most Frequent Causes of Workplace Deaths and Injuries

Injury

Overexertion: Working beyond physical limitations
Impact accidents: Being struck by or against an object
Falls
Bodily reaction to chemicals
Compression
Motor vehicle accidents
Exposure to radiation or caustics
Rubbing or abrasions
Exposure to extreme temperatures

Deaths

Motor-vehicle related
Falls
Electrical current
Drowning
Fire related
Air transport related
Poison
Water transport related
Other

SOURCE: Wickens, Gordon, and Liu (1998).

SAFETY REGULATION

In 1970 Congress passed the **Occupational Safety and Health Act.** The purpose of that act was to ensure safe and healthful working conditions for every working man and woman in the United States. Two federal agencies were established to maintain and enforce this act. The first was the **Occupational Safety and Health Administration (OSHA).** OSHA's role is regulatory: It establishes standards and enforces them. The second agency was the **National Institute of Occupational Safety and Health (NIOSH).** Its responsibility is to conduct safety-related research; a great deal of the recent research in the area of work-related stress has been funded by NIOSH.

However, while legislation may be a necessary condition for worker safety, it is not a sufficient condition, as you can see from the accident and injury statistics cited in the last section. Employers and I-O psychologists still need to develop better ways of preventing work-related illness, injury, and accidents.

TRADITIONAL APPROACHES TO WORKPLACE SAFETY

A Model of Unsafe Behavior

The commonsense view of an accident is that someone was in the wrong place at the wrong time. The implication is that the accident was a random event and could not have been foreseen or prevented. I-O psychologists do not subscribe to this view. To be sure, there are chance events that enter into the making of an accident, but these events are independent of the behavior of the person to whom the accident will occur. An accident requires both a hazard and a behavior. The behavior is an unsafe act. If that act occurs when no hazard is present, no accident will occur. If the unsafe behavior occurs in the presence of a hazard, an accident is much more likely to occur. If a firefighter enters a burning building without a breathing apparatus in place, and there are no toxic fumes, there may be no health consequences. If that same firefighter enters the same building and toxic fumes are present, the result could be serious injury or death.

Figure 16.6 depicts in detail all of the variables that might enter into unsafe behavior. This model is meant to show that there is never "one" cause of an accident but multiple factors that interact. Take our hypothetical firefighter. The unsafe behavior might be attributed to inadequate training and a supervisor's lack of attention to safe behaviors. In addition, there might have been a great deal of noise and confusion at the fire scene, with reports of children trapped inside. The firefighter might have been awakened at 3:00 A.M. to respond to this call, after having fought another fire for six hours prior to the alarm. Fellow firefighters might have expressed criticism that valuable seconds were wasted while finding and donning the apparatus. All of these factors might have combined to yield the ultimate unsafe behavior. Ultimately, regardless of the presence of toxic fumes—the "chance" factor in the model—unless the firefighter engaged in an unsafe act, no injury from the toxic fumes could have resulted.

Rather than reviewing each of the factors in Figure 16.6 in detail, we will look at the general approaches that have been taken to increase safety in the workplace.

The Engineering Approach

The **engineering approach to safety** is based on the principles we reviewed earlier in this chapter. It might involve making a display (e.g., a pressure gauge) more visible or making a control (e.g., gear selector for a forklift) easier to activate. This approach assumes that an individual will engage in an action that might lead to injury unless the environment prevents that action. Acting upon this assumption, the engineering approach employs three levels of "prevention." The first and most direct is the design level: The hazard is engineered

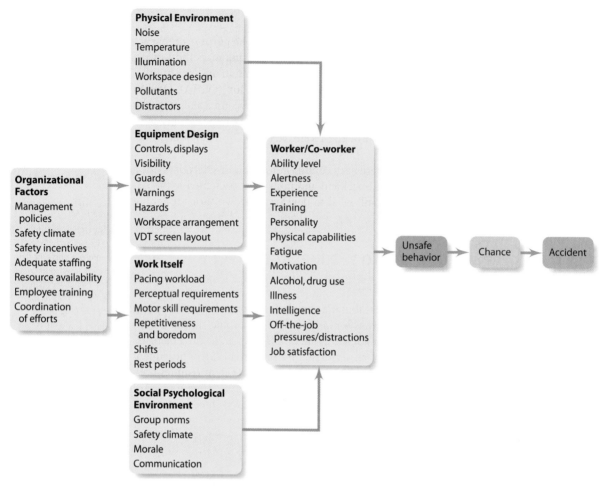

FIGURE 16.6 **A Model of Factors Contributing to Workplace Accidents** SOURCE: Adapted from Sanders & McCormick (1993).

out of the environment. The second level is the **safeguard** level; it acknowledges that although a hazard cannot be designed out of an environment, safeguards can be put in place which will eliminate the possibility of an injury. An example of such a safeguard is the tire cage, devised in response to the frequent separation of truck tire rims when tires are being mounted. When they do separate, parts of the rim explode with tremendous force, capable of killing the person changing the tire. The tire cage, standard equipment at most commercial tire dealerships, acts as a safeguard against such injuries. When a tire is to be inflated, it is placed in a restraining cage which protects the worker from the effects of a possible tire failure and explosion during inflation. The third level of prevention is the "warning" level. If we can't design a hazard out of the environment or develop a reasonable safeguard for the hazard, then the least we can do is to warn the user against it.

Figure 16.7 presents some examples of hazard warnings. As you can see, the warning designs are easy to understand and can be effective in reducing accidents. The design of warnings is a well developed but technical area; there are a number of excellent sources on the principles of warning design (Edworthy & Adams, 1996; Laughery & Wogalter, 1997; Peters & Peters, 1999). At a basic level, an effective warning has four characteristics:

1. It must catch the worker's attention.
2. It must identify the hazard.

(a)

(b)

(c)

(d)

FIGURE 16.7 Examples of Pictorials Conveying Hazard Information Source: Laughery & Wogalter (1997).

3. It must inform the worker of the consequences of not avoiding the hazard.

4. It must tell the worker how to avoid the hazard.

Figure 16.8 presents two examples of warnings. The text in the two boxes on the left would be considered inadequate, while the text in the two boxes on the right would be more appropriate.

A recent tragedy at a hockey game highlights the various engineering approaches that might be applied in a given situation. Brittanie Cecil was celebrating her 14th birthday by attending a professional hockey game in Columbus, Ohio. A slap shot by one of the players was deflected into the stands and hit her in the forehead. Slap shots have been known to travel at speeds in excess of 100 miles per hour. Brittanie was rushed to the hospital, where she died the next day (Wong, 2002). A debate ensued between social observers, on the one hand, and National Hockey League and stadium officials, on the other, about how to ensure the safety of spectators at hockey matches. There was little possibility of designing the slap shot out of the game or making the hockey puck softer, so the debate was over warnings and safeguards. The safeguard approach would be to increase the height of the protective glass that surrounds the hockey rink or, alternatively, to stretch nets above the glass, as is done in major league baseball to protect fans behind home plate from pitches that are fouled back.

The warning approach would be to display more prominent warnings about pucks leaving the ice and to have announcers remind fans of that hazard. In this case, the warning approach would be useless. A slap shot produces a projectile (the puck) that travels 50 feet in less than $\frac{25}{100}$ths of a second. The fastest simple reaction time for a human (e.g., to initiate a ducking movement) is about $\frac{35}{100}$ths of a second. For Brittanie, the puck was simply moving faster than she could hope to react; all the warnings in the world would not change that reality. Goalies are highly trained and well paid to stop slap shots aimed at the

Dangerous environment
Health hazard
Take precautionary measures

Mechanical hazard
You could be injured
Exercise care

Alternatives that would be considered more explicit and appropriate are:

Toxic fumes
Breathing fumes can lead to servere lung damage
Always wear type 1234 respirator in this area

Moving parts, pinch point hazard
Your hand could be caught in rollers and severely crushed
Do not operate without guard X in place

FIGURE 16.8 Two Kinds of Hazard Warnings Source: Laughery & Wogalter (1997).

FIGURE 16.9

A Low-Back Biomechanical Model of Static Coplanar Lifting
SOURCE: Chaffin & Andersson (1991).

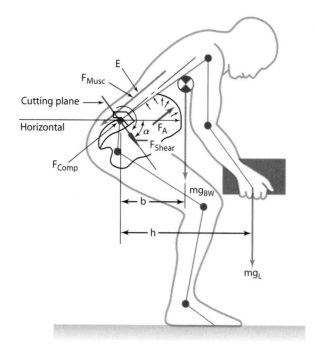

goal, and they are "warned" that the pucks are coming, but they are not always successful in stopping them. Why would a hockey fan be expected to perform as well as, or better than, a goalie?

Ergonomics Although the term "ergonomics" has come to be synonymous with human factors engineering, the term has another, narrower use. Historically, ergonomics meant the study of the physical demands of work such as reaching, stretching, lifting, and carrying (Grandjean, 1988), and it has close connections with the field of exercise physiology (McArdle, Katch, & Katch, 2001). For example, ergonomists have developed elaborate physiologically based computer models that can accurately calculate the forces on the lower back and joints when a person of a given height and weight lifts a box of certain dimensions and weight to a specified height from a lower height (Chaffin, 1997). Figure 16.9 presents an example of a schematic that would be used for predicting these forces. There are many excellent and detailed treatments of the ergonomic design of physically demanding jobs (e.g., Salvendy, 1997).

With respect to workplace safety, the most commonly studied injuries are lower back and upper extremity disorders. These are commonly referred to as musculoskeletal injuries. The National Research Council (2001) recently completed an extensive review of research on these injuries and their prevention. Consider the devices depicted in Figure 16.10, intended to help prevent back injuries resulting from picking up heavy boxes from the floor. The specially designed table can lift a box to waist level and tilt the box for packing or lifting. The other common form of injury, particularly involving the upper extremities (e.g., arm, shoulder, wrist), is known as the **cumulative trauma disorder (CTD)** (Wickens, Gordon, & Liu, 1998). The best known CTD is **carpal tunnel syndrome** of the hand and wrist. There is a tunnel in the wrist through which tissues, nerves, and blood vesssels pass. Various hand tools, keyboards, and computer "mice" can place stress on that tunnel, resulting in inflammation and swelling with accompanying pain and numbness (Wickens, Gordon, & Liu, 1998). The correct design of tools, keyboards, and motions can greatly reduce the risk of cumulative trauma disorders.

CUMULATIVE TRAUMA DISORDER (CTD)

Common form of workplace injury involving the upper extremities (arm, shoulder, wrist).

CARPAL TUNNEL SYNDROME

Injury of the hand and wrist caused by stress from various tools, keyboards, and computer "mice," resulting in inflammation, swelling, pain, and numbness.

(a)

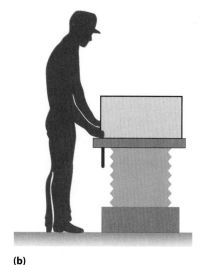

(b)

FIGURE 16.10

A Typical Lift-and-Tilt Table and Pallet Lift The lift-and-tilt table (A) and pallet lift (B) are used to avoid stooped lifting of large or heavy packages. SOURCE: Chaffin (1997).

The Personnel Approach

The concept of accident proneness has always been a popular one. It assumes that certain individuals are more likely to have accidents than others. Were this true, safety would be a simple case of selection. An organization would simply not hire accident-prone individuals. But **accident proneness** is a myth founded on the statistical properties of accidents. Some individuals do have more accidents than others because they work in hazardous occupations like fishing, forestry, or mining, or because they are exposed to hazards at a more frequent rate (e.g., auto assemblers versus account clerks in the auto industry). Another potentially misleading factor is this: In a given year, for a given location, there are usually many more people than there are accidents. Consider a plant with 1,000 employees that experiences 500 accidents in a given year. Of the workers who do experience accidents, the vast majority will have only one. Some smaller number of workers will have two, and an even smaller number will have three. Assume that we could randomly distribute 500 accidents to 1,000 workers by drawing their names out of a hat. Each time we drew a name, this would represent an "accident." We would put that name back into the hat for a subsequent drawing; this would mirror accident histories at plants, with the exception of a worker who is killed or permanently disabled. Using such a procedure to "assign" accidents, a small number of names would be drawn from the hat more than once. This would not mean that those individuals were "accident prone"; it would simply be an expression of the laws of probability.

Although accident proneness does not exist as a general syndrome, it is reasonable to assume that certain demographic characteristics, abilities, and personality characteristics may be associated with unsafe behavior—and recall that unsafe behavior is one of the components of an accident. Mihal and Barrett (1976) found that utility company drivers with highly developed perceptual skills experienced fewer accidents. Earlier, Barrett and Thornton (1968) found similar results in a simulated driving task involving the avoidance of pedestrians. Avolio, Kroeck, and Panek (1985) found associations between several information processing measures and motor vehicle accidents. Arthur, Barrett, and Alexander (1991) conducted a meta-analysis of the relationship between vehicular accidents and a number of individual difference variables such as cognitive ability and personality. They found that both cognitive ability and certain personality variables (e.g., internal locus of control and general activity level) were negatively related to accidents; the greater the amount of these attributes in a person, the fewer the number of accidents.

Some occupations tend to attract individuals who have feelings of invulnerability.

It is well known that the vehicular accident rate for young males tends to be the highest of any demographic group (U.S. Dept. of Transportation, 1996). The primary reason for this seems to be the tendency among these drivers to speed (Nell, 2002). Young males see themselves as invulnerable to injury or death (in almost any environment) and have an unrealistically high assessment of their skills and abilities. As a result, they see little risk in driving fast. There is ample evidence that men take more risks than women, particularly in the age group of 18 to 21 (Byrnes, Miller, & Schafer, 1999). These differences appear in the relative accident rates of employed male and female adolescents as well, with males experiencing more accidents on the job than their female counterparts (Frone, 1998).

Organizations using the **personnel approach** to reducing accidents would emphasize the selection of particular groups of individuals as they are identified by various individual difference characteristics, and/or would provide training to overcome potential risk factors prevalent in some individuals.

PERSONNEL APPROACH

Emphasizes the selection of particular groups of individuals identified by individual difference characteristics, or provides training to overcome potential risk factors prevalent in some individuals.

MOTIVATIONAL APPROACH

Assumes that a worker is capable of behaving safely but may choose not to, so the worker must be motivated to behave safely.

The Motivational Approach

The **motivational approach** assumes that a worker is *capable* of behaving safely, but may choose not to; the worker therefore must be motivated to behave safely. A worker might choose not to behave safely for any number of reasons: It is too much effort to retrieve safety goggles and put them on, co-workers will make fun of him or her for taking extra precautions, and so forth. The motivational approach to safety tries to change worker preferences for and satisfactions with safe behavior.

Ludwig and Geller (1997) presented an example of the motivational approach in their research on pizza delivery drivers. The accident rate of pizza delivery drivers is estimated to be three times higher than the national average (Ludwig & Geller, 1997; Meagher, 1989). There are a number of reasons for this. The typical delivery driver is a young male, and we have already seen that this demographic group drives faster and perceives less risk than other drivers. In addition, pizza delivery businesses market speed. They promise or imply that your food will arrive quickly, and piping hot. In addition, since the drivers depend heavily on tips for their income, the more pizzas they can deliver, the more money they make.

Ludwig and Geller introduced a motivational program to improve pizza delivery driver safety based on the goal-setting approaches we studied in Chapter 9. Employees at one store participated in goal setting, while employees at a second store were simply assigned goals. A third store was used as a control store, with no goals of any type introduced. The goals were directed toward coming to a complete stop at intersections, but two other behaviors were observed as well (with no goals involved): signaling for turns and wearing the seat belt. It was assumed that if the drivers practiced these three safe behaviors, accidents would decrease. Drivers in both experimental conditions were shown a poster with the percentage of complete stops every four days for a month (the intervention period). At the end of the month, posters were removed and replaced with congratulatory signs for meeting the goals for four more days (the withdrawal period), then the signs were removed and data were collected for the next five and one-half months (the follow-up period).

TABLE 16.7	**Means and Standard Deviations for Each Driving Behavior across Phases and within Groups, and for the Postmeeting Questionnaire Items**							
	OVERALL		PARTICIPATIVE		ASSIGNED		CONTROL[a]	
MEASURE AND PHASE	**M**	**SD**	**M**	**SD**	**M**	**SD**	**M**	**SD**
Complete stops (%)								
Baseline	51.4	15.9	54.1	11.6	45.2	23.4	48.7	17.1
Intervention	58.2	21.8	65.9	12.9	68.5	12.8	49.0	31.9
Withdraw	52.5	22.6	60.0	18.5	59.0	18.2	38.6	23.2
Follow-up	48.3	19.5	53.5	18.5	41.8	14.6	46.6	23.9
Turn signal use (%)								
Baseline	64.4	21.5	68.1	17.2	66.3	13.5	56.4	16.4
Intervention	65.1	25.3	76.1	14.6	61.8	21.7	54.6	32.1
Withdraw	63.9	26.3	78.5	19.4	52.7	23.1	47.7	24.2
Follow-up	62.5	23.0	71.6	14.6	51.3	16.5	53.5	30.9
Safety belt use (%)								
Baseline	58.8	38.8	75.4	28.4	57.0	39.8	38.6	43.6
Intervention	62.5	39.9	84.9	21.8	56.2	36.9	31.0	44.7
Withdraw	63.9	34.2	83.8	24.1	58.3	33.0	37.0	31.3
Follow-up	71.7	35.8	88.9	18.5	60.6	44.8	35.8	40.7
Meeting participation[b]	1.65	4.9	1.31	.48	1.92	.28		
Goal participation[c]	3.15	1.31	3.69	1.38	2.61	1.04		
Discussion participation[d]	3.65	0.98	0.40	1.0	3.3	.85		
Intention to stop[e]	4.58	0.76	4.3	.95	4.8	.38		

[a]Did not participate in postmeeting questionnaire.   [b]1 = *no* and 2 = *yes*.   [c]1 = *not at all* and 5 = *very much*.   [d]1 = *not at all* and 5 = *very much*.   [e]1 = *never* and 5 = *every time*.

SOURCE: Ludwig & Geller (1997).

As Table 16.7 shows, the effect of participative goal setting was positive and substantial. All three safe behaviors increased for the participative goal-setting group, and to a lesser extent for the assigned goal group. Even though the only targeted behavior was coming to a complete stop at intersections, there was a spillover effect on the other two behaviors as well. In addition, you can see that the effects of the goal setting generally remained high even after the intervention period was over.

This motivational intervention would be considered a success. It depended on changing the preferences and behavioral choices of the drivers, rather than on selecting different drivers (i.e., the personnel approach) or on changing the design of the work (e.g., making "hurrying" of lesser value by hiring more drivers, or permitting drivers only two deliveries an hour).

We have presented these three approaches as if they were mutually exclusive, but the best way to ensure success would be to include elements of all three approaches. The safe environment starts with design issues and safeguard considerations. It is also appropriate to provide warnings for hazardous environment and operations. Next, we would

Although we expressed skepticism about the concept of "accident proneness" earlier in this module, the following incident makes one wonder whether there are indeed individual difference characteristics that can consistenly predict unsafe behaviors.

One of your authors was performing a job analysis of a cabinet maker's job when he noticed that the supervisor whom he was interviewing was missing a finger on his left hand. Since safety was an issue in this job, it made sense to ask whether the loss of the finger was work-related. The supervisor got an embarrassed look on his face and said that it had happened, ironically, while he was instructing a new employee on the safe use of a band saw. He then proceeded to go over to the saw and demonstrate to the psychologist how it had happened—and promptly cut off two fingers on his other hand!

want to select and train the most capable applicants based on a job analysis, particularly with an emphasis on the successful performance of hazardous tasks. Finally, we would want to provide a social-psychological atmosphere that encouraged safe behavior through various motivational approaches.

NEWER APPROACHES TO SAFETY

The traditional approaches to safety all tend to focus on the individual. The engineering approach is designed to prevent an individual from performing an unsafe act. The personnel approach assumes that "safe" individuals can be selected or trained. The motivational approach is directed toward changing the choices that an individual worker makes. To be fair, it is always the individual worker who actually engages in an unsafe act, but it would be incorrect to imply that this act occurs in a social vacuum. There are other, broader forces at work as well (Hofmann & Stetzer, 1996). These forces include attitudes and behaviors of supervisors and fellow workers toward safety, management and organizational commitment toward safe behavior, and a general climate and culture in the workplace that favors or disfavors safe behavior.

Hofmann, Jacobs, and Landy (1995) have suggested that an organization has three levels, and that each level plays a role in safe behavior. The first level is the traditional one—the individual level. It includes employee attitudes, employee behavior, and employee knowledge. The second level is called the microorganizational level and includes management attitudes, the presence of accountability mechanisms, a willingness on the part of the organization to self-regulate rather than depend on external compliance agencies for regulation, and the presence of joint labor-management groups such as safety committees. The third level, the macroorganizational level, includes communication channels, centralization versus decentralization of decision making, technological complexity, redundancy backup systems, and workforce specialization. For the present discussion, we will concentrate on the second level, microorganizational issues.

The Role of Leaders in Safety

Hofmann and Morgeson (1999) devised a model to describe how leaders influence accidents (see Figure 16.11). The model proposes that the quality of the relationship between the leader and the group members determines the extent of communication about safety-related issues. You will recall from Chapter 12 on leadership that the quality of the supervisor-subordinate relationship was a key component of the leader-member exchange (LMX) theory. In the case of accident avoidance, this communication may be in the form of safety planning before a particular task or piece of work, or in the form of reviewing accidents or unsafe behaviors

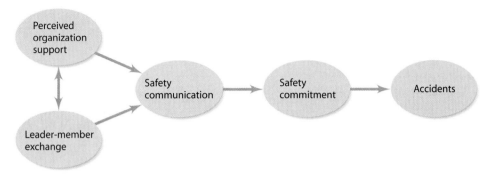

FIGURE 16.11

Leader Influence on Accidents SOURCE: Hofmann & Morgeson (1999).

after they have occurred. In environments lacking an open and supportive relationship between the leader and group members, accidents and unsafe behavior tend to be attributed to events and the environment (e.g., equipment failures), rather than to individual workers. Even when the worker is clearly at fault, unless the supervisor has established a pattern of open and nonjudgmental communication, workers will not see any direct connection between their behavior and accidents (Hofmann & Morgeson, 1999; Hofmann & Stetzer, 1998). Zohar (2002) provided confirming evidence of this link between leader behavior and subordinate safety. In a study of 420 workers and supervisors in a heavy equipment repair facility, he found that by increasing safety-oriented communication between supervisors and their managers on the one hand, and supervisors and their subordinates on the other hand, the company was able to achieve a significant increase in safe behaviors.

Safety Climate and Culture

Organizations can be characterized by their respective internal **safety cultures**—they fall along a continuum from placing strong emphasis on safety to disregarding it. No one would characterize the National Football League (NFL) or the National Hockey League (NHL) as valuing safety above entertainment or winning. Players are expected to sacrifice their bodies for the sake of victory. In contrast, most of us would agree that regulated industries such as nuclear power, petrochemicals, and commercial aviation are committed to safety above all else. It is this organizational commitment (or lack thereof) that shapes the attitudes of managers, supervisors, and workers. If the NFL or NHL fined owners and coaches for the frequency of injuries among their team members, or awarded championship rings or the Stanley Cup for injury-free seasons, the nature of football and hockey would change considerably.

Establishing a safety culture in an organization is not a simple task. It is not enough simply to include safety as one of the stated values of the organization. As the saying goes, "Talk is cheap." It takes hard work to establish and maintain a safety culture. There must be a commitment at every level of the organization. Examples of this cross-level commitment would include:

- Establishing safety committees with members from all levels of the organization.
- Establishing a budget for safety that does not disappear during periods of economic crisis.
- Including safety-related behaviors in the evaluation of performance of employees at all levels of the organization.
- Establishing high-quality leader/subordinate relationships that foster open discussion of safety-related issues.
- Developing a shared attitude toward self-regulation of safety-related behavior at all levels of the organization.

SAFETY CULTURE

Type of culture in an organization ranging along a continuum from a strong emphasis on safety to disregard for it.

As Hofmann and Stetzer (1996) suggested, organizational safety is not the responsibility of any single group (e.g., workers *or* supervisors *or* managers *or* executives). The safety climate must pervade all levels of the organization, and all levels of the organization must be involved in a constant dialogue about those issues if the commitment to safety is to be effective.

It is tempting to think of a culture as universal within an organization—either a safety culture exists or it doesn't. But that is not necessarily the case. Once again, the group leader seems to be central to the process by which a culture is adopted by individual work groups. For example, Clarke (1999) found that even though representatives at various levels of the British Rail Corporation (e.g., drivers, supervisors, and executives) shared a perception that safety was important, they varied in terms of how important they thought that perception was to *other* levels. Drivers did not believe that supervisors or executives understood the influence of working conditions on safety. And supervisors did not believe that executives were aware of the importance of working conditions. Thus, despite the commitment of all parties to safety in the workplace, they tended to doubt each other's level of understanding of the most important factors in creating a safe workplace. If each level of an organization doubts the level of understanding or commitment of the other levels, it is less likely that a truly safe workplace can be established. The belief that others "may not get it" is likely to put a damper on individual safety efforts.

The importance of the connection between organizational level culture and work group culture is underlined by research conducted by Zohar (2000) on 53 different work groups in a metal-processing plant. He found that each work group developed its own shared perception of the safety climate of the organization, and that substantial differences existed among the work groups on this perception. In essence, there were **microcultures** in the organization. Remember from our discussion in Chapter 1 that a culture is represented by a consensus or shared set of values or perceptions. Zohar found a culture operating at the work group level. More importantly, he found that the group culture predicted accident frequency within that group. He concluded, as did Clarke (1999), that it is insufficient simply to examine an organizational level climate or culture in the hopes of increasing safety. We must consider the interaction of all levels of the organization with respect to safety. It starts with the individual worker, but also includes the work group, the leader, and the upper-level managers and executives. Safety does not rest on the shoulders of any one person or level of the organization; instead, it must have the support of all levels.

MICROCULTURE

Occurs when a work group develops its own view of a particular culture (e.g., safety) in an organization.

SAFETY FROM THE INTERNATIONAL PERSPECTIVE

Safety has been a topic of interest for I-O psychologists in many different countries. Here is a sampling of recent work done outside the United States (Griffin & Kabanoff, 2001). We have included the affiliations of the researchers to allow you to explore their research in greater detail by contacting them directly.

Israel   Dov Zohar at the Technion University is doing research on safety climates and cultures, group leadership, and leadership training as they relate to organizational safety.

Australia   Researchers at the University of New South Wales are examining the effect on safety practices of having contingent (i.e., part-time or temporary) workers.

England   Psychologists at the Institute of Work Psychology in Sheffield are studying the effects of organizational design on safety as well as the impact of semiautonomous teams versus traditionally managed work groups. They are also looking at the possible effects of deregulation on safety, that is, whether plants that adopt a self-regulatory posture will be as safe as those that depend on regulatory agencies for guidance.

Scotland   Psychologists at the University of Aberdeen are concentrating on issues of safety in high-reliability organizations, including nuclear power plants, commercial aviation, and hospitals. They are particularly focused on issues of safety culture and climate.

Germany   The Division of Work and Organizational Psychology of the Berlin University of Technology is studying the relationship between system breakdown and accidents and near misses. In addition, they are performing a comparative analysis of safety cultures in East European high-reliability organizations such as nuclear power plants.

As you can see, international safety research is thriving. It is interesting to note, however, that most of these efforts go well beyond the traditional individual-focused efforts in U.S. safety research. It is clear that future contributions to creating safer environments will include considerations of culture, climate, leadership, and multicultural influences.

MODULE 16.3 SUMMARY

- The Occupational Safety and Health Act of 1970 requires employers to provide safe and healthful working conditions for employees.
- The major concern of the I-O psychologist in promoting safety in the workplace is the study of unsafe behavior.
- Three common behavioral approaches to increasing worker safety are the engineering, personnel, and motivational approaches. The engineering approach emphasizes the design of the workplace. The personnel approach emphasizes the selection and training of workers to enhance safety. The motivational approach attempts to increase safety by changing goals and attitudes.
- Recent approaches to safety have emphasized organizational climate and culture, as well as the effect of leaders and group attitudes on safe behavior.

KEY TERMS

Occupational Safety and Health Act

Occupational Safety and Health Administration (OSHA)

National Institute of Occupational Safety and Health (NIOSH)

engineering approach to safety

safeguard

cumulative trauma disorder (CTD)

carpal tunnel syndrome

accident proneness

personnel approach

motivational approach

safety culture

microculture

CRITICAL THINKING EXERCISES

16.5 Tire repair can be a dangerous activity, particularly for large truck tires. Often, the tire will explode while being inflated or cause the rim to separate, resulting in catastrophic injuries to a worker. One way of reducing these injuries is to have the worker inflate the tire within a cage, thus physically protecting the worker from the tire and the rim. But workers often don't want to take the time or suffer the inconvenience of using the cage arrangement. Using one of the three approaches we have described for influencing safety—engineering, personnel, motivational—suggest an intervention that would reduce accidents related to this activity.

16.6 If we accept the notion that leaders have an influence on the safety of their subordinates, how can we be sure that safety remains an important issue for leaders?

VIOLENCE AT WORK

A man shot four co-workers to death at an aircraft parts plant Friday, then fired at police from a stolen company van during a high-speed chase that ended with him killing himself . . . The gunman opened fire during a meeting, targeting particular co-workers. "He used to get in little squabbles with them because he didn't get his merchandise in time to ship it out. He was kind of rigid, a lone wolf. He was afraid of losing his job" (Coyne, 2002, p. 11A).

In the past, the workplace was seen as a protected environment, one in which workers could feel safe. That is no longer the case (Barling, 1996). Violence is becoming more common in the workplace and therefore more important than ever to I-O psychologists (Bulatao & Vandenbos, 1996). Work-related violence falls into two different categories. The first deals with violent actions carried out by a nonemployee against an employee. Examples include armed robberies of convenience stores or gas stations in which a clerk is threatened, and often assaulted, by a robber. Similarly, workers in certain occupations, such as corrections and police officers, deal with violence as an essential function of their jobs. The second category of violence is perpetrated by employees and directed toward fellow employees. It is the second form of violence that we will consider. Several excellent reviews cover both types of violence (Kinney, 1995; Vandenbos & Bulatao, 1996).

There have been many hypotheses about why we have seen the workplace become more violent since the early 1990s (Elliott & Jarrett, 1994; Mack, Shannon, Quick, & Quick, 1996), including the following:

- The surge of layoffs, mergers, and acquisitions has radically increased stress at the workplace.
- As a result of the baby boom, fewer jobs are available as people strive to move up in the organization.
- Increasingly multicultural workplaces make it more likely that prejudices and biases will enter into worker interactions.
- There is a greater tendency for workers to abuse drugs and alcohol, thus lowering inhibitions that prevent violent behavior.
- In attempts to become leaner, organizations have eliminated layers of management, resulting in reduced opportunities for communication with employees about frustrating situations.

As we saw in Chapter 15, stress is often associated with violent actions by individuals. To the extent that work is stressful, then, it should not come as a total shock to see violent behavior at work such as the incident at the aircraft parts plant described above. Although to date there has been little careful and systematic research on workplace violence, a great deal of descriptive, anecdotal, and theoretical work exists on the topic.

LEVELS OF VIOLENCE

Shootings, such as the incident described above, tend to grab the headlines. But most violent acts in the workplace are far less dramatic. They include acts like verbal threats, insults, and bullying. Table 16.8 presents a three-level description of the most common forms of workplace violence. Kinney (1995) suggested that managerial and supervisory responses such as counseling, discipline, and referral to employee assistance programs (EAPs) are often the most appropriate reactions to level one behaviors. More formal responses, often including psychological assessment and law enforcement involvement, might be required for level two, and certainly for level three behaviors.

TABLE 16.8   **Incidents or Behaviors Associated with Levels One, Two, and Three Violence and Responses**

Level One Violence

- Refuses to cooperate with immediate supervisor.
- Spreads rumors and gossip to harm others.
- Consistently argues with co-workers.
- Belligerent toward customers or clients.
- Constantly swears at others.
- Makes inappropriate sexual comments.

Available Responses

- Discipline or referral to EAP.

Level Two Violence

- Argues increasingly with customers, vendors, co-workers, and management.
- Refuses to obey company policies and procedures.
- Sabotages or destroys equipment or property of employer or co-worker.
- Verbalizes wishes to hurt co-workers or management.
- Sends sexual or violent notes to co-workers or management.
- Sees self as victimized by management ("me vs. them").

Level Three Violence

Frequent displays of intense anger resulting in:

- Recurrent physical fights.
- Destruction of property.
- Recurrent suicidal threats.
- Utilization of weapons to harm others.
- Murder, rape, or arson.

Available Responses

- Psychological assessment, discipline, or law enforcement intervention.

SOURCE: National Safe Workplace Institute (1989); reproduced in Kinney (1995).

FIGURE 16.12

Routine Experiential Sequence of Violence Perpetrators
SOURCE: Based on Kinney, (1995).

1. Individual suffers trauma which creates extreme tension or anxiety; may be a single major event (e.g., job loss or divorce) or cumulative minor events.

2. Individual thinks that problems are unsolvable.

3. Individual projects all responsibility onto the situation.

4. Individual's frame of reference becomes increasingly egocentric.

5. Self-preservation and self-protection gradually become sole objectives.

6. Violent act perceived as only way out.

7. Violent act is attempted or committed.

THE EXPERIENTIAL SEQUENCE OF VIOLENCE

Kinney (1995) outlined a common thought process that precedes the commission of a violent act in the workplace. The sequence is presented in Figure 16.12. The key steps in the sequence include an "event" in the individual's life (e.g., a poor performance appraisal), a belief that a "problem" cannot be resolved, and a perceived threat to the individual's self-esteem or well-being. We will consider the issue of self-esteem in greater detail shortly.

THE "TYPICAL" VIOLENT WORKER

With the exception of the worker who is suffering from a serious mental disorder (e.g., one who hears "voices" telling him to kill his supervisor), most cases of workplace violence involve some feeling of being treated unfairly, and the perpetrator has some real or imagined grievance against the organization or a person in the organization. In addition, experts in workplace violence have assembled a laundry list of possible characteristics of a perpetrator. Any given perpetrator is not likely to have *all* of the characteristics listed below, but will certainly have some of them (Paul & Townsend, 1998). Similarly, just because an individual has many, or even all, of these characteristics, it does not necessarily mean that he or she will engage in violence.

- Does not participate in organizational events.
- Has few outside interests.
- Has worked for the company for some time.
- Has a history of violence.
- Is a white male between 25 and 50 years of age.
- Has lost or is worried about losing his or her job.
- Has a history of conflicts with co-workers, supervisors, or both.
- Has difficulty accepting authority.
- Commonly violates company policies and rules.
- Works in a company or work group with an authoritarian management style.
- Abuses alcohol.

This list emphasizes the characteristics of the individual violent employee, but several of these individual factors (e.g., job loss, authoritarian management style) indicate that organizational characteristics may also be associated with workplace violence. These characteristics would include high levels of job-related stress (e.g., role conflict and role ambiguity), a continuing threat of layoff, few opportunities for communication between management and employees, and lack of a formal or informal appeal process for questioning management actions such as performance appraisals, compensation decisions, and transfers (Paul & Townsend, 1998). It would also seem logical to include the absence of group work or teamwork, since environments without them usually provide less opportunity for communication among workers. Poor communication between a worker and a supervisor or between co-workers seems to be central to many instances of workplace violence.

THEORIES OF WORKPLACE VIOLENCE

I-O psychologists commonly examine workplace violence using one of two theoretical approaches. The first is a variation on a traditional approach to all aggressive behavior, regardless of where it occurs. Its premise is that the individual worker has been frustrated—prevented from achieving some important goal or outcome—which results in aggression directed toward a co-worker or supervisor. The second approach is more specific to industrial situations and invokes the concept of justice (see Chapter 11). We will briefly consider these two approaches.

Frustration-Aggression Hypothesis

More than 60 years ago, Dollard, Doob, Miller, Mowrer, and Sears (1939) proposed a simple hypothesis: Frustration leads to aggression. They cited laboratory and field data to support that proposition. The initial **frustration-aggression hypothesis** proved to be far too broad. It became clear that aggression was only one possible response to frustration and that not everyone responded to frustration with aggression. Further, it became clear that aggression has many different roots, only one of which is represented by frustration. To put it simply, not all frustrated individuals act aggressively, and not all aggressive acts are a result of frustration.

> **FRUSTRATION-AGGRESSION HYPOTHESIS**
>
> *Argues that frustration leads to aggression; ultimately found to be too broad—aggression was only one possible response to frustration and not everyone responded to frustration with aggression.*

Spector (1975) adapted the frustration-aggression hypothesis to issues of work behavior, particularly counterproductive behavior, which we discussed in Chapter 5. Spector defined frustrating events as "situational constraints in the immediate work situation that block individuals from achieving valued work goals or attaining effective performance" (Fox & Spector, 1999, p. 917). The modern view of the frustration-aggression connection is that frustration leads to a stress reaction and that the individual expends energy to relieve this stress, often in the form of destructive or counterproductive behavior.

The key to whether or not an individual engages in destructive behavior is thought to be the extent to which he or she believes that the obstacle to goal attainment—and thus the frustration—can be eliminated through constructive behavior. If the individual does not believe that constructive behavior will eliminate the frustration, then aggressive action may be taken instead (Fox & Spector, 1999; Spector, 2000). And this belief, of course, depends to some extent on the prior history of the individual. If constructive behavior has not worked before, the individual is less likely to try it again. Spector's model of this process is presented in Figure 16.13. Recently, Fox and Spector (1999) identified several personality variables and beliefs that seem to intervene in the process by which frustration becomes aggression. The first of these variables is locus of control. As you will recall from our discussion in Chapter 15, individuals with an external locus of control believe that events are controlled by forces outside of themselves, while internals believe that they are in control of their fate. Fox and Spector found that when confronted with obstacles, externals were more likely to report unpleasant emotions and

FIGURE 16.13

Constructive and Destructive Employee Behavior as a Result of Frustration and Employee Control
SOURCE: Spector (2000).

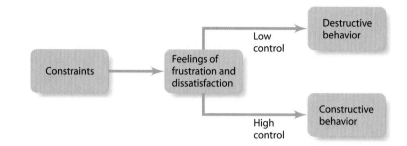

engage in aggressive action than internals. They also found that levels of anger and anxiety, as well as beliefs that counterproductive behaviors would be punished, affected the likelihood that a worker would engage in counterproductive behaviors. Anger is a commonly observed emotion that appears to accompany violence—domestic or workplace. But anger is very often the by-product of anxiety or fear. This is particularly true in the workplace. When violence breaks out, fear of something (e.g., loss of a job, "losing face" in front of fellow workers) is often at the root of the violence.

Baumeister, Smart, and Boden (1996) identified another personality variable that appears to be associated with violence: self-esteem. The conventional wisdom has been that individuals with low self-esteem are most likely to engage in violent behavior. In reviewing the literature on violence, Baumeister et al. found exactly the opposite. Individuals and groups who believe in their own superiority are those most likely to engage in aggressive and violent actions. This positive self-image is often unrealistically positive, and this is where the problem arises. When individuals receive information that challenges this positive self-appraisal, they reject it and react against the source of this conflicting information, often violently. Thus, a realistic performance evaluation with some negative information can trigger a violent response in an individual with an unrealistically high opinion of his or her work. Similarly, an individual who believes that he or she is central to the success of an organization will find it hard to accept or understand a layoff notice. Two of the most common precipitating events in instances of workplace violence are the loss of a job and a negative performance review, both of which challenge one's self-image as an effective and valuable employee.

The "Justice" Hypothesis

JUSTICE HYPOTHESIS OF WORKPLACE VIOLENCE

Proposes that some violent acts can be understood as reactions by an employee against perceived injustice.

Folger and Baron (1996) argued compellingly that at least some violent acts can be understood as reactions against perceived injustice by an employee. This is the conceptual basis for the **justice hypothesis of workplace violence.** You will recall from Chapter 11 that workers generally evaluate events in the workplace according to three types of justice. Procedural justice relates to issues of due process and whether all individuals are treated equally. Distributive justice relates to actual outcomes, such as layoffs, and whether a particular individual believes that he or she deserved the outcome. Interpersonal justice deals with the manner by which decisions are communicated, whether compassionate and respectful or callous and demeaning. Folger and Baron suggested some ways that an organization can reduce the likelihood of violent acts when individuals are laid off or given negative performance reviews. As shown in Table 16.9, the issues associated with each aspect of justice are different. The prudent employer will pursue ways to create justice perceptions in each of the three areas. Even when workplace violence is not the issue, organizations should be aware that these prevention strategies represent best practices; the same initiatives that can maintain a satisfied and productive workforce can also reduce the possibility of violence.

TABLE 16.9	Distributive, Procedural, and Interpersonal Justice Actions to Prevent Workplace Aggression

DISTRIBUTIVE JUSTICE

Layoffs and firings

    Do not raise chief executive officer's pay when downsizing

    Try other financial alternatives to layoffs

    If firing by performance ratings, check their validity

Performance appraisal

    Use job-related, relevant criteria

    Develop criteria based on job analysis

PROCEDURAL JUSTICE

Layoffs and firings

    Use employee voice or input where possible

        Details on severance, and so on

        Suggestions on avoiding bias

        Consistently applied guidelines

        Timeliness of feedback

        Adequate explanations

Performance appraisal

    Clarify in advance standards and expectations

    Solicit employee's own opinion about performance (e.g., self-appraisal)

    Explain and discuss ratings (explore discrepancies)

INTERPERSONAL JUSTICE

Layoffs and firings

    Notify in a timely manner

    Explain sincerely and with sincere concern

    Express sincere remorse

    Avoid distancing and aloofness

    Treat with dignity and respect

Performance appraisal

    Same as for layoffs and firings

Source: Folger & Baron (1996).

Greenberg and Barling (1999) examined the role of procedural justice in employee aggression among nonfaculty employees of a Canadian university. Their results not only confirm the hypotheses of Folger and Baron regarding the role of justice perceptions, but also extend them in interesting ways. They found that perceptions of procedural injustice were associated with aggression against supervisors. They also found that alcohol consumption interacted with these feelings of injustice. If procedures were considered fair, then alcohol consumption was unrelated to aggression. On the other hand, if procedures were considered unfair, then alcohol consumption increased the likelihood of aggression toward a supervisor. (Virtually every examination of workplace violence has identified alcohol consumption as a substantial risk factor.) Greenberg and Barling also found that increased workplace surveillance was associated with a greater likelihood of aggressive acts directed toward supervisors. This last finding, however, is hard to interpret. In some organizations, increased surveillance may be the result of a history of counterproductive behavior. Thus, it is difficult to tell if surveillance is a cause of aggressive behavior or part of a vicious circle in which it is as much an effect as a cause.

Although job loss seems to be involved in many acts of workplace violence and aggression, Catalano, Novaco, and McConnell (1997) reported some intriguing findings about the effects of widespread job loss. They designed a study to examine the relationship between the reported number of layoffs on a weekly basis in San Francisco for a one-year period, and civil commitments for danger to others during the same period. This type of civil commitment is a court order that permits an individual whom mental health professionals deem likely to commit an act of violence against another to be held in custody for up to 72 hours. If, after 72 hours, the detainee is still perceived as a threat to another person, he or she may be held for longer periods after a hearing.

Catalano et al. discovered that as layoffs increased, so did violent and threatening behavior (as defined by increases in civil commitments) but *only up to a point*. As layoffs continued to increase, violent and threatening behavior began to diminish. The researchers explained this phenomenon as one of protecting one's job. As jobs became more scarce, workers were more likely to inhibit aggressive acts that might jeopardize those jobs. This suggests a dilemma for employers. In an attempt to reduce the potential for violence by reducing layoffs, an organization may very well be *increasing* the potential. Thus, it might be more harmful for an organization to implement a series of small layoffs rather than one large layoff.

A way out of this dilemma may be in the manner by which layoffs are handled. Both Folger and Baron (1996) and Greenberg and Barling (1999) suggested that justice perceptions are crucial to preventing violent employee responses. With appropriate justice mechanisms in place, it is possible that studies such as those done by Catalano et al. would find little or no relationship between layoffs and the threat of violence. Some of these mechanisms might include the consistent application of layoff policies (Hemingway & Conte, in press), treating those to be laid off with dignity and respect—for example, informing them in person rather than by e-mail or written memo (Greenberg, 1994)—and providing clear explanations of the criteria used to make layoff decisions.

A SPECIAL TYPE OF VIOLENCE: BULLYING

The topic of bullying, particularly as experienced by children and teenagers in school, has achieved some prominence in recent years. Sadly, the prominence has come from violent outbursts such as the killings at Columbine High School in Littleton, Colorado, in the spring of 1999. Two students who had been bullied by fellow students brought weapons to school and killed 12 fellow students and a teacher. But bullying is not confined to schools; it is just as likely to occur at the workplace. In light of what appears to be an increase in workplace violence in the United States, some understanding of the phenomenon of bullying might prove very useful in reducing such violence.

Strangely, the topic of bullying at work has received virtually no attention by American I-O psychologists. Most of the research has been carried out by European scholars. The *European Journal of Work and Organizational Psychology* published a special issue on the topic in December 2001, summarizing what is known about the phenomenon of bullying. In addition, a text by Einarson, Hoel, Zapf, and Cooper (2002) covered much of the same ground, but in somewhat greater detail. Since many who have worked in the United States have experienced at least one encounter with a workplace bully, the likely reason for the lack of interest among American scholars is cultural. In other cultures, power and its use often has negative connotations, particularly in countries characterized as collectivist. On the other hand, the United States is characterized as an individualist country where each worker might expected to fend for him- or herself, without recourse to group support as a protection from an abusive co-worker or supervisor.

Despite the virtual lack of U.S. data on this topic, the increasing body of knowledge from non-U.S. workplaces provides us with some foundation for introducing the topic. We feel that this is an important area of research for future I-O psychologists and, as a result, we will use the European experience as a way of introducing the topic.

Bullying has been defined as subjecting a victim to:

> being harassed, offended, socially excluded, [having] to carry out humiliating tasks; [the victim] is in an inferior position. To call something bullying, it must occur repeatedly (e.g., at least once per week) and over a long time (e.g., at least six months). It is not bullying if it is a single event. Also, it is not bullying if two equally strong parties are in conflict. (Zapf and Gross, 2001, p. 498)

Most surveys that have examined the prevalence of bullying have concluded that it is widespread (e.g., Einarson, 2000; Zapf, 1999). Mikkelsen and Einarson (2001) reported rates as high as 25 percent in the workforce. Hoel, Cooper and Faragher (2001) reported that when the period of time covered is five years, the rate rises to almost 50 percent in Great Britian. Zapf and Gross (2001) noted that bullying has seriously affected the health of between 1 percent and 4 percent of the victims. Even though the definition above cites a minimum period of 6 months before a situation can be called bullying, Leymann (1996) found that in Sweden the more common duration is 15 months; in Germany, Zapf (1999) found episodes lasting as long as 46 months. Note that the definition adopted by the European researchers for bullying requires weekly encounters over six months or more. If the definition were less stringent (e.g., one incident in the last three months, or three times in the last year), it is safe to say that the majority of workers would report either having seen bullying or been the victim of a bully.

In many European countries, the legal system makes it more difficult to terminate an employee than it is in the United States, while at the same time it ensures less protection for the rights of individual workers. Because U.S. workers can more easily be terminated if bullying is a problem, and may very well sue the company if they are the victim of a bully, the duration, though not the severity, of bullying is likely to be less in the United States than in other countries. Hubert and Veldhoven (2001) and Salin (2001) reported that the prevalence of bullying is just as great in professional and white-collar positions as it is for blue-collar workers.

From an organizational point of view, bullying can be seen as the escalation of conflict (Leymann, 1996; Zapf & Gross, 2001). The steps in this escalation are:

1. A critical incident: There is a work-related dispute between two individuals.
2. Bullying and stigmatizing: The person in the inferior position is stigmatized and subjected to increasingly aggressive acts by the bully. The intent of the bully is to damage the victim in some way.
3. Organizational intervention: The organization steps in and makes the dispute "official."
4. Expulsion: The victim—not the bully!—by now stigmatized and possibly acting in ineffective and traumatized ways, is separated from the organization.

In most instances, the victim of bullying has been rendered powerless by the stigmatization. Once the bully has developed a head of steam, the victim can take very few actions that might be considered effective.

The actual bullying behavior has also been broken down into three phases (Einarsen, 2000). First, the bully may spread rumors about the victim or engage in subtle acts of

BULLYING

Harassing, offending, socially excluding, or assigning humiliating tasks to a person of subordinate status repeatedly and over a long period of time.

sabotage to make the victim look less effective. Next, the victim is singled out for public humiliation and ridicule. Finally, the victim may be directly threatened or characterized as emotionally unstable. Even though the victim might attempt to behave rationally at an early stage in the process by discussing the conflict or defusing it with humor or a concession, the bully will have none of it, and increases his or her aggressive behavior. The victim eventually sees that the single goal of the bully is to drive the victim out of the organization (Zapf, 1999).

In a study of victims who "successfully" coped with bullying, Knorz and Zapf (1996) found that successful coping was invariably the result of a third-party intervention, rather than any behavior pattern of the victim, and in most cases the intervention was some form of physical separation of the bully and the victim (e.g., the transfer of the bully or the victim to a different department or work unit). By far, the single most common piece of advice given by victims to those experiencing bullying is to leave the organization (Zapf & Gross, 2001). If the third party confronts the bully in an attempt to restore order without taking administrative action such as transfer or termination, the most likely effect is simply an increase in the bullying behavior. The bully now sees the victim as having "declared war" and feels justified in increasing his or her aggression.

The critical finding in bullying research is that victims are often in a position of noncontrol. There is little they can do to improve their position other than to leave the work unit. Bullying scenarios require strong and immediate action by an organization. First, managers and supervisors need to be sensitive to the presence of bullying. Then they need to take steps to separate the victim and the bully from each other, either by terminating the bully, or physically separating the bully and victim through internal transfer. Allowing the parties to "work it out themselves" is likely to end in failure, and possibly even tragedy. The irony is that the first level of intervention is usually a manager who, at least in Great Britain, is more often than not the bully! (Hoel, Cooper, & Faragher, 2001).

One cannot ignore the parallels between the phenomenon of bullying as described above, and the phenomenon of sexual harassment as considered in Chapter 8. Not all sexual harassment can be thought of as a special case of bullying; harassment is a more complex phenomenon. Nevertheless, the tactics of the bully are often the tactics of the harasser. Similarly, the woman who is the target of a harasser often experiences the same sense of powerlessness as does the more generic victim of a bully. Finally, the harasser is often a manager, as is the bully (Zellars, Tepper, & Duffy, 2002).

There is no happy ending to this topic. We will simply return to our original point. When American I-O psychologists decide to elevate bullying to the level of a work behavior worth studying, they will find that it is widespread, damaging to both individuals and organizations, and difficult to eradicate. This will likely lead to more informative research related to situational and organizational variables that allow bullying to thrive (e.g., work group climates), research on individual differences directed toward identifying the personality characteristics of bullies (and possibly victims), and interventions to reduce the incidence of bullying in the workplace.

There is some indication that American researchers are indeed becoming interested in bullying, although cultural influences are apparent. Zellars et al. (2002), who examined the effect of bullying behavior by the military supervisors of an Air National Guard unit, were interested in whether supervisor bullying would reduce the willingness of subordinates to engage in organizational citizenship behaviors (OCB) or contextual performance. For subordinates who defined these OCBs as falling outside normal role expectations, this was exactly the effect. The authors concluded that

> A number of studies suggest that OCBs benefit organizations in terms of sales, performance quality and quantity, and operating efficiency. Hence, our data suggesting that abused subordinates perform fewer OCBs than their non-abused counterparts provides further motivation for organizations to be concerned about allowing abusive supervisor to go unchecked (Zellars et al., 2002, p. 1074).

American I-O psychology has a tradition of concentrating on the "bottom line." As we saw in Chapter 10, new work on emotions by I-O researchers is a departure from that tradition. European I-O psychologists study the phenomenon of bullying because it is morally wrong and has dreadful consequences on the well-being of the worker. We hope that American researchers will follow that lead and study abusive work environments because they are wrong, not simply because they are correlated with organizational efficiency. We hope to have more promising news on the topic of bullying in later editions of this book.

WHAT CAN WE CONCLUDE ABOUT WORKPLACE VIOLENCE?

There is every reason to believe that you are at greater risk of being the victim of an aggressive act at the workplace than your parents were. In part, this is the result of the changing nature of work. There is greater uncertainty about stable employment, and rapidly changing technologies and the increasing importance of work–life balance represent stressors. Several themes emerge from the study of workplace violence. The first is that employees need avenues for communicating concerns about the fairness of organizational decisions that affect them. Second, managers need to be sensitive to signs of potential trouble in the form of individual worker behaviors. Perceived justice—distributive, procedural, and interpersonal—seems to be central to many, if not most, instances of workplace violence. Violent acts are often precipitated by an organizational action such as a layoff, termination, or negative performance review. Whenever an action of this kind is contemplated, it would be wise to analyze the action from the point of view of the person or persons likely to be affected by that action, with a particular emphasis on justice issues. At this point, there are no data that directly connect bullying in the workplace with worker violence. Nevertheless, the anecdotal and logical connections seem apparent. In extreme situations in a school environment, students who are bullied by fellow students appear to resort to violence to achieve some sense of control. One explanation of the tragic killings at Columbine was that the two protagonists had been the target of relentless bullying by fellow students. To be sure, it takes a unique and pathological personality to react in such a destructive manner to bullying, but given the increasing interest in violence at the workplace, it would be valuable to examine the role of bullying.

MODULE 16.4 SUMMARY

- Most violent acts in the workplace stop well short of life-threatening acts, but violence at the workplace does seem to be on the increase.

- Problems in the workplace, accompanied by a belief that the problem cannot be resolved and that it threatens the self-esteem of an individual, often lead to an act of violence by that individual.

- One theory of workplace violence is the frustration-aggression theory, which proposes that work-related events lead to stress, which in turn leads to aggressive and counterproductive acts. An alternative theory suggests that violent workplace behavior results from perceived injustice by a worker.

- Bullying is a special type of workplace violence, one that is widespread. The bully is often in a position of superiority to the victim. One of the most effective resolutions to bullying is to traansfer either the victim or the bully to another work group or department.

KEY TERMS

frustration-aggression hypothesis

justice hypothesis of workplace violence

bullying

CRITICAL THINKING EXERCISES

16.7 The violation of some aspect of justice is often involved in acts of workplace violence. Knowing that, what might a supervisor do to reduce the probability of violent behavior in his or her work group?

16.8 It is reasonable to assume that bullying is commonplace in the American workplace. In which occupational groups might you expect bullying to be more common? Why? With respect to demographic characteristics (e.g., age, race, gender, experience), would you expect that some individuals would be more likely to be victims than others? Why?

A

absenteeism Type of counterproductive behavior that involves failure of an employee to report for or remain at work as scheduled.

accident proneness The general notion that certain individuals are more likely to have accidents than others. Although accident proneness does not exist as a general syndrome, research indicates that certain individual difference characteristics may be associated with unsafe behavior.

accommodation Adjustments or modifications to the work environment provided by an employer to enable people with disabilities to have equal employment opportunities. A reasonable accommodation must be provided if a person with a disability needs one in order to apply for a job, perform a job, or enjoy benefits equal to those offered to other employees.

achievement A facet of conscientiousness consisting of hard work, persistence, and the desire to do good work.

achievement strivings (AS) Type A behavior pattern subcomponent involving the tendency to be active and to work hard in achieving one's goals.

action process Process that starts with a goal, proceeds to a consideration of events that may occur in the future, then to the development of several alternative plans, the selection of a plan, the execution and monitoring of the chosen plan, and the processing of information resulting from the execution of the plan. The last step, feedback, influences goal development once again.

action structure Structure that includes the notion that (1) observable action is the result of a number of prior events and plans, hierarchically arranged and (2) the feedback and resulting regulation of actions occur at different levels.

action theory (Rubicon theory) Theory that includes broad consideration of the role of intention in motivated behavior as well as the connection between intention and action.

active practice Practice that involves actively participating in a training or work task rather than passively observing someone else performing the task.

activity inhibition Psychological term used to describe a person who is not impulsive.

actual criterion The actual measure of job performance obtained.

adaptive performance Performance component that includes flexibility and the ability to adapt to changing circumstances.

adverse (or disparate) treatment Type of discrimination in which the plaintiff attempts to show that the employer actually treated the plaintiff differently than majority applicants or employees; intentional discrimination.

adverse impact Type of discrimination that acknowledges that the employer may not have *intended* to discriminate against a plaintiff, but a practice implemented by the employer had the *effect* of disadvantaging (i.e., had an adverse impact on) the group to which the plaintiff belongs.

adverse impact ratio Obtained by dividing the selection ratio of the protected group by the selection ratio of the majority group. If this ratio is lower than 80 percent, then there is evidence of adverse impact.

affect The conscious, subjective aspect of emotion.

affect circumplex Figure in which opposite emotions appear directly across from each other in the circle.

affective commitment An element of commitment representing an emotional attachment to an organization.

affective outcome A type of learning outcome that includes attitudes or beliefs that predispose a person to behave in a certain way.

affiliation need Need for approval or connections with others.

affirmative action Program that acknowledges that particular demographic groups may be underrepresented in the work environment; provides specific mechanisms for reducing this underrepresentation.

agreeableness Likable, easy to get along with, friendly.

alarm reaction Stage of the General Adaptation Syndrome in which the body mobilizes resources to cope with added stress.

altruism Helpful behaviors directed toward individuals or groups within the organization, such as offering to help a co-worker who is up against a deadline.

American Psychological Association (APA) The major professional organization for psychologists of all kinds in the United States.

Americans with Disabilities Act of 1990 Federal legislation that requires employers to give applicants and employees with disabilities the same consideration as other applicants and employees, and to make certain adaptations in the work environment to accommodate disabilities. Applies to a person who has a physical or mental impairment that substantially limits one or more major life activities (e.g., sitting, standing, or sleeping).

apprenticeship A formal program used to teach a skilled trade.

assessment center Collection of procedures for evaluation that is administered to groups of individuals; assessments are typically done by multiple assessors.

assimilation model Model for addressing diversity that recruits, selects, trains, and motivates employees so that they all share the same values and culture.

attempted leadership Leader accepts the goal of changing the behavior of a follower, and can be observed attempting to change the follower.

attitudes Relatively stable feelings or beliefs that are directed toward specific persons, groups, ideas, jobs, or other objects.

attraction-selection-attrition (ASA) model Model that proposes that organizations and individuals undergo a process of jointly assessing probable fit based primarily on personality characteristics. Through a process of attraction, selection, and attrition, the goal is to make the workforce homogeneous with respect to personality characteristics.

autocratic climate Organization described by Lewin as highly structured with little opportunity for individual responsibility or risk taking at the lowest levels.

automaticity Occurs when tasks can be performed with limited attention; likely to be developed when learners are given several extra learning opportunities even after they have demonstrated mastery of a task.

automation A method of completing work through the use of mechanical or electrical devices rather than through direct human action.

autonomous work group A specific kind of production team that has control over a variety of functions, including planning shift operations, allocating work, determining work priorities, performing a variety of actual work tasks, and recommending new hires as work group members.

autonomy The extent to which employees can control how and when they perform the tasks of their job.

B

base rate The percentage of the current workforce that is performing successfully.

behavior modification A training and motivational method that is based primarily on reinforcement theory; involves identifying, measuring, rewarding, and evaluating employee behaviors aimed at performance improvement.

behavioral approach Approach begun by a group of leadership researchers at Ohio State University; focused on the kinds of behavior engaged in by people in leadership roles and identified two major types of leader behavior: consideration and initiating structure.

behavioral criteria Measures of how well the behaviors learned in training transfer to the job.

behavioral modeling Learning approach that consists of observing actual job incumbents (or videos of job incumbents) that demonstrate positive modeling behaviors, rehearsing the behavior using a role-playing technique, receiving feedback on the rehearsal, and finally trying out the behavior on the job.

behavioral observation scale (BOS) Rating scale that asks the rater to consider how frequently an employee has been seen to act in a particular way.

behaviorally anchored rating scales (BARS) Rating format that includes behavioral anchors that describe what a worker has done, or might be expected to do, in a particular duty area.

behaviorist approach Approach developed by B. F. Skinner that placed the emphasis for behavior and directed activity on the environment rather than on any internal needs or instincts.

bias A technical and statistical term that deals exclusively with a situation in which a given test results in errors of prediction for a subgroup.

Big Five A taxonomy of five personality factors; the five factor model (FFM).

biodata Information collected on an application blank or in a standardized test that includes questions about previous jobs, education, specialized training, and personal history; also known as biographical data.

biofeedback Stress management technique that teaches individuals to control certain body functions such as heart rate, blood pressure, and even skin temperature by responding to feedback from an electronic instrument.

biological approach Approach to work design and redesign used to reduce injuries and increase the physical comfort of the workers through the reduction of fatigue and discomfort.

branching programming A type of programmed instruction that provides a customized approach enabling each learner to practice material he or she had difficulty with when it was first presented.

buffer or moderator hypothesis Hypothesis that social support moderates or reduces health problems by protecting individuals from the negative effects of work stressors.

bullying Harassing, offending, socially excluding, or assigning humiliating tasks to a person of subordinate status repeatedly and over a long period of time.

bureaucracy Proposed by Max Weber in the 1940s to be the ideal form of organization; included a formal hierarchy, division of labor, and clear set of operating procedures.

burnout   An extreme state of psychological strain resulting from a prolonged response to chronic job stressors that exceed an individual's resources to cope with them.

C

cardiac psychology   Field that combines the expertise of medical doctors (cardiologists) and psychologists in an effort to reduce heart disease by changing the thought processes of Type A heart patients.

carpal tunnel syndrome   Injury of the hand and wrist caused by stress from various tools, keyboards, and computer "mice," resulting in inflammation, swelling, pain, and numbness.

central tendency error   Error in which raters choose a middle point on the scale as a way to describe performance, even though a more extreme point might better describe the employee.

changing   Second stage in the process of changing an organization in which individuals adopt new values, beliefs, and attitudes.

charisma   A personal attribute of a leader that hypnotizes followers and compels them to identify with and attempt to emulate the leader.

charismatic leader   Leader with followers who are emotionally attached to the leader, never question the leader's beliefs or actions, and see themselves as integral to the accomplishment of the leader's goals.

charismatic leadership theory   Approach with many different versions of the notion that charisma is related to leadership; (1) in a crisis situation, followers will perceive charismatic characteristics in an individual and accept that person as a leader; (2) certain leader behaviors (use of innovative strategies) contribute to a charismatic aura.

checklist   A list of behaviors presented to a rater who is asked to place a check next to each of the items that best (or least) describe the ratee.

circadian cycle   The 24-hour physiological cycle in which humans tend to be active during hours of light and inactive (e.g., sleeping or resting) during hours of darkness.

class certification   Judge's decision based on several criteria that help determine whether individual plaintiffs can file together under a class action suit.

classic organizational theory   Theory that assumes there is one best configuration for an organization, regardless of its circumstances; places a premium on control of individual behavior by the organization.

classroom lecture   Training method in which the trainer communicates through spoken words and audiovisual materials what trainees are supposed to learn; also commonly used to efficiently present a large amount of information to a large number of trainees.

climate   A shared perception among employees regarding a particular work entity (organization or division, department, or even work group). Examples include safety climate and service climate.

climate/culture strength   The extent to which members of an organization share a perception (in the case of climate or a value/belief pattern (in the case of culture).

clinical decision making   Decision making that uses judgment to combine information and to make a decision about the relative value of different candidates or applicants.

coaching   A practical, goal-focused form of personal, one-on-one learning for busy employees that may be used to improve performance, enhance a career, or to work through organizational issues or change initiatives.

cognitive ability   The capacity to reason, plan, and solve problems; mental ability.

cognitive ability test   Test that allows individuals to demonstrate what they know, perceive, remember, understand, or can work with mentally; includes problem identification, problem-solving tasks, perceptual skills, the development or evaluation of ideas, and remembering what one has learned through general experience or specific training.

cognitive outcome   A type of learning outcome that includes declarative knowledge, or knowledge of rules, facts, and principles.

cognitive restructuring   Type of stress intervention that focuses on changing perceptions and thought processes that lead to stress; reduces stress by changing the individual's perception of, or capacity to meet the demands of, the work environment.

cognitive task analysis   Consists of methods for decomposing job and task performance into discrete, measurable units, with special emphasis on eliciting mental processes and knowledge content.

cognitive test battery   A collection of tests that assess a variety of cognitive aptitudes or abilities; often called Multiple Aptitude Test Batteries.

cohesion   The degree to which team members desire to remain in the team and are committed to team goals.

collectivist culture   A culture that values the group more than the individual.

commitment   The psychological and emotional attachment an individual feels to a relationship, an organization, a goal, or an occupation.

comparable worth   Notion that people who are performing jobs of comparable worth to the organization should receive comparable pay.

comparison other   Co-workers or other idealized persons to whom the individual compares him or herself in determining perceived equity.

compensable factors   Factors in a job evaluation system that are given points that are later linked to compensation for various jobs within the organization. These factors usually include skills, responsibility, effort, and working conditions.

compensatory system   Model in which a good score on one test can compensate for a lower score on another test.

competencies   Sets of behaviors that are instrumental in the delivery of desired organizational results or outcomes.

competency modeling   Process that identifies the characteristics desired across all individuals and jobs within an organization. These characteristics should predict behavior across a wide variety of tasks and settings, and provide the organization with a set of core characteristics that distinguish it from other organizations; involves integrating individual characteristics with the organization's strategy.

complexity   Property of automated systems that typically replace the functions of many individuals and, as a result, represents a "job" that is much more complicated than the work done by any one individual.

comprehensive staffing model   Model that gathers enough high-quality information about candidates to predict the likelihood of their success on the varied demands of the job.

compressed workweek   Schedule that permits an employee to work for longer than eight hours a day and fewer than five days a week; most common is the 4/10 plan, which permits the worker to accumulate the 40 hours of the workweek in four days.

computer adaptive testing (CAT)   Testing approach in which every candidate does not need to answer every test item for adequate assessment; approach that presents a test taker with a few items that cover the range of difficulty of the test, identifies a test taker's approximate level of ability, and then asks only questions that will further refine the test taker's position within that ability level.

computer-based training   Training that includes text, graphics, and/or animation presented via computer for the express purpose of teaching job-relevant knowledge and skills.

concurrent validity design   Criterion-related validity design in which there is no time lag between gathering the test scores and the performance data.

conscientiousness   The quality of having positive intentions and carrying them out with care.

consideration   Type of behavior identified in the Ohio State Leadership Studies; included behavior indicating mutual trust, respect, and a certain warmth and rapport between the supervisor and his or her group.

construct   A psychological concept or characteristic that a predictor or criterion is intended to measure. Examples of constructs are intelligence, personality, and leadership.

construct validity   Validity approach in which investigators gather evidence to support decisions or

inferences about psychological constructs; often begins with the investigators demonstrating that a test designed to measure a particular construct correlates with other tests in the predicted manner.

constructive work dissatisfaction   A type of dissatisfaction that arouses or energizes individuals and is beneficial for motivating them to join attempts at organizational change.

content-related validation design   Design that demonstrates that the content of the selection procedure represents an adequate sample of important work behaviors and activities and/or worker KSAOs defined by the job analysis.

context   Includes both the announced purpose and other, nonannounced agendas of the circumstances surrounding performance ratings.

context of the work   Conditions or characteristics of work that can change the demands on the incumbent; includes interpersonal relationships, physical work conditions, and structural job characteristics.

contextual performance   Activities that are not typically part of job descriptions but support the organizational, social, and psychological environment in which the job tasks are performed; similar to organizational citizenship behavior.

contingency approach   Approach that was proposed to take into account the role of the situation in the exercise of leadership.

contingency theories of organization   Approaches that propose that the best way to structure an organization actually depends on the circumstances of the organization.

contingent reward   System in which a reward depends on or is contingent upon a particular response.

continuance commitment   An element of commitment representing the perceived cost for leaving an organization.

continuous change   Ongoing, evolving, and cumulative, organizational change characterized by small continuous adjustments, created simultaneously across units, that add up to substantial change.

continuous process organization   An organization that depends on a continuous process for output or product.

continuous reward   System in which a reward is presented every time a correct response occurs.

control   Device such as a keyboard or mouse that permits an individual to take actions.

control theory   Theory based on the principle of a feedback loop which assumes that an individual compares a standard to an actual outcome and adjusts behavior to bring the outcome into agreement with the standard.

coordination loss   Reduced group performance that occurs when team members expend their energies in different directions or fail to synchronize or coordinate their work.

core evaluations   Assessments that individuals make of their circumstances. Elements of core evaluations include self-esteem, self-efficacy, locus of control, and the absence of neuroticism.

coronary-prone personality   Alternative name given to the Type A behavior pattern (TABP) because of its links to coronary heart disease and heart attacks.

correlation coefficient   Statistic assessing the bivariate, linear association between two variables. Provides information about both the magnitude (numerical value) and the direction (+ or −) of the relationship between two variables.

counterproductive performance   Voluntary behavior that violates significant organizational norms and in so doing, threatens the well-being of the organization, its members, or both.

criterion   An outcome variable that describes important aspects or demands of the job; the variable that we predict when evaluating the validity of a predictor.

criterion contamination   Occurs when an actual criterion includes information that is unrelated to the behavior that one is trying to measure.

criterion deficiency   Occurs when an actual criterion is missing information that is part of the behavior that one is trying to measure.

criterion-referenced cut score   Cut score that is established by considering the desired level of performance for a new hire and finding the test score that corresponds to that desired level of performance; sometimes called "domain-referenced" cut score.

criterion-related validity   Validity approach that is demonstrated by correlating a test score with a performance measure. Improves researcher's confidence in the inference that people with higher test scores have higher performance.

critical incident technique   Approach in which subject matter experts are asked to identify critical aspects of behavior or performance in a particular job that led to success or failure.

critical incidents   Examples of behavior that appear "critical" in determining whether performance would be good, average, or poor in specific performance areas.

critical thinking skills   Skills that require active involvement in applying the principles under discussion.

cross-cultural training   Training designed to prepare individuals from one culture to interact more effectively with individuals from different cultures. The goal is to develop trainees' understanding of basic differences in values and communication styles.

cross-training   Training that involves rotating team members through different positions on the team so that they can acquire an understanding of the duties of their teammates and an overview of the teams task.

cross-validation   Process used with multiple regression techniques in which a regression equation developed on a first sample is tested on a second sample to determine if it still fits well; usually carried out with an incumbent sample, and the cross-validated results are then used to weight the predictor scores of an applicant sample.

cultural assimilator   A written or computer-based tool for individual use which presents a collection of scenarios describing challenging, cross-cultural critical incidents.

culture   A system in which individuals share meanings and common ways of viewing events and objects. In organizations it refers to the shared beliefs and values among employees that are created and communicated by the managers and leaders of the organization.

culture shock   A condition typically experienced four to six months after expatriates arrive in a foreign country; symptoms include homesickness, irritability, hostility toward host nationals, and the loss of ability to work effectively.

culture-general assimilator   An assimilator used to sensitize people to cross-cultural differences they may encounter across a wide variety of cultures.

culture-specific assimilator   An assimilator developed for a particular culture.

culture-specific characteristics   Leader characteristics that are more acceptable in some countries than others.

cumulative trauma disorder (CTD)   A common form of workplace injury involving the upper extremities (arm, shoulder, wrist).

cut score   A specified point in a distribution of scores below which candidates are rejected; also known as a "cutoff score."

D

Daubert challenge   Challenge in which opposing lawyers may ask the judge to prevent the expert witness from voicing an opinion in front of a jury, arguing that the jury will be swayed by an expert testifying about a topic that cannot be considered a legitimate scientific topic.

declarative knowledge   The familiarity with facts or abstract concepts, often acquired through direct instruction; understanding what is required to perform a job or task.

deep acting   A type of emotional labor that consists of managing one's feelings, including the emotions required by the job.

delegation of authority   Refers to information about which lower-level employees report to employees above them in an organization.

deliberate practice   Individualized training on tasks selected by a qualified teacher.

Demand-Control model   A model suggesting that two factors are prominent in producing job stress: job demands and individual control; developed by Robert Karasek.

democratic climate Organization described by Lewin and colleagues that emphasizes a less structured organization, with greater opportunity for individual responsibility and risk taking.

demographic diversity Differences in observable attributes or demographic characteristics such as age, gender, and ethnicity.

dependability A facet of conscientiousness, consisting of being disciplined, well organized, respectful of laws and regulations, honest, trustworthy, and accepting of authority.

depersonalization Type of burnout that occurs when individuals become hardened by their job and tend to treat clients or patients like objects.

deposition An interview under oath taken by an opposing attorney in a lawsuit.

descriptive statistics Statistics that summarize, organize, and describe a sample of data.

destructive criticism Negative feedback that is cruel, sarcastic, and offensive; usually general rather than specific and often directed toward personal characteristics of the employee rather than job-relevant behaviors.

determinants of performance The basic building blocks or causes of performance, which are declarative knowledge, procedural knowledge, and motivation.

development Refers to formal education, job experiences, mentoring relationships, and assessments of personality and abilities that help employees prepare for the future.

Dictionary of Occupational Titles (D.O.T.) Document that includes job analysis and occupational information that is used to match applicants with job openings; one major purpose of the D.O.T was, and still is, for use in occupational counseling.

differential psychology The scientific study of differences between or among two or more people.

discovery Process in which lawyers are given access to potential witnesses who will be called by the other side, as well as any documents relevant to the complaints.

dishonesty Involves employee theft of goods as well as theft of time (e.g., arriving late, leaving early, taking unnecessary sick days) or dishonest communications with customers, co-workers, or management.

disinterestedness Characteristic of scientists who should be objective and uninfluenced by biases or prejudices when conducting research.

display Device such as a computer screen that provides an individual with information.

dissonance theory Festinger's theory that tension exists when individuals hold "dissonant cognitions" (incompatible thoughts). This approach assumes that individuals always seek some sense of "balance" (i.e., absence of tension) and that they will direct their behavior toward reducing the tension resulting from dissonant cognitions.

distance learning Approach that allows trainees to interact and communicate with an instructor by using audio and video (e.g., television, computer, or radio) links that allow for learning from a distant location.

distress A type of stress resulting from chronically demanding situations that produce negative health outcomes.

distributed practice Provides individuals with rest intervals between practice sessions, which are spaced over a longer period of time.

distributive justice Type of justice that focuses on the perceived fairness of the allocation of outcomes or rewards to organizational members.

diversity Traditionally refers to differences in demographic characteristics, but also includes differences in values, abilities, interests, and experiences.

division of labor The tasks performed in an organization can be divided into specialized jobs and departmental functions.

drive Nonhuman equivalent of motives and needs.

duties Groups of similar tasks; each duty involves a segment of work that is directed at one of the general goals of a job.

E

ecology model Underlying model for life history biodata instruments. Proposes that the events that make up a person's history represent choices made by the individual to interact with his or her environment. These choices can signal abilities, interests, and personality characteristics.

effective leadership Leader changes a follower's behavior, resulting in both leader and follower feeling satisfied and effective.

effectiveness The evaluation of the results of performance; often controlled by factors beyond the actions of an individual.

"80 percent" or "4/5ths" rule Guideline for assessing whether there is evidence of adverse impact. If it can be shown that a protected group received less than 80 percent of the desirable outcomes (e.g., job offers, promotions) received by a majority group, the plaintiffs can claim to have met the burden of demonstrating adverse impact.

electronic performance monitoring Monitoring work processes with electronic devices; can be cost effective and has the potential for providing detailed and accurate work logs.

emotion An affect or feeling, often experienced and displayed in reaction to an event or thought and accompanied by physiological changes in various systems of the body, often intense enough to disrupt thought processes.

emotional exhaustion Type of burnout that occurs when individuals feel emotionally drained by work.

emotional intelligence (EI) A proposed kind of intelligence that is focused on our awareness of our own and others' emotions.

emotional intelligence quotient (EQ) Parallels the notion of intelligence quotient (IQ); a score on a test of emotional intelligence.

emotional labor Regulation of one's emotions to meet job or organizational demands. Such regulation can be achieved through surface acting and deep acting.

emotional stability Displaying little emotion or showing the same emotional response in various situations.

emotion-focused coping Type of coping that involves reducing the emotional response to a problem by avoiding, minimizing, or distancing oneself from the problem.

employee assistance program (EAP) Counseling provided by an organization to deal with work stress, alcohol or drug difficulties, and problems stemming from outside the job; originally developed by organizations to address alcohol and drug problems, but subsequently broadened to include stress management interventions.

employee comparison methods Form of evaluation that involves the direct comparison of one person to another.

engineering approach to safety Approach that assumes an individual will engage in an action that might lead to injury unless the environment prevents that action.

episodic change Organizational change characterized as infrequent, discontinuous, and intentional; often launched with fanfare, with senior leaders clearly articulating pathways to change and disseminating information about the process and desired end state.

EQ Abbreviation for *emotional intelligence quotient.*

Equal Pay Act of 1963 Law that prohibits discrimination on the basis of sex in the payment of wages or benefits, where men and women perform work of similar skill, effort, and responsibility for the same employer under similar working conditions.

equality norm Definition of fairness based on the view that people should receive approximately equal rewards; most common foundation for defining fairness in Scandinavian and Asian countries.

equity theory Motivational theory developed by Adams suggesting that individuals look at their world in terms of comparative inputs and outcomes. Individuals compare their inputs and outcomes with others (e.g., peers, co-workers) by developing an input/outcome ratio.

equivalent forms reliability Form of reliability calculated by correlating measurements from a sample of individuals who complete two different forms of the same test.

ERG theory Alderfer's theory of human needs that proposes that human needs are best thought of as arranged in three levels: existence, relatedness, and growth.

ergonomics The study of the physical demands of work such as reaching, stretching, lifting, and carrying.

ethnocentrism A multinational model in which the values of the parent company predominate.

ethnographically informed design Type of user-centered design that takes into account power relationships, tacit knowledge of the organization and its procedures, and organizational climate and culture.

eustress Type of stress that provides challenges that motivate individuals to work hard and meet their goals.

evolutionary/ecological approach Approach that adopts a biological model and concentrates on explaining why some types of organizations thrive and diversify, while others atrophy and disappear.

exhaustion A stage of the General Adaptation Syndrome in which overall resistance drops and adverse consequences (e.g., burnout, severe illness, and even death) can result unless stress is reduced.

expatriate Manager or professional assigned to work in a location outside of his or her home country.

expectancy An individual's belief that a particular behavior (e.g., effort, hard work) will lead to a particular outcome (e.g., a promotion).

expectancy framework Approach in which employees expectations about the relationship between how much effort they expend and how well they perform are important to employee motivation and learning.

experience Direct participation in, or observation of, events and activities that serves as a basis for knowledge.

experimental control Characteristic of research in which possible confounding influences that might make results less reliable or harder to interpret are eliminated; often easier to establish in laboratory studies than in field studies.

experimental design Design in which participants are randomly assigned to different conditions.

expert performance Performance exhibited by those who have been practicing for at least 10 years and have spent an average of four hours per day in deliberate practice.

expert witness Witness in a lawsuit who is permitted to voice opinions about organizational practices.

external criteria Criteria that assess whether changes as a result of training occur when trainees are back on the job.

extrinsic satisfaction Concerns aspects of satisfaction that are extrinsic, or external, to job tasks, such as pay or benefits.

F

facet satisfaction Information related to specific facets or elements of job satisfaction.

fairness A value judgment about actions or decisions based on test scores.

false negative   Decision in which an applicant was rejected but would have performed adequately or successfully. The decision is *false* because of the incorrect prediction that the applicant would not have performed successfully and *negative* because the applicant was not hired.

false positive   Decision in which an applicant was accepted but performed poorly. The decision is *false* because of the incorrect prediction that the applicant would have performed successfully and *positive* because the applicant was hired.

feedback   Knowledge of the results of one's actions; enhances learning and performance in training and on the job.

feedback loop   Connection between knowledge of results and the intermediate states that occur between goal commitment and performance.

fidelity   The extent to which the task trained is similar to the task required on the job.

field theory   Kurt Lewin's approach proposing that various forces in the psychological environment interacted and combined to yield a final course of action.

fight-or-flight reaction   Adaptive response to stressful situations exhibited by animals and humans in which they choose to either fight or attempt to escape.

Five Factor Model (FFM)   A taxonomy of five personality factors, comprised of conscientiousness, extraversion, agreeableness, emotional stability, and openness to experience.

fixed band system   System in which candidates in lower bands are not considered until higher bands have been completely exhausted.

fixed shift   Workers are permanently assigned to a particular shift.

flextime   Schedule in which individual workers are given discretion over the time they report to work and the time they leave work on a given day.

Flynn effect   The phenomenon in which new generations appear to be smarter than their parents by a gain of 15 points in average intelligence test score per generation; named after the political scientist who has done extensive research on the topic.

forced choice format   Rating format that requires the rater to choose two statements out of four that could describe the ratee.

forced distribution rating system   System requiring evaluators to place employees into performance categories based on a predetermined percentage of employees in different categories (low, moderate, high).

frame-of-reference (FOR) training   Rater training based on the assumption that a rater needs a context or "frame" for providing a rating; includes (1) providing information about the multidimensional nature of performance, (2) ensuring that raters understand the meaning of the

anchors on the scale, (3) engaging in practice rating exercises of a standard performance by means of videotape, and (4) providing feedback on practice exercises.

frustration-aggression hypothesis   Argues that frustration leads to aggression, a hypothesis which ultimately was found to be too broad when it became clear that aggression was only one possible response to frustration and that not everyone responded to frustration with aggression.

full-range theory of leadership   Hierarchical model that ranges from laissez-faire leadership through transactional leadership to transformational leadership.

functional personality at work   The way that an individual behaves, handles emotions, and accomplishes tasks in a work setting; a combination of **Big Five** personality factors.

G

"g"   The abbreviation for *general mental ability*.

General Adaptation Syndrome (GAS)   A nearly identical response sequence to almost any disease or trauma (e.g., poisoning, injury, psychological stress); identified by Hans Seyle.

general mental ability   The nonspecific capacity to reason, learn, and solve problems in any of a wide variety of ways and circumstances.

generalizability theory   A sophisticated approach to the question of reliability that simultaneously considers all types of error in reliability estimates (e.g., test-retest, equivalent forms, and internal consistency).

generalize   To apply the results from one study or sample to other participants or situations.

generalized compliance   Behavior that is helpful to the broader organization, such as upholding company rules.

geocentrism   A multinational model in which a new corporatewide policy is developed to handle issues in a way that creates a global perspective.

Global Leadership and Organizational Behavior Effectiveness (GLOBE)   A large-scale cross-cultural study of leadership that involves the efforts of 170 social scientists and management researchers in over 60 countries.

goal setting   Motivational approach in which specific, difficult goals direct attention and improve performance in training and on the job.

goal-setting theory   Approach proposed by Locke and colleagues in which the general concept of a goal is adapted to work motivation. A goal is seen as a motivational force, and individuals who set specific, difficult goals perform better than individuals who simply adopt a "do your best" goal or no goal at all.

g-ocentric model   The tendency to understand and predict the behavior of workers simply by examining "g"; coined by Sternberg and Wagner (1993).

graphic rating scale Scale that graphically displays performance scores that run from high on one end to low on the other end.

graphology A technique that presumes that traits can be assessed from various characteristics of a person's handwriting; also known as handwriting analysis.

great man/great woman theory Theory developed by historians who examined the life of a respected leader for clues leading to his or her greatness; often focused on a galvanizing experience or an admirable trait (persistence, optimism, or intelligence) that the leader possesses to a singular degree.

group dynamics Approach that grew out of the application of Kurt Lewin's field theory to industry.

group polarization The tendency for groups to make more extreme decisions (e.g., more cautious or more risky) than those made by individuals.

group test Test that can be administered to large groups of individuals; often valuable in reducing the costs (both in time and money) of testing many applicants.

groupthink A mode of thinking engaged in by people deeply involved in a cohesive group and when group members' desire for agreement overrides their motivation to appraise alternative courses of action realistically.

H

halo error Error that occurs when a rater assigns the same rating to an employee on a series of dimensions, creating a *halo* or aura that surrounds all of the ratings, causing them to be similar.

hands-on performance measurement Evaluation that requires an employee to engage in work-related tasks; usually includes carefully constructed simulations of central or critical pieces of work that involve single workers.

hardiness A set of personality characteristics that provide resistance to stress. Hardy individuals feel in control of their lives, have a sense of commitment to their family and their work goals and values, and see unexpected change as a challenge.

Hawthorne effect Refers to a change in behavior or attitudes that was the simple result of increased attention.

Hawthorne studies Research done at the Hawthorne, Illinois, plant of the Western Electric Company that began as attempts to increase productivity by manipulating lighting, rest breaks, and work hours. This research showed the important role that workers' attitudes played in productivity.

high performance work practices Practices that include the use of formal job analyses, selection from within for key positions, merit-based promotions, and the use of formal assessment devices for selection.

hobo syndrome Refers to the tendency of some workers to be more prone to change jobs than others.

horizontal culture A culture that minimizes distances between individuals.

hostile working environment sexual harassment Harassment that occurs when a pattern of conduct, which is perceived as offensive and is related to sex or gender, unreasonably interferences with work performance.

hostility Type A behavior pattern subcomponent associated with increased secretion of stress hormones as well as increased risk of coronary heart disease and other long-term, harmful health outcomes.

human engineering or human factors psychology The study of the capacities and limitations of humans with respect to a particular environment.

human error The view that if humans can be taken out of the system, the threat of accidents will be greatly reduced; often used as an explanation for a catastrophic accident.

human factors Approach that uses knowledge of human capabilities and limitations to design systems, organizations, jobs, machines, tools, and consumer products for safe, efficient, and comfortable human use; synonymous with human factors engineering or human factors psychology.

Human Relations Movement The results of the Hawthorne studies ushered in this movement, which focused on work attitudes and the newly discovered emotional world of the worker.

human relations theory Approach that adds a personal or human element to the study of organizations; considers the interrelationship between an organization's requirements and the characteristics of its members.

human resources management (HRM) Practices such as recruiting, selection, retention, training and development of people (human resources) in order to achieve individual and organizational goals.

human-computer interface (HCI) The interaction between a human and a computer.

hurdle system A noncompensatory strategy in which an individual has no opportunity to compensate at a later assessment stage for a low score in an earlier stage of the assessment process.

hurry sickness Severe and chronic feelings of time urgency that negatively affect one's lifestyle.

hygiene needs Lower-level needs described in Herzberg's two-factor theory, which proposed that meeting these needs would eliminate dissatisfaction, but would not result in motivated behavior or a state of positive satisfaction.

hypothesis Prediction about relationship(s) among variables of interest.

I

idealized influence Leaders display conviction, emphasize trust, take stands on difficult issues, emphasize the importance of commitment and purpose, and are aware of the ethical consequences of their decisions.

impatience/irritability (II) Type A behavior pattern subcomponent that reflects intolerance and frustration resulting from being slowed down.

incremental validity The value in terms of increased validity of adding a particular predictor to an existing selection system.

indicators Quantitative measures of how well each objective is being met in the ProMES approach.

individual assessment Situation in which only one candidate (or a very few) is assessed on many different attributes.

individual differences The dissimilarities between or among two or more people.

individual test Test that can be given only on an individual basis.

individualism/collectivism The degree to which individuals are expected to look after themselves compared to remaining integrated into groups.

individualist culture A culture that values the individual more than the group.

individualized consideration Leaders deal with others as individuals; consider individual needs, abilities, and aspirations; listen attentively; and advise, coach, and teach.

industrial-organizational (I-O) psychology The application of psychological principles, theory, and research to the work setting.

inferential statistics Statistics used to aid the researcher in testing hypotheses and making inferences from sample data to a larger sample or population.

informal training Training experiences that occur outside of formal training programs; can include specific job assignments, experiences, and activities outside work.

in-group members Followers who have high-quality relationships with their leader and high latitude for negotiating their work roles.

initiating structure Type of behavior identified in the Ohio State Leadership Studies; included behavior in which a supervisor organizes and defines group activities and his or her relation to the group.

input component Component that provides information to a human or computer.

input/outcome ratio Ratio that results when employees compare their inputs and outcomes to those of others (e.g., peers, co-workers) to determine if they are being treated equitably.

input-process-output model of team effectiveness Model that provides links among team inputs, processes, and outputs, thereby providing a way to understand how teams perform and how to maximize their performance.

inputs The training, effort, skills, and abilities that employees bring to or invest in their work.

inspirational motivation Leaders articulate an appealing vision of the future, challenge followers with high standards, talk optimistically with enthusiasm, and provide encouragement and meaning for what needs to be done.

instinct Inborn tendency that is thought to direct behavior.

instrumentality The perceived relationship between performance and the attainment of a certain outcome.

integrity The quality of being honest, reliable, and ethical, as in an employee.

intellectual stimulation Leaders question old assumptions, values, and beliefs; stimulate new ways of doing things, and encourage expression of ideas and reasons.

intelligence The ability to learn and adapt to an environment; often refers to general intellectual capacity, as opposed to cognitive ability or mental ability which often refer to more specific abilities such as memory or reasoning.

intelligence quotient (IQ) The measure of intelligence obtained by giving a subject a standardized "IQ" test. The score is obtained by multiplying by 100 the ratio of the subject's mental age to chronological age.

intelligence test Instrument designed to measure the ability to reason, learn, and solve problems.

interactional justice Type of justice concerned with the sensitivity with which employees are treated; associated with the extent to which an employee feels respected by the employer.

intercultural sensitivity The ability to interpret events in the same way as those from other cultures.

interests Preferences or likings for broad ranges of activities.

intermittent reward System in which only a portion of correct responses are rewarded.

internal consistency Form of reliability that assesses how consistently the items of a test measure a single construct. Affected by the number of items in the test and the correlations among the test items.

internal criteria Criteria that assess trainee reactions to and learning in the training program; generally assessed before trainees leave the training program.

interpersonal competence Includes social awareness and social skills such as the ability to resolve conflict and foster a spirit of cooperation.

interpersonal conflict Negative interactions with co-workers, supervisors, or clients which can range from heated arguments to subtle incidents of unfriendly behavior.

interpersonal justice Justice that focuses on the respectfulness and personal tone of the communications surrounding the evaluation, particularly the feedback and performance planning that follows the evaluation.

intrinsic satisfaction Concerns aspects of satisfaction that are central, or intrinsic, to the job or work itself such as responsibility.

introspection Early scientific method in which the participant was also the experimenter, who would record his or her experiences in completing an experimental task; considered very subjective by modern standards.

IQ Abbreviation for *intelligence quotient.*

J

job analysis   A process used by I-O psychologists to develop an understanding of a job by identifying the duties of the job and the human attributes necessary to perform them.

job control   Component of Demand-Control model that refers to a combination of autonomy in the job and discretion for using different skills.

job demand   Component of demand-control model that refers to the workload or intellectual requirements of the job.

Job Descriptive Index (JDI)   One of the most extensively researched and documented job satisfaction instruments; assesses satisfaction with five distinct areas of work: the work itself, supervision, people, pay, and promotion.

job embeddedness   Refers to the many and varied types of commitment that individuals feel toward co-workers, teams, organizations, and careers.

job enrichment   A motivational approach that involves increasing the responsibility and interest level of jobs in order to increase the motivation and job satisfaction of employees performing those jobs.

job evaluation   A method for making internal pay decisions by comparing job titles to one another and determining their relative merit by way of these comparisons.

job ladder or job family   Cluster of positions that are similar in terms of the human attributes needed to be successful in those positions or in terms of the tasks that are carried out in those positions.

job maturity   A subordinate's job-related ability, skills, and knowledge.

job psychograph   Early form used in a job analysis to display the mental requirements of the job.

job rotation   Approach that involves moving employees to various departments or areas of a company, or to various jobs within a single department.

job satisfaction   Positive attitude or emotional state resulting from the appraisal of one's job or job experience.

job withdrawal   Represents an individual's willingness to sever ties to an organization and the work role; includes intentions to quit or retire.

judgmental performance measure   Evaluation made of the effectiveness of an individual's work behavior, most often by supervisors in the context of a yearly performance evaluation.

justice hypothesis of workplace violence   Hypothesis that proposes that some violent acts can be understood as reactions by an employee against perceived injustice.

just-in-time (JIT) production   System that depends on the detailed tracking of materials and production so that the materials and human resources necessary for production arrive just in time. Central to the reduction of waste in lean production processes.

K

knowledge   A collection of specific and interrelated facts and information about a particular topical area.

knowledge test   Test that assesses the extent to which individuals understand course or training materials; also administered for licensing and certification purposes.

KSAOs   Individual attributes of knowledge, skills, abilities, and other characteristics that are required to perform job tasks successfully, grouped as follows: *k*nowledge—a collection of discrete but related facts and information about a particular domain which is acquired through formal education or training, or accumulated through specific experiences; *s*kill—a practiced act; *a*bility—The stable capacity to engage in a specific behavior; and *o*ther characteristics—personality variables, interests, training and experience.

L

laissez-faire leadership   The lowest level of leadership identified by Bass who contrasted it with transactional leadership and transformational leadership.

large batch and mass production organization   An organization that produces large numbers of discrete units, often using assembly-line operations.

layoff   Job loss due to employer downsizing or reductions in the workforce; often comes without warning, or with a generic warning that the workforce will be reduced.

leader   The individual in a group given the task of directing and coordinating task-relevant group activities or, in the absence of a designated leader, carries the primary responsibility for performing these functions in the group.

leader development   Training that concentrates on developing, maintaining, or enhancing individual leader attributes such as knowledge, skills, and abilities.

leader emergence   The study of the characteristics of individuals who become leaders, thereby examining the basis on which they were elected, appointed, or simply accepted.

leader-member exchange (LMX) theory   Leadership theory that proposed that leaders adopt different behaviors with individual subordinates and that the particular behavior pattern of the leader develops over time and depends to a large extent on the quality of the leader-subordinate relationship.

leadership development   Training that concentrates on the leader-follower relationship and on developing an environment in which the leader can build networked relationships among individuals that enhance cooperation and resource exchange in creating organizational value.

leadership effectiveness   The study of which behaviors on the part of a designated leader (regardless of how that position was achieved) lead to an outcome valued by the work group or organization.

lean production   Method that focuses on reducing waste in every form including overproduction, lengthy waiting times for materials, excessive transportation costs, unnecessary stock, and defective products.

learning   A relatively permanent change in behavior and human capabilities that is produced by experience and practice.

learning criteria   Measures that assess how much was learned in the training program.

learning organization   Company that emphasizes continuous learning, knowledge sharing, and personal mastery.

leniency error   Error that occurs with raters who are unusually easy in their ratings.

level of specificity   A method used to gauge experience according to task, job, and organizational characteristics.

"life-cycle" of a leader-follower relationship   Describes recent versions of leader-member exchange (LMX) theory that include a dynamic process in which the task of the leader is to drive the relationship from a tentative first-stage relationship to a deeper, more meaningful one.

limited rationality   The inability of humans to reason and make decisions in perfectly rational ways.

linear   Relationship between two variables that can be depicted by a straight line.

linear programming   A type of programmed instruction in which all trainees proceed through the same material.

locus of control (LOC)   A construct that refers to the belief of individuals that what happens to them is under their control (internal LOC) or beyond their control (external LOC).

long-term versus short-term orientation   The extent to which members of a culture expect immediate rather than delayed gratification of their material, social, and emotional needs.

Lordstown syndrome   Act of sabotage named after a General Motors plant plagued with acts of sabotage, including workers' intentional dropping of nuts and bolts into an engine, or neglecting to anchor parts to a car body appropriately.

low personal accomplishment   A type of burnout in which individuals feel they cannot deal with problems effectively and understand or identify with others' problems.

M

management by objectives (MBO)   A concept introduced in the mid-1950s to define and measure employee performance; proposed a plan to direct the efforts of workers and managers through a plan that includes objectives and methods to meet those performance objectives.

masculinity/femininity   The distribution of emotional roles between the genders with the masculine role perceived as "tough" and the feminine role as "tender."

Maslow's need theory   Theory that proposed that all humans have a basic set of needs that express themselves over the life span of the individual as internal "pushes" or drives; identified five basic need sets: physiological, security, love or social, esteem, and self-actualization.

massed practice   Conditions in which individuals practice a task continuously and without rest.

mastery orientation   Orientation in which individuals are concerned with increasing their competence for the task at hand; they view errors and mistakes as part of the learning process.

matrix organization   Organization in which individuals have dual reporting relationships: reporting to a project (product) manager and to a home department (functional) manager.

mean   The arithmetic average of the scores in a distribution; obtained by summing all of the scores in a distribution and dividing by the sample size.

measure of central tendency   Statistic that indicates where the center of a distribution is located. Mean, median, and mode are measures of central tendency.

measurement   Assigning numbers to characteristics of individuals or objects according to rules.

measurement modes   The unit of measurement used to assess experience.

mechanistic approach   Approach to work design and redesign that is used to increase productive efficiency through the modification of tasks or equipment.

mechanistic organization   An organization that depends on formal rules and regulations, makes decisions at higher levels of the organization, and has small spans of control.

median   The middle score in a distribution.

mental ability   The capacity to reason, plan, and solve problems; cognitive ability.

Mental Measurements Yearbook   A widely used source that includes an extensive listing of tests as well as reviews of those tests.

mental test   An instrument designed to measure a subject's ability to reason, plan, and solve problems; an intelligence test.

merit or equity norm   Definition of fairness based on the view that the people who work hardest or produce the most should get the greatest rewards; most common foundation for defining fairness in the United States.

meta-analysis   A statistical method for combining and analyzing the results from many studies to draw a general conclusion about relationships among variables.

metric   A standard of measurement; a scale.

microculture   Occurs when a work group develops its own view of a particular culture (e.g., safety) in an organization.

Minnesota Satisfaction Questionnaire (MSQ) A commonly used job satisfaction instrument that assesses particular aspects of work (e.g., achievement, ability utilization) as well as scores for extrinsic satisfaction and intrinsic satisfaction.

mixed standard scale Method of performance rating that is like a checklist, except that it includes behavioral expectation statements like those found in BARS scales; includes three statements for each dimension that describe good, average, and poor performance.

mode The most common or frequently occurring score in a distribution.

modesty bias Occurs when raters give themselves lower ratings than are warranted.

mood Generalized state of feeling not identified with a particular stimulus and not sufficiently intense to interrupt ongoing thought processes.

motivation Concerns the conditions responsible for variations in intensity, quality, and direction of ongoing behavior.

motivational approach to work place safety Approach to work design and redesign that is used to increase worker satisfaction and reduce turnover through modification of motivational levels.

motivational approach to work design Approach that assumes that a worker is capable of behaving safely, but may choose not to, so the worker must be motivated to behave safely.

Motivational Trait Questionnaire (MTQ) A questionnaire that provides a standardized method of assessing six distinct aspects of general performance motivation.

motivator needs Higher-level needs described in Herzberg's two-factor theory, which proposed that meeting such needs resulted in the expenditure of effort as well as satisfaction.

motor abilities The physical functions of movement, associated with coordination, dexterity, and reaction time; also called psychomotor or sensorimotor abilities.

Multifactor Leadership Questionnaire (MLQ) Self-report instrument used in the development and validation of the theory of transformational leadership.

multinational staffing Procedures that involve staffing for organizations in more than one country.

multiple correlation coefficient Statistic that represents the overall linear association between several variables (e.g., cognitive ability, personality, experience) on the one hand, and a single variable (e.g., job performance) on the other hand.

multiple hurdle system Constructed from multiple hurdles so that candidates who do not exceed each of the minimum dimension scores are excluded from further consideration.

multiple regression analysis Analysis that results in an equation for combining test scores into a composite based on the correlations among the test scores and the correlations of each test score with the performance score.

muscular endurance The physical ability to continue to use a single muscle or muscle group repeatedly over a period of time.

muscular power The physical ability to lift, pull, push, or otherwise move an object; unlike endurance, this is a one-time maximum effort.

muscular tension The physical quality of muscular strength.

musculoskeletal disorders Disorders of the lower back and upper extremities (arm, shoulder, wrist) which are the most commonly studied injuries related to workplace safety.

N

National Institute of Occupational Safety and Health (NIOSH) One of two federal agencies established to maintain and enforce the Occupational Safety and Health Act; responsible for conducting research on safety and work stress.

need Internal motivation that is thought to be inborn and universally present in humans.

need norm Definition of fairness based on the view that people should receive rewards in proportion to their needs.

negative affectivity (NA) Characteristic in which individuals are prone to experience a diverse array of negative mood states (e.g., anxiety, depression, hostility, and guilt).

negative valence A continuum of unfavorable personality characteristics running from normal to abominable.

nonexperimental design Design that does not include any "treatment" or assignment to different conditions.

nonlinear Relationship between two variables that cannot be depicted by a straight line; sometimes called "curvilinear" and most easily identified by examining a scatterplot.

norm group The group whose tests scores are used to compare and understand an individual's test score.

normative commitment An element of commitment representing an obligation to remain in the organization.

norming Comparing a test score to other relevant test scores.

norm-referenced cut score Cut score that is based on some index of the test-takers' scores rather than any notion of job performance.

norms The informal and sometimes unspoken rules that teams adopt to regulate members' behavior.

O

O*NET Abbreviation for *Occupational Information Network*.

objective performance measure Usually a quantitative count of the results of work such as sales volume, complaint letters, and output.

observational design Design in which the researcher observes employee behavior and systematically records what is observed.

occupational commitment Commitment to a particular occupational field; includes affective, continuance, and normative commitment to the occupation.

occupational health psychology Field that involves the application of psychology to improving the quality of work life, and to protecting and promoting the safety, health, and well-being of workers.

Occupational Information Network (O*NET) A collection of electronic databases, based on well-developed taxonomies, that has updated and replaced the D.O.T.; expert computer systems have been developed to allow the databases to be combined in ways that will facilitate person-job matches.

Occupational Safety and Health Act Federal law passed in 1970 to ensure, as far as possible, that every working man and woman in the nation has safe and healthful working conditions.

Occupational Safety and Health Administration (OSHA) One of two federal agencies established to maintain and enforce the Occupational Safety and Health Act; plays a regulatory role in terms of establishing and enforcing health and safety standards.

on-the-job training Training that involves assigning trainees to jobs and encouraging them to observe and learn from more experienced employees.

opponent process theory Theory of job satisfaction that proposes that every emotional reaction is accompanied by an opposing emotional reaction.

organic organization An organization that has a large span of control, less formal procedures, and decision making at middle levels.

organization A group of people who have common goals and who follow a set of operating procedures to develop products and services.

organizational analysis Component of training needs analysis that examines organizational goals, available resources, and the organizational environment; helps to determine where training should be directed.

organizational chart A diagram of an organization's structure.

organizational citizenship behavior (OCB) Behavior that goes beyond what is expected.

organizational development (OD) Action-oriented approach providing techniques that work to help a client organization grow or change.

organizational fit model Model that accounts for the way people choose jobs by examining the match between the personality and values of the individual and the organization.

organizational justice Type of justice that is composed of organizational procedures, outcomes, and interpersonal interactions.

organizational psychology Field of psychology that combines research from social psychology and organizational behavior and addresses the emotional and motivational side of work.

outcomes The compensation, satisfaction, and other benefits employees derive from their work.

out-group members Members who have low-quality relationships with their leader and little latitude for negotiating their work roles.

output component Component that receives information from a human or computer and converts that information to action.

overall satisfaction An overall assessment of job satisfaction that results either from mathematically combining scores based on satisfaction with specific important aspects of work or a single overall evaluative rating of the job.

overt integrity test Test that asks questions directly about past honesty behavior (e.g., stealing) as well as attitudes toward various behaviors such as employee theft.

P

paired comparison Technique in which each employee in a work group or a collection of individuals with the same job title is compared with each other individual in the group on the various dimensions being considered.

paper and pencil test One of the most common forms of industrial testing that requires no manipulation of any objects other than the instrument used to respond.

part learning Training approach in which subtasks are practiced separately and later combined.

participative behavior Behavior identified in the Michigan Leadership Studies; allows subordinates more participation in decision making and encourages more two-way communication.

participatory design Design adopted in usability engineering that is stated in user-directed terms.

path-goal leadership theory Leadership theory proposed by House and his colleagues that includes both the characteristics of the subordinate and the characteristics of the situation. It assumes that the leader's responsibility is to show the subordinate the path to valued goals.

path-goal motivation theory First formal work motivation theory to suggest that people weighed options before choosing among them (Georgopolus, Mahoney, & Jones, 1957). Reasoned that if a worker saw high productivity as a path to the goal of desired rewards or personal goals (e.g., a pay increase or promotion, or increased power, prestige, or responsibility), that worker would likely be a high producer.

peer reviewed   Process in which research is subjected to scientific scrutiny by peer researchers who evaluate the research and consider plausible alternative explanations.

people skills   A nontechnical term that includes negotiating skills, communication skills, and conflict resolution skills.

perceptual-motor abilities   Physical attributes that combine the senses (e.g., seeing, hearing, smell) and motion (e.g., coordination, dexterity).

perceptual-motor approach   Approach to work design and redesign that is used to reduce errors or accidents through knowledge of perceptual motor skills and abilities.

performance   Actions or behaviors that are relevant to the organization's goals and measurable in terms of each individual's proficiency.

performance components   Types of performance that may appear in different jobs and that result from the determinants of performance. John Campbell and colleagues identified eight performance components, some or all of which can be found in every job.

performance management   System that emphasizes the link between individual behavior and organizational strategies and goals by defining performance in the context of those goals; jointly developed by managers and the people who report to them.

performance orientation   Orientation in which individuals are concerned about doing well in training and being evaluated positively.

performance test   Test that requires the individual to make a response by manipulating a particular physical object or piece of equipment.

person analysis   Component of training needs analysis that identifies which individuals within the organization should receive training and what kind of instruction they need.

"person as godlike" metaphor   Metaphor that suggests that people are perfectly rational and intentional rather than automatic or reflexive.

person-as-intentional approach   Motivational approach that assumes individuals are intentional in their behavior.

"person as judge" metaphor   Metaphor in which an individual seeks information about the extent to which the person and others are perceived as responsible for positive and negative events. The person looks for evidence of intent in the actions of others and considers those intentions in choosing a personal course of action.

"person as machine" metaphor   Metaphor that suggests that people's behaviors and actions are reflexive and involuntary and are performed without conscious awareness.

"person as scientist" metaphor   Metaphor that suggests that people are active information gatherers and analysts who seek knowledge and understanding as a way of mastering their environment.

personality   An individual's behavioral and emotional characteristics, generally found to be stable over time and in a variety of circumstances; an individual's habitual way of responding.

personality based integrity test   Test that infers honesty and integrity from questions dealing with broad constructs such as conscientiousness, reliability, and social responsibility and awareness.

Personality-Related Position Requirements Form (PPRF)   A job analysis instrument devoted to identifying personality predictors of job performance.

person-job (P-J) fit   Extent to which the skills, abilities, and interests of an individual are compatible with the demands of the job.

personnel approach   Approach that emphasizes the selection of particular groups of individuals identified by individual difference characteristics, or that provides training to overcome potential risk factors prevalent in some individuals.

personnel measure   Measure typically kept in a personnel file, including absences, accidents, tardiness, rate of advancement, disciplinary actions, and commendations or notes of meritorious behavior.

personnel psychology   Field of psychology that addresses issues such as recruitment, selection, training, performance appraisal, promotion, transfer, and termination.

person-organization (P-O) fit   Extent to which the values of an employee are consistent with the values held by most others in the organization.

physical abilities   Bodily powers such as muscular strength, flexibility, and stamina.

physical fidelity   The extent to which the training task mirrors the physical features of the task performed on the job.

policy capturing   Technique that allows researchers to code various characteristics and determine which weighed most heavily in raters' decision making.

polycentrism   A multinational model in which the values of the local company are accepted.

polygraph   Machine that measures a person's physiological reactions. Approach assumes that when people are being dishonest, their physiological reactions will signal that they are being deceptive; often known as a "lie detector" test.

positive affectivity (PA)   Characteristic in which individuals are prone to describe themselves as cheerful, enthusiastic, confident, active, and energetic.

positive reinforcement   Occurs when desired behavior is followed by a reward, which increases the probability that the behavior will be repeated.

positive valence   A continuum of favorable personality characteristics running from normal to exceptional.

power approach   An approach to leadership that examines the types of power wielded by leaders.

power distance   The degree to which less powerful members of an organization accept and expect an unequal distribution of power.

power motive   Motive to attain control or power that results from people learning that the exercise of such control over others or the environment is pleasing.

power test   Test that has no rigid time limits; enough time is given for a majority of the test takers to complete all of the test items.

predictive validity design   Criterion-related validity design in which there is a time lag between collection of the test data and the criterion data.

predictor   The test chosen or developed to assess attributes (e.g., abilities) identified as important for successful job performance.

pretest posttest control group design   Design that generally includes random assignment of participants to conditions, a control group, and measures obtained both before and after training has occurred.

primary prevention strategy   Stress prevention strategy concerned with modifying or eliminating stressors in the work environment.

problem-focused coping   A type of coping directed at managing or altering a problem causing the stress.

procedural justice   Perceived fairness of the process (or procedure) by which rewards are distributed, decisions made, or evaluations conducted.

procedural knowledge   Knowing how to perform a job or task; often developed through practice and experience.

process emotion   Emotional reaction that can result from a consideration of the tasks one is currently doing.

production team   Team that consists of frontline employees who produce tangible output.

productivity   The ratio of effectiveness (output) to the cost of achieving that level of effectiveness (input).

programmed instruction   Approach in which trainees are given instructional materials in written or computer-based forms that positively reinforce them as they move through the material at their own pace.

progression hypothesis   Hypothesis that there is a progression of withdrawal behaviors that start with tardiness, increase to absenteeism, and eventually result in a decision to quit or retire.

progressive muscle relaxation   Stress management technique to relax the muscles, by moving through each major muscle group in the body, thereby helping to progressively relax the entire body.

project team   Team created to solve a particular problem or set of problems and disbanded after the project is completed or the problem is solved; also called an ad hoc committee, a task force, or a cross-functional team.

ProMES   The Productivity Measurement and Enhancement System, a motivational approach that utilizes goal setting, rewards, and feedback to increase motivation and performance.

prospective emotion   Emotional reaction that can result from a consideration of the tasks one anticipates doing.

protection model   Model for addressing diversity that identifies disadvantaged and underrepresented groups and provides special protections for them.

psychological diversity   Refers to differences in underlying attributes such as skills, abilities, personality characteristics, attitudes, beliefs, and values; may also include functional, occupational, and educational backgrounds.

psychological fidelity   The extent to which the training task helps trainees to develop the knowledge, skills, abilities, and other characteristics (KSAOs) necessary to perform the job.

psychological maturity   The self-confidence and self-respect of a subordinate.

psychometric training   Training that makes raters aware of common rating errors (central tendency, leniency/severity, and halo) in the hope that this will reduce the likelihood of errors.

psychometrician   A psychologist trained in measuring characteristics such as mental ability.

psychometrics   The practice of measuring a characteristic such as mental ability, placing it on a scale or metric.

psychomotor abilities   The physical functions of movement, associated with coordination, dexterity, and reaction time; also called motor or sensorimotor abilities.

Q

qualitative methods   Methods that rely on observation, interview, case study, and analysis of diaries or written documents and that produce flow diagrams and narrative descriptions of events or processes.

quality circle   Work group arrangement that typically involves 6 to 12 employees who meet regularly to identify work-related problems and generate ideas to increase productivity or product quality.

quantitative methods   Methods that rely on tests, rating scales, questionnaires, and physiological measures, and that yield numerical results.

quasi-experimental design   Design in which participants are assigned to different conditions, but random assignment to conditions is not possible.

quid pro quo sexual harassment   Harassment that involves direct requests for sexual favors—for example, when sexual compliance is mandatory for promotions or retaining one's job.

R

ranking Employees are ranked from top to bottom according to their assessed proficiency on some dimension, duty area, or standard.

rating errors Inaccuracies in ratings that may be actual errors or intentional or systematic distortions.

rational economic model Model that accounts for the way people choose jobs that views the individual as an accountant who sums potential economic losses and gains in making the best choice.

rational psychological model Model that accounts for the way people choose jobs that infers a bookkeeper mentality on the part of the applicant, but also includes calculations that depend on psychological factors.

reaction criteria Measures of trainee impressions of the training program.

realistic job preview (RJP) Technique for providing practical information about a job to prospective employees; includes information about the task and context of the work.

rebalance Stage in the freeze-rebalance-unfreeze continuous change process. This phase is intended to reframe what has happened and produce a cognitive framework that gives change a deeper meaning.

refreezing Third stage in the process of changing an organization in which the new attitudes and values of individuals are stabilized.

regiocentrism A multinational model which has a blend of the values of the parent organization and the local company.

regression line Straight line that best "fits" the scatterplot and describes the relationship between the variables in the graph; can also be presented as an equation that specifies where the line intersects the vertical axis and what the angle or slope of the line is.

reinforcement theory A theory that proposes that behavior depends on three simple elements: stimulus, response, and reward. If a response in the presence of a particular stimulus is rewarded (i.e., reinforced), that response is likely to occur again in the presence of that stimulus.

relational demography Refers to the relative makeup of various demographic characteristics in particular work groups.

relations-oriented behavior Type of behavior identified by University of Michigan researchers as an important part of a leader's activities; similar to consideration in the Ohio State model.

reliability The consistency or stability of a measure.

research design Design that provides the overall structure or architecture for the research study; allows investigators to conduct scientific research on a phenomenon of interest.

resigned work satisfaction Satisfaction associated with a reduced work effort and a reduced willingness to change or adapt.

resistance Stage of the General Adaptation Syndrome in which the body copes with the original source of stress, but resistance to other stressors is lowered.

resource theory Theory proposing that an organization must be viewed in the context of its connections to other organizations. The key to organizational survival is the ability to acquire and maintain resources.

results criteria Measures of how well training can be related to organizational outcomes such as productivity gains, cost savings, error reductions, or increased customer satisfaction.

retrospective emotion Emotional reaction that can result from a consideration of the tasks one has already completed.

revery obsession Australian psychologist Elton Mayo proposed that this mental state resulted from the mind-numbing, repetitive and difficult work that characterized U.S. factories in the early 20th century, causing factory workers to be unhappy, prone to resist management attempts to increase productivity, and sympathetic to labor unions.

RIASEC The acronym for Holland's (1973) model of vocational interests which proposes six interest types: *Realistic*—asocial, conforming, frank, genuine, hard-headed, materialistic, natural, normal, persistent, practical, self-effacing, inflexible, thrifty, uninsightful, uninvolved; *Investigative*—analytical, cautious, critical, complex, curious, independent, intellectual, introspective, pessimistic, precise, rational, reserved, retiring, unassuming, unpopular; *Artistic*—complicated, disorderly, emotional, expressive, idealistic, imaginative, impractical, impulsive, independent, introspective, intuitive, nonconforming, original, sensitive, open; *Social*—ascendant, cooperative, patient, friendly, generous, helpful, idealistic, empathic, kind, persuasive, responsible, sociable, tactful, understanding, warm; *Enterprising*—acquisitive, adventurous, agreeable, ambitious, domineering, energetic, exhibitionistic, excitement-seeking, extroverted, flirtatious, optimistic, self-confident, sociable, talkative; and *Conventional*—careful, conforming, conscientious, defensive, efficient, inflexible, inhibited, methodical, obedient, orderly, persistent, practical, prudish, thrifty, unimaginative.

risky-shift phenomenon The tendency for groups to make more risky decisions than individuals; related to the more general phenomenon of group polarization.

role The expectations regarding the responsibilities and requirements of a particular job.

role ambiguity Stressor that occurs when employees lack clear knowledge of what behavior is expected in their job.

role conflict Stressor that occurs when demands from different sources are incompatible.

role overload   Stressor that occurs when an individual is expected to fulfill too many roles at the same time.

role stressors   Collective term for stressors resulting from the multiple task requirements or roles of employees.

rotating shift   Workers are moved from shift to shift over a certain period of time.

routing test   The preliminary test used in computer adaptive testing that identifies a test taker's approximate level of ability before providing additional questions to refine the test taker's position within that ability level.

S

sabotage   Acts that damage, disrupt, or subvert an organization's operations for personal purposes of the saboteur by creating unfavorable publicity, damage to property, destruction of working relationships, or harming of employees or customers.

safeguard   Part of the engineering approach to safety; acknowledges that although a hazard cannot be designed out of an environment, guards can be put in place that will eliminate the possibility of an injury.

safety culture   Type of culture in an organization that can range along a continuum from a strong emphasis on safety to disregard for it.

scatterplot   Graph that is used to plot the scatter of scores on two variables. Used to display the correlational relationship between two variables.

science   Approach that involves the understanding, prediction, and control of some phenomenon of interest.

Scientific Management   A movement based on principles developed by Frederick W. Taylor who suggested that there was one best and most efficient way to perform various jobs.

score banding   Approach in which individuals with similar test scores are grouped together in a category or score band, and selection within the band is then made based on other considerations. The logic is that if two individuals have similar, but not identical, scores, it is likely that the differences are a result of measurement error rather than true differences in the attribute being measured.

screen in test   A test used to add information about the positive attributes of a candidate that might predict outstanding performance; tests of normal personality are examples of screen in tests in the employment setting.

screen out test   A test used to eliminate candidates who are clearly unsuitable for employment; tests of psychopathology are examples of screen out tests in the employment setting.

secondary prevention strategy   Stress prevention strategy that involves modifying responses to inevitable demands or stressors.

selection ratio (SR)   Index ranging from 0 to 1 that reflects the ratio of positions to applicants; calculated by dividing the number of positions available (i.e., the number of hires to be made) by the number of applicants.

self-efficacy   The belief in one's capability to perform a specific task or reach a specific goal; also, the belief that one can overcome obstacles and accomplish difficult tasks.

self-esteem   A positive self-worth or self-concept that is an important resource for coping.

self-presentation   A person's public face or "game face."

self-regulation   Process by which individuals take in information about behavior, and make adjustments or changes based on that information. These changes, in turn, affect subsequent behavior (e.g., strategies, goal commitment).

sensorimotor abilities   The physical functions of movement, associated with coordination, dexterity, and reaction time; also called psychomotor or motor abilities.

sensory abilities   The physical functions of vision, hearing, touch, taste, smell, and kinesthetic feedback (e.g., noticing changes in body position).

settlement discussions   Discussions that are often conducted by the parties in a lawsuit in an attempt to reach a mutually satisfying resolution of the complaint before proceeding with all of the other steps that lead to a trial.

severity error   Error that occurs with raters who are unusually harsh in their ratings.

sexual harassment   Unwelcome sexual advances, requests for sexual favors, and other conduct of a sexual nature constitute sexual harassment when submission to or rejection of this conduct explicitly or implicitly affects an individual's employment, unreasonably interferes with an individual's work performance, or creates a hostile work environment. See also *quid pro quo sexual harassment* and *hostile working environment sexual harassment.*

shared mental model   Organized way for team members to think about how the team will work; helps team members understand and predict the behavior of their teammates.

shift work   The scheduling of work into temporal shifts; common in particular occupational groups such as nurses, blue-collar workers, and public safety personnel.

simulator   Teaching tool designed to reproduce the critical characteristics of the real world in a training setting that produces learning and transfer to the job.

situational interview   Asks the interviewee to describe in specific and behavioral detail how he or she would respond to a hypothetical situation.

situational judgment test   Commonly a paper and pencil test that presents the candidate with a written scenario and asks the candidate to choose the best response from a series of alternatives.

Six Sigma systems   An approach to quality management that provides training for employees and managers in statistical analysis, project management, and problem-solving methods to reduce the defect rate of products.

skew The extent to which scores in a distribution are lopsided or tend to fall on the left or right side of the distribution.

skill-based outcome A type of learning outcome that concerns the development of motor or technical skills.

skills Practiced acts, such as shooting a basketball, using a computer keyboard, or persuading someone to buy something.

sliding band system System that permits the band to be moved down a score point (or to slide) when the highest score in a band is exhausted.

small batch organization An organization that produces specialty products one at a time.

social desirability The desire to be appealing to others.

social learning theory A cognitive theory that proposes that there are many ways to learn, including observational learning which occurs when people watch someone perform a task and then rehearse those activities mentally until they have an opportunity to try them out.

social loafing Reduced motivation and performance in groups that occurs when there is a diminished feeling of individual accountability or a reduced opportunity for evaluation of individual performance.

social support The comfort, assistance, or information an individual receives through formal or informal contacts with individuals or groups.

social undermining Behaviors such as a leader's criticism that indicate a dislike for another individual, as well as actions that tend to present an obstacle to that individual's goal-directed behavior.

socialization The process by which a new employee becomes aware of the values and procedures of the organization.

Society for Industrial and Organizational Psychology (SIOP) An association to which many I/O psychologists, both practitioners and researchers, belong. Designated as Division 14 of the American Psychological Association (APA).

sociotechnical approach Approach that uncovered a number of dramatic changes in the social patterns of work that accompanied technological change; developed at Tavistock Institute of Human Relations in England in the late 1940s.

Solomon four-group design A rigorous evaluation design that includes random assignment of participants to four groups, pretests for training and control groups, and posttests for all four groups.

span of control Refers to the number of positions or people reporting to a single individual—the width—in an organization.

speed test Test that has rigid and demanding time limits such that most test takers will be unable to finish the test in the allotted time.

staffing decisions Decisions associated with recruiting, selecting, promoting, and separating employees.

stamina The physical ability to supply muscles with oxygenated blood through the cardiovascular system; also known as cardiovascular strength or aerobic strength or endurance.

standard deviation A measure of the extent of spread in a set of scores.

standard error of measurement (SEM) Statistic that provides a measure of the amount of error in a test score distribution. The function of the reliability of the test and the variability in test scores.

Stanford-Binet test A well-known intelligence test designed for testing one individual at a time. Originally developed by Alfred Binet and Theodore Simon in 1905, the Binet-Simon test was updated starting in 1916 by Lewis Terman and colleagues at Stanford University, which led to the test's current name.

statistical artifacts Characteristics (e.g., small sample size, unreliable measures) of a particular study that distort the observed results. Researchers can correct for artifacts to arrive at a statistic that represents the "true" relationship between the variables of interest.

statistical control Using statistical techniques to control for the influence of certain variables. Such control allows researchers to concentrate exclusively on the primary relationships of interest.

statistical decision making Combines decision-making information according to a mathematical formula.

statistical power The likelihood of finding a statistically significant difference when a true difference exists.

statistical significance Indicates that the probability of the observed statistic is less than the stated significance level adopted by the researcher (commonly p = .05). A statistically significant finding indicates that, if the null hypothesis were true, the results found are unlikely to occur by chance, and the null hypothesis is rejected.

strains Reaction or response to stressors.

stress hormone Chemical (e.g., adrenalin, noradrenalin, epinephrine, or cortisol) released in the body when a person encounters stressful or demanding situations.

stress inoculation Common type of stress management training that usually combines primary prevention and secondary prevention strategies.

stress management training A training program useful for helping employees deal with workplace stressors that are difficult to remove or change.

stressors Physical or psychological demands to which an individual responds.

structure Refers to the formal way that an organization is designed in terms of division of labor, delegation of authority, and span of control; represented by the number of levels—the height—in an organization.

structured interview   Interview that consists of very specific questions that are asked of each candidate; includes tightly crafted scoring schemes with detailed outlines for the interviewer with respect to assigning ratings or scores based on interview performance.

subgroup norming   Approach that involves developing separate lists for individuals within different demographic groups, then ranking the candidates within their respective demographic group.

subject matter expert (SME)   Employee (incumbent) who provides information about a job in a job analysis interview or survey.

successful leadership   Follower changes his or her behavior as a function of the leader's effort.

surface acting   A type of emotional labor that consists of managing or faking one's expressions or emotions.

survey design   Research strategy in which participants are asked to complete a questionnaire or survey.

T

tacit knowledge   Action-oriented, goal-directed knowledge, acquired without direct help from others; colloquially called "street smarts".

task analysis   Component of training needs analysis that examines what employees must do to perform the job properly.

task performance   The proficiency with which job incumbents perform activities that are formally recognized as a part of their job.

task-oriented behavior   Type of behavior identified by University of Michigan researchers as an important part of a leader's activities; similar to initiating structure from the Ohio State studies.

task-oriented job analysis   Approach that begins with a statement of the actual tasks as well as what is accomplished by those tasks.

taxonomy   An orderly, scientific system of classification.

team   An interdependent collection of individuals who work together toward a common goal and who share responsibility for specific outcomes for their organizations.

team composition   Refers to the attributes of team members, including skills, abilities, experiences, and personality characteristics.

team coordination training   Training that involves teaching team members about sharing information, managing conflict, solving problems, clarifying roles, and making decisions; used to help team members learn to employ the resources of the entire team effectively.

team leader training   Training the team's leader in conflict resolution and team coordination.

team-role theory   Belbin's proposal that effective teams contain a combination of individuals capable of working in nine team roles; used by organizations and management consultants in Europe and Australia to assess and develop teams.

telecommuting   Accomplishing work tasks from a distant location using electronic communication media.

termination for cause   Situation in which an individual is fired from an organization for a particular reason. The individual has usually been warned one or more times about a problem, and either cannot or will not correct it.

tertiary prevention strategy   Stress prevention strategy focused on healing the negative effects of stressors.

test   An objective and standardized procedure for measuring a psychological construct using a sample of behavior.

test battery   A collection of tests that usually assesses a variety of different attributes.

test-retest reliability   Form of reliability calculated by correlating measurements taken at time one with measurements taken at time two.

Theory X   Approach developed by McGregor to described the contrasting beliefs that managers hold about their subordinates. Theory X managers believe that subordinates must be controlled to meet organizational ends.

Theory Y   The contrasting approach developed by McGregor. Theory Y managers believe that subordinates would be motivated to meet goals in the absence of organizational controls.

think-aloud protocol   Approach used by cognitive psychologists to investigate the thought processes of experts who achieve high levels of performance. An expert performer describes in words the thought process that he or she uses to accomplish a task, and an observer/interviewer takes notes and may ask some follow-up questions.

360 degree feedback   The process of collecting and providing an employee with feedback that comes from many sources including supervisors, peers, subordinates, customers, and suppliers.

time and motion studies   Studies that broke every action down into its constituent parts, timed those movements with a stopwatch, and developed new and more efficient movements that would reduce fatigue and increase productivity.

time horizon   Cultural dimension that affects whether managers and employees focus on short-term or long-term goals.

time urgency   Type A behavior pattern subcomponent that refers to the feeling of being pressured by inadequate time.

TIP (The Industrial-Organizational Psychologist)   Quarterly newsletter published by the Society for Industrial and Organizational Psychology; provides I-O psychologists and those interested in I-O psychology with the latest relevant information about the field.

Title VII of Civil Rights Act of 1964   Federal legislation that prohibits employment discrimination on the basis of race, color, religion, sex, or national origin, which define what are known as protected groups. Prohibits not only intentional discrimination, but also practices that have the unintentional effect of discriminating against individuals because of their race, color, national origin, religion, or sex.

total quality management (TQM)   Approach that proposes a unique way of organizing productive effort by emphasizing team-based behavior directed toward improving quality and meeting customer demands.

trainee motivation   The extent to which trainees are interested in attending training, learning from training, and transferring the skills and knowledge acquired in training back to the job.

trainee readiness   Refers to whether employees have the personal characteristics necessary to acquire knowledge from a training program and apply it to the job.

training   The systematic acquisition of skills, concepts, or attitudes that results in improved performance in another environment.

training evaluation   Approach that involves the systematic collection of descriptive and judgmental information that can be used to make effective training decisions.

training needs analysis   A three-step process of organizational, task, and person analysis; required to develop a systematic understanding of where training is needed, what needs to be taught or trained, and who will be trained.

trait approach   Approach that attempts to show that leaders possessed certain characteristics that nonleaders did not.

transactional leadership   Process by which leaders show followers how they can meet their personal goals by adopting a particular behavior pattern. The leader develops social contracts with followers in which certain behaviors will be rewarded.

transfer of training   The degree to which trainees apply the knowledge, skills, and attitudes gained in training to their jobs.

transfer of training climate   Workplace characteristics that either inhibit or facilitate the transfer to the job of what has been learned in training.

transformational leadership   Concept that describes the behavior of inspirational political leaders who transform their followers by appealing to nobler motives such as justice, morality, and peace.

triangulation   Approach in which the researchers seek converging information from different sources.

true negative   Decision in which an applicant was rejected and would have performed poorly if he or she were hired. The decision is *true* because of the correct prediction that the applicant would not be a good performer and *negative* because the applicant was not hired.

true positive   Decision in which an applicant was accepted and performed successfully. The decision is *true* because of the correct prediction that the applicant would be a good performer and *positive* because the applicant was hired.

trust   A belief about how a person or an organization will act on some future occasion.

two-factor theory   Herzberg's theory proposed that there were really two basic needs, not five as suggested by Maslow, and that they were not so much hierarchically arranged as independent of one another.

Type A behavior pattern (TABP)   A set of characteristics exhibited by individuals who are engaged in a chronic struggle to obtain an unlimited number of poorly defined things from their environment in the shortest period of time. Characteristics or subcomponents of TABP include hostility, achievement strivings, impatience/irritability, and time urgency.

U

ultimate criterion   An ideal measure of all of the relevant aspects of job performance.

uncertainty avoidance   The extent to which members of a culture feel comfortable in unpredictable situations.

unfreezing   First stage in the process of changing an organization in which individuals become aware of their values and beliefs.

Uniform Guidelines on Employee Selection Procedures   Official government guidelines designed to assist employers, labor organizations, employment agencies, and licensing and certification boards to comply with federal requirements prohibiting employment practices that discriminate on the grounds of race, color, religion, sex, and national origin.

unstructured interview   Interview that includes questions that may vary by candidate and that allow the candidate to answer in any form he or she may prefer.

usability engineering   Approach that involves an iterative process in which a basic system is designed and then redesigned with input from users.

user friendliness   Positive characteristic of machines, tools, and consumer products that are designed to be comfortable, easy to use, and compatible with human capacities and limitations.

user-centered design   Approach to human-computer interaction research that focuses on the user during system development.

utility analysis   A technique that assesses the economic return on investment of human resource interventions such as staffing or training.

V

valence   The strength of a person's preference for a particular outcome.

validity   The accurateness of inferences made based on test or performance data; also addresses the issue of whether a measure accurately and completely represents what was intended to be measured.

validity coefficient   A correlation coefficient between a test score (predictor) and a performance measure (criterion).

value model   Model for addressing diversity in which each element of an organization is valued for what it uniquely brings to the organization.

value theory   Job satisfaction theory proposed by Locke, in which the relative importance of a particular job aspect to a given worker influenced the range of that worker's responses to it.

variability   The extent to which scores in a distribution vary.

vertical culture   A culture that accepts and depends upon distances between individuals.

VIE theory   Motivation theory that assumes individuals will rationally estimate the relative attractiveness and unattractiveness of different rewards or outcomes (valence), the probability that performance will lead to particular outcomes or rewards (instrumentality), and the probability that effort will lead to performance (expectancy).

virtual team   Team that has widely dispersed members working together toward a common goal and linked through computers and other technology.

virtual-collaboration behaviors   Behaviors used in virtual team interactions that include exchanging ideas without criticism, agreeing on responsibilities, and meeting deadlines.

virtual-communication skills   Skills used in virtual team interactions that include rephrasing unclear sentences or expressions so that all team members understand what is being said, acknowledging the receipt of messages, and responding within one business day.

virtual-socialization skills   Skills used in virtual team interactions that include soliciting team members' feedback on the work process used to accomplish team goals, expressing appreciation for ideas and completed tasks, and apologizing for mistakes.

vocational interest   A preference or liking for a particular activity or setting (as in a job or occupational setting).

voice   The possibility of challenging, influencing, or expressing an objection to a process or outcome.

W

walk-through testing   Method that requires an employee to describe to an interviewer in detail how to complete a task or job-related behavior. Employee may literally walk through the facility (e.g., a nuclear power plant) answering questions as he or she actually sees the displays or controls in question.

weighted checklist   Checklist that includes items that have values or weights assigned to them that are derived from the expert judgments of incumbents and supervisors of the position in question.

welfare-to-work program   Program that requires individuals to work in return for government subsidies.

"West versus the Rest" mentality   Tendency for researchers to develop theories that are relevant to U.S. situations with less concern about their applicability in other countries.

whole learning   Training approach in which the entire task is practiced at once.

withdrawal behaviors   Behaviors such as absenteeism, turnover, tardiness, and retirement that may be different manifestations of a larger construct called withdrawal.

work diary   Job analysis approach that requires workers and/or supervisors to keep a log of their activities over a prescribed period of time.

Work Profiling System (WPS)   PC-based job analysis instrument that can be used to streamline the job analysis process, reducing costs to the organization, minimizing distractions to the SMEs, and increasing the speed and accuracy of the process.

work sample test   Assessment procedure that measures job skills by taking samples of behavior under realistic joblike conditions.

work withdrawal   Includes lateness and **absenteeism** and represents an attempt by the individual to withdraw from work but maintain ties to the organization and the work role.

worker-oriented job analysis   Approach that focuses on the attributes of the worker necessary to accomplish the tasks.

work–family balance   Area of research that investigates whether the satisfaction that one experiences at work is in part affected by the satisfaction that one experiences in nonwork and vice versa.

work-family conflict   Conflict that occurs when workers experience conflict between the roles they fulfill at work and in their personal lives.

work–life balance   Area of research that investigates whether the satisfaction that one experiences at work is in part affected by the satisfaction that one experiences in nonwork and vice versa, particularly to the extent that one environment has demands that conflict with the other.

REFERENCES

Academy of Management. (1990). *The Academy of Management code of conduct.* Ada, OH: Author.

Ackerman, P. L. (1992). Predicting individual differences in complex skill acquisition: Dynamics of ability determinants. *Journal of Applied Psychology, 77,* 598–614.

Ackerman, P. L., & Cianciolo, A. T. (1999). Psychomotor abilities via touch-panel testing: Measurement innovations, construct and criterion validity. *Human Performance, 12* (3/4), 231–273.

Ackerman, P. L., & Cianciolo, A. T. (2002). Ability and task constraint determinants of complex task performance. *Journal of Experimental Psychology: Applied, 8* (3), 194–208.

Adams, J. D. (2001). Managing dispersed work effectively. *OD Practitioner, 33* (1), 381–391.

Adams, J. S. (1965). Inequity in social exchange. In K. Berkowitz (Ed.), *Advances in experimental social psychology* (Vol. 2, pp. 267–299). New York: Academic Press.

Adelmann, P. K. (1995). Emotional labor as a potential source of job stress. S. L. Sauter & L. R. Murphy (Eds.), *Organizational risk factors for job stress* (pp. 371–381). Washington, DC: American Psychological Association.

Aguinis, H., & Henle, C. A. (2002). The search for universals in cross-cultural organizational behavior. In J. Greenberg (Ed.), *Organizational behavior: The state of the science* (2nd ed.). Mahwah, NJ: Erlbaum.

Aguinis, H., & Roth, H. (2002). *Teaching in China: Culture-based challenges.* Unpublished manuscript. University of Colorado at Denver.

Aiello, J. R., & Kolb, K. J. (1995). Electronic performance monitoring and social context: Impact on productivity and stress. *Journal of Applied Psychology, 80,* 339–353.

Alderfer, C. P. (1969). An empirical test of a new theory of human needs. *Organizational Behavior and Human Performance, 4,* 142–175.

Alderfer, C. P. (1972). *Existence, relatedness and growth: Human needs in organizational settings.* New York: Free Press.

Aldrich, H. E. (1999). *Organizations evolving.* London: Sage.

Alexander, S., & Ruderman, A. (1987). The role of procedural and distributive justice in organizational behavior. *Social Justice Research, 1,* 177–198.

Alge, B. J. (2001). Effects of computer surveillance on perceptions of privacy and procedural justice. *Journal of Applied Psychology, 86,* 797–804.

Allalouf, A., & Ben-Shakhar, G. (1998). The effect of coaching on the predictive validity of scholastic aptitude tests. *Journal of Educational Measurement, 35,* 31–47.

Allan, R., & Scheidt, S. (1996). *Heart and mind: The practice of cardiac psychology.* Washington, DC: American Psychological Association.

Allen, T. D., Herst, D. E., Bruck, C. S., & Sutton, M. (2000). Consequences associated with work-to-family conflict: A review and agenda for future research. *Journal of Occupational Health Psychology, 5,* 278–308.

Allen, T. D., McManus, S. E., & Russell, J. E. (1999). Newcomer socialization and stress: Formal peer relationships as a source of support. *Journal of Vocational Behavior, 54,* 453–470.

Alliger, G. M., Tannenbaum, S. I., Bennett, W., Traver, H., & Shotland, A. (1997). A meta-analysis of the relations among training criteria. *Personnel Psychology, 50,* 341–358.

Allport, G. W., Vernon, P. E., Lindzey, G. (1960). *Study of values* (3rd ed.). Manual. Chicago: Riverside.

Amalfe, C. A., & Adelman, H. A. (2001, August 13). Forced rankings: Latest plaintiffs' target. *The New Jersey Lawyer,* 1–10.

American Educational Research Association, American Psychological Association, and National Council on Measurement in Education. (1999). *Standards for educational and psychological testing.* Washington, DC: American Educational Research Association.

American Heart Association. (2002). *American Heart Association statistical facts.* Dallas, TX: Author.

American Psychological Association. (2002). Ethical principles of psychologists and code of conduct. *American Psychologist, 47,* 1597–1611.

Americans with Disabilities Act. (1990, July 26). PL 101–336, 104 Statute 327.

Anastasi, A. (1982). *Psychological testing* (5th ed.). New York: Macmillan.

Anastasi, A., & Urbina, S. (1997). *Psychological testing* (7th ed.). Upper Saddle River, NJ: Prentice Hall.

Anderson, N., Born, M., & Cunningham-Snell, N. (2001). Recruitment and selection: Applicant perspectives and outcomes. In N. Anderson, D. Ones, H. Sinangil and C. Viswesvaran (Eds.), *Handbook of industrial, work, and organizational psychology* (Vol. 1, pp. 200–218). London: Sage.

Anderson, N., & Ostroff, C. (1997). Selection as socialization. In N. Anderson and P. Herriott (Eds.), *Handbook of selection and appraisal* (2nd ed., pp. 413–440). London: John Wiley.

Antonakis, J., & Avolio, B. J. (2003) Examining contextual moderators of the full range leadership theory using the Multifactor Leadership Questionnaire (MLQ Form 5X). In C. Pearce & J. Conger (Eds.), *Shared leadership.* Thousand Oaks, CA: Sage.

Applied Ergonomics. (1974). *Applied ergonomics handbook.* Surrey, England: IPC Science and Technology Press.

Argyris, C. (1965). *Organization and innovation.* Homewood, IL: Irwin.

Argyris, C. (1972). *The applicability of organizational sociology.* Cambridge, England: Cambridge University Press.

Argyris, C. (1990). *Overcoming organizational defenses: Facilitating organizational learning.* Boston: Allyn & Bacon.

Arnold, J. D., Rauschenberger, J. M., Soubel, W. G., & Guion, R. M. (1982). Validation and utility of a strength test for selecting steelworkers. *Journal of Applied Psychology, 67,* 588–604.

Arthur, W., Jr., Barrett, G. V., & Alexander, R. A. (1991). Prediction of vehicular accident involvement: A meta-analysis. *Human Performance, 4,* 89–105.

Arthur, W., Jr., Fuentes, R., & Doverspike, D. (1990). Relationships among personnel tests, age, and job performance. *Experimental Aging Research, 16,* 11–16.

Arvey, R. D. (1986). Sex bias in job evaluation procedures. *Personnel Psychology, 39,* 315–335.

Arvey, R. D. (1992). Constructs and construct validation: Definitions and issues. *Human Performance, 51* (1–2), 59–69.

Arvey, R. D., & Bouchard, T. J. (1994). Genetics, twins and organizational behavior. *Research in Organizational Behavior, 16,* 47–82.

Arvey, R. D., Bouchard, T. J., Carroll, J. B., Cattell, R. B. Cohen, D. B., Dawis, R. U., et al. (1995). Mainstream science on intelligence. *The Industrial-Organizational Psychologist, 32* (4), 67–72.

Arvey, R. D., Bouchard, T. J., Segal, N. L., & Abraham, L. M. (1989). Job satisfaction: environmental and genetic components. *Journal of Applied Psychology, 74,* 187–192.

Arvey, R. D., Landon, T. E., Nutting, S. M., & Maxwell, S. E. (1992). Development of physical ability tests for police officers: A construct validation approach. *Journal of Applied Psychology, 77,* 996–1009.

Arvey, R. D., & Murphy, K. R. (1998). Performance evaluation in work settings. *Annual Review of Psychology, 49,* 141–168.

Ash, P. (1976). The assessment of honesty in employment. *South African Journal of Psychology, 6,* 68–79.

Ashkenasy, N. M., & Holmes, S. (1995). Perceptions of organizational ideology following merger: A longitudinal study of merging accounting firms. *Accounting, Organizations and Society, 20,* 19–34.

Ashkenasy, N. M., & Jackson, C. R. A. (2001). Organizational climate and culture. In N. Anderson, D. Ones, H. Sinangil, and C. Viswesvaran (Eds.), *Handbook of industrial, work, and organizational psychology* (pp. 332–345). London: Sage.

Ashkenasy, N. M., Wilderom, C. P. M., & Peterson, M. F. (Eds.). (2000). *Handbook of organizational climate and culture.* Thousand Oaks, CA: Sage.

Associated Press, (2000, October 4). New chief vows to change LAPD. *Denver Post,* p. 7a.

Athey, T. R., & McIntyre, R. M. (1987). Effect of rater training on rater accuracy: Levels of processing theory and social facilitation theory perspectives. *Journal of Applied Psychology, 72,* 567–572.

Atkins, P. W. B., Wood, R. E., & Rutgers, P. J. (2002). The effects of feedback format on dynamic decision making. *Organizational Behavior and Human Decision Processes, 88,* 587–604.

Atwater, L. E. (1998). The advantages and pitfalls of self-assessment in organizations. In J. W. Smither (Ed.). *Performance appraisal: State of the art in practice* (pp. 331–369). San Francisco: Jossey-Bass.

Austin, J. T., & Klein, H. J. (1996). Work motivation and goal striving. In K. R. Murphy (Ed.), *Individual differences and behavior in organizations* (pp. 209–256). San Francisco: Jossey-Bass.

Austin, J. T., Scherbaum, C. A., & Mahlman, R. A. (2002). History of research methods in industrial and organizational psychology: Measurement, design, and analysis. In S. G. Rogelberg (Ed.), *Handbook of research methods in industrial and organizational psychology* (pp. 3–33). Cambridge, MA: Blackwell.

Austin, J. T., & Vancouver, J. B. (1996). Goal constructs in psychology: Structure, process and content. *Psychological Bulletin, 120,* 338–375.

Avery, D. R., & Quinones, M. A. (2002). Disentangling the effects of voice: The incremental roles of opportunity, behavior, and instrumentality in predicting procedural fairness. *Journal of Applied Psychology, 87,* 81–86.

Avolio, B. J., & Bass, B. M. (1991). *The full range leadership development program: Basic and advanced manuals.* Binghamton, NY: Bass, Avolio, and Associates.

Avolio, B. J., Bass, B. M., & Jung, D. I. (1999). Re-examining the components of transformational and transactional leadership using the Multifactor Leadership Questionnaire. *Journal of Occupational and Organizational Psychology, 72,* 441–462.

Avolio, B. J., Kahai, S., Dumdum, R., & Sivasubramaniam, N. (2001). Virtual teams: Implications for e-leadership and team development. In M. London (Ed.), *How people evaluate others in organizations.* Mahwah, NJ: Erlbaum.

Avolio, B. J., Kroeck, K. G., & Panek, P. E. (1985). Individual differences in information processing ability as a predictor in motor vehicle accidents. *Human Factors, 27,* 577–588.

Avolio, B. J., & Sivasubramaniam, N. (2002). Re-examining the components of the multifactor leadership theory: When too few is probably not enough. Unpublished manuscript, Binghamton University.

Aycan, Z., & Kanungo, R. N. (2001). Cross cultural industrial and organizational psychology: A critical appraisal of the field and future directions. In N. Anderson, D. S. Ones, H. K. Sinangil, & C. Viswesvaran (Eds.), *Handbook of industrial, work, and organizational psychology* (Vol. 1, pp. 385–408). London: Sage.

Aycan, Z., Kanungo, R. N., Mendonca, M., Yu, K., Deller, J., Stahl, G., & Kurshid, A. (2000). Impact of culture on human resource management practices: A 10-country comparison. *Applied Psychology: An International Review, 49* (1), 192–221.

Bachiochi, P. D., & Weiner, S. P. (2002). Qualitative data collection and analysis. In S. G. Rogelberg (Ed.), *Handbook of research methods in industrial and organizational psychology* (pp. 161–183). Cambridge, MA: Blackwell.

Baer, M., & Frese, M. (2002). Innovation is not enough: Climate for initiative and psychological safety, process innovation, and firm performance. *Journal of Organizational Behavior, 24,* 45–68.

Baldamus, W. (1951). Type of work and motivation. *British Journal of Sociology, 2,* 44–58.

Baldwin, T. T. (1992). Effects of alternative modeling strategies on outcomes of interpersonal-skills training. *Journal of Applied Psychology, 77,* 147–154.

Baldwin, T. T., Danielson, C., & Wiggenhorn, W. (1997). The evolution of learning strategies in organizations: From employee development to business redefinition. *Academy of Management Executive, 11,* 47–58.

Baldwin, T. T., & Ford, J. K. (1988). Transfer of training: A review and directions for future research. *Personnel Psychology, 41,* 63–105.

Baltes, B. B., Briggs, T. E., Huff, J. W., Wright, J. A., Neuman, G. A. (1999). Flexible and compressed workweek schedules: A meta-analysis of their effects on work-related criteria. *Journal of Applied Psychology, 84,* 496–513.

Balzer, W. K., Smith, P.C., Kravitz, D. A., Lovell, S. E., Paul, K. B., Reilly, B. A., & Reilly, C. E. (1990). *User's manual for the Job Descriptive Index (JDI) and the Job In General (JIG) scales.* Bowling Green, OH: Bowling Green State University.

Bandura, A. (1986). *Social foundation of thought and action: A social cognitive theory.* Englewood Cliffs, NJ: Prentice Hall.

Bandura, A. (1991). Social cognitive theory of self-regulation. *Organizational behavior and human decision processes, 50,* 248–287.

Bandura, A. (1997). *Self-efficacy: The exercise of control.* New York: W. H. Freeman.

Banks, C. G., & May, K. E. (1999). Performance management: The real glue in organizations. In A. I. Kraut & A. K. Korman (Eds.), *Evolving practices in human resource management* (pp. 118–145). San Francisco: Jossey-Bass.

Banks, C. G., & Murphy, K. R. (1985). Toward narrowing the research-practice gap in performance appraisal. *Personnel Psychology, 38,* 335–345.

Barbian, J. (2000, March). A little help from your friends. *Training, 39,* 38–41.

Barge, B. N., & Hough, L. M. (1988). Utility of interest assessment for predicting job performance. In L. M. Hough (Ed.), *Utility of temperament, biodata, and interest assessment for predicting job performance: A review and integration of the literature* (ARI Research note 88-02). Alexandria, VA: U.S. Army Research Institute for the Behavioral and Social Sciences.

Baritz, L. (1960). *Servants of power.* Middletown, CT: Wesleyan University Press.

Barling, J. (1996). The prediction, experience, and consequences of workplace violence. In G. R. Vandenbos, & E. Q. Bulatao, (Eds.) *Violence on the job: Identifying risks and developing solutions* (pp. 29–50). Washington, DC: American Psychological Association.

Barling, J., & Boswell, R. (1995). Work performance and the achievement strivings and impatience-irritability dimensions of Type A behavior. *Applied Psychology: An International Review, 44,* 143–153.

Barling, J., Dupre, K. E., & Hepburn, C. G. (1998). Effects of parents' job insecurity on children's work beliefs and attitudes. *Journal of Applied Psychology, 83,* 112–118.

Barling, J., Kelloway, E. K., & Cheung, D. (1996). Time management and achievement striving interact to predict car sales performance. *Journal of Applied Psychology, 81,* 821–826.

Barling, J., & Mendelson, M. B. (1999). Parents' job insecurity affects children's grade performance through the indirect effects of beliefs in an unjust world and negative mood. *Journal of Occupational Health Psychology, 4,* 347–355.

Barling, J., Zacharatos, A., & Hepburn, C. G. (1999). Parents' job insecurity affects children's academic performance through cognitive difficulties. *Journal of Applied Psychology, 84,* 437–444.

Barnes-Farrell, J. L., & Weiss, H. M. (1984). Effects of standard extremity on mixed standard scale performance ratings. *Personnel Psychology, 37,* 301–316.

Barnett, R. C., & Hyde, J. S. (2001). Women, men, work, and family. *American Psychologist, 56,* 781–796.

Barney, M. (2002). Six Sigma. *The Industrial-Organizational Psychologist, 39* (4), 104–107.

Baron, R. A. (1988). Negative effects of destructive criticism: Impact on conflict, self-efficacy, and task performance. *Journal of Applied Psychology, 73,* 199–207.

Baron, R. A. (1990). Countering the effects of destructive criticism: The relative efficacy of four interventions. *Journal of Applied Psychology, 75,* 235–245.

Baron, H., & Chaudry, A. (1997). A multi-media approach to assessing customer service potential. *SHL Research Division: Research Note.*

Barrett, G. V. (2001). *Emotional intelligence: The Madison Avenue approach to professional practice.* Paper presented at the 16th annual conference of the Society for Industrial and Organizational Psychology, San Diego, CA.

Barrett, G. V., & Kernan, M. C. (1987). Performance appraisal and termination: A review of court decisions since *Brito v. Zia* with implications for personnel practices. *Personnel Psychology, 40,* 489–503.

Barrett, G. V., Phillips, J. S., & Alexander, R. A. (1981). Concurrent and predictive validity designs: A critical re-analysis. *Journal of Applied Psychology, 66,* 1–6.

Barrett, G. V., & Thornton, C. L. (1968). The relationship between perceptual style and driver reaction to an emergency situation. *Journal of Applied Psychology, 52,* 169–176.

Barrick, M. R., & Mount, M. K. (1991). The Big Five personality dimensions and job performance. A meta-analysis. *Personnel Psychology, 44,* 1–26.

Barrick, M. R., & Mount, M. K. (1993). Autonomy as a moderator between the Big Five personality dimensions and job performance. *Journal of Applied Psychology, 78,* 111–118.

Barrick, M. R., Mount, M. K., & Judge, T. A. (2001). Personality and performance at the beginning of the new millennium: What do we know and where do we go next. *International Journal of Selection and Assessment, 9,* 9–30.

Barrick, M. R., Stewart, G. L., Neubert, M. J., & Mount, M. K. (1998). Relating member ability and personality to work-team processes and team effectiveness. *Journal of Applied Psychology, 83,* 377–391.

Barry, B., & Stewart, G. L. (1997). Composition, process, and performance in self-managed groups: The role of personality. *Journal of Applied Psychology, 82,* 62–78.

Bartel, A. P. (1994). Productivity gains from the implementation of employee training programs. *Industrial Relations, 33,* 411–425.

Bartlett, J. (1998). In J. Kaplan (Ed.) (1998). *Familiar quotations: A collection of passages, phrases, and proverbs traced to their sources in ancient and modern literature* (p. 752). Boston: Little, Brown.

Barton, J. (1994). Choosing to work at night: A moderating influence on individual tolerance to shift work. *Journal of Applied Psychology, 79,* 449–454.

Bartram, D. (2002, March). Assessment center validity: Has it dropped? *SHL Research Division* Research Note.

Baruch-Feldman, C., Brondolo, E., Ben-Dayan, D., & Schwartz, J. (2002). Sources of social support and burnout, job satisfaction, and productivity. *Journal of Occupational Health Psychology, 7,* 84–93.

Bass, B. M. (1957). Faking by sales applicants of a forced choice personality inventory. *Journal of Applied Psychology, 41,* 403–404.

Bass, B. M. (1960). *Leadership, psychology, and organizational behavior.* New York: Harper & Row.

Bass, B. M. (1985). *Leadership and performance beyond expectations.* New York: Free Press.

Bass, B. M. (1997). Does the transactional-transformational leadership paradigm transcend organizational boundaries? *American Psychologist, 52,* 130–139.

Bass, B. M., & Avolio, B. J. (1997). *Full range leadership development: Manual for the Multifactor Leadership Questionnaire.* Palo Alto, CA: Mindgarden.

Bassi, L., & McMurrer, D. P. (1998). Training investment can mean financial performance. *Training and Development, 52,* 40–42.

Bauer, T. N., & Green, S. G. (1998). Testing the combined effects of newcomer information seeking and manager behavior on socialization. *Journal of Applied Psychology, 83,* 72–83.

Bauer, T. N., Maertz, C. P., Jr., Dolen, M. R., & Campion, M. A. (1998). Longitudinal assessment of applicant reactions to employment testing and test outcome feedback. *Journal of Applied Psychology, 83,* 892–903.

Bauer, T. N., & Taylor, S. (2001). Toward a globalized conceptualization of organizational socializations. In N. Anderson, D. Ones, & C. Viswesvaran (Eds.), *Handbook of industrial, work, and organizational psychology* (Vol. 1, pp. 409–423). London: Sage.

Baumeister, R. F., Smart, L., & Boden, J. M. (1996). Relation of threatened egotism to violence and aggression: The dark side of self-esteem. *Psychological Review, 103,* 5–33.

Beckhard, R. (1969). *Organization development: Source strategies and models.* Reading, MA: Addison-Wesley.

Beer, M., Eisenstat, R. A., & Spector, B. (1990). *The critical path to corporate renewal.* Boston: Harvard Business School.

Beer, M., & Walton, A. E. (1987). Organization change and development. *Annnual Review of Psychology, 38,* 339–367.

Belbin, R. M. (1981). *Management teams: Why they succeed or fail.* London: Heinemann.

Belbin, R. M. (1993). *Team roles at work.* London: Butterworth-Heinemann.

Bell, B. S., & Kozlowski, S. W. J. (2002). A typology of virtual teams: Implications for effective leadership. *Group and Organization Management, 27,* 12–49.

Bellarosa, C., & Chen, P. Y. (1997). The effectiveness and practicality of occupational stress management interventions: A survey of subject matter expert opinions. *Journal of Occupational Health Psychology, 2,* 247–262.

Benjamin, L. T. (1997). A history of Division 14 (The Society for Industrial and Organizational Psychology). In D. A. Dewsbury (Ed.), *Unification through division: Histories of the divisions of the American Psychological Association* (Vol. 2, pp. 459–466). Washington, DC: American Psychological Association.

Bennett, G. K. (1980). *Test of mechanical comprehension.* New York: The Psychological Corporation.

Bennett, J. B., & Lehman, W. E. (2001). Workplace substance abuse prevention and help seeking: Comparing team-oriented and informational training. *Journal of Occupational Health Psychology, 6,* 243–254.

Ben-Shukhar, G., Bar-Hillel, M., Bilu, Y., Ben-Abba, E., & Flug, A. (1986). Can graphology predict occupational success? Two empirical studies and some methodological ruminations. *Journal of Applied Psychology, 71,* 645–653.

Bentley, R., Hughes, J. A., Randall, D., Rodden, T., Sawyer, P. (1992). Ethnographically-informed system design for air traffic control. *Proceedings of CSCW 1994 Conference on Computer Supported Cooperative Work* (pp. 123–129). New York: Associate Computer Machinery.

Bernardin, H. J., & Beatty, R. W. (1984). *Performance appraisal: Assessing human behavior.* Boston: Kent.

Bernardin, H. J., Dahmus, S. A., & Redmon, G. (1993). Attitudes of first-line supervisors toward subordinate appraisals. *Human Resource Management Journal, 32,* 315–324.

Bernardin, H. J., Hagan, C. M., Kane, J. S., & Villanova, P. (1998). Effective performance management: A focus on precision, customers, and situational constraints. In J. W. Smither (Ed.), *Performance appraisal: State of the art in practice* (pp. 3–44). San Francisco: Jossey-Bass.

Bernardin, H. J., Hennessey, H. W., & Peyfritte, J. (1995). Age, racial, and gender bias as a function of criterion specificity: A test of expert testimony. *Human Resource Management Review, 5,* 63–77.

Bernardin, H. J., & Pence, E. C. (1980). Effects of rater training: Creating new response sets and decreasing accuracy. *Journal of Applied Psychology, 65,* 60–66.

Bettenhausen, K. L. (1991). Five years of groups research: What we have learned and what needs to be addressed. *Journal of Management, 17,* 345–381.

Bhawuk, D. P. S. (1998). The role of culture theory in cross-cultural training: A multimethod study of culture-specific, culture-general, and culture theory-based assimilators. *Journal of Cross-Cultural Psychology, 29,* 630–655.

Bhawuk, D. P. S. (2001). Evolution of culture assimilators: Toward theory-based assimilators. *International Journal of Intercultural Relations, 25,* 141–163.

Bhawuk, D. P. S., & Brislin, R. W. (2000). Cross-cultural training: A review. *Applied Psychology: An International Review, 49,* 162–191.

Bies, R. J., & Moag, J. S. (1986). Interaction justice: Communication criteria for fairness. *Research on Negotiation in Organization, 1,* 43–55.

Bingham, W. V., & Moore, B. V. (1931). *How to interview.* New York: Harper Brothers.

Binney, G. (1992). *Making quality work: Lessons from Europe's leading companies.* London: Economist Intelligence Unit.

Binning, J. F., & Barrett, G. V. (1989). Validity of personnel decisions: A conceptual analysis of the inferential and evidential bases. *Journal of Applied Psychology, 74,* 478–494.

Birnbaum, M. H. (1983). Perceived equity of salary policies. *Journal of Applied Psychology, 68,* 49–59.

Black, J. S., & Mendenhall, M. (1990). Cross-cultural training effectiveness: A review and a theoretical framework for future research. *Academy of Management Review, 15,* 113–136.

Blackburn, R., & Rosen, B. (1993). Total quality and human resource management: Lessons learned from Baldridge award-winning companies. *Academy of Management Executive, 7,* 49–65.

Blakely, G. L., Blakely, E. H., & Moorman, R. H. (1998). The effects of training on perceptions of sexual harassment allegations. *Journal of Applied Social Psychology, 28,* 71–83.

Blanz, F., & Ghiselli, E. E. (1972). The mixed standard scale: A new rating scale. *Personnel Psychology, 25,* 185–199.

Blau, G. (1994). Developing and testing a taxonomy of lateness behavior. *Journal of Applied Psychology, 79,* 959–970.

Blau, G., & Lunz, M. (1999). Testing the impact of shift schedules on organizational variables. *Journal of Organizational Behavior, 20,* 933–942.

Bluedorn, A. C. (2002). *The human organization of time: Temporal realities and experience.* Stanford, CA: Stanford University Press.

Bluen, S. D., Barling, J., & Burns, W. (1990). Predicting sales performance, job satisfaction, and depression by using the achievement strivings and impatience-irritability dimensions of Type A behavior. *Journal of Applied Psychology, 75,* 212–216.

Bluestone, B., & Rose, S. (1997). Overworked and underemployed: Unraveling an economic engine. *The American Prospect On-line, 31.* Retrieved (2003, March 6), from www.prospect.org/archives/31/31bluefs.html

Bobko, P. & Colella, A. (1994). Employee reactions to employment standards: A review of related literatures and identification of future research needs. *Personnel Psychology, 47,* 1–30.

Bobko, P., Roth, P. L., & Potosky, D. (1999). Derivation and implications of meta-analytic matrix incorporating cognitive abilities, alternative predictors, and job performance. *Personnel Psychology, 52,* 561–589.

Bohle, P., & Tilley, A. J. (1998). Early experience on shiftwork: Influences on attitudes. *Journal of Occupational and Organizational Psychology, 71,* 61–79.

Bommer, W. H., Johnson, J. L., Rich, G. A., Podsakoff, P. M., & McKenzie, S. B. (1995). On the interchangeability of objective and subjective measures of employee performance: A meta-analysis. *Personnel Psychology, 48,* 587–605.

Booth-Kewley, S., Edwards, J. E., & Rosenfeld, P. (1992). Impression management, social desirability, and computer administration of attitude questionnaires: Does the computer make a difference? *Journal of Applied Psychology, 77,* 562–566.

Booth-Kewley, S., & Friedman, H. S. (1987). Psychological predictors of heart disease: A quantitative review. *Psychological Bulletin, 101,* 343–362.

Borman, W. C. (1982). Validity of behavioral assessment for predicting military recruiter performance. *Journal of Applied Psychology, 67,* 3–9.

Borman, W. C., & Brush, D. H. (1993). More progress toward a taxonomy of managerial performance requirements. *Human Performance, 6,* 1–21.

Borman, W. C., & Motowidlo, S. J. (1993). Expanding the criterion domain to include elements of contextual performance. In N. Schmitt and W. C. Borman (Eds.), *Personnel selection in organizations* (pp. 71–98). San Francisco: Jossey-Bass.

Borman, W. C., & Motowidlo, S. J. (1997). Task performance and contextual performance: The meaning for personnel selection research. *Human Performance, 10,* 91–109.

Borman, W. C., Motowidlo, S. J., & Hanser, L. M. (1983). A model of individual performance effectiveness: Thoughts about expanding the criterion space. In N. K. Eaton & J. P. Campbell (Chairs). *Integrated criterion measurement for large-scale computerized selection and classification.* Symposium conducted at the 91st annual convention of the American Psychological Association, Anaheim, CA.

Borman, W. C., White, L. A., Pulakos, E. D., & Oppler, S. H. (1991). Models of supervisory job performance ratings. *Journal of Applied Psychology, 76,* 863–872.

Botan, C. (1996). Communication work and electronic surveillance. *Communication Monographs, 63,* 293–313.

Bouchard, T. J., Arvey, R. D., Keller, L. M., & Segal, N. L. (1992). Genetic influences on job satisfaction. *Journal of Applied Psychology, 77,* 89–93.

Boudreau, J. W. (1991) Utility analysis for decisions in human resource management. In M. D. Dunnette & L. M. Hough (Eds.), *Handbook of industrial and organizational psychology* (2nd ed., Vol. 2, pp. 621–745). Palo Alto, CA: Consulting Psychologists Press.

Bowen, D. E., & Waldman, D. A. (1998). Customer driven employee performance. In D. R. Ilgen & E. D. Pulakos (Eds.), *The changing nature of performance* (pp. 154–191). San Francisco: Jossey-Bass.

Braver, M. C., & Braver, S. L. (1988). Statistical treatment of the Solomon four-group design: A meta-analytic approach. *Psychological Bulletin, 104,* 150–154.

Bray, D. W., Campbell, R. J., & Grant, D. L. (1974). *Formative years in business: A long-term AT&T study of managerial lives.* New York: John Wiley.

Brayfield, A. H., & Crockett, W. H. (1955). Employee attitudes and employee performance. *Psychological Bulletin, 52,* 396–424.

Brett, J. F., & Atwater, L. E. (2001). 360 degree feedback: Accuracy, reactions, and perceptions of usefulness. *Journal of Applied Psychology, 86,* 930–942.

Brett, J. M., Tinsley, C. H., Janssens, M., Barsness, Z. I., & Lytle, A. L. (1997). New approaches to the study of culture in industrial/organizational psychology. In P. C. Earley and M. Erez (Eds.), *New perspectives on international industrial/organizational psychology* (pp. 75–129). San Francisco: Jossey-Bass.

Brett, J. F., & VandeWalle, D. (1999). Goal orientation and goal content as predictors of performance in a training program. *Journal of Applied Psychology, 84,* 863–873.

Bretz, R. D., & Thompsett, R. E. (1992). Comparing traditional and integrative learning methods in organizational training programs. *Journal of Applied Psychology, 77,* 941–951.

Brief, A. J., & Motowidlo, S. J. (1986). Prosocial organizational behaviors. *Academy of Management Review, 11,* 710–725.

Brief, A. P., & Weiss, H. M. (2002). Organizational behavior: Affect in the workplace. *Annual Review of Psychology, 53,* 279–307.

Briner, R. B., & Reynolds, S. (1999). The costs, benefits, and limitations of organizational level stress interventions. *Journal of Organizational Behavior, 20,* 647–664.

Brockner, J., & Weisenfeld, B. M. (1996). An integrative framework for explaining reactions to decisions: Interactive effects of outcomes and procedures. *Psychological Bulletin, 120,* 189–208.

Brodbeck, F. (1996). Work group performance and effectiveness: Conceptual and measurement issues. In M. A. West (Ed.), *Handbook of work group psychology.* Chichester, England: John Wiley.

Brodbeck, F. C., Frese, M., Akerblom, S., Audia, G., Bakacsi, G., Bendova, H., Bodega, D., et al. (2000). Cultural variation of leadership prototypes across 22 European countries. *Journal of Occupational and Organizational Psychology, 73,* 1–29.

Brotheridge, C. M., & Grandey, A. A. (2002). Emotional labor and burnout: Comparing two perspectives of "people work." *Journal of Vocational Behavior, 60,* 17–39.

Brown, D. C. (1994) Subgroup norming: Legitimate testing practice or reverse discrimination? *American Psychologist, 49,* 927–928.

Brown, K. G. (2001). Using computers to deliver training: Which employees learn and why? *Personnel Psychology, 54,* 271–296.

Brown, K. G., & Ford, J. K. (2002). Using computer technology in training: Building an infrastructure for active learning. In K. Kraiger (Ed.), *Creating, implementing, and managing effective training and development* (pp. 192–233). San Francisco: Jossey-Bass.

Browning, L. (2002, September 15). MBA programs now screen for integrity too. *New York Times,* p. 4B.

Bruchon-Schweitzer, M. (2002). Must one use graphology in personnel selection. In C. Levy-Leboyer, M. Huteau, C. Louche, and J. Rolland (Eds.), *RH: Les apports de la psychologie du travail.* Paris: Editions d'Organisation.

Bruggemann, A., Groskurth, P., & Ulich, E. (1975). *Arbeitszufriedenheit.* Bern, Switzerland: Huber.

Brunet v. City of Columbus. 58 F. 3d 251 (6th Cir., 1995).

Brutus, S., Leslie, J. B., & McDonald-Mann, D. (2001). Cross-cultural issues in multisource feedback. In D. W. Bracken, C. W. Timmreck, & A. H. Church (Eds.), *The handbook of multisource feedback* (pp. 433–446). San Francisco: Jossey-Bass.

Buchanan, B. (1974). Building organizational commitment: The socialization of managers in work organizations. *Administrative Science Quarterly, 19,* 533–546.

Buchanan, D. A., & Boddy, D. (1983). Advanced technology and the quality of working life: The effects of computerized controls on biscuit making operators. *Journal of Occupational Psychology, 56,* 109–119.

Bulatao, E. Q., & VandenBos, G. R. (1996). Workplace violence: Its scope and issues. In G. R. VandenBos, & E. Q. Bulatao, *Violence on the job: Identifying risks and developing solutions* (pp. 1–23). Washington, DC: American Psychological Association.

Bunce, D. (1997). What factors are associated with the outcome of individual-focused worksite stress management interventions? *Journal of Occupational & Organizational Psychology, 70,* 1–17.

Burke, M. J., & Day, R. R. (1986). A cumulative study of the effectiveness of managerial training. *Journal of Applied Psychology, 71,* 232–245.

Burke, R. J., & Greenglass, E. R. (1987). Work-family conflict, spouse support, and nursing staff well being during organizational restructuring. *Journal of Occupational Health Psychology, 4,* 327–336.

Burlington Industries v. Ellerth (1998). 118 S. Ct. 2257.

Burns, J. M. (1978). *Leadership.* New York: Harper & Row.

Burns, T., & Stalker, G. M. (1961). *The management of innovation.* London: Tavistock.

Buros, O. K. (1938). *The First mental measurements yearbook.* Hyland Park, NJ: Gryphon.

Burt, R., & Knez, M. (1995). Kinds of third party effects on trust. *Journal of Rational Sociology, 7,* 255–292.

Bush, D. F., & O'Shea, P. (1996). Workplace violence: Comparative use of prevention practices and policies. In G. R. VandenBos & E. Q. Bulatao (Eds). *Violence on the job: Identifying risks and developing solutions* (pp. 283–297). Washington, DC: American Psychological Association.

Büssing, A. (1992). A dynamic view of job satisfaction. *Work and Stress, 6,* 239–259.

Büssing, A. (2002). Motivation and satisfaction. In A. Sorge (Ed.), *Organization* (pp. 371–387). London: Thomson Learning.

Büssing, A., & Bissels, T. (1998). Different forms of work satisfaction: Concept and qualitative research. *European Psychologist, 3,* 209–218.

Büssing, A., Bissel, T., Herbig, B., and Krusken, J. (1998). An analysis of forms of work satisfaction and latitudes at work in a computer-aided laboratory study: Method development and first results (Rep. No. 43 of the Chair of Psychology). Munich, Germany: Technical University.

Büssing, A., Bissels, T., Herbig, B., & Krusken, J. (1999). Motivation in different forms of job satisfaction: When nursing knowledge is transferred into action and when it is not. In P. M. LeBlanc, M. C. W. Peters, A. Büssing, and W. B. Schaufeli (Eds.), *Organizational psychology and health care: European contributions* (pp. 45–64). Munich, Germany: Rainer Hampp Verlag.

Bycio, P., Hackett, R. D., & Allen, J. S. (1995). Further assessments of Bass' conceptualization of transactional and transformational leadership. *Journal of Applied Psychology, 80,* 468–478.

Byrnes, J. P., Miller, D. C., & Schafer, W. D. (1999). Gender differences in risk taking: A meta-analysis. *Psychological Bulletin, 125,* 367–383.

Cable, D. M. (2002). Personal Communication.

Cable, D. M., Aiman-Smith, L., Mulvey, P. W., & Edwards, J. R. (2000). The sources and accuracy of job applicants' beliefs about organizational culture. *Academy of Management Journal, 43,* 1076–1085.

Cable, D. M., & Judge, T. A. (1996). Person-organization fit, job choice decisions, and organizational entry. *Organizational Behavior and Human Decision Processes, 67,* 294–311.

Cable, D. M., & Judge, T. A. (1997). Interviewers' perceptions of person-organization fit and organizational selection decisions. *Journal of Applied Psychology, 82,* 562–577.

Cable, D. M., & Parsons, C. K. (2001). Socialization tactics and person-organization fit. *Personnel Psychology, 54,* 1–23.

Cades, E. (1924). The textile industry in Philadelphia. *Psych. Clin., 15,* 203–228.

Callinan, M., & Robertson, I. T. (2000) Work sample testing. *International Journal of Selection and Assessment, 8,* 248–260.

Caligiuri, P. M. (2000). The Big Five personality characteristics as predictors of expatriate's desire to terminate the assignment and supervisor-rated performance. *Personnel Psychology, 53,* 67–88.

Caligiuri, P. M., Hyland, M. M., Bross, A.S., & Joshi, A. (1998). Testing a theoretical model for examining the relationship between family adjustment and expatriate's work adjustment. *Journal of Applied Psychology, 83,* 598–614.

Campbell, J. P. (1990a). The role of theory in industrial and organizational psychology. In M. D. Dunnette and L. M. Hough (Eds), *Handbook of industrial and organizational psychology* (pp. 39–74). Palo Alto, CA: Consulting Psychologists Press.

Campbell, J. P. (1990b). An overview of the Army selection and classification project (Project A). *Personnel Psychology, 43,* 231–239.

Campbell, J. P. (1990c). Modeling the performance prediction problem in industrial and organizational psychology. In M. D. Dunnette & L. M. Hough (Eds.), *Handbook of industrial and organizational psychology* (Vol. 2, 2nd ed., pp. 687–732). Palo Alto, CA: Consulting Psychologists Press.

Campbell, J. P. (1999). The definition and measurement of performance in the new age. In D. R. Ilgen & E. D. Pulakos (Eds.), *The changing nature of performance* (pp. 399–430). San Francisco: Jossey-Bass.

Campbell, J. P. & Campbell, R. J. (1988). *Productivity in organizations: New perspectives from industrial and organizational psychology.* San Francisco: Jossey-Bass.

Campbell, J. P., Dunnette, M. D., Lawler, E. E., Jr., & Weick, K. (1970). *Managerial behavior, performance and effectiveness.* New York: McGraw-Hill.

Campbell, J. P., Gasser, M. B., & Oswald, F. L. (1996). The substantive nature of job performance variability. In K. R. Murphy (Ed.), *Individual differences and behavior in organizations* (pp. 258–299). San Francisco: Jossey-Bass.

Campbell, J. P., McCloy, R. A., Oppler, S. H., & Sager, C. E. (1993). A theory of performance. In N. Schmitt & W. C. Borman (Eds.), *Personnel selection in organizations* (pp. 35–70). San Francisco: Jossey-Bass.

Campbell, J. P., McHenry, J. J., & Wise, L. L. (1990). Modeling job performance in a population of jobs. *Personnel Psychology, 43,* 313–333.

Campbell, J. P., & Zook, L. M. (1990). *Improving the selection, classification, and utilization of army enlisted personnel: Final report on Project A.* Alexandria, VA: U. S. Army Research Institute for the Behavioral and Social Sciences.

Campion, M. A. (1983). Personnel selection for physically demanding jobs: Review and recommendations. *Personnel Psychology, 36,* 527–550.

Campion, M. A. (1988). Interdisciplinary approaches to job design: A constructive replication with extensions. *Journal of Applied Psychology, 73,* 467–481.

Campion, M. A. (1989). Ability requirement implications of job design: An interdisciplinary perspective. *Personnel Psychology, 42,* 1–24.

Campion, M. A., Cheraskin, L., & Stevens, M. J. (1994). Career-related antecedents and outcomes of job rotation. *Academy of Management Journal, 37,* 1518–1542.

Campion, M. A., Medsker, G. J., & Higgs, A. C. (1993). Relations between work group characteristics and effectiveness: Implications for designing effective work groups. *Personnel Psychology, 46,* 823–850.

Campion, M. A., Outtz, J. L., Zedeck, S., Schmidt, F. L., Kehoe, J. F., Murphy, K. R., & Guion, R. M. (2001). The controversy over score banding in personnel selection: Answers to 10 key questions. *Personnel Psychology, 54,* 147–185.

Campion, M. A., Papper, E. M., & Medsker, G. J. (1996). Relations between work team characteristics and effectiveness: A replication and extension. *Personnel Psychology, 49,* 429–452.

Campion, M. A., & Thayer, P. W. (1985). Development and field evaluation of an interdisciplinary measure of job design. *Journal of Applied Psychology, 70,* 29–43.

Campion, M. A., & Thayer, P. W. (1987). Job design: Approaches, outcomes, and trade-offs. *Organizational Dynamics, 15,* 66–79.

Cannon, W. B. (1929). *Bodily changes in pain, hunger, fear, and rage.* New York: Appleton-Century.

Cannon-Bowers, J. A., Oser, R., & Flanagan, D. L. (1992). Work teams in industry: A selected review and a proposed framework. In R. W. Swezey & E. Salas (Eds.), *Teams: Their training and performance* (pp. 355–378). Stamford, CT: Ablex.

Cannon-Bowers, J. A., & Salas, E. (1997). Teamwork competencies: The interaction of team member knowledge, skills, and attitudes. In H. F. O'Neil (Ed.), *Workforce readiness: Competencies and assessment* (pp. 151–174). Mahwah, NJ: Erlbaum.

Cannon-Bowers, J. A., Tannenbaum, S. I., Salas, E., & Volpe, C. E. (1995). Defining competencies and establishing team training requirements. In R. A. Guzzo & E. Salas (Eds.), *Team effectiveness and decision making in organizations* (pp. 333–380). San Francisco: Jossey-Bass.

Caplan, R. (1992). Disabled by design. *Interior Design, 63,* 88–91.

Caro, R. A. (2002). *Master of the Senate: The years of Lyndon Johnson.* New York: Knopf.

Carroll, J. B. (1993). *Human cognitive abilities: A survey of factor-analytic studies.* Cambridge, England: Cambridge University Press.

Carroll, J. M. (1997). Human-computer interaction: Psychology as a science of design. *Annual Review of Psychology, 48,* 61–83.

Cartwright, S., & Cooper, C. L. (1997). *Managing workplace stress.* Thousand Oaks, CA: Sage.

Cascio, W. F. (1982). *Applied psychology in personnel management* (2nd ed.). Reston, VA: Reston Publishing, a Prentice Hall Company.

Cascio, W. F. (1995). Whither industrial and organizational psychology in a changing world of work? *American Psychologist, 50,* 928–939.

Cascio, W. F. (1998). *Applied psychology in human resource management* (5th ed.). Englewood Cliffs, NJ: Prentice Hall.

Cascio, W. F. (1998). *Managing human resources* (5th ed.). New York: McGraw-Hill.

Cascio, W. F. (1998). The virtual workplace: A reality now. *The Industrial-Organizational Psychologist, 35* (4), 32–36.

Cascio, W. F. (1999). Data-based remodeling of the electronic cottage. *The Industrial-Organizational Psychologist, 36* (3), pp. 25–27.

Cascio, W. F. (2000). *Costing human resources: The financial impact of behavior in organizations* (4th ed). Cincinnati, OH: Southwestern.

Cascio, W. F. (2000). Managing a virtual workplace. *Academy of Management Executive, 14,* 81–90.

Cascio, W. F. (2003). *Managing human resources: Productivity, quality of work life, and profits,* (6th ed.). New York: McGraw-Hill.

Cascio, W. F., & Morris, J. R. (1990). A critical re-analysis of Hunter, Schmidt & Coggin's "Problems and pitfalls in using capital budgeting and financial accounting techniques in assessing the utility of personnel programs." *Journal of Applied Psychology, 75,* 410–417.

Cascio, W. F., Outtz, J., Zedeck, S., & Goldstein, I. L. (1991). The implications of six methods of score use in personnel selection. *Human Performance, 4* (4), 233–264.

Catalano, R., Novaco, R., & McConnell, W. (1997). A model of the net effect of job loss on violence. *Journal of Personality and Social Psychology, 72,* 1440–1447.

Cawley, B. D., Keeping, L. M., & Levy, P. E. (1998). Participation in the performance appraisal process and employee reactions: A meta-analytic review of field investigations. *Journal of Applied Psychology, 83,* 615–633.

Centra, J. A. (1993). *Reflective faculty evaluation.* San Francisco: Jossey-Bass.

Chadwick-Jones, J. K., Nicholson, N., & Browne, C. (1982). *The social psychology of absenteeism.* New York: Praeger.

Chaffin, D. B. (1997). Biomechanical aspects of workplace design. In G. Salvendy, *Handbook of human factors and ergonomics* (2nd ed., pp. 772–789). New York: John Wiley.

Chaffin, D. B., & Andersson, G. B. J. (1991). *Occupational biomechanics* (2nd ed.). New York: John Wiley.

Chan, D., & Schmitt, N. (1997). Video based versus paper and pencil method of assessment in situational judgment tests: Subgroup differences in test performance and face validity perceptions. *Journal of Applied Psychology, 82,* 143–159.

Chan, D., & Schmitt, N. (2002). Situational judgment and job performance. *Human Performance, 15,* (3), 233–254.

Chan, D., Schmitt, N., Sacco, J., & DeShon, R. P. (1998). Understanding pretest and posttest reactions to cognitive ability and personality tests. *Journal of Applied Psychology, 83,* 471–485.

Chan, K., & Drasgow, F. (2001). Toward a theory of individual differences and leadership: Understanding the motivation to lead. *Journal of Applied Psychology, 86,* 481–498.

Charness, N. (Ed.). (1985). *Aging and human performance.* New York: John Wiley.

Chee, L. S. (1994). Singapore Airlines: Strategic human resource initiatives. In D. Torrington (Ed.), *International human resource management: Think globally, act locally* (pp. 143–159). Upper Saddle River, NJ: Prentice Hall.

Chen, P. Y., & Spector, P. E. (1992). Relationships of work stressors with aggression, withdrawal, theft, and substance abuse: An exploratory study. *Journal of Occupational and Organizational Psychology, 65,* 177–184.

Cherrington, D. J. (1980). *The work ethic: Working values and values that work.* New York: Amacom.

Chicago to Pay $2.6 million for race norming exam. (2002, April 2). *National Law Journal,* p. B2.

Chmiel, N. (2000). History and context for work and organizational psychology. In N. Chmiel (Ed.), *Introduction to work and organizational psychology: a European perspective.* Malden, MA: Blackwell.

Chrobot-Mason, D., & Ruderman, M. N. (2003). Leadership in a diverse workplace. In M. S. Stockdale & F. J. Crosby (Eds.), *The psychology and management of workplace diversity* (pp. 100–121). Oxford, England: Blackwell.

Clark, L. K., & Miller, S. M. (1990). Self-reliance and desire for control in the Type A behavior pattern. *Journal of Social Behavior & Personality, 5,* 405–418.

Clarke, S. (1999). Perceptions of organizational safety: Implications for the development of safety culture. *Journal of Organizational Behavior, 20,* 185–198.

Cleveland, J. N., & Murphy, K. R. (1992). Analyzing performance appraisal as goal-directed behavior. In G. Ferris & K. Rowland (Eds.), *Research in personnel and human resources management* (Vol. 10, pp. 121–185). Greenwich, CT: JAI Press.

Cleveland, J. N., Stockdale, M., & Murphy, K. R. (2000). *Women and men in organizations.* Mahwah, NJ: Erlbaum.

Clevenger, J., Pereira, G. M., Weichmann, D., Schmitt, N., and Harvey, V. S. (2001). Incremental validity of situational judgment tests. *Journal of Applied Psychology, 86,* 410–417.

Cohen, A. (1999). Relationship among five forms of commitment: An empirical assessment. *Journal of Organizational Behavior, 20,* 285–308.

Cohen, J. (1988). *Statistical power analysis for the behavioral sciences* (2nd Ed). Hillsdale, NJ: Erlbaum.

Cohen, J. (1994). The earth is round (p < .05). *American Psychologist, 49,* 997–1003.

Cohen, M. S., Freeman, J. T., Thompson, B. (1998). Critical thinking skills in tactical decision making: A model and a training strategy. In J. A. Cannon-Bowers & E. Salas (Eds.), *Making decisions under stress: Implications for individual and team training* (pp. 155–189). Washington, DC: American Psychological Association.

Cohen, R. J., & Swerdlik, M. E. (2002). *Psychological testing and assessment: An introduction to test and measurement* (5th ed.). New York: McGraw-Hill.

Cohen, S., & Edwards, J. R. (1989). Personality characteristics as moderators of the relationship between stress and disorder. In R. W. Neufeld (Ed.), *Advances in the investigation of psychological stress* (pp. 235–283). New York: John Wiley.

Cohen, S., Evans, G. W., Stokols, D., & Krantz, D. S. (1986). *Behavior, health, and environmental stress.* New York: Plenum.

Cohen, S., & Hebert, T. B. (1996). Psychological factors and physical disease from the perspective of psychoimmunology. *Annual Review of Psychology, 47,* 113–142.

Cohen, S., & Wills, T. A. (1985). Stress, social support, and the buffering hypothesis. *Psychological Bulletin, 98,* 310–357.

Cohen, S. G., & Bailey, G. E. (1997). What makes teams work? Group effectiveness from the shop floor to the executive suite. *Journal of Management, 23,* 239–290.

Cohen, S. G., & Ledford, G. E. (1994). The effectiveness of self-managing teams: A quasi-experiment. *Human Relations, 47,* 13–43.

Cole, M., Gay, J., Glick, J., & Sharpe, D. W. (1971). *The cultural context of learning and thinking.* New York: Basic Books.

Collins, J. (1998). Conscientiousness: Is that all there is? *The Industrial-Organizational Psychologist, 36* (2), 27–28.

Colquitt, J. A. (2001). On the dimensionality of organizational justice: A construct validation of a measure. *Journal of Applied Psychology, 86,* 386–400.

Colquitt, J. A., Conlon, D. E., Wesson, M. J., Porter, C. O., & Ng, K. Y. (2001). Justice at the millennium: A meta-analytic review of 25 years of organizational justice research. *Journal of Applied Psychology, 86,* 425–445.

Colquitt, J. A., LePine, J. A., & Noe, R. A. (2000). Toward an integrative theory of training motivation: A meta-analytic path analysis of 20 years of research. *Journal of Applied Psychology, 85,* 678–707.

Confessore, S. J., & Kops, W. J. (1998). Self-directed learning and the learning organization: Examining the connection between the individual and the learning environment. *Human Resource Development Quarterly, 9,* 365–375.

Conger, J. A., & Kanungo, R. (1987). Toward a behavioral theory of charismatic leadership in organizational settings. *Academy of Management Review, 12,* 637–647.

Conte, J. M., Landy, F. J., & Mathieu, J. E. (1995). Time urgency: Conceptual and construct development. *Journal of Applied Psychology, 80,* 178–185.

Conte, J. M., Mathieu, J. E., & Landy, F. J. (1998). The nomological and predictive validity of time urgency. *Journal of Organizational Behavior, 18,* 1–13.

Conte, J. M., Schwenneker, H. H., Dew, A. F., & Romano, D. M. (2001). The incremental validity of time urgency and other Type A subcomponents in predicting behavioral and health criteria. *Journal of Applied Social Psychology, 31,* 1727–1748.

Conway, J. M. (1999). Distinguishing contextual performance from task performance for managerial jobs. *Journal of Applied Psychology, 84,* 3–13.

Cook, T. D., Campbell, D. T., & Peracchio, L. (1990). Quasi-experimentation. In M. D. Dunnette & L. M. Hough (Eds.), *Handbook of industrial and organizational psychology* (2nd ed., Vol. 1, pp. 491–576). Palo Alto, CA: Consulting Psychologists Press.

Cooke, R. A., & Lafferty, J. C. (1989). *Organizational culture inventory.* Plymouth, MI: Human Synergistics.

Cooke, R. A., & Rousseau, D. M. (1988). Behavioral norms and expectations: A quantitative approach to the assessment of organizational culture. *Group and Organizational Studies, 13,* 245–273.

Cooke, R. A., & Szumal, J. L. (2000). Using the organizational culture inventory to understand the operating cultures of organizations. In N. M. Ashkenasy, C. P. M. Wilderom, and M. F. Peterson (Eds.), *Handbook of Organizational Climate and Culture* (pp. 147–162). Thousand Oaks, CA: Sage.

Cooney, R., & Sohal, A. (2003). The human impact of total quality management. In D. Holman, T. Wall, C. Clegg, P. Sparrow, and A. Howard (Eds.), *The new workplace: A guide to the human impact of modern working practices.* Chichester, England: John Wiley.

Cooper, C. L., & Cartwright, S. (1994). Healthy mind, healthy organization: A proactive approach to occupational stress. *Human Relations, 47,* 455–471.

Cooper, C. L., & Cartwright, S. (2001). A strategic approach to organizational stress management. In P. A. Hancock & P. A. Desmond (Eds). *Stress, workload, and fatigue. Human factors in transportation* (pp. 235–248). Mahwah, NJ: Erlbaum.

Cooper, C. L. & Locke, E. A. (Eds.) (2000). *Industrial and organizational psychology.* Malden, MA: Blackwell.

Cooper C. L., & Sadri, G. (1991). The impact of stress counseling at work. *Journal of Social Behavior and Personality, 6,* 411–423.

Cooper, C. L., Dewe, P. J., & O'Driscoll, M. P. (2001). *Organizational stress: A review and critique of theory, research, and applications.* Thousand Oaks, CA: Sage.

Cordery, J. L. (1996). Autonomous work groups and quality circles. In M. A. West (Ed.), *Handbook of work group psychology.* (pp. 225–246). Chichester, England: John Wiley.

Cordery, J. L., Mueller, W. S., & Smith, L. M. (1991). Attitudinal and behavioral effects of autonomous group working: A longitudinal field study. *Academy of Management Journal, 34,* 464–476.

Cordes, C., & Dougherty, T. (1993). A review and integration of research on job burnout. *Academy of Management Review, 18,* 621–656.

Costa, P. T., & McCrae, R. R. (1997). Longitudinal stability of personality. In R. Hogan, J. Johnson, & S. Briggs (Eds.), *Handbook of personality psychology,* pp. 123–139. San Diego, CA: Academic Press.

Coyne, T. (2002, March 23). Employee kills four colleagues in Indiana. *Rocky Mountain News,* p. 11A.

Craiger, J. P. (2000). Traveling in cyberspace: Psychology of software design, Part II–usability evaluation. *The Industrial-Organizational Psychologist, 37* (3), 101–107.

Craiger, J. P., & Weiss, R. J. (1998). Traveling in cyberspace, the final frontier: An interview with Donald Norman. *The Industrial-Organizational Psychologist, 35* (4), 47–53.

Crino, M. D. (1994). Employee sabotage: a random or preventable phenomenon? *Journal of Managerial Issues, 6* (3), 311–330.

Cronbach, L. J., Gleser, G. C., Nanda, H., & Rajaratnam, N. (1972). *The dependability of behavioral measurements: Theory of generalizability for scores and profiles.* New York: John Wiley.

Cronbach, L. J., & Meehl, P. W. (1955). Construct validity in psychological tests. *Psychological Bulletin, 52,* 281–302.

Cronshaw, S. F. (1997). Lo! The stimulus speaks: The insider's view on Whyte and Latham's "The futility of utility analysis." *Personnel Psychology, 50,* 611–615.

Cronshaw, S. F., & Alexander, R. A. (1985). One answer to the demand for accountability: Selection utility as an investment decision. *Organizational Behavior and Human Decision Processes, 35,* 102–118.

Cropanzano, R. (2001). *Justice in the workplace: From theory to practice* (Vol 2). Mahwah, NJ: Erlbaum.

Cropanzano, R., Byrne, Z. S., & Prehar, C. A. (1999). *How workers manage relationships in a complex social world: A multi-foci approach to procedural and interactional justice.* Paper presented at the First International Round Table: Innovations in organizational justice, Nice, France.

Cropanzano, R., & James, K. (1990). Some methodological considerations for behavioral genetic analysis of work attitudes. *Journal of Applied Psychology, 75,* 433–439.

Cropanzano, R., James, K., & Konovosky, M. A. (1993). Dispositional affectivity as a predictor of work attitudes and job performance. *Journal of Organizational Behavior, 14,* 595–606.

Cummings, T., & Worley, C. (2001). *Organizational development and change* (7th ed.). St. Paul, MN: West Publishing.

Cummins, R. (1989). Locus of control and social support: Clarifiers of the relationship between job stress and job satisfaction. *Journal of Applied Social Psychology, 19,* 772–788.

Cunningham, J. W., Boese, R. R., Neeb, R.W., & Pass, J. J. (1983). Systematically derived work dimensions: Factor analysis of the Occupational Analysis Inventory. *Journal of Applied Psychology, 68,* 232–252.

Cushner, K., & Brislin, R. W. (1996). *Intercultural relations: A practical guide* (2nd ed.). Thousand Oaks, CA: Sage.

D.A.T. Spatial Relations Test Manual (1973, 1974). New York: The Psychological Corporation.

d'Appolonia, S. & Abrami, P. C. (1997). Navigating student ratings of instruction. *American Psychologist, 52,* 1198–1208.

Dachler, H. P. (2000). Taking qualitative methods a (radical) step forward? *European Journal of Work and Organizational Psychology, 9* (4), 575–583.

Dalessio, A. T. (1998). Using multi-source feedback for employee development and personnel decisions. In J. W. Smither (Ed.), *Performance appraisal: State of the art in practice* (pp. 278–330). San Francisco: Jossey-Bass.

Dalessio, A. T., & Silverhart, T. A. (1994). Combining biodata test and interview information: Predicting decisions and performance criteria. *Personnel Psychology, 47,* 303–315.

Daniels, C. (2000, May 1). The man in the tan khaki pants. *Fortune, 141* (9), 338–339.

Dansereau, F., Graen, G., & Haga, W. J. (1975). A vertical dyad linkage approach to leadership within formal organizations: A longitudinal investigation of the role-making process. *Organizational Behavior and Human Performance, 13,* 46–78.

Daubert v. Merrell Dow Pharm., Inc. 509 U.S. 579 (1993).

Davidson, W. N., III, Worrell, D. L., & Fox, J. B. et al (1996). Early retirement programs and firm performance. *Academy of Management Journal, 39,* 970–984.

Davies, M., Stankov, L., & Roberts, R. D. (1998). Emotional intelligence: In search of an elusive construct. *Journal of Personality and Social Psychology, 75,* 989–1015.

Davis, D. D. (1998). International performance measurement and management. In J. W. Smither (Ed.), *Performance appraisal: State of the art in practice* (pp. 95–131). San Francisco: Jossey-Bass.

Davis, S. M., & Lawrence, P. R. (1977). *Matrix.* Reading, MA: Addison-Wesley.

Davis, S. M., & Lawrence, P. R. (1978). Problems of matrix organizations. *Harvard Business Review, 56* (3), 131–142.

Dawes, R. M. (1988). *Rational choice in an uncertain world.* San Diego, CA: Harcourt, Brace, Jovanovich.

Dawis, R. V., & Lofquist, L. H. (1984). *A psychological theory of work adjustment: An individual differences model and its applications.* Minneapolis: University of Minnesota Press.

Day, A. L., & Livingstone, H. A. (2001). Chronic and acute stressors among military personnel: Do coping styles buffer their negative impact on health? *Journal of Occupational Health Psychology, 6,* 348–360.

Day, D. V. (2001a). Assessment of leadership outcomes. In S. Zaccaro & R. Klimoski (Eds.), *The nature of organizational leadership: Understanding the performance imperatives confronting today's leaders* (pp. 384–412). San Francisco: Jossey-Bass.

Day, D. V. (2001b). Leadership development: A review in context. *Leadership Quarterly, 11* (4), 581–613.

Day, D. V., & Sulsky, L. M. (1995). Effects of frame-of-reference training and information configuration on memory organization and rating accuracy. *Journal of Applied Psychology, 80,* 158–167.

DeFrank, R. S., & Ivancevich, J. M. (1998). Stress on the job: An executive update. *Academy of Management Executive, 12,* 55–66.

Delbridge, R. (2003). Workers under lean manufacturing. In D. Holman, T. Wall, C. Clegg, P. Sparrow, and A. Howard (Eds.), *The new workplace: A guide to the human impact of modern working practices* (pp. 19–36). Chichester, England: John Wiley.

Delbridge, R., & Turnbull, P. (1992). Human resource maximization: The management of labour under a JIT system. In P. Blyton and P. Turnbull (Eds.), *Reassessing human resource management* (pp. 56–73). London: Sage.

Demerouti, E., Bakker, A. B., Nachreiner, F., & Schaufeli, W. B. (2001). The job demands-resources model of burnout. *Journal of Applied Psychology, 86,* 499–512.

Deming, W. E. (1986) *Out of crisis.* Cambridge, MA: MIT, Center for Advanced Engineering Study.

Den Hartog, D. N., Emics and etics of culturally endorsed implicit leadership theories: Are attributes of charismatic and transformational leadership universally endorsed? Unpublished manuscript.

Den Hartog, D. N., & Koopman, P. L. (2001). Leadership in organizations. In N. Anderson, D. S. Ones, H. K. Sinangil, & C. Viswesvaran (Eds.), *Handbook of Industrial, work, and organizational psychology* (Vol. 2, pp. 166–187). London: Sage.

Deshpande, S. P., & Viswesvaran, C. (1992). Is cross-cultural training of expatriate managers effective? A meta-analysis. *International Journal of Intercultural Relations, 16,* 295–310.

Devine, D. J., Clayton, L. D., Philips, J. L., Dunford, B. B., & Melner, S. B. (1999). Teams in organizations: Prevalence, characteristics, and effectiveness. *Small Group Research, 30,* 678–711.

Digman, J. M. (1990). Personality structure: Emergence of the five factor model. *Annual Review of Psychology, 41,* 417–440.

Dollard, J., Doob, L., Miller, N., Mowrer, D., & Sears, R. (1939). *Frustration and aggression.* New Haven, CT: Yale University Press.

Donaldson, S. I., & Weiss, R. (1998). Health, well being and organizational effectiveness in the virtual workplace. In M. Igbaria and M. Tan (Eds.), *The virtual workplace* (pp. 24–44). Hershey, PA: IDEA Publishing.

Donovan, J. J. (2001). Work motivation. In N. Anderson, D. S. Ones, H. K. Sinangil, and C. Visvesvaran (Eds.), *Handbook of industrial, work, and organizational psychology* (pp. 53–76). London: Sage.

Donovan, J., & Radosevich, D. (1999). A meta-analytic review of the distribution of practice effect: Now you see it, now you don't. *Journal of Applied Psychology, 84,* 795–805.

Donovan, M. A., Drasgow, F., & Munson, L. J. (1998). The perceptions of fair interpersonal treatment scale: Development and validation of a measure of interpersonal treatment in the workplace. *Journal of Applied Psychology, 83,* 683–692.

Donovan, M. A., Drasgow, F., & Probst, T. M. (2000). Does computerizing paper and pencil attitude scales make a difference? New IRT analyses offer insight. *Journal of Applied Psychology, 85,* 305–313.

Douglas, C. A., & McCauley, C. D. (1999). Formal developmental relationships: A survey of organizational practices. *Human Resource Development Quarterly, 10,* 203–220.

Douthitt, E. A., & Aiello, J. R. (2001). The role of participation and control in effects of computer monitoring on fairness perceptions, task satisfaction, and performance. *Journal of Applied Psychology, 86,* 867–874.

Drasgow, F., & Olson-Buchanan, J. B. (Eds.) (1999). *Innovations in computerized assessment.* Mahwah, NJ: Erlbaum.

Drath, W. H., & Palus, C. J. (1994). *Making common sense: Leadership as meaning-making in a community of practice.* Greensboro, NC: Center for Creative Leadership.

Driskell, J. E., Willis, R. P., & Copper, C. (1992). Effect of overlearning on retention. *Journal of Applied Psychology, 77,* 615–622.

Droege, R. C. (1988). Department of Labor analysis methodology. In S. Gael (Ed.), *The job analysis handbook for business, industry, and government* (Vol. 2, pp. 993–1018). New York: John Wiley.

Drucker, P. (1954). *The practice of management.* New York: Harper & Row.

Dubois, D. A., Shalin, V. L., Levi, K. R., & Borman, W. C. (1998). A cognitively-oriented approach to task analysis. *Training Research Journal, 3,* 103–142.

DuBois, D. D. (1999). Competency modeling. In D. G. Landon, K. S. Whiteside, & M. M. McKenna, (Eds.), *Intervention Resource Guide: 50 performance improvement tools.* San Francisco: Jossey-Bass.

Duffy, M. K., Ganster, D. C., & Pagon, M. (2002). Social undermining in the workplace. *Academy of Management Journal, 45,* 331–351.

Dunbar, E. (1996). Sociocultural and contextual challenges of organizational life in Eastern Europe. In D. Landis & R. S. Bhagat (Eds.), *Handbook of intercultural training* (2nd ed., pp. 349–365). Thousand Oaks, CA: Sage.

Duncan, T. S. (1995, April). Death in the office: Workplace homicides. *The FBI Law Enforcement Bulletin.* Retrieved 2003, June 6, from http://www.nsi.org/tips/workdeth.txt

Dunn, W. L. S. (1993). *Managers' perceptions of the validity of personality and general mental ability.* Unpublished doctoral dissertation, University of Iowa.

Dunnette, M. D. (1966). Fads, fashions and folderol. *American Psychologist, 21,* 343–352.

Dunnette, M. D. (1999). Introduction. In N. G. Peterson, M. D. Mumford, W. C. Borman, P. R. Jeanneret, and E. A. Fleishman (Eds.), *An occupational information system for the 21st century* (pp. 3–8). Washington, DC: American Psychological Assoication.

Duxbury, L., Higgins, C., and Neufeld, D. (1998). Telework and the balance between work and family. In M. Igbaria and M. Tan (Eds.), *The virtual workplace* (pp. 218–255). Hershey, PA: IDEA Publishing.

Dye, D., & Silver, M. (1999). The origins of O*NET. In N. G. Peterson, M. D. Mumford, W. C. Borman, P. R. Jeanneret, and E. A. Fleishman (Eds.), *An occupational information system for the 21st century* (pp. 9–20). Washington, DC: American Psychological Association.

Eagly, A. H. (1995). The science and politics of comparing men and women. *American Psychologist, 50,* 145–158.

Eagly, A. H., & Johnson, B. T. (1990). Gender and leadership style: A meta-analysis. *Psychological Bulletin, 108,* 233–256.

Eagly, A. H., Karau, S. J., & Makhijani, M. G. (1995). Gender and the effectiveness of leaders: A meta-analysis. *Psychological Bulletin, 117,* 125–145.

Eagly, A. H., Makhijani, M. G., & Klonsky, B. G. (1992). Gender and the evaluation of leaders: A meta-analysis. *Psychological Bulletin, 111,* 3–22.

Earley, P. C. (1989). Social loafing and collectivism: A comparison of the United States and the People's Republic of China. *Administrative Science Quarterly, 34,* 565–581.

Earley, P. C. (1993). East meets West meets Mideast: Further explorations of collectivistic and individualistic work groups. *Academy of Management Journal, 36,* 319–348.

Earley, P. C., Connolly, T., & Ekegren, G. (1989). Goals, strategy development, and task performance. *Journal of Applied Psychology, 74,* 24–33.

Earley, P. C. & Erez, M. (1997). Introduction. In P. C. Earley and M. Erez (Eds.), *New perspectives on international industrial/organizational psychology* (pp. 1–10). San Francisco: Jossey-Bass.

Eby, L. T., Freeman, D. M., Rush, M. C., & Lance, C. E. (1999). Motivational bases of affective organizational commitment: A partial test of an integrative theoretical model. *Journal of Occupational and Organizational Psychology, 72,* 463–483.

Edelstein, B. C., & Armstrong, D. J. (1993). A model for executive development. *Human Resource Planning, 16,* 46–51.

Eden, D. (2002). Personal Communication.

Edwards, J. R. (1996). An examination of competing versions of the person-environment fit approach to stress. *Academy of Management Journal, 39,* 292–339.

Edwards, J. R., & Rothbard, N. P. (1999). Work and family stress and well-being: An examination of person-environment fit in the work and family domains. *Organizational Behavior & Human Decision Processes, 77,* 85–129.

Edwards, J. R., Scully, J. A., & Brtek, M. D. (2000). The nature and outcomes of work: A replication and extension of interdisciplinary work design research. *Journal of Applied Psychology, 85,* 860–868.

Edworthy, J., & Adams, A. (1996). *Warning designs: A research perspective.* London: Taylor & Francis.

Eelles, K. (1951). *Intelligence and cultural differences.* Chicago: University of Chicago Press.

Einarsen, S. (2000). Harassment and bullying at work: A review of the Scandanavian approach. *Aggression and Violent Behavior: A Review Journal, 4,* 371–401.

Einarsen, S., Hoel, H., Zapf, D., and Cooper, C. (Eds). (2002). *Bullying and emotional abuse in the workplace.* London: Taylor & Francis.

Eliot, R. S., & Buell, J. C. (1983). The role of the central nervous system in sudden cardiac death. In T. M. Dembroski, T. Schmidt, & G. Blunchen (Eds.), *Biobehavioral bases of coronary-prone behavior.* New York: Karger.

Elkins, T. J., & Phillips, J. S. (2000). Job context, selection decision outcome, and the perceived fairness of selection tests: Biodata as an illustrative case. *Journal of Applied Psychology, 85,* 479–484.

Ellemers, N., de Gilder, D., & van den Heuvel, H. (1998). Career-oriented vs. team-oriented commitment and behavior at work. *Journal of Applied Psychology, 83,* 717–730.

Ellin, A. (2000, March 29). Training programs often miss the point on the job. *New York Times,* p. C12.

Elliott, R. H., & Jarrett, D. T. (1994). Violence in the workplace: The role of human resource management. *Public Personnel Management, 23,* 287–299.

Englebrecht, A. S., & Fischer, A. H. (1995). The managerial performance implications of a developmental assessment center process. *Human Relations, 48,* 387–404.

Erez, M. A. (1997). Culture based model of work motivation. In P. C. Earley and M. Erez (Eds.), *New perspectives on international industrial and organizational psychology* (pp. 193–242.). San Francisco: New Lexington Press.

Erez, M. A., & Eden, D. (2001). Introduction: Trends reflected in work motivation. In M. Erez, U. Kleinbeck, and H. Thierry (Eds.), *Work motivation in the context of a globalizing economy* (pp. 1–12). Mahwah, NJ: Erlbaum.

Ericsson, K. A., & Charness, N. (1994). Expert performance: Its structure and acquisition. *American Psychologist, 49,* 725–747.

Ericsson, K. A., Krampe, R. T., & Tesch-Romer, C. (1993). The role of deliberate practice in acquisition of expert performance. *Psychological Review, 100,* 363–406.

Ericsson, K. A., & Lehman, A. C. (1996). Expert and exceptional performance: Evidence of maximal adaptation to task constraints. *Annual Review of Psychology, 47,* 273–305.

Ericsson, K. A., & Simon, H. A. (1993). *Protocol analysis: Verbal reports as data.* Cambridge, MA: MIT Press.

Estrada, C. A., Isen, A. M., Young, M. J. (1997). Positive affect facilitates integration of information and decreases anchoring among physicians. *Organizational Behavior and Human Decision Processes, 72,* 117–135.

Etzion, D., & Westman, M. (1994). Social support and sense of control as moderators of the stress-burnout relationship in military careers. *Journal of Social Behavior & Personality, 9,* 639–656.

Evans, G. W. (1994). Working on the hot seat: Urban bus operators. *Accident and Analysis Prevention, 26,* 181–193.

Evans, G. W., & Carrere, S. (1991). Traffic congestion, perceived control, and psychophysiological stress among urban bus drivers. *Journal of Applied Psychology, 76,* 658–663.

Evans, G. W., & Johnson, D. (2000). Stress and open-office noise. *Journal of Applied Psychology, 85,* 779–783.

Ewen, R. B., Smith, P. C., Hulin, C. L., & Locke, E. A. (1966). An empirical test of the Herzberg two-factor theory. *Journal of Applied Psychology, 50,* 544–550.

Eyde, L. D., Moreland, K. L., Robertson, G. J., Primoff, E. S., & Most, R. B. (1988). *Test user qualifications: A data based approach to promoting good test use.* Washington, DC: American Psychological Association.

Fahr, J. L., Dobbins, G. H., & Cheng, B. S. (1991). Cultural relativity in action: A comparison of self-ratings made by Chinese and U.S. workers. *Personnel Psychology, 44,* 129–147.

Faragher v. City of Boca Raton, 118 S. Ct. 2275 (1998).

Farr, J. L., Hofmann, D. A., & Ringenbach, K. L. (1993). Goal orientation and action control theory: Implications for industrial and organizational psychology. In C. L. Cooper & I. T. Robertson (Eds.), *International review of industrial and organizational psychology* (pp. 193–232). New York: John Wiley.

Farr, J. L., & Ringseis, E. L. (2002). The older worker in organizational context: Beyond the individual. In C. Cooper and I. Robertson (Eds.), *International review of industrial and organizational psychology* (Vol. 17, pp. 31–76). Chichester, England: John Wiley.

Feild, H. S., & Holley, W. H. (1982). The relationship of performance appraisal system characteristics to verdicts in selected employment discrimination cases. *Academy of Management Journal, 25,* 392–406.

Feingold, A. (1994). Gender differences in personality: A meta-analysis. *Psychological Bulletin, 116,* 429–456.

Feldman, D. C. (1984). The development and enforcement of group norms. *Academy of Management Review, 9,* 47–53.

Feldman, D. C. (1989). Socialization, resocialization, and training: Reframing the research agenda. In I. L. Goldstein (Ed.), *Training and development in organizations. Frontiers of industrial and organizational psychology* (pp. 376–416). San Francisco: Jossey-Bass.

Feldman, J. M. (1981). Beyond attribution theory: Cognitive processes in performance appraisal. *Journal of Applied Psychology, 66,* 127–148.

Feldman, T. B., & Johnson, P. W. (1994, August). *Violence in the workplace: A preliminary investigation.* Paper presented at the annual meeting of the American Bar Association, New Orleans, LA.

Ferguson, L. (1965). *The heritage of industrial psychology.* Hartford, CT: Finlay Press.

Ferster, C. B., & Skinner, B. F. (1957). *Schedules of reinforcement.* New York: Appleton-Century-Crofts.

Festinger, L. (1957). *A theory of cognitive dissonance.* Evanston, IL: Row Peterson.

Fiedler, F. E. (1967). *A theory of leadership effectiveness.* New York: McGraw-Hill.

Filipczak, B. (1996, September). Training on the intranets: The hope and the hype. *Training, 33,* 24–32.

Fine, S. A. (1988). Functional job analysis. In S. Gael (Ed.), *Job analysis for business, industry, and government* (Vol. 2, pp. 1019–1035). New York: John Wiley.

Finkle, R. B. (1976). Managerial assessment centers. In M. D. Dunnette (Ed.), *Handbook of industrial and organizational psychology* (pp. 861–888). Chicago: Rand McNally.

Finnigan, A. (2001). The 100 best companies for working women: The inside story. *Working Woman.* Retrieved 2003, March 6, from http://www.workingwoman.com/oct_2001/inside_01.shtml

Fisher, C. D., & Ashkanasy, N. M. (2000). The emerging role of emotions in work life: An introduction. *Journal of Organizational Behavior, 21,* 123–129.

Fisher, S. G., Hunter, T. A., & Macrosson, W. D. (2001). A validation study of Belbin's team roles. *European Journal of Work and Organizational Psychology, 10,* 121–144.

Flanagan, J. C. (1954). The critical incidents technique. *Psychological Bulletin, 51,* 327–358.

Flannery, R. B. (1995). *Violence in the workplace.* New York: Crossroad Press.

Fleishman, E. A. (1967). Performance assessment based on an empirically derived task taxonomy. *Human Factors, 9,* 349–366.

Fleishman, E. A. (1975). Toward a taxonomy of human performance. *American Psychologist, 30,* 1127–1149.

Fleishman, E. A. (1992). *Fleishman Job Analysis Survey (F-JAS).* Bethesda, MD: Management Research Institute.

Fleishman, E. A., Costanza, D. P., & Marshall-Mies, J. (1999). Abilities. In N. G. Peterson, M. D. Mumford, W. C. Borman, P. R. Jeanneret, & E. A. Fleishman, (Eds.), *An occupational information system for the 21st century,* pp. 175–195. Washington, DC: American Psychological Association.

Fleishman, E. A., & Harris, E. F. (1962). Patterns of leadership behavior related to employee grievances and turnover. *Personnel Psychology, 15,* 43–56.

Fleishman, E. A., & Mumford, M. D. (1989). Individual attributes and training performance. In I. L. Goldstein (Ed.), *Training and development in organizations,* pp. 183–255. San Francisco: Jossey Bass.

Fleishman, E. A., Quaintance, M. K., & Broedling, L. A. (1984). *Taxonomies of human performance: The description of human tasks.* San Diego, CA: Academic Press.

Fleishman, E. A., & Reilly, M. E. (1992). *Handbook of human abilities: Definitions, measurements, and job task requirements.* Palo Alto, CA: Consulting Psychologists Press.

Fleishman, E. A., & Zaccaro, S. J. (1992). Toward a taxonomy of team performance functions. In R. W. Swezey & E. Salas (Eds.), *Teams: Their training and performance* (pp. 31–56). Stamford, CT: Ablex.

Flynn, J. R. (1984). The mean IQ of Americans: Massive gains 1932 to 1978. *Psychological Bulletin, 92,* 29–51.

Flynn, J. R. (1987). Massive gains in 14 nations: What IQ tests really measure. *Psychological Bulletin, 101,* 171–191.

Flynn, J. R. (1999). Searching for justice. *American Psychologist, 54,* 5–20.

Folger, R. (1977). Distributive and procedural justice: Combined impact of "voice" and improvement of experienced inequity. *Journal of Personality and Social Psychology, 35,* 108–119.

Folger, R., & Baron, R. A. (1996). Violence and hostility at work: A model of reactions to perceived injustice. In G. R. VandenBos, & E. Q. Bulatao, *Violence on the job: Identifying risks and developing solutions* (pp. 51–86). Washington, DC: American Psychological Association.

Folger, R., & Cropanzano, R. (1998). *Organizational justice and human resource management.* Thousand Oaks, CA: Sage.

Folger, R., & Konovsky, M. A. (1989). Effects of procedural and distributive justice on reactions to pay raise decisions. *Academy of Management Journal, 32,* 115–130.

Folkman, S. (1984). Personal control and stress and coping processes: A theoretical analysis. *Journal of Personality and Social Psychology, 46,* 839–852.

Ford, D. L. (1985). Job-related stress of the minority professional. In T. A. Beehr & R. S. Bhagat (Eds), *Human stress and cognition in organizations.* New York: John Wiley.

Ford, J. D., & Ford, L. W. (1994). Logics of identity, contradiction, and attraction in change. *Academy of Management Review, 19,* 756–785.

Ford, J. K., Smith, E. M., Weissbein, D. A., Gully, S. M., & Salas, E. (1998). Relationships of goal orientation, metacognitive activity, and practice strategies with learning outcomes and transfer. *Journal of Applied Psychology, 83,* 218–233.

Forsyth, D. R. (1999). *Group dynamics* (3rd ed.). Belmont, CA: Brooks/Cole/Wadsworth.

Fowers, B. J., & Richardson, F. C. (1996). Why is multiculturalism good? *American Psychologist, 51,* 609–621.

Fox, M. L., Dwyer, D. J., & Ganster, D. C. (1993). Effects of stressful job demand and control on physiological and attitudinal outcomes in a hospital setting. *Academy of Management Journal, 36,* 289–318.

Fox, S., & Spector, P. E. (1999). A model of work frustration-aggression. *Journal of Organizational Behavior, 20,* 915–931.

Freedman, J. L., & Edwards, D. R. (1988). Time pressure, task performance, and enjoyment. In J. E. McGrath (Ed.), *The social psychology of time* (pp. 113–133). Newbury Park, CA: Sage.

French, J. R. P., & Raven, B. H. (1959). The bases of social power. In D. Cartwright (Ed.), *Studies of social power* (pp. 150–157). Ann Arbor, MI: Institute for Social Research.

French, J. R. P., Caplan, R. D., & Harrison, R. V. (1982). *Mechanisms of job stress and strain.* New York: John Wiley.

Frese, M. (1999). Social support as a moderator of the relationship between work stressors and psychological dysfunctioning: A longitudinal study with objective measures. *Journal of Occupational Health Psychology, 3,* 179–192.

Frese, M., & Sabini, J. (1985). *Goal directed behavior: The concept of action in psychology.* Hillsdale, NJ: Erlbaum.

Frese, M., & Zapf, D. (1994). Action as core of work psychology: A German approach. In M. Dunnette, L. Hough, & H. C. Triandis (Eds.), *Handbook of industrial and organizational psychology* (2nd ed., vol. 4, pp. 271–340). Palo Alto, CA: Consulting Psychologists Press.

Fried, Y. (1991). Meta-analytic comparison of the Job Diagnostic Survey and Job Characteristics Inventory as correlates of work satisfaction and performance. *Journal of Applied Psychology, 76,* 690–697.

Fried, Y., Tiegs, R. B., & Bellamy, A. R. (1992). Personal and interpersonal predictors of supervisors' avoidance of evaluating subordinates. *Journal of Applied Psychology, 77,* 462–468.

Friedlander, F. (1980). The facilitation of change in organizations. *Professional Psychology, 11,* 520–530.

Friedman, M., & Rosenman, R. (1959). Association of specific overt behavior pattern with blood and cardiovascular findings. *Journal of the American Medical Association, 169,* 1286–1296.

Friedman, M., & Rosenman, R. (1974). *Type A behavior and your heart.* New York: Knopf.

Friedman, S. D., & Greenhaus, J. H. (2000). *Work and family—Allies or enemies? What happens when business professionals confront life choices?* Oxford, England: Oxford University Press.

Frisch, M. H. (1998). Designing the individual assessment process. In R. Jeanneret and R. Silzer (Eds.), *Individual psychological assessment* (pp. 135–177). San Francisco: Jossey-Bass.

Frone, M. R. (1998). Predictors of work injuries among employed adolescents. *Journal of Applied Psychology, 83,* 565–576.

Frone, M. R. (2000a). Interpersonal conflict at work and psychological outcomes: Testing a model among young workers. *Journal of Occupational Health Psychology, 5,* 246–255.

Frone, M. R. (2000b). Work-family conflict and employee psychiatric disorders: The National Comorbidity Survey. *Journal of Applied Psychology, 85,* 888–895.

Fryer, D. (1931). *Measurement of interest.* New York: Henry Holt.

Fulkerson, J. R., & Tucker, M. F. (1999). Diversity: Lessons from global human resource practices. In A. I. Kraut and A. K. Korman (Eds.), *Evolving practices in human resource management* (pp. 249–274). San Francisco: Jossey-Bass.

Fullerton, H. N. (1995). The 2005 labor force. *Monthly Labor Review, 118* (11), 29–44.

Gaddy, C. D., & Wachtel, J. A. (1992). Team skills training in nuclear power plant operations. In R. W. Swezey & E. Salas (Eds.), *Teams: Their training and performance* (pp. 379–396). Stamford, CT: Ablex.

Gael, S. (1979). *Job analysis.* New York: John Wiley.

Gael, S. (1988). *The job analysis handbook for business, industry, and government.* New York: John Wiley.

Gallagher, J. (2002, March 13). Judge likely to OK Ford payouts. *Detroit Free Press.*

Ganster, D. C., Fox, M. L., & Dwyer, D. J. (2001). Explaining employees' health care costs: A prospective examination of stressful job demands, personal control, and physiological reactivity. *Journal of Applied Psychology, 86,* 954–964.

Ganster, D. C., Mayes, B. T., Sime, W. E., & Tharp, G. D. (1982). Managing organizational stress: A field experiment. *Journal of Applied Psychology, 67,* 533–542.

Ganster, D. C., & Murphy, L. R. (2000). Workplace interventions to prevent stress-related illness: Lessons from research and practice. In C. L. Cooper & E. A. Locke (Eds.), *Industrial and organizational psychology: Linking theory with practice.* Malden, MA: Blackwell.

Ganster, D. C., & Schaubroeck, J. (1995). The moderating effects of self-esteem on the work stress–employee health relationship. In R. Crandall & P. L. Perrewe (Eds.), *Occupational stress: A handbook* (pp. 167–177). London: Taylor & Francis.

Ganzach, Y. (1995). Negativity (and positivity) in performance evaluation: Three field studies. *Journal of Applied Psychology, 80,* 491–499.

Gardiner, M., & Tiggemann, M. (1999). Gender differences in leadership style, job stress, and mental health in male- and female-dominated industries. *Journal of Occupational and Organizational Psychology, 72,* 301–315.

Gardner, H. (1983). *Frames of mind: The theory of multiple intelligences.* New York: Basic Books.

Gardner, H. (1993). *Multiple intelligences: The theory in practice.* New York: Basic Books.

Gardner, H. (2002, February 22). Good work, well done: A psychological study. *The Chronicle of Higher Education,* p. B7(3).

Gardner, H., Csikszentmihalyi, M., & Damon, W. (2001). *Good work: When excellence and ethics meet.* New York: Basic Books.

Garonzik, R., Brockner, J., & Siegel, P. A. (2000). Identifying international assignees at risk for premature departure: The interactive effect of outcome favorability and procedural fairness. *Journal of Applied Psychology, 85,* 13–20.

Garson, B. (1972, June). Luddites in Lordstown. *Harpers Magazine,* pp. 67–73.

Garson, B. (1994). *All the livelong day* (2nd ed.). New York: Penguin Books.

Gastorf, J. W. (1980). Time urgency of the Type A behavior pattern. *Journal of Consulting and Clinical Psychology, 48,* 299.

Gatewood, R. D., & Feild, H. S. (2001). *Human resource selection* (5th ed.). New York: Harcourt.

Gaugler, B. B., Rosenthal, D. B., Thornton, G. C., & Bentson, C. (1987). Meta-analysis of assessment center validity. *Journal of Applied Psychology, 72,* 493–511.

George, J. (1989). Mood and absence. *Journal of Applied Psychology, 74,* 317–324.

George, J. (1990). Personality, affect and behavior in groups. *Journal of Applied Psychology, 75,* 107–116.

George, J. (1991). State or trait: Effects of positive mood on prosocial behaviors at work. *Journal of Applied Psychology, 76,* 299–307.

George, J., & Brief, A. P. (1992). Feeling good—doing good: A conceptual analysis of the mood at work–organizational spontaneity relationship. *Psychological Bulletin, 112,* 310–329.

Georgopolous, B. S., Mahoney, G. M., & Jones, N. W. (1957). A path-goal approach to productivity. *Journal of Applied Psychology, 41,* 345–353.

Gersick, C. J. (1988). Time and transition in work teams: Toward a new model of group development. *Academy of Management Journal, 31,* 9–41.

Gersick, C. J. (1989). Marking time: Predictable transition in task groups. *Academy of Management Journal, 32,* 274–309.

Gersick, C. J. (1990). The bankers. In J. R. Hackman (Ed.), *Groups that work (and those that don't),* pp. 112–125. San Francisco: Jossey-Bass.

Gersick, C. J., & Davis-Sacks, M. L. (1990). Summary: Task forces. In J. R. Hackman (Ed.), *Groups that work (and those that don't),* pp. 146–153. San Francisco: Jossey-Bass.

Gerstner, C., & Day, D. V. (1997). Meta-analytic review of leader-member exchange theory: Correlates and construct issues. *Journal of Applied Psychology, 82,* 827–844.

Ghiselli, E. E. (1974, February). Some perspectives for industrial psychology. *American Psychologist,* 80–87.

Ghiselli, E. E., & Brown, C. W. (1955). *Personnel and industrial psychology* (2nd ed.). New York: McGraw-Hill.

Ghorpade, J., Hattrup, K., & Lackritz, J. R. (1999). The use of personality measures in cross-cultural research: A test of three personality scales across two countries. *Journal of Applied Psychology, 84,* 670–679.

Gibson, J. W., & Tesone, D. V. (2001). Management fads: Emergence, evolution, and implications for managers. *Academy of Management Executive, 15,* 122–133.

Gigone, D., & Hastie, R. (1997). Proper analysis of the accuracy of group judgments. *Psychological Bulletin, 121,* 149–167.

Gilbreth, F. B., & Carey, E. G. (1948). *Cheaper by the dozen.* New York: Thomas Y. Crowell.

Gilliland, S. W. (1993). The perceived fairness of selection systems: An organizational justice perspective. *Academy of Management Review, 18,* 694–734.

Gilliland, S. W. (1994). Effects of procedural and distributive justice on reactions to a selection system. *Journal of Applied Psychology, 79,* 691–701.

Gilliland, S. W., Benson, L., III, & Schepers, D. H. (1998). A rejection threshold in justice evaluations: Effects on judgment and decision making. *Organizational Behavior and Human Decision Processes, 76,* 113–131.

Gilliland, S. W., & Chan, D. (2001). Justice in organizations. In N. Anderson, D. Ones, H. Sinangil and C. Viswesvaran (Eds.), *Handbook of industrial, work, and organizational psychology* (Vol. 2, pp. 143–165). London: Sage.

Gilliland, S. W., & Cherry, B. (2000). Managing "customers" of selection processes. In J. Kehoe (Ed.), *Managing selection in changing organizations* (pp. 158–195). San Francisco: Jossey-Bass.

Gilliland, S. W., Groth, M., Baker, R. C., Dew, A. F., Polly, L. M., & Langdon, J. C. (2001). Improving applicants' reactions to rejection letters: An application of fairness theory. *Personnel Psychology, 54,* 699–703.

Gilliland, S. W., & Langdon, J. C. (1998). Creating performance management systems that promote perceptions of fairness. In J. W. Smither (Ed.), *Performance appraisal: State of the art in practice* (pp. 209–243). San Francisco: Jossey-Bass.

Ginnett, R. C. (1990). Airline cockpit crew. In J. R. Hackman (Ed.), *Groups that work (and those that don't)*. San Francisco: Jossey Bass.

Gist, M. E., & McDonald-Mann, D. (2000). Advances in leadership training and development. In C. L. Cooper & E. A. Locke (Eds.), *Industrial and organizational psychology: Linking theory with practice.* Malden, MA: Blackwell.

Gist, M. E., Schwoerer, C., & Rosen, B. (1989). Effects of alternative training methods on self-efficacy and performance in computer software training. *Journal of Applied Psychology, 74,* 884–891.

Gladstein, D. L. (1984). Groups in context: A model of task group effectiveness. *Administrative Science Quarterly, 29,* 499–517.

Glass, D. C. (1977). *Behavior patterns, stress and coronary disease.* Hillsdale, NJ: Erlbaum.

Glass, G. V. (1976). Primary, secondary, and meta-analysis of research. *Educational Researcher, 5,* 3–8.

Gleick, J. (1999). *Faster: The acceleration of just about everything.* New York: Pantheon Books.

Glomb, T. M., Munson, L. J., Hulin, C. L., Bergman, M. E., & Drasgow, F. (1999). Structural equation models of sexual harassment: Longitudinal explorations and cross-sectional generalizations. *Journal of Applied Psychology, 84,* 14–28.

Goetsch, D. L. (1996). *Occupational Safety and Health* (2nd ed.). Englewood Cliffs, NJ: Prentice Hall.

Goff, S. J., Mount, M. K., & Jamison, R. L. (1990). Employer supported child care, work/family conflict, and absenteeism: A field study. *Personnel Psychology, 43,* 793–809.

Goffin, R. D., Rothstein, M. G., & Johnston, N. G. (1996). Personality testing and the assessment center: Incremental validity for managerial selection. *Journal of Applied Psychology, 81,* 746–756.

Goldstein, I. L., & Ford, J. K. (2002). *Training in organizations: Needs assessment, development, and evaluation* (4th ed.). Belmont, CA: Wadsworth.

Goldstein, I. L., Zedeck, S., & Schneider, B. (1993). An exploration of the job analysis-content validity process.

In N. Schmitt & W. C. Borman (Eds.), *Personnel selection in organizations* (pp. 3–34). San Francisco: Jossey-Bass.

Goleman, D. (1995). *Emotional intelligence.* New York: Bantam Books.

Goleman, D. (1995). What's your EQ? The UTNE Lens, *UTNE Reader* (online). Retrieved March 6, 2003 from http://www.utne.com/lens/bms/eq.html

Gollwitzer, P. M. (1990). Action phases and mind sets. In E. T. Higgins and R. M. Sorrentino (Eds.), *Handbook of motivation and cognition: Foundations of social behavior* (Vol. 2, pp. 53–92). New York: Guilford Press.

Gollwitzer, P. M. (1993). Goal achievement: The role of intentions. In W. Strobe and M. Hewstone (Eds.), *European Review of Social Psychology* (Vol. 4, pp. 141–185). London: John Wiley.

Gollwitzer, P. M. (1999). Implementation intentions: Strong effects of simple plans. *American Psychologist, 54,* 493–503.

Gollwitzer, P. M., Heckhausen, H., & Ratajczak, H. (1990). From weighing to willing: Approaching a change decision through pre- or post-decisional mentation. *Organizational Behavior and Human Decision Processes, 45,* 41–65.

Goodman, P. S. (1986). The impact of task and technology on group performance. In P. S. Goodman (Ed.), *Designing effective work groups* (pp. 120–167). San Francisco: Jossey-Bass.

Goodman, P. S., Ravlin, E., & Schminke, M. (1987). Understanding groups in organizations. *Research in Organizational Behavior, 9,* 121–173.

Gottfredson, L. S. (1994). The science and politics of race norming. *American Psychologist, 49,* 955–963.

Graen, G. B. (1969). Instrumentality theory of work motivation. *Journal of Applied Psychology, 52* (2), 261–280, Part 2.

Graen, G. B., Liden, R. C., & Hoel, W. (1982). Role of leadership in the employee withdrawal process. *Journal of Applied Psychology, 67,* 868–872.

Graen, G. B., & Scandura, T. (1987). Toward a psychology of dyadic organizing. *Research in Organizational Behavior, 9,* 175–208.

Graen, G. B., & Uhl-Bein, M. (1991). The transformation of work group professionals into self-managing and partially self-designing contributors: Toward a theory of leadership making. *Journal of Management Systems, 3* (3), 33–48.

Graen, G. B., & Uhl-Bein, M. (1995). Relationship-based approach to leadership: Development of the leader-member (LMX) exchange theory over 25 years. Applying a multi-level domain approach. *Leadership Quarterly, 6,* 219–247.

Graham, M. E., & Welbourne, T. M. (1999). Gainsharing and women's and men's relative pay satisfaction. *Journal of Organizational Behavior, 20,* 1027–1042.

Grandey, A. (2000). Emotional regulation in the workplace: A new way to conceptualize emotional labor. *Journal of Occupational Health Psychology, 5*, 95–110.

Grandjean, E. (1988). *Fitting the task to the man* (4th ed.). London: Taylor & Francis.

Green, B., Kingsbury, G., Lloyd, B., Mills, C., Plake, B., Skaggs, et al. (1995). *Guidelines for Computerized Adaptive-Test (CAT) development and use in education* (Credit by Examination Program). Washington, DC: American Council on Education.

Greenberg, J. (1982). Approaching equity and avoiding inequity in groups and organizations. In J. Greenberg and R. L. Cohen (Eds.), *Equity and Justice in social behavior* (pp. 389–345). New York: Academic Press.

Greenberg, J. (1986). Determinants of perceived fairness of performance evaluations. *Journal of Applied Psychology, 71*, 340–342.

Greenberg, J. (1986). The distributive justice of organizational performance evaluations. In H. W. Bierhof, R. L. Cohen, and J. Greenberg (Eds.), *Justice in social relations*. New York: Plenum.

Greenberg, J. (1993). The social side of fairness: interpersonal and informational classes of organizational justice. In R. Cropazano (Ed.), *Justice in the workplace: Approaching fairness in human resource management* (pp. 79–103). Hillsdale, NJ: Erlbaum.

Greenberg, J. (1994). Using socially fair treatment to promote acceptance of a work site smoking ban. *Journal of Applied Psychology, 79*, 288–297.

Greenberg, J. (2002). *Managing behavior in organizations* (3rd ed.). Upper Saddle River, NJ: Prentice Hall.

Greenberg, J., & Scott, K. S. (1996). Why do workers bite the hands that feed them? Employee theft as a social exchange process. *Research in Organizational Behavior, 18*, 111–156.

Greenberg, J. A. (1990). Employee theft as a reaction to underpayment inequity: The hidden cost of pay cuts. *Journal of Applied Psychology, 75*, 561–568.

Greenberg, L., & Barling, J. (1999). Predicting employee aggression against co-workers, subordinates, and supervisors: The roles of person behaviors and perceived workplace factors. *Journal of Organizational Behavior, 20*, 897–913.

Greenfield, P. M. (1997). You can't take it with you: Why ability assessments don't cross cultures. *American Psychologist, 52*, 115–124.

Greenhaus, J. H., & Beutell, N. J. (1985). Sources of conflict between work and family roles. *Academy of Management Review, 10*, 76–88.

Greenwald, A. G. (1997). Validity concerns and usefulness of student ratings of instruction. *American Psychologist, 52*, 1182–1186.

Greenwald, A. J., & Gillmore, G. M. (1997). Grading leniency is a removable contaminant of student ratings. *American Psychologist, 52*, 1209–1217.

Greg, W. R. (1877). *Life at high pressure.* Boston: Osgood Publishing.

Griffin, M. A., & Kabanoff, B. (2001). Global vision: The psychology of safety. *The Industrial-Organizational Psychologist, 38*, 123–127.

Griffin, M. A., Landy, F. L., & Mayocchi, L. (2002). Australian influences on Elton Mayo: The construct of revery in industrial society. *History of Psychology, 5* (4), 356–375.

Griffin, R. W. (1988). Consequences of quality circles in an industrial setting: A longitudinal assessment. *Academy of Management Journal, 31*, 338–358.

Gross, M. L. (1962). *The brain watchers.* New York: Random House.

Grovier, T. (1994). An epistemology of trust. *International Journal of Moral Social Studies, 8*, 155–174.

Guernsey, L. (2000, March 2). Bookbag of the future. *New York Times,* pp. D1, D7.

Guion, R. M. (1965). *Personnel testing.* New York: McGraw-Hill.

Guion, R. M. (1980). On Trinitarian doctrines of validity. *Professional Psychology, 11*, 385–398.

Guion, R. M. (1998). *Assessment, measurement and prediction for personnel decisions.* Mahwah, NJ: Erlbaum.

Guion, R. M. (2002). Personal Communication.

Guion, R. M., & Cranny, C. J. (1982). A note on concurrent and predictive validity designs: A critical re-analysis. *Journal of Applied Psychology, 67* (2), 239–244.

Gulino et al., v. Board of Education of the New York City School District of the City of New York and the New York State Education Department. New York, NY, 86 Civ. 8414 (CBM).

Gully, S. M., Payne, S. C., Koles, K. L., & Whiteman, J. K. (2002). The impact of error training and individual differences on training outcomes: An attribute-treatment interaction perspective. *Journal of Applied Psychology, 87*, 143–155.

Gutierres, S. E., Saenz, D. S., & Green, B. L. (1994). Job stress and health outcomes among white and Hispanic employees: A test of the person-environment fit model. In G. P. Keita & J. J. Hurrell (Eds.), *Job stress in a changing workforce: Investigating gender, diversity, and family issues* (pp. 107–125). Washington, DC: American Psychological Association.

Gutman, A. (2000). *EEO law and personnel practices* (2nd ed.). Thousand Oaks, CA: Sage.

Gutman, A. (2001). On the legal front—so what's new at the EEOC? *The Industrial-Organizational Psychologist, 39*, 78–84.

Guzzo, R. A. (1995). Introduction: At the intersection of team effectiveness and decision making. In R. A. Guzzo & E. Salas (Eds.), *Team effectiveness and decision making in organizations*, pp. 1–8. San Francisco: Jossey-Bass.

Guzzo, R. A., & Dickson, M. W. (1996). Teams in organizations: Recent research on performance and effectiveness. *Annual Review of Psychology, 46*, 307–338.

Guzzo, R. A., & Shea, G. P. (1992). Group performance and intergroup relations in organizations. In M. D. Dunnette & L. M. Hough (Eds.), *Handbook of industrial and organizational psychology* (2nd ed., Vol. 3, pp. 269–313). Palo Alto, CA: Consulting Psychologists Press.

Haccoun, R. R., & Hamtiaux, T. (1994). Optimizing knowledge tests for inferring learning acquisition levels in single group training evaluation designs: The Internal Referencing Strategy. *Personnel Psychology, 47*, 593–604.

Hacker, W. (1992). *Expertkönnen: Erkönnen und vermitteln.* Göttingen, Germany: Hogrefe Verlag für Angewandte Psychologie.

Hackman, J. R. (1987). The design of work teams. In J. W. Lorsch (Ed.), *Handbook of Organizational Behavior* (pp. 315–342). Englewood Cliffs, NJ: Prentice Hall.

Hackman, J. R. (1990). *Groups that work (and those that don't).* San Francisco: Jossey-Bass.

Hackman, J. R. (1992). Group influences on individuals in organizations. In M. D. Dunnette & L. M. Hough (Eds.), *Handbook of industrial and organizational psychology* (2nd ed., Vol. 3, pp. 199–267). Palo Alto, CA: Consulting Psychologists Press.

Hackman, J. R., & Oldham, G. R. (1975). Development of the job diagnostic survey. *Journal of Applied Psychology, 60*, 159–170.

Hackman, J. R., & Oldham, G. R. (1976). Motivation through the design of work: Test of a theory. *Organizational Behavior and Human Performance, 16*, 250–279.

Hackman, J. R., & Oldham, G. R. (1980). *Work redesign.* Reading, MA: Addison-Wesley.

Hall, D. T., & Nougaim, K. E. (1968). An examination of Maslow's need hierarchy in an organizational setting. *Organizational Behavior and Human Performance, 3*, 12–35.

Hall, D. T., Otazo, K. L., & Hollenbeck, G. P. (1999). Behind closed doors: What really happens in executive coaching. *Organizational Dynamics, 27*, 39–53.

Hall, E. T. (1983). *The dance of life.* Garden City, NY: Anchor Press.

Hallam, G. (2001). Multisource feedback for teams. In D. W. Bracken, C. W. Timmreck, & A. H. Church (Eds.), *The handbook of multisource feedback*, pp. 289–300. San Francisco: Jossey-Bass.

Halpern, D. F. (1998). Teaching critical thinking for transfer across domains. *American Psychologist, 53*, 449–455.

Hancock, P. A., Lesch, M., & Simmons, L. (2003). The distraction effects of phone use during a crucial driving maneuver. *Accident Analysis and Prevention, 35*, 501–514.

Hanges, P. J., Schneider, B., & Niles, K. (1990). Stability of performance: an interactionist perspective. *Journal of Applied Psychology, 75*, 658–667.

Hanisch, K. A. (1992). The Job Descriptive Index revisited: Questions about the question mark. *Journal of Applied Psychology, 77*, 377–382.

Hanisch, K. A., & Hulin, C. L. (1990). Job attitudes and organizational withdrawal: An examination of retirement and other voluntary withdrawal behaviors. *Journal of Vocational Behavior, 37*, 60–78.

Hanisch, K. A., & Hulin, C. L. (1991). General attitudes and organizational withdrawal: An evaluation of a causal model. *Journal of Vocational Behavior, 39*, 110–128.

Hannafin, K. M., & Hannafin, M. J. (1995). The ecology of distance learning environments. *Training Research Journal, 1*, 49–69.

Hannan, M. T., & Carroll, G. R. (1992). *Dynamics of organizational populations: Density, legitimation, and competition.* New York: Oxford University Press.

Hannan, M. T., & Freeman, J. (1977). The population ecology of organizations. *American Journal of Sociology, 82*, 929–964.

Harris, D. A. (1987). Joint service job performance measurement enlistment standards project. *The Industrial-Organizational Psychologist, 24*, 36–42.

Harris, G., & Hogan, J. (1992). *Perceptions and personality correlates of managerial effectiveness.* Paper presented at the 13th annual Psychology in the Department of Defense Symposium, Colorado Springs, CO.

Harris, M. (1998). Competency modeling: Viagraized job analysis or impotent imposter. *The Industrial-Organizational Psychologist, 36* (2), 37–42.

Harris, M., & Heft, R. (1993). Pre-employment urinalysis drug testing: A critical review of psychometric and legal issues and effects on applicants. *Human Resource Management Review, 3*, 271–191.

Harris, M. M. (1998). The structured interview: What constructs are being measured? In R. Eder and M. Harris (Eds.), *The employment interview: Theory, research and practice* (2nd ed.). Thousand Oaks, CA: Sage.

Harris, M. M. (2000). *Human resource management: A practical approach* (2nd ed.). New York: Dryden Press.

Harrison, D. A., Kravitz, D. A., & Lev-Arey, D. (2001). Attitudes toward affirmative action programs: A meta-analysis of 25 years of research on government mandated approaches to reducing employment discrimination. In D. Kravitz (Facilitator). *Affirmative Action: Some New Perspectives.* Symposium at the annual meeting of the Academy of Management, Washington, DC.

Harrison, D. A., Price, K. H., & Bell, M. P. (1998). Beyond relational demography: Time and the effects of surface- and deep-level diversity on work group cohesion. *Academy of Management Journal, 41*, 96–107.

Harrison, D. A., Price, K. H., Gavin, J. H., & Florey, A. T. (2002). Time, teams, and task performance: Changing effects of surface- and deep-level diversity on group functioning. *Academy of Management Journal, 45*, 1029–1045.

Harrison, J. K. (1992). Individual and combined effects of behavior modeling and the cultural assimilator in cross-cultural management training. *Journal of Applied Psychology, 77*, 952–962.

Hartigan, J., & Wigdor, A. K. (1989). *Fairness in employment testing: Validity generalization, minority issues, and the general aptitude test battery.* Washington, DC: National Academies Press.

Hartley, J. (2002). Organizational change and development. In P. B. Warr (Ed.), *Psychology at Work* (5th ed., pp. 399–425). London: Penguin Books.

Harvey, R. J. (1991). Job analysis. In M. D. Dunnette & L. M. Hough (Eds.), *Handbook of industrial and organizational psychology* (2nd ed., Vol. 1, pp. 71–163). Palo Alto, CA: Consulting Psychologists Press.

Hattrup, K., & Jackson, S. E. (1996). Learning about individual differences by taking situations seriously. In K. R. Murphy (Ed.), *Individual differences and behavior in organizations* (pp. 507–547). San Francisco: Jossey-Bass.

Hattrup, K., O'Connell, M. S., & Wingate, P. H. (1998). Prediction of multidimensional criteria: Distinguishing task and contextual performance. *Human Performance, 11*, 305–319.

Hauenstein. N. M. A. (1998). Training raters to increase the accuracy of appraisals and the usefulness of feedback. In J. W. Smither (Ed.), *Performance appraisal: State of the art in practice* (pp. 404–443). San Francisco: Jossey-Bass.

Hawkridge, D. (1999). Distance learning: International comparisons. *Performance Improvement Quarterly, 12*, 9–20.

Heckhausen, H. (1977). Achievement motivation and its constructs. A cognitive model. *Motivation and Emotion, 1*, 283–329.

Heckhausen, H., Gollwitzer, P. M., & Weinert, F. E. (Eds.) (1987). *Jenseits des Rubikon: Der Wille in den Humanwissenschaften.* Berlin: Springer Verlag.

Heckhausen, J. (1997). Developmental regulation across adulthood. Primary and secondary control of age-related challenges. *Developmental Psychology, 33*, 176–187.

Hedge, J. W., & Borman, W. C. (1995). Changing conceptions and practices in performance appraisal. In A. Howard (Ed.), *The changing nature of work* (pp. 451–481). San Francisco: Jossey-Bass.

Hedge, J. W., & Teachout, M. S. (1992). An interview approach to work sample criterion measurement. *Journal of Applied Psychology, 77*, 453–461.

Hedge, J. W., Teachout, M. S., & Laue, F. J. (1990). *Interview testing as a work sample measure of job proficiency* (AFHRL-TP-89-60). Brooks Air Force Base, TX: Air Force Systems Command.

Heggestad, E. D., & Kanfer, R. (2001). Individual differences in trait motivation: Development of the Motivational Trait Questionnaire. *International Journal of Educational Research, 33*, 751–776.

Heilman, M. E., & Alcot, V. B. (2001). What I think you think of me: Women's reactions to being viewed as beneficiaries of preferential selection. *Journal of Applied Psychology, 86*, 574–582.

Heilman, M. E., Battle, W. S., Keller, C. E., & Lee, R. A. (1998). Type of affirmative action policy: A determinant of reactions to sex-based preferential selection? *Journal of Applied Psychology, 83*, 190–205.

Heilman, M. E., & Blader, S. L. (2001). Assuming preferential selection when admissions policy is unknown: The effects of gender rarity. *Journal of Applied Psychology, 86*, 188–193.

Heilman, M. E., Block, C. J., & Lucas, J. A. (1992). Presumed incompetent? Stigmatization and affirmative action efforts. *Journal of Applied Psychology, 77*, 536–544.

Heilman, M. E., McCullough, W. F., & Gilbert, D. (1996). The other side of affirmative action: Reactions of non-beneficiaries to sex-based preferential selection. *Journal of Applied Psychology, 81*, 346–357.

Helander, M. (1997). The human factors profession. In G. Salvendy, *Handbook of human factors and ergonomics* (2nd ed., pp. 3–17). New York: John Wiley.

Heller, E. (2002, January 21). Chief Witness: A cellphone. *National Law Journal*, p. B10.

Hemingway, M. (2001). Qualitative research in I-O psychology. *The Industrial-Organizational Psychologist, 38* (3), 45–51.

Hemingway, M. A., & Conte, J. M. (in press). The perceived fairness of layoff practices. *Journal of Applied Social Psychology.*

Hemphill, J. K. (1959). Job descriptions for executives. *Harvard Business Review, 37*, 55–67.

Heneman, R. L. (1986). The relationship between supervisory ratings and results-oriented measures of performance: A meta-analysis. *Personnel Psychology, 39*, 811–826.

Heneman, R. L., Ledford, G. E., Jr., & Gresham, M. T. (2000). The changing nature of work and its effects on compensation design and delivery. In S. L. Rynes & B. Gerhart (Eds.), *Compensation in organizations* (pp. 195–240). San Francisco: Jossey-Bass.

Herlihy, B. (1977). Watch out, IQ myth: Here comes another debunker. *Phi Delta Kappan, 59*, 298.

Hermans, H. J. M., & Kempen, H. J. G. (1998). Moving cultures: The perilous problems of cultural dichotomies in a globalizing society. *American Psychologist, 53*, 1111–1120.

Herriot, P., & Pemberton, C. (1995). *Competitive advantage through diversity*. London: Sage.

Hersey, P., & Blanchard, K. H. (1977). *The management of organizational behavior* (3rd ed.). Englewood Cliffs, NJ: Prentice Hall.

Hershberger, S. L., Lichenstein, P., & Knox, S. S. (1994). Genetic and environmental influences on perceptions of organizational climates. *Journal of Applied Psychology, 79* (1), 24–33.

Herzberg, F. (1966). *Work and the nature of man.* Cleveland: World Publishing.

Herzberg, F., Mausner, B., Peterson, R. O., & Capwell, D. F. (1957). *Job attitudes: Review of research and opinion*. Pittsburgh, PA: Psychological Service of Pittsburgh.

Herzberg, F., Mausner, B., & Snyderman, B. (1959). *The motivation to work.* New York: John Wiley.

Hewitt Associates, LLC (1995). *Work and family benefits provided by major U.S. employers in 1994*. New York: Author.

Hewlett, S. A. (2002). *Creating a life: Professional women and the quest for children*. New York: Talk Miramax Books.

Hill, E. J., Miller, B. C., Weiner, S. P., & Colihan, J. (1998). Influences of the virtual office on aspects of work and work/life balance. *Personnel Psychology, 51*, 667–683.

Hinrichs, J. R., & Mischkind, L. A. (1967). Empirical and theoretical limitations of the two factor hypothesis of job satisfaction. *Journal of Applied Psychology, 51*, 191–200.

Hnath, E. A. (2002). Personal Communication.

Hochschild, A. R. (1983). *The managed heart: Commercialization of human feeling*. Berkeley: University of California Press.

Hoel, H., Cooper, C. L., & Faragher (2001). The experience of bullying in Great Britain: The impact of organizational status. *European Journal of Work and Organizational Psychology, 10*, 485–496.

Hoffmann, C. C. (1999). Generalizing physical ability test validity: A case study using test transportability, validity generalization, and construct-related validation evidence. *Personnel Psychology, 52*, 1019–1041.

Hofmann, D. A., Jacobs, R. R., & Landy, F. J. (1995). High reliability process industries: Individual, micro, and macro organizational influences on safety performance. *Journal of Safety Research, 26*, 131–149.

Hofmann, D. A., & Morgeson, F. P. (1999). Safety-related behavior as a social exchange: The role of perceived organizational support and leader-member exchange. *Journal of Applied Psychology, 84*, 286–296.

Hofmann, D. A., & Stetzer, A. (1996). A cross-level investigation of factors influencing unsafe behaviors and accidents. *Personnel Psychology, 49*, 307–339.

Hofmann, D. A., & Stetzer, A. (1998). The role of safety climate and communication in accident interpretation: implication from negative events. *Academy of Management Journal, 41*, 644–657.

Hofstede, G. (1980a). *Culture's consequences: International differences in work-related values*. Beverly Hills, CA: Sage.

Hofstede, G. (1980b). Motivation, leadership and organizations: Do American theories apply abroad? *Organizational Dynamics, 9*(1) 42–63.

Hofstede, G. (1984). *Culture's consequences: International differences in work-related values*. Newbury Park, CA: Sage.

Hofstede, G. (1991). *Culture and organizations: Software of the mind*. New York: McGraw-Hill.

Hofstede, G. (1993). Cultural constraints in management theories. *Academy of Management Executive, 7*, 91.

Hofstede, G. (2001). *Culture's consequences: Comparing values, behaviors, institutions, and organizations across nations*. Thousand Oaks, CA: Sage.

Hogan, J. (1991a). Physical abilities. In M. D. Dunnette & L. M. Hough (Eds). *Handbook of industrial and organizational psychology* (2nd ed., Vol. 2, pp. 753–831). Palo Alto, CA: Consulting Psychologists Press.

Hogan, J. (1991b). Structure of physical performance in occupational tasks. *Journal of Applied Psychology, 76*, 495–507.

Hogan, J., & Hogan, R. (1989). How to measure employee reliability. *Journal of Applied Psychology, 74*, 273–279.

Hogan, J., & Roberts, B. W. (1996). Issues and non-issues in the fidelity-bandwidth trade-off. *Journal of Organizational Behavior, 17*, 627–637.

Hogan, R., & Blake, R. J. (1996). Vocational interests: Matching self concept with the work environment. In K. R. Murphy (Ed.), *Individual differences and behavior in organizations* (pp. 89–144). San Francisco: Jossey-Bass.

Hogan, R., Curphy, G. J., & Hogan, J. (1994). What we know about leadership: Effectiveness and personality. *American Psychologist, 49*, 493–504.

Hogan, R., Hogan, J., & Roberts, B. W. (1996). Personality measurement and employment decisions. *American Psychologist, 51*, 469–477.

Holland, B., & Hogan, R. (1998). Remodeling the electronic cottage. *The Industrial-Organizational Psychologist, 36* (2), 21–22.

Holland, J. L. (1973). *Making vocational choices: A theory of careers*. Englewood Cliffs, NJ: Prentice Hall.

Holland, J. L. (1985). *Making vocational choices: A theory of careers* (2nd ed.) Englewood Cliffs, NJ: Prentice Hall.

Holland, J. L. (1994). *Self directed search Form R*. Lutz, FL: Psychological Assessment Resources.

Hollander, E. P., & Julian, J. W. (1969). Contemporary trends in the analysis of the leadership process. *Psychological Bulletin, 71,* 387–397.

Hollenbeck, G. P. (2001). Coaching executives: Individual leader development. In R. F. Silzer (Ed.), *The 21st century executive: Innovative practices for building leadership at the top.* San Francisco: Jossey-Bass.

Hollenbeck, G. P., & McCall, M. W. (1999). Leadership development: Contemporary practices. In A. I. Kraut & A. K. Korman (Eds.), *Evolving practice in human resource management.* San Francisco: Jossey-Bass.

Hom, P. W., & Griffeth, R. W. (1995). *Employee turnover.* Cincinnati, OH: Southwestern.

Hoppock, R. (1935). *Job satisfaction.* New York: Harper & Row.

Horner, K. L. (1996). Locus of control, neuroticism, and stressors: Combined influences on reported physical illness. *Personality & Individual Differences, 21,* 195–204.

Hosking, D. M. (1988). Chairperson's address: Organizing through skillful leadership. *British Psychological Society: The Occupational Psychologist, 4,* 4–11.

Hough, L. M. (1992). The "Big Five" personality variables—construct confusion: Description vs. prediction. *Human Performance, 5,* 139–155.

Hough, L. M. (1998). Effects of intentional distortion in personality measurement and evaluation of suggested palliatives. *Human Performance, 11,* 209–244.

Hough, L. M., Eaton, N. K., Dunnette, M. D., Kamp, J. D., & McCloy, R. A. (1990). Criterion-related validities of personality constructs and the effect of response distortions on those validities. *Journal of Applied Psychology [Monograph] 75,* 581–595.

Hough, L. M., & Ones, D. S. (2001). The structure, measurement, validity and use of personality variables in industrial, work, and organizational psychology. In N. Anderson, D. S. Ones, H. K. Siningal, and C. Viswesvaran (Eds.), *Handbook of industrial, work, and organizational psychology* (pp. 233–277). London: Sage.

Hough, L. M., & Schneider, R. J. (1996). Personality traits, taxonomies, and applications in organizations. In K. R. Murphy (Ed.), *Individual differences and behavior in organizations* (pp. 31–88). San Francisco: Jossey-Bass.

House, J. S. (1981). *Work stress and social support.* Reading, MA: Addison-Wesley.

House, R. J. (1971). A path-goal theory of leader effectiveness. *Administrative Science Quarterly, 16,* 321–339.

House, R. J. (1977). A 1976 theory of charismatic leadership. In J. G. Hunt & L. L. Larson (Eds.), *Leadership: The cutting edge.* Carbondale: Southern Illinois University Press.

House, R. J., & Dessler, G. (1974). The path-goal theory of leadership: Some post hoc and a priori tests. In J. Hunt & L. Larson (Eds.), *Contingency approaches to leadership.* Carbondale: Southern Illinois University Press.

House, R. J., Hanges, P. J., Ruiz-Quintanilla, S. A., Dorfman, P. W. Javidian, M., Dickson, M., et al. (1999). Cultural influences on leadership and organization: Project GLOBE. In W. Mobley, J. Gessner, and V. Arnold (Eds.), *Advances in global leadership* (Vol. 1, pp. 171–234). Stamford, CT: JAI Press.

House, R. J., Javidian, M., & Dorfman, P. (2001). Project GLOBE: An introduction. *Applied Psychology: An International Review, 50* (4), 489–505.

House, R. J., & Mitchell, T. R. (1974). Path-goal theory of leadership. *Contemporary Business, 3* (Fall), 81–98.

House, R. J., & Singh, J. V. (1987). Organizational behavior: Some new directions for I-O psychology. *Annual Review of Psychology, 38,* 669–718.

House, R. J., Wright, N. S., & Aditya, R. N. (1997). Cross-cultural research on organizational leadership: A critical analysis and proposed theory. In P. C. Early & M. Erez (Eds.), *New perspectives on international industrial and organizational psychology,* pp. 535–625. San Francisco: Jossey-Bass.

Houser, J. D. (1927). *What the employer thinks.* Cambridge: Harvard University Press.

Howard, A. (1990). *The multiple facets of industrial/ organizational psychology: Membership survey results.* Arlington Heights, IL: Society for Industrial and Organizational Psychology.

Howard, A. (1991). New directions for human resources practice. In D. W. Bray (Ed.), *Working with Organizations and their people: A guide to human resources practice,* pp. 219–251. New York: Guilford Press.

Howard, A. (2001). Identifying, assessing, and selecting senior leaders. In S. J. Zaccaro and R. J. Klimoski (Eds.), *The nature of organizational leadership: Understanding the performance imperatives confronting today's leaders* (pp. 305–346). San Francisco: Jossey-Bass.

Howard, A., & Associates (1991). *Diagnosis for organizational change: Methods and models.* New York: Guilford Press.

Howell, W. C. (1993). Engineering psychology in a changing world. *Annual Review of Psychology, 44,* 231–263.

Hubbard, A. (2002, June). Successful ethics training. *Mortgage Banking, 62,* 104–108.

Hubert, A. B., & Veldhoven, M. (2001). Risk sectors for undesirable behavior and mobbing. *European Journal of Work and Organizational Psychology, 10,* 415–424.

Huffcutt, A. I., & Arthur, W., Jr. (1994). Hunter and Hunter (1984) revisited: Interview validity for entry level jobs. *Journal of Applied Psychology, 79,* 184–190.

Huffcutt, A. I., Conway, J. M., Roth, P. L., & Stone, N. J. (2001). Identification and meta-analytic assessment of psychological constructs measured in employment interviews. *Journal of Applied Psychology, 86,* 897–913.

Huffcutt, A. I., & Roth, P. L. (1998). Racial group differences in employment interview evaluations. *Journal of Applied Psychology, 83,* 179–189.

Huffcut, A. I., & Woehr, D. J. (1999). Further analysis of the employment interview validity: A quantitative evaluation of interviewer-related structuring methods. *Journal of Organizational Behavior, 20,* 549–560.

Hui, C. H., & Yee, C. (1999). The impact of psychological collectivism and workgroup atmosphere on Chinese employees' job satisfaction. *Applied Psychology: An International Review, 48,* 175–185.

Hulin, C. L. (1991). Adaptation, persistence, and commitment in organizations. In M. D. Dunnette & L. M. Hough (Eds.), *Handbook of industrial and organizational psychology* (2nd ed., Vol. 2, pp. 445–505). Palo Alto, CA: Consulting Psychologists Press.

Hulin, C. L., & Mayer, L. J. (1986). Psychometric equivalence of a translation of the Job Descriptive Index into Hebrew. *Journal of Applied Psychology, 71,* 83–94.

Hull, C. L. (1928). *Aptitude testing.* Yonkers, NY: World Book.

Human Dynamics Associates. *Team Jumpstart: 1-800-Skyjump.* Pepperill, MA: Author.

Hunter, J. E., & Hunter, R. F. (1984). Validity and utility of alternative predictors of job performance. *Psychological Bulletin, 96,* 72–98.

Hunter, J. E., Schmidt, F. L., & Jackson, G. B. (1982). *Meta-analysis: Cumulating research findings across studies.* Beverly Hills, CA: Sage.

Hunter, J. E., Schmidt, F. L., & Pearlman, K. (1979). *Assessing the impact of intervention programs in workforce productivity.* Washington, DC: Office of Personnel Management.

Hurrell, J. J. (1985). Machine-paced work and the Type A behaviour pattern. *Journal of Occupational Psychology, 58,* 15–25.

Hurrell, J. J., Nelson, D. L., & Simmons, B. L. (1998). Measuring job stressors and strains: Where we have been, where we are, and where we need to go. *Journal of Occupational Health Psychology, 3,* 368–389.

Hurrell, J. J., Worthington, K. A., & Driscoll, R. J. (1996). Job stress, gender, and workplace violence: Analysis of assault experiences of state employees. In G. R. VandenBos & E. Q. Bulatao (Eds.), *Violence on the job: Identifying risks and developing solutions* (pp. 163–170). Washington, D.C.: American Psychological Association.

Hurtz, G. M., & Donovan, J. J. (2000). Personality and job performance: The Big Five revisited. *Journal of Applied Psychology, 85,* 869–879.

Huselid, M. A. (1995). The impact of human resource management practices on turnover, productivity, and corporate financial performance. *Academy of Management Journal, 38,* 635–672.

Hyde, J. S., & Plant, E. A. (1995). Magnitude of psychological gender differences: Another side to the story. *American Psychologist, 50,* 159–161.

Iacono, W. G., & Lykken, D. T. (1997). The validity of the lie detector: Two surveys of scientific opinion. *Journal of Applied Psychology, 82,* 426–433.

Igalens, J., & Roussel, P. (1999). A study of the relationships between compensation package, work motivation, and job satisfaction. *Journal of Organizational Behavior, 20,* 1003–1025.

Igbaria, M., & Tan, M. (1998). *The virtual workplace.* Hershey, PA: IDEA Publishing.

Ilgen, D. R. (1990). Health issues at work: Opportunities for industrial/organizational psychologists. *American Psychologist, 45,* 273–283.

Ilgen, D. R. (1999). Teams embedded in organizations: Some implications. *American Psychologist, 54,* 129–139.

Ilgen, D. R., & Pulakos, E. D. (1999). Employee performance in today's organizations. In D. R. Ilgen & E. D. Pulakos (Eds.), *The changing nature of performance: Implications for staffing, motivation, and development.* San Francisco: Jossey-Bass.

Impara, J. C., & Plake, B. S. (Eds.) (1998). *The thirteenth mental measurements yearbook.* Lincoln, NE: Buros Institute of Mental Measurements, University of Nebraska.

Isen, A. (1999). Positive affect and creativity. In S. Russ (Ed.), *Affect, creative experience, and psychological adjustment* (pp. 3–17). Philadelphia: Bruner/Mazel.

Isen, A. M., & Baron, R. A. (1991). Positive affect as a factor in organizational behavior. *Research in Organizational Behavior, 13,* 1–53.

Ivancevich, J. M., & Matteson, M. T. (2002). *Organizational behavior and management* (6th ed.). New York: McGraw-Hill.

Ivancevich, J. M., Matteson, M. T., & Richards, E. P. (1985). Who's liable for stress at work. *Harvard Business Review* (Vol. 63, pp. 60–72).

Jablonski, J. R. (1991). *Implementing Total Quality Management: An Overview.* San Francisco: Pfeiffer.

Jackson, M. (2002, September 8). Can a test gauge the value of an MBA? *New York Times,* p. B12.

Jackson, S. E. (1983). Participation in decision making as a strategy for reducing job related strain. *Journal of Applied Psychology, 68,* 3–19.

Jackson, S. E. (1991). Team composition in organizational settings: Issues in managing an increasingly diverse workforce. In S. Worchel, W. Wood, & J. A. Simpson (Eds.), *Group process and productivity* (pp. 138–173). Newbury Park, CA: Sage.

Jackson, S. E. (1996). The consequences of diversity in multidisciplinary work teams. In M. A. West (Ed.),

Handbook of work group psychology. Chichester, England: John Wiley.

Jackson, S. E., Brett, J. F., Sessa, V. I., Cooper, D. M., Julin, J. A., & Peyronnin, K. (1991). Some differences make a difference: Individual dissimilarity and group heterogeneity as correlates of recruitment, promotions, and turnover. *Journal of Applied Psychology, 76,* 675–689.

Jackson, S. E., & Joshi, A. (2001). Research on domestic and international diversity in organizations: A merger that works? In N. Anderson, D. Ones, H. Sinangil, and C. Viswesvaran (Eds.), *Handbook of industrial, work, and organizational psychology* (Vol. 1, pp. 206–231). London: Sage.

Jackson, S. E., May, K. E., & Whitney, K. (1995). Understanding the dynamics of diversity in decision-making teams. In R. Guzzo and E. Salas (Eds.), *Team effectiveness and decision-making in organizations* (pp. 204–261). San Francisco: Jossey-Bass.

Jackson, S. E., & Schuler, R. S. (1985). A meta-analysis and conceptual critique of research on role ambiguity and role conflict in work settings. *Organizational Behavior & Human Decision Processes, 36,* 16–78.

Jacobs, R. R., Hofmann, D. A., & Kriska, S. D. (1990). Performance and seniority. *Human Performance, 3,* 107–121.

Jaeger, R. M. (1989). Certification of student competence. In R. L. Linn (Ed.), *Educational Measurement* (3rd ed.), pp. 485–514. New York: American Council on Education/Macmillan.

Jahoda, M. (1981). Work, employment and unemployment: Values, theories and approaches in social research. *American Psychologist, 36,* 184–191.

James, K. (1994). Social identity, work stress, and minority workers' health. In G. P. Keita & J. J. Hurrell (Eds.), *Job stress in a changing workforce: Investigating gender, diversity, and family issues* (pp. 127–145). Washington, DC: American Psychological Association.

James, K. (1997). Worker social identity and health-related costs for organizations: A comparative study between ethnic groups. *Journal of Occupational Health Psychology, 2,* 108–117.

James, L. A., & James, L. R. (1989). Integrating work environment perceptions: Explorations in the measurement of meaning. *Journal of Applied Psychology, 69,* 85–98.

James, L. R., & McIntyre, M. D. (1996). Perceptions of organizational climate. In K. R. Murphy (Ed.), *Individual differences and behavior in organizations* (pp. 416–450). San Francisco: Jossey-Bass.

Janis, I. L. (1982). *Groupthink: A study of foreign policy decisions and fiascos* (2nd ed.). Boston: Houghton Mifflin.

Jeanneret, P. R. (1992). Applications of job component/synthetic validity to construct validity. *Human Performance, 5,* 81–96.

Jentsch, F., & Bowers, C. A. (1998). Evidence for the validity of PC-based simulations in studying aircrew coordination. *International Journal of Aviation Psychology, 8,* 243–260.

Jeppensen, J. C. (2002). Creating and maintaining the learning organization. In K. Kraiger (Ed.), *Creating, implementing, and managing effective training and development* (pp. 302–330). San Francisco: Jossey-Bass.

Jex, S. M. (1998). *Stress and job performance: Theory, research, and implications for managerial practice.* Thousand Oaks, CA: Sage.

Jex, S. M. (2002). *Organizational psychology: A scientist-practitioner approach.* New York: John Wiley.

Johns, G. (2001). The psychology of lateness, absenteeism, and turnover. In N. Anderson, D. Ones, H. Sinangil, & C. Viswesvaran (Eds.), *Handbook of industrial, work, and organizational psychology* (Vol 2, pp. 233–252). London: Sage.

Johnson, J. W. (2001). The relative importance of task and contextual performance dimensions to supervisor judgments of overall performance. *Journal of Applied Psychology, 86,* 984–996.

Johnson, L. C., Tepas, D. I., Colquhoun, W. P., & Colligan, M. J. (1981). *Biological rhythms, sleep, and shift work.* New York: Spectrum.

Johnson, M. (1999, October). Use anti-harassment training to shelter yourself from suits. *HR Magazine, 44,* 76–81.

Joinson, C. (2002, June). Managing virtual teams. *HR Magazine, 47,* 68–73.

Jones, G. R. (1984). Task visibility, free riding, and shirking: Explaining the effect of structure and technology on employee behavior. *Academy of Management Review, 9,* 684–695.

Jones, J. M. (1988). Cultural differences in temporal perspectives: Instrumental and expressive behaviors in time. In J. E. McGrath (Ed.), *The social psychology of time: New perspectives* (pp. 21–38). Thousand Oaks, CA: Sage.

Jones, J. W., Barge, B. N., Steffy, B. D., Fay, L. M., Kunz, L. K., & Wuebker, L. J. (1988). Stress and medical malpractice: Organizational risk assessment and intervention. *Journal of Applied Psychology, 73,* 727–735.

Jones, R. G., & Whitmore, M. D. (1995). Evaluating developmental assessment centers as interventions. *Personnel Psychology, 48,* 377–388.

Jones, R. G., Stevens, M. J., & Fischer, D. L. (2000). Selection in team contexts. In J. Kehoe (Ed.), *Managing selection in changing organizations* (pp. 210–241). San Francisco: Jossey-Bass.

Jones, S., & Moffett, R. G. (1999). Measurement and feedback for teams. In E. Sundstrom (Ed.), *Supporting team effectiveness: Best management practices for fostering high performance.* San Francisco: Jossey-Bass.

Judge, T. A., & Bono, J. E. (2000). Five factor model of personality and transformational leadership. *Journal of Applied Psychology, 85,* 751–765.

Judge, T. A., & Bono, J. E. (2001). Relationship of core self evaluations traits—self esteem, generalized self efficacy, locus of control, and emotional stability—with job satisfaction and job performance: A meta-analysis. *Journal of Applied Psychology, 86,* 80–92.

Judge, T. A., Bono, J. E., & Locke, E. A. (2000). Personality and job satisfaction: The mediating role of job characteristics. *Journal of Applied Psychology, 85,* 237–249.

Judge, T. A., Bono, J. E., Ilies, R., & Gerhardt, M. W. (2002). Personality and Leadership: A qualitative and quantitative review. *Journal of Applied Psychology, 87,* 765–780.

Judge, T. A., & Cable, D. M. (1997). Applicant personality, organizational culture, and organization attraction. *Personnel Psychology, 50,* 359–394.

Judge, T. A., & Ferris, G. R. (1993). Social context of performance evaluation decisions. *Academy of Management Journal, 36,* 80–105.

Judge, T. A., & Hulin, C. L. (1993). Job satisfaction as a reflection of disposition: A multiple source causal analysis. *Organizational Behavior and Human Decision Processes, 56,* 388–421.

Judge, T. A., & Ilies, R. (2002). Relationship of personality to performance motivation: A meta-analytic review. *Journal of Applied Psychology, 87,* 797–807.

Judge, T. A., Locke, E. A., & Durham, C. C. (1997). The dispositional causes of job satisfaction: A core evaluations approach. *Research in Organizational Behavior, 19,* 151–188.

Judge, T. A., Locke, E. A., Durham, C. C., & Kluger, A. N. (1998). Dispositional effects on job and life satisfaction: The role of core evaluations. *Journal of Applied Psychology, 83,* 17–34.

Judge, T. A., Parker, S., Colbert, A. E., Heller, D., & Ilies, R. (2001). Job satisfaction: A cross-cultural review. In N. Anderson, D. Ones, H. Sinangil, and C. Viswesvaran (Eds.), *Handbook of industrial, work, and organizational psychology* (Vol. 2, pp. 25–52). London: Sage.

Judge, T. A., Thoreson, C. J., Bono, J. E., & Patton, G. K. (2001). The job satisfaction—job performance relationship: A qualitative and quantitative review. *Psychological Bulletin, 127,* 376–407.

Judge, T. A., Thoreson, C. J., Pucik, V., & Welbourne, T. M. (1999). Managerial coping with organizational change: A dispositional perspective. *Journal of Applied Psychology, 84,* 107–122.

Judge, T. A., & Watanabe, S. (1995). Is the past prologue? A test of Ghiselli's Hobo syndrome. *Journal of Management, 21,* 211–229.

Judge, T. A., & Welbourne, T. M. (1994). A confirmatory investigation of the dimensionality of the pay satisfaction questionnaire. *Journal of Applied Psychology, 79,* 461–466.

Juran, J. M. (1992). *Juran on quality by design: The new steps for planning quality into goods and services.* New York: Free Press.

Kabanoff, B. (1991). Equity, equality, power, and conflict. *Academy of Management Review, 16,* 416–441.

Kabanoff, B. (1997). Organizational justice across cultures: Integrating organization-level and culture-level perspectives. In P. C. Earley & M. Erez (Eds.), *New perspectives on international industrial/organizational psychology* (pp. 676–712). San Francisco: Jossey-Bass.

Kaeter, M. (1993). Cross-training: The tactical view. *Training, 30* (3), 35–36.

Kanfer, R., & Kantrowitz, T. M. (2002). Ability and nonability predictors of job performance. In S. Sonnentag (Ed.), *Psychological management of individual performance* (pp. 27–50). New York: John Wiley.

Kahn, R. L., & Byosiere, P. (1992). Stress in organizations. In M. D. Dunnette & L. M. Hough (Eds.), *Handbook of industrial and organizational psychology* (2nd ed., Vol. 3 571–650). Palo Alto, CA: Consulting Psychologists Press.

Kahn, R. L., Wolfe, D. M., Quinn, R. P., Snoek, J. D., & Rosenthal, R. A. (1964). *Organizational stress: Studies in role conflict and ambiguity.* New York: John Wiley.

Kahneman, D., Slovic, P., & Tversky, A. (Eds.) (1982). *Judgment under uncertainty: Heuristics and biases.* New York: Cambridge University Press.

Kanfer, R. (1992). Work motivation: New directions in theory and research. *International Review of Industrial and Organizational Psychology, 7,* 2–53.

Kanfer, R., & Ackerman, P. L. (1989). Motivation and cognitive abilities: An integrative adaptive treatment interaction approach to skill acquisition. *Journal of Applied Psychology, 74,* 657–690.

Kanfer, R., & Ackerman, P. L. (2000). Individual differences in work motivation: Further explorations of a trait framework. *Applied Psychology: An International Review, 49,* 470–482.

Kanfer, R., Ackerman, P. L., Murtha, T. C., & Dugdale, B. (1994). Goal setting, conditions of practice, and task performance: A resource allocation perspective. *Journal of Applied Psychology, 79,* 826–835.

Kanfer, R., & Heggestad, E. D. (1997). Motivational traits and skills: A person centered approach to work motivation. *Research in Organizational Behavior, 19,* 1–56.

Kanter, R., Stein, B., & Jick, T. (1992). *The challenge of organizational change.* New York: Free Press.

Kaplan, R. M., & Saccuzzo, D. P. (2001). *Psychological testing: Principles, applications, and issues* (5th ed.). Belmont, CA: Wadsworth.

Karasek, R. A. (1979). Job demands, job decision latitude, and mental strain: Implications for job redesign. *Administrative Sciences Quarterly, 24,* 285–308.

Karasek, R. A., Russell, R. S., & Theorell, T. (1982). Physiology of stress and regeneration in job related cardiovascular illness. *Journal of Human Stress, 8,* 29–42.

Karasek, R. A., & Theorell, T. (1990). *Healthy work.* New York: Basic Books.

Katkowski, D. A., & Metsker, G. J. (2001). SIOP income and employment: Income and employment of SIOP members in 2000. *The Industrial-Organizational Psychologist, 39* (1), 21–36.

Katz, D., & Kahn, R. L. (1978). *The social psychology of organizations* (2nd ed.). New York: John Wiley.

Katz, M. R. (1987). Theory and practice: The rationale for a career guidance workbook. *Career Guidance Quarterly, 36,* 31–44.

Katzell, R. A., & Austin, J. T. (1992). From then to now: The development of industrial-organizational psychology in the United States. *Journal of Applied Psychology, 77,* 803–835.

Katzell, R. A., & Thompson, D. E. (1990). An integrative model of work attitudes, motivation, and performance. *Human Performance, 3* (2), 63–85.

Katzell, R. A., Thompson, D. E., & Guzzo, R. A. (1992). How job satisfaction and job performance are and are not linked. In C. J. Cranny, P. C. Smith, and E. F. Stone (Eds.), *Job satisfaction: How people feel about their work and how it affects their performance* (pp. 195–217). New York: Lexington Books.

Kay, E., Meyer, H., & French, J. (1965). Effects of threat in a performance interview. *Journal of Applied Psychology, 49,* 311–317.

Keita, G. P., & Hurrell, J. J. (1994). *Job stress in a changing workforce: Investigating gender, diversity, and family issues.* Washington, DC: American Psychological Association.

Keller, F. J., & Viteles, M. S. (1937). *Vocational guidance throughout the world.* New York: W. W. Norton.

Kelley, H. (1967). Attribution theory in social psychology. In D. Levine (Ed.), *Nebraska symposium on motivation.* Lincoln: University of Nebraska Press.

Kennish, J. W. (1995). Violence in the workplace. *Professional Safety, 40,* 34–36.

Kenny, D. A., & DePaulo, B. M. (1993). Do people know how others view them? An empirical and theoretical account. *Psychological Bulletin, 114,* 145–161.

Kernan, M. C., & Hanges, P. J. (2002). Survivor reactions to reorganization: Antecedents and consequences of procedural, interpersonal, and informational justice. *Journal of Applied Psychology, 87,* 916–928.

Kiker, D. S., & Motowidlo, S. J. (1999). Main and interaction effects of task and contextual performance

on supervisory reward decisions. *Journal of Applied Psychology, 84,* 602–609.

King, M. L., Jr. (1956, August 11). Speech to Alpha Phi Alpha fraternity. Chicago, IL.

King, N. (1970). Clarification and evaluation of the two factor theory of job satisfaction. *Psychological Bulletin, 74,* 18–31.

Kinicki, A. J., McKee-Ryan, F. M., Schriesheim, C. A., & Carson, K. P. (2002). Assessing the construct validity of the Job Descriptive Index: A review and meta-analysis. *Journal of Applied Psychology, 87,* 14–32.

Kinney, J. A. (1995a). *Essentials of managing workplace violence.* Charlotte, NC: Pinkerton Services.

Kinney, J. A. (1995b). *Violence at work: How to make your company safer for employees and customers.* Englewood Cliffs, NJ: Prentice Hall.

Kinney, J. A. (1996). The dynamics of threat management. In G. R. VandenBos, & E. Q. Bulatao (Eds.), *Violence on the job: Identifying risks and developing solutions* (pp. 299–314). Washington, DC: American Psychological Association.

Kirchner, W. W., Dunnette, M. D., & Mousely, N. (1960). Use of the Edwards Personal Preference Schedule in the selection of salesmen. *Personnel Psychology, 13,* 421–424.

Kirkpatrick, D. L. (1959). Techniques for evaluating training programs. *Journal of the American Society of Training Directors, 13,* 3–9.

Kirkpatrick, D. L. (1998). *Evaluating training programs: The four levels* (2nd ed.). San Francisco: Berrett-Koehler.

Klahr, D., & Simon, H. A. (1999). Studies of scientific discovery: Complementary approaches and convergent findings. *Psychological Bulletin, 125,* 524–543.

Klein, H. J. (1991a). Control theory and understanding motivated behavior: A different conclusion. *Motivation and Emotion, 15,* 29–44.

Klein, H. J. (1991b). Further evidence on the relationship between goal setting and expectancy theories. *Organizational Behavior and Human Decision Processes, 49,* 230–257.

Klimoski, R., & Brickner, M. (1987). Why do assessment centers work? The puzzle of assessment center validity. *Personnel Psychology, 40,* 243–260.

Kluger, A. N., & DeNisi, A. (1996). Effects of feedback intervention on performance: A historical review, a meta-analysis, and a preliminary feedback intervention theory. *Psychological Bulletin, 119,* 254–284.

Knorz, C., & Zapf, D. (1996). Mobbing: An extreme form of social stressors at the workplace. *Zeitschrift für Personalforschung, 12,* 352–362.

Ko, J., Price, J. L., & Mueller, C. W. (1997). Assessment of Meyer and Allen's three component model of organizational commitment in South Korea. *Journal of Applied Psychology, 82,* 961–973.

Kobasa, S. C. (1979). Stressful life events, personality, and health: An inquiry into hardiness. *Journal of Personality & Social Psychology, 37,* 1–11.

Kobasa, S. C., Maddi, S. R., & Kahn, S. (1982). Hardiness and health: A prospective study. *Journal of Personality & Social Psychology, 42,* 168–177.

Kohn, J. P., Friend, M. A., & Winterberger, C. A. (1996). *Fundamentals of occupational safety and health.* Rockville, MD: Government Institutes.

Konrad, A. M., Ritchie, J. E., Lieb, P., & Corrigal, E. (2000). Sex differences and similarities in job attribute preferences: A meta-analysis. *Psychological Bulletin, 112,* 593–641.

Koppes, L. L. (1997). American female pioneers of industrial and organizational psychology during the early years. *Journal of Applied Psychology, 82,* 500–515.

Korabik, K., & McDonald, L. M. (1991). Sources of stress and ways of coping among male and female managers. *Journal of Social Behavior and Personality, 6,* 1–14.

Korman, A. (1971). *Industrial and organizational psychology.* Englewood Cliffs, NJ: Prentice Hall.

Kornhauser, A. W. (1929). Industrial psychology in England, Germany and the United States. *Personnel Journal, 8,* 421–434.

Kotter, J. P. (1995, March–April). Leading change: Why transformation efforts fail. *Harvard Business Review, 73,* 59–67.

Koys, D. J. (2001). The effects of employee satisfaction, organizational citizenship behavior, and turnover on organizational effectiveness: A unit-level, longitudinal study. *Personnel Psychology, 54,* 101–114.

Kozlowski, S. W. J., Chao, G. T., & Morrison, R. F. (1998). Games raters play: Politics, strategies, and impression management in performance appraisal. In J. W. Smither (Ed.), *Performance appraisal: State of the art in practice* (pp. 163–208). San Francisco: Jossey-Bass.

Kozlowsky, M., Sagie, A., Krausz, M., & Singer, A. (1997). Correlates of employee lateness: Some theoretical considerations. *Journal of Applied Psychology, 82,* 79–88.

Kraiger, K. (2002a). Decision-based evaluation. In K. Kraiger (Ed.), *Creating, implementing, and managing effective training and development* (pp. 331–375). San Francisco: Jossey-Bass.

Kraiger, K. (2002b). Training and development in organizations. In W. C. Borman, D. R. Ilgen, & R. J. Klimoski (Eds.), *Comprehensive handbook of psychology: Vol. 12. Industrial and Organizational Psychology.* New York: John Wiley.

Kraiger, K., Ford, J. K., & Salas, E. (1993). Application of cognitive, skill-based, and affective theories of learning outcomes to new methods of training evaluation. *Journal of Applied Psychology, 78,* 311–328.

Kraiger, K., & Smith-Jentsch, K. (2002). Evidence of the reliability and validity of collective climates in work teams. Unpublished manuscript.

Kramer, R. M. (1999). Trust and distrust in organizations: Emerging perspectives, enduring questions. *Annual Review of Psychology, 50,* 569–598.

Krantz, D. S., & Manuck, S. B. (1984). Acute psychophysiologic reactivity and risk of cardiovascular disease: A review and methodologic critique. *Psychological Bulletin, 96,* 435–464.

Krantz, D. S., & McCeney, M. K. (2002). Effects of psychological and social factors on organic disease: A critical reassessment of research on coronary heart disease. *Annual Review of Psychology, 53,* 31–369.

Kraut, A. I., and Korman, A. K. (1999). The DELTA forces causing change in human resource management. In A. I. Kraut and A. K. Korman (Eds.), *Evolving practices in human resource management* (pp. 3–22). San Francisco: Jossey-Bass.

Kravitz, D. A., Harrison, D. A., Turner, M. E., Levine, E. L., Chaves, W., Brannick, M., et al. (1997). *Affirmative action: A review of psychological and behavioral research.* Bowling Green, OH: Society for Industrial and Organizational Psychology.

Kravitz, D. A., & Klineberg, S. L. (2000). Reactions to two versions of affirmative action among whites, blacks and Hispanics. *Journal of Applied Psychology, 85,* 597–611.

Kravitz, D. A., Klineberg, S. L., Avery, D. R., Nguyen, A. K., Lund, C., & Fu, E. J. (2000). Attitudes toward affirmative action: Correlations with demographic variables and with beliefs about targets, actions and economic effects. *Journal of Applied Social Psychology, 30,* 1109–1136.

Kravitz, D. A., Stinson, V., & Chavez, T. L. (1996). Evaluations of tests used for making selection and promotion decisions. *International Journal of Selection and Assessment, 4,* 24–34.

Krueger, J. (2001). Null hypothesis significance testing: On the survival of a flawed method. *American Psychologist, 56,* 16–26.

Kuder, G. F. (1966). The occupational interest survey. *Personnel and Guidance Journal, 45,* 72–77.

Kuder, G. F., & Diamond, E. E. (1979). *Kuder occupational interest survey general manual.* Chicago: Science Research Associates.

Kudish, J. D., Rotolo, C. T., Avis, J. M., Fallon, J. D., Roberts, F. E., Rollier, T. J., & Thibodeaux, H. F. (1998). *A preliminary look at assessment center practices worldwide: What's hot and what's not.* Paper presented at the 26th annual meeting of the International Congress on Assessment Center Methods, Pittsburgh, PA.

Kuhl, J. (1992). A theory of self-regulation: Action versus state orientation, self-discrimination, and some applications. *Applied Psychology: An International Review, 41* (2), 97–129.

Kuhl, J., & Kraska, K. (1989). Self-regulation and meta-motivation: Computational mechanisms, development and assessment. In R. Kanfer, P. L. Ackerman, & R. Cudek (Eds.), *Abilities, motivation, and methodology* (pp. 343–374). Hillsdale, NJ: Erlbaum.

Kunin, T. (1955). The construction of a new type of attitude measure. *Personnel Psychology, 8,* 70–71.

Kunin, T. (1998). The construction of a new type of attitude measure. *Personnel Psychology, 51,* 823–824. (Reprinted from 1955).

Kupperschmidt, B. R. (2000). Multigenerational employees: Strategies for effective management. *The Health Care Manager, 19,* 65–76.

Kurz, R., & Bartram, D. (2002). Competency and individual performance: Modeling the world of work. In I. T. Robertson, M. Callinan, & D. Bartram (Eds.), *Organizational effectiveness: The role of psychology* (pp. 227–255). New York: John Wiley.

Laabs, J. J. (1992) Surveillance: Tool or trap. *Personnel Journal, 71,* 96–104.

Lance, C. E., Newbolt, W. H., Gatewood, R. D., Foster, M. R., French, N. R., & Smith, D. E. (2000). Assessment center exercise factors represent cross-situational specificity, not method bias. *Human Performance, 13,* 323–353.

Landsberger, H. A. (1958). *Hawthorne revisited: Management and the worker, its critics and developments in human relations in industry.* Ithaca: New York State School of Industrial and Labor Relations.

Landy, F. J. (1978). An opponent process theory of job satisfaction. *Journal of Applied Psychology, 63,* 533–547.

Landy, F. J. (1986). Stamp collecting versus science: Validation as hypothesis testing. *American Psychologist, 41,* 1183–1192.

Landy, F. J. (1987). *Psychology: The science of people* (2nd ed.). Englewood Cliffs, NJ: Prentice Hall.

Landy, F. J. (1988). Selection procedure development and usage. In S. Gael (Ed.), *The job analysis handbook for business, industry, and government* (Vol. 1, pp. 271–287). New York: John Wiley.

Landy, F. J. (1989). *Psychology of work behavior* (4th ed.). Pacific Grove, CA: Brooks Cole.

Landy, F. J. (1992). Hugo Munsterberg: Victim or visionary. *Journal of Applied Psychology, 77,* 787–802.

Landy, F. J. (1993). Early influences on the development of industrial and organizational psychology. In American Psychological Association, *Exploring applied psychology* (pp. 81–118). Washington, DC: Author.

Landy, F. J. (1997). Early influences on the development of industrial and organizational psychology. *Journal of Applied Psychology, 82,* 467–477.

Landy, F. J. (2001). Age, race and gender in organizations. In N. J. Smelser & P. B. Baltes (Eds.), *International encyclopedia of social and behavioral sciences* (pp. 271–275). Oxford, England: Pergamon.

Landy, F. J. (2002a). Legal implications of web-based applicant screening. Paper presented at the annual meeting of the Society for Industrial and Organizational Psychology, Toronto, Canada, April 12–14.

Landy, F. J. (2002b). Does classical measurement theory apply to I-O Psychology? The reliability of job performance ratings. Paper presented at the annual meetings of the Society for Industrial and Organizational Psychology, Toronto, Canada, April 12–14.

Landy, F. J. (2002c). Validity generalization theory then and now. In K. R. Murphy (Ed.), *Validity generalization: A critical review.* Mahwah, NJ: Erlbaum.

Landy, F. J., Barnes, J., & Murphy, K. (1978). Correlates of perceived fairness and accuracy of performance appraisals. *Journal of Applied Psychology, 63,* 751–754.

Landy, F. J., Barnes-Farrell, J., & Cleveland, J. N. (1980). Perceived fairness and accuracy of performance evaluation: A follow-up. *Journal of Applied Psychology, 65,* 355–356.

Landy, F. J., Bland, R. E., Buskirk, E. R., Daly, R. E., Debusk, R. F., Donavan, E. J., et al. (1992). *Alternatives to chronological age in determining standards of suitability for public safety jobs.* University Park, PA: Center for Applied Behavioral Sciences.

Landy, F. J., & Farr, J. L. (1980) Performance rating. *Psychological Bulletin, 87,* 72–107.

Landy, F. J., & Farr, J. L. (1983). *The measurement of work performance: methods, theory, and applications.* New York: Academic Press.

Landy, F. J., Farr, J. L., & Jacobs, R. R. (1982). Utility concepts in performance measurement. *Organizational Behavior & Human Decision Processes, 30,* 15–40.

Landy, F. J., & Guion, R. M. (1970). Development of scales for the measurement of work motivation. *Organizational Behavior and Human Performance, 5,* 93–103.

Landy, F. J., Quick, J. C., & Kasl, S. (1994). Work, stress, and well-being. *International Journal of Stress Management, 1,* 33–73.

Landy, F. J., Rastegary, H., Thayer, J., & Colvin, C. (1991). Time urgency: The construct and its measurement. *Journal of Applied Psychology, 76,* 644–657.

Landy, F. J., Rosenberg, B. G., & Sutton-Smith, B. (1969). The effect of limited father absence on the cognitive development of children. *Child Development, 40,* 941–944.

Landy, F. J., Shankster, L. J., & Kohler, S. S. (1994). Personnel selection and placement. *Annual Review of Psychology, 45,* 261–296.

Landy, F. J., Zedeck, S., & Cleveland, J. N. (1983). *Performance measurement and theory.* Hillsdale, NJ: Erlbaum.

Landy, Jacobs and Associates (1997, November). *TOSS-LESS project final report.* State College, PA: Author.

Langewiesche, W. (2002). *American ground: Unbuilding the World Trade Center.* New York: North Point Press.

Lanning v. *SEPTA,* U.S. Dist. LEXIS, 9388 (1998).

Lanning v. *SEPTA,* 181, F.3d 478 (3rd Cir. 1999); *cert. Denied,* 120 S. Ct. 970 (2000).

Lanning v. *SEPTA,* U.S. Dist. LEXIS 17612. (2000).

Larson, J. R., & Callahan, C. (1990). Performance monitoring: How it affects work productivity. *Journal of Applied Psychology, 75,* 530–538.

Latané, B., Williams, K., & Harkins S. (1979). Many hands make light the work: The causes and consequences of social loafing. *Journal of Personality and Social Psychology, 37,* 822–832.

Latham, G. P. (1986). Job performance and appraisal. In C. Cooper and I. Robertson (Eds.), *International review of industrial and organizational psychology.* Chichester, England: John Wiley.

Latham, G. P., & Skarlicki, C. P. (1996). The effectiveness of situational, patterned behaviour, and conventional structured interviews in minimizing in-group favouritism of Canadian francophone managers. *Applied Psychology: An International Review, 45,* 177–184.

Latham, G. P., & Wexley, K. N. (1981). *Increasing productivity through performance appraisal.* Reading, MA: Addison-Wesley.

Latham, G. P., & Whyte, G. (1994). The futility of utility analysis. *Personnel Psychology, 47,* 31–46.

Laughery, K. R, Sr., & Wogalter, M. S. (1997). Warnings and risk perception. In G. Salvendy (Ed.), *Handbook of human factors and ergonomics* (2nd ed., pp. 1174–1198). New York: John Wiley.

Lauver, K. J., & Kristof-Brown, A. (2001). Distinguishing between employees' perceptions of person–job and person–organization fit. *Journal of Vocational Behavior, 59,* 454–470.

Law, K. S., & Wong, C. (1998). Relative importance of referents on pay satisfaction: A review and test of a new policy-capturing approach. *Journal of Occupational and Organizational Psychology, 71,* 47–60.

Lawler, E. E. (1971). *Pay and organizational effectiveness: A psychological review.* New York: McGraw-Hill.

Lawler, E. E. (1973). *Motivation in work organizations.* Monterey, CA: Brooks/Cole.

Lawler, E. E., & Suttle, J. L. (1972). A causal correlational test of the need hierarchy concept. *Organizational Behavior and Human Performance, 7,* 265–287.

Lawler, E. E., Mohrman, S. A., & Ledford, G. (1992). *Employee involvement and TQM: Practice and results in Fortune 500 companies.* San Francisco: Jossey-Bass.

Lawrence, P. R., & Lorsch, J. (1967). *Organization and environment.* Cambridge: Harvard University Press.

Lazarus, R. S. (1991). Progress on a cognitive-motivational-relational theory of emotion. *American Psychologist, 46,* 819–834.

Lazarus, R. S. (2000). Toward better research on stress and coping. *American Psychologist, 55,* 665–673.

LeBlanc, M. M., & Kelloway, E. K. (2002). Predictors and outcomes of workplace violence and aggression. *Journal of Applied Psychology, 87,* 444–453.

Lee, K., Carswell, J. J., & Allen, N. J. (2000). A meta-analytic review of occupational commitment: Relations with person- and work-related variables. *Journal of Applied Psychology, 85,* 799–811.

Lee, R. T., & Ashforth, B. E (1996). A meta-analytic examination of the correlates of the three dimensions of job burnout. *Journal of Applied Psychology, 81,* 123–133.

Lefkowitz, J. (1994). Sex-related differences in job attitudes and dispositional variables: Now you see them. . . *Academy of Management Journal, 37,* 323–349.

Leib, J., Morgan, R., & Hughes, J (2003, January 3). Mechanic disables jet, citing safety concerns. *Denver Post,* pp. 1A, 9A.

Levine, R. L., West, L. J., & Reis, H. T. (1980). Perceptions of time and punctuality in the United States and Brazil. *Journal of Personality and Social Psychology, 38,* 541–550.

Levine, R. V. (1997). *A geography of time: The temporal misadventures of a social psychologist, or how every culture keeps time just a little bit differently.* New York: HarperCollins.

Levine, R. V., Lynch, K., Miyake, K., Lucia, M. (1989). The Type A city: Coronary heart disease and the pace of life. *Journal of Behavioral Medicine, 12,* 509–524.

Levine, R. V., & Norenzayan, A. (1999). The pace of life in 31 countries. *Journal of Cross-Cultural Psychology, 30,* 178–205.

Lewin, K. (1935). *A dynamic theory of personality.* New York: McGraw-Hill.

Lewin, K. (1938). *The conceptual representation and the measurement of psychological forces.* Durham, NC: Duke University Press.

Lewin, K. (1951). *Field theory in social psychology.* New York: Harper.

Lewin, K., Lippitt, R., & White, R. K. (1939). Patterns of aggressive behavior in experimentally created "social climates." *Journal of Social Psychology, 10,* 271–299.

Lewin, T. (2002, June 28). College Board announces an overhaul for the SAT. *New York Times,* p. A12.

Lewis, S., & Cooper, C. L. (1999). The work-family research agenda in changing contexts. *Journal of Occupational Health Psychology, 4,* 382–393.

Leymann, H. (1996). The content and development of mobbing at work. *European Journal of Work and Organizational Psychology, 5,* 165–184.

Likert, R. (1961). *New patterns of management.* New York: McGraw-Hill.

Likert, R. (1967) *The human organization: Its management and value.* New York: McGraw-Hill.

Litwin, G. H., & Stringer, R. A. (1966). *Motivation and organizational climate.* Cambridge: Harvard University, Graduate School of Business Administration, Division of Research.

Locke, E. A. (1968). Toward a theory of task motivation and incentives. *Organizational Behavior and Human Performance, 3,* 157–189.

Locke, E. A. (1976). The nature and causes of job satisfaction. In M. D. Dunnette (Ed.), *Handbook of industrial and organizational psychology* (pp. 1297–1343). Chicago: Rand McNally.

Locke, E. A. (1980). Latham vs. Komaki: A tale of two paradigms. *Journal of Applied Psychology, 65*(1), 16–23.

Locke, E. A. (1986). *Generalizing from laboratories to field settings.* Lexington, MA: Lexington Books.

Locke, E. A. (2001). Self-set goals and self-efficacy as mediators of incentives and personality. In M. Erez, U. Kleinbeck, and H. Thierry (Eds.), *Work motivation in the context of a globalizing economy* (pp. 13–26). Mahwah, NJ: Erlbaum.

Locke, E. A., & Henne, D. (1986). Work motivation theories. In C. L. Cooper & I. T. Robertson (Eds.), *International review of industrial and organizational psychology* (pp. 1–35). Chichester, England: John Wiley.

Locke, E. A., & Latham, G. P. (1990). *A theory of goal setting and task performance.* Englewood Cliffs, NJ: Prentice Hall.

Locke, E. A., & Latham, G. P. (1994). Goal setting theory. In H. F. O'Neil, Jr., & M. Drilling (Eds.), *Motivation: Theory and research* (pp. 13–29). Hillsdale, NJ: Erlbaum.

Locke, E. A., & Latham, G. P. (1996). Goal setting theory: An introduction. In R. M. Steers, L. W. Porter, and G. A. Bigley (Eds.), *Motivation and leadership at work* (pp. 95–122). New York: McGraw-Hill.

Locke, E. A., Shaw, K. N., Saari, L. M., & Latham, G. P. (1981). Goal setting and task performance. *Psychological Bulletin, 90,* 125–152.

Locke, K., & Golden-Biddle, K. (2002). An introduction to qualitative research. In S. Rogelberg (Ed.), *Handbook of research methods in industrial and organizational psychology* (pp. 99–118). Cambridge, MA: Blackwell.

Loher, B. T., Hazer, J. T., Tsai, A., Tilton, K., & James, J. Letters of reference: A process approach. *Journal of Business and Psychology, 11,* 339–355.

London, M. (2002). *Leadership development: Paths to self-insight and professional growth.* Mahwah, NJ: Erlbaum.

London, M., & Mone, E. M. (1999). Continuous learning. In D. R. Ilgen & E. D. Pulakos (Eds.), *The changing nature of performance: Implications for staffing, motivation, and development.* San Francisco: Jossey-Bass.

Longnecker, C. O., Sims, H. P., & Gioia, D. A. (1987). Behind the mask: The politics of performance appraisal. *Academy of Management Executive 1,* 183–193.

Lord, R. G., & Gradwohl-Smith, W. (1999). Leadership and the changing nature of performance. In D. R. Ilgen & E. D. Pulakos (Eds.), *The changing nature of performance: Implications for staffing, motivation, and development* (pp. 192–239). San Francisco: Jossey-Bass.

Love, K. G., Bishop, R. C., Heinisch, D. A., & Montei, M. S. (1994). Selection across two cultures: Adapting the selection of American assemblers to met Japanese job performance demands. *Personnel Psychology, 47,* 837–846.

Lovelace, K., & Rosen, B. (1996). Differences in achieving person-organization fit among diverse groups of managers. *Journal of Management, 22,* 703–722.

Lowman, R. L. (1985a). *Casebook on ethics and standards for the practice of psychology in organizations.* Bowling Green, OH: Society for Industrial and Organizational Psychology.

Lowman, R. L. (1985b). Ethical practice of psychological consultation: Not an impossible dream. *Counseling Psychologist, 13*(3), 466–472.

Lowman, R. L. (1989). *Pre-employment screening for psychopathology: A guide to professional practice.* Sarasota, FL: Professional Resource Exchange.

Lowman, R. L. (1991a). Ethical issues in applying psychology in organizations. In J. J. Jones, B. P. Steffy, & D. W. Bray (Eds.), *Applying psychology in organizations* (pp. 40–47). Lexington, MA: Lexington Books.

Lowman, R. L. (1991b). Ethical human resources practice in organizational settings. In D. W. Bray (Ed.), *Working with organizations and their people* (pp. 194–218). New York: Guilford Press.

Lowman, R. L. (1998). *The ethical practice of psychology in organizations.* Washington, DC and Bowling Green, OH: American Psychological Association and Society for Industrial and Organizational Psychology.

Lubinski, D. (2000). Scientific and social significance of assessing individual differences: Sinking shafts at a few critical points. *Annual Review of Psychology, 51,* 405–444.

Ludwig, T. D., & Geller, E. S. (1997). Assigned versus participative goal setting and response generalization: Managing injury control among professional pizza drivers. *Journal of Applied Psychology, 82,* 253–261.

Lundberg, U., & Frankenhauser, M. (1999). Stress and workload of men and women in high-ranking positions. *Journal of Occupational Health Psychology, 4,* 142–151.

Luthans, F., Paul, R., & Baker, D. (1981). An experimental analysis of the impact of contingent reinforcement on sales persons' performance behavior. *Journal of Applied Psychology, 66,* 314–323.

Lykken, D. T., (1981). *A tremor in the blood: Uses and abuses of the lie detector.* New York: McGraw-Hill.

Lykken, D. T., (1983). Polygraph prejudice. *Monitor, 14,* p. 4.

Lykken, D. T., Bouchard, T. J., Jr., McGue, M., & Tellegen, A. (1993). Heritability of interests: A twin study. *Journal of Applied Psychology, 78,* 649–661.

Lykken, D. T., McGue, M., Tellegen, A., & Bouchard, T. J., Jr. (1992). Emergenesis: Genetic traits that may not run in families. *American Psychologist, 47,* 1565–1577.

Macan, T. H. (1994). Time management: Test of a process model. *Journal of Applied Psychology, 79,* 381–391.

Macan, T. H., Avedon, M. J., Paese, M., & Smith, D. E. (1994). The effects of applicants' reactions to cognitive ability tests and an assessment center. *Personnel Psychology, 47,* 715–738.

MacCoun, R. J. (1998). Biases in interpretation and use of test results. *Annual Review of Psychology, 49,* 259–287.

Machin, M. A. (2002). Planning, managing, and optimizing transfer of training. In K. Kraiger (Ed.), *Creating, implementing, and managing effective training and development* (pp. 263–301). San Francisco: Jossey-Bass.

Mack, D. A., Shannon, C., Quick, J. D., & Quick, J. C. (1998). Stress and the preventative management of workplace violence. In R. W. Griffin, A. O'Leary-Kelly, & J. Collins (Eds.), *Dysfunctional behavior in organizations: Violent and deviant behavior* (pp. 119–141). Stamford, CT: JAI Press.

Maddi, S. R., & Kobasa, S. C. (1984). *The hardy executive: Health under stress.* Homewood, IL: Dow Jones-Irwin.

Mael, F. A. (1991). A conceptual rationale for the domain and attribute of bio data items. *Personnel Psychology, 44,* 763–792.

Mael, F. A., Connerly, M., & Morath, M. A. (1996). None of your business: Parameters of biodata invasiveness. *Personnel Psychology, 49,* 613–650.

Magjuka, R. J., & Baldwin, T. T. (1991). Team-based employee involvement programs: Effects of design and administration. *Personnel Psychology, 44,* 793–812.

Mahoney, T. A. (1988). Productivity defined: The relativity of efficiency, effectiveness, and change. In J. P. Campbell & R. J. Campbell (Eds.), *Productivity in Organizations.* San Francisco: Jossey-Bass.

Malamut, A. B., & Offermann, L. R. (2001). Coping with sexual harassment: Personal, environmental, and cognitive determinants. *Journal of Applied Psychology, 86,* 1152–1166.

Malos, S. B. (1998). Currrent legal issues in performance appraisal. In J. W. Smither (Ed.), *Performance appraisal: State of the art in practice* (pp. 49–94). San Francisco: Jossey-Bass.

Maranto, D. B. (2001). National Academy reviewing scientific evidence for polygraphs. *The Industrial-Organizational Psychologist, 38*(4), 159–160.

Markos, V. H. (2001). Developing executives. In R. F. Silzer (Ed.), *The 21st century executive: Innovative practices for building leadership at the top.* San Francisco: Jossey-Bass.

Marks, M. A., Mathieu, J. E., & Zaccaro, S. J. (2001). A temporally based framework and taxonomy of team processes. *Academy of Management Review, 26,* 356–376.

Marks, M. A., Sabella, M. J., Burke, C. S., & Zaccaro, S. J. (2002). The impact of cross-training on team effectiveness. *Journal of Applied Psychology, 87,* 3–13.

Marsh, H. W. (1984). Students' evaluations of university teaching: Dimensionality, reliability, validity, potential biases, and utility. *Journal of Educational and Psychological Measurement, 76,* 707–754.

Marsh, H. W., & Roche, L. A. (1997). Making students' evaluations of teaching effectiveness effective. *American Psychologist, 52,* 1187–1197.

Marshall, A. E. (1985). Employment qualifications of college graduates: How important are they? *Employment Counseling, 22*(4), 136–143.

Martin, C. L., & Bennett, N. (1996). The role of justice judgments in explaining the relationship between job satisfaction and organizational commitment. *Group and Organization Management, 21,* 84–104.

Martinko, M. J., & Zellars, K. L. (1998). Toward a theory of workplace violence and aggression: A cognitive appraisal perspective. In R. W. Griffin, A. O'Leary-Kelly, & J. Collins (Eds.), *Dysfunctional behavior in organizations: Violent and deviant behavior.* Stamford, CT: JAI Press.

Maryland: Driver in crash was using cell phone. (2002, February 5). National Briefing, *New York Times,* p. A21.

Maslach, C., Jackson, S. E., & Leiter, M. P. (1996). *Maslach Burnout Inventory manual* (3rd ed.). Palo Alto, CA: Consulting Psychologists Press.

Maslach, C., Schaufeli, W. B., & Leiter, M. P. (2001). Job burnout. *Annual Review of Psychology, 52,* 397–422.

Maslow, A. H. (1943). A theory of motivation. *Psychological Review, 50,* 370–396.

Maslow, A. H. (1971). *The farthest reaches of human nature.* New York: Viking Press.

Mathieu, J. E., Heffner, T. S., Goodwin, G. F., Salas, E., & Cannon-Bowers, J. A. (2000). The influence of shared mental models on team process and performance. *Journal of Applied Psychology, 85,* 273–283.

Mathieu, J. E., & Leonard, R. L. (1987). Applying utility concepts to a training program in supervisory skills: A time-based approach. *Academy of Management Journal, 30,* 828–847.

Mathieu, J. E., & Martineau, J. W. (1997). Individual and situational influences in training motivation. In J. K. Ford, S. W. J. Kozlowski, K. Kraiger, E., Salas, & M. S. Teachout, (Eds.), *Improving training effectiveness in work organizations.* Mahwah, NJ: Erlbaum.

Matthews, K. A. (1982). Psychological perspectives on the Type A behavior pattern. *Psychological Bulletin, 91,* 293–323.

Maurer, H. (1979). *Not working.* New York: Holt, Rinehart, & Winston.

Maurer, T. J., & Alexander, R. A. (1992). Methods of improving employment test critical scores derived by judging test content: A review and critique. *Personnel Psychology, 45,* 727–762.

Maurer, T. J., Alexander, R. A., Callahan, C. M., Bailey, J. J., & Dambrot, F. H. (1991). Methodological and psychometric issues in setting cutoff scores using the Angoff method. *Personnel Psychology, 44, 235–262.*

Maurer, T. J., & Rafuse, N. E. (2001). Learning, not litigating: Managing employee development and avoiding claims of age discrimination. *Academy of Management Executive, 15,* 110–121.

May, G. L., & Kahnwieler, W. M. (2000). The effect of mastery practice design on learning and transfer behavior in behavior modeling training. *Personnel Psychology, 53,* 353–374.

May, K. (1998). Work in the 21st century: The role of I-O in work-life programs. *The Industrial-Organizational Psychologist, 36*(2), 79–82.

Mayo, E. (1923a). The irrational factor in society. *Journal of Personnel Research, 1,* 419–426.

Mayo, E. (1923b). Irrationality and revery. *Journal of Personnel Research, 1,* 477–483.

Mayo, E. (1923c). The irrational factor in human behavior. *Annals of the American Academy of Political and Social Science, 110,* 117–130.

Mazzeo, J., & Harvey, A. L. (1988). The equivalence of scores from automated and conventional educational tests: A review of the literature. *College board report,* No. 88-8, New York: College Entrance Examination Board.

McArdle, W. D., Katch, F. I., & Katch, V. L. (2001). *Exercise physiology: Energy, nutrition, and human performance.* (5th ed.). Philadelphia: Lippincott, Williams and Wilkins.

McBride, J. R. (1998). Innovations in computer based ability testing: Promise, problems and perils. In M. D. Hakel (Ed.), *Beyond multiple choice: evaluating alternatives to traditional testing for selection* (pp. 23–39). Mahwah, NJ: Erlbaum.

McCall, M. W., Lombardo, M. M., & Morrison, A. M. (1988). *The lessons of experience: How successful executives develop on the job.* Lexington, MA: Lexington Books.

McCauley, C. D. (2001). Leader training and development. In S. J. Zaccaro & R. J. Klimoski (Eds.), *The nature of organizational leadership: Understanding the performance imperatives confronting today's leaders* (pp. 347–383). San Francisco: Jossey-Bass.

McCauley, C. D., Ruderman, M. N., Ohlott, P. J., & Morrow, J. E. (1994). Assessing the developmental components of managerial jobs. *Journal of Applied Psychology, 79,* 544–560.

McClelland, D. C. (1975). *Power: The inner experience.* New York: Irvington.

McClelland, D. C. (1979). Inhibited power motivation and high blood pressure in men. *Journal of Abnormal Psychology, 88,* 182–190.

McClelland, D. C. (1982). The need for power, sympathetic activation, and illness. *Motivation and Emotion, 6,* 31–41.

McClelland, D. C. (1985). *Human motivation.* Glenview, IL: Scott Foresman.

McCloy, R. A., Campbell, J. P., & Cudek, R. (1994). A confirmatory test of a model of performance determinants. *Journal of Applied Psychology, 79,* 493–503.

McCluskey, D. W., & Igbaria, M. (1998). A review of empirical research on telecommuting and directions for future research. In M. Igbaria & M. Tan (Eds.), *The virtual workplace* (pp. 338–358). Hershey, PA: IDEA Publishing.

McCormick, E. J., Jeanneret, P. R., & Mecham, R. C. (1972). A study of job characteristics and job dimensions as based on the Position Analysis Questionnaire. *Journal of Applied Psychology* [Monograph], *56,* 347–368.

McCrae, R. R., & Costa, P. T., Jr. (1985). Updating Norman's "adequate taxonomy": Intelligence and personality dimensions in natural language and in questionnaire. *Journal of Personality and Social Psychology, 49,* 710–721.

McCrae, R. R., & Costa, P. T., Jr. (1987). Validation of the five factor model of personality across instruments and observers. *Journal of Personality and Social Psychology, 52,* 81–90.

McDaniel, M. A., Morgeson, F. P., Finnegan, E. B., Campion, M. A., & Braverman, E. P. (2001). Use of situational judgment tests to predict job performance: A clarification of the literature. *Journal of Applied Psychology, 86,* 730–740.

McDaniel, M. A., Whetzel, D. L., Schmidt, F. L., & Maurer, S. D. (1994). The validity of employment interviews: A comprehensive review and meta-analysis. *Journal of Applied Psychology, 79,* 599–616.

McEvoy, G. M., & Cascio, W. F. (1989). Cumulative evidence of the relationship between employee age and job performance. *Journal of Applied Psychology, 74,* 11–17.

McFarlin, D. B., & Sweeney, P. D. (1992). Distributive and procedural justice as predictors of satisfaction with personal and organizational outcomes. *Academy of Management Journal, 35,* 626–637.

McGrath, J. E., & O'Conner, K. M. (1996). Temporal issues in work groups. In M. A. West (Ed.), *Handbook of work group psychology.* Chichester, England: John Wiley.

McGrath, J. J. (1984). *Groups: Interaction and performance.* Englewood Cliffs, NJ: Prentice Hall.

McGregor, D. (1960). *The human side of enterprise.* New York: McGraw-Hill.

McIntyre, R. M., Smith, D., & Hassett, C. E. (1984). Accuracy of performance ratings as affected by rater training and perceived purpose of rating. *Journal of Applied Psychology, 69,* 147–156.

McKeachie, W. J. (1997). Student ratings: The validity of use. *American Psychologist, 52,* 1218–1225.

McManus, M. A., & Kelly, M. L. (1999). Personality measures and biodata: Evidence regarding their incremental predictive value in the life insurance industry. *Personnel Psychology, 52,* 137–148.

Mead, A. D., & Drasgow, F. (1993). Equivalence of computerized and paper-and-pencil cognitive ability tests: A meta-analysis. *Psychological Bulletin, 114,* 449–458.

McMurrer, D. P., Van Buren, M., & Woodwell, W. (2000). *The 2000 ASTD state of the industry report.* Washington, DC: American Society for Training and Development.

Meagher, M. (1989, February). Death in the delivery zone (Television show). *Inside edition.* New York: American Broadcasting Company.

Meehl, P. E. (1954). *Clinical vs. statistical prediction.* Minneapolis: University of Minnesota Press.

Meehl, P. E. (1957). When shall we use our heads instead of a formula? *Journal of Counseling Psychology, 4,* 268–273.

Meehl, P. E. (1965). Seer over sign: The first good example. *Journal of Experimental Research in Personality, 1,* 27–32.

Meglino, B. M., Ravlin, E. C., & Adkins, C. L. (1989). A work values approach to corporate culture: A field test of the value congruence process and its relationship to individual outcomes. *Journal of Applied Psychology, 74,* 424–432.

Meglino, B. M., Ravlin, E. C., & Adkins, C. L. (1991). Value congruence and satisfaction with a leader: An examination of the role of interaction. *Human Relations, 44,* 481–495.

Meindl, J. R. (1990). On leadership: An alternative to conventional wisdom. In B. M. Staw & L. L. Cummings (Eds.), *Research in organizational behavior* (Vol., 12 pp. 159–203). Greenwich, CT: JAI Press.

Meister., J. C. (1994). *Corporate quality universities: Lessons in building a world class workforce.* New York: McGraw-Hill.

Mellers, B. A. (1982). Equity judgment: A revision of Aristotelian views. *Journal of Experimental Psychology, 111,* 242–270.

Menon, S., Narayanan, L., & Spector, P. E. (1996). The relation of time urgency to occupational stress and health outcomes for health care professionals. In C. D. Spielberger & I. G. Sarason (Eds.), *Stress and emotion: Anxiety, anger, and curiosity* (Vol. 16). London: Taylor & Francis.

Merritt, A. C., & Helmreich, R. L. (1996). Human factors on the flight deck: The influence of national culture. *Journal of Cross-Cultural Psychology, 27,* 5–24.

Merton, R. K. (1973). *The sociology of science.* Chicago: University of Chicago Press.

Messick, S. (1995). Validity of psychological assessment: Validation of inferences from person's responses and performances as scientific inquiry into score meaning. *American Psychologist, 50,* 741–749.

Messick, S., & Jungeblut, A. (1981). Time and method in coaching for the SAT. *Psychological Bulletin, 89,* 191–216.

Meyer, J. P., & Allen, N. J. (1991). A three component conceptualization of organizational commitment. *Resource Management Review, 1,* 61–98.

Meyer, J. P., Allen, N. J., & Smith, C. A. (1993). Commitments to organizations and occupations: Extension and test of a three component conceptualization. *Journal of Applied Psychology, 78,* 538–551.

Michael, R. T., Hartmann, H. I., & O'Farrell, B. (Eds.) (1989). *Pay equity: Empirical inquiries.* Washington, DC: National Academy Press.

Michaelis, W., & Eysenck, H. J. (1971). The determination of personality inventory factor patterns and intercorrelations by changes in real-life motivation. *Journal of Genetic Psychology, 118,* 223–234.

Micklethwait, J., & Wooldridge, A. (1996). *The witch doctors.* New York: Times Books.

Mihal, W. L., & Barrett, G. V. (1976). Individual differences in perceptual information processing and their relation to automobile accident involvement. *Journal of Applied Psychology, 61,* 229–233.

Mikkelsen, E. G., & Einarson, S. (2001). The role of victim personality in workplace bullying. Unpublished manuscript. Psykologisk Institut, Risskov, Denmark.

Mikula, G., Scherer, K. R., & Athenstaedt, U. (1998). The role of injustice in the elicitation of differential emotional reactions. *Personality and Social Psychology Bulletin, 24,* 769–783.

Militello, L. G., & Hutton, R. J. (1998). Applied cognitive task analysis (ACTA): A practitioner's toolkit for understanding cognitive task demands. *Ergonomics, 41,* 1618–1641.

Miller, D. (1993). The architecture of simplicity. *Academy of Management Review, 18,* 116–138.

Miller, D. (1994). What happens after success: The perils of excellence. *Journal of Management Studies, 31,* 325–358.

Miller, D. T. (2001). Disrespect and the experience of injustice. *Annual Review of Psychology, 52,* 527–553.

Miller, T. Q., Smith, T. W., Turner, C. W., Guijarro, M. L., Hallet, A. J. (1996). Meta-analytic review of research on hostility and physical health. *Psychological Bulletin, 119,* 322–348.

Milliken, F. J., & Martins, L. L. (1996). Searching for common threads: Understanding the multiple effects of diversity in organizational groups. *Academy of Management Review, 21,* 402–433.

Milne, S. H., Blum, T. C., & Roman, P. M. (1994). Factors influencing employees' propensity to use an employee assistance program. *Personnel Psychology, 47,* 123–145.

Miner, J. B. (2002). *Organizational behavior: Foundations, theories, and analyses.* Oxford, England: Oxford University Press.

Mitchell, J. L. (1978). *Structured job analysis of professional and managerial positions.* Unpublished doctoral dissertation. Purdue University, West Lafayette, IN.

Mitchell, T. R., Holtom, B. C., Lee, T. W., Sablynski, C. J., & Erez, M. (2001). Why people stay: Using job embeddedness to predict voluntary turnover. *Academy of Management Journal, 44,* 1102–1121.

Mitchell, T. R., Thompson, K. R., & George-Falvy, J. (2000). Goal setting: Theory and practice. In C. L. Cooper, & E. A. Locke (Eds.), *Industrial and organizational Psychology* (pp. 216–243). Malden, MA: Blackwell.

Mitchell, T. W. (1994). The utility of biodata. In G. S., Stokes, & M. D. Mumford (Eds.), *Biodata handbook: Theory, research, and the use of biographical information in selection and performance prediction* (pp. 485–516). Palo Alto, CA: Consulting Psychologists Press.

Mobley, W. H. (1977). Intermediate linkages in the relationship between job satisfaction and employee turnover. *Journal of Applied Psychology, 62,* 237–240.

Mohrman, S. A., Cohen, S. G., & Mohrman, A. M. (1995). *Designing team-based organizations.* San Francisco: Jossey-Bass.

Moon, H. (2001). The two faces of conscientiousness: Duty and achievement striving in escalation of commitment dilemmas. *Journal of Applied Psychology, 86,* 533–540.

Moorman, C., & Miner, A. S. (1998). Organizational improvisation and organizational memory. *Academy of Management Review, 23,* 698–723.

Moran, S. K., Wolff, S. C., & Green, J. E. (1995). Workers' compensation and occupational stress: Gaining control. In L. R. Murphy & J. J. Hurrell (Eds.), *Job stress interventions* (pp. 355–368). Washington, DC: American Psychological Association.

Morehead, G., Ference, R., & Neck, C. P. (1991). Group decision fiascos continue: Space shuttle *Challenger* and a revised groupthink framework. *Human Relations, 44,* 539–550.

Moreland, J. L., Eyde, L. D., Robertson, G. J., Primoff, E. S., & Most, R. B. (1995). Assessment of test user qualifications. *American Psychologist, 50,* 14–23.

Morgan, B. B., & Lassiter, D. L. (1992). Team composition and staffing. In R. W. Swezey & E. Salas (Eds.), *Teams: Their training and performance* (pp. 75–100). Stamford, CT: Ablex.

Morgeson, F. P., & Campion, M. A. (1997). Social and cognitive sources of inaccuracy in job analysis. *Journal of Applied Psychology, 82,* 627–655.

Morris, J. A., & Feldman, D. C. (1996). The dimensions, antecedents, and consequences of emotional labor. *Academy of Management Review, 21,* 986–1010.

Morris, M. A., & Robie, C. (2001). A meta-analysis of the effects of cross-cultural training on expatriate performance and adjustment. *International Journal of Training & Development, 5,* 112–125.

Morrow, C. C., Jarrett, M. Q., & Rupinski, M. T. (1997). An investigation of the effect and economic utility of corporate-wide training. *Personnel Psychology, 50,* 91–119.

Morrow, P. C. (1993). *The theory and measurement of work commitment.* Greenwich, CT: JAI Press.

Motowidlo, S. J., Borman, W. C., & Schmit, M. J. (1997). A theory of individual differences in task and contextual performance. *Human Performance, 10,* 71–83.

Motowidlo, S. J., Dunnette, M. D., & Carter, G. W. (1990). An alternative selection procedure: The low fidelity simulation. *Journal of Applied Psychology, 75,* 640–647.

Motowidlo, S. J., Packard, J. S., & Manning, M. R. (1986). Occupational stress: Its causes and consequences for job performance. *Journal of Applied Psychology, 71,* 618–629.

Motowidlo, S. J., & Tippins, N. (1993). Further studies of the low fidelity simulation in the form of a situational inventory. *Journal of Occupational and Organizational Psychology, 66,* 337–344.

Motowidlo, S. J., & Van Scotter, J. R. (1994). Evidence that task performance should be distinguished from contextual performance. *Journal of Applied Psychology, 79,* 475–480.

Mount, M. K., & Barrick, M. R. (1995). The Big Five personality dimensions: Implications for research and practice in human resources management. In G. R. Ferris (Ed.), *Research in personnel and human resources management* (Vol. 13, pp. 153–200). Greenwich, CT: JAI Press.

Mount, M. K., Barrick, M. R., & Stewart, G. L. (1998). Five-factor model of personality and performance in jobs involving interpersonal interactions. *Human Performance, 11,* 145–165.

Mount, M. K., Witt, L. A., & Barrick, M. R. (2000). Incremental validity of empirically keyed bio-data scales over GMA and the five factor personality constructs. *Personnel Psychology, 53,* 299–323.

Mowday, R. T., Porter, L.W., & Steers, R. M. (1982). *Employee-organization linkages: The psychology of commitment, absenteeism, and turnover.* New York: Academic Press.

Moyer, R. S., & Nath, A. (1998). Some effects of brief training interventions on perceptions of sexual harassment. *Journal of Applied Social Psychology, 28,* 333–356.

Mullen, B., & Cooper, C. (1994). The relation between group cohesiveness and performance: An integration. *Psychological Bulletin, 115,* 210–227.

Mumford, M. D., Baughman, W. A., Supinski, E. P., & Anderson, L. E. (1998). A construct approach to skill assessment: Procedures for assessing complex cognitive skills. In M. D. Hakel (Ed.), *Beyond multiple choice: Evaluating alternatives to traditional testing for selection* (pp. 75–112). Mahwah, NJ: Erlbaum.

Mumford, M. D., & Owens, W. A. (1982). Life history and vocational interests. *Journal of Vocational Behavior, 21,* 330–348.

Mumford, M. D., & Peterson, N. G. (1999). The O*NET content model: Structural considerations in describing jobs. In N. G. Peterson, M. D. Mumford, W. C. Borman, P. R. Jeanneret, & E. A. Fleishman (Eds.), *An occupational information system for the 21st century* (pp. 21–30). Washington, DC: American Psychological Association.

Mumford, M. D., Snell, A. F., Reiter-Palmon, R. (1994). Personality and background data: Life history and self concepts in an ecological system. In G. S. Stokes, M. D. Mumford, & W. A. Owens (Eds.), *Handbook of background data research: Theories, measures, and applications* (pp. 122–147). Palo Alto, CA: Consulting Psychologists Press.

Mumford, M. D., & Stokes, G. S. (1991). Developmental determinants of individual action: Theory and practice in applying background measures. In M. D. Dunnette, & L. M. Hough (Eds.), *Handbook on industrial and organizational psychology* (2nd ed., Vol. 3, pp. 61–138). Palo Alto, CA: Consulting Psychologists Press.

Mumford, M. R., Uhlman, C. E., & Kilcullen, R. N. (1992). The structure of life history: Implications for the construct validity of background data scales. *Human Performance, 5,* 109–137.

Munsterberg, H. (1912). *Psychologie und Wirtschaftsleben* [Psychology and industrial efficiency]. Leipzig, Germany: J. A. Barth.

Munsterberg, H. (1913). *Psychology and industrial efficiency.* Boston: Houghton Mifflin.

Murphy, G. C., & Athanasou, J. A. (1999). The effect of unemployment on mental health. *Journal of Occupational and Organizational Psychology, 72,* 83–99.

Murphy, K. R. (1993). *Honesty in the workplace.* Pacific Grove, CA: Brooks/Cole.

Murphy, K. R. (1996a). *Individual differences and behavior in organizations.* San Francisco, CA: Jossey-Bass.

Murphy, K. R. (1996b). Individual differences and behavior: Much more than "g." In K. R. Murphy (Ed.), *Individual differences and behavior in organizations* (pp. 3–30). San Francisco: Jossey-Bass.

Murphy, K. R. (1997). Editorial. *Journal of Applied Psychology, 82,* 1–3.

Murphy, K. R. (1999). The challenge of staffing a post-industrial workplace. In D. R. Ilgen & E. D. Pulakos (Eds.), *The changing nature of performance: Implications for staffing, motivation, and development* (pp. 295–324). San Francisco: Jossey-Bass.

Murphy, K. R. (2002a). Using power analysis to evaluate and improve research. In S. Rogelberg (Ed.), *Handbook of research methods in industrial and organizational psychology.* London: Blackwell.

Murphy, K. R. (2000b). *Validity generalization: A critical review.* Mahwah, NJ: Erlbaum.

Murphy, K. R., & Balzer, W. K. (1986). Systematic distortions in memory based behavior ratings and performance evaluation: Consequences for rating accuracy. *Journal of Applied Psychology, 71,* 39–44.

Murphy, K. R., & Cleveland, J. N. (1995). *Understanding performance appraisal: Social, organizational, and goal-based perspectives.* Thousand Oaks, CA: Sage.

Murphy, K. R., & Constans, J. I. (1987). Behavioral anchors as a source of bias in rating. *Journal of Applied Psychology, 72,* 573–579.

Murphy, K. R., & Davidshofer, C. O. (2001). *Psychological testing: Principles and application* (5th ed.). Upper Saddle River, NJ: Prentice Hall.

Murphy, K. R., & DeShon, R. (2000a). Interrater correlations do not estimate the reliability of job performance ratings. *Personnel Psychology, 53,* 873–900.

Murphy, K. R., & DeShon, R. (2000b). Progress in psychometrics: can industrial and organizational psychology catch up? *Personnel Psychology, 53,* 913–924.

Murphy, K. R., Garcia, M., Kerkar, S., Martin, C., & Balzer, W. K. (1982). Relationship between observational accuracy and accuracy in evaluating performance. *Journal of Applied Psychology, 67,* 320–325.

Murphy, K. R., & Myors, B. (1998). *Statistical power analysis: A simple and general model for traditional and modern hypothesis tests.* Mahwah, NJ: Erlbaum.

Murphy, K. R., Thornton, G. C., & Prue, K. (1991). Influence of job characteristics on the acceptability of employee drug testing. *Journal of Applied Psychology, 76,* 447–453.

Murphy, K. R., Thornton, G. C., & Reynolds, D. H. (1990). College students' attitudes toward employee drug testing programs. *Personnel Psychology, 43,* 615–631.

Murphy, L. L., Plake, B. S., Impara, J. C., & Spies, R. A. (2002). *Tests in print VI.* Lincoln: University of Nebraska Press.

Murphy, L. R. (1996). Stress management in work settings: A critical review of the health effects. *American Journal of Health Promotion, 11,* 112–135.

Myers, D. G., & Lamm, H. (1976). The group polarization phenomenon. *Psychological Bulletin, 83,* 602–627.

Nadler, D. A. (1987). The effective management of organizational change. In J. W. Lorsch (Ed.), *Handbook of organizational behavior* (pp. 358–369). Upper Saddle River, NJ: Prentice Hall.

National Evaluation Systems, Inc. (2002). *The Liberal Arts and Sciences Test (LAST).* Amherst, MA: Author.

National Research Council (1999). *The changing nature of work.* Washington, DC: National Academies Press.

National Research Council (2001). *Musculoskeletal disorders and the workplace.* Washington, DC: National Academies Press.

National Research Council (2002). *The polygraph and lie detection.* Wshington, DC: National Academies Press.

National Safety Council (1996). *Accident facts.* Chicago: Author.

Neisser, U., Boodoo, G., Bouchard, T. J., Boykin, A. W., Brody, N., Ceci, S. J., et al. (1996). Intelligence: Knowns and unknowns. *American Psychologist, 51,* 77–101.

Nell, V. (2002). Why young men drive dangerously: Implications for injury prevention. *Current Directions in Psychological Science, 11* (2), 75–78.

Netemeyer, R. G., Johnston, M. W., & Burton, S. (1990). Analysis of role conflict and role ambiguity in a structural equations framework. *Journal of Applied Psychology, 75,* 148–157.

Neter, E., & Ben-Shakhar, G. (1989). The predictive validity of graphological inferences: A meta-analytic approach. *Personality and Individual Differences, 10,* 737–745.

Neuman, G. A., & Wright, J. (1999). Team effectiveness: Beyond skills and cognitive ability. *Journal of Applied Psychology, 84,* 376–389.

Nicholson, N. (1977). Absence behavior and attendance motivation: A conceptual synthesis. *Journal of Management Studies, 14,* 231–252.

Nicholson, N., Brown, C. A., & Chadwick-Jones, J. K. (1976). Absence from work and job satisfaction. *Journal of Applied Psychology, 61,* 728–737.

Nicholson, N., & Johns, G. (1985). The absence culture and the psychological contract—who's in control of absence? *Academy of Management Review, 10,* 397–407.

Nieve, V. F., & Gutek, B. A. (1981). *Women and work: A psychological perspective.* New York: Praeger.

Noe, R. A. (2002). *Employee training and development* (2nd ed.). New York: McGraw-Hill.

Noe, R. A., & Colquitt, J. A. (2002). Planning for training impact: Principles of training effectiveness. In K. Kraiger (ed.), *Creating, implementing, and managing effective training and development* (pp. 53–79). San Francisco: Jossey-Bass.

Noe, R. A., Hollenbeck, J. R., Gerhart, B., & Wright, P. M. (2000). *Human resource management* (3rd ed). New York: McGraw-Hill.

Noer, D. M. (1999). Helping organizations change: Coping with downsizing, mergers, reengineering, and reorganizations. In A. I. Kraut & A. K. Korman (Eds.), *Evolving practices in human resource management* (pp. 275–301). San Francisco: Jossey-Bass.

Normand, J., Salyards, S. D., & Mahoney, J. J. (1990). An evaluation of pre-employment drug testing. *Journal of Applied Psychology, 75,* 629–639.

Northrup, L. C. (1989). *The psychometric history of selected ability constructs.* Washington, DC: Office of Personnel Management.

Nyfield, G., & Baron, H. (2000). Cultural context in adapting selection practices across borders. In J. Kehoe (Ed.), *Managing selection in changing organizations: Human resource strategies* (pp. 242–268). San Francisco: Jossey-Bass.

O'Connor, G. T., & Ryan, A. M. (1996). *Multiple facets of industrial-organizational psychology* II. Results of the 1995 membership survey. Bowling Green, OH: Society for Industrial and Organizational Psychology.

Ohno, T. (1998). *Just-in-time: For today and tomorrow.* Cambridge, England: Productivity Press.

Oldham, G. R., Cummings, A., Mischel, L. J., Schmidtke, J. M., & Jhou, J. (1995). Listen while you work? Quasi-experimental relations between personal stereo-headset use and employee work responses. *Journal of Applied Psychology, 80,* 547–564.

Olea, M. M., & Ree, M. J. (1994). Predicting pilot and navigator criteria: Not much more than "g". *Journal of Applied Psychology, 79,* 845–851.

Olson-Buchanan, J. B. (2001). Computer-based advances in assessment. In F. Drasgow & N. Schmitt (Eds.), *Measuring and analyzing behavior in organizations* (pp. 44–87). San Francisco: Jossey-Bass.

Olson-Buchanan, J. B., Drasgow, F., Moberg, P. J., Mead, A. D., Kennan, P. A., & Donovan (1998). Conflict resolution skills assessment: A model-based, multi-media approach. *Personnel Psychology, 51,* 1–24.

Ones, D. S., & Viswesvaran, C. (1996). Bandwidth-fidelity dilemma in personality measurement for personnel selection. *Journal of Organizational Behavior, 17,* 609–626.

Ones, D. S., & Viswesvaran, C. (1998). The effects of social desirability and faking on personality and integrity assessment for personnel selection. *Human Performance, 11,* 245–269.

Ones, D. S., & Viswesvaran, C. (1999). Relative importance of personality dimensions for expatriate selection: A policy capturing study. *Human Performance, 12* (3–4), 275–294.

Ones, D. S., Viswesvaran, C., & Schmidt, F. L. (1993). Comprehensive meta-analysis of integrity test validities: Findings and implications for personel selection and theories of job performance. *Journal of Applied Psychology, 78* [Monograph], 679–703.

Oppler, S. H., Campbell, J. P., Pulakos, E. D., & Borman, W. C. (1992). Three approaches to the investigation of subgroup bias in performance measurement: Review, results, and conclusions. *Journal of Applied Psychology, 77,* 201–217.

Organ, D. W. (1988). *Organizational citizenship behavior: The good soldier syndrome.* Lexington, MA: Lexington Books.

Organ, D. W., & Ryan, K. (1995). A meta-analytic review of attitudinal and dispositional predictors of organizational citizenship behavior. *Personnel Psychology, 48,* 775–802.

Oser, R. L., Salas, E., Merket, D. C., & Bowers, C. A. (2001). Applying resource management training in naval aviation: A methodology and lessons learned. In E. Salas, C. A. Bowers, & E. Edens (Eds.), *Improving teamwork in organizations: Applications of resource management training* (pp. 283–301). Mahwah, NJ: Erlbaum.

Ostroff, C. (1992). The relationship between satisfaction, attitudes and performance: An organizational level analysis. *Journal of Applied Psychology, 77,* 963–974.

Ouchi, W. (1981). *Theory Z: How American business can meet the Japanese challenge.* Reading, MA: Addison-Wesley.

Owens, W. A., & Schoenfeldt, L. F. (1979). Toward a classification of persons. *Journal of Applied Psychology, 64,* 569–607.

Parker, S. K., Chmiel, N., & Wall, T. D. (1997). Work characteristics and employee well being within a context of strategic downsizing. *Journal of Occupational Health Psychology, 2,* 289–303.

Parkes, K. R. (1999). Shiftwork, job type, and the work environment as joint predictors of health-related outcomes. *Journal of Occupational Health Psychology, 4,* 256–268.

Paterson, D. G. (1923). Methods of rating human qualities. *Annual Proceedings of the American Academy of Political and Social Scientists, 110,* 81–93.

Paul, R. J., & Townsend, J. B. (1998). Violence in the workplace: A review with recommendations. *Employee Responsibilities & Rights Journal, 11,* 1–14.

Pearce, J. A., & Ravlin, E. C. (1987). The design and activation of self-regulating work groups. *Human Relations, 40,* 751–782.

Pekrun, R., & Frese, M. (1992). Emotions in work and achievement. *International Review of Industrial and Organizational Psychology, 7,* 153–200.

Perotta, T. (2002, January 21). NY Cell phone ban passes court test. *National Law Journal,* p. A4.

Perry, E. L., Kulik, C. T., & Schmidtke, J. M. (1998). Individual differences in the effectiveness of sexual harassment awareness training. *Journal of Applied Social Psychology, 28,* 698–723.

Personnel Decisions International (1991b). *A blueprint for individual assessment, executive success profile.* Minneapolis: Author.

Personnel Decisions International (1991a). *Competency factors, executive success profile.* Minneapolis: Author.

Peters, G. A., & Peters, B. J. (1999). *Warnings, instructions, and technical communications.* Tucson, AZ: Lawyers and Judges Publishing.

Peterson, D. B. (2002). Management development: Coaching and mentoring programs. In K. Kraiger (Ed.), *Creating, implementing, and managing effective training and development* (pp. 160–191). San Francisco: Jossey-Bass.

Peterson, M. F., Smith, P. B., Akande, A., Ayestaran, S., Bochner, S., Callan, V., et al. (1995). Role conflict, ambiguity, and overload: A 21-nation study. *Academy of Management Journal, 38,* 429–452.

Peterson, N. G., Borman, W. C., Hanson, M. A., & Kubisiak, U. C. (1999). Summary of results, implications for O*NET applications and future directions. In N. G. Peterson, M. D. Mumford, W. C. Borman, P. R. Jeanneret, & E. A. Fleishman (Eds.), *An occupational information system for the 21st century* (pp. 289–296). Washington, DC: American Psychological Association.

Peterson, N. G., Hough, L. M., Dunnette, M. D., Rosse, R. L., Houston, J. S., Toquam, J. S., et al. (1990). Project A: Specification of the predictor domain and development of new selection/classification tests. *Personnel Psychology, 43,* 247–276.

Peterson, N. G., Mumford, M. D., Borman, W. C., Jeanneret, P. R., & Fleishman, E. A. (1999). *An occupational information system for the 21st century.* Washington, DC: American Psychological Association.

Pfeffer, J. (1977). The ambiguity of leadership. *Academy of Management Review, 2,* 104–112.

Pfeffer, J. (1981). *Power in organizations.* Marshfield, MA: Pitman.

Pfeffer, J. (1983). Organizational demography. *Research in Organizational Behavior, 5,* 299–357.

Pfeffer, J. (1990). Incentives in organizations: The importance of social relations. In O. E. Williamson (Ed.), *Organization theory from Chester Barnard to the present and beyond* (pp. 72–97). New York: Oxford University Press.

Pfeffer, J., & Salancik, G. R. (1975). Determinants of supervisory behavior: A role set analysis. *Human Relations, 28,* 139–153.

Pfeffer, J., & Salancik, G. R. (1978). *The external control of organizations: A resource dependence perspective.* New York: Harper & Row.

Phillips, J. M., (1998). Effects of realistic job previews on multiple organizational outcomes: A meta-analysis. *Academy of Management Journal, 41,* 673–690.

Phillips, J. M., & Gully, S. A. (1997). Role of goal orientation, ability, need for achievement, and locus of control in the self-efficacy and goal-setting process. *Journal of Applied Psychology, 82,* 792–802.

Piller, C. (1993). Bosses with X-ray eyes. *MacWorld, 10* (7), 118–123.

Pinto, J. K., & Prescott, J. E. (1988). Variations in critical success factors over the stages in the project life cycle. *Journal of Management, 14,* 5–18.

Pitariu, H. D. (1992). I/O psychology in Romania: Past, present and intentions. *The Industrial-Organizational Psychologist, 29* (4), 29–33.

Plake, B. S., Impara, J. C., & Spies, R. A. (2003). *The fifteenth mental measurements yearbook.* Lincoln, NE: Buros Institute of Mental Measurements, University of Nebraska.

Ployhart, R. E., Ryan, A. M., & Bennett, M. (1999). Explanations for selection decisions: Applicants' reactions to informational and sensitivity features of explanations. *Journal of Applied Psychology, 84,* 87–106.

Porras, J., & Silvers, R. (1991). Organizational development and transformation. *Annual Review of Psychology, 42,* 51–78.

Porter, L. W., & Lawler, E. E. (1968). *Managerial attitudes and performance.* Homewood, IL: Irwin.

Porter, L. W., Steers, R. M., Mowday, R. T., & Boulian, P. V. (1974). Organizational commitment, job satisfaction, and turnover among psychiatric technicians. *Journal of Applied Psychology, 59,* 603–609.

Posthuma, R. A., Morgeson, F. P., & Campion, M. A. (2002). Beyond employment interview validity: A comprehensive narrative review of recent research and trends over time. *Personnel Psychology, 55,* 1–82.

Powers, D. E. (1993). Coaching for the SAT: A summary of the summaries and an update. *Educational Measurement: Issues and Practice, 7,* 24–39.

Powers, D. E., & Rock, D. A. (1999). Effects of coaching on SAT I: Reasoning test scores. *Journal of Educational Measurement, 36,* 93–118.

Prichard, J. S., & Stanton, N. A. (1999). Testing Belbin's team role theory of effective groups. *Journal of Management Development, 18,* 652–665.

Priem, R. L., Harrison, D. A., & Muir, N. K. (1995). Structured conflict and consensus outcomes in group decision making. *Journal of Management, 21,* 691–710.

Prince, C., Chidester, T. R., Bowers, C., & Cannon-Bowers, J. A. (1992). Aircrew coordination: Achieving teamwork in the cockpit. In R. W. Swezey & E. Salas (Eds.), *Teams: Their training and performance* (pp. 355–378). Stamford, CT: Ablex.

Pritchard, R. D. (1990). *Measuring and improving organizational productivity: A practical guide.* New York: Praeger.

Pritchard, R. D. (1992). Organizational productivity. In M. Dunnette & L. Hough (Eds.), *Handbook of Industrial and Organizational Psychology* (2nd ed., Vol. 3, pp. 443–471). Palo Alto: Consulting Psychologists Press.

Pritchard, R. D. (1995). *Productivity measurement and improvement: Organizational case studies.* New York: Praeger.

Pritchard, R. D., Jones, S. D., Roth, P. L., Steubing, K. K., & Ekeberg, S. E. (1988). Effects of group feedback, goal setting and incentives on organizational productivity [Monograph]. *Journal of Applied Psychology, 73,* 337–358.

Pritchard, R. D., Paquin, A. R., DeCuir, A. D., McCormick, M. J., & Bly, P. R. (2001). The measurement and improvement of organizational productivity: An overview of ProMES, the productivity measurement and enhancement system. In R. D. Pritchard, H. Holling, F. Lammers, & B. D. Clark (Eds.), *Improving organizational performance with the Productivity Measurement and Enhancement System: An international collaboration.* Huntingdon, NY: Nova Science.

Pritchard, R. D., & Ramstad, P. M. (2003). *Managing motivation.* Unpublished manuscript. Texas A & M.

Probst, T. M. (2000). Wedded to the job: Moderating effects of job involvement on the consequences of job insecurity. *Journal of Occupational and Health Psychology, 5,* 63–73.

Pugh, S. D. (2001). Service with a smile: Emotional contagion in the service encounter. *Academy of Management Journal, 44,* 1018–1027.

Pugliesi, K. (1999). The consequences of emotional labor: Effects on work stress, job satisfaction, and well-being. *Motivation & Emotion, 23,* 125–154.

Pulakos, E. D. (1984). A comparison of rater training programs: Error training and accuracy training. *Journal of Applied Psychology, 69,* 581–588.

Pulakos, E. D., Arad, S., Donovan, M. A., & Plamandon, K. E. (2000). Adaptability in the workplace: Development of a taxonomy of adaptive performance. *Journal of Applied Psychology, 85,* 612–624.

Pulakos, E. D., & Schmitt, N. (1995). Experience-based and situational interview questions: Studies of validity. *Personnel Psychology, 48,* 289–308.

Pulakos, E. D., White, L. A., Oppler, S. H., & Borman, W. C. (1989). Examination of race and sex effects in performance ratings. *Journal of Applied Psychology, 74,* 770–780.

Pyle, C. (2002). Personal Communication.

Quick, J. C., Quick, J. D., Nelson, D. L., & Hurrell, J. J. (1997). *Preventative stress management in organizations.* Washington, DC: American Psychological Association.

Quinones, M. A., Ford, J. K., & Teachout, M. S. (1995). The relationship between work experience and job performance: A conceptual and meta-analytic review. *Personnel Psychology, 48,* 887–910.

Rafaeli, A. (1999). Pre-employment screening and applicants' attitudes toward an employment opportunity. *Journal of Social Psychology, 139* (6), 700–712.

Rafaeli, A., & Klomoski, R. J. (1983). Predicting sales success through handwriting analysis: An evaluation of the effects of training and handwriting sample content. *Journal of Applied Psychology, 68,* 212–217.

Ralston, D. A. (1989). The benefits of flextime: Real or imagined? *Journal of Organizational Behavior, 10,* 369–373.

Randall, D. M., & Cote, J. A. (1991). Interrelationships of work commitment constructs. *Work and Occupation, 18,* 194–211.

Rastegary, H., & Landy, F. J. (1993). The interactions among time urgency, uncertainty, and time pressure. In O. Svenson & A. J. Maule (Eds.), *Time pressure and stress in human judgment and decision making* (pp. 217–239). New York: Plenum.

Rauschenberger, J., Schmitt, N., & Hunter, J. E. (1980). A test of the need hierarchy concept by a Markov model of change in need strength. *Administrative Science Quarterly, 25,* 654–670.

Raymark, P. H., Schmit, M. J., & Guion, R. M. (1997). Identifying potentially useful personality constructs for employee selection. *Personnel Psychology, 50,* 723–736.

Ree, M. J., & Carretta, T. R. (2002). g2K. *Human Performance, 15,* 3–23.

Ree, M. J., & Earles, J. A. (1991). Predicting training success: Not much more than g. *Personnel Psychology, 44,* 321–332.

Ree, M. J., & Earles, J. A. (1992). Intelligence is the best predictor of job performance. Psychological Science, 1, 86–89.

Ree, M. J., Earles, J. A., & Teachout, M. S. (1994). Predicting job performance: Not much more than "g". *Journal of Applied Psychology, 79,* 518–524.

Reichers, A. E., & Schneider, B. (1990). Climate and culture: An evolution of constructs. In B. Schneider (Ed.), *Organizational climate and culture* (pp. 5–39). San Francisco: Jossey-Bass.

Reilly, R. R., & McGourty, J. (1998). Performance appraisal in team settings. In J. W. Smither (Ed.), *Performance appraisal: State of the art in practice.* San Francisco: Jossey-Bass.

Reilly, R. R., Zedeck, S., & Tenopyr, M. (1979). Validity and fairness of physical ability tests for predicting performance in craft jobs. *Journal of Applied Psychology, 64,* 262–274.

Rentsch, J. R. (1990). Climate and culture: Interaction and qualitative differences in organizational meanings. *Journal of Applied Psychology, 75,* 668–681.

Rice, A. K. (1958). *Productivity and social organization: The Ahmedabad experiment.* London: Tavistock.

Rice, R. W., Gentile, D. A., & McFarlin, D. B. (1991). Facet importance and job satisfaction. *Journal of Applied Psychology, 76,* 31–39.

Richman-Hirsch, W. L., Olson-Buchanan, J. B., & Drasgow, F. (2000). Examining the impact of administration medium on examinee perceptions and attitudes. *Journal of Applied Psychology, 85,* 880–887.

Ricklefs, R. (1997, September 2). Computer training of disabled expands its commercial reach. *The Wall Street Journal* (Interactive Edition).

Ringlemann, M. (1913). Research on animate sources of power: The work of man. *Annales de l'Institut National Agronomique,* 2nd series, Vol. 12, pp. 1–40.

Rizzo, J. R., House, R. J., & Lirtzman, S. I. (1970). Role conflict and ambiguity in complex organizations. *Administrative Science Quarterly, 15,* 150–163.

Robb, D. (2002). Virtual workplace. *HR Magazine, 47,* 105–114.

Robbins, T. L., & DeNisi, A. S. (1998). Mood vs. interpersonal affect: Identifying process and rating distortions in performance appraisal. *Journal of Business and Psychology, 12,* 313–325.

Robert, C., Probst, T. M., Martocchio, J. J., Drasgow, F., & Lawler, J. L. (2000). Empowerment and continuous improvement in the United States, Mexico, Poland, and India: Predicting fit on the basis of the dimensions of power distance and individualism. *Journal of Applied Psychology, 85,* 643–658.

Roberts, R. D., Zeidner, M., & Matthews, G. (2001). Does emotional intelligence meet traditional standards for an intelligence? Some new data and conclusions. *Emotion, 1*(3), 196–231.

Robinson, M. (1999, September 8). Ford agrees to pay $7.75 million to settle sexual harassment case. *The Oregonian,* p. D2.

Robinson, S. L., & Bennett, R. J. (1995). A typology of deviant workplace behaviors: A multidimensional scaling study. *Academy of Management Journal, 38,* 555–572.

Roethlisberger F. J., & Dickson, W. J. (1939). *Management and the worker.* Cambridge: Harvard University Press.

Rogelberg, S. G. (2002). *Handbook of research methods in industrial and organizational psychology.* Cambridge, MA: Blackwell.

Rogelberg, S. G., & Brooks-Laber, M. E. (2002). Securing our collective future: Challenges facing those designing and doing research in industrial and organizational psychology. In S. G. Rogelberg (Ed.), *Handbook of research methods in industrial and organizational psychology* (pp. 479–485). Cambridge, MA: Blackwell.

Rogers, W., Maurer, T., Salas, E., & Fisk, A. (1997). Task analysis and cognitive theory: Controlled and automatic processing. Task analytic methodology. In J. K. Ford, S. W. J., Kozlowski, K., Kraiger, E., Salas, M. S. Teachout (Eds.), *Improving training effectiveness in work organizations.* Mahwah, NJ: Erlbaum.

Romanov, K., Appelberg, K., Honkasalo, M., & Koskenvuo, M. (1996). Recent interpersonal conflict at work and psychiatric morbidity: A prospective study of 15,530 employees aged 24–64. *Journal of Psychosomatic Research, 40,* 169–176.

Ronen, S. (1981). Arrival and departure patterns of public sector employees before and after implementation of flexitime. *Personnel Psychology, 34,* 817–822.

Ronen, S. (1997). Personal reflections and projections: International industrial/organizational psychology at a crossroads. In P. C. Earley & M. Erez (Eds.), *New perspectives on industrial/organizational psychology* (pp. 715–731). San Francisco: Jossey-Bass.

Rorty, R. (1989). *Contingency, irony, and solidarity.* New York: Cambridge University press.

Rosca, A., & Voicu, C. (1982). *A concise history of psychology in Romania.* Bucharest: Editura Stiintifica Psychologica si Enciclopedica.

Rosse, J. G. (1988). Relations among lateness, absence, and turnover: Is there a progression of withdrawal? *Human Relations, 41*(7), 517–531.

Roth, P. L., & Bobko, P. (2000). College grade point average as a personnel selection device: Ethnic group differences and potential adverse impact. *Journal of Applied Psychology, 85*(3), 399–406.

Roth, P. L., BeVier, C. A., Switzer, F. S., & Schippmann, J. S. (1996). Meta-analyzing the relationship between grades and job performance. *Journal of Applied Psychology, 81,* 548–556.

Rosse, J. G., Miller, J. L., & Stecher, M. D. (1994). A field study of job applicants' reactions to personality and cognitive ability testing. *Journal of Applied Psychology, 79,* 987–992.

Rothstein, H. R. (1990). Interrater reliability of job performance ratings: Growth to asymptote level with increasing opportunity to observe. *Journal of Applied Psychology, 75,* 322–327.

Rotter, J. B. (1996). Generalized expectancies for internal versus external control of reinforcement. *Psychological Monographs, 80* (1, Whole No. 609).

Rotundo, M., & Sackett, P. R. (2002). The relative importance of task, citizenship, and counterproductive performance to global ratings of job performance: A policy capturing approach. *Journal of Applied Psychology, 87,* 66–80.

Rouillier, J. Z., & Goldstein, I. L. (1993). The relationship between organizational transfer climate and positive transfer of training. *Human Resource Development Quarterly, 4,* 377–390.

Rousseau, D. M. (1988). The construction of climate in organizational research. In C. L. Cooper & I. Robertson (Eds.), *International review of industrial and organizational psychology* (pp. 137–158). London: John Wiley.

Roy, M. P., Kirschbaum, C., & Steptoe, A. (2001). Psychological, cardiovascular, and metabolic correlates of individual differences in cortisol stress recovery in young men. *Psychoneuroendocrinology, 26,* 375–391.

Russell, C. J., Collela, A., & Bobko, P. (1993). Expanding the context of utility: The strategic impact of personnel selection. *Personnel Psychology, 46,* 781–801.

Russell, J. A. (1991). Culture and categorization of emotions. *Psychological Bulletin, 110,* 426–450.

Ryan, A. M., Chan, D., Ployhart, R. E., & Slade, L. A. (1999). Employee attitude surveys in a multinational organization: Considering language and culture in assessing measurement equivalence. *Personnel Psychology, 52,* 37–58.

Ryan, A. M., & Greguras, G. J. (1998). Life is not multiple choices. In M. Hakel (Ed.), *Alternatives to traditional assessment* (pp. 183–202). Mahwah, NJ: Erlbaum.

Ryan, A. M., McFarland, L., Baron, H., & Page, R. (1999). An international look at selection practices: Nation and culture as explanations for variability in practice. *Personnel Psychology, 52,* 359–391.

Ryan, A. M., Ployhart, R. E., Greguras, G. J., & Schmit, M. J. (1998). Test preparation programs in selection contexts: Self-selection and program effectiveness. *Personnel Psychology, 51,* 599–621.

Ryan, A. M., & Sackett, P. R. (1987). Pre-employment honesty testing: Fakability, reactions of test takers, and company image. *Journal of Business and Psychology, 1,* 248–256.

Ryan, A. M., & Sackett, P. R. (1992). Relationships between graduate training, professional affiliation, and individual psychological assessment practices for personnel decisions. *Personnel Psychology, 45,* 363–387.

Ryan, A. M., & Sackett, P. R. (1998). Individual assessment: The research base. In R. Silzer & P. R. Jeanneret (Eds.). *Individual psychological assessment: Predicting behavior in organizational settings* (pp. 54–87). San Francisco: Jossey-Bass.

Ryan, A. M., Schmit, M. J., & Johnson, R. (1996). Attitudes and effectiveness: Examining relations at an organizational level. *Personnel Psychology, 49,* 853–882.

Ryan, T. A. 1970. *Intentional behavior.* New York: Ronald Press.

Rynes, S. L., & Gerhart, B. (2001). *Compensation in organizations.* San Francisco: Jossey-Bass.

Saal, F. E. (1979). Mixed standard rating scale: A consistent system for numerically coding inconsistent response combinations. *Journal of Applied Psychology, 64,* 422–428.

Sackett, P. R., & Arvey, R. D. (1993). Selection in small N settings. In N. Schmitt & W. C. Borman (Eds.), *Personnel selection in organizations* (pp. 418–447). San Francisco: Jossey-Bass.

Sackett, P. R., Burris, L. R., & Ryan, A. M. (1989). Coaching and practice effects in personnel selection. In C. L. Cooper & I. T. Robertson (Eds.), *International review of industrial and organizational psychology.* Chichester, England: John Wiley.

Sackett, P. R., & Decker, P. J. (1979). Detection of deception in the employment context: A review and critical analysis. *Personnel Psychology, 32,* 487–506.

Sackett, P. R., & DeVore, C. J. (2001). Counterproductive behaviors at work. In N. Anderson, D. S. Ones, H. K. Sinangil, & C. Viswesvaran (Eds.), *Handbook of industrial, work, and organizational psychology* (Vol. 1, pp. 145–164). London: Sage.

Sackett, P. R., & DuBois, C. L. (1991). Rater-ratee race effects on performance evaluation: Challenging meta-analytic conclusions. *Journal of Applied Psychology, 76,* 873–877.

Sackett, P. R., & Harris, M. M. (1984). Honesty testing for personnel selection: A review and critique. *Personnel Psychology, 37,* 221–246.

Sackett, P. R., & Mullen, E. J. (1993). Beyond formal experimental design: Towards an expanded view of the training evaluation process. *Personnel Psychology, 46,* 613–627.

Sackett, P. R., Schmitt, N., Elsington, J. E., & Kabin, M. B. (2001). High stakes testing in employment, credentialing, and higher education. *American Psychologist, 56,* 302–318.

Sackett, P. R., & Tuzinski, K. A. (2001). The role of dimensions and exercises in assessment center judgments. In M. London (Ed.), *How people evaluate others in organizations* (pp. 111–134). Mahwah, NJ: Erlbaum.

Sackett, P. R., & Wanek, J. E. (1996). New developments in the use of measures of honesty, integrity, conscientiousness, dependability, trustworthiness, and reliability for personnel selection. *Personnel Psychology, 49,* 787–829.

Sackett, P. R., & Wilk, S. L. (1994). Within group norming and other forms of score adjustment in pre-employment testing. *American Psychologist, 49,* 929–954.

Saks, A. M., & Ashforth, B. E. (1997). A longitudinal investigation of the relationships between job information sources, applicant perceptions of fit, and work outcomes. *Personnel Psychology, 50,* 395–426.

Saks, A. M., & Waldman, D. A. (1998). The relationship between age and job performance evaluations for entry-level professionals. *Journal of Organizational Behavior, 19,* 409–419.

Salancik, G. R., & Pfeffer, J. (1977). Who gets power and how they hold on to it: A strategic contingency model of power. *Organizational Dynamics, 5,* 3–21.

Salas, E., Burke, S. C., Bowers, C. A., & Wilson, K. A. (2001). Team training in the skies: Does crew resource management (CRM) training work? *Human Factors, 43,* 641–674.

Salas, E., Burke, S. C., & Cannon-Bowers, J. A. (2002). What we know about designing and delivering team training: Tips and guidelines. In K. Kraiger (Ed.), *Creating, implementing, and managing effective training and development* (pp. 234–259). San Francisco: Jossey-Bass.

Salas, E., & Cannon-Bowers, J. A. (1997). Strategies for team training. In M. Quinones & A. Dutta (Eds.), *Training for 21st century technology: Applications for psychology research.* Washington, DC: American Psychological Association.

Salas, E., & Cannon-Bowers, J. A. (2001). The science of training: A decade of progress. *Annual Review of Psychology, 52,* 471–499.

Salgado, J. F. (1997). The five factor model of personality and job performance in the European Community. *Journal of Applied Psychology, 82,* 30–43.

Salgado, J. F. (1998). Big Five personality dimensions and job performance in army and civil occupations: A European perspective. *Human Performance, 11,* 271–288.

Salgado, J. F., & Moscoso, S. (2002). Comprehensive meta-analysis of the construct validity of the employment interview. *European Journal of Work and Organizational Psychology, 11,* 299–324.

Salgado, J. F., Viswesvaran, C., & Ones, D. S. (2001). Predictors used for personnel selection: An overview of constructs, methods and techniques. IN N. Anderson, D. S. Ones, H. K. Sinangil, & C. Viswesvaran (Eds.), *Handbook of industrial, work, and organizational psychology* (pp. 165–199). Thousand Oaks, CA: Sage.

Salin, D. (2001). Prevalence and forms of bullying among professionals: A comparison of two different strategies for measuring bullying. *European Journal of Work and Organizational Psychology, 10,* 425–442.

Salovey, P., & Mayer, J. D. (1990). Emotional intelligence. *Imagination, Cognition and Personality, 9* (3), 185–211.

Salovey, P., Mayer, J. D., Goldman, S. L., Turvey, C., & Palfai, T. P. (1995). Emotional attention, clarity, and repair: Exploring emotional intelligence using Trait

Meta-Mood Scale. In J. W. Pennebaker (Ed.), *Emotion, disclosure and health* (pp. 135–154). Washington, DC: American Psychological Association.

Salvendy, G. (1997). *Handbook of human factors and ergonomics* (2nd ed.). New York: John Wiley.

Sanchez, J. I., & Levine, E. L. (1999). Is job analysis dead, misunderstood, or both? New forms of work analysis and design. In A. I. Kraut & A. K. Korman (Eds.), *Evolving practices in human resource management* (pp. 43–68). San Francisco: Jossey-Bass.

Sanders, M. S., & McCormick, E. J. (1993). *Human factors in engineering and design* (7th ed.). New York: McGraw-Hill.

Sapolsky, R. M. (1998). *Why zebras don't get ulcers: An updated guide to stress, stress-related diseases, and coping.* New York: W. H. Freeman.

Sauter, S., Murphy, L. R., & Hurrell, J. J. (1990). A national strategy for the prevention of work related psychological disorders. *American Psychologist, 45,* 1146–1158.

Saville & Holdsworth Limited (1998). *The work profiling system (WPS) technical manual.* Boulder, CO: Author.

Saville & Holdsworth Limited (2001). *The work profiling system (WPS) technical manual.* Boulder, CO: Author.

Schachter, S. (1964). The interaction of cognitive and physiological determinants of emotional state. In L. Berkowitz (Ed.), *Advances in experimental-social psychology* (Vol. 1). New York: Academic Press.

Schachter, S., & Singer, J. E. (1962). Cognitive, social, and physiological determinants of emotional state. *Psychological Review, 69,* 379–399.

Schaffer, R. H. (1953). Job satisfaction as related to need satisfaction in work. *Psychological Monographs, 67* (No. 304).

Schalk, R., & Rousseau, D. M. (2001). Psychological contracts in employment. In N. Anderson, D. Ones, H. Sinangil, & C. Viswesvaran (Eds.), *Handbook of industrial, work, and organizational psychology* (Vol. 2, pp. 133–142). London: Sage.

Schaubroeck, J., & Kuehn, K. (1992). Research design in industrial and organizational psychology. In C. L. Cooper & I. T. Robertson (Eds.), *International review of industrial and organizational psychology* (Vol. 7, pp. 99–121). Chichester, England: John Wiley.

Schaufeli, W. B., & Enzmann, D. (1998). *The burnout companion to study and practice: A critical analysis.* London: Taylor & Francis.

Schaufeli, W. B., Leiter, M. P., Maslach, C., & Jackson, S. E. (1996). Maslach Burnout Inventory-General Survey. Palo Alto, CA: Consulting Psychologists Press.

Schein, E. (1981). Does Japanese management style have a message for managers? *Sloan Management Review, 23,* 55–68.

Schein, E. (1985). *Organizational culture and leadership: A dynamic view.* San Francisco: Jossey-Bass.

Schein, E. (1992). *Organizational culture and leadership* (2nd ed.). San Francisco: Jossey-Bass.

Schein, E. (1996). Kurt Lewin's change theory in the field and in the classroom: Notes toward a model of managed learning. *Systems Practice, 9,* 27–47.

Schendel, J. D., & Hagman, J. D. (1982). On sustaining procedural skills over a prolonged retention interval. *Journal of Applied Psychology, 67,* 605–610.

Schmidt, F. L. (1991). Why all banding procedures are logically flawed. *Human Performance, 4,* 265– 277.

Schmidt, F. L. (1992). What do the data really mean? Research findings, meta-analysis, and cumulative knowledge in psychology. *American Psychologist, 47,* 1173–1181.

Schmidt, F. L. (1996). Statistical significance testing and cumulative knowledge in psychology: Implications for training of researchers. *Psychological Methods, 1,* 115–129.

Schmidt, F. L., & Hunter, J. E. (1992). Development of causal models of processes determining job performance. *Current Directions in Psychological Sciences, 1,* 89–92.

Schmidt, F. L., & Hunter, J. E. (1998). The validity and utility of selection methods in personnel psychology: Practical and theoretical implications of 85 years of research findings. *Psychological Bulletin, 124,* 262–274.

Schmidt, F. L., & Hunter, J. E. (2002a). History, development, and impact of validity generalization and meta-analysis methods, 1975–2001. In K. R. Murphy (Ed.), *Validity generalization: A critical review.* Mahwah, NJ: Erlbaum.

Schmidt, F. L., & Hunter, J. E. (2002b). Are there benefits from NHST? *American Psychologist, 57,* 65–66.

Schmidt, F. L., Viswesvaran, C., & Ones, D. S. (2000). Reliability is not validity is not reliability. *Personnel Psychology, 53,* 901–911.

Schminke, M., Ambrose, M. L., & Cropanzano, R. (2000). The effect of organizational structure on perceptions of procedural fairness. *Journal of Applied Psychology, 85,* 294–304.

Schmit, M. J., & Alscheid, S. P. (1995). Employee attitudes and customer satisfaction: Making theoretical and empirical connections. *Personnel Psychology, 48,* 521–536.

Schmit, M. J., & Ryan, A. M. (1992). Test taking dispositions: A missing link? *Journal of Applied Psychology, 77,* 629–937.

Schmit, M. J., & Ryan, A. M. (1993). The Big Five in personnel selection: Factor structure in applicant and non-applicant populations. *Journal of Applied Psychology, 78,* 966–974.

Schmitt, N. (1976). Social and situational determinants of interview decisions: Implications for the employment interview. *Personnel Psychology, 29,* 79–101.

Schmitt, N., Gooding, R. Z., Noe, R. A., & Kirsch, M. (1984). Meta-analysis of validity studies published between 1964 and 1982 and the investigation of study characteristics. *Personnel Psychology, 37*, 407–422.

Schmitt, N., Gilliland, S. W., Landis, R. S., & Devine, D. (1993). Computer based testing applied to selection of secretarial applicants. *Personnel Psychology, 46*, 149–165.

Schmitt, N., & Landy, F. J. (1993). The concept of validity. In N. Schmitt & W. C. Borman (Eds.), *Personnel selection in organizations.* San Francisco: Jossey-Bass.

Schmitt, N., & Pulakos, E. (1998). Biodata and differential prediction: Some reservations. In M. D. Hakel (Ed.), *Beyond multiple choice: Evaluating alternatives to traditional testing for selection* (pp. 167–182). Mahwah, NJ: Erlbaum.

Schmitt, N., Sacco, J. M., Ramey, S., Ramey, C., & Chan, D. (1999). Parental employment, school climate, and children's academic and social development. *Journal of Applied Psychology, 84*, 737–753.

Schneider, B. (1987). The people make the place. *Personnel Psychology, 40*, 437–454.

Schneider, B. (1996). When individual differences aren't. In K. R. Murphy (Ed.), *Individual differences and behavior in organizations* (pp. 548–571). San Francisco: Jossey-Bass.

Schneider, B. (2000). Organizational culture and climate: The psychological life of organizations. In N. Ashkenasy, C. Wilderom, & M. Peterson (Eds.), *Handbook of organizational culture and climate* (pp. xvii–xxi). London: Sage.

Schneider, B., Ashworth, S. D., Higgs, A. C., & Carr, L. (1996). Design, validity, and use of strategically focused employee attitude surveys. *Personnel Psychology, 49*, 695–705.

Schneider, B., Bowen, D. E., Ehrhart, M. G., & Holcombe, K. M. (2000). The climate for service: Evolution of a construct. In N. Ashkenasy, C. Wilderom, & M. Peterson (Eds.), *Handbook of organizational culture and climate* (pp. 21–36). London: Sage.

Schneider, B., Goldstein, H. W., & Smith, D. B. (1995). The ASA framework: An update. *Personnel Psychology, 48*, 747–773.

Schneider, B., Salvaggio, A. M., & Subarits, M. (2002). Climate strength: A new direction for climate research. *Journal of Applied Psychology, 87*, 220–229.

Schneider, B., & Schmitt, N. (1986). *Staffing organizations.* Glenview, IL: Scott Foresman.

Schneider, B., Smith, D. B., & Sipe, W. B. (2000). Personnel selection psychology. In K. Klein & S. W. J. Kozlowski (Eds.), *Multi-level theory, research, and methods in organizations: Foundations, extensions, and new directions* (pp. 91–120). San Francisco: Jossey-Bass.

Schneider, B., Smith, D. B., Taylor, S, & Fleenor, J. (1998). Personality and organizations: A test of the homogeneity of personality hypothesis. *Journal of Applied Psychology, 83*, 462–470.

Schneider, R. J., Hough, L. M., & Dunnette, M. D. (1996). Broadsided by broad traits: How to sink science into five dimensions of less. *Journal of Organizational Behavior, 17*, 639–655.

Schroth, H. A., & Shah, P. P. (2000). Procedures: Do we really want to know them? An examination of the effects of procedural justice on self-esteem. *Journal of Applied Psychology, 85*, 462–471.

Schuler, H., Moser, K., & Funke, U. (1994). *The moderating effect of rater-ratee acquaintance on the validity of an assessment center.* Paper presented at the 23rd International Congress of Applied Psychology, Madrid, Spain.

Schuler, R. S., & Jackson, S. E. (1996). *Human resource management: Positioning for the 21st century* (6th ed.). Minneapolis, MN: West Publishing.

Scott, S. G., & Einstein, W. O. (2001). Strategic performance appraisal in team-based organizations. *Academy of Management Executive, 15*, 107–116.

Selye, H. (1956). *The stress of life.* New York: McGraw-Hill.

Semmer, N. (1996). Individual differences, work stress, and health. In M. J. Schabracq, J. A. Winnubst, & C. L. Cooper. *Handbook of work and health psychology* (pp. 51–86). Chichester, England: John Wiley.

Senge, P. M. (1990). *The fifth discipline: The art and practice of learning organizations.* New York: Doubleday.

Senior, B. (1997). Team roles and team performance: Is there "really" a link? *Journal of Occupational and Organizational Psychology, 70*, 241–258.

Shaffer, M. A., & Harrison, D. A. (2001). Forgotten partners of international assignments: Development and test of a model of spouse adjustment. *Journal of Applied Psychology, 86*, 238–254.

Shamir, B., House, R. J., & Arthur, M. B. (1993). The motivational effects of charismatic leadership: A self-concept based theory. *Organizational Science, 4*, 1–17.

Shanteau, J., & Dino, G. A. (1993). Environmental stressor effects on creativity and decision-making. In O. Svenson & A. J. Maule (Eds.), *Time pressure and stress in human judgment and decision making* (pp. 293–308). New York: Plenum.

Sharf, J. C., & Jones, D. P. (2000). Employment risk management. In J. Kehoe (Ed.), *Managing selection in changing environments: Human resource strategies* (pp. 271–318). San Francisco: Jossey-Bass.

Shephard, L. (Ed.) (1978). Setting standards. *Journal of Educational Measurement: Special Issue, 15* (4), 237–327.

Shepperd, J. (1993). Productivity loss in performance groups: A motivation analysis. *Psychological Bulletin, 113*, 67–81.

Shimmin, S., & van Strien, P. J. (1998). History of the psychology of work and organization. In P. J. D. Drenth H. Thierry & C. J. de Wolff (Eds.), *Handbook of work and organizational psychology* (pp. 71–99). Hove, England: Psychology Press.

Shimmin, S., & Wallis, D. (1994). *Fifty years of occupational psychology.* Leicester, England: British Psychological Society.

Shippmann, J. S., Ash, R. A., Battista, M., Carr, L., Eyde, L. D., Hesketh, B., et al. (2000). The practice of competency modeling. *Personnel Psychology, 53,* 703–740.

Silzer, R. (2002). *The 21st century executive: Innovative practices for building leadership at the top.* San Francisco: Jossey-Bass.

Silzer, R., & Jeanneret, P. R. (1998). *Individual psychological assessment: Predicting behavior in organizational settings.* San Francisco: Jossey-Bass.

Simon, H. A. (1960). *The new science of management decision.* New York: Harper & Row.

Simon, S. J., & Werner, J. M. (1996). Computer training through behavior modeling, self-paced, and instructional approaches: A field experiment. *Journal of Applied Psychology, 81,* 648–659.

Simonetti, S. H., & Weitz, J. (1972). Job satisfaction: Cross cultural effects. *Personnel Psychology, 25,* 107–118.

Skarlicki, D. P., & Folger, R. (1997). Retaliation in the workplace: The role of procedural, distributive and interactional justice. *Journal of Applied Psychology, 82,* 434–443.

Skarlicki, D. P., & Latham, G. P. (1996). Increasing citizenship behavior within a labor union: A test of organizational justice theory. *Journal of Applied Psychology, 81,* 161–169.

Skarlicki, D. P., & Latham, G. P. (1997). Leadership training in organizational justice to increase citizenship behavior within a labor union: A replication. *Personnel Psychology, 50,* 617–633.

Skinner, B. F. (1938). *The behavior of organisms.* Englewood Cliffs, NJ: Prentice Hall.

Skinner, B. F. (1954). Science of learning and the art of teaching. *Harvard Educational Review, 24,* 86–97.

Slovic, P. (1993). Perceived risk, trust, and democracy. *Risk Analysis, 13,* 675–682.

Smith, A. (1990). Stress and information processing. In M. Johnston & L. Wallace (Eds.), *Stress and medical procedures: Oxford medical publications* (pp. 58–79). Oxford, England: Oxford University Press.

Smith, C. A., Organ, D. W., & Near, J. P. (1983). Organizational citizenship behavior: Its nature and antecedents. *Journal of Applied Psychology, 68,* 653–663.

Smith, C. S., Robie, C., Folkard, S., Barton, J., MacDonald, I., Smith, I. et al. (1999). A process model of shiftwork and health. *Journal of Occupational and Health Psychology, 4,* 207–218.

Smith, P. B., & Noakes, J. (1996). Cultural differences in group processes. In M. A. West (Ed.), *Handbook of work group psychology.* Chichester, England: John Wiley.

Smith, P. C., & Kendall, L. M. (1963). Retranslation of expectations: An approach to the construction of unambiguous anchors for rating scales. *Journal of Applied Psychology, 47,* 149–155.

Smith, P. C., Kendall, L. M., & Hulin, C. L. (1969). *Job satisfaction in work and retirement: A strategy for the study of attitudes.* Chicago: Rand McNally.

Smith, T., & Anderson, N. (1986). Models of personality and disease: An interactional approach to Type A behavior and cardiovascular risk. *Journal of Personality and Social Psychology, 50,* 1166–1173.

Smither, J. W., London, M., Vasilopoulos, N. L., Reilly, R. R., Millsap, R. E., & Salvemini, N. (1995). An examination of the effects of an upward feedback program over time. *Personnel Psychology, 48,* 1–34.

Smither, J. W., Reilly, R. R., Millsap, R. E., Pearlman, K. & Stoffey, R. W. (1993). Applicant reactions to selection procedures. *Personnel Psychology, 46,* 49–76.

Smith-Jentsch, K. A., Jentsch, F. G., Payne, S. C., & Salas, E. (1996). Can pretraining influences explain individual differences in learning? *Journal of Applied Psychology, 81,* 110–116.

Smith-Jentsch, K. A., Salas, E., & Brannick, M. T. (2001). To transfer or not to transfer? Investigating the combined effects of trainee characteristics, team leader support, and team climate. *Journal of Applied Psychology, 86,* 279–292.

Smola, K. W., & Sutton, C. D. (2002). Generational differences: Revisiting generational work values for the new millennium. *Journal of Organizational Behavior, 23,* 363–382.

Snow, C. C. & Snell, S. A. (1993). Staffing as strategy. In N. Schmitt & W. C. Borman (Eds.), *Personnel selection in organizations* (pp. 448–480). San Francisco: Jossey-Bass.

Society for Human Resources Management (1990). *Code of ethics.* Alexandria, VA: Author.

Society for Industrial and Organizational Psychology (in press). *Principles for the validation and use of personnel selection techniques* (4th ed.). Bowling Green, OH: Author.

Society for Personnel Administration and the American Compensation Association (1981). *Elements of sound base pay administration.* Scottsdale, AZ: Author.

Sokal, M. M. (1982). James McKeen Cattell and the failure of anthropometric mental testing: 1890–1901. In W. R. Woodward & M. G. Ash (Eds.), *The problematic science: Psychology in nineteenth century thought* (pp. 322–345). New York: Praeger.

Solomon, R. L. (1949). An extension of control group design. *Psychological Bulletin, 46,* 137–150.

Sonnentag, S. (1996). Individual well-being. In M. A. West (Ed.), *Handbook of work group psychology.* Chichester, England: John Wiley.

Sothmann, M., Saupe, K., Jesenof, D., Blaney, J., Fuhrman, S., Woulfe, T. et al. (1990). Advancing age and cardiorespiratory stress of fire suppression: Determining a minimum standard for aerobic fitness. *Human Performance, 3,* 217–236.

Sparks, K., Cooper, C., Fried, Y., & Shirom, A. (1997). The effects of hours of work on health: A meta-analytic review. *Journal of Occupational and Organizational Psychology, 70,* 391–408.

Spearman, C. (1927). *The abilities of man.* New York: Macmillan.

Spector, P. E. (1975). Relationships of organizational frustration with reported behavioral reactions of employees. *Journal of Applied Psychology, 60,* 635–637.

Spector, P. E. (1986). Perceived control by employees: A meta-analysis of studies concerning autonomy and participation at work. *Human Relations, 39,* 1005–1016.

Spector, P. E. (2000). *Industrial and organizational psychology: Research and practice* (2nd ed.). New York: John Wiley.

Spector, P. E. (2001). Research methods in industrial and organizational psychology: Data collection and data analysis with special consideration to international issues. In N. Anderson, D. S. Ones, H. K. Sinangil, & C. Viswesvaran (Eds.), *Handbook on industrial, work, and organizational psychology* (pp. 10–26). London: Sage.

Spence, J. T., Helmreich, R. L., & Pred, R. S. (1987). Impatience versus achievement strivings on the Type A pattern: Differential effects on students' health and academic achievement. *Journal of Applied Psychology, 72,* 522–528.

Spychalski, A. C., Quinones, M. A., Gaugler, B. B., & Pohley, K. (1997). A survey of assessment center practices in organizations in the United States. *Personnel Psychology, 50,* 71–90.

Srull, T. K. & Wyer, R. S. (1980). Category accessibility and social perception: Some implications for the study of person memory and interpersonal judgment. *Journal of Personality and Social Psychology, 38,* 841–856.

Srull, T. K. & Wyer, R. S. (1989). Person memory and judgment. *Psychological Review, 96,* 58–83.

Stajkovic, A. D., & Luthans, F. (1997). A meta-analysis of the effects of organizational behavior modification on task performance, 1975–1995. *Academy of Management Journal, 40,* 1122–1149.

Stajkovic, A. D., & Luthans, F. (2001). Differential effects of incentive motivators on work performance. *Academy of Management Journal, 44,* 580–590.

Stanton, J. M. (1998). An empirical assessment of data collection using the Internet. *Personnel Psychology, 51,* 709–725.

Stanton, J. M., & Barnes-Farrell, J. L. (1996). Effects of electronic performance monitoring on personal control, task satisfaction, and task performance. *Journal of Applied Psychology, 81,* 738–745.

Staw, B. M., Bell, N. E., & Clausen, J. A. (1986). The dispositional approach to job satisfaction: A lifetime longitudinal test. *Administrative Science Quarterly, 31,* 56–77.

Steers, R. M., Porter, L. W., & Bigley, G. A. (1996). *Motivation and leadership at work.* New York: McGraw-Hill.

Steiner, D. D. (2002). Personal Communication.

Steiner, D. D., & Gilliland, S. W. (1996). Fairness reactions to personnel selection techniques in France and the United States. *Journal of Applied Psychology, 81,* 134–141.

Steiner, D. D., & Gilliland, S. W. (2001). Procedural justice in personnel selection: International and cross-cultural perspectives. *International Journal of Selection and Assessment, 9*(1/2), 124–137.

Sternberg, R. J., & Kaufmann, J. C. (1998). Human abilities. *Annual Review of Psychology, 49,* 479–502.

Sternberg, R. J., & Wagner, R. K. (1986). *Practical intelligence: Nature and origins of competence in the everyday world.* New York: Cambridge University Press.

Sternberg, R. J., & Wagner, R. K. (1993). The g-ocentric view of intelligence and job performance is wrong. *Current Directions is Psychological Science, 2,* 1–5.

Sternberg, R. J., Wagner, R. K., & Okagaki, L. (1993). Practical intelligence: The nature and role of tacit knowledge in work and at school. In H. Reese and J. Puckett (Eds.), *Advances in lifespan development* (pp. 205–227). Hillsdale, NJ: Erlbaum.

Sternberg, R. J., Wagner, R. K., Williams, W. M., & Horvath, J. A. (1995). Testing common sense. *American Psychologist, 50,* 912–927.

Stevens, M. J., & Campion, M. A. (1993). *The Teamwork-KSA Test.* Chicago: NCS-London House.

Stevens, M. J., & Campion, M. A. (1994). The knowledge, skill, and ability requirements for teamwork: Implications for human resource management. *Journal of Management, 20,* 503–530.

Stevens, M. J., & Campion, M. A. (1999). Staffing work teams: Development and validation of a selection test for teamwork settings. *Journal of Management, 25,* 207–228.

Stewart, G. (2002, April 3). Golfers' children handled with care. *Los Angeles Times,* p. D3.

Stewart, G. L. (1999). Trait bandwidth and stages of job performance: Assessing individual effects for conscientiousness and its subtraits. *Journal of Applied Psychology, 84,* 959–968.

Stokes, G. S., & Mumford, M. D. (Eds.) (1994). *Biodata handbook: Theory, research, and the use of biographical information in selection and performance prediction* (pp. 485–516). Palo Alto, CA: Consulting Psychologists Press Books.

Stone-Romero, E. F. (2002). The relative validity and usefulness of various empirical research designs. In S. G. Rogelberg (Ed.), *Handbook of research methods in industrial and organizational psychology* (pp. 77–98). Cambridge, MA: Blackwell.

Strayer, D. L., & Johnston, W. A. (2001). Driven to distraction: Dual task studies of simulated driving and conversing on a cellular telephone. *Psychological Science, 12*(6), 462–466.

Strong, M. H., Jeanneret, P. R., McPhail, S. M., Blakley, B. R., & D'Egidio, E. L. (1999). Work context: taxonomy and measurement of work environment. In N. G. Peterson, M. D. Mumford, W. C. Borman, P. R. Jeanneret, & E. A. Fleishman (Eds.), *An occupational information system for the 21st century* (pp. 127–146). Washington, DC: American Psychological Association.

Strube, M. J., Lott, C. L., Heilizer, R., & Gregg., B. (1986). Type A behavior pattern and the judgment of control. *Journal of Personality & Social Psychology, 50*, 403–412.

Sun, L. H. (2002, April 20). Anthrax patients' ailments lingering. *Washington Post*, p. A1.

Sundstrom, E., Demuse, K. P., & Futrell, D. (1990). Work teams: Applications and effectiveness. *American Psychologist, 45*, 120–133.

Sundstrom, E., McIntyre, M., Halfhill, T., & Richards, H. (2000). Work groups: From the Hawthorne studies to work teams of the 1990s and beyond. *Group Dynamics: Theory, Research, and Practice, 1,* 44–67.

Super, D. E. (1973). The work values inventory. In D. Zytowski (Ed.), *Contemporary approaches to interest measurement*. Minneapolis: University of Minnesota Press.

Sutton, R. I. (1991). Maintaining norms about expressed emotions: The case of bill collectors. *Administrative Science Quarterly, 36*, 245–268.

Sutton-Smith, B., Rosenberg, B. G., & Landy, F. J. (1968). Father absence effects in families of differing sibling compositions. *Child Development, 39*, 1213–1221.

Svenson, O., & Maule, J. A. (1993). *Time pressure and stress in human judgment and decision-making*. New York: Plenum.

Svyantek, D. J., Goodman, S. A., Benz, L. L., & Gard, J. A. (1999). The relationship between organizational characteristics and team building success. *Journal of Business & Psychology, 14*, 265–283.

Swezey, R. W., & Salas, E. (1992). Guidelines for use in team-training development. In R. W. Swezey & E. Salas (Eds.), *Teams: Their training and performance* (pp. 219–245). Stamford, CT: Ablex.

Symon, G., Cassell, C., & Dickson, R. (2000). Expanding our research and practice through innovative research methods. *European Journal of Work and organizational Psychology, 9*(4), 457–462.

Tannenbaum, S. I. (2002). A strategic view of organizational training and learning. In K. Kraiger (Ed.), *Creating, implementing, and managing effective training and development*. San Francisco: Jossey-Bass.

Tannenbaum, S. I. (1997). Enhancing continuous learning: Diagnostic findings from multiple companies. *Human Resource Management, 36*, 437–452.

Task Force on Assessment Center Guidelines. (1989). *Guidelines and ethical considerations for assessment center operations*. Pittsburgh, PA: Author.

Taylor, M. S., Fisher, C. D., & Ilgen, D. R. (1984). Individuals' reactions to performance feedback in organizations: A control theory perspective. In K. M. Rowland & G. R. Ferris (Eds.), *Research in personnel and human resources management* (Vol. 2 161–187), Greenwich, CT: JAI Press.

Taylor, M. S., Locke, E. A., Lee, C., & Gist, M. E. (1984). Type A behavior and faculty research productivity: What are the mechanisms? *Organizational Behavior and Human Performance, 34*, 402–418.

Tellegen, A. (1993). Folk concepts and psychological concepts in personality and personality disorder. *Psychological Inquiry, 4*, 122–130.

Tellegen, A., Grove, W., & Waller, N. G. (1991). Inventory of personality characteristics, #7 (IPC7). Unpublished manuscript, Department of Psychology, University of Minnesota, Minneapolis.

Tellegen, A., & Waller, N. G. (2000). Exploring personality through test construction: Development of the Multidimensional Personality Questionnaire. In S. R. Briggs & J. M. Cheek (Eds.), *Personality measures: Development and evaluation* Greenwich, CT: JAI Press.

Tepas, D. I., Paley, M. J., & Popkin, S. M. (1997). Work schedules and sustained performance. In G. Salvendy, *Handbook of human factors and ergonomics* (2nd ed., pp. 1021–1058). New York: John Wiley.

Terkel, S. (1974). *Working: People talk about what they do all day and how they feel about what they do*. New York: Pantheon Books.

Tesluk, P. E., & Jacobs, R. R. (1998). Toward an integrated model of work experience. *Personnel Psychology, 51,* 321–355.

Tett, R. P. (1995). Is conscientiousness ALWAYS positively related to job performance? *The Industrial-Organizational Psychologist, 36(1)*, 24–29.

Tett, R. P., Guterman, H. A., Bleir, A., & Murphy, P. J. (2000). Development and content validation of a "hyperdimensional" taxonomy of managerial competence. *Human Performance, 13*, 205–251.

Thayer, P. W. (1997). A rapidly changing world: Some implications for training systems in the year 2001 and beyond. In M. A. Quinones & A. Ehrenstein (Eds.), *Training for a rapidly changing workplace*. Washington, DC: American Psychological Association.

Thomas, A. (1998). Scientific and practical aspects of cross-cultural cooperation and management in the context of European integration. *Studia Psychologica, 40* (1–2), 69–78.

Thomas, K. M. (1996). Psychological privilege and ethnocentrism as barriers to cross-cultural adjustment and effective intercultural interactions. *Leadership Quarterly, 2,* 215–228.

Thomas, K. M. (1998). Psychological readiness for multicultural leadership. *Management Development Forum, 1*(2), 99–112.

Thomas, K. W. (1992). Conflict and negotiation processes in organizations. In M. D. Dunnette & L. M. Hough (Eds.), *Handbook of industrial and organizational psychology* (2nd ed., Vol. 3, pp. 651–717). Palo Alto, CA: Consulting Psychologists Press.

Thomas, R. R., Jr. (1992). Managing diversity: A conceptual framework. In S. E. Jackson & Associates (Eds.), *Diversity in the workplace: Human resource initiatives* (pp. 306–317). New York: Guilford Press.

Thornton, G. C., & Byham, W. C. (1982). *Assessment centers and managerial performance.* New York: Academic Press.

Threlkeld, R., & Brzoshka, K. (1994). Research in distance education. In B. Willis (Ed.), *Distance education: Tools and strategies.* Englewood Cliffs, NJ: Educational Technology Publications.

Thurley, K. (1982, February). The Japanese model: Practical reservations and surprising opportunities. *Personnel Management,* pp. 36–39.

Thurstone, L. L. (1938). Primary mental abilities. *Psychometric Monographs, 1.*

Tierney, P., Farmer, F. M., & Graen, G. B. (1999). An examination of leadership and employee creativity: The relevance of traits and relationships. *Personnel Psychology, 52,* 591–620.

Tolbert, A. S., & McLean, G. N. (1995). Venezuelan culture assimilator for training United States professionals conducting business in Venezuela. *International Journal of Intercultural Relations, 19,* 111–125.

Tolbert, A. S., McLean, G. N., & Myers, R. C. (2002). Creating the global learning organization. *International Journal of Intercultural Relations, 26,* 463–472.

Tornow, W. W., & Pinto, P. R. (1976). The development of a managerial job taxonomy: A system for describing, classifying, and evaluating executive positions. *Journal of Applied Psychology, 61,* 410–418.

Towler, A. J., & Dipboye, R. L. (2001). Effects of trainer expressiveness, organization, and trainee goal orientation on training outcomes. *Journal of Applied Psychology, 86,* 664–673.

Townsend, A. M., Demarie, S. M., & Hendrickson, A. R. (1998). Virtual teams: Technology and the workplace of the future. *Academy of Management Executive, 12,* 17–29.

Tracey, J. B., Tannenbaum, S. I., & Kavanagh, M. J. (1995). Applying trained skills on the job: The importance of the work environment. *Journal of Applied Psychology, 80,* 239–252.

Trahair, R. C. S. (1984). *The humanist temper: The life and work of Elton Mayo.* New Brunswick, NJ: Transaction.

Treimann, D. J., & Hartmann, H. I. (1981). *Women, work, and wages: Equal pay for jobs of equal value.* Washington, DC: National Academy Press.

Triandis, H. C. (1995a). Culture specific assimilators. In S. M. Fowler (Ed.), *Intercultural sourcebook: Cross-cultural training methods* (Vol. 1, pp. 179–186). Yarmouth, ME: Intercultural Press.

Triandis, H. C. (1995b). *Individulism and collectivism.* Boulder, CO: Westview.

Triandis, H. C., & Bhawuk, D. P. S. (1997). Culture theory and the meaning of relatedness. In P. C. Earley & M. Erez (Eds.), *New perspectives on international industrial/organizational psychology* (pp. 13–51). San Francisco: Jossey-Bass.

Triandis, H. C., & Brislin, R. (1984). Cross-cultural psychology. *American Psychologist, 39,* 1006–1016.

Trist, E. L., & Bamforth, K. W. (1951). Some social and psychological consequences of the longwall method of coal-getting. *Human Relations, 4,* 3–38.

Trompenaars, F., & Hampden-Turner, C. (1998). *Riding the waves of culture: Understanding cultural diversity in global business* (2nd ed.). New York: McGraw-Hill.

Truxillo, D. M., & Bauer, T. N. (1999). Applicant reactions to test score banding in entry-level and promotional contexts. *Journal of Applied Psychology, 84,* 322–339.

Tsui, A. S., Egan, T. D., & O'Reilly, C. A. (1991). Being different: Relational demography and organizational attachment. *Academy of Management Best Paper Proceedings, 37,* 183–187.

Tsui, A. S., Egan, T. D., & O'Reilly, C. A. (1992). Being different: Relational demography and organizational attachment. *Administrative Science Quarterly, 37,* 549–579.

Tsui, A. S., & O'Reilly, C. A. (1989). Beyond simple demographics: The importance of relational demography in superior-subordinate dyads. *Academy of Management Journal, 32,* 402–423.

Tubre, T. C., & Collins, J. M. (2000). Jackson and Schuler (1985) revisited: A meta-analysis of the relationships between role ambiguity, role conflict, and job performance. *Journal of Management, 26,* 155–169.

Tuckman, B. W., & Jensen, M. A. (1977). Stages of small-group development revisited. *Group & Organization Studies, 2,* 419–427.

Turnage, J. J. (1990). The challenge of new workplace technology for psychology. In L. Offermann & M. Gowing (Eds.) [Special issue]. *American Psychologist, 45,* 171–178.

Turner, N., Barling, J., Epitropaki, O., Butcher, V., & Milner, C. (2002). Transformational leadership and moral reasoning. *Journal of Applied Psychology, 87,* 304–311.

Tziner, A., & Eden, D. (1985). Effects of crew composition on crew performance: Does the whole equal the sum of its parts? *Journal of Applied Psychology, 70,* 85–93.

Uchino, B. N., Cacioppo, J. T., & Kiecolt-Glaser, J. K. (1996). The relationship between social support and physiological processes: A review with emphasis on underlying mechanisms and implications for health. *Psychological Bulletin, 119,* 488–531.

Ulmer, D. K., & Schwartzburd, L. (1996). Treatment of time pathologies. In R. Allan & S. Scheidt (Eds.), *Heart and mind: The practice of cardiac psychology.* Washington, DC: American Psychological Association.

Ulrich, L., & Trumbo, D. (1965). The selection interview since 1949. *Psychological Bulletin, 63,* 100–116.

Uniform Guidelines on Employee Selection Procedures (1978). *Federal Register, 43,* 38290–38315.

Unsworth, K. L., & West, M. A. (2000). Teams: The challenges of cooperative work. In N. Chmiel (Ed.), *Introduction to work and organizational psychology.* Oxford, England: Blackwell.

U.S. Department of Transportation. (1996). *Traffic Safety CD-ROM, 1975–1994* (BTS-CD-10). Washington, DC: Bureau of Transportation Statistics.

Van Buren, M., (2001). *The 2001 ASTD state of the industry report.* Alexandria, VA: American Society for Training and Development.

Van Buren, M., & King, S. (2000). *The 2000 ASTD international comparisons report.* Alexandria, VA: American Society for Training and Development.

Vandenberg, R. J., & Self, R. M. (1993). Assessing newcomers' changing commitments to organizations during the first 6 months of work. *Journal of Applied Psychology, 78* (4), 557–568.

VandenBos, G. R., & Bulatao, E. Q. (1996). *Violence on the job: Identifying risks and developing solutions.* Washington, DC: American Psychological Association.

Vanderheiden, G. C. (1997). Design for people with functional limitations resulting from disability, aging, and circumstance. In G. Salvendy, *Handbook of human factors and ergonomics* (2nd ed., pp. 2010–2052). New York: John Wiley.

van der Klink, J. J., Blonk, R. W., Schene, A. H., van Dijk, F. J. (2001). The benefits of interventions for work-related stess. *American Journal of Public Health, 91,* 270–276.

Van Dierendonck, D., Schaufeli, W. B., & Buunk, B. P. (2001). Burnout and inequity among human service professionals. *Journal of Occupational Health Psychology, 6,* 43–52.

van Drunen, P., & van Strien, P. J. (1999). Psychology in the Netherlands: Recent trends and current situation *European Psychologist, 4,* 263–271.

Van Eerde, W., & Thierry, H. (1996). Vroom's expectancy models and work-related criteria: A meta-analysis. *Journal of Applied Psychology, 81,* 575–586.

Van Mannen, J., & Schein, E. H. (1979). Toward a theory of organizational commitment. In B. M. Staw (Ed.), *Research in Organizational Behavior* (Vol. 1, pp. 197–216). Greenwich, CT: JAI Press.

Van Scotter, J. R., & Motowidlo, S. J. (1996). Interpersonal facilitation and job dedication as separate facets of contextual performance. *Journal of Applied Psychology, 81* (5), 525–531.

Van Scotter, J. R., Motowidlo, S. J., & Cross, T. C. (2000). Effects of task performance and contextual performance on systemic rewards. *Journal of Applied Psychology, 85* (4), 526–535.

van Strien, P. J. (1998). Psychotechnics in the Netherlands. *Revista de Historia de la Psicologia, 19,* 121–141.

Vecchio, R. P. (1981). An individual differences interpretation of the conflicting interpretations generated by equity theory and expectancy theory. *Journal of Applied Psychology, 66,* 470–481.

Velocci, A. L., Jr. (1998). Pursuit of Six Sigma emerges as an industry trend. *Aviation Week and Space Technology, 149* (20), 52–58.

Vinacke, E. (1962). Motivation as a complex problem. *Nebraska Symposium on Motivation, 10,* 1–45.

Vincente, K. (1999). *Cognitive work analysis.* Mahwah, NJ: Erlbaum.

Vinchur, V. J., Schippmann, J. S., Switzer, F. S., & Roth, P. L. (1998). A meta-analytic review of predictors of job performance for salespeople. *Journal of Applied Psychology, 83,* 586–597.

Vinokur, A. D., & van Ryn, M. (1993). Social support and undermining in close relationships: Their independent effect on the mental health of unemployed persons. *Journal of Personality and Social Psychology, 65,* 350–359.

Viswesvaran, C., & Ones, D. S. (1999). Meta-analyses of fakability estimates: Implications for personality measurement. *Educational and Psychological Measurement, 59,* 197–210.

Viswesvaran, C., Ones, D. S., & Schmidt, F. L. (1996). Comparative analysis of the reliability of job performance ratings. *Journal of Applied Psychology, 81,* 557–574.

Viswesvaran, C., Sanchez, J. I., & Fisher, J. (1999). The role of social support in the process of work stress: A meta-analysis. *Journal of Vocational Behavior, 54,* 314–334.

Viteles, M. S. (1922). Job specifications and diagnostic tests of job competency designed for the auditing division of a street railway company. *Psychological Clinic, 14,* 83–105.

Viteles, M. S. (1926). Psychology in industry. *Psychological Bulletin, 23,* 631–680.

Viteles, M. S. (1928). Psychology in industry. *Psychological Bulletin, 25,* 309–340.

Viteles, M. S. (1930). Psychology in industry. *Psychological Bulletin, 27,* 567–635.

Viteles, M. S. (1932). *Industrial psychology.* New York: W. W. Norton.

Viteles, M. S. (1953). *Motivation and morale in industry.* New York: W. W. Norton.

Vroom, V. H. (1964). *Work and motivation.* New York: John Wiley.

Vroom, V. H., & Jago, A. G. (1988). *The new leadership: managing participation in organizations.* Englewood Cliffs, NJ: Prentice Hall.

Vroom, V. H., & Yetton, P. W. (1973). *Leadership and decision-making.* Pittsburgh, PA: University of Pittsburgh Press.

Waclawski, J. (1999). The real world: Generation X or generation gap? *The Industrial-Organizational Psychologist, 37* (1), 79–90.

Waclawski, J., & Church, A. H. (2002). *Organizational development: A data-driven approach to organizational change.* San Francisco: Jossey-Bass.

Wagner, R. (1949). The employment interview: A critical review. *Personnel Psychology, 2,* 17–46.

Wahba, M. A., & Bridwell, L. B. (1976). Maslow reconsidered: A review of research on the need hierarchy theory. *Organizational Behavior and Human Performance, 15,* 212–240.

Waldman, D. A. (1997). Predictors of employee preferences for multirater and group-based performance appraisal. *Group & Organization Management, 22,* 264–287.

Waldman, D. A., & Atwater, L. E. (2001). Attitudinal and behavioral outcomes of an upward feedback process. *Group & Organization Management, 26,* 189–205.

Walker, A. (1999). Combating age discrimination at the workplace. *Experimental Aging Research, 25,* 367–377.

Walker, A. G., & Smither, J. W. (1999). A five-year study of upward feedback: What managers do with their results matters. *Personnel Psychology, 52,* 393–423.

Walker, E., Bonsall, R., & Walder, D. (2002). Plasma hormones and catecholamine metabolites in monozygotic twins discordant for psychosis. *Neuropsychiatry, Neuropsychology, and Behavioral Neurology, 15* (1), 10–17.

Wall, T. D., Kemp, N. J., Jackson, P. R., & Clegg, C. W. (1986). Outcomes of autonomous work groups: A field experiment. *Academy of Management Journal, 29,* 280–304.

Waller, M. J., Conte, J. M., Gibson, C., & Carpenter, M. (2001). The impact of individual time perception on team performance under deadline conditions. *Academy of Management Review, 26,* 586–600.

Wanberg, C. R., & Kammeyer-Mueller, J. D. (2000). Predictors and outcomes of proactivity in the socialization process. *Journal of Applied Psychology, 85,* 373–385.

Wanous, J. P., & Dean, R. A. (1984). The effect of realistic job previews on hiring bank tellers. *Journal of Applied Psychology, 69,* 335–344.

Wanous, J. P., Reichers, A. E., & Hundy, M. J. (1997). Overall job satisfaction: How good are single-item measures? *Journal of Applied Psychology, 82,* 247–252.

Wanous, J. P., & Zwany, A. (1977). A cross sectional test of need hierarchy theory. *Organizational Performance and Human Behavior, 18,* 78–89.

Warr, P. B. (1990). The measurement of well-being and other aspects of mental health. *Journal of Occupational Psychology, 63,* 93–210.

Warr, P. B. (1983). Work, jobs and unemployment. *Bulletin of the British Psychological Society, 36,* 305–311.

Warr, P. B. (1987). *Work, unemployment and mental health.* Oxford, England: Clarendon Press.

Warr, P. B. (1999). Well-being in the workplace. In D. Kahneman, E. Diener, & N. Schwarz (Eds.), *Well being: The foundations of hedonic psychology* (pp. 392–412), New York: Russell Sage Foundation.

Warr, P. B., Allan, C., & Birdi, K. (1999). Predicting three levels of training outcome. *Journal of Occupational and Organizational Psychology, 72,* 351–375.

Watson, W. E., Kumar, K., & Michaelsen, L. K. (1993). Cultural diversity's impact on interaction process and performance: Comparing homogenous and diverse task groups. *Academy of Management Journal, 36,* 590–602.

Weber, M. (1947). *The theory of social and ecomomic organization.* In A. R. Henderson and T. Parsons (Eds.), New York: Oxford University Press.

Weber, Y. (2000). Measuring cultural fit in mergers and acquisitions. In N. Ashkenasy, C. Wilderom, & M. Peterson (Eds.), *Handbook of organizational culture and climate* (pp. 309–320). London: Sage.

Webster, E. C. (1982). *The employment interview: A social judgment process.* Schomberg, Ontario, Canada: SIP Publications.

Webster, J., & Hackley, P. (1997). Teaching effectiveness in technology-mediated distance learning. *Academy of Management Journal, 40,* 1282–1309.

Wedderburn, A. A. I. (1981). How important are the social effects of shift work? In L. C. Johnson, D. I. Tepas, W. P. Colquhoun, & M. J. Colligan (Eds.), *Biological rhythms, sleep, and shift work.* New York: Spectrum.

Weekly, J. A., & Jones, C. (1997). Video based situational testing. *Personnel Psychology, 50,* 25–49.

Weick, K., & Quinn, R. (1999). Organizational change and development. *Annual Review of Psychology, 50,* 361–386.

Weiner, B. (1991). Metaphors in motivation and attribution. *American Psychologist, 46* (9), 921–930.

Weiner, B. (1992). *Human motivation: Metaphors, theories, and research*. London: Sage.

Weiss, D. J., Dawis, R. V., England, G. W., & Lofquist, L. H. (1967). *Manual for the Minnesota Satisfaction Questionnaire*. Minneapolis: Industrial Relations Center, University of Minnesota.

Weiss, H. M. (2002). Conceptual and empirical foundations for the study of affect at work. In R. G. Lord, R. L. Klimoski, & R. Kanfer (Eds.), *Emotions in the workplace: Understanding the structure and role of emotions in organizational behavior* (pp. 20–63). San Francisco: Jossey-Bass.

Weiss, H. M. (in press). Deconstructing job satisfaction: Separating evaluations, beliefs, and affective experiences. *Human Resource Review*.

Weiss, H. M., & Cropanzano, R. (1996). Affective events theory: A theoretical discussion of the structure, causes, and consequences of affective experiences at work. *Research in Organizational Behavior, 18,* 1–74.

Weiss, H. M., Suckow, K., & Cropanzano, R. (1999). Effects of justice conditions on discrete emotions. *Journal of Applied Psychology, 84,* 786–794.

Welbourne, T. M., & Andrews, A. O. (1996). Predicting the performance of initial public offerings: Should human resource management be in the equation. *Academy of Management Journal, 39,* 891–919.

Wells, D., & Schminke, M. (2001). Ethical development and human resource training. *Human Resource Management Review, 11,* 135–158.

Wentworth, D. K. (2002). The schizophrenic organization. *The Industrial-Organizational Psychologist, 39* (4), 39–41.

Werner, J. M., & Bolino, M. C. (1997). Explaining U.S. Courts of Appeals decisions involving performance appraisal: Accuracy, fairness, and validation. *Personnel Psychology, 50,* 1–23.

West, M. A., & Anderson, N. R. (1996). Innovation in top management teams. *Journal of Applied Psychology, 81,* 680–693.

West, M. A., Borrill, C. S., & Unsworth, K. L. (1998). Team effectiveness in organizations. In C. L. Cooper & I. T. Robertson (Eds.), *International Review of Industrial and Organizational Psychology, 13,* 1–48.

Westman, M., & Eden, D. (1996). The inverted-U relationship between stress and performance: A field study. *Work & Stress, 10,* 165–173.

Wexley, K. N., & Latham, G. P. (2002). *Developing and training human resources in organizations* (3rd ed.). Upper Saddle River, NJ: Prentice Hall.

Wheatley, M. J. (1992). *Leadership and the new science*. San Francisco: Berrett-Koehler.

Whitney, D. J., & Schmitt, N. (1997). Relationship between culture and response to biodata items. *Journal of Applied Psychology, 82,* 113–129.

Whyte, W. H. (1956). *The organization man.* New York: Simon & Schuster.

Whyte, G., & Latham, G. P. (1997). The futility of utility analysis revisited. *Personnel Psychology, 50,* 601–610.

Wickens, C. D., Gordon, S. E., & Liu, Y. (1998). *An introduction to human factors engineering.* New York: Longman.

Wickens, C. D., & Hollands, J. G. (2000). *Engineering psychology and human performance* (3rd ed.). Upper Saddle River, NJ: Prentice Hall.

Wiesner, W. H., & Cronshaw, S. F. (1988). A meta-analytic investigation of the impact of interview format and degree of structure on the validity of the employment interview. *Journal of Occupational Psychology, 61,* 275–290.

Wigdor, A. K., & Green, B. F. (1991). *Performance assessment in the workplace.* Washington, DC: National Academy Press.

Wilkerson, J. M. (1999). The impact of job level and prior training on sexual harassment labeling and remedy choice. *Journal of Applied Social Psychology, 29,* 1605–1623.

Williams, K. J., Suls, J., Alliger, G. M., Learner, S. M., & Wan, C. K. (1991). Multiple role juggling and daily mood states in working mothers: An experience sampling study. *Journal of Applied Psychology, 76,* 664–674.

Williams, R. E. (1956). *A description of some executive abilities by means of a critical incident technique.* Unpublished doctoral dissertation. Columbia University, New York.

Williams, R. L. (1972). *The BITCH-100: A culture-specific test.* Paper presented at the annual convention of the American Psychological Association. Honolulu, HI.

Winefield, A. H., & Tiggemann, M. (1990). Employment status and psychological well-being: A longitudinal study. *Journal of Applied Psychology, 75,* 455–459.

Winefield, A. H., Winefield, H. R., Tiggemann, M., & Godney, R. D. (1991). A longitudinal study of the psychological effects of unemployment and unsatisfactory employment on young adults. *Journal of Applied Psychology, 76,* 424–431.

Witt, L. A., & Nye, L. G. (1992). Gender and the relationship between perceived fairness of pay or promotion and job satisfaction. *Journal of Applied Psychology, 77,* 910–917.

Woehr, D. J. (1994). Understanding frame-of-reference training: The impact of training on the recall of performance information. *Journal of Applied Psychology, 79,* 525–534.

Woehr, D. J., & Feldman, J. (1993). Processing objective and question order effects on the causal relationship between memory and judgment in performance appraisal: The tip of the iceberg. *Journal of Applied Psychology, 78,* 232–241.

Woehr, D. J., & Huffcut, A. I. (1994). Rater training for performance appraisal: A quantitative review. *Journal of Occupational and Organizational Psychology, 67,* 189–205.

Wong, E. (2002, March 20). 13-year-old girl dies after being struck by puck at NHL game. *New York Times,* p. C19.

Wood, R. E., Atkins, P., & Tabernero, C. (2000). Self efficacy and strategy on complex tasks. *Applied Psychology: An International Review, 49,* 430–446.

Wood, R. E., & Bandura, A. (1989). Impact of conceptions of ability of self-regulatory mechanisms and complex decision making. *Journal of Personality and Social Psychology, 56,* 407–415.

Wood, R. E., George-Falvy, J., & Debowsky, S. (2001). Motivation and information search on complex tasks. In M. Erez, U. Kleinbeck, & H. Thierry (Eds.), *Work motivation in the context of a globalising economy* (pp. 33–57). Hillsdale, NJ: Erlbaum.

Woodward, J. (1958). *Management and technology.* London: Her Majesty's Stationery Office.

Worren, N. (1996). Management fashion. *Academy of Management Review, 21,* 613–614.

Wright, L. (1988). The Type A behavior pattern and coronary artery disease. *American Psychologist, 43,* 2–14.

Wright, T. A., & Cropanzano, R. (1998). Emotional exhaustion as a predictor of job performance and voluntary turnover. *Journal of Applied Psychology, 83,* 486–493.

Wright, T. A., & Cropanzano, R. (2000). Psychological well-being and job satisfaction as predictors of job performance. *Journal of Occupational Health Psychology, 5,* 84–94.

Xiao, Y., & Vincente, K. J. (2000). A framework for epistemological analysis in empirical (laboratory and field) studies. *Human Factors, 42,* 87–101.

Xie, J. L. (1996). Karasek's model in the People's Republic of China: Effects of job demands, control, and individual differences. *Academy of Management Journal, 39,* 1594–1618.

Yarnold, P. R., & Grimm, L. G. (1982). Time urgency among coronary-prone individuals. *Journal of Abnormal Psychology, 91,* 175–177.

Yerkes, R. M., & Dodson, J. D. (1908). The relation of strength of stimulus to rapidity of habit-formation. *Journal of Comparative Neurology and Psychology, 18,* 459–482.

Yukl, G. (1981). *Leadership in organizations.* Englewood Cliffs, NJ: Prentice Hall.

Yukl, G. (1987). *A new perspective for integrating diverse perspectives on managerial behavior.* Paper presented at the annual meeting of the American Psychological Association, New York.

Yukl, G. (1998). *Leadership in organizations* (4th ed.). Upper Saddle River, NJ: Prentice Hall.

Zapf, D. (1999). Organizational, work group related, and personal causes of mobbing/bullying at work. *International Journal of Manpower, 20,* 70–85.

Zapf, D., & Einarsen, S. (2001). Bullying in the workplace: Recent trends in research and practice. *European Journal of Work and Organizational Psychology, 10* (4), 369–373.

Zapf, D., & Gross, C. (2001). Conflict escalation and coping with workplace bullying: A replication and extension. *European Journal of Work and Organizational Psychology, 10* (4), 497–522.

Zaslow, J. (2002, October 16). Moving on: The sniper's other victims. *The Wall Street Journal,* p. D1.

Zedeck, S. (1992). Introduction: Exploring the domain of work and family concerns. In S. Zedeck (Ed.), *Work, families and organizations* (pp. 1–32). San Francisco: Jossey-Bass.

Zedeck, S., Cascio, W. F., Goldstein, I. L., & Outtz, J. (1996). Sliding bands: An alternative to top-down selection. In R. S. Barrett (Ed.), *Fair employment strategies in human resource management* (pp. 222–234). Westport, CT: Quorum.

Zellars, K. J., Tepper, B. J., & Duffy, M. K. (2002). Abusive supervision and subordinates' organizational citizenship behaviors. *Journal of Applied Psychology, 87,* 1068–1078.

Zhang, S., & Fulford, C. (1994). Are time and psychological interactivity the same thing in distance learning television classroom? *Educational Technology, 34,* 58–64.

Zimmer, T. (1972). The impact of Watergate on the public trust in people and confidence in the mass media. *Social Science Quarterly, 59,* 743–751.

Zohar, D. (2000). A group-level model of safey climate: Testing the effect of group climate on microaccidents in manufacturing jobs. *Journal of Applied Psychology, 85,* 587–596.

Zohar, D. (2002). Modifying supervisory practices to improve subunit safety: A leadership-based intervention model. *Journal of Applied Psychology, 87,* 156–163.

Chapter 1: What Is Industrial and Organizational Psychology?

Pp. 3, 5: Quotes from Gardner, H. (2002). Good work, well done: A psychological study. *The Chronicle of Higher Education,* Feb. 22, pp. B7(3). Reprinted by permission of Howard Gardner.

P. 4: Box 1.1 from Terkel, S. (1974). *Working: People talk about what they do all day and how they feel about what they do.* New York: Pantheon Press, pp. 758–759. Copyright 1974 by Studs Terkel. Reprinted by permission of Donadio & Olson, Inc.

P. 5: Box 1.2 from Garson, B. (1975). *All the livelong day,* #1 from p.19; #2 from p. 250–251. New York: Penguin Books. Copyright © Barbara Garson. Used by permission of the author.

P. 6: Box 1.3 from Maurer, H. (1979). *Not working,* p. 103–104. New York: Holt, Rinehart & Winston. © 1979 by Harry Maurer. Reprinted by permission of Henry Holt and Company, LLC.

P. 7: Quote from SIOP, and Table 1.1. Used by permission of the Society for Industrial & Organizational Psychology.

P. 9: Figure 1.1 adapted from 2002 SIOP Survey. Used by permission of the Society for Industrial & Organizational Psychology.

P. 24: Cartoon ID #32865, published in *The New Yorker* 4/29/1996. © The New Yorker Collection 1996 Tom Cheney from cartoonbank.com. All Rights Reserved.

P. 28: Table 1.6 from Hostede, G. (2001). *Culture's consequences: Comparing values, behaviors, institutions, and organizations across nations,* 2nd ed. Thousand Oaks, CA: Sage Publications. Table based on Hofstede, G. (1991). The implications of cultural dimensions for human resource management. In G. Hofstede, *Cultures and organizations:Software of the mind.* New York: McGraw-Hill. Reproduced with permission of Geert Hofstede.

P. 29: Figure 1.3 from Hofstede, G. (1993). Cultural constraints in management theories. *Academy of Management Executive 7,* p. 91. Copyright 1993. Reprinted by permission of *Academy of Management Executive* via the Copyright Clearance Center.

P. 30: Figure 1.4 adapted from Triandis, H. C. and Bhawuk, D. P. S. (1997). Cultural theory and the meaning of relatedness. In P. C. Earley and M. Erez (Eds.), *New perspectives on international industrial/organizational psychology,* pp. 13–51. San Francisco: Jossey-Bass. This material is used by permission of John Wiley & Sons, Inc.

Chapter 2: Studying and Interpreting Worker Behavior

P. 46: Table 2.1 adapted from Spector, P. E. (2001). Research methods in industrial and organizational psychology: Data collection and data analysis with special consideration to international issues. In N. Anderson, D. S. Ones, H. K. Sinangil, & C. Viswesvaran (Eds.), *Handbook of industrial, work, and organizational psychology* (10–26). London: Sage Publications. Reprinted by permission of Sage Publications, Ltd.

P. 53: Cartoon ID #33515. © The New Yorker Collection 1989 Mick Stevens from cartoonbank.com. All Rights Reserved.

Pp. 69, 70: Quotes from SIOP (in press). Draft *Principles for the validation and use of personnel selection procedures.* Used by permission of the Society for Industrial & Organizational Psychology.

P. 72: Figure 2.11 from Arvey, R. D. (1992). Constructs and construct validation: Definitions and issues. *Human Performance, 51 (1&2),* pp. 59–69, Fig. 3 on p. 65. Used by permission of Lawrence Erlbaum Associates, Inc.

Chapter 3: Individual Differences

P. 79: Figure 3.1 from Murphy, K. R. (Ed.) (1996). *Individual differences and behavior in organizations,* p. 47. San Francisco: Jossey-Bass. This material is used by permission of John Wiley & Sons, Inc.

Pp. 83–89: Table 3.1, adapted in part from Fleishman, E. A., Costanza, D. P., & Marshall-Mies, J. (1999). Abilities. In Peterson, N. G, Mumford, M. D., Borman, W. C., Jeanneret, P. R., & Fleishman, E. A. (1999). *An occupational information system for the 21st century.*

Washington, D. C.: American Psychological Association. Copyright © 1999 by the American Psychological Association. Reprinted with permission. And adapted in part from Fleishman, E. A. (1992). Definitions of abilities in the taxonomy with task examples. In E. A. Fleishman & M. E. Reilly, *Handbook of human abilities: Definitions, measurements, and job task requirements.* Palo Alto, CA: Consulting Psychologists Press. See also Fleishman & Quaintance (1984); Fleishman & Reilly (1992); Fleishman, Costanza, & Marshall-Meis (1999). The *Fleishman Job Analysis Survey (F-JAS)* measures the extent to which each of these abilities is required in different jobs (Fleishman, 1992). Reprinted by permission of Edwin A. Fleishman, Management Research Institute, Inc. Publications.

P. 92: Figure 3.2 from Carroll, J. B. (1993). *Human cognitive abilities: A survey of factor-analytic studies.* Cambridge, UK: Cambridge University Press. Reprinted with the permission of Cambridge University Press.

P. 94: Figure 3.3 from Guion, R. M. (1998). *Assessment, measurement, and prediction,* Fig. 3.7, p. 148. Mahwah, NJ: Lawrence Erlbaum Associates. Reprinted by permission of Lawrence Erlbaum Associates, Inc.

P. 95: Table 3.3, adapted in part from Fleishman, E. A., Costanza, D. P., & Marshall-Mies, J. (1999). Abilities. In Peterson, N. G, Mumford, M. D., Borman, W. C., Jeanneret, P. R., & Fleishman, E. A. (1999). *An occupational information system for the 21st century.* Washington, D. C.: American Psychological Association. Copyright © 1999 by the American Psychological Association. Reprinted with permission. And adapted in part from Fleishman, E. A. (1992). Definitions of abilities in the taxonomy with task examples. In E. A. Fleishman & M. E. Reilly, *Handbook of Human Abilities: Psychomotor abilities.* Palo Alto, CA: Consulting Psychologists Press. Extracted from Figure 4.1; see also Fleishman (1972); Fleishman & Reilly (1992). Reprinted by permission of

Edwin A. Fleishman, Management Research Institute, Inc. Publications.

P. 106: Table 3.5 and Figure 3.4 from Hogan, R., & Blake, R. J. (1996). Vocational interests: Matching self-concept with the work environment. In K. R. Murphy (Ed.), *Individual differences and behavior in organizations,* pp. 98, 99. San Francisco, CA: Jossey-Bass. This material is used by permission of John Wiley & Sons, Inc.

Pp. 110–114: Table 3.6 adapted from Peterson, N. G., Mumford, M. D., Borman, W. C., Jeanneret, P. R., & Fleishman, E. A. (1999). *An occupational information system for the 21st century,* pp. 77–79. Copyright © 1999 by the American Psychological Association. Reprinted with permission.

Chapter 4: Assessing Individuals

P. 123: Quote from Guion, R. M. (1998). *Assessment, measurement, and prediction,* p. 485. Mahwah, NJ: Lawrence Erlbaum Associates. Reprinted by permission of Lawrence Erlbaum Associates, Inc.

P. 125: Table 4.1 from Moreland, J. L., et al. (1995). Assessment of test user qualifications. *American Psychologist, 50,* pp. 14–23; table on p. 16. Copyright © 1995 by the American Psychological Association. Reprinted with permission.

P. 125: Cartoon ID #36185. © The New Yorker Collection 1987 Dana Fradon from cartoonbank.com. All Rights Reserved.

P. 128: Table 4.2 from Impara, J. C., & Plake, B. S. (Eds.) (1998). *The thirteenth mental measurements yearbook,* p. 287. Lincoln, NE: Buros Institute of Mental Measurements, University of Nebraska. A review of the above test is available from the Buros Institute at: http://www.unl.edu/buros/; used by permission.

P. 130: Quote from Greenfield, P. M. (1997). You can't take it with you: Why ability assessments don't cross cultures. *American Psychologist, 52,* p. 1116. Copyright © 1997 by the American Psychological Association. Reprinted with permission.

P. 132: Quote from Guion, R. M. (1998). *Assessment, measurement, and prediction,* p. 486. Mahwah, NJ: Lawrence Erlbaum Associates. Reprinted by permission of Lawrence Erlbaum Associates, Inc.

P. 132: Figure 4.2 from *Bennett Mechanical Comprehension Test,* Form BB, Item Y. Copyright © 1942, 1967–1970, 1980 by The Psychological Corporation, a Harcourt Assessment Company. Reproduced by permission. All rights reserved.

P. 135: Figure 4.4 from *Crawford Small Parts Dexterity Test.* Copyright © 1946, 1956, 1998 by The Psychological Corporation, a Harcourt Assessment Company. Reproduced by permission. All rights reserved.

P. 137: Figure 4.5 from Occupational Personality Questionnaire (OPQ32). Boulder, CO: SHL. © SHL Group PLC. Used by permission of Saville Holdsworth Limited: www.shlgroup.com/home.asp

P. 138: Table 4.5 from Spector, P. E. (2000). *Industrial and organizational psychology,* 2nd ed., p. 107. New York: John Wiley & Sons. Copyright © 2000. This material is used by permission of John Wiley & Sons, Inc.

P. 141: Table 4.6 from Ryan, A. M., & Sackett, P. R. (1992). Relationships between graduate training, professional affiliation, and individual psychological assessment practices for personnel decisions. *Personnel Psychology, 45,* pp. 363–387; Table 4 on p. 371. Copyright 1992. Used by permission.

P. 142: Figure 4.6, "A Blueprint for Individual Assessment," Executive Success Profile. Personnel Decisions International © 1991.

P. 142: Figure 4.7 from Competency Factors, THE PROFILOR® for Executives. Copyright © 1991 Personnel Decisions International Corporation. Used by permission.

P. 144: Table 4.7 from Schneider, B., & Schmitt, N. (1986). *Staffing organizations,* 2nd ed. Original copyright © 1986, 1976 by Scott, Foresman and Company. Copyright © 1991 by Benjamin Schneider and Neal Schmitt. Used by permission.

P. 146: Table 4.9 from Bray, D. W., Campbell, R. J., & Grant, D. L. (1974). *Formative years in business: A long-term AT&T study of managerial lives.* New York: John Wiley & Sons. Copyright © 1974. This material is used by permission of John Wiley & Sons, Inc.

P. 147: Photo from Poffenberger, A. T. (1929). *Applied psychology: Its principles and methods,* facing p. 322. New York: D. Appleton.

P. 150: Figure 4.9 from Mumford, M. D., & Stokes, G. S. (1991). Developmental determinants of individual action: Theory and practice in applying background measures. In M. D. Dunnette & L. M. Hough (Eds.), *Handbook of industrial and organizational psychology,* 2nd ed., Vol. 3, p. 84. Palo Alto, CA: Consulting Psychologists Press. Modified and reproduced by special permission of the Publisher, CPP, Inc., Palo Alto,

CA 94303. Copyright 1992 by CPP, Inc. All rights reserved. Further reproduction is prohibited without the Publisher's written consent.

Pp. 150–151: Quote from Guion, R. M. (1998). *Assessment, measurement, and prediction.* Mahwah, NJ: Lawrence Erlbaum Associates. Reprinted by permission of Lawrence Erlbaum Associates, Inc.

P. 151: Table 4.11 from Mael, F. A. (1991). A conceptual rationale for the domain and attribute of biodata items. *Personnel Psychology, 44,* p. 773. Used by permission of Personnel Psychology, Bowling Green, OH.

P. 157: Table 4.12 adapted from Cascio, W. F. (1998b). *Managing human resources,* 5th ed., p. 214. New York: McGraw Hill. Reproduced with permission of The McGraw Hill Companies.

P. 161: Quote and Figure 4.11 from Murphy, K. R., & Davidshofer, C. O. (2001*). Psychological testing: Principles and application,* 5th ed., p. 242. Upper Saddle River, N. J.: Prentice Hall. © 2001. Reprinted by permission of Pearson Education, Inc., Upper Saddle River, NJ.

Chapter 5: Understanding Performance

Pp. 174, 175: Tables 5.2 & 5.3 adapted from Pulakos, E. D., Arad, S., Donovan, M. A., & Plamandon, K. E. (2000). Adaptability in the workplace: Development of a taxonomy of adaptive performance. *Journal of Applied Psychology, 85 (4),* Tables 1 & 2, p. 617. Copyright © 2000 by the American Psychological Association. Reprinted with permission.

P. 182: Figure 5.6 from Cades, E. (1924). The textile industry in Philadelphia. *Psych. Clin., 15,* 203–228; cited in Viteles (1932), pp. 151–152.

P. 183: Figure 5.7 from Viteles, M. S. (1932). *Industrial psychology,* p. 153. New York: W. W. Norton. Copyright 1932 by W. W. Norton & Company, Inc. Used by permission of W. W. Norton & Company, Inc.

P. 194: Table 5.5 & Figure 5.9 from Guion, R. M. (1998). *Assessment, measurement, and prediction,* pp. 81–82, 83. Mahwah, NJ: Lawrence Erlbaum Associates. Reprinted by permission of Lawrence Erlbaum Associates, Inc.

Pp. 196, 197: Figure 5.10 & 5.11 from Saville Holdsworth Limited (2001). *The Work Profiling System (WPS) technical manual,* pp. 29, 23. Boulder, CO: SHL. © 2001 SHL Group PLC. Used by permission of Saville Holdsworth Limited: www.shlgroup.com/home.asp

P. 199: Figure 5.12 from Mumford, M. D., & Peterson, N. G. (1999). The O*NET content model: Structural considerations in describing jobs. In N. G. Peterson, M. D. Mumford, W. C. Borman, P. R. Jeanneret, & E. A. Fleishman (Eds.) (1999). *An occupational information system for the 21st century*, p. 25. Washington, D.C.: American Psychological Association. Copyright © 1999 by the American Psychological Association. Reprinted with permission.

Chapter 6: Performance Measurement

P. 219: Figure 6.1 from Landy, F. J., & Farr, J. L. (1980). Performance rating. *Psychological Bulletin, 87*, 72–107. Copyright © 1980 by the American Psychological Association. Reprinted with permission.

P. 220: Figure 6.2 adapted from Borman, W. C., White, L. A., Pulakos, E. D., & Oppler, S. H. (1991). Models of supervisory job performance ratings. *Journal of Applied Psychology, 76*, pp. 863–872; figure on p. 870. Copyright © 1991 by the American Psychological Association. Adapted with permission.

P. 223: Figure 6.3 from Guion, R. M. (1965). *Personnel testing*, p. 114. New York: McGraw Hill. Reprinted by permission of R.M. Guion.

P. 228: Table 6.8 from Latham, G. P., & Wexley, K. N. (1981). *Increasing productivity through performance appraisal*, Fig. 3-8 on p. 56. Copyright 1981, Addison-Wesley Publishing Co., Inc. Reprinted by permission of Pearson Education, Inc., Upper Saddle River, NJ.

P. 235: Cartoon ID #25227, Published in *The New Yorker* 5/17/1993. © The New Yorker Collection 1993 J. B. Handelsman from cartoonbank.com. All Rights Reserved.

P. 244: Box 6.2 from *Chronicle of Higher Education* (1978). A dramatic example of the connections between feedback and behavior. *Chronicle of Higher Education, 46*, p. 129, #2. Copyright 1978, The Chronicle of Higher Education. Reprinted with permission.

Pp. 248, 249: Tables 6.9 & 6.10 from Malos, S. B. (1998). Current legal issues in performance appraisal. In J. W. Smither (Ed.), *Performance appraisal: State of the art in practice*, Table 2.2, p. 80, & Table 2.3, p. 83. San Francisco: Jossey-Bass. This material is used by permission of John Wiley & Sons, Inc.

Chapter 7: Staffing Decisions

P. 254: Figure 7.1 from from Guion, R. M. (1998). *Assessment, measurement, and prediction*, p. 6. Mahwah, NJ: Lawrence

Erlbaum Associates. Reprinted by permission of Lawrence Erlbaum Associates, Inc.

P. 255: Figure 7.2 from Howard, A. (1991). Current influences on the staffing process. In D. W. Bray (Ed.), *Working with organizations and their people: A guide to human resources practice*. New York: Guilford Press. Used by permission.

Pp. 225, 256: Tables 7.1 & 7.2 from Snow, C. C., & Snell, S. A. (1993). Staffing as strategy. In N. Schmitt & W. C. Borman (Eds.), *Personnel selection in organizations*, p. 448–480; tables on pp. 451, 467. San Francisco: Jossey-Bass. This material is used by permission of John Wiley & Sons, Inc.

P. 258: Table 7.3 from Gilliland, S. W., & Cherry, B. (2000). Managing "customers" of selection processes. In J. Kehoe (Ed.), *Research and practice in personnel selection*, pp. 158–195; table on p. 165. San Francisco: Jossey-Bass. Copyright © 2000. This material is used by permission of John Wiley & Sons, Inc.

P. 279: Table 7.6 from Cascio, W. (1982). *Applied psychology in personnel management*, 2nd ed. (c) 1982. Reston Publishing Co., a Prentice Hall Company. Reprinted by permission of Pearson Education, Inc., Upper Saddle River, N.J. and The McGraw-Hill Companies.

Chapter 8: Training and Development

P. 294: Figure 8.1 adapted from Goldstein, I. L., & Ford, J. K. (2002). *Training in organizations: Needs assessment, development, and evaluation*, 4th ed. Belmont, CA: Wadsworth. © 2002. Reprinted with permission of Wadsworth, a division of Thomson Learning: www.thomsonrights.com

P. 297: Figure 8.2 extrapolated from Baldwin, T. T., & Ford, J. K. (1988). Transfer of training: A review and directions for future research. *Personnel Psychology, 41*, pp. 63–105. Used by permission of Personnel Psychology, Bowling Green, OH.

P. 305: Table 8.3 from Tannenbaum, S. I. (1997). Enhancing continuous learning: Diagnostic findings from multiple companies. *Human Resource Management, 36*, pp. 437–452. John Wiley & Sons, Inc. Copyright © 1997. Reprinted by permission of John Wiley & Sons, Inc.

P. 306: Figure 8.3 from Tolbert A. S., McLean, G. N., & Myers, R. C. (2002). Creating the global learning organization. *International Journal of Intercultural Relations, 26*, pp. 463–472. Oxford, UK: Elsevier Science. Used by permission.

P. 317: Table 8.5 from Alliger, G. M., Tannenbaum, S. I., Bennett, W., Traver, H., & Shotland, A. (1997). A meta-analysis of the relations among training criteria. *Personnel Psychology, 50*, pp. 341–358. Copyright by Personnel Psychology, Inc. Used by permission of Personnel Psychology, Bowling Green, OH.

P. 320: Table 8.7 from Simon, S. J., & Werner, J. M. (1996). Computer training through behavior modeling, self-paced, and instructional approaches: A field experiment. *Journal of Applied Psychology, 81*, 648–659. Copyright © 1996 by the American Psychological Association. Reprinted with permission.

P. 328: Table 8.9 from Peterson, D. B. (2002). Management development: Coaching and mentoring programs. In K. Kraiger (Ed.), *Creating, implementing, and managing effective training and development*, pp. 160–191. San Francisco: Jossey-Bass. This material is used by permission of John Wiley & Sons, Inc.

P. 321: Box 8.2 from Harrison, J. K. (1992). Individual and combined effects of behavior modeling and the cultural assimilator in cross-cultural management training. *Journal of Applied Psychology, 77*, 952–962. Copyright © 1992 by the American Psychological Association. Reprinted with permission.

Chapter 9: The Motivation to Work

P. 338: Lyrics from Taylor, James V. (1978). "Mill Work." Copyright 1978 Country Road Music, Inc.: wbpsales@warnerchappell.com Used by permission.

P. 343: Cartoon #22453 © The New Yorker Collection 2003 Bob Zahn from cartoonbank.com. All Rights Reserved.

P. 348: Box 9.1 from Adams, S. (1996). *Dogbert's top secret management handbook*. New York: HarperCollins. Copyright © 1996 by United Features Syndicate. Reprinted by permission of HarperCollins Publishers Inc.

P. 353: Table 9.2 from Steers, R. M., Porter, L. W., & Bigley, G. A. (Eds.) (1979). *Motivation and work behavior*, 2nd ed. Copyright © 1979. New York: McGraw Hill. Reprinted by permission of The McGraw-Hill Companies.

P. 357: Figure 9.4 from Austin, J. T., & Klein, H. J (1996). Work motivation and goal striving. In K. R. Murphy (Ed.), *Individual differences and behavior in organizations*, p. 215. San Francisco: Jossey-Bass. This material is used by permission of John Wiley & Sons, Inc.

P. 359: Figure 9.5 from Locke, E. A., & Latham, G. P. (1996). Goal setting theory:

Chapter 10: Attitudes, Emotions, and Work

Chapter 11: Fairness and Diversity in the Workplace

international diversity in organizations: A merger that works? In N. Anderson, D. Ones, H. Sinangil, & C. Viswesvaran (Eds.), *Handbook of industrial, work, and organizational psychology,* Vol. 1, p. 223. London: Sage. Reprinted by permission of Sage Publications Ltd.

Chapter 12: Leadership

P. 450: Quote from Fleishman, E. A. (1967). Performance assessment based on an empirically derived task taxonomy. *Human Factors, 9,* pp. 349–366; quote on p. 362.
Pp. 450–452: Quote from Fleishman, E. A., & Harris, E. F. (1962). Patterns of leadership behavior related to employee grievances and turnover. *Personnel Psychology, 15,* pp. 43–56.
Pp. 451, 453, 454: Table 12.4; Figures 12.1, 12.2, 12.3, & 12.4 from Yukl, G. (1998). *Leadership in organizations,* 4th ed., p. 197, 271, 267, 268. Upper Saddle River, N.J.: Prentice Hall. © 1998. Reprinted by permission of Pearson Education, Inc., Upper Saddle River, NJ.
Pp. 457, 458: Table 12.5 & Figure 12.5 from Vroom, V. H., & Yetton, P. W. (1973). *Leadership and decision-making.* Pittsburgh: University of Pittsburgh Press. © 1973 by University of Pittsburgh Press. Reprinted by permission.
P. 473: Table 12.6 from Yukl, G. (1998). *Leadership in organizations,* 4th ed., p. 342. Upper Saddle River, N.J.: Prentice Hall. © 1998. Reprinted by permission of Pearson Education, Inc., Upper Saddle River, NJ.
Pp. 473, 474: Tables 12.7 & 12.8 adapted from Brodbeck, F. C., Frese, M., et al.(2000). Cultural variation of leadership prototypes across 22 European countries. *Journal of Occupational and Organizational Psychology, 73,* pp. 1–29; tables p. 15. © The British Psychology Society. Reproduced with permission.

Chapter 13: Teams in Organizations

P. 488: Figure 13.1 adapted from Gladstein, D. L. (1984). Groups in context: A model of task group effectiveness. *Administrative Sciences Quarterly, 29,* pp. 499–517. Used by permission.
P. 490: Table 13.1 from Stevens, M. J., & Campion, M. A. (1999). Staffing work teams: Development and validation of a selection test for teamwork settings. *Journal of Management, 25,* pp. 207–228. Copyright 1999. Reprinted with permission from Elsevier.
P. 491: Table 13.2 from Stevens, M. J., & Campion, M. A. (1993). *The teamwork-*

KSA test. Chicago: NCS-London House. Copyright 1993 M. J. Stevens and M. A. Campion. All rights reserved. Used by permission of NCS Pearson, Inc.
P. 496: Cartoon ID # 38625, published in *The New Yorker* 4/23/1979. © The New Yorker Collection 1979 Henry Martin from cartoonbank.com. All Rights Reserved.
P. 501: Table 13.3 adapted from Belbin, R. M. (1993). *Team roles at work,* p. 22. London: Butterworth-Heinemann. Copyright 1993. Reprinted with permission from Elsevier.
P. 504: Table 13.4 from Forsyth, D. R. (1999). *Group dynamics,* 3rd ed., Table 6-2, p. 155. Belmont, CA: Brooks/Cole/Wadsworth. © 1999. Reprinted with permission of Wadsworth, a division of Thomson Learning: www.thomsonrights.com

Chapter 14: The Organization of Work Behavior

P. 515: Figure 14.2 adapted from Argyris, C. (1965). *Organization and innovation,* pp. 230–237. Homewood, IL: R. D. Irwin. Used by permission of The McGraw-Hill Companies. Adapted in Korman, A. (1971). *Industrial and organizational psychology.* Englewood Cliffs, N.J.: Prentice Prentice Hall. © 1971. Reprinted by permission of Pearson Education, Inc., Upper Saddle River, NJ.
P. 523: Figure 14.3 from James, L. A., & James, L. R. (1989). Integrating work environment perceptions: Explorations in the measurement of meaning. *Journal of Applied Psychology, 74,* p. 741. Copyright © 1989 by American Psychological Association. Reprinted with permission.
Pp. 524–525: Table 14.2 adapted from Cooke, R. A., & Lafferty, J. C. (1989). *Organizational culture inventory.* Plymouth, MI: Human Synergistics, Inc. Copyright © 1987, 1989 by Human Synergistics, Inc. The OCI instructions and items may not be reproduced without the express written permission of Human Synergistics. Used by permission.
Pp. 530, 531: Figures 14.4 & 14.5; Table 14.3 from Greenberg, J. (2002). *Managing behavior in organizations,* 3rd ed., pp. 172, 176, 178. Upper Saddle River, N.J.: Prentice Hall. © 2002. Reprinted by permission of Pearson Education, Inc., Upper Saddle River, NJ.
P. 533: Figure 14.6 from Dawis, R. V., & Lofquist, L. H. (1984). *A psychological theory of work adjustment: An individual differences model and its applications,* Figure 5.3, p. 62. Minneapolis: University of Minnesota Press. Reprinted by permission of René Dawis.

P. 538: DILBERT cartoon by Scott Adams 9/7/94 reprinted by permission of United Feature Syndicate, Inc. (c) 1994 United Feature Syndicate, Inc.
Pp. 539, 540: Quotes from Weick, K., & Quinn, R. (1999). Organizational change and development. *Annual Review of Psychology, 50,* pp. 369, 370, 375. © 1999 by Annual Reviews. With permission from Annual Review of Psychology: www.annualreviews.org
P. 543: Figure 14.8 supplied by Gene Larson, Advanced Technology Laboratories.
P. 544: Table 14.5 from Blackburn, R., & Rosen, B. (1993). Human Resource Management. *Academy of Management Executive, 7,* pp. 49–65. Copyright 1993. Reprinted by permission of Academy of Management Executive via the Copyright Clearance Center.
P. 549: Quote from Weick, K., & Quinn, R. (1999). Organizational change and development. *Annual Review of Psychology, 50,* pp. 361–386. © 1999 by Annual Reviews. With permission from Annual Review of Psychology: www.annualreviews.org

Chapter 15: Stress and Workplace Health

P. 554: Figure 15.1 adapted from Kahn, R. L., & Byosiere, P. (1992). Stress in organizations. In M. D. Dunnette & L. M. Hough (Eds.), *Handbook of industrial and organizational psychology,* 2nd ed., Vol. 3. Palo Alto, CA: Consulting Psychologists Press. Modified and reproduced by special permission of the Publisher, CPP, Inc., Palo Alto, CA 94303. Copyright 1992 by CPP, Inc. All rights reserved. Further reproduction is prohibited without the Publisher's written consent.
P. 561: Table 15.2 adapted from Quick, J. C., Quick, J. D., Nelson, D. L., & Hurrell, J. J. (1997). *Preventative stress management in organizations,* Fig. 4.1, p. 66. Washington, DC: American Psychological Association. Copyright © 1997 by American Psychological Association. Reprinted with permission.
P. 562: Figure 15.2 from Jex, S. M. (1998). *Stress and job performance: Theory, research, and implications for managerial practice.* Thousand Oaks, CA: Sage. Copyright © 1998. Reprinted by Permission of Sage Publications, Inc.
P. 562: Table 15.3 from Schaufeli, W. B., Leiter, M. P., Maslach, C., & Jackson, S. E. (1996). *Maslach Burnout Inventory-General Survey.* Palo Alto, CA: Consulting Psychologists Press. Excerpted and reproduced by special permission of the

Publisher, CPP, Inc., Palo Alto, CA 94303. Copyright 1996 Consulting Psychologists Press, Inc. All rights reserved. Further reproduction is prohibited without the Publisher's written consent.

P. 567: Figure 15.3 adapted from Karasek, R. A. (1979). Job demands, job decision latitude, and mental strain: Implications for job redesign. *Administrative Sciences Quarterly*, 24, 285–308. Used by permission.

P. 572: Table 15.4 adapted from Landy, F. J., Rastegary, H., Thayer, J., & Colvin, C. (1991). Time urgency: The construct and its measurement. *Journal of Applied Psychology*, 76, 644–657. Copyright © 1991 by the American Psychological Association. Reprinted with permission.

P. 575: Cartoon #24904 © 1993 The New Yorker Collection Edward Koren from cartoonbank.com. All Rights Reserved.

P. 576: Table 15.5 adapted from Cooper, C. L., Dewe, P. J., & O'Driscoll, M. P. (2001). *Organizational stress: A review and critique of theory, research, and applications*. Thousand Oaks, CA: Sage. Copyright © 2001. Reprinted by permission of Sage Publications, Inc.

Chapter 16: Designing Work for People

P. 587: Figure 16.1 from Applied Ergonomics (1974). *Applied ergonomics handbook.*, p. 3. Surrey, UK: IPC Science and Technology Press. Used by permission of Elsevier Science/Harcourt.

P. 588: Figure 16.2 based on *Esquire* (2002, January), p. 60.

P. 588: Table 16.1 from Howell, W. C. (1993). How human factors addresses challenges: Engineering psychology in a changing world. *Annual Review of Psychology*, 44, pp. 231–263. © 1993. Used by permission of Annual Reviews www.annualreviews.org

P. 589: Figures 16.3 & 16.4 from Applied Ergonomics (1974). *Applied ergonomics handbook.*, pp. 10, 12. Surrey, UK: IPC Science and Technology Press. Used by permission of Elsevier Science/Harcourt.

P. 590: Figure 16.5 from Helander, M. (1997). The human factors profession. In

G. Salvendy, *Handbook of human factors and ergonomics*, 2nd ed., pp. 3–17; Fig. 1.1, p. 6. New York: John Wiley & Sons. Copyright © 1997. This material is used by permission of John Wiley & Sons, Inc.

P. 605: Table 16.4 adapted from Vanderheiden, G. C. (1997). Design for people with functional limitations resulting from disability, aging, and circumstance. In G. Salvendy, *Handbook of human factors and ergonomics*, 2nd ed.; Table 60.1, p. 2019. New York: John Wiley & Sons. Copyright © 1997. This material is used by permission of John Wiley & Sons, Inc.

P. 608: Table 16.6 from Wickens, C. D., Gordon, S. E., & Liu, Y. (1998). *An introduction to human factors engineering*, p. 411. New York: Longman. © 1998. Reprinted by permission of Pearson Education, Inc., Upper Saddle River, NJ.

P. 610: Figure 16.6 adapted from Sanders, M. S., & McCormick, E. J. (1993). *Human factors in engineering and design*, 7th ed., p. 321. New York: McGraw-Hill. Used by permission of The McGraw-Hill Companies.

P. 611: Figures 16.7 & 16.8 from Laughery, K. R, Sr., & Wogalter, M. S. (1997). Warnings and risk perception. In G. Salvendy, *Handbook of human factors and ergonomics*, 2nd ed., pp. 1184, 1188. New York: John Wiley & Sons. Copyright © 1997. This material is used by permission of John Wiley & Sons, Inc.

P. 612: Figure 16.9 adapted from *UAW-Ford Job Improvement Guide*, copyright © 1988, The Regents of the University of Michigan. Adapted in Chaffin, D. B., & Andersson, G. B. J. (1991). *Occupational Biomechanics*, 2nd ed. New York: John Wiley & Sons, Inc. Copyright © 1991. This material is used by permission of John Wiley & Sons, Inc.

P. 613: Figure 16.10 from Chaffin, D. B. (1997). Biomechanical aspects of workplace design. In G. Salvendy, *Handbook of human factors and ergonomics*, 2nd ed., p. 772–789. New York: John Wiley & Sons. Copyright © 1997. This material is used by permission of John Wiley & Sons, Inc.

P. 615: Table 16.7 from Ludwig, T. D., & Geller, E. S. (1997). Assigned

versus participative goal setting and response generalization: Managing injury control among professional pizza drivers. *Journal of Applied Psychology, 82(2)*, pp. 253–261; table on p. 257. Copyright © 1997 by the American Psychological Association. Reprinted with permission.

P. 617: Figure 16.11 from Hofmann, D. A., & Morgeson, F. P. (1999). Safety-related behavior as a social exchange: The role of perceived organizational support and leader-member exchange. *Journal of Applied Psychology, 84(2)*, p. 292. Copyright © 1999 by the American Psychological Association. Reprinted with permission.

P. 620: Quote from Coyne, T. (2002). Employee kills four colleagues in Indiana. *Rocky Mountain News*, March 23, p. 11A. Reprinted with permission of The Associated Press.

P. 621: Table 16.8 from National Safe Workplace Institute (1989). Reproduced in Kinney, J. A. (1996). The dynamics of threat management. In G. R. VandenBos & E. Q. Bulatao, *Violence on the job: Identifying risks and developing solutions*, pp. 307–308. Washington, D.C: American Psychological Association.

P. 623: Quote from Fox, S., & Spector, P. E. (1999). A model of work frustration-aggression. *Journal of Organizational Behavior, 20*, p. 917. Copyright 1999 © John Wiley & Sons Limited. Reproduced with permission.

P. 624: Figure 16.13 from Spector, P. E. (2000). *Industrial and organizational psychology: Research and practice*, 2nd ed., p. 242. New York: John Wiley & Sons, Inc. Reproduced with permission.

P. 625: Table 16.9 from Folger, R., & Baron, R. A. (1996). Violence and hostility at work: A model of reactions to perceived injustice. In G. R. VandenBos & E. Q. Bulatao, *Violence on the job: Identifying risks and developing solutions*, p. 73. Washington, D.C: American Psychological Association. Cpyright © 1996 by American Psychological Association. Reprinted with permission.

PHOTO CREDITS

PRE-1900

SOCIAL AND PSYCHOLOGICAL ENVIRONMENT

- Psychology emerges as a science distinct from philosophy and physiology; dominated by research on the senses and consciousness
- The APA is founded in 1892
- Clinical psychology emerges as one of the few applications of psychology to real world problems

- F. Galton develops the science of fingerprinting as a way of demonstrating the principles of Darwin's theory of evolution
- Typical Americans and Europeans are fascinated with phrenology (assessing personality from bumps on the skull) and hypnotism

1900 – 1920

SOCIAL AND PSYCHOLOGICAL ENVIRONMENT

- Scientific Management captivates the United States, Europe, and Japan
- Time and motion studies become popular in industry
- World War I begins and ends
- Elton Mayo asserts that unions are examples of psychopathology in Australia
- The Eugenics movement (the improvement of races through breeding) attracts many psychologists, including

J. McK. Cattell
- The success of the psychological testing of army recruits is used to promote employment testing in industry, and eventually, to justify immigration quotas for many central and southern European ethnic groups
- University-based and private I-O consulting firms begin to appear

1920 – 1940

SOCIAL AND PSYCHOLOGICAL ENVIRONMENT

- Social psychology, child psychology and behaviorism attract great attention
- A major economic depression affects employment
- America prepares for a new war in Europe
- Manufacturing processes become more technically sophisticated

- Scientific techniques for attitude measurement are introduced
- Race discrimination in housing, immigration, and employment become important national topics

1940 – 1960

SOCIAL AND PSYCHOLOGICAL ENVIRONMENT

- Social psychologists begin to emphasize groups, teams, and attitudes
- World War II begins and ends; the Korean war begins
- Industry experiences frequent and disruptive strikes
- Behaviorism wanes and cognitive psychology emerges
- APA forms a committee to establish technical and scientific standards for tests

- The United States Employment Service publishes the *Dictionary of Occupational Titles*, a comprehensive description of thousands of job
- The assessment center is introduced by the U.S. Office of Strategic Services as a method for selecting spies and sabotage agents

1960-1980

SOCIAL AND PSYCHOLOGICAL ENVIRONMENT

- Personality theory and research migrate from clinical to social psychology
- John and Robert Kennedy, Martin Luther King, and Malcolm X are assassinated
- The Vietnam war begins and ends
- The transistor replaces the vacuum tube, which is then replaced by the computer chip
- Racially based riots occur in most large cities

- The Civil Rights Act of 1964 addresses discrimination in employment
- The federal government issues administrative guidelines defining adverse impact and employment discrimination
- Three Mile Island nuclear accident raises questions about safety cultures

1980-PRESENT

SOCIAL AND PSYCHOLOGICAL ENVIRONMENT

- Class action lawsuits brought by ethnic minority and female workers become common
- Laws protecting older workers (ADEA) and disabled workers (ADA) are passed
- The Civil Rights Act of 1964 is amended by the Civil Rights Act of 1991 to prohibit quota hiring
- Downsizings, acquisitions, and mergers become commonplace

- The workplace becomes more diverse and multinational
- Terrorists destroy the World Trade Center in New York
- The *Challenger* and *Columbia* disasters raise questions about safety cultures
- The communist bloc in Europe dissolves; NAFTA is passed; The European Common Market is formed